Cookbook Writers

James Beard
Marian Burros
Julia Child
Craig Claiborne
M. F. K. Fisher
Pierre Franey
Jean D. Hewitt
Graham Kerr
Margaret Romagnoli
Raymond Sokolov
Jane Stern
. . . and more

Dance Critics

William Como
Arlene Croce
Edwin Denby
John Gruen
Deborah Jowitt
Marcia B. Siegel
Tobi Tobias
. . . and more

Dancers

George Balanchine
Christopher d'Amboise
Katherine Dunham
Margot Fonteyn
Jose Greco
Natalia Makarova
Peter Martins
Valery Panov
. . . and more

Diet Specialists

Stuart Berger
Jane Brody
Martin Katahn
Jean Nidetch
Nathan Pritikin
Lendon Smith
Herman Tarnower
Roy L. Walford
. . . and more

Drama Critics

Clive Barnes
Eric Bentley
Robert S. Brustein
Martin Esslin
Brendan Gill
Walter Kerr
Joseph Wood Krutch

John Simon
Stark Young
. . . and more

Economists

Alfred D. Chandler, Jr.
Martin S. Feldstein
Milton Friedman
John Kenneth Galbraith
L. St. Clare Grondona
Robert L. Heilbroner
Ursula Kathleen Hicks
Jean Monnet
Felix G. Rohatyn
Walt W. Rostow
Herbert A. Simon
Herbert Stein
James Tobin
Friedrich August von
   Hayek
Barbara Ward
. . . and more

Educators

J. D. Bernal
Joseph A. Califano, Jr.
Marva Collins
Robert Lyons Danly
Thomas Flanagan
Ronald Gross
Theodore M. Hesburgh
Jonathan Kozol
A. S. Neill
Neil Postman
Anne Rogovin
Richard B. Sewall
Norman R. Shapiro
Ellease Southerland
Daniel H. Yergin
. . . and more

Entrepreneurs

Walt Disney
Malcolm Forbes
J. Paul Getty
Mary Kay
Ray Kroc
Dan Lundberg
Ted Turner
. . . and more

Essayists

G. K. Chesterton
Bryan F. Griffin

Edward Hoagland
John McPhee
Joseph Mitchell
George Orwell
Calvin Trillin
E. B. White
Ellen Willis
Tom Wolfe
. . . and more

Explorers

Edwin E. Aldrin, Jr.
Michael Collins
Jacques Yves Cousteau
Thor Heyerdahl
Edmund Hillary
John Hunt
Peter Matthiessen
Alfred M. Worden
. . . and more

Feminists

Simone de Beauvoir
Susan Brownmiller
Andrea Dworkin
Barbara Ehrenreich
Betty Friedan
Germaine Greer
Kate Millet
Gloria Steinem
Rebecca West
. . . and more

Film Critics

Andre Bazin
Vincent Canby
Judith Crist
Roger Ebert
Pauline Kael
Stanley Kauffmann
Leonard Maltin
Harry Medved
Michael Medved
Rex Reed
Andrew Sarris
Richard Schickel
Gene Siskel
. . . and more

Folklorists

Roger Abrahams
Dan Ben-Amos

Jan Harold Brunvand
Richard M. Dorson
David King Dunaway
Alan Dundes
Barbara Kirshenblatt-
   Gimblett
Maria Leach
Alan Lomax
Stith Thompson
. . . and more

Gossip Columnists

Rona Barrett
Sheilah Graham
Hedda Hopper
Diana McLellan
Louella Parsons
Liz Smith
. . . and more

Historians

Herbert Aptheker
Jacques Benoist-Mechin
Anthony Blunt (art)
Daniel J. Boorstin
Fernand Braudel
Arthur Bryant
Bruce Catton
Kenneth Clark
Alessandra Comini
Merle Eugene Curti
Robert Darnton
David Brion Davis
Bern Dibner
Ariel Durant
Will Durant
Antonia Fraser
Peter Gay
Eugene D. Genovese
Richard Hofstadter
Hugh Honour (art)
Paul Horgan
Rhys L. Isaac
Emmanuel Le Roy
   Ladurie
Golo Mann
Thomas K. McCraw
Edmund Morgan
Thomas Pakenham
Erwin Panofsky (art)
Meyer Schapiro
Arthur Schlesinger, Jr.
C. V. Wedgwood
Theodore H. White
C. Vann Woodward
Louis Booker Wright
. . . and more

Horror and Occult Writers

Peter Benchley
William Peter Blatty
Edgar E. Cayce
John Coyne
Stephen King
Richard Burton
   Matheson
Ruth Shick
   Montgomery
Anne Rice
John Sand
John Saul
Jess Stearn
Whitley Strieber
. . . and more

Humorists

Roy Blount
Erma Bombeck
Art Buchwald
Peter De Vries
Ogden Nash
S. J. Perelman
James Stevenson
James Thurber
. . . and more

Jazz Artists

Louis Armstrong
Duke Ellington
Dizzy Gillespie
Benny Goodman
Charles Mingus
Art Taylor
Mel Torme
. . . and more

Lexicographers

Tana de Gamez
J. L. Dillard
Stuart Flexner
E. Arsenio Manuel
Leo C. Rosten
. . . and more

Literary Critics

M. H. Abrams
R. P. Blackmur

Literary Critics

(continued)

Harold Bloom
Cleanth Brooks
Malcolm Cowley
Jonathan Culler
David Daiches
Richard Ellmann
William Empson
Leslie A. Fiedler
Northrop Frye
Helen Gardner
Alfred Kazin
Frank Kermode
H. D. F. Kitto
F. R. Leavis
Q. D. Leavis
Percy Lubbock
John Crowe Ransom
I. A. Richards
Christopher Ricks
Lionel Trilling
Helen Hennessy Vendler
Rene Wellek
Edmund Wilson
W. K. Wimsatt, Jr.
. . . and more

Magazine and Journal Editors

Uri Avnery
Gray Davis Boone
Charles Brasch
Helen Gurley Brown
Tina Brown
Norman Cousins
Martha Foley
Tatyana Mamonova
Victoria Ocampo
William S. Schlamm
William Shawn
Jann S. Wenner
. . . and more

Media Figures and Celebrities

Alan Alda
Lauren Bacall
Joseph Bologna
Anita Bryant
George Burns
Rosalyn Carter
Dick Cavett
Charlie Chaplin
Sammy Davis, Jr.
Ruby Dee
Phil Donahue
Mike Douglas
Buddy Ebsen
Redd Foxx
Arlene Francis
David Frost
Chief Dan George
Julie Harris
Sterling Hayden
Charlton Heston
Bob Hope
Ann Jackson
Lady Bird Johnson
Angela Lansbury
Norman Lear
Shirley MacLaine
Mary Martin
Groucho Marx
Ed McMahon
Bette Midler
Roger George Moore
Nancy Davis Reagan
Robert Redford
Mister Rogers
Roy Rogers
Rosalind Russell
Margaret Truman
Liv Ullmann
Diana Dalziel Vreeland
John Wayne
Shelley Winters
. . . and more

Memoirists and Autobiographers

Quentin Crisp
Betty Ford
Helen Hanff
Billy Hayes
Nadezhda Mandelstam
Joyce Maynard
Veljko Micunovic
Richard Rodriguez
. . . and more

Military Scientists

Dwight D. Eisenhower
Basil Henry Liddell Hart
Daniel Lang
S. L. A. Marshall
John Cecil Masterman
C. Northcote Parkinson
William C. Westmoreland
Elmo Russell Zumwalt, Jr.
. . . and more

Music Critics

Lester Bangs
Robert Christgau
Jonathan Cott
Gary Giddins
Nat Hentoff
Greil Marcus
Dave Marsh
Hugues Panassie
Harold Schonberg
Nat Shapiro
Ritchie Yorke
. . . and more

Mystery and Suspense Writers

Edward S. Aarons
Eric Ambler
Gwendoline Williams Butler
James M. Cain
Agatha Christie
Mary Higgins Clark
Len Deighton
Ian Fleming
Ken Follet
Dick Francis
Sarah Gainham
Erle Stanley Gardner
John Edmund Gardner
Martha Grimes
Dashiell Hammett
Joseph Hansen
P. D. James
H. R. F. Keating
Harry Kemelman
William X. Kienzle
Emma Lathen
John le Carre
Elmore Leonard
Robert Ludlum
John D. MacDonald
Kenneth Millar
Margaret Millar
L. A. Morse
Bernard Newman
Ruth Rendell
Dorothy L. Sayers
Trevanian
. . . and more

Naturalists and Environmentalists

Cleveland Amory
Wendell Berry
Rachel Carson
Barry Commoner
Claude L. Fly
Euell Gibbons
Anne W. Simon
Victor Wolfgang Von Hagen
. . . and more

Novelists

Chinua Achebe
Alice Adams
Vassily Aksyonov
Jorge Amado
Kingsley Amis
Ivo Andric
Harriet Simpson Arnow
Miguel Angel Asturias
Margaret Atwood
James Baldwin
Djuna Barnes
John Barth
Donald Barthelme
Saul Bellow
Heinrich Boell
Jorge Luis Borges
Elizabeth Bowen
Anita Brookner
Pearl S. Buck
Anthony Burgess
Erskine Caldwell
Italo Calvino
Truman Capote
Angela Carter
Adolfo Bioy Casares
Louis-Ferdinand Celine
John Cheever
Julio Cortazar
Robertson Davies
Joan Didion
Isak Dinesen
Jose Donoso
John Dos Passos
Sergei Dovlatov
Margaret Drabble
Marguerite Duras
Lawrence Durrell
Ralph Ellison
William Faulkner
E. M. Forster
John Fowles
Ladislav Fuks
William Gaddis
Gabriel Garcia Marquez
Jean Genet
Jose Maria Gironella
Janusz Glowacki
Gail Godwin
William Golding
Nadine Gordimer
Mary Gordon
Guenter Grass
Shirley Ann Grau
Graham Greene
Jiri Grusa
Knut Hamsun
Peter Handke
Elizabeth Hardwick
John Hawkes
Joseph Heller
Ernest Hemingway

(continued on back endsheets)

**Check the *Contemporary Authors* Cumulative Index
to Locate Sketches on These and Thousands of Other Authors**

Contemporary Authors®

ISSN 0010-7468

Contemporary

Authors®

**A Bio-Bibliographical Guide to
Current Writers in Fiction, General Nonfiction,
Poetry, Journalism, Drama, Motion Pictures,
Television, and Other Fields**

HAL MAY
SUSAN M. TROSKY
Editors

**NANCY H. EVANS
LOUISE MOONEY
POLLY A. VEDDER**
Associate Editors

LES STONE
Senior Writer

volume 125

Gale Research Inc. • Book Tower • Detroit, Michigan 48226

STAFF

Hal May and Susan M. Trosky, *Editors, Original Volumes*

Nancy H. Evans, Louise Mooney, and Polly A. Vedder, *Associate Editors*

Les Stone, *Senior Writer*

Christa Brelin and Elizabeth Thomas, *Senior Assistant Editors*

Thomas Kozikowski, Nancy Pear, and Joanne M. Peters, *Assistant Editors and Writers*

Barbara K. Carlisle, Barbara A. Cicchetti, Emily J. Compagnone, Carol Lynn DeKane, Janice E. Drane, Jeremy Kane, and Linda S. Smouse, *Assistant Editors*

Arlene True, *Sketchwriter*

Peter Benjaminson and Jean W. Ross, *Interviewers*

Diane L. Dupuis, David G. Holborn, Linda Hubbard, Anne Janette Johnson, Frances Locher, Paulette Petrimoulx, Curtis Skinner, and Dennis Wepman, *Contributing Editors*

James G. Lesniak, *Index Coordinator*

Linda Metzger, *Senior Editor, Contemporary Authors*

Mary Rose Bonk, *Research Supervisor*

Alysa I. Hunton, *Research Coordinator*

David Esse Salamie, *Assistant Research Coordinator*

Reginald A. Carlton, Jane Cousins-Clegg, and Norma Sawaya, *Senior Research Assistants*

John P. Dodt, Shirley Gates, Shirelle Goss, Clare Kinsman, Timothy P. Loszewski, Andrew Guy Malonis, Sharon McGilvray, and Tracey Head Turbett, *Research Assistants*

Special recognition is given to the staff of
Young People's Literature Department, Gale Research Inc.

Library of Congress Catalog Card Number 62-52046
ISBN 0-8103-1950-0
ISSN 0010-7468

Computerized photocomposition by
Typographics, Incorporated
Kansas City, Missouri

Contents

Authors and Media People
Featured in This Volume

Robert Sam Anson (American journalist)—A prominent reporter and writer, Anson is well known for his journalistic books. They include *"They've Killed the President!," Exile: The Unquiet Oblivion of Richard M. Nixon,* and *Best Intentions: The Education and Killing of Edmund Perry.* (Sketch contains interview.)

Tony Brown (American broadcaster)—Since 1970 Brown has been producer, scriptwriter, and host of "Tony Brown's Journal," a highly acclaimed newsmagazine carried by stations of the Public Broadcasting Service.

Martin Buber (Austrian-born Israeli philosopher who died in 1965)—One of this century's major existentialists, Buber is widely known for his masterwork *I and Thou.* He was deeply influenced by the Hasidic branch of Judaism and in turn profoundly influenced the thinking of Christian theologians.

Shirley Christian (American journalist)—While reporting from Central America for the *Miami Herald* Christian won both a Pulitzer Prize and the George Polk Memorial Award. Now with the *New York Times,* she wrote the critically acclaimed *Nicaragua: Revolution in the Family* in 1985. (Sketch contains interview.)

Birago Diop (Senegalese veterinarian and writer)—One of Africa's most widely read authors, Diop is best known for writing short stories inspired by the folktales of West Africa. Among his award-winning collections is *Tales of Amadou Koumba.*

Sheila Fugard (British-born author)—As a young girl Fugard moved to South Africa, which provides the settings for her novels *A Revolutionary Woman, The Rite of Passage,* and *The Castaways,* winner of two prestigious South African prizes.

William Greaves (American filmmaker)—Greaves is regarded as a first-rate filmmaker whose documentaries and feature productions focus primarily on aspects of the black experience. His scriptwriting credits include "In the Company of Men," "Voice of La Raza" and "Ali the Fighter."

Nicolas Guillen (Cuban poet)—Considered Cuba's greatest living poet, Guillen is a master of the Afro-Cuban style. A synthesis of Spanish, black Cuban, and African elements, Guillen's poems are available to readers in English in his volumes *Tengo, El gran Zoo,* and *Man-Making Words.*

Paul Carter Harrison (American playwright)—Writer in residence at Chicago's Columbia College, Harrison won an Obie Award for his play "The Great MacDaddy." His book of essays, *The Drama of Nommo,* has influenced others writing for and about black theater. (Sketch contains interview.)

Geoffrey H. Hartman (American literary theorist)—Hartman has been the Karl Young Professor of English and Comparative Literature at Yale since 1974. He is best known for his radical and difficult books on the deconstruction theory of literary criticism, such as *Beyond Formalism, The Fate of Reading,* and *Criticism in the Wilderness.*

Adam Hochschild (American writer)—Co-founder and editor of *Mother Jones* magazine, Hochschild has long contributed to periodicals such as *Ramparts* and *Village Voice.* In addition, he is the author of *Half the Way Home,* in which he recounts his relationship with his father, wealthy entrepreneur Harold Hochschild. (Sketch contains interview.)

A. E. Housman (British scholar, educator, and poet who died in 1936)—Although Housman wrote the enormously popular *Shropshire Lad* and two other volumes of poems, he is probably most revered as one of the world's foremost classical scholars. Housman edited the five-volume *Astronomica* of Manilius as well as works by Juvenal and Lucan.

Keri Hulme (New Zealand writer)—Hulme won international praise for her first novel, *The Bone People,* for which she received Britain's prestigious Booker McConnell Prize in 1985. Centering on the stormy relationship of three social outcasts, the book is considered a masterpiece of New Zealand fiction. (Sketch contains interview.)

Lee Iacocca (American entrepreneur)—The man who took charge of Chrysler Corporation when it was on the verge of bankruptcy and turned its fortunes around, Iacocca has been called America's first corporate folk hero. His memoirs, *Iacocca: An Autobiography* and *Talking Straight,* were both best-sellers.

Jamaica Kincaid (Antiguan-born American writer)—Kincaid is the widely praised author of *Annie John* and *At the Bottom of the River.* Her short stories about life on the island of Antigua employ a highly poetic literary style and have established the author as a prominent voice in American literature.

Diane Kurys (French screenwriter and director)—Kurys came recently to filmmaking and already has three acclaimed films to her credit, "Peppermint Soda," "Cocktail Molotov," and "Entre Nous." Popular both in Europe and America, her films have garnered the Prix Louis Delluc and an Academy Award nomination.

R. M. Lamming (British writer)—The author of two novels, Lamming won the David Higham Award for her first work, *The Notebook of Gismondo Cavalletti,* which is set in Renaissance Italy. *In the Dark,* about a modern-day octogenarian, was also well received. (Sketch contains interview.)

Andrea Lee (American author)—Lee, who is a staff writer for *New Yorker* magazine, has produced two successful books, the novel *Sarah Phillips* and *Russian Journal,* a nonfiction account of the author's stay in the Soviet Union. The latter volume was nominated for an American Book Award in 1981.

Spike Lee (American filmmaker)—Deemed one of the most promising comedic filmmakers to appear in the late 1980s, Lee is notable for addressing issues of the black community. He wrote and directed "She's Gotta Have It" and "School Daze," which have earned him a reputation as a provocative and important talent.

Nelson and Winnie Mandela (South African political activists)—Nelson Mandela, a lawyer imprisoned since 1962, and his wife Winnie, harassed and periodically jailed for her outspokenness, are living symbols of the anti-apartheid struggle in South Africa. Winnie's autobiography, *Part of My Soul Went With Him,* was published in 1985, and collections of Nelson's statements were published as *No Easy Walk to Freedom* and *The Struggle Is My Life.*

James Melville (British novelist)—James Melville is the pseudonym of Peter Martin, author of popular crime fiction featuring Japanese police superintendent Tetsuo Otani. Martin served twice in Japan as a cultural affairs officer. His books include *The Wages of Zen* and *The Chrysanthemum Chain.* (Sketch contains interview.)

H. L. Mencken (American journalist who died in 1956)—Mencken exercised enormous influence on the life and letters of his time, and is still considered the epoch's premier satirist. His writings include books on philosophy and literary criticism, a series of volumes titled *Prejudices,* and the autobiographical *Days of H. L. Mencken: Happy Days, Newspaper Days, Heathen Days.*

Margaret Mitchell (American writer who died in 1949)—Mitchell worked as a journalist for the *Atlanta Journal* early in her career, but she achieved enduring fame when her only novel, *Gone With the Wind,* was published in 1936. A perennial favorite, the novel sells a quarter of a million copies each year.

Pauli Murray (American activist who died in 1985)—Murray began fighting for racial and sexual equality in the late 1930s and went on to become an educator, an attorney, and an Episcopal priest. She wrote such books as *Proud Shoes: The Story of an American Family* and the autobiographical *Song in a Weary Throat: An American Pilgrimage.*

Sembene Ousmane (Senegalese writer and filmmaker)—Since publication of his first novel in 1956, Ousmane has become widely acclaimed for both his books and for his films. Among his most popular works are the two novellas published together in translation as *The Money Order, With White Genesis,* and his films "Mandabi" and "Xala."

Dora Russell (British activist who died in 1986)—Russell campaigned for feminist and social causes all her life and was an early advocate of free love, birth control, and open marriage. With her first husband, philosopher Bertrand Russell, she founded the progressive Beacon Hill School. She wrote several books, including her three-volume autobiography, *The Tamarisk Tree.*

Leopold Sedar Senghor (Senegalese intellectual, statesman, and writer)—Senghor, who helped establish and shape negritude in the 1930s and 1940s, was president of the Republic of Senegal from its independence in 1960 until 1980. He is considered one of Africa's leading intellectuals and is revered for his literary and political accomplishments. His works include *On African Socialism* and the poetry collections *Ethiopiques* and *Nocturnes.*

Raymond M. Smullyan (American professor of mathematics and philosophy)—A man "whose mind seems to have been largely his own invention," Smullyan has written several unusual and challenging puzzle books for the general reader. His volumes include *Alice in Puzzle-Land, To Mock a Mockingbird,* and *The Chess Mysteries of Sherlock Holmes.* (Sketch contains interview.)

Gary Soto (American poet)—An award-winning poet and prose writer often associated with the Fresno school of poets, Soto garnered an American Book Award in 1985 for his book of prose memoirs, *Living up the Street.* Soto's other well-received volumes include *The Elements of San Joaquin* and *The Tales of Sunlight.* (Sketch contains interview.)

Dale Spender (Australian writer)—A full-time writer since 1978, Spender has published several nonfiction works celebrating women's achievements. Among her titles are *Women of Ideas and What Men Have Done to Them, Feminist Theorists: Three Centuries of Key Women Theorists,* and *Invisible Women: The Schooling Scandal.* (Sketch contains interview.)

Art Spiegelman (Swedish-born artist and writer)—Spiegelman is the author of *Maus,* a critically acclaimed comic saga originally published in the underground work *Funny Animals* and subsequently issued by Pantheon. The artist, who "redefines the comic book," also publishes *Raw,* an annual magazine of avant-garde comics.

George Stevens, Jr. (American filmmaker)—Stevens apprenticed under his famous father, George Stevens, and later wrote, produced, and directed the critically acclaimed biographical film "George Stevens: A Filmmaker's Journey." (Sketch contains interview.)

Desmond M. Tutu (South African prelate and social reformer)—The Nobel Peace Prize received by Tutu in 1984 gave worldwide visibility to his efforts to abolish apartheid in South Africa. Many of Tutu's orations have been collected in *Hope and Suffering: Sermons and Speeches.*

Nathanael West (American novelist and screenwriter who died in 1940)—West's best-known work is the novel *Miss Lonelyhearts,* about a young advice columnist who becomes personally involved in the lives of his unhappy readers. West's reputation languished until the late 1950s, when his brand of brooding humor began appearing in the works of other American writers.

Preface

The nearly 900 entries in *Contemporary Authors* (*CA*), Volume 125, bring to more than 91,000 the number of authors now represented in the *Contemporary Authors* series. *CA* includes nontechnical writers in all genres—fiction, nonfiction, poetry, drama, etc.—whose books are issued by commercial, risk publishers or by university presses. Authors of books published only by known vanity or author-subsidized firms are ordinarily not included. Since native language and nationality have no bearing on inclusion in *CA*, authors who write in languages other than English are included in *CA* if their works have been published in the United States or translated into English.

Although *CA* focuses primarily on authors of published books, the series also encompasses prominent persons in communications: newspaper and television reporters and correspondents, columnists, newspaper and magazine editors, photojournalists, syndicated cartoonists, screenwriters, television scriptwriters, and other media people.

Starting with Volume 104, the editors of *CA* began to broaden the series' scope to encompass authors deceased since 1900 whose works are still of interest to today's readers. (Previously, *CA* covered only living writers and authors deceased 1960 or later.) Since the great poets, novelists, short story writers, and playwrights of the early twentieth century are popular writers for study in today's high school and college curriculums, and since their writings continue to be analyzed by literary critics, these writers are in many ways as contemporary as the authors *CA* has regularly featured.

Each volume of *CA*, therefore, includes a limited number of entries on authors deceased before 1960. Providing commentary about writers' lives and literary achievements, these sketches in addition offer both a historical and contemporary review of the authors' critical reputations. The entries in this volume on A. E. Housman, H. L. Mencken, Margaret Mitchell, and Nathanael West reflect the variety of early twentieth-century authors to be featured in future *CA* volumes.

No charge or obligation is attached to a *CA* listing. Authors are included in the series solely on the basis of the above criteria and their interest to *CA* users.

Compilation Methods

The editors make every effort to secure information directly from the authors through questionnaires and personal correspondence. If writers of special interest to *CA* users are deceased or fail to reply to requests for information, material is gathered from other reliable sources. Biographical dictionaries are checked (a task made easier through the use of Gale's *Biography and Genealogy Master Index* and other volumes in the "Gale Biographical Index Series"), as are bibliographical sources such as *Cumulative Book Index* and *The National Union Catalog*. Published interviews, feature stories, and book reviews are examined, and often material is supplied by the authors' publishers. All sketches, whether prepared from questionnaires or through extensive research, are sent to the biographees for review prior to publication. Sketches on recently deceased authors are sent to family members, agents, etc., if possible, for a similar review.

Format

CA is designed to present, clearly and concisely, biographical and bibliographical information in three kinds of listings: sketches, brief entries, and obituary notices. The series' easy-to-use format ensures that a reader needing specific information can quickly focus on the pertinent portion of an entry. Sketches, for instance, contain individual paragraphs with rubrics identifying addresses, memberships, and awards and honors. Furthermore, in sketch sections headed "Writings," the title of each book, play, and other published or unpublished work appears on a separate line, clearly distinguishing one title from another. This same convenient bibliographical presentation is featured in the "Biographical/Critical Sources" sections of sketches and brief entries and in the "Obituaries and Other Sources" sections of obituary notices where individual book and periodical titles are also listed on separate lines. *CA* readers can therefore quickly scan these often-lengthy bibliographies to find the titles they need.

Informative Sidelights

Numerous *CA* sketches contain sidelights, which provide personal dimensions to the listings, supply information about the critical reception the authors' works have received, or both. Some authors presented in Volume 125 worked closely with *CA*'s editors to develop interesting, incisive sidelights. Educator, musician, and composer David Michael Hertz, for example, tells *CA* that his goal "is to live the double life of artist and scholar," adding that "from both a scholarly and artistic point of view, I believe that real originality must happen organically, from within, and must never be self-conscious."

CA's editors also compile sidelights when authors and media people of particular interest do not supply sidelights material or when demand for information about the critical reception accorded their writings is especially high. Volume 125, for instance, profiles Leopold Sedar Senghor, poet and former president of the Republic of Senegal, who in the 1920s sparked a new black cultural consciousness called "negritude." For this, writes a *CA* editor, Senghor "is credited with contributing to Africa's progress toward independence from colonial rule." Also featured in this volume is feminist screenwriter and director Lizzie Borden, whose independently produced films "Born in Flames" and "Working Girls" have generated the interest of Hollywood studios.

We hope these sketches, as well as others with sidelights compiled by *CA*'s editors, provide informative and enjoyable reading.

Exclusive Interviews

CA provides exclusive, primary information on certain writers in the form of interviews. Prepared specifically for *CA,* the never-before-published conversations presented in the section of the sketch headed "*CA* Interview" give users the opportunity to learn the authors' thoughts, in depth, about their craft. Subjects chosen for interviews are, the editors feel, authors who hold special interest for *CA*'s readers.

Writers and journalists in this volume whose sketches include interviews are Robert Sam Anson, Shirley Christian, Paul Carter Harrison, Adam Hochschild, Keri Hulme, R. M. Lamming, James Melville, Raymond M. Smullyan, Gary Soto, Dale Spender, and George Stevens, Jr.

Brief Entries

CA also includes short entries on authors of current popular appeal or literary stature whose full-length sketches are not yet ready for publication. Identified by the heading "Brief Entry," these short listings highlight the authors' careers and writings and often include a few sources where additional information may be found.

Obituary Notices Make *CA* Timely and Comprehensive

To be as timely and comprehensive as possible, *CA* publishes obituary notices on deceased authors within the scope of the series. These notices provide date and place of birth and death, highlight the author's career and writings, and list other sources where additional biographical information and obituaries may be found. To distinguish them from full-length sketches, obituaries are identified with the heading "Obituary Notice."

CA includes obituary notices for writers who already have full-length entries in earlier *CA* volumes—47 percent of the obituary notices in this volume are for such authors—as well as for authors who do not yet have sketches in the series. Deceased writers of special interest currently represented only by obituary notices will be scheduled for full-length sketch treatment in forthcoming *CA* volumes.

Contemporary Authors New Revision Series

A major change in the preparation of *CA* revision volumes began with the first volume of *Contemporary Authors New Revision Series.* No longer are all of the sketches in a given *CA* volume updated and published together as a revision volume. Instead, entries from a number of volumes are assessed, and only those sketches requiring *significant change* are revised and published in a *New Revision Series* volume. This enables us to provide *CA* users with updated information about active writers on a more timely basis and avoids printing entries in which there has been little or no change. As always, the most recent *CA* cumulative index continues to be the user's guide to the location of an individual author's revised listing.

Contemporary Authors Autobiography Series

Designed to complement the information in *CA* original and revision volumes, the *Contemporary Authors Autobiography Series* provides autobiographical essays written by important current authors. Each volume contains twenty to thirty specially commissioned autobiographies and is illustrated with numerous personal photographs supplied by the authors. The range of contemporary writers describing their lives and interests in the *Autobiography Series* encompasses authors such as Dannie Abse, Vance Bourjaily, Doris Grumbach, Elizabeth Forsythe Hailey, Marge Piercy, Frederik Pohl, Alan Sillitoe, William Stafford, Diane Wakoski, and Elie Wiesel. Though the information presented in the autobiographies is as varied and unique as the authors, common topics of discussion include their motivations for writing, the people and experiences that shaped their careers, the rewards they derive from their work, and their impressions of the current literary scene.

Autobiographies included in the *Contemporary Authors Autobiography Series* can be located through both the *CA* cumulative index and the *Contemporary Authors Autobiography Series* cumulative index, which lists not only personal names but also titles of works, geographical names, subjects, and schools of writing.

Contemporary Authors Bibliographical Series

The *Contemporary Authors Bibliographical Series* is a comprehensive survey of writings by and about the most important authors since World War II in the United States and abroad. Each volume concentrates on a specific genre and nationality and features approximately ten major writers. Volume 1, for instance, covers the American novelists James Baldwin, John Barth, Saul Bellow, John Cheever, Joseph Heller, Norman Mailer, Bernard Malamud, Carson McCullers, John Updike, and Eudora Welty. *Bibliographical Series* entries consist of three parts: a primary bibliography that lists works written by the author, a secondary bibliography that lists works about the author, and an analytical bibliographical essay that thoroughly discusses the merits and deficiencies of major critical and scholarly works. Complementing the information in other *CA* volumes, the *Bibliographical Series* is a new key to finding and evaluating information on the lives and writings of those authors who have attracted significant critical attention.

Each author's entry in the *Contemporary Authors Bibliographical Series* can be located through both the *CA* cumulative index and, beginning with Volume 2, the *Contemporary Authors Bibliographical Series* cumulative author index. A cumulative index to the critics discussed in the bibliographical essays also appears in each *Bibliographical Series* volume.

CA Numbering System

Occasionally questions arise about the *CA* numbering system. Despite numbers like "97-100" and "125," the entire *CA* series consists of only 87 physical volumes with the publication of Volume 125. The following information notes changes in the numbering system, as well as in cover design, to help users better understand the organization of the entire *CA* series.

CA First Revisions
- 1-4R through 41-44R (11 books)
  Cover: Brown with black and gold trim.
  There will be no further *First Revisions* because revised entries are now being handled exclusively through the more efficient *New Revision Series* mentioned below.

CA Original Volumes
- 45-48 through 97-100 (14 books)
  Cover: Brown with black and gold trim.
- 101 through 125 (25 books)
  Cover: Blue and black with orange bands.
  The same as previous *CA* original volumes but with a new, simplified numbering system and new cover design.

CA New Revision Series
- *CANR*-1 through *CANR*-25 (25 books)
  Cover: Blue and black with green bands.
  Includes only sketches requiring extensive change; **sketches are taken from any previously published *CA* volume.**

CA Permanent Series
- *CAP*-1 and *CAP*-2 (2 books)
  Cover: Brown with red and gold trim.
  There will be no further *Permanent Series* volumes be-

cause revised entries are now being handled exclusively through the more efficient *New Revision Series* mentioned above.

CA Autobiography Series

- *CAAS*-1 through *CAAS*-8 (8 books)
  Cover: Blue and black with pink and purple bands.
  Presents specially commissioned autobiographies by leading contemporary writers.

CA Bibliographical Series

- *CABS*-1 and *CABS*-2 (2 books)
  Cover: Blue and black with blue bands.
  Provides comprehensive bibliographical information on published works by and about major modern authors.

Retaining *CA* Volumes

As new volumes in the series are published, users often ask which *CA* volumes, if any, can be discarded. The Volume Update Chart on page xiii is designed to assist users in keeping their collections as complete as possible. All volumes in the left column of the chart should be retained to have the most complete, up-to-date coverage; volumes in the right column can be discarded if the appropriate replacements are held.

Cumulative Index Should Always Be Consulted

The key to locating an individual author's listing is the *CA* cumulative index bound into the back of alternate original volumes (and available separately as an offprint). Since the *CA* cumulative index provides access to *all* entries in the *CA* series, the latest cumulative index should always be consulted to find the specific volume containing an author's original or most recently revised sketch.

For the convenience of *CA* users, the *CA* cumulative index also includes references to all entries in these related Gale literary series: *Authors in the News, Children's Literature Review, Concise Dictionary of American Literary Biography, Contemporary Literary Criticism, Dictionary of Literary Biography, Short Story Criticism, Something About the Author, Something About the Author Autobiography Series, Twentieth-Century Literary Criticism,* and *Yesterday's Authors of Books for Children.*

Acknowledgments

The editors wish to thank Judith S. Baughman for her assistance with copy editing.

Suggestions Are Welcome

The editors welcome comments and suggestions from users on any aspects of the *CA* series. If readers would like to suggest authors whose entries should appear in future volumes of the series, they are cordially invited to write: The Editors, *Contemporary Authors,* Gale Research Inc., Book Tower, Detroit, MI 48226-1822; or call toll-free at 1-800-521-0707.

Volume Update Chart

IF YOU HAVE:	YOU MAY DISCARD:
1-4 First Revision (1967)	1 (1962) 2 (1963) 3 (1963) 4 (1963)
5-8 First Revision (1969)	5-6 (1963) 7-8 (1963)
Both 9-12 First Revision (1974) AND *Contemporary Authors Permanent Series,* Volume 1 (1975)	9-10 (1964) 11-12 (1965)
Both 13-16 First Revision (1975) AND *Contemporary Authors Permanent Series,* Volumes 1 and 2 (1975, 1978)	13-14 (1965) 15-16 (1966)
Both 17-20 First Revision (1976) AND *Contemporary Authors Permanent Series,* Volumes 1 and 2 (1975, 1978)	17-18 (1967) 19-20 (1968)
Both 21-24 First Revision (1977) AND *Contemporary Authors Permanent Series,* Volumes 1 and 2 (1975, 1978)	21-22 (1969) 23-24 (1970)
Both 25-28 First Revision (1977) AND *Contemporary Authors Permanent Series,* Volume 2 (1978)	25-28 (1971)
Both 29-32 First Revision (1978) AND *Contemporary Authors Permanent Series,* Volume 2 (1978)	29-32 (1972)
Both 33-36 First Revision (1978) AND *Contemporary Authors Permanent Series,* Volume 2 (1978)	33-36 (1973)
37-40 First Revision (1979)	37-40 (1973)
41-44 First Revision (1979)	41-44 (1974)
45-48 (1974) 49-52 (1975) ↓ ↓ 125 (1989)	NONE: These volumes will not be superseded by corresponding revised volumes. Individual entries from these and all other volumes appearing in the left column of this chart will be revised and included in the *New Revision Series.*
Volumes in the *Contemporary Authors New Revision Series*	NONE: The *New Revision Series* does not replace any single volume of *CA*. All volumes appearing in the left column of this chart must be retained to have information on all authors in the series.

Contemporary Authors

ABBEY, Lloyd (Robert) 1943-

PERSONAL: Born April 4, 1943, in London, Ontario, Canada; married, 1976. *Education:* McMaster University, B.A., 1966; University of Western Ontario, M.A., 1968; University of Toronto, Ph.D., 1971.

ADDRESSES: Office—Victoria College, University of Toronto, Toronto, Ontario, Canada M5S 1K7.

CAREER: McMaster University, Hamilton, Ontario, assistant professor of English, 1971-72; University of British Columbia, Vancouver, assistant professor of English, 1972-77; University of Toronto, Toronto, Ontario, assistant professor of English, 1977—.

MEMBER: Modern Language Association of America.

WRITINGS:

Flies (poems), Oberon Press, 1973.
Braindances (poems), Oberon Press, 1979.
Destroyer and Preserver: Shelley's Poetic Skepticism, University of Nebraska Press, 1979.
The Antlered Boy (poems), Oberon Press, 1984.

Contributor to journals, including *English Studies in Canada, Mosaic,* and *Keats-Shelley Journal.**

*　　　*　　　*

ABRAHAM, Gerald Ernest Heal 1904-1988

OBITUARY NOTICE—See index for *CA* sketch: Born March 9, 1904, in Newport, Isle of Wight, England; died March 18, 1988. British educator, radio programmer, composer, editor, critic, and author. Abraham, a noted authority on Russian classical music, published his first book, *Borodin: The Composer and His Music,* in 1927. In his long and varied career he edited periodicals, including *Radio Times* and *Listener,* and was associated with the British Broadcasting Corporation (BBC) in the 1940s and 1960s, eventually becoming assistant controller of music. Between his stints with the BBC he was professor of music at the University of Liverpool; he later taught at the University of California, Berkeley. Abraham composed reconstructions for missing or unfinished pieces of classical music such as Richard Wagner's *Siegfried Idyll* and Franz Schubert's "Unfinished Symphony," edited books on classical music, and penned books on philosophers and Russian novelists in addition to those he wrote in his field of specialization. His writings include *This Modern Stuff: A Fairly "Plaine and Easie" Introduction to Contemporary Music, Masters of Russian Music, Chopin's Musical Style, Rimsky-Korsakov: A Short Biography,* and *Slavonic and Romantic Music: Essays and Studies.* In 1979 he published the *Concise Oxford History of Music.*

OBITUARIES AND OTHER SOURCES:

BOOKS

International Who's Who in Music and Musicians' Directory, 9th edition, Melrose, 1980.
Who's Who, 140th edition, St. Martin's, 1988.
The Writers Directory: 1988-1990, St. James Press, 1988.

PERIODICALS

Times (London), March 18, 1988.

*　　　*　　　*

ACKER, Alison 1928-

PERSONAL: Born October 8, 1928, in London, England; daughter of William (an insurance agent) and Ruth (a music teacher; maiden name, Sterland) Sutherland; married Philip Hunt, September 1, 1955 (died, 1964); married Harold Acker (a sculptor), August 12, 1969 (deceased); children: (second marriage) John. *Education:* University of London, B.A. (with honors), 1952; University of Toronto, M.A., 1968. *Politics:* Socialist. *Religion:* None.

ADDRESSES: Home—38 Howland Ave., Toronto, Ontario, Canada M5R 3B3. *Office*—c/o Ryerson Polytechnic Institute, 350 Victoria St., Toronto, Ontario, Canada.

CAREER: Journalist in London, England, Winnipeg, Manitoba, Vancouver, British Columbia, and Toronto, Ontario, 1950-65; professor at Ryerson Polytechnic Institute, Toronto, 1969—.

MEMBER: Association of Canadian University Teachers of English, Centre for Investigative Journalism.

WRITINGS:

Children of the Volcano, Lawrence Hill, 1986.

Also author of *A History of Honduras,* in press. Contributor to periodicals.

SIDELIGHTS: Alison Acker's *Children of the Volcano* records the author's travels through Central America in 1984. Acker visited Guatemala, El Salvador, Honduras, and Nicaragua. She wrote profiles of the people she met, both the old and young, soldiers as well as civilians, and the prosperous as well as the poor. Ronald Wright commented in the *Globe and Mail* that it was a "relief to read a book that brings us face to face with the people themselves. . . . Her own voice is calm, and her selections balanced. She avoids sentimentality and political moralizing." *Children of the Volcano* reveals the effects of politics and war upon all the people of Central America. The author emphasizes, however, the endurance of the people and their potential for survival. She sees reason for optimism, even in ravaged Nicaragua. Wright concluded: "This is a most commendable book; it is impressionistic yet accurate, provocative yet balanced, simple but not oversimplified, horrifying and uplifting."

Acker told *CA:* "I write mainly on Latin America because of an affinity to and respect for the Latin American people. I believe in committed writing as a force for change."

BIOGRAPHICAL/CRITICAL SOURCES:

PERIODICALS

Globe and Mail [Toronto], January 17, 1987.

*   *   *

ADAMS, Christopher
See HOPKINS, (Hector) Kenneth

*   *   *

ADAMS, Leonie (Fuller)   1899-1988

OBITUARY NOTICE—See index for *CA* sketch: Born December 9, 1899, in Brooklyn, N.Y.; died of heart disease, June 27, 1988, in New Milford, Conn. Educator, consultant, editor, and poet. Adams was best known for her lyric poetry reminiscent of both the romantic and metaphysical periods, which won her several awards, including the Harriet Monroe Poetry Award, the Shelley Memorial Award, and the Bollingen Prize. She served in editorial capacities for both Wilson Publishing and the Metropolitan Museum of Art in New York City during the 1920s and later taught English or lectured at various colleges and universities, such as Sarah Lawrence College, Bennington College, and Columbia University. From 1948 to 1949 Adams worked as a poetry consultant for the U.S. Library of Congress. Her writings include *Those Not Elect, High Falcon and Other Poems, This Measure,* and *Poems: A Selection.*

OBITUARIES AND OTHER SOURCES:

BOOKS

American Women Writers: A Critical Reference Guide From Colonial Times to the Present, Volume I, Ungar, 1979.
Contemporary Poets, 3rd edition, St. Martin's, 1980.
Dictionary of Literary Biography, Volume 48: *American Poets, 1880-1945, Second Series,* Gale, 1986.
The International Who's Who, 51st edition, Europa, 1987.

PERIODICALS

New York Times, June 30, 1988.

ADAMS, Phoebe-Lou   1918-

PERSONAL: Born December 18, 1918, in Hartford, Conn.; daughter of Harold Irving and Alice Maria (Burlingame) Adams; married Edward Augustus Weeks (an editor), 1971. *Education:* Radcliffe College, A.B. (cum laude), 1939.

ADDRESSES: Office—*Atlantic Monthly,* 8 Arlington St., Boston, Mass. 12116.

CAREER: Hartford Courant, Hartford, Conn., reporter, 1942-45; *Atlantic Monthly,* Boston, Mass., member of editorial staff and staff writer, 1945—.

WRITINGS:

A Rough Map of Greece, Little, Brown, 1965.

Contributor of articles and reviews to magazines.

WORK IN PROGRESS: Book reviews.

BIOGRAPHICAL/CRITICAL SOURCES:

PERIODICALS

New York Times Book Review, May 9, 1965.

*   *   *

AFTON, Effie
See HARPER, Frances Ellen Watkins

*   *   *

Al-AMIN, Jamil Abdullah   1943-
(H. Rap Brown)

PERSONAL: Name originally Hubert Gerold Brown; became known as H. Rap Brown; assumed present name during 1970s; born October 4, 1943, in Baton Rouge, La.; son of a worker for an oil company; married Lynne Doswell (a schoolteacher), May 3, 1968. *Education:* Attended Southern University, 1960-64.

CAREER: U.S. Department of Agriculture, Washington, D.C., librarian, 1964-65; Nonviolent Action Group, Washington, D.C., chairman, beginning in 1964; neighborhood worker in government poverty program in Washington, D.C., beginning in 1965; Student Nonviolent Coordinating Committee (SNCC; renamed Student National Coordinating Committee, 1969), organizer in Greene County, Ala., beginning in 1966, Alabama state project director, beginning in 1966, chairman, beginning in 1967; imprisoned for robbery in state of New York, 1971-76; operator of a small grocery in Atlanta, Ga., c. 1976—.

WRITINGS:

(Under name H. Rap Brown) *Die Nigger Die!* (autobiography), Dial, 1969.

SIDELIGHTS: Jamil Abdullah Al-Amin was an outspoken young black leader who came to prominence in the late 1960s, when he was widely known as H. Rap Brown. In the aftermath of the struggle by Martin Luther King, Jr., to win black civil rights through nonviolent protest, some in Brown's generation believed that a more direct confrontation with white racism was necessary. Brown became known for his belief that black people should be prepared to use guns to assert their rights, and many charged that he was an advocate of violence. Brown countered that his views were necessitated by the virulence of racism. "I preach a response to violence," he wrote in his 1969 autobiography, *Die Nigger Die!*—"Meet violence with violence.'' If someone deprives you of your human rights, Brown contended, he is being violent. ''It's your responsibility to jump back'' at your oppressor, because ''if you don't, he knows that you're scared and that he can control you.'' The reactions to Brown varied widely. *Newsweek* magazine accused him of ''hate-mongering,'' for instance, while Kiarri Cheatwood in *Black World* called him ''a young man of deep sensibilities.''

In his autobiography Brown recounted some of the experiences that led him to such controversial views. During the early 1960s he studied sociology at Southern University, a black college in his hometown of Baton Rouge, Louisiana. He concluded, however, that the school's administration was unwilling to stand up to racial injustice. He worked briefly in a government antipoverty program in Washington, D.C., but sensed that blacks were being co-opted there. ''The poverty program,'' he wrote, ''was designed to take those people whom the government considered threatening to the structure and buy them off. It didn't address itself to the causes of poverty but to the effects of poverty.''

Brown increasingly looked outside of traditional American institutions to change society. While chairman of the Washington, D.C., Nonviolent Action Group in 1965, he joined several black leaders at a meeting with U.S. President Lyndon Johnson. He gained notoriety for berating the strong-willed president. ''I'm not happy to be here,'' he remembered telling Johnson, ''and I think it's unnecessary that we have to be here protesting against the brutality that Black people are subjected to.'' The next year Brown went to Greene County, Alabama, as an organizer for the Student Nonviolent Coordinating Committee (SNCC), facing the hostility of white citizens and police as he encouraged local black people to exercise their rights to vote and to hold public office. He became the SNCC's Alabama project director a few months later and in 1967 was elected chairman of the entire organization.

Brown's post brought him national attention. He made repeated statements about the need for a violent confrontation with racism, becoming widely known for such remarks as ''violence is as American as cherry pie.'' He suggested that the riots sweeping America's poor black neighborhoods heralded a political insurrection, and riots broke out in the cities of Dayton, Ohio, East St. Louis, Illinois, and Cambridge, Maryland, shortly after he spoke there. Authorities in Maryland indicted Brown for inciting the Cambridge riot and engaging in arson, and for the next few years he was mired in a succession of highly publicized legal battles involving such charges as illegally possessing a gun and violating the terms of his bail. Supporters of Brown argued that he was being harassed for his political beliefs.

At the height of his fame Brown wrote *Die Nigger Die!*, and the book garnered mixed reactions, as had its author. John Leonard of the *New York Times* found the work unsatisfactory both as autobiography and as political commentary, charging that Brown was ''so busy proving his *machismo* that his material never comes into focus.'' But in the *New York Times Book Review*, Shane Stevens asserted that *Die Nigger Die!* expressed the author's ''essential humanism . . . , cloaked though it may be in fear and hate.'' Citing Brown's ability to combine his outrage with an irreverent sense of humor, Stevens wrote that ''the cutting edge of deep pain is there. But so is the raucous, sometimes slightly hysterical, laughter of life.'' Cheatwood stressed Brown's political analyses, lauding his ''depth,'' ''historically-shaped consciousness,'' and ''mature thought.'' As an example, Cheatwood observed that ''perhaps better than anyone before him,'' the author outlined ''the responsibilities of Black students to their people.''

In 1970 Brown went into hiding, delaying the start of his riot trial in Maryland. The Federal Bureau of Investigation (FBI) promptly placed him on its list of most-wanted criminals. The next year New York City police took him into custody near the scene of a barroom robbery. He remained imprisoned while he was tried and convicted of taking part in the holdup and was sentenced to further time in jail. When he pleaded guilty to eluding his Maryland trial, authorities in that state dropped their riot and arson charges.

During his incarceration Brown converted to Islam and adopted his current name. Paroled in 1976, he moved to Atlanta, Georgia, where he operates a small grocery. Though no longer in the national headlines, he has given occasional interviews to journalists. In 1985 he met with *Washington Post* columnist George F. Will, who found him ''enveloped in a strange serenity.'' Brown's life, Will suggested, was now centered on his Muslim faith, and the onetime political activist was working with neighbors on plans for a religious school. ''Many people reckon time from the '60s,'' Brown observed, because ''time stopped for them then.'' He added, ''I don't miss the '60s.''

BIOGRAPHICAL/CRITICAL SOURCES:

BOOKS

Brown, H. Rap, *Die Nigger Die!*, Dial, 1969.

PERIODICALS

Black World, October, 1975.
Chicago Tribune Book World, May 11, 1969.
New Republic, June 14, 1969.
Newsweek, August 7, 1967, June 3, 1968, February 12, 1973.
New York Times, August 13, 1967, April 30, 1969, November 7, 1973, September 25, 1976.
New York Times Book Review, June 15, 1969.
Saturday Review, May 3, 1969.
Village Voice, November 2, 1967.
Washington Post, June 15, 1978, September 19, 1985.*

—Sketch by Thomas Kozikowski

*   *   *

ALBRIGHT, Daniel 1945-

PERSONAL: Born October 29, 1945, in Chicago, Ill.; son of Frank J. (a negotiator) and Leone (a teacher; maiden name, Hinze) Albright; married Karin Larson (a teacher), June 19, 1977; children: Christopher. *Education:* Rice University, B.A., 1967; Yale University, M.Phil., 1969, Ph.D., 1970.

ADDRESSES: Office—Department of English, University of Rochester, Rochester, N.Y. 14627.

CAREER: University of Virginia, Charlottesville, assistant professor, 1970-75, associate professor, 1975-81, professor of English, 1981-87; University of Rochester, Rochester, N.Y., professor of English, 1987—.

MEMBER: Modern Language Association of America.

WRITINGS:

The Myth Against Myth: Yeats's Imagination in Old Age, Oxford University Press, 1972.

Personality and Impersonality: Lawrence, Beckett, Maua, University of Chicago Press, 1978.

Representation and the Imagination: Beckett, Kafka, Nabokov, and Schoenberg, University of Chicago Press, 1981.

Lyricality in English Literature, University of Nebraska Press, 1985.

Tennyson: The Muses' Tug-of-War, University Press of Virginia, 1986.

Americanische Lyrik: Texte und Deutungen (title means "American Poetry: Texts and Interpretations"), Wissenschaftliche Buchgesellschaft, in press.

Contributor to literature journals.

WORK IN PROGRESS: A Companion to Comparative Literature; Stravinsky.

* * *

ALCOCK, John 1942-

PERSONAL: Born November 13, 1942, in Charlottesville, Va.; son of John Powell (a chemical engineer) and Mariana (a housewife; maiden name, Collins) Alcock; married Susanne Eleanor Coates (a housewife), October 26, 1968; children: John, Nicholas. *Education:* Amherst College, B.A., 1965; Harvard University, Ph.D., 1969. *Politics:* Democrat. *Religion:* Society of Friends (Quakers).

ADDRESSES: Home—705 East Loyola Dr., Tempe, Ariz. 85282. *Office*—Department of Zoology, Arizona State University, Tempe, Ariz. 85287-1501.

CAREER: Associated with University of Washington, Seattle, Wash., 1969-72; Arizona State University, Tempe, assistant professor, 1972-74, associate professor, 1974-80, professor of zoology, 1980—.

WRITINGS:

Animal Behavior: An Evolutionary Approach, Sinauer Associates, 1975.

The Evolution of Insect Mating Systems, Harvard University Press, 1983.

Sonoran Desert Spring, University of Chicago Press, 1985.

The Kookaburra's Song, University of Arizona Press, in press.

* * *

ALDRIDGE, Alan 1943-

PERSONAL: Born in 1943 in Aylesbury, Buckinghamshire, England. *Education:* Attended Romford Technical College.

CAREER: Worked previous to 1963 in various positions, including insurance clerk and repertory actor; free-lance illustrator and graphic designer, 1963—. Designs and illustrations exhibited in museums and galleries, including Galerie Priebut, Amsterdam, Netherlands, 1967; Galerie Germain, Paris, France, 1969; Seibu Gallery, Tokyo, Japan, 1970; Galerie Bijenkorf, Amsterdam, 1971; Arthur Tooth & Sons, London, England, 1972; Institute of Contemporary Arts, London, 1973; and The Minories, Colchester, England, 1978.

AWARDS, HONORS: Whitbread Award from Booksellers Association of Great Britain and Ireland, 1973, for *The Butterfly Ball and the Grasshopper's Feast;* Children's Book of the Year Award, 1974; silver medals from Designers and Art Directors Association; Scotsman International Awards.

WRITINGS:

(Editor with George Perry) *The Penguin Book of Comics,* Penguin Books, 1967, revised edition, 1971.

(Editor and contributor of illustrations) *The Beatles Illustrated Lyrics,* illustrations by Julian Allen and others, Delacorte, 1969.

(Editor with Mike Dempsey) *Bernie Taupin: The One Who Writes the Words for Elton John; Complete Lyrics From 1968 Through to "Goodbye Yellow Brick Road,"* Knopf, 1976.

(Author with George E. Ryder; illustrator with Harry Willock) *The Peacock Party: A Sequel to the Butterfly Ball and the Grasshopper's Feast* (juvenile), Viking, 1979.

(And illustrator; with Ted Walker) *The Lion's Cavalcade* (juvenile), J. Cape, 1980.

(And illustrator; with Willock) *Phantasia of Dockland, Rockland, and Dodos* (juvenile), J. Cape, 1981, Ballantine, 1982.

ILLUSTRATOR

William Plomer and Richard Fitter, *The Butterfly Ball and the Grasshopper's Feast* (juvenile), J. Cape, 1973, Grossman, 1975.

(With Willock) Richard Adams, *The Adventures and Brave Deeds of the Ship's Cat on the Spanish Maine: Together With the Most Lamentable Losse of the Alcestis and Triumphant Firing of the Port of Chagres* (juvenile), Random House, 1977.

Also designer of album covers for recording artists such as the Beatles, the Rolling Stones, and Elton John. Contributor of illustrations to periodicals, including *Esquire, Melody Maker,* and *Daily Telegraph Magazine.*

BIOGRAPHICAL/CRITICAL SOURCES:

PERIODICALS

Listener, December 21, 1967.
New Republic, November 8, 1969.
Times Literary Supplement, December 21, 1967.*

* * *

ALLEN, Daniel 1947-

PERSONAL: Born December 13, 1947, in Brooklyn, N.Y. *Education:* Massachusetts Institute of Technology, B.S., 1969; University of Toronto, M.L.S., 1972.

ADDRESSES: Box 929, Adelaide Station, Toronto, Ontario, Canada M5C 2K3.

CAREER: Business manager of Coda Publications, 1973—. Owner of Walter C. Allen of Canada, 1975—.

MEMBER: International Society for Jazz Research.

WRITINGS:

Bibliography of Discographies, Volume II: *Jazz,* Bowker, 1981.

Contributor to library journals.*

* * *

ALLEN, Martha Mitten 1937-

PERSONAL: Born June 12, 1937, in Youngstown, Ohio; daughter of Joe A. (a school principal) and Helen (a teacher; maiden name, Boyd) Mitten; children: Shannon, Matthew. *Ed-*

ucation: Southern Methodist University, B.A. (summa cum laude), 1958, M.A., 1960; University of Texas at Austin, Ph.D., 1972.

ADDRESSES: Office—Department of History, Southwestern University, Box 6008, Georgetown, Tex. 78626.

CAREER: Southwestern University, Georgetown, Tex., assistant professor, 1960-74, associate professor, 1974-82, professor of history, 1982—, dean of women, 1960-67. Executive director of Handcrafts Unlimited, 1983-87; president of Georgetown Heritage Society, 1987-88.

MEMBER: American Studies Association, National Trust for Historic Preservation, Western History Association, Sierra Club, Phi Beta Kappa.

WRITINGS:

(Editor) *Georgetown's Yesteryears,* four volumes, Georgetown Heritage Society, 1985-87.
Traveling West: Nineteenth-Century Women on the Overland Routes, Texas Western Press, 1986.

SIDELIGHTS: Martha Mitten Allen told *CA:* "I began researching western women travelers in 1968, before the great outpouring of women's history really began. I read more than two hundred published travel accounts by women, most of which were out of print. I later supplemented these with manuscript diaries and journals. My focus was on what women thought of the West, not what it was like to travel. It took fifteen years to get the study published because the concept was not what publishers were ready to accept.

"*Georgetown's Yesteryears* is a four-volume series of local history, which grew out of an oral history project for the Texas Sesquicentennial. My other interests are quilting and helping the elderly to market their handmade items. I organize a quilt show every year in our town, and I serve as a volunteer executive director of Handcrafts Unlimited. This is an all-volunteer, nonprofit shop that markets the arts and crafts of our senior citizens."

*   *   *

ALLEN, Robert Day   1927-1986

OBITUARY NOTICE—See index for *CA* sketch: Born August 28, 1927, in Providence, R.I.; died of pancreatic cancer, March 23, 1986. Biologist, educator, editor, and author. Allen is best remembered as a pioneering biologist in areas of research that include cell motility and video-enhanced contrast microscopy. He began his teaching career in 1954 as an instructor at the University of Michigan before moving, in 1956, to Princeton University, where he was an associate professor. He subsequently became a full professor at the State University of New York at Albany, and in 1972 began teaching at Dartmouth College. With Noburu Kamiya, Allen edited *Primitive Motile Systems in Cell Biology,* and he wrote the 1977 book *The Science of Life.* He also served as the editor of periodicals such as *Microscopica Aeta* and *Journal of Mechanochemistry and Cell Motility.*

OBITUARIES AND OTHER SOURCES:

BOOKS

International Authors and Writers Who's Who, 10th edition, International Biographical Centre, 1986.
Who's Who in America, 43rd edition, Marquis, 1984.

PERIODICALS

Nature, June 12, 1986.

*   *   *

ALLENDE, Isabel   1942-

BRIEF ENTRY: Surname is pronounced "Ah-*yen*-day"; born in 1942 in Lima, Peru; immigrated to Venezuela, c. 1973. Chilean journalist, playwright, and novelist. Best known for her widely reviewed and highly praised international best-seller, *The House of Spirits* (Knopf, 1985), Allende also had a career as a journalist in Chile, working on the staff of a radical feminist magazine, reporting in film newsreels, and conducting television interviews. In addition, she wrote plays for children. In 1973 a military coup resulted in the death of her uncle, Chilean president Salvador Allende, and brought an end to his coalition government, forcing Isabel Allende to take refuge in Caracas, Venezuela, where she wrote a weekly column for the newspaper *El Nacional.* In Venezuela, Allende began work on *House of Spirits,* which features the magical realism technique made popular by Latin American author Gabriel Garcia Marquez and tells the story of three generations in an unnamed Latin American country shaken by a coup d'etat. Her second novel, *Of Love and Shadows* (Knopf, 1987), concerns two lovers who uncover scandals in a dictatorship. Allende's writings also include *Eva Luna* (Knopf, 1988).

BIOGRAPHICAL/CRITICAL SOURCES:

BOOKS

Contemporary Literary Criticism, Volume 39, Gale, 1986.
Current Biography, H. W. Wilson, 1988.

PERIODICALS

New York Review of Books, July 18, 1985.
New York Times Book Review, May 12, 1985, July 12, 1987.
People, June 10, 1985.
Publishers Weekly, May 17, 1985.
Times Literary Supplement, July 5, 1985, July 10, 1987.
Washington Post Book World, May 12, 1985, May 24, 1987.

*   *   *

ANDERS, Donna Carolyn   1938-
(Donna Carolyn Anders Crefeld)

PERSONAL: Born July 22, 1938, in Tacoma, Wash.; daughter of David Edward and Lorna (Ivarsen) Anderson; married Emil E. Crefeld, October 30, 1956 (divorced); children: Ruth Crefeld Aeschliman, Lisa, Tina. *Education:* Attended Fort Steilacoom Community College, 1970-72. *Politics:* Democrat. *Religion:* Protestant.

ADDRESSES: Home—Seattle, Wash. *Office*—10718 166th Court N.E., Redmond, Wash. 98052. *Agent*—Ruth Cohen Inc. Literary Agents, P.O. Box 7626, Menlo Park, Calif. 94025.

CAREER: General Contracting Co., Tacoma, Wash., co-owner, 1965-70; Writer's Digest School, Seattle, Wash., instructor, 1972—. Pacific Northwest Writer's Conference, vice-president, 1975, member of board of directors, 1975-80.

MEMBER: Romance Writers of America, Seattle Freelances.

WRITINGS:

(Under name Donna Carolyn Anders Crefeld) *From This Land* (historical novel), Pinnacle Books, 1980.

North to Destiny (historical novel), Bantam, 1986.

Also author of two historical novels, for Harlequin, in press. Author of two coloring books, *Visiting Washington State* and *Wicked Wacky Wilda Witch,* published by Coffee Break Press, 1985.

Contributor of more than three hundred stories, articles, poems, and plays to national magazines, under name Donna Carolyn Anders Crefeld.

WORK IN PROGRESS: Sun of the Morning, a historical novel.

AVOCATIONAL INTERESTS: Painting, bicycling, swimming, theatre.

*   *   *

ANDERSON, C. Farley
  See MENCKEN, H(enry) L(ouis)
  and NATHAN, George Jean

*   *   *

ANDERSON, Lindsay (Gordon)   1923-

BRIEF ENTRY: Born April 17, 1923, in Bangalore, India; British citizen born abroad. British stage, television, and film director and actor, editor, film critic, and author. Best known for his portrayals of the English common people, Anderson has directed stage plays including "Billy Liar," "The Diary of a Madman," "Julius Caesar," "The Cherry Orchard," "In Celebration," and "The Bed Before Yesterday"; the British television series "Robin Hood"; and films such as "Thursday's Children," "Pleasure Garden," "Wakefield Express," the satirical "O Lucky Man!" and "Britannia Hospital," and the 1987 "The Whales of August." He has also acted on stage and in film and television, and during his early career served as an editor of the antiestablishment film periodical *Sequence.* In addition, Anderson has critiqued the art of filmmaking for magazines, including *Sight and Sound.* His writings include *Making a Film: The Story of "Secret People"* (Allen & Unwin, 1952; Garland Publishing, 1977) and the portrait of a fellow screen director, *About John Ford* (Plexus, 1981; McGraw-Hill, 1983). *Addresses: Home*—9 Stirling Mansions, Canfield Gardens, London NW6, England. *Office*— LGA Services Ltd., c/o M. L. White, 1st Floor, Linton House, 39 Highgate Rd., London NW5, England.

BIOGRAPHICAL/CRITICAL SOURCES:

BOOKS

Contemporary Literary Criticism, Volume 20, Gale, 1982.
Contemporary Theatre, Film, and Television, Volume 2, Gale, 1986.
Current Biography, H. W. Wilson, 1975.
Who's Who, 140th edition, St. Martin's, 1988.
Who's Who in the World, 8th edition, Marquis, 1986.

PERIODICALS

New York Times, March 6, 1983.
Times (London), January 10, 1987.
Times Literary Supplement, June 11, 1982.

*   *   *

ANDREWS, Lynn V.

BRIEF ENTRY: American spiritual counselor and author. An-

drews published her first book, *Medicine Woman* (Harper & Row), in 1981. The work details the author's spiritual quest for identity with a Canadian Cree Indian shaman woman named Agnes Whistling Elk and emphasizes feminist principles. Since becoming associated with Whistling Elk, Andrews has seen many clients as a spiritual counselor in Beverly Hills, California, and has written several additional books that deal with shaman women around the world. Her writings in this vein also include *Flight of the Seventh Moon: The Teaching of the Shields* (Harper, 1984), *Jaguar Woman and the Wisdom of the Butterfly Tree* (Harper, 1985), *Star Woman: We Are Made From Stars and to the Stars We Must Return* (Warner Books, 1986), and *Crystal Woman: The Sisters of the Dreamtime* (Warner Books, 1987).

BIOGRAPHICAL/CRITICAL SOURCES:

PERIODICALS

Los Angeles Times, February 20, 1985, October 4, 1985, November 23, 1987.

*   *   *

ANON, Charles Robert
  See PESSOA, Fernando (Antonio Nogueira)

*   *   *

ANSON, Robert Sam   1945-

PERSONAL: Born March 12, 1945, in Cleveland, Ohio; son of Sam B. and Virginia Anson; married Amanda Kay Kyser (an artist), August 17, 1986; children: Christian Kennedy, Sam Gideon, Georgia Kay. *Education:* University of Notre Dame, B.A. (cum laude), 1967. *Religion:* Catholic.

ADDRESSES: Home and office—P.O. Box 2009, Sag Harbor, N.Y. 11963. *Agent*—Peter Shepherd, Harold Ober Associates, 40 East 49th Street, New York, N.Y. 10017.

CAREER: Writer. *Time,* New York City, correspondent in Chicago, Los Angeles, New York City, and Indochina, 1966-72; WNET-TV, New York City, producer and anchorman, 1972-78; *New Times,* New York City, senior writer, 1975-78; *Esquire,* New York City, contributing editor, 1978-81; *Manhattan, Inc.,* New York City, contributing editor, 1985-87.

WRITINGS:

McGovern, Holt, 1972.
"They've Killed the President!": The Search for the Murderers of John F. Kennedy, Bantam, 1975.
Gone Crazy and Back Again: The Rise and Fall of the Rolling Stone Generation, Doubleday, 1981.
Exile: The Unquiet Oblivion of Richard M. Nixon, Simon & Schuster, 1984.
Best Intentions: The Education and Killing of Edmund Perry, Random House, 1987.

Contributor to periodicals, including *Esquire* and *Life.*

WORK IN PROGRESS: A memoir of the Vietnam War.

SIDELIGHTS: Robert Sam Anson is a prominent figure in American journalism. He entered the field as a correspondent for *Time* while he was still a student at the University of Notre Dame in the mid-1960s, and upon graduation he worked for the magazine's *Chicago* and *Los Angeles* bureaus. Anson eventually covered the Vietnam War, and in 1970 he was captured by the North Vietnamese soldiers fighting with Cambodia's Communist forces, the Khmer Rouge. He initially feared for his life, particularly since other American journalists had already been killed by the Communists. But Anson succeeded in befriending his captors, and after three weeks he was freed in a ceremony led by ranking Cambodian and Vietnamese officers. Prior to the ceremony he supplied comments on his captivity to North Vietnamese radio for later broadcast—the comments, however, were never used. Once released, Anson was also interviewed by the Western press, to whom he conveyed his impressions of his captors as dedicated and compassionate. "They treated me like a brother," he declared in announcing that he would no longer cover the war. "I have friends on both sides now. I don't want to see my friends dead."

In 1972 Anson left *Time* and began working as an anchorman and producer for WNET-TV, New York City's public television station. That same year he published *McGovern,* a biography of the Democratic party's presidential candidate, U.S. Senator George S. McGovern. Anson's book appeared prior to the 1972 election—which McGovern lost, overwhelmingly, to incumbent Richard M. Nixon—and was commended as a reasoned, unflinching account of McGovern's career. A critic for the *Times Literary Supplement* reported that *McGovern* afforded readers a frank appraisal of the senator's career, and L. W. Koenig, writing in the *Saturday Review,* praised Anson's book as a "shrewd and informing study."

While working at WNET-TV Anson also began writing for the investigative magazine *New Times.* He became one of the periodical's leading political writers, and in his years with the magazine—from 1975 to 1978, when it ceased publication— he produced incisive pieces on prominent political figures such as Hubert H. Humphrey, Ronald Reagan, and Jimmy Carter. His best-known articles, however, are probably those exploring the 1963 assassination of President John F. Kennedy. As author of an article entitled "The Greatest Cover-up of All," Anson cited flagrant distortions in the official investigation, which concluded that Lee Harvey Oswald was the sole assassin of the president, and he presented evidence that Kennedy was the victim of a conspiracy most probably involving right-wing Cubans and members of organized crime. Anson's piece gained notoriety for its accompanying cover illustration featuring a shaken Kennedy with blood spraying from a head wound, but the article was nonetheless important for delineating various aspects of the assassination, including Oswald's ties to right-wing extremists and to both Soviet and American espionage organizations.

In 1975, the same year of the *New Times* report, Anson presented a more detailed investigation of the Kennedy assassination and its related controversies in *"They've Killed the President!": The Search for the Murderers of John F. Kennedy.* The book, like the aforementioned article, explores the possibility that Kennedy's death resulted from conspiracy and presents evidence that at least one individual—and possibly more—posed as Oswald. In addition, Anson argues that a 1966 investigation conducted by Jim Garrison, who was then district attorney of New Orleans, had the effect of besmirching the integrity of sincere conspiracy theorists.

In a field rife with preposterous speculation and misinformation, Anson's *"They've Killed the President!"* is among the more plausible and keenly researched reports. D. C. Anderson, writing in the *New York Times Book Review,* called Anson's book "a powerful piece of journalistic scholarship" and praised Anson's "exhaustive documentation." In addition,

Anderson commended Anson's "thoroughness" and cited his "capacity for backbreaking research."

By 1978 *New Times* had ceased publication and Anson had resigned his position at WNET-TV. His next important work as a writer was *Gone Crazy and Back Again: The Rise and Fall of the Rolling Stone Generation,* an entertaining analysis of the 1960s counterculture as it was reflected in the development of *Rolling Stone* magazine. The book was dismissed as trivial by some reviewers and considered highly readable, if not particularly profound, by others.

Anson followed *Gone Crazy and Back Again* with the more incisive *Exile: The Unquiet Oblivion of Richard M. Nixon,* which detailed Nixon's life in the decade following his resignation from the American presidency. Anson was unable to secure Nixon's cooperation on *Exile* and thus relied heavily on research and interviews. Despite this seeming drawback, the book elicited positive responses from critics such as J. Anthony Lukas, who wrote in the *New York Times Book Review* that Anson's inclusion of voluminous notes constituted "a model of journalist attribution," and the *Los Angeles Times*'s reviewer, who called *Exile* a "fascinating account" and a "fast-paced, colorful, highly readable narrative."

Anson's most recent book is *Best Intentions: The Education and Killing of Edmund Perry,* in which he explores the circumstances behind the 1985 death of a Harlem youth killed while attempting to rob a plainclothes policeman. The seeming contradiction of Perry's action—a criminal act perpetrated by an admired Exeter Academy student—led Harlem residents to accuse New York City's police of racist violence. But Anson traces Perry's life in Harlem and at the exclusive Exeter preparatory school and discovers that Perry was a confused, angry youth capable of both earning an academic scholarship and committing a violent crime. Anson reports that Perry was perceived in Harlem as a model citizen and an inspiration to others hoping to avoid a life of poverty and crime. But Anson also discloses that at Exeter the usually soft-spoken Perry portrayed himself as a streetwise militant who used and sold drugs. *Best Intentions* ultimately portrays Perry as a confused young man whose inability to sustain conflicting life-styles led to self-destruction. As one of his friends disclosed to Anson: "Eddie didn't get killed. He committed suicide." *Best Intentions* earned Anson further recognition as a keen reporter of provocative subjects. *Newsweek*'s David Gates found the book "engrossing," and a *People* reviewer described it as "profoundly moving."

CA INTERVIEW

CA interviewed Robert Sam Anson by phone on December 2, 1986, at his home in Sag Harbor, N.Y.

CA: When you were an undergraduate at Notre Dame you started a student newspaper. What was it like?

ANSON: It was an irresponsible left-wing rag, but it's still there twenty years later.

CA: What's its name?

ANSON: The Observer.

CA: How did you become a reporter for Time *while still an undergraduate?*

ANSON: I was a campus stringer for *Time* at Notre Dame. I also worked for the magazine during the summer of my junior year, and whenever I had a few days to spare while in college, I would just go down to Chicago and work for the *Time* bureau there. Also, I come from a journalistic family.

CA: Who were the other journalists in your family?

ANSON: My grandfather, Sam Anson, who later adopted me, was publisher of the Columbus (Ohio) *Monitor* and was city editor of all three Cleveland newspapers at one time or another. And my mother was a teacher who wrote free-lance magazine articles.

CA: You were captured by the North Vietnamese Army and the Khmer Rouge while working for Time *in Cambodia. You described the whole experience in a* Time *article, but briefly, how were you captured?*

ANSON: I was driving somewhere I shouldn't have been, they fired a burst over the car, and I stopped. I was held less than one month.

CA: Did being captured change your opinion of the North Vietnamese?

ANSON: No.

CA: What was your opinion of the United States' excursion into Cambodia and the opponents it fought there?

ANSON: I thought we had no business being there, and I was not unhappy when the other side won the war. They've made quite a mess of the country since then, however.

CA: Why did you then leave Time? *Were you unhappy there?*

ANSON: They treated me well, and I was moderately happy there, but I wanted to go off and write a book. I took a leave to write a book, and I wrote the book and then came back. Then [former Congressman] Al Lowenstein asked me to write a book with him on American politics. At that point I thought it was time to leave *Time.*

CA: Did you write the book with Lowenstein?

ANSON: It never got written. It was a series of conversations on the way to the airport with him.

CA: So after you left Time *you free-lanced and then became a senior writer for* New Times, *which was far to the left of* Time *politically. Did the move indicate that you were also moving to the political left?*

ANSON: In some respects I think I've moved progressively right since I was eighteen. And *Time,* believe it or not, accommodated divergent views. They just didn't print any. But I thought it was a terrific place to work.

CA: You also worked at public station WNET-TV. What sort of shows did you produce there?

ANSON: I produced a lot of documentaries at WNET-TV, and then I was an anchorman there for a long time on the station's weekly show about city politics.

CA: Why did you leave the station?

ANSON: Although it was certainly the easiest job I ever had, I think public television is an astonishing waste of the taxpayer's money. Management at the time was fantastically incompetent. It was most unpleasant working there, and it was very hard to get straight answers from a lot of people. I know many talented producers and reporters at WNET-TV, but, given the overall product, I'm astounded that people still contribute money to the station.

CA: How does public television compare to commercial television?

ANSON: I think commercial television does much better news reporting. When you get to the point where ABC-TV is producing tougher documentaries than public television, it's time to get out. There was a time when I thought public television did wonderful shows—such as "The Great American Dream Machine" and "The Fifty-First State," a program that I worked on. While that was a really terrific program, it was terrific largely because of the executive producer—the very talented guy who ran it. He left, and the show, for a variety of reasons, became a lot less freewheeling and a lot more corporate.

The station's managers were also sensitive to political pressures from the state and also didn't want to offend the federal government, which provided the money. For example, we had done a series of person-to-person conversations with such individuals as New York's gubernatorial candidates Hugh Carey and Howard Samuels. Both these interviews took place in the subjects' homes. But there was an appropriation for WNET-TV of about $150,000, and it was pending in the New York State Assembly, so I was dispatched to do an interview with Stanley Steingut, who was speaker of the assembly at the time. There was no good news-related reason to do that at all, and management told me certain questions they did not want me to ask. I asked the questions nonetheless. The show ran, though, and I think the station got the money.

CA: Did you think your biography McGovern *favorably biased towards McGovern, or did you think it a balanced assessment?*

ANSON: It was a campaign biography. That is, it was commissioned as a campaign biography, but I was told that I could write whatever I wanted and that McGovern would give me complete access to his files and people. And I thought it was in some respects very tough on him. I've read a lot of campaign biographies and mine was one of the toughest I ever read. McGovern was not happy about all of it, but he let it go out. He was that kind of guy.

CA: You then wrote about President Kennedy's assassination. What gave you the idea to write on that subject?

ANSON: I saw Abraham Zapruder's film of the assassination when the film first came out, and it changed my view of the Warren Commission's official report. But the Kennedy assassination is an unbelievably dark hole for a reporter. I promised myself to limit my involvement in that investigation. Some people are a little bit whacky because they've been working on it too long.

CA: Your book theorized that President Kennedy was most probably a victim of a conspiracy that included anti-Castro Cubans and the Mafia, and that Oswald—whether he fired at the president or not—had ties to U.S. intelligence.

ANSON: Well, it didn't come right out and say so, but I indicated that organized crime was the leading suspect. It's always been known that these folks were mixed up with all the principals, but how the anti-Castro Cubans and intelligence people linked up with the Mafia was never clear until it was found out about Sam Giancana and company.

CA; What was the Giancana link?

ANSON: Among other things, Giancana and Johnny Roselli accepted a contract from the CIA to kill [Cuban leader] Fidel Castro.

CA: Has anything come up since your book was published that would make you doubt your theory about the assassination?

ANSON: No. That theory got quite popular. Bob Blakey, a former U.S. attorney who taught at Cornell and Notre Dame, became chief counsel for the House Assassination Investigation, and he wrote a book along the same lines. A couple of other books have come out that also espouse that theory. I don't think it will ever be proven though.

CA: After writing about President Kennedy's assassination you wrote about the 1960s counterculture and Rolling Stone *magazine.*

ANSON: I didn't think much of that book [*Gone Crazy and Back Again*]. The problem was that it was schizophrenic: half about the 1960s and half about [*Rolling Stone* editor] Jann Wenner. I was trying to use Wenner and *Rolling Stone* as a metaphor for the 1960s—as a way of looking at the 1960s—but I wasn't happy with the way it came out. It only sold about ten thousand hardcover copies and never came out in paperback.

CA: What about the idea of Wenner personifying the 1960s?

ANSON: I don't think there was a problem with the idea. I just should have gone on at greater depth. It turned into *The Sixties' Greatest Hits.* I think it had a definite point of view, and the point of view was that you can base a revolution on culture. But I was distressed then, and am increasingly so now, by.... How does that Jackson Browne song go? "We started out so young and strong, only to surrender." *Rolling Stone* really embodies that. It's not only a metaphor for the 1960s, it's one for the 1980s.

CA: How about as a metaphor for the human condition?

ANSON: I suppose that happens to everybody, but I'd prefer not to think about it.

CA: The Los Angeles Times *reviewer, writing about* Gone Crazy and Back Again, *said you were addicted to forty-line, thumbnail biographies of people mentioned in the book. Do you think that is a fair criticism?*

ANSON: I just finished a twenty-five-thousand-word article on someone. The reviewer you quote is Carolyn See, who's a highly intelligent reviewer, but I don't agree with her on that point, although I'd rather write too short than too long.

CA: Your book on Nixon, Exile, *earned largely favorable reviews. One of the few criticisms of it was that you relied more on anecdotes than on analysis of his recent pronouncements on world affairs. What do you think of that criticism?*

ANSON: I wasn't interested in analyzing Nixon's view of world affairs because I don't think it has changed substantially since he was president. I didn't set out to do that. I think sometimes reviewers get caught up in what they would have done had they written the book. The work I wrote was a chronicle of how Nixon managed to pull himself together and, more than survive, prevail. It was supposed to be the human story of the guy.

CA: Could you have called your book about Nixon Gone Crazy and Back Again?

ANSON: But Nixon wasn't crazy.

CA: He was accused of being paranoid.

ANSON: Well he's certainly wired differently than the rest of the population. I think he's just as fascinated by himself as we're fascinated by him.

CA: But does he know more about himself than we do?

ANSON: I think he knows an enormous amount about himself. He doesn't make one spontaneous move. He's a fascinating character, and if you forget about the Vietnam War and Watergate—which I can't—he was a great president. I would certainly trade him for any we've had since. His conduct as president was, in many respects, really very extraordinary. He started a lot of social programs. Then there's the opening to China, detente with the Soviet Union, the volunteer army, and the Environmental Protection Agency, which he started.

CA: You're working on a book about the Vietnam War, aren't you?

ANSON: I'm doing a memoir about Vietnam.

CA: A great number of books about Vietnam are being published these days.

ANSON: Most of the other Vietnam books are about how terrible it was, but I had a good time there. The dirty little secret is that a lot of people had a good time there. You really lived on your nerve endings and, although I've never picked up a gun in my life, there is a certain jolt in seeing someone step out of a hole and take a shot at you. It's a turn-on in a sick sort of way.

CA: You never fired a gun yourself?

ANSON: No. I think it's appalling, shooting people. But to be shot at is another thing entirely. The other books, and television, show Vietnam as ghastly, with everyone coming back with long hair and nightmares. But for a lot of people it was just a walk in the sun. A lot of people who were in Vietnam now have, in the French phrase, "nostalgie de la boue," a fondness for the war.

CA: Finally, which do you prefer writing, books or magazine articles?

ANSON: Actually, I don't prefer writing at all. I prefer reporting. To answer your question, though, magazine articles are a narcotic; they must be resisted. On the other hand, although it's satisfying when you finish a book, it's a pretty lonely business.

9

CA: Which of your books did you like best?

ANSON: Exile, the Nixon book, was the best written. *"They've Killed the President!"* was the most important and was done the quickest. But *Best Intentions* will get the most attention and will unsettle many people. It's about Eddie Perry, the honors graduate of Exeter who wanted to go to Stanford University. He was a black kid from Harlem who was shot to death while trying to mug a police officer in June, 1985. The whole book is pretty depressing. It will upset liberals, conservatives, and blacks. It's about what's going on today in places such as Harlem. It's about profound racism and anger in the black community and profound racism in the white community. It's a book about how a kid tries to negotiate his way in two radically different worlds and how he gets chewed up by both. No one comes out looking too good.

BIOGRAPHICAL/CRITICAL SOURCES:

PERIODICALS

Chicago Tribune Book World, August 26, 1984.
Los Angeles Times, February 26, 1981, July 1, 1984.
Newsweek, September 7, 1970, June 1, 1987.
New Times, April 18, 1975, March 19, 1976.
New York Times, February 10, 1981, June 28, 1984.
New York Times Book Review, June 4, 1972, January 4, 1976, July 1, 1984.
People, August 3, 1987.
Saturday Review, June 3, 1972.
Time, September 7, 1970, August 17, 1987.
Times Literary Supplement, June 30, 1972.
Washington Post, March 14, 1981.

—*Sketch by Les Stone*

—*Interview by Peter Benjaminson*

* * *

ARBUTHNOTT, Hugh (James) 1936-

PERSONAL: Born December 27, 1936 in Ceylon (now Sri Lanka); son of James Gordon and Margaret (Hyde) Arbuthnott; married Vanessa Rose Dyer, May 24, 1964; children: three sons. *Education:* New College, Oxford, M.A., 1960.

ADDRESSES: Office—Foreign and Commonwealth Office, London SW1A 2AH, England.

CAREER: Foreign and Commonwealth Office, London, England, 1960—, third secretary in Tehran, Iran, 1962-64, second and first secretary in London, 1964-66, private secretary to minister of state for foreign affairs, 1966-68, served in Lagos, Nigeria, 1968-71, first secretary and head of chancery in Tehran, 1971-74, assistant in European integration department (external), 1974-75, head of department, 1975-77, agricultural and economic counselor and head of chancery in Paris, France, 1978-83, under-secretary of Overseas Development Administration, 1983-86, ambassador to Romania, 1986—. *Military service:* British Army, Black Watch Regiment, 1955-57; became second lieutenant.

MEMBER: United Oxford and Cambridge University Club.

AWARDS, HONORS: Commander of Order of St. Michael and St. George.

WRITINGS:

(Editor with Geoffrey Edwards) *A Common Man's Guide to the Common Market,* Holmes & Meier, 1979.

WORK IN PROGRESS: Revising *A Common Man's Guide to the Common Market.*

* * *

ARCHER, Herbert Winslow
See MENCKEN, H(enry) L(ouis)

* * *

ARCHER, W(illiam) G(eorge) 1907-1979

OBITUARY NOTICE—See index for *CA* sketch: Born November 2 (some sources say February 11), 1907, in London, England; died March 6, 1979. Civil servant, museum curator, editor, and author. Archer was affiliated with the Indian Civil Service in Bihar from 1931 to 1948, holding such posts as district magistrate, deputy commissioner, and provincial census superintendent. In 1949 he became keeper of the Indian section of the London's Victoria and Albert Museum, and in 1959 was named keeper emeritus. Made a member of the Order of the British Empire in 1947, Archer also served as the editor of *Man in India* from 1942 to 1948. His writings include *The Blue Grove: The Poetry of the Uraons, Indian Paintings From Rajasthan, India and Modern Art, An Anthology of Sinhalese Literature,* the two-volume *Indian Paintings From the Punjab Hills,* and *The Hill of Flutes: Life, Love, and Poetry in Tribal India; A Portrait of the Santals.*

OBITUARIES AND OTHER SOURCES:

BOOKS

Who's Who in the World, 3rd edition, Marquis, 1976.
Who Was Who, Volume VII: *1971-1980,* A. & C. Black, 1981.

* * *

AREY, James A(rthur) 1936-1988

OBITUARY NOTICE—See index for *CA* sketch: Born September 23, 1936, in Brookline, Mass.; died of pancreatic cancer, April 23, 1988, in Scarsdale, N.Y. Public relations executive, editor, and author. Arey served as the assistant night editor for United Press International in Boston, Massachusetts, from 1961 until 1966, when he became director of corporate public relations for Pan American World Airways. He was a contributing editor of *Dictionary of American History,* and he wrote a book about airplane hijacking titled *The Sky Pirates.*

OBITUARIES AND OTHER SOURCES:

PERIODICALS

New York Times, April 28, 1988.

* * *

AREY, Leslie Brainerd 1891-1988

OBITUARY NOTICE: Born February 15, 1891, in Camden, Me.; died of a heart attack, March 23, 1988. Anatomist, educator, and author. A teacher at Northwestern University for seventy-two years, Arey held one of the longest tenures of any medical school professor. After receiving a Ph.D. from Harvard University in 1915, he began teaching at Northwestern, where he eventually became head of the anatomy department and was appointed the Robert Laughlin Rea Professor of Anatomy. Arey was named professor emeritus in 1956, and, although he formally retired the same year, he continued to teach histology and embryology on a voluntary basis until 1987. He wrote and co-authored various editions of textbooks, including *Developmental Anatomy: A Textbook and Laboratory Manual of Embryology, Human Histology: A Textbook in Outline Form, Special Cytology, Cytology and Cellular Pathology of the Nervous System,* and *Morris' Human Anatomy.*

OBITUARIES AND OTHER SOURCES:

BOOKS

Who's Who in America, 42nd edition, Marquis, 1982.
Who Was Who Among North American Authors, 1921-1939, Gale, 1976.

PERIODICALS

Chicago Tribune, March 26, 1988.

*   *   *

ARNOLD, Catharine   1959-

PERSONAL: Born August 25, 1959, in Wales; daughter of Robert St. Alban Gladwyn (an actor, musician, and lecturer in English) and Morfa (Rees) Arnold. *Education:* Cambridge University, B.A. (with honors), 1982, M.A., 1986.

ADDRESSES: Home—7 Harvard House, Rivermead, Wilford Lane, Nottingham, England. *Agent*—Amanda Little, Watson, Little Ltd., 26 Charing Cross Rd., Suite 8, London WC2H 0DG, England.

CAREER: Advertising writer, 1985—; Pork Farms, Nottingham, England, technical writer and secretary, 1986—; *Reader's Digest,* London, England, sub-editor of special books, 1987—; free-lance writer, 1987—.

MEMBER: Society of Authors, British Film Institute.

AWARDS, HONORS: Betty Trask Award from Society of Authors, 1987, for *Lost Time.*

WRITINGS:

Lost Time (novel), Hodder & Stoughton, 1986, Viking, 1987.
Changeling (novel), Hodder & Stoughton, 1987.
Hello Stranger (novel), Hodder & Stoughton, 1988.

SIDELIGHTS: "It is difficult to come up with a definitive statement about my artistic intentions," Catharine Arnold told *CA.* "If I knew why I wrote, I wouldn't have to sit down and turn out a novel once a year. There is also the anxiety that to inquire too deeply into my motivation would destroy the subconscious and the no doubt deeply sinister impulses which drive me to write in the first place.

"When I was growing up in a haphazard bohemian household in Nottingham, I had three ambitions: to be a novelist, a film director, or a rock musician. I opted for the novels, but music is still an extremely important factor in my life. I usually put in two to three hours a day practicing on the piano after a morning's writing, and have been studying electric guitar for the past six months. I'm one of the few writers who work while listening to loud music.

"Writing my latest novel involved listening to a variety of albums from the 1970s. *Hello Stranger* is a historical novel about the 1970s, reproducing the prevailing atmosphere of cocaine-induced euphoria and gin-soaked melancholy of that decade. It examines the friendship between two women, a writer

and a musician, who meet at art school, and traces their fortunes over the following fifteen years. I found that the music of Roger Waters of Pink Floyd produced the necessary atmosphere of lyrical cosmic despair which I needed to write the book.

"I am interested in the supernatural and the spiritual, as they give me a focus for the characters' sensations of loneliness and alienation. My protagonists are generally outsiders, who consider themselves to be both apart from and at the mercy of the rest of the world. I seem to write about love a great deal, and there is a dark streak of romance in my novels to date, though it is romance of a sinister variety. My major interest at the moment is in presenting the way that our lives are absurd, passionate, tender, and rather touching, and our relationships conducted above an icy abyss of panic and despair."

BIOGRAPHICAL/CRITICAL SOURCES:

PERIODICALS

London Portrait, September, 1986.
Sky, July 2, 1987.
Times (London), May 22, 1986.
Times Literary Supplement, December 25-31, 1987.

*   *   *

ASHE, Mary Ann
See LEWIS, Mary (Christianna)

*   *   *

AUBIGNY, Pierre d'
See MENCKEN, H(enry) L(ouis)

*   *   *

AXINN, Donald E(verett)   1929-

PERSONAL: Born July 13, 1929, in New York, N.Y.; son of Michael and Ann (Schneider) Axinn; married Joan Fingold; children: four. *Education:* Middlebury College, B.A., 1951; Hofstra University, M.A. (wtih distinction), 1975.

ADDRESSES: Home—Sands Point, N.Y. *Office*—Donald E. Axinn Companies, 131 Jericho Turnpike, Jericho, N.Y. 11753.

CAREER: Vice-president of Axinn & Sons Lumber Co., 1951-58; Donald E. Axinn Companies (developers of office and industrial parks), Jericho, N.Y., founder and chairman, 1958—. Creator of Axinn-Levine Associates, 1959-65; partner of stock investment firm, Alexander Associates, 1960—, and art investment firm, William Pall Associates, 1972-78; director and partner of publishing company, Farrar, Straus & Giroux, 1971—. Hofstra University, director of Institute of the Arts and associate dean of College of Liberal Arts, 1971-72, past vice-chairman of board of trustees. Chairman of Nassau County Fine Arts Commission, 1970-73; trustee of Waldemar Cancer Research Institute, 1966-68, Pro-Arte Symphony Orchestra, 1967-70, New York Ocean Sciences Laboratories, 1969-71, New York State Nature and Historical Preserve Trust, 1978-83, and Friends for Long Island's Heritage, 1980—; director of New York Quarterly Poetry Review Foundation, 1969-76. Member of advisory board of Outward Bound, Inc., 1974-78; member of Governor's Task Force on Cultural Life and Arts, 1975—; member of Interfaith Nutrition Network, 1983-85, and Long Island Regional Economic Development Council, 1985—. *Military service:* U.S. Army Reserve, Strategic Intelligence, 1951-58. Civil Air Patrol, 1953-59; became first lieutenant.

MEMBER: International P.E.N., Poetry Society of America (member of board of governors, 1987), Academy of American Poets, Poets and Writers (member of executive committee, 1980—), National Pilots Association, Aircraft Owners and Pilots Association, Middlebury College Alumni Association (vice-president, 1978), Delta Upsilon, Players Club, Long Island Early Fliers Club, Old Westbury Raquet Club.

AWARDS, HONORS: Awards for architectural design and community enhancement; Brotherhood Award from National Conference of Christians and Jews, 1977; honor award from Beta Gamma Sigma, 1978; Long Island Humanitarian Award

from American Jewish Committee, 1978; Tennessee Williams fellow at Bread Loaf Writer's Conference, 1979; Citizen's Award from Mental Health Association of Nassau County, 1984; George M. Estabrook Distinguished Service Award from Hofstra University, 1987.

WRITINGS:

Sliding Down the Wind (poems), Swallow Press, 1978.
The Hawk's Dream and Other Poems, Grove, 1982.
Against Gravity (poems), Grove, 1986.

Contributor of articles and poems to magazines and newspapers, including *Confrontation, SunStorm, Maine Times, Newsday, New York Quarterly,* and *New England Review.*

WORK IN PROGRESS: The Orphan, a novel.

B

BAILEY, D. F.   1950-

PERSONAL: Born October 1, 1950, in Montreal, Quebec, Canada; son of Kenneth (a businessman) and Mary (Kydd) Bailey; married Audrey Ilich; children: Adam, Lauren. *Education:* University of New Brunswick, B.A. (with honors), 1971; Simon Fraser University, Teaching Certificate, 1974; University of British Columbia, M.Ed., 1978.

ADDRESSES: Agent—Bella Pomer, 22 Shallmar, No. PH2, Toronto, Ontario, Canada M5N 2Z8.

CAREER: Greater Victoria School District, Victoria, British Columbia, English teacher, 1978—. Counselor at Eric Martin Psychiatric Institute, 1978-81; president of Altext Communications, Inc., 1983—.

WRITINGS:

Fire Eyes (novel), Douglas & McIntyre, 1987.

SIDELIGHTS: Fire Eyes was described in the *Globe and Mail* as "a taut psychological thriller with literary overtones, a very contemporary terrorist romance." Critic William French reported that it was D. F. Bailey's experience as a psychologist that allowed him to create the believable but flawed character of Billy Deerborn, the protagonist of *Fire Eyes,* who was abandoned as a baby and grew up unloved and unwanted. In the army Billy was trained as a demolitions expert, and it was a job from which the young man derived great personal satisfaction. He then became infatuated with an adventurous young woman who had a decidedly terrorist approach to resolving the world's nuclear issue. French wrote in the *Globe and Mail* that Bailey's first novel is authentic, graphic, and explosive. "Among its major strengths," the critic added, "is a nice sense of ambiguity; things could really be as they seem, but surface events could just as easily be hiding more complex and sinister motivations."

BIOGRAPHICAL/CRITICAL SOURCES:

PERIODICALS

Globe and Mail (Toronto), April 4, 1987.

*   *   *

BAILEY, Victor   1948-

PERSONAL: Born August 14, 1948, in Keighley, Yorkshire, England; son of Fred (a painter) and Lily (a weaver; maiden name, Meadows) Bailey; married Sheila Blackburn, 1971 (divorced); married Jennifer Donnelly (a journalist), October 12, 1985. *Education:* University of Warwick, B.A., 1969, Ph.D., 1975; Jesus College, Cambridge, M.Phil., 1970. *Religion:* Methodist.

ADDRESSES: Office—Department of History, University of Kansas, Lawrence, Kan. 66045.

CAREER: Centre for Criminology, Oxford, England, research officer, 1975-78; Oxford University, Oxford, senior research fellow at Worcester College, 1978-82; University of Rochester, Rochester, N.Y., R. T. French Visiting Professor of History, 1982-83; University of Hull, Hull, England, lecturer in economic and social history, 1983-87; member of faculty, University of Kansas, Lawrence, 1988—.

MEMBER: Society for the Study of Labour History, Social History Society.

WRITINGS:

(Editor) *Policing and Punishment in Nineteenth Century Britain,* Rutgers University Press, 1981.
Delinquency and Citizenship: Reclaiming the Young Offender, 1914-1948, Clarendon Press, 1987.
"To Take Arms Against a Sea of Troubles": Suicide in Victorian Hull, Harvester, in press.

Contributor to history, criminology, and sociology journals.

WORK IN PROGRESS: Crime and Society in England, 1890 to Present, for Longman, completion expected in 1990; *Robert Blatchford and the Culture of Labour,* for Harvester, completion expected in 1992.

SIDELIGHTS: Victor Bailey told *CA:* "My research on crime and punishment started with a study of the police, magistracy, and law enforcement in late Victorian England, under the influence of the unique academic collective at Warwick University's Centre for the Study of Social History that was examining various aspects of law and society in England from the eighteenth century. Thereafter I focused attention on the period from the late eighteenth to the mid-nineteenth century, looking at the persons and socio-economic forces responsible for the rise of probation, the establishment of the juvenile court, and the development of the Borstal reformatory system.

"Robert Blatchford, who lived between 1851 and 1943, was a socialist journalist who is best known in labor history circles for editing the *Clarion,* one of the most popular radical journals of the late Victorian and Edwardian era, and for writing *Merrie England,* his famous propagandist work in the cause of making socialists. Making socialists was preface to the implementation of the Co-operative Commonwealth, Blatchford's notion of the ideal socialist society. In his advocacy of Empire and tariff reform, however, he gradually lost touch with mainstream radicalism. My biography of Blatchford will examine the events which converted him to socialism in the 1880s, the contribution of his writings to the socialist movement, and his political ideas and activity between 1890 and 1918.''

AVOCATIONAL INTERESTS: "Escorting my wife to antique auctions, exercising our boxer dog.''

BIOGRAPHICAL/CRITICAL SOURCES:

PERIODICALS

Times Literary Supplement, July 3, 1987.

*   *   *

BAKER, James C(alvin)   1935-

PERSONAL: Born March 10, 1935, in Windfall, Ind.; son of Clyde M. and Lillian (Shaw) Baker; married Phyllis J. Harris, March 4, 1955; children: Janet, Ralph, Jolie. *Education:* Indiana University—Bloomington, B.S., 1961, M.B.A., 1962, D.B.A., 1966.

ADDRESSES: Home—707 Crain Ave., Kent, Ohio 44240. *Office*—Department of Finance, Kent State University, Kent, Ohio 44242.

CAREER: University of Maryland at College Park, assistant professor of business administration, 1965-68; San Francisco State College (now University), San Francisco, Calif., associate professor of world business, 1968-71; Kent State University, Kent, Ohio, professor of finance, 1971—, chairman of department, 1971-75. Member of Regional Export Expansion Council, 1967-73; international finance adviser to Federal Deposit Insurance Corp. (FDIC), 1975-77. *Military service:* U.S. Army, 1954-58.

MEMBER: Academy of International Business, Academy of Management, Eastern Finance Association, Southern Finance Association, Beta Gamma Sigma.

AWARDS, HONORS: Fellow of American Assembly of Collegiate Schools of Business and Sears Foundation, 1975-76.

WRITINGS:

(With J. K. Ryans) *World Marketing,* Wiley, 1967.
The International Finance Corporation: Origin, Operations, and Evaluation, Praeger, 1968.
The German Stock Market: Its Operations, Problems, and Prospects, Praeger, 1970.
(With Thomas H. Bates) *Financing International Business Operations,* Intext Educational Publishers, 1971.
(With M. Gerald Bradford) *American Banks Abroad: Edge Act Companies and Multinational Banking,* Praeger, 1974.
(With Ryans and A. R. Neghandi) *Trading with China, the U.S.S.R., and Eastern Europe,* Kent State University Press, 1974.
(With Ryans) *Multinational Marketing: Dimensions in Strategy,* Grid, 1975.

International Bank Regulation, Praeger, 1978.
(With Ryans and D. R. Howard) *International Business Classics,* Lexington, 1988.

Contributor of about eighty articles to business and finance journals. Member of editorial board of *Journal of International Business Studies,* 1970-75, 1980-82.

WORK IN PROGRESS: A textbook on international banking, publication by Reston expected in 1990.

SIDELIGHTS: James C. Baker told *CA:* "The subjects of my books have varied but one constant remains: most of them have something to do with international finance. My Praeger books have been about the International Finance Corporation, the German stock markets (the subject of my doctoral dissertation), Edge Act banking in the United States, and international bank regulation—a subject in which I was involved while working at the Federal Deposit Insurance Corporation (FDIC). *Financing International Business Operations* was a short paperback supplementary textbook on international financial management. The other books are readers or conference proceedings and cover general areas of international business or, in the case of the conference proceedings, East-West trade and business. However, my contribution to them generally pertained to international finance subjects.

"My views about writing have slowly evolved from dealing with general topics in international finance to writing about subjects, some of them very narrow and obscure in terms of the subject matter, in which I have found some very strong interest. I have become quite interested, for example, in institutions such as the International Centre for Settlement of Investment Disputes (ICSID), the Society for Worldwide Interbank Financial Telecommunications (SWIFT), the Migros Cooperative in Switzerland, expatriate managerial training in the United States, and bank deregulation. Thus, I have become more eclectic in my writing interests and have adopted a philosophy of aiming my articles at specific journals in which I am interested in publishing. This eclecticism has, of course, benefited my teaching because I have been able to present a host of ideas and up-to-date real world, practical case examples to my students. It has also benefited the doctoral students whom I have advised on their dissertation committees.

"My present views on international banking and international finance have also been slowly evolving. The world has become more integrated and financial institutions and markets and financial operations have become more globalized and interrelated. This was certainly confirmed by the October 19, 1987, bloodbath worldwide on securities exchanges when stock prices made record declines. This is also true of multinational business operations. Future research on international business and international finance topics must take this fact into consideration.''

*   *   *

BALTHASAR, Hans Urs von
See von BALTHASAR, Hans Urs

*   *   *

BANHAM, (Peter) Reyner   1922-1988

OBITUARY NOTICE—See index for *CA* sketch: Born March 2, 1922, in Norwich, England; died of cancer, March 19 (one source says March 18), 1988, in London, England. Architectural critic, educator, editor, and author. Though well known even outside of architectural circles, Banham will be best remembered for his critical studies of modern architecture, including *Los Angeles, The New Brutalism: Ethic or Aesthetic?* and *The Architecture of the Well-Tempered Environment.* He began his career as a member of the *Architectural Review*'s editorial staff in 1952, becoming assistant executive editor by 1964, when he left to serve as a full-time lecturer in architectural history at the University of London. Banham also taught at the State University of New York at Buffalo and the University of California at Santa Cruz. His other writings include *Theory and Design in the First Machine Age, Guide to Modern Architecture,* and *Megastructure.*

OBITUARIES AND OTHER SOURCES:

BOOKS

Who's Who, 140th edition, St. Martin's, 1988.
The Writers Directory: 1988-1990, St. James Press, 1988.

PERIODICALS

Los Angeles Times, March 23, 1988.
New York Times, March 22, 1988.
Times (London), March 22, 1988.

*   *   *

BARKER, Elliott S(peer)   1886-1988

OBITUARY NOTICE—See index for *CA* sketch: Born December 25, 1886, in Moran, Tex.; died April 3, 1988, in Santa Fe, N.M. Conservationist, rancher, and author. Barker was known as the man who in 1950 rescued the bear cub that became the United States's symbol for forest fire prevention, Smokey the Bear. After a stint as a professional guide and hunter, Barker joined the U.S. Forest Service in 1909, serving as a forest ranger and forest supervisor until becoming a rancher in 1919. He eventually worked for the New Mexico Department of Game and Fish as a state game warden, becoming director of the department, until he retired in 1953 to write about his experiences. Barker's *Western Life and Adventures, 1889-1970* won a Golden Spur Award from Western Writers of America in 1972. His other writings include *When the Dogs Barked "Treed": A Year on the Trail of the Longtails; Beatty's Cabin: Adventures in the Pecos High Country; Outdoors, Faith, Fun, and Other Poems; Ramblings in the Field of Conservation;* and *Eighty Years With Rod and Rifle.*

OBITUARIES AND OTHER SOURCES:

PERIODICALS

Los Angeles Times, April 5, 1988.
New York Times, April 5, 1988.
Times (London), April 7, 1988.
Washington Post, April 5, 1988.

*   *   *

BARKER, W(illiam) Alan   1923-1988(?)

OBITUARY NOTICE—See index for *CA* sketch: Born October 1, 1923, in Edinburgh, Scotland; died c. 1988. Educator, editor, and author. Barker served as headmaster of British schools such as the Leys School and University College School. Also active in local Conservative politics, he contributed to the two-volume *General History of England* and helped edit both volumes of *Documents of English History.* Barker's own writings include *Religion and Politics, 1558-1603* and *The Civil War in America.*

OBITUARIES AND OTHER SOURCES:

BOOKS

Who's Who, 140th edition, St. Martin's, 1988.

PERIODICALS

Times (London), May 17, 1988.

*   *   *

BARKER, Wendy B.   1942-

PERSONAL: Born September 22, 1942, in Summit, N.J.; daughter of G. Clarke (a banker) and Pamela (a homemaker; maiden name, Dodwell) Bean; married Laurence Barker (a choral music conductor and university professor), August 11, 1962; children: Clarke David. *Education:* Arizona State University, B.A. (with honors), 1966, M.A., 1974; University of California, Davis, Ph.D., 1981.

ADDRESSES: Home—Route 1, Box 1639, Boerne, Tex. 78006. *Office*—Division of English, Classics, and Philosophy, University of Texas at San Antonio, San Antonio, Tex. 78285.

CAREER: High school English teacher in Scottsdale, Ariz., and Berkeley, Calif., 1966-72; University of Texas at San Antonio, assistant professor of English, 1982—. Co-founder of alternative school for gifted students in Berkeley, 1972. Gives poetry readings and workshops.

MEMBER: National Society of Arts and Letters (member of advisory board).

AWARDS, HONORS: Poetry award from Southwest Women Artists and Writers, 1982, for "Winter Chickens"; fellow of National Endowment for the Arts, 1986.

WRITINGS:

(Contributor) Jane Cooper, Gwen Head, and other editors, *The Iowa Review Collection of Contemporary Women Writers: Extended Outlooks,* Macmillan, 1982.
(Contributor) Joanna Bankier and Deirdre Lashgari, editors, *Women Poets of the World,* Macmillan, 1983.
Lunacy of Light: Emily Dickinson and the Experience of Metaphor, Southern Illinois University Press, 1987.
(Contributor) Martha Nell Smith, editor, *Titanic Opera: Contemporary Women Poets and Emily Dickinson,* Oxford University Press, in press.

Work represented in anthologies, including *Green Rain: A Collection for Young People of All Ages,* edited by Cyra Sweet Dumitru, San Antonio Independent School District, 1983; *Crossing the River: Poets of the American West,* edited by Ray Gonzalez, Second Chance; *Anthology of Magazine Verse and Yearbook of American Poetry, 1986/87,* edited by Alan F. Pater, Monitor Book. Contributor of more than fifty articles, poems, and reviews to magazines, including *Poetry, Southern Poetry Review, Nimrod, Viaztlan, American Scholar,* and *Cedar Rock.* Member of poetry editorial board of *California Quarterly,* 1979.

WORK IN PROGRESS: Death Blows, Life Blows: Women Writers in Nineteenth-Century America (tentative title), publication by Indiana University Press expected in 1993; *Winter Chickens,* poems.

BIOGRAPHICAL/CRITICAL SOURCES:

PERIODICALS

San Antonio Light, August 2, 1987.
The Women's Review of Books, December, 1987.

* * *

BARMINE, Alexander (G.)   1899-1987

OBITUARY NOTICE: Some sources spell given name Alexandre; born in 1899 in Mogilev, Byelorussia (now of the U.S.S.R.); died of complications from a stroke, December 25, 1987, in Rockville, Md. Military leader, government official, journalist, and author. Barmine was recognized as one of the earliest high-level Soviet defectors. After fighting civil wars in his native country following the Russian Revolution, Barmine was appointed commissar at the age of nineteen and eventually became a brigadier general in the Soviet Army. He held several government posts in the Soviet Union and abroad, and from 1929 to 1932 he headed the Soviet trade delegations to Paris and Milan.

Barmine defected from the U.S.S.R. in 1937. While serving as Soviet charge d'affaires in Athens, Greece, he learned that one of his mentors had been killed in a purge by the Joseph Stalin regime; Barmine feared a similar fate and fled to Paris. There he occasionally wrote articles for the *New York Times* concerning the terror under Stalin's rule. He moved to New York City in 1940 and served in the U.S. Army from 1942 to 1943. After writing for several magazines, he joined the radio program "Voice of America," where he was chief of its Russian branch for sixteen years. In 1964 he became the officer in charge of Soviet affairs for the U.S. Information Agency, serving as a special adviser to the agency from 1969 to the time of his retirement in 1972. Barmine chronicled his life as a Soviet soldier and diplomat in his highly acclaimed 1945 book, *One Who Survived: The Life Story of a Russian Under the Soviets.*

OBITUARIES AND OTHER SOURCES:

PERIODICALS

Newsweek, January 11, 1988.
New York Times, December 28, 1987.
Washington Post, December 28, 1987.

* * *

BARNETT, Sanford   1909(?)-1988

OBITUARY NOTICE: Born c. 1909 in East Orange, N.J.; died of complications from a stroke, April 14, 1988, in Oxnard, Calif. Public relations specialist, journalist, and radio, television, and film scriptwriter. Barnett was known for his varied writing accomplishments, which include the Academy Award-winning screenplay for "Father Goose," a 1964 comedy film starring Cary Grant. Barnett started out as an errand boy for radio stations, eventually becoming a newspaper reporter and contributor to Rudy Vallee's radio show. He later wrote for the "Believe It or Not" radio series, and he went on to become one of the first writers adapting films and Broadway plays to radio for the series "The Lux Radio Theater," broadcast from 1936 to 1955. He is said to have completed six hundred radio and television scripts throughout his career. Beginning in 1970, Barnett served as a public relations specialist, writing press releases and speeches for the Los Angeles Police Department.

OBITUARIES AND OTHER SOURCES:

PERIODICALS

Los Angeles Times, April 16, 1988.

* * *

BARON de TEIVE
See PESSOA, Fernando (Antonio Nogueira)

* * *

BARRETT, Lois (Yvonne)   1947-

PERSONAL: Born November 9, 1947, in Enid, Okla.; daughter of H. Preston (a minister) and Audrey (a homemaker; maiden name, Wilson) Barrett; married Thomas B. Mierau (a teacher), June 26, 1977; children: Barbara, Susanna, John. *Education:* University of Oklahoma, B.A. (with highest honors), 1969; Mennonite Biblical Seminary, Elkhart, Ind., M.Div., 1983.

ADDRESSES: Home—1508 Fairview, Wichita, Kan. 67203.

CAREER: Ordained Mennonite minister, 1985; *Wichita Eagle,* Wichita, Kan., reporter, 1969-70; *The Mennonite,* Newton, Kan., associate editor, 1971-77; free-lance writer, 1977-79; Bethel College, North Newton, Kan., instructor in communications, 1979-80; Mennonite Church of the Servant, Wichita, minister, 1983—. Member of executive council of Institute of Mennonite Studies, 1983—. Member of central planning committee of New Call to Peacemaking, 1977-80, of U.S. Peace Section of Mennonite Central Committee, 1980-83, and of steering committee of Wichita's Churches United for Peacemaking, 1984—. President of Wichita's Midtown Citizens Association, 1978-79.

AWARDS, HONORS: Award from American Bible Society, 1983.

WRITINGS:

The Vision and the Reality, Faith and Life, 1983.
Building the House Church, Herald Press, 1986.
The Way God Fights, Herald Press, 1987.

Contributor to magazines, including *Gospel Herald, Builder, Sojourners, Other Side,* and *Friends Journal.*

WORK IN PROGRESS: A book on biblical justice, publication by Herald Press expected in 1988; research on Ursula Jost and apocalyptic Anabaptism in the sixteenth century.

AVOCATIONAL INTERESTS: Music (performance and composition).

BIOGRAPHICAL/CRITICAL SOURCES:

BOOKS

Wolseley, Roland E., *Careers in Religious Communications,* Herald Press, 1977.

* * *

BARTELL, Linda Lang   1948-

PERSONAL: Born January 1, 1948, in Cleveland, Ohio; daughter of Edward William (a plumber) and Ethel (a secretary; maiden name, Vaigle) Lang; married Robert Bartell (in marketing), October 2, 1971; children: Heather Lauren. *Education:* Cleveland State University, B.A., 1970.

ADDRESSES: Office—c/o Avon Books, 105 Madison Ave., New York, N.Y. 10016. *Agent*—Ellen Levine Literary Agency, Inc., 432 Park Ave., Suite 1205, New York, N.Y. 10016.

CAREER: Taught French and history at high schools in Ohio, 1970-78; writer, 1985—.

MEMBER: Romance Writers of America (served on board of directors, 1984-86), Detroit Women Writers.

AWARDS, HONORS: Romance Writers of America Golden Heart Award for *Brianna*, 1985.

WRITINGS:

HISTORICAL ROMANCES

Brianna, Avon, 1986.
Alyssa, Avon, 1987.
Marisa, Avon, 1988.
Brittany, Avon, in press.

WORK IN PROGRESS: A historical romance, tentatively titled *Wake Not the Lion*, to be published by Onyx.

SIDELIGHTS: Linda Lang Bartell told *CA:* "My interest in European history and romantic adventure prompted me to write historical fiction, especially set in England and France. I am fluent in French and have traveled to Belgium and France."

AVOCATIONAL INTERESTS: Sports ("I am a former gymnast and gymnastics instructor"), dancing, music—classical as well as rock.

*   *   *

BARTLETT, Robert (John)   1950-

PERSONAL: Born November 27, 1950, in London, England; immigrated to the United States, 1986; son of Leonard F. and Mabel (Adams) Bartlett; married Honora Elaine Hickey (a writer); children: Gabriel, Penelope, Brian. *Education:* Peterhouse, Cambridge, B.A., 1972, M.A., 1976; graduate study at Princeton University, 1976-77; St. John's College, Oxford, D.Phil., 1978.

ADDRESSES: Office—Department of History, University of Chicago, 1126 East 59th St., Chicago, Ill. 60637.

CAREER: University of Edinburgh, Edinburgh, Scotland, lecturer in history, 1980-86; University of Chicago, Chicago, Ill., professor of medieval history, 1986—. Member of Institute for Advanced Study and fellow at Davis Center, Princeton, N.J., 1983-84.

MEMBER: Royal Historical Society (fellow), Historical Association, Ecclesiastical History Society, Pipe Roll Society, Mediaeval Academy of America.

AWARDS, HONORS: Fellow at University of Michigan, 1979-80; Fulbright scholar at Princeton University, 1983-84.

WRITINGS:

Gerald of Wales, 1146-1223, Oxford University Press, 1982.
Trial by Fire and Water: The Medieval Judicial Ordeal, Oxford University Press, 1986.

Contributor to history journals.

WORK IN PROGRESS: The Dynamics of Expansion in the High Middle Ages: Conquest, Colonization, and Cultural Change, 900-1300, completion expected in 1992.

SIDELIGHTS: In a *Times Literary Supplement* review of Robert Bartlett's *Gerald of Wales, 1146-1223*, Gwyn Jones main-

tained that "Dr. Bartlett's bibliographical rather than biographical approach to his subject, together with his detailed characterization of Gerald's ideas, attitudes, and intellectual milieu, can leave no one in doubt that here was an intriguing man . . . and an author of considerable skill, eloquence and diversity." Gerald of Wales was a Latin historian of the twelfth century. He was born into nobility, both Norman and Welsh, and became a controversial figure in English history. He served the church as archdeacon of Brecon; Gerald's goal was to become bishop of St. David's and establish that parish as a metropolitan see, independent of the Archbishop of Canterbury. This effort was doomed, in part because of Gerald's stormy relationship with the Angevin kings of England, particularly King John. In defeat, Gerald allied himself with the cause of his native Wales and retired from public life. His last years were spent in writing, both about himself and the history of his times. His writing was both erudite and relatively readable for the modern scholar. Jones wrote of Bartlett's study: "*Gerald of Wales* is a useful contribution to the history of ideas at a particular time and in respect of a remarkable man."

In *Trial by Fire and Water*, Bartlett made the rather surprising comment that, hideous as the practice may have been, the ordeal was as rational to the medieval mind as any other known method of criminal procedure. Witnesses lied routinely, evidence was rarely indisputable, and only God's will was unquestionably reliable. The ordeal was employed widely from the eighth through the twelfth centuries, and its popularity waned only when the clergy was forbidden to serve as judges, particularly in cases where the death of the accused was a likely result. The practice was abandoned in 1215, and Europe was left with no clear-cut criminal procedure for several hundred years. *Times Literary Supplement* critic Jonathan Sumption lauded *Trial by Fire and Water:* "A monograph which not only covers the whole chronological and geographical range, but does so as elegantly and thoughtfully as this one, is a considerable achievement."

BIOGRAPHICAL/CRITICAL SOURCES:

PERIODICALS

Times Literary Supplement, October 29, 1982, April 17, 1987.

*   *   *

BARTON, Jon
See HARVEY, John (Barton)

*   *   *

BARWOOD, Hal

BRIEF ENTRY: American film producer, director, and screenwriter. Author of scripts with writer-director Matthew Robbins, Barwood has six screen credits to his name, the earliest of which include "The Sugarland Express" (Universal, 1974), "The Bingo Long Traveling All-Stars and Motor Kings" (Universal, 1976), and "MacArthur" (Universal, 1977). Continuing his writing in collaboration with Robbins, Barwood also produced some of the team's scripts, including "Corvette Summer" (United Artists, 1978) and the fantasy adventure "Dragonslayer" (United Artists, 1981). He made his directorial debut in 1985 with "Warning Sign" (Twentieth Century-Fox), a film about a deadly germ which, unleashed during a laboratory accident, turns its victims into depraved zombies. While "Warning Sign" received mixed reviews, Barwood's fast-paced direction and fair representation of minor characters were cited among the film's assets by Jon Pareles in the *New York Times*.

BIOGRAPHICAL/CRITICAL SOURCES:

BOOKS

International Motion Picture Almanac, Quigley, 1988.

PERIODICALS

Los Angeles Times, August 23, 1985.
New York Times, July 1, 1977, August 4, 1978, June 26, 1981, August 23, 1985.

*   *   *

BASCOM, William R(ussel) 1912-1981

OBITUARY NOTICE—See index for *CA* sketch: Born May 23, 1912, in Princeton, Ill.; died from complications following open-heart surgery, September 11, 1981, in San Francisco, Calif.; buried in Sunset View Cemetery, Berkeley, Calif. Anthropologist, museum director, educator, and author. An authority on African art, Bascom will also be remembered for his studies of Nigeria's Yoruba people, including *The Sociological Role of the Yoruba Cult-Group* and *The Yoruba of Southwestern Nigeria*. He began his academic career as an anthropology instructor at Northwestern University in 1939 and became a full professor by 1954. Bascom left Northwestern in 1957 for the University of California, Berkeley, where, in addition to teaching classes, he served as the director of the Robert H. Lowie Museum of Anthropology. His other writings include *Ponape: A Pacific Economy in Transition*, *Ifa Divination: Communications Between Gods and Men in West Africa*, *African Art in Cultural Perspective: An Introduction*, and *African Dilemma Tales*.

OBITUARIES AND OTHER SOURCES:

BOOKS

American Men and Women of Science: The Physical and Biological Sciences, 13th edition, Bowker, 1976.
The Writers Directory: 1986-1988, St. James Press, 1986.

PERIODICALS

Journal of American Folklore, October-December, 1982.

*   *   *

BASSET, Bernard 1909-1988

OBITUARY NOTICE—See index for *CA* sketch: Born March 21, 1909, in London (one source says Westminster), England; died June 13, 1988. Clergyman, educator, and author. Basset entered the Society of Jesus (Jesuits) in 1927 and was ordained a Roman Catholic priest in 1941. He taught history at England's Stonyhurst and Beaumont colleges and later lectured throughout the United States. Basset's best-known writings are his humorous "Margery" stories, collected in the volumes *Margery and Me* and *The Seven Deadly Virtues, and Other Stories*. He also wrote *We Neurotics: A Handbook for the Half-Mad*, *Born for Friendship: The Spirit of Sir Thomas More*, *We Agnostics: On the Tightrope to Eternity*, and *Let's Start Praying Again: Field Work in Meditation*. He was the author of a column appearing in *Catholic Herald* and contributed to the British Catholic publication *Stella Maris*.

OBITUARIES AND OTHER SOURCES:

PERIODICALS

Times (London), June 20, 1988.

*   *   *

BATEY, Mavis 1921-

PERSONAL: Born May 5, 1921, in London, England; daughter of Frederick (a civil servant) and Lilian (Day) Lever; married Keith Batey (an academic); children: Elizabeth, Christopher, Deborah. *Education:* Attended University of London, 1937-39. *Religion:* Church of England.

ADDRESSES: Home—Aldwick, West Sussex, England.

CAREER: Worked as reader in German at University of London and as cryptographer until 1946; Oxford University, Oxford, England, tutor in external studies, 1972—. Trustee of Lewis Carroll Birthplace Trust.

MEMBER: Garden History Society (president).

AWARDS, HONORS: Veitch Memorial Medal, 1986; member of Order of the British Empire, 1987; Gold Medal from Royal Horticultural Society.

WRITINGS:

Alice's Adventures in Oxford, Pitkin, 1978.
Oxford Gardens, Avebury, 1982, Scolar Press, 1986.
(With Sandra Raphael, Christopher Thacker, and Denis Wood) *Of Oxfordshire Gardens*, illustrations by Meriel Edmunds, Oxford Polytechnic Press, 1982.
Oxford and Cambridge Gardens, Macmillan, 1988.

Contributor to *Country Life*, *Garden History*, and *Oxoniensia*.

WORK IN PROGRESS: Further work on Lewis Carroll.

SIDELIGHTS: Mavis Batey told *CA:* "My chief work has been in conservation, for the Council for the Protection of Rural England, English Heritage, the Oxford Civic Society, the Oxford Preservation Trust, and many historic garden trusts. I am also much involved in adult education, particularly American summer schools in Oxford."

Oxford Gardens provides not only a history of the gardens at Oxford University but also a glimpse of the men and women who created them. London *Times* critic Ruth Stungo commented that Batey "covers all aspects of the life of the university which have influenced garden history in its widest sense." The author concentrates on the Commonwealth and Restoration periods, when creativity in garden design was at its height, but she also examines the decline of the Oxford garden and the ideas of designers like Capability Brown, whose plans were never realized. Stungo recommended, "For anyone with an interest in garden history or the history of Oxford, this is an essential book."

Of Oxfordshire Gardens is a collection of essays in which Batey and her co-authors point out the importance Oxford has held in garden history because of its many gardens and the prominent designers who worked there. They present information on gardens now vanished, with an emphasis on the eighteenth century, and they discuss the impact of these decorative gardens on the writers and artists of the day. John Buxton of the *Times Literary Supplement* deemed it "a delightfully produced and elegantly adorned book for the relaxed perusal of anyone who has delighted in gardens anywhere."

BIOGRAPHICAL/CRITICAL SOURCES:

PERIODICALS

Times (London), September 20, 1986.
Times Literary Supplement, July 20, 1982.

*   *   *

BATSON, Wade Thomas 1912-

PERSONAL: Born May 7, 1912, in Marietta, S.C.; married in 1939; children: two. *Education:* Furman University, B.S., 1934; Duke University, M.A., 1949, Ph.D., 1952.

ADDRESSES: *Office*—Department of Biology, University of South Carolina—Columbia, Columbia, S.C. 29208.

CAREER: Biology teacher at high school in South Carolina, 1937-41, principal, 1941-44; civilian readjustment officer for Thirteenth Naval District, 1947; Duke University, Durham, N.C., instructor in botany, 1950-52; University of South Carolina—Columbia, assistant professor of biology, 1952-54; Oak Ridge Institute for Nuclear Studies, Oak Ridge, Tenn., assistant chairman of University Relations Division, 1954-55; University of South Carolina—Columbia, associate professor, 1955-59, professor of biology, 1959—, acting head of department, 1958-59. Chairman of South Carolina Governor's Beautification Committee, c. 1975-76, and Cayce Beautification Committee. *Military service:* U.S. Naval Reserve, active duty; became lieutenant commander.

MEMBER: American Bryological and Lichenological Society, Southern Appalachian Botanical Club, South Carolina Association of Biology Teachers (past president), South Carolina Academy of Science (past president), Sigma Xi (past president).

AWARDS, HONORS: Distinguished Teaching Award from Association of Southeastern Biologists, 1968.

WRITINGS:

Wild Flowers in South Carolina, University of South Carolina Press, 1964.
Genera of the Eastern Plants, University of South Carolina Press, 3rd edition, 1977.
Genera of the Western Plants, University of South Carolina Press, 1982.
Landscape Plants for the Southeast, University of South Carolina Press, 1984.
For Plant Lovers: Everything You Need to Know to Identify Plants, Shrubs, and Trees!, University of South Carolina Press, 1984.
Wild Flowers in the Carolinas, University of South Carolina Press, 1987.

Contributor to scientific journals.

*   *   *

BAUMANN, Gerd 1953-

PERSONAL: Born November 13, 1953, in Aachen, West Germany; son of Arno (a physician) and Marianne (Undorf) Baumann. *Education:* Attended Cologne Conservatory and University of Cologne, 1972-75; Queen's University, Belfast, Ph.D., 1980. *Politics:* "Liberty, equality, fraternity." *Religion:* "Ex-Roman Catholic."

ADDRESSES: *Office*—Department of Human Sciences, Brunel University of West London, Uxbridge UB18 3PH, England.

CAREER: Queen's University, Belfast, Northern Ireland, lecturer in social anthropology, 1978-81; Oxford University, Oxford, England, junior research fellow at Wolfson College, 1982-85; Brunel University of West London, Uxbridge, England, lecturer in social anthropology, 1986—.

MEMBER: International Council for Traditional Music (member of council), Royal Anthropological Institute, Association of Social Anthropologists of the Commonwealth, British Society for Middle Eastern Studies, Society for Ethnomusicology.

WRITINGS:

(Editor) *The Written Word: Literacy in Transition*, Oxford University Press, 1987.
National Integration and Local Integrity, Oxford University Press, 1988.

Contributor to academic journals and literary magazines in England, Germany, and the United States.

WORK IN PROGRESS: Research in a London suburb, on immigrants from India and the Caribbean, with a monograph expected to result; research on the literary implications of social research, with a book of essays expected to result.

SIDELIGHTS: Gerd Baumann told *CA:* "While working in academia, my research and writing are concerned less with adding to what is called 'social science,' and more with contributing to a humanistic project of understanding and translating the human condition as it is perceived by individuals in nonindependent societies. This involves attention to intangibles such as affect, artistic expression, and styles of communicating. To describe these in purely academic language is inadequate. To describe them in a literary idiom that retains academic precision would be important, but would require more freedom from academic constraints than my circumstances have so far allowed."

*   *   *

BAUMEL, Judith 1956-

PERSONAL: Born October 9, 1956, in Bronx, N.Y.; daughter of Abraham (an educator) and Betty (an educator; maiden name, Fogel) Baumel; married David Ghitelman (a journalist), July 4, 1985. *Education:* Harvard University, B.A. (magna cum laude), 1977; Johns Hopkins University, M.A., 1978.

ADDRESSES: *Home*—New York, N.Y. *Office*—Poetry Society of America, 15 Gramercy Park, New York, N.Y. 10003.

CAREER: Poetry Society of America, New York, N.Y., director, 1985—.

AWARDS, HONORS: Walt Whitman Award from the Academy of American Poets, 1987, for *The Weight of Numbers*; New York Foundation for the Arts fellowship for poetry, 1987.

WRITINGS:

The Weight of Numbers (poems), Wesleyan University Press, 1988.

Contributor of poems to periodicals, including *New Yorker*, *Paris Review*, and *American Poetry Review*.

*   *   *

BEACH, Frank Ambrose 1911-1988

OBITUARY NOTICE—See index for *CA* sketch: Born April 13, 1911, in Emporia, Kansas; died of congestive heart failure,

June 15, 1988, in Berkeley, Calif. Educator, museum curator, editor, and author. A noted expert on sexual behavior, Beach taught psychology at Yale University from 1946 to 1958 and at the University of California, Berkeley, from 1958 to 1978. Previous to becoming a professor, he was a curator for the American Museum of Natural History in New York City. Beach served as a scientific adviser to William H. Masters and Virginia E. Johnson in their work on the 1966 book, *Human Sexual Response,* and he edited *Sex and Behavior* and *Human Sexuality in Four Perspectives.* His writings include *Hormones and Behavior* and *Patterns of Sexual Behavior.*

OBITUARIES AND OTHER SOURCES:

BOOKS

The International Who's Who, 51st edition, Europa, 1987.
Who's Who in America, 44th edition, Marquis, 1986.

PERIODICALS

New York Times, June 18, 1988.

*   *   *

BEALES, H(ugh) L(ancelot)   1889-1988

OBITUARY NOTICE: Born February 18, 1889; died April 19, 1988. Historian, educator, preacher, editorial adviser, editor, and author. Beales was best known for his nearly thirty years of teaching at the London School of Economics and Political Science. He began his academic career as a reader of medieval history at the University of Manchester. After serving in the infantry during World War I he became a lecturer in economic history at Sheffield University, where he was an avid supporter of the Workers' Educational Association. He lectured from 1926 to 1954 at the London School of Economics and Political Science, where he was made an honorary fellow in 1971. Additionally, Beales was a preacher who advocated a secular, humanist socialism. He also served as an editorial adviser for Penguin and Pelican books, as well as for International Thomson Organization. Among his writings are *The Industrial Revolution: 1750-1850* and *The Early English Socialists.* He also co-edited *Memoirs of the Unemployed.*

OBITUARIES AND OTHER SOURCES:

BOOKS

Who's Who, 140th edition, St. Martin's, 1988.
Who Was Who Among English and European Authors, 1931-1949, Gale, 1978.

PERIODICALS

Times (London), April 22, 1988.

*   *   *

BEARDEN, Romare (Howard)   1914(?)-1988

OBITUARY NOTICE—See index for *CA* sketch: Born September 2, 1914 (some sources say 1912) in Charlotte, N.C.; died following a stroke (one source says cancer), March 11 (some sources say March 12), 1988, in New York, N.Y. Artist, social worker, semi-professional athlete, composer, and author. Bearden will be best remembered for his highly acclaimed artwork, particularly his collages featuring themes from black life. One of the first critically and financially successful black artists in the United States, Bearden nevertheless periodically served as a social worker in New York to supplement his painting income. While in college he played for a time with the Boston Tigers, an all-black baseball team. Bearden also composed songs, including the jazz classic "Seabreeze." Bearden exhibited his art in many one-man shows at locations such as New York City's Museum of Modern Art and the Albert Loeb Gallery in Paris, France. Credited with doing a great deal to promote black art, Bearden and some of his associates founded the Cinque Gallery in the 1960s to feature the work of minority artists. He illustrated Samuel Allen's *Poems From Africa,* penned the foreword to Elton Clay Fox's *Black Artists of the New Generation,* and co-authored *The Painter's Mind: A Study of the Relations of Structure and Space in Painting* and *Six Black Masters of American Art.*

OBITUARIES AND OTHER SOURCES:

BOOKS

Current Biography, H. W. Wilson, 1988.
Who's Who in American Art, 17th edition, Bowker, 1986.

PERIODICALS

Chicago Tribune, March 15, 1988.
Los Angeles Times, March 14, 1988.
New York Times, March 13, 1988.
Washington Post, March 14, 1988.

*   *   *

BECKER, William H(enry)   1943-

PERSONAL: Born March 28, 1943, in New York, N.Y.; son of Henry W. and Dorothy M. (Wach) Becker; married Ruth Anne Neal (an archivist), June 19, 1965; children: Megan L., Lauren L. *Education:* Muhlenberg College, B.A., 1964; Johns Hopkins University, Ph.D., 1969.

ADDRESSES: Office—Department of History, George Washington University, 2121 I St. N.W., Washington, D.C. 20052.

CAREER: University of Maryland, Baltimore County, Catonsville, assistant professor, 1969-73, associate professor of history, 1973-80; George Washington University, Washington, D.C., visiting associate professor, 1980-82, associate professor, 1982-83, professor of history, 1983—, chairman of department, 1987—. Business history consultant.

MEMBER: American Historical Association, Organization of American Historians, Economic History Association, Society of Historians of American Foreign Relations, Business History Conference.

AWARDS, HONORS: Thomas Newcomen Award in Business History from Newcomen Society in North America, 1982, for *The Dynamics of Business-Government Relations.*

WRITINGS:

The Dynamics of Business-Government Relations: Industry and Exports, 1893-1921, University of Chicago Press, 1982.
(Editor with Samuel F. Wells, Jr.) *Economics and World Power: An Assessment of American Diplomacy Since 1789,* Columbia University Press, 1984.
From the Atlantic to the Great Lakes: The Corps of Engineers' Role in the St. Lawrence Seaway, U.S. Government Printing Office, 1984.
A History of American Business Management in the Twentieth Century, Oxford University Press, 1988.

General editor of *Encyclopedia of American Business History and Biography,* Bruccoli Clark, 1987—. Contributor to history journals.

SIDELIGHTS: William H. Becker informed *CA:* "I have been interested in the history of business-government relations, but through teaching business history at a business school, I have become more interested in the history of management and business in the twentieth century. In view of the role of business in American history and contemporary life, the subject has not received the kind of scholarly attention it deserves.

"Business, especially the large corporation, has often been controversial in twentieth-century America, and historians have tended to reflect the negative public views of business and business leaders. While business and the large corporation are far from being above reproach, it is important to study business on its own terms. Why do the people who create and lead businesses behave the way they do? Why do they hold the views that they do of their workers, communities, politics, competitors, and so on? Such understanding is necessary because the large corporation has an enormous impact on the lives not only of the people corporate management employs, but also of those in the broader society. If government would change the behavior of corporate management, it must understand how managers view their world. Much regulation in the past has been good politics but not necessarily good economics."

BIOGRAPHICAL/CRITICAL SOURCES:

PERIODICALS

Annals of the American Academy of Political and Social Science, November, 1982.
New York Times, March 27, 1987.

*   *   *

BEILENSON, Laurence W.   1899-1988

OBITUARY NOTICE—See index for *CA* sketch: Born May 31, 1899, in Helena, Ark.; died following a stroke, June 27, 1988. Attorney, union organizer, and author. Beilenson will be best remembered for his role in helping found the Screen Actors Guild, the Writers Guild of America, the Directors Guild of America, and the American Federation of Television and Radio Artists. While also maintaining a private law practice, Beilenson served as legal counsel for the Screen Actors Guild and penned its first constitution and bylaws. After his retirement in 1965, he began writing books on diplomacy and nuclear issues, including *The Treaty Trap, Power Through Subversion,* and *Survival and Peace in the Nuclear Age.*

OBITUARIES AND OTHER SOURCES:

PERIODICALS

Los Angeles Times, July 1, 1988.

*   *   *

BELL, W. L. D.
See MENCKEN, H(enry) L(ouis)

*   *   *

BELLAMY, Atwood C.
See MENCKEN, H(enry) L(ouis)

*   *   *

BENJAMIN, Ruth   1934-

PERSONAL: Born March 5, 1934, in Tacoma, Wash.; daughter of David (a social worker) and Rebecca (a writer; maiden name, Shallit) Turteltaub; married Arthur Rosenblatt (an architect), August 5, 1956; children: Paul, Judith. *Education:* Sarah Lawrence College, B.A., 1956.

ADDRESSES: Home—1158 Fifth Ave., 5D, New York, N.Y. 10029.

CAREER: Poets and Writers, Inc., New York, N.Y., assistant to director of development, 1983-86.

MEMBER: National Writers Union, Authors Guild.

WRITINGS:

Naked at Forty (novel), Horizon Press, 1984.

WORK IN PROGRESS: A novel, tentatively titled *The Doll House Job.*

BIOGRAPHICAL/CRITICAL SOURCES:

PERIODICALS

New York Times Book Review, June 24, 1984.

*   *   *

BENNETT, Elizabeth
See MITCHELL, Margaret (Munnerlyn)

*   *   *

BENNETT, Gwendolyn B.   1902-1981

PERSONAL: Born July 8, 1902, in Giddings, Tex.; died May 30, 1981; daughter of Joshua (a teacher) and Maime (a teacher) Bennett; married Alfred Jackson (a physician) in 1927 (died in early 1930s); married Richard Crosscup (an antiques collector and dealer; died c. 1980). *Education:* Graduated from Pratt Institute in 1924; attended Columbia University, 1921-24; studied at Academie Julian and Ecole du Pantheon, Paris, 1925.

ADDRESSES: Home—Kutztown, Pa.

CAREER: Howard University, Washington, D.C., instructor in watercolor and design, 1924 and 1926; taught art education and English at Tennessee State College in 1927; Work Progress Administration (W.P.A.; U.S. Government agency), associated with Federal Works Project during 1930s and with Federal Art Project's Harlem Community Art Center in New York, N.Y., as assistant director, 1937, and director, 1938-41; teacher and member of administrative staff of Jefferson School for Democracy, beginning in 1941; director of George Washington Carver School, beginning in 1943; worked as secretary for Consumer's Union during the mid-1940s; became antiques dealer in Kutztown, Pa. Cover illustrator for *Crisis* and *Opportunity* magazines, 1923-31.

HONORS, AWARDS: Received Alfred C. Barnes Foundation fellowship, 1926.

WRITINGS:

CONTRIBUTOR

James Weldon Johnson, editor, *The Book of American Negro Poetry,* Harcourt, 1922, revised edition, 1931.
Alain LeRoy Locke, editor, *The New Negro: An Interpretation,* Boni, 1925.
William Stanley Braithwaite, editor, *Anthology of Magazine*

Verse for 1925 and Yearbook of American Poetry, B. J.
   Brimmer, 1926.
Braithwaite, editor, *Anthology of Magazine Verse for 1926
   and Yearbook of American Poetry,* B. J. Brimmer, 1927.
Countee Cullen, editor, *Caroling Dusk: An Anthology of Verse
   by Negro Poets,* Harper, 1927.
Charles S. Johnson, editor, *Ebony and Topaz: A Collectanea,*
   National Urban League, 1927.
Victor Francis Calverton, editor, *Anthology of American Ne-
   gro Literature,* Modern Library, 1929.
Robert Burns Eleazer, editor, *Singers in the Dawn: A Brief
   Supplement to the Study of American Literature,* Confer-
   ence on Education and Race Relations, 1934, published
   as *Singers in the Dawn: A Brief Anthology of American
   Negro Poetry,* Commission on Interracial Cooperation,
   1942.
Rosey E. Pool and Eric Walrond, editors, *Black and Unknown
   Bards: A Collection of Negro Poetry,* Hand and Flower
   Press, 1958.
Arna Wendell Bontemps, editor, *American Negro Poetry,* Hill
   & Wang, 1963.
Lindsay Patterson, editor, *An Introduction to Black Literature
   in America From 1746 to the Present,* Volume 10 of "The
   International Library of Negro Life and History," Asso-
   ciation for the Study of Negro Life, 1969.
Bontemps and Langston Hughes, editors, *The Poetry of the
   Negro, 1946-1970: An Anthology,* revised edition (Ben-
   nett was not associated with earlier edition), Doubleday,
   1970.
Arnold Adoff, editor, *The Poetry of Black America: Anthology
   of the Twentieth Century,* Harper, 1973.

Contributor to *Afro-American Literature,* 1979. Also contributor of poetry, short stories, and articles to periodicals, including *Crisis, Fire!!, Gypsy, Howard University Record,
Messenger, Opportunity, Palms,* and *Southern Workman.*

OTHER

Author of monthly column "The Ebony Flute" for *Opportunity,* 1926-28, assistant editor, 1926-28.

SIDELIGHTS: A minor literary figure and artist associated
with the Afro-American artistic movement known as the Harlem Renaissance, Gwendolyn B. Bennett was considered a
promising young writer by her peers. Her poetry received favorable reviews from critics, though only a few of the poems
appeared in print and no collection was ever compiled. The
majority of Bennett's published writings appeared in "The
Ebony Flute," her literary and fine arts column written for
Opportunity magazine. The monthly column offered news and
commentary about contemporary black artists and their works
and eventually proved to be an important chronicle of Afro-
American cultural history. In addition, Bennett was a graphic
artist and illustrated several magazine covers for *Crisis* and
Opportunity; she worked in a variety of media, principally pen
and ink, watercolor, oil, batik, and woodcuts.

BIOGRAPHICAL/CRITICAL SOURCES:

BOOKS

Dictionary of Literary Biography, Volume 51: *Afro-American
   Writers From the Harlem Renaissance to 1940,* Gale, 1987.
Fax, Elton C., *Seventeen Black Artists,* Dodd, 1971.
Perry, Margaret, *Silence to the Drums: A Survey of the Lit-
   erature of the Harlem Renaissance,* Greenwood Press,
   1976.

BENNIGSEN, Alexandre (A.)   1913-1988(?)

OBITUARY NOTICE: Born March 20, 1913, in St. Petersburg, Russia (now Leningrad, U.S.S.R.); immigrated to France,
1924; naturalized citizen; died c. 1988. Historian, educator,
and author. A leading Western authority on Soviet Islamic
studies, Bennigsen was the first scholar to discover the existence of an underground Islamic culture in the Soviet Union.
After immigrating to France in 1924, he earned his Ph.D. from
the University of Paris in 1935. He soon developed an interest
in Soviet Central Asian studies, and in the mid-1950s he was
elected to a personal chair of history of non-Arabic Islam at
the Ecole des Hautes Etudes en Sciences Sociales, a position
he held until his retirement in 1983. Bennigsen was also a
director of the Russian center at the Maison des Sciences de
L'Homme in Paris and was a visiting professor of history at
the University of Chicago, beginning in 1970. His book *Muslim National Communism in the Soviet Union: A Revolutionary
Strategy for the Colonial World* has become a standard work
on the Muslim national movements that began in Soviet Russia
at the beginning of the twentieth century. His other writings
include *The Evolution of the Muslim Nationalities of the U.S.S.R.
and Their Linguistic Problems, Islam in the Soviet Union,* and
Mystics and Commissars: Sufism in the Soviet Union.

OBITUARIES AND OTHER SOURCES:

BOOKS

Directory of American Scholars, Volume I: *History,* 7th edition, Bowker, 1978.

PERIODICALS

Times (London), June 24, 1988.

*   *   *

BENTLEY, Ursula   1945-

PERSONAL: Born September 18, 1945, in Sheffield, England;
daughter of Bertram James (in inland revenue) and Ursula (a
teacher; maiden name, Liston) Bentley; married Alan Thompson (a professor), April 12, 1969 (divorced, 1987); children:
Alexis (son), Ishbel (daughter). *Education:* Received B.A. (with
honors) from Manchester University. *Politics:* Social Democrat. *Religion:* "Lapsed Catholic."

CAREER: University College Hospital, London, England, student nurse, 1964; teacher of English and drama in Middleton,
England, 1970-71; Manchester University, Manchester, England, map curator and librarian, 1971-72. Writer. Worked
odd jobs as a stapling machine operator, secretary, cosmetic
salesperson, and domestic help.

AWARDS, HONORS: Named best of young British writers,
1982.

WRITINGS:

The Natural Order (novel), Secker & Warburg, 1982.
Private Accounts (novel), Secker & Warburg, 1986.

WORK IN PROGRESS: A film adaptation of *Private Accounts;*
a novel, tentatively titled *Stifling Domestic Novel.*

SIDELIGHTS: In her first novel, *The Natural Order,* Ursula
Bentley depicts three young women who attempt to recreate
the bond that existed between the nineteenth-century authors
Charlotte, Emily, and Anne Bronte. *Times Literary Supplement* critic Lindsay Duguid commented that "in the end [Bent-
ley] does not seem sufficiently committed to the idea of three

modern girls trying to act out the genius of the Bronte sisters,'' but other critics deemed *The Natural Order* a funny and elegant first novel. Bentley depicts another trio of women in her second novel, *Private Accounts*. As an American married woman meets two other married women in Switzerland, affairs occur, marital roles are challenged, and worlds clash in this story of humor, aggression, and insecurity.

Bentley told *CA:* ''I started writing to cover my aversion to going out to work. I am now cured, although unemployable, and feel obliged to go on writing.''

BIOGRAPHICAL/CRITICAL SOURCES:

PERIODICALS

New Yorker, February 14, 1983.
Spectator, August 21, 1982.
Times Literary Supplement, July 2, 1982.

*   *   *

BERKOWITZ, Leonard 1926-

PERSONAL: Born August 11, 1926, in New York, N.Y.; son of Morris and Goldie (Berkowitz) Berkowitz; married Nettie Shankler, January 30, 1949 (died January, 1975); married Norma P. Nesbitt, December 13, 1975; children: (first marriage) Marti Anne, Phyllis Joan. *Education:* New York University, B.A., 1948; University of Michigan, Ph.D., 1951. *Religion:* Jewish.

ADDRESSES: Home—5818 Anchorage Ave., Madison, Wis. 53705. *Office*—Department of Psychology, University of Wisconsin—Madison, Madison, Wis. 53706.

CAREER: Human Resources Research Center, Randolph Air Force Base, Tex., research psychologist, 1951-55; University of Wisconsin—Madison, 1955—, began as assistant professor, became professor of psychology, 1962—, Vilas Research Professor, 1969—, chairman of department, 1968-70. Visiting associate professor at Stanford University, 1960-61; visiting professor at Cornell University, 1966-67, and University of Edinburgh, 1979. Researcher at Oxford University, 1964-65; fellow at Center for Advanced Study in the Behavioral Sciences, Palo Alto, Calif., 1970-71; overseas fellow of Churchill College, Cambridge, 1974 and 1976. Consultant to Presidential Commission on the Causes and Prevention of Violence. *Military service:* U.S. Army Air Forces, 1945-46.

MEMBER: International Society for Research on Aggression (president, 1981-83), American Association for the Advancement of Science (fellow), American Psychological Association (president of Personality and Social Psychology Division, 1971-72), Society for the Psychological Study of Social Issues, Society of Experimental Social Psychology.

AWARDS, HONORS: Honorary Ph.D. from University of Louvain, 1979.

WRITINGS:

Aggression: A Social-Psychological Analysis, McGraw, 1962.
The Development of Motives and Values in the Child, Basic Books, 1964.
(Contributor) Albert R. Gilgen, editor, *Contemporary Scientific Psychology*, Academic Press, 1970.
Social Psychology, Scott, Foresman, 1972.
A Survey of Social Psychology, Dryden, 1975, revised edition, Holt, 1980.

EDITOR

Roots of Aggression: A Re-Examination of the Frustration-Aggression Hypothesis, Atherton Press, 1969.
(With Jacqueline Macaulay) *Altruism and Helping Behavior: Social Psychological Studies of Some Antecedents and Consequences*, Academic Press, 1970.
(With Elaine Hatfield Walster) *Equity Theory: Toward a General Theory of Social Interaction*, Academic Press, 1976.
Cognitive Theories in Social Psychology: Papers From the Advances in Experimental Social Psychology, Academic Press, 1978.
Group Processes: Papers From the Advances in Experimental Social Psychology, Academic Press, 1978.

Editor of series ''Advances in Experimental Social Psychology,'' Academic Press, 1963—. Associate editor of *Journal of Personality and Social Psychology*, 1967-68.*

*   *   *

BERLAND, Alwyn 1920-

PERSONAL: Born July 31, 1920, in Chicago, Ill.; son of Jacob and Elizabeth (Berg) Berland; married Jayne Epstein (a poet), August 3, 1941; children: four. *Education:* University of Chicago, M.A., 1948; Cambridge University, M.Litt., 1953.

ADDRESSES: Office—Department of English, McMaster University, 1280 Main St. W., Hamilton, Ontario, Canada L8S 4K1.

CAREER: University of Saskatchewan, Regina, professor of English and chairman of department, 1963-67, dean of arts and science, 1967-68; executive secretary of Canadian Association of University Teachers, 1968-72; McMaster University, Hamilton, Ontario, dean of humanities, 1973-81; writer. *Military service:* U.S. Navy, 1942-46.

MEMBER: Humanities Association of Canada (president, 1969-70), Humanities Research Association of Canada.

AWARDS, HONORS: Fulbright fellow in Cambridge, England, 1951-52 and 1952-53; Canada Council grant, 1968, fellowship, 1978-79.

WRITINGS:

Culture and Conduct in the Novels of Henry James, Cambridge University Press, 1981.

Editor of *Wascana Review*, 1966-71. Contributor of articles and stories to literature journals and other magazines in the United States and Canada.

WORK IN PROGRESS: A book on William Faulkner's *Light in August;* a chapter on Henry James, to be included in *The Penguin History of American Literature*, for Penguin.

BIOGRAPHICAL/CRITICAL SOURCES:

PERIODICALS

Times Literary Supplement, August 14, 1981.

*   *   *

BERNSTEIN, Paula 1944-

PERSONAL: Born October 20, 1944, in New York, N.Y.; daughter of Meyer and Anna (Sissman) Kreisman; married Uri Bernstein (a physicist), June 23, 1968; children: Danielle. *Education:* Barnard College, B.A., 1965; Columbia University,

M.A., 1966; California Institute of Technology, Ph.D., 1970; University of Miami, M.D., 1976.

ADDRESSES: Office—8635 West Third St., Los Angeles, Calif. 90048.

CAREER: Cedars-Sinai Medical Center, Los Angeles, Calif., intern and resident, 1976-80; obstetrician and gynecologist in Los Angeles, 1980—.

WRITINGS:

Alive and Well Woman to Woman: A Gynecologist's Guide to Your Body, Bantam, 1984.

SIDELIGHTS: Paula Bernstein told *CA:* "My book grew out of a series of interviews on gynecological topics that I did for the 'Alive and Well' television show. It tries to answer some of the most common gynecological questions and problems encountered in practice."

*　　*　　*

BETTENBENDER, John (I.)   1921-1988

OBITUARY NOTICE: Born April 18, 1921, in Chicago, Ill.; died of cancer, June 24, 1988, in New Brunswick, N.J. Educator, administrator, director, and editor. Bettenbender is remembered for his affiliation with Rutgers University, where he served as both theater director and dean of its art school. He taught drama at various universities before joining the faculty of Rutgers in 1970. There he served as dean of the Mason Gross School of the Arts from its founding in 1976 to the time of his death. He was also founder and director of Chicago's Academy Festival Theater and the Levin Theater Company at Rutgers. In addition to directing more than two hundred theatrical productions throughout his career, Bettenbender edited *Three English Comedies* and *Poetry Festival* and co-edited *Famous Battles.* He also contributed to the Dell editions of *West Side Story, Romeo and Juliet,* and *Man of La Mancha.*

OBITUARIES AND OTHER SOURCES:

BOOKS

Directory of American Scholars, Volume II: *English, Speech, and Drama,* 8th edition, Bowker, 1982.

PERIODICALS

New York Times, June 26, 1988.

*　　*　　*

BIEBEL, David B.   1949-

PERSONAL: Born August 13, 1949, in Boston, Mass.; son of Warren C., Jr. (a minister) and Marian Lois (a housewife; maiden name, Miller) Biebel; married Ann Marie Becker (a housewife), July 5, 1969; children: Jonathan (deceased), Allison, Christopher, Dana. *Education:* Gordon College, B.A., 1970; Gordon Conwell Theological Seminary, M.T.S., 1973, D.Min. (with distinction), 1986.

ADDRESSES: Home and office—Christian Medical Society, New England Regional Office, Stage Rd., Plainfield, N.H. 03781. *Agent*—Helen Hosier, 4943 Seneca Park Loop, Fremont, Calif. 94538.

CAREER: Ordained minister of Evangelical Free Church of America, 1979; songwriter, free-lance photographer, and outdoor editor, 1970-74; associate pastor of Evangelical Free Church of America in Windsor, Vt., 1974-75, and Muskego,

Wis., 1975-78; pastor of Evangelical Free Church of America in Carney, Mich., 1978-81; co-director of Singing Hill Christian Fellowship in Plainfield, N.H., 1981-87; Christian Medical Society, Richardson, Tex., New England regional director, 1987—.

MEMBER: Ministerial Association of the Evangelical Free Church of America.

WRITINGS:

Jonathan, You Left Too Soon, Thomas Nelson, 1981.
(Editor with Howard W. Lawrence) *Pastors Are People, Too,* Regal Books, 1986.

Contributor to magazines.

WORK IN PROGRESS: Pain Is Pain; co-authoring *Christian Medical Ethics Study Guide* and *Layman's Guide to Christian Medical Ethics.*

SIDELIGHTS: David B. Biebel told *CA:* "I was privileged to be a 'preacher's kid,' which provided early foundations for knowing Christ. My personal pilgrimage of faith included grappling with the death of my college friend and former roommate, as well as struggling to resolve other typical adolescent issues amid the turmoil of the late 1960s.

"My faith commitment was challenged by the 1976 death of my mentor, the senior pastor with whom I worked, but that was just a preface to the 1978 death of our first son, Jonathan. This was the event that produced my first book, *Jonathan, You Left Too Soon.* The year 1986 brought another test of faith for our family, through the debilitating illness of our son Christopher, then six years old. Apparently it was the same extremely rare disorder that had killed Jonathan.

"The long-term result of all these things has been to strengthen our resolve to work with God in redeeming power from the pain that life can bring. We have learned through personal experience that, while losses are inevitable in this life, despair is not. We wish to bring this message of hope, faith, and power to people who are hurting."

*　　*　　*

BIRKNER, Michael John   1950-

PERSONAL: Born March 26, 1950, in Teaneck, N.J.; son of John J. and Mildred D. (Marsilio) Birkner; married Robin Wagner (a college reference librarian), October 6, 1979. *Education:* Gettysburg College, B.A., 1972; University of Virginia, M.A., 1973; Ph.D., 1981. *Religion:* Roman Catholic.

ADDRESSES: Home—930 Martha Ave., Lancaster, Pa. 17601. *Office*—Department of History, Millersville University, Millersville, Pa. 17551.

CAREER: Gettysburg College, Gettysburg, Pa., instructor in history, 1978-79; University of Kentucky, Lexington, visiting assistant professor of history, 1979-81; Dartmouth College, Hanover, N.H., adjunct assistant professor of history and associate editor of "The Papers of Daniel Webster," 1981-83; *Concord Monitor,* Concord, N.H., editor of editorial page, 1983-85; Millersville University, Millersville, Pa., assistant professor of history, 1985—.

MEMBER: Organization of American Historians, Society of Historians of the Early Republic.

AWARDS, HONORS: John A. Booth Prize from New Jersey Historical Society, 1987.

WRITINGS:

(Contributor) Paul A. Stellhorn, editor, *Jacksonian New Jersey,* New Jersey Historical Commission, 1979.
(Editor with Paul A. Stellhorn) *The Governors of New Jersey, 1664-1974,* New Jersey Historical Commission, 1982.
Samuel L. Southard: Jeffersonian Whig, Fairleigh Dickinson University Press, 1984.
(Editor with Charles M. Wiltse) *The Papers of Daniel Webster: Correspondence,* Volume VII: *1850-1852,* University Press of New England, 1986.

Contributor to newspapers. Editor of *Pennsylvania History,* 1987—.

WORK IN PROGRESS: The Lion in Winter: Daniel Webster and the Crisis of the Union, 1850.

SIDELIGHTS: Michael John Birkner told *CA:* "A two-year sabbatical from academe to write editorials for the *Concord Monitor* broadened my view of the historian's mission. The public is starved for good history, written with verve and grace. If history is to avoid irrelevance, it must reach a general readership. That's why my current project, focusing on Daniel Webster's last years, will seek a wider audience than scholars. Marrying factual accuracy and lively narrative is the challenge historians must meet."

*   *   *

BIRNBAUM, Louis   1909-1983

PERSONAL: Born February 20, 1909, in London, England; immigrated to the United States, 1914, naturalized citizen, 1925; died of cancer, June 13, 1983; son of Julius I. (a metal smith) and Jane (a housewife) Birnbaum; married Ruth L. Bay (an educational psychologist), May 17, 1940; children: Philip H., Carol J. Birnbaum Sutton. *Education:* University of Denver, B.A., 1931; University of Southern California, M.S., 1942, Ed.D., 1966.

ADDRESSES: Agent—Julian Bach Literary Agency, Inc., 747 Third Ave., New York, N.Y. 10017.

CAREER: Los Angeles Unified School District, Los Angeles, Calif., teacher of U.S. history and government and head football coach, 1951-74, social studies consultant, 1974-76. Training officer for Veterans Administration, 1945-47. *Military service:* U.S. Navy, 1945-69, active duty, 1943-45; became lieutenant commander.

WRITINGS:

Red Dawn at Lexington: "If They Mean to Have a War, Let It Begin Here!" Houghton, 1986.

Contributor to *Mankind.*

WORK IN PROGRESS: At time of death—research to complete the history of the American Revolution; research on Colonel John Stark.

AVOCATIONAL INTERESTS: U.S. history and government; football strategy as it relates to the strategy of battles.

[Sketch verified by wife, Ruth L. Birnbaum.]

*   *   *

BIRNBAUM, Philip   1904-1988

OBITUARY NOTICE—See index for *CA* sketch: Born April 15, 1904, in Zarnowiec, Poland; immigrated to United States, 1923; died March 19, 1988, in New York, N.Y. Educator, editor, translator, and author. Birnbaum spent most of his career teaching and serving as director in Hebrew schools in locations such as Wilmington, Delaware, Birmingham, Alabama, and Camden, New Jersey, before becoming an editor and consultant for Hebrew Publishing Company. Producing the largest-selling translations of Hebrew to English, Birnbaum edited or translated several works of Jewish cultural significance, including *Mishnen Torah, The Daily Hebrew Prayer Book,* and *The Passover Haggadah.* His own writings include *The Arabic Commentary of Yefet ben Ali, the Karaite, on the Book of Hosea; A Book of Jewish Concepts;* and *Death and Mourning in Jewish Tradition.*

OBITUARIES AND OTHER SOURCES:

BOOKS

International Authors and Writers Who's Who, 9th edition, [and] *International Who's Who in Poetry,* 6th edition, Melrose, 1982.

PERIODICALS

New York Times, March 22, 1988.

*   *   *

BIRNBAUM, Stephen (Norman)   1937-
(Steve Birnbaum)

BRIEF ENTRY: Born March 28, 1937, in New York, N.Y. American advertising agent, radio and television commentator, columnist, editor, and author. Regarded as one of the foremost travel authorities in the United States, Birnbaum is probably best known for his appearances as travel editor on such morning television news shows as "Good Morning America" and "Today." He is also editor and author, sometimes under the name Steve Birnbaum, of a highly acclaimed series of annually revised guidebooks, including *Birnbaum's Europe, Birnbaum's Florida for Free, Birnbaum's Hawaii, Birnbaum's South America,* and *U.S.A. for Business Travelers,* all published by Houghton beginning in 1977. From 1971 to 1975 he was managing editor of the popular Fodor travel guide series. Birnbaum stresses personal participation in his guidebooks, which reviewers generally consider to be reliable, practical, and informative. In addition, Birnbaum is a daily commentator on travel subjects for radio networks, writes a syndicated newspaper column on travel, and serves as travel editor for several magazines, including *Esquire, Good Housekeeping,* and *Playboy.* During the 1960s he founded Chamberlain Properties and served as creative director for DePerri Advertising in New York City from 1967 to 1972. *Addresses: Home*—151 East 83rd St., New York, N.Y. 10165. *Office*—Diversion Communications, Inc., 60 East 42nd St., New York, N.Y. 10165.

BIOGRAPHICAL/CRITICAL SOURCES:

BOOKS

Who's Who in America, Supplement to 44th edition, Marquis, 1987.

PERIODICALS

Publishers Weekly, February 13, 1987.
Village Voice Literary Supplement, April, 1982.

BIRNBAUM, Steve
   See BIRNBAUM, Stephen (Norman)

*   *   *

BI Shang-guan
   See SHEN Congwen

*   *   *

BLAIR, Gwenda (Linda)   1943-

PERSONAL: Born May 10, 1943, in Washington, D.C.; daughter of Newell and Greta (Flinterman) Blair; married Richard Goldensohn, October 11, 1975 (deceased); married Charles Cameron Mann (a writer), July 26, 1984; children: (first marriage) Sasha Blair-Goldensohn; (second marriage) Newell Blair-Mann. *Education:* Attended Wheaton College, Norton, Mass., 1960-61; University of Michigan, B.A., 1964; graduate study at Columbia University, 1968-69, and University of California, Berkeley, 1971.

ADDRESSES: Home—365 West End Ave., New York, N.Y. 10024. *Agent*—Gloria Loomis, 150 East 35th St., New York, N.Y.

CAREER: University of Michigan, Ann Arbor, research assistant, 1964-67; teacher at public schools in Sumpter, Mich., 1965-66, New York City, 1969, and Oakland, Calif., 1970; *Liberation,* New York City, editor, 1971-74; *Seven Days,* New York City, editor, 1974-77; free-lance writer, 1977-79; *Attenzione,* New York City, editor, 1979-81; *Mademoiselle,* New York City, editor, 1981-83; free-lance writer, 1983—. Member of board of directors of Dick Goldensohn Fund.

MEMBER: National Writers Union.

WRITINGS:

Laura Ingalls Wilder (juvenile biography), Putnam, 1983.

Author of monthly column in *Mademoiselle.* Contributor to magazines and newspapers. Contributing editor of *Liberation,* 1974-77, *Mother Jones,* 1978-79, *Manhattan, Inc.,* 1984-87.

WORK IN PROGRESS: Almost Golden, a book on television journalist Jessica Savitch and the television news business, publication by Simon & Schuster expected in 1988.

SIDELIGHTS: Gwenda Blair told *CA:* "I devoured the 'Little House' books as a child and was always curious about their author, Laura Ingalls Wilder. My book on her introduces Wilder to her prime audience, children aged six to nine. An extraordinarily gifted writer who did not start to write until she was in her sixties, she revealed an amazing ear and perceptive eye.

"My book *Almost Golden,* on the late television newscaster Jessica Savitch, covers not only her career but the evolution of television news itself. Savitch entered that industry in 1971, at the point when it was coming into full flower as a true broadcast medium: one that could—for better or worse—supplement the facts and figures with a whole new range of eye-catching, show-business-oriented possibilities. My subject is how Jessica Savitch fit into this new definition of 'the news.' "

*   *   *

BLAISDELL, Anne
   See LININGTON, (Barbara) Elizabeth

BLAKELY, Allison   1940-

PERSONAL: Born March 31, 1940, in Clinton, Ala.; son of Ed Walton (a farmer) and Alice Blakely (a seamstress); married Shirley Ann Reynolds (a nutritional scientist), July 5, 1968; children: Shantel, Andrei. *Education:* University of Oregon, B.A., 1962; University of California, Berkeley, M.A., 1964, Ph.D., 1971.

ADDRESSES: Home—8 Belmont Court, Silver Spring, Md. 20910. *Office*— Department of History, Howard University, Washington, D.C. 20059.

CAREER: Stanford University, Stanford, Calif., instructor in history, 1970-71; Howard University, Washington, D.C., assistant professor, 1971-77, associate professor, 1977-87, professor of history, 1987—. Member of test development committee of Educational Testing Service, 1984-88. Member of board of directors of Extended Hand of Montgomery County, Md.; youth sports official in Montgomery County. *Military service:* U.S. Army, 1966-68; became captain; received Bronze Star and Purple Heart.

MEMBER: World History Association, American Historical Association, American Association for the Advancement of Slavic Studies, American Association for Netherlandic Studies, Association for the Study of Negro Life and History.

AWARDS, HONORS: Andrew Mellon fellow, 1976-77; Fulbright fellow, 1985-86; Ford Foundation fellow, 1987-88; American Book Award, 1988.

WRITINGS:

(Contributor) Michael Conniff, editor, *Latin American Populism in Comparative Perspective,* University of New Mexico Press, 1982.
Russia and the Negro: Blacks in Russian History and Thought, Howard University Press, 1987.

Contributor to *Modern Encyclopedia of Russian and Soviet History.* Contributor to history and black studies journals.

WORK IN PROGRESS: The Image of Blacks in the Dutch World.

SIDELIGHTS: Allison Blakely told *CA:* "My research and writing have centered on topics which I consider very important, but which have been neglected. This is true of Russian populism, which as I view as the prototype for twentieth-century revolutionary movements. The role and significance of blacks in European history and culture is also neglected. Russia and the Netherlands are both countries of global importance which have been omitted in previous studies of this subject."

*   *   *

BLOOM, Allan (David)   1930-

BRIEF ENTRY: Born September 14, 1930, in Indianapolis, Ind. American philosopher, educator, editor, and author. Although he is best known for his thought-provoking and controversial best-seller *The Closing of the American Mind: How Higher Education Has Failed Democracy and Impoverished the Souls of Today's Students* (Simon & Schuster, 1987), Bloom considers himself a teacher rather than a writer. A professor of philosophy and political science at the University of Chicago since 1979, Bloom presents his critique of the contemporary university from an educator's point of view. He has also taught political science and liberal arts at the universities of Toronto, Tel Aviv, Chicago, and Paris as well as Cornell and Yale universities. Bloom's writings include *The Political Philosophy of Isocrates* (University of Chicago, 1955), *Shakespeare's Politics* (with Harry V. Jaffa; Basic Books, 1964), and translations of Plato's *Republic* (Basic Books, 1968) and Jean-Jacques Rousseau's *Emile* (Basic Books, 1979). Bloom also edited Alexandre Kojeve's *Introduction to the Reading of Hegel: Lectures on the "Phenomenology of Spirit"* (Cornell University Press, 1980). *Addresses: Home*—5807 Dorchester Ave., Apt. 10E, Chicago, Ill. 60637. *Office*—1126 East 59th St., Chicago, Ill. 60637.

BIOGRAPHICAL/CRITICAL SOURCES:

BOOKS

Current Biography, H. W. Wilson, 1988.
Who's Who in America, 42nd edition, Marquis, 1982.

PERIODICALS

Insight, May 11, 1987.
Nation, May 30, 1987.
New York Times, January 3, 1988.
Publishers Weekly, July 3, 1987.

*   *   *

BLOOMER, Kent C(ress) 1935-

PERSONAL: Born May 31, 1935, in Mount Vernon, N.Y.; son of Harold F. (in the sugar business) and Allene (Cress) Bloomer; married Leonor Golay (a librarian), June 13, 1959; children: Mark Clifford, May Saenz. *Education:* Attended Massachusetts Institute of Technology, 1953-57; Yale University, B.F.A., 1959, M.F.A., 1961.

ADDRESSES: Home—988 Leetes Island Rd., Guilford, Conn. 06437. *Office*—School of Architecture, Yale University, New Haven, Conn. 06520.

CAREER: Carnegie Institute of Technology (now Carnegie-Mellon University), Pittsburgh, Pa., instructor, 1961-63, assistant professor of architecture, 1963-66; Yale University, New Haven, Conn., assistant professor, 1966-69, adjunct associate professor, 1969-74, adjunct professor of architectural design and director of undergraduate studies in architecture, 1974—. Architect with firms of Coffin & Coffin, summers, 1957-58, and Henry S. Kelly, summer, 1960. Sculptor, with nearly fifty exhibitions in the United States and abroad, 1958—; work represented in permanent collections; juror of architecture and sculpture awards. Lecturer at colleges and museums in the United States, Canada, Mexico, and England; member of National Architecture Accrediting Board, 1984-85, and Guilford Building Code Board of Appeals, 1984—.

MEMBER: Association of Collegiate Schools of Architecture, Connecticut Association of Historic Theaters (member of executive board, 1982-84), Sculptors Guild of New York.

AWARDS, HONORS: Art Medal from *Hartford Courant*, 1952; four awards from Association of Artists of Pittsburgh, including first in show and first in sculpture, both 1963; shared Honor Award for design excellence from U.S. Department of Health, Education, and Welfare, 1970; shared citation for estate design from Pittsburgh chapter of American Institute of Architects, 1981; winner of national art competition for design of new physics complex at University of Oregon, 1986.

WRITINGS:

(With Charles W. Moore) *Body, Memory, and Architecture*, Yale University Press, 1977.

Contributor of articles and reviews to journals, including *Carnegie Review, American Scientist, Interiors, Dichotomy, Places, Audubon*, and *Perspecta*. Guest editor of *Journal of Architectural Education*, 1975.

WORK IN PROGRESS: "Robert Kerr, Architect of Bearwood" to be included in *Architect's People*, edited by Russ Ellis and Dana Cuff, for Oxford University Press; *A Study of Ornaments in Architectural Space*.

SIDELIGHTS: In *Harper's* magazine, John Fischer described *Body, Memory, and Architecture* as "the most heretical book on architecture published in many years." Kent C. Bloomer and his co-author have presented an overview of architectural history that emphasizes increasing dehumanization of buildings over the centuries. They point to the development of fortresses as feats of engineering, factories as homes for machinery, and futuristic high-rise apartment complexes as homes for a future in which environmental concerns displace human, emotional needs. In *Body, Memory, and Architecture*, Bloomer proposes the "heretical" thesis that perhaps, after all, the single-unit dwelling with its yard and fireplace is the most appropriate home for a family of human beings. The *Harper's* critic responded: "The authors develop their theses with an erudition I have hardly hinted at. . . . Nearly every page of the book is wittily illustrated with cartoons, drawings, and photographs." Fischer concluded: "If the coming generation of architects—and their clients—pay attention to it, America may someday be a much more agreeable place."

Kent C. Bloomer told *CA*: "My background is both as a sculptor and as an architectural designer. I have been attempting in my practice, in my writings, and in my teaching to combine, or I should say re-combine, properties of sculpture (as art) and building (as architecture) into a concept of ornament, in which certain subject matter normally found in art becomes a fixed property of architecture. My present scholarly interest is in theory of ornament, that is, examining ornament in light of ornaments as figures or things distributed throughout buildings."

BIOGRAPHICAL/CRITICAL SOURCES:

PERIODICALS

Harper's, May, 1978.
New York Times, July 12, 1978, January 14, 1979, April 22, 1979, February 17, 1980, August 7, 1981, August 28, 1983.

*   *   *

BLUM, William (Henry) 1933-

PERSONAL: Born March 6, 1933, in Brooklyn, N.Y.; son of Isadore (a factory worker) and Ruth (a housewife; maiden name, Katz) Blum; living with Adelheid Zoefel (a translator) since 1975; children: Alexander. *Education:* City College (now of the City University of New York), B.B.A., 1955. *Politics:* Socialist.

ADDRESSES: Home—1531 North Fuller Ave. No. 12, Los Angeles, Calif. 90046.

CAREER: Accountant in New York City, 1955-60; International Business Machines Corp., New York City, computer systems analyst and programmer, 1960-64; U.S. State Department, Washington, D.C., computer systems analyst and programmer, 1964-67; *Washington Free Press*, Washington, D.C., founder, editor, and columnist, 1967-69; free-lance journalist in the United States, South America, and Europe, 1970-76; Radio Station KPFA, Berkeley, Calif., business manager and news writer, 1976-80; *Daily Californian*, Berkeley, Calif., general manager and writer, 1981-82; writer, 1982—.

MEMBER: Media Alliance.

WRITINGS:

The CIA: A Forgotten History—U.S. Global Interventions Since World War II, Zed, 1986.
(Contributor) Barbara Rogers, *For Men Only*, Pandora Press, 1988.

Contributor of articles to periodicals, including *San Francisco Chronicle*, *Los Angeles Times*, *People's Almanac*, and *To the Point*.

WORK IN PROGRESS: A revised edition of *The CIA: A Forgotten History*, publication expected in 1988; preparing film documentary based on *The CIA: A Forgotten History* with director and producer Oliver Stone, release expected in 1988; contributing to a book about terrorism and the West, edited by Alexander George, publication by Zed expected in 1988.

SIDELIGHTS: William Blum told *CA:* "My political writing is aimed principally at dispelling the myths—particularly the anti-Communist myths—that all Americans are raised to believe. This is a formidable task, for I have to do battle with no less than a lifetime of indoctrination of my potential audience."

* * *

BOBER, Harry 1915-1988

OBITUARY NOTICE: Born in 1915; died of complications from liver cancer, June 17, 1988. Art historian, educator, and author. Bober was considered a notable authority on the art, architecture, and historiography of the Middle Ages and the early Renaissance period. A professor at the Institute of Fine Arts at New York University beginning in 1954, he was named the school's first Avalon Professor of the Humanities in 1965. Bober also taught at Queens and Smith colleges and at Harvard and Johns Hopkins universities. His writings include the two-volume *Catalogue of Astrological and Mythological Illuminated Manuscripts of the Latin Middle Ages: English Libraries, The St. Blasien Psalter, The Mortimer Brandt Collection of Medieval Manuscript Illuminations*, and *Medieval Objects in the Guennal Collection*. He also wrote *The Passover: An Exhibition by Harry Bober*, the companion volume to a display he arranged at New York City's Metropolitan Museum of Art in 1975.

OBITUARIES AND OTHER SOURCES:

PERIODICALS

New York Times, June 20, 1988.

* * *

BODEEN, DeWitt 1908-1988

OBITUARY NOTICE—See index for *CA* sketch: Born July 25, 1908, in Fresno, Calif.; died of bronchial pneumonia, March 12, 1988, in Woodland Hills, Calif. Actor, screenwriter, playwright, biographer, and novelist. Bodeen began his career as an actor in Pasadena, California, while writing his own plays. He obtained a position as a research assistant to author Aldous Huxley, who was working on the script of the film "Jane Eyre," and this led to Bodeen's becoming first a script reader and then a staff writer with RKO Pictures. In the 1940s he wrote the screenplays for such films as "Cat People," "I Remember Mama," and "Mrs. Mike"; he also co-authored the 1962 filmscript "Billy Budd." In addition to screenwriting, Bodeen wrote for television and the stage, penned the novel *Thirteen Castle Walk*, and published biographies and other factual works about film and the people involved in them. These include *The Films of Cecil B. DeMille* and *Chevalier: The Films and Career of Maurice Chevalier*, both of which he wrote with Gene Ringgold, and his own *Ladies of the Footlights*, *From Hollywood*, and *More From Hollywood*.

OBITUARIES AND OTHER SOURCES:

PERIODICALS

Los Angeles Times, March 18, 1988.

* * *

BOIME, Albert 1933-

PERSONAL: Born March 17, 1933, in St. Louis, Mo.; son of Max (a salesman) and Dorothy (a homemaker; maiden name, Rubin) Boime; married Myra Block (a teacher and sociologist), June 27, 1964; children: Robert, Eric. *Education:* University of California, Los Angeles, B.A., 1961; Columbia University, M.A., 1963, Ph.D., 1968. *Politics:* "Political and economic justice for all."

ADDRESSES: Office—Department of Art Design, University of California, 405 Hilgard Ave., Los Angeles, Calif. 90024.

CAREER: State University of New York at Stony Brook, instructor, 1967-68, associate professor, 1969-70; State University of New York at Binghamton, professor, 1971-78; University of California, Los Angeles, professor of art history, 1978—. *Military service:* U.S. Army, 1955-58.

MEMBER: College Art Association of America, Academy of Rome.

AWARDS, HONORS: Guggenheim fellow, 1974 and 1984; Rome Fellowship prize, 1979.

WRITINGS:

The Academy and French Painting in the Nineteenth Century, Phaidon, 1971, revised edition, Yale University Press, 1986.
Thomas Couture and the Eclectic Vision, Yale University Press, 1980.
Hollow Icons: Politics of Sculpture in Nineteenth-Century France, Kent State University Press, 1987.
A Social History of Modern Art, 1750-1914, University of Chicago Press, Volume I: *Art in the Age of Revolution*, 1987, Volume II: *Art in the Age of Bonapartism*, in press.

Contributor to art journals.

SIDELIGHTS: Albert Boime told *CA:* "I somehow have the conviction that what I write contributes to making the world a saner place to live. Others may dispute this claim, but I am grateful for the feeling. I am also grateful for the opportunity to acknowledge the influence of my dear brother, Jerome Philip Boime, whose rare, provocative mind inspired me with the sheer joy of intellectual pursuit. Whatever present success I have, I owe to my capacity to enjoy my work thoroughly, to exult in ideas and the unboundedness of scholarly activity, and to commit this love to my developing engagement with political, social, and philosophical issues.''

The Academy and French Painting in the Nineteenth Century was welcomed by Christopher Thompson of the *Cambridge Review* as ''the first detailed description of standard teaching practice in France.'' Boime's work represents an attempt to show that, despite its resistance to the independent painters of the day, the French Academy was more important to artistic innovation than previous historians have believed. Thompson wrote, ''Boime has ... given us an irreplaceable description of teaching procedures between 1815 and 1863, with a wonderful selection of little known and interesting works by painters too often thought of as purely conservative.'' A *Times Literary Supplement* critic agreed: ''This excellently researched work makes a very important contribution to the study of modern painting and one which future historians of the French Impressionists will be unable to overlook with impunity.''

One of the most radical independent painters and teachers who aroused the ire of the Academy was Thomas Couture. Boime's lengthy and detailed study *Thomas Couture and the Eclectic Vision* describes the social milieu in which the artist lived and places his development as a painter within this social context. It examines his relationships with other artists, including his famous pupil Edouard Manet, and examines the effect of his teaching on later artistic develoments in France. Benedict Read wrote in the *Times Literary Supplement:* ''Professor Boime has now put Couture in his place, and reminded us that if we are properly to comprehend the art of this period we must also interpret its lesser lights.''

BIOGRAPHICAL/CRITICAL SOURCES:

PERIODICALS

American Historical Review, October, 1981.
Cambridge Review, October 22, 1971.
New York Review of Books, May 27, 1982.
New York Times Book Review, September 14, 1980.
Times Literary Supplement, January 29, 1971, April 3, 1981.

*   *   *

BONES, James C., Jr.   1943-
(Jim Bones, Jr.)

PERSONAL: Born November 1, 1943, in Monroe, La.; son of James (an officer of the U.S. Air Force) and Nell (DeLee) Bones; divorced; children: Paul Daniel. *Education:* Attended University of Texas at Austin, 1962-67.

ADDRESSES: Home and office—P.O. Box 22, Tesuque, N.M. 87574.

CAREER: Free-lance photographer, until 1968; Texas A&M University, College Station, research photographer and consultant for Programma de Education Inter-Americana, 1968; free-lance photographer, 1968-70; Corporation for Public Broadcasting, KERA-TV, Dallas, Tex., environmental filmmaker and producer, 1970-71; Laguna Gloria Art Museum, Austin, Tex., photography teacher, 1972; University of Texas at Austin, artist in residence, 1972-73; free-lance photographer, 1973-75; printing assistant to photographer Eliot F. Porter, 1975-78; free-lance photographer and writer, 1978—.

Wilderness river guide; teacher at photography workshops. Photographs widely exhibited in solo and group shows throughout the southwestern United States.

AWARDS, HONORS: Fellow of Corporation for Public Broadcasting, 1970-71; Dobie-Paisano fellow at University of Texas at Austin, 1972-73.

WRITINGS:

UNDER NAME JIM BONES, JR.

Texas Earth Surfaces, Encino Press, 1970.
Texas Heartland: A Hill Country Year, Texas A&M University Press, 1975.
(With Richard Phelan) *Texas Wild*, Dutton, 1976.
Texas West of the Pecos, Texas A&M University Press, 1981.
Rio Grande: Mountains to the Sea, Texas Monthly, 1985.
Texas: Images of the Landscape, Westcliffe Publishers, 1986.

Contributor of articles and photographs to magazines, including *Audubon, True West, Texas Monthly, Texas Highways, Frontier Times, New Mexico, Outside, Backpacker, Natural History,* and *Sierra.*

WORK IN PROGRESS: Islands of Wilderness, on ''the major life zones of North America, from Mexico to Alaska,'' publication by Westcliffe Publishers expected in 1990 or 1991.

SIDELIGHTS: James C. Bones, Jr., told *CA:* ''My career in photography began when I was a child, with pictures made of models placed in miniature sandbox landscapes. Throughout my high school years, I continued to work with photography, covering missile launches at Vandenberg Air Force Base, in California, for the school newspaper and science club. While waiting for the often delayed early rocket launches, I had time to observe and become interested in the natural events that occurred along the wild stretches of coast within the Pacific Test Range.

''Between my junior and senior high school years I held jobs at some of the launch sites. One evening I assisted in the mating of a test nuclear warhead to a Minuteman missile, slender, pale, green, efficiently designed to kill. The experience woke in me a vague discontent that eventually developed into a conscious attitude toward life and individual responsibility.

''At sundown, I went alone to cliffs overlooking the ocean, where I considered the terrifying and at the same time fascinating images of the procedure. It reminded me in strange way of the procreative activities of a giant mechanical beast, standing apart from the biological world that produced it. Embedded in the headlands around me were tapered fossil shells, left by snails that lived millions of years before, which bore a remarkable resemblance to the missile warhead.

''As I reflected on the immense longevity of life and the swift destruction I was employed to perfect, it became impossible to reconcile my growing curiosity about the natural world with my aspirations to build and fly rockets into space.

''In 1962 I entered the University of Texas at Austin and pursued a complex academic career that included geology, biology, and anthropology, with concentrations in art and literature. I continued to make photographs of the fields I studied, with the aim of improving my ability to communicate what I was learning about the earth and our human position in the web of life.

''After college I went to work for Ron Perryman, a filmmaker, who was producing a film for the U.S. Health, Education, and

Welfare Department about the problems of urban crowding. As a research photographer for Texas A&M University, I traveled in South America to photograph cultural textures for use in public schools. At KERA-TV in Dallas, I filmed and produced several short video programs and an eight-part series called 'Images and Memories' that is now included in the permanent archives of the Corporation for Public Broadcasting.

"During a fellowship at J. Frank Dobie's Hill Country Ranch in 1972, I produced several thousand photographs that explored the thesis that as much can be realized from the microcosmic study of an intimate location as can be learned from a more superficial survey of an entire region. The distillation of those photographs became the illustrations for my second book, *Texas Heartland*. My fourth book, *Texas West of the Pecos*, represents the culmination of fifteen years of work, developing the thesis that natural solitude can be catalytic in precipitating an understanding of the fact that we are all part of one immense body of life.

"I believe life is art, all else is simply artifact. The life of the artist is his great work, and whatever is left behind only reflects how well he did that work. Today the life of the earth is threatened, and I believe that artists working without a social and world consciousness are wasting their time."

BIOGRAPHICAL/CRITICAL SOURCES:

PERIODICALS

Popular Photography, December, 1982.

*   *   *

BONES, Jim, Jr.
   See BONES, James C., Jr.

*   *   *

BONN, Robert Lewis   1937-

PERSONAL: Born October 19, 1937, in Oceanside, N.Y.; son of Walter R. and Elizabeth C. Bonn; married June 18, 1967; children: Timothy, Eti. *Education:* Columbia University, B.A., 1959; New York University, M.A., 1966, Ph.D., 1970.

ADDRESSES: Home—Bronx, N.Y. *Office*—Department of Sociology, John Jay College of Criminal Justice of the City University of New York, 445 West 56th St., New York, N.Y. 10019.

CAREER: Columbia University, New York City, lecturer in sociology, 1969-70; John Jay College of Criminal Justice of the City University of New York, New York City, 1970—, began as assistant professor, became professor of sociology, 1984—.

MEMBER: American Sociological Association, American Criminal Justice Society, American Society of Criminology.

WRITINGS:

Criminology, McGraw, 1984.

Contributor to law and sociology journals.

WORK IN PROGRESS: Images of Society, Imprisonment in the United States.

SIDELIGHTS: Robert Lewis Bonn told *CA:* "I came to criminology out of an interest in social behavior generally and out of having taught the subject for more than five years. After

using several different texts, I concluded that I could write one that was clearer and that would take a distinctly sociological rather than legalistic viewpoint. In my opinion crime is a social problem and can best be seen as a social problem. At the same time, my book is most comprehensive in that it covers all phases of criminology, and it is balanced in that it presents competing viewpoints whenever possible.

"Concerning imprisonment in the United States, I feel that we need to understand why the rate of imprisonment—the number per 100,000—has more than doubled in the last fifteen years and now stands at a record high. Such an understanding means seeing the rate in terms of the enormous social changes which have taken place as our high technological, post-industrial society has emerged. At this point we are left with a big question: In order to keep us safe from ourselves, is it really necessary to maintain—at great cost—a twenty-four-hour surveillance of a "surplus population" now numbering over half-a-million young males?"

*   *   *

BORDEN, Linda   1951(?)-
   (Lizzie Borden)

PERSONAL: Born c. 1951 in Detroit, Mich. *Education:* Attended Wayne State University; received B.A., Wellesley College; received M.F.A., Queens College of the City University of New York.

ADDRESSES: Office—c/o Miramax Films, 18 East 48th St., New York, N.Y. 10017.

CAREER: Screenwriter and director of motion pictures. Writer for *Artforum* in New York City; film editor in New York City.

AWARDS, HONORS: Grants from New York State Council of the Arts and from National Endowment for the Humanities; prize from United States Film Festival, 1987, for "Working Girls."

WRITINGS:

UNDER NAME LIZZIE BORDEN; SCREENPLAYS

(And director) "Born in Flames," First Run Features, 1983.
(With Sandra Kay; and director) "Working Girls," Miramax Films, 1987.

WORK IN PROGRESS: Collaborating with cartoonist Lynda Barry on a motion picture about a cartoonist.

SIDELIGHTS: Lizzie Borden is a feminist filmmaker known for her radical works "Born in Flames" and "Working Girls." She was born in Detroit, Michigan, and studied art there at Wayne State University before transferring to Wellesley College, where she majored in art. She continued her art studies at New York City's Queens College and eventually earned an M.F.A. After receiving her graduate degree she remained in New York City and worked both as a painter and as a critic for the magazine *Artforum*. At that time, according to Borden, she became increasingly "politicized by feminism." She also found her own artwork less and less worthwhile, and after seeing the free-spirited, quasi-experimental films of Jean-Luc Godard she abandoned painting for filmmaking.

Borden later revealed that she had been greatly impressed by the more experimental aspects of Godard's works and was generally intrigued by film's potential as a forum for political debate. "I saw Godard's films and thought, 'Experimentation. Why not?,' " she told the *Detroit Free Press* in 1987. "You can take the graphic and bring it up to the surface. You can deal politically and have people talk as if they're giving essays. . . . On some level, I came into film thinking of it more as essay than entertainment.''

After deciding to become a filmmaker Borden began securing financial backing through a process she described as ''beg, borrow or steal.'' The constant hustling for production funds prevented her from filming regularly, but Borden compensated by concentrating on other technical aspects, notably editing. ''My first film took four years to produce and cost $40,000,'' she related in the *Detroit Free Press* profile. ''I financed it myself and shot once a month. When I taught myself film, that's where I found editing really great. Because it's like the logic of writing. That's where you take the raw material and turn it into what you want it to be.''

In 1983 Borden completed her first film, ''Born in Flames,'' an ambitious fantasy/comedy set in the United States ten years after a socialist revolution. Although ostensibly devoted to equality, the new government has apparently implemented few tenets of feminism, thus compelling New York City's more militant females to band together as the Women's Army. Members of this gang patrol the city to protect fellow women from a seeming multitude of male assailants. The army's efforts prove successful, though their means are sometimes violent. And the enthusiasm with which they execute their duties prompts the American media to construe that the women are actually waging a war against men.

Political and philosophical dissension is rife within the women's organization, however. Much of ''Born in Flames'' actually consists of women debating the merits of their particular feminist perspective. Race, class distinction, and even sexual preference are all subjects of avid debate. But when federal law enforcers accelerate their opposition to the Women's Army, the feminists overcome their ideological differences and join in overthrowing the sexist government.

''Born in Flames'' was not widely reviewed among major American publications, with the notable exceptions of the *New York Times* and *Ms.* Janet Maslin, in her review for the *Times*, described Borden's film as ''inventive'' but ultimately ''too diffuse and overcrowded.'' Maslin acknowledged that the work was ''livelier than might be expected, with its militancy even accompanied by a modicum of topical humor,'' but she added that Borden failed to develop the various politico-feminist conflicts. In addition, Maslin found the characters long-winded, but contended that the excessive rhetoric was actually an asset to the film, resulting in ''an aggressive energy.'' *Ms.* reviewer Martha Nelson was more positive in her assessment of Borden's film, calling it a ''funny, gutsy break in independent feminist filmmaking.'' For Nelson, ''Born in Flames'' was ''not a blueprint for action, but an inspiration to smile and imagine a different future.''

In her next film, ''Working Girls,'' Borden maintained a more sober perspective as she detailed the surprisingly monotonous world of middle-class prostitution. She became intrigued with the subject after meeting prostitutes' rights advocate Margo St. James while filming ''Born in Flames.'' Through St. James, Borden befriended several other members of prostitutes' organizations. Afterwards, she discovered that ''a couple of women I knew . . . worked in brothels.''

Borden eventually accompanied two prostitutes to a middle-class brothel and observed their daily activities. She discovered that prostitution, as it exists in New York City's middle-class brothels, was ''ordinary . . . like the other aspects of middle-class life.'' Borden soon decided to make a film about life in such a brothel, but before she commenced filming she conducted interviews with more than three hundred employees of such places. ''I was fascinated by the subject,'' she later confessed.

Borden's interest resulted in ''Working Girls,'' her film about one day in the life of Molly, a lesbian Yale graduate working as a prostitute in one of New York City's many middle-class brothels. Molly is a kind, witty woman, and much of the film details the dull, stifling repetition of her job. For Borden, life as a middle-class prostitute consists of working and waiting. She thus renders prostitution in a far more believable, though less exotic, manner than is usual in commercial films. When Molly or her co-workers are actually servicing customers, their attitude seems one of reserved compliance. When Molly and the others are waiting for customers, they behave in the same manner as other workers awaiting work—they talk about their lives and their work and engage in generally mundane conversations and activities.

What becomes obvious in ''Working Girls'' is that prostitution is, first and foremost, a job—a dull but lucrative means of livelihood. For the prostitutes, the male clients are merely a means to an end, though some of the men perceive themselves—and encourage the prostitutes to see them—from a more romantic perspective. If there is a villain in the film, it is the house proprietor, Lucy, a former prostitute whose apparent sincerity fails to obscure her coldhearted and calculated manipulation of her employees. Lucy is the catalyst for Molly's decision to quit the brothel. Having already worked her normal shift, Molly is coerced into overtime service by the unsympathetic Lucy. But in the face of Lucy's increasingly irritating intimidation Molly abruptly leaves and bicycles home to her female lover. More than one critic has noted that Molly's decision seems prompted more from disgust over being treated as a commodity than from distaste for her actual profession.

''Working Girls'' divided critical opinion upon its release in early 1987. Some reviewers found the film monotonous and thematically obvious, while others considered it insightful and even entertaining. Among the work's detractors was *Time*'s Richard Schickel, who complained that Borden's movie was not ''novel or shocking.'' Another critic, Rita Kempley, wrote in the *Washington Post* that Borden possessed ''noodlehead notions'' and that the film makes its point ''in the first fifteen minutes.'' But critics such as the *New York Times*'s Vincent Canby asserted that ''Working Girls'' was a worthwhile and provocative work. He called Borden ''a good, disciplined filmmaker'' and praised her skill as a realist. '''Working Girls,' though a work of fiction, sounds as authentic as might a documentary about coal miners,'' he wrote. And even Schickel conceded that ''Working Girls'' possessed ''down-to-earthiness'' in some of its dialogues.

Some critics complained that Borden had depicted prostitution as a sexual power struggle. Schickel, for example, speculated that Borden perceived prostitution as ''a paradigm of the male-female relationship'' and criticized that perception as ''closer to feminist propaganda than to home truth.'' To Borden, however, the film depicted prostitution as a quintessentially capitalist enterprise, and she contended that her film's perspective was both provocative and valid. ''Prostitution is perhaps the lowest form of selling yourself in this culture,'' she told the *Los Angeles Times;* ''but within capitalism, one is always selling an aspect of oneself.'' She asked, ''Who can decide whether renting your body is worse than renting your brain?''

Owing to the attention accorded ''Working Girls,'' Borden has gained increasing respect from Hollywood film studios. She noted to the Toronto *Globe and Mail* that various studios had expressed interest in her forthcoming works, including a collaboration with cartoonist Lynda Barry. ''I'm getting calls from the studios,'' she enthused. ''They say, 'Bring us your next project.''' For Borden, the newfound popularity is welcome.

BIOGRAPHICAL/CRITICAL SOURCES:

PERIODICALS

Detroit Free Press, May 13, 1987.
Film Quarterly, winter, 1986-87.
Globe and Mail (Toronto), May 16, 1987.
Los Angeles Times, March 13, 1987, April 7, 1987.
Metro Times (Detroit), May 6, 1987.
Ms., January, 1984.
New York Times, November 10, 1983, February 27, 1987.
Time, April 27, 1987.
Times (London), March 20, 1987.
Washington Post, March 20, 1987, March 22, 1987, March 25, 1987.*

—*Sketch by Les Stone*

*   *   *

BORDEN, Lizzie
   See BORDEN, Linda

*   *   *

BOTTIGHEIMER, Ruth B.   1939-

PERSONAL: Born July 14, 1939, in Salem, N.J.; daughter of Louis E. (an engineer) and Edna Gabell (a homemaker; maiden name, Wiest) Ballenger; married Karl S. Bottigheimer (a university professor), August 4, 1960; children: John Nathaniel, Hannah Louise. *Education:* Attended Wellesley College, 1957-59, and University of Munich, 1959-60; University of California, Berkeley, B.A. (with honors), 1961, M.A., 1964; further graduate study at University of London, 1962-63; State University of New York at Stony Brook, D.A., 1981.

ADDRESSES: Home—61 Cedar St., Stony Brook, N.Y. 11790. *Office*—Department of Comparative Literature, State University of New York at Stony Brook, Stony Brook, N.Y. 11794.

CAREER: Princeton University, Princeton, N.J., lecturer in German, 1981-84; State University of New York at Stony Brook, assistant professor of comparative literature, 1984—. Member of Environmental Centers of Smithtown-Setauket, Inc.

MEMBER: International Germanistic Association, International Society for Folk Narrative Research, Modern Language Association of America, American Association of Teachers of German, Women in German, German Studies Association, Brothers Grimm Society, League of Women Voters, Frauen in der Literaturwissenschaft, Phi Beta Kappa.

WRITINGS:

(Editor) *Fairy Tales and Society: Illusion, Allusion, and Paradigm* (essays), University of Pennsylvania Press, 1986.
Grimms' Bad Girls and Bold Boys: The Moral and Social Vision of the Tales, Yale University Press, 1987.

WORK IN PROGRESS: An editorial history of Grimms' tales, publication expected in 1990; research on illustration theory, children's Bibles, and illustration history of Grimms' tales.

SIDELIGHTS: Ruth B. Bottigheimer told *CA:* ''I have long been interested in the short narrative in its many forms: medieval epics and tales, fairy tales, short stories, and tale collections like those of Chaucer and Boccaccio. What especially fascinates me—apart from the imaginative plots—are the different ways in which these tales both mirror the society out of which they grow and in turn become a pattern for subsequent tellings of the same tale by storytellers in following generations and centuries, even in very different societies. I work with stories in English, German, French, Spanish, and Italian, and I am beginning to sort out Dutch, Danish, and Norwegian, though I can only claim fluency in speaking German.

''Fairy tales for children in the nineteenth and twentieth centuries offer a special opportunity to see what the adult world wants to impress on its young. This varies considerably according to social, educational, and economic levels, country and century of origin, and religious belief. My work with the tales of the brothers Grimm is part of my efforts to understand the relationships between culture, society, and narrative.''

AVOCATIONAL INTERESTS: History and politics, art and literature, European travel, biology and medicine.

BIOGRAPHICAL/CRITICAL SOURCES:

PERIODICALS

Christian Science Monitor, January 21, 1988.
Detroit Free Press, July 8, 1987.
Los Angeles Times, April 13, 1986.
New York Review of Books, December 3, 1987.
New York Times, March 5, 1985.
Princeton, September, 1982.
Times Literary Supplement, November 20-26, 1987.

*   *   *

BOVE, Paul A(nthony)   1949-

PERSONAL: Surname is pronounced ''Bo-*vay*''; born January 7, 1949, in Philadelphia, Pa.; son of Mario (a salesman) and Carmella (a manager; maiden name, Caspanello) Bove; married Carol Ann Mastrangelo (a professor of French), August 16, 1970; children: Laura M. *Education:* St. Joseph's University, A.B. (magna cum laude), 1970; State University of New York at Binghamton, Ph.D., 1976.

ADDRESSES: Home—11 Gateway Rd., New Wilmington, Pa. 16142. *Office*—Department of English, University of Pittsburgh, 4200 Fifth Ave., Pittsburgh, Pa. 15260.

CAREER: Columbia University, New York, N.Y., assistant professor of English and comparative literature, 1975-78; University of Pittsburgh, Pittsburgh, Pa., professor of English, 1978—.

MEMBER: Modern Language Association of America, English Institute, Society for Critical Exchange (member of board of directors).

AWARDS, HONORS: Chamberlain fellow, 1978; grants from American Council of Learned Societies, 1978-79 and 1984, and University of Pittsburgh, 1981.

WRITINGS:

Destructive Poetics: Heidegger and Modern American Poetry, Columbia University Press, 1980.

(Editor with William V. Spanos and Daniel O'Hara, and author of introduction) *The Question of Textuality: Strategies of Reading in Contemporary American Criticism*, Indiana University Press, 1982.

(Contributor) Jonathan Arac and other editors, *The Yale Critics: Deconstruction in America*, University of Minnesota Press, 1983.

(Contributor) Ronald Schleifer, editor, *Kierkegaard and Literature*, University of Oklahoma Press, 1984.

(Contributor) Daniel O'Hara, editor, *Why Nietzsche Now?*, Indiana University Press, 1985.

Intellectuals in Power: A Genealogy of Critical Humanism, Columbia University Press, 1986.

(Contributor) Jonathan Arac, editor, *Postmodernism and Marxism*, University of Minnesota Press, 1986.

(Contributor) Jonathan Arac, editor, *Philosophy After Foucault*, University of Minnesota Press, 1986.

(Contributor) Joseph Buttigieg, editor, *Shaping the Foundations*, University of Notre Dame Press, 1986.

(Contributor) Frank Lentricchia and Thomas McLaughlin, editors, *Critical Terms for Literary Study*, University of Chicago Press, 1987.

The Politics of the New Criticism, University of Wisconsin Press, in press.

Contributor to *Postmodern Studies in Modern Fiction*, edited by Leonard Orr.

Contributor of articles and reviews to literary journals, including *Contemporary Literature, Criticism, Genre, Minnesota Review, Sub-Stance*, and *Union Seminary Quarterly Review*. Associate editor and contributor to *Boundary 2* and member of editorial board of *Cultural Critique*.

WORK IN PROGRESS: A book on R. P. Blackmur for the "American Writers" series of University of Wisconsin Press; a book on Edmund Wilson for the "American Culture" series of University of Minnesota Press; a book on Henry Adams.

SIDELIGHTS: Paul A. Bove's book *Destructive Politics* is, according to *World Literature Today* critic Edouard Morot-Sir, "a description-justification of deconstructive criticism" and "a sort of rehabilitation-defense of deconstructive poetry of our times." The author discusses New Criticism in great detail, from the perspective of one who would replace it by deconstructionism. Morot-Sir wrote: "Bove's book is important, provocative. It calls for a serious reading from those who like poetry as well as all those who may wonder today about the future of literary criticism."

BIOGRAPHICAL/CRITICAL SOURCES:

BOOKS

Graff, Gerald, *Professing Literature*, University of Chicago Press, 1987.

Leitch, Vincent, *Deconstruction: An Advanced Introduction*, Columbia University Press, 1983.

Melville, Stephen, *Philosophy Beside Itself*, University of Minnesota Press, 1986.

PERIODICALS

Times Literary Supplement, January 2, 1981.
World Literature Today, autumn, 1981.

*   *   *

BRADY, Dave   1913(?)-1988

OBITUARY NOTICE: Born c. 1913; died after a heart attack,

April 1, 1988. Journalist. A sports reporter for the *Washington Post* for more than thirty years, Brady is recognized as one of the first and most knowledgeable writers to cover professional football. After attending St. Joseph's College in Pennsylvania, he was a sportswriter and editor for New Jersey's *Camden Courier-Post* from 1930 to 1943 and again in 1946. He then joined the *Washington Post*, where he was a sports desk reporter and an authority on boxing before becoming renowned for his year-round and exclusive coverage of football. Brady broke many important stories concerning both the game and the business of the National Football League (NFL), and he was respected and admired by fellow journalists, as well as members of the NFL, who found him to be a tough yet fair reporter.

OBITUARIES AND OTHER SOURCES:

PERIODICALS

Washington Post, April 3, 1988.

*   *   *

BRADY, William S.
    See HARVEY, John (Barton)

*   *   *

BRAITHWAITE, William Stanley (Beaumont)   1878-1962

PERSONAL: Born December 6, 1878, in Boston, Mass.; died following a brief illness, June 8, 1962; son of William Smith and Emma (DeWolfe) Braithwaite; married Emma Kelly, June 30, 1903; children: Fiona Lydia Rossetti (Mrs. Merrill Carter), Katherine Keats (Mrs. William J. Arnold), William Stanley Beaumont, Edith Carman, Paul Ledoux, Arnold DeWolfe, Francis Robinson. *Education:* Self-educated; apprenticed to a typesetter at Ginn and Company.

CAREER: Colored American Magazine, Boston, Mass., editor, 1901-02; *Boston Evening Transcript*, Boston, literary editor and columnist, beginning in 1905; Atlanta University, Atlanta, Ga., professor of creative literature, 1935-45. Publisher of *The Poetic Journal in Boston*, 1912-14; editor of *Poetry Review*, 1916-17; founder and editor of B. J. Brimmer Publishing Co., 1921-27; member of editorial board of *Phylon*.

MEMBER: Poetry Society of America, New England Poetry Society, Boston Authors' Club.

AWARDS, HONORS: Spingarn Medal from the National Association for the Advancement of Colored People for outstanding achievement by a member of the colored race, A.M. from Atlanta University, and Litt.D. from Talladega College, all 1918.

WRITINGS:

POETRY

Lyrics of Life and Love (collection), H. B. Turner, 1904, reprinted, University Microfilms, 1971.

(Editor) *The Book of Elizabethan Verse*, introduction by Thomas Wentworth Higginson, H. B. Turner, 1906, reprinted, Folcroft/Norwood, 1980.

The House of Falling Leaves (collection), J. W. Luce, 1908, reprinted, Mnemosyne Publishing, 1969.

(Editor) *The Book of Georgian Verse*, Brentano's, 1909, reprinted, Books for Libraries Press, two volumes, 1969.

(Editor) *The Book of Restoration Verse*, Brentano's, 1910.

(Editor) *Anthology of Magazine Verse and Yearbook of American Poetry*, seventeen volumes, G. Sully, 1913-29, reprinted, Books for Libraries Press, 1972—.

(Editor with Henry Thomas Schnittkind) *Representative American Poetry*, R. G. Badger, 1916.

(Editor) *The Poetic Year for 1916: A Critical Anthology*, Small, Maynard, 1917.

(Editor) *The Golden Treasury of Magazine Verse*, Small, Maynard, 1918.

(Author of introduction) Georgia Douglas Johnson, *The Heart of a Woman and Other Poems*, Cornhill, 1918.

(Editor) *The Book of Modern British Verse*, Small, Maynard, 1919.

(Editor) *Victory! Celebrated by Thirty-eight American Poets*, introduction by Theodore Roosevelt, Small, Maynard, 1919.

(Editor) *Anthology of Massachusetts Poets*, Small, Maynard, 1922.

(Editor) *Our Lady's Choir: A Contemporary Anthology of Verse by Catholic Sisters*, foreword by Hugh Francis Blunt, introduction by Ralph Adams Cram, B. Humphries, 1931.

Selected Poems (collection), Coward-McCann, 1948.

(Editor) *Anthology of Magazine Verse for 1958*, Pentelic, 1959.

Also author of the collection *Sandy Star*, 1926.

OTHER

The Canadian (novel), Small, Maynard, 1901.

The Story of the Great War (juvenile; essays), F. A. Stokes, 1919.

Going Over Tindal: A Fragment Wrenched From the Life of Titus Jabson (novel), B. J. Brimmer, 1924.

The Bewitched Parsonage: The Story of the Brontes, Coward-McCann, 1950.

The William Stanley Braithwaite Reader, edited by Philip Butcher, University of Michigan Press, 1972.

Also author of *Our Essayists and Critics of Today*, 1920, *Frost on the Green Tree* (stories), 1928, and *The Story of the Years Between, 1918-1939*, 1940.

Contributor of book reviews, verse, essays, and articles to periodicals, including *Alexander's Magazine, American Magazine, Atlantic Monthly, Bookman, Book News Monthly, Boston Courant, Century, Christian Endeavor Herald, Crisis, Forum, Independent, Lippincott's, National Magazine, New England Magazine, New Era, New Republic, Opportunity, Poet Lore, Scribner's*, and *Voice of the Negro*. Braithwaite's autobiography, ''The House Under Arcturus,'' was serialized in *Phylon*, 1941-42.

SIDELIGHTS: A major force behind the American poetry revival of the first three decades of the twentieth century, William Stanley Braithwaite was a respected columnist at the *Boston Evening Transcript* and editor of annual poetry anthologies. For seventeen years he introduced many fine poets to the general reading public through his verse compilations and critical writings, and he attempted to widen his audience's understanding of poetry by prefacing his anthologies with educational, up-to-date information on literary trends. He was also a skillful poet in his own right. Introduced to literature while apprenticed to a typesetter, Braithwaite was so moved by English romantic poetry, especially John Keats's ''Ode on a Grecian Urn,'' that he began studying the great writers and composing his own verse.

Braithwaite published his first collection of poetry, *Lyrics of Life and Love*, in 1904. In it he paid homage to his idol through the sonnets ''Keats Was an Unbeliever'' and ''On a Pressed Flower in My Copy of Keats.'' Four years later Braithwaite published a second volume of poems, *House of Falling Leaves*, which celebrated New England nature and included a number of sonnet sequences. The volume also contained ''White Magic: An Ode Read at the Centenary Celebration of the Birth of John Greenleaf Whittier at Faneuil Hall, December 17, 1907,'' in which the poet commends the abolitionist Whittier for giving up composing poetry to write about Negro emancipation in prose. ''White Magic'' offers an important clue to Braithwaite's poetical philosophy, indicating that he thought sociopolitical subject matter incompatible with aesthetics; that poetry, an art form, should be written only for its own sake.

Braithwaite's third collection, *Selected Poems*, was published in 1948, forty years after *The House of Falling Leaves*. Appearing in *Selected Poems* are works from his first two books of verse and others that were previously published in periodicals, as well as new poems. The later verse shows a continuing romantic influence on the author's themes and forms, and critics also cite a new obscurity—a dreamy, otherworldliness—in Braithwaite's work, especially in the poems ''Ascension'' and ''Myths of the Circumference,'' that are reminiscent of the early romantic poet William Blake.

As a whole, Braithwaite's poetry explores typically romantic themes—life and death, nature, innocent love—through skillfully sounded rhyme schemes and traditional verse forms, especially the sonnet. Yet, unlike the romantic poets, Braithwaite never addressed social and political issues, which prompted a number of his contemporaries, unaware of his aesthetic view of poetry, to claim that he was ashamed of being black. In fact, Braithwaite felt that race did not have to direct one's creativity. Even the poet Countee Cullen—whom Braithwaite respected but feared was mired in racial issues—concurred with Braithwaite on this point, writing in *Caroling Dusk: An Anthology of Verse by Negro Poets*, which he dedicated to Braithwaite, that American Negro poetry does not exist; only poetry written by American Negroes.

Braithwaite's talent as a poet and his unwillingness to address black issues elicited responses from critics such as Newman Ivey White, who, in *Anthology of Verse by American Negroes*, claimed that much of Braithwaite's verses in *Lyrics of Life and Love* possess ''a technical finish well above average. Some are rather exquisite; many have a delicate beauty, but . . . there is no interest in racial questions at all, nor in much else that implies stress or conflict.'' This detachment was also evident in Braithwaite's second collection, *The House of Falling Leaves*, prompting the critic to observe that its poetry has ''a somewhat pale and graceful estheticism with no feeling of 'mission' or racial self-consciousness.'' Black writer James Weldon Johnson agreed, stating in *The Book of American Negro Poetry*: ''As an Afroamerican poet [Braithwaite] is unique; he has written no poetry motivated or colored by race. . . . It is simply that race has not impinged upon him as it has upon other Negro poets.''

Braithwaite joined the staff of the *Boston Evening Transcript* in 1905, at the beginning of a poetic renaissance that would excite the country for the next twenty-five years. As literary editor he wrote a column on contemporary poetry, analyzing the genre that previously had been used only as filler in magazines. In 1913 he began culling through magazines and journals to gather works by various poets for an annual anthology, which would also feature his criticism on authors. Yearly, until 1929, the *Anthology of Magazine Verse and Yearbook of American Poetry* brought to the general reading public good verse before it was published in book form. Keeping abreast of the literary trends and focusing on the yet undiscovered poets, Braithwaite wrote in these anthologies prefaces on the art of poetry, in hopes of educating his audience. Today these prefaces and newspaper columns are considered invaluable tools for analyzing past American poetical works and movements.

Although Braithwaite favored the traditional and romantic in his own verse, he was extremely broad-minded and could recognize literary ability. He published works by experimental and avant-garde poets, even when he did not accept their philosophies. For example, Braithwaite included works by the imagist writers, although some of those poets were known for their outspoken prejudice against blacks. And though he was criticized for not mentioning his being black in his own poetry, Braithwaite did introduce many Negro writers to the nation, especially during the Harlem Renaissance of the 1920s. Indeed, he helped black literary criticism emerge by reviewing works by Negroes rather than just providing biographical information on them, as was done previously. Braithwaite included biographical indexes in his anthologies with statements on the authors' lives and influences, but he never mentioned nationality or race. Aware that black works were judged by lower standards than white works because critics at the time deemed literature by Negroes novel and exotic, Braithwaite attempted to evaluate literature strictly by merit and to teach his readers to do the same.

As Braithwaite's influence grew, to be included in one of his anthologies was to have gained acceptance in the literary world. An article in *Phylon* claimed the editor "Made American Writers Famous," yet he had his adversaries, including Conrad Aiken, who claimed in his *Scepticisms: Notes on Contemporary Poetry* that Braithwaite's poetic tastes tended toward the mundane and sentimental, or "marshmallows and tears." In his *Negro Poetry and Drama*, Sterling A. Brown disagreed with Aiken's description of Braithwaite as an editor, claiming that because of Braithwaite's numerous anthologies and objective eye, he "was one of the pioneers in the poetry revival in America."

BIOGRAPHICAL/CRITICAL SOURCES:

BOOKS

Aiken, Conrad, *Scepticisms: Notes on Contemporary Poetry,* Knopf, 1919.
Brown, Sterling A., *Negro Poetry and Drama,* Associates in Negro Folk Education, 1937, reprinted with *The Negro in American Fiction,* Atheneum, 1969.
Cullen, Countee, editor, *Caroling Dusk: An Anthology of Verse by Negro Poets,* Harper, 1927, reprinted, 1974.
Daniels, John, *In Freedom's Birthplace: A Study of the Boston Negroes,* Houghton, 1914.
Dictionary of Literary Biography, Gale, Volume 46: *American Literary Publishing Houses, 1900-1980: Trade and Paperback,* 1986, Volume 50: *Afro-American Writers Before the Harlem Renaissance,* 1986, Volume 54: *American Poets, 1880-1945, Third Series,* 1987.
Johnson, James Weldon, editor, *The Book of American Negro Poetry,* Harcourt, 1922, revised edition, 1931, reprinted, 1983.
Robinson, William H., *Black New England Letters,* Boston Public Library, 1977.
Wagner, Jean, *Black Poets of the United States,* translation by Kenneth Douglas, University of Illinois Press, 1973.
White, Newman Ivey, editor, *An Anthology of Verse by American Negroes,* Trinity College Press, 1924, reprinted, Folcroft, 1975.
Who's Who of the Colored Race, reprinted, Gale, 1976.

PERIODICALS

CLA Journal, December, 1971, September, 1973.
New England Magazine, December, 1905.
Poetry, January, 1917.
Southern Literary Journal, spring, 1971.

OBITUARIES:

PERIODICALS

Negro History Bulletin, January, 1963, April, 1963.
New York Times, June 9, 1962.
Phylon, summer, 1969.
Publishers Weekly, June 18, 1962.*

—*Sketch by Carol Lynn DeKane*

*   *   *

BRAND, Christianna
   See LEWIS, Mary (Christianna)

*   *   *

BRAWLEY, Benjamin (Griffith)   1882-1939

PERSONAL: Born April 22, 1882, in Columbia, S. C.; died after a brief illness following a stroke, February 1, 1939, in Washington, D. C.; son of Edward MacKnight (a clergyman and an educator) and Margaret Sophronia (Dickerson) Brawley; married Hilda Damaris Prowd, July 20, 1912. *Education:* Atlanta Baptist College (now Morehouse College), B.A., 1901; University of Chicago, B.A., 1906; Harvard University, M.A., 1908.

ADDRESSES: Home—1201 Harvard St. N. W., Washington, D. C. 20009.

CAREER: Educator and author. Taught in a rural one-room school in Georgetown, Fla., 1901-02; Morehouse College, Atlanta, Ga., instructor in English, history, and Latin, 1902-10; Howard University, Washington, D. C., professor of English, 1910-12; Morehouse College, professor of English and dean, 1912-20; ordained to Baptist ministry, 1921; Messiah Baptist Church, Brockton, Mass., pastor, 1921-22; Shaw University, Raleigh, N. C., professor of English, 1923-31, dean, 1930-31; Howard University, professor of English, 1931-39. President of Association of Colleges for Negro Youth, 1919-20. Conducted a study of educational and social conditions on the west coast of Africa in 1930; gave lectures to various colleges and universities.

AWARDS, HONORS: Recipient of honorary doctorates from Shaw University, 1927, and Morehouse College, 1937.

WRITINGS:

A Toast to Love and Death (poems), Atlanta Baptist College, 1902.
The Problem, and Other Poems (poems), Atlanta Baptist College, 1905.

A Short History of the American Negro, Macmillan, 1913, 4th revised edition, 1939.

History of Morehouse College, Morehouse College (Atlanta, Ga.), 1917, reprinted, McGrath Publishing, 1970.

The Negro in Literature and Art in the United States, Duffield, 1918, revised edition, 1921, reprinted, Scholarly Press, 1972.

Women of Achievement, Woman's American Home Baptist Mission Society, 1919, reprinted, University Microfilms (Ann Arbor, Mich.), 1978.

A Short History of the English Drama, Harcourt, 1921, reprinted, Books for Libraries, 1969.

A Social History of the American Negro, Macmillan, 1921, reprinted, AMS Press, 1971.

New Survey of English Literature: A Textbook for Colleges, Knopf, 1925, reprinted, 1930.

Doctor Dillard of the Jeanes Fund, with an introduction by Anson Phelps Stokes, Revell, 1930, reprinted, Books for Libraries, 1971.

History of the English Hymn, Abingdon, 1932.

(Editor) *Early Negro American Writers,* University of North Carolina Press, 1935, reprinted, Books for Libraries, 1968.

Paul Laurence Dunbar, Poet of His People, University of North Carolina Press, 1936, reprinted, Kennikat, 1967.

Negro Builders and Heroes, University of North Carolina Press, 1937, reprinted, 1965.

The Negro Genius: A New Appraisal of the Achievement of the American Negro in Literature and the Fine Arts, Dodd, 1937, reprinted, Biblo & Tannen, 1966.

The Seven Sleepers of Ephesys (poems), Foote & Davis (Atlanta, Ga.), 1971.

Also author of short stories and other poems and editor of *The Best Stories of Paul Laurence Dunbar,* 1938. Contributor of scholarly articles to the *Dictionary of American Biography* and of historical essays, social commentaries, poems, and book reviews to *Crisis, Dial, Lippincott's Magazine, Christian Advocate, Bookman, Southern Workman, Opportunity, Journal of Negro History, Harvard Monthly, Sewanee Review,* the *Springfield Republican,* and other publications. Editor of *Home Mission College Review* for several years.

SIDELIGHTS: Regarded as one of the most prolific writers of all Afro-American educators, Benjamin Brawley is best known for his works in literary and social history. Several of his books are considered standard texts in college and university curriculums. Among these are *The Negro in Literature and Art in the United States, New Survey of English Literature,* and Brawley's two biographical volumes, *The Negro Genius,* which focuses on black artists and literary figures, and *Negro Builders and Heroes,* which covers a wider field of black notables.

BIOGRAPHICAL/CRITICAL SOURCES:

BOOKS

Brown, Sterling A., Arthur P. Davis, and Ulysses Lee, editors, *The Negro Caravan,* Arno, 1969.

Hughes, Langston, and Arna Bontemps, editors, *Poetry of the Negro, 1746-1949,* Doubleday, 1949.

Thorpe, Earl Endris, *Black Historians,* Morrow, 1971.

PERIODICALS

Afro-American, February 11, 1939.

New York Times, February 7, 1939.

Phylon, Volume X, number 1, 1949.*

BRENNAN, Gale (Patrick) 1927-

PERSONAL: Born March 12, 1927, in Manitowoc, Wis.; son of Harold and Irene (Cavanaugh) Brennan; married Mary Elizabeth Casey, January 31, 1953; children: Katherine (Mrs. Tom Dillig), Bridget Gale, John Patrick, Brian Daniel, Peter Thomas (deceased), Patrick Cavanaugh, Maura Casey, Margaret Mary, Shiela Marie, Therese Elizabeth, Joel Thomas, Sarah Mauve. *Education:* Marquette University, Ph.B., 1951.

ADDRESSES: Home and office—8419 Stickney Ave., Wauwatosa, Wis. 53226.

CAREER: Milwaukee Catholic Charities, Milwaukee, Wis., writer, 1951; Miller Brewing Co., Milwaukee, editor, 1951-55, publications director, 1953-55; Robin Press Publishers, Milwaukee, writer and editor, 1955-58; president of Communications, Inc., 1958-77; Book World Promotions, Newark, N.J., writer, 1977-78; owner of Gale Brennan Enterprises, 1987—. President and creative director of Gale Brennan & Associates, Milwaukee, 1965-74; president of Brennan Books, Inc., Milwaukee, 1972-77; writer and editor for Ideals Publishing and Reiman Publishing. *Military service:* U.S. Army, 1945-47.

MEMBER: National Writers Association, Milwaukee Press Club.

WRITINGS:

The XXII Summer Olympic Games, Moscow, 1980, Ideals, 1980.

Household Energy Saving Guide, Ideals, 1981.

CHILDREN'S BOOKS

(With Tom LaFleur) *Bingo the Bear,* Brennan Books, 1981.

Earl the Squirrel, Brennan Books, 1981.

(With LaFleur) *Isadore the Dinosaur,* Brennan Books, 1981.

Toulouse the Mouse, Brennan Books, 1981.

(With LaFleur) *Spunky the Monkey,* Brennan Books, 1981.

(With LaFleur) *Woolly the Wolf,* Brennan Books, 1981.

(With LaFleur) *Henry the Hound,* Brennan Books, 1982.

(With LaFleur) *Tuffy the Tiger,* Brennan Books, 1982.

Also author of *The 1980 Winter Olympics, Vegetable Gardening Guide, Family First Aid Guide, About Alcohol and Alcoholics, Elihu the Elephant, Gloomy Gus the Hippopotamus, Dugan the Duck, Ulysses S. Ant and Robert E. Flea, Terry the Canary, Hugh the Gnu, Myrtle the Turtle, What If . . . , Here Come the Clowns, In the Land of Sniggl de-Bloop, Alone: A Story for Children About Abortion,* and *I Know They Love Me Anyway.*

Editor of *Freddie the Frog* and *Emil the Eagle.*

WORK IN PROGRESS: Parsimonious T. Prattle . . . Who Loves to Hear His Money Rattle; a mystery novel; research on alcohol and drug abuse and treatment.

SIDELIGHTS: Gale Brennan told *CA:* ''I have discovered that the only thing children like to do more than eat is laugh—which, I suppose, is one reason I try to write children's books that incorporate humor. These days, in view of television, publishers are loath to invest money in books that do *not* feature television characters. The result is lousy children's books written by amateurs who crank out stories about Disney-like characters. These have been 'pre-sold' on the tube. There's no need for quality, and that's a pity. For the most part, except for a few writers and storytellers who can also illustrate their material—Mercer Meyer, Theodore Geisel—children's book writers starve.

"The 'Brennan Animal Stories' were translated into French, Scandinavian, and Dutch."

AVOCATIONAL INTERESTS: Golf; curling; politics; antique furniture; the life, times, and style of Ring Lardner; people (especially those to whom others pay little attention); his Irish ancestry; the Milwaukee and Wisconsin lifestyle.

*   *   *

BRITTEN, Milton R(eese) 1924-1985

PERSONAL: Born December 17, 1924, in Wilkes-Barre, Pa.; died after an apparent heart attack, March 19, 1985, in Memphis, Tenn.; son of Isaac Milton and Marguerite (Reese) Britten; married Virginia Butler (a junior high school teacher), November 11, 1951; children: Ann George, Jonathan B., Martha, Anthony. *Education:* Yale University, B.A. (with honors), 1949.

ADDRESSES: Home—5170 Shady Grove Rd., Memphis, Tenn. 38117.

CAREER: Memphis Press-Scimitar, Memphis, Tenn., reporter, 1949-56, Washington correspondent, 1956-63; Scripps-Howard Newspaper Alliance, Washington, D.C., night editor, 1963-66, assistant managing editor, 1966-74, managing editor, 1974-76; *Memphis Press-Scimitar,* editor, 1976-83. Washington correspondent for *Knoxville News-Sentinel,* 1956-63. Trustee of Scripps-Howard Foundation, beginning in 1969. *Military service:* U.S. Army, 1942-45; served in European theater.

AWARDS, HONORS: Christopher Award, 1953.

WRITINGS:

(With Andrew Tully) *Where Did Your Money Go? The Foreign Aid Story,* Simon & Schuster, 1964.

OBITUARIES:

PERIODICALS

Chicago Tribune, March 21, 1985.
New York Times, March 21, 1985.
Washington Post, March 25, 1985.*

*   *   *

BROCKWAY, (Archibald) Fenner 1888-1988

OBITUARY NOTICE—See index for *CA* sketch: Born November 1, 1888, in Calcutta, India; died April 28 (one source says April 29), 1988, in Hertfordshire, England. Politician, activist, and author. First elected to the British Parliament's House of Commons in 1929 as a member of the Labour party, Brockway fought all his life for the causes of socialism, peace, Indian and African independence, and nuclear disarmament. Active in establishing links with Socialist groups in other countries, he also helped found the Campaign for Nuclear Disarmament, taking part in many protest marches. Though he advocated the abolition of the House of Lords because it represented to him a last bastion of special privilege, Brockway was created a life peer by Queen Elizabeth II in 1964, and thus gained a seat in the House of Lords. He wrote novels and plays as well as political works, including *Labour and Liberalism, English Prisons Today: Being the Report of the Prison System Enquiry Committee, Purple Plague: A Tale of Love*

and Revolution, Pacifism and the Left Wing, an autobiography titled *Towards Tomorrow,* and *98 Not Out.*

OBITUARIES AND OTHER SOURCES:

BOOKS

International Who's Who, 51st edition, Europa, 1987.
The Writers Directory: 1988-1990, St. James Press, 1988.

PERIODICALS

Globe and Mail (Toronto), April 30, 1988.
Los Angeles Times, April 30, 1988.
New York Times, May 1, 1988.
Times (London), April 30, 1988.
Washington Post, April 30, 1988.

*   *   *

BROGAN, Jacqueline Vaught 1952-
(Jacque Vaught)

PERSONAL: Born July 23, 1952, in Odessa, Tex.; daughter of N. R. (a professor) and M. I. (a professor; maiden name, Alcorn) Vaught; married T. V. F. Brogan (a professor), June 28, 1981; children: Jessica Leigh, Evan Lloyd. *Education:* Southern Methodist University, B.A. (magna cum laude), 1974, M.A., 1975; attended Tufts University, 1976; University of Texas at Austin, Ph.D., 1982.

ADDRESSES: Office—Department of English, University of Notre Dame, Notre Dame, Ind. 46556.

CAREER: Midland College, Midland, Tex., and Odessa College, Odessa, Tex., instructor in world literature, 1977; University of Texas at Austin, assistant instructor in English, 1977-82; University of Hawaii at Manos, Honolulu, assistant professor of English, 1983-86; University of Notre Dame, Notre Dame, Ind., assistant professor of English, 1986—.

MEMBER: Modern Language Association of America, Wallace Stevens Society, Phi Beta Kappa, Phi Kappa Phi.

WRITINGS:

Stevens and Simile: A Theory of Language, Princeton University Press, 1986.
(Editor) *Part of the Climate: An Anthology of American Cubist Poetry,* University of California Press, 1988.

Contributor of articles, poems (under name Jacque Vaught), and reviews to magazines, including *American Literature, American Poetry, Wallace Stevens Journal, Bamboo Ridge,* and *Trinity Review.* Assistant editor of *Texas Quarterly,* 1978-79, 1979-80.

WORK IN PROGRESS: Intricate Evasions, on language theory, completion expected in 1990.

SIDELIGHTS: Jacqueline Vaught Brogan told *CA:* "Despite the rather abstract nature of my book on Stevens, what prompted my work on Stevens and simile was actually quite personal: the question of what I was doing to myself and how I was naming myself and the world in writing my own poetry. I was especially perplexed by what seemed to be the power of language to make personal problems disappear and, conversely, the power of language to make things appear by naming them. I began to take classes in the philosophy of language as a sidelight to my work as an English graduate student.

"My poetry is probably most colored by growing up in the west Texas desert—a place full, as it were, of vast empty spaces, a constant wind, and mental freedom. Living for three years in Hawaii, a place as different from west Texas culturally as geographically, changed my writing completely. My most recent work is much less private or confessional than my earlier work. I've yet to see what direction it will take now.''

* * *

BRONTE, D(iana) Lydia 1938-

PERSONAL: Surname is pronounced "*Bron*-ty"; born December 27, 1938, in Memphis, Tenn.; daughter of Paul (a businessman) and Dorothy Vivian (a journalist; maiden name, Hamilton) Bronte. *Education:* Hendrix College, B.A. (with high honors), 1960; graduate study at University of Aix-Marseille, 1960-61; University of North Carolina at Chapel Hill, Ph.D., 1969. *Politics:* Democrat. *Religion:* Protestant.

ADDRESSES: Home—111 East 88th St., New York, N.Y. 10128. *Office*—Carnegie Corporation of New York, 437 Madison Ave., New York, N.Y. 10022.

CAREER: George Washington University, Washington, D.C., instructor, 1965-70, assistant professor of French and English, 1969-71; Woodrow Wilson National Fellowship Foundation, Princeton, N.J., director of research for National Humanities Series, 1971-73; Rockefeller Foundation, New York City, consultant in humanities, 1973-74, assistant director for humanities, 1974-77, associate director for humanities, 1977-79, program officer for Central Administration, 1979-80; MacArthur Foundation, Chicago, Ill., consultant to Program Policy Committee, 1980-82; Carnegie Corporation of New York, New York City, consultant, 1982—, staff director of Aging Society Project, 1983—. Special assistant to the director of Folger Shakespeare Library, 1970-71.

MEMBER: Modern Language Association of America, Coffee House, Princeton Club, Women's City Club of New York, Cosmopolitan Club.

AWARDS, HONORS: Fulbright fellow, 1960-61; Woodrow Wilson fellow, 1961-62 and 1962-63.

WRITINGS:

(Editor and author of introduction, with Alan Pifer) *Our Aging Society: Paradox and Promise*, Norton, 1986.

Guest editor of *Mademoiselle*.

WORK IN PROGRESS: Two books about the third quarter of life and long careers.

SIDELIGHTS: D. Lydia Bronte told *CA*: "People always ask about this, so for the record, I am a cousin of Charlotte and Emily Bronte, descended from their uncle William Bronte (their father Patrick was the oldest of ten children, William the next child after Patrick in an Irish family from County Down). Patrick traveled to England to attend St. John's College, Cambridge, at the age of fifteen and stayed. The rest of the family remained in Ireland, except for William's son John who emigrated to the United States probably around 1840 and thereby unwittingly became my ancestor. In one of those amazing accidents of heredity, I inherited Emily's profile. It would have been nice if along with that I had inherited her gift for fiction writing, but my interests have always gone instead into nonfiction. But there's more of a connection than might appear on the surface: there were not many intellectual and creative outlets available to women in the nineteenth century, and even novel-writing was somewhat daring. Charlotte's and Emily's

novels show a powerful concern for human rights and equality and for social justice. If they have twentieth-century reincarnations, Emily is probably a brilliant psychotherapist, and Charlotte is probably in the Senate or the House of Representatives. The 'real world' was always the center of their interest; they just weren't as free to translate that interest into action, as women in the twentieth century fortunately have been. So they created a magnificent alternative—perhaps ultimately more powerful and long-lasting than action in the 'real world' would have been.''

AVOCATIONAL INTERESTS: Tennis, collecting American antiques and Bronte novels.

* * *

BROOKS, Elston (Harwood) 1930-

PERSONAL: Born February 18, 1930, in Kansas City, Mo.; son of Amos E. and Dorothy Miller (Gale) Brooks; married, 1953 (divorced); married Pamela Gilbert; children: (previous marriage) David Bryan. *Education:* Attended Texas Christian University, 1957-58.

ADDRESSES: Home—1951 Shelman Trail, Fort Worth, Tex. 76112. *Office*—*Fort Worth Star-Telegram*, Fort Worth, Tex. 76102.

CAREER: Fort Worth Press, Fort Worth, Tex., reporter, 1947-48; *Fort Worth Star-Telegram*, Fort Worth, author of "The Elston Brooks Column," 1948—. Star of "Ballads by Brooks," (currently titled "The Elston Brooks Show"), on KXOL-Radio and WBAP-Radio, 1947-80. *Military service:* U.S. Army, 1950-52.

MEMBER: Sigma Delta Chi.

AWARDS, HONORS: Journalism awards include three Texas Headliners Awards, seven awards from Associated Press, and five awards from Sigma Delta Chi; won NBC-TV's "The Big Story," 1956; Pulitzer Prize nomination, 1957.

WRITINGS:

Don't Dry-clean My Blackjack, Branch-Smith, 1979.
I've Heard Those Songs Before: The Weekly Top Ten Tunes of the Last Fifty Years, Morrow, 1981.
With a Cast of Thousands, Branch-Smith, 1982.
Column, Write!, Eakin Publications, 1986.

WORK IN PROGRESS: The Man Who Ruined Football, a novel, publication expected in 1989; *The Yesterday Man,* a novel, publication expected in 1990.

* * *

BROWN, Dorothy M. 1932-

PERSONAL: Born December 23, 1932, in Baltimore, Md.; daughter of Basil F. (an accountant) and Marie (a housewife; maiden name, Hooper) Brown. *Education:* College of Notre Dame of Maryland, A.B., 1954; Georgetown University, M.A., 1959, Ph.D., 1962.

ADDRESSES: Home—3611 O St. N.W., Washington, D.C. 20007. *Office*—Department of History, Georgetown University, Washington, D.C. 20057.

CAREER: High school English teacher in Baltimore, Md., 1954-57; College of Notre Dame of Maryland, Baltimore, assistant professor of history, 1958-66; Georgetown University, Washington, D.C., assistant professor, 1966-72, associate professor, 1973-81, professor of American history, 1981—, chairman of department of history, 1973-79, coordinator of academic planning, 1979-87. Member of District of Columbia Community Humanities Council.

MEMBER: American Historical Association, Organization of American Historians, Society for Values in Education, Danforth Associates.

AWARDS, HONORS: Certificate of Merit from American Bar Association, 1985, for *Mabel Walker Willebrandt*.

WRITINGS:

(Contributor) W. Richard Walsh and William L. Fox, editors, *Maryland's History*, Maryland Historical Society, 1974.
Mabel Walker Willebrandt: Power, Loyalty, and Law, University of Tennessee Press, 1984.
Setting a Course: American Women in the 1920s, G. K. Hall, 1987.

Contributor to history journals.

WORK IN PROGRESS: Research for a book on American women in the 1960s.

SIDELIGHTS: Dorothy M. Brown told *CA:* ''Trained in political and cultural history, I have gradually moved into women's history in the 1980s. My biography on Mabel Walker Willebrandt resulted from two factors: an assignment for her article in *Notable American Women: The Modern Period;* and the dedication of her daughter who had been seeking a biographer almost since her death in 1963. Willebrandt, throughout most of the 1920s, was the highest ranking woman in the federal government—an assistant attorney general with responsiblity for prohibition cases, federal income tax litigation, and the federal prison system. She was a master of networking and a redoubtable but reluctant campaigner for the Republicans. In 1928 her speeches for Herbert Hoover earned her the title 'Mrs. Firebrand' and led to the conclusion of a commentator in *Collier's:* 'No other woman has ever had so much influence upon a Presidential campaign as Mrs. Willebrandt has had upon this one.' Her friend Judge John Sirica observed that 'if Mabel had worn trousers, she could have been President.' What she really wanted was a federal judgeship, but this 'first' was not to be hers. Frustrated with the leadership of Hoover and believing that she had been left in no-man's land by the party during the 1928 campaign, she left the Justice Department and pioneered in air and radio law. For more than twenty years she represented the Screen Directors Guild, and for years she was the attorney for Metro-Goldwyn-Mayer and for Hollywood stars ranging from Jeanette MacDonald to Charlie Chaplin.

''The Willebrandt biography led to an invitation from Barbara Haber, the editor of the Twayne series on American women in the twentieth century, to undertake a study of women in the 1920s. *Setting a Course: American Women in the 1920s* was the result.''

*   *   *

BROWN, H. Rap
    See Al-AMIN, Jamil Abdullah

*   *   *

BROWN, Rustie   1930(?)-1988

OBITUARY NOTICE: Born c. 1930; died of a heart attack,

January 14, 1988, in Los Angeles, Calif. Magazine columnist and author. Brown was known for her writings concerning nautical subjects. After interviewing a survivor from the shipwrecked *Titanic*, she became interested in marine books and wrote *The Mariner's Trivia Book* and *The Titanic, the Psychic, and the Sea*. Brown also compiled *Women as We See Ourselves*, a collection of the columns she contributed to magazines.

OBITUARIES AND OTHER SOURCES:

PERIODICALS

Los Angeles Times, January 20, 1988.

*   *   *

BROWN, Tony
    See BROWN, William Anthony

*   *   *

BROWN, Wesley   1945-

PERSONAL: Born May 23, 1945, in New York, N.Y. *Education:* Oswego State University, B.A. in political science and history, 1968.

ADDRESSES: Home—103 West 141st St., New York, N.Y. 10030.

CAREER: Writer.

WRITINGS:

Tragic Magic (novel), Random House, 1978.

Work represented in anthologies, including *Poetry* and *We Be Word Sorcerers*. Contributor of poems and short stories to *Essence, Black Creation*, and other periodicals.

SIDELIGHTS: Wesley Brown's first novel, *Tragic Magic*, is the story of Melvin Ellington, a well-educated, young black man who returns to his Queens, New York, neighborhood after serving two years in prison as a conscientious objector to the Vietnam War. The narrative covers the events of Ellington's first day home, interspersed with recollections of prison life and college days. Trying to get all the pieces of his life back together, Melvin rejoins his family for dinner, and later in the evening he goes out with a high school friend on a nighttime excursion that turns catastrophic.

Tragic Magic won the attention and praise of many critics. They particularly admired Brown's ability to evoke urban black America and his sensitivity to man's search for meaning and identity in life. ''Wesley Brown has a careful eye for the details and nuances of urban black existence,'' remarked a *Choice* contributor, who then hailed Brown as ''a gifted writer, capable of exploring a wide range of human emotions'' and judged *Tragic Magic* ''an impressive first novel.'' Likewise, a reviewer of the novel for *New Yorker* assessed Brown's portrait of Ellington as ''effective and original'' and lauded the author's recording of ''the provocative, singsong slang of the street and prison.'' *Village Voice* contributor Lin Rosechild Harris complimented Brown for creating ''a wonderful addition to the pantheon of heroic young initiates'' while also observing that ''the book sings with images and rhythms of urban black America,'' and Alan Cheuse, writing in *New York Times Book Review*, described *Tragic Magic* as a ''jaunty prose version of the urban blues'' that ''deserves an attentive audience.''

BIOGRAPHICAL/CRITICAL SOURCES:

PERIODICALS

American Book Review, summer, 1979.
Choice, February, 1979.
Nation, December 29, 1979.
New Yorker, October 23, 1978.
New York Times Book Review, February 11, 1979.
Village Voice, November 20, 1978.*

*   *   *

BROWN, William Anthony   1933-
(Tony Brown)

PERSONAL: Known professionally as Tony Brown; born April 11, 1933, in Charleston, W.Va.; son of Royal and Catherine (Davis) Brown; divorced; children: Byron Anthony. *Education:* Wayne State University, B.A., 1959, M.S.W., 1961.

CAREER/WRITINGS: Detroit Courier, began as drama critic, became city editor; WTVS-TV, Detroit, Mich., worked variously as producer, host, and writer of series, including "C. P. T.," "For Whites Only," and "Free Play"; WNET-TV, New York City, producer and host of series "Black Journal," 1970-77; Howard University, Washington, D.C., founder and dean of school of communications and chairman of board of WHUR-FM Radio, 1971-74, later became professor; Tony Brown Productions, president, and producer and host of "Tony Brown's Journal," 1977-81; WRC-TV, Washington, D.C., producer and host of "Tony Brown at Daybreak"; WNET-TV, New York City, producer and host of "Tony Brown's Journal," 1982—.

Owner of public relations and advertising firm; publisher and editor of periodicals. Visiting professor at Central Washington State University, 1971-72. Member of communications advisory committee of National Institute of Mental Health, beginning in 1972, Congressional Black Caucus Communications Brain Trust, beginning in 1977, advisory board of National Council for Black Studies, beginning in 1977; member of board of directors of National Center of Afro-American Artists, National Black United Fund. Author of a syndicated column; lecturer. Helped coordinate March to Freedom With Dr. Martin Luther King, Jr., in Detroit, 1963; associated with Project '80 Coalition for Black Colleges, and Black College Day in Washington, D.C., 1980. *Military service:* U.S. Army, 1953-55.

MEMBER: National Communications Council (member of board of governors), Alpha Phi Alpha.

AWARDS, HONORS: "Black Journal" series nominated for Emmy Award by National Academy of Television Arts and Sciences, 1972; Business Achievement Award from Black Retail Action Group, 1972; Media Workshop Award, 1972; Communicator for Freedom Award from OPERATION PUSH, 1973; national achievement award from Nebraska Urban League, 1973; named one of one hundred most influential black Americans by *Ebony* magazine, 1973; Frederick Douglass Liberation Award from Howard University, 1974; named Communicator of the Year by National Association of Market Developers, 1976; public service award from National Urban League, 1977; award from International Key Women of America, 1977. Honorary LL.D. from University of Michigan, 1975.

SIDELIGHTS: Praised by *Black Enterprise* for his "provocative interviewing and analytical wit," Tony Brown is producer and host of the long-running television series "Tony Brown's Journal" (known until 1977 as "Black Journal"). As Bettelou Peterson observed in the *Detroit Free Press,* the program has special importance to television because it is "produced by and for blacks with an uncompromisingly black point of view." Within a newsmagazine format Brown presents documentaries, commentaries, interviews, and discussions covering a wide range of subjects. Over the years his viewers have learned about black colleges, seen rare footage from the early days of blacks in film, and heard President Ronald Reagan defend his controversial economic policies.

Originally Brown studied psychology, sociology, and social work at Wayne State University in Detroit, but after earning a master's degree in 1961 he sought work in the communications industry. Hired by Detroit's public television station, WTVS, Brown produced its first series for a black audience, "C. P. T." ("Colored People's Time"). He proceeded to both produce and host a community-oriented program for the station titled "Free Play."

Brown gained national attention in 1970 when he became the new producer-host of "Black Journal." The series, produced under the auspices of WNET-TV in New York City, had been broadcast on public television stations across the country since 1968 and had already received an Emmy award. Brown was outspoken about the goals he held for his new job. As he told Charlayne Hunter in the *New York Times,* he did not intend "to sit there and outline racism so that some white liberal can sit at home and understand it. They want me to produce a show so that they can sit up in their suburban hi-rises and see an addict up in Harlem laying out in the alley with a needle in his arm." Instead of "show[ing] white people how awful it is to be Black," Brown hoped to present a positive vision of black life to a black audience, publicizing accomplishments and showing viewers how to improve their lives. "In all our programs we want to show blacks how to work for themselves," he told Peterson. "To be respected we must have something to be respected for. We should have learned long ago, we can't depend on anyone but ourselves."

As part of such self-reliance Brown sought to increase the number of blacks in the communications field, where they had traditionally been underrepresented both as performers and technicians. He looked outside the membership of white-dominated trade unions for much of his New York City staff, and although he sometimes needed white production companies to do on-location filming for the "Journal," he insisted that they work with black apprentices and producers. In 1971 Howard University, a prominent black institution, hired Brown to establish its school of communications. For the next few years he worked simultaneously as television producer in New York and as dean of Howard's communications faculty in Washington, D.C. While at the university Brown instituted an annual Careers in Communications Conference, designed to alert young people to opportunities in his field.

Although "Black Journal" drew praise from blacks and whites alike—garnering a second Emmy nomination in 1972—it also prompted controversy. As James D. Williams quoted Brown in *Black Enterprise,* "because 'Black Journal' insists on first-class citizenship in television, we are a threat." Many public broadcasting stations in the South refused to carry the program, an action Brown considered racist. Near the end of 1972 the Corporation for Public Broadcasting (CPB), which allocated government money to public television programs, left the "Journal" off the list of shows it would fund for the upcoming season. Critics immediately accused the corporation of trying to please conservatives in the administration of President Richard Nixon. Organizations such as the Congressional Black Caucus, the Newspaper Publishers Association, the Urban League—even local groups styling themselves "Friends of Black Journal"—protested vehemently. The CPB relented, but at an open meeting of its board of directors in November of 1973, Brown joined Jesse Jackson and other prominent blacks in criticizing the corporation's treatment of minority programming.

In 1977, with assistance from corporate sponsor Pepsi-Cola, Brown took "Black Journal" off public television and into commercial syndication, renaming it "Tony Brown's Journal." (The program was subsequently produced by Brown's own company, Tony Brown Productions, Inc.) He hoped that commercial television would bring a wider audience to the series, which soon topped the A. C. Nielsen ratings for syndicated educational and talk shows. Brown grew frustrated, however, by the limited number of stations that carried the program and the odd hours they sometimes chose to broadcast it, and in 1982 he returned the "Journal" to public television.

After Brown's syndication venture he spoke with C. Gerald Fraser of the *New York Times,* acknowledging that he had lost some illusions about his work. "Producing is a business," he observed. "When I started, I saw it [as] more of a creative enterprise than a business. It is creative in the sense that money can be attracted if you posture what you're doing in some kind of innovative context." As a friend had warned him, "money makes things happen." And, Brown added, "money makes people give you things—if you don't need it."

But Brown remained confident about his future in television. Whites in the medium might "have run out of ideas," he said, but black culture "hasn't even been scratched. . . . Everything black in this country is just sitting there reserved for me because white people are not interested." He expected to keep digging "into this gold mine of black history—into this gold mine of black contributions."

BIOGRAPHICAL/CRITICAL SOURCES:

PERIODICALS

Black Enterprise, January, 1974, September, 1979.
Detroit Free Press, September 24, 1971.
Essence, October, 1980.
Jet, February 15, 1979.
New York Times, November 29, 1970, February 7, 1982.
Sepia, March, 1972.

—*Sketch by Thomas Kozikowski*

*   *   *

BROWNING, J(ohn) D.   1942-

PERSONAL: Born June 30, 1942, in London, England. *Education:* University of London, B.A., 1963, M.Phil., 1970; University of Essex, Ph.D., 1973.

ADDRESSES: Office—Department of Modern Languages, McMaster University, 1289 Main St. S.W., Hamilton, Ontario, Canada L8S 4K1.

CAREER: Affiliated with department of modern languages, McMaster University, Hamilton, Ontario.

WRITINGS:

(Editor) *Biography in the Eighteenth Century,* Garland Publishing, 1981.
Vida e ideologia de Antonio Jose de Irisarri, Editorial Universitaria Guatemala, 1986.

Editor in chief of the "Publications of the McMaster University Association for Eighteenth-Century Studies" series, which includes such titles as *The Stage in the Eighteenth Century,* Garland Publishing, 1981, and *Satire in the Eighteenth Century,* Garland Publishing, 1983.

WORK IN PROGRESS: A chapter on Creole nationalism in the eighteenth century, to be included in the five-volume work *Historia general de Guatemala.*

*   *   *

BRUCE, Maurice   1913(?)-1988

OBITUARY NOTICE: Born c. 1913; died May 7, 1988. Educator and author. Bruce was best known as an advocate of higher education among the British working class. Upon earning a degree in history from King's College, London, Bruce was appointed to a lectureship in adult education at Cambridge University. He traveled throughout England in the 1930s, stressing to the general public the importance of a college education. In 1947 he became director of extramural studies at Sheffield University, where he was also a professor from 1968 to 1975. His contributions to the university helped to educate many working-class people, several of whom went on to become members of Parliament, local councillors, and trade union officials. Bruce's writings include *The Coming of the Welfare State* and *The Shaping of the Modern World: 1870-1939.*

OBITUARIES AND OTHER SOURCES:

PERIODICALS

Times (London), May 25, 1988.

*   *   *

BRUCE, Richard
   See NUGENT, Richard Bruce

*   *   *

BUBER, Martin   1878-1965

PERSONAL: Surname pronounced "*Boo*-ber"; born February 8, 1878, in Vienna, Austria; died June 13, 1965, in Jerusalem, Israel; son of Carl (a farmer) and Elise Buber; married Paula Winkler (a novelist who published under the pseudonym George Mundt [one source says Georg Munk]), 1899 (died, 1958); children: Rafael, Eva Buber Strauss. *Education:* Attended the universities of Vienna, Leipzig, Zurich, and Berlin, 1897-1904; University of Vienna, Ph.D., 1904.

CAREER: Author, editor, scholar, lecturer, and Zionist activist in Austria, Germany, and Switzerland, 1904-23; University of Frankfurt, Frankfurt am Main, Germany, professor of comparative religion, 1923-33; Central Office for Jewish Adult Education, Frankfurt, director, 1933-38; Frankfurter Juedische Lehrhaus (Free Jewish Academy), Frankfurt, director, 1933-38; Hebrew University, Jerusalem, Israel, professor of social philosophy, 1938-51, professor emeritus, beginning in 1951. Institute for Adult Education, Jerusalem, founder and director, 1949-53.

Edited *Die Welt* (Zionist weekly periodical), Berlin, 1901, and *Der Jude* (Zionist monthly periodical), Berlin, 1916-24; co-edited *Die Kreatur* (quarterly religious journal), Berlin, 1926-30.

AWARDS, HONORS: Honorary doctoral degrees from Hebrew Union College, Hebrew University, and the universities of Aberdeen and Paris (Sorbonne); nominated by Hermann Hesse for the Nobel Prize in Literature, 1949; Goethe Prize from the University of Hamburg, 1953, and Peace Prize from the German Book Trade Association, 1955, both recognizing achievement as a writer of prose fiction in German.

WRITINGS:

(Editor) *Juedische Kuenstler*, Juedischer Verlag, 1903.

Die Geschichten des Rabbi Nachman, Ruetten & Loening, 1906, translation by Maurice Friedman published as *Tales of Rabbi Nachman*, Horizon, 1968.

(Editor) *Die Gesellschaft: Sammlung sozialpsychologischer Monographien*, Ruetten & Loening, 1906-12.

Die Legende des Baalschem, Ruetten & Loening, 1908, translation by Lucy Cohen published as *Jewish Mysticism and the Legends of Baalshem*, Dent, 1931; translation by Maurice Friedman published as *The Legend of the Baal-Shem*, Harper, 1955.

Ekstatische Konfessionen, Eugen Diedrichs Verlag, 1909.

Chinesische Geister- und Liebesgeschichten, Ruetten & Loening, 1911.

Drei Reden ueber das Judentum, Ruetten & Loening, 1911.

Buberheft: Neue Blaetter, Verlag der Neuen Blaetter, 1913.

Daniel: Gespraeche von der Verwirklichung, Insel Verlag, 1913, translation by Maurice Friedman published as *Daniel: Dialogues on Realization*, Holt, 1964.

Kalewala, Georg Mueller, 1914.

Reden und Gleichnisse des Tschuang-Tse, Insel Verlag, 1914.

(Editor) *Die vier Zweige des Mabinogi*, Insel Verlag, 1914.

Die juedische Bewegung: Gesammelte Aufsaetze und Ansprachen, Juedischer Verlag, Volume I: *1900-1914*, 1916, Volume II: *1916-1920*, 1921.

Vom Geist des Judentums, Kurt Wolff Verlag, 1916.

Voelker, Staaten und Zion, R. Loewit Verlag, 1917.

Ereignisse und Begegnungen, Insel Verlag, 1917.

Mein Weg zum Chassidismus, Ruetten & Loening, 1918.

Cheruth: Ein Rede ueber Jugend und Religion, R. Loewit Verlag, 1919.

Worte an die Zeit, Dreilander Verlag, Volume I: *Grundsaetze*, 1919, Volume II: *Gemeinschaft*, 1919.

Der Heilige Weg, Ruetten & Loening, 1919.

Die Rede, die Lehre, und das Lied, Insel Verlag, 1920.

Der grosse Maggid und seine Nachfolge, Ruetten & Loening, 1922.

Ich und Du, Insel Verlag, 1923, translation by Ronald Gregor Smith published as *I and Thou*, T. & T. Clark, 1937, Scribner, 1957.

Reden ueber das Judentum, Ruetten & Loening, 1923.

Das verborgene Licht, Ruetten & Loening, 1924.

(With Franz Rosenzweig) *Die Schrift*, fifteen volumes, Schocken Verlag, 1925-38, revised edition published in four volumes by Jakob Hegner Verlag, Volume I: *Die fuenf Buecher der Weisung*, 1954, Volume II: *Buecher der Geschichte*, 1958, Volume III: *Buecher der Kundung*, 1958, Volume IV: *Die Schriftwerke*, 1961.

Des Baal-Schem-Tow Unterweisung im Umgang mit Gott, Jakob Hegner Verlag, 1927.

Die chassidischen Buecher: Gesamtausgabe, Jakob Hegner Verlag, 1928, translation by Olga Marx published as *Tales*

of the Hasidim, Schocken, 1948, Volume I: *The Early Masters*, Volume II: *The Later Masters*.

(Editor with Ina Britschgi-Schimmer) *Gustav Landauer: Sein Lebensgang in Briefen*, two volumes, Ruetten & Loening, 1929.

Hundert chassidische Geschichten, Schocken Verlag, 1930.

Koenigtum Gottes, Schocken Verlag, 1932, third revised edition, Lambert Schneider Verlag, 1956, translation by Richard Scheimann published as *Kingship of God*, Harper, 1967.

Zwiesprache, Schocken Verlag, 1932, Lambert Schneider Verlag, 1978, translation by Ronald Gregor Smith published as *Between Man and Man*, Macmillan, 1948, new edition translated by Maurice Friedman with an afterword by Buber, 1965.

Kampf um Israel: Reden und Schriften, Schocken Verlag, 1933.

Die Troestung Israels, Schocken Verlag, 1933.

Erzaehlungen von Engelm, Geistern und Daemonen, Schocken Verlag, 1934, translation by David Antin and Jerome Rothenberg published as *Tales of Angels, Spirits, and Demons*, Hawk's Well Press, 1958.

Deutung des Chassidismus, Schocken Verlag, 1935, translation by Maurice Friedman published as *Hasidism and Modern Man*, Horizon Press, 1958.

Aus Tiefen rufe ich Dich: Dreiundzwanzig Psalmen in der Urschrift mit der Verdeutschung von Martin Bubers, Schocken Verlag, 1936.

Die Frage an den Einzelnen, Schocken Verlag, 1936.

Die Stunde und die Erkenntnis: Reden und Augsaetze, 1933-1935, Schocken Verlag, 1936.

Zion als Ziel und Aufgabe, Schocken Verlag, 1936.

Die Forderung des Geistes und die geschichtliche Wirklichkeit: Antrittsvorlesung gehalten am 25. April 1938 in der Hebraischen Universitaet, Schocken Verlag (Jerusalem), 1938.

Worte an die Jugend, Schocken Verlag, 1938.

(With Judah Magnes) *Two Letters to Gandhi*, Rubin Mass (Jerusalem), 1939.

Ba'yat ha-adam, [Tel-Aviv], 1942-43.

Ha-Ruah veha-metziut, [Tel-Aviv], 1942.

Torat ha-nevi'im, [Tel-Aviv], 1942.

Gog u-Magog, [Jerusalem], 1943, translation from the German manuscript by Ludwig Lewisohn published as *For the Sake of Heaven*, Jewish Publication Society, 1945, Harper, 1953.

Ben'am le-artso, [Jerusalem], 1944, translation from the German manuscript by Stanley Godman published as *On Zion: The History of an Idea*, Schocken, 1973.

Chassidismus, 1945, translation by Greta Hort published as *Hasidism*, Philosophical Library, 1948.

Be-pardes ha-hasidut, [Tel-Aviv], 1945.

Or ha-ganuz, [Tel-Aviv], 1946, selection translated by Haim Shachter and edited by David Harden published as *From the Treasurehouse of Hassidism: A Selection from 'Or haganuz' by Martin Buber*, Organizacion Sionista Mundial, [Jerusalem], 1969.

Mamre: Essays in Religion, translation by Greta Hort, Oxford University Press, 1946.

Moses: The Revelation and the Covenant, East West Library, 1946.

Netivot be-utopiyah, [Tel-Aviv], 1947, translation by R.F.C. Hull published as *Paths in Utopia*, Routledge & Kegan Paul, 1949.

(With Judah Magnes) *Arab-Jewish Unity*, Victor Gollancz, 1947.

Dialogisches Leben: Gessamelte philosophische und paeda-gogische Schriften (includes *Ich und Du, Zwiesprache, Die Frage an den Einzelnen, Ueber das Erzieherische, Das Problem des Menschen*), Gregor Mueller Verlag, 1947.

(With Franz Rosenzweig) *Der Knecht Gottes: Schicksal, Augfage, Trost*, Pulvis Viarum, 1947.

Ten Rungs: Hasidic Sayings, translation from the Hebrew manuscript by Olga Marx, Schocken, 1947.

(Editor with J. L. Magnes and E. Simon) *Towards Union in Palestine: Essays on Zionism and Jewish-Arab Cooperation*, Ihud Association (Jerusalem), 1947, Greenwood, 1972.

Israel and the World: Essays in a Time of Crisis, Schocken, 1948.

Das Problem des Menschen, Lambert Schneider Verlag, 1948.

Der Weg des Menschen: Nach der chassidischen Lehre, [Jerusalem], 1948, Lambert Schneider Verlag, 1960, translation by Maurice Friedman published as *The Way of Man According to the Teachings of Hasidism*, Routledge & Kegan Paul, 1950.

The Prophetic Faith, translated from the Hebrew by Carlyle Witton-Davies, Macmillan, 1949.

Die Erzaehlungen der Chassidim, Manesse Verlag, 1950.

Zwei Glaubensweisen, Manesse Verlag, 1950, translation by Norman P. Goldhawk published as *Two Types of Faith*, Macmillan, 1952.

Israel und Palaestina: Zur Geschichte einter Idee, Artemis Verlag, 1950, translation by Stanley Godman published as *Israel and Palestine: The History of an Idea*, Farrar, Straus, 1952, reprinted as *On Zion*.

Urdistanz und Beziehung, Lambert Schneider Verlag, 1951.

At the Turning: Three Addresses on Judaism, Farrar, Straus, 1952.

Bilder von Gut und Boese, Jakob Hegner Verlag, 1952, translation by Michael Bullock published as *Images of Good and Evil*, Routledge & Kegan Paul, 1952.

Die chassidische Botschaft, Lambert Schneider Verlag, 1952.

Right and Wrong: An Interpretation of Some Psalms, translated by Ronald Gregor Smith, S.C.M. Press, 1952.

Zwischen Gesellschaft und Staat, Lambert Schneider Verlag, 1952.

Einsichten: Aus den Schriften gesammelt, Insel Verlag, 1953.

Gottesfinsternis, Manesse Verlag, 1953, translation by Maurice Friedman and others published as *Eclipse of God: Studies in the Relation Between Religion and Philosophy*, Harper, 1952.

Good and Evil: Two Interpretations (includes *Right and Wrong* and *Images of Good and Evil*), Scribner, 1953.

Hinweise: Gesammelte Essays, Manesse Verlag, 1953, translation by Maurice Friedman published as *Pointing the Way: Collected Essays*, Harper, 1957.

Die Schriften ueber das dialogische Prinzip, Lambert Schneider Verlag, 1954, revised edition, 1973.

Zu einer neuen Verdeutschung der Schrift: Beilage zu dem Werk, Jakob Hegner, 1954.

Der Mensch und sein Gebild, Lambert Schneider Verlag, 1955, translation by Maurice Friedman and Ronald Gregor Smith published as *The Knowledge of Man*, Harper, 1965.

Das Sehertum: Anfang und Ausgang, Jakob Hegner, 1955.

Stationen des Glaubens, Insel Verlag, 1956, published in English as *To Hallow This Life*, Harper, 1958.

The Writings of Martin Buber, selected and edited by Will Herberg, World Publishing Co., 1956, New American Library, 1974.

Pirke hasidut, [Jerusalem], 1957.

Schuld und Schuldgefuhle, Lambert Schneider Verlag, 1958.

Be-sod siah, [Jerusalem], 1959.

Te'udah ve-yi'ud, [Jerusalem], 1959.

Begegnung: Autobiographische Fragmente, W. Kohlhammer Verlag, 1960, translation by Maurice Friedman published as *Encounter: Autobiographical Fragments*, Open Court, 1972.

The Origin and Meaning of Hasidism, translated by Maurice Friedman, Horizon Press, 1960.

(With Nahum Goldmann) *Die Juden in der UdSSR*, translated from the English manuscript by Wilfried Freiherr von Bredon, Ner-Tamid Verlag, 1961.

Pene adam, [Jerusalem], 1962.

Werke, Koesel Verlag and Lambert Schneider Verlag, Volume I: *Schriften zur Philosophie*, 1962, Volume II: *Schriften zur Bibel*, 1964, Volume III: *Schriften zum Chassidismus*, 1963.

Elija: Ein Mysterienspiel, Lambert Schneider Verlag, 1963, translation published as "Elijah: A Mystery Play" in *Martin Buber and the Theater*, edited by Maurice Friedman, Funk & Wagnalls, 1969.

Der Jude und sein Judentum: Gesammelte Aufsaetze und Reden, Joseph Melzer Verlag, 1963.

Nachlese, Lambert Schneider Verlag, 1965.

The Way of Response: Martin Buber, Selections from His Writings, edited by Nahum N. Glatzer, Schocken, 1966.

A Believing Humanism: Gleanings, translated by Maurice Friedman, Simon & Schuster, 1967.

On the Bible, edited by Nahum N. Glatzer, Schocken, 1968.

On Judaism (includes translation of lectures from *Reden ueber das Judentum* by Eva Jospe and lectures from *At the Turning*), Schocken, 1968.

Briefwechsel aus sieben Jahrzehnten, Lambert Schneider Verlag, Volume I (1897-1918), 1972, Volume II (1918-1938), 1973, Volume III (1938-1965), 1975.

Meetings, edited and translated by Maurice Friedman, Open Court, 1973.

SIDELIGHTS: The Austrian-born Israeli philosopher Martin Buber was one of the major religious existentialist thinkers of the twentieth century. His teaching, a kind of spiritual humanism best expressed in his philosophical masterwork *I and Thou*, has deeply influenced both Jewish and Christian theologians and secular moral philosophers. Buber's life-affirming "philosophy of dialogue" draws on sources as diverse as the anti-religious German philosopher Friedrich Nietzsche and the mystical Hasidic Jewish sect and centers on the proposition that the individual's concrete interaction with others reveals spiritual truth. In addition to his many philosophical works, Buber wrote numerous books on Hasidism and biblical interpretation and produced an acclaimed translation, into German, of the complete Hebrew Bible. Committed to putting his ideas into practice, Buber led a life that enabled him to combine philosophy and career in his roles as educator, Zionist activist, and communitarian socialist.

Martin Buber was born in Vienna in 1878 but grew up in the home of his paternal grandfather, Salomon Buber, in Lemberg, Galicia, then part of the Austro-Hungarian empire and now the city of Lvov in the Soviet Union's Ukrainian Republic. Salomon Buber, a noted Hebrew scholar, thoroughly educated the boy in Jewish culture and religion and introduced him to the mystically inclined Hasidic movement in Galicia, which would later deeply influence Buber's religious philosophy. Buber went on to study philosophy and art history at the universities of Leipzig, Zurich, Berlin, and finally Vienna, where he took his doctoral degree with a dissertation on German mysticism in 1904. As a student, Buber immersed himself in the classic literature of nineteenth-century German idealism and romanticism, and he was profoundly impressed by the existentialist moral philosophy of Nietzsche, as well as Soren Kierkegaard and Fyodor Dostoyevsky.

While still a student, Buber became active in Theodore Herzl's newly organized Zionist movement, which had the goal of reconstituting a Jewish state in Palestine. From the beginning of his association with the Zionist cause, Buber took the position that the movement could not succeed if it were limited to secular nationalism but that it must entail a spiritual and cultural renewal of world Jewry. Only a return to Judaism's cultural roots, he insisted, could effectively unify Diaspora Jews—those living outside the Holy Land—as a people in the quest for a national homeland and legitimize this goal in the eyes of the rest of the world. Buber urged this viewpoint as editor of the Berlin-based Zionist journal *Die Welt* in 1901, but his ideas were decisively rejected in favor of a purely political movement at the Fifth Zionist Congress held that year.

This defeat prompted Buber to withdraw from active participation in the Zionist movement for a period of several years and to turn his private efforts to achieving the Jewish spiritual renewal he advocated. He began this quest with an intensive study of Hasidism, the joyously communitarian Orthodox movement that had impressed him as a youth in Galicia. To grasp the essence of the Hasidic teaching, Buber turned from the debased and declining present-day Hasidic communities to the writings of the sect's eighteenth-century founder, Baal-Shem-Tov (Israel ben Eliezer) and his great-grandson Nachman ben Simcha. These spiritual leaders stressed the importance of achieving a direct and personal communication with God and of recognizing the divine by "hallowing everyday life" and creating true human community. Hasidism's world-affirming mysticism, which encouraged religious expression through music and dance and judged purity of heart more pleasing to God than learning, emerged partly as a reaction to the legalistic rationalism of rabbinical Judaism, which in turn declared the Hasidic movement heretical. Buber found in Hasidism a spiritual movement capable of rejuvenating the Jewish people, one in which the emphasis on life-enhancing values and the personal encounter with God had certain affinities to the existentialist philosophy that had so impressed him.

Inspired by this discovery, Buber set about the task of collecting and translating into modern German the rich trove of Hasidic literature that was virtually unknown outside of the tiny European Hasidic communities. In Berlin in 1906 he published *The Tales of Rabbi Nachman* and in 1908 *The Legend of the Baal-Shem*. Many other books interpreting and translating the Hasidic teachings followed in later years, including the two-volume *Tales of the Hasidim, The Origin and Meaning of Hasidism*, and *Hasidism and Modern Man*. Buber also set his only novel, *For the Sake of Heaven*, in an early Russian Hasidic community at the time of the Napoleonic wars and filled the book with Hasidic philosophy. Buber's evocative and stylistically imaginative adaptations of Hasidic tales into the German earned him the Goethe Prize in 1953 and the German Book Trade Association Peace Prize in 1955.

While producing his works on Hasidism in the years before the First World War, Buber also published some collections of mystical writings from other religions, including *Ekstatische Konfesionen*, and delivered influential speeches in several European capitals on the meaning of Jewishness, the most important of which are included in his 1911 work *Drei Reden ueber das Judentum*. At the time, Buber held a rather mystical view of Jewishness that was influenced by the German neo-romantic *volk* movement and located both the unique Jewish spirit and its affinity for the land of Palestine in the racial characteristics or "blood" of the Jewish people. Buber elaborated this view along with his general call for spiritual renewal in *Der Jude*, a widely circulated Zionist journal that he edited from 1916 to 1924. Buber's Zionism was confirmed and strengthened by his conclusion that the eighteenth-century European Hasidic communities had failed to achieve true community because they lacked the legal and territorial independence that would result from national self-determination.

Even as he engaged in these specifically Jewish tasks, Buber was developing a distinctly nonmystical religious philosophy that would appeal to Jews and non-Jews alike and earn him worldwide renown. Buber's emerging "philosophy of dialogue" drew on the Hasidic concerns with "hallowing the everyday" and building a loving spiritual community as well as on the personal commitment and active self-definition central to the existentialist philosophies of Kierkegaard and Nietzsche. Buber planted the seeds of this philosophy in his 1913 book *Daniel*, which counterposed two basic attitudes toward the world: that of "orientation," the objective ordering of the environment for knowledge and use, and that of "realization," the subjective, metaphysical emergence of life's inner meaning.

Buber recast these two basic worldviews in dialogical form in his 1923 philosophical masterwork, *I and Thou*. In this slim but highly influential volume, Buber suggests that the individual confronts the world either as subject-to-object ("I-It") or subject-to-subject ("I-Thou"). The I-It relation objectifies and grasps the world in terms of utilities and is essential to physical survival, while the I-Thou—true relation—involves opening one's full being to meet another spiritual subject. According to Buber, the three types of worldly spiritual subjects with whom one can enter the I-Thou relation are nature, "intelligible forms" or art, and other individuals. Meeting another subject entails meeting oneself because one must surrender one's whole being to the relation; the I of I-Thou, then, is a deeper and richer I than the I of I-It, in which only part of one's being seeks a utility. Whereas objects and the I-It essentially subsist in the past—in terms that have been defined—the I-Thou relation is true presentness: it is open-ended and suspends the movement of time to give a glimpse of eternity. Each particular I-Thou relation is exclusive, since true dialogue is only possible between two subjects at a time, but each radiates universal meaning because it intimates the Eternal Thou, or God.

Buber describes meeting the worldly Thou and meeting God as something of a circular process. Both the love of God and the consciousness of God's love give us the power to love our neighbor; at the same time, meeting our neighbor's Thou helps to reveal God. The Eternal Thou—God—is further intimated by the necessary collapse of every particular I-Thou relation into an I-It relation, which Buber describes as a basic tragedy in the human condition. We are unable to indefinitely sustain our original spiritual relation with a person, a painting, or a landscape, but inevitably begin to analyze it, define it, limit it, and reduce it to an object—in short, we make its Thou into an It and bring it into the world of instrumentalities. The yearning for God is the yearning for the Thou who can never be limited or reduced to an It.

Entering the I-Thou relation, according to Buber, involves both choosing and being chosen; it is paradoxically both an act of God's grace and a product of one's actions and attitude. Similarly, revelation, or the encounter with the Eternal Thou, cannot be sought as such; one can only prepare for this supreme meeting by engaging in the world with an active love, that is, by seeking to live with one's full being. Each one of us must discover the truth of God in the concrete conditions of our own lives, and fundamentally in our relations with others. "Men do not find God if they stay in the world," Buber remarks in *I and Thou*. "They do not find him if they leave the world. He who goes out with his whole being to meet his Thou, and carries to it all being that is in the world, finds him who cannot be sought." In a later work, *At the Turning*, the philosopher adds, "*You must yourself begin*. Existence will remain meaningless for you if you yourself do not penetrate into it with active love and if you do not in this way discover its meaning for yourself.... Meet the world with the fullness of your being, and you shall meet God.... If you wish to believe, love."

Buber consequently rejects the traditional religious notion that material and spiritual worlds oppose each other; rather, "there is only the world—which appears to us as twofold in accordance with our twofold attitude." Engaging in the I-It relation, even with people, is necessary for survival, but the morally good individual, says Buber, places greater emphasis on the I-Thou in the overall course of his or her human relations. Evil emerges from the failure to achieve the spiritual self-unification that allows one to live a directed life with one's full being.

"Evil cannot be done with the whole soul; good can only be done with the whole soul," Buber writes in his book *Good and Evil*. Love must see the whole of another being, but hate is "by nature blind," he asserts; only part of one's person hates, and only part of another person can be hated. Evil is accomplished either as a result of simple decisionlessness, allowing oneself to fall passively under the dominance of I-It, or, in its more sinister form, by willful wrong decision, or the deliberate suppression of self-knowledge and spiritual truth in an attempt to create oneself apart from man and God. The good man "stakes his life on his thinking" and lives according to the spiritual truth that is revealed in his concrete interactions with others. Buber stresses that it is not sufficient to mechanically apply moral rules to life's problems; rather, one must confront each moral situation with full creative freedom and openness in the I-Thou dialogue.

Though his dialogical form is unique, Buber's moral thinking has much in common with that of several other modern philosophers in the Judeo-Christian tradition. The I-Thou relation is evocative of Immanuel Kant's "categorical imperative" to treat one's fellow "as an end in himself and never as a means only." Buber's emphasis on dialogue and his assertion that "the fundamental fact of existence is not man, but man-with-man," also closely parallels the thinking of his contemporary, Karl Jaspers, a German religious existentialist who similarly regarded the "loving strife" of true human communication as the opening to transcendence.

The true wellspring of Buber's philosophy, though, is that great dialogue between God and man recorded in the Hebrew Bible. Of Buber's numerous books of biblical interpretation, *Moses* and *The Prophetic Faith* most cogently develop his dialogical themes. A principal goal in these works is to re-establish the basis of true biblical faith, which the author sees as continually threatened by magical, gnostic, and legalistic distortions, both within organized religion and without. In Buber's interpretation, the biblical dialogue is an intensely personal one between "the 'I' of the speaking God and the 'Thou' of the hearing Israel," considered both collectively and individually. The biblical God becomes flesh in order to meet man, and the story of the Bible is basically the chronicle of successive efforts to strengthen, deepen, and more fully personify the dialogue between God and man, which culminates in the promise of the messiah. As Buber sees it, faith in the God of the Bible is not a consoling faith in any superficial sense; on the contrary, God makes an absolute demand on the totality of one's life and being, and shatters all human self-sufficiency and security. Therefore man is under a constant injunction to sustain his part of the dialogue by seeking to interpret and do the will of God in every concrete situation. Because of the difficulties of God's demands and his loving confidence in humankind, men and women meet him in both fear and love—the two attitudes are inextricably merged in divine love.

Buber's deep commitment to the Bible inspired him to initiate a prolonged and fruitful dialogue with the other great biblical religion: Christianity. He helped found the influential religious journal *Die Kreatur* in 1926 and co-edited it for four years with Joseph Wittig, a Catholic, and Viktor von Weizsaecker, a Protestant. In later years, Buber kept up a mutually productive correspondence with the great American Christian existentialist theologians Paul Tillich and Reinhold Niebuhr, the latter of whom acknowledged his specific debt to *I and Thou* for instructing "me and many others on the uniqueness of human selfhood and on the religious dimension of the person." Buber's outstanding work on the relation between Judaism and Christianity is *Two Types of Faith*, published in English in 1952.

In addition to his works of interpretation, Buber's biblical scholarship encompassed the massive project of translating the entire Old Testament from Hebrew into German. The philosopher collaborated with the renowned German Jewish scholar Franz Rosenzweig on this task after the First World War and continued with it on his own after Rosenzweig died in 1929. The fifteen-volume *Die Schrift* was acclaimed for its success in capturing much of the spirit of the Hebrew original lost in previous translations. Rather than adapt the Hebrew to the demands of modern German, Buber managed to twist the German into a form that resembled the ancient text but still remained intelligible.

In keeping with his philosophy, Buber not only wrote about the life of dialogue but pursued it actively as a teacher and educational administrator. As professor of comparative religion at Frankfurt University, he held the only chair of Jewish philosophy at a German university from 1923 until 1933, when the Nazi regime excluded Jews from German educational institutions. For the next five years, Buber directed the Central Office for Jewish Adult Education in Germany and the Frankfurter Juedische Lehrhaus, a free college for Jews. His educational work was credited with helping to spiritually strengthen German Jews at a time of terrible trial for his people. Buber was finally forced to flee Germany in 1938 for Palestine, where he became professor of social philosophy at Hebrew University in Jerusalem. When Israel became an independent state in 1948, the philosopher was appointed director of the Institute for Adult Education in Jerusalem, which trained teachers in the instruction of newly arrived immigrants.

In Palestine, Buber was deeply impressed by the Jewish rural commune movement, which he believed had great potential for helping to realize the full life of the I-Thou dialogue. A "communitarian" socialist since early adulthood, Buber advocates a social philosophy that is closely linked to his religious teaching. In his view, true community emerges out of the I-Thou relationship and must have both a religious foundation, wherein community members are unified in their individual relation with a "divine center," and a socioeconomic foundation, wherein cooperative units maintain the cycle of production and consumption. Buber judged these conditions best realized in the Palestine kibbutzes—small living and working groups—where members could exert real cooperative control over their conditions of life and bond effectively with one another in the I-Thou relationship while maintaining a healthy degree of individual privacy. These basic social units would in turn associate with one another and with larger socioeconomic units to create an ascending "community of communities" that would ultimately constitute a world society. In his writings on the subject, Buber acknowledges that this decentralized society must develop new and radically different technologies from those already predominant in contemporary urban society and that the optimum balance between local autonomy and centralism will have to be worked out by trial and error in each concrete instance. Buber counterposes this social vision—which bears some affinities to anarchist communitarianism and the contemporary "bioregionalist" movement—to the individualism of modern capitalism and the collectivism of Soviet communism and Western European state socialism. "Individualism understands only a part of man, collectivism understands man only as a part: neither advances to the wholeness of man," the philosopher explains in *Between Man and Man*. "Individualism sees man only in relation to himself, but collectivism does not see man at all; it sees 'society.'" Buber further develops his social views with particular reference to the kibbutz in his 1949 work *Paths in Utopia*.

The example of the kibbutz movement also influenced Buber's later Zionist thinking. Although he never abandoned the mystical view that the Holy Land was uniquely suited to the Jews because of their religious heritage, Buber insisted in the years before the nation of Israel was born that Zionism could only succeed as a form of "Hebrew humanism" that would bring supernatural values into the world. In his 1942 book *Ha-Ruah veha-Metziut*, the philosopher contrasts this view "to that Jewish nationalism which regards Israel as a nation like unto other nations, and recognizes no task for Israel save that of preserving and asserting itself. But no nation in the world has this as its only task, for just as an individual who wishes merely to preserve and assert himself leads an unjustified and meaningless existence, so a nation with no other aim deserves to pass away." According to Buber, the specifically Jewish task is to endeavor to realize "the attributes of God revealed to it, justice and love" in concrete life by building the I-Thou relation and examples of true community. Buber decided that fulfilling this task required forming a binational state representing both Jews and Palestinian Arabs, and he collaborated with Hebrew University chancellor Judah Magnes to draft a program advocating the formation of such a state in 1946. After Israel was created a Jewish state two years later, Buber spoke out vigorously to defend the civil and political rights of what had become a largely dispossessed Arab minority in the new country. In a unique gesture that bridged the often bitter divisions between the two peoples in modern Israel, Arab students from Hebrew University placed a wreath on Buber's bier when the great Jewish philosopher died in 1965.

BIOGRAPHICAL/CRITICAL SOURCES:

BOOKS

Arnett, Ronald C., *Communication and Community: Implications of Martin Buber's Dialogue*, Southern Illinois University Press, 1986.

Balthazar, Hans Urs von, *Martin Buber and Christianity*, Harvill, 1958.

Beek, Martinus Adrianus and J. Sperna Weiland, *Martin Buber, Personalist and Prophet*, Newman Press, 1968.

Berkovitz, Eliezer, *A Jewish Critique of the Philosophy of Martin Buber*, Yeshiva University Press, 1962.

Berry, Donald L., *Mutuality: The Vision of Martin Buber*, State University of New York Press, 1985.

Buber, Martin, *The Writings of Martin Buber*, edited by Will Herberg, World Publishing Co., 1956, New American Library, 1974.

Buber, Martin, *Meetings*, edited by Maurice Friedman, Open Court, 1973.

Cohen, Arthur A., *Martin Buber*, Hillary House, 1957.

Diamond, Malcolm, *Martin Buber, Jewish Existentialist*, Oxford University Press, 1960.

Edwards, Paul, *Buber and Buberism: A Critical Evaluation*, University of Kansas Press, 1971.

Friedman, Maurice, *Martin Buber: The Life of Dialogue*, Harper, 1960, third edition, University of Chicago Press, 1976.

Friedman, Maurice, *Martin Buber's Life and Work*, Dutton, Volume I: *The Early Years, 1878-1923*, 1982, Volume II: *The Middle Years, 1923-1945*, 1983, Volume III: *The Later Years, 1945-1965*, 1984.

Friedman, Maurice, *Martin Buber and the Eternal*, Human Sciences, 1986.

Gordon, Haim and Jochanan Bloch, *Martin Buber: A Centenary Volume*, Ktav Publishing House, 1984.

Hodes, Aubrey, *Martin Buber, an Intimate Portrait*, Viking, 1971.

Kohanski, Alexander S., *Martin Buber's Philosophy of Interhuman Relation*, Associated University Presses, 1982.

Manheim, Werner, *Martin Buber*, Twayne, 1974.

Martin, Bernard, editor, *Great Twentieth-Century Jewish Philosophers: Shestov, Rosenzweig, Buber, With Selections From Their Writings*, Macmillan, 1969.

Moore, Donald J., *Martin Buber, Prophet of Religious Secularism*, Jewish Publication Society of America, 1974.

Oliver, Roy, *Wanderer and the Way: The Hebrew Humanism in the Writings of Martin Buber*, Cornell University Press, 1968.

Schlipp, Paul Arthur and Maurice Friedman, editors, *The Philosophy of Martin Buber*, Open Court, 1967.

Schneider, Grete, *The Hebrew Humanism of Martin Buber*, Wayne State University Press, 1973.

Simon, Akiva Ernst, editor, *Martin Buber, 1878-1978* (library exhibition catalogue), Raphael Haim Hachonen Press (Jerusalem), 1978.

PERIODICALS

Newsweek, April 1, 1957.
New York Times, December 3, 1961.
New York Times Book Review, March 16, 1969.
Times Literary Supplement, December 28, 1973.

OBITUARIES:

PERIODICALS

Commonweal, July 2, 1965.
Newsweek, June 28, 1965.

New York Times, June 14, 1965, June 15, 1965.
Saturday Review, July 24, 1965.
Time, June 25, 1965.*

—*Sketch by Curtis Skinner*

*   *   *

BUCHANAN, Edna (Rydzik) 1946(?)-

BRIEF ENTRY: Born c. 1946 (one source says c. 1939) in Paterson, N.J. American journalist and author. A police crime reporter for the *Miami Herald* since 1970, Buchanan won a Pulitzer Prize in 1986 for general reporting and the Green Eye Shade Award in 1982 for deadline reporting. Her first book, *Carr: Five Years of Rape and Murder; From the Personal Account of Robert Frederick Carr III* (Dutton, 1979), profiles the confessed murderer and describes the motivation behind his violent actions. In 1987 the journalist recounted her professional experiences in *The Corpse Had a Familiar Face: Covering Miami, America's Hottest Beat* (Random House). Buchanan also contributes articles to periodicals, including *Cosmopolitan, Rolling Stone,* and *Family Circle. Addresses: Office*—Miami Herald, 1 Herald Plaza, P. O. Box 615, Miami, Fla. 33152.

BIOGRAPHICAL/CRITICAL SOURCES:

PERIODICALS

Chicago Tribune, October 16, 1987, December 27, 1987.
Los Angeles Times, December 4, 1987.
New Yorker, February 17, 1986.
People, January 18, 1988.
Washington Post, November 8, 1987, December 10, 1987.

*   *   *

BUCKNELL, Howard III 1924-1986

PERSONAL: Born February 3, 1924, in Canton, China; died October 7, 1986, in La Jolla, Calif.; son of Howard (an American foreign service officer) and Lucy (Taylor) Bucknell; married Susanne Potter, June 19, 1976; children: (previous marriage) Howard, Lawrence, Lucy, Nathaniel, David; (stepchildren) Susanne, Margaret, Dickson. *Education:* U.S. Naval Academy, B.S., 1944; graduate of U.S. Naval Submarine School, 1948, U.S. Naval War College, 1958, and U.S. Navy Nuclear Power Engineering Training Program, 1960; University of Georgia, M.A., 1974, Ph.D., 1977.

CAREER: U.S. Navy, career officer, 1944-71, assigned as instructor at Gunfire Support School, Coronado, Calif., 1946-47, liaison officer with 187th Airborne Division, 1946, commander of U.S.S. *Remora,* 1955-57, head of plans and policy section of Submarine Warfare Branch, Office of the Chief of Naval Operations, 1958-59, commander of U.S.S. *Snook,* 1960-63, and U.S.S. *Theodore Roosevelt,* 1963-67, chief of nuclear operations and safety on staff of the commander in chief of the Pacific, 1967-69, assistant chief of staff of 14th Naval District, Honolulu, Hawaii, 1969-70, coordinator of student research programs at U.S. Naval War College, Newport, R.I., 1970, retiring as captain; University of Georgia, Athens, instructor in political science, 1977; Ohio State University, Columbus, lecturer and research association at Mershon Center and director of Energy and National Security Project, both 1977-80; John Addison Cobb Associates (energy analysts), East Hampton, N.Y., president, beginning in 1980. Member of national advisory board of Alliance to Save Energy; member

of energy task force of American Society for Public Administration, 1977; member of National Research Council's Committee on Federal Research on the Biological and Health Effects of Ionizing Radiation, 1980.

AWARDS, HONORS—Military: Commendation Medals from Secretary of the Navy, 1953 and 1970; Special Commendation from commander in chief of U.S. Pacific Fleet, 1962; U.S. Navy Presidential Commendation Medal, 1970. Other: Ford Foundation fellow, 1976.

WRITINGS:

Command at Sea, 3rd edition, U.S. Naval Institute, 1966.
Energy Policy and Naval Strategy, Sage Publications, 1975.
(Contributor) James E. Bailey, editor, *Energy Systems: An Analysis for Engineers and Policy Makers,* Dekker, 1978.
Energy and the National Defense, University Press of Kentucky, 1983.

Contributor to magazines and newspapers, including *World Trade Journal, U.S. Naval Institute Proceedings, Energy Communications Journal, Marine Corps Gazette,* and *Our Navy.**

*   *   *

BUDZISZEWSKI, J(ay Dalton) 1952-

PERSONAL: Surname is pronounced "Boo-jee-*shef*-skee"; born April 19, 1952, in Milwaukee, Wis.; son of Wes J. (a purchasing agent) and Esther Ruth (Chrzanowski) Budziszewski; married Sandra Lynn Hall (an interior designer), September 4, 1971; children: Anastasia, Alexandra. *Education:* University of South Florida, B.A., 1975; University of Florida, M.A., 1977; Yale University, Ph.D., 1981. *Religion:* Christian.

ADDRESSES: Office—Department of Government, University of Texas at Austin, Austin, Tex. 78712.

CAREER: University of Texas at Austin, assistant professor of political philosophy, 1981—.

MEMBER: North American Society for Social Philosophy, American Political Science Association, Southern Political Science Association, Conference Group on Political Economy.

WRITINGS:

The Resurrection of Nature: Political Theory and the Human Character, Cornell University Press, 1986.
The Nearest Coast of Darkness: A Vindication of the Politics of Virtues, Cornell University Press, in press.

Contributor to political science journals.

WORK IN PROGRESS: True Tolerance, for Cornell University Press.

SIDELIGHTS: J. Budziszewski told *CA* that he believes that an understanding of human nature is essential to political and philosophical reflection. He added, "From this theme branches a number of sub-themes. One of the most important is the classical idea that the character of the citizens is the central concern of the statesman. Thinking about that requires, first, an investigation of just what good character is, and second, a reappraisal—not of the value of tolerance—but of the *idea* that having this virtue means being morally 'neutral.' My earlier work concentrated on the meaning of good character. My more recent work investigates the meaning of tolerance."

BUKOWCZYK, John J(oseph) 1950-

PERSONAL: Born June 16, 1950, in Perth Amboy, N.J. *Education:* Northwestern University, B.A., 1972; Harvard University, A.M., 1973, Ph.D., 1980.

ADDRESSES: Office—Department of History, 809 Mackenzie Hall, Wayne State University, 5950 Cass Ave., Detroit, Mich. 48202.

CAREER: Connecticut College, New London, visiting instructor, 1978-79, visiting assistant professor of history, 1979-80; Wayne State University, Detroit, Mich., assistant professor, 1980-86, associate professor of history, 1986—. Member of board of directors of Preservation Detroit, 1984-86.

MEMBER: Polish American Historical Association (second vice-president, 1986), Immigration History Society.

AWARDS, HONORS: Reverend Joseph P. Swastek Prize, 1985, for article "Polish Rural Culture and Immigrant Working Class Formation, 1880-1914" and award for *And My Children Did Not Know Me: A History of the Polish Americans,* 1988, both from Polish-American Association; Richard P. McCormick Prize from New Jersey Historical Commission, 1985, for article "The Transformation of Working-Class Ethnicity: Corporate Control, Americanization, and the Polish Immigrant Middle Class in Bayonne, N.J., 1915-1925"; doctoral dissertation award from Kosciuszko Foundation, 1985; achievement award from Probus Club, 1985.

WRITINGS:

(Contributor) Stanislaus Blejwas and Mieczyslaw Boleslaw Biskupski, editors, *Pastor of the Poles: Polish American Essays,* Central Connecticut State College, 1982.
And My Children Did Not Know Me: A History of the Polish-Americans, Indiana University Press, 1987.
(Contributor) James Obelkevich, Lyndal Roper, and Raphael Samuel, editors, *Disciplines of Faith: Studies in Religion, Politics, and Patriarchy,* Routledge & Kegan Paul, 1987.
(Editor with Douglas Aikenhead, and contributor) *Detroit Images: The Changing City,* Wayne State University Press, 1988.

Contributor of more than twenty articles and reviews to history and international studies journals.

WORK IN PROGRESS: The formation of the immigrant middle class in Polish Brooklyn, 1880-1940; a study of the political economy of neighborhood formation focusing on Detroit's eastside, 1850-present.

*   *   *

BUNCHE, Ralph J(ohnson) 1904-1971

PERSONAL: Born August 7, 1904, in Detroit, Mich.; died after a long series of illnesses, December 9, 1971, in New York, N.Y.; son of Fred (a barber) and Olive Agnes (a musician; maiden name Johnson) Bunche; married Ruth Ethel Harris, June 23, 1930; children: Ralph, Jr., Joan, Jane (Mrs. Burton Pierce; died in 1966). *Education:* University of California, Los Angeles, B.A. (summa cum laude), 1927; Harvard University, M.A., 1928, Ph.D., 1934; postdoctoral study at Northwestern University, 1936, London School of Economics and Political Science, London, 1937, and Capetown University, 1937. *Religion:* Nonsectarian. *Politics:* Independent.

ADDRESSES: Home—Kew Gardens, New York, N.Y.

CAREER: Howard University, Washington, D.C., instructor, 1928, assistant professor and department chairman, beginning in 1929, special assistant to the president of the university, 1931-32, professor of political science, 1937-42; staff member serving as chief aide to Swedish sociologist Gunnar Myrdal at Carnegie Corporation of New York, 1938-40; Office of the Coordinator of Information (later Office of Strategic Services), Washington, D.C., senior social science analyst, beginning in 1941, principal research analyst in the Africa and Far East section, 1942-43, chief of the Africa Section of the Research and Analysis Branch, 1943-44; U.S. State Department, Washington, D.C., divisional assistant for colonial problems in the Division of Political Studies and area specialist on Africa and dependent areas in the Division of Territorial Studies, both 1944, acting associate chief, 1945, and associate chief of the Division of Dependent Area Affairs (also serving some months as acting chief), 1945-47, assistant secretary to the U.S. delegation at Dumbarton Oaks conference, 1944, technical expert on trusteeship for the U.S. delegation at the conference on International Organization at San Francisco, 1945, appointed by President Truman to membership on Anglo-American Caribbean Commission, 1945, adviser to the U.S. delegation to the United Nations General Assembly in London, 1946, adviser to the U.S. delegation to International Labor conferences in Paris and Philadephia; United Nations Secretariat, Washington, D.C., director of the Trusteeship Division, 1947-55, undersecretary, 1955-57, undersecretary for special political affairs serving under Secretary-General Dag Hammarskjold, 1957-67, undersecretary-general serving under Secretary-General U Thant, 1967-71. Special assistant to the Secretary-General's Special Committee on Palestine, and appointed principal secretary of the Palestine Commission, both 1947, head of the Palestine Commission, 1948, directed peace-keeping operations in such areas as Suez, 1956, Congo, 1960, Yemen, 1962-64, Cyprus, 1964, and India and Pakistan, 1965. Founder of National Negro Congress, 1936. Co-director of Institute of Race Relations at Swarthmore College, 1936; member of faculty of Harvard University, 1950-52; became trustee of Oberlin College, 1950, and the Rockefeller Foundation, 1955; member of the Harvard University board of overseers, 1958-65.

MEMBER: American Political Science Association (member of executive council; president, 1953-54), National Association for the Advancement of Colored People (member of board of directors, c. 1949-71), William Allen White Committee, Phi Beta Kappa.

AWARDS, HONORS: New York's Town Hall Distinguished Service Award, 1949; awarded citation by the American Association for the United Nations, 1949, for "distinguished and unselfish service in advancing the ideas of the United Nations"; Spingarn Award of the National Association for the Advancement of Colored People, 1949, and the Nobel Peace Prize, 1950, both for negotiating the 1949 armistice between Arab and Israeli states; One World Award; Franklin D. Roosevelt Four Freedoms Award from Four Freedoms Foundation, Inc.; Medal of Freedom, 1963; Ozias Goodwin fellowship from Harvard University, Rosenwald Field fellowship, and Social Science Research Council fellowship for anthropology and colonial policy; more than fifty honorary degrees from colleges and universities.

WRITINGS:

A World View of Race, Association in Negro Folk Education, 1936, reprinted, Kennikat, 1968.

Peace and the United Nations, Leeds University, 1952.
The Political Status of the Negro in the Age of FDR (collection of interviews), edited and with an introduction by Dewey W. Grantham, University of Chicago Press, 1973.

Contributor of articles on colonial policy, trusteeship, and race relations to periodicals, including *New Republic, National Municipal Review, Annals, Journal of Negro History,* and *Journal of Negro Education.* Also contributor to trusteeship sections of the United Nations Charter, 1945.

SIDELIGHTS: The highest ranking American official in the United Nations and the first black recipient of the Nobel Peace Prize, Ralph J. Bunche was "an ideal international civil servant, a black man of learning and experience open to men and ideas of all shades," according to Robert D. McFadden of the *New York Times.* For his leading role in negotiating peace talks between Arab and Israeli states in 1949 and his direction of numerous peace-keeping forces around the world, Bunche is considered one of the most significant American diplomats of the twentieth century.

Born in Detroit in 1904, Bunch moved to Los Angeles at the age of thirteen upon the death of his parents. After graduating from the University of California at Los Angeles in 1927 and receiving his master's degree in government at Harvard University the following year, he began teaching at the all-black Howard University in Washington, D.C., soon becoming the head of the political science department there. He returned to Harvard where he obtained a doctorate in government and international relations in 1934. His later postdoctoral work in anthropology and colonial policy led to worldwide travel, field work in Africa, and completion of his 1937 book *A World View of Race.* Concerned with racial problems, Bunche went on to work with Swedish sociologist Gunnar Myrdal from 1938 to 1940 surveying the conditions of the Negro in America. Their interview work in the South—which caused them to be chased out of some Alabama towns and almost lynched by a mob of angry whites—led to the publication of Myrdal's widely acclaimed 1944 *An American Dilemma,* a massive study of race relations.

Bunche eventually became known as an expert on colonial affairs. During World War II he served as a specialist in African and Far Eastern affairs for the Office of Strategic Services before moving to the U.S. State Department, where he soon became associate chief of its Division of Dependent Area Affairs. He was the first black to hold a desk job in the department. For his expertise on trusteeship, Bunche was recommended by Secretary-General Trygve Lie to direct the Trusteeship Division at the United Nations in 1947. Later that year the diplomat was appointed special assistant to the Secretary-General's Special Committee on Palestine, and in 1948 he became head of the Palestine Commission when its original appointee, Count Folke Bernadotte of Sweden, was assassinated. Bunche consequently was faced with the great challenge of continuing cease-fire talks between the long-time fighting Arab and Israeli nations.

"As it turned out," commented Homer Metz of *New Review,* "he was exactly suited for the difficult task of bringing Arabs and Jews together." Hailed for his endless patience, sensitivity, and optimism, Bunche, after eighty-one days of negotiations on the island of Rhodes, worked out the "Four Armistice Agreements" which resulted in an immediate cessation of the hostilities between the two combatants. "The art of his compromise," lauded McFadden, "lay in his seemingly boundless energy and the order and timing of his moves." A writer for

Time further praised the diplomat: "It required painstaking, brilliant diplomacy to bring the Arabs and Israelis together on the island of Rhodes; Bunche's forceful personality . . . helped to keep them there." Garnering worldwide praise for his successful peace-keeping efforts, Bunche won the 1950 Nobel Peace Prize, becoming the first black recipient of the coveted award.

Bunche did not consider his work on Rhodes, however, his most fulfilling mission. McFadden quoted Bunche from a 1969 interview: "'The Peace Prize attracted all the attention, but I've had more satisfaction in the work I've done since.'" For example, the statesman went on to conduct peace forces in the Congo, Yemen, Cyprus, India, and Pakistan, and he regarded his work in the Suez area of Egypt—where he organized and directed the deployment of a 6,000-man neutral force which maintained peace there from 1956 to 1967—as his most satisfying accomplishment. About that mission, Bunche was quoted in *Time:* "'For the first time . . . we have found a way to use military men for peace instead of war.'"

Bunche's peace-keeping efforts for the United Nations soon earned the diplomat the position of undersecretary in 1955, the highest post held by an American in the world organization. And by the time he became undersecretary-general in 1967 (the post he held until his retirement in 1971), Bunche's "diplomatic skills—a masterwork in the practical application of psychology—[had] became legendary at the United Nations," noted McFadden. But the international civil servant was not only valuable to the United Nations; Bunche was considered an inspiration to millions of Americans and was what *Newsweek* called "the foremost Negro of his generation—the distinguished symbol of how far a black man could rise in the Establishment." Furthermore, concluded *Time,* "Bunche had achieved a unique status: a black without color and an American who belonged to all the nations." His book *Peace and the United Nations* appeared in 1952, and *The Political Status of the Negro in the Age of FDR*—a collection of more than five hundred interviews conducted in the American South—was published posthumously in 1973.

BIOGRAPHICAL/CRITICAL SOURCES:

BOOKS

Kugelmass, J. Alvin, *Ralph J. Bunche: Fighter for Peace,* Messner, 1962.
Mann, Peggy, *Ralph Bunche: UN Peacemaker,* Coward, McCann & Geoghegan, 1975.

PERIODICALS

American History Review, June, 1974.
Journal of American History, June, 1974.
New Review, May 30, 1949.

OBITUARIES:

PERIODICALS

Nation, December 27, 1971.
Newsweek, December 20, 1971.
New York Times, December 10, 1971.
Time, December 20, 1971.*

—*Sketch by Janice E. Drane*

*   *   *

**BURNEY, Anton
See HOPKINS, (Hector) Kenneth**

BURNHAM, Linda Frye   1940-

PERSONAL: Born in 1940. *Education:* University of Southern California, B.A., 1962; University of California, Irvine, M.F.A., 1974.

ADDRESSES: Home—240 South Broadway, Los Angeles, Calif. 90012.

CAREER: University of California, Irvine, editor in Public Information Office, 1973-78; editor of *High Performance*, 1978—; performance artist. Co-owner of Astro Artz Publishing, 1980-83.

WRITINGS:

Bob and Bob: The First Five Years, Astro Artz, 1980.

Staff writer for *Artforum*, 1981—. Contributor to *Performance Anthology*, 1980.

*   *   *

BURNS, Allan P.   1935-

PERSONAL: Born May 18, 1935, in Baltimore, Md.; son of Donald L. (a lawyer) and Pauline D. Burns; married Joan Bailey (a writer), June 11, 1964; children: Eric C., Matthew M. *Education:* Attended University of Oregon, 1953-57. *Politics:* Democrat.

ADDRESSES: Home—4024 Radford Ave., Studio City, Calif. 91604.

CAREER: Screen and television writer.

AWARDS, HONORS: Emmy Awards for comedy series writing, 1968, for "He and She," 1971 and 1977, for "The Mary Tyler Moore Show," and for comedy series production, 1974, 1976, and 1977, for "The Mary Tyler Moore Show"; Writers Guild Award for television comedy, 1970, for "Room 222"; Oscar nomination from Academy of Motion Picture Arts and Sciences, 1979, for "A Little Romance."

WRITINGS:

"Butch and Sundance: The Early Days" (screenplay), Twentieth Century-Fox, 1979.
"A Little Romance" (screenplay), Orion, 1979.
"I Won't Dance" (screenplay), Metro-Goldwyn-Mayer, 1983.
"Just the Way You Are" (screenplay), Metro-Goldwyn-Mayer, 1984.
"Just Between Friends" (screenplay; also director and co-producer), Orion, 1986.

Creator of and writer for "The Mary Tyler Moore Show," "Rhoda," "Lou Grant," and "Eisenhower and Lutz," all on CBS-TV, and "The Duck Factory," NBC-TV; head writer for "Get Smart," NBC-TV and CBS-TV, and "He and She," CBS-TV.

WORK IN PROGRESS: Two screenplays, "Trust Me" and "Parental Guidance."

BIOGRAPHICAL/CRITICAL SOURCES:

PERIODICALS

Box Office, May, 1986.
Times (London), February 6, 1987.

BURNS, Tex
See L'AMOUR, Louis (Dearborn)

*   *   *

BUSH, Frederic W(illiam)   1929-

PERSONAL: Born August 7, 1929, in Vancouver, British Columbia, Canada; immigrated to United States, 1948, naturalized citizen, 1961; son of Sidney F. (a police officer) and Violet (Piper) Bush; married Jerel Calkins, June, 1954 (died June 6, 1969); married Bernice Fern Spencer (an advertising agency executive), December 13, 1969; children: (first marriage) Perry J., Preston F., Piper Rae (Mrs. Paul Cartland). *Education:* University of Washington, Seattle, B.A., 1954; Fuller Theological Seminary, B.D., 1958, Th.M., 1960; Brandeis University, M.A., 1962, Ph.D., 1964. *Politics:* Democrat. *Religion:* Presbyterian.

ADDRESSES: Home—16621 Edgewater Lane, Huntington Beach, Calif. 92649. *Office*—Department of Old Testament, Fuller Theological Seminary, Pasadena, Calif. 91101.

CAREER: Brandeis University, Waltham, Mass., instructor in Mediterranean studies, 1964-65; Fuller Theological Seminary, Pasadena, Calif., instructor, 1965-66, assistant professor, 1966-84, associate professor of Old Testament, 1984—.

MEMBER: Institute for Biblical Research, Society of Biblical Literature.

WRITINGS:

Old Testament Survey: The Message, Form, and Background of the Old Testament, Eerdmans, 1981.

Contributor to scholarly journals.

WORK IN PROGRESS: A Commentary on Ruth and Esther, publication by Word, Inc., expected in 1990.

*   *   *

BUSSELL, Harold L.   1941-

PERSONAL: Born August 14, 1941, in California. *Education:* Bethany College, B.A., 1963; University of Santa Clara, M.A., 1973; Andover Newton Theological School, D.Min., 1980.

ADDRESSES: Office—Chapel, Gordon College, 255 Grapevine Rd., Wenham, Mass. 01984.

CAREER: Ordained Congregational minister; Gordon College, Wenham, Mass., dean of chapel, 1976—. Pastor of First Congregational Church of Hamilton, 1986—; family counselor; member of board of directors of American Family Foundation.

WRITINGS:

Unholy Devotion: Why Cults Lure Christians, Zondervan, 1983.
Lord, I Can Resist Everything But Temptation, Zondervan, 1986.
The Ethics of Evangelism, Inter-Varsity Press, in press.

Author of monthly column in *New England Church Life*.

*   *   *

BUTTERWORTH, Neil   1934-

PERSONAL: Born September 4, 1934, in London, England; son of Philip (an engineer) and Phyllis (a musician; maiden name, Lovett) Butterworth; married Anna Mary Barnes (a lecturer in music), April 23, 1960; children: Clare, Alexandra, Eleanor. *Education:* University of Nottingham, B.A. (English), 1957, B.A. (music), 1958, M.A., 1965; graduate study at University of London, 1958-59, and Guildhall School of Music, 1960-62. *Politics:* None. *Religion:* None.

ADDRESSES: Home—White House, Inveresk, Musselburgh, Midlothian EH21 7TG, Scotland. *Office*—Napier College, Sighthill Court, Edinburgh EH11 4BD, Scotland.

CAREER: Kingston College of Education, Surrey, England, lecturer in English, 1962-68; Napier College, Edinburgh, Scotland, head of department of music, 1968-87; writer. Conductor of Glasgow Orchestral Society, 1975-83; regular broadcaster on BBC-Radio; chairman of Edinburgh Centre.

MEMBER: Incorporated Society of Musicians (chairman), Performing Rights Society, Society of Scottish Composers.

AWARDS, HONORS: Winston Churchill traveling fellow, 1975; fellow of London College of Music, 1982.

WRITINGS:

Four Hundred Aural Training Exercises, Novello, 1966.
English for Business and Professional Students, McGraw, 1967.
Music Quiz, Banks, 1970.

Haydn: His Life and Times, Midas, 1976.
Dvorak, Midas, 1980.
Dictionary of American Composers, Garland Publishing, 1983.
The Music of Aaron Copland, Toccata, 1985.
The Music of Samuel Barber, Toccata, 1988.
Vaughan Williams: A Research Manual, Garland Publishing, 1988.

Music critic for Scotland's *Times Educational Supplement*.

SIDELIGHTS: Neil Butterworth told *CA:* "My books on Aaron Copland and Samuel Barber are the first critical studies to be issued on these composers for over thirty years. My enthusiasm for their work is such that I felt it was essential that some recognition should be paid to them. My writing has grown out of my teaching of music history. The Joseph Haydn and Antonin Dvorak books are lavishly illustrated biographies for the layman. My future books will include studies of the music of Leonard Bernstein and Gian Carlo Menotti, whose work has been largely ignored in favor of their private lives."

AVOCATIONAL INTERESTS: Hellenic studies, collecting records and books, collecting autographs, the life of Emily Dickinson.

C

CAEIRO, Alberto
See PESSOA, Fernando (Antonio Nogueira)

* * *

CALHOUN, Charles W(illiam) 1948-

PERSONAL: Born February 24, 1948, in South Bend, Ind.; son of Robert C. (a molder) and Juanita (Johnson) Calhoun; married Mary Bankhead Foord (a teacher), August 29, 1972. *Education:* Yale University, B.A., 1970; Columbia University, M.A., 1972, M.Phil., 1974, Ph.D., 1977.

ADDRESSES: Home—545 Beechwood Dr., Clarksville, Tenn. 37040. *Office*—Department of History, Austin Peay State University, College St., Clarksville, Tenn. 37044.

CAREER: Austin Peay State University, Clarksville, Tenn., assistant professor, 1978-83, associate professor, 1983-87, professor of history and chairman of department, 1987—. Trustee of Clarksville-Montgomery County Historical Museum.

MEMBER: American Historical Association, Organization of American Historians, Society of Historians of American Foreign Relations, Indiana Historical Society, Phi Kappa Phi, Phi Alpha Theta.

AWARDS, HONORS: National Endowment for the Humanities fellowship, 1988-89.

WRITINGS:

(With Rebecca A. Shepherd) *Biographical Directory of the Indiana General Assembly, 1816-1899,* Indiana Historical Bureau, 1980.
Gilded Age Cato: The Life of Walter Q. Gresham, University Press of Kentucky, 1987.

Contributor of articles and reviews to history journals. Member of editorial advisory board of *Hayes Historical Journal: A Journal of the Gilded Age.*

WORK IN PROGRESS: The Ideology of the Republican Party in the Gilded Age.

SIDELIGHTS: Charles W. Calhoun told *CA:* "My current research is an examination of the ideology of the Republican party in the Gilded Age. It has been convention to deny that ideology played much part in the politics of that period and to conclude that the quest for offices, not ideas, guided the politicians' behavior. This impression has enjoyed currency, in large measure, because historians have neglected to pose the kinds of questions that would lead to a clearer understanding of the larger thinking of these political leaders. What, for instance, did these people conceive to be the nature of American society? What were their ambitions and goals for that society? To what extent did history, tradition, and an idealization of the early Republic influence their ideas? How did the triumph of Union arms and the apotheosis of Lincoln affect their political thinking? What did they see as the purposes of government? What were the sources of the government's legitimacy and power? What was the proper relationship between the government and the economy, between the state and the individual? What was the true nature of federalism? Was the Constitution a liberating document or a confining one? In short, what vision and philosophy, explicit or implicit, underlay the actions of Blaine, Garfield, Harrison, Sherman, and others, and in what ideational terms did they justify those actions to themselves, their countrymen, and the world? These are the kinds of questions that inform my study of the ideology of the Republican party in the Gilded Age.''

* * *

CALKINS, Lucy McCormick

PERSONAL: Born in Boston, Mass.; daughter of Evan and Virginia Calkins; married John Skorpen; children: Miles Evan. *Education:* Attended Mount Holyoke College, 1969-71; Williams College, B.A., 1973; University of Hartford, M.A., 1974; New York University, Ph.D., 1982.

ADDRESSES: Home—2 Dawn Lane, Ridgefield, Conn. 06877. *Office*—The Writers Project, P.O. Box 77, Teachers College, Columbia University, 525 West 121st St., New York, N.Y. 10027. *Agent*—John Wright, 112 Shelbank Pl., Rockville Centre, N.Y. 11570.

CAREER: High school English teacher in Hartford, Conn., 1973-74; teacher at primary school in Oxfordshire, England, 1974-75; teacher and program leader at junior high school in Durham/Middlefield, Conn., 1975-76; co-founder and teacher at public alternative elementary school in Durham/Middlefield, 1976-78; University of New Hampshire, Durham, research associate for National Institute of Education project,

"How Children Change as Writers," 1978-80; Columbia University, Teachers College, New York, N.Y., began as assistant professor, became associate professor of English Education and director of the Writers Project, 1982—. Member of summer writing faculty at University of New Hampshire, 1981-82, and Northeastern University, 1982; speaker in more than one hundred school districts in the United States and Canada; interviewed on radio and television programs; consultant to *Time, Learning,* and "Sesame Street."

MEMBER: International Reading Association, National Council of Teachers of English, National Conference on Research in English, Commission on Composition.

AWARDS, HONORS: Grants from New York City Board of Education, 1984-88, Morgan Guaranty Trust Co., 1984-85, 1985-86, 1987-88, Hazen Foundation, 1984-85, Conrad Hilton Foundation, 1984-85, Edwin Gould Foundation, 1984-85, 1985-87, 1987-89, New York Times Foundation, 1985-86, 1986-87, and Valentine Perry Snyder Foundation, 1985-86.

WRITINGS:

(Contributor) R. D. Walshe, editor, *Donald Graves in Australia,* Primary English Teaching Association, 1981.
Lessons From a Child: On the Teaching and Learning of Writing, Heinemann Educational, 1983.
(Contributor) Angela Jaggar, editor, *Child-Watching: Observing the Language Learner,* International Reading Association, 1984.
(Contributor) B. McClelland, editor, *New Perspectives on Composition Research,* Modern Language Association of America, 1985.
The Art of Teaching Writing, Heinemann Educational, 1985.
The Writing Workshop, Heinemann Educational, 1988.

Contributor to *Classroom Practices in Teaching English,* National Council of Teachers of English, 1980, and education journals.

SIDELIGHTS: In a *New York Times* book review, Fred M. Hechinger wrote that *The Art of Teaching Writing* "is a book for all teachers and parents who cherish writing, reading and children." Lucy McCormick Calkins believes that the successful writing teacher must be a person who loves both reading and writing and focuses on the child rather than the textbook. The writing classroom must become a writing workshop where children can share their work. The teacher must listen to the child and be aware of the ways in which his needs change as he grows older. Calkins's book provides guidelines for accomplishing these objectives, emphasizing the art rather than the skills of teaching.

BIOGRAPHICAL/CRITICAL SOURCES:

PERIODICALS

New York Times, December 3, 1985.

*   *   *

CAMBON, Glauco (Gianlorenzo)   1921-1988

OBITUARY NOTICE—See index for *CA* sketch: Born May 7, 1921, in Pusiano, Italy; died of a heart attack, March 31, 1988, in North Windham, Conn. Educator, translator, and author. Cambon taught English in Italian schools before coming to the United States as a visiting professor at the University of Michigan in 1958. Eventually he became a professor of Italian and comparative literature at institutions including Rutgers University and the University of Connecticut, Storrs. Cambon translated into Italian such works as William Faulkner's *Absalom, Absalom!* and Robert Penn Warren's *World Enough and Time.* His own writings include *Tematica e sviluppo della poesia americana, Recent American Poetry, The Inclusive Flame, Dante's Craft, Ugo Foscolo: Poet of Exile,* and *Eugenio Montale's Poetry.*

OBITUARIES AND OTHER SOURCES:

BOOKS

Directory of American Scholars, Volume III: *Foreign Languages, Linguistics, and Philology,* 8th edition, Bowker, 1982.

PERIODICALS

New York Times, April 8, 1988.

*   *   *

CAMEJA, Pedro
    See CAMEJO, Peter (Miguel)

*   *   *

CAMEJO, Pedro
    See CAMEJO, Peter (Miguel)

*   *   *

CAMEJO, Pedro M.
    See CAMEJO, Peter (Miguel)

*   *   *

CAMEJO, Peter (Miguel)   1939-
    (Pedro Cameja, Pedro Camejo, Pedro M. Camejo)

PERSONAL: Born December 31, 1939, in New York, N.Y.; son of Daniel Camejo and Elvia (Guanche) Octavio. *Education:* Attended Massachusetts Institute of Technology, 1958-61, and University of California, Berkeley, 1967.

CAREER: New England director of the Fair Play for Cuba Committee, 1960-61; member of national committee, 1963—, presidential candidate, 1976, and national field organizer for the Southwest, 1977—, for the Socialist Workers party. Member of national coordinating committee of Anti-War Student Mobilization Committee, 1966-72.

WRITINGS:

Guevara's Guerrilla Strategy: Why It Failed, Pathfinder Press (New York, N.Y.), 1972.
(Author of introduction and notes) Hugo Blanco, *Tierra o muerte: Las luchas campesinas en Peru,* Siglo Vientiuno Editores, 1972.
Racism, Revolution, Reaction, 1861-1877: The Rise and Fall of Radical Reconstruction, Monad Press, 1976.
(With Michael Harrington) *The Lesser Evil? The Left Debates the Democratic Party and Social Change,* Pathfinder Press (New York, N.Y.), 1978.
(Editor, under name Pedro Camejo, with Fred Murphy) *The Nicaraguan Revolution,* Pathfinder Press (New York, N.Y.), 1979.

Author of political pamphlets, sometimes under names Pedro M. Camejo and Pedro Cameja.

CAMERON, Peter 1959-

PERSONAL: Born November 29, 1959, in Pompton Plains, N.J., son of Donald O. (an economist) and Sally (a homemaker; maiden name, Shaw) Cameron. *Education:* Hamilton College, B.A., 1982.

ADDRESSES: Home—New York, N.Y. *Agent*—Candida Donadio & Associates, Inc., 231 West 22nd St., New York, N.Y. 10011.

CAREER: St. Martin's Press, New York City, subsidiary rights assistant, 1982-83; Trust for Public Land, New York City, word processor, 1983—. Assistant professor at Oberlin College, Oberlin, Ohio, 1987.

MEMBER: P.E.N., Authors Guild.

AWARDS, HONORS: Short stories included in *Prize Stories: O. Henry Awards:* "Homework," 1985, and "Excerpts from Swanlake," 1986; National Endowment for the Arts Grant fellowship, 1987; P.E.N.-Hemingway Award, honorable mention, 1987.

WRITINGS:

One Way or Another (short stories), Harper, 1986.

WORK IN PROGRESS: The Half You Don't Know, a novel; *Leap Year,* a novel; stories.

SIDELIGHTS: Peter Cameron received widespread critical attention for his first book, *One Way or Another,* a collection of what reviewers characterized as sensitive, well-crafted short stories that focus on the crises and decisions ordinary people have to face in their everyday lives. Often compared to the works of minimalist writers Ann Beattie and Raymond Carver, Cameron's stories present such crises in a bare, blunt way, according to a number of critics. In *Boston Review,* for instance, Rosellen Brown argued that his style, like that of "[most] postsixties fiction writers," is "unabashedly impersonal" and "attempts to defy the inevitability of point-of-view" with a "concomitant reduction in emotional volume," while Victor Kantor Burg, in the *New York Times Book Review,* noted that events in Cameron's stories occasionally happen "abruptly and unpredictably."

A major theme in Cameron's work is the sense of isolation and disaffectation people experience when faced with dilemmas for which they can find no solution. Divorced from the emotional support of close relationships with family or friends, the central characters in *One Way or Another* reflect what David Leavitt, as quoted by Amy Hempel in the *Los Angeles Times Book Review,* described as "an attitude of angry betrayal" born of a world where "marriages and families, rather than providing havens, are themselves the fulcrums of the most sweeping upheavals." In "Memorial Day," for example, a teenage boy is dismayed when his divorced mother quickly remarries a man only thirteen years his senior, while a young woman in "Fear of Math," taking a summer course in calculus to enter college, retreats from her parents' arguing, and thinks, when her mother begins to confide in her, "Don't tell me this, don't say any of this. I don't want to know you're unhappy." Such are the preoccupations of the author's characters; they are "young adults," according to Alice H. G. Phillips in the *Times Literary Supplement,* "wrapped up in their own problems, surprised that other people can feel pain." But in spite of the apparent self-centeredness of his characters—a condi-

tion that led Brown to charge that his stories end "one after the other, in emotional disengagement"—critics applauded Cameron for his handling of what Phillips called the "serious unhappiness and vague hopes" of his heroes, especially when he "allows himself to be swept away by [their] uncertainties [and makes] them his own."

BIOGRAPHICAL/CRITICAL SOURCES:

BOOKS

Contemporary Literary Criticism, Volume 44, Gale, 1986.

PERIODICALS

Boston Review, August, 1986.
Tribune Books, October 5, 1986.
Los Angeles Times Book Review, May 11, 1986.
Newsweek, September 15, 1986.
New York Times Book Review, June 22, 1986, October 25, 1987.
Times Literary Supplement, September 5, 1986.

*   *   *

CAMPOS, Alvaro de
See PESSOA, Fernando (Antonio Nogueira)

*   *   *

CANIFF, Milton (Arthur) 1907-1988

OBITUARY NOTICE—See index for *CA* sketch: Born February 28, 1907, in Hillsboro, Ohio; died of lung cancer, April 3 (one source says April 4), 1988, in New York, N.Y. Artist, actor, and cartoonist. Caniff will be best remembered as the creator of the comic strips "Terry and the Pirates" and "Steve Canyon." He began drawing for newspapers at the age of thirteen and also landed small parts in a few films before settling on writing comic strips full time. Caniff's first strips for the Associated Press were "Dickie Dare" and "The Gay Thirties," but he caught the public's imagination in 1934 with his adventure strip about a boy, Terry Lee, and his tutor, Pat Ryan, who traveled throughout the Orient encountering such villains as the Dragon Lady. By 1946, dissatisfied because he did not own the rights to "Terry," Caniff allowed George Wunder to take over the strip while he went on to create "Steve Canyon," an Air Force colonel who had many exciting adventures. Caniff also created a special strip, "Male Call," to boost morale in the armed forces during World War II. He also painted in oils, and some of his paintings have been exhibited in galleries in New York.

OBITUARIES AND OTHER SOURCES:

BOOKS

Current Biography, H. W. Wilson, 1988.
Who's Who in America, 44th edition, Marquis, 1986.
Who's Who in American Art, 17th edition, Bowker, 1986.

PERIODICALS

Chicago Tribune, April 5, 1988.
Los Angeles Times, April 4, 1988.
New York Times, April 5, 1988.
Washington Post, April 5, 1988.

*   *   *

CARAWAY, Charless 1888-1977

PERSONAL: Born November 20, 1888, in Raleigh, Ill.; died

July 13, 1977; son of Merritt M. (a farmer) and Melvina (a housewife; maiden name, Powell) Caraway; married Bessie Mae Rowan, February 23, 1910 (deceased); children: Lester (deceased), George, Wayne (deceased), Ethel Caraway Miller, Cleo, Charley, Betty Lou Caraway Nettland. *Education:* Attended elementary schools in Saline and Jackson Counties, Ill.

CAREER: Farmer in Makanda and Murphysboro, Ill., 1910-71.

WRITINGS:

Foothold on a Hillside: Memories of a Southern Illinoisan, Southern Illinois University Press, 1986.

Contributor to history journals.

[Sketch verified by daughter Cleo Caraway]

*   *   *

CARLOCK, Lynn
See CUNNINGHAM, Marilyn

*   *   *

CARMICHAEL, Ann G(ayton) 1947-

PERSONAL: Born August 28, 1947, in Virginia; daughter of Gordon Gayton (a surgeon) and Pauline (a radiologist; maiden name, Davis) Carmichael; married James W. Mold, March 10, 1974 (divorced, 1976); children: Gibson. *Education:* DePauw University, B.A., 1969; Duke University, Ph.D., 1978, M.D., 1978.

ADDRESSES: Home—Bloomington, Ind. *Office*—Department of History, Indiana University—Bloomington, Bloomington, Ind. 47405.

CAREER: Indiana University—Bloomington, assistant professor, 1979-85, associate professor of history, 1985—.

MEMBER: American Historical Association, American Association for the History of Medicine, Renaissance Society of America, Italian Historical Association, Indiana Historical Society.

AWARDS, HONORS: Grant from National Endowment for the Humanities.

WRITINGS:

Plague and the Poor in Renaissance Florence, Cambridge University Press, 1987.

Associate editor of *American Historical Review,* 1986—.

WORK IN PROGRESS: Morbidity and Mortality in Early Modern Milan, completion expected in 1991; *New Diseases in the Sixteenth Century,* completion expected in 1992.

*   *   *

CARTER, Arthur M. 1911-1988

OBITUARY NOTICE: Born September 2, 1911, in Washington, D.C.; died of cancer, May 22, 1988, in Washington, D.C. Journalist, editor, and publisher. An award-winning newsman, Carter was known for his association with the *Afro-American* chain of publications. He began working for *Afro-American* newspapers in 1937 as a sports correspondent and police reporter, and in 1939 he became sports editor of the Baltimore, Maryland, *Afro American.* During World War II Carter was one of America's few black war correspondents, reporting in northern Africa and Italy. He continued his journalism career after the war, serving as national correspondent, assistant managing editor, and managing editor of *Afro-American* publications in Baltimore, Washington, D.C., and Richmond, Virginia. In 1970 he became editor and publisher of the *Washington Afro-American and Tribune,* serving in that capacity until his retirement in 1986. For his extensive journalistic achievements, Carter received numerous awards, including editor of the year honors from both the National Newspaper Publishers Association and the Capital Press Club (of which he was a founder and past president); a meritorious service award of Sigma Delta Chi in 1985; and a citation from the American Cancer Society in 1986.

OBITUARIES AND OTHER SOURCES:

BOOKS

Who's Who Among Black Americans, 5th edition, Who's Who Among Black Americans, 1988.

PERIODICALS

Chicago Tribune, May 27, 1988.
New York Times, May 25, 1988.
Washington Post, May 24, 1988.

*   *   *

CARTER-HARRISON, Paul
See HARRISON, Paul Carter

*   *   *

CARTIER, Xam Wilson 1949(?)-

PERSONAL: Born in St. Louis, Mo.

ADDRESSES: Home—San Francisco, Calif.

CAREER: Artist, pianist, dancer, and writer.

WRITINGS:

Be-Bop, Re-Bop (novel), Available Press/Ballantine, 1987.

SIDELIGHTS: The unnamed black woman who narrates Xam Wilson Cartier's first novel *Be-Bop, Re-Bop* recalls significant moments in her childhood and young adulthood and reflects on the liberating presence of jazz in her life. Like her father before her, the narrator finds that cares surrender—at least momentarily—to the lyrics and melodies of black music; "jazz seems to mirror key elements in black culture: spontaneity, improvisation," related Cartier, "because your situation is always in flux." Discussing *Be-Bop, Re-Bop* in the *New York Times Book Review,* Valerie Smith wrote: "Jazz informs the style as well as the subject of Ms. Cartier's novel. Metaphors and rhymes resonate off one another, off alliterative phrases with all the intensity of an inspired riff." While the critic did find "minor difficulties" in the novel's singular focus ("the easy way in which music alleviates grief and fear and anxiety at times seems simplistically upbeat"), she nevertheless decided that "the power of the language . . . is so compelling one can overlook these minor shortcomings." Smith added, "This marvelous first novel . . . demonstrate[s] the deep connections between music and narrative."

BIOGRAPHICAL/CRITICAL SOURCES:

PERIODICALS

New York Times Book Review, December 13, 1987.

CASSAVANT, Sharron Greer 1939-

PERSONAL: Born July 22, 1939, in Pendleton, Ore.; daughter of Arthur G. (a farmer) and Christena (a housewife; maiden name, Baker) Greer; married Roland J. Cassavant, Jr. (an attorney), August 20, 1972; children: Stephen Roland, Sara Eileen. *Education:* College of Idaho, B.A., 1961; University of Utah, M.A., 1964; University of London, Certificate, 1969; Tufts University, Ph.D., 1979. *Religion:* Unitarian-Universalist.

ADDRESSES: Home—90 Pleasant St., Wakefield, Mass. 01880. *Office*—Department of English, Simmons College, 300 The Fenway, Boston, Mass. 02115.

CAREER: Glendale Community College, Glendale, Ariz., instructor in literature and composition, 1964-67; American College for Girls, Istanbul, Turkey, instructor in literature and composition, 1967-70; teaching fellow at Tufts University, 1970-79; Northeastern University, Boston, Mass., lecturer in literature and composition, 1979-82; Simmons College, Boston, instructor in literature and composition, 1982—. Director of communications for Insurance Cost Control, Inc.; member of finance committee of city of Wakefield.

MEMBER: Modern Language Association of America, National Council of Teachers of English, Conference on College Composition and Communication, Alliance of Independent Scholars.

WRITINGS:

John Middleton Murry: The Critic as Moralist, University of Alabama Press, 1983.

WORK IN PROGRESS: Research on the fiction of Rebecca West.

SIDELIGHTS: Sharron Greer Cassavant told *CA:* "Although John Middleton Murry was best known in the 1920s as a literary critic and editor (and even more widely as the husband of Katherine Mansfield and the friend of D. H. Lawrence), he thought and wrote about broader cultural issues. He was a failed creative writer, a spokesman for causes, and a founder of enterprises, including a communal farm for pacifists in England during World War II. He wrote more than forty books and scores of pamphlets, essays, and reviews during a complicated, energetic life.

"My interest in Murry grew out of considering the entanglement of idea and personality in his work and the extent to which private values, experiences, and personal oddities shaped the frequently controversial paths he took. As Murry confesses in his autobiography *Between Two Worlds,* he felt socially displaced by the stresses attendent upon moving, with the first wave of scholarships available to bright boys of the British lower classes, from the lower middle class to public school and university. Since I grew up on a subsistence farm in Idaho and similarly moved to another world in the course of gaining intellectual credentials, I understand something of the tension Murry felt in encountering the assured world of Bloomsbury, the aristocratic power vested in Ottoline Morrell's Garsington Manor, and the intellectual decorum of Oxford. Although Murry was well able to succeed in these milieus, he quite deliberately decided not to walk in the paths of literary or academic establishments, choosing an iconoclastic path and focusing on a middlebrow audience. He saw great literature as the source of moral vision and the breath of life itself."

CAUNITZ, William J. 1935-

BRIEF ENTRY: Born in 1935 in Brooklyn, N.Y. American police officer and author. Caunitz is known for his best-selling action thrillers *One Police Plaza* (Crown, 1984) and *Suspects* (Crown, 1986), works based on his nearly thirty years of experience with the New York City police force. Selling more than one million copies, *One Police Plaza,* the author's first novel, earned praise for its convincing and unglamorized portrayal of dedicated policemen working in the violent and seamy world of New York City crime. The book depicts Lieutenant Dan Malone, a middle-aged officer whose obsession with his job renders his personal life virtually nonexistent. Involved in the homicide case of a young girl, Malone uncovers conspiracy and corruption in various organizations, including the New York Police Department. Although some reviewers claimed Caunitz courted sales by filling the novel with an abundance of sex and violence, *One Police Plaza* was well received for its vivid descriptions and the author's unpretentious prose. It was subsequently adapted as a television movie. Caunitz drew further on his police experiences for his second novel, *Suspects,* in which protagonist Lieutenant Anthony Scanlon investigates the murder of co-worker Lieutenant Joseph P. Gallagher—a seemingly exemplary police officer—and discovers Gallagher's sordid secret life, as well as other oddities within the police department. *Suspects,* like *Plaza,* was lauded for its authenticity and gritty realism.

BIOGRAPHICAL/CRITICAL SOURCES:

BOOKS

Contemporary Literary Criticism, Volume 34, Gale, 1985.

PERIODICALS

Los Angeles Times Book Review, July 29, 1984.
Newsweek, March 19, 1984.
People, November 10, 1986.

* * *

CAVERS, David F(arquhar) 1902-1988

OBITUARY NOTICE—See index for *CA* sketch: Born September 3, 1902, in Buffalo, N.Y.; died of prostate cancer, March 4, 1988, in Cambridge, Mass. Attorney, educator, editor, and author. Admitted to the bar of New York State in 1928, Cavers spent most of his career as a professor of law at Harvard University. Previously, he taught law at such institutions as West Virginia University and Duke University. Cavers specialized in resolving legal conflicts between different jurisdictions. He served as editor of the periodical *Law and Contemporary Problems,* and his writings include *Electric Power Regulation in Latin America, The Choice-of-Law Process,* and *Contemporary Conflicts: Law in American Perspective.*

OBITUARIES AND OTHER SOURCES:

BOOKS

The International Year Book and Statesmen's Who's Who, Thomas Skinner Directories, 1982.

PERIODICALS

New York Times, March 12, 1988.

* * *

CHAMBERS, Lucille Arcola 1909(?)-1988

OBITUARY NOTICE: Born c. 1909; died March 22, 1988, in

New York, N.Y. Author. Chambers was known for her writings on black history. In addition to producing a series of coloring books on black pioneers, she wrote a chronology of black achievers in the United States titled *America's Tenth Man: A Pictorial Review of One-Tenth of a Nation*. The volume featured a foreword by American senator and statesman Henry Cabot Lodge.

OBITUARIES AND OTHER SOURCES:

PERIODICALS

Los Angeles Times, March 29, 1988.

*   *   *

CHARLES, Will
See WILLEFORD, Charles (Ray III)

*   *   *

CHARLESWORTH, Edward A(llison) 1949-

PERSONAL: Born March 23, 1949, in New Orleans, La.; son of Albert Ernest and Wilma Nadine (Wright) Charlesworth; married Robin Elaine Rupley, December 7, 1974. *Education:* University of Houston, B.S., 1974, M.S., 1978, Ph.D., 1980; additional training at National Institute for Mental Health, 1976-78, and Veterans Administration Hospital, 1978. *Politics:* Democrat. *Religion:* Presbyterian.

ADDRESSES: Home—11401 Hylander, Houston, Tex. 77070. *Office*—Willowbrook Psychological Associates, 9725 Louedd Ave., Houston, Tex. 77070.

CAREER: Baylor University, Houston, Tex., research associate at College of Medicine, 1970-81, psychologist and instructor in psychology, 1981-82; Willowbrook Psychological Associates, Houston, director, 1982—. Diplomate of American Academy of Behavioral Medicine; president of Stress Management Research Associates, Inc., 1977—; founder and sponsor of Forest Lake Teens in Action, 1978-80; chairman and chief editor of Biobehavioral Press, 1980—; instructor in local school district Wellness Program, 1982.

MEMBER: American Psychological Association, American Society of Biofeedback Clinicians, Mensa, Texas Psychological Association, Harris County Biofeedback Society, Houston Psychological Association, Willowbrook Rotary Club (director of community service, 1984-86; president-elect, 1988-89).

WRITINGS:

(With Ronald G. Nathan) *Stress Management: A Conceptual and Procedural Guide*, Biobehavioral Press, 1980.
(With Nathan) *Stress Management: A Comprehensive Guide to Wellness*, Biobehavioral Press, 1982.

*   *   *

CHASE, Richard 1904-1988

OBITUARY NOTICE—See index for *CA* sketch: Born February 15, 1904, near Huntsville, Ala.; died February 2, 1988, in Huntsville, Ala. Folklorist, editor, and author. Chase traveled to many educational institutions throughout the United States, lecturing on Appalachian folklore and telling stories. He edited several books of folktales, including *Old Songs and Singing Games; The Jack Tales: Told by R. M. Ward and His Kindred in the Beech Mountain Section of Western North Carolina and by Other Descendants of Council Harmon (1803-*

1896) Elsewhere in the Southern Mountains: With Three Tales From Wise County, Virginia; Grandfather Tales: American-English Folk Tales; and *American Folk Tales and Songs, and Other Examples of English-American Tradition as Preserved in the Appalachian Mountains and Elsewhere in the United States.* Chase's own works include *Jack and the Three Sillies* and *Wicked John and the Devil.*

OBITUARIES AND OTHER SOURCES:

BOOKS

Who's Who in America, 41st edition, Marquis, 1980.

PERIODICALS

School Library Journal, June/July, 1988.

*   *   *

CHEN Jia
See SHEN Congwen

*   *   *

CHERRY, Gordon E(manuel) 1931-

PERSONAL: Born February 6, 1931, in Barnsley, Yorkshire, England; son of Emanuel (a former tenant farmer and a bank clerk) and Nora (a housewife) Cherry; married Margaret May London Cox (a housewife), June 8, 1957; children: Shona Margaret, Shelagh Louise, Iain Gordon. *Education:* Queen Mary College, London, B.A. (with honors), 1953.

ADDRESSES: Home—Quaker Ridge, 66 Meriden Rd., Hampton in Arden, West Midlands B92 0BT, England. *Office*—Department of Geography, University of Birmingham, Birmingham B15 2TT, England.

CAREER: City planner in Durham, Hull, Doncaster, and Sheffield, 1956-63; City Planning Department, Newcastle upon Tyne, England, research officer, 1963-68; University of Birmingham, Birmingham, England, deputy director of Centre for Urban and Regional Studies, 1968-85, senior lecturer, 1968-76, professor of urban and regional planning, 1976—, dean of faculty of commerce and social science, 1981-85, head of department of geography, 1986—. Member of Bournville Village Trust, 1979—, Local Government Boundary Commission for England, 1979—, and Advisory Committee on Landscape Treatment of Trunk Roads for Ministry of Transport, 1984—. *Military service:* British Army, Royal Army Education Corps, 1954-56.

MEMBER: Royal Town Planning Institute (fellow and president, 1978-79), Royal Institution of Chartered Surveyors (fellow), Planning History Group (chairman).

AWARDS, HONORS: D.Sc. from Heriot-Watt University, 1984.

WRITINGS:

Town Planning in Its Social Context, Leonard Hill Books, 1970, revised edition, 1973.
(With T. L. Burton) *Social Research Techniques for Planners*, Allen & Unwin, 1971.
Urban Change and Planning, G. T. Foulis, 1972.
The Evolution of British Town Planning, Leonard Hill Books, 1974.
Environmental Planning, Volume II: *National Parks and Recreation in the Countryside*, H.M.S.O., 1976.
The Politics of Town Planning, Longman, 1982.

(With J. L. Penny) *Holford: A Study in Architecture, Planning, and Civic Design,* Mansell, 1986.
Cities and Plans, Edward Arnold, 1988.

EDITOR

Urban Planning Problems, Leonard Hill Books, 1974.
Rural Planning Problems, Leonard Hill Books, 1976.
Shaping the Urban World, Mansell, 1980.
Pioneers in British Planning, Architectural Press, 1981.

Co-editor of "Studies in History, Planning, and the Environment," Mansell, 1980—. Co-editor of *Planning Perspectives: An International Journal of History, Planning, and the Environment,* 1986—.

WORK IN PROGRESS: Research on the history of town planning.

SIDELIGHTS: Gordon E. Cherry told *CA:* "I was trained as a geographer and made an easy transition into town planning (British style). I practiced as a town planner in local government. Since then I have taught the subject and analyzed it politically and historically. I am a curious observer of world cities: what they look like, how they function, how they change, how people live in them, and what life chances these people have."

*   *   *

CHESNUTT, Charles W(addell)   1858-1932

PERSONAL: Born June 20, 1858, in Cleveland, Ohio; died November 15, 1932, in Cleveland, Ohio; son of Andrew Jackson (in grocery business) and Ann (one source says Anne) Maria (Sampson) Chesnutt; married Susan Utley Perry (a teacher), June 6, 1878; children: Ethel, Helen Maria, Edwin, Dorothy. *Education:* Educated at schools in Cleveland, Ohio, and Fayetteville, N.C.

ADDRESSES: 9719 Lamont Ave., Cleveland, Ohio.

CAREER: Teacher, lawyer, businessman, and writer. Taught at public schools in Spartanburg, S.C., Charlotte, N.C., and Fayetteville, N.C., 1872-77; New State Normal School, Fayetteville, assistant principal, 1877-80, principal, 1880-83; worked as a reporter for Dow Jones & Co., 1883; *New York Mail and Express,* New York, N.Y., stenographer, reporter, and author of daily column "Wall Street Gossip," 1883; Nickel Plate Railroad Co., Cleveland, Ohio, 1884-89, began as clerk, became stenographer for the firm's legal counsel; admitted to the Bar of Ohio, 1887; private practice of court reporting, beginning in 1890. Active in community affairs and social causes; served on General Committee of National Association for the Advancement of Colored People (NAACP).

AWARDS, HONORS: Spingarn Medal from NAACP, 1928.

WRITINGS:

The Conjure Woman (short stories; contains "The Goophered Grapevine," "Po' Sandy," "Mars Jeems's Nightmare," "The Conjurer's Revenge," "Sis' Becky's Pickaninny," "The Gray Wolf's Ha'nt," and "Hot-Foot Hannibal"), Houghton, 1899, deluxe edition with a foreword by Joel Elias Spingarn, 1929, reprinted, Gregg, 1968, retold for young readers by Ray Anthony Shepard as *Conjure Tales,* with illustrations by John Ross and Clare Romano, Dutton, 1973.
The Wife of His Youth, and Other Stories of the Color Line (short stories; contains "The Wife of His Youth," "Her

Virginia Mammy," "The Sheriff's Children," "A Matter of Principle," "Cicely's Dream," "The Passing of Grandison," "Uncle Wellington's Wives," "The Bouquet," and "The Web of Circumstance"), Houghton, 1899, reprinted with illustrations by Clyde O. DeLand, Gregg, 1967.
Frederick Douglass (biography), Small, Maynard, 1899, reprinted, Johnson Reprints, 1970.
The House Behind the Cedars (novel), Houghton, 1900, reprinted, Gregg, 1968, reprinted with an introduction by Darwin Turner, P. F. Collier, 1969.
The Marrow of Tradition (novel), Houghton, 1901, reprinted, Gregg, 1968.
The Colonel's Dream (novel), Doubleday, Page, 1905, reprinted, Gregg, 1968.
The Short Fiction of Charles W. Chesnutt, edited with an introduction by Sylvia Lyons Render, Howard University Press, 1974.

Work represented in anthologies.

Contributor to periodicals, including *Alexander's Magazine, Boston Evening Transcript, Family Fiction, Puck, Youth's Companion, Cleveland News and Herald, Atlantic Monthly, Crisis, Overland Monthly, Chicago Ledger, Century, New Haven Register, New York Independent, Outlook,* and *Southern Workman.*

SIDELIGHTS: In her biography, *Charles W. Chesnutt: Pioneer of the Color Line,* Helen M. Chesnutt describes her father as "a pioneer Negro author, the first to exploit in fiction the complex lives of men and women of mixed blood." Similarly, Sylvia Lyons Render writes admiringly in her introduction to *The Short Fiction of Charles W. Chesnutt* of his "extraordinary ability to blend his African and European heritages into distinctly American forms." Because of his fair complexion, Render pointed out, Chesnutt could have "passed" for white; instead "he chose to remain identified as an Afro-American and sought to remove rather than to avoid various forms of discrimination." Chesnutt also merits recognition as one of the first black American fiction writers to receive serious critical attention and acclaim for portraying blacks realistically and sensitively, shunning condescending characterizations and nostalgia for antebellum days of slavery in the South.

Chesnutt was born in 1858 in Cleveland, Ohio, the son of free Negro parents who had moved from Fayetteville, North Carolina, before the Civil War in flight from increasingly severe restrictions imposed on the free colored population of North Carolina. In 1866 the family returned to Fayetteville, and Chesnutt's father started a grocery store there. When young Charles wasn't working in the store, he attended the Howard School for blacks, founded by the Freedman's Bureau in 1865. Pressed to help support his family, Chesnutt was forced to end his formal education when he was only fourteen. However, Robert Harris, the school's principal, prevailed upon Charles's father to let his son stay at the school as a pupil-teacher and turn his modest salary over to his father. At sixteen Chesnutt went to Charlotte as a full-time teacher, and in 1877 he returned to Fayetteville as assistant principal of Howard School, becoming upon Harris's death three years later its principal. Concomitantly Chesnutt commenced a vigorous program of reading and study that led to his proficiency in Latin, German, French, mathematics, and stenography. In 1883 Chesnutt resigned his school-administrator post and struck out alone in search of more lucrative employment in the North. He found a job in New York City as a stenographer and journalist on Wall Street, then later returned to Cleveland, where he was hired as a railway clerk and, in 1884, settled with his family.

Chesnutt eventually became a stenographer for the railway company's lawyer, Judge Samuel E. Williamson, in whose office he studied law, and in 1887 he passed the Ohio Bar at the top of his class. Judge Williamson offered to finance a law practice for Chesnutt in Europe, which was less racist than the United States, but Chesnutt declined the offer. He also turned down the invitation of George Washington Cable, a prominent American writer, to become his private secretary.

Instead, in 1890 Chesnutt chose to support his growing family by establishing a court reporting business and devoting his evenings to his longtime avocation, writing fiction. His first stories were generally light in tone and dealt with conventional subjects of appeal to lesser magazines ranging from *Puck* to *Youth's Companion* and to newspaper syndicates such as S. S. McClure's. These early efforts were crowned by *Atlantic Monthly*'s acceptance of his stories "The Goophered Grapevine" in 1887 and "Po' Sandy" in 1888. At Cable's urging he also contributed commentary to the *New York Independent* and other liberal publications, and by 1889 Chesnutt had completed his first novel, eventually published in 1900 as *The House Behind the Cedars*.

Most of the stories Chesnutt produced after 1890, according to Render, "differ in form, tone, and focus from earlier works. The mood is more serious, the humor increasingly subtle and satirical, the irony more apparent, and the action [focused] largely upon Afro-Americans." Furthermore, instead of using contemporary settings, Chesnutt placed his characters in times of slavery or Reconstruction in the Cape Fear River area of North Carolina, where he had lived from age eight to age twenty-five. In so doing, he displayed such fidelity to his settings and to the idiosyncrasies of the people of the area—including their folkways, dialects, and superstitions—as to prompt critics to compare his work to that of leading nineteenth-century local colorists Bret Harte and Mark Twain.

Chesnutt's first published volume, *The Conjure Woman*—issued in 1899 by Houghton Mifflin—was a collection of dialect stories told by an old Negro gardener, "Uncle" Julius McAdoo, to his Northern employer. Ostensibly simple tales of metamorphosis, voodoo, and conjuring, they nonetheless illuminate the dynamics of master-slave relationships and the injustices of slavery. One slave-owner, for instance, resorts to conjuring his grapevine to protect his grapes from thieving slaves. That idea misfires when a new slave mistakenly eats some of the "goophered" grapes. Even after he has tried a magic antidote, the unlucky slave has strange tendrils of grapes growing all over his head—grapes that appear every spring and die down in the winter along with his strength and youth, which also wax and wane with the seasons. Yet his owner profits from this, selling the slave in the spring, when he is young and vigorous, and buying him back cheaply in the fall, when he looks about to die. As several critics noted, these stories convey a very different picture of Southern society from those in the Uncle Remus stories of Joel Chandler Harris, in which happy slaves cheerfully tell animal fables about mischievous Brer Rabbit.

In *The Wife of His Youth, and Other Stories of the Color Line*, a second collection of short stories also published in 1899, Chesnutt portrays the dilemma of mulattoes who felt alien in the black community and excluded from the white. Chesnutt satirized the race-conscious Blue Veins of Cleveland—people of Negro descent with skin light enough to show the blueness of their veins—for snubbing their darker-skinned relatives and mimicking middle-class whites. A third 1899 Chesnutt publication was *Frederick Douglass*, a biography of the prominent abolitionist, for the series "Beacon Biographies of Eminent Americans."

In September, 1900, buoyed by the favorable initial reception given *The Conjure Woman*, *The Wife of His Youth*, and *Frederick Douglass*, Chesnutt closed down his stenography business so that he could write and lecture full time. Financial success, however, did not match critical acclaim and recognition. His first two novels, *The House Behind the Cedars* and *The Marrow of Tradition*, published in 1900 and 1901 respectively, attracted more controversy than sales. Reviewers who had applauded *The Conjure Woman* became disenchanted with Chesnutt when he began to treat taboo themes such as miscegenation and racial hatred. His sympathetic treatment of erotic love in *The House Behind the Cedars* and his pessimism toward the likelihood of racial harmony in *The Marrow of Tradition* outraged critics. Even William Dean Howells, the distinguished American novelist and critic who in 1900 had praised Chesnutt for "sound[ing] a fresh note, boldly, not blatantly" and placed him in the top rank of American short story writers, declared in a 1901 issue of *North American Review* that "at his worst, [Chesnutt] is no worse than the higher average of the ordinary novelists, but he ought always to be very much better, for he began better."

Chesnutt's earnings from the sales of his two novels and from his free-lance journalism and speaking engagements proved inadequate to the financial needs of his family. Consequently in 1902 he reopened the stenography firm he had closed two years earlier. Chesnutt continued writing, however, and in 1905 he published *The Colonel's Dream*, a novel examining the futility of amoral schemes for the economic regeneration of the South. *The Colonel's Dream* received less attention than *The Marrow of Tradition* and garnered even fewer sales. It was to be Chesnutt's last book-length work to appear during his lifetime.

In 1910, five years after the publication of *The Colonel's Dream*, Chesnutt collapsed in his Cleveland office, and he remained unconscious for several days. His recovery was slow, necessitating curtailment of his strenuous schedule of social, public, and professional engagements. In 1920 he suffered an attack of appendicitis followed by peritonitis that left his health permanently impaired.

The 1920s brought some belated recognition to Chesnutt for his literary labors at the turn of the century. In 1928 the NAACP awarded him its Spingarn Medal for his "pioneer work as a literary artist depicting the life and struggles of Americans of Negro descent, and for his long and useful career as scholar, worker, and freeman." And in 1929 Houghton Mifflin reprinted *The Conjure Woman* in a deluxe edition that restored Chesnutt to print thirty years after he had first become an author.

Chesnutt's last published work was an article titled "Post-Bellum—Pre-Harlem" that appeared in *Colophon* a year before his death in 1932. In the article Chesnutt reflected on his literary life and on the history of Afro-American writing in general. He summarized his various books and commented on the ambivalence of his publishers toward revealing his racial identity during the early years of his career. He accepted the fact that literary fashion had passed him by, but he proudly noted that Afro-American literature and the attitude of the white literary world had advanced considerably since the days of his earliest publications. Once possibly the only black American to write serious fiction about Negroes, Chesnutt had devoted his art to reorienting his readers toward what he considered the real issues of race in America.

History has at least partially restored Chesnutt's place as one of the most important figures in the early history of black literature in the United States. Critics now acknowledge that Chesnutt helped establish a truly Afro-American literary heritage in the short story and novel, and they credit him with making the broad range of black experience his artistic domain and considering practically everything within it worthy of treatment. Chesnutt is also remembered as a brilliant, gifted man endowed with an indefatigable capacity for hard work and self-discipline and as an ardent crusader for civil rights and equal opportunity. Among the tributes paid Chesnutt at the time of his death was that of American Negro civil rights leader W.E.B. DuBois, who wrote in the January, 1933, *Crisis:* "[Chesnutt] was not a Negro; he was a man. . . . If his white friends could not tolerate colored friends, they need not come to Mr. Chesnutt's home. If colored friends demanded racial segregation and hatred, he had no patience with them. Merit and friendship in his broad and tolerant mind knew no lines of color or race, and all men, good, bad, and indifferent, were simply men."

BIOGRAPHICAL/CRITICAL SOURCES:

BOOKS

Andrews, William L., *The Literary Career of Charles W. Chesnutt*, Louisiana State University Press, 1980.
Bigsby, E.W.E., editor, *The Black American Writer*, Everett/Edwards, 1969.
Bone, Robert A., *The Negro Novel in America*, Yale University Press, 1965.
Brown, Sterling, *The Negro in American Fiction*, Associates in Negro Folk Education, 1937.
Chesnutt, Helen M., *Charles Waddell Chesnutt: Pioneer of the Color Line*, University of North Carolina Press, 1952.
Dictionary of Literary Biography, Volume 12: *American Realists and Naturalists*, Gale, 1982, Volume 50: *Afro-American Writers Before the Harlem Renaissance*, Gale, 1986.
Ellison, Curtis W. and E. W. Metcalf, Jr., *Charles W. Chesnutt: A Reference Guide*, G. K. Hall, 1977.
Heermance, J. Noel, *Charles W. Chesnutt: America's First Great Black Novelist*, Shoe String, 1974.
Keller, Frances Richardson, *An American Crusade: The Life of Charles Waddell Chesnutt*, Brigham Young University Press, 1978.
Render, Sylvia Lyons, editor, *The Short Fiction of Charles W. Chesnutt*, Howard University Press, 1974.
Twentieth-Century Literary Criticism, Gale, Volume 5, 1981.

PERIODICALS

American Literature, May, 1975.
American Scholar, winter, 1972.
Atlantic Monthly, May, 1900.
Books and Bookmen, December, 1975.
CLA Journal, March, 1972, December, 1974.
Colophon, Volume II, number 5, 1931.
Crisis, January, 1933.
Growing Point, January, 1976.
Kirkus Reviews, September 15, 1973, December 15, 1973.
Kliatt, winter, 1979.

New Republic, March 1, 1975.
New York Times Book Review, November 4, 1973, January 17, 1974.
Observer, December 7, 1975.
Phylon, spring, 1971.
Saturday Review, June 21, 1969, October 25, 1969.
Southern Literary Journal, fall, 1982.
Spectator, March 21, 1969, August 16, 1979.
Times Literary Supplement, December 5, 1975.*

—*Sketch by Joanne M. Peters*

*   *   *

CHIPPERFIELD, Richard   1904-1988

OBITUARY NOTICE: Born in 1904; died March 3, 1988. Circus performer, animal trainer, and author. As head of a famous circus family that has been performing since the seventeenth century, Chipperfield was known as one of England's most experienced breeders of lions, tigers, and leopards. He began working as a clown at the age of five and at eighteen started training horses and elephants. Chipperfield eventually worked with big cats, developing a stock that at times exceeded that of most British zoos, to which he often supplied animals. He also helped to maintain stocks of endangered big-game species in different areas of the world, and he exported circus-trained lions and tigers to European countries where the practice of animal training was becoming extinct. He recorded his memoirs in *My Friends the Animals*, which appeared in 1963.

OBITUARIES AND OTHER SOURCES:

PERIODICALS

Times (London), March 7, 1988.

*   *   *

CHRISTIAN, Shirley (Ann)   1938-

PERSONAL: Born January 16, 1938, in Windsor, Mo.; daughter of Herbert Walsh and Minnie Lucille (Acker) Christian. *Education:* Pittsburg State University, Pittsburg, Kan., B.A., 1960; Ohio State University, M.A., 1966; graduate study at Harvard University, 1973-74. *Politics:* "Independent." *Religion:* Congregational United Church of Christ.

ADDRESSES: Home—Luis Agote 2445, 7th piso, 1425 Buenos Aires, Argentina. *Office*—Corrientes 456, Oficina 182, 1366 Buenos Aires, Argentina. *Agent*—Elizabeth McKee Purdy, 279 Fifth Ave., New York, N.Y. 10017.

CAREER: Associated Press, United Nations correspondent, 1970-73, copy editor and foreign desk reporter, 1974-77, chief of bureau in Santiago, Chile, 1977-79; *Miami Herald*, Miami, Fla., Latin American correspondent, 1979-83; *New York Times*, foreign affairs reporter in Washington, D.C., 1985-86, chief of bureau in Buenos Aires, Argentina, 1986—. Adjunct professor of journalism at Columbia University, 1977; visiting professor of journalism at Baylor University, 1985.

AWARDS, HONORS: Pulitzer Prize for international reporting from Columbia University Graduate School of Journalism, and George Polk Memorial Award for foreign reporting from Long Island University's journalism department, both 1981.

WRITINGS:

Nicaragua: Revolution in the Family (nonfiction), Random House, 1985.

Contributor to periodicals, including *Atlantic Monthly* and *New Republic.*

SIDELIGHTS: After ten years in her field, Shirley Christian won the Pulitzer Prize for international reporting in 1981. The journalist began as a correspondent to the United Nations for the Associated Press and was a Latin American correspondent for the *Miami Herald* at the time she received the Pulitzer. After writing her critically acclaimed first book, *Nicaragua: Revolution in the Family,* Christian signed on as a foreign affairs reporter with the *New York Times* and has served as that paper's bureau chief in Buenos Aires, Argentina.

Christian added research to the background experience she had gained in Central America to produce *Nicaragua: Revolution in the Family.* The book deals with much of Nicaragua's past history but focuses primarily on the activities and motivations of the ruling Sandinista government. As an important backdrop to this focus, however, Christian also discusses the previous dictatorship ruled by the allegedly corrupt Somoza family. Though her book concerns a controversial subject—the communist nature of the Sandinistas and their conflict with the resistance or *contras*—most critics applauded Christian's objectivity. In reference to the noisy arguments and sensationalized charges often encountered on both sides of the Nicaragua issue, Gabriel Zaid announced in the *New Republic* that "Shirley Christian chose to attend to something less clamorous, but more revealing: the reality behind the rhetoric.... She lets events, slowly assembled, speak for themselves." Similarly, Timothy Garton Ash declared in the *New York Times Book Review* that "it is marvelous to find a book that spends most of its considerable length just telling us what actually happened—facts, dates, names, quotations recorded by a professional journalist." Ash further noted that "anyone seriously interested in contemporary Nicaragua will have to read it."

Even critics who saw Christian's book as unfair to the Sandinistas had praise for her. While advancing the accusation that "in order to make the sins of the Sandinistas stand out in bold relief, the author first mutes and softens the grim record of the Somoza dynasty," Robert E. White affirmed in *Commonweal* that "there is much that is valuable in *Nicaragua.*" He went on to laud Christian's practice of juxtaposing speakers with opposing views—the words of *contra* leaders follow upon those of Sandinista revolutionaries—admitting that "these voices . . . have an authentic ring" and that "Shirley Christian writes wonderfully well."

Christian's thesis in *Nicaragua,* according to most reviewers, is summarized in her epilogue to the book. There she writes: "The leaders of the Sandinista Front intended to establish a Leninist system from the day they marched into Managua whether they called it that or not. Their goal was to assure themselves the means to control nearly every aspect of Nicaraguan life, from beans and rice to religion." Also deemed integral to the work by critics was her statement that the *contras* "represented what little hope there was to force the Sandinista Front into accepting major structural changes toward an open political system."

Christian was deemed "far from uncritical in [her] approach to the efforts of the [U.S. President Ronald] Reagan administration to deal with the [Nicaraguan] situation," by Richard L. Millett in a *Washington Post Book World* review. But she does not hold Reagan's predecessor, President Jimmy Carter, blameless either. As Ash pointed out, the Pulitzer Prize-winner's "first major conclusion is that the Carter administration missed a real opportunity to bring to power a civilian, moderate and pluralistic regime" in place of Nicaraguan President Anastasio Somoza Debayle's. Christian claims in *Nicaragua* that "moderate political alternatives to Somoza" were looking to the United States for help in setting up a government—a government which in her opinion would have been much less repressive than the Marxist Sandinistas. The Carter administration's policy toward Nicaragua, however, was "shaped by the Vietnam experience" and therefore "unwilling to use U.S. influence to effect change," according to Christian. Instead, it continued dealing with Nicaragua under the Somoza dictatorship "basically as a human rights problem," in her words. Susan Kaufman Purcell summarized the administration's actions thus in the *New York Times:* "By withholding aid and using other pressures, it hoped to liberalize the [Somoza] regime and thereby make it more tolerable." By 1979, however, Somoza's dictatorship had fallen and the revolutionary *Frente Sandinista de Liberacion Nacional* (Sandinista National Liberation Front; FSLN)—which many perceive as being closely allied to the Soviet Union and Cuba and thus antagonistic to the United States—had assumed power. The United States, argues Christian, should learn from the Nicaraguan revolution that it "should not allow itself to fall into the trap of having to accept, in an area as closely tied to it as Central America, either a repressive right-wing dictatorship because it is not threatening to U.S. national security or a repressive left-wing dictatorship in exchange for commitments not to overthrow a neighboring government or acquire MiGs [Soviet aircraft]."

In addition to making strong declarations about U.S. policy, *Nicaragua: Revolution in the Family* contains much information about Nicaragua's social climate. Christian discusses the various sectors of Nicaraguan society and how they perceive the Sandinista government. She has garnered praise for her examination of the discord between the Sandinistas and the market vendors, which "provides illuminating evidence of the gap between Sandinista rhetoric and actual practice," according to Millett. Christian also covers the story of the minority Miskito Indians and, as Lawrence Pezzullo asserted in the *Los Angeles Times,* "documents how the Sandinista's compulsion to control drove the fiercely independent Miskitos to violence and exile." White noted *Nicaragua*'s chapter on the Catholic church, lauding it as "particularly informative and contain[ing] good description and sound analysis of the conflicts within the Catholic church in Nicaragua."

Christian also makes it clear that Nicaragua is a divided country not only socially and politically, but familially—even its families often have members on both sides of the conflict. For instance, in Zaid's words, "Ernesto and Fernando Cardenal, brothers, priests, and Sandinista ministers (in charge of culture and education), are the cousins of Pablo Antonio Cuadra, the director of *La Prensa,* the opposition's sole daily newspaper. They are also related to Jose Francisco Cardenal, who is in armed opposition to the Sandinista regime." Uncles and nephews, parents and children, brothers and sisters sometimes find themselves in factious opposition to one another. Claudia Chamorro Barrios, an official in the Sandinista Ministry of Culture, has a brother, Pedro Joaquin, now "in civil opposition in Costa Rica," as Zaid put it. Pezzullo summed up Christian's volume as "a book that succeeds in holding up a mirror reflecting a true image of a revolution in the Nicaraguan family."

CA INTERVIEW

CA interviewed Shirley Christian by telephone on February 3, 1987, while she vacationed in Miami, Florida.

CA: You were a United Nations (UN) correspondent for the Associated Press (AP) from 1970 to 1973. Was the UN covered differently then than it is now?

CHRISTIAN: Well, at one time the AP had eight full-time journalists there. When I left, they had four, two of them year-round, and now, I'm certain, they have fewer. The *New York Times* has maintained a fair amount of interest in the UN over the years. Part of the reason, I think, is that Abe Rosenthal, who recently retired as executive editor, had been a UN correspondent early in his career and always thought the UN was very important. I think in general there's less day-to-day coverage of the UN, though. It's increasingly used as a place to make contacts for stories, particularly with countries that don't have good relations with the United States. People might not be able to make good contacts in those countries in Washington, or by traveling to them.

CA: Why did you move from the Associated Press to the Miami Herald?

CHRISTIAN: Well, for one thing, the *Herald* made me an offer. I was in Chile at the time, waiting to be transferred to Europe. Partly it was my feeling that I wanted to stay in Latin America. Also, I liked the AP, but a big newspaper gives you a lot more freedom in terms of room to write.

CA: How does working at the New York Times *differ from working at the* Miami Herald?

CHRISTIAN: The *Herald* has a freer writing style, but in terms of what you can write there's no difference. I like both papers very much. The *Herald* has marvelous coverage of Latin America; other correspondents, particularly network correspondents, follow the *Herald* very carefully. The reach of the *Times* is much more global and for going elsewhere in the world, it's better to be at the *Times*. The *Herald* has correspondents elsewhere, but it's known for its Latin coverage. The *Times* is without peer and in a way you worry more about what you write for the *Times* because it will get read and interpreted every which way.

CA: Chile has had an oppressive regime for some time now. What is it like working as a journalist in a country with such an oppressive regime?

CHRISTIAN: I have been living in Chile, or going there to work, for twenty years, under various Chilean administrations. I spend a lot of time there now, because Chile has been part of my territory for the *Times* for the past year. And even though I technically live in Buenos Aires, I spend about 40 percent of my time in Chile, because there's quite a lot of interest in Chile these days.

It's not a difficult place to work in. The government, the little nucleus of political and military people around Chilean leader General Augusto Pinochet Ugarte, don't particularly like the foreign press, and they will continually tell you that. But Chileans, as a people, are open and friendly to foreigners. In comparison to most other Latin Americans, Chileans are open to talking to foreign journalists. And a little of that comes over into the government. Also, individual ministers are given a great deal of leeway in running their departments. In Argentina or Ecuador, even those countries that have elected presidents, everyone waits for the president or someone immediately around him to make the decision. Chile is more like working in Washington in the sense of getting to government people. But that's

Chilean tradition. The Chilean opposition, even though they've been illegal until recently, still always talk to the press. So, for a journalist, whatever the country's political situation at the time, Chile has always been a good place to work.

CA: How does it compare with Nicaragua as a place to work?

CHRISTIAN: It's almost at the opposite extreme. Nicaragua is a little country with a very low educational level, and it's not going to change overnight. It can't. Nicaragua's still a place where if you make the right connection, everybody will help you. In that sense, Nicaraguans are like Chileans: very open, very friendly. Even General Pinochet once told me in an interview, "I don't give interviews to the *New York Times* or the *Washington Post*." And he was talking to me while he was saying this. Those in power in Nicaragua, the Sandinistas, are a little bit the same way. They're constantly saying they don't like the American media, but they're open and friendly to "gringos." The problem for journalists in Nicaragua is the incredible bureaucracy that has developed. We used to say only partly in jest that every year the Sandinista government became more organized, the worse it got for journalists because it took that many more days to get an interview with somebody. In 1979 when they came in you could catch somebody on the street. Now that they've built up this vast structure, it's hardly that easy. In some ways it's the same as in Chile. The opposition, what's left of it, basically likes to talk to the foreign press and will try, some way or another, to do it.

CA: Do you miss Nicaragua?

CHRISTIAN: It's easy to become saturated with Central America. It's a small place. I really love the area, and I like the people. It's just that after a while you're one of the family and I think it's good to get away from that for a while. Also, I'm extremely interested in the Southern Cone, especially in Chile.

CA: Why?

CHRISTIAN: Chile has the potential of becoming a domestic and foreign policy issue for the United States in the same way South Africa has. A lot depends on how much the insurgency grows—it's very small at the moment—and how the government responds. I hope I'm wrong. It may all end very quietly.

CA: Many newspapers, and the wire services, have been accused of covering only the coups and earthquakes in other countries, while not covering anything more subtle going on in those places. Do you think that accusation has merit?

CHRISTIAN: One of my former AP colleagues, Mort Rosenblum, wrote a book on that subject, called, appropriately, *Coups and Earthquakes*, about Third World coverage. I cannot deny that some of that attitude exists. Most people closely involved in foreign coverage are constantly fighting against that, both correspondents and the editors who directly supervise them. It's a constant battle in their minds to write about the things that are significant for the long term, political or economic or whatever, that may not grab today's headlines, and having to balance those subjects with the earthquakes and the coups and the hijackings and all of those things that actually occur. I think it's partially a space thing. The amount of foreign news that can get in most papers, unfortunately, is not very great, so the editors must often make choices that fit into the coup/earthquake syndrome. The *Miami Herald* had a particular focus on and strong interest in Latin America, so we were more successful in getting space, although we didn't always get it on page one. And the *New York Times* thinks a lot about whether it is presenting a full package of coverage. I cover five countries—Uruguay, Paraguay, Argentina, Bolivia, and Chile—and obviously I can't be there every time something happens. And sometimes there's more interest in two or three of those countries than in the others. But I never fail to get a sympathetic hearing from an editor when I propose a story about any country. For instance, I have a piece in New York, which has been waiting to go in the "Arts and Leisure" section for a month, about filmmaking in Argentina. There has been an incredible renaissance and flowering in filmmaking in Argentina in just the past couple of years. And for Argentina today, that's the kind of coverage that's very important. True, the *Times* has held it for a month, but it will get into the paper eventually and run for two thousand words. Now that's a pretty big commitment.

CA: You've written magazine articles. Is that because you had thoughts or opinions that you couldn't get into the paper?

CHRISTIAN: I wanted to write longer pieces, even though the *Herald* allows longer pieces than a lot of papers. It wasn't frustration with what I could write in the paper. Also, I was tired. In November of 1982 I was riding in the back of a truck in northern Nicaragua with a group of correspondents. We were going about five miles an hour. Each and every jolt of the truck was pulling my body apart. I said to myself, "You're past forty and have two college degrees and can't you do something else for a living?" So I took a leave to write magazine articles. I wanted to write a book, but I didn't have a contract because at that point I hadn't been able to convince publishers in New York that Nicaragua was a worthy topic.

CA: How did you convince the publishers Nicaragua was a worthwhile subject for a book?

CHRISTIAN: It was a combination of timing and finding a good agent. The first agent I had was really not convinced that writing a book about Nicaragua was a good idea. She kept trying to convince me to come up with a different kind of proposal. But I really had Nicaragua on the brain. From the end of 1979 on, I was thinking of a Nicaragua book, but I kept thinking somebody else would do it. I had not been there for the fall of President Anastasio Somoza Debayle so I kept thinking someone who had been around longer would do it. Then those people all left the area and pretty soon I was the one who had been there the longest. Finally at the beginning of 1983 I found this wonderful agent at Harold Matson Company, a woman who had been around New York forever and ever. Whatever I wanted to write, she wanted to handle.

CA: Were you pleased with the reaction to your book?

CHRISTIAN: If I had written the book in a different way, I could have dealt with some of the criticisms. Basically I was happy with the reviews and the reaction I got.

CA: Some of the reviewers pointed out that in your book you urged the United States to avoid accepting either repressive right-wing dictatorships or repressive left-wing dictatorships. How should the United States go about not accepting them if they're already there?

CHRISTIAN: I don't believe we should have a policy based on a principle such as "We are never going to support such and such a government" or "We are never going to support loans for such and such a government if such and such an element is present." We have to have a lot of latitude and different policies for different countries and situations. I think we ought to have general things that we stand for. But the way we accomplish what we stand for, or the way we seek to accomplish it, may not be the same for each country. In the case of Nicaragua, we had reached this point that we should have preferred not to reach, where we were faced with a choice of only one thing, which we didn't want. I'm not in favor of invading Nicaragua. I wouldn't rule it out completely. I don't think you should ever rule those things out. But I think we ought to fashion policy over the long term that's supportive of democratic rule. We also ought to weigh how much influence the United States has had historically in that country. Even if we were to conclude that we should intervene in Nicaragua, that doesn't necessarily mean we should intervene elsewhere in the region, even though people in the region have always, rightly or wrongly, looked to us for help in solving things.

CA: Could former U.S. President Jimmy Carter have replaced Somoza with a democratic moderate?

CHRISTIAN: I think there was a small chance. Somoza was a difficult man, no doubt. It's not as if the whole problem was Carter's. Some people in Carter's administration will argue that it could have been done as late as 1978, but I think that would have been very difficult, in part because Cuban leader Fidel Castro was already supplying the rebels. By then, you were already having a serious insurgency. Earlier on it would have been possible. Preferable would have been a longer-term policy going back to the 1960s to favor a transition.

CA: What kind of policy would that have been?

CHRISTIAN: Making our position clear to Somoza that we were not going to close our eyes to a fraudulent election. And encouraging the political opposition and the other political parties to develop. That goes on over the long term.

CA: Do you think that U.S. support of the anti-Sandinista contras *will move the Sandinistas toward opening up their system at all?*

CHRISTIAN: I thought that a couple of years ago. I couldn't see that anything else would work. I didn't think being nice to the Sandinistas would work. At this point I really don't know. The Sandinistas have very strongly held convictions. I think some of them are quite willing to die or suffer the destruction of their country in defense of their principles. But I couldn't really see what other options there were besides supporting the *contras*.

CA: For Central America as a whole, is there an option besides right-wing dictatorships or left-wing dictatorships?

CHRISTIAN: I think there is. There are analysts who say that the countries in the region which have had the best experiences along these lines are the basically white countries: Costa Rica, Chile (historically), and Uruguay (historically). But Argentina's basically a white country and it has had a bad experience. So I don't think that narrows it down. Maybe a homogeneous population helps. But I really don't see Latin America as destined for totalitarian regimes either of the left or the right.

Spain settled most of Latin America and although it has been behind the rest of Europe for a long time, it's now steadily evolving and that may have an influence on Latin America. In any case, it's necessary to look at each country individually, and most of them have evolved somewhat. That makes me hopeful about some of them.

CA: What do you think will happen eventually in Nicaragua?

CHRISTIAN: It'll be clear in the next few months whether or not the *contras* will be successful. At that point the United States will weigh an invasion on one hand against an accommodation on the other. It's also possible that once the Democrats come in they'll invade, after studying the problem. I know the point to which the thinking of some of the people in the Carter Administration had evolved near the end of Carter's term. If some of those same people are back directing Latin policy they'll be having the same sort of internal debate the Reagan people are having now and may well decide to invade.

CA: Did winning the Pulitzer Prize change your life or career at all?

CHRISTIAN: It gave me a lot more options. I don't think it made me any better. Like most people who get it, I don't think I deserved it.

BIOGRAPHICAL/CRITICAL SOURCES:

BOOKS

Christian, Shirley, *Nicaragua: Revolution in the Family*, Random House, 1985.
Rosenblum, Mort, *Coups and Earthquakes: Reporting the World to America*, Harper, 1981.

PERIODICALS

Chicago Tribune, July 21, 1985.
Commonweal, November 1, 1985.
Los Angeles Times, August 18, 1985.
New Republic, September 30, 1985.
New York Times, July 20, 1985.
New York Times Book Review, July 28, 1985.
Washington Post Book World, July 14, 1985.

—*Sketch by Elizabeth Thomas*

—*Interview by Peter Benjaminson*

*   *   *

CLANCY, Thomas L., Jr.   1947-
(Tom Clancy)

BRIEF ENTRY: Born in 1947 in Baltimore, Md. American insurance broker and author. Although he never served in the armed forces, Tom Clancy has gained recognition for his best-selling works containing detailed and realistic accounts of military operations. He has thus been credited with creating and becoming the master of what one critic labeled the "technico-military thriller" genre. Clancy's highly acclaimed first novel, *The Hunt for Red October* (Naval Institute Press, 1984), concerns a Lithuanian sea captain's attempt to defect to the United States in one of the Soviet Union's most advanced nuclear submarines. Protagonist Jack Ryan, an American CIA analyst and expert on Soviet intentions, tracks the submarine, discovering Soviet military secrets. Garnering praise from reviewers and defense experts alike—President Ronald Reagan called the book "the perfect yarn" and invited the author to the White

House—*The Hunt for Red October* sold more than two million copies.

Also a best-seller is Clancy's second work, *Red Storm Rising* (Putnam, 1986), a story about a Soviet attack on NATO that leads to World War III. *Patriot Games* (Putnam, 1987), Clancy's third novel, features central character Jack Ryan in London, where he saves the Prince and Princess of Wales from an Irish revolutionary group only to become the terrorists' next target. Critics generally praised Clancy for his mastery of plot and suspense and found that his works are characterized by a fascination with machines, systems, and procedures; the idealization of the soldier's life; and sarcastic humor. Another book, *The Cardinal of the Kremlin*, is expected to be published by Putnam in 1988.

BIOGRAPHICAL/CRITICAL SOURCES:

BOOKS

Contemporary Literary Criticism, Volume 45, Gale, 1987.

PERIODICALS

Los Angeles Times Book Review, December 9, 1984, July 26, 1987.
New York Times Book Review, July 27, 1986, August 2, 1987.
New York Times Magazine, May 1, 1988.
Washington Post Book World, October 21, 1984, July 27, 1986.

*   *   *

CLANCY, Tom
See CLANCY, Thomas L., Jr.

*   *   *

CLARKE, D(erek) A(shdown)   1921-

PERSONAL: Born July 8, 1921, in West Bromwich, England; son of Alfred George (a schoolmaster) and Olive Evelyn (a schoolmistress; maiden name, Ashdown) Clarke; married Pauline Francesca Mitchell, January 11, 1964. *Education:* Oriel College, Oxford, M.A., 1967; University of London, Diploma in Librarianship, 1969. *Religion:* Anglican.

ADDRESSES: Home—Stretton Lodge, Birch Grove, West Hill, Ottery St. Mary, Devonshire EX11 1XP, England.

CAREER: British Museum, London, England, assistant keeper of printed books, 1947-53; University of Leeds, Leeds, England, deputy librarian, 1953-55; University College of Rhodesia and Nyasaland (now University of Zimbabwe), Harare, founding librarian, 1955-61; University of Liverpool, Liverpool, England, chief librarian, 1961-66; British Library of Political and Economic Science, London, chief librarian, 1966-84. *Military service:* British Army, 1941-45.

MEMBER: Library Association (associate), Bibliographical Society, Royal Society of Arts (fellow).

AWARDS, HONORS: Fulbright fellow in the United States, 1950-51.

WRITINGS:

(Editor) *A London Bibliography of the Social Sciences*, Volumes 15-41, Mansell, 1970-84.
(Editor) *Acquisition of Publications From the Third World*, Mansell, 1974.

Contributor to *Short Title Catalogue of Books Printed in Italy From 1465 to 1600*, 1958, and to *Chambers's Encyclopaedia*. Contributor of articles and reviews to library journals.

WORK IN PROGRESS: Publications of Political Parties in Africa; research on printing in Venice in the sixteenth century.

SIDELIGHTS: D. A. Clarke told *CA:* "My special interest is the early history of printing. As a Fulbright fellow, I spent a year in distinguished rare book libraries in the United States, including the Library of Congress, the Henry E. Huntington Library in San Marino, California, and the Pierpont Morgan Library in New York City. From 1963 to 1972 I contributed an annual review of publications in this field to the University of Virginia periodical *Studies in Bibliography*.

"Another concern is interlibrary cooperation. In Britain I was active in the Standing Conference of National and University Libraries, serving as chairman of its committees on buildings and on Latin American materials. Internationally I was active in the International Federation of Library Associations and Institutions as the chairman of its Section of Social Science Libraries and chairman of the Division of Special Libraries. I was also a member of the UNESCO International Committee for Social Science Information and Documentation from 1968 to 1984.

"I am also interested in African affairs. From 1955 to 1961 I was responsible for establishing the library of the University College of Rhodesia and Nyasaland (now the University of Zimbabwe), which was set up to provide higher education for what was then the Central African Federation. My present research project concerns the publications of political parties in Africa.

"Though my main responsibility has been the management of information services for social sciences, my university education was in Greek and Latin languages and literatures, as well as philosophy and ancient history. Additionally, I have a general interest in linguistic studies and am competent in most of the languages of Western Europe."

*   *   *

CLAY, Edith   1910-

PERSONAL: Born February 23, 1910, in Burley-in-Wharfedale, England; daughter of Percival Travis and Elizabeth (Hutchinson) Clay. *Education:* Attended girls' high school in Bridlington, Yorkshire, England. *Politics:* Conservative. *Religion:* Church of England.

ADDRESSES: Home—128A Ashley Gardens, London SW1P 1HL, England.

CAREER: British School of Archaeology at Athens, Athens, Greece, administrative secretary, 1937-62. Worked for Foreign Office, London, England, 1939-44; assistant secretary of British Committee on the Preservation and Restitution of Works of Art, Archives, and Other Material in Enemy Hands, 1944-46.

MEMBER: Society of Antiquaries of London (fellow).

WRITINGS:

(Editor) Craufurd Tait Ramage, *Ramage in South Italy: The Nooks and By-Ways of Italy*, Longman, 1965, Academy Chicago, 1987.
(Editor) Richard Chandler, *Travels in Asia Minor, 1764-1765*, British Museum, 1971.

(Editor) *Sir William Gell in Italy: Letters to the Society of Dilettanti, 1831-1835*, Hamish Hamilton, 1976.
Lady Blessington at Naples, Hamish Hamilton, 1979.

Contributor to scholarly journals.

SIDELIGHTS: Edith Clay told *CA:* "On retiring from the British School at Athens, I decided to buy a house in Magna Graecia (Southern Italy) and did so at Agropoli, 60 miles south of Naples. I had the intention of writing books whose subjects would be connected with that region and would be personages who had not been written about for a long time and whom I wished to bring again to public notice. The subjects of three of my books—Craufurd Tait Ramage, Sir William Gell, and Lady Blessington—had lived in Naples in the early nineteenth century. I wrote about Richard Chandler because he led the first expedition to Ionia (Asia Minor) on behalf of the Society of Dilettanti, with whom Sir William Gell was associated many years later."

*   *   *

CLAY, Jenny Strauss

PERSONAL: Born in Cairo, Egypt; immigrated to United States, 1946, naturalized citizen, 1953; natural daughter of Paul and Bettina (Strauss) Kraus; adopted daughter of Leo (a professor) and Miriam (Bernsohn) Strauss; married Diskin Clay (divorced); children: Andreia. *Education:* Reed College, B.A.; University of Chicago, M.A.; University of Washington, Seattle, M.A., Ph.D. *Religion:* Jewish.

ADDRESSES: Home—1014 Glendale Rd., Charlottesville, Va. 22901. *Office*—Department of Classics, N Cabel H1141, University of Virginia, Charlottesville, Va. 22903.

CAREER: Johns Hopkins University, Baltimore, Md., assistant professor of classics, 1975-77; University of California, Irvine, assistant professor of classics, 1979-80; University of Virginia, Charlottesville, assistant professor, 1980-86, associate professor of classics, 1987—.

MEMBER: American Philological Association, Classical Association of the Midwest and South.

WRITINGS:

The Wrath of Athene: Gods and Men in the Odyssey, Princeton University Press, 1984.

WORK IN PROGRESS: The Politics of Olympus: Form and Meaning in the Major Homeric Hymns, publication expected in 1988.

*   *   *

CLEWES, Howard (Charles Vivian)   1912(?)-1988

OBITUARY NOTICE: Born October 27, 1912 (one source says 1916), in York, England; died January 29, 1988. Military officer, dramatist, screenwriter, and novelist. A prolific author of novels, plays, and screenplays, Clewes was probably best known for his screenwriting role in the 1962 remake of "Mutiny on the Bounty," a film starring Marlon Brando and Trevor Howard. He worked for various advertising agencies in the 1930s before becoming a major in the Green Howards during World War II. Following the war Clewes was a press and information officer for northern Italy in the Foreign Office but quit when his novel *Dead Ground* became a success. As a full-time writer, Clewes lived in and traveled to different parts of the world, including Italy, South America, and Tahiti. Among his other writings are the novels *The Unforgiven* and *I, The King;* the plays "Quay South" and "Image in the Sun"; and the filmscripts "The Long Memory" and "The Day They Robbed the Bank of England."

OBITUARIES AND OTHER SOURCES:

BOOKS

The Author's and Writer's Who's Who, 6th edition, reprinted, Burke's Peerage, 1971.
International Authors and Writers Who's Who, 9th edition, [and] *International Who's Who in Poetry,* 6th edition, Melrose, 1982.
Who's Who, 140th edition, St. Martin's, 1988.

PERIODICALS

Times (London), February 3, 1988.

* * *

CLIFFORD, Craig Edward 1951-

PERSONAL: Born July 9, 1951, in Lafayette, La.; son of Edward Lehr Clifford; married Gloria Lorraine Leach. *Education:* University of Texas at Austin, B.A., 1974; State University of New York at Buffalo, Ph.D., 1981.

ADDRESSES: Home—231 South McIlhaney, Stephenville, Tex. 76401. *Office*—Department of Social Sciences, Tarleton State University, Stephenville, Tex. 76402.

CAREER: Tarleton State University, Stephenville, Tex., assistant professor of philosophy and university scholar, 1985—.

MEMBER: American Philosophical Association, Western Literature Association.

WRITINGS:

In the Deep Heart's Core: Reflections on Life, Letters, and Texas (essays), Texas A&M University Press, 1985.

Guest columnist for *Fort Worth Star-Telegram* and *San Antonio Light.* Contributor to newspapers.

WORK IN PROGRESS: A second collection of essays, tentatively titled *The Rooted Intellect.*

* * *

CLIFTON-TAYLOR, Alec 1907-1985

PERSONAL: Born August 2, 1907, in Cheam, Surrey, England; died April 1, 1985; son of Stanley E. (a corn merchant) and E. E. (Hills) Taylor. *Education:* Received diploma in *civilisation francaise* from Sorbonne, University of Paris, 1929; Queen's College, Oxford, M.A., 1932; Courtauld Institute of Arts, London, B.A. (first class honors), 1934.

ADDRESSES: Home—15 Clareville Grove, London SW7 5AU, England.

CAREER: University of London, Institute of Education and Royal College of Art, London, England, lecturer in history of art, 1934-39; extramural lecturer in London, 1946-57; freelance lecturer at universities, art galleries, and museums throughout the world, 1956-85. Guest speaker on historical buildings on British Broadcasting Corporation (BBC) programs; member of the board of trustees of Historic Churches Preservation Trust, Patron of Avoncroft Museum of Building. *Wartime service:* British Admiralty, 1940-46; served as private secretary to parliamentary secretary, 1943-46.

MEMBER: Society of Antiquaries (fellow), Royal Institute of British Architects (honorary fellow), Kensington Society (past president), Society for Italic Handwriting (past vice-president), Men of the Stones (past vice-president), Oxford Union Society, Art Workers Guild (honorary broker).

AWARDS, HONORS: Officer, Order of the British Empire, 1982.

WRITINGS:

(With A. S. Ireson) *The Pattern of English Building,* Batsford, 1962, 3rd edition, Faber, 1972.
The Cathedrals of England, photographs by Martin Huerlimann and others, Thames & Hudson, 1967, Association Press, 1970.
(Contributor) Miles Hadfield, editor, *A Book of Country Houses,* Country Life Books, 1969.
English Parish Churches as Works of Art, Batsford, 1974.
(With others) *Spirit of the Age* (an expanded version of the BBC television series), BBC Publications, 1975.
(With Ronald Brunskill) *English Brickwork,* Ward Lock, 1977.
Six English Towns, photographs by Geoff Howard, BBC Publications, 1978.
Six More English Towns, BBC Publications, 1981.
English Stone Building, Gollancz, 1983.
Another Six English Towns, BBC Publications, 1984.

Contributor to magazines and art journals, including *Architectural Review, Encounter, Connoisseur,* and *House and Garden.*

SIDELIGHTS: In reviewing *The Cathedrals of England,* a *Times Literary Supplement* critic praised Alec Clifton-Taylor for examining English cathedrals "historically in a sensible, workmanlike way" that "blows a lot of cobwebs off a subject that might seem to have been overexplored already." "Clifton-Taylor both knows and loves his cathedrals," the review concluded, "and his book is an informative and reliable introduction, which is full of infectious enthusiasm."

Clifton-Taylor told *CA:* "My life's work has been devoted to trying to help people to respond visually to the world around them. I feel very strongly that visual responses do not receive nearly enough prominence in our education. So every one of my books is primarily an exercise in looking. In the arts, to *see* is surely at least as important as to *know.*"

AVOCATIONAL INTERESTS: Gazing at mountains, quizzing old churches and houses, painting, gardening, writing limericks.

BIOGRAPHICAL/CRITICAL SOURCES:

PERIODICALS

Times Literary Supplement, October 17, 1968.

OBITUARIES:

PERIODICALS

Times (London), April 4, 1985.

* * *

CLINE, Gloria Griffen 1929-1973

OBITUARY NOTICE—See index for *CA* sketch: Born March 21, 1929, in San Francisco, Calif.; died April 12, 1973, in Ireland. Educator and author. Cline taught history at Sacramento State College and was a visiting lecturer at various other universities before becoming a full-time writer in 1966. Her first work, *Exploring the Great Basin,* was nominated for a

Pulitzer Prize in 1963. Besides contributing to two volumes of *Mountain Men and the Fur Trade*, Cline wrote *The Hudson's Bay Company as a Source for North American Research* and *Peter Skene Ogden and the Hudson's Bay Company*.

OBITUARIES AND OTHER SOURCES:

PERIODICALS

Western Historical Quarterly, July, 1975.

* * *

COATES, David   1946-

PERSONAL: Born December 24, 1946, in Bury, England; son of Robert (a police officer) and Edna (a housewife; maiden name, Todd) Coates; divorced; children: Emma, Ben, Anna, Thomas, Edward. *Education:* University of York, B.A. (with first class honors), 1967; Oxford University, D.Phil., 1970. *Politics:* Socialist. *Religion:* None.

ADDRESSES: Home—14 Grove Park Walk, Harrogate, North Yorkshire, HG1 4BP, England. *Office*—Department of Politics, University of Leeds, Leeds LS2 9JT, England.

CAREER: University of York, Heslington, England, lecturer in politics, 1970-77, chairman of Graduate School, 1976-77; University of Leeds, Leeds, England, lecturer, 1977-83, senior lecturer in politics, 1983—, head of department, 1984-87.

WRITINGS:

Teacher Unions and Interest Group Politics, Cambridge University Press, 1972.
(With George Bain and Valerie Ellis) *Social Stratification and Trade Unionism*, Heinemann, 1973.
The Labour Party and the Struggle for Socialism, Cambridge University Press, 1975.
Labour in Power? A Study of the Labour Government, 1974-1979, Longman, 1980.
(Editor) *A Socialist Primer*, Volume I (with Gordon Johnson): *Socialist Arguments*, Martin Robertson, 1983, Volume II (with Johnson): *Socialist Strategies*, Martin Robertson, 1983, Volume III (with Johnson and Ray Bush): *A Socialist Anatomy of Britain*, Polity Press, 1984, Volume IV (with Johnson and Bush): *Two World Orders: Socialist Perspectives*, Polity Press, 1987.
The Context of British Politics, Hutchinson, 1984.
(Editor with John Hillard) *The Economic Decline of Modern Britain: The Debate Between Left and Right*, Wheatsheaf, 1987.
(Editor with Hillard) *The Economic Revival of Modern Britain: The Debate Between Left and Right*, Edward Elgar Publications, 1987.

CONTRIBUTOR

Anthony King, editor, *Why Is Britain Becoming Harder to Govern?*, BBC Publications, 1976.
Andrew Cox, editor, *Politics, Policy, and the European Recession*, Macmillan, 1982.
Ralph Miliband and John Saville, editors, *The Socialist Register 1983*, Merlin, 1983.
Malcolm Harrison, editor, *Corporatism and the Welfare State*, Gower, 1984.
James Anderson, editor, *The Rise of the Modern State*, Wheatsheaf, 1986.

Contributor to *Dictionary of Marxist Thought* and the annual, *World View*. Contributor to political science journals.

WORK IN PROGRESS: Class Conflict and Industrial Capitalism, with R. J. Looker, for Wheatsheaf.

BIOGRAPHICAL/CRITICAL SOURCES:

PERIODICALS

Times Literary Supplement, November 19, 1987, January 8-14, 1988.

* * *

COBURN, L. J.
See HARVEY, John (Barton)

* * *

COCHRANE, A(rchibald) L(eman)   1909(?)-1988

OBITUARY NOTICE: Born c. 1909 in Galashiels, Scotland; died June 18, 1988. Epidemiologist and author. Cochrane is best remembered for his work involving the detailed measurement of disease patterns in industrial populations, particularly among the coal mining community of South Wales. After treating prisoners in Crete, Greece, and Germany for tuberculosis during World War II, he joined the Medical Research Council's epidemiology unit in Cardiff, Wales, where he specialized in pneumoconiosis research. Treating coal mine workers for chest diseases, Cochrane helped to demonstrate that field epidemiology could produce the same high level of scientific accuracy as that achieved in research laboratories. He went on to hold the chair of chest disease and tuberculosis at the Welsh National School of Medicine, beginning in 1958, and returned to the Medical Research Council in 1969 as a full-time director. His writings include *Effectiveness and Efficiency: Random Reflections on Health Services*.

OBITUARIES AND OTHER SOURCES:

PERIODICALS

Times (London), June 22, 1988.

* * *

CODY, Liza

BRIEF ENTRY: British novelist. Cody is best known for her series of mystery novels featuring private detective Anna Lee. Her first novel, *Dupe* (Collins, 1980), met with enthusiastic reviews and received the John Creasey Award for the best first mystery novel published in England in 1980. The book portrays resourceful heroine Anna Lee, a former policewoman who works for a London detective agency. Taking a seemingly straightforward case of a fatal car accident, Anna finds herself investigating the illegal and seedy side of London's filmmaking industry. Critics were impressed with Cody's characterization of Anna, finding the detective both intelligent and endearing. Subsequent books in Cody's mystery series—*Bad Company* (Scribner, 1982), *Stalker* (Scribner, 1984), *Head Case* (Collins, 1985), and *Under Contract* (Collins, 1986)—depict Anna Lee in other harrowing adventures in the streets of London. Although critics felt that these books were less successful than *Dupe*, they consistently hailed Cody's novels for their low-key and realistic approach to the mystery genre and for their smoothness and economy of presentation.

BIOGRAPHICAL/CRITICAL SOURCES:

PERIODICALS

New York Times Book Review, April 10, 1983, August 2, 1987.
Times Literary Supplement, January 3, 1986.
Washington Post Book World, October 18, 1981.

* * *

CODY, Morrill   1901-

PERSONAL: Born April 10, 1901, in Lake Forest, Ill.; son of Sherwin (a writer) and Marion Teresa (Hurley) Cody; married Frances Ryan, March 2, 1923 (divorced, 1926); married Marion Holbrook, June 1, 1935 (died, 1952); married Verna Feuerhelm, February 7, 1953 (died, 1958); married Jane Hoster, November 3, 1960; children: (first marriage) Peter Malcolm; (second marriage) Judith Alden; (fourth marriage) Gabrielle Hamilton. *Education:* Amherst College, B.A., 1921.

ADDRESSES: Home—9310 Caroline Ave., Silver Spring, Md. 20901.

CAREER: Foreign correspondent, 1924-34; magazine editor, 1934-41; U.S. Foreign Service, Washington, D.C., cultural attache in Asuncion, Paraguay, 1941-45, Buenos Aires, Argentina, 1945-46, and Mexico City, Mexico, 1946-48, assigned to U.S. Department of State, Washington, D.C., 1948-50, information liaison officer at American embassy in Paris, France, 1950-53, public affairs officer in Stockholm, Sweden, 1951, first secretary at American embassy in Madrid, Spain, 1953-55, counselor for public affairs at American embassy in Paris, 1955-61; U.S. Information Agency, Washington, D.C., assistant director, 1961-63; Radio Liberty, consultant in New York, N.Y., and Paris, 1963-65, bureau manager in Paris, 1965-76. *Military service:* U.S. Army, 1918.

MEMBER: Anglo-American Press Club, Dacor Club.

WRITINGS:

This Must Be the Place (first published in the United Kingdom, 1934), Lee Furman, 1937.
Passing Stranger, Macaulay, 1936.
Hemingway's Paris, Tower Books, 1965.
The Favorite Restaurants of an American in Paris, Nouveau Quartier Latin, 1966.
(With Hugh Ford) *The Women of Montparnasse: The Americans in Paris,* Cornwall Press, 1984.

Contributor to magazines and newspapers. Past art editor of *Literary Digest.*

SIDELIGHTS: Morrill Cody no longer pursues a writing career. His daughter, Judith Alden Cody, told *CA:* "My father attended primary and secondary school in Paris. He lived in Paris for more than twenty-five years altogether and is fluent in French. Considered an expert on the artistic and literary movement in Paris in the 1920s, my father has researched and written about the subject at great length. He is also a lover of good food and wine and of beautiful objects, of which he has a great collection."

* * *

COHN, Samuel Kline, Jr.   1949-

PERSONAL: Born April 13, 1949, in Birmingham, Ala.; son of Samuel Kline (a physician) and Mildred (an artist; maiden name, Hiller) Cohn. *Education:* Attended University of London, 1969-70; Union College, Schenectady, N.Y., B.A., 1971; University of Wisconsin—Madison, M.A., 1972; Harvard University, Ph.D., 1978. *Politics:* Socialist.

ADDRESSES: Home—63 Mount Vernon St., Cambridge, Mass. 02140. *Office*—Department of History, Brandeis University, 415 South St., Waltham, Mass. 02154.

CAREER: Wesleyan University, Middletown, Conn., assistant professor of history, 1978-79; Brandeis University, Waltham, Mass., assistant professor, 1979-85, associate professor of history, 1985—.

WRITINGS:

The Laboring Classes in Renaissance Florence, Academic Press, 1982.
Death and Property in Siena, 1205-1799: Strategies for the Afterlife, Johns Hopkins University Press, 1988.

WORK IN PROGRESS: A comparative history of reactions to the Black Death, publication in 1990.

BIOGRAPHICAL/CRITICAL SOURCES:

PERIODICALS

Times Literary Supplement, January 15, 1982.

* * *

COKER, Carolyn
(Allison Cole)

PERSONAL: Born in Tulsa, Okla.; daughter of Samuel Bennet (an owner of a wholesale business) and Bernice (a teacher; maiden name, Woods) Cole; married Franklin C. Coker (a tax consultant; divorced); children: Cal C. *Education:* University of Oklahoma, B.A.; graduate study at Southern Methodist University and Tulane University.

ADDRESSES: Home—90 Coburn Ave., Sierra Madre, Calif. 91024. *Office*—California Institute of Technology, 1201 East California Blvd., Pasadena, Calif. 91125. *Agent*—Shelly Wile, Triad Artists, 10100 Santa Monica Blvd., Los Angeles, Calif. 90067.

CAREER: Writer.

WRITINGS:

The Other David (novel), Dodd, 1984.
(Under pseudonym Allison Cole) *Back Toward Lisbon* (novel), Dodd, 1985.
The Vines of Ferrara (novel), Dodd, 1986.
The Hand of the Lion, Dodd, 1988.

* * *

COLE, Allison
See COKER, Carolyn

* * *

COLE, C. Donald   1923-

PERSONAL: Born June 25, 1923, in Kansas City, Mo.; son of Paul Edwards and Margaret (Ross) Cole; married Naomi Sutton, April 26, 1947; children: Stephanie Cole Gray, Paul D., J. Andrew. *Education:* Received B.G.S. from Roosevelt University; received M.A. from DePaul University; attended Northern Baptist Theological Seminary. *Religion:* Evangelical.

ADDRESSES: Home—196 Ivy Lane, Bloomingdale, Ill. 60108. *Office*—Moody Broadcasting Network, Moody Bible Institute, Chicago, Ill. 60610.

CAREER: Ordained minister; missionary in Angola, 1947-66; editor of *Interest* magazine, 1966-70; faculty member at Emmaus Bible College; Moody Bible Institute, Chicago, Ill., radio pastor for Moody Broadcasting Network and host of radio program "Open Line," 1971—. *Military service:* U.S. Army, 1943-46; became staff sergeant.

WRITINGS:

Christian Perspectives on Controversial Issues, Moody, 1983.
I Believe . . . , Moody, 1983.
Have I Committed the Unpardonable Sin? and Other Questions You Were Afraid to Ask About the Christian Faith, Crossway, 1984.
Basic Christian Faith, Good News, 1985.
Thirsting for God: A Devotional Study of the Psalms in Light of Their Historical Background, Good News, 1986.

Also author of *Abraham.*

*   *   *

COLE, Gordon
    See COLE, Gordon H(enry)

*   *   *

COLE, Gordon H(enry)   1912-1988
(Gordon Cole)

OBITUARY NOTICE: Born January 11, 1912, in Providence, R.I.; died of bone cancer, April 29, 1988, in Virginia. Labor union official, educator, journalist, editor, and author. The editor for thirty years of the workers' publication *Machinist,* Cole is remembered for his strong commitment to labor relations. He began his career in 1934 as a reporter for the Syracuse *Post-Standard,* later working in Washington, D.C., for the *Wall Street Journal,* the *Labor Relations Reporter,* and *PM.* He also held offices in various organizations, including the Washington Newspaper Guild, the American Newspaper Guild, and the International Labor Press Association. From 1947 to 1977 Cole served as public relations director of the International Association of Machinists and Aerospace Workers with the AFL-CIO, concurrently editing the *Machinist,* the organization's newspaper. He later taught labor communications at the George Meany Center for Labor Studies in Silver Spring, Maryland. In addition to writing numerous articles concerning the trade union movement, Cole co-edited *Labor's Story as Reported by the American Labor Press* and was co-author of *Picnic Meals: It's a Picnic to Pack a Lunch* and *When You Gamble You Risk More Than Your Money.*

OBITUARIES AND OTHER SOURCES:

BOOKS

Who's Who in America, Supplement to 44th edition, Marquis, 1987.
Who's Who in Labor, Arno, 1976.

PERIODICALS

New York Times, May 7, 1988.

COLIN, Ann
    See URE, Jean

*   *   *

COLLINS, Linda   1931-

PERSONAL: Born May 20, 1931, in New York, N.Y.; daughter of Morris A. (a bank analyst) and Alma (a painter; maiden name, Cahn) Schapiro; married Arthur W. Collins (a professor of philosophy), October 9, 1953; children: Rufus, Jacob. *Education:* Attended Smith College; Barnard College, B.A., 1952; Columbia University, M.A., 1971.

ADDRESSES: Home—635 Park Ave., New York, N.Y. 10021. *Agent*—Candida Donadio, 231 West 22nd St., New York, N.Y. 10011.

CAREER: Writer. Teacher of literature at Columbia University and New York University, 1968-85.

WRITINGS:

Going to See the Leaves (stories), Viking, 1987.

Contributor to magazines.

WORK IN PROGRESS: A novel, for Viking; a collection of short stories.

SIDELIGHTS: "I like to take a quite ordinary situation and press it until it gives up its meaning," Linda Collins told *CA.* "I like to write about how life feels to people, how they receive its pleasures and unhappinesses. So far I have written only about certain kinds of people, but I hope to think about other kinds soon. I love to think about the weather when I write, what the light looks like outside the room where the people are talking or dreaming as they look out the window, and what time of day it is. When I was young I wrote some stories, but after a while I stopped, thinking I had nothing to say. I didn't write for fifteen years, but when I started again it seemed I had no end of things to say."

Collins's book, *Going to See the Leaves,* is a collection of eight stories variously describing experiences of ordinary life. In particular, a number of the selections focus on mid-life crisis and on the "difficulties and fragility of intimacy," wrote Joe David Bellamy in the *New York Times Book Review.* In the title story, for example, a middle-aged couple and their grown son and his spouse struggle "with the disparity between youthful expectations and the responsibilities of adulthood," Bellamy related, as they traverse New England on a weekend trip to view the fall colors. While outwardly pleasant and enjoyable, the journey proves simultaneously "full of anguish," continued the reviewer, due to the uncompromising personal barriers distancing the family members from one another. Having a similar theme is the narrative "Intimacy," in which Bellamy observed "tensions . . . helplessness," and underlying obstacles making for strained domestic relationships. Even the surreal tale "The Doctor's House," which offers an extraordinary bent, serves as an exercise in self-realization and the maturing process. Described by Amy Hempel in the *Chicago Tribune Book World* as the "showpiece" of *Going to See the Leaves,* this novella-length story features a Manhattan attorney who—suffering with abdominal discomfort and dizziness—discovers he is pregnant. While reminiscent of the bizarre "Metamorphosis" written by Franz Kafka, as Bellamy pointed out, Collins's story of physical transformation "tugs at the heart with unexpected force."

Overall, *Going to See the Leaves* impressed critics as a skillful display of seasoned talent. Reviewing the collection, Bellamy found the prose infused with "spiritual implications" and noted the "penetrating vision" and psychological acuity characterizing the stories. He opined further that the strength of Collins's writing derives from her "ability to evoke . . . elusive feelings with delicacy and credibility." Hempel likewise commended Collins, remarking that "she illumines the fragility and complexity of 'ordinary' life with confidence and skill." According to Bellamy, Collins achieves "sobering precision" in presenting this diverse account of everyday living.

BIOGRAPHICAL/CRITICAL SOURCES:

BOOKS

Contemporary Literary Criticism, Volume 44, Gale, 1987.

PERIODICALS

Chicago Tribune Book World, July 13, 1986.
New York Times Book World, March 9, 1986.

*   *   *

COLQUHOUN, Ithell   1906-1988

OBITUARY NOTICE—See index for *CA* sketch: Born October 9, 1906, in Shillong, Assam, India; died April 11, 1988, in Cornwall, England. Artist and author. Colquhoun is best remembered as a major painter of the British surrealist movement, having had over twenty one-woman exhibitions of her art in her lifetime. She also wrote poetry, novels, and nonfiction and illustrated many of her books, including *The Crying of the Wind: Ireland, The Living Stones: Cornwall, Goose of Hermogenes, Grimoire of the Entangled Thicket,* and *Sword of Wisdom: MacGregor Mathers and the Golden Dawn.*

OBITUARIES AND OTHER SOURCES:

BOOKS

International Authors and Writers Who's Who, 9th edition, [and] *International Who's Who in Poetry,* 6th edition, Melrose, 1982.

PERIODICALS

Times (London), April 14, 1988.

*   *   *

COLUMBU, Franco   1941-

PERSONAL: Born August 7, 1941, in Sardinia, Italy; immigrated to United States, 1969, naturalized citizen, 1987; son of Antonio and Maria Columbu. *Education:* Received Ph.D. in 1982. *Religion:* Roman Catholic.

ADDRESSES: Office—2947 South Sepulveda Blvd., Los Angeles, Calif. 90064.

CAREER: Actor, athlete, doctor of chiropractic, and writer. Staff writer for *Muscle and Fitness* and *Flex.* Actor in the films "Pumping Iron," "Conan the Barbarian," "Terminator," "Stay Hungry," "Getting Physical," "Raw Deal," "Circle Man," "The Running Man," and "Big Top"; television appearances in "Streets of San Francisco," "Hustler of Muscle Beach," and "Shepherd to Superstar"; guest on numerous television and radio programs. Lecturer on bodybuilding and health in Australia, Canada, Central America, Europe, Japan, South Africa, and Mexico.

MEMBER: International Federation of Bodybuilders, American Chiropractic Association (member of council on sports injuries), National Health Federation, American Federation of Television and Radio Artists, Screen Actors Guild, California Chiropractic Association.

AWARDS, HONORS: Bodybuilding titles include Mr. Olympia, Mr. Universe, Mr. World, Mr. International, Mr. Europe, and Mr. Italy; world champion and European champion powerlifter; boxing champion of Italy in amateur division.

WRITINGS:

Winning Bodybuilding, CBI Publishing, 1977.
Coming On Strong, CBI Publishing, 1978.
Starbodies: The Women's Weight Training Book, Dutton, 1978.
Weight Training for the Young Athlete, CBI Publishing, 1979.
Winning Powerlifting and Weightlifting, CBI Publishing, 1979.
Bodybuilding for the Young Athlete, Simon & Schuster, 1979.
Franco Columbu's Complete Book of Bodybuilding, CBI Publishing, 1982.
The Businessman's Minutes-a-Day Guide to Shaping Up, CBI Publishing, 1983.
Redesign Your Body, Dutton, 1985.
The Bodybuilder's Nutrition Book, CBI Publishing, 1985.

WORK IN PROGRESS: An exercise video, release expected in 1988.

SIDELIGHTS: Franco Columbu is a doctor of chiropractic who specializes in sports injuries and kinesiology. He is also a professional athlete, and he has worked as a trainer for such actors as Sylvester Stallone, Gary Busey, Kevin Dobson, and Fred Dryer.

AVOCATIONAL INTERESTS: Growing roses, maintaining his aviary, horseback riding, running, rope climbing, karate, soccer, tennis.

*   *   *

COMAROFF, John L(ionel)   1945-

PERSONAL: Born January 1, 1945, in Cape Town, South Africa; immigrated to United States, 1978, naturalized citizen, 1986; son of Lionel (a shopkeeper) and Jane (a housewife; maiden name, Miller) Comaroff; married Jean Rakoff (a professor of anthropology), January 15, 1967; children: Joshua, Jane. *Education:* University of Cape Town, B.A., 1966; London School of Economics and Political Science, London, Ph.D., 1973. *Religion:* Jewish.

ADDRESSES: Home—5327 South University Ave., Chicago, Ill. 60615. *Office*—Department of Anthropology, University of Chicago, Chicago, Ill. 60637.

CAREER: University of Wales, University College of Swansea, lecturer in anthropology, 1971-72; Victoria University of Manchester, Manchester, England, lecturer in anthropology, 1972-78; University of Chicago, Chicago, Ill., assistant professor, 1978-81, associate professor, 1981-87, professor of anthropology and sociology, 1987—. Member of anti-apartheid organizations.

MEMBER: American Anthropological Association (fellow), American Ethnological Society, African Studies Association (United States), African Studies Association (England), Association of Social Anthropologists (England; fellow), Royal Anthropological Institute (fellow).

WRITINGS:

(Editor) *The Diary of Solomon T. Plaatje: An African at Mafeking,* Macmillan, 1973.
(Editor) *The Meaning of Marriage Payments,* Academic Press, 1980.
(With Simon Roberts) *Rules and Processes: The Cultural Logic of Dispute in an African Context,* University of Chicago Press, 1981.
(Editor with Eileen Jensen Krige) *Essays on African Marriage in South Africa,* Juta, 1981.
(With wife, Jean Comaroff) *From Revelation to Revolution: Christianity, Colonialism, and Black Consciousness in South Africa,* University of Chicago Press, in press.

Contributor to African studies and anthropology journals. Member of editorial boards of *American Ethnologist, Africa,* and *Annual Reviews of Anthropology.*

WORK IN PROGRESS: Research for a book on the relationship between culture and power, completion expected in 1990.

SIDELIGHTS: John L. Comaroff told *CA:* "My theoretical concerns are to explore and develop the relationship between history and anthropology, to develop the methodology of a generic historical anthropology, and to investigate the nature of colonial domination and popular resistance. As an emigre from South Africa, I want to document and analyze the history and anthropology of political and economic domination and black resistance. To me, this is at once a moral, political, and intellectual project."

BIOGRAPHICAL/CRITICAL SOURCES:

PERIODICALS

Times Literary Supplement, May 7, 1982.

*   *   *

COOK, Elsa E(stelle)   1932-

PERSONAL: Born January 29, 1932, in Belleville, Ill.; daughter of Walter (a florist) and Elsa (a nurse; maiden name, Adler) Ogle; married Frank S. Cook, Jr. (a computer systems analyst), July 5, 1974; children: Patricia Sue Grant, Barbara Lynn Larson. *Education:* University of Missouri, Columbia, B.J., 1955; St. Louis University, M.A., 1969. *Religion:* "Ethical Society."

ADDRESSES: Home and office—8112 Pershing, Clayton, Mo. 63105. *Agent*—Joyce A. Flaherty, 816 Lynda Ct., St. Louis, Mo. 63122.

CAREER: Sears, Roebuck & Co., St. Louis, Mo., copywriter, 1962-63; Ferguson-Florissant school district, Florissant, Mo., teacher of history, 1963-88.

MEMBER: National Council for the Social Studies, Romance Writers of America, St. Louis Writers Guild.

AWARDS, HONORS: Fulbright scholarship, 1980; grant from National Endowment for the Humanities, 1986.

WRITINGS:

(Contributor) *Best Places to Stay in America's Cities,* Harvard Common, 1985.
Satin Dolls (novel), Pocket Books, 1987.

WORK IN PROGRESS: Research into nineteenth-century women's suffrage for a novel, *Shadows in a Winter Garden.*

SIDELIGHTS: Elsa Cook told *CA:* "The civil rights movement, the black experience, and black music coalesce in *Satin Dolls,* a generational saga concerning five black women and their dreams for a better life in a better world. Lucy, a slave, realizes her personal dream when she is given her freedom at age seventeen. Her hope for a better world is realized when all slaves are freed after the Civil War. Her daughter Sarah is jubilant when she becomes a star in a minstrel show at the turn of the century, but later, Sarah's dreams are shattered when her husband is killed in the East St. Louis race riot. Sarah's daughter Bobbie becomes a jazz singer in the 1920s. Although her life changes radically when the stock market crashes in 1929, she sees the struggle for equality and freedom continue through her daughter Tess, who becomes involved in the civil rights movement of the 1960s. The last of the five women, Carmen, triumphs as a popular rhythm and blues singer. Both *Satin Dolls* and my next novel, *Shadows in a Winter Garden,* reflect my interest in history.

"Research is my passion. Besides using libraries for research, I travel extensively, studying people, places, and historical sites. Travel brings history to life and makes the historical novel relevant to modern readers. Since I love to travel and do research in libraries, historical novels are the most exciting forms of writing for me."

*   *   *

COOMER, Joe   1958-

PERSONAL: Born November 3, 1958, in Fort Worth, Tex.; son of Rufus (a business owner) and Linda (a business owner; maiden name, Dennis) Coomer; married Heather Hutton (an antiques dealer and writer), April 5, 1986. *Education:* Southern Methodist University, B.A., 1981.

ADDRESSES: Home and office—101 Ash Creek Dr. W., Azle, Tex. 76020. *Agent*—Elaine Markson, Elaine Markson Literary Agency, Inc., 44 Greenwich Ave., New York, N.Y. 10011.

CAREER: Writer, 1981—; owner of antiques malls in Fort Worth, Tex., 1986—.

MEMBER: Texas Institute of Letters, Phi Beta Kappa.

AWARDS, HONORS: Texas Institute of Letters award for fiction and Jesse Jones Award for fiction, both 1983, both for *The Decatur Road.*

WRITINGS:

The Decatur Road (novel), St. Martin's, 1983.
Kentucky Love (novel), St. Martin's, 1985.
A Flatland Fable (novel), Texas Monthly, 1986.

WORK IN PROGRESS: A nonfiction book about building a house by a pond, completion expected in 1988.

SIDELIGHTS: Joe Coomer's award-winning first novel, *The Decatur Road,* is set in the Appalachian hills of eastern Kentucky and was described by critic Ivan Gold of the *New York Times Book Review* as "a gentle story of mountain domesticity." Spanning some six decades, *The Decatur Road* centers primarily on the enduring relationship of Mitchell and Jenny Parks and their ongoing struggle to survive persistent hard times, with the dusty, twisted road of the title serving as a metaphor for that struggle. Coomer's subsequent novels, *Kentucky Love* and *A Flatland Fable,* received favorable reviews and were recommended by critics, who praised their charm and powerful imagery.

Coomer told *CA:* "I wake up every morning appalled that things have changed. It's still hard to believe at midday, and by nightfall I've got to write about it. Sometimes I feel like I'm the only one who's noticed, but that's not so; I tell the same old story, different only in that I've forgotten some of the details and added my own to fill in the gaps. I find great joy in passing the story on."

BIOGRAPHICAL/CRITICAL SOURCES:

PERIODICALS

Los Angeles Times Book Review, July 14, 1985.
New York Times Book Review, January 8, 1984.

*   *   *

COOPER, J. California

PERSONAL: Born in Berkeley, Calif.; daughter of Joseph C. and Maxine Rosemary Cooper; children: Paris A. Williams. *Education:* Attended technical high school and various colleges. *Politics:* None. *Religion:* Christian.

CAREER: Writer.

WRITINGS:

A Piece of Mine (stories), Alice Walker, 1984.
Homemade Love, St. Martin's, 1986.
Some Soul to Keep, St. Martin's, 1987.

Also author of plays in anthology *Center Stage.*

WORK IN PROGRESS: A novel; a collection of short stories for children; a collection of stories for adults.

*   *   *

COPE, Lewis   1934-

PERSONAL: Born June 24, 1934, in Sweetwater, Tex.; son of Millard L. (a newspaper editor) and Margaret Wallace (Kilgore) Cope; married Betty Joan Ball, June 28, 1958; children: Margaret, Elizabeth, Mary Amelia. *Education:* Washington and Lee University, B.A., 1955; graduate study at Columbia University, 1963-64. *Religion:* Episcopalian.

ADDRESSES: Home—5217 West 91st St., Bloomington, Minn. 55437. *Office*—*Minneapolis Tribune,* 425 Portland Ave., Minneapolis, Minn. 55488.

CAREER: Greenville Herald-Banner, Greenville, Tex., reporter, 1957-60; *Richmond Times-Dispatch,* Richmond, Va., copy editor, 1960-62; *San Antonio Express,* San Antonio, Tex., 1962-66, began as copy editor, became news editor; *Minneapolis Tribune,* Minneapolis, Minn., science reporter, 1966—. Writer in residence of Council for the Advancement of Science Writing at National Cancer Institute, 1976. *Military service:* U.S. Army, 1955-57.

MEMBER: National Association of Science Writers (member of executive committee, 1982), Sigma Delta Chi (president of Minnesota chapter, 1973-74; deputy regional director, 1974—).

AWARDS, HONORS: Award of Merit from American Association of Blood Banks, 1974; Journalism Award from American Academy of Family Physicians, 1976 and 1979; Penney Award for lifestyle reporting from University of Missouri, 1977; National Media Award from American Cancer Society, 1977; Blakeslee Award from American Heart Association, 1979; Cecil Award from Arthritis Foundation, 1982.

WRITINGS:

Save Your Life: A Handbook for Preventing Heart Attacks, Cancer, Strokes, Minneapolis Tribune, 1979.

*   *   *

COPELAND, James E(verett)   1937-

PERSONAL: Born June 6, 1937, in Texas; son of William (a minister) and Golda (Stern) Copeland; married, 1965; children: Kimberly Gayle. *Education:* University of Colorado, B.A., 1961; Cornell University, Ph.D., 1965.

ADDRESSES: Office—Department of Linguistics and Semiotics, Rice University, Box 1892, Houston, Tex. 77251.

CAREER: Cornell University, Ithaca, N.Y., instructor in German, 1964-65; University of California, Davis, assistant professor of linguistics and German, 1965-66; Rice University, Houston, Tex., assistant professor, 1966-69, associate professor, 1969-83, professor of linguistics and semiotics, 1983—, chairman of department, 1969-82. Visiting assistant professor at Cornell University, summer, 1967; visiting professor at University of Saarbruecken, 1984; visiting scholar at University of Arizona, 1986.

MEMBER: Modern Language Association of America, Linguistic Society of America, Linguistic Association of Canada and the United States, South Central Modern Language Association.

WRITINGS:

A Stepmatricial Generative Phonology of German, Mouton, 1970.
(Editor with Philip W. Davis, and contributor) *Papers in Cognitive Stratificational Linguistics,* Volume LVI, Rice University Press, 1980.
(Editor with others, and contributor) *The Seventh Linguistic Association of Canada and the United States Forum,* Hornbeam, 1981.
(Editor) *New Directions in Linguistics and Semiotics,* John Benjamins, 1984.

Contributor to linguistic journals. Editor of *Forum linguisticum.*

WORK IN PROGRESS: Discourse on Relational Networks; research on cognitive linguistics.

*   *   *

CORBALIS, Judy   1941-

PERSONAL: Born March 29, 1941, in Dannevirke, New Zealand; daughter of Robert and June (Hales) Mintoft; married Jonathan James Corbalis, April 21, 1962 (divorced, 1974); children: Toby Jonathan James. *Education:* Victoria University of Wellington, B.A., 1961; attended London Academy of Music and Dramatic Art, 1973-74. *Politics:* "Left wing."

ADDRESSES: Home—London, England. *Agent*—Jane Gregory, 4 Westwick Gardens, London W.14, England.

CAREER: Teacher of English language and literature, history, French, and physical education at high schools in London, England, and Wanganui, Rotorua, and Whangarei, New Zealand, 1962-73; actress working in theatre and on television in New Zealand, Australia, and England, 1974—; garden design consultant, 1976—; children's book writer, 1983—.

MEMBER: British Actors' Equity, Writers Guild.

AWARDS, HONORS: Fortnight Top Children's Book Choice, 1986, for *The Wrestling Princess and Other Stories.*

WRITINGS:

The Wrestling Princess and Other Stories (juvenile), Deutsch, 1986.
Porcellus, Flying Pig (juvenile), J. Cape, 1987, Dial, 1988.
Oskar and the Icepick (juvenile), Deutsch, 1988.
The Cuckoo Bird (juvenile), Deutsch, 1988.

WORK IN PROGRESS: A sequel to *Porcellus, Flying Pig;* an adult novel; a television adaptation of an adult novel; a children's play; a second book of children's short stories, publication expected in 1989; a younger children's picture book; a television adaptation of "The Enchanted Toad", from *The Wrestling Princess* collection.

SIDELIGHTS: Judy Corbalis told *CA:* "I write because I enjoy it and I like having the freedom to create fantasy. I find I want to start a story from a believable point or incident and move from there further and further into fantasy while keeping the storyline intact. The traditional fairy story is good as a basis because everyone already knows all the elements in it. The stories in *The Wrestling Princess* are based on traditional ideas that have been adapted and changed and have modern-day elements spliced in. I also find I can only write from the basis of what I know or have experienced, or want to experience, and expand from there.

"I don't set out to write specifically anti-sexist or anti-racist books because doing so seems rather moralistic and a bit self-defeating. I hope that what I believe and think and feel comes into the books automatically and naturally. I like the possibility of a world where neither sex, race, age, income, nor any kind of handicap precludes anyone from doing anything he or she wants very much. If there's a common theme to the books I've written so far, it's the possibility of realizing one's dreams. By finding the right kind of power, something you really long for can be made to happen.

"Compared to acting, the feedback from writing is a lot slower in coming and you can't adapt your performance to your audience to suit a particular occasion. A book is written and finished by the time you get your response. That's why I find the follow-up of meeting and talking with children on school and library visits very valuable and stimulating."

AVOCATIONAL INTERESTS: Travel, music.

* * *

CORBIN, Richard 1911-1988

OBITUARY NOTICE—See index for *CA* sketch: Born November 4, 1911, in Schenectady, N.Y.; died of heart disease, April 20, 1988, in Peekskill, N.Y. Educator, editor, and author. Known for his work on textbooks, Corbin began his career teaching English at Bay Shore High School in New York in 1933. He moved to Peekskill High School in 1937 and eventually became chairman of its English department. Corbin was also chair of English at New York City's Hunter College High School from 1960 to 1972, in addition to lecturing at many universities. He co-authored the "Guide to Modern English" textbook series, and edited anthologies such as *Poetry I, Surprises: Twenty Stories by O. Henry,* and *Twelve American Plays.* Corbin's other writings include *What Parents Should Know About the Teaching of Writing in Our Schools* and *Research Papers: A Guided Writing Experience for Senior High School Students,* which he wrote with his son, Jonathan.

OBITUARIES AND OTHER SOURCES:

BOOKS

Directory of American Scholars, Volume II: *English, Speech, and Drama,* 8th edition, Bowker, 1982.

PERIODICALS

New York Times, April 23, 1988.

* * *

CORNISH, Geoffrey (St. John) 1914-

PERSONAL: Born August 6, 1914, in Winnipeg, Manitoba, Canada; immigrated to United States, 1947, naturalized citizen, 1955; son of Clifford and Mary Cornish; married Carol Burr Gawthrop, March 31, 1951. *Education:* University of British Columbia, B.S.A., 1935; University of Massachusetts at Amherst, M.S., 1952. *Religion:* Episcopalian.

ADDRESSES: Home and office—Fiddlers Green, Amherst, Mass. 01002.

CAREER: Thompson-Jones and Co., Toronto, Ontario, golf course architect, 1935-37; University of Massachusetts at Amherst, instructor in golf course design and maintenance, 1947-52; private practice of golf course architecture in Amherst, 1952—. Visiting lecturer at University of Massachusetts at Amherst. *Military service:* Canadian Army, 1940-45; became major.

MEMBER: American Society of Golf Course Architects (president, 1975), Soil Science Society of America, British Association of Golf Course Architects (honorary member), Sigma Xi, Phi Kappa Phi.

AWARDS, HONORS: Distinguished Service Award from Golf Course Superintendents of America, 1981; Donald Ross Award from American Society of Golf Course Architects, 1982; Outstanding Service Award from National Golf Foundation; Honorary D.Sc. from University of Massachusetts at Amherst, 1987.

WRITINGS:

(With Ronald E. Whitten) *The Golf Course,* W. H. Smith, 1981, revised edition, 1987.

Contributor to journals.

BIOGRAPHICAL/CRITICAL SOURCES:

PERIODICALS

Interview, April, 1987.

* * *

CORRIN, Jay P(atrick) 1943-

PERSONAL: Born December 18, 1943, in Duluth, Minn.; son of John J. and Patricia M. Corrin; married Nancy Jean Kuch, December 30, 1967. *Education:* Michigan State University, B.A., 1966; University of Hawaii at Manoa, M.A., 1968; Boston University, Ph.D., 1976.

ADDRESSES: Office—College of Basic Studies, Boston University, 871 Commonwealth Ave., Boston, Mass. 02215.

CAREER: English teacher with the Peace Corps at preparatory school in Misurata, Libya, 1968-69; Boston University, Boston, Mass., assistant professor of liberal arts, 1976-77, assistant professor of social science, 1977-81, associate professor, 1981—.

MEMBER: American Historical Association, New England Historical Association, Association of General and Liberal Studies, Chesterton Society.

WRITINGS:

G. K. Chesterton and Hilaire Belloc: The Battle Against Modernity, Ohio University Press, 1981.

Contributor to journals.

WORK IN PROGRESS: A textbook on modern China, with June Grasso and Michael Kort, for M. E. Sharpe; research on Catholic intellectuals and the crises of the 1930s; research on Catholics and social action.

SIDELIGHTS: Jay Corrin told *CA:* "I became interested in G. K. Chesterton and Hilaire Belloc because they were two of the most prolific and versatile writers in the English-speaking world and also, in their day, the best known. Yet no book attempted to explain their social and political philosophy or assess its impact on modern thought. Distributism, their philosophy, is not easy to define. It was not simply an economic theory but an approach to life that called for a return to a small-scale society where the individual could experience a close sense of involvement with his community and where he could reach his full potential as a creative being by working with his hands and his mind. This social philosophy was influenced by the papal encyclical *Rerum Novarum,* which castigated the evils of both unrestrained capitalism and socialism and recognized small proprietorship as a prerequisite for a just and stable society. It is in this sense that distributism gave battle to 'modernity,' since it took issue with the social and psychological tendencies generated when society shifted from a rural base with peasant labor to an urban society based on proletarian and professional labor. As a sociopolitical philosophy, distributism has had enormous influence (especially on post-industrial thinking, the 'small is beautiful' movement, neo-liberalism, and so forth).

"My current major project is to study Anglo-American Catholic intellectuals and their commitment to social action as called for in the papal encyclicals from *Rerum Novarum* and *Quadragesimo Anno.* These labor encyclicals were a response to the social disruptions caused by industrialism, capitalism, and socialism. A corporative government was recommended as the best means to heal the social ills produced by these changes. In particular, I propose to explore how the encyclicals informed the reactions of Catholic intellectuals to the turmoils of the 1930s and 1940s. For example: Was there a 'Catholic political view' that emerged during these decades? If so, what relationship did it have with the labor encyclicals? If not, what positions developed concerning fascism and social and economic reform? Were the differences of opinion in Catholic circles derivatives of nineteenth-century left- and right-wing political orientations? Is there any relationship between Catholic social thought and liberation theology in the Third World today? Was there a cross-fertilization of ideas between American and English Catholic intellectuals during this time? Finally, to what extent did these experiences inform a Catholic critique of modernity?"

COSTABEL, Eva Deutsch   1924-
(Eva Costabel-Deutsch)

PERSONAL: Born November 20, 1924, in Zagreb, Yugoslavia; immigrated to United States, 1949; daughter of Arnold (a chemical merchant) and Ann (in business; maiden name, Weinberger) Deutsch. *Education:* Attended the Academy of Fine Arts, Rome, Italy, and Pratt Institute, Brooklyn, N.Y. *Politics:* Democrat. *Religion:* Jewish.

ADDRESSES: Home—33-43 Crescent St., Long Island City, N.Y. 11106.

CAREER: Artist and writer. Assistant to art director for Barton's Bonbonniere, Inc., 1953-55; package designer for Mitchell Studios, 1955-65; senior graphic and package designer for J. C. Penney Co., 1965-68; senior package designer for Clairol, Inc., 1968-71; instructor at Parsons School of Design, New York, N.Y., 1982-85.

MEMBER: Graphic Artists Guild, Greater Astoria Historical Society, American Museum of Natural History, Appalachian Mountain Club.

WRITINGS:

JUVENILE; SELF-ILLUSTRATED

(Under name Constabel-Deutsch) *Full-Color Floral Needlepoint Designs: Charted for Easy Use,* Dover, 1976.
(Under name Costabel-Deutsch) *Design and Make Your Own Floral Applique,* Dover, 1976.
A New England Village (historical), Atheneum, 1983.
The Pennsylvania Dutch: Craftsmen and Farmers, Atheneum, 1986.

*   *   *

COSTABEL-DEUTSCH, Eva
See COSTABEL, Eva Deutsch

*   *   *

COULETTE, Henri Anthony   1927-1988

OBITUARY NOTICE—See index for *CA* sketch: Born November 11, 1927, in Los Angeles, Calif.; died of apparent heart failure, March 26, 1988. Educator, editor, and poet. Best known for his traditionally metered poetry, Coulette taught English at California State University, Los Angeles, for almost thirty years. Formerly he had been a high school English teacher and an instructor at the University of Iowa's writer's workshop. Coulette's first volume of poetry, *The War of the Secret Agents and Other Poems,* won the Lamont Poetry Award. He edited *Midland: Twenty-five Years of Fiction and Poetry From Writing Workshops of the State University of Iowa, The Unstrung Lyre: Interviews With Fourteen Poets,* and *Character and Crisis: A Contemporary Reader.* Coulette also wrote *The Family Goldschmitt* and *The Attic.*

OBITUARIES AND OTHER SOURCES:

BOOKS

The Writers Directory: 1988-1990, St. James Press, 1988.

PERIODICALS

Los Angeles Times, April 14, 1988.

COX, G. William   1949(?)-1988

OBITUARY NOTICE: Born c. 1949 in Owensboro, Ky.; died of complications from acquired immune deficiency syndrome (AIDS), May 20, 1988, in Manhattan Beach, Calif. Journalist. As managing editor of the Honolulu *Star Bulletin,* Cox became well known when he resigned from his post after writing an editorial column announcing that he had AIDS. Upon graduating from the University of Missouri in 1971, Cox joined the staff of the *Courier-Journal* in Louisville, Ky. He left the paper in 1978 to work for the *Miami Herald* but returned to the *Courier* in less than a year to become the publication's city editor, holding that position for five years. In 1984 he moved to Hawaii where he became managing editor of the *Star-Bulletin.* During his tenure there, Cox avidly supported reporters' rights in having access to government records and meetings, and he was a chairman of the Freedom of Information Committee of the Society of Professional Journalists. Shortly after his 1986 column appeared that disclosed he was suffering from AIDS, Cox resigned from the paper maintaining he did not feel well enough to continue supervising his staff. He subsequently moved to California where he lectured to professional journalism groups on the coverage of AIDS.

OBITUARIES AND OTHER SOURCES:

PERIODICALS

Chicago Tribune, May 24, 1988.
Los Angeles Times, May 22, 1988.
New York Times, May 21, 1988.
Washington Post, May 22, 1988.

*   *   *

CRANE, Jacob L(eslie)   1892-1988

OBITUARY NOTICE: Born September 14, 1892, in Benzonia, Mich.; died following a stroke, March 19, 1988, in Washington, D.C. Town planning consultant, federal housing official, and author. Crane was best known for his skills in urban planning. After graduating from the University of Michigan and studying landscape architecture at Harvard, he established a private practice in Chicago during the 1930s. He moved to Washington, D.C., in 1937 and became an assistant to the administrator of what is now the Housing and Home Finance Agency (HHFA). During World War II Crane served as co-ordinator of housing for the president and was also an adviser on international housing matters. He retired from the HHFA in 1954, returning to a private consulting practice where he assisted in the planning of several U.S. towns. Additionally, Crane was involved in city-planning projects in foreign countries and was a consultant on housing and urban renewal for the United Nations and the Organization of American States. His writings include *Urban Planning—Illusion and Reality: A New Philosophy for Planned City Building.*

OBITUARY NOTICES AND OTHER SOURCES:

BOOKS

International Who's Who, 40th edition, Europa, 1976.

PERIODICALS

Washington Post, March 20, 1988.

*   *   *

CREESE, Walter L(ittlefield)   1919-

PERSONAL: Born December 19, 1919, in Danvers, Mass.; son of Guy Talbot (a manufacturer) and Avis (a housewife; maiden name, Littlefield) Creese; married Eleanor Roberts (a housewife), June 16, 1945; children: Guy. *Education:* Brown University, A.B. (magna cum laude), 1941; Harvard University, M.A., 1945, Ph.D., 1950.

ADDRESSES: Home—1817 Moraine Dr., Champaign, Ill. 61821.

CAREER: Wellesley College, Wellesley, Mass., instructor in art and architectural history, 1945; University of Louisville, Louisville, Ky., 1946-58, began as instructor, became professor at Hite Art Institute; University of Illinois at Urbana-Champaign, Urbana, professor of architecture, 1958-63; University of Oregon, Eugene, dean of School of Architecture and Allied Arts, 1963-68; University of Illinois at Urbana-Champaign, chairman of Division of Architectural History and Preservation, 1968-87. Visiting professor at Harvard University, 1961. Chairman of Louisville Planning and Zoning Commission, 1952-55; consultant to National Park Service, 1972-79.

MEMBER: American Institute of Architects (honorary member), College Art Association of America (member of board of directors, 1951-55), Society of Architectural Historians (president, 1958-60), Phi Beta Kappa, Phi Kappa Phi, Sphinx Society.

AWARDS, HONORS: Fellow of American Council of Learned Societies, 1951-52; Fulbright fellow at University of Liverpool, 1955-56; Rehmann fellow of American Institute of Architects, 1963; Smithsonian fellow, 1969-70; Guggenheim fellow, 1972-73; Rockefeller fellow, 1976-77; special teaching award from Gargoyle Society, 1978; Cultural Achievement Award from U.S. Department of the Interior, 1979; Excellence in Education Award from Illinois Council of American Institute of Architects, 1987.

WRITINGS:

The Search for Environment, Yale University Press, 1966.
The Legacy of Raymond Unwin, MIT Press, 1967.
The Crowning of the American Landscape, Princeton University Press, 1985.

Editor of journal of Society of Architectural Historians, 1950-53.

WORK IN PROGRESS: The Tennessee Valley Authority as an Allegory, publication expected in 1989.

SIDELIGHTS: Walter L. Creese told *CA:* "Although I was trained as an art and architectural historian, my publications, especially the books, have been mostly about environmental history in Britain and the United States.

"Buildings are designed as entities—single, contained units—but they always have surroundings in which humans are forced to act, so only half the result occurs inside. Industry and technology have brought forth many and larger buildings, but there has been no corresponding enlargement of the aesthetics of such scenes, hence the titles of my books: the 'search' meaning a more outward look at human settlement, epitomized by the British garden city; the 'legacy' of Sir Raymond Unwin, the greatest and most humane thinker and doer for that movement; and the 'crowning,' meaning that landscape architecture and building architecture have only rarely been pushed to their ultimate potential in the United States, and only then when we have had the sense to pay attention to the loftiest visionaries in this country—like Thomas Jefferson, Frederick Law Olmsted, and Frank Lloyd Wright. The architectural professions have aimed too low, especially in light of the wonderful continental territory that opened up in the nineteenth century, from the Revolution on, really, and the high caliber of native geniuses that were then produced. The absorption in international problems and challenges since World War II has tended to obscure those earlier traditions and accomplishments—the internal achievements of a democracy imprinting themselves upon the land.

"The Tennessee Valley Authority was the largest of such dreams, but unfortunately, although it had success in many ways, it was put forward in the midst of a depression and great poverty and so did not render as integrated and positive a result as it might have in better economic circumstances. It is an allegory of what might have been for the rest of America."

*   *   *

CREFELD, Donna Carolyn Anders
See ANDERS, Donna Carolyn

*   *   *

CRONE, Moira 1952-

PERSONAL: Born August 10, 1952, in Goldsboro, N.C.; daughter of James Clarence (an accountant) and Ethel (an executive assistant; maiden name, Donnelly) Crone; married Rodger L. Kamentz (a poet and writer), October 14, 1979; children: Anya Miriam, Kezia Vida. *Education:* Smith College, B.A. (with high honors), 1974; Johns Hopkins University, M.A., 1977.

ADDRESSES: Office—c/o Mary Ingraham Bunting Institute, 34 Concord Ave., Cambridge, Mass. 02138. *Agent*—Ellen Levine, 432 Park Ave. S., Suite 1205, New York, N.Y. 10016.

CAREER: Enoch Pratt Free Library, Baltimore, Md., tutor in reading and English as a second language, 1977-78; Goucher College, Towson, Md., lecturer in English, 1979-81; Louisiana State University, Baton Rouge, instructor, 1981-83, assistant professor, 1983-86, associate professor of English, 1986—. Lecturer at Johns Hopkins University, 1979-81; member of board of directors of Bethesda Writers' Center, 1981, and Fiction Collective, New York, N.Y.

MEMBER: Authors Guild, Associated Writing Programs, Phi Kappa Phi.

AWARDS, HONORS: Fellow at Mary Ingraham Bunting Institute, Radcliffe College, 1987-88.

WRITINGS:

The Winnebago Mysteries and Other Stories, Fiction Collective, 1982.
A Period of Confinement (novel), Putnam, 1986.

Work represented in anthologies, including *American Made,* Fiction Collective, 1986. Contributor of stories to magazines, including *New Yorker, Mademoiselle, Western Humanities Review,* and *Southern Review.*

WORK IN PROGRESS: Remember Who Loves You, a novel, completion expected in 1988.

SIDELIGHTS: Moira Crone told *CA:* "I was born in the tobacco country of North Carolina in 1952. My father was a native of the region, and my mother was from Brooklyn, New York. I spent my childhood in the same house where my father

was born, with frequent visits to New York City to visit my grandmother and other relatives. In 1970 I entered Smith College, where I worked with V. S. Pritchett.

"After graduation, I lived in Boston and studied with another British author, Penelope Mortimer. In 1976 I was offered a fellowship for the Johns Hopkins Writing Seminars, where John Barth and Leslie Epstein taught. From 1977 to 1980 I worked as a teacher of English as a second language to Spanish-speaking adults in the Fells Point section of Baltimore and as a fiction workshop teacher. I also began publishing in literary magazines. Since 1981 I have lived in Louisiana, with extended stays out of the country—in France in 1983 and Jerusalem in 1986.

"My first book, *The Winnebago Mysteries and Other Stories,* was accepted for publication in 1980. It is a novella and a collection of stories I wrote during the late seventies. The strong reception of my book of stories helped me find a place for my novel, *A Period of Confinement,* a book about pregnancy and motherhood, and art.

"My next book is about the way a second generation absorbs the intentional and unintentional inflictions they receive as children and how their parents' losses and disappointments are transmuted into their own. It is a coming-of-age novel, concerning the attachments that threaten people and the need for separation, and for betrayal, as well as for forgiveness.

"My primary concerns as a writer have always been the questions of separation—questions about difference and individuation. I am centrally obsessed with motherhood and the conundrum of identity motherhood presents to mothers and children."

*   *   *

CRONIN, Audrey Kurth 1958-

PERSONAL: Born January 14, 1958, in Jacksonville, Fla.; daughter of Ronald James (a naval officer) and E. Charlene (a music teacher; maiden name, Schaefer) Kurth; married Patrick M. Cronin (a defense analyst), June 8, 1985. *Education:* Attended Bowdoin College, 1977-79; Princeton University, A.B. (summa cum laude), 1981; St. Antony's College, Oxford, M.Phil., 1983, D.Phil., 1984.

ADDRESSES: Home—Burke, Va. *Office*—Department of Government and Foreign Affairs, 232 Cabell Hall, University of Virginia, Charlottesville, Va. 22903.

CAREER: U.S. Embassy, Moscow, U.S.S.R., administrative assistant, 1976-77; Office of the Secretary of the Navy, Washington, D.C., assistant to speechwriter for secretary of the navy, 1981; University of Virginia, Charlottesville, assistant professor of international relations, 1987—. Consultant to Office of the Secretary of Defense.

MEMBER: International Studies Association, American Political Science Association, Committee on Atlantic Studies, Oxford University Strategic Studies Group (president, 1983-84).

AWARDS, HONORS: Marshall scholar at Oxford University, 1981-84; Certificate of Commendation from Secretary of the Navy, 1981; grant from Cyril Foster Fund, 1983; postdoctoral fellow at Harvard University's Center for International Affairs, 1984-85; Herman Kahn Visiting Fellow at Hudson Institute, 1987-88.

WRITINGS:

Great Power Politics and the Struggle Over Austria, 1945-1955, Cornell University Press, 1986.

WORK IN PROGRESS: Research for a book on "strategic stalemate and neutralization in the pre-nuclear and nuclear eras."

SIDELIGHTS: Audrey Kurth Cronin told *CA:* "My book on the negotiations over Austria arose out of a long-standing interest in the U.S.-Soviet relationship since 1945. It focuses on the nature of the conflict between the two superpowers and how the Austrian State Treaty, a unique compromise between East and West, came to be signed. In particular, I try to answer two questions: Why did the Soviet Union withdraw its troops from Austria? and what lessons do the eight years of talks over Austria provide for future East-West negotiations?"

*   *   *

CROSS, George Lynn   1905-

PERSONAL: Born May 12, 1905, in Woonsocket, S.D.; son of George Washington and Jemima Jane (Dawson) Cross; married Cleo Sikkink, October 28, 1926; children: Mary-Lynn, George W., Braden Riehl. *Education:* South Dakota State College (now University), B.S., 1926, M.S., 1927; University of Chicago, Ph.D., 1929. *Religion:* Presbyterian.

ADDRESSES: Home—812 Mockingbird Lane, Norman, Okla. 73071.

CAREER: University of South Dakota, Vermillion, professor of botany, 1930-34; University of Oklahoma, Norman, professor of botany, 1934-38, head of department, 1938-42, acting dean of Graduate College and acting director of Research Institute, 1942-44, president of university, 1944-68, president emeritus, 1968—. President of Oklahoma Health Sciences Foundation, 1968-80. Member of public panel of Eighth District War Labor Board, 1942. Chairman of Federal Home Loan Bank of Topeka, 1960-68, and member of Federal Home Loan Bank Board; chairman of board of directors of American Exchange Bank, Norman, 1964-86; member of board of directors of Oklahoma Medical Research Foundation, and of Friendly National Bank, and Central National Bank, both Oklahoma City, Okla. Member of board of university presidents of William Rockhill Nelson Trust, 1944-68; member of executive council of University of Oklahoma Research Institute; trustee of Cottey College, 1969-75. Director of Midwest Research Institute.

MEMBER: American Association for the Advancement of Science (fellow), National Association of State Universities (president, 1959-60), Association of Scientific University Professors, National Farm Chemurgic Council, Botanical Society of America, National Education Association, National Geographic Society, American Society of Naturalists, Newcomen Society, Oklahoma Academy of Sciences, Oklahoma Historical Society, Torrey Botanical Club, Norman Chamber of Commerce, Lions Club, Phi Beta Kappa, Sigma Xi, Phi Sigma, Alpha Phi Omega.

AWARDS, HONORS: American Citation from B'nai B'rith, 1950; member of Oklahoma Hall of Fame, 1951; citation from American Conference of Christians and Jews, 1952; citation for public service from University of Chicago Alumni Association, 1956; Human Relations Award from Southwestern Anti-Defamation League, 1956; member of Oklahoma Medical Sciences Hall of Fame, 1958; D.Sc. from South Dakota State College (now University), 1959; LL.D. from Oberlin College, 1960; fellow of University of Oklahoma Academy of Science, 1971.

WRITINGS:

Blacks in White Colleges, University of Oklahoma Press, 1975.
Presidents Can't Punt, University of Oklahoma Press, 1977.
The University of Oklahoma and World War II, University of Oklahoma Press, 1980.
Professors, Presidents, and Politicians, University of Oklahoma Press, 1981.
Letters to Bill: On University Administration, University of Oklahoma Press, 1983.
Seeds of Excellence, University of Oklahoma Press, 1986.
The University of Oklahoma Research Institute, University of Oklahoma Press, 1986.

WORK IN PROGRESS: Magazine articles on the history of the University of Oklahoma.

SIDELIGHTS: George Lynn Cross told *CA:* "I have attempted to prepare histories of the most important issues that developed during my twenty-five years as president of the University of Oklahoma."

*   *   *

CSIKSZENTMIHALYI, Mihaly   1934-

PERSONAL: Born September 29, 1934, in Fiume, Italy; immigrated to United States, 1956, naturalized citizen, 1968; son of Alfred (a diplomat) and Edith (Jankovich) Csikszentmihalyi; married Isabella Selega (a writer), December 30, 1960; children: Mark, Christopher. *Education:* University of Chicago, B.A., 1959, Ph.D., 1965. *Religion:* Roman Catholic.

ADDRESSES: Home—5333 South Hyde Park, Chicago, Ill. 60615. *Office*—Department of Behavioral Sciences, University of Chicago, Chicago, Ill. 60637. *Agent*—John Brockman, John Brockman Associates, Inc., 2307 Broadway, New York, N.Y. 10024.

CAREER: Lake Forest College, Lake Forest, Ill., instructor, 1965-67, assistant professor, 1967-68, associate professor of sociology and anthropology, 1968-69, chairman of department, 1967-69; University of Chicago, Chicago, Ill., associate professor, 1969-79, professor of human development, 1980—, chairman of department of behavioral sciences, 1985—. Member of board of advisers of Getty Museum and *Encyclopaedia Britannica*.

WRITINGS:

Beyond Boredom and Anxiety, Jossey-Bass, 1975.
(With J. W. Getzels) *The Creative Vision*, Wiley, 1976.
(With Eugene Rochberg Halton) *The Meaning of Things*, Cambridge University Press, 1981.
(With Reed Larson) *Being Adolescent: Conflict and Growth in the Teenage Years*, Basic Books, 1985.
(With wife, Isabella Csikszentmihalyi) *Optimal Experience: Studies of Flow in Consciousness*, Cambridge University Press, 1988.
The Psychology of Optimal Experience, Harper, in press.

WORK IN PROGRESS: A longitudinal study of talented teenagers; studies of museum audiences.

SIDELIGHTS: Being Adolescent is the result of a project in which seventy-five high school students were equipped with beepers. At frequent but random intervals over a one-week period, the students were paged and required to record their activities and feelings. The book reveals that most of these teenagers were unhappy and alienated most of the time. According to the authors, their happiest moments seemed to involve escapist activity with friends, such as drinking and smoking marijuana. Most teenagers, they discovered, spend less than three hours a week alone with a parent, and less than two percent of their time is spent with adult role models other than parents. Yet the authors are optimistic about the future of these young people. From the frustrating chaos of adolescence, they claim, many teenagers will learn to impose an order of their own that will allow them to make sense of life. The successful ones will be the young people who can consciously direct their energy and mold a negative or boring experience into a stimulating challenge. "This is a hopeful book," wrote Elizabeth Crow in the *Washington Post Book World*. "For frightened, confused parents whose children haven't yet emerged on the sunny side of adolescence, *Being Adolescent* is useful on-the-job training."

Csikszentmihalyi told *CA:* "My research and writing focuses on the positive dimensions of experience—creativity, enjoyment, productive involvement. Psychology has dealt almost exclusively with pathology, neglecting the positive side of mental life. This one-sided view distorts the actual state of affairs. My work attempts to redress somewhat this glum view. In the volume *Optimal Experience,* for instance, which I edited with my wife, we include many chapters by researchers in the United States as well as in Japan, Korea, Australia, and Europe, which show how similarly people around the world describe the most enjoyable times in their lives."

BIOGRAPHICAL/CRITICAL SOURCES:

PERIODICALS

Washington Post Book World, June 10, 1984.

*   *   *

CUMING, Geoffrey John   1917-1988

OBITUARY NOTICE—See index for *CA* sketch: Born September 9, 1917, in Gilston, Hertfordshire, England; died March 25, 1988, in Texas. Clergyman, administrator, editor, and author. An Anglican minister who served in Burnley and Billesdon, England, and a former vice-principal of St. John's College, Cuming was an expert on the Anglican liturgy. He was also greatly interested in recorded music. Cuming edited several volumes of *Studies in Church History* in addition to *The Durham Book* and *Prayers of the Eucharist: Early and Reformed.* His own writings include *The World's Encyclopaedia of Recorded Music, A History of Anglican Liturgy,* and *The Liturgy of St. Mark.*

OBITUARIES AND OTHER SOURCES:

PERIODICALS

Times (London), March 28, 1988.

*   *   *

CUMMINGS, Gary   1941(?)-1987

OBITUARY NOTICE: Born c. 1941; died of complications from melanoma (a type of skin cancer), October 31, 1987, in Chicago, Ill. Business executive, educator, and journalist. Working his way up from newspaper reporter to vice-president and general manager of the Chicago affiliate of Columbia

Broadcasting System (CBS-TV), Cummings was recognized as one of the most successful journalists to make the transition from newspapers to television. He began his career writing for United Press International in Concord, N.H., and in 1965 he joined the Chicago *American,* where he was a reporter and rewrite man. After joining CBS-TV's Chicago affiliate, WBBM-TV, as assistant news director in 1972, Cummings moved to WCBS-TV in New York in 1981. The next year he was named vice-president of the CBS Television Stations Division, and in 1984 he accepted the position of general manager of WBBM-TV. For his journalistic achievements, Cummings received a number of professional honors, including Emmy awards in 1974, 1980, and 1981. Following his resignation from the station in 1986, he joined the faculty of Medill School of Journalism as an associate professor and director of the broadcast division. He also wrote a monthly column for the *Washington Journalism Review.*

OBITUARIES AND OTHER SOURCES:

PERIODICALS

Chicago Tribune, November 2, 1987.
New York Times, November 3, 1987.

*   *   *

CUNEO, Ernest (L.)   1905-1988

OBITUARY NOTICE: Born in 1905 in East Rutherford, N.J.; died following a heart attack, March 1 (one source says March 2), 1988, in Washington, D.C. Lawyer, business owner, intelligence officer, military analyst, journalist, and author. Cuneo was probably best known for his ownership and administration of the North American Newspaper Alliance (NANA) from the mid-1950s to 1963. After his admission to the New York Bar in 1932, he moved to the Washington, D.C., area where he was a legal assistant to then Republican congressman and future New York City mayor Fiorello LaGuardia. Cuneo soon established a private law practice and from 1936 to 1940 was associate counsel to the Democratic National Committee. During World War II he served with the Office for Strategic Services as a liaison officer for the White House, the FBI, and British intelligence. He continued practicing law after the war and in the 1950s bought NANA, serving as the news service's president until he sold it in 1963. Cuneo, however, continued to work for the organization as a syndicated columnist and military analyst until 1980. He retired from practicing law the following year. His writings include *Science and History, Life With Fiorello: A Memoir,* and *Dynamics of World History.*

OBITUARIES AND OTHER SOURCES:

BOOKS

Who's Who in America, Supplement to 44th edition, Marquis, 1987.

PERIODICALS

Chicago Tribune, March 8, 1988.
New York Times, March 5, 1988.
Washington Post, March 3, 1988.

*   *   *

CUNEY, Waring
See CUNEY, William Waring

CUNEY, William Waring   1906-1976
(Waring Cuney)

PERSONAL: Born May 6, 1906, in Washington, D. C.; died June 30, 1976; son of Norris Cuney II and Madge Louise Baker. *Education:* Attended Howard University and Lincoln University; studied music at the New England Conservatory of Music in Boston and at the Conservatory in Rome.

CAREER: Writer. *Military service:* U. S. Army; served more than three years in the South Pacific as a technical sergeant during World War II; received Asiatic Pacific Theater Ribbon and three Bronze Stars.

AWARDS, HONORS: Poem ''No Images'' won first prize in *Opportunity* magazine contest in 1926.

WRITINGS:

POEMS

Chain Gang Chant, [Norman, Okla.], 1930.
Puzzles, selected and introduced by Paul Breman, woodcuts by Ru van Rossem, De Roos (Utrecht, Holland), 1960.
Storefront Church, P. Breman (London), 1973.

OTHER

(Editor under name Waring Cuney, with Langston Hughes and Bruce McM. Wright) *Lincoln University Poets: Centennial Anthology, 1854-1954*, foreword by Horace Mann Bond, introduction by J. Saunders Redding, Fine Editions, 1954.

Also author of several songs and broadsides, including *The Alley Cat Brushed His Whiskers, Two Poems: ''Darkness Hides His Throne'' [and] ''We Make Supplication,''* and *Women and Kitchens.*

Work represented in anthologies, including *American Negro Poetry, An Anthology of Magazine Verse for 1926, Negro Caravan, Caroling Dusk, Cavalcade, Book of American Negro Poetry, Negro Poets and Their Poems,* and *Beyond the Blues.* Contributor of poems and criticism to periodicals, including *Crisis, Harlem Quarterly, Negro Quarterly, Opportunity,* and *Black World.*

SIDELIGHTS: One of the poets of the Harlem Renaissance, a period of burgeoning black American literary activity during the 1920s and 1930s, Cuney is best known for his widely anthologized poem ''No Images.'' Though the rest of his work has been largely overlooked, a number of critics regard his poetry as both unprecedented and unsurpassed in its reflection of the language and tempo of the ghetto-dweller.

BIOGRAPHICAL/CRITICAL SOURCES:

BOOKS

Bontemps, Arna, *The Harlem Renaissance Remembered*, Dodd, 1972.
Dictionary of Literary Biography, Volume 51: *Afro-American Writers From the Harlem Renaissance to 1940*, Gale, 1987.

PERIODICALS

Black World, November, 1970, March, 1973.
Negro History Bulletin, February, 1948, March, 1948.*

*   *   *

CUNNINGHAM, Marilyn   1927-
(Lynn Carlock)

PERSONAL: Born April 18, 1927, in Boise, Idaho; daughter of Charles Henry (a logger) and Esther (a teacher; maiden name, Seaman) Carlock; married A. Bruce Cunningham (died February, 1980); children: Cheryl June Cunningham DeJong, A. Bryce, Aric B. *Education:* Attended Boise State University. *Politics:* Liberal. *Religion:* ''Humanist.''

ADDRESSES: Home and office—259 Oleander Dr., San Rafael, Calif. 94903. *Agent*—Robin Kaigh, 300 East 54th St., New York, N.Y. 10022.

CAREER: Held managerial positions for twenty years in Social Security Administration at Baltimore, Md., and San Francisco, Calif.; full-time writer, 1980—. Member of League of Women Voters' Tutor in Literacy Program.

MEMBER: Romance Writers of America, California Writers Club.

WRITINGS:

Paint the Thief Green (young adult novel), Academic Therapy Publications, 1985.
Nugget (young adult novel), Academic Therapy Publications, 1985.
(Under name Lynn Carlock) *Daughter of the Moon* (young adult romance novel), Silhouette, 1986.
The Thrill of His Kiss (romance novel), Dell, 1986.
Under the Northern Lights (romance novel), Dell, 1987.
Forbidden Passion (romance novel), Dell, 1987.

Contributor of more then a dozen stories and articles to magazines, including *True Story, Alaska, Secrets, Wooden Boat, True Love,* and *Pacific Sun.*

WORK IN PROGRESS: North Wind Rising, a romantic suspense novel; *Seasons of the Heart*, a historical saga set in Idaho.

SIDELIGHTS: Marilyn Cunningham told *CA:* ''I have traveled to nearly every state in the United States, to Canada, Mexico, and Australia, and I use these settings in my books. Central to my writing is my childhood in the mountains of Idaho, where I was exposed to a place and culture like few others that exist today: a close-knit community, isolation, involvement with nature, and the rhythms of the seasons. That background encouraged a strain of mysticism which surfaced early, balanced by the harsh realities of life in a logging community.

''I grew up during the Depression years, seeing the struggle of hard-working, intelligent people trying to escape the clutches of poverty. This helped to make me a lifelong liberal with a strong skepticism toward authority figures and institutions. Probably the writings that were most influential in shaping my philosophy were Ralph Waldo Emerson's essays, Thomas Paine's *Age of Reason*, and the works of Thomas Jefferson, including the Declaration of Independence.

''One of the changes that living has brought is to make me a little less political and a bit more cognizant of the enduring value of relationships—which is why I like writing romance novels.''

AVOCATIONAL INTERESTS: ''I spend much of my time in my home in Marin County, California, where I garden and hike when I'm not writing. I usually spend two months each summer in my cabin in the high country of Idaho, or traveling to Alaska to visit my two sons.''

CUSUMANO, Michael A. 1954-

PERSONAL: Born September 5, 1954, in Glen Ridge, N.J.; son of Michael and Mary (Fortunato) Cusumano. *Education:* Princeton University, A.B. (high honors), 1976; Harvard University, Ph.D., 1984.

ADDRESSES: Home—65C Dana St., Cambridge, Mass. 02138. *Office*—Alfred P. Sloan School of Management, Massachusetts Institute of Technology, Cambridge, Mass. 02139.

CAREER: Massachusetts Institute of Technology, Cambridge, assistant professor of management, 1986—.

MEMBER: Strategic Management Society, Japan Business History Society, Phi Beta Kappa.

AWARDS, HONORS: Princeton-in-Asia Teaching Fellow at International Christian University, Tokyo, 1976-78; Fulbright fellow, 1980-83; postdoctoral fellow at Harvard Business School, 1984-86.

WRITINGS:

The Japanese Automobile Industry: Technology and Management at Nissan and Toyota, Harvard University Press, 1985.

Contributor to periodicals, including *California Management Review.*

WORK IN PROGRESS: A study of software engineering management in the United States and Japan, focusing on the implementation of ''factory'' models.

BIOGRAPHICAL/CRITICAL SOURCES:

PERIODICALS

New York Times, April 2, 1986.

CUTRATE, Joe
See SPIEGELMAN, Art

*   *   *

CYR, Arthur 1945-

PERSONAL: Born March 1, 1945, in Los Angeles, Calif.; son of Irving Arthur and Frances Mary Cyr; married Betty Jean Totten; children: David Arthur, Thomas Harold, James Price. *Education:* University of California, Los Angeles, B.A., 1966, M.A., 1967; Harvard University, A.M., 1969, Ph.D., 1971.

ADDRESSES: Office—Chicago Council on Foreign Relations, 116 South Michigan Ave., Chicago, Ill. 60603.

CAREER: Ford Foundation, New York, N.Y., program officer in international and education/research divisions, 1971-74; University of California, Los Angeles, assistant professor of political science and administrator of international studies, 1974-76; Chicago Council on Foreign Relations, Chicago, Ill., program director, 1976—, vice-president, 1981—. Lecturer at University of Chicago and University of Illinois.

MEMBER: International Institute for Strategic Studies, American Political Science Association, New York Council on Foreign Relations, Phi Beta Kappa, University Club (Chicago), Arts Club, Economic Club, Quadrangle Club.

WRITINGS:

Liberal Party Politics in Britain, Transaction Books, 1977.
British Foreign Policy and the Atlantic Area, Holmes & Meier, 1979.
U.S. Foreign Policy and European Security, St. Martin's, 1987.

Contributor to journals.

WORK IN PROGRESS: Revising *Liberal Party Politics in Britain.*

D

DABYDEEN, David 1955-

PERSONAL: Born December 9, 1955, in Guyana; immigrated to England, 1969; son of Krishna Prasad and Vera Dabydeen. *Education:* Cambridge University, B.A. (with honors), 1978; University of London, Ph.D., 1981; postdoctoral study at Oxford University, 1983-87.

ADDRESSES: Home—London, England. *Office*—Wolfson College, Oxford University, Oxford OX2 6UD, England.

CAREER: Community education officer in Wolverhampton, England, 1982-84; University of Warwick, Coventry, England, lecturer in Caribbean studies, 1984-86.

MEMBER: Association for the Teaching of Caribbean, African, and Asian Literature (president, 1985-87), Society for Caribbean Studies (executive member), Black Media Research Committee (honorary consultant).

AWARDS, HONORS: Quiller-Couch Prize from Cambridge University, 1978, for poetry; resident fellowship from Yale University's Centre for British Art, 1982, and postdoctoral research fellowship from Oxford University, 1983; Commonwealth Poetry Prize, 1984, for *Slave Song*.

WRITINGS:

Slave Song (poems), Dangaroo Press, 1984.
Hogarth's Blacks: Images of Blacks in Eighteenth Century English Art, Dangaroo Press, 1985, University of Georgia Press, 1987.
(Editor and contributor) *The Black Presence in English Literature,* Manchester University Press, 1985.
Caribbean Literature: A Teacher's Handbook, Heinemann, 1986.
Hogarth and Walpoleian England, Swan Publications, 1988.

Also author of television program "Britain and Its Empire," 1986.

WORK IN PROGRESS: A poem collection, *Coolie Odyssey*.

SIDELIGHTS: Marking David Dabydeen's debut as a poet and earning him the 1984 Commonwealth Poetry Prize, the poem collection *Slave Song* was critically acclaimed for its passionate and revealing portrayal of life on the sugar plantations in Guyana and, in particular, its author's lyrical use of Guyanese Creole—a language derived from African, English, East Indian, French, and Spanish dialects. Reviewers such as Faustin Charles of the *Caribbean Times* praised *Slave Song*'s language as "raw, earthly, controlled and spun," and lauding Dabydeen for his rhythmic verse, the critic asserted that the "intensity of speech-patterns" places the reader "within the action of things. The poet's capacity to feel is near miraculous." Charles declared that Dabydeen is "convincing by his music, and most of all, he has kept the people's language as it should always be, a strong, living, imaginative expression." In what the reviewer labeled "a powerful piece of Caribbean writing," the Guyanese-born poet displays a concern for the social and political oppression of his country's peasant workers while evoking both the fullness and the despair of Caribbean culture.

In his introduction to *Slave Song*, Dabydeen proclaims that "the poems . . . (a jumble of fact and myth, past and present) are largely concerned with an exploration of the erotic energies of the colonial experience, ranging from a corrosive to a lyrical sexuality." Depicting the experience of black Guyanese canecutters degraded in their servitude to colonial white rule, the poet explores the passion, toil, and brutality of their existence. He achieves this largely through his use of the Creole dialect, which the author describes as "angry, crude, energetic." Stressing that his poems are meant to be read aloud in order for their tone to come through, Dabydeen maintains that he has "retained the full vulgarity of the language for it is a profound element in Guyanese life." And in his "recognition and expression of the uniqueness of the people, the particularity of their being," the poet additionally notes in his introduction that he employed the Guyanese Creole in *Slave Song* to express "the full experience of its users which is a very deep one, deep in suffering, cruelty, drunken merriment and tenderness."

Dabydeen further extols the cultural importance and value of blacks in a subsequent work, *Hogarth's Blacks: Images of Blacks in Eighteenth-Century English Art*. In the study, which *Times Literary Supplement* reviewer Roy Porter called a "revelation," Dabydeen explains the significance of the recurring presence of blacks in British artist William Hogarth's paintings. Although the eighteenth-century painter seemed to stereotypically portray blacks in such figures as the kneeling Sambo-like servant, Dabydeen, according to Porter, argues that "[Hogarth's] blacks weren't just 'invisible men' or conventional symbols. He meant their presence as contrasts to provoke, threaten and subvert.'' Dabydeen, Porter continued, believes that Hogarth intentionally incorporated bestial or unnatural images of blacks in his works in order to challenge the viewer, for the figures ''hold up the mirror to the barbarity of polite society,'' serving as emblems of the dark side of humanity. The reviewer assessed the author's explorations in *Hogarth's Blacks* as ''invigorating, his interpretation powerful and his judgment secure.'' He concluded that Dabydeen ''shows what can be achieved with sound historical research and a sharp pair of eyes.''

Another study of the significance of blacks in history is Dabydeen's *The Black Presence in English Literature*. A compilation of essays originally delivered by various authors at a 1982 conference Dabydeen organized in Wolverhampton, England, the work addresses the often-ignored contributions by and existence of black people in famous works of literature. ''Polemical rather than scholarly, [Dabydeen's] contributors aim to provoke a reappraisal of the literature taught in British schools by pointing out some of the gaps and mistaken assumptions in English studies today,'' expressed *Times Literary Supplement* reviewer Dennis Walder. Including Dabydeen's own essay dealing with slavery and commerce in eighteenth-century poetry, the book embraces discussions of black characters in Renaissance drama, the ''Afro-Black'' in nineteenth-century Australian literature, and the manipulation of Africa in contemporary adventure fiction, among others. The work was hailed as rich and instructive, and Walder noted that *The Black Presence in English Literature* ''does some justice'' to a timely subject that has ''received disappointingly little attention outside specialist circles.''

BIOGRAPHICAL/CRITICAL SOURCES:

BOOKS

Contemporary Literary Criticism, Volume 34, Gale, 1985.
Dabydeen, David, *Slave Song,* Dangaroo Press, 1984.

PERIODICALS

Caribbean Times, May 10, 1984, November 30, 1984.
Times Literary Supplement, September 13, 1985, June 13, 1986.

*   *   *

DALEY, Janet 1944-

PERSONAL: Born March 21, 1944, in Boston, Mass.; immigrated to England, 1965; daughter of Morris and Irma (Vandernoot) Klatskin; married Michael Daley (an artist), August 12, 1967; children: Emma, Melissa. *Education:* University of California, Berkeley, B.A., 1965; graduate study at University of London, 1966-69.

ADDRESSES: Home—East Barnet, England. *Office*—Royal College of Art, Kensington Gore, London S.W.7, England. *Agent*—Anthony Sheil Associates Ltd., 43 Doughty St., London WC1N 2LF, England.

CAREER: Lecturer at Kingston Polytechnic, University of London, and Open University, 1969-77; Royal College of Art, London, England, lecturer in cultural history, 1977—.

WRITINGS:

All Good Men (novel), Chatto & Windus, 1987.

Contributor of art criticism to *Arts Review, Art and Artist,* and *Studio International* and literary criticism to *Literary Review*

and *Times Educational Supplement;* contributor of articles to *Guardian, New Society,* London *Times,* and *London Magazine.*

WORK IN PROGRESS: Another novel.

*   *   *

DAMAS, Leon-Gontran 1912-1978

PERSONAL: Born March 28, 1912, in Cayenne, French Guiana; died January 23 (some sources say January 22), 1978, in Washington, D.C.; married wife, Marieth. *Education:* Attended the Universite de Paris in the early 1930s.

CAREER: Poet, 1934-78. Worked in various positions, including editor for the overseas department of Editions Fasquelles, co-founder of *L'Etudiant noir,* and researcher on African culture in the Caribbean and Brazil. Represented French Guiana in the French National Assembly, beginning in 1948, and represented the Societie Africanine de Culture of the United Nations Educational, Scientific, and Cultural Organization (UNESCO). Taught modern and African literature at Federal City College and Howard University in Washington, D.C.

AWARDS, HONORS: Made Officer of National Orders of Honor and Merit by the Republic of Haiti.

WRITINGS:

POETRY; EXCEPT AS NOTED

Pigments (includes ''The Black Man's Lament,'' ''They Came That Night,'' ''Sell Out,'' ''Blues,'' ''Reality,'' ''If Often,'' ''Whitewashed,'' ''Shine,'' ''Like the Legend,'' ''Obsession,'' ''There Are Nights,'' ''Position,'' *''Et Cetera,''* and ''Hiccups''), [Paris], 1937, revised edition, Presence Africaine, 1962 (also see below).
Veillees noires (short stories), 2nd edition, Stock, 1943.
(Editor) *Poetes d'expression francaise d'Afrique Noire, Madagascar, Reunion, Guadeloupe, Martinique, Indochine, Guyane: 1900-1945,* Seuil, 1947.
Poems negres sur des airs africains, GLM, 1948.
Graffiti, Seghers, 1952.
Black-Label, Gallimard, 1956.
African Songs of Love, War, Grief, and Abuse, translation by Miriam Koshland and Ulli Beier, illustrations by Georgina Betts, Mbari Publications, 1961.
Nevralgies, Presence Africaine, c. 1965 (also see below).
(With Claude Souffrant, Roger Bastide, and Peter D. Thomas) *Hommage a Jean Price-Mars* [and] *A Touch of Negritude* (nonfiction; the former by Damas, Souffrant, and Bastide, the latter by Thomas) Presence Africaine, 1969.
Pigments [and] *Nevralgies,* Presence Africaine, 1972 (also see above).

Contributor of poems to French periodicals, including *Esprit.*

SIDELIGHTS: In the 1930s, Leon-Gontran Damas banded together with fellow French-speaking black writers Aime Cesaire and Leopold Sedar Senghor in Paris to form the literary movement that later became known as Negritude. They founded the journal *L'Etudiant noir* (title means, ''The Black Student'') as a forum for Negritude, which derived some of its ideals from the Harlem Renaissance in the United States but expressed its emphasis on black culture in French. Damas was the first of the movement's founders to publish a book of poems—his famous *Pigments,* which came out in 1937. In addition to producing several other volumes of poetry and a collection of short stories entitled *Veillees noires,* Damas represented his native French Guiana in the French National Assembly for a brief period before coming to the United States to teach literature at the college level in Washington, D.C.

"*Pigments* is an attack, a cry of pain, an anguished inventory of the personal loss of Africa, of Black identity, of discomfort and revolt at the inauthenticity of being 'whitewashed,'" asserted critic Ellen Conroy Kennedy in *Black World*. The poems in *Pigments* range from the very specific, such as "*Et Cetera*," which urges the Senegalese soldiers fighting for the French army to turn on the French and fight for their own independence, to those, like "The Black Man's Lament," "Sell Out," and "Shine," which Kennedy claimed "could well have been written by a Black American today." Still other pieces, such as "Obsession," "There Are Nights," and "Position," have more universal, non-racial themes—depression and despair. Kennedy praised the "blunt, dry, vivid style" of *Pigments*, concluding that "marked by fresh images, unashamedly plain language, staccato rhythms and acridly witty puns, Damas'[s] short poems lay bare their author's often violent rejection of white European [civilization]."

BIOGRAPHICAL/CRITICAL SOURCES:

BOOKS

Racine, Daniel L., editor, *Leon-Gontran Damas, 1912-1978: Founder of Negritude; A Memorial Casebook*, University Press of America, 1979.

PERIODICALS

Black World, January, 1972.*

* * *

DAMATA, Ted   1909(?)-1988

OBITUARY NOTICE: Born c. 1909; died following a lingering illness, May 22, 1988, in Elk Grove Village, Ill. Journalist. A sports reporter in Chicago for more than sixty years, Damata was known for his coverage of professional hockey. He began his career in 1929 working for the Chicago *Daily News,* later becoming an assistant sports editor for the former *Chicago Daily Times.* When the *Times* and the *Chicago Sun* merged in the 1940s, Damata joined the staff of the *Chicago Tribune.* He was respected for his dedication and objectivity, and in 1984 he was inducted into the Hockey Hall of Fame in Toronto, Canada, for his reporting and writing.

OBITUARIES AND OTHER SOURCES:

PERIODICALS

Chicago Tribune, May 24, 1988.

* * *

DANCER, J. B.
See HARVEY, John (Barton)

* * *

DANDRIDGE, Ray G.
See DANDRIDGE, Raymond Garfield

* * *

DANDRIDGE, Raymond Garfield   1882-1930
(Ray G. Dandridge)

PERSONAL: Born in 1882 in Cincinnati, Ohio; died February 24, 1930; son of Ellen C. Dandridge. *Education:* Attended high school in Cincinnati, Ohio.

ADDRESSES: Home—Cincinnati, Ohio.

CAREER: Poet. House painter and decorator; solicited phone orders for Roger Kemper Rogan's coal company.

WRITINGS:

POETRY

(Under name Ray G. Dandridge) *Penciled Poems,* Powell & White, 1917.
The Poet and Other Poems, Powell & White, 1920, reprinted, AMS Press, 1975.
(Contributor) Robert T. Kerlin, *Negro Poets and Their Poems,* Associated Publishers, 1923.
(Contributor) Newman Ivey White and Walter Clinton Jackson, editors, *An Anthology of Verse by American Negroes,* Trinity College Press, 1924.
Zalka Peetruza and Other Poems, McDonald, 1928.
(Contributor) James Weldon Johnson, editor, *The Book of American Negro Poetry,* expanded edition, Harcourt, 1931.
(Contributor) Robert B. Eleazer, *Singers in the Dawn: A Brief Anthology of American Negro Poetry,* Conference on Education and Race Relations, 1934.

Poetry also represented in anthology *The Poetry of Black America* and in periodicals.

OTHER

Literary editor for *Cincinnati Journal.*

SIDELIGHTS: Most known for his poetry written in the black dialect tradition, Raymond Garfield Dandridge aligned himself with other Harlem Renaissance writers of the 1920s whose poetry expressed discovery, affirmation, achievement, and opportunity for their race. After suffering paralysis of both legs and his right arm from a stroke in 1912, Dandridge taught himself to write verse with his left hand while lying on his back. It is said that his poetry was, perhaps, born out of a courageous spirit to give his thoughts the movement his body had been denied. Optimistic in spirit, the poet was attracted to the charm, humor, and spontaneity of humble people, incorporating their situations and especially the rhythms of their speech into such poems as "De Drum Majah," "Sprin' Fevah," and "Close Mouf." Although his dialect poetry was sometimes considered imitative and erratic, Dandridge's work was popular because of the poet's good-natured approach to life and avoidance of life's more difficult aspects. Dandridge was also able to exhibit the racial protest and militant vigor that marked the 1920s in such later poems as "Time to Die," "Supplication, Brother Mine," and "Awake and Forward." Although he was never considered a great poet such as contemporaries Paul Laurence Dunbar or Alain Locke, his work is said to reflect the democratic, optimistic, and proud spirit characteristic of the black race of his era.

BIOGRAPHICAL/CRITICAL SOURCES:

BOOKS

Dictionary of Literary Biography, Volume 51: *Afro-American Writers From the Harlem Renaissance to 1940,* Gale, 1987.*

* * *

DANIEL, Lee
See REID, Daniel P. (Jr.)

DANIELS, Douglas Henry 1943-

PERSONAL: Born October 12, 1943, in Chicago, Ill.; son of
Henry E. (a worker) and Eleanora W. (a seamstress) Daniels;
children: two. *Education:* University of Chicago, B.A., 1964;
University of California, Berkeley, M.A., 1969, Ph.D., 1975.

ADDRESSES: Office—Department of Black Studies, University of California, Santa Barbara, Calif. 93106.

CAREER: University of Texas at Austin, assistant professor
of U.S. history, 1975-79; University of California, Santa Barbara, assistant professor, 1979-83, associate professor, 1983-
87, professor of history and black studies, 1987—.

MEMBER: American Historical Association, Organization of
American Historians, American Studies Association, Sonneck
Society, Association for the Study of Afro-American Life and
History.

AWARDS, HONORS: Fellow of Ford Foundation, 1971-73,
National Endowment for the Humanities, 1975, John Hay
Whitney Foundation, 1974-75, and Danforth Foundation, 1978-
83; fellow of Smithsonian Institution, 1980-81; Mellon fellow,
1982-83.

WRITINGS:

*Pioneer Urbanites: A Social and Cultural History of Black
San Francisco,* Temple University Press, 1980.

*WORK IN PROGRESS: Blue Lester: The Life and Times of
Pres Young, Saxophone Stylist,* publication expected in 1990.

*   *   *

DARBY, Edwin Wheeler 1922-

PERSONAL: Born January 7, 1922, in Oakland, Md.; son of
John Dade and Nell (Bosley) Darby; married Susan E. Kroening, March 14, 1970; children: (from previous marriage) Ann
Wheeler, John Dade; (from second marriage) George Kroening. *Education:* Ohio University, B.S., 1942.

ADDRESSES: Home—2703 West Logan Blvd., Chicago, Ill.
60647. *Office*—Chicago *Sun-Times,* Chicago, Ill. 60611.

CAREER: Time, New York, N.Y., White House correspondent, 1948-55, Midwest correspondent, 1956-58; Chicago *Sun-Times,* Chicago, Ill., financial editor and columnist, 1958—.
Midwest correspondent for *Fortune,* 1956-58.

MEMBER: Tavern Club, Attic Club.

AWARDS, HONORS: Marshall Field Award, 1974; Gerald Loeb
Award for Distinguished Business and Financial Journalism
from Graduate School of Management at University of California, Los Angeles, 1975.

WRITINGS:

The Fortune Builders, Doubleday, 1986.

*   *   *

DARRELL, R(obert) D(onaldson) 1903-1988

OBITUARY NOTICE: Born December 13, 1903, in Newton,
Mass.; died following a stroke, May 1, 1988. Music critic,
editor, publisher, and author. As one of the first critics to focus
primarily on electronically recorded music, Darrell became

nationally known for his expertise in the field of high fidelity
sound. He studied music at Harvard University and the New
England Conservatory before co-founding *Phonograph Monthly
Review* in 1927; Darrell was the sole music critic for the publication and in 1930 became its editor and publisher. After
moving to New York and writing reviews for *Music Lovers'
Guide,* he worked as record researcher and consultant for the
Gramophone Shop beginning in 1934, subsequently becoming
the editor of *The Gramophone Shop Supplement* from 1937 to
1939. Darrell's 1936 book, *Gramophone Shop Encyclopedia
of Recorded Music,* was the first comprehensive discography
published in the United States and, as such, earned its author
nationwide recognition. He continued to work as editor for
various publications and, specializing in classical music, contributed reviews to magazines, including *down beat, Saturday
Review,* and *High Fidelity,* where he was a columnist from
1954 to 1987. His other books on music include *The Highroad
to Musical Enjoyment, Schirmer's Guide to Books on Music
and Musicians: A Practical Bibliography, Good Listening,* and
Tapes in Review.

OBITUARIES AND OTHER SOURCES:

BOOKS

Current Biography, H. W. Wilson, 1955, June, 1988.
Who's Who in America, 44th edition, Marquis, 1986.

PERIODICALS

New York Times, May 7, 1988.

*   *   *

DASENBROCK, Reed Way 1953-

PERSONAL: Born September 18, 1953, in Detroit, Mich. *Education:* McGill University, B.A. (with honors), 1974; Oxford
University, B.Phil., 1977; Johns Hopkins University, M.A.,
1980, Ph.D., 1982.

ADDRESSES: Office—Department of English, Box 3E, New
Mexico State University, Las Cruces, N.M. 88003.

CAREER: New Mexico State University, Las Cruces, member
of English faculty, 1981—.

WRITINGS:

*The Literary Vorticism of Ezra Pound and Wyndham Lewis:
Towards the Condition of Painting,* Johns Hopkins University Press, 1986.
(Editor) Wyndham Lewis, *The Art of Being Ruled,* Black Sparrow Press, 1988.
(Editor) *Redrawing the Lines: Deconstruction, Analytical Philosophy, and Literary Theory,* University of Minnesota
Press, 1988.

*   *   *

DASH, Irene G(olden)

PERSONAL: Born in New York, N.Y.; daughter of Samuel
and Bella (Lasker) Golden; married Martin Dash; children:
Deborah Dash Moore, Deena Dash Kushner. *Education:* Beaver College, B.A.; Columbia University, M.A. and Ph.D.,
1972.

ADDRESSES: Office—Hunter College of the City University
of New York, 695 Park Ave., New York, N.Y. 10021.

CAREER: Queensborough Community College of the City
University of New York, Bayside, N.Y., lecturer in English,

1970-71; Hunter College of the City University of New York, New York, N.Y., lecturer, 1972-74, adjunct assistant professor of English, 1974-86, adjunct professor, 1986—. Co-chair of Shakespeare seminar at Columbia University, 1985-88.

MEMBER: Shakespeare Association of America, American Society for Eighteenth-Century Studies, American Name Society, National Council of Teachers of English, American Society for Theatre Research, Northeast Modern Language Association (director of executive council, 1985-88).

AWARDS, HONORS: National Endowment for the Humanities, fellowship, 1983, travel grant, 1986.

WRITINGS:

(Contributor) Lina Mainiero, editor, *Guide to American Women's Writings*, Volume II, Ungar, 1979.
(Contributor) E. M. Broner and Cathy Davidson, editors, *The Lost Tradition: Mothers and Daughters in Literature*, Ungar, 1980.
(Contributor) Carolyn Ruth Swift Lenz and others, editors, *The Woman's Part: Feminist Criticism of Shakespeare*, University of Illinois Press, 1980.
Wooing, Wedding, and Power: Women in Shakespeare's Plays, Columbia University Press, 1981.
(Contributor) Irene Thompson and Audrey Roberts, editors, *The Road Retaken: Women Reenter the Academy*, Modern Language Association of America, 1985.

Contributor to literature journals.

WORK IN PROGRESS: A book, tentatively titled *To Thine Own Self Be True: Shakespeare's Women in Text and Theatrical Context*, publication expected in 1989.

SIDELIGHTS: Irene G. Dash told *CA:* "I guess I've always been a feminist without realizing it. However, the way I became involved in writing on women in William Shakespeare's plays grew out of an assignment in graduate school concerning 'The Winter's Tale.' In conflict with contemporary mythos critics, I perceived the drama's women characters to be amazingly lifelike, not symbols at all. As strong women, they appealed to me. Why had this work so seldom been performed? Researching its stage history in the eighteenth century, I discovered that the women's roles had been condensed, shifted, and transformed. This led to my current interest—the influence of stage history and patriarchal values on criticism of Shakespeare's plays."

*   *   *

DAUGHERTY, Carroll R(oop)   1900-1988

OBITUARY NOTICE: Born December 3, 1900, in Annville, Pa.; died of liver cancer, May 11, 1988, in La Jolla, Calif. Economist, educator, labor arbitrator, and author. A strong advocate of peaceful labor-management relations, Daugherty was perhaps best known for the noncontributory pension plan he helped devise for steel employees in 1949. He began his academic career at Mercersburg Academy in Pennsylvania, going on to teach at such institutions as the Wharton School of Finance, the universities of Alabama and Pittsburgh, and New York's Hunter College. He joined the staff of Northwestern University in 1946 as professor of business economics, serving in that capacity until 1968, when he was named professor emeritus.

Concurrent with his teaching positions was Daugherty's prolific career as a consultant and adviser to several governmental economic and labor bodies. Among other posts, he served as the chief economist of the Bureau of Labor Statistics and of the wage and hour division of the U.S. Department of Labor, and his job as wage stabilization director of the War Labor Board from 1942 to 1945 is considered his most important wartime work. In 1949 Daugherty was appointed chairman of President Truman's fact-finding committee that headed the contract dispute between the nation's sixty-four steel companies and the United Steelworkers of America. Daugherty proposed a plan involving management-paid pensions and welfare benefits for workers, and a strike was avoided. He subsequently was a referee for the National Railroad Adjustment Board and served as an arbitrator for numerous other labor disputes. Among his writings are *The Development of Horsepower Equipment in the United States, Labor Problems in American Industry, Labor Under the N.R.A., The Economics of the Iron and Steel Industry,* and *Principles of Political Economy.*

OBITUARIES AND OTHER SOURCES:

BOOKS

Current Biography, H. W. Wilson, 1949, June, 1988.
Who's Who in the World, 6th edition, Marquis, 1982.

PERIODICALS

New York Times, May 13, 1988.

*   *   *

DAUNTON, M(artin) J(ames)   1949-

PERSONAL: Born February 7, 1949, in Cardiff, Wales; son of Ronald J. (a bank official) and Dorothy (a housewife; maiden name, Bellett) Daunton; married Claire Gobbi (an archivist), January 7, 1984. *Education:* University of Nottingham, B.A., 1970; University of Kent at Canterbury, Ph.D., 1973.

ADDRESSES: Home—88 Park Ave. S., London N8 8LS, England. *Office*—University College London, Gower St., London WC1E 6BT, England.

CAREER: University of Durham, Durham, England, lecturer in economic history, 1973-79; University College London, London, England, lecturer, 1979-85, reader in history, 1985—.

MEMBER: Royal Historical Society (treasurer, 1986—), Economic History Society (member of council, 1985—).

WRITINGS:

Coal Metropolis: Cardiff, 1870-1914, Leicester University Press, 1977.
House and Home in the Victorian City: Working Class Housing, 1850-1914, Edward Arnold, 1983.
Councillors and Tenants, Leicester University Press, 1985.
Royal Mail: The Post Office Since 1840, Athlone Press, 1986.
A Property Owning Democracy? Faber, 1987.

Contributor to economic and history journals. Assistant editor of *Economic History Review.*

WORK IN PROGRESS: A social history of the city of London, 1810-1890, publication by Oxford University Press expected in 1989; an international study of urban architecture in the nineteenth century, publication by Leicester University Press expected in 1990; a textbook on British economic history from 1700 to 1914, publication by Oxford University Press expected in 1991.

SIDELIGHTS: M. J. Daunton told CA: "My main interest has been in the interface between social and architectural history, which has informed three of my books. This is to extend the history of the built environment from a simple description of design and style, to consider how it was affected by, and in turn influenced, the life it contained. Although this focus continues, I am now involved in considering the historical background to certain current concerns in Britain: the overturning of the housing market and the deregulation of the city [London's financial community]."

Daunton's first book, Coal Metropolis, was welcomed by critics as a much-needed and long overdue history of the Welsh city of Cardiff. The author considered the economic development of the city since 1870 and its social evolution as a city, extending his research into the areas of social culture and politics. Kenneth O. Morgan wrote in the Times Literary Supplement: "The result is impressive—a precise, fully documented, lucidly written and beautifully illustrated book which will be of great value and interest to historians . . . of the British urban experience."

House and Home in the Victorian City enjoyed a similar reception. In a Times Literary Supplement review, P. J. Waller commented that Daunton's second book "combines very different perspectives to illuminate a complex topic: those of physical form, class culture, distinctive local habit, and particular personal preference." The author analyzes various approaches to planning and housing, and studies the nineteenth-century trends which resulted in sweeping changes in the relationships between public and private space. Daunton surveys the types of housing that characterized various localities, examines housing from the perspective of rents and investment values, and considers the political issues involved in the relationships of landlords to tenants and public officials. According to Waller, "Daunton integrates the subject better than any historian before him," providing "a more complete picture than we have yet had."

BIOGRAPHICAL/CRITICAL SOURCES:

PERIODICALS

Times Literary Supplement, March 4, 1977, January 20, 1984, November 29, 1985.

*   *   *

DAVIS, (William) Allison   1902-1983

PERSONAL: Born October 14 (some sources say October 10), 1902, in Washington, D.C.; died following heart surgery, November 21, 1983, in Chicago, Ill.; son of John Abraham and Gabrielle Dorothy (Beale) Davis; married Alice Elizabeth Stubbs, June 23, 1929 (died, 1966); married Lois L. Mason, January 7, 1969; children: (first marriage) Allison Stubbs, Gordon Jamison. Education: Williams College, A.B., 1924; Harvard University, M.A. (English), 1925, M.A. (anthropology), 1932; graduate study at London School of Economics and Political Science, London, 1932-33; University of Chicago, Ph.D., 1942.

CAREER: Harvard University, Cambridge, Mass., co-director of field research in social anthropology, 1933-35; Dillard University, New Orleans, La., professor of anthropology, 1935-38; Yale University Institute of Human Relations, New Haven, Conn., research associate in psychology, 1938-39; University of Chicago, Chicago, Ill., research associate and assistant professor of human development at Center on Child Develop-

ment, 1939-42, assistant professor, 1942-47, associate professor, 1947-48, professor of education, 1948-70, John Dewey Distinguished Service Professor, 1970-78, retired as professor emeritus, 1978. Member of President's Commission on Civil Rights, 1966-67; vice-chairman for Commission on Manpower Retraining for U.S. Department of Labor, 1968-72; director of Great Books Foundation, beginning in 1970. Lecturer at Harvard University, Smith College, University of Pittsburgh, University of Wisconsin, and University of Rochester.

MEMBER: American Academy of Arts and Sciences (first fellow elected from the field of education), American Psychiatric Association, Center for Advanced Study in the Behavioral Sciences (fellow, 1959-60), Phi Beta Kappa, Sigma Xi, Phi Delta Kappa.

AWARDS, HONORS: Elected George E. Miller Distinguished Professor at University of Illinois, 1965; elected Prentiss M. Brown Distinguished Service Professor at Albion College, 1970; elected John Dewey Distinguished Service Professor at University of Chicago, 1970; Teachers College Medal from Columbia University, 1977, for distinguished service in education; Solomon Carter Fuller award from American Psychiatric Association, 1977; grants from Spencer Foundation, 1978-80 and 1981-82.

WRITINGS:

(With John Dollard) Children of Bondage: The Personality Development of Negro Youth in the Urban South, American Council on Education, 1940, special educational edition, 1956.
(With Burleigh B. Gardner and Mary R. Gardner) Deep South: A Social Anthropological Study of Caste and Class, directed by W. Lloyd Warner, University of Chicago Press, 1941, abridged edition, with foreword by James W. Silver, 1965, reprinted, University of California Press, 1988.
(With Robert J. Havighurst) Father of the Man: How Your Child Gets His Personality, Houghton, 1947.
Social-Class Influences Upon Learning, Harvard University Press, 1948.
(With Kenneth Eells) Davis-Eells Games, World Book, 1953.
(With Eells) Davis-Eells Test of General Intelligence or Problem-Solving Ability: Directions for Administering and Scoring, World Book, 1953.
(With Eells) Davis-Eells Test of General Intelligence or Problem-Solving Ability: Manual, World Book, 1953.
Psychology of the Child in the Middle Class, University of Pittsburgh Press, 1960.
(With Benjamin S. Bloom and Robert Hess) Compensatory Education for Cultural Deprivation, Department of Education, University of Chicago, c. 1964.
(With Hess) Relationships Between Achievement in High School, College, and Occupation: A Follow-up Study, University of Chicago Press, 1965.
Leadership, Love, and Aggression, Harcourt, c. 1983.

Also author of The Motivation of the Underprivileged Worker, The Relation Between Color Caste and Economic Stratification in Two "Black" Plantation Counties, and, with J. J. G. St. Clair Drake, The Negro Church and Associations in the Lower South: Research Memorandum [and] The Negro Church and Associations in Chicago. Supervised production of Intelligence and Cultural Differences: A Study of Cultural Learning and Problem-Solving, by Kenneth Walter Eells and others. Contributor to newspapers, journals, and magazines.

SIDELIGHTS: Allison Davis was a respected psychologist, social anthropologist, and educator. As assistant professor at the University of Chicago beginning in 1939, Davis was one of the first blacks to hold a full-time teaching position at a major northern university. In 1970 he was named John Dewey Distinguished Service Professor by the University of Chicago, and eight years later he retired as professor emeritus. Many of his writings, including *Children of Bondage: The Personality Development of Negro Youth in the Urban South, Psychology of the Child in the Middle Class,* and *Compensatory Education for Cultural Deprivation,* reflect the author's interest in the psychological development and educational opportunities of children in various social and economic classes.

One of Davis's first works, co-authored by Burleigh B. Gardner and Mary R. Gardner, was the 1941 *Deep South: A Social Anthropological Study of Caste and Class.* The book details the authors' observations and conclusions about the lives of black and white residents in a small southern town. Social psychologist John Dollard determined in *American Anthropologist* that "there is no other single book which does such an excellent job of portraying the social and economic systems of a community," and renowned anthropologist Margaret Mead predicted in 1941 that *Deep South* would "prove an effective background for the kind of thinking which leads to social change." Although the analysis was limited to only one community, stated L. C. Copeland in *American Journal of Sociology,* "the series of studies represented by [*Deep South*] bids fair to extend our knowledge of culture as a whole and of society as a functioning system."

In his 1948 study *Social-Class Influences Upon Learning,* Davis challenged the validity of intelligence tests, asserting that children from lower-class families consistently scored lower than those from middle-class families not because of an intelligence difference, but because the tests were biased toward middle-class culture and educational methods. His findings prompted a re-evaluation of teaching and testing procedures and the development of learning programs such as Head Start for economically disadvantaged children.

In his last book, *Leadership, Love, and Aggression,* Davis analyzes the lives and accomplishments of four prominent black men: Frederick Douglass, W. E. B. Du Bois, Richard Wright, and Martin Luther King, Jr. Citing anger as a common motivating factor in the men's lives, Davis demonstrates how each transformed the negative emotion into positive action. Calling *Leadership, Love, and Aggression* "an extraordinary piece of research," a reviewer in *West Coast Review of Books* stated: "This work is more than a psychobiography of the four but is also a descriptive analysis of the suffering of the American Black at the hands of the government and the larger society."

BIOGRAPHICAL/CRITICAL SOURCES:

PERIODICALS

American Anthropologist, October, 1942.
American Journal of Sociology, November, 1942.
New York Herald Tribune Books, December 7, 1941.
West Coast Review of Books, November, 1983.

OBITUARIES:

PERIODICALS

Chicago Tribune, November 24, 1983.
Newsweek, December 5, 1983.

New York Times, November 22, 1983.
Washington Post, November 23, 1983.*

* * *

DAVIS, Charles T(witchell) 1918-1981

PERSONAL: Born April 29, 1918, in Hampton, Va.; died in 1981; married; children: two. *Education:* Dartmouth College, A.B., 1939; University of Chicago, A.M., 1942; New York University, Ph.D., 1951.

CAREER: New York University, New York, N.Y., began as instructor, became assistant professor of English, 1948-55; Princeton University, Princeton, N.J., assistant professor, 1955-61; Pennsylvania State University, University Park, Pa., began as associate professor, became professor, 1961-70; University of Iowa, Iowa City, professor of English, 1970-76; Yale University, New Haven, Conn., professor of English and chairman of Afro-American studies, 1972-81, master of Calhoun College, 1973-81. Chairman of the Senate Committeee on Student Affairs at Pennsylvania State University during the 1960s; member of supervisory committee, English Institute, 1962-65; Fulbright professor at the University of Turin, 1966-67; fellow, Center for Advanced Study in Behavioral Science in Stanford, Calif., 1976-77; member of advisory council, Center of Independent Study in New Haven, 1977-81; member of board of trustees, National Humanities Center in Research Triangle Park, N.C., 1978-81; member of board, State of Connecticut's academic awards, 1979-81.

MEMBER: Modern Language Association of America, American Studies Association, Society for the Study of Southern Literature.

AWARDS, HONORS: Rockefeller Humanities Fellowship.

WRITINGS:

(With Gay Wilson Allen) *Walt Whitman's Poems: Selections With Critical Aids,* New York University Press, 1955.
(Editor) E. A. Robinson, *Selected Early Poems and Letters,* Holt, 1960.
(Editor) Lucy Larcom, *A New England Girlhood,* Corinth Books, 1961.
(Editor) *On Being Black: Writings by Afro-Americans From Frederick Douglass to the Present,* Fawcett, 1970.
(With Michel Fabre) *Richard Wright: A Primary Bibliography,* G. K. Hall, 1982.
Black Is the Color of the Cosmos: Essays on Afro-American Literature and Culture, 1942-1981, edited by Henry Louis Gates, Jr., foreword by A. Bartlett Giamatti, Garland Publishing, 1982.
(Editor with Gates) *The Slave's Narrative,* Oxford University Press, 1985.

WORK IN PROGRESS: The Shaping of the Afro-American Literary Tradition, a two-volume history, left unfinished at time of death.

SIDELIGHTS: Charles T. Davis, professor of English and chairman of the Afro-American studies department at Yale University for the last years of his life, had become one of the most influential scholars of black American literature by the time of his death in 1981. Also an expert on nineteenth-century white American authors such as poet Walt Whitman, Davis is now best known for his posthumously published works—his collection of writings on black literature and culture, *Black Is the Color of the Cosmos,* and a compilation of critical essays he edited with Henry Louis Gates, Jr., *The Slave's Narrative.*

Lauded as "a fine critical mind" by reviewer Peter Nazareth in *World Literature Today,* Davis was mourned by Ishmael Reed in the *Yale Review* as "the critic of tomorrow," whose "biculturalism, which enabled him to move comfortably through both black and white American literary and cultural traditions," would be missed.

Black Is the Color of the Cosmos discusses many issues in the field of black literature with "original insight and clarity," according to Reed. Davis opines on the relation of the 1960s Black Arts Movement to nineteenth-century American romanticism, asserts the precedence of black lecturer and writer Frederick Douglass's *Narrative* over those published by most other former slaves, and declares that Charles Chestnutt—one of the first black novelists to be published in the United States—produced an "achievement in fiction . . . superior to that of any other Negro artist until the time of the Harlem Renaissance." Davis also explores the Harlem Renaissance itself, and holds forth on the work of later black authors Richard Wright, Ralph Ellison, and James Baldwin. To these and other writers, "he brings a superior intelligence and the perspectives of a sophisticated humanist," summed reviewer P. Butcher in *World Literature Today.* Davis's work was perceived by some, however, as too greatly influenced by white, Western cultural tradition. "When Davis suggests the appropriateness of reading [authors] Gwndolyn Brooks and Robert Hayden on Western grounds," complained critic R. Baxter Miller in *Black American Literature Forum,* "he hardly considers any other way of reading to be possible."

The Slave's Narrative, which Davis edited with Gates, was labeled "an impressive collection" by Frances Smith Foster in *The New York Times Book Review,* who upheld "the book's rightful claim as a contribution to the re-evaluation of slave narratives." The essays which Davis and Gates compiled address issues such as the literary and historical merits of autobiographical accounts by former slaves. The book also includes reviews published shortly after the narratives themselves, and moved critic William L. Andrews to conclude in *Black American Literature Forum:* "It is unlikely that any single collection of essays could do greater justice than *The Slave's Narrative* has to the breadth, vitality, and untapped potential of this topic and the discourse it has generated."

BIOGRAPHICAL/CRITICAL SOURCES:

BOOKS

Davis, Charles T., *Black Is the Color of the Cosmos: Essays on Afro-American Literature and Culture, 1942-1981,* Garland Publishing, 1982.

PERIODICALS

Black American Literature Forum, winter, 1984, spring, 1986.
New York Times Book Review, July 7, 1985.
World Literature Today, summer, 1983, autumn, 1983.
Yale Review, summer, 1983.*

* * *

DAVIS, Frank Marshall 1905-1987

PERSONAL: Born December 31, 1905, in Arkansas City, Kan.; died July 26, 1987, in Honolulu, Hawaii; married; children: Lynn, Beth, Jeanne, Jill, Mark. *Education:* Attended Friends University, 1923; attended Kansas State Agricultural College (now Kansas State University of Agricultural and Applied Science), 1924-27, 1929.

CAREER: Worked for various newspapers in Illinois, including the *Chicago Evening Bulletin, Whip,* and *Gary American,* 1927-29; *Atlanta Daily World,* Atlanta, Ga., editor and cofounder, 1931-34; Associated Negro Press, Chicago, Ill., executive editor, 1935-47; *Chicago Star,* Chicago, executive editor, 1946-48; owned wholesale paper business in Honolulu, Hawaii, beginning c. 1948. Served as a jazz radio disc jockey in the early 1940s. Authored weekly column for *Honolulu Record.* Toured black colleges as a lecturer, 1973.

MEMBER: League of American Writers, Allied Arts Guild, Southside Chicago Writers Group.

AWARDS, HONORS: Julius Rosenwald Foundation grant, 1937.

WRITINGS:

Black Man's Verse (poems; includes "Giles Johnson, Ph.D.," "Lynched [Symphonic Interlude for Twenty-One Selected Instruments]," "Mojo Mike's Beer Garden," "Cabaret," and "Ebony Under Granite"), Black Cat, 1935.
I Am the American Negro (poems; includes "I Am the American Negro," "Flowers of Darkness," "To One Who Would Leave Me," "Awakening," "Come to Me," "Modern Man—The Superman: A Song of Praise for Hearst, Hitler, Mussolini, and the Munitions Makers," "'Mancipation Day," "Onward Christian Soldiers," "Christ Is a Dixie Nigger," "Note Left by a Suicide," "Ebony Under Granite," and "Frank Marshall Davis: Writer"), Black Cat, 1937.
Through Sepia Eyes (poems; includes "Chicago Skyscrapers," "To Those Who Sing America," "Life Is a Woman," and "Coincidence"), Black Cat, 1938.
47th Street: Poems (includes "47th Street," "Pattern for Conquest," "Egotistic Runt," "Tenement Room," "Black Weariness," "Snapshots of the Cotton South," "Peace Quiz for America," "For All Common People," "War Zone," "Nothing Can Stop the People," "Peace Is a Fragile Cup," and "Self-Portrait"), Decker, 1948.
Awakening, and Other Poems, Black Cat, 1978.

Also author of poem "Chicago's Congo" and of a volume of poetry entitled *Jazz Interlude,* 1985; author of the unpublished manuscript "That Incredible Waikiki Jungle." Poems published in anthologies, including *The Negro Caravan,* Dryden, 1942; *Kaleidoscope: Poems by American Negro Poets,* Harcourt, 1967; *Black Voices: An Anthology of Afro-American Literature,* New American Library, 1968; *The Poetry of the Negro, 1746-1970,* Anchor Books, 1970; *Black Insights,* Ginn, 1971; *Understanding the New Black Poetry,* Morrow, 1973; and *The New Negro Renaissance: An Anthology,* Holt, 1975. Contributor to periodicals, including *National, Light and Heebie Jeebies,* and *Voices.*

SIDELIGHTS: Frank Marshall Davis's poetry "not only questioned social ills in his own time but also inspired blacks in the politically charged 1960s," according to John Edgar Tidwell in the *Dictionary of Literary Biography.* Davis, who has been compared to poets such as Walt Whitman and Carl Sandburg, published his first volume, *Black Man's Verse,* in 1935. The book met with much applause from critics, including Harriet Monroe, who concluded in *Poetry* that its author was "a poet of authentic inspiration, who belongs not only among the best of his race, but who need not lean upon his race for recognition as an impassioned singer with something to say." Davis concerned himself with portraying black life, protesting racial inequalities, and promoting black pride. The poet described his work thus in the poem "Frank Marshall Davis: Writer" from his *I Am the American Negro:* "When I wrote / I dipped my pen / In the crazy heart / Of mad America."

Davis grew up in Arkansas City, Kansas, surrounded by racism. Tidwell reports that when the poet was five years old he was nearly killed by some older white children who had heard stories of lynchings and wanted to try one for themselves. The result of this incident and others was that Davis hated whites in his youth. He gained some relief, according to Tidwell, when he left the prejudiced, small-town atmosphere of Arkansas City in 1923 to attend Friends University in Wichita; he eventually transferred to Kansas State Agricultural College's school of journalism. There, because of a class assignment, Davis received his first introduction to writing free verse—his preferred poetic form. When he left Kansas State, he traveled to Chicago where he wrote free-lance articles for magazines and worked for several black newspapers while continuing to produce poems. After a brief return to Kansas State, Davis moved to Atlanta, Georgia, to take an editing post on a semi-weekly paper. With the help of his leadership, the periodical became the *Atlanta Daily World,* the first successful black daily newspaper in America. Meanwhile, one of Davis's published poems, "Chicago's Congo," which concerns the underlying similarities between the blacks of Chicago and those still living the tribal life of the African Congo, attracted the attention of bohemian intellectual Frances Norton Manning. When Davis returned to Chicago, Manning introduced him to Norman Forgue, whose Black Cat Press subsequently published Davis's *Black Man's Verse.*

A critical success, *Black Man's Verse* "is experimental, cacophonous, yet sometimes harmonious," according to Tidwell. The volume includes poems such as "Giles Johnson, Ph.D.," in which the title character starves to death in spite of his four college degrees and knowledge of Latin and Greek because he did not wish to teach and was incapable of doing the manual labor that made up the majority of work available to blacks. Other pieces in *Black Man's Verse*—"Lynched," "Mojo Mike's Beer Garden," and "Cabaret," for example—make use of Davis's expertise on the subject of jazz to combine "the spirit of protest in jazz and free verse with . . . objections to racial oppression, producing a poetry that loudly declaims against injustice," explained Tidwell. Another well-known part of the volume is entitled "Ebony Under Granite." Likened to author Edgar Lee Masters's *Spoon River Anthology,* this section discusses the lives of various black people buried in a cemetery. Characters include Reverend Joseph Williams, who used to have sex with most of the women in his congregation; Goldie Blackwell, a two-dollar prostitute; George Brown, who served life in prison for voting more than once—in Mississippi he had seen white voters commit the same crime many times without punishment; and Roosevelt Smith, a black writer who was so frustrated by literary critics that he became a postman.

I Am the American Negro, Davis's second collection of poems, was published two years after his first. While drawing generally favorable reviews, it did not attract as much attention as *Black Man's Verse,* and some critics complained that it was too similar to the earlier book. For example, Tidwell quotes black critic Alain Locke's assertion that *I Am the American Negro* "has too many echoes of the author's first volume. . . . It is not a crescendo in the light of the achievement of [*Black Man's Verse*]." One of the obvious similarities between the two collections is that Davis also included an "Ebony Under Granite" section in the second. Members of this cast are people like the two Greeley sisters—the first's earlier promiscuous life-style did not prevent her from marrying respectably, while the second's lack of sexual experience caused her husband to be unfaithful; Nicodemus Perry, killed by loiterers for accidentally bumping into a white woman while, ironically, lost in memories of the sexual abuse his female relatives suffered at the hands of white men; and Mrs. Clifton Townsend, prejudiced against the darker-skinned members of her own race, who dies after giving birth to a baby much blacker than herself. Other poems featured in *I Am the American Negro* are "Modern Man—The Superman," which laments the state of modern civilization and has mock musical notations in its margins such as "Eight airplane motors, each keyed to a different pitch, are turned on and off to furnish musical accompaniment within the range of an octave"; and the title poem, which is a diatribe against Southern laws treating blacks differently from whites. Davis also placed love poems such as "Flowers of Darkness" and "Come to Me" in this book.

The poems of Davis's limited-edition third volume, *Through Sepia Eyes,* were later published along with others in his 1948 collection, *47th Street.* Though Tidwell described *47th Street* as "the culmination of Davis's thought and poetic development," Davis himself remarked on the time span between *I Am the American Negro* and his fourth book in a 1973 interview for *Black World:* "I was going through a number of changes during that particular time and I had to wait for these changes to settle and jell before I produced other work which I thought would be suitable to appear in a volume. And, of course, some critics naturally have thought that I would have been better off had I just continued to jell indefinitely." *47th Street* is composed of poems such as "Coincidence," which narrates the life stories of Donald Woods, a white man, and Booker Scott, a black man, who shared their dates of birth and death—by the poem's end the reader discovers that they also shared the same white biological father. The title poem, "unlike [Davis's] previous descriptions of Southside Chicago as exclusively black," noted Tidwell, "presents a 'rainbow race' of people." Indeed, Tidwell saw the whole of *47th Street* as having more universal concerns than his earlier works. When questioned about this issue Davis declared: "I am a Black poet, definitely a Black poet, and I think that my way of seeing things is the result of the impact of our civilization upon what I like to think of as a sensitive Black man. . . . But I do not think the Black poet should confine himself exclusively to Black readership. I think poetry, if it is going to be any good, should move members of all groups, and that is what I hope for."

In the same year that *47th Street* was published, Davis left Chicago for Honolulu, Hawaii. What began as a vacation turned into permanent residency. Except for a few poems that appeared in *Voices* in 1950, Davis virtually disappeared from the literary world until going on a college lecture tour in 1973. He later published other volumes of poetry, and at the time of his death in 1987 he had been working on a manuscript called "That Incredible Waikiki Jungle," about his Hawaiian experiences. When asked why he decided to remain in Hawaii, Davis cited the relative lack of racial problems and added, "I think one of the reasons why was that this [was] the first time that I began to be treated as a man instead of a Black curiosity. That was important to me, for my feeling of dignity and self-respect."

BIOGRAPHICAL/CRITICAL SOURCES:

BOOKS

Davis, Frank Marshall, *I Am the American Negro,* Black Cat, 1978.

Dictionary of Literary Biography, Volume 51: *Afro-American Writers From the Harlem Renaissance to 1940,* Gale, 1987.

PERIODICALS

Black World, January, 1974.
Poetry, August, 1936.

OBITUARIES:

PERIODICALS

Chicago Tribune, August 9, 1987.*

—Sketch by Elizabeth Thomas

*   *   *

DAVIS, Sara deSaussure   1943-

PERSONAL: Born May 7, 1943, in Columbia, S.C.; daughter of Richard Champion (an engineer) and Ella (a housewife; maiden name, Hunter) Davis. *Education:* Mississippi State College (now Mississippi University) for Women, B.A., 1965; Tulane University, M.A., 1969, Ph.D., 1974.

ADDRESSES: Home—1702 Ninth St., Tuscaloosa, Ala. 35401. *Office*—Department of English, University of Alabama, Tuscaloosa, Ala. 35487.

CAREER: Jay Scott Associates (advertising and public relations firm), Memphis, Tenn., copywriter, 1966-67; University of Alabama, Tuscaloosa, 1973—, began as assistant professor, became associate professor of English, assistant dean of arts and sciences, 1985—. Senior Fulbright lecturer at University of Heidelberg and University of Mannheim, 1980-81. Vice-president and member of board of directors of Tuscaloosa Symphony Guild and Druid City Historic District.

MEMBER: Modern Language Association of America, South Atlantic Modern Language Association (Women's Caucus), Tuscaloosa County Preservation Society (vice-president and member of board of directors).

WRITINGS:

(Editor with Philip D. Beidler) *The Mythologizing of Mark Twain,* University of Alabama Press, 1984.

Assistant editor of *South Atlantic Bulletin,* 1977-79; book review editor of *South Atlantic Review,* 1987—.

WORK IN PROGRESS: Kate Chopin's "A Vocation and a Voice"; research on neurasthenia as cultural metaphor.

*   *   *

DEADMAN, Ronald   1919-1988(?)

OBITUARY NOTICE: Born in 1919 in Shoeburyness, Essex, England; died c. 1988. Educator, editor, and author. Deadman gained recognition for his dedication to bringing higher and more imaginative standards of education to the schools in which he taught. After serving in World War II in the air and sea rescue service, he attended teachers' training college. His years of teaching experience between 1950 and 1966 included a Fulbright scholarship in 1957 to the United States—where he was influenced by American methods of teaching and reading—and a lecturing position for two years at Brentwood College of Education. A teacher at both the secondary and college levels, Deadman also educated middle-aged black and Asian immigrants in the London area. He became features editor of *The Teacher* in 1966, and from 1968 to 1976 he was editor of

Teacher's World. Resuming his teaching career, Deadman became a tutor in adult education beginning in 1985. His writings for juveniles include the multivolume *Enjoying English, The Happening, Wanderbodies,* and *The Pretenders.* He also edited the two-volume *Round the World Folk Tales* and *English Language Texts.*

OBITUARIES AND OTHER SOURCES:

BOOKS

International Authors and Writers Who's Who, 7th edition, Melrose, 1976.
Who's Who, 140th edition, St. Martin's, 1988.

PERIODICALS

Times (London), May 10, 1988.

*   *   *

DEAR, William (C.)   1937-

PERSONAL: Born August 1, 1937, in Miami, Fla.; son of James E. and Lucille Dear; children: Michael.

ADDRESSES: Home and office—Route 1, Box 237B, De Soto, Tex. 75115.

CAREER: Florida Highway Patrol, Miami, patrolman, 1955-62; William C. Dear and Associates (private investigators), Dallas, Tex., president, 1962—. Co-producer of feature film based on his book *The Dungon Master,* for Disney/Touchstone, 1988. *Military service:* U.S. Air Force, 1955.

WRITINGS:

The Dungeon Master: The Disappearance of James Dallas Egbert III (nonfiction), Houghton, 1984.

WORK IN PROGRESS: Please Don't Kill Me, a tentatively titled book about "a murder case I solved in Ohio, in which the police had no clues and I provided information leading to the arrests of eleven people," publication expected in 1988.

SIDELIGHTS: William Dear is a self-described millionaire who says, according to the *Washington Post's* Carla Hall, that the British call him "the real James Bond." He is "one of the most successful and best-known private investigators of our time, a man who has solved routine and bizarre cases from Britain and Italy to Thailand and Hong Kong," Robert Mills asserted in the *New York Times Book Review.* Some of Dear's work is familiar to the public: his investigation of the Milo fratricide in Ohio, for instance, is documented in Dan E. Moldea's *The Hunting of Cain.* The case that is perhaps Dear's most notorious, however, involved the disappearance of student James Dallas Egbert III from the Michigan State University campus in East Lansing in 1979. Dear based *The Dungeon Master,* his first book, on his investigation of this disappearance.

Egbert was sixteen years old and a college sophomore when he vanished. A computer genius who had few friends, he apparently became obsessed with a fantasy and adventure role-playing game called Dungeons and Dragons and began acting out the game's usually imaginary proceedings in the steam tunnels beneath the university campus. When Egbert disappeared, his relatives quickly summoned Dear. His approach to locating the missing teenager was to try to recreate Egbert's state of mind. The "flamboyant" detective, as Hall described him, hung from a railroad trestle while a locomotive passed overhead, just as Egbert had often done; he immersed himself in a Dungeons and Dragons game and found it disturbingly seductive.

Dear's account in *The Dungeon Master* of his search for Egbert gains power, Chris Goodrich related in the *Los Angeles Times*, because Dear and Egbert are "such opposites. [Egbert]—small, shy, intelligent and leaning toward homosexuality—is pursued by Dear—robust, bullying, *macho*. And yet we sense a connection between the hunter and his prey; each of them is a game player. [Egbert] plays games to escape reality; Dear has done the reverse, making his life's work a game of pursuit." After a month passed, Egbert reappeared—he telephoned Dear from Louisiana and the investigator flew to meet him in his private plane. Dear determined through talks with Egbert that the teenage genius had succumbed to family pressure and loneliness, and he strove to help him. A year later, having moved back to his parents' home in Ohio, Egbert killed himself. Reflecting on the death, Dear told Hall, "I took such an interest in the boy . . . became so wrapped up . . . tried to get his life straightened out. It was a very tragic time for me when he died."

Many reviewers praised the thoroughness of Dear's treatment of the case and found his writing style well suited to the material. "While he does not have or even attempt a polished . . . style," Mills wrote, Dear "does unfold his story in a brisk, convincing manner." Goodrich found Dear's "passion" for solving mysteries, which asserts itself through his "workmanlike" writing, to be compelling. Comparing *The Dungeon Master* to "a good detective novel," *Newsweek*'s Gene Lyons noted that "the fascination of Dear's book lies in the description of the investigation itself." Mills concurred: "Dear's account has all the trappings of high-gloss detective fiction."

Dear told *CA:* "I enjoy working as an international investigator solving major crimes, and I have been to some interesting cities, including East Berlin, Naples, Rome, Bangkok, London, and Paris. My motivation for writing *The Dungeon Master* was that I thought it would be extremely interesting to the general public and also that I wanted to alert parents and their children to the dangers of fantasy role-playing games."

MEDIA ADAPTATIONS: Dear's nonfiction book, *The Dungeon Master*, was adapted as the 1988 feature film of the same title, released by Disney/Touchstone.

BIOGRAPHICAL/CRITICAL SOURCES:

BOOKS

Moldea, Dan E., *The Hunting of Cain: A True Story of Money, Greed, and Fratricide*, Atheneum, 1983.

PERIODICALS

Los Angeles Times, November 15, 1984.
Newsweek, November 12, 1984.
New York Times Book Review, December 23, 1984.
Washington Post, November 28, 1984.

*   *   *

de HEVESY, Paul   1883-1988

OBITUARY NOTICE: Name originally Pal Bischitz; born April 9, 1883; died March 15, 1988. Diplomat and author. Until his death at age 104, de Hevesy was one of the last surviving diplomats from the Austro-Hungarian Empire. In 1908 he enlisted in the Diplomatic Service in London, where his first posting was under the reign of Edward VII. When the Austro-

Hungarian Empire dissolved with the 1919 Treaty of Versailles, de Hevesy continued his career in the Royal Hungarian Diplomatic Service, where he was Hungary's delegate to the League of Nations. He resigned from that post when Hitler annexed Austria. Throughout his career, de Hevesy concerned himself with such issues as war and peace, the promotion of a world government, and how better to feed a growing world population. His writings include *Alarming Discontents in Europe and the Danger of a Second World War*, *World Wheat Planning*, and *The Unification of the World*.

OBITUARIES AND OTHER SOURCES:

PERIODICALS

Times (London), March 21, 1988.

*   *   *

DELAPLANE, Stanton Hill   1907-1988

OBITUARY NOTICE—See index for *CA* sketch: Born October 12, 1907, in Chicago, Ill.; died of emphysema, April 18, 1988, in San Francisco, Calif. Editor, columnist, and author. Famed for his humorous travel column, Delaplane began his career as an editor for *Aperitif* magazine but soon joined the staff of the *San Francisco Chronicle* as a reporter in 1936. While at the *Chronicle*, he won a Pulitzer Prize for his 1941 series of articles on a group of California and Oregon counties threatening to secede and form a new state. In 1953 he became a syndicated travel columnist, spending at least half of each year abroad to furnish material for his column, which appeared six days a week. Delaplane is also credited with popularizing Irish coffee in the United States. His writings include *Postcards From Delaplane*, *The Little World of Stanton Delaplane*, *Delaplane in Mexico*, *And How She Grew*, *Pacific Pathways*, and *Stan Delaplane's Mexico*.

OBITUARIES AND OTHER SOURCES:

BOOKS

Who's Who in America, 44th edition, Marquis, 1986.

PERIODICALS

Los Angeles Times, April 19, 1988.
New York Times, April 21, 1988.
Washington Post, April 20, 1988.

*   *   *

DELAUNAY, Charles   1911-1988

OBITUARY NOTICE: Born in 1911; died of complications from Parkinson's disease, February 16, 1988, near Paris, France. Jazz music scholar and author. Delaunay was well known as one of the founding fathers of "Le Jazz Hot," a movement in France during the 1930s that fostered the love of American jazz music, previously shunned by Europeans. The son of famed French artists Robert and Sonia Delaunay, Charles was exposed to jazz at an early age, and he eventually teamed with Hugues Panassie to amass the largest collection of jazz recordings in Europe at that time. The two men subsequently founded the Hot Club of France, an association of jazz enthusiasts that promoted concerts, record dates, and radio programs. In 1934 Delaunay and Panassie started what is now the world's oldest jazz magazine, *Le Jazz Hot*, which Delaunay edited for many years. He later was director of the French record label, Vogue Records. His 1936 book *Hot Discography* was the first comprehensive anthology of recorded jazz music and musicians and is continually updated. Delaunay also wrote *De la vie et du jazz*, and the biography *Django Reinhardt*.

OBITUARIES AND OTHER SOURCES:

PERIODICALS

Los Angeles Times, February 18, 1988.
New York Times, February 20, 1988.

*　　*　　*

DeLEEUW, Adele (Louise) 1899-1988

OBITUARY NOTICE—See index for *CA* sketch: Born August 12, 1899, in Hamilton, Ohio; died of cancer of the colon, June 12, 1988, in Plainfield, N.J. Librarian and author. DeLeeuw will be best remembered for her many books for children and teenagers, some of which were illustrated or co-authored by her sister, Cateau DeLeeuw. She began writing after starting a children's story hour at the public library in Plainfield where she was employed as an assistant librarian, and by 1926 writing was her sole occupation. DeLeeuw penned over seventy-five volumes, including *The Expandable Browns*, *Where Valor Lies* (a 1959 Catholic Youth Book Club selection), *Casey Jones Drives an Ice Cream Train*, *Maria Tallchief: American Ballerina*, *Carlos P. Romulo: The Barefoot Boy of Diplomacy*, and *Remembered With Love*.

OBITUARIES AND OTHER SOURCES:

BOOKS

The Writers Directory: 1988-1990, St. James Press, 1988.

PERIODICALS

New York Times, June 14, 1988.

*　　*　　*

De MARLY, Diana 1939-

PERSONAL: Born May 25, 1939, in Malta. *Education:* Lady Margaret Hall, Oxford, B.A. (with honors), 1959, M.A., 1969; attended Central School of Art, London, England, 1964-66; Courtauld Institute of Art, London, C.C.H.D., 1969. *Politics:* Moderate. *Religion:* None.

ADDRESSES: Home—London, England. *Office*—Courtauld Institute of Art, 20 Portman Square, London W1H 0BE, England.

CAREER: University of London, Courtauld Institute of Art, London, England, lecturer in fashion history, 1970—. Lecturer at London College of Fashion Technology, 1971-73, and Croydon College of Art, 1973-75; Susette Taylor research fellow at Lady Margaret Hall, Oxford, 1977-78. Member of planning subcommittee for St. Marylebone and Regent's Park.

MEMBER: Society of Authors, Costume Society, St. Marylebone Society.

WRITINGS:

The History of Haute Couture, 1850-1950, Batsford, 1980.
Worth: Father of Haute Couture, Elm Tree Books, 1980, second edition, Holmes & Meier, 1988.
Costume on the Stage, 1600-1940, Batsford, 1982.
Fashion for Men, Batsford, 1985.
Working Dress, Batsford, 1986.
Louis XIV at Versailles, Batsford, 1987.
Christian Dior, Batsford, in press.

Also author, with Roger Dalladay, M. D. Anderson, and Stella Mary Newton, of educational filmstrips for Visual Publications, 1971. Contributor to *Contemporary Designers*, Macmillan, 1984. Contributor to art and theater journals.

WORK IN PROGRESS: Volume I of *Costume in North America*, publication by Holmes & Meier expected in 1989 or 1990.

SIDELIGHTS: Diana De Marly told *CA:* "Students report that *The History of Haute Couture* is a book all fashion and textile students are told to read as the best introduction to the subject that there is. It covers the rise of the couturier, Charles Frederick Worth and fashion, *la belle epoque*, the Poiret revolution, the revolt against fashion by art and medicine, the structure of a couture house, finance and promotion, the clientele and the clothes, Paris from 1914 to 1939, developments in London, and the war and after, in an attempt to give as full and as broad a picture of the industry as possible within one book.

"Strangely enough, there was no serious study of the founder of the French haute couture industry, the Englishman Charles Frederick Worth, who turned the traditional dressmaker with forty seamstresses into a mammoth establishment with twelve hundred employees on an industrial scale. Therefore I wrote one. *Worth: Father of Haute Couture* clearly answered a need, for the book sold out in the year of its publication. It covers Worth's youth in England, his move to Paris during a very changeable period that saw a monarchy giving way to a republic only to be replaced by an empire. Despite this, Worth had successes at international exhibitions with his first gowns and opened his own house in 1858, becoming couturier to the Empress Eugenie in 1860. Thus he became the court couturier, dealing with its masquerades, its official events, launching fashions for the empress, and establishing an artistic policy toward design. When the empire collapsed in 1870, Worth carried on, sustained by new American custom and other European monarchies and courts. He also dressed many leading ladies of the theater and ended his days, in 1895, as *le grand doyen* of the whole industry of dress.

"*Costume on the Stage, 1600-1940* was an attempt to look at the reform movements in theater costume in relation to artistic theory, but the underlying theme was that all attempts to be accurate over historical dress will be compromised by contemporary attitudes. Every period imposes its own look on its productions, even when it is claiming to be antique. Actresses in particular are expected to conform to the latest look, as if no woman could exist outside the date stamp of fashion. The book covers the Renaissance and Baroque ideals, the clothing system in England and France, the voices for reform, the abundance of romantic productions, the developments in ballet costume, the battle between spectacle and ideas, and it ends by contrasting the new cinematic extravaganza with the streamlined look of the stage. There is an appendix on theater collections around the globe.

"One of my aunts observed that reading my books is like hearing me talk, which amounts to a very accurate statement because I do regard writing as talking and trying to explain questions to people. One is telling a story even when it involves providing the documentation and evidence to support one's interpretation. Thus one should be aware of readability in one's text. It is not enough to present the facts. It must be done in a style that flows along at a comfortable pace and makes learning an enjoyable experience.

"Another interest of mine is the study of the position of clothes in art, by investigating the policies laid down over costuming by different artistic movements in history. This is an area that has been neglected by male scholars. My long article 'The Establishment of Roman Dress in Seventeenth-Century Portraiture' in *Burlington Magazine* received much academic welcome, for the simple reason that it was the very first attempt to discover why the period insisted on Roman clothing in official portraits. This remains an area where there is still much work for us to do, and where I ought to produce an authoritative book some day.''

BIOGRAPHICAL/CRITICAL SOURCES:

BOOKS

Wright, Christopher, *The Art of the Forger*, Gordon Fraser, 1984.

PERIODICALS

British Book News, August 22, 1980.
Country Life, November 20, 1980.
Economist, July 12, 1980.
Fashion Weekly, April 18, 1980.
Financial Times, July 12, 1980.
Lady, July 3, 1980.
Times Literary Supplement, September 12, 1980.
Woman's World, June, 1980.
World Times, July, 1980.

*   *   *

DENNING, Candace   1946-

PERSONAL: Born June 24, 1946, in Champaign, Ill.; daughter of Doyle Lavern (a pilot and building contractor) and Esther Carolyn (a teacher and housewife; maiden name, Phipps) Howell; married Daniel Burke Denning (a government executive), December 29, 1975; children: Burke Carolyn. *Education:* Indiana University—Bloomington, B.A., 1968, M.A., 1971; Warren Wilson College, M.F.A., 1984.

ADDRESSES: Agent—Robert Lescher, Lescher & Lescher Ltd., 67 Irving Place, New York, N.Y. 10003.

CAREER: Kennesaw Junior College, Marietta, Ga., instructor in French, 1971-73; Dekalb Community College, Clarkston, Ga., instructor in French, 1973-75; *Europe*, Washington, D.C., assistant editor, 1976-81; free-lance writer and editor, 1981—. Reporter for *Cherokee Tribune*, Canton, Ga., 1974-75.

MEMBER: Women's National Book Association.

AWARDS, HONORS: Fellow at MacDowell Colony, 1984, and Virginia Center for the Creative Arts, 1985; Virginia Prize for Literature in fiction, 1987.

WRITINGS:

Adventures With Julia (novel), North Point Press, 1986.
The Women in Her Dreams (novel), North Point Press, in press.

WORK IN PROGRESS: A novel.

SIDELIGHTS: Candace Denning told *CA:* "*Adventures With Julia* explores the contradictions of Julia Murphy's character. Julia's sense of menace in the everyday world makes living seem dangerous. Yet her life is weird, funny, and relentless. At the age of thirty-five, she has everything that someone else might want. But something is wrong. Julia sometimes feels

inhabited by another woman. She recognizes the voices and hands of strangers. There is something she wants to say, someone she is looking for. She works out a system for finding people in the yellow pages. A talent agent, a psychiatrist, a divorce lawyer: who has the answer? *Adventures With Julia* is a book of humor and insight. It is about foolishness and courage and the small inner moves that change minds and lives.

"*The Women in Her Dreams* is a story about living within the confines and chaos of a loving family. It is about being an identical twin and the confusing boundaries of self, other, and love. Twenty-two-year-old Sarah Broderhouse doesn't need anyone to tell her that Jack Summers is dangerous—he's married, for one thing, and he wants her to leave with him on a motorcycle to go live in a hut on a beach somewhere. But danger may be what Sarah needs. She refuses to live like her twin sister Laura, who wants to get married and be happy. 'Having a twin,' Sarah tells someone, 'is like having a part of yourself out of control.' Nor does she wish to be like her mother Irene, a good and reasonable person who always does the right thing. Sarah *wants* to do the right thing, but the right thing bores her. If she doesn't get away, Sarah thinks, she'll die.

"I am fascinated by how people behave in the relationships of their lives, and so I write about behavior, actions, reactions. My first two books have also been about loneliness and rebellion. To me, the challenge in writing a novel is to make sense of the characters' lives and also to make a novel with style, integrity, and a life of its own.

"I had a wonderful teacher once who encouraged me to move steadily in the direction of my own impulses, to listen for the sound of my own voice, and to be true to that voice. That was when I started listening to the voice inside me. I picked up its rhythm, its pitch, and density. I heard the shapes that vowels give to words. I listened for the sounds of trueness and falseness in dialogue and narration, and I learned to write by using my intuition. Writing is also the process of taming language. Language must be vigorously shaped, and it must be shaped in tune with the work as a whole. Writing is a discipline of self and discipline of language. I learned to shape language with my own sense of economy and rightness.

"My obsession in writing is to convey as much as possible with the greatest economy. I am fascinated by how much can be left out because of the edge that gives to what is then said. I rarely describe what a character is feeling, but try instead to show feeling through gesture, action, and dialogue. This keeps my writing close to the surface of the story. I only dig into the characters' backgrounds when a past event seems irresistible or essential. I believe every moment contains the past. Julia's behavior implies the emotional experiences that have brought her to the moment. Therefore, in my first two novels, the characters act and react without a lot of narrative explanation. The dialogue is brief, and the sentences are short. The chapters are compressed. The books are accumulations of moments, episodes that convey more than the space they occupy.''

BIOGRAPHICAL/CRITICAL SOURCES:

PERIODICALS

Library Journal, October 1, 1986.
New Yorker, February 23, 1987.
New York Times Book Review, December 14, 1986.
Philadelphia Inquirer, December 29, 1986.
Publishers Weekly, August 22, 1986.

DENNIS, Ian 1952-

PERSONAL: Born August 10, 1952, in Kingston, Ontario, Canada; son of Frederick J. (a manager) and Patricia (a legal secretary; maiden name, Murphy) Dennis. *Education:* University of Toronto, B.A., 1975, M.A., 1976.

ADDRESSES: Home—26 Tichester Rd., Toronto, Ontario, Canada M5P 1P1. *Agent*—Bella Pomer, Bella Pomer Agency, Inc., 22 Shallmar Blvd., Penthouse 2, Toronto, Ontario, Canada M5N 2Z8.

CAREER: Ministry of Government Services, Queen's Park Computing Centre, Toronto, Ontario, computer operator and supervisor, 1977-86; free-lance computer consultant, 1986—.

AWARDS, HONORS: Norma Epstein National Award, 1976.

WRITINGS:

Bagdad (romance), Allen & Unwin, 1986, also published with *The Prince of Stars* (also see below).
The Prince of Stars (romance), Allen & Unwin, 1987, also published with *Bagdad* (also see below).
The Prince of Stars (contains *Bagdad* and *The Prince of Stars*), Overlook Press, 1987.

WORK IN PROGRESS: Disasters of Love, stories; *Miriam and the Mysteries of the Universe*, a romance and tragedy; *Rupert and Clara*, a romance.

SIDELIGHTS: Ian Dennis told *CA:* "I set out determined to do something 'different.' From the vantage of twenty years of age I clearly perceived the exhaustion of the naturalistic novel, the staleness of current forms and the futility (this at least was practical) of writing from my limited personal experience. I wrote stories, therefore, of every conceivable non-naturalistic sort, which won me undergraduate writing prizes both at my own university and then at a national level. These were praised for their variety, their inventiveness. The judges also noted that the weakest efforts were those that attempted to picture contemporary realities and social relations.

"By the time I had finished my schooling I had come to the conclusion that both personal predilection and my evolving ideas about genre agreed I should write romance. Romance was what the world—the small part of it that read books, at any rate—now needed most. As this has meant no end of trouble, I have recently, some eleven years later, been asking myself what on earth sent me off in this direction.

"The only answer that makes sense is that my aspirations reflected my own experience of books. I was not simply being difficult or defensive about my callow youth: the great tradition of social novels did not deeply excite me. The treasure house of other forms from every period did. They seemed full of limitless potential, full of a vast resource of other ways of looking at human life and character. They were an expanding perspective, not fully exploited. Genre, I thought, was the aspect of writing where innovation would be most welcome. Wasn't the explosive success of books like *The Lord of the Rings* evidence that readers were eager for something different?

"I suppose dichotomy appeals to immature minds: mine was the novel and romance. If all fiction was a spectrum from science to dream, novel was closer to the former, romance to the latter. The novel was concerned with society (and individuals that reflected social truths); the romance focused on individuals and their journeys through trouble and confusion toward greater understanding. The novel threatened always to become storyless (as E. M. Forster hoped it would!), as the novelist simply used plot to deliver his insights and observations. The romancer, on the other hand, believed that his form knew more than he did and contained, like a genetic code embedded in its ever-repeated story shape, an ageless human wisdom. The novel was shapeless, by comparison, and limited in time. The romance resonated still with the quality of religious ritual. The novel was finally static, descriptive; the romance dynamic, full of the promise and challenge of personal change.

"Northrop Frye once said that for a certain number of people in any era suspensions of disbelief are simply impossible—beyond the reach of their wills. He noted the Elizabethan diarist who walked out of a performance of 'A Midsummer Night's Dream.' No fairies for him, whatever the literary pretensions of the author. But I can't help feeling that the full-blown chauvinism of our day—the same chauvinism that superciliously dismisses all of fantasy and science fiction, airily talking of a 'lack of seriousness'—is something more than the voice of that predictable proportion of the audience. This is a matter Ursula Le Guin speaks of, for example, in *The Language of the Night*, when she asks why Americans are afraid of dragons and speaks of the intense moral disapproval of her chosen genre. It has to do with the condition of the collective imagination, and with, I suppose, current notions about the social utility of art.

"At any rate, it seems clear that I was asking for more trouble than I knew when I set out to try to 'moralize Tolkien,' to try to blend genres, and to try to achieve serious and meaningful and lasting books in a new, 'evolved' form. That I should try to do this, of course, by no means assured that the results would be any good. Despite my genre advocacy I believed, and believe, that quality is the only measure of a book—the style, the thought, the harmony of design, the life and interest of the story, the beauty of the thing. This is always difficult to gauge, especially in new and unknown writers. People take shortcuts, and one of the favorites is the mindless rejection—or acceptance—of the genre. For the kind of writing I do it has been difficult to get critical or editorial response that is not heavily colored by reaction to my form.

"It is at once gratifying and frustrating to see the larger literary scene to a greater and greater extent mirroring my preoccupations with genre. More and more of the 'important' and successful books of our day are being written in new forms and mixtures of forms, in 'evolved' genres, and while this was doubtless underway long before I ever started thinking about it I do feel some sense of justification. The list of authors who have produced work that expands or grafts genres is a Who's Who of 'serious' contemporary literature: John Barth, Donald Bartheleme, Kingsley Amis, Margaret Atwood, Doris Lessing, John Updike, Norman Mailer, Anthony Burgess, Theroux, and on and on and on. But it is frustrating to see the double standard which is applied to all this writing. If authors venture into new ground from the mainstream side of the fence, as it were, they are daring and inventive. If they come from the other direction—well, there are still plenty of us who'll have nothing to do with fairies.''

*   *   *

DENT, Thomas C(ovington) 1932-
(Tom Dent)

PERSONAL: Born March 20, 1932, in New Orleans, La.; son

of Albert (a university president) and Jessie (a teacher and concert pianist; maiden name, Covington) Dent. *Education:* Morehouse College, B.A., 1952; Goddard College, M.A., 1974.

ADDRESSES: Home—Box 50584, New Orleans, La. 70150. *Agent*—Lawrence Jordan, 2067 Broadway, Suite 41, New York, N.Y. 10023.

CAREER: Houston Informer, Houston, Tex., reporter, 1950-52; *New York Age,* New York, N.Y., reporter, 1959; National Association for the Advancement of Colored People (NAACP), New York City, public information worker for Legal Defense Fund, 1961-63; Free Southern Theater, New Orleans, La., associate director, 1966-70; Total Community Action, New Orleans, public relations officer, 1971-73; public lecturer. Co-publisher of political newspaper *On Guard for Freedom,* 1960; co-founder of Umbra Workshop, New York City, 1962, and co-publisher of poetry magazine *Umbra;* co-founder of literary journal *Callaloo,* 1978; founder of Congo Square Writers Union, New Orleans, 1974; free-lance writer and poetry reader. Instructor at Mary Holmes College, 1968-70, University of New Orleans, 1979-81. Executive director of New Orleans Jazz and Heritage Foundation. *Military service:* U.S. Army, 1957-59.

MEMBER: Modern Language Association, African Literature Association.

AWARDS, HONORS: Whitney Young fellow, 1973-74.

WRITINGS:

(Editor with Richard Schechner and Gilbert Moses) *The Free Southern Theater, by the Free Southern Theater,* Bobbs-Merrill, 1969.
(Under name Tom Dent) *Magnolia Street* (poems), privately printed, 1976, reprinted, 1987.
(Under name Tom Dent) *Blue Lights and River Songs: Poems,* Lotus Press, 1982.

PLAYS

"Negro Study No. 34A" (one-act), first produced in New Orleans, La., at Free Southern Theater, 1970.
"Snapshot" (one-act), first produced in New Orleans at Free Southern Theater, 1970.
"Ritual Murder" (one-act), first produced in New Orleans at Ethiopian Theater, 1976.

Also author, with Val Ferdinand, of one-act play "Song of Survival."

OTHER

"The Ghetto of Desire" (prose narrative), Columbia Broadcasting System (CBS-TV), 1966.

Writings represented in anthologies, including *Anthology of the American Negro in the Theatre, Black Culture, An Introduction to Black Literature in America,* and *New Black Voices.* Contributor of poetry, short stories, and drama to *Callaloo, Nkombo, Umbra,* and *Pacific Moana Quarterly;* of articles and critical reviews to *Black American Literature Forum, Black Creation, Black River Journal, Crisis, Black World, Freedomways, Jackson Advocate, Negro Digest, Obsidian,* and others. Editor, *Black River Journal,* 1976; co-editor of *Nkombo,* 1968-74.

WORK IN PROGRESS: With Andrew Young, under name Tom Dent, an autobiography, for Bantam.

SIDELIGHTS: Born into a prominent, socially committed family, Tom Dent was educated in both public and private schools in New Orleans. He earned a degree in political science from Morehouse College, where he began his literary career as editor of the *Maroon Tiger;* during summer vacations he also worked as a cub reporter for the *Houston Informer.* "Certainly," Dent remembered, "I had no concept of what it meant to be a black writer. . . . We were taught and prepared to *belong.* . . . We had been taught that race as a subject was limiting, something to escape from if possible, and the further one escaped the more successful one became."

Dent's move to New York City in 1959, however, brought a new race-consciousness as he lived and worked among other black writers. A reporter for the black paper *New York Age,* Dent became involved with the political publication *On Guard for Freedom* and—with Calvin Hernton and David Henderson—founded the influential Umbra Workshop. A collective of black artists, activists, and thinkers on the lower east side of New York City, the workshop explored the interface of politics, art, and social reality with black identity. Publishers of the poetry magazine *Umbra,* workshop writers gave public readings, "continuing a trend popularized by the 'beat generation' poets of the 1950s," commented Lorenzo Thomas in the *Dictionary of Literary Biography,* "challeng[ing] their audiences' cultural preconceptions." Recalling that theirs was the first group to use "the language black people speak," Dent wrote: "Umbra was my introduction to the Black Arts Movement; it turned me into viewing reality through a black lens."

Like the Umbra Workshop, New Orleans's Free Southern Theater was a cultural project conceived to challenge the status quo. Comprised of theater professionals and political activists, the organization assailed racism and segregation in the Deep South. When Dent returned to New Orleans in 1965 he joined the ranks of the Free Southern Theater, eventually becoming its associate director. Among his controversial projects was a program of poetry readings, "The Ghetto of Desire," for the CBS television show "Look Up and Live" in 1966. Objecting to the presentation's bleak portrayal of black life in New Orleans, the city's housing authority tried to prevent a national broadcast by pressuring the program's sponsor. Rejecting censorship, the National Council of Churches presented "The Ghetto of Desire" intact, although some southern stations refused to air it.

While earning considerable attention as a dramatist and poet, Dent has focused more on the organization and distribution of the works and ideas of other black artists. Seeing the office of the poet as essential to the life of a community—uncovering the "subliminal truth" that lies beyond "surface reality"—Dent believes that art can effect social change. Yet he also acknowledges that it is the individual, and not the community, who creates; in the arts collectives he has formed or directed (including New Orleans's Congo Square Writers Union) Dent has addressed the tension that exists between community consciousness and individual vision. Lorenzo Thomas reflected: "It is pertinent to view Tom Dent's first twenty years of literary activity as an attempt to design viable models of collective work. . . . Urging his community to attend the writer's personal vision, forcing artists' collectives to confront their members' individualism, Dent has attempted to solve philosophical and practical problems of organization."

It is to the community, however, that Dent looks for black survival. "He opposes the idea that economic and political advancement of the black American depends upon a middle class that can achieve integration into the larger society," Lorenzo Thomas related; "Dent's alternative depends upon race pride and a collective solidarity, in opposition to narrow self-interest.'' The poems collected in Dent's *Magnolia Street* and *Blue Lights and River Songs,* the *Dictionary of Literary Biography* writer continued, ''affirm [that] . . . black people can only find their true identities within a community founded on recognition of their African heritage and common historical experience.'' Capturing the improvisational quality of jazz music, Dent's verse focuses on the struggle for racial and self-identity in contemporary urban America. Much of his drama explores the desperation that springs from a lack of identity; in the 1976 play ''Ritual Murder,'' for example, the dramatist shows how young black men, denied a legitimate heritage and most common avenues of self-esteem, turn their rage inward and violently upon one another.

BIOGRAPHICAL/CRITICAL SOURCES:

BOOKS

Dictionary of Literary Biography, Volume 38: *Afro-American Writers After 1955: Dramatists and Prose Writers,* Gale, 1985.

PERIODICALS

Callaloo, November 4, 1978.
Drama Review, fall, 1987.
World Literature Today, autumn, 1982.
Xaiver Review, Volume 6, No. 1, 1986.

* * *

DENT, Tom
    See DENT, Thomas C(ovington)

* * *

DEUTSCH, Eva Costabel
    See COSTABEL, Eva Deutsch

* * *

DEWDNEY, Christopher   1951-

PERSONAL: Born May 9, 1951, in London, Ontario, Canada; son of Selwyn (an ethnoarchaeologist) and Irene (an art therapist; maiden name, Donner) Dewdney; married Suzanne Dennison (marriage ended); married Lise Downe (an artist); children: Calla Xanthoria Kirk, Tristan Alexander Downe. *Education:* Attended art school and collegiate schools in London, Ontario.

ADDRESSES: Office—Winters College, York University, Downsview, Ontario, Canada M3J 1P3.

CAREER: Writer and artist, with solo and group exhibitions of sculpture and collages. Teacher of creative writing, 1984—; member of board of directors of Provincial Essays; associate fellow of Winters College, York University.

MEMBER: League of Canadian Poets, Forest City Gallery Artists Association (president, 1978, 1979).

AWARDS, HONORS: Award of Excellence from *Design Canada,* 1974, for *A Palaeozoic Geology of London, Ontario;* finalist for Canadian Governor General's Award for poetry, 1984, for *Predators of the Adoration: Selected Poems, 1972-1982;* first prize for poetry from Canadian Broadcasting Corp. literary competition, 1986.

WRITINGS:

POETRY, EXCEPT AS NOTED

Golders Green, privately printed, 1971, Coach House Press (Toronto, Ontario), 1972.
A Paleozoic Geology of London, Ontario: Poems and Collages, Coach House Press (Toronto), 1973, revised edition, 1974.
Fovea Centralis, Coach House Press (Toronto), 1975.
Spring Trances in the Control Emerald Night, Figures, 1978.
Alter Sublime, Coach House Press (Toronto), 1980.
The Cenozoic Asylum, Delires, 1983.
Predators of the Adoration: Selected Poems, 1972-1982, McClelland & Stewart, 1983.
The Immaculate Perception (theoretical prose), self-illustrated, House of Anansi, 1986.

Work represented in anthologies, including *The Poets of Canada, The New Oxford Book of Canadian Verse,* and *The Contemporary Canadian Poem Anthology.* Also contributor to periodicals, including *Descant, Impulse, Tamarack Review,* and *Capilano Review* in Canada; *Sulfur, Notas,* and *Hambone* in the United States; *Die Horen* in Germany; *Grosseteste Review* and *One* in England.

WORK IN PROGRESS: A Natural History of Southwestern Ontario.

BIOGRAPHICAL/CRITICAL SOURCES:

BOOKS

Dictionary of Literary Biography, Volume 60: *Canadian Writers Since 1960, Second Series,* Gale, 1987.

PERIODICALS

Books in Canada, February, 1984.
Globe and Mail (Toronto), January 31, 1987.

* * *

DIAMANO, Silmang
    See SENGHOR, Leopold Sedar

* * *

DIAMOND, I(sidore) A. L.   1920-1988

OBITUARY NOTICE—See index for *CA* sketch: Name originally Itek Dommnici; born June 27, 1920, in Ungheni, Romania; came to United States, 1929; died of multiple myeloma (a form of cancer), April 21, 1988, in Beverly Hills, Calif. Screenwriter. Diamond began his career as a junior writer at Paramount Studios for seventy-five dollars a week in 1941. He was soon writing films such as the 1944 ''Murder in the Blue Room,'' but his biggest successes were his collaborations with writer-director Billy Wilder, which included ''Some Like It Hot'' in 1959 and the Oscar-winning ''The Apartment'' in 1960. Diamond's other screen credits include ''Irma La Douce,'' ''The Fortune Cookie,'' and ''Buddy Buddy.''

OBITUARIES AND OTHER SOURCES:

BOOKS

Who's Who in America, 44th edition, Marquis, 1986.

PERIODICALS

Los Angeles Times, April 22, 1988.
New York Times, April 22, 1988.

Times (London), April 23, 1988.
Washington Post, April 23, 1988.

*   *   *

DiFEDERICO, Frank R.   1933(?)-1987

OBITUARY NOTICE: Born c. 1933 in Southbridge, Mass.; died of cancer, December 1, 1987, in Washington, D.C. Educator, publisher, editor, and author. DiFederico was publisher and editor of Decatur House Press, which he founded in the mid-1970s. He served in the U.S. Air Force during the late 1950s as a Chinese language specialist, received a doctorate in art history from New York University's Institute of Fine Arts in 1970, and became professor of art history at the University of Maryland in 1971, specializing in seventeenth- and eighteenth-century Roman art. DiFederico also wrote three art history books: *Francesco Trevisani, Eighteenth-Century Painter in Rome, The Mosaics in the National Shrine of the Immaculate Conception,* and *Mosaics of St. Peter's: Decorating the New Basilica.*

OBITUARIES AND OTHER SOURCES:

PERIODICALS

Washington Post, December 4, 1987.

*   *   *

DILKE, Christopher Wentworth   1913(?)-1987

OBITUARY NOTICE: Born December 15, 1913 (one source says 1930), in London, England; died November 1, 1987. Broadcaster, linguist, translator, journalist, and author. Dilke studied languages at Freiburg University and after World War II helped reestablish a free press in Germany. During his years with the British Broadcasting Corporation (BBC) he was an organizer, writer, and broadcaster for the German Language Service and broadcasts to southern Europe. In addition he expanded the English by Radio service to include television and pioneered English-Teaching by Television. Among his writings are *The Road to Dalmatia,* the novels *The Bridgehead, France Is a Star, The Eye of the Night,* and *The Rotten Apple,* and articles on wine and food. Dilke also translated a seventeenth-century petition written by an Inca chief to his Spanish conquerors.

OBITUARIES AND OTHER SOURCES:

BOOKS

The Author's and Writer's Who's Who, 6th edition, reprinted, Burke's Peerage, 1971.
International Authors and Writers Who's Who, 7th edition, Melrose, 1976.
Who Was Who Among English and European Authors, 1931-1949, Gale, 1978.

PERIODICALS

Times (London), November 5, 1987.

*   *   *

DIOP, Birago (Ismael)   1906-
(Max, d'Alain Provist)

PERSONAL: Some sources spell middle name "Ismail"; born December 11, 1906, in Ouakam (some sources say Dakar), Senegal; son of Ismael (a master mason) and Sokhna (Dia-wara) Diop; married Marie-Louise Pradere (an accountant), 1934 (deceased); children: Renee, Andree. *Education:* Received doctorate from Ecole Nationale Veterinaire de Toulouse, 1933; attended Institut de Medecine Veterinaire Exotique, c. 1934, and Ecole Francaise des Cuirs et Peaux.

ADDRESSES: B.P. No. 5018, Dakar, Senegal.

CAREER: Head of government cattle inspection service in Senegal and French Sudan (now Mali), c. 1934-42; employed at Institut de Medecine Veterinaire Exotique in Paris, France, 1942-44; interim head of zoological technical services in Ivory Coast, 1946; head of zoological technical services in Upper Volta (now Burkina Faso), 1947-50, in Mauritania, 1950-54, and in Senegal, 1955; administrator for Societe de la Radio-diffusion d'Outre-Mer (broadcasting company), 1957; ambassador from Senegal to Tunisia during early 1960s; veterinarian in private practice in Dakar, Senegal, c. 1964—. Vice-president of Confederation Internationale des Societes d'Auteurs et Compositeurs, 1982; president of reading board of Nouvelles Editions Africaines (publisher); official of Institut des Hautes Etudes de Defense Nationale (French national defense institute). *Military service:* Nurse in military hospital in St.-Louis, Senegal, 1928-29.

MEMBER: Association des Ecrivains du Senegal (president), Bureau Senegalais des Droits d'Auteur (president of administrative council), Societe des Gens de Lettres de France, Pen-Club, Rotary-Club de Dakar, Anemon.

AWARDS, HONORS: Grand Prix Litteraire de l'Afrique-Occidentale Francaise, for *Les Contes d'Amadou Koumba;* Grand Prix Litteraire de l'Afrique Noire from Association des Ecrivains d'Expression Francaise de la Mer et de l'Outre Mer (now Association des Ecrivains de Langue Francaise), 1964, for *Contes et lavanes.* Officier de la Legion d'Honneur; commandeur des Palmes Academiques; chevalier de l'Etoile Noire; chevalier du Merite Agricole; chevalier des Arts et des Lettres; grand-croix de l'Ordre National Senegalais; grand officier de l'Ordre de la Republique Tunisienne; grand officier de l'Ordre National Ivoirien.

WRITINGS:

SHORT STORIES

Les Contes d'Amadou Koumba (includes "Maman-Caiman," "Les Mamelles," and "Sarzan"), Fasquelle, 1947, reprinted, Presence Africaine, 1978.
Les Nouveaux Contes d'Amadou Koumba (title means "The New Tales of Amadou Koumba"; includes "L'Os de Mor Lam"), preface by Leopold Sedar Senghor, Presence Africaine, 1958.
Contes et lavanes (title means "Tales and Commentaries"), Presence Africaine, 1963.
Tales of Amadou Koumba (collection; includes "A Judgment"), translation and introduction by Dorothy S. Blair, Oxford University Press, 1966.
Contes choisis (collection), edited with an introduction by Joyce A. Hutchinson, Cambridge University Press, 1967.
Contes d'Awa, illustrations by A. Diallo, Nouvelles Editions Africaines, 1977.
Mother Crocodile—Maman-Caiman, translation and adaptation by Rosa Guy, illustrations by John Steptoe, Delacorte Press, 1981.

PLAYS; ADAPTED FROM HIS SHORT STORIES

"Sarzan," performed in Dakar, Senegal, 1955.

L'Os de Mor Lam (performed at Theatre National Daniel So-rano, Senegal, 1967-68), Nouvelles Editions Africaines, 1977.

Also adapted "Maman-Caiman" and "Les Mamelles."

OTHER

Leurres et lueurs (poems; title means "Lures and Lights"; includes "Viatique"), Presence Africaine, 1960.
Birago Diop, ecrivain senegalais (collection), commentary by Roger Mercier and M. and S. Battestini, F. Nathan, 1964.
Memoires (autobiography), Presence Africaine, volume 1: *La Plume raboutee* (title means "The Piecemeal Pen"), 1978, volume 2: *A Rebrousse-temps* (title means "Against the Grain of Time"), 1982, volume 3: *A Rebrousse-gens: Epissures, entrelacs, et reliefs,* 1985.

Work represented in anthologies, including *Anthologie de la nouvelle poesie negre et malagache de langue francaise,* edited by Leopold Sedar Senghor, Presses Universitaires de France, 1948; *A Book of African Verse,* Heinemann, 1964; *An Anthology of African and Malagasy Poetry in French,* Oxford University Press, 1965.

Contributor to periodicals, including *L'Echo des etudiants* (sometimes under pseudonyms Max and d'Alain Provist), *L'Etudiant noir,* and *Presence africaine.*

SIDELIGHTS: Birago Diop is an author and poet best known for short stories inspired by the folktales of West Africa. Born and raised in Senegal, formerly a French colony, Diop writes in French, although some of his works have been translated into English and other languages. As a young man Diop left Senegal for France, where he studied veterinary science at the Ecole Nationale Veterinaire in Toulouse. After receiving his doctorate in 1933 he went to Paris, where he encountered a community of black writers from the French colonial empire that included Aime Cesaire of Martinique and Leopold Sedar Senghor of Senegal. Senghor and Cesaire led the Negritude movement, which rejected the assimilation of black colonial peoples into French culture, asserting instead the value of the black heritage. Inspired by the movement, Diop wrote poems such as "Viatique," a vivid portrayal of the initiation cere-mony of an African tribe. His work appeared in two of Sen-ghor's groundbreaking efforts at publishing Franco-African authors: the journal *L'Etudiant noir* and the book *Anthologie de la nouvelle poesie negre et malagache de langue francaise.*

Later in the 1930s Diop returned to French West Africa, and in his work as a government veterinarian he traveled widely throughout the region, sometimes into remote areas of the in-terior. He turned from poetry to the short story, "the most traditional form of African literature," as Joyce A. Hutchinson observed in her introduction to *Contes choisis.* For centuries African literature was primarily spoken, and storytellers such as the *griots* of West Africa found the short story a convenient form in which to provide moral lessons or to discuss the human condition. When Diop published his first collection of stories, *Les Contes d'Amadou Koumba,* he said they were drawn ver-batim from a *griot* named Amadou whom he had met during his travels. In a later interview for *Le Soleil,* however, he acknowledged that Amadou was a composite of many story-tellers he had encountered, including members of his own family.

In fact many commentators, including Senghor, have sug-gested that Diop's stories succeed on the printed page because they are a skillful combination of African oral tradition and

the author's own considerable talent as a writer. Diop "uses tradition, of which he is proud," Hutchinson wrote, "but he does not insist in an unintelligent fashion on tradition for tra-dition's sake. He resuscitates the spirit and the style of the traditional *conte* [tale] in beautiful French, without losing all the qualities which were in the vernacular version."

Diop's tales have often been praised for their varied and skill-ful observations on human nature. In "L'Os de Mor Lam," for instance, a selfish man prefers to be buried alive rather than share his supper with a neighbor. The author often draws upon traditional animal tales, which put human foibles on dis-play by endowing animals with exaggerated forms of human characteristics. In one African story cycle, which Diop uses extensively, a physically strong but foolish hyena is repeatedly bested by a hare who relies on intelligence rather than strength.

Reviewers generally note that Diop prefers laughter to melo-drama in his stories, and in *The African Experience in Liter-ature and Ideology* Abiola Irele stressed the "gentle" quality of Diop's humor. But other commentators agreed with Doro-thy S. Blair, who in her foreword to *Tales of Amadou Koumba* held that some stories contain a sharper element of social sat-ire. In "Sarzan," for example, Diop describes the comeup-pance of an African villager who returns from service in the French Army and tries to impose French culture on his people. And in "A Judgment," according to John Field of *Books and Bookmen,* a couple with marital problems must endure first the "pompous legalism" of the village elders and then the "arbitrary and callous" judgment of a Muslim lord.

In adapting the oral folktale to a written form, Diop strives to maintain the spontaneity of human speech, and to do so he intersperses his prose with dialogue, songs, and poems—all part of the African storyteller's technique, as Hutchinson noted. "Diop's use of dialogue," she remarked, "is masterly. He uses the whole range of human emotional expression: shouts, cries, tears, so vividly that one can without difficulty imagine and supply the accompanying gestures and the intonation of the voice." Accordingly, Diop has adapted several of his sto-ries for the stage, including "Sarzan" and "L'Os de Mor Lam." Writing in *World Literature Today,* Eileen Julien praised Diop's adaptation of "L'Os" for "depict[ing] in a warm and colorful style the manners of an African village," including "gatherings, prayers, communal rites and . . . ubiquitous, compelling chatter." "All of these," she averred, "are the matter of which theatre is made."

Diop's adaptations of the folktale have made him one of Af-rica's most widely read authors, and he has received numerous awards and distinctions. His first volume of tales promptly won the Grand Prix Litteraire de l'Afrique-Occidentale Fran-caise, and for his second volume Senghor, who had become one of Senegal's most prominent writers and political leaders, wrote a laudatory preface. After Senghor led Senegal to in-dependence in 1960 he sought Diop as the country's first am-bassador to Tunisia. Since 1978 Diop has produced three highly detailed volumes of memoirs, including his account of the early days of the Negritude movement in Paris. Summarizing Diop's literary achievement, Hutchinson praised the author for showing that short stories in the traditional African style are "not just children's tales, not just sociological or even histor-ical material, but a work of art, part of Africa's cultural heritage."

BIOGRAPHICAL/CRITICAL SOURCES:

BOOKS

Diop, Birago, *Contes choisis,* edited with an introduction by Joyce A. Hutchinson, Cambridge University Press, 1967.

Diop, Birago, *Les Nouveaux Contes d'Amadou Koumba*, preface by Leopold Sedar Senghor, Presence Africaine, 1958.

Diop, Birago, *Tales of Amadou Koumba*, translation and introduction by Dorothy S. Blair, Oxford University Press, 1966.

Irele, Abiola, *The African Experience in Literature and Ideology*, Heinemann, 1981.

PERIODICALS

Books and Bookmen, October, 1986.
Le Soleil, December 11, 1976.
World Literature Today, winter, 1979, autumn, 1986.*

—Sketch by Thomas Kozikowski

*   *   *

DIOP, Cheikh Anta   1923-1986

PERSONAL: Born in 1923 in Diourbel, Senegal; died February 7, 1986, in Dakar, Senegal. *Education:* Received a Litt.D. in France.

CAREER: Historian. Headed the carbon-14 dating laboratory for the Institut Fondamentale d'Afrique Noire in Senegal. Founder of two political parties in the 1960s, the Bloc des Masses Senegalaises and the Front Nationale Senegalaise.

AWARDS, HONORS: Honored by the World Festival of Negro Arts in 1966 as the black intellectual who had exercised the most fruitful influence in the twentieth century.

WRITINGS:

Nations negres et culture, Editions Africaines, 1955, two-volume edition published as *Nations negres et culture: De l'antiquite negre egyptienne aux problemes culturels de l'Afrique noire d'aujourd'hui*, Presence Africaine, 1979, partial translation by Mercer Cook in *The African Origin of Civilization: Myth or Reality*, Lawrence Hill, 1974 (also see below).

L'Unite culturelle de l'Afrique noire: Domaines du patriarcat et du matriarcat dans l'antiquite classique, Presence Africaine, 1959, translation published as *The Cultural Unity of Negro Africa: The Domains of Patriarchy and of Matriarchy in Classical Antiquity*, Presence Africaine, 1962, translation with introduction by John Henrik Clarke and afterword by James G. Spady published as *The Cultural Unity of Black Africa: The Domains of Patriarchy and of Matriarchy in Classical Antiquity*, Third World Press, 1978.

Les Fondements culturels, techniques et industriels d'un futur etat federal d'Afrique noire, Presence Africaine, 1960, revised edition published as *Les Fondements economiques et culturels d'un etat federal d'Afrique noire*, Presence Africaine, 1974, translation by Harold Salemson published as *Black Africa: The Economic and Cultural Basis for a Federated State*, Lawrence Hill, 1978.

L'Afrique noire pre-coloniale: Etude comparee des systemes politiques et sociaux de l'Europe et de l'Afrique noire, de l'antiquite a la formation des etats modernes, Presence Africaine, 1960.

Anteriorite des civilisations negres: Myth ou verite historique? Presence Africaine, 1967, partial translation by Cook in *The African Origin of Civilization: Myth or Reality*, Lawrence Hill, 1974 (also see below).

Le Laboratoire de radiocarbone de l'IFAN, Institut Fondamentale d'Afrique Noire, 1968.

Physique nucleaire et chronologie absolue, Institut Fondamentale d'Afrique Noire, 1974.

The African Origin of Civilization: Myth or Reality (translation of portions of *Anteriorite des civilisations negres* and *Nations negres et culture* by Cook), Lawrence Hill, 1974 (also see above).

Parente genetique de l'egyptien pharaonique et des langues negro-africaines: Processus de semitisation, Nouvelles Editions Africaines, 1977.

SIDELIGHTS: Cheikh Anta Diop began the first carbon-14 dating laboratory in Africa and founded two political parties in his native Senegal that were later banned, but he is best remembered for his historical works about Africa. His books attempt to prove that blacks had a larger role in the beginnings of civilization than was previously accorded them. Diop argued that the ancient Egyptians, extremely advanced in science and culture, were black; he also held that the first steps toward civilization began south of the Sahara Desert.

OBITUARIES:

PERIODICALS

Publishers Weekly, March 7, 1986.*

*   *   *

DODGSHON, Robert A(ndrew)   1941-

PERSONAL: Surname is pronounced ''*Dodge*-shon''; born August 12, 1941, in Bangor, Wales; son of Robert Cyril and Dorothy (Owens) Dodgshon; married Katherine Simmons (a university tutor), August 16, 1969; children: Clare Louise, Lucy Richenda. *Education:* University of Liverpool, B.A., and Ph.D., 1966. *Politics:* Social Democrat.

ADDRESSES: Home—25 Pen-y-graig, Aberystwyth SY23 2JA, Wales. *Office*—Department of Geography, University College of Wales, University of Wales, Aberystwyth SY23 3DB, Wales. *Agent*—F. Kelly, Clifton Rd., Kingston-upon-Thames, Surrey KT2 6PL, England.

CAREER: University of Reading, Reading, England, assistant keeper at Museum of English Rural Life, 1966-70; University of Wales, University College of Wales, Aberystwyth, senior lecturer, 1970-84, reader in geography, 1984—.

WRITINGS:

(Editor with R. A. Butlin) *An Historical Geography of England and Eales*, Academic Press, 1978.
The Origins of British Field Systems, Academic Press, 1981.
Land and Society in Early Scotland, Clarendon Press, 1981.

Also author of *The European Past: Social Evolution and Spatial Order*, Macmillan. Editor of ''Historical Geography Research'' series, HGRG, 1978-82.

WORK IN PROGRESS: Celtic Landscapes; The Geographical Basis of Societal Change.

*   *   *

DOOLING, Dave
See DOOLING, David, Jr.

*   *   *

DOOLING, David, Jr.   1950-
(Dave Dooling)

PERSONAL: Born March 26, 1950, in Patuxent River, Md.; son of David (a personnel manager) and Martha Ann (Moseley) Dooling; married Jo Sharon Church (a co-owner of a store), November 19, 1977; children: Holly Ann Church. *Education:* Attended Florida Institute of Technology, 1968-69, and Old Dominion University, 1971-73.

ADDRESSES: Home—3806 Timwood Dr., Huntsville, Ala. 35810. *Office*—Alabama Space and Rocket Center, Huntsville, Ala. 35807.

CAREER: Newport News Daily Press, Newport News, Va., copy editor, 1974-76; *UJF News*, Norfolk, Va., managing editor, 1976; *Huntsville Times*, Huntsville, Ala., science editor, 1977-85; Essex Corp., Huntsville, research associate, 1985-86; employed with Alabama Space and Rocket Center, Huntsville, 1986—. Managing editor of *Canopus*.

MEMBER: American Institute of Aeronautics and Astronautics, National Space Club.

AWARDS, HONORS: Press Award from National Space Club, 1980; Goddard History Essay Prize, 1982; Ralph Coats Roe Medal from American Society of Mechanical Engineers, 1985.

WRITINGS:

UNDER NAME DAVE DOOLING

(Editor) *Shuttle to the Next Space Age*, American Institute of Aeronautics and Astronautics, 1979.
(With wife, Sharon Dooling) *Huntsville: A Pictorial History*, Donning, 1980.
Space Travel: A History, Harper, 1985.

Contributor to *Encyclopaedia Britannica* and to magazines, including *Spaceflight* and *Journal of the British Interplanetary Society*. Editor of *Space World*, 1981-84.

WORK IN PROGRESS: The Next Space Age, on future space missions.

SIDELIGHTS: David Dooling, Jr., told *CA:* "I am now specializing in space-oriented writing and developing space curricula for high school and college students and interested adults. My concern at the Alabama Space and Rocket Center is the same one I had when I was in the newspaper business. I want to contribute toward proper public understanding of aerospace technology and issues."

*　　*　　*

DOREN, Marion (Walker)   1928-

PERSONAL: Born July 10, 1928, in Glen Ridge, N.J.; daughter of Robert M. S. (in advertising) and Marion (an artist; maiden name, Lockwood) Walker; married George V. Doren (a musician and teacher), April 15, 1950; children: Anne Doren Krupsky, Martin V., Keith D., Laurie Doren Camillucci. *Education:* Connecticut College for Women (now Connecticut College), B.A., 1949; graduate study at Framingham State College, 1963-80, and College of Charleston, 1983.

ADDRESSES: Home—1107 Liberty Court, Mount Pleasant, S.C. 29464.

CAREER: Elementary schoolteacher in Madison, Conn., 1949-50; Missouri Historical Society, St. Louis, lecturer, 1950; housewife, 1950-62; elementary schoolteacher in Marlborough, Mass., 1962-64, and Southborough, Mass., 1965-81; writer, 1981—.

MEMBER: National League of American Pen Women (historian), Society of Children's Book Writers, Charleston Women's Network, Newcomers East of the Cooper.

AWARDS, HONORS: Fiction Award from South Carolina Arts Commission, 1986, for short story "Green Wishes"; Christopher Award, 1987, for *Borrowed Summer*.

WRITINGS:

Borrowed Summer (juvenile), Harper, 1986.

Contributor of articles and stories to magazines, including *Berkshire Sampler*, *Discovery*, *Today's Christian Parent*, *True Love*, and *Horsemen's Yankee Pedlar*, and newspapers.

WORK IN PROGRESS: Rich Little Poor Girl; Nell of Blue Harbor; A Pony in the Field.

SIDELIGHTS: Marion Doren told *CA:* "When I hit New York, diploma in hand, I was ready to write copy for anyone. Instead I was advised to go to Katie Gibbs, work for fifteen years in the secretarial pool, and then I might be chosen to write. I took a course in education, married, had four children, and wrote in secret. For most of my adult life I was involved with my own children and the children in my classes, so it was natural to begin by writing for them.

"After so many years of being controlled by school bells, it is a new experience to set my own schedule. I have been influenced mainly by women writers who have faced the same dilemmas I have: balancing child-raising, working, and writing. *Borrowed Summer*, the result of having to put my mother in a nursing home, spent three years traveling from editor to editor. I write for children, not markets or editors, and this will probably make me the Grandma Moses of the writing world."

*　　*　　*

DOTTO, Lydia   1949-

PERSONAL: Surname is pronounced "*Dott*-o"; born May 29, 1949, in Cadomin, Alberta, Canada; daughter of August Joseph and Assunta (Paron) Dotto. *Education:* Attended University of Alberta, 1968-69; Carleton University, B.J. (with honors), 1971.

ADDRESSES: Office—52 Three Valleys Dr., No. 9, Don Mills, Ontario, Canada M3A 3B5.

CAREER: Globe and Mail, Toronto, Ontario, science writer, 1972-78; free-lance writer, 1978—. Executive co-editor of Canadian Science News Service, 1983—; reporter for *Edmonton Journal*, summer, 1969, and *Toronto Star*, summers, 1970-71; public speaker.

MEMBER: Canadian Science Writers Association (president, 1979-80).

AWARDS, HONORS: Citation from Canadian National Newspaper Awards, 1974, for article on diving in the Arctic; Canadian Science Writers Association, science and technology awards, 1974, for article on nuclear terrorism, and 1981, for article on high energy physics, science and society award, 1984, for article on women in science; award from Canadian Meteorological Society, 1975, for articles on weather and climate; Sandford Fleming Medal from Royal Canadian Institute, 1983, for promoting understanding of science among the Canadian public.

WRITINGS:

(With Harold Schiff) *The Ozone War*, Doubleday, 1978.
Planet Earth in Jeopardy: The Environmental Consequences of Nuclear War, Wiley, 1986.

Canada in Space, foreword by Marc Garneau, Irwin, 1987.
One Third of a Lifetime: The Impact of Sleep on Waking Life, Irwin, 1989.

Contributor to magazines and newspapers, including *Quest, Canadian Geographic, High Technology, enRoute*, and *Canadian Business*.

FILMS

"The First Canadian Astronaut" (television film), Filmcentre Productions, 1984.
"The Space Experience" (six-part television series), Filmcentre Productions, 1987.

WORK IN PROGRESS: A science fiction novel.

SIDELIGHTS: Lydia Dotto told *CA:* "When people ask me why I became a writer, I tell them that I did not choose writing; writing chose me. I started writing when I was about eight years old and had my first free-lance newspaper article published when I was fourteen. Until then, I'd been telling myself to choose a 'practical' profession, like teaching, but seeing my byline in print for the first time sealed my fate.

"I got my first part-time newspaper job when I was in high school and continued to work as a newspaper reporter while attending journalism school. While I was in university, I became interested in the space program and decided I wanted to become a science writer. After graduation, I was lucky enough to be hired as the science and space writer for Canada's national newspaper, the *Globe and Mail*.

"In the six years I worked there, I had many fascinating assignments. I wrote a story on the development of Arctic diving techniques which gave me an opportunity to participate in two dives under six feet of Arctic ice. I also covered manned space missions, including the Apollo, Skylab, and space shuttle programs and planetary missions. One of the highlights was being selected by the National Aeronautics and Space Administration (NASA) as a member of the press pool aboard the aircraft carrier *Ticonderoga* for the recovery of the first Skylab crew in 1974. This was the first time a woman had been on board a U.S. aircraft carrier at sea. Later I participated in a flight aboard a NASA zero gravity training plane, which allowed me to experience the same kind of weightlessness experienced by astronauts in space.

"While I was at the *Globe*, I also did a great deal of writing about environmental issues, especially the controversy over the impact of fluorocarbons (spray can propellants) on the earth's protective ozone shield. In 1978, I wrote a book on the subject with Harold Schiff, a Canadian atmospheric scientist.

"Although I enjoyed my job at the *Globe*, I felt a need to move beyond newspaper writing and particularly to do more in-depth coverage of important scientific issues. Newspaper reporting allows you to cover a wide range of interesting topics, but rarely allows you to do more than skate across the surface of issues. I found this increasingly frustrating, so, in 1978, I decided to become a free-lancer and devote my efforts to writing magazine articles and books.

"At the beginning of the 1980s, the space program started to pick up again. I had long wanted to do a book about the Canadian space program, and the selection of Canada's first astronauts in 1983 provided exactly the focal point I needed. For the next four years, I devoted most of my time to writing the book *Canada in Space*, which is about Canada's involvement in the manned space program, particularly our contri-

bution to the U.S. shuttle and space station programs. The book features a unique, behind-the-scenes account of the astronaut training program and details Canada's plans for the future, including our participation in the space station.

"My interest in science writing stems from my curiosity about how the world works and my fascination with the unknown. I am particularly intrigued with the role played by science and technology in shaping the future. For this reason, I am also an avid science fiction fan. I am also concerned about the impact of scientific and technological discoveries on people's lives. I believe that, on the whole, the impact has been good, but this does not blind me to the fact that there have been many bad side effects of modern industrialization—particularly increased global pollution, climate modification, and the arms race. However, I don't believe that stopping the march of science and technology is the solution to these problems—rather, the solution, or at least part of it, lies in an informed and knowledgeable public. This is why I believe that the job of disseminating information about scientific and technological discoveries is particularly important in today's world. People have a right to information about the impact of these discoveries on their daily lives, on their health, and on the environment. Such knowledge puts people in a better position to defend themselves and to bring pressure to bear on the political and industrial system to minimize the risks inherent in our use of new technologies and the fruits of new scientific knowledge."

Dotto's first book, *The Ozone War*, describes the controversy that erupted in 1974, when two scientists from the University of California announced that the earth's protective ozone layer was disappearing into space and that the culprits were the fluorocarbons in popular aerosol products. Dotto and co-author Schiff describe the development of this theory, the scientific debate and the personalities of the people involved in it, and the reactions of the regulatory agencies and aerosol manufacturers which were forced to deal with the tenuous problem. In the *Washington Post Book World* Colin Norman wrote, "*The Ozone War* helps to put the whole debate into perspective." Adding that "Dotto and Schiff do a particularly fine job in reconstructing the scientific debate over the theory," the critic commended their "enterprising and lively manner." According to Norman, the authors concluded "that products should not be granted the same rights as people. They should not be assumed innocent until proven guilty." In *New Republic*, Nicholas Wade described the book as a lively and "pertinent political primer for those interested in knowing what to believe when groups of equally qualified experts issue flatly contradictory statements." The critic felt that "Dotto and Schiff have an acute understanding of the scientific decision-making process."

Canada in Space is the story of Canada's manned space program, concentrating on the contributions of Canadian industry and science to the development of the space station and shuttle program. Bill Knapp of the *Globe and Mail* found in the book "a colorful tapestry, rich with detail," and he described Dotto's style as "straightforward and down-to-earth, . . . very easy to read, with a delicate sprinkling of wonderfully wry humor." He summarized it as "an excellent book" and concluded that it "sets the standard" for future studies of the Canadian space program.

BIOGRAPHICAL/CRITICAL SOURCES:

PERIODICALS

Globe and Mail (Toronto), March 21, 1987.

New Republic, October 7, 1978.
Washington Post Book World, May 10, 1978.

* * *

DOWDEN, Wilfred S(ellers) 1917-

PERSONAL: Born April 5, 1917, in Sebree, Ky.; son of Roy Houston and Bessie Grace Dowden; married Betty Rose Dillon in 1944 (died in 1977); married Sumarie Larson Sutton in 1979; children: one. *Education:* Vanderbilt University, A.B., 1939, M.A., 1940; University of North Carolina at Chapel Hill, Ph.D., 1949.

ADDRESSES: Office—Department of English, Rice University, Box 1892, Houston, Tex. 77251.

CAREER: Rice University, Houston, Tex., began as assistant professor, 1950, professor of English, 1960-87, professor emeritus, 1987—, chairman of department, 1963-68. Fulbright lecturer at University of Vienna, 1952-53.

MEMBER: Modern Language Association of America, South Central Modern Language Association (president, 1966).

WRITINGS:

(Editor) *The Letters of Thomas Moore*, Oxford University Press, 1965.
Joseph Conrad: The Imaged Style, Vanderbilt University Press, 1970.
(Editor) *The Journal of Thomas Moore*, Associated University Presses, Volume I, 1983, Volume II, 1984, Volume III, 1986, Volume IV, 1987, Volume V, 1988, Volume VI, in press.

Contributor to literature journals.

BIOGRAPHICAL/CRITICAL SOURCES:

PERIODICALS

Times Literary Supplement, January 1-7, 1988.

* * *

DRAGLAND, Stan L(ouis) 1942-

PERSONAL: Born December 2, 1942, in Calgary, Alberta, Canada; son of Kenneth Arthur (a gambler) and Mydra (a teacher; maiden name, Roberts) Dragland; married Truus Alberta Schalk, May 15, 1965 (divorced May, 1987); married Marnie Margaret Parsons (a teacher), May 30, 1987; children: Michael Tobias, Simon Jesse, Rachel Emily. *Education:* University of Alberta, B.A., 1964, M.A., 1966; Queen's University, Kingston, Ontario, Ph.D., 1970.

ADDRESSES: Home—47 Briscoe St. W., London, Ontario, Canada N6J 1M4. *Office*—Department of English, University of Western Ontario, London, Ontario, Canada N6A 3K7.

CAREER: University of Alberta, Edmonton, lecturer in English, 1965-66; English teacher and department head at grammar school in Sudbury, England, 1966-67; University of Alberta, lecturer in English, 1967-68; University of Western Ontario, London, assistant professor, 1970-77, associate professor of English, 1977—.

MEMBER: Writers Union of Canada.

WRITINGS:

Wilson MacDonald's Western Tour, Coach House Press, 1975.
Peckertracks, Coach House Press, 1978.

Simon Jesse's Journey (juvenile), Groundwood, 1984.
Journeys Through Bookland, Coach House Press, 1985.

WORK IN PROGRESS: A book on Duncan Campbell Scott and Treaty Number Nine.

SIDELIGHTS: Stan L. Dragland told *CA:* "Across Depot Creek from the cottage north of Kingston, Ontario—where I have spent the last fifteen summers—I have built a small writing hut. The hut replaces the 'dining' tent which replaced another in its turn. In those tents, pitched under two oaks for shade and cool, all of my creative writing has been done. That is the place of my soul, quiet and creatured and green, where I write fictions about the life I lead in the gentle and savage books I read and in the houseless fascinating world."

* * *

DRAYHAM, James
See MENCKEN, H(enry) L(ouis)

* * *

DREISS, Joseph G. 1949-

PERSONAL: Born December 30, 1949, in Jersey City, N.J.; son of Louis John (a banker) and Dorothy Ann (an executive; maiden name, Corcoran) Dreiss; married Carol Ann Kennedy (a housewife), October 12, 1974; children: Erik Ryan, James Louis. *Education:* Fairleigh Dickinson University, B.A., 1972; Rutgers University, M.A., 1974; State University of New York at Binghamton, Ph.D., 1980.

ADDRESSES: Home—809 Sylvania Ave., Fredericksburg, Va. 22401. *Office*—Mary Washington College, Fredericksburg, Va. 22401.

CAREER: Art historian at Mary Washington College, Fredericksburg, Va. Partner of Dreiss & Grover, fine arts consultants and appraisers.

MEMBER: College Art Association of America.

WRITINGS:

Gari Melchers: His Works in the Belmont Collection, University Press of Virginia, 1984.

WORK IN PROGRESS: Research on American sculpture, 1880-1930.

SIDELIGHTS: Joseph G. Dreiss told *CA:* "My primary interests are art and literature. I am a professional art historian and critic, and my goal is to become a full-time writer and sculptor."

* * *

DRIVER, Donald 1922-1988

OBITUARY NOTICE: Born October 21, 1922, in Portland, Ore.; died of acquired immune deficiency syndrome (AIDS), June 27, 1988, in New York, N.Y. Broadcaster, actor, dancer, director, playwright, and author. Driver earned a Tony nomination in 1967 for his first directing effort on Broadway, a restaging of "Marat-Sade" by Peter Weiss. Beginning his career as a radio announcer in Seattle, Washington, he moved to New York City in 1948 to study ballet; he performed as a dancer and actor on stage for several years before his interest turned to directing and writing. In addition to "Marat-Sade," Driver directed "Jimmy Shine," starring Dustin Hoffman, and a revival of Thornton Wilder's "Our Town," which starred

Henry Fonda. His writings include the co-authored Off-Broadway musical "Your Own Thing," "Status Quo Vadis," which he also directed, the 1981 musical "Oh Brother!" which was acquired by Cablevision for production in 1989, and "In the Sweet Bye and Bye," first produced in Buffalo, New York, in 1988. Among Driver's non-theater projects were "G.I. Jive," written for the Public Broadcasting Service, and a screenplay of Desmond Morris's book *The Naked Ape,* which he also directed.

OBITUARIES AND OTHER SOURCES:

BOOKS

Contemporary Dramatists, 3rd edition, St. Martin's, 1982.
Who's Who in America, 40th edition, Marquis, 1978.
Who's Who in the Theatre: A Biographical Record of the Contemporary Stage, 17th edition, Gale, 1981.

PERIODICALS

New York Times, June 28, 1988.
Washington Post, June 29, 1988.

*   *   *

DRURY, William 1918-

PERSONAL: Born December 24, 1918, in Middlesbrough, England; son of Walter A. and Ethel (Maugham) Drury; married Winifred A. Foulkes (a nurse), December 26, 1964. *Education:* Constantine College, B.A., 1930. *Politics:* None. *Religion:* None.

ADDRESSES: Home and office—1326 20th Ave., No. 201, San Francisco, Calif. 94122. *Agent*—Richard Curtis Associates, Inc., 164 East 64th St., Suite 1, New York, N.Y. 10021.

CAREER: Daily Mail, London, England, drama critic, 1945-52; *Singapore Standard,* Singapore, editor, 1952-58; *Honolulu Star-Bulletin,* Honolulu, Hawaii, columnist, 1958-64; *San Francisco News Call-Bulletin,* San Francisco, Calif., columnist, 1964-66; Fiji Visitors Bureau, Suva, Fiji, executive director, 1966-68; free-lance writer, 1968—. *Military service:* Royal Air Force, 1939-45.

WRITINGS:

Chindit Column 76 (war memoirs), Longmans, Green, 1945.
Norton I: Emperor of the United States, Dodd, 1986.

Editor of *Pacific,* 1964.

*   *   *

DRYSDALE, Helena 1960-

PERSONAL: Born May 6, 1960, in London, England, daughter of Andrew (an insurance underwriter) and Merida (a conservationist; maiden name, Gascoigne) Drysdale; married Richard Pomeroy (an art dealer). *Education:* Trinity College, Cambridge, M.A., 1982.

ADDRESSES: Home—Basement, 176 Stockwell Rd., London SW9 9TG, England. *Agent*—Imogen Parker, Curtis Brown Ltd., 162-168 Regent St., London W1R 5TB, England.

CAREER: Artscribe, London, England, editor, journalist, and art critic, 1982-84; free-lance writer, photographer, and lecturer, 1984—. Arts editor for *Richmond Times* and *Twickenham Times,* 1982-84.

WRITINGS:

Alone Through China and Tibet, Constable, 1986.

Contributor of articles and photographs to magazines and newspapers.

WORK IN PROGRESS: A novel set in a meditation center in Sri Lanka.

SIDELIGHTS: Helena Drysdale told *CA:* "*Alone Through China and Tibet* recounts a five-month journey starting in Canton during the new year festivities in February, 1985, continuing down to the remote hills of Hainan Island, across the wastelands of northwest China to Tibet, and thence to Nepal. The journey was undertaken purely in a spirit of adventure, and it is this that I have tried to capture in the book. My experiences along the way ranged from the hilarious to the macabre: I was hailed as a visiting VIP in Hainan, took part in a spectacular Lantern Festival, and witnessed the dawn Sky Burial in Tibet. Exploring back streets, markets, temples, on bicycles, buses, and trains, I traveled and lived with ordinary people—teachers, sailors, black marketeers, monks—made friends and visited their families, at a time when China was just beginning to open its doors to the West and when the lives of these peoples were changing dramatically.

"I discovered the exhilaration—and occasional anxiety—of traveling alone: the contradictory urge to go on, and yet also to turn and run back for home. This too I tried to capture, as honestly and straightforwardly as possible: the loneliness and discomfort, the thrill, the sadness. Reviewers have pointed out the candor of the book, and emphasized the personal nature of the account.

"Travel is one of my major interests, and I have visited the United States, Eastern and Western Europe, Turkey, India, Nepal, Burma, Thailand, Hong Kong, China, Sri Lanka, and Bangladesh. Travel, however, is becoming more of an inspiration for writing, both travel books and novels, than purely an end in itself."

BIOGRAPHICAL/CRITICAL SOURCES:

PERIODICALS

Catholic Herald, October 31, 1986.
New Statesman, November 28, 1986.
Times Literary Supplement, January 16, 1987.

*   *   *

DUBAN, James 1951-

PERSONAL: Born March 14, 1951, in Paris, France; American citizen born abroad; son of Edmund Irving and Sylvia (Mould) Duban; married in 1981; children: one. *Education:* University of Massachusetts at Amherst, B.A., 1972; Cornell University, M.A., 1975, Ph.D., 1976.

ADDRESSES: Office—Department of English, University of Texas at Austin, Austin, Tex. 78712.

CAREER: Cornell University, Ithaca, N.Y., lecturer in English and American literature, 1976-77; University of Texas at Austin, assistant professor, 1977-82, associate professor of American literature, 1982—.

MEMBER: Modern Language Association of America, Nathaniel Hawthorne Society, Herman Melville Society.

AWARDS, HONORS: Grant from American Council of Learned Societies, 1978; distinguished teaching awards from University of Texas, 1981 and 1986.

WRITINGS:

Melville's Major Fiction, Northern Illinois University Press, 1983.

Contributor to literature journals, including *American Literature, New England Quarterly,* and *Nineteenth-Century Fiction.*

WORK IN PROGRESS: Herman Melville and Henry Whitney Bellows: On and Beyond the Consensus Ideology of Nineteenth-Century America.

*   *   *

Du BRUL, Paul   1938(?)-1987

OBITUARY NOTICE: Born c. 1938 in Brooklyn, N.Y.; died of cardiac arrest due to complications of cystic fibrosis, December 18, 1987, in New York, N.Y. Labor organizer, social and political activist, civil servant, and author. Known for his fight to ban the use of lead-based paint in New York City apartments, Du Brul successfully lobbied for legislation to outlaw the practice. He began his career as a union leader and civil rights worker, and during the late 1970s he served as special assistant to New York State Attorney General Robert Abrams. Later he served as special assistant to the state social services commissioner of New York. With former Hunter College classmate Jack Newfield, Du Brul wrote about the abuse of power in *The Permanent Government.* According to Du Brul's *New York Times* obituary, American economist and writer John Kenneth Galbraith considered the book possibly "the best piece of urban journalism since Lincoln Steffens."

OBITUARIES AND OTHER SOURCES:

PERIODICALS

New York Times, December 20, 1987.

*   *   *

DUCHIN, Faye   1944-

PERSONAL: Born January 20, 1944, in Bayonne, N.J.; daughter of Jules (a printer) and Mary (a teacher) Duchin; married Micha Brym (a manager), March 2, 1973; children: Moon, Maya. *Education:* Cornell University, B.A., 1965; University of California, Berkeley, M.A., 1972, Ph.D., 1973.

ADDRESSES: Office—Institute for Economic Analysis, New York University, 269 Mercer St., New York, N.Y. 10003.

CAREER: Mathematica, Inc., Princeton, N.J., economist, 1974-78; New York University, New York, N.Y., associate research scientist at Institute for Economic Analysis, 1978-80, senior research scientist, 1980-81, associate director of institute, 1981-86, director, 1986—, research professor, 1987—.

MEMBER: American Economic Association, American Association for the Advancement of Science, New York Academy of Science.

WRITINGS:

(With Wassily Leontief) *Military Spending: Facts, Figures, Worldwide Implications and Future Outlook,* Oxford University Press, 1983.
(With Leontief) *The Future Impact of Automation on Workers,* Oxford University Press, 1986.

Contributor to economic journals.

WORK IN PROGRESS: "Over the next couple of years I expect to examine in detail the technological options facing individual sectors of the U.S. economy and the economic and other considerations for choosing among them. My colleagues and I will cover the entire economy in this way as a basis for analyzing the interactions among decisions taken in different parts of the economy; we will give particular attention to the activities of different types of households."

SIDELIGHTS: Faye Duchin told *CA:* "I feel that considerable progress can be made through a scientific approach to understanding and anticipating economic and social changes. The key to this progress is combining the power of formal mathematical models with detailed, systematic observation and description of the day-to-day activities carried out within the society. Using such computer models and data bases it is possible to anticipate now the likely future implications of alternative lines of action. This analysis can help identify the most important areas where public and private decisions can make a discernible difference and provide information to improve the quality of such decisions.

"My writing is based on my technical research, but I believe it is also accessible to the non-specialized reader who is willing and able to take the time to understand the framework and logic of the analysis. This is the type of nonfiction I find stimulating to read—by contrast with a popularized treatment that relies more on opinion and persuasion than reason.

"The fundamental concepts underlying the work of my research institute are based on input-output economics, and I have had the good fortune to work for more than a decade with the person who created this approach, Wassily Leontief. We are now carrying this approach forward in new directions."

*   *   *

DUMENIL, Lynn   1950-

PERSONAL: Born October 9, 1950, in Houston, Tex.; daughter of Joe B. and Margaret (Brosius) Dumenil. *Education:* Attended Rice University, 1968-70; University of Southern California, B.A., 1974; University of California, Berkeley, M.A., 1976, Ph.D., 1981.

ADDRESSES: Home—Pasadena, Calif. *Office*—Department of History, Claremont McKenna College, Claremont, Calif. 91711.

CAREER: University of California, Berkeley, visiting lecturer in history, 1981-83; Whitman College, Walla Walla, Wash., assistant professor of history, 1983-85; Claremont McKenna College, Claremont, Calif., assistant professor of history, 1985—.

MEMBER: American Historical Association, Organization of American Historians, American Studies Association.

WRITINGS:

Freemasonry and American Culture, 1880-1930, Princeton University Press, 1985.

WORK IN PROGRESS: The Modern Temper: American Culture in the 1920s, completion expected in 1990; research on Roman Catholics in twentieth-century America.

SIDELIGHTS: Lynn Dumenil has written what critic Lewis L. Gould called "a solid contribution in a fresh field of history."

Her study covers the history of the Scottish Rite Masons from the late nineteenth century, when it was largely a religious organization, to the period between the world wars. Dumenil shows that Masonry functioned not only as a Protestant religious lay order but as a cohesive socializing force for the middle classes. At the end of the nineteenth century, Masons had a haven from social unrest, religious issues, and political controversy. After World War I the elaborate religious ritual of the order faded, and Masons turned more and more to community service and social activities. The order gained social status, as prominent members of the community sought its Christian fellowship and public benevolence. Gould wrote in the *Times Literary Supplement:* "Lynn Dumenil has done Masonry the credit of taking it seriously as a cultural force, and her book provides fascinating insights into an important yet little-known aspect of American history."

BIOGRAPHICAL/CRITICAL SOURCES:

PERIODICALS

Times Literary Supplement, March 15, 1985.
Virginia Quarterly Review, spring, 1985.

*   *   *

DUNBAR, Leslie W(allace) 1921-

PERSONAL: Born January 27, 1921, in Lewisburg, W.Va.; son of Marion Leslie and Minnie Lee (Crickenberger) Dunbar; married Peggy Rawls, July 5, 1942; children: Linda Dunbar Kravitz, Anthony Paul. *Education:* Cornell University, M.A., 1946, Ph.D., 1948.

ADDRESSES: Home and office—10 Whitburn Pl., Durham, N.C. 27705.

CAREER: Emory University, Atlanta, Ga., assistant professor of political science, 1948-51; Atomic Energy Commission, Aiken, S.C., chief of community affairs at Savannah River plant, 1951-54; Mount Holyoke College, South Hadley, Mass., assistant professor of political science, 1955-58; Southern Regional Council, Atlanta, director of research, 1958-61, executive director, 1961-65; Field Foundation, New York, N.Y., executive director and secretary, 1965-80. Visiting professor at University of Arizona, 1981. Member of board of directors of Franklin and Eleanor Roosevelt Institute, 1976—, and Winston Foundation for World Peace, 1984—; past president of Nation Institute; past chairman of advisory board of Center for National Security Studies; past member of board of directors of Amnesty International, U.S.A. and Field Foundation; past chairman of Children's Foundation and Minority Rights Group of New York City; past member and chairman of board of directors of Pelham Village library.

AWARDS, HONORS: Guggenheim fellow, 1954-55.

WRITINGS:

A Republic of Equals, University of Michigan Press, 1966.
(Editor) *Minority Report: What Has Happened to Blacks, Hispanics, American Indians, and Other American Minorities in the Eighties*, Pantheon, 1984.

Contributor to magazines.

WORK IN PROGRESS: A book on U.S. social welfare policies, publication by Pantheon expected in 1988; a study of "constitutionalism," publication by Norton expected in 1990.

DUNCAN, Helen (Harger Bodwell) 1902-

PERSONAL: Born June 11, 1902, in St. Mary's, Ontario, Canada; daughter of Wilber Franklin (a physician) and Effie Charlotte (a schoolteacher; maiden name, Bodwell) Brown; married William Henry Duncan (a librarian), July 5, 1933 (deceased). *Education:* University of Toronto, B.A., 1925, M.A., 1928; attended Sorbonne, University of Paris, 1926-27; Pratt Institute, degree in library science, 1932; attended Columbia University, 1940. *Politics:* "Mostly Liberal." *Religion:* "Liberal."

ADDRESSES: Home—7 Relmar Rd., Toronto, Ontario, Canada M5P 2Y4.

CAREER: Brooklyn Museum, New York City, librarian assistant, 1937-38; *Reader's Digest*, New York City, art librarian and researcher, 1957-71.

MEMBER: Royal Ontario Museum.

AWARDS, HONORS: Canada Arts Council grant for *The Treehouse*, 1975; Ontario Arts Council grant, 1988.

WRITINGS:

The Treehouse (novel), Simon & Pierre, 1975.
Kate Rice: Prospector (biography), Simon & Pierre, 1985.
Across the Bridge (novel), Simon & Pierre, 1988.
Enigmatic Night (novel), Simon & Pierre, in press.

Also author of unpublished manuscript, "Roosters on Peel Street," 1977. Short story "A Little Patience" broadcast by Canadian Broadcasting Corporation, 1960.

WORK IN PROGRESS: Brooklyn at War, a novel, publication by Simon & Pierre expected in 1991.

SIDELIGHTS: Helen Duncan's *Kate Rice: Prospector* is a loosely biographical account of the life and times of Canadian prospector Kathleen Rice. A gifted mathematician who took to the Manitoba wilderness and the male world of mineral prospecting in 1907, Rice forged a singular lifestyle that included wearing men's clothing, carrying a shotgun, and living with business partner Dick Woosey. Reviewing the book for the Toronto *Globe and Mail*, Nancy Wigston determined that "meticulous research and a measure of poetic licence" create a "lively evocation of the milieu in which Kate lived. . . . The seductive promise of hidden deposits of gold, copper and nickel, . . . the incessant danger of rapids, storms and marauding animals—all are brought to life in this compelling narrative in its exploration of the physical and psychic rhythms of our eccentric past."

Duncan told *CA:* "I began as a 'closet' writer turning out short stories that did not sell; in the late 1940's, for example, I traveled twice to Hudson Bay and—appalled by the plight of the Cree Indian—wrote a series of stories relating how educational, religious, civil, and health authorities were trying to make the Indians into proper Canadians while the government was passing laws restricting centuries-old hunting and fishing rites—a catch-22. Macmillan kept these stories for a year before finally refusing to publish them: the decision was they presented too discouraging a picture of Indian life, although it later surfaced that the Indian situation was even more disastrous than what I had portrayed. Of this series only one was produced on radio by the Canadian Broadcasting Corporation—the only amusing story of the lot about an old swampy Cree at Berens River Mission in northern Manitoba who 'takes on' the Mother Superior, and wins. Another story on a different subject concerned the effect of the writings of Karl Marx on an enlightened Michigan farmer, 1899-1900. While the usual comment generated by this story was that Marx was unknown in America at that time, it is based on my own farmer grandfather's terrible shock at encountering Marx's *Manifesto* at the turn of the century.

"My first novel, *The Treehouse,* evokes a doctor's family where the wife dies and a neighbor tries, by hook or by crook, to marry and supplant her—thwarted by the intrigues of an older son. *Kate Rice: Prospector* took five years to research, and about as long to write. Only bits and snatches could be gleaned from still-living prospectors about Kate and her business partner Dick Woosey (they shared a cabin). Parts of the story are fictionalized, but always based on the characters of Kate and her companion. Not a true biography, it is a recreation of a life, a time, and a place. Woosey was a noncommissioned British Army officer and Kate was a 1906 gold medalist in mathematics at the University of Toronto. Several film companies are interested in their story.

"*Kate Rice* is a direct result of my great interest in the frontiers of the United States and Canada; I am a great lover of North America and of U.S. and Canadian histories, and am descended from colonial stock on both sides. I find all the old names fascinating: Daniel Boone, Kit Carson, George Washington, Benjamin Franklin, John Butler and his son Walter. My reading leans heavily towards the historical. My third book, *Across the Bridge,* is a novel about spies in Canada before World War I. While the story is based on my own mother's unwitting acquaintanceship with two spies in 1939, I have changed the date to 1914, equating it with Canada's loss of innocence."

Duncan continued: "I have traveled to France many times, living there one year during Sorbonne days, and taking a house in St. Remy-en-Provence in the summer of 1965. I am bilingual (French and English). I am still a 'closet' writer."

BIOGRAPHICAL/CRITICAL SOURCES:

PERIODICALS

Globe and Mail (Toronto), March 9, 1985.

*   *   *

DUNNIGAN, Alice Allison   1906-1983

PERSONAL: Born April 27, 1906, in Russellville, Ky.; died of ischemic bowel disease, May 6, 1983, in Washington, D.C.; daughter of Willie and Lena Pittman; married Charles Dunnigan, January 8, 1932; children: Robert William. *Education:* Attended Western Kentucky Industrial College, 1930-32; Louisville Municipal College, 1935; Tennessee Agricultural and Industrial State College (now Tennessee State University), 1936-37; Howard University, 1943.

ADDRESSES: Home—1462 Ogden St., Washington, D.C. 20010. *Office*—801 19th St., Washington, D.C. 20006.

CAREER: Teacher in Kentucky public schools, 1924-42; federal government employee, 1942-46; Associated Negro Press, Washington, D.C., bureau chief and member of Senate and House of Representatives press galleries, 1947-61, White House correspondent, 1948-61; U.S. Department of Labor, Washington, D.C., information officer, 1965-67. Writer for several Kentucky newspapers, including the *Louisville Defender, Kentucky Reporter,* and *Hopkinsville Globe,* from 1920, and the *Atlanta Daily World.* Served on speaker's bureau of the Dem-

ocratic National Committee during the 1948 presidential election campaign; member of the Inaugural Public Relations Committee, 1949. Educational consultant to the President's Commission on Equal Employment Opportunity, 1961-65; associate editor for the President's Council on Youth Opportunity, 1967-70; member of the Presidential Committee for "National Employ the Physically Handicapped Week."

MEMBER: National Council of Negro Women, Women's National Press Club, Writer's Association, Capital Press Club, White House Correspondent's Association, State Department Correspondent's Association, First Lady's Press Association, Sigma Gamma Rho.

AWARDS, HONORS: Elected to the University of Kentucky's Journalism Hall of Fame; recipient of more than fifty journalism awards.

WRITINGS:

A Black Woman's Experience: From Schoolhouse to White House, Dorrance, 1974.
The Fascinating Story of Black Kentuckians: Their Heritage and Traditions, Associated Publishers, 1982.

Contributor of articles to various magazines and newspapers.

SIDELIGHTS: Following an early career as a public school teacher and newspaper writer in Kentucky, Alice Allison Dunnigan moved to Washington, D.C., in 1942. While in the capital she worked for the federal government but maintained her interest in journalism by contributing articles, on a freelance basis, to several Kentucky newspapers. Her appointment as chief of the Washington bureau of the Associated Negro Press, in 1947, signaled her full-time commitment to journalism as a career.

During her fourteen years with the bureau, Dunnigan had the distinction of becoming the first black female member of the Senate and House of Representatives press galleries, in 1947, the first black female White House correspondent in 1948, and the first black elected to the Women's National Press Club. Her reputation as a journalist grew steadily throughout the 1940s, reaching a peak with her reporting of President Harry S. Truman's election campaign of 1948 when, as one of only three black newspaper reporters with the Truman entourage, she became the only woman to accompany the president throughout his entire western campaign.

In addition to her career in journalism, Dunnigan was a committed member of several social policy advisory organizations, including the Presidential Committee on Equal Employment Opportunity between 1967 and 1970, lending her own accomplishments to the community as a fine example of minority achievement. After her retirement in 1970 Dunnigan continued to contribute articles to newspapers and completed two books: her autobiography, *A Black Woman's Experience,* and *The Fascinating Story of Black Kentuckians: Their Heritage and Traditions.*

OBITUARIES:

PERIODICALS

New York Times, May 9, 1983.
Washington Post, May 8, 1983.*

*   *   *

DuPONT, Robert L(ouis), Jr.   1936-

PERSONAL: Born March 25, 1936, in Toledo, Ohio; son of

Robert Louis (in sales) and Martha Ireton (a teacher; maiden name, Lancashire) DuPont; married Helen Gayden Spink (a manager), July 14, 1962; children: Elizabeth, Caroline. *Education:* Emory University, B.A., 1958; Harvard University, M.D., 1963.

ADDRESSES: Home—8708 Susanna Lane, Chevy Chase, Md. 20815. *Office*—6191 Executive Blvd., Rockville, Md. 20852.

CAREER: Western Reserve University (now Case Western Reserve University), Cleveland, Ohio, intern, 1963-64; Harvard Medical School, Boston, Mass., resident in psychiatry, 1964-66; National Institutes of Health, Bethesda, Md., clinical associate, 1966-68; private practice of psychiatry, 1969—. Diplomate of American Board of Psychiatry and Neurology; president of Institute for Behavior and Health, Inc., 1978—, and American Council for Drug Education, 1980-84; director of Center for Behavioral Medicine, 1978—; vice-president of Bensinger, DuPont Associates, Inc., 1983—. Research psychiatrist and acting associate director for community services at District of Columbia Department of Corrections, 1968-70; administrator of Narcotics Treatment Administration, District of Columbia Department of Human Resources, 1970-73; U.S. Department of Health, Education and Welfare, director of National Institute on Drug Abuse, 1973-78, acting administrator of Alcohol, Drug Abuse, and Mental Health Administration, 1974; director of Special Action Office for Drug Abuse Prevention, Executive Office of the President, 1973-75; U.S. delegate to United Nations Commission on Narcotic Drugs, 1973-78; member of Coordinating Council on Juvenile Justice and Delinquency Prevention, U.S. Department of Justice, 1974-78. Associate clinical professor at George Washington University, 1972-80; visiting associate professor at Harvard University, 1978—; clinical professor at Georgetown University, 1980—; guest on television programs, including "Good Morning, America." Member of advisory committee of Washington Junior League, 1972-76. *Military service:* U.S. Public Health Service, surgeon, 1966-68; became major.

MEMBER: World Psychiatric Association, Pan American Medical Association, American Psychiatric Association (fellow), Phobia Society of America (president, 1982-84), Washington Psychiatric Society, Washington Society for Performing Arts (member of board of directors, 1972-76).

WRITINGS:

Getting Tough on Gateway Drugs: A Guide for the Family, American Psychiatric Press, 1984.

Contributor to medical journals.

SIDELIGHTS: Robert L. DuPont, Jr., told *CA:* "My current interests include drugs in the workplace and the use of benzodiapines (like Valium and Xanax) in the treatment of anxiety. My long-term interests include a variety of 'behavioral disorders' ranging from panic/phobia and eating disorders to delinquency and chemical dependency. My focus is often on the positive roles that can be played by family and community in both prevention and treatment. The self-help movement built around Alcoholics Anonymous is one of the most remarkable, wise, and compassionate expressions of the American spirit. I use this tradition in much of my work with my patients and in the public policy area."

*   *   *

DUPREE, Robert S(cott)   1940-

PERSONAL: Born May 4, 1940, in Alexander, La.; son of

Benoit Henri and Margaret (Buxton) Dupree; married Susan MacKenzie, December 22, 1973; children: Pierre, Caroline, Christian. *Education:* University of Dallas, B.A., 1962; Yale University, M.A., 1964, Ph.D., 1966.

ADDRESSES: Office—Department of English, University of Dallas, Irving, Tex. 75061.

CAREER: University of Dallas, Irving, Tex., assistant professor, 1966-73, associate professor of English, 1973—. Visiting professor at University of Besancon, 1986-87, and Internationale Akademie fuer Philosophie im Fuerstentum Liechtenstein, 1987. Fellow at Dallas Institute of Humanities and Culture.

MEMBER: South Central Renaissance Conference.

WRITINGS:

Allen Tate and the Augustinian Imagination: A Study of the Poetry, Louisiana State University Press, 1982.
(Editor, translator, and contributor) Gaston Bachelard, *Lautreamont,* Dallas Institute of Humanities and Culture, 1986.

WORK IN PROGRESS: Research on the planning and poetry of the city, particularly "the way in which cities are imagined, both by poets and by those who build them"; a book about Lewis Carroll that "seeks to approach his writings from a fresh perspective—in the light of the history of education."

SIDELIGHTS: Robert S. Dupree told *CA:* "My work on Allen Tate was inspired by my association and friendship with Caroline Gordon, from whom I intuited the importance of St. Augustine in his work. I had wanted to do a thorough reading of the whole of Tate's poetry, and this Augustinian perspective allowed me to organize my own interpretations of the poems. In the end, however, the main focus of the book emerged from a study of the poems and five drafts of the complete manuscript; it was not a schema that was imposed on the poetry but the last stage of an attempt to see what story Tate's work was telling."

BIOGRAPHICAL/CRITICAL SOURCES:

PERIODICALS

Times Literary Supplement, September 21, 1984.

*   *   *

DURYEE, Mary Ballard   1896-1988

OBITUARY NOTICE: Born January 21, 1896, in Philadelphia, Pa.; died after a stroke, March 27, 1988, in Medford, N.J. Civic activist and poet. Duryee was active in the civic affairs of New York City, serving terms as president of the Women's City Club and the Cosmopolitan Club. She published several collections of poems, including *Songs and Sonnets, Avenues of Song, No Special Pleading, Free Enterprise,* and *Signs and Wonders.* In addition, Duryee contributed to periodicals, including *New Yorker* and *Voices.*

OBITUARIES AND OTHER SOURCES:

BOOKS

Who's Who of American Women, 2nd edition, Marquis, 1961.

PERIODICALS

New York Times, April 1, 1988.

DYER, Geoff   1958-

PERSONAL: Born June 5, 1958, in Cheltenham, England; son of Arthur John (a metal worker) and Mary (a cleaner; maiden name, Tudor) Dyer. *Education:* Corpus Christi College, Oxford, B.A. (with honors), 1980.

ADDRESSES: Home—4 Crownstone Ct., London SW2 1LS, England. *Agent*—Xandra Hardie, 14 Elsworthy Ter., London NW3 3DR, England.

CAREER: Writer. Jonathan Cape Ltd., London, England, literary consultant, 1987—.

MEMBER: National Union of Journalists.

WRITINGS:

Ways of Telling: The Work of John Berger, Pluto, 1986.

Contributor of articles to periodicals, including *New Statesman, Listener, City Limits,* and *New Society.*

WORK IN PROGRESS: A fictional memoir of Brixton in the 1980s, publication by J. Cape expected in 1989.

BIOGRAPHICAL/CRITICAL SOURCES:

PERIODICALS

Times Literary Supplement, April 24, 1987.

E

EADE, Alfred Thompson 1891-1988

OBITUARY NOTICE: Born November 17, 1891, in London, England; immigrated to United States; died April 7, 1988, in Grants Pass, Ore. Educator, illustrator, and author. Originally a commercial artist and art teacher, Eade used his talent to illustrate various biblical events as an aid in Bible studies. His creations resulted in *The New Panorama Bible Study Course,* which has been printed in fourteen languages and ten dialects; first published in 1941, the book has sold more than two hundred thousand copies. Eade also wrote and illustrated the multivolume *Expanded Panorama Bible Study Course.*

OBITUARIES AND OTHER SOURCES:

PERIODICALS

New York Times, April 23, 1988.

* * *

EAMES, Elizabeth Ramsden 1921-

PERSONAL: Surname is pronounced like the name "Ames"; born February 18, 1921, in Toronto, Ontario, Canada; immigrated to United States, 1948, naturalized citizen, 1957; daughter of Francis Cleave and Vera (Frances) Ramsden; married S. Morris Eames (a professor of philosophy), 1952 (deceased); children: Ivan Lee, Anne Eames Adamczyk. *Education:* University of Toronto, A.B., 1943, M.A., 1944; Bryn Mawr College, Ph.D., 1951.

ADDRESSES: Office—Department of Philosophy, Southern Illinois University, 3026 Faner Hall, Carbondale, Ill. 62901.

CAREER: Smith College, Northampton, Mass., instructor in philosophy, 1946-47; University of Missouri—Columbia, instructor, 1948-51, assistant professor, 1951-52; Washington University, St. Louis, Mo., lecturer in philosophy, 1952-63; Southern Illinois University, Carbondale, lecturer, 1963-65, associate professor, 1965-71, professor of philosophy, 1971—.

MEMBER: American Philosophical Association (past member of executive committee), Society for Women in Philosophy, Illinois Philosophy Association (past president).

AWARDS, HONORS: Grants from American Philosophical Society, 1971, and National Endowment for the Humanities, 1977-78.

WRITINGS:

(With husband, S. Morris Eames) *Logical Methods,* Stipes, 1966.
Bertrand Russell's Theory of Knowledge, Allen & Unwin, 1969.
(Contributor) Walter Robert Corti, editor, *The Philosophy of G. H. Mead,* Archiv fuer genetische Philosophie, 1972.
(Contributor) Corti, editor, *The Philosophy of William James,* Meiner, 1976.
(With S. M. Eames) *Lectures in the Far East,* New Asia College of Hong Kong, 1980.
(Editor with Kenneth Blackwell) Bertrand Russell, *Theory of Knowledge: The 1913 Manuscript* (volume 7 of Russell's collected papers), Allen & Unwin, 1984.
Bertrand Russell's Dialogue With His Contemporaries, Southern Illinois University Press, 1988.

Contributor to philosophy journals.

WORK IN PROGRESS: Contributing to *Bertrand Russell's Philosophy of Science,* for University of Minnesota Press; with son, Ivan Lee Eames, editing *Democracy,* by her late husband, S. Morris Eames.

BIOGRAPHICAL/CRITICAL SOURCES:

PERIODICALS

Times Literary Supplement, December 7, 1984.

* * *

EARLE, Timothy K. 1946-

PERSONAL: Born August 10, 1946, in New Bedford, Mass.; son of Osborne (a professor) and Eleanor (Clark) Earle; married Eliza Howe (a landscape designer), June 14, 1969; children: Caroline, Hester. *Education:* Harvard University, B.A., 1969; University of Michigan, M.A., 1970, Ph.D., 1973.

ADDRESSES: Home—Los Angeles, Calif. *Office*—Department of Anthropology, 341 Haines Hall, University of California, 405 Hilgard Ave., Los Angeles, Calif. 90024.

CAREER: University of California, Los Angeles, assistant professor, 1973-80, associate professor, 1980-86, professor of anthropology, 1986—. Visiting fellow at Clare Hall, Cambridge, 1986-87.

MEMBER: American Anthropological Association (member of executive committee of Archaeology Unit), Society for American Archaeology, Society of Economic Anthropology (member of executive board, 1985-88).

WRITINGS:

(With Jonathon Ericson) *Exchange Systems in Prehistory,* Academic Press, 1977.

Economic and Social Organization of a Complex Chiefdom, Museum of Anthropology, University of Michigan, 1978.

(With Andrew Christenson) *Modeling Prehistoric Subsistence Change,* Academic Press, 1980.

(With Ericson) *Contexts for Prehistoric Exchange,* Academic Press, 1982.

(With Allen W. Johnson) *The Evolution of Human Societies,* Stanford University Press, 1987.

(With Elizabeth Brumfiel) *Specialization, Exchange, and Complex Societies,* Cambridge University Press, 1987.

Member of editorial board of "New Directions in Archaeology" series, Cambridge University Press. Contributor of about twenty articles to anthropology journals.

WORK IN PROGRESS: A cross-cultural study of social complexity in prestate societies, comparing pre-Roman Britain, pre-conquest Peru, and prehistoric Hawaii.

SIDELIGHTS: Timothy K. Earle told *CA:* "In my writings and research, I seek to unravel the ways in which human society evolved from simple, family-level groups to massive modern states. I have concentrated on the ways in which the economy creates opportunities for freedom, requirements for cooperation, justification for war, and powers for exploitation. In my book with Allen W. Johnson we attempt to understand the common human experience and the reasons people have become domesticated (civilized) as members of settled communities and then incarcerated in a system of inequality. The driving force behind the evolutionary change appears to be a tragic interplay between population growth, technology, and social complexity."

*   *   *

EBERLE, Nancy (Oates)   1935(?)-1988

OBITUARY NOTICE: Born c. 1935; died June 25, 1988, in Chicago, Ill. Administrator, journalist, and author. Eberle worked for the Chicago *Sun-Times* as a general assignment reporter before serving on the Chicago Board Options Exchange as vice-president in charge of advertising and marketing from 1975 to 1977. In 1978 she moved with her husband and family from a Chicago suburb to a two-hundred-acre farm in the country. She based her book *Return to Main Street: A Journey to Another America* on that experience. Eberle also wrote *Our Houses, Our Lives* and contributed articles to periodicals, including *McCall's* and *Redbook.*

OBITUARIES AND OTHER SOURCES:

PERIODICALS

Chicago Tribune, June 29, 1988.

*   *   *

EDMONDS, (Sheppard) Randolph   1900-1983

PERSONAL: Born April 30, 1900, in Lawrenceville, Va.; died March 28, 1983; son of George Washington (a tenant farmer and sharecropper) and Frances (Fisherman) Edmonds; married

Irene Colbert, 1931 (died, 1968); children: Henriette Highland Garnett, S. Randolph, Jr. *Education:* Oberlin College, B.A., 1926; Columbia University, M.A., 1932; further graduate study at Yale University, University of Dublin, and London School of Speech Training and Dramatic Art.

CAREER: Morgan State College, Baltimore, Md., instructor in English and drama, 1926-1935; Dillard University, New Orleans, La., chairman of speech and theatre department, 1935-47; Florida Agricultural and Mechanical University, Tallahassee, Fla., chairman of theatre arts department, 1947-70. Founder and president of Negro Intercollegiate Drama Association, 1930; organized Morgan College Dramatic Club, Southern Association of Drama and Speech Arts, 1936 (now National Association of Dramatic and Speech Arts; president, 1936-43), and Southeastern Theatre Conference. President of Crescent Concerts Company, New Orleans, 1942-43.

MEMBER: American Educational Theatre Association (fellow).

AWARDS, HONORS: Rockefeller Foundation scholarship, 1934-35; Rosenwald Fellowship, 1938; first prize in a contest from Foundation of Expressive Arts, 1941, for *The Land of Cotton;* Litt.D. from Bethune-Cookman College, 1947; special citation from the American Theatre Association, 1972.

WRITINGS:

PLAYS

"Rocky Roads" (three-act), first produced in Oberlin, Ohio, at Oberlin High School, May 15, 1926.

"Job Hunting" (one-act), first produced in Baltimore at Morgan College, February 18, 1928.

Shades and Shadows (contains "Shades and Shadows," "The Devil's Price," "Hewers of Wood," "Everyman's Land," "The Tribal Chief," and "The Phantom Treasure"), Meador, 1930, reprinted, University Microfilms, 1971.

"Shades and Shadows" (first produced in Baltimore at Douglass High School, April 24, 1931), published in *Shades and Shadows,* Meador, 1930 (also see above).

"Bad Man" (one-act; first produced in New York on NBC-Radio, February 26, 1932), published in *Six Plays for a Negro Theatre,* Walter H. Baker, 1934 (also see below).

Six Plays for a Negro Theatre (contains "Bad Man," "Old Man Pete," "Nat Turner," "Breeders," "Bleeding Hearts," and "The New Window"), foreword by Frederick H. Koch, Walter H. Baker, 1934, reprinted, University Microfilms, 1974.

"Nat Turner" (first produced in New Orleans at Dillard University Theatre, January 17, 1936), published in *Six Plays for a Negro Theatre,* Walter H. Baker, 1934 (also see above).

"The High Court of Historia" (first produced in New Orleans at Dillard University Workshop Theatre, February, 1939), published in *The Land of Cotton, and Other Plays,* Associated, 1942 (also see below).

"The Land of Cotton" (four-act; first produced in New Orleans at Longshoreman's Hall, March 20, 1941), published in *The Land of Cotton, and Other Plays,* Associated, 1942 (also see below).

The Land of Cotton, and Other Plays (contains "The Land of Cotton," "Gangsters Over Harlem," "Yellow Death," "Silas Brown," and "The High Court of Historia"), Associated, 1942, University Microfilms, 1974.

"Simon in Cyrene" (four-act), first produced in New Orleans at Dillard University Little Theatre, February 11, 1943.

"Earth and Stars" (first produced in New Orleans at Dillard University Little Theatre, February 13, 1946), revised version published in *Black Drama in America*, Fawcett, 1971.

"Whatever the Battle Be: A Symphonic Drama," first produced in Tallahassee at Lee Auditorium, November 3, 1950.

Also author of more than twenty-five unproduced and unpublished plays, including "A Merchant in Dixie," "For Fatherland," "Shadow Across the Path," "The Shape of Wars to Come," "The Trial and Banishment of Uncle Tom," and "Prometheus and the Atom."

Work represented in anthologies, including *Negro History in Thirteen Plays*, edited by Willis Richardson and May Miller, Associated, 1935; *The Negro Caravan*, edited by Sterling A. Brown, Arthur P. Davis, and Ulysses Lee, Dryden, 1941; and *The American Theatre: A Sum of Its Parts*, edited by Henry B. Williams, Samuel French, 1971. Contributor to periodicals, including *Arts Quarterly*, *Crisis*, *Florida A & M University Bulletin*, *Messenger*, *Opportunity*, *Pittsburgh Courier*, and *University of North Carolina Playbook*.

SIDELIGHTS: As a playwright, critic, teacher, and leader in theatre organizations, Randolph Edmonds was a driving force behind academic dramatics in Afro-American universities for more than four decades. He published many articles in journals to help foster an appreciation for collegiate and regional theatre, to educate its audience, and to urge others to take an active role in it. In his own popular plays Edmonds addressed issues ranging from civil rights to slavery, dramatized lives of prominent black historical figures, and looked to the daily experiences of blacks for subject matter.

Edmonds began writing plays while a student at Oberlin College during the 1920s. His first full-length work, "Rocky Roads," a farce about a medical student at Howard University, was produced in 1926 while he was a senior. Following graduation Edmonds taught English at Morgan State College in Baltimore, Maryland, and organized there the first drama department in any black university in the country. He also founded a student acting club that distinguished itself by being the first college players ever to appear on Broadway. After teaching at Morgan State for nine years Edmonds moved to Dillard University in New Orleans, Louisiana, where he established and directed its speech and theatre arts department. At Dillard he founded the Southern Association of Dramatic and Speech Arts and acted as its president for seven years.

Edmonds realized that a major drawback of the black American theatre was that it lacked skillful playwrights. To contend with this problem he compiled six plays that he had written while a student at Oberlin. The collection, *Shades and Shadows*, was published in 1930. Although a reviewer for the *Pittsburgh Post Gazette* wrote that the dialogue featured in the plays was "somewhat amateurish," he predicted that "with further experience [Edmonds] will be able to make important contributions to the literature of his race." The playwright's next collection, *Six Plays for a Negro Theatre*, proved the critic right, for reviewers held that the quality of Edmonds's writing was much improved. Writing in the preface the dramatist explained that his plays were meant to be staged at the "Negro Little Theatres, where there has been for many years a great need for plays of Negro life written by Negroes."

Intrigued by the folk plays that a professor at the University of North Carolina and his students were writing, Edmonds based the plays for his second collection on the experiences of Southern Negroes, who would also be the primary audience for them. The plays utilize incidents from the daily lives, legends, and language of the common people. By writing the plays in dialect, Edmonds intended to lend authenticity to the drama but was later condemned by critics who thought it degraded Negroes. The playwright defended his writing in the vernacular, however, believing that tragedy is grievous regardless of the language in which it is written. More important to Edmonds were universal themes to which the audience could relate, thought-provoking conflicts, dynamic characterization, and melodrama.

Critics praised the folk dramas of *Six Plays for a Negro Theatre* for their vivid imagery, exciting plots, and interesting characters. Most of the plays were melodramatic and sentimental, and some depicted blacks victimized by white society as well as by other members of the black community. In "Breeders," for example, Edmonds decries the practice of forcing slaves to mate so that they could produce able bodies to work the fields and in "Bad Man" he tells the tale of an innocent black man who was lynched by a mob of whites bent on avenging the murder of a white man. The playwright also explores the difficulties in adjusting to city life that many Southern Negroes and whites faced when migrating to the North during the first three decades of the twentieth century in "Old Man Pete," and the historical drama "Nat Turner" chronicles the life of the folk hero who led a slave revolt on a Virginia plantation in 1831.

In 1942 Edmonds published a third collected book of dramas with socially relevant and historical subjects, *The Land of Cotton, and Other Plays*. The work "Simon in Cyrene" is a rendering of the life of the African who helped Jesus Christ carry his cross to Calvary. The title play, "The Land of Cotton," tells the story of two men attempting to unionize black tenant farmers in the South against the resistance of the racist Ku Klux Klan, while "The High Court of Historia" is a condemnation of historians who either are not proud of their African heritage or do not instruct their students in black history.

In honor of his outstanding contributions to the development of interest in the theatre and his organizing drama departments and associations in predominately black colleges of the southern United States, Edmonds was named by the National Association of Dramatic and Speech Arts "Dean of Black Academic Theatre" in 1970. In his nearly forty-five years as an active critic and teacher he not only inspired and educated audiences and playwrights alike, but also entertained playgoers who were moved by seeing their ancestors—or even themselves—on the stage in the characters Edmonds portrayed.

BIOGRAPHICAL/CRITICAL SOURCES:

BOOKS

Abramson, Doris, *Negro Playwrights in the American Theatre, 1925-1959*, Columbia University Press, 1969.

Bond, Frederick, *The Negro and the Drama*, Associated Press, 1940.

Brawley, Benjamin G., *Negro Genius*, Dodd, 1937.

Dictionary of Literary Biography, Volume 51: *Afro-American Writers From the Harlem Renaissance to 1940*, Gale, 1987.

Dreer, Herman, *American Literature by Negro Authors*, Macmillan, 1950.

Isaacs, Edith J. R., *The Negro in the American Theatre*, McGrath, 1947.

Turner, Darwin T., editor, *Black American Literature: Essays, Poetry, Fiction, Drama*, three volumes, Merrill, 1970.
Wallace, Karl R., editor, *The History of Speech Education in America*, Appleton-Century, 1954.

PERIODICALS

Freedomways, 3rd quarter, 1982.
Pittsburgh Post Gazette, May 2, 1931.
Washington Post, February 21, 1979.*

—*Sketch by Carol Lynn DeKane*

* * *

EDWARDS, Margaret (Alexander) 1902-1988

OBITUARY NOTICE—See index for *CA* sketch: Born October 23, 1902, in Childress, Tex.; died following a stroke, April 19, 1988. Educator, librarian, and author. Though she taught high school English and Latin in Texas and Maryland, Edwards will be best remembered for her service as coordinator of young adult services for the Enoch Pratt Free Library in Baltimore, Maryland, from 1932 to 1962. An authority on library services for teenagers, she gave lectures on the subject for students of library science at many universities. Edwards wrote *The Fair Garden and the Swarm of Beasts: The Library and the Young Adult*.

OBITUARIES AND OTHER SOURCES:

BOOKS

A Biographical Directory of Librarians in the United States and Canada, 5th edition, American Library Association, 1970.

PERIODICALS

School Library Journal, June/July, 1988.

* * *

EDWARDS, Raoul D(urant) 1928-1987

OBITUARY NOTICE: Born November 3, 1928, in New York, N.Y.; died of a heart attack, December 18, 1987, in Harrison, N.Y. Administrator, consultant, journalist, and author. Edwards began his career as a reporter for *American Banker*, later serving as the trade journal's bureau manager in Washington, D.C. In 1963 he became head of the information office of the Federal Deposit Insurance Corporation and three years later joined the Bank Administration Institute as director of public relations. Edwards formed his own consulting company in 1970 and in 1977 became associate editor of *U.S. Banker*, advancing to editor in 1983. His other editorial work included posts with *Issues and Innovations* and *Financial Computing*. Edwards contributed to several books on banking and co-authored *The Changing World of Banking*.

OBITUARIES AND OTHER SOURCES:

BOOKS

Who's Who in the South and Southwest, 20th edition, Marquis, 1986.

PERIODICALS

Washington Post, December 20, 1987.

EGAN, Lesley
See LININGTON, (Barbara) Elizabeth

* * *

EGER, Jeffrey 1946-

PERSONAL: Born February 26, 1946, in Jersey City, N.J.; son of Marvin (a city administrator) and Edith (a hospital personnel director; maiden name, Seciow) Eger; married Miriam Szamosi (a real estate agent), April 18, 1969; children: Erik Kino, Alexander Asa. *Education:* Rutgers University, B.A., 1968; London School of Film Technique, Certificate, 1969; Jersey City State College, M.A., 1972. *Religion:* Jewish.

ADDRESSES: Home—42 Blackberry Lane, Morristown, N.J. 07960.

CAREER: Film producer, director, and writer, 1969—. Manager of film production company in Israel, 1974-81.

MEMBER: Writers Guild of America East, Thomas Nast Society (vice-president; director of publications).

AWARDS, HONORS: Numerous film awards, including CINE Gold Eagle from Council on International Nontheatrical Events; Emmy Award from Academy of Television Arts and Sciences.

WRITINGS:

The Statue of Liberty Enlightening the World, New York Bound Books, 1984.
Statue of Liberty Postcards, Dover, 1985.
The Statue in the Harbor: A Story of Two Apprentices (juvenile), Silver Burdett, 1986.
Uncle Sam and Friends: American Political Symbols and Cartoons, Silver Burdett, 1988.

WORK IN PROGRESS: A book and a one-hour film about political cartoons; a film series on children and cooking; a film about Louis C. Tiffany.

* * *

EHRENREICH, John H. 1943-

PERSONAL: Born February 20, 1943, in Philadelphia, Pa.; son of Joseph and Freda (Steinbrook) Ehrenreich; married first wife, Barbara, August 6, 1966 (divorced, 1981); married Sharon McQuaide (a psychotherapist), February 14, 1987; children: Rosa, Benjamin. *Education:* Harvard University, B.A., 1964; Rockefeller University, Ph.D., 1969.

ADDRESSES: Office—Department of American Studies, State University of New York College at Old Westbury, Box 210, Old Westbury, N.Y. 11568.

CAREER: State University of New York College at Old Westbury, instructor, 1972-74, assistant professor, 1974-77, associate professor, 1977-81, professor of American studies, 1981—. Lecturer in social policy at Smith College, 1979-87.

WRITINGS:

(With wife, Barbara Ehrenreich) *Long March, Short Spring: The Student Movements at Home and Abroad*, Monthly Review Press, 1969.
(With B. Ehrenreich) *The American Health Empire: Power, Profits, and Politics*, Random House, 1971.
(Editor) *The Cultural Crisis of Modern Medicine*, Monthly Review Press, 1977.

The Altruistic Imagination: A History of Social Work and Social Policy in the United States, Cornell University Press, 1985.

Contributor to magazines.

* * *

EHRENWALD, Jan   1900-1988

OBITUARY NOTICE—See index for *CA* sketch: Born March 13, 1900, in Bratislava, Czechoslovakia; immigrated to United States, 1946; died of a heart attack, June 15, 1988, in Somers, N.Y. Psychiatrist, educator, and author. Ehrenwald practiced psychiatry in Czechoslovakia, England, and the United States and served on the faculty of the University of Vienna and the State University of New York. His books include *From Medicine Man to Freud, Neurosis in the Family and Patterns of Psychosocial Defense, The ESP Experience: A Psychiatric Validation,* and *The History of Psychotherapy: From Healing Magic to Encounter,* which he edited. Ehrenwald also contributed many articles on psychiatry, neurology, psychoanalysis, and parapsychology to professional journals.

OBITUARIES AND OTHER SOURCES:

PERIODICALS

New York Times, June 18, 1988.

* * *

EISLER, Paul (Erich)   1922-1978

OBITUARY NOTICE—See index for *CA* sketch: Born September 3, 1922, in New York, N.Y.; died December 12, 1978, in New York, N.Y. Musician, administrator, educator, and author. Eisler, a faculty member of a number of colleges and universities, including the Manhattan School of Music, Concordia College, and New York University, served as dean of arts and sciences at New England College from 1960 to 1965. He was also a conductor and pianist for operas and symphonies and author of *History of the Metropolitan Opera, 1883-1908,* and the multivolume *World Chronology of Music History.*

OBITUARIES AND OTHER SOURCES:

BOOKS

Who's Who in the East, 17th edition, Marquis, 1979.

* * *

ELDER, Rob(ert Laurie)   1938-

PERSONAL: Born June 23, 1938, in Nashville, Tenn.; son of Charles Jerome and Dorothea Eloise (Calhoun) Elder; married Betty Ann Doak, September 1, 1958 (divorced May, 1969); married wife, Sarah (divorced); married Gloria Charmian Duffy, September 30, 1984; children: (first marriage) Mark Christopher, Jeffrey Cathcart. *Education:* Washington and Lee University, B.A., 1960; Vanderbilt University, M.A., 1966; graduate study at Stanford University, 1976-77. *Religion:* Episcopalian.

ADDRESSES: Office—c/o *San Jose Mercury News,* 750 Ridder Park Dr., San Jose, Calif. 95190.

CAREER: Tennessean, Nashville, Tenn., reporter, 1964-68; Southern Newspaper Publishers Association Foundation, Atlanta, Ga., assistant director, 1969; *Miami Herald,* Miami, Fla., reporter, 1970-76; *San Jose Mercury News,* San Jose,

Calif., editor, 1978—. Member board of directors of the World Affairs Council, 1984—. *Military service:* U.S. Army, 1960-62.

AWARDS, HONORS: Distinguished Achievement Award from Florida Society of Newspaper Editors, 1973.

WRITINGS:

(With wife, Sarah Elder) *Crash* (nonfiction), Atheneum, 1977.

BIOGRAPHICAL/CRITICAL SOURCES:

PERIODICALS

Washington Post Book World, March 27, 1977.

* * *

ELGOOD, Robert (Francis Willard)   1948-

PERSONAL: Born July 9, 1948, in Cardiff, Wales; son of F. R. M. (a pediatrician) and M. M. (Peat) Elgood. *Education:* School of Oriental and African Studies, London, received B.A. *Politics:* Conservative.

ADDRESSES: Home—18 Hyde Park Sq., London W.2., England. *Office*—Sotheby's, 34-35 New Bond St., London W1A 2AA, England.

CAREER: Islamic department consultant for Sotheby's, London, England; lecturer.

MEMBER: United Kingdom Falkland Islands Association (executive committee member).

WRITINGS:

(Editor) *Islamic Arms and Armour,* Scolar Press, 1979.

WORK IN PROGRESS: Research on Islamic swords and on Archibald Percival Wavell, viceroy of India.

SIDELIGHTS: The essay collection *Islamic Arms and Armour,* edited by Robert Elgood, indicates a growing interest in this comparatively neglected field of Islamic art. "Arms and armour were esteemed by the elites of [the Islamic world] not only for their value in maintaining contending claims to power but also as *objets de grand luxe,* of exquisite craftsmanship and lavish and expensive ornamentation," explained Simon Digby in the *Times Literary Supplement.* The essays explore such aspects as manufacture, use, attribution, and collection, and while noting that *Islamic Arms and Armour* "is a far from comprehensive survey of the field," Digby commended its "exacting standards of scholarship." The reviewer concluded: "On all these topics the volume has something to add to previous knowledge."

Elgood told *CA:* "From my viewpoint the most important circumstance in my career must be my birth, followed by my nationality. I have always been acutely grateful for both. For the rest I have merely responded to the virtues and vices of the age."

BIOGRAPHICAL/CRITICAL SOURCES:

PERIODICALS

Times Literary Supplement, August 1, 1980.

* * *

ELLIS, Dan C.   1949-

PERSONAL: Born October 10, 1949, in Norman, Okla.; son

of Robert E. (a pharmacist) and Mary (a loan officer; maiden name, Lundquist) Ellis; married first wife, Rosemary, August 9, 1975 (divorced, 1980); married Ruth Wendl (an ultrasonographer), September 21, 1985; children: Abby. *Education:* Northern Arizona University, B.S., 1971, M.A., 1972; Union Graduate School, Cincinnati, Ohio, Ph.D., 1980. *Religion:* Roman Catholic.

ADDRESSES: Home—1530 South 143rd St., Omaha, Neb. 68144. *Office*—Hudson Center, 12111 Pacific St., Omaha, Neb. 68154.

CAREER: Alcoholism Counselor Training Institute, Lincoln, Neb., executive director, 1978-82; Catholic Social Services, Omaha, Neb., psychotherapist, 1982-83; Hudson Center, Omaha, psychotherapist, 1983—. Member of faculty at University of Nebraska, 1978-85.

WRITINGS:

Essentials of Chemical Dependency Counseling, Aspen Systems Corp., 1984.
Growing Up Stoned: Coming To Terms With Teen-age Drug Abuse in Modern America, Health Communications, 1986.

Also author of novel, *Drunken Destiny,* as yet unpublished.

Contributor to psychology journals.

WORK IN PROGRESS: Two novels, including one set in the counterculture of the early 1970s; research on multi-generational influences on the development of chemical dependency.

SIDELIGHTS: Dan C. Ellis told *CA:* "I am very interested in the generational influences on present and future behavior—family legacies. I recently returned from India, where I studied alcoholism and the Indian family.

"I fell into the field of chemical dependency by accident in 1974. Since then I have progressively focused my attention upon adolescents and families. Over the years I have collected a portfolio, you might say, of profoundly dramatic stories about real people. Many of these stories I would have said were the creations of a screenwriter if I had not heard and seen them played out in true life.

"With chemical dependency *affecting* one in every four people, it seems that many of us have realized some of these gut-wrenching stories first hand. Such a common phenomenon should be interesting reading to a large segment of the American population. This realization lead to me write my first novel, *Drunken Destiny,* about a three-generational alcoholic family. Now I am working on two other novels. One, which I am most interested in, takes place in the early 1970s. It is about the counterculture—drugs and people seeking the 'truth.' I have woven in some of my own experiences from that period, when I lived in a variety of communes.

"We have learned much in the past twenty years about drug abuse, but the problem seems to be just as serious as ever. Each generation coming up must learn for itself the dangers of drugs. Our early prevention efforts have proven to be mostly ineffectual. Recently I was involved in a project to develop a state-of-the-art school prevention program. It involved translating my second book, *Growing Up Stoned,* to a video format. I am excited about this project as I believe it is breaking some new ground in the drug prevention field."

ELLIS, John H. 1931-

PERSONAL: Born September 29, 1931, in Memphis, Tenn.; son of John H. and Esther (Sides) Ellis; married Wanda Roper, July 1, 1949; children: Elaine Ann Ellis Tucci, John L., Suzanne. *Education:* Memphis State University, B.S., 1955, M.A., 1957; Tulane University, Ph.D., 1962. *Religion:* Christian.

ADDRESSES: Home—1431 Dalehurst Dr., Bethlehem, Pa. 18018. *Office*—Department of History, Lehigh University, Bethlehem, Pa. 18015.

CAREER: Memphis State University, Memphis, Tenn., assistant professor of history, 1960-64; Georgia State University, Atlanta, assistant professor of history, 1964-65; U.S. Public Health Service, National Institute of General Medical Sciences, Bethesda, Md., postdoctoral research fellow, 1965-67; Georgetown College, Georgetown, Ky., associate professor of history and director of institutional research, 1967-71; Lehigh University, Bethlehem, Pa., associate professor, 1971-79, professor of history, 1979—. *Military service:* U.S. Air Force, 1948-51; became sergeant.

MEMBER: American Association for the History of Medicine, Association for the History of Chiropractic, Southern Historical Association.

WRITINGS:

Medicine in Kentucky, University Press of Kentucky, 1977.

WORK IN PROGRESS: A nonfiction book, tentatively titled *The D.C.s: A History of Chiropractic in America.*

SIDELIGHTS: John H. Ellis told *CA:* "My book *Medicine in Kentucky* was solicited by the University Press of Kentucky as part of its 'Bicentennial Bookshelf' series during the 1970s. There were thirty or forty titles in the series, I believe, on Kentucky subjects such as bourbon whiskey, thoroughbred horses, the Shakers, and so forth. I was asked to do the one on medicine. Kentucky was the first state established after the original thirteen colonies, so I guess the distinctive or unique feature of medicine there was that of medicine in a frontier, pioneer westward-moving society. It is an interesting story and I very much enjoyed doing it.

"As a teacher of medical history, I noticed some years ago that there is no reliable scholarly, objective history of chiropractic. This is a major deficiency in the history of medicine and the healing arts. As a historian of medicine, I hope to fill that gap with my forthcoming study on the history of chiropractic in America, which hopefully I will complete in time for the centennial of the founding of chiropractic in 1995. While my book will be primarily a history of the chiropractic profession and its institutions—licensure, schools, professional organizations, and so forth—it will also feature chiropractic as a social phenomenon and its relationship to the development of scientific medicine during the past one hundred years. I consider this work an extremely important undertaking, and I am encouraged by peers who hold the same view."

*   *   *

El-SHABAZZ, El-Hajj Malik
See LITTLE, Malcolm

ELWOOD, Ann 1931-

PERSONAL: Born January 3, 1931, in Ridgewood, N.J.; daughter of E. S. (a carpenter) and Helen (a housewife; maiden name, Buhlman) Elwood. *Education:* Fairleigh Dickinson University, B.A., 1952; graduate study at University of California, San Diego, 1981—.

ADDRESSES: Home—2442 Montgomery Ave., Cardiff, Calif. 92007.

CAREER: Glencoe Press (publishing company), Beverly Hills, Calif., advertising manager, 1967-72; free-lance writer, 1952-67, 1972—.

AWARDS, HONORS: Windows in Space was named a "distinguished work of nonfiction" by Southern California Council on Literature for Children and Young People, 1983.

WRITINGS:

FOR YOUNG PEOPLE

(With John Raht) *Walkin' Out,* Grosset, 1979.
(With Carol Orsag and Sidney Solomon) *The Macmillan Illustrated Almanac for Kids,* Macmillan, 1981.
(With Linda C. Wood) *Windows in Space,* Walker and Co., 1982.
(With Carol Madigan) *Brainstorms and Thunderbolts,* Macmillan, 1983.
(With Madigan) *Kids' World,* Macmillan, in press.

WORK IN PROGRESS: A biography of Elizabeth Ranfaing, founder of convents for "fallen women," completion expected in 1989; research on French nuns, 1630-1792.

SIDELIGHTS: Ann Elwood told *CA:* "When I was in France in 1985-1986, I spent most of my time in the provincial archives, primarily in Avignon, Nancy, and Besancon. In Avignon I lived in a cheap motel with my dog (who had accompanied me on the trip), where from the backyard through clotheslines and junk I could see the Papal Palace on the other side of the river. Besancon and Nancy were cold in the winter, but the sense of neighborhood gave them emotional warmth. Living abroad, one feels always to be a stranger, even when one speaks the language; however, this also gives the sense of distance and marginality that often are the source of insight into a culture.

"I became interested in French nuns because as a francophile, I wanted to do research in France rather than some other country, and as a social historian, I wanted to study women who were not in families. The Notre Dame du Refuge left behind excellent records in several cities; partly because the nuns took in fallen women and women of all levels of society, sometimes in uneasy proximity. The founder, Elisabeth de Ranfaing, was a young widow who became possessed by the devil (in the early 1600s), then, having recovered, started the Refuge. She was the central figure in a Jesuit cult that was suppressed by Rome. After her death, she was responsible for several miraculous cures, or so people said.

"It is difficult to say at this point what my final conclusions will be, but I hope to find some correlation between the nuns' changing mentalities, as revealed in funeral biographies and other documents, and the changing status of the convents (downward), and I want to show how society's attitudes toward 'bad women' shifted over the seventeenth and eighteenth centuries and what this meant to Notre Dame du Refuge."

EMMONS, Nuel 1927-

PERSONAL: Born September 17, 1927, in Non, Okla.; son of Sidney Emmons and Christena (a seamstress; maiden name, Folsom) Emmons Melton; married Virginia Fessenden, November 10, 1946 (divorced January 30, 1966); married Elizabeth Wilson Quiett (an accountant and auditor), May 16, 1966; children: (first marriage) Terry White, Cynthia Flaherty, Ron Melton; Bob Quiett, Doug Quiett (stepchildren). *Education:* Took courses through College of Puget Sound (now University of Puget Sound), 1961-62.

ADDRESSES: Office—Emmons, Inc., P.O. Box 446, Nice, Calif. 95464. *Agent*—Writers House, Inc., 21 West 26th St., New York, N.Y. 10010.

CAREER: Self-employed autobody repairman and painter, 1946-78; *Clear Lake Observer,* Clear Lake, Calif., sports and feature writer, 1978-79; *Lake County Record Bee,* Lakeport, Calif., correspondent, 1978-79; *Ukiah Daily Journal*/Donrey Media, Ukiah, Calif., sports and feature writer, 1979-82; free-lance photojournalist, 1984-88. Member of Lake County drug advisory board, 1985—; youth counselor. *Wartime service:* Seaman in U.S. Army Transport Service, 1945-46.

MEMBER: Golf Writers Association of America.

WRITINGS:

(With Charles Manson) *Manson in His Own Words,* Grove, 1986 (published in England as *Without Conscience: Charles Manson in His Own Words,* Grafton & Co., 1987).

Author of golf column "Meet the Pros" in *Ukiah Journal,* 1981-83. Contributor to *Score* and *Woman's World.*

WORK IN PROGRESS: Dear Mom and Dad, a nonfiction book dealing with parent/child relationships; *The Other Side of Fame,* a novel exploring the struggles and pitfalls of fame and glory seekers; *Third Life of a Black Athlete,* examining the difficult childhoods, sports stardom, and postcareer letdowns of three black athletes.

SIDELIGHTS: Nearly two decades ago cult leader Charles Manson and other members of his communal family were convicted of the brutal slayings of eight California residents. Known as the Tate-La Bianca murders, the case focused on the disturbing figure of Manson and the ominous power he held over the troubled young men and women who shared his world of sex and drugs and followed his orders for random murder. Appearing in the media as the embodiment of evil, Manson "would come to symbolize," wrote Gary L. Cunningham in the *Los Angeles Times Book Review,* "the end of the '60s and what went wrong with them." *Manson in His Own Words,* as told to Nuel Emmons (a reformed car thief and Manson jailmate during the mid-fifties), is an autobiographical account of the murderer's life. Based on seven years of interviews and correspondences, the book is an attempt—according to Emmons—to demystify the monster. Calling the volume "fascinating" in the *Times Literary Supplement,* Patricia Highsmith determined, "This book explains, as far as patient inquiry and frank answers can, why Charles Manson's curious yet banal life-story led to the violence that was to land him in jail for the rest of his life." "It is likely that this book, as it claims, gives us a portrait close to the truth," *New York Times Book Review* critic Alison Friesinger agreed.

Like its inscrutable narrator, *Manson in His Own Words* stirred a variety of interpretations; the convict's claim that he is a reflector—and not an originator—of evil drew particular comment. An unwanted child raised with abuse in institutions, Manson presents himself as a mirror of society's ills, a kid who never stood a chance. Finding the man manipulative and "surprisingly cowardly," Friesinger decided, "finally, and most importantly, he seems crazy." Yet in the *New York Times* Christopher Lehmann-Haupt judged Manson far more astute: "Passages detailing how adroitly he manipulated his group do not exactly square with his impassioned renunciations of the roles of evil genius and charismatic leader," wrote the critic, adding that transfusing blame will do little to "reduce the dimensions of his myth by much, or greatly ease what is apparently the burden of his guilt." Similarly relating that the convict "reveals a surprisingly canny view of the world and a realistic understanding of what he has done," *Washington Post* reviewer David Black reiterated, "It is easy to see how he commanded the attention and loyalty of others." *Manson in His Own Words* "is a worthwhile document, a glimpse of part of the American experience that is rarely described from the inside," continued the critic. "It is not literature, but neither is it merely exploitation. It compels both interest and horror." And Cunningham expressed this concern: "The real unanswered question is whether the specter of Charles Manson is just a frightening aberration or a true product of our juvenile and criminal systems."

Emmons told *CA:* "As a youth I was a better-than-average athlete. I excelled at golf and baseball, but at sixteen (during World War II) I started to get into trouble. It wasn't until 1964 (at age thirty-six) that I realized what a mess I had made, not only of my life, but of my family's. I took a hold of my life—doing right—and the rewards were so self-satisfying. Gratified, I wanted to reach out and help others. Writing something of essence for every reader—regardless of subject matter—is my motivation.

"The Manson book is not written in a sensational manner. It is a true look at an unsuccessful man (at everything) who—through other writings and sensationalized media coverage—has become so notorious that he is considered intriguing and mystifying. For those fascinated by Manson's notoriety, the simplicity of my narrative presents a less complicated view. And if those who despise the man can get past their hostilities, they can find clues in the book that might prevent another Charles Manson.

"Certainly, like any writer, I reach into my own past for emotions that relate to my writing subjects. Unfortunately (for me, but I hope valuable to my readers), I have been closely associated with some of the societal ills of which I write.

"My sportswriting is, again, a throwback to my past. The better part! But whether a story is about a well-known sports celebrity or the world's most notorious villain, something can be gained by each reader.

"I think a reformed felon is very much like a born-again Christian. He or she is always trying to straighten someone out, or relate something that will shed some light on people's lives."

MEDIA ADAPTATIONS: Manson in His Own Words is being adapted by Heritage Entertainment as a film of the same name, with release expected in 1989.

BIOGRAPHICAL/CRITICAL SOURCES:

PERIODICALS

Los Angeles Times Book Review, January 4, 1987, July 5, 1987.
New York Times, January 19, 1987.

New York Times Book Review, January 25, 1987.
Times Literary Supplement, June 12, 1987.
Washington Post, February 6, 1987.

*   *   *

ENDELMAN, Todd M(ichael)   1946-

PERSONAL: Born November 10, 1946, in Fresno, Calif.; son of Albert L. (a merchant) and Marcelle N. (a housewife; maiden name, Todresic) Endelman; married Judith Epstein (a librarian), June 16, 1968; children: Michael, Flora. *Education:* University of California, Berkeley, B.A., 1968; Hebrew Union College-Jewish Institute of Religion, Los Angeles, Calif., B.H.L., 1972; Harvard University, A.M., 1972, Ph.D., 1976.

ADDRESSES: Home—3519 Paisley Court, Ann Arbor, Mich. 48105. *Office*—Department of History, University of Michigan, Ann Arbor, Mich. 48109.

CAREER: Yeshiva University, New York, N.Y., assistant professor of Jewish history, 1976-79; Indiana University—Bloomington, assistant professor, 1979-81, associate professor of modern Jewish and European history, 1981-85; University of Michigan, Ann Arbor, professor of Jewish history, 1985—.

MEMBER: American Historical Association, Jewish Historical Society of England, Leo Baeck Institute, Association for Jewish Studies.

AWARDS, HONORS: A. S. Diamond Memorial Prize from Jewish Historical Society of England and National Jewish Book Award, both 1980, both for *The Jews of Georgian England, 1714-1830.*

WRITINGS:

The Jews of Georgian England, 1714-1830: Tradition and Change in a Liberal Society, Jewish Publication Society, 1979.
(Editor and contributor) *Jewish Apostasy in the Modern World,* Holmes & Meier, 1987.

CONTRIBUTOR

David Berger, editor, *The Legacy of Jewish Migration: 1881 and Its Impact,* Brooklyn College Press, 1983.
Harry S. Allen and Ivan Volgyes, editors, *The Middle East, Israel, and U.S. National Interests,* Praeger, 1983.
Shlomo Simonsohn and Robert Rockaway, editors, *Michael: On the History of the Jews in the Diaspora,* Volume X, Diaspora Research Institute, University of Tel Aviv, 1986.
Jacob Katz, editor, *Toward Modernity: The European Jewish Model,* Transaction Books, 1986.
Berger, editor, *History and Hate: The Dimensions of Anti-Semitism,* Jewish Publication Society, 1986.
Jehuda Reinharz, editor, *Living With Antisemitism: Modern Jewish Responses,* University Press of New England, 1987.

Contributor to history and Jewish studies journals.

WORK IN PROGRESS: Radical Assimilation in Anglo-Jewish History: Conversion and Intermarriage From the Resettlement to World War II.

*   *   *

EPPSTEIN, John   1895-1988

OBITUARY NOTICE: Born in 1895; died April 2, 1988. International relations activist, administrator, and author. Active in international relations for more than fifty years, Eppstein was the first secretary-general of the Atlantic Treaty Association (ATA), which he helped establish; at one time he also served as ATA's director of education, working closely with the Atlantic Information Centre for Teachers. He began his career after World War II as an officer of the League of Nations Union, serving as an assistant secretary in the organization, and for a time was attached to the League of Nations section of the foreign office. Eppstein also founded the British Society for International Understanding in 1938 and, as a proponent of collective security, devoted his later years to the cause of the North Atlantic Treaty Organization (NATO). In 1935 Eppstein wrote *The Catholic Tradition of the Law of Nations*, which American Catholic universities adopted as a standard text, and in 1972, in response to the Second Vatican Council, published *Has the Catholic Church Gone Mad?*

OBITUARIES AND OTHER SOURCES:

PERIODICALS

Times (London), April 7, 1988.

*   *   *

ERENBERG, Lewis A.   1944-

PERSONAL: Born September 30, 1944, in Los Angeles, Calif.; son of Isidore (a cab driver) and Shirley (a bookkeeper; maiden name, Zientz) Erenberg; married Phyllis Vine, June 12, 1966 (divorced); married Susan E. Hirsch (a professor), October 15, 1978; children: Jesse, Joanna. *Education:* University of California, Los Angeles, B.A. (cum laude), 1966; University of Michigan, Ph.D., 1974.

ADDRESSES: Home—Chicago, Ill. *Office*—Department of History, Loyola University, 820 North Michigan Ave., Chicago, Ill. 60611.

CAREER: Loyola University, Chicago, Ill., assistant professor, 1976-80, associate professor of history, 1980—. Visiting assistant professor at Bowdoin College, spring, 1975, and University of Virginia, 1975-76.

MEMBER: American Historical Association, Organization of American Historians, American Studies Association, Phi Beta Kappa.

WRITINGS:

Steppin' Out: New York Nightlife and the Transformation of American Culture, 1890-1930, Greenwood Press, 1981.

WORK IN PROGRESS: A history of popular musical culture from 1920 to 1950.

SIDELIGHTS: Lewis A. Erenberg's *Steppin' Out* compares the entertainments of Victorian America, which were centered around the home and family, with the colorful nightlife that had developed in urban areas by 1920. Cabarets and other public places of entertainment were not considered respectable in the last years of the nineteenth century, but after the turn of the century, American entertainers and other colorful public figures began to patronize New York City's glamorous cabarets, restaurants, and lobster palaces. Gradually, these opulent night spots came within the reach of middle-class Americans, and by the 1920s the social stigma of such public display had disappeared. Robert Dawidoff wrote in the *Los Angeles Times Book Review:* "*Steppin' Out* shows how people's fun reveals interesting things about their lives." Frances Taliaferro told readers of the *New York Times Book Review,* "The general

reader will find much of interest in its lively material and workable thesis."

BIOGRAPHICAL/CRITICAL SOURCES:

PERIODICALS

Los Angeles Times Book Review, September 6, 1981.
New York Times Book Review, August 16, 1981.

*   *   *

ERLICH, Gloria C.

PERSONAL: Born in Baltimore, Md.; daughter of Daniel M. (an optometrist) and L. Blanche (a philanthropist; maiden name, Nessel) Chasson; married Philip Erlich (a psychiatrist), May 24, 1953; children: Julie, Austin. *Education:* Goucher College, B.A. (with honors), 1946; Stanford University, M.A., 1950; Princeton University, Ph.D., 1977.

ADDRESSES: Home and office—41 Littlebrook Rd., Princeton, N.J. 08540.

CAREER: Rutgers University, New Brunswick, N.J., Douglass College, instructor in English, 1965-69; Rider College, Lawrenceville, N.J., lecturer in English, 1969-71; Dickinson College, Carlisle, Pa., assistant professor of English, 1978-79; Rutgers University, visiting assistant professor of English, 1986-87. Princeton Research Forum, founding member, vice-president, 1985-87, president, 1987—; member of biography seminars at New York University's Institute for the Humanities, 1980—; visiting scholar at Douglass College, Rutgers University, 1986; visiting fellow at Beinecke Library, Yale University, 1987.

MEMBER: Modern Language Association of America, Nathaniel Hawthorne Society (member of executive board, 1981-86), Edith Wharton Society, Melville Society, Northeast Modern Language Association, Phi Beta Kappa.

AWARDS, HONORS: Prize for Independent Scholars from Modern Language Association of America and House of Seven Gables Hawthorne Award, both 1985, for *Family Themes and Hawthorne's Fiction;* grant from National Endowment for the Humanities, 1987; fellow of American Council of Learned Societies, 1988-89.

WRITINGS:

Family Themes and Hawthorne's Fiction: The Tenacious Web, Rutgers University Press, 1984, revised edition, 1986.

Contributor to literature journals. Member of editorial board of *Nathaniel Hawthorne Review*, 1983—.

WORK IN PROGRESS: Double Mothers and the Creative Imagination: Freud, Wharton, Faulkner; The Sexual Education of Edith Wharton.

SIDELIGHTS: Gloria C. Erlich told *CA* that "the structure of the life course" is one of her major interests, as are "biographical theory, paradigms for writing lives, and subjectivity in interpretation." Her other concerns include "the imprint of the family constellation on the creative imagination." The author added that her curiosity about "the ways in which selves are constructed and represented" provides the driving question that motivates her work.

"Regarding my *Double Mothers* book," she continued, "in it, as I did in *Family Themes,* I trace the creative transformations of a psychic design experienced first within the family constellation by individuals with unique kinds of receptivity and perception and later modified by social expectations and experience. But in *Double Mothers* I study the imprint of secondary nurturing figures, such as nannies, nursemaids, or mammies, on the lives and works of a selected group of writers. The project explores specific instances in which creative people experienced a divided perception of maternal care. I try to bring together human individuality, general psychological principles, and family systems theory (all operating within particular social and historical contexts) in order to illuminate not the creative gift itself but how the creativity found its particular channel and course.''

BIOGRAPHICAL/CRITICAL SOURCES:

PERIODICALS

Christian Science Monitor, July 10, 1986.
Journal of Personality, March, 1988.
New York Review of Books, May 9, 1985.

*   *   *

ETTLING, John 1944-

PERSONAL: Born October 30, 1944, in Poplar Bluff, Mo.; son of Albert J. (a clergyman) and Emily (Tucker) Ettling; married Jennifer Tarlin, September 30, 1974; children: Sarah, Rachel. *Education:* University of Virginia, B.A., 1966; Harvard University, A.M., 1972, Ph.D., 1978.

ADDRESSES: Office—Department of History, University of Houston, Houston, Tex. 77004.

CAREER: Northwestern University, Evanston, Ill., visiting assistant professor of history, 1978-79; University of Houston, Houston, Tex., assistant professor, 1979-83, associate professor of history, 1983—, chairman of department, 1984—. *Military service:* U.S. Air Force, 1966-71; became captain.

MEMBER: American Historical Association, Organization of American Historians, American Association for the History of Medicine.

AWARDS, HONORS: Allan Nevins Prize from Society of American Historians, 1979, and Friends of the Dallas Public Library Award from Texas Institute of Letters, 1982, both for *The Germ of Laziness.*

WRITINGS:

The Germ of Laziness: Rockefeller Philanthropy and Public Health in the New South, Harvard University Press, 1981.

*   *   *

EVANS, G. B.
See EVANS, Gwynne Blakemore

*   *   *

EVANS, G. Blakemore
See EVANS, Gwynne Blakemore

*   *   *

EVANS, Gwynne B.
See EVANS, Gwynne Blakemore

EVANS, Gwynne Blakemore 1912-
(G. B. Evans, G. Blakemore Evans, Gwynne B. Evans)

PERSONAL: Born March 31, 1912, in Columbus, Ohio; son of Marshall Blakemore and Theodora (Grose) Evans; married Florence Elizabeth Richey, June 1, 1943; children: Michael Blakemore, Pamela Grose. *Education:* Ohio State University, A.B., 1934; University of Cincinnati, M.A., 1936; Harvard University, Ph.D., 1940.

ADDRESSES: Home—985 Memorial Dr., No. 201, Cambridge, Mass. 02138. *Office*—Warren House, Harvard University, Cambridge, Mass. 02138.

CAREER: University of Wisconsin—Madison, instructor, 1941-42 and 1945-46, assistant professor of English, 1946-47; University of Illinois at Urbana-Champaign, Urbana, assistant professor, 1947-51, associate professor, 1951-56, professor of English, 1956-67; Harvard University, Cambridge, Mass., professor of English literature, 1967-75, Cabot Professor of English Literature, 1975—. *Military service:* U.S. Army, Signal Corps Intelligence, 1942-45.

MEMBER: Renaissance English Text Society, Academy for Literary Studies, Phi Beta Kappa.

AWARDS, HONORS: Dexter traveling fellow, 1940; Guggenheim fellow, 1948-49.

WRITINGS:

EDITOR UNDER NAME G. BLAKEMORE EVANS, EXCEPT AS NOTED

(And author of introduction) Cartwright, William, *Plays and Poems,* University of Wisconsin Press, 1951.
Shakespeare, William, *The Tragedy of Richard the Third* (play), Penguin, 1959, revised, 1969.
Shakespearean Prompt-books of the Seventeenth Century, six volumes, Bibliographical Society of the University of Virginia, 1960-1980.
(With others) *Milton Studies: In Honor of Harris Francis Fletcher* (essays), University of Illinois Press, 1961, reprinted, Folcroft, 1974, reprinted, Norwood, 1977.
(Under name Gwynne Blakemore Evans, with George Walton Williams) Shakespeare, William and Sir Edward Dering, *The History of King Henry the Fourth, as Revised by Sir Edward Dering, Bart.* (play), University Press of Virginia, 1974.
Shakespeare, William, *The Riverside Shakespeare* (collected works), Houghton, 1974.
(Under name G. B. Evans) *Shakespeare: Aspects of Influence* (essays), Harvard University Press, 1976.
Shakespeare, William, *Romeo and Juliet* (play), Cambridge University Press, 1984.
(Assistant editor) Chapman, George, *The Plays of George Chapman: The Tragedies,* edited by Alan Holaday and others, Boydell & Brewer, 1987.

OTHER

Contributor, sometimes under name Gwynne B. Evans, of monographs, articles, and reviews to literature journals, including *Shakespeare Quarterly* and *Library.* Editor of *Journal of English and Germanic Philology,* 1955-62; member of editorial board of *Proceedings of the Modern Language Association,* 1963-69.

WORK IN PROGRESS: Elizabethan-Jacobean Drama: A New Mermaid Background Book; Volumes VII and VIII of *Shakespearean Prompt-books.*

EWING, John A(lexander) 1923-

PERSONAL: Born March 17, 1923, in Largo, Fife, Scotland; immigrated to United States, 1951, naturalized citizen, 1959; son of James Anderson and Esther Stratton (Turner) Ewing; married Janet S. G. Combe, October 31, 1946; children: Christine, Ian James. *Education:* University of Edinburgh, M.B., Ch.B., 1946, M.D., 1954; University of London, Diploma in Psychological Medicine, 1950; additional study at Washington Psychoanalytic Institute and University of North Carolina at Chapel Hill, 1959-69.

ADDRESSES: Office—2311 Canterwood Dr., Wilmington, N.C. 28401.

CAREER: Royal Infirmary, Preston, Scotland, intern, 1946-47; Gogarburn Hospital, Edinburgh, Scotland, intern, 1947; University of Durham, Durham, England, resident in psychiatry at university hospital, 1947-50; Cherry Knowle Hospital, Sunderland, England, senior registrar, 1950-51; North Carolina Alcoholic Rehabilitation Center, Butner, psychiatrist, 1951-54; University of North Carolina at Chapel Hill, clinical instructor, 1953-54, instructor, 1954-56, assistant professor, 1956-59, associate professor, 1959-63, professor of psychiatry, 1963-84, professor emeritus, 1984—, chairman of department, 1965-70, chairman of staff of university hospital, 1965-67, director of Center for Alcohol Studies, 1970-84. Assistant physician at Psychiatric Clinic, Royal Infirmary, Sunderland, and S. Shields General Hospital, both 1949-51; senior physician at John Umstead Hospital, Butner, 1951-54; director of Psychiatric In-Patient Service, North Carolina Memorial Hospital, 1957-64; consultant psychiatrist at Watts Hospital, Durham, N.C., 1957—.

MEMBER: American College of Psychiatrists (fellow), American Psychiatric Association (fellow; president, 1965-67), American Academy of Psychoanalysis (fellow), American Medical Association, American Medical Society on Alcoholism, American Association of Social Psychiatry, American Association for the Advancement of Science, American Psychosomatic Association, American Orthopsychiatric Association, Royal College of Psychiatrists (fellow), British Medical Association, Caribbean Psychiatric Association, Association for the Advancement of Psychotherapy, North Carolina Medical Society, North Carolina Neuropsychiatric Association, Alpha Omega Alpha.

WRITINGS:

(Editor with Beatrice A. Rouse) *Law and Drinking Behavior,* Center for Alcohol Studies, University of North Carolina at Chapel Hill, 1971.

(Editor with Rouse) *Drinking: Alcohol in American Society; Issues and Current Research,* Nelson-Hall, 1978.

Drinking to Your Health, Reston, 1981.

(With R. W. McNichol and M. D. Faiman) *Disulfiram (Antabuse): A Unique Medical Aid to Sobriety,* Thomas, 1987.

Contributor to medical journals.

WORK IN PROGRESS: Updating *Drinking to Your Health.*

SIDELIGHTS: John A. Ewing told *CA:* "I was prompted to do research on alcoholism and drug dependence because we knew so little about the origins of these diseases. Now we know we are dealing with the interplay of biological, psychological, and environmental forces and that genetic factors are important. The chemistry of the brain is proving to be another key to our understanding. My book *Drinking to Your Health* was written as a guide for lay people and to show that alcoholic beverages do not necessarily have to cause damage or induce alcoholism. Virtually all of my other writings are technical and medical."

F

FAIRWEATHER, Eileen 1954-

PERSONAL: Born June 6, 1954, in London, England; daughter of Arthur (a clerk) and Mary (McCauley) Fairweather; children: Katarina Fairweather Holmberg. *Education:* University of Sussex, B.A., 1975. *Politics:* "Feminist and liberal socialist." *Religion:* "Lapsed Catholic."

ADDRESSES: Home—Brighton, England.

CAREER: Actress and playwright, 1975-79; *Spare Rib* (feminist journal), London, England, member of editorial collective, 1979-80; free-lance writer, 1980—.

MEMBER: National Union of Journalists, Writers Guild of Great Britain.

AWARDS, HONORS: Catherine Pakenham/*Evening Standard* Award for Young Women Journalists from London *Evening Standard,* 1983, for an article on prostitution; *Only the Rivers Run Free* was among the Selected Twenty of the International Feminist Book Fair, 1985.

WRITINGS:

(With Roisin McDonough and Melanie McFadyean) *Only the Rivers Run Free: Northern Ireland, the Women's War,* Pluto, 1984.
French Letters: The Life and Loves of Miss Maxine Harrison, Form 4A (young adult novel), Women's Press, 1987.
French Leave (young adult novel), Women's Press, in press.

Work represented in anthologies, including *Hard Feelings: Fiction From Spare Rib,* Women's Press, 1979; *The Other Britain: Twenty Years of Writing From New Society,* Routledge & Kegan Paul, 1982; *Fathers: Reflections by Daughters,* Virago, 1983, Pantheon, 1985; and *Women's Health: A Spare Rib Reader,* Pandora, 1987.

Author of plays and film scripts; radio writer. Contributor to magazines and newspapers, including *New Society.* Contributing editor of British edition of *Cosmopolitan;* children's book reviewer for *Good Housekeeping.*

SIDELIGHTS: Eileen Fairweather described herself to *CA* as "a Gemini with a compulsive need to communicate; a woman of Catholic background, which leads to interesting hang-ups and the constant need to question 'the meaning of life'; and a woman in a world which still doesn't always hear us." The author added: "I have traveled widely, and I lived for four years in Finland. I love the theater, funny people, and the license journalism gives one to indulge being one hundred percent nosy."

She continued: "As a journalist, and an English-born woman of Irish descent, I find the British media's censorship of the truth about the war in Northern Ireland reprehensible. The majority of people in Britain wish that the entire place could be bombed. There is almost no understanding in Britain of the historical origins of the war, or of the continuing oppression which fuels it. Ireland was Britain's first colony, and, bloodily, remains our last.

"That said, neither I nor my co-authors on *Only the Rivers Run Free,* which is based on interviews with women in the Catholic and Protestant ghettoes of Belfast, are romantic about Irish nationalism. We wrote the book partly because we know that women's interests are very often considered secondary in nationalist and anti-imperialist struggles. Yet the status of women in Ireland, on both sides of the sectarian divide, is unenviable. Religion bans contraception, abortion, and divorce; the war encourages macho attitudes and domestic violence; and poverty makes motherhood heartbreaking.

"Feminists are now writing for young adults because so much of what they are offered is pap—especially, I am afraid, the American imports which are now flooding Britain. The heroine of *French Letters,* Maxine, has been widely compared to the hugely successful Adrian Mole books by Sue Townsend. She too lusts for romance, is a compulsive fantasizer, a bright working class girl who longs for more than she is supposed to long for within Prime Minister Margaret Thatcher's Britain. I had never imagined myself writing for teenagers but in fact loved doing so. The book has been very well received—hence the sequel, *French Leave.* It is, I should add, more than a little autobiographical!"

BIOGRAPHICAL/CRITICAL SOURCES:

BOOKS

Ursula Owen, editor, *Fathers: Reflections by Daughters,* Virago, 1983, Pantheon, 1985.

FAITH, (Richard) Mack 1944-

PERSONAL: Born December 7, 1944, in Wichita, Kan.; son of Robert Hayes (in sales) and Rosemary (an educator) Faith; married Diane Thomass (a student; divorced, 1970); married Ellen Schouler Heard (an educator); children: Cheree LeAnn, Ana Maria, Nathan Henry. *Education:* Attended Mesa Junior College, 1962-64; Western State College of Colorado, B.A., 1966; graduate study at University of Idaho, 1967-70; Western Washington University, M.A., 1981; Vermont College, M.F.A., 1986. *Religion:* Catholic.

ADDRESSES: Home—P.O. Box 2085, University Station, Murray, Ky. 42071.

CAREER: High school teacher of drama in Paonia, Colo., 1966-68; Portland Community College, Portland, Ore., instructor in adult basic education, 1971-74; substitute teacher in Spokane, Wash., and Coeur d'Alene, Idaho, 1974-76; Western Washington University, Bellingham, composition teacher and project teacher, 1981-84, academic counselor, 1984, summer workshop director, 1985 and 1986; Murray State University, Murray, Ky., creative writing teacher, 1986-87; Vermont College, Montpelier, creative writing teacher, 1987—. Public lecturer on writing in British Columbia, 1981; conducted writing workshops in Oregon, Washington, and British Columbia, 1982-85.

AWARDS, HONORS: Associated Writing Programs Award, 1985, for *The Warrior's Gift.*

WRITINGS:

"Lost in Boy" (short story), published in *Jeopardy,* spring, 1980.
"Tight Against the Rail" (short story), published in *Intro 13,* summer, 1982.
The Warrior's Gift (novel), University of Iowa Press, 1986.

Contributor of articles to periodicals.

WORK IN PROGRESS: A novel, tentatively titled *Desperado.*

SIDELIGHTS: Mack Faith's complex, award-winning first novel, *The Warrior's Gift,* is set in the 1960s and narrated by sixteen-year-old Louis. Orphaned shortly after the story begins, Louis sets out on a journey through the Midwest and his narration focuses primarily on the array of characters he meets and the disturbing events he witnesses. In her review of *The Warrior's Gift,* critic Elaine Kendall of the *Los Angeles Times* wrote that "Faith has tackled themes of vengeance, illicit sexual passion and racial hatred, setting these forces against the restorative powers of innocence, charity and love."

Faith told *CA:* "I am interested in the history of radical political movements and revolutionary movements, especially those little-known individuals for whom such dreams are so important as to shape and control their lives. I am also interested in the history of race relations in America. I believe that the failure to resolve the problems created by slavery and racism continues to be the country's central problem."

BIOGRAPHICAL/CRITICAL SOURCES:

PERIODICALS

Los Angeles Times, July 10, 1986.

*   *   *

FARMER, David Hugh 1923-

PERSONAL: Born January 30, 1923, in Ealing, London, England; son of Charles (a publisher) and Madeleine (a housewife; maiden name, Beard) Farmer; married Ann Widgery (a teacher); children: Paul, John. *Education:* Studied at Quarr Abbey, 1941-58; attended St. Benet's Hall, Oxford, 1959-60; Linacre College, Oxford, B.Litt., 1967.

ADDRESSES: Office—Department of History, University of Reading, Reading RG6 2AA, England.

CAREER: Entered Prinknash Abbey (Benedictine), 1939; Benedictine monk at Quarr Abbey, Isle of Wight, 1941-58; University of Reading, Reading, England, lecturer, 1967-77, reader in history, 1977—. Broadcaster for British Broadcasting Corp., Radio Telefis Eirann, and local radio stations.

MEMBER: Royal Historical Society (fellow), Society of Antiquaries (fellow).

AWARDS, HONORS: Grant from British Academy, 1987; Emeritus Research Fellowship, 1988.

WRITINGS:

The Magna Vita of St. Hugh of Lincoln, Oxford University Press, Volume I, 1961, Volume II, 1962, 2nd edition, revised, 1985.
The Monk of Farne, Darton, Longman & Todd, 1962.
The Rule of St. Benedict, Rosenkild & Bagger, 1968.
The Oxford Dictionary of Saints, Oxford University Press, 1978, 2nd edition, 1987.
(Editor and contributor) *Benedict's Disciples,* Fowler Wright Books, 1980.
(With J. F. Webb) *The Age of Bede,* Penguin, 1983, revised, 1988.
St. Hugh of Lincoln (biography), Darton, Longman & Todd, 1985.

Work represented in anthologies, including *The Amesbury Millennium Lectures* and *East Anglian and Other Studies.*

WORK IN PROGRESS: The Conversion of the Vikings, publication expected in 1990; *The Gesta Pontificum of William of Malmesbury,* for Oxford University Press.

SIDELIGHTS: David Hugh Farmer described himself as "a medieval historian, with a special interest in the church." He has concentrated his research on the Anglo-Saxons, Vikings, and Normans, in the fields of monasticism, hagiography, and historiography. He likes to speak to, and write for, a wider audience than academics alone.

AVOCATIONAL INTERESTS: Travel (France, Italy, and Scandinavia), walking, swimming, music, exploring old buildings and art galleries.

BIOGRAPHICAL/CRITICAL SOURCES:

PERIODICALS

Times Literary Supplement, January 9, 1981.

*   *   *

FARRELL, Cliff 1899-1977

OBITUARY NOTICE—See index for *CA* sketch: Born November 20, 1899, in Zanesville, Ohio; died in 1977. Journalist and author. Farrell was an award-winning author of numerous western and historical novels and more than six hundred short stories contributed to fiction magazines. Prior to writing full time, Farrell worked for the *Los Angeles Examiner* as telegraph, night news, and sports new editor. His books include

Ride the Wild Country, Treachery Trail, The Renegade, The Mighty Land, Terror in Eagle Basin, and *The Devil's Playground.* In 1970 Farrell won a Golden Spur Award from Western Writers of America.

OBITUARIES AND OTHER SOURCES:

Date of death provided by wife, Mildred Farrell.

* * *

FASICK, Adele M(ongan)　1930-

PERSONAL: Born March 18, 1930, in New York, N.Y.; daughter of Stephen (an optometrist) and Florence (a teacher; maiden name, Geary) Mongan; divorced; children: Pamela, Laura, Julia. *Education:* Cornell University, B.A., 1951; Columbia Univeristy, M.A., 1954, M.L.S., 1956; Case Western Reserve University, Ph.D., 1970.

ADDRESSES: Home—4351 Bloor St. W., No. 40, Etobicoke, Ontario, Canada M9C 2A4. *Office*—Faculty of Library and Information Science, University of Toronto, Toronto, Ontario, Canada M5S 1A1.

CAREER: New York Public Library, New York, N.Y., librarian, 1955-56; Long Island University, Brooklyn, N.Y., librarian, 1956-58; homemaker, 1958-67; Rosary College, River Forest, Ill., assistant professor of library science, 1970-71; University of Toronto, Toronto, Ontario, professor of library science, 1971—.

MEMBER: International Federation of Library Associations (chairman of Children's Libraries Section), Canadian Library Association, American Library Association, Association of Library Service to Children, Association of Library and Information Science Education (member of board of directors), Ontario Library Association.

WRITINGS:

(With Claire England) *Childview: Evaluating and Reviewing Materials for Children,* Libraries Unlimited, 1987.

Contributor to library journals.

WORK IN PROGRESS: A book on the administration of library services for children, publication by Libraries Unlimited expected in 1990; editing a book in honor of children's librarian Lillian H. Smith, publication by Scarecrow expected in 1988.

SIDELIGHTS: Adele M. Fasick told *CA:* "I became interested in library services for children during the 1960s, when psychologists and educators began writing about how a child's attitude toward books and learning is influenced by his or her experience during preschool years. During these years I was also able to observe my own children and to see the way in which they enjoyed and learned from books, reading, and library services. The public library is one of the primary sources of enrichment for preschool children.

"Children's services in libraries have been both successful and popular for almost one hundred years and are an essential element of the success of public libraries in general. In recent years there have been suggestions that, because of the aging of the population, libraries ought not to spend as much time and money on children's services as they have in the past. It seems to me that the smaller proportion of children in the population means that services to them are of greater, not lesser, importance. While it is necessary to provide good sup-

port services for aging adults, the future of society still depends on the children who will grow up to be the leaders of the future. With fewer children in the population, everyone has a greater stake in the success of each of those children. Public education and public services such as libraries are the only ways in which we can be sure that every child has an equal opportunity to become a productive adult.

"The costs of services to children are far less than the cost of care for unproductive adults. Although the emphasis in the past few years has been on the privatization of opportunity, I think that this will change because it is not economically feasible for even middle-class parents to provide all of the resources that children need. As many families delay having children and have fewer of them, they will demand that those children have the opportunity for information and cultural activities that libraries provide. The demands by middle-class families will lead to greater support for children's services and will eventually benefit the children of poor parents. We are in great danger of raising two classes of children—the pampered children of affluent families and the impoverished children of poor and often young mothers. Public services such as libraries can help to bridge the gap between these two groups so that all children will be able to develop their abilities."

* * *

FAULKNER, Christopher G(raham)　1942-

PERSONAL: Born October 4, 1942, in Westbury, Wiltshire, England; son of Alwyn (a civil engineer) and Audrey (a housewife; maiden name, Pinfield) Faulkner; married Debra Wittenberg (a secretary), June 4, 1964; children: Ursula, Graham, Jason, Gwen. *Education:* Sir George Williams University, B.A., 1964; University of Western Ontario, M.A., 1967; graduate study at Victoria University of Manchester, 1968-70.

ADDRESSES: Office—Department of Film Studies, Carleton University, Colonel By. Dr., Ottawa, Ontario, Canada K1S 5B6.

CAREER: Carleton University, Ottawa, Ontario, assistant professor, 1971-79, associate professor, 1979-87, professor of film studies, 1987—, chairman of department, 1980-85.

MEMBER: Film Studies Association of Canada, Society for Cinema Studies.

AWARDS, HONORS: Canada Council grant, 1975-76; Social Science and Humanities Research Council of Canada fellowship, 1979-80, grant, 1985-86.

WRITINGS:

Jean Renoir: A Guide to References and Resources, G. K. Hall, 1979.
The Social Cinema of Jean Renoir, Princeton University Press, 1986.

WORK IN PROGRESS: A historical study of Jean Renoir's "La Regle du jeu"; an English-language collection of Renoir's essays.

SIDELIGHTS: Christopher G. Faulkner told *CA:* "The reason I became interested in Jean Renoir (rather than some other filmmaker) is beyond my conscious apprehension. For many years, antedating my interest in Renoir, I have also been interested in Robert Graves and the literature of the First World War. To my conscious awareness, the common ground is a concern with the social function of artistic practice. In this very general respect I believe my views on Renoir's work do differ from those of others in the field, for this position allows me to engage theoretical questions (largely from poststructuralist thought) surrounding cultural production and historical processes. Renoir (or Graves) is thus a particular instance for a general preoccupation.''

BIOGRAPHICAL/CRITICAL SOURCES:

PERIODICALS

Globe and Mail (Toronto), November 29, 1986.

*   *   *

FEAR, Richard Arthur 1909-

PERSONAL: Born March 4, 1909, in Gloversville, N.Y. *Education:* Middlebury College, B.S., 1931; Boston College, Ed.M., 1940.

ADDRESSES: Home and office—R.D.3, Box 220, Pittstown, N.J. 08867.

CAREER: Staff member of Psychological Corp., beginning in 1941, became director of Industrial Division, 1956, and vice-president, 1964. Interview Training Service, Pittstown, N.J., president, 1968—. Lecturer at Newark College of Engineering (now New Jersey Institute of Technology), 1942-43, and Columbia University, 1942-47.

MEMBER: American Psychological Association.

AWARDS, HONORS: The Evaluation Interview was named an outstanding book in human resource management by American Society for Personnel Administration, 1973.

WRITINGS:

Employee Evaluation for Interviewers, Psychological Corp., 1943.
The Evaluation Interview, McGraw, 1958, 3rd edition, 1984.
(With James F. Ross) *Jobs, Dollars, and EEO: How to Hire More Productive Entry-Level Workers,* McGraw, 1982.

WORK IN PROGRESS: Revising *The Evaluation Interview.*

AVOCATIONAL INTERESTS: Breeding horses and ponies; travel (Japan, China, Russia, Australia and New Zealand, the South Seas islands, Iceland, most of South America, safaris in East and South Africa, most of Europe).

*   *   *

FELD, Bernard (David III) 1947-

PERSONAL: Born May 29, 1947, in Birmingham, Ala.; son of Bernard David, Jr. (a newspaper executive) and Anna May (a homemaker; maiden name, Levy) Feld; married Susanna Van Hoose (a writer and editor), May 24, 1985; children: Gil Rogers. *Education:* Washington and Lee University, B.A. (magna cum laude), 1969; Columbia University, M.A. (with honors), 1970, Ph.D. (with distinction), 1978.

ADDRESSES: Home—Birmingham, Ala. *Agent*—Sobel Weber Associates Inc., 146 East 19th St., New York, N.Y. 10003

CAREER: University of Alabama in Birmingham, Birmingham, lecturer, 1974-77, assistant professor of English, 1978-81; free-lance writer and advertising creative consultant, 1981—. Gives readings.

MEMBER: Phi Beta Kappa.

AWARDS, HONORS: Prize from Academy of American Poets, 1969, for a series of poems; Emily Clark Balch Creative Writing Fellowship, 1973-74; ''A Winter Story'' listed among distinctive stories of *The Best American Short Stories,* 1975; creative writing fellowship from Southern Federation of State Arts Agencies, 1977.

WRITINGS:

Blood Relations (novel), Little, Brown, 1987.

Contributor of short stories to publications including *Cavalier, Prairie Schooner,* and *Shenandoah;* also contributor to *Collier's Encyclopedia* and *Folio.*

WORK IN PROGRESS: A novel set in the contemporary South, completion expected between 1989 and 1990; short stories for a collection.

SIDELIGHTS: Bernard Feld told *CA:* ''Until about six years ago, I had spent much of my life in a university, either as student or teacher. More recent jobs, however, have provided richer material for my writing. I drew on my experience as a newspaper reporter for the central character in *Blood Relations,* my first novel, while my recent experience as an advertising writer and consultant reflects in a character in the book I am currently writing.

''I have lived much of my life in Birmingham, Alabama, and my family has roots in the region. For better and for worse, the deep South has been a kind of place unto itself. In certain ways, I think this remains true today. In other ways, however, much of the South, particularly the urban South, is becoming indistinguishable from any other American city. The tension inherent in this split identity, and in the transition from one to the other, provides fertile ground for a writer.

''Like many southern writers, I have always been concerned with the special influence of the place. *Blood Relations* is a southern novel of a particular kind. Its setting is not the rural landscape of the older agrarian South, but the modern urban landscape of the new industrial South. While the book evokes some sense of the South's mythic past, it depicts a society that is losing its special identity, and a world where, beneath a veneer of southern gentility, status is based on money and power, which lead to exploitation and corruption.

''*Blood Relations* draws upon the shape and narrative structure of a mystery to explore the complex fabric of relationships within a southern family and the manners and morals of an entire society. In many ways, it can be seen as an initiation novel, in which the main character, like F. Scott Fitzgerald's Nick Carraway in *The Great Gatsby,* begins as a detached observer, and is gradually drawn deeper into a world that both attracts and repels him. As he unravels the book's central mystery, he learns the truth not only about the other characters, but about himself, and he must then find his own moral balance and values.''

BIOGRAPHICAL/CRITICAL SOURCES:

PERIODICALS

New York Times Book Review, March 29, 1987.

*   *   *

FELDMAN, Egal 1925-

PERSONAL: Born April 9, 1925, in New York, N.Y.; son of Morris Feldman; married Mary Kalman (an insurance agent),

June 30, 1959; children: Tyla, Auora, Naomi. *Education:* Brooklyn College (now of the City University of New York), B.A., 1950; New York University, M.A., 1954; University of Pennsylvania, Ph.D., 1959. *Religion:* Jewish.

ADDRESSES: Home—2019 Weeks Ave., Superior, Wis. 54880. *Office*—Department of History, University of Wisconsin—Superior, Superior, Wis. 54880.

CAREER: University of Texas at Arlington, assistant professor of history, 1960-66; University of Wisconsin—Superior, associate professor, 1966-67, professor of history, 1968—, director of Area Research Center, 1970-74, chairman of department, 1973-77, dean of College of Letters and Science, 1977-81, coordinator of history program, 1982—.

MEMBER: American Historical Association, Organization of American Historians, American Professors for Peace in the Middle East, American Jewish Historical Society, Wisconsin Humanities Committee.

AWARDS, HONORS: YIVO-Institute for Jewish Research essay award, 1954, for "The Impact of the American Revolution on the Jewish Community in America"; Teacher of the Year award, 1968, from University of Wisconsin; Max H. Lavine awards from University of Wisconsin, 1975, 1982, 1985, for "scholarly contributions to contemporary concerns"; grants from Wisconsin Humanities Committee, 1977, 1980; Chancellor's Award for scholarly interpretations, 1982, from University of Wisconsin; travel grant from the National Endowment for the Humanities, 1984.

WRITINGS:

Fit for Men: A History of New York's Clothing Trade, Public Affairs Press, 1960.
The Dreyfus Affair and the American Conscience, Wayne State University Press, 1981.
A Dual Destiny: Protestants and Jews in American History, University of Illinois Press, in press.

CONTRIBUTOR

Leonard Dinnerstein and Kenneth T. Jackson, editors, *American Vistas,* Volume II, Oxford University Press, 1971.
Lloyd Gartner, editor, *Documentary History of the Jews in the United States,* University of Tel Aviv Press, 1975.
David A. Gerber, editor, *Anti-Semitism in American History,* University of Illinois Press, 1986.

Also author of introduction to *The Dreyfus Case: The Ben Shahn Prints,* Crossroad Books, 1984. Contributor to *Encyclopedia of Southern History* and *Encyclopedia Judaica.* Contributor of articles and reviews to history journals.

WORK IN PROGRESS: On the Frontiers of Jewish-Christian Relations; Reinhold Niebuhr and the Jews.

SIDELIGHTS: Egal Feldman told *CA:* "The Dreyfus Affair, the subject of my recent book, was too important an event to be left to the French. The false conviction of the Jewish French Army officer, Capt. Alfred Dreyfus, was the first conspicuous sign that Jews could not rely upon Western liberal institutions at the end of the nineteenth century for their safety. Its impact was broad and deep, affecting Catholics, Protestants, and Jews in this country and abroad, and touched and shaped the lives of a generation. As a classic moment in human affairs, it should be remembered and reflected upon for years to come.

"Being aware of the cosmic importance of the Dreyfus event, I was surprised to learn that despite the countless books written about it, not a single publication existed that examined America's reaction to it. By the mid-1970s I was well on my way to correcting this situation.

"Actually, my interest in the Dreyfus Affair was an outgrowth of a wider pursuit—a desire to understand the evolution of Jewish-Christian relations in the United States. This interest began more than two decades ago, during the 'ecumenical revolution' of the mid-sixties. Here, too, I was surprised to discover how little attention American historians have devoted to this important subject. I decided to devote my spare time to the history of Jewish-Christian relations in the United States. Since those days I have published studies dealing with the theologians George F. Moore, Reinhold Niebuhr, and A. Roy Eckardt and their views of Judaism. I have also examined the impact of the Social Gospel and Christian orthodoxy upon Jewish-Christian relations. My forthcoming book, *A Dual Destiny: Protestants and Jews in American History,* will be the first full-length study of the entire subject.

"My advice to young historians seeking satisfaction and some success with their life's work is: first, find a problem worth grappling with; second, be prepared for hard work and some discouragement; and finally, devote some time each day to their research and writing."

BIOGRAPHICAL/CRITICAL SOURCES:

PERIODICALS

American Historical Review, June, 1982.
Gazette (Montreal), August 21, 1982.
History: Review of New Books, May, 1982.
Journal of American History, fall, 1982.
Reform Judaism, September, 1981.

*   *   *

FELIX-TCHICAYA, Gerald
   See TCHICAYA, Gerald Felix

*   *   *

FENNELLY, Parker W.   1891-1988

OBITUARY NOTICE: Born in 1891 in Northeast Harbor, Me.; died after a brief illness, January 22, 1988, in Cortlandt (one source says Peekskill), N.Y. Actor, playwright, and author. Fennelly specialized in playing old Yankee characters and is best known for his radio portrayal of New England codger Titus Moody on "The Fred Allen Show" during the 1930s and 1940s. He also had parts in radio's "Stebbins Boys of Bucksport Point," "Snow Village Sketches," "Grand Central Station," "Mystery Theater," and "Route 66." Trained in classical theater, Fennelly began his stage career as a Shakespearean actor before performing on Broadway in shows such as "Mr. Pitt," "Our Town," "Carousel," and "The Southwest Corner" and in films including "The Trouble With Harry," "Angel in My Pocket," "The Russians Are Coming, the Russians Are Coming," and "How to Frame a Figg." In addition, Fennelly gained recognition during the 1970s as the folksy, Moody-like spokesman in Pepperidge Farm radio and television commercials. He wrote several plays, including "Cuckoos on the Hearth" and, with George M. Cohan, "Fulton of Oak Falls."

OBITUARIES AND OTHER SOURCES:

BOOKS

Who's Who in Hollywood, 1900-1976, Arlington House, 1976.

PERIODICALS

Chicago Tribune, January 27, 1988.
Los Angeles Times, January 24, 1988.
New York Times, January 23, 1988.
Washington Post, January 24, 1988.

*   *   *

FERGUS, Jan   1943-

PERSONAL: Born April 5, 1943, in Bronxville, N.Y.; daughter of John and Charlotte Fergus. *Education:* Stanford University, B.A., 1964; City University of New York, Ph.D., 1975.

ADDRESSES: Office—Department of English, Lehigh University, Bethlehem, Pa. 18015.

CAREER: Lehigh University, Bethlehem, Pa., assistant professor, 1976-82, associate professor of English, 1982—. Visiting associate professor at New York University, 1985-86.

MEMBER: Modern Language Association of America, Association for the Study of Eighteenth Century Studies, Jane Austen Society, Phi Beta Kappa.

WRITINGS:

Jane Austen and the Didactic Novel: Northanger Abbey; Sense and Sensibility; and Pride and Prejudice, Macmillan, 1983.
Jane Austen: The Literary Career, Macmillan, in press.

Contributor to literature journals.

WORK IN PROGRESS: Readers and Fictions, a study of the eighteenth-century English provincial reading public.

*   *   *

FEWSTER, Kevin (John)   1953-

PERSONAL: Born December 1, 1953, in Perth, Australia; son of Geoffrey Edson (a public servant) and Audrey Irene (a homemaker; maiden name, Gledell) Fewster. *Education:* Australian National University, B.A. (with honors), 1975; University of New South Wales, Ph.D., 1980.

ADDRESSES: Home—23 Melbourne Pl., Alberton, South Australia 5014. *Office*—South Australian Maritime Museum, P.O. Box 555, Port Adelaide, South Australia 5015.

CAREER: Monash University, Victoria, Australia, senior tutor in history, 1981-84; South Australian Maritime Museum, Port Adelaide, director, 1984—.

WRITINGS:

(Editor) *Gallipoli Correspondent: The Frontline Diary of C.E.W. Bean*, Allen & Unwin, 1983.
(With V. Basarin and H. H. Basarin) *A Turkish View of Gallipoli: Chanakkale*, Hodja, 1985.

SIDELIGHTS: Kevin Fewster's 1983 book, *Gallipoli Correspondent*, contains selections from the detailed diaries of C.E.W. Bean, the journalist who spent four years as the official press correspondent of the Australian Imperial Force during World War I. As such, he was part of the first landing at Gallipoli in 1915. Bean not only sent regular reports to Sydney's *Morning Herald*, he also recorded for posterity the history of the war. His diaries include interviews with the survivors of the battle, sketches of the land, and numerous photographs.

BIOGRAPHICAL/CRITICAL SOURCES:

PERIODICALS

Times Literary Supplement, October 7, 1983.

*   *   *

FEYNMAN, R. P.
See FEYNMAN, Richard Phillips

*   *   *

FEYNMAN, Richard
See FEYNMAN, Richard Phillips

*   *   *

FEYNMAN, Richard P.
See FEYNMAN, Richard Phillips

*   *   *

FEYNMAN, Richard Phillips   1918-1988
(R. P. Feynman, Richard Feynman, Richard P. Feynman)

OBITUARY NOTICE: Born May 11, 1918, in New York, N.Y.; died of abdominal cancer, February 15, 1988, in Los Angeles, Calif. Scientist, educator, and author. Considered one of the most brilliant and influential theoretical physicists of his generation, Feynman was a member of the scientific team that developed the atomic bomb during World War II, and in 1965 he shared a Nobel Prize for physics. He also received several other honors and awards, including Princeton University's Albert Einstein Award, the Atomic Energy Commission's E. O. Lawrence Award, the Neils Bohr International gold medal, and the Albert Einstein College of Medicine's Einstein Award. Feynman taught theoretical physics at Cornell University from 1945 to 1950, then joined the faculty at the California Institute of Technology. In addition, the physicist gained national attention after the tragic 1986 explosion of space shuttle *Challenger* when, as a member of the presidential investigation committee, he emerged as a leading critic of the National Aeronautics and Space Administration. Under various forms of his name, Feynman wrote *Theory of Fundamental Processes*, *The Character of Physical Law*, *Photon-Hadron Interactions*, *QED: The Strange Theory of Light and Matter*, and his autobiography, *Surely You're Joking, Mr. Feynman! Adventures of a Curious Character*, which became a bestseller. He also co-authored *The Feynman Lectures on Physics*.

OBITUARIES AND OTHER SOURCES:

BOOKS

Current Biography, H. W. Wilson, 1966, April, 1988.

PERIODICALS

Chicago Tribune, February 17, 1988.
New York Times, February 17, 1988.
Times (London), February 17, 1988.
Washington Post, February 17, 1988.

*   *   *

FIGUEROA, John
See FIGUEROA, John J(oseph Maria)

FIGUEROA, John J(oseph Maria)   1920-
(John Figueroa)

PERSONAL: Born August 4, 1920, in Kingston, Jamaica; immigrated to England, 1979, dual British and Jamaican citizenship; son of Rupert Aston (an insurance salesman) and Isclena (a teacher; maiden name, Palomino) Figueroa; married Dorothy Grace Murray Alexander (a teacher and author), August 3, 1944; children: Dorothy Anna Jarvis, Catherine, J. Peter, Robert P. D., Mark F. E., Esther M., Thomas Theodore (deceased). *Education:* College of the Holy Cross, A.B. (cum laude), 1942; University of London, teachers diploma, 1947, M.A., 1950; graduate study at University of Indiana—Bloomington, 1964. *Religion:* Catholic.

ADDRESSES: Home—77 Station Rd., Woburn Sands, Buckinghamshire MK17 8SH, England.

CAREER: Water Commission, Kingston, Jamaica, clerk, 1937-38; teacher at secondary schools in Jamaica, 1942-46, and London, England, 1946-48; University of London, Institute of Education, London, lecturer in English and philosophy, 1948-53; University College of the West Indies, Kingston, senior lecturer, 1953-57, professor of education, 1957-73, dean of faculty of education, 1966-69; University of Puerto Rico, Rio Piedras and Cayey, professor of English and consultant to the president, 1971-73; El Centro Caribeno de Estudios Postgraduados, Carolina, Puerto Rico, professor of humanities and consultant in community education, 1973-76; University of Jos, Jos, Nigeria, professor of education and acting dean, 1976-80; Bradford College, Yorkshire, England, visiting professor of humanities and consultant in multicultural education, 1980; Open University, Milton Keynes, England, member of Third World Studies Course Team, 1980-83; Manchester Education Authority, Manchester, England, adviser on multicultural studies, West Indian language and literature, and Caribbean heritage students, 1983-85; fellow at Warwick University's Center of Caribbean studies, 1988. British Broadcasting Corporation, London, sports reporter and general broadcaster for programs including "Reflections" and poetry readings, 1946-60. Consultant to Ford and Carnegie foundations; consultant to Organization of American States and to West Indian governments. External examiner, Africa and West Indies. Has lectured and read his poetry in Africa, Canada, Europe, South America, the United Kingdom, and the United States.

MEMBER: Linguistic Society of America, Caribbean Studies Association, Society for the Study of Caribbean Affairs, Athenaeum Club.

AWARDS, HONORS: British Council fellowship, 1946-47; L.H.D. from College of the Holy Cross, 1960; Carnegie fellowship, 1960; Guggenheim fellowship, 1964; Lilly Foundation grant, 1973; Institute of Jamaica Medal, 1980.

WRITINGS:

Blue Mountain Peak (poetry and prose), Gleaner, 1944.
Love Leaps Here (poetry), privately printed, 1962.
Staffing and Examinations in British Caribbean Secondary Schools: A Report of the Conference of the Caribbean Heads, Evans, c. 1964.
(Editor under name John Figueroa) *Caribbean Voices: An Anthology of West Indian Poetry,* Evans, Volume I: *Dreams and Visions,* 1966, second edition, 1982, Volume II: *The Blue Horizons,* 1970; published in one volume, Evans, 1971, Luce, 1973.

Society, Schools, and Progress in the West Indies, Pergamon, 1971.
(Author of introduction) Edgar Mittelhoelzer, *A Morning at the Office,* Heinemann, 1974.
(Under name John Figueroa) *Ignoring Hurts: Poems* (includes "Cosmopolitan Pig" and "The Grave Digger"), introduction by Frank Getlein, Three Continents Press, 1976.
(Editor and author of introduction under name John Figueroa) Sonny Oti, *Dreams and Realities: Six One-Act Comedies,* J. West, 1978.
(Editor with Donald E. Herdeck and others) *Caribbean Writers,* Three Continents, 1979.
(Editor) *An Anthology of African and Caribbean Writing in English,* Heinemann, 1982.
(Editor under name John Figueroa) *Third World Studies: Caribbean Sampler,* Open University Press, 1983.

Screenwriter with Ed Milner of film, "St. Lucia: Peoples and Celebrations," for British Broadcasting Corporation. Translator of works by Horace. Contributor to *Whose Language?* 1985, and *The Caribbean in Europe,* Cass, 1986; contributor to periodicals, including *Commonweal, Dorenkamp, London Magazine, Universities Quarterly, Caribbean Studies, Cross Currents,* and *Caribbean Quarterly.* General editor of "Caribbean Writers" series for Heinemann. Editor of recording *Poets of the West Indies Reading Their Own Works,* Caedmon, 1972.

WORK IN PROGRESS: Articles on the role of London as a magnet for West Indian and other colonial writers in the 1940s and 1950s and on the attitude toward slavery expressed in *Tom Cringle's Log;* memoirs.

SIDELIGHTS: West Indian poet and scholar John J. Figueroa is known for his original verse, the anthologies he has edited, and his critical and academic writings. He draws on classical literature, such as the poetry of Virgil and Horace, as well as on the rhythms of Jamaican speech and calypso music for his poems, which at their best are regarded as sensual, spiritual, and unusually well crafted. His nonfiction writings reflect more than forty years of commitment to the academic field.

Figueroa commented: "It has been good to have grown up with and to have been part of the development and flowering of Caribbean literature, painting, and music. But it is a pity that there is so little appreciation of the *variety* as well as the achievement in these fields. People are much too quick to look for something they call identity, and to disown anyone who does not abjectly follow the tribe on the grounds that right or wrong doesn't matter—all that matters is whether it's 'one of us' who is involved.

"I have also been very lucky to have traveled and lived among various peoples in Africa, Europe, and the Americas, and to have seen the kinds of space explorations which have not, alas, made it clearer to dwellers on the Earth that caring for one's neighbor is not 'other worldly' but an imperative for life, and for living more abundantly."

AVOCATIONAL INTERESTS: Travel, Creole linguistics, cricket, Caribbean studies, music, painting, and lay theology and liturgy.

BIOGRAPHICAL/CRITICAL SOURCES:

PERIODICALS

Times Literary Supplement, January 28, 1972.
World Literature Today, spring, 1977.

FILREIS, Alan 1956-

PERSONAL: Surname is pronounced "*Phil*-reese"; born March 25, 1956, in Newark, N.J.; son of Samuel H. (an engineer) and Lois (a teacher; maiden name, Gainsburg) Filreis. *Education:* Colgate University, B.A., 1978; University of Virginia, M.A., 1980, Ph.D., 1985.

ADDRESSES: Home—2318 Spurce St., Philadelphia, Pa. 19103. *Office*—Department of English, University of Pennsylvania, Philadelphia, Pa. 19104.

CAREER: University of Pennsylvania, Philadelphia, assistant professor of English, 1985—.

AWARDS, HONORS: Huntington Library fellowship, 1986; grant from National Endowment for the Humanities, 1987-88.

WRITINGS:

(Editor with Beverly Coyle) *Secretaries of the Moon: The Letters of Wallace Stevens and Jose Rodriguez Feo,* Duke University Press, 1987.

WORK IN PROGRESS: A book on the life and work of Wallace Stevens, publication expected in 1988; a political literary history of the American fifties.

SIDELIGHTS: Alan Filreis told *CA:* "My work on Wallace Stevens has made me realize that even a poet whose writing resists being read as the record of a life is in fact deeply marked by time, place, culture, and occasion. The career is an American career. All my work aims to present a coherent criticism of the literary career, which I like to read not as a set of individual works but as a motion through them, and to understand the human and historical force that impels that motion."

BIOGRAPHICAL/CRITICAL SOURCES:

PERIODICALS

Times Literary Supplement, July 10, 1987.

*   *   *

FINK, William
See MENCKEN, H(enry) L(ouis)

*   *   *

FINSON, Jon W(illiam) 1950-

PERSONAL: Born November 4, 1950, in Chicago, Ill. *Education:* University of Colorado, Boulder, B.Mus., 1973; University of Wisconsin—Madison, M.A., 1975; University of Chicago, Ph.D., 1980.

ADDRESSES: Office—Department of Music, University of North Carolina at Chapel Hill, Chapel Hill, N.C. 27514.

CAREER: University of North Carolina at Chapel Hill, assistant professor, beginning in 1978, became associate professor of music. Director of International Mendelssohn-Schumann Conference, 1981-82; member of Orange County board of directors of North Carolina Symphony, 1982-85.

MEMBER: American Musicological Society (chairman of Southeast chapter, 1981-82).

WRITINGS:

(Editor with Larry Todd) *Mendelssohn and Schumann,* Duke University Press, 1985.

WORK IN PROGRESS: The Genesis of Robert Schumann's First Symphony.*

*   *   *

FLANAGAN, Mary 1943-

PERSONAL: Born May 20, 1943, in Rochester, N.H.; immigrated to England, 1969; daughter of Martin James (a housing director) and Mary (a housewife and secretary; maiden name, Nesbitt) Flanagan. *Education:* Brandeis University, B.A., 1965. *Politics:* Labour. *Religion:* Roman Catholic.

ADDRESSES: Home—London, England. *Office*—c/o Bloomsbury Publishing, 2 Soho Sq., London W1, England.

CAREER: Writer.

MEMBER: Authors Guild.

WRITINGS:

Bad Girls (stories), edited by Liz Calder, J. Cape, 1984, Atheneum, 1985.
Trust (novel), Bloomsbury Publishing, 1987, Atheneum, 1988.

Contributor to literary magazines and newspapers.

WORK IN PROGRESS: Another novel, publication by Bloomsbury Publishing expected in 1989; an introduction for the novel *The Land of Spices,* by Kate O'Brien, Virago, 1988; a screenplay, "Strang."

SIDELIGHTS: Mary Flanagan, who was born in the United States to Irish parents, settled in England after spending a year in Morocco between 1968 and 1969. Her first book, *Bad Girls,* is a collection of short stories chronicling the morally "bad" behavior of a number of young women victimized by their own illusions. Assessing the work as an "impressive debut," Roz Kaveney in the *Times Literary Supplement* further observed that "Flanagan writes well of the delicate balances by which friendship is constructed and maintained."

In her first novel, *Trust,* Flanagan examines both the elusive nature of and the quest for trust. Reviewing the book for the London *Times,* Chris Peachment compared this "excellent" debut to the works of novelists Henry James and sisters Charlotte, Emily, and Anne Bronte. In Kaveney's opinion, *Trust* brings to mind the fiction of Iris Murdoch, featuring "a world of high sensibility, profitable artistic taste, private incomes and . . . interlockings of familial and sexual intrigue." It is a "moral tale," wrote the reviewer, "in which solidarity between the more or less virtuous makes it possible for them to capture . . . some moments of pleasure in a world in which the selfish and unreliable usually make the running."

Flanagan told *CA:* "I write about people in extremes who are forced to satisfy the demands of both instinct and conscience. What interests me is the resultant play of conflicting elements in a character's nature, such as desire opposing ethics, the child and the beast straining against their social conditioning."

AVOCATIONAL INTERESTS: Gardening and playing the piano.

BIOGRAPHICAL/CRITICAL SOURCES:

PERIODICALS

Independent, April 2, 1987.
Irish Times, April 8, 1987.
Punch, April 15, 1987.
Times (London), April 2, 1987.
Times Literary Supplement, November 9, 1984, April 3, 1987.

FLANAGAN, Owen J. 1949-

PERSONAL: Born January 30, 1949, in Bronxville, N.Y.; son of Owen J., Sr. (an accountant) and Virginia (a housewife; maiden name, Lyons) Flanagan; married Joyce Walworth, May, 1980; children: Ben, Kate. *Education:* Fordham University, B.A., 1970; Boston University, M.A., 1973, Ph.D., 1977.

ADDRESSES: Home—16 Cottonwood Rd., Wellesley, Mass. 02181. *Office*—Department of Philosophy, Wellesley College, Wellesley, Mass. 02181.

CAREER: Wellesley College, Wellesley, Mass., assistant professor, 1977-83, associate professor of philosophy, 1983—. Visiting associate professor at Duke University, 1985-86. Visiting scholar at Harvard University, 1987-88.

WRITINGS:

The Science of the Mind, MIT Press, 1984.

WORK IN PROGRESS: Varieties of Moral Personality: Explorations in Moral Psychology and Moral Philosophy, for Harvard University Press.

SIDELIGHTS: The Science of the Mind was described in the *Times Literary Supplement* as "a series of essays examining the foundations of the science(s) of the mind." Critic P. N. Johnson-Laird described these sciences as "a confederation of disciplines" which have emerged during the last ten years, and which include "linguistics, philosophy of mind, cognitive anthropology, neuroscience, artificial intelligence, and psychology." In order to demonstrate that each of these disciplines provides mutual support to all the others, Owen J. Flanagan has analyzed the seemingly disparate work of such scholars and scientists as the philosopher Rene Descartes and the psychologists Sigmund Freud, William James, B. F. Skinner, Jean Piaget, and Lawrence Kohlberg. Johnson-Laird informed the reader: "*The Science of the Mind* touches upon many . . . challenges to the cognitive sciences—rationality, free will, and the extent to which genes determine mental phenomena." He added that the author has managed, as a result of his interdisciplinary studies, "to solve a series of intriguing puzzles."

BIOGRAPHICAL/CRITICAL SOURCES:

PERIODICALS

Times Literary Supplement, December 14, 1984.

* * *

FLETCHER, Bramwell 1904(?)-1988

OBITUARY NOTICE: Born February 20, 1904 (some sources say 1906), in Bradford, Yorkshire, England; immigrated to United States; died June 22, 1988, in Westmoreland, N.H. Insurance clerk, actor, lecturer, and playwright. A seasoned actor of stage, screen, and television, Fletcher specialized in playing roles written by George Bernard Shaw and was the understudy for Rex Harrison as Professor Henry Higgins in the long-running Broadway hit "My Fair Lady." He was best known for his portrayal of the Irish playwright in the one-man production "The Bernard Shaw Story," which Fletcher also wrote. A theatrical portrait of Shaw based on anecdotes and the playwright's essays, the highly acclaimed show toured widely during the 1960s and 1970s. Fletcher worked as an office boy for a London insurance firm before making his first stage appearance in 1927 with a Shakespearean company at Stratford-

on-Avon; a year later he made his film debut. His acting credits include plays by Anton Chekhov, Henrik Ibsen, Moliere, and Sean O'Casey, films such as "The Millionaire," "Svengali," "The Scarlet Pimpernel," and "Immortal Sergeant," and more than two hundred television plays. In 1971 Fletcher collaborated on the play "Operation Gadfly" for the Educational Theater Project, which was written for college performances and sponsored by the National Endowment for the Humanities.

OBITUARIES AND OTHER SOURCES:

BOOKS

Film Encyclopedia, Crowell, 1979.
Who's Who in the Theatre: A Biographical Record of the Contemporary Stage, 17th edition, Gale, 1981.

PERIODICALS

New York Times, June 24, 1988.

* * *

FLOOGLEBUCKLE, Al
See SPIEGELMAN, Art

* * *

FOOSANER, Samuel J. 1907(?)-1988

OBITUARY NOTICE: Born c. 1907; died of prostate cancer, May 19, 1988, in Cocoa Beach, Fla. Tax lawyer, consultant, and author. A graduate of Rutgers University School of Law, Foosaner was a tax law expert and often served as adviser to members of congressional tax panels. He was also a former chairman of the National Federal Tax Lawyers Committee. Foosaner wrote more than one hundred books and articles about taxes, including *The Frustrated American* and *Your Will, Don't Leave Life Without It*.

OBITUARIES AND OTHER SOURCES:

PERIODICALS

New York Times, May 21, 1988.

* * *

FORBES-BOYD, Eric 1897-1979

OBITUARY NOTICE—See index for *CA* sketch: Born August 29, 1897, in Addlestone, Surrey, England; died October 21, 1979. Author of several novels, travel books, and plays. Forbes-Boyd was a regular monthly contributor and reviewer for the *Christian Science Monitor* for many years and gave lectures on medieval Greece. His works include the novels *A Stranger in These Parts* and *The General in Retreat;* the travel books *In Crusader Greece* and *Aegean Quest;* and the plays *Maripoza Bung* and *The Seventeenth Highwayman*.

OBITUARIES AND OTHER SOURCES:

Date of death provided by wife, Aileen Forbes-Boyd.

BOOKS

The Writers Directory: 1980-1982, St. Martin's, 1979.

* * *

FORCADE, Robert J. 1935-

PERSONAL: Surname is pronounced "For-*kade*"; born November 26, 1935, in Edmonton, Alberta, Canada; son of Joseph G. (a cook) and Rose (a housewife; maiden name, Duffet) Forcade; married Jean A. McAurthur (a personnel clerk), June 3, 1961; children: Michele Forcade Mackenzie, Janice. *Education:* University of Alberta, Personnel Certification, 1971.

ADDRESSES: Home—11620 32 ''A'' Ave., Edmonton, Alberta, Canada T6J 3G8.

CAREER: Gulf Canada Ltd., laboratory technician at refinery in Edmonton, Alberta, 1954-67, personnel clerk, 1967-71, labor relations adviser at main office in Toronto, Ontario, 1971-77, manager of human resources at Edmonton refinery, 1977-87; writer, 1987—.

AWARDS, HONORS: First prize for nonfiction from *Edmonton Journal,* 1965.

WRITINGS:

Watch for the Breaking of Day (juvenile novel), Fitzhenry & Whiteside, 1986.

Also author of unpublished manuscript, *To a Distant Place.*

WORK IN PROGRESS: Research for another novel.

SIDELIGHTS: Robert J. Forcade told *CA:* ''The desire to write has been with me for most of my life. As a boy in grade school, when I was about twelve, I wrote a surprising number of pages for a cowboy novel. It was fun but hard work, so I eventually quit. There were better things for a twelve-year-old boy to do.

''It wasn't until after I was married in 1961 that I really took up writing as a hobby. For the first few years I played with short stories and such and had only one small success: winning the local newspaper's award for nonfiction. After that I wanted to try writing a novel, but I had no idea how to go about it. It never entered my head to take a writing course. Instead, I simply sat down and started to write, but there were about six false starts—one of about twenty thousand words—before I finally completed the manuscript. I called it *To a Distant Place.* It made the rounds of all the Canadian publishers and now sits in the bottom drawer of my desk.

''*Watch for the Breaking of Day* is my second novel. I must say that I'm proud of this book. In my opinion it is for people of all ages, from nine to ninety, and it leans very heavily on human relationships. Most of the story is set in the Canadian Rockies, and I think that my own love for the mountains shows through in many of the chapters.

''I firmly believe that good literature is effortless to read. At the same time, good literature allows the reader not only to see the scene but to hear, taste, touch, and smell it as well. This is what I tried to accomplish in *Watch for the Breaking of Day.* Whether I was successful or not remains to be seen.''

*   *   *

FORSTER, Kent   1916-1981

OBITUARY NOTICE—See index for *CA* sketch: Born December 4, 1916, in New York, N.Y.; died in January, 1981. Educator and author. Forster, who was a faculty member at Pennsylvania State University beginning in 1941, became professor of history there in 1954 and chairman of the history department in 1970. Notable among his writings are *The Failures of Peace: The Search for a Negotiated Peace During the First World War, World Affairs: Problems and Prospects, Recent Europe:*

A Twentieth Century History, Man and Civilization, and *World Tensions: Conflict and Accommodation.*

OBITUARIES AND OTHER SOURCES:

Date of death provided by the secretary of the history department of Pennsylvania State University.

BOOKS

Directory of American Scholars, Volume I: *History,* 7th edition, Bowker, 1978.

*   *   *

FOSSEDAL, Gregory
See FOSSEDAL, Gregory A.

*   *   *

FOSSEDAL, Gregory A.   1959-
(Gregory Fossedal)

PERSONAL: Born June 18, 1959, in Williamsport, Pa.; son of Donald E. (in business) and Ruth (in education; maiden name, Vosburg) Fossedal; married Elizabeth Sullivan (a homemaker), March 1, 1986. *Education:* Received B.A. (summa cum laude) from Dartmouth College. *Religion:* Roman Catholic.

ADDRESSES: Office—Hoover Institution, Stanford University, Stanford, Calif. 94305. *Agent*—Carol Mann, 174 Pacific St., Brooklyn, N.Y. 11201.

CAREER: Wall Street Journal, New York City, editorial writer, 1983-86; syndicated columnist at Copley News Service, 1986—.

MEMBER: Phi Beta Kappa.

AWARDS, HONORS: Worst Editorial of the Year award from Wisconsin Senator William Proxmire, 1984; media fellow at Hoover Institution on War, Revolution, and Peace, beginning in 1986.

WRITINGS:

(With Daniel O. Graham) *A Defense That Defends: Blocking Nuclear Attack,* Devin-Adair, 1984.
(With Dinesh D'Souza; under name Gregory Fossedal) *My Dear Alex: Letters From a KGB Agent* (satire), Kampmann, 1987.

Contributing editor, *Harper's,* 1986—; regular contributor to *American Spectator* and *Wall Street Journal.*

WORK IN PROGRESS: A book on U.S. foreign policy.

SIDELIGHTS: Citing U.S. military weakness, Daniel O. Graham and Gregory A. Fossedal argue for the development of space-based nuclear defenses in their book *A Defense That Defends: Blocking Nuclear Attack* and predict a new foreign policy directed at containing the Soviet Union. In a critique for the *New York Times Book Review,* Mark A. Uhlig questioned the authors' ''implicit assumption regarding the utility of nuclear weapons,'' adding, ''The book's central, if forgivable, weakness is its inability to resolve the most basic uncertainty of 'Star Wars' technologies—will they work?'' *My Dear Alex: Letters From a KGB Agent* is a satiric look at how Westernized Soviet representatives use U.S. journalists and politicians and our own goodwill and self-criticism to further their objectives. ''To [authors] D'Souza and Fossedal . . . the answer is self-evident: Americans should not do anything that may give comfort to the Soviets,'' determined Dimitri K. Simes in the *Los Angeles Times Book Review;* yet noting how subterfuge and restraint have "led . . . Soviet society only to stagnation and corruption," the critic decided, "I would settle for the American propensity for masochistic self-expose anytime."

BIOGRAPHICAL/CRITICAL SOURCES:

PERIODICALS

Insight, August 17, 1987.
Los Angeles Times Book Review, June 28, 1987.
New York Times Book Review, March 11, 1984.

*   *   *

FOSTER, Henry H(ubbard), Jr.   1911-1988

OBITUARY NOTICE—See index for *CA* sketch: Born December 3, 1911, in Norman, Okla.; died of heart failure, June 24, 1988, in New York, N.Y. Lawyer, educator, and author. A specialist in matrimonial and family law, Foster served both government and academia with distinction. In the 1930s and 1940s he worked with the antitrust division of the U.S. Justice Department and on the staff of the National Labor Relations Board in Washington, D.C. From 1946 to 1962 Foster served the law faculties of the universities of Idaho, Oklahoma, Nebraska, and Pittsburgh respectively, culminating his academic career as professor of law at New York University from 1962 until his retirement as professor emeritus in 1977. Among Foster's many publications are *Society and the Law,* the multi-volume *Law and the Family, A "Bill of Rights" for Children,* and articles contributed to reference books and professional journals.

OBITUARIES AND OTHER SOURCES:

BOOKS

Who's Who in American Law, 3rd edition, Marquis, 1983.

PERIODICALS

New York Times, June 25, 1988.

*   *   *

FOX, John Roger   1896-1987

OBITUARY NOTICE: Born November 26, 1896, in Honiton Clyst, Devon, England; died November 24, 1987, in Switzerland. Clergyman and author. Originally ordained into the Church of England in 1925, Fox converted to Catholicism in 1926 and was ordained a Catholic priest in 1933. A member of the Order of St. Augustine, he served the church in many foreign countries, including Nepal, India, and China. He wrote an autobiography, *Bridging the Gulf,* for which novelist Graham Greene wrote the foreword.

OBITUARIES AND OTHER SOURCES:

PERIODICALS

Times (London), November 28, 1987.

*   *   *

FOX, Kenneth   1944-

PERSONAL: Born April 3, 1944, in St. Louis, Mo.; son of Robert A. (a physician) and Diana (a social worker; maiden name, Bricks) Fox; married Susan E. Logston (a professor), February 11, 1981; children: Zachary James. *Education:* Columbia University, A.B. (magna cum laude), 1966; University of Pennsylvania, Ph.D., 1972.

ADDRESSES: Home—627 Quinnipiac Ave., New Haven, Conn. 06513.

CAREER: University of Massachusetts, Amherst, professor of history and politics, 1972-76; State University of New York at Binghamton, professor of history and politics, 1977-78; Seton Hall University, South Orange, professor of history and politics, 1985-87; Yale University, New Haven, Conn., professor of history and politics, 1988—.

WRITINGS:

Better City Government: Innovation in American Urban Politics, 1850-1937, Temple University Press, 1977.
Metropolitan America: Urban Life and Urban Policy in the United States, 1940-1980, University Press of Mississippi, 1986.

WORK IN PROGRESS: America's Diffuse Economy: Strategies for the Post-Industrial Age, with Evan Stark, publication expected in 1989.

SIDELIGHTS: According to critic Peter Hall of the *Times Literary Supplement,* Kenneth Fox sees the American city of the 1980s as "an embarrassing historical relic." In his book *Metropolitan America* Fox analyzes the declining importance of the American metropolis. He points to the emergence of a new suburban middle class in the 1950s, which left in America's cities an even newer "underclass" of unemployed blacks and poor who do not vote or contribute to the urban tax base. The author explains further that federal policies under presidents Johnson, Nixon, Ford and Carter were aimed at shifting responsibility for urban America to the cities themselves. Hall reported that, according to Fox, "Carter was simply recognizing that the cities were now a spent force, of little political value and that the time had come to say goodbye to Metropolis."

BIOGRAPHICAL/CRITICAL SOURCES:

PERIODICALS

Times Literary Supplement, May 30, 1986.

*   *   *

FRANCIS, Gloria A(ileen)   1930-1988

OBITUARY NOTICE: Born November 2, 1930, in Detroit, Mich.; died February 28, 1988, in Dearborn Heights, Mich. Librarian and editor. After receiving a master's degree in library science from the University of Michigan, Francis began her career in 1960 as a reference librarian for the Dearborn Public Library. She then joined the staff of the Detroit Public Library in 1964, working in the catalog department, and in 1966 became chief of the rare books room. Active in library organizations, Francis held offices with the Association of College and Research Libraries and the Book Club of Detroit. With Artem Lozynsky she compiled *Whitman at Auction, 1899-1972.*

OBITUARIES AND OTHER SOURCES:

PERIODICALS

Detroit Free Press, March 1, 1988.

FRANKEN, Rose (Dorothy)   1895(?)-1988
(Margaret Grant, Franken Meloney, joint pseudonyms)

OBITUARY NOTICE: Born December 28, 1895 (some sources say 1898), in Gainesville, Tex.; died June 22, 1988, in Tucson, Ariz. Producer, director, playwright, screenwriter, and author. Best known for her "Claudia" series of eight novels begun in 1939, Franken adapted the first two books into the highly acclaimed 1941 Broadway play "Claudia," which she also directed, a 1943 film version, and the 1946 movie sequel "Claudia and David." First serialized in magazines such as *Redbook* and *Good Housekeeping*, the stories were later adapted for radio and television. Franken co-produced several of her plays, notably "Another Language," which was later filmed, "Doctors Disagree," which she directed, "Soldier's Wife," and "The Wing"; she also co-authored a screenplay, "Beloved Enemy." Her short stories, sometimes written with her husband William Brown Meloney, appeared in periodicals, and some of her plays have been included in the Burns Mantle "Best Plays" series. Franken wrote *Call Back Love* with Meloney under the joint pseudonym Margaret Grant and, under the joint pseudonym Franken Meloney, *Strange Victory, American Bred*, and *Doctors Disagree*. Her books under her own name include *Pattern, The Antic Years, You're Well Out of the Hospital*, and an autobiography, *When All Is Said and Done*.

OBITUARIES AND OTHER SOURCES:

BOOKS

Current Biography, H. W. Wilson, 1947.
Dictionary of Literary Biography Yearbook: 1984, Gale, 1985.
Franken, Rose, *When All Is Said and Done: An Autobiography*, Allen & Unwin, 1962, Doubleday, 1963.
Who's Who, 140th edition, St. Martin's, 1988.

PERIODICALS

Los Angeles Times, June 25, 1988.
New York Times, June 24, 1988.
Washington Post, June 25, 1988.

*   *   *

FRANKLIN, Jill (Leslie)   1928-1988

OBITUARY NOTICE: Architectural historian, educator, and author. Franklin is best known for her pioneering book *The Gentleman's Country House and Its Plan, 1835-1914*, which discusses the effect of social stratification and other practices on the construction of Victorian and Edwardian homes. She taught at Keele and Boston universities and was a part-time tutor for the University of London's department of extramural studies. Franklin was also a recipient of the Gilchrist Prize.

OBITUARIES AND OTHER SOURCES:

PERIODICALS

Times (London), April 2, 1988.

*   *   *

FRANKLIN, Penelope (Florence)   1948-

PERSONAL: Born February 3, 1948, in New York, N.Y.; daughter of Anthony S. (a teacher) and Judith (a teacher; maiden name, Luttinger) Florence; married Thomas R. Franklin, October 30, 1971 (separated, 1980; divorced, 1986). *Education:*

Columbia University, B.A., 1973; also attended University of New Mexico, 1965-66, 1967-68, and New York University, 1966-67.

ADDRESSES: Home and office—New York, N.Y. *Agent*—Lynn Seligman, 400 Highland Ave., Upper Montclair, N.J. 07043.

CAREER: Burt Franklin & Co., New York, N.Y., editor, 1973-80; free-lance writer and editor, 1980—. Producer at WBAI-FM Radio, 1978-82; New York Feminist Art Institute, member of board of directors, 1979—, instructor, 1980-83; editorial director of UNICEF Flag Stamps Program, 1983—.

MEMBER: National Writers Union.

WRITINGS:

(Editor) *Private Pages: Diaries of American Women, 1830s-1970s*, Ballantine, 1986.

General editor of "American Women's Diary" series, Burt Franklin, 1978-80. Contributor to magazines and newspapers.

WORK IN PROGRESS: Aftermath: The Human Dimension of the UFO Phenomenon, with Budd Hopkins; *Viki: The Journals and Letters of a Young Writer*.

SIDELIGHTS: Penelope Franklin told *CA*: "I'm a versatile writer with a variety of interests. For years I have supported myself with different types of commercial writing—publisher's catalogs, book jackets, advertisements, press releases, brochures, etc. Many of my magazine pieces have been satirical; I've also published poetry, stories, interviews, and features on food and art. Currently I do a great deal of writing for UNICEF. This has been an eye-opener for me, in terms of exposing me to life beyond my own sheltered society.

"The lives of ordinary people, especially women, are a consistent theme in my work. Some years ago, while an editor at Burt Franklin & Company, I initiated the 'American Women's Diary' series because of my strong belief that the voices of women needed to be heard. This was a projected series of twelve volumes. I acquired and edited six manuscripts, two of which were published in 1980, when I left the company. Two of the remaining manuscripts were subsequently brought out by other publishers.

"My interest in women's diaries continued, and I edited *Private Pages: Diaries of American Women, 1830s-1970s*. In this work I delved deeper into what I term the 'inner landscape' of women, selecting entries from thirteen diaries that dealt with feelings on such issues as self-image, independence, duty, religion, sex, and aging. I'm now working on a related project—which has a very personal meaning to me—editing the diaries of my sister Viki Florence, who died in March of 1987.

"I also have an interest in psychology and what is sometimes called the 'paranormal'—although I dislike that term. This has led me to the fascinating area of UFO studies. With Budd Hopkins, author of *Intruders* (Random House, 1987), I'm now writing a book about people who believe they've been abducted by alien beings. Whether or not one subscribes to the 'abduction' hypothesis, such accounts constitute a widespread phenomenon that cannot be simply explained away. I have interviewed dozens of these 'abductees' and find them to be ordinary people struggling to deal with a major trauma that they don't understand and that society doesn't accept (tests reveal them to be psychologically normal). I'm interested in the ways that these experiences have affected these people's basic values, relationships, and views of themselves. Again, I'm dealing with the 'inner landscape'—aspects of the self generally kept hidden from others. It is my hope that the book will encourage more widespread inquiry into the meaning of such accounts."

BIOGRAPHICAL/CRITICAL SOURCES:

PERIODICALS

Albuquerque Tribune, February 16, 1987.
Book-of-the-Month Club News, December, 1978.
Chicago Tribune, November 19, 1978.
Morning Call (Allentown, Pa.), November 9, 1986.
New York Times Book Review, June 25, 1978.
San Antonio Express-News (San Antonio, Tex.), December 30, 1986.

*   *   *

FRANKLIN, Wayne S(teven)   1945-

PERSONAL: Born July 28, 1945, in Albany, N.Y.; son of William F. (a mail clerk) and Harriet A. (Denny) Franklin; married Karin A. White (an urban planner), March 11, 1966; children: Nathaniel White. *Education:* Union College, Schenectady, N.Y., B.A., 1967; University of Pittsburgh, M.A., 1968, Ph.D., 1972. *Politics:* Democrat.

ADDRESSES: Home—R.R. 7, Box 62, Iowa City, Iowa 52240. *Office*—Department of English, University of Iowa, Iowa City, Iowa 52242.

CAREER: Washington and Jefferson College, Washington, Pa., assistant professor of English, 1972-73; University of Iowa, Iowa City, assistant professor, 1973-77, associate professor, 1977-82, professor of English and American studies, 1982—.

MEMBER: American Studies Association, American Association of University Professors, New York State Historical Association.

WRITINGS:

(Contributor) Merrill Lewis, editor, *The Westering Experience in American Literature,* Western Washington State University Press, 1977.
Discoverers, Explorers, Settlers: The Diligent Writers of Early America, University of Chicago Press, 1979.
(Contributor) Steven E. Kagle, editor, *America: Exploration and Travel,* Bowling Green Popular Press, 1979.
The New World of James Fenimore Cooper, University of Chicago Press, 1982.

Contributor to literature journals. Member of editorial board of *Winterthur Portfolio: A Journal of American Material Culture.*

WORK IN PROGRESS: A Carpenter's World, a book on rural crafts in nineteenth-century America; research on American vernacular architecture and the American landscape.

SIDELIGHTS: Wayne S. Franklin told *CA:* "The ordinary or 'vernacular' architecture of the United States includes the kinds of houses most Americans have lived in: log cabins, immigrant cottages, bungalows, ranches, and even mobile homes. By studying this subject, usually neglected by architectural historians, one hopes to learn how Americans have lived, what kinds of values they have expressed in their dwellings, and what their typical home has looked and felt like.

"Similarly, the study of the American landscape—from the surviving remnants of colonial times to the 'megafarms' of the contemporary midwest or the San Joaquin valley—directs attention to the often eloquent record which our lives have written, not in books or other great moments, but rather in the open spaces of the land itself.

"My interest in these topics dates from my work in the 1970s with the 'diligent writers' of early America: those discoverers, explorers, and settlers who wrote down, in the nearly breathless spaces of their otherwise extraordinarily practical lives, the first, often sketchy installments of an American literature. Theirs was a literature intimately associated with the land and with their tenuous lives on it, a kind of imaginative dwelling composed of words to house them in the long initial American night. From Christopher Columbus, John Smith, William Bradford, and William Byrd, to Hector St. John de Crevecoeur, William Bartram, and Thomas Jefferson, these writers worked in the spirit of the instructions given to Henry Hudson when he sailed for the New World in 1609: 'Send those on land,' he was told, 'who will prove themselves diligent writers'—writers who would live up to the challenge of recording the extraordinary events enacted in America."

BIOGRAPHICAL/CRITICAL SOURCES:

PERIODICALS

Los Angeles Times, October 26, 1979.

*   *   *

FRANKS, Felix   1926-

PERSONAL: Born March 21, 1926, in Berlin, Germany; immigrated to England; married Hedy Werner in 1950; children: Suzanne, Carolyn. *Education:* University of London, B.Sc., 1951, Ph.D., 1958, D.Sc., 1971. *Politics:* Social Democrat. *Religion:* Jewish.

ADDRESSES: Home—7 Wootton Way, Cambridge CB3 9LX, England. *Office*—Pafra Ltd., Biopreservation Division, 150 Science Park, Cambridge CB4 4GG, England.

CAREER: University of Bradford, Bradford, Yorkshire, England, senior lecturer in physics and chemistry, 1959-60; Unilever (research lab), Bedford, England, senior research manager, 1966-77; University of Nottingham, Nottingham, England, special professor of biophysics, 1973—. Visiting professor at Australian National University, 1977, and at University of Waterloo in Canada, 1979 and 1984. Director of Pafra Ltd. Course director for Center for Professional Advancement, New Brunswick, N.J., 1981—. Consultant to General Foods Corp., Philip Morris USA, and British Oxygen Company. Has done radio and television programs on topics related to water. *Military service:* British Army, 1943-48, served in reconnaissance and intelligence corps.

MEMBER: Royal Society of Chemistry (council member of industrial division), Society for Cryobiology (member of board of governors).

AWARDS, HONORS: National Aeronautics and Space Administration (NASA) fellow in Pittsburgh, Pa., 1963-64; fellow of Girton College, Cambridge, 1979—.

WRITINGS:

(Editor and contributor) *Water: A Comprehensive Treatise,* seven volumes, Plenum, 1971-82.
Protein Characterization, Symposium Press, 1979.

Polywater, MIT Press, 1981.
Biophysics and Biochemistry at Low Temperatures, Cambridge University Press, 1985.

Author of numerous research papers and reviews.

CONTRIBUTOR

A. J. Morris and A. Clarke, editors, *Biological Membranes at Low Temperatures*, Academic Press, 1981.
Walter Lorch, editor, *Handbook of Water Purification*, McGraw, 1982.
C. A. Finch, editor, *Chemistry and Technology of Water-Soluble Polymers*, Plenum Press (London), 1983.
D. Simatos and J. L. Multon, editors, *Properties of Water in Foods in Relation to Quality and Stability*, Martinus Nijhoff (Netherlands), 1985.
Gerald L. Dring, D. L. Ellas, and G. W. Gould, editors, *Fundamental and Applied Aspects of Bacterial Spores*, Academic Press (London), 1985.
K. Bowler and B. J. Fuller, editors, *Animal Cells and Temperature*, Society for Experimental Biology (London), 1987.

OTHER

Editor and publisher of *Cryo-Letters*, 1979—; editor of *Water Science Review*.

SIDELIGHTS: In his 1981 book, *Polywater*, biophysicist Felix Franks recounts how, during the late 1960s and early 1970s, the purported discovery of a new and more stable form of ordinary water by a Russian chemist ignited the international scientific community. Called polywater, the revolutionary liquid was later found to be simply contaminated water, its strange properties springing from its impurities; yet in the four years before it was decisively disproved, countless research hours and dollars were spent in polywater's pursuit. "Felix Franks, an acknowledged expert on the physics and chemistry of water, here examines the rise and fall of polywater as a cautionary tale of how science is done," wrote one critic in the *New York Review of Books*. "[He] considers events in the light of the late Sixties when science was riding high, but also when the very idea that the Russians were on to something could spark instant action."

Reviewing *Polywater* for the *Chicago Tribune Book World*, Clarence Petersen related that it "can be studied as scientific history and enjoyed as a good yarn." "Mr. Franks' story is arresting, and he tells it well," concurred Stephen Jay Gould in the *New York Times Book Review*. "But when Mr. Franks tries to infuse deeper meaning and turn his tale into a warning or a moral lesson, then I demur." Feeling that the polywater case is neither as alarming nor as aberrant as the author makes it out to be," the reviewer reflected: "For once, science really worked as scientists say it should. . . . You [can't] expect scientists to act as robots devoid of emotional involvement. . . . Science isn't supposed to be right all the time; it is only supposed to be able to test its claims. And it did, and with dispatch." "It wasn't as bad as Franks makes out—but he also makes of it an intriguing, unusual book," the *New York Review of Books* writer agreed.

Franks told *CA* that his interests include the sociology of scientists and the interface between industry and academia. He is also an amateur musician (piano and cello) and speaks fluent German and "adequate" French. A keen hiker, he has traveled extensively in Europe and North America and has visited Australia and Argentina.

BIOGRAPHICAL/CRITICAL SOURCES:

PERIODICALS

Chicago Tribune Book World, May 29, 1983.
New York Review of Books, October 8, 1981.
New York Times Book Review, August 30, 1981.

*　　*　　*

FRANKS, Marlene Strong 1955-

PERSONAL: Born May 31, 1955, in Baltimore, Md.; daughter of Theodore J. Strong (a building manager) and Gertrude (a teacher; maiden name, Stasiak) Strong; married Grant H. Franks (an attorney), June 4, 1977. *Education:* St. John's College, Annapolis, Md., B.A, 1977; University of California, Berkeley, M.P.P., 1982, doctoral candidate beginning in 1984.

ADDRESSES: Home—Berkeley, Calif. *Office*—Berkeley Planning Associates, 3200 Adeline St., Berkeley, Calif. 94703.

CAREER: Berkeley Planning Associates (private consulting firm engaged in research and evaluation for government agencies), Berkeley, Calif., senior analyst, 1983—.

MEMBER: American Public Welfare Association, Association for Public Policy Analysis and Management.

WRITINGS:

(With David L. Kirp and Mark G. Yudof) *Gender Justice*, University of Chicago Press, 1986.

WORK IN PROGRESS: Suffer the Children: The Specter of AIDS in America's Schoolhouses, "about how school districts around the country are handling acquired immune deficiency syndrome and what this tells us about the definition of community in our time," publication expected in 1989.

SIDELIGHTS: In *Gender Justice* Marlene Strong Franks and co-authors David L. Kirp and Mark G. Yudof look at gender-related public policy in America. "The authors . . . insist that American institutions are constitutionally and morally obligated to promote the equality of the sexes," observed Maimon Schwarzschild in the *New York Times Book Review;* but while removing impediments to free choice for men and women, the state is not required to shape social outcomes. Equal liberty, not equality, they maintain, should be the focus of laws and policies—guaranteeing process, not results. Schwarzschild related: "Liberty itself, the authors argue, requires the preservation of the private sphere of life in which people can make intimate choices without public interference."

Disavowing rightist views of biological determinism and feminism's focus on the force of socialization, *Gender Justice* stirred strong reader reactions. *Los Angeles Times Book Review* critic Laura J. Lederer objected to the authors' dismissal of all feminist writings as radical; it shows "a profound ignorance . . . concerning feminist theory," the reviewer stated, and overlooks that "most of the gender-related policy that has emerged in the last 10 years has been a direct result of, and reaction to, the theories of sexual politics that were put forth by early feminists." Reviewing the book for the *Washington Post Book World*, Suzanne Gordon criticized its exclusion of "the most recent and sophisticated feminist thinking" as well. The reviewer found the authors' "animating vision—a world where autonomous individuals reject collective solutions to major social problems"—oblivious to the interdependency that marks human society, adding: "Alas for most ordinary folk, results . . . are far more important than process. . . . The authors of . . . *Gender Justice* fail . . . because their single-minded devotion to the ethos of individualism has blinded them to the needs of real life individuals." Yet Schwarzschild, conversely, welcomed this provocative philosophical investigation by Franks, Kirp, and Yudof. "'Gender Justice' has the rarity value of being a book about public policy that is literate, jargon-free and even entertaining," wrote the critic. "The authors make a fascinating case for a gender policy centered on personal liberty. Freedom of choice rightly appeals to most Americans, whatever the reservations."

Franks told *CA:* "I juggle several different personas: the day-to-day analyst working on specific policy problems (Does this child abuse prevention program work?), the researcher investigating broader but still policy-relevant concerns (What is gender justice? How is community defined?), and the thinker who still pursues 'big questions' as a member of a seminar group of St. John's College (the 'Great Books School') alumni (latest reading: Virginia Woolf's *To the Lighthouse*)."

BIOGRAPHICAL/CRITICAL SOURCES:

PERIODICALS

Los Angeles Times Book Review, November 17, 1985.
New York Times Book Review, June 15, 1986.
Washington Post Book World, February 2, 1986.

*   *   *

FRASER, Keath 1944-

PERSONAL: Born December 25, 1944, in Vancouver, British Columbia, Canada; son of Lyle and Cecelia (Penland) Fraser; married Lorraine Horsman (a teacher), May 31, 1969; children: Robin (son). *Education:* University of British Columbia, B.A., 1966, M.A., 1969; University of London, Ph.D., 1973.

ADDRESSES: Home—3091 West 12th Ave., Vancouver, British Columbia, Canada V6K 2R4. *Agent*—David Colbert, Colbert Agency, 303 Davenport Rd., Toronto, Ontario, Canada M5R 1K5.

CAREER: University of Calgary, Calgary, Alberta, assistant professor of English literature, 1973-78; writer, 1978—.

MEMBER: P.E.N. International.

AWARDS, HONORS: Annual contributor's prize from *Canadian Fiction Magazine,* 1981, for "This Is What You Were Born For"; Governor-General's Award nomination for fiction from Canada Council and Ethel Wilson Prizes for fiction from British Columbia Book Prizes, both 1986, both for *Foreign Affairs; Western Magazine* award for fiction, 1987, for "Bones."

WRITINGS:

Taking Cover (story collection), Oberon Press, 1982.
Foreign Affairs (story and novella collection), Stoddart, 1985.

Work represented in anthologies, including *Canadian Writers in 1984,* edited by W. H. New, University of British Columbia Press, 1984; *Best Canadian Stories; Best Canadian Short Fiction; On Middle Ground; The Methuen Anthology to Canadian Poetry and Short Fiction; The Macmillan Anthology.* Contributor of travel essays, literary reviews, and fiction to periodicals, including *Canadian Literature, Malahat Review, Descant, Essays on Canadian Writing, Prism International,* and *Literary Review.*

WORK IN PROGRESS: A novel, *Popular Anatomy; Writers' Worst Journeys,* an edition of travel essays by various authors.

SIDELIGHTS: Keath Fraser's *Foreign Affairs* is a collection of short stories and novellas that interconnect through repeated themes and similar situations. "Many of the characters in Foreign Affairs seem to be seeking redemption, but it is only occasionally possible and always difficult," detailed Antanas Sileika in a review for the Toronto *Globe and Mail;* like the journalist tortured by her foreign captors in one story, or the diplomat betrayed by his diseased body in another, all are compatriots in a world marked by "lurking horror and shattered dreams." But "the tone is far from depressing," insisted the critic, relating that *Foreign Affairs* "is the kind of book whose themes keep coming back, and whose symmetry suddenly becomes clear." Deeming it "one of the finest pieces of fiction to appear in a long time," Sileika added: "Fraser's remarkable facility with language and image gives many of these stories the density of poetry."

Fraser told *CA* that he has traveled widely in Europe, Asia, Australia, New Zealand, and Central and South America. Discussing his art in the essay "Notes Toward a Supreme Fiction," the author stated: "I am talking about fiction that overturns expectation by jextaposition, nexus, dislocation. I am talking about fiction that aspires to be an understanding of cultural anorexy; fiction that creates the complexity capable of engaging our imaginations; fiction capable of perceiving the many ways that our received culture, for all its splendors of cohesion, for all our diplomacy, is suffering from edema of the soul."

BIOGRAPHICAL/CRITICAL SOURCES:

BOOKS

David, Jack, and Robert Lecker, editors, *The Methuen Anthology to Canadian Poetry and Short Fiction,* Methuen (Toronto), 1988.
Metcalf, John, editor, *On the Edge: Canadian Short Stories,* Vehicule Press (Montreal), 1987.

PERIODICALS

Canadian Fiction Magazine, spring, 1988.
Canadian Forum, February, 1986.
Globe and Mail (Toronto), September 30, 1982, January 4, 1986, October 25, 1986.
Toronto Star, November 10, 1985, October 19, 1987.

*   *   *

FREEMAN, T(homas) W(alter) 1908-1988

OBITUARY NOTICE—See index for *CA* sketch: Born December 27, 1908, in Congleton, Cheshire, England; died March 11, 1988. Geographer, educator, and author. Freeman taught geography at the University of Manchester from 1949 to 1976, retiring as professor emeritus. His many publications include *Ireland: Its Physical, Historical, Social, and Economic Geography; Geography and Planning; One Hundred Years of Geography; The Geographer's Craft; The Writing of Geography;* and *A History of Modern British Geography.* Freeman also served as editor of *Irish Geography* from 1945 to 1949 and as a reviewer for *Geographical Journal,* and he contributed articles to reference books.

OBITUARIES AND OTHER SOURCES:

BOOKS

International Authors and Writers Who's Who, 8th edition, Melrose, 1977.

The Writers Directory, 1988-1990, St. James Press, 1988.

PERIODICALS

Times (London), March 14, 1988.

*   *   *

FREER, Coburn   1939-

PERSONAL: Born November 5, 1939, in New Orleans, La.; son of W. C. (an air force officer) and Lillian Jackson (Hicks) Freer; married Ramona Salminen, June 10, 1961; children: Meagan, Elinor. *Education:* Lewis and Clark College, B.A., 1960; University of Washington, Seattle, Ph.D., 1967.

ADDRESSES: Home—370 Duncan Springs Rd., Athens, Ga. 30606. *Office*—Department of English, University of Georgia, Athens, Ga. 30602.

CAREER: University of Arizona, Tucson, instructor in English, 1965-67; University of Montana, Missoula, assistant professor, 1967-72, associate professor, 1972-76, professor of English, 1976-80; University of Georgia, Athens, professor of English and head of department, 1980—. Senior Fulbright lecturer at University of Oulu, 1971-72.

MEMBER: International Association of Professors of English, Modern Language Association of America, Milton Society, South Atlantic Modern Language Association, Southeastern Renaissance Society.

AWARDS, HONORS: Fellow of National Endowment for the Humanities in London, England, 1974-75, and American Council of Learned Societies, 1975.

WRITINGS:

Music for a King: George Herbert's Style and the Metrical Psalms, Johns Hopkins University Press, 1972.
The Poetics of Jacobean Drama, Johns Hopkins University Press, 1981.

Contributor to collections of essays, including *A Poet and A Filthy Play-Maker: New Essays on Christopher Marlowe,* 1986; *Concord in Discord; A Spenser Encyclopedia;* and *Renaissance Women Writers,* 1987.

*   *   *

FRICKER, E(dward) G(eorge)   1910-

PERSONAL: Born March 8, 1910, in London, England; son of Arthur Edwin (a printer) and Emily (a homemaker) Fricker; married Alice Grace Morley (a homemaker); children: Derek Edward, Rita Margaret Fricker Solomon, Theresa Christina Fricker Starling. *Education:* Educated in England.

ADDRESSES: Home—Barnet, Herts, England. *Agent*—Eric Glass Ltd., 28 Berkeley Sq., London W1X 6HD, England.

CAREER: Worked as a butcher, barrow boy, and shop assistant in London, England, 1926-39; in business in London, 1947-51; Fricker's Healing Centre, London, spiritual healer, 1952—. *Military service:* British Army, 1940-46; became sergeant major; received George VI War Medal, Defence Medal, and France and Germany Star.

WRITINGS:

God Is My Witness: The Story of the World-Famous Healer, Stein & Day, 1977.

Also author of *Why God Put Us on Earth.*

SIDELIGHTS: In his autobiography *God Is My Witness* psychic healer E. G. Fricker recounts how he came to discover and develop his healing gift. After his mother's death from cancer Fricker prayed that he might be able to heal others; a medium-channeled voice contacted a team of physicians in the spirit world whose insights empowered him to heal more than one million people over the next three decades. Today operating a London clinic, the spiritualist treats nearly two hundred people daily, including well-known British personalities.

Fricker told *CA:* "Having been told by a voice, as a child, to carry out the healing mission, I have devoted my life—since middle age, when extraordinary circumstances led me into this—to helping others. I believe that people can cure their loved ones by the laying-on of hands—a gift from God—and I have traveled on healing missions to the United States and the Netherlands, although my main work has been confined to the United Kingdom."

BIOGRAPHICAL/CRITICAL SOURCES:

BOOKS

Barbanell, Maurice, *I Hear a Voice: A Biography of E. G. Fricker, the Healer,* Spiritualist Press, 1962.

*   *   *

FRIEDMAN, Alan J(acob)   1942-

PERSONAL: Born November 15, 1942, in Brooklyn, N.Y.; son of George (a salesman) and Eleanor (Goldberger) Friedman; married Mickey Thompson (a novelist), December 26, 1966. *Education:* Georgia Institute of Technology, B.S., 1964; Florida State University, Ph.D., 1970.

ADDRESSES: Home—New York, N.Y. *Office*—New York Hall of Science, 47-01 111th St., Flushing Meadows-Corona Park, N.Y. 11368.

CAREER: Hiram College, Hiram, Ohio, instructor, 1969-70, assistant professor of physics, 1970-74; University of California, Berkeley, director of astronomy and physics at Lawrence Hall of Science, 1973-84; New York Hall of Science, Flushing Meadows-Corona Park, director, 1984—. Research fellow in English at University of California, Berkeley, 1972-73; visiting lecturer at San Francisco State University, 1974-75; visiting assistant professor at Temple University, 1975; senior planning consultant to Cite des Sciences et de l'Industrie, Paris, 1982-84.

MEMBER: International Planetarium Society (president, 1985-86), American Association of Physics Teachers, Phi Beta Kappa, Sigma Pi Sigma.

AWARDS, HONORS: Younger humanist fellow of National Endowment for the Humanities, 1972-73; Distinguished Service Award from Mid-Atlantic Planetarium Society, 1982; Professional Award of Merit from Astronomical Association of Northern California, 1983.

WRITINGS:

(Contributor) Richard Pearce, editor, *Critical Essays on Thomas Pynchon,* G. K. Hall, 1981.
(Contributor) Zipporah W. Collins, editor, *Museums, Adults, and the Humanities,* American Association of Museums, 1981.
(Contributor) Charles Clerc, editor, *Approaches to Gravity's Rainbow,* Ohio State University Press, 1983.

(With Carol Donley) *Einstein as Myth and Muse,* Cambridge University Press, 1985.
(Contributor) David Evered and Maeve O'Connor, editors, *Communicating Science to the Public,* Wiley, 1987.

Contributor to scientific and museum journals. Member of editorial board of *Museum Studies Journal,* 1984—.

WORK IN PROGRESS: Strategies for Public Science-Technology Centers; research on the cultural influences of science and technology.

SIDELIGHTS: Alan J. Friedman told *CA:* "I have loved literature since my mother started reading to me when I was a small child. High school English courses, however, convinced me that a career in literature would be perilous. An essay I thought was great might get an A or a D; you never could tell what the teacher would like. Science, on the other hand, seemed to have simply right or wrong answers; you could always tell what would get an A and what would flunk. So I became a physicist, although I took all the English courses Georgia Institute of Technology had to offer.

"By the time I got to graduate school at Florida State I had learned that real physics is not just right or wrong answers but involves judgment, taste, inspiration, and lots of disagreement, just like literature. But I stayed in physics through my Ph.D. I married an English major, however, who has since published five novels.

"I learned from our English professors that some writers were fascinated by science and used their fascination in their work. William Shakespeare, John Donne, William Wordsworth, Joseph Conrad, Virginia Woolf, Vladimir Nabokov, E. E. Cummings, W. H. Auden, Charles Wilbert Snow, William Pynchon—as well as a host of science fiction writers—all got to think about both science *and* literature.

"So starting with my first job at Hiram College I combined my two interests and taught a course on science and literature, with my wife as co-teacher. I've since collaborated with other scientists and other literary people on a variety of projects.

"Professor Carol Donley and I wrote *Einstein as Myth and Muse,* which surveys the remarkably broad range of interesting connections between physicist Albert Einstein, his work, and other aspects of culture such as poetry and novels. Einstein has inspired a great variety of experiments in literary form and subject. He has also served to represent intellect in general and scientific intelligence in particular. We found that in this latter role images of Einstein reveal a strong ambiguity towards science, with Einstein—a modern Prometheus—single-handedly and unexpectedly bringing us an atomic fire we are not ready to handle. This is cockeyed history but a powerful myth nonetheless.

"My regular profession has been communicating science to the general public. I've not written much science popularization—though I've been tempted—but have spent most of my career in the new generation of science museums, known as science-technology centers. These are instruments to present science through real, hands-on experiences. With colleagues, I've worked on exhibits ('Star Games'), activity kits ('Sky Challenger,' published by the Lawrence Hall of Science in Berkeley), and new teaching techniques (participatory planetarium shows).

"For slow writers like me, lectures are an easy way to communicate verbally. I've greatly enjoyed developing several popular-level, lecture-demonstration courses wth astronomer Andrew Fraknoi on science and its cultural relations: 'Einstein: The Man and His Legacy,' 'Science and the Science Fiction Film,' and 'Science and . . .' (a course for college teachers).

"After working on the staffs of two major science-technology centers—the Lawrence Hall of Science and the Cite des Sciences et de l'Industrie, Paris—I decided to try administration so that I would have to live with only my own mistakes. I can now report that it is far easier to live with someone else's mistakes. Thanks to some very talented and patient colleagues and public officials, however, we have created a new science-technology museum in New York City.

"I have a collection of essays I've written, mostly in Paris, about strategies for communicating science and technology to the public. My experience here in New York, putting some of those strategies to test, has proven the need to rewrite most of those essays. But a book might emerge, I think. I've found that communicating through museums involves judgment, taste, inspiration, and disagreement—just like physics and literature."

* * *

FRIEDMAN, John Block 1934-

PERSONAL: Born December 8, 1934, in Troy, N.Y.; son of Favius Louis (a writer) and Maxine (a writer; maiden name, Block) Friedman; children: Anna Francesca, Cordalie. *Education:* Reed College, B.A., 1960; Johns Hopkins University, M.A., 1961; Michigan State University, Ph.D., 1965.

ADDRESSES: Department of English, University of Illinois, Urbana, Ill. 61801.

CAREER: Connecticut College, New London, assistant professor of English, 1965-68; Sir George Williams University, Montreal, Quebec, associate professor of English, 1968-71; University of Illinois, Urbana, professor of English, 1971—, associate of Center for Advanced Studies, 1975-76. Resident at Center for the Study of Medieval Civilization, Poitiers, France, 1973.

MEMBER: Mediaeval Academy of America, New Chaucer Society, Illinois Medieval Association.

AWARDS, HONORS: Woodrow Wilson fellow, 1960-61; fellow at Southeastern Institute of Medieval and Renaissance Studies, 1975; Guggenheim Memorial Foundation fellow, 1979-80; American Council of Learned Societies grant-in-aid, 1983-84.

WRITINGS:

Orpheus in the Middle Ages, Harvard University Press, 1970.
The Monstrous Races in Medieval Art and Thought, Harvard University Press, 1981.
John de Foxton's Liber Cosmographiae (1408): An Edition and Codicological Study, E. J. Brill (Leiden), 1988.

Contributor to scholarly journals, including *Journal of Warburg and Courtauld Institutes, Journal of English and German Philology, Scriptorium, Studies in Philology, Modern Philology, Traditio, Studies in the Age of Chaucer, Chaucer Review, Studies in Iconography,* and *Library Quarterly.*

WORK IN PROGRESS: "*Fer in the North, I Kan Nat Telle Where*": Manuscript Book Production in Yorkshire, 1375-1450, completion expected about 1992.

SIDELIGHTS: In *The Monstrous Races in Medieval Art and Thought* John Block Friedman explores the appeal of the monstrous races—deformed species of men living beyond the civilized world—to the medieval mind. According to T. A. Shippey in the *Times Literary Supplement,* human monsters like Cyclops, Sciopods, Amazons, and Pygmies represent more than the gullibility of past ages; Friedman looks at the reasons behind the myths, suggesting that escapism, xenophobia, the misapprehension of actual phenomena (the one-legged Sciopods, for example, are a misperception of contorted Yogis) helped build the durable tradition of monstrous races. Reviewing the book for the *New York Times,* John Leonard determined, "Mr. Friedman is a graceful and witty writer." While regretting some exclusions and "loose ends," the critic decided, "What [Friedman] has given us, for which I am grateful, is first-class intellectual history." "With droll style and broad erudition, Professor Friedman has produced a lively chronicle of these curious creatures," *Newsweek* writer Jim Miller concurred. "But his book is not just about them; it is also about our enduring inability to view other cultures without prejudice."

BIOGRAPHICAL/CRITICAL SOURCES:

PERIODICALS

Newsweek, July 27,1981.
New York Times, June 16, 1981.
Times Literary Supplement, November 13, 1981.

*   *   *

FRIEDMAN, Max Motel   1899(?)-1988
   (Morris "Red" Rudensky)

OBITUARY NOTICE: One source cites birth-given name as Macy Motie Friedman; known professionally as Morris "Red" Rudensky; born c. 1899 (one source says 1908) in New York, N.Y.; died April 21, 1988, in St. Paul, Minn. Criminal, security consultant, editor, and author. After beginning his career as a juvenile delinquent, Rudensky became renowned as a free-lance safecracker and thief during the 1920s, accepting assignments from the criminal gangs of George "Bugs" Moran and Al Capone. He acquired his professional name when arresting officers mistook him for another safecracker, and he kept the alias to elude prosecution for his own, more serious, crimes. Among Rudensky's prison cellmates were Capone and Robert Stroud, the so-called "Birdman of Alcatraz."

While in jail Rudensky changed from a troublesome escapee to a model prisoner, editing the Atlanta penitentiary's newspaper and organizing prisoners across the country to make clothing and equipment for soldiers during World War II. Paroled in 1944, he became a copy editor at Brown & Bigelow in St. Paul, Minnesota, later transferring to the 3M Company as a lock consultant and alarm expert. A respected humanitarian, Rudensky entertained hospitalized children and the inmates of nursing homes. His autobiography, published under the name Morris "Red" Rudensky, was titled *The Gonif*—Yiddish for "thief." Rudensky's other writings include poetry for Boy Scout calendars.

OBITUARIES AND OTHER SOURCES:

BOOKS

The Directory of Infamy: The Best of the Worst, Mills & Boon, 1980.
Rudensky, Morris "Red" and Don Riley, *The Gonif,* edited by John M. Sullivan, Jr., Piper Publishing, 1970.

PERIODICALS

Chicago Tribune, April 24, 1988.
Globe & Mail (Toronto), April 23, 1988.
Los Angeles Times, April 23, 1988.
New York Times, April 24, 1988.
Washington Post, April 23, 1988.

*   *   *

FRIER, Bruce W(oodward)   1943-

PERSONAL: Born August 31, 1943, in Chicago, Ill.; son of Bill E. (an engineer) and Jane (Davies) Frier. *Education:* Trinity College, Hartford, Conn., B.A., 1964; Princeton University, Ph.D., 1970.

ADDRESSES: Office—Department of Classical Studies, University of Michigan, Ann Arbor, Mich. 48109.

CAREER: Bryn Mawr College, Bryn Mawr, Pa., lecturer in Latin, 1968-69; University of Michigan, Ann Arbor, assistant professor, 1969-75, associate professor, 1975-83, professor of classical studies, 1983—, professor of law, 1986—.

MEMBER: American Philological Association, American Society for Legal History.

AWARDS, HONORS: Godwin Award of Merit from American Philological Association, 1983, for *Landlords and Tenants in Imperial Rome.*

WRITINGS:

Landlords and Tenants in Imperial Rome, Princeton University Press, 1981.
The Rise of the Roman Jurists: Studies in Cicero's "pro Caecina," Princeton University Press, 1985.

WORK IN PROGRESS: A Casebook on the Roman Law of Delict, for American Philological Association.

SIDELIGHTS: Bruce W. Frier told *CA:* "My publications in Roman law center on one question: What can be said, with some degree of definiteness, about the relationship of Roman law to Roman society? It is widely agreed that Roman law ranks among the greatest and most enduring achievements of Roman culture, but the origins of this achievement in the historical context of the Roman empire remain far more mysterious. Through the close study of specific examples, I am trying to unravel this thorny issue."

BIOGRAPHICAL/CRITICAL SOURCES:

PERIODICALS

American Historical Review, December, 1981, January, 1986.
Times Literary Supplement, December 13, 1985.

*   *   *

FRIESNER, Esther M.
   See FRIESNER-STUTZMAN, Esther M.

*   *   *

FRIESNER-STUTZMAN, Esther M.   1951-
   (Esther M. Friesner)

PERSONAL: Born July 16, 1951, in New York; daughter of David R. (a teacher) and Beatrice (a teacher; maiden name, Richter) Friesner; married Walter Stutzman (a software specialist), December 22, 1974; children: Michael Jacob, Anne

Elizabeth. *Education:* Vassar College, B.A., 1972; Yale University, M.A., Ph.D., 1977.

ADDRESSES: Home and office—53 Mendingwall Circle, Madison, Conn. 06443. *Agent*—Richard Curtis, 164 East 64th St., New York, N.Y. 10021.

CAREER: Yale University, New Haven, Conn., instructor in Spanish, 1977-79, and 1983.

MEMBER: Science Fiction Writers of America.

AWARDS, HONORS: Named Outstanding New Fantasy Writer by *Romantic Times*, 1986.

WRITINGS:

UNDER NAME ESTHER M. FRIESNER

Mustapha and His Wise Dog, Avon, 1985.
Harlot's Ruse, Warner Books, 1986.
Spells of Mortal Weaving, Avon, 1986.
The Silver Mountain, Warner Books, 1986.
New York by Knight, New American Library, 1986.
"The Shame of Maudie Jones" (play), first produced in 1986.
Witchwood Cradle, Avon, 1987.
Here Be Demons (fantasy novel), Berkley Publications, 1988.

WORK IN PROGRESS: Two fantasy novels, *Elf Defense* and *The Groves of Academon.*

SIDELIGHTS: Esther M. Friesner-Stutzman told *CA:* "I can never resist a challenge, particularly to the imagination. I enjoy drawing the quirkier aspects of real life into the world of fantasy. With so many ideas surrounding us, why limit fantasy to the cloners of established classics? This betrays the very essence of fantastic literature—and literature in general—which is to explore and expand our vision of life and its infinite possibilities."

* * *

FUGARD, Sheila 1932-

PERSONAL: Born February 25, 1932, in Birmingham, England; daughter of Ernest (a physician) and Elizabeth (Kerley) Meiring; married Athol Fugard (a playwright and director), September 22, 1956; children: Lisa. *Education:* Attended University of Cape Town, 1950-52. *Politics:* Liberal. *Religion:* Buddhist.

ADDRESSES: Home—P.O. Box 5090, Walmer, Port Elizabeth, South Africa; or, Drewville Rd., Carmel, N.Y. 10512. *Agent*—Elaine Markson Literary Agency, 44 Greenwich Ave., New York, N.Y. 10011.

CAREER: Writer.

AWARDS, HONORS: Central News Agency Literary Award (South Africa), 1972, and Olive Schreiner Prize from English Academy of Southern Africa, 1973, both for *The Castaways.*

WRITINGS:

The Castaways (novel), Macmillan (South Africa), 1972.
Threshold (poems), Donker (South Africa), 1975.
Rite of Passage (novel), Donker, 1976.
Mythic Things (poems), Donker, 1981.
A Revolutionary Woman (novel), Virago Press, 1984, Braziller, 1985.

Contributor to anthologies, including *Sometimes When It Rains,* Methuen, 1987.

WORK IN PROGRESS: A novel, *Faces of the Ancestors;* a memoir about a Tibetan Buddhist nun, *Lady of Realization;* short stories; poems.

SIDELIGHTS: Born in England, Sheila Fugard moved to Africa when she was a young girl; her writings reflect a concern with clashing cultures, racial tension, decaying civilization, and revolutionary nonviolence and retaliation. Fugard's first novel, *The Castaways,* is narrated by a patient in a psychiatric hospital whose hallucinations return him to the time of his ancestors—South Africa's first white settlers; after his escape from the sanatorium the narrator encounters an equally mad revolutionary awaiting that country's liberation. "In part a meditation of spiritual and political power, [*The Castaways*] moves with sure imaginative conviction from 1770 to the present and looks farther into the future than most South African writers dare," described one *Times Literary Supplement* critic. Deeming its prose "'poetic' in the best sense," the reviewer judged this first book "a highly original work."

According to Eileen Julien in *World Literature Today,* Fugard "expresses more intensely ideas first explored in her novel *The Castaways*" in the poetry collection *Threshold.* Reflecting on modern tragedies like Hiroshima and Auschwitz that have negated traditional concepts of civilization, the poet explores the individual's search for meaningful new patterns to succeed the old. "*Threshold* contains many eloquent and memorable poems," determined Julien. "Fugard experiments with syntax and employs a beautiful, eclectic metaphor while retaining prosaic tones. This first collection of verse reveals a promising, sensitive poet."

In the novel *Rite of Passage* Fugard contemplates South Africa's primitive past, suggesting that there lie solutions to the country's troubled present. A doctor accused of malpractice travels to Pedi country to study that tribe's rite of passage for adolescent males; while there he helps a white boy who has run away after a traumatic homosexual experience undergo the rite and purge himself of sexual guilt. Reviewing the book for the *New Statesman,* Hermione Lee decided that "the power of this mythic tale stems from its well sustained, bare, lyric, descriptive voice." The critic added: "Sheila Fugard's brief, intense novel . . . undermines South African civilisation not from within but, more daringly, from the vantage point of primitivism. . . . Life there is so stricken that the only cure may be in primitive ritual, in the I-Ching and the reading of the bones."

Fugard's first book to appear in the United States was the novel *A Revolutionary Woman.* Set in South Africa in 1920, the story is told by an Englishwoman who teaches at a segregated school in an isolated enclave for non-whites. A disciple of Gandhi, Christina Ransome envisions a classless South Africa implemented by revolutionary nonviolence; she shares these dreams with a sensitive student named Ebrahim, whom she comes to see as an adopted son and inheritor of the vision. Things go tragically awry, however, when the youth seduces a retarded white girl and the townspeople gather for his lynching. "The final section of the book is a rhetorical dialogue between the twelve men of the posse, the narrator and the Coloured victim, each justifying his actions and point of view, rather like the chorus of a Greek play," detailed David Wright in a review for the *Times Literary Supplement.* "It is here that the emotional validity of this odd book is manifest."

Attending this story of racial injustice is a look at sexual injustice as well. Christina is troubled by a former romance complicated by her Indian lover's child bride; greater still is her confusion over Gandhi's submissive wife Kasterbai, prohibited from participating in his political life. Discussing the concurrent themes of *A Revolutionary Woman* in the *New York Times Book Review*, Paula Bonnell found them overly ambitious. "The author seems undecided about whether to present an inner, almost hallucinatory vision, or an outer, detail-filled narrative," she commented. "The dialogue combines the realistic and the symbolic." Wright, likewise, noted that "there is little attempt at realism, or even fidelity to the period." Still, "the novel works," decided the reviewer. "It's driving emotional energy forces conviction even though the characters hardly ever seem to coincide with reality. They are types, symbols, larger and less complex than life."

Other critics agreed that it is this mythic, poetic quality that gives *A Revolutionary Woman* its strange appeal. Citing the book's "stylized prose, ritualist dialogues, [and] chorus of raging characters," Maureen Connell remarked in the *Los Angeles Times Book Review* that "a poet's sensibility touches each page." "The novel alternates between ritualized formal dialogue and shimmering imagery," reiterated *Washington Post Book World* reviewer Frances A. Koestler. "Short declarative sentences set up a rhythmic, dirgelike beat as events march to their inexorable culmination. Scenes are deftly captured in a few sentences." And assessing the novel in *Ms.*, Elinor Langer concluded: "Constructed like poetry, with recurring rhythms and refrains, it sweeps past the clutter of personality and works directly with its characters' souls."

Fugard told *CA:* "My novels usually depend on some historical South African background, which is then fictionalized into an imaginative piece of writing. In *A Revolutionary Woman* I also deal with women's issues. As for my work in progress, *Faces of the Ancestors*, I've had difficulty in finding the right tone for the book, particularly as the poetic resonances of my style are so necessary for the success of the work. I think I've broken through that barrier by giving my characters—black tribal women in Angola caught up in a war situation—more elevated and complex speech than they would normally use. It's a question of my characters being slightly larger than life, and moving away from realism and more towards an imaginative fictional world. I feel that I am achieving this now. I am also becoming interested in writing short stories, or as I would rather say 'fictions.' This form allows me to make a dense and subtle statement and is not nearly as exhausting as a novel. In addition, I'm working on a collection of poems—as yet untitled—which are varied and reflect my own feelings over the last decade. The poems are about contemporary South Africa, women, and landscapes in Africa, Asia, and America. I'm refining the poems and also seeking a cohesion to the collection.

"South Africa is a very difficult country to live in, and always a challenge to me as a writer. I find it abrasive, and it's a struggle now to live there, while I really enjoy being in my adopted land, the United States. Firstly, I find that I still live with the unresolved problems of coming to South Africa from England, where I was born, just before the outbreak of World War II. My South African father and Irish mother had a bitter divorce, which affected me deeply as a child. In a way, I still find myself a stranger in South Africa. The daily trauma of that land and its peoples takes its toll. On recent stays in South Africa, I have found that I struggled too with the paternalism inherent in apartheid, which damages and restricts, not only blacks and people of colour, but in a subtle sense, also women. Yet, I remain attached to South Africa and feel compelled to write about it.

"I appreciate the great freedom which the United States offers to those who live here. I'm also provoked by events here, but they don't have the barbs that I experience in South Africa.

"A word about my Buddhism. I don't belong to organizations or any political party because I feel that a committment to Buddhism is sufficient. It's a religion that asks for a certain self-discipline and compassion for others. Within this broad framework, one encompasses not only the homeless and those without a political voice, but also the ecology, the animal of the earth, in fact every living being. Another work in progress is a memoir which I wrote ten years ago about my original Buddhist teacher, an Englishwoman who was a Tibetan Buddhist nun. The memoir is titled *Lady of Realization,* and now, with so much interest in women in religious life, I am trying to expand the book."

BIOGRAPHICAL/CRITICAL SOURCES:

PERIODICALS

Los Angeles Times Book Review, September 29, 1985.
Ms., November, 1985.
New Statesman, December 9, 1977.
New York Times Book Review, October 6, 1985.
Times Literary Supplement, November 10, 1972, February 15, 1985.
Washington Post Book World, November 24, 1985.
World Literature Today, winter, 1977.

—Sketch by Nancy Pear

*   *   *

FULLER, Jack (William) 1946-

BRIEF ENTRY: Born October 12, 1946, in Chicago, Ill. American journalist, editor, and author. *Chicago Tribune* editorial page editor and winner of a 1985 Pulitzer Prize for his editorials on constitutional issues, Fuller garnered considerable acclaim for his first novel, an action-packed spy thriller titled *Convergence* (Doubleday, 1982). Fuller was introduced to the world of intelligence operations in 1975 while working for the U.S. Justice Department as special assistant to Attorney General Edward Levi. Likened to the works of contemporary espionage novelists John le Carre and Graham Greene, *Convergence* was hailed "the most plausible, and perhaps the best, spy novel ever written by an American" by Arthur Maling in *Chicago Tribune Book World*. Fuller's second novel, *Fragments* (Morrow, 1984), earned him a 1987 Friends of American Writers Award for its cogent, realistic, and perceptive account of the Vietnam war experience. The author returned to the spy thriller genre in *Mass* (Morrow, 1985), the story of a murdered Soviet defector. Fuller's fourth book, the 1987 detective story *Our Fathers' Shadows* (Morrow, 1987), was praised for its fast pace and tight prose—two of the author's stylistic trademarks. *Addresses: Office—Chicago Tribune,* 435 North Michigan Ave., Chicago, Ill. 60611. *Agent*—Peter Shepherd, 40 East 49th St., New York, N.Y. 10017.

BIOGRAPHICAL/CRITICAL SOURCES:

BOOKS

Who's Who in America, 44th edition, Marquis, 1986.

PERIODICALS

Chicago Tribune Book World, October 3, 1982, January 8, 1984.

New York Times, February 13, 1984.
Washington Post, January 9, 1984.

*   *   *

FULLER, Ken 1946-

PERSONAL: Born January 11, 1946, in Reading, England; son of Violet East; married and divorced twice; married third wife, Firma Rizalado Delusa, October 24, 1983. *Education:* Attended secondary schools in Reading and Twickenham, England. *Politics:* Socialist. *Religion:* None.

ADDRESSES: Home—155 The Avenue, Tottenham, London N17 6JJ, England.

CAREER: Baker and confectioner, 1961-68; merchant seaman, 1968-70; baker and confectioner, 1970-72; bus driver in London, England, 1972-83; Transport and General Workers Union, London, district officer, 1983—.

WRITINGS:

Radical Aristocrats: London Busworkers from the 1880s to the 1980s, Lawrence & Wishart, 1985.

Author of pamphlets on public transport. Contributor to Caribbean newspapers.

WORK IN PROGRESS: Reality Never Wears Off, a novel; *Oh Jamaica!*, a political travelogue; another novel.

SIDELIGHTS: Ken Fuller told *CA:* "*Radical Aristocrats* grew out of my own years as a London bus driver and my trade union activity. *Oh Jamaica!* is a result of several visits to Jamaica. If one single experience can be said to have made me a socialist, it was seeing Jamaica and its people. I have been writing fiction since my early twenties. It is only recently, however, with the accumulation of experience and the dawning of political and literary maturity, that I have completed something publishable."

In his history of London bus workers, Fuller explained that the city's "radical aristocrats" began as relatively well-paid blue-collar workers. The period of unionization in the 1920s was characterized by an upsurge of political activity and the growth of Marxism within the British labor movement. The system in which they worked, assignment to organized garages, fostered a certain amount of responsibility for fellow workers. After World War II, London's bus workers suffered from raises in fares and a decline in bus traffic. The power of their union, of which the London bus section was once associated with Britain's Communist party, was unable to protect the workers' wages, and the "radical aristocrats" entered the present decade further down the pay scale. Patrick Renshaw of the *Times Literary Supplement* commented that Fuller's book "fills an important gap and tells a fascinating tale."

BIOGRAPHICAL/CRITICAL SOURCES:

PERIODICALS

Times Literary Supplement, May 30, 1986.

G

GALDOS, Benito Perez
See PEREZ GALDOS, Benito

*   *   *

GANLY, Helen (Mary)   1940-

PERSONAL: Born March 7, 1940, in Cookham, England; daughter of Geoffrey Favatt (an artist and publisher) and Helen (a teacher; maiden name, Whatley) Robinson; married Charles Fabian Ware (divorced); married Michael Roy Ganly, March 11, 1967; children: Daniel, Benjamin. *Education:* Attended Slade School of Fine Art, 1958-62.

ADDRESSES: Home—Oxford, England.

CAREER: Artist and art teacher, 1962—.

MEMBER: National Association of Artists (member of management committee), Institute of Contemporary Arts, Oxford Printmakers, Oxford Artists Group, Friends of the Royal Academy of Arts, Friends of the Museum of Modern Art (Oxford).

WRITINGS:

Jyoti's Journey (self-illustrated juvenile), Deutsch, 1986.
(Illustrator) Phillippa Pearce, *The Toothball* (juvenile), Deutsch, 1987.

WORK IN PROGRESS: Writing and illustrating another children's book for Deutsch; a series of paintings and prints "inspired by Virginia Woolf's *A Room of One's Own.*"

SIDELIGHTS: Helen Ganly has had solo exhibitions of her work since 1973 and has participated in group shows since 1959. She has been featured on "The Summer of '76," which was produced by the British Broadcasting Corporation, "Guardian Women," on Associated Television, and "Helen Ganly: The Many Faces of a Woman Artist," a documentary produced by the Arts Council of Great Britain in 1986.

*   *   *

GARLAND, Hazel (Barbara)   1913-1988

OBITUARY NOTICE: Born January 28, 1913, in Terre Haute (one source says Burnette), Ind.; died of a heart attack, April 5, 1988, in McKeesport, Pa. Consultant and journalist. Recognized by the National Negro Press Association as the first black woman to edit a periodical with national circulation, Garland served as editor in chief of the *Pittsburgh Courier* from 1974 to 1977. She began her career with the publication in 1943 and through the years worked in a variety of positions, including general assignment reporter, consultant, feature editor, and associate magazine editor. During her tenure she was honored with the National Sojourner Truth Award, an editor of the year award from the National Newspaper Publishers Association, and a National Headliner Award from Women in Communication. In 1979 Garland served as a member of the Pulitzer Prize selection committee, and, in 1987, she lent her name to the Garland-Goode journalism scholarship.

OBITUARIES AND OTHER SOURCES:

BOOKS

Who's Who Among Black Americans, 4th edition, Who's Who Among Black Americans, 1985.

PERIODICALS

Ebony, August, 1968.
New York Times, April 11, 1988.
Washington Post, April 7, 1988.

*   *   *

GARNETT, Henrietta (Catherine Vanessa)   1945-

PERSONAL: Born May 15, 1945, in London, England; daughter of David (a writer) and Angelica (a painter; maiden name, Bell) Garnett; married Lytton Burgo Partridge, December 22, 1962 (deceased, September 7, 1963); married John Baker (a writer), December 16, 1986; children: Sophie Vanessa Partridge Gelpke. *Education:* Attended Dartington School of Drama, 1961-63, and University of London, 1977-78. ("I was so lazy that my education was really nonexistent except that I had the great luck to be brought up in exceptionally civilized surroundings of great beauty, and my father, in particular, always encouraged me.")

ADDRESSES: Home—Les Sapins, Brachy, 76730 par Bacqueville-en-Caux, France. *Agent*—Anthony Sheil Associates, 46 Doughty St., London WC1N 2LF, England.

CAREER: Writer. Has worked as restaurateur in Spain, 1963-65, language tutor (French, Spanish, and English), drama coach, and reader. Executor of paintings and writings of Duncan Grant.

MEMBER: British Museum Library, Irish Georgian Society, London Library, New York City Public Library, Charleston Restoration Trust (committee member).

WRITINGS:

(Contributor) Milos Keynes, editor, *Lydia Lopokova,* Weidenfeld & Nicolson, 1983.
Family Skeletons (novel), Gollancz, 1986, Knopf, 1987.
(Contributor) *Charleston Past and Present,* Chatto & Windus, 1987.

Contributor to *Canada Today, Harpers and Queen,* and *Lookout* (Spain). Editor of *Sunday Scandal,* 1953-59.

WORK IN PROGRESS: The Rest Is Silence and *Love at First Sight,* both novels; scriptwriting for Biblimus animated film company.

SIDELIGHTS: Born into a distinguished artistic family, Bloomsbury scion Henrietta Garnett is the great-niece of Virginia Woolf, the grandchild of Vanessa Bell and Duncan Grant, and the daughter of David and Angelica Garnett. Yet in her first novel, *Family Skeletons*—wrote London *Times* reporter Liz Hodgkinson—"the overwhelming impression is of a totally new voice, one untouched by any obvious literary heritage." Owing more to Daphne du Maurier's *Rebecca* and Victorian novels like *Wuthering Heights, Family Skeletons* is a gothic tale about a young woman grappling with isolation, tragedy, and madness. Raised by an eccentric uncle on a secluded estate after the drowning deaths of her parents, Catherine married a mysterious older cousin who also dies in a boating accident; left homeless by a fire, she falls into debilitating despair, conquering it only through a new love relationship and the inevitable confrontation with her family's secret past.

Reviewing *Family Skeletons* for the *Times Literary Supplement,* Patricia Craig described it as "one of those novels that play with the idea of fiction. A good many elements of the plot come at full strength—death, obsession, destruction and so forth—and the book is cast in an agreeably romantic mode." Michiko Kakutani reached a similar assessment in the *New York Times,* remarking that "it's often hard to read 'Family Skeletons' without feeling that it's an unconscious parody—a compendium of every cliche in the body of romantic fiction." And discussing the novel in the *New York Times Book Review,* Nina Auerbach commented: "Like a well-preserved doll's house, 'Family Skeletons' is both eerily alive and repellently alien to life. . . . This novel is lost in beautiful fabrications, cut off from any times at all."

Still, some critics determined that *Family Skeletons* works as entertainment. "The prose is competent . . . it's a quick read . . . a mildly entertaining way to spend a few hours," decided *Washington Post* reviewer Susan Wood. "Henrietta Garnett has a natural gift for story-telling; and much of this novel is so good that it is easy to forgive the occasional archness and pretentiousness," wrote Isabel Raphael approvingly in a critique for the London *Times.* "Hers is a rare ability to create characters that breathe, conversations that one can listen in to, and places that have an authentic life of their own. . . . This is not yet the formidable talent that her publishers claim, but it is a promising beginning."

Garnett told *CA:* "Because I was brought up by painters and writers, writing comes naturally as a most important means of expression. I may well have been infuenced very early by the writings of my relations, although I do not believe that my work bears any resemblance to theirs. Individuals who have influenced me have been Cyril Connolly, my father and my mother-in-law, Frances Partridge, Robert Kee, and my uncle, Quentin Bell. Perhaps the writers who have influenced me most are Wyatt, Lord Byron, Henry James, Sir Thomas Malory, John Stuart Mill, Alexander Pope, John Locke, Campion, the Bronte sisters, philosopher George Moore, and the authors of Early and Middle English and Anglo-Saxon poetry.

"I have traveled extensively in Europe, Africa, and North America and speak French, Spanish, and some Italian. Currently I am living between London, France, and Italy. My hobbies include music (piano and cello), botany, painting, and gardening. I am passionately interested in the behavior of the human race, collectively and individually: its folly, comedy, tragedy, beauty, stupidity, and love. I am also deeply concerned, sometimes actively, by the plight of people in pain and how to help reeducate them in pleasurable ways—mainly through music, which can return the agony of the individual to his own physical and spiritual harmony."

BIOGRAPHICAL/CRITICAL SOURCES:

PERIODICALS

New York Times, March 7, 1987.
New York Times Book Review, June 14, 1987.
Times (London), October 24, 1986, November 6, 1986.
Times Literary Supplement, December 12, 1986.
Washington Post, March 13, 1987.

*   *   *

GARRARD, Mary D(ubose) 1937-

PERSONAL: Born July 25, 1937, in Greenwood, Miss.; daughter of W. M. and Lucile C. (Clark) Garrard. *Education:* Newcomb College, B.A., 1958; Radcliffe College, M.A., 1960; Johns Hopkins University, Ph.D., 1970.

ADDRESSES: Home—2915 University Ter. N.W., Washington, D.C. 20016. *Office*—Art Department, American University, 4400 Massachusetts Ave. N.W., Washington, D.C. 20016.

CAREER: American University, Washington, D.C., assistant professor, 1964-70, associate professor, 1971-76, professor of art, 1977—.

MEMBER: American Association of University Professors, National Women's Caucus for Art (president, 1974-76), College Art Association (member of board of directors, 1978-81).

AWARDS, HONORS: Fulbright grant, 1963-64; grants from American Association of University Women and American Council of Learned Societies, both 1978-79, and Fund for the Improvement of Postsecondary Education, 1982.

WRITINGS:

(Editor) *Slides of Works by Women Artists: A Sourcebook,* Women's Caucus for Art, 1974.
(Editor with Norma Broude) *Feminism and Art History: Questioning the Litany,* Harper, 1982.
Artemisia Gentileschi (1593-1652), Princeton University Press, 1988.

Contributor to art journals, including *Art Bulletin, Journal of Warburg and Courtauld Institutes,* and *Viator.*

SIDELIGHTS: Feminism and Art History: Questioning the Litany is a collection of seventeen illustrated essays based on research papers delivered to the College Art Association's Women's Caucus for Art in the late 1970's. Edited by Norma Broude and Mary D. Garrard, the writings encourage an alternate reading of male-dominated Western art history that integrates female accomplishments and viewpoints; contributors discuss the social and sexual mores that have shaped art interpretation over the centuries, as well as neglected female artists and art forms. "The cumulative effect of these essays is to turn art history inside out," observed Carrie Rickey in the *Village Voice Literary Supplement*. "Eminently readable and compelling for specialists as well as lay readers, . . . it's not comprehensive, and it doesn't pretend to be a unified overview, yet it touches on every historical epoch and art historiographical methodology . . . bristling with provocative questions and scholarship. . . . If you buy one art book this year, make it *Feminism and Art History*." Writing in the *Los Angeles Times Book Review*, Suzanne Muchnic showed equal enthusiasm for the volume's "provocative and absorbing" essays, recommending *Feminism and Art History* as "a lively supplemental text for art history courses still taught according to a conventionally male litany."

BIOGRAPHICAL/CRITICAL SOURCES:

PERIODICALS

Los Angeles Times Book Review, August, 1, 1982.
Village Voice Literary Supplement, September, 1982.

*   *   *

GARRISON, Dee   1934-

PERSONAL: Born October 18, 1934, in Cleburne, Tex.; daughter of James R. (a ginner) and Clara M. (a teacher; maiden name, Martin) White; children: Traywick, Martin. *Education:* California State University, Fullerton, B.A., 1968; University of California, Irvine, Ph.D., 1972.

ADDRESSES: Home—Highland Park, N.J. *Office*—Department of History, Rutgers University, New Brunswick, N.J. 08903.

CAREER: Rutgers University, New Brunswick, N.J., assistant professor, 1972-79, associate professor of history, 1979—.

MEMBER: American Historical Society, Berkshire Conference of Women Historians.

WRITINGS:

(Contributor) Sidney Jackson, editor, *A Century of Service: Librarianship in the United States and Canada*, American Library Association, 1976.
Apostles of Culture: The Public Librarian and American Society, Macmillan, 1979.
(Editor and author of introduction) *Rebel Pen: The Writings of Mary Heaton Vorse*, Monthly Review Press, 1986.

Contributor to periodicals, including *Signs, American Quarterly, Journal of Social History*, and *American Historical Review*.

WORK IN PROGRESS: Rises Like the Tide: The Life of Mary Heaton Vorse, publication expected in 1988; a study of attacks on women's organizations during the Red Scare, 1919-22.

SIDELIGHTS: Rebel Pen: The Writings of Mary Heaton Vorse is an anthology of labor journalism written by twentieth-cen-

tury author Mary Heaton Vorse (1881-1966). Although better known for her popular fiction and articles, Vorse was committed to many radical and feminist causes during her lifetime, championing—according to Daniel J. Leab in the *New York Times Book Review*—"the downtrodden, the exploited, the oppressed." Leab reflected: "Some of her writing about women in this anthology demonstrates convincingly that [Vorse] was more than just a vigorous advocate who can be relegated to a footnote in history."

Garrison told *CA:* "My chief scholarly interest is American social history, especially the history of women, of labor, and of radicalism. Like millions of other women, I have been greatly influenced by the socialist feminist movement of the 1960s."

BIOGRAPHICAL/CRITICAL SOURCES:

PERIODICALS

New York Times Book Review, January 12, 1986.

*   *   *

GIBNEY, Sheridan   1904(?)-1988

OBITUARY NOTICE: Born c. 1904; died of cancer, April 10, 1988, in Missoula, Mont. Producer, playwright, screenwriter, and literary critic. Gibney, who shared two 1936 Academy Awards with co-author Pierre Collings for the original story and screenplay for "The Story of Louis Pasteur," began his career in the 1920s as a playwright and critic. After he signed with Warner Brothers he wrote numerous screenplays, including "I Am a Fugitive From a Chain Gang," "Green Pastures," "Anthony Adverse," "The Locket," and "Our Hearts Were Young and Gay," which he produced as well. He also wrote for television, including episodes for "Bachelor Father," "The Man From U.N.C.L.E.," "The Six Million Dollar Man," and "Police Woman."

OBITUARIES AND OTHER SOURCES:

PERIODICALS

Los Angeles Times, April 23, 1988.

*   *   *

GIBSON, Anne (E.)   1954-

PERSONAL: Born November 13, 1954, in Clinton, Mass.; daughter of George W. (a librarian) and Marjorie (a secretary; maiden name, Hubbell) Gibson. *Education:* College of William and Mary, B.A., 1976; Clark University, M.A., 1987, doctoral study.

ADDRESSES: Home—34 Wagon Wheel Rd., Sudbury, Mass. 01776.

CAREER: University of Massachusetts at Amherst, assistant editor for design and production of Atlas of Massachusetts Project, 1985—. Instructor at Mount Holyoke College, 1986.

MEMBER: American Congress on Surveying and Mapping, Canadian Cartographic Association.

AWARDS, HONORS: National Geographic Society intern, 1982.

WRITINGS:

(With Timothy Fast) *The Women's Atlas of the United States*, Facts on File, 1986.

WORK IN PROGRESS: Research on the use of color for data structuring on maps.

SIDELIGHTS: Anne Gibson told CA: "When Timothy Fast and I initially conceived of The Women's Atlas of the United States, no other atlas focusing specifically on women in the U.S. was in print. There is now one other. We felt it was important to deal with women specifically because statistical patterns for women are often different from those for men; frequently the two get lumped together, obscuring significant differences. The geographical perspective offered in the map format allowed us to show important regional differences in women's experience within the U.S. Many people are fascinated by maps; we hoped the combination of colorful maps and a humorous touch would catch the interest of people who might not normally be interested in feminist issues. We were surprised to discover that much of the data was easily available and accessible. There is a great deal of statistical information that is gathered and broken down according to sex."

BIOGRAPHICAL/CRITICAL SOURCES:

PERIODICALS

Chicago Tribune, July 5, 1977.
Los Angeles Times Book Review, March 1, 1987.

*   *   *

GIDDINGS, Paula   1948-

PERSONAL: Born in 1948; daughter of a teacher and a school administrator. Education: Attended Howard University.

ADDRESSES: Office—Department of Social Science, Spelman College, 350 Spelman Lane, Atlanta, Ga. 30314.

CAREER: Free-lance writer. Served as Paris bureau chief for Encore America and Worldwide News; affiliated with Random House, New York, N.Y.; affiliated with Howard University Press, Washington, D.C.

WRITINGS:

(Contributor) John A. Williams and Charles F. Harris, editors, Amistad Two, Howard University Press, 1971.
When and Where I Enter: The Impact of Black Women on Race and Sex in America, Morrow, 1984.

Work represented in anthologies, including We Speak As Liberators: Young Black Poets, edited by Orde Coombs, Dodd, 1970, and A Rock Against the Wind. Contributor to Black World. Editor of Afro-American Review.

SIDELIGHTS: When and Where I Enter: The Impact of Black Women on Race and Sex in America is journalist Paula Giddings's detailed history of black women's contributions to racial and sexual equality. Arguing that the assertiveness and organization of black women furthered the cause of all women as well as all blacks, Giddings traces the development of black women's clubs, suffrage associations, and civil rights groups from the early 1890s to the 1940s. The book is "a jarringly fresh and challenging interpretation," judged New York Times Book Review contributor Gloria Naylor, who commended Giddings's realistic view of current women's and black rights and her account of gains made.

Giddings shows how black women's activism began before the Civil War, when slave women used contraceptives and abortions to avoid bearing children who would be slaves, and continued after the war with formation of the National Association of Colored Women. She explains how the Victorian ideal of womanhood—which insisted that women be submissive and confined to domestic life—conflicted with black

women's need to work to help support their families, since jobs for black men were scarce. Such conflicts resulted in the redefinition of womanhood by blacks: as Jacqueline Trescott remarked in the Washington Post, "These women became the models for modern womanhood." Black women fought racism from whites both male and female, even where women's rights in general were at stake, and struggled against the sexism of black men who shared with whites the belief that women should remain at home. "Inherent in the Black women's defense of their integrity was a challenge to the Victorian ideas that kept all women oppressed," asserts Giddings. The author opens "our eyes to the relationship of racism and sexism in America," commented Wendy Kaminer in Village Voice; Ms. reviewer Margo Jefferson deemed the book "a readable, generally clear-sighted overview."

BIOGRAPHICAL/CRITICAL SOURCES:

PERIODICALS

Ms., May, 1984.
New York Times Book Review, July 8, 1984.
Village Voice, August 28, 1984.
Washington Post, February 28, 1985.*

*   *   *

GILRAY, J. D.
   See MENCKEN, H(enry) L(ouis)

*   *   *

GJERTSEN, Derek   1933-

PERSONAL: Born October 13, 1933, in Grimsby, England; son of Rasmus Munthe-kaas (a merchant) and Anne (Allan) Gjertsen; married Elspeth Kirstan Roy; children: Polly Megan, Christopher James, Veronica Kate. Education: Attended University of Leeds, 1955-58, and Queen's College, Oxford, 1958-60. Politics: Libertarian. Religion: Atheist.

ADDRESSES: Home and office—1 Ash Grove, Formby, Merseyside L37 2DT, England.

CAREER: University of Ghana, Legon, lecturer in philosophy, 1960-78; writer. Military service: British Army, Royal Army Education Corps, 1952-54; became sergeant.

WRITINGS:

The Classics of Science, Lilian Barber, 1984.
The Newton Handbook, Routledge & Kegan Paul, 1986.

Also author of a book on the philosophy of science, Penguin, 1988.

*   *   *

GLASSMAN, Joyce
   See JOHNSON, Joyce

*   *   *

GODBOUT, Jacques   1933-

BRIEF ENTRY: Born November 27, 1933, in Montreal, Quebec, Canada. Canadian filmmaker, poet, and novelist. A film producer in his native Montreal for more than three decades, Godbout began writing highly symbolic poetry and prose as a teenager. While his poems have been collected and published in volumes, including Carton-pate (Seghers, 1956) and C'est *la chaude loi des hommes* (Editions de l'Hexagone, 1960), Godbout is best known for his novels that explore Quebec's political and social problems through a blend of fantasy and realism. The first of these, *L'Aquarium* (Seuil, 1962), won the Prix France-Quebec and established a theme of revolution that pervades many of his subsequent writings. The 1965 work *Le Couteau sur la table* (Seuil), translated as *Knife on the Table* (McClelland & Stewart, 1968), highlights the cultural differences between French and English-speaking North Americans by focusing on an ill-fated romance between a French-Canadian army deserter and a wealthy English-Canadian girl. Godbout expanded on this dichotomy in the satiric comedy *Les Tetes a Papineau* (Seuil, 1981), in which a two-headed infant born to a couple in Quebec represents the bilingual nature of the province. The author's most successful novel, however, is *Salut Galarneau!* (Seuil, 1967), translated as *Hail Galarneau!* (Longman, 1970), the award-winning memoir of a fictional hot dog stand proprieter. Godbout's imaginative storytelling, nonsequential plot development, and penchant for linguistic experimentation have placed him among the literary avante-garde in French Canada. *Addresses: Home*—815 Pratt, Outremont, Montreal, Quebec, Canada H2V 2T7. *Office*—P.O. Box 6100, Montreal, Quebec H4N 2N4.

BIOGRAPHICAL/CRITICAL SOURCES:

BOOKS

The Canadian Who's Who, Volume XXII, University of Toronto Press, 1987.
Dictionary of Literary Biography, Volume 53: *Canadian Writers Since 1960, First Series*, Gale, 1986.
The Oxford Companion to Canadian History and Literature, reprinted with corrections, Oxford University Press (Toronto), 1967.

*   *   *

GOLDEN, Harry, Jr.   1928(?)-1988

OBITUARY NOTICE: Born c. 1928; died after a long illness, May 1, 1988. Editor and journalist. A veteran reporter for the Chicago *Sun-Times* known as the "dean" of the City Hall press corps, Golden was noted for his concise, polished leads and an old-fashioned style of journalism that avoided interpretation and opinion. He began his career after the Korean War as a city hall reporter for the *Charlotte Observer* then worked for the *Detroit Free Press*. Golden edited nine of his father's books based on the elder Golden's editorial columns for the *Carolina Israelite*, including the best-selling *Only in America*.

OBITUARIES AND OTHER SOURCES:

PERIODICALS

Chicago Tribune, May 3, 1988.

*   *   *

GOLDMAN, Louis   1925-

PERSONAL: Born June 8, 1925, in Frankfurt, Germany; immigrated to the United States, 1955, naturalized citizen, 1963; son of Paul (in textiles) and Mina (a housewife) Goldman; married Leah Ildiko (a fashion coordinator), March 30, 1970; children: Daniela, Adina, David. *Education:* Attended high school in Montpellier, France. *Religion:* Jewish.

ADDRESSES: Home—40 Waterside Plaza, New York, N.Y. 10010. *Agent*—Photo-Researchers, 60 East 56th St., New York, N.Y. 10022.

CAREER: Professional photographer.

MEMBER: Cinematographers and Photographers Union.

WRITINGS:

AUTHOR AND PHOTOGRAPHER

The Burning Bush, Holy Land Publishers, 1957.
A Week in the World of Hagar, Crowell-Collier, 1969.
A Week in the World of Samil, Crowell-Collier, 1973.
Lights, Camera, Action! Behind the Scenes, Making Movies, Abrams, 1986.
Friends for Life (novel), Holocaust, 1988.

SIDELIGHTS: Louis Goldman told *CA:* "I am pleasantly surprised to find myself listed among writers. By profession and love of it I have been a photographer for over forty years. Writing grew out of the necessity to supply elaborate captions for photo assignments from magazines.

"*The Burning Bush* is a collection of photographs documenting aspects of a reborn nation in the making—Israel in its early statehood. *A Week in the World of Hagar* and *A Week in the World of Samil* were part of a book series commissioned by Crowell-Collier to show American first- and second-graders how children live and function in other societies. Hagar is a girl living on a kibbutz in Israel with her parents and grandparents; Samil is the son of a family living in Istanbul, Turkey.

"*Lights, Camera, Action!* reflects twenty-five years of photographic coverage on seventy major feature films. The concept for the book gestated in my mind for many years. I wanted to give the average moviegoer an idea of the tremendous amounts of not just money but also hard work, skill, dedication, tension, and lunacy that go into putting a film on the screen. When it came to writing the accompanying text, the publisher decided that my own accumulated firsthand experiences and personal observations would be preferable to what a hired writer could do.

"*Friends for Life* is a novelized account of true events. It focuses on the extraordinary efforts by a group of young Catholic priests. On their own initiative, putting themselves in great danger, they saved the lives of many Jews during the Nazi occupation of Italy."

BIOGRAPHICAL/CRITICAL SOURCES:

PERIODICALS

New York Times, October 18, 1981.

*   *   *

GOLDSMITH, John   1947-

PERSONAL: Born April 9, 1947, in London, England; son of Allen (an eye surgeon) and Rosemary (Porter) Goldsmith; married Anthea Ionides (a teacher), November 11, 1978; children: Theodore John Ionides. *Education:* University of Aix-Marseille, received Diplome de Langue et Lettres Francaises. *Politics:* Green Party. *Religion:* Church of England.

ADDRESSES: Home and office—8 Well Walk, Hampstead, London NW3 1LD, England. *Agent*—Ed Victor Ltd., 162 Wardour St., London W1V 3AT, England.

CAREER: Writer.

MEMBER: Writer's Guild of Great Britain (deputy chairman, 1984; chairman, 1985), Society of Authors, Authors Lending and Copyright Society (director), Savile Club.

WRITINGS:

FICTION

Mrs. Mount Ascendant, Hogarth, 1968.
The Icing of Balthazar, Cassell, 1977.
Exodus, Genesis, Sidgwich & Jackson, 1981 (published in the United States as *Exodus '43,* Coward, 1982).
(With Gordon Briggs and Don Bernard) *Bullion,* Sidgwich & Jackson, 1982.
Return to Treasure Island, Pan Books, 1985.

NONFICTION

Voyage in the Beagle, Chatto & Windus, 1978.
(Editor) Roger Hinks, *The Gymnasium of the Mind: Journals, 1933-1963,* Michael Russell, 1984.
(Editor) *Stephen Spender, Journals, 1939-1983,* Faber, 1985.

JUVENILE

Tarkina the Otter (nonfiction), Pelham Books, 1981.
The Rajah of Bong (nonfiction), Pelham Books, 1981.
Oliver and His Magic Hat (fiction), MacDonald & Co., 1983.

Also author of the "Mrs. Babcary" fiction series for Pelham Books and the "It's Easy To" nonfiction series, Lothrop, 1980.

OTHER

Author of television scripts for the series "Return to Treasure Island," "A Waltz Through the Hills," and the British Broadcasting Company series "Great Expectations"; author of television documentaries "Mrs. Livingstone, I Presume" and "A Secret Place." Contributor to various television series, including "The Protectors," "Space 1999," "Return of the Saint," "The New Avengers," and "The Professionals."

SIDELIGHTS: Author of *Bullion,* a successful novel that remained on the British best-seller list for fourteen weeks in 1982, and a well-known writer for television, Goldsmith has also won acclaim for his editing of the journals of British diplomat Roger Hinks and poet Stephen Spender.

BIOGRAPHICAL/CRITICAL SOURCES:

Los Angeles Times, June 30, 1983.
Times Literary Supplement, June 29, 1984, November 22, 1985.
Washington Post Book World, July 31, 1983.

*   *   *

GOLIARD, Roy
See SHIPLEY, Joseph T(wadell)

*   *   *

GOOD, David F(ranklin) 1943-

PERSONAL: Born March 2, 1943, in Rockford, Ill.; son of Everett Oliver (a furniture retailer) and Gladys (a housewife; maiden name, Hackman) Good; married Rosemary Hekman (a musician), June 11, 1966; children: Allison, Adam. *Education:* Wesleyan University, Middletown, Conn., B.A., 1965; University of Chicago, M.B.A., 1967; University of Pennsylvania, M.A., 1968, Ph.D., 1972.

ADDRESSES: Office—Department of Economics, Temple University, Broad and Montgomery, Philadelphia, Pa. 19122.

CAREER: Stockton State College, Pomona, N.J., assistant professor of economics, 1971-74; Temple University, Philadelphia, Pa., assistant professor, 1974-77, associate professor, 1977-86, professor of economics, 1986—.

MEMBER: American Economic Association, Economic History Society, Economic History Association.

AWARDS, HONORS: University of Vienna, Fulbright graduate fellow, 1969-70, honorary professor of economic history, 1986—.

WRITINGS:

The Economic Rise of the Habsburg Empire, 1750-1914, University of California Press, 1984.

Contributor to economic history journals.

WORK IN PROGRESS: Regional Inequalities Within National Economies During the Transition to Modern Economic Growth.

SIDELIGHTS: In *The Economic Rise of the Habsburg Empire, 1750-1914,* David F. Good opposes the traditional view of economic historians who assert that the Habsburg Empire never managed to achieve economic unity prior to World War I and that its commercial and industrial achievements compared poorly to those of other European countries. Utilizing a regional analysis rather than the socio-political theories influencing similar studies, Good proves the empire's economic integration by way of newly established criteria. This includes studying some unusual factors such as personal bank deposits, infant mortality rates, literacy, and the ratio of physicians to the population they served. The result, according to Good, supports the author's contention that the Habsburg Empire did in fact achieve economic unity and a level of production that compared favorably with that of its European neighbors. Reviewing the book in the *Times Literary Supplement,* Michael Hurst defended Good's regional approach, stating that he starts "from square one and work[s] his way systematically through the chronology," thereby "introducing a steadily increasing degree of sophistication." Furthermore, Good makes his case "with distinction," assessed Hurst, and in the process he provides a "highly proficient and useful book."

Good told *CA:* "Many American scholars write on European topics because of family ties. I have no known ancestral link to East-Central Europe that might explain my intellectual interest in the Habsburg Empire. My first exposure to its history was at Wesleyan University. Curiosity about how a powerful empire could disappear so quickly prompted me to spend the summer of 1964 at the Hope College Vienna Summer School, where I deepened my knowledge of the former monarchy by experiencing life in Vienna first-hand.

"Subsequent years brought an academic detour, but I eventually returned to Habsburg history at the dissertation stage of my graduate work in economic history at the University of Pennsylvania. Formerly, I paid little attention to the economic side of the Habsburg story since most scholars focused on the political developments, leaving the economic history literature quite thin. For a budding economic historian, the gap provided a clear-cut opportunity. I learned that I was not alone, for research in Habsburg economic history—although sparse—was growing rapidly. Important work had already been done in the 1960s, and the 1970s proved to accelerate this bent. Over time the work became more 'cliometric,' as scholars began to use economic theory and statistical techniques in their historical research. The new work generated data and findings which were increasingly at odds with the accepted view of Habsburg economic backwardness. My book, *The Economic Rise of the Habsburg Empire,* synthesizes, reinterprets, and extends the specialized literature for a wider audience.

"My forthcoming work, *Regional Inequalities Within National Economies,* grew out of my first book. Uneven regional development is a major theme in Habsburg economic history. Some scholars believe that regional disparities contributed to the empire's decline by stimulating the ethnic conflict that paralyzed political life in the empire's final years. But the Habsburg case is not unique as a case of uneven development. Regional economic disparities and political conflict along sectional lines were common in other nineteenth-century contemporaries (Germany, Italy, and the United States) and today plague Third World countries (India, China, and Brazil) as well. I analyze uneven development in several nineteenth-century cases in my forthcoming work and trace the policy implications for today's developing economies."

BIOGRAPHICAL/CRITICAL SOURCES:

PERIODICALS

American Historical Review, June, 1985.
Economic History Review, summer, 1985.
Journal of Modern History, September, 1986.
Southern Economic Journal, October, 1985.
Times Literary Supplement, August 2, 1985.

*   *   *

GOODSTEIN, Marvin (Elias)   1927-

PERSONAL: Born May 20, 1927, in New York, N.Y.; son of Elliot M. (an insurance broker) and Jessie (a homemaker; maiden name, Silverstein) Goodstein; married Anita Shafer (a teacher), June 14, 1953; children: Sarah, Eban. *Education:* New York University, B.S., 1950; Cornell University, Ph.D., 1961.

ADDRESSES: 6 Louisiana Cir., Sewanee, Tenn. 37375.

CAREER: University of the South, Sewanee, Tenn., assistant professor, 1955-63, associate professor, 1963-72, professor of economics, 1972-87. Consultant to U.S. Agency for International Development in Manila and Southern Regional Education Board.

WRITINGS:

(Editor with Sidney Weintraub) *Reaganomics in the Stagflation Economy,* University of Pennsylvania Press, 1983.

*   *   *

GORALSKI, Robert   1928-1988

OBITUARY NOTICE—See index for *CA* sketch: Born January 2, 1928, in Chicago, Ill.; died of cancer, March 18, 1988, in McLean, Va. Information director, lecturer, consultant, journalist, and author. Goralski, a news correspondent for the National Broadcasting Company (NBC) from 1961 to 1975, covered the Vietnam War, the Middle East War of 1967, the White House, and the U.S. State and Defense departments during his career. He left NBC News in 1975 to join the Gulf Oil Corporation as public relations director, where he remained until 1983, when he became a senior adviser to the American Petroleum Institute. Goralski was author of *World War II Almanac, 1931-1945: A Political and Military Record,* co-author of *Oil and War,* and a contributor to such publications as the *New Republic, Washington Post, American Heritage,* and the *Encyclopaedia Britannica Book of the Year* from

1966 to 1975. Sought after as a lecturer for university, business, and government organizations, Goralski was the recipient of several awards and honors, among them a 1970 Emmy Award from the National Academy of Television Arts and Sciences for his war coverage of Southeast Asia.

OBITUARIES AND OTHER SOURCES:

BOOKS

Who's Who in America, 44th edition, Marquis, 1986.

PERIODICALS

Chicago Tribune, March 22, 1988.
Los Angeles Times, March 23, 1988.
New York Times, March 21, 1988.
Washington Post, March 20, 1988.

*   *   *

GORE, Christopher   1946(?)-1988

OBITUARY NOTICE: Born c. 1946 (one source says c. 1943) in Fort Lauderdale, Fla.; died of cancer, May 18, 1988, in Santa Monica, Calif. Screenwriter and playwright. Gore wrote the screenplay for the hit movie "Fame," which centers on the struggles and triumphs of the students at New York City's High School of the Performing Arts. Gore also created the scripts for the successful television series based on it. The film earned five Academy Award nominations in 1981, including best screenplay written directly for the screen. Gore began his writing career after graduating from Northwestern University, and one of his first works was the 1967 musical "Mary," focusing on Mary, Queen of Scots. His other musicals included the 1972 Broadway science-fiction rock musical "Via Galactica," which he wrote with Judith Ross and Galt MacDermot, and "Nefertiti," a production about the ancient Egyptian queen, for which Gore provided both the book and lyrics.

OBITUARIES AND OTHER SOURCES:

PERIODICALS

Chicago Tribune, May 24, 1988.
Los Angeles Times, May 20, 1988.
New York Times, May 20, 1988.

*   *   *

GOTTLIEB, Alan M(erril)   1947-

PERSONAL: Born May 2, 1947, in Los Angeles, Calif.; son of Seymour and Sherry (Schutz) Gottlieb; married Julie Hoy Versnel, 1979; children: Amy, Sarah, Merril. *Education:* Attended Georgetown University, 1970; University of Tennessee, B.S., 1971.

ADDRESSES: Home—12500 Northeast 10th Pl., Bellevue, Wash. 98005.

CAREER: Merril Associates, Bellevue, Wash., president, 1974—. Director of United States Ammunition Company; chairman of Citizens Committee for the Right to Keep and Bear Arms. *Military service:* Army National Guard, 1968-74.

AWARDS, HONORS: Freedom Award from Young Americans for Freedom, 1974, for work protecting individual rights; Roy Rogers Award, 1987, from the National Antique Arms Association for Protecting Gun Rights.

WRITINGS:

The Gun Owner's Political Action Manual, Green Hill, 1976.
The Rights of Gun Owners, Caroline House, 1981.
The Gun Grabbers, Merril Press, 1986.
Guns for Women, Merril Press, 1987.

*   *   *

GOTTLIEB, Robert A(dams)   1931-

BRIEF ENTRY: Born April 29, 1931, in New York, N.Y. American publishing executive and editor. Appointed editor of *New Yorker* in 1987, Gottlieb became the focus of a controversy over the magazine's future. Traditionalists on the *New Yorker* staff feared that Gottlieb, at the behest of the magazine's new parent company, Newhouse Publications, would imperil *New Yorker*'s reputation for valuing fine writing above profits. Advocates of change, however, contended that the magazine had become editorially self-indulgent and that its sense of tradition had left it unable to adapt to a changing literary marketplace. But as Edwin Diamond noted in *New York,* "Gottlieb specifically stated when he became editor that he had no 'master plan' and foresaw no 'radical' changes," and in the first few months of Gottlieb's tenure observers in the press seemed to view his effects on the editorial content of the magazine as moderate.

Gottlieb began his career in book publishing with Simon & Schuster in 1955. As a young editor there he assisted author Joseph Heller with the completion of the novel *Catch-22;* the book's immense success brought Gottlieb renown and respect in the industry and in his firm, where he soon rose to vice-president and editor in chief. Moreover, Gottlieb's editorial skill was so highly prized by authors that after he became editor in chief of Alfred A. Knopf, Inc., in 1968, such prominent writers as Ray Bradbury, Anthony Burgess, John Cheever, John le Carre, and Margaret Drabble signed with the publishing house so they could work with him. Gottlieb also served Knopf as executive vice-president from 1968 to 1973, when he became president. *Addresses: Office*—New Yorker, 25 West 43rd St., New York, N.Y. 10036.

BIOGRAPHICAL/CRITICAL SOURCES:

BOOKS

Current Biography, H. W. Wilson, 1987.
Who's Who in America, 44th edition, Marquis, 1986.

PERIODICALS

Chicago Tribune, January 14, 1987.
Esquire, August, 1987.
Los Angeles Times, January 13, 1987, January 15, 1987, February 12, 1987.
New York, January 26, 1987, June 8, 1987.
New York Times, January 13, 1987, January 14, 1987, January 26, 1987, November 9, 1987.
Washington Post, January 15, 1987, January 18, 1987, January 19, 1987, January 26, 1988.

*   *   *

GOURVISH, T(erry) R.   1943-

PERSONAL: Born March 13, 1943, in Leicester, England; son of Assir (a company director) and Catherine Mercy (Lond) Gourvish; married Susan Phillips (a lecturer); children: Peter Louis, Matthew Patric. *Education:* King's College, London,

B.A., 1964; London School of Economics and Political Science, London, Ph.D., 1967.

ADDRESSES: Office—School of Economic and Social Studies, University of East Anglia, Norwich, Norfolk NR4 7TJ, England.

CAREER: University of Glasgow, Glasgow, Scotland, assistant lecturer, 1967-69, lecturer in economic and social history, 1969-70; University of East Anglia, Norwich, England, lecturer, 1971-74, senior lecturer in economic and social history, 1974—, dean of School of Economic and Social Studies, 1986—. Member of National Council on Inland Transport, 1971-77, and Norfolk County Council Adoption Panel, 1985—.

MEMBER: Economic History Society, Scottish Railway Development Association (Scottish Association for Public Transport).

AWARDS, HONORS: First Prize in Business History Awards from Newcomen Society of North America, 1974, for "A British Business Elite: The Chief Executive Managers of the Railway Industry, 1850-1922."

WRITINGS:

Mark Huish and the London and North Western Railway, Leicester University Press, 1972.
"A British Business Elite: The Chief Executive Managers of the Railway Industry, 1850-1922" (article), published in *Business History Review,* autumn, 1973.
Railways and the British Economy, 1830-1914, Macmillan, 1980.
British Railways, 1948-1973: A Business History, Cambridge University Press, 1986.
Norfolk Beers From English Barley, Centre of East Anglian Studies, 1987.
(Editor with Alan O'Day, and contributor) *Later Victorian Britain, 1867-1900,* Macmillan, 1988.

Also author of a comparative study of nationalized transport enterprises, Angeli, 1988.

Co-editor of *Journal of Transport History,* 1979—.

WORK IN PROGRESS: Research on the emergence of managerial capitalism.

SIDELIGHTS: T. R. Gourvish's book *British Railways, 1948-1973* was described by T. C. Barker in the *Times Literary Supplement* as a clear presentation on the decline of England's railway system after nationalization. The author is outspoken in his criticism of the government officials who have controlled the British Transport Commission. He is also sympathetic toward the younger generation of administrators who inherited an unwieldy and inefficient system and attempted to improve it. "Dr. Gourvish has written an honest, sympathetic and detailed study which makes an important contribution to any debate on nationalization and will serve as a valuable work of reference," Barker commented. "This vast wealth of material . . . has been pulled together with great skill."

Gourvish told *CA:* "My work on the management of one of the world's largest mid-nineteenth-century companies, the London and North Western Railway, was supervised by Professor Donald Coleman, one of Britain's leading business historians. Thereafter, I considered myself to be both a transport *and* a business historian, and I think my work reflects this. Work on brewing and banking was an extension of my interest in management and the corporate economy. At the same time,

I have taken part in the standard-of-living debate that surrounds the assessment of the Industrial Revolution. I also have an interest in the rise of professional occupations in the nineteenth century, in which the railways played a part.

"When I was asked to undertake a commissioned business history of nationalized railways by the British Railways Board, I was delighted to accept. The rail system had been run down during World War II, and recovery was painful. On top of that, the British Transport Commission, with over 850,000 workers, was Britains's largest corporation, and its management problems were collosal. Public sector enterprises shared fully in the transformation of British business techniques generally from the 1950s, despite government interference and the conflict of 'profit' and 'service' goals. At the present time, the railway busines is being managed with a determination to keep the government subsidy as low as possible—a situation in marked contrast to that of many other rail systems, for example in Japan."

AVOCATIONAL INTERESTS: Cricket, walking, beer.

BIOGRAPHICAL/CRITICAL SOURCES:

PERIODICALS

Times Literary Supplement, April 3, 1987.

*   *   *

GRADWOHL, David M(ayer)   1934-

PERSONAL: Born January 22, 1934, in Lincoln, Neb.; son of Bernard Sam (a lawyer) and Elaine (a housewife; maiden name, Mayer) Gradwohl; married Hanna Rosenberg (a social worker), December 29, 1957; children: Steven, Jane, Kathryn. *Education:* University of Nebraska, B.A. (with highest distinction), 1955; graduate study at University of Edinburgh, 1955-56; Harvard University, Ph.D., 1967. *Politics:* Liberal. *Religion:* Jewish.

ADDRESSES: Home—606 Lynn Ave., Ames, Iowa 50010. *Office*—Department of Sociology and Anthropology, 4 East Hall, Iowa State University, Ames, Iowa 50011.

CAREER: Iowa State University, Ames, instructor, 1962-66, assistant professor, 1966-67, associate professor, 1967-72, professor of anthropology, 1972—, coordinator of anthropology, 1968-75, chairman of American Indian Studies Program, 1981-85, faculty adviser to American Indian Rights Organization. Field worker and archaeological field supervisor in South Dakota and Nebraska for Nebraska State Historical Society, 1952-59; conducted field work in Nebraska, Wyoming, and Montana for University of Nebraska State Museum, 1953; archaeological field worker in Scotland, 1955, and at Stonehenge, 1956; director of Red Rock Reservoir Archaeological Project, 1964—, Ames Reservoir Archaeological Project, 1971—, and Saylorville Reservoir Archaeological Project, 1967—. Member of Iowa advisory committee of National Register of Historic Sites and Places, 1969—; member of advisory committee of Office of the State Archaeologist of Iowa, 1983—; member of Iowa Conservation Commission's Ledges State Park Task Force, 1977-81; member of Iowa's First Farmers Committee, a joint project of Iowa Natural Heritage Foundation and Living History Farms, 1979—. *Military service:* U.S. Army, 1957-59; served in Europe.

MEMBER: American Anthropological Association (fellow), Current Anthropology (associate), Society for American Archaeology, American Interprofessional Institute, Society for

Historical Archaeology, Conference on Historic Sites Archaeology, National Association for Ethnic Studies, United Native American Student Association, Plains Anthropologist (member of board of directors, 1969-72; vice-president, 1971; president, 1972), Plains Anthropological Society (member of board of directors, 1987—), Association of Iowa Archaeologists (fellow; chairperson, 1977-78), Iowa Archaeological Society (member of board of trustees, 1966-69, 1971-74), Missouri Archaeological Society, Nebraska State Historical Society, Nebraska Jewish Historical Society (charter member), Nebraska Association of Professional Archaeologists (fellow; charter member), Phi Beta Kappa, Sigma Xi, Phi Kappa Phi, Alpha Kappa Delta, Sigma Gamma Epsilon, Delta Sigma Rho.

AWARDS, HONORS; Fulbright fellow in Scotland, 1955-56; Woodrow Wilson fellow, 1955-56; grants from National Science Foundation, 1961-62, U.S. Army Corps of Engineers, 1976—, National Park Service, 1977—, and National Endowment for the Humanities, 1985—.

WRITINGS:

(Contributor) Eldon Johnson, editor, *Aspects of Upper Great Lakes Anthropology: Papers in Honor of Lloyd A. Wilford*, Minnesota Historical Society, 1974.
(Editor with Gretchen M. Bataille and Charles L. P. Silet, and contributor) *The Worlds Between Two Rivers: Perspectives on American Indians in Iowa*, Iowa State University Press, 1978.
(With Nancy M. Osborn) *Exploring Buried Buxton: Archaeology of an Abandoned Iowa Coal Mining Town With a Large Black Population*, Iowa State University Press, 1984.
(With Nancy M. Osborn) *Blacks and Whites in Buxton: A Site Explored, a Town Remembered*, Media Resources Center, Iowa State Unversity, 1986.
(Contributor with Hanna Rosenberg) Walter P. Zenner, editor, *Persistence and Flexibility: Anthropological Studies of American Jewish Identities and Institutions*, State University of New York Press, 1988.

Contributor to *Plains Indian Studies: A Collection of Essays in Honor of John C. Evans and Waldo R. Wedel*. Also contributor of articles and reviews to scholarly journals. Member of editorial board of *Ethnic Reporter, Explorations in Sights and Sounds*, and *Explorations in Ethnic Studies*, 1987—.

WORK IN PROGRESS: A study of Jewish cemeteries in Des Moines; research on the archaeology of Buxton; research on the ethnoarchaeology of Jewish cemeteries.

SIDELIGHTS: David M. Gradwohl told *CA:* "I am continuing my research projects (prehistoric and ethnoarchaeology), teaching interests (the American Indian, North American archaeology, and cultural continuity and change in the Prairie Plains), and social-activist involvements in American Indian studies. I serve as the faculty adviser to the recently formed American Indian Rights Organization (AIRO) at Iowa State University in addition to participating in the United Native American Student Association (UNASA), which I helped co-found in 1971. Each year on campus we sponsor the Iowa State University American Indian Symposium dealing with social and political issues as well as literary programs and art exhibits.

"Our archaeological work at Buxton, Iowa, resulted in the placement of the townsite on the National Register of Historic Places. Research verified the fact that both blacks and whites enjoyed a relatively high standard of living, had a well-ordered and appointed community, and lived together in a notably harmonious fashion. Our book and audiovisual program are aimed at getting this message across to people today in the hope of creating better interracial and cross-cultural understanding.

"My wife's and my recent ethnoarchaeological studies of Jewish cemeteries continue our research interests in historical traditions and ethnicity. More specifically, the studies show some of the dimensions of *intra*group diversity in regard to theology, national origin, and different sociocultural factors. Ultimately our understanding of the importance of ethnicity and individual identities must take into account *intra*group variations as well as *inter*group differences."

* * *

GRANT, Margaret
See FRANKEN, Rose (Dorothy)

* * *

GRANT, Skeeter
See SPIEGELMAN, Art

* * *

GREAVES, William 1926-

PERSONAL: Born October 8, 1926, in New York, N.Y.; son of Garfield (a cab driver and minister) and Emily (Muir) Greaves; married Louise Archambault, August 23, 1959; children: David, Taiyi, Maiya. *Education:* Attended New School of Social Research and New York Actors Studio, 1948, City College of New York (now City College of City University of New York), 1949-51, and New Institute for Film and Television, 1950.

ADDRESSES: Office—William Greaves Productions, Inc., 80 Eighth Ave., Suite 1703, New York, New York 10011.

CAREER: Performer, songwriter, producer, director, scriptwriter, and independent filmmaker. Began theatrical career with Sierra Leonian Asadata Dafora Dance Company as an African dancer, joined Pearl Primus Dance Troupe, then worked as an actor on stage, radio, television, and screen from 1943 to 1952. Actor in stage productions, including "Three's a Family," 1943, "Henri Christophe," 1945, "A Young American," 1946, "Finian's Rainbow," 1946, "John Loves Mary," (black cast), 1948, "Lost in the Stars," 1949, and "Arsenic and Old Lace," (black cast); actor in films, including "Miracle in Harlem," 1948, and "Lost Boundaries," 1949.

National Film Board of Canada, Ottawa, Ontario, film production staff, 1952-60; United Nations International Civil Aviation Organization (ICAO), Montreal, Quebec, public information officer, 1962-63, writer and producer, 1965-66; United Nations Television, New York, N.Y., producer and director, 1963-68; National Educational Television, New York City, executive producer, scriptwriter, and host of "Black Journal" television series, 1968-71; associated with "Black News" television series, 1975; William Greaves Productions, Inc., New York City, founder and president, producer, director, and scriptwriter, 1964—. Director and/or producer of documentary and feature films, c. 1952-81, including "Roads in the Sky" for International Civil Aviation Organization; "Emergency Ward" with Wolf Koening and "Four Religions, Part 2: Islam and Christianity" with James Beveridge for National Film Board of Canada; "The Life and Legacy of Booker T. Washington" for National Parks Service; "Cleared for Takeoff" with Alistair Cooke for United Nations Televi-

sion; "Still a Brother: Inside the Negro Middle Class" and "Wealth of a Nation" for United States Information Agency; "Family Dream," for Universal Pictures; and "Choice of Destinies," "Deathgrip," "Liberty: On Being Black," and "Putting It Straight."

Founder and director, Canadian Drama Studio, Montreal, Quebec, and Toronto and Ottawa, Ontario, 1952-63; drama teacher, Lee Strasberg Theatre Institute, New York City, beginning in 1973; teacher, New York Actors Studio, New York City; visiting professor of film, Boston University, Boston, Mass.; lecturer at numerous institutions, including Boston, Brandeis, Columbia, Harvard, and Howard universities, City College of City University of New York, universities of Buffalo, Michigan, and Vermont, and Williams College. Member of Emmy Award panel, National Academy of Television Arts and Sciences; media panel judge for National Endowment for the Arts and National Endowment for the Humanitites, both beginning in 1979; member of media committee, Indo-American sub-commission on education and culture; chairman of film committee and council member, Massachusetts Foundation for the Humanities and Public Policy; film panelist, American Film Institute; vice-president of AMAS Repertory Theatre, Inc.

MEMBER: American Federation of Television and Radio Artists, American Guild of Authors and Composers, Directors Guild of America, National Association of Black Media Producers (co-founder, 1970), Writers Guild of America, Equity Association, New York Actors Studio (member of auditioning committee), Screen Actors Guild, National Urban League (member of communications committee).

AWARDS, HONORS: Won membership in New York Actors Studio, 1948; American Film Festival Award, c. 1964, for documentary "Still a Brother: Inside the Negro Middle Class"; Emmy Award nomination, c. 1964, for "Still a Brother: Inside the Negro Middle Class," Emmy Award, 1970, as executive producer of "Black Journal" television series, and three Emmy Award nominations, 1973, for documentary film "Voice of La Raza," all from National Academy of Television Arts and Sciences; Silver Medal, International Film and Television Festival, 1969; Atlanta International Film Festival Award, Chicago International Film Festival Award, and Randy Award from Job Film Fair Competition, all in 1969 for documentary "In the Company of Men"; John Russwurm Award from National Newspaper Publishers Association of America, 1970, for "Black Journal"; Special Gold Medal Award from Atlanta International Film Festival, Blue Ribbon American Festival Award, and San Francisco International Film Festival Award, all in 1970 for "In the Company of Men"; Oscar Michaud Award, 1980, for induction into the Black Filmmakers Hall of Fame; Hommage award, Festival of Black Independent American Cinema 1920-1980 (Paris, France), 1980; Dusa Award from New York Actors Studio, 1980; Doctor of Humane Letters from King Memorial College; recipient of more than sixty awards from International Film Festival for documentary and feature films.

WRITINGS:

FILM SCRIPTS

(And director) "First World Festival of Negro Arts," National Film Board of Canada for United States Information Agency, 1966.

(And director) "In the Company of Men" (documentary), William Greaves Productions for *Newsweek* magazine, 1969.

(And director) "Ali, the Fighter" (feature), William Greaves Productions, 1971.

(And director) "The Fighters" (documentary), William Greaves Productions, 1971.

(With Jose Garcia) "Voice of La Raza" (documentary), William Greaves Productions for Equal Employment Opportunity Commission, 1971.

"From These Roots" (documentary), William Greaves Productions, 1974.

(With Woody Robinson) "The Marijuana Affair" (feature documentary), 1975.

"Space for Women," National Aeronautics and Space Administration, 1981.

Also author of film scripts "The Magic Mineral," "Smoke and Weather," and "Symbiopsychotaxiplasm: Take One." Also composed more than one hundred popular songs, including "African Lullaby" with lyrics in both English and Swahili, recorded by Eartha Kitt in 1952.

SIDELIGHTS: In an autobiographical essay written in 1969 for *Sightlines* magazine, independent filmmaker William Greaves stated: "My interest in film stems from three basic sources. First, I have always had a deep interest in Africa and Afro-American history . . . [and I decided] to enter the mass media as a producer in order to disseminate information on the black experience. Secondly, I became infuriated by the racially degrading sterotypes of black people that white film producers threw up on American screens. . . . It became quite clear to me that unless we black people . . . began to produce information for screen and television, there would probably always be a distortion of the 'black image.' My third reason for entering the production side of films was . . . [the] need to channel my diverse interests. It occurred to me that film was a medium where many different talents could be employed while feigning to be a specialist. Somehow, these three reasons have become inextricably intertwined and I'm now simply a filmmaker with rambling interests, committed only to the expression of consciousness: mine and others."

Considered one of America's finest independent film producers during the 1960s and 1970s, Greaves actually learned his craft in Canada. Facing what he considered insurmountable racial barriers during the early 1950s, Greaves was forced to leave the United States in order to acquire the skills and experience necessary to pursue his career in documentary filmmaking. He worked ten years for Canada's National Film Board as a writer, editor, and director of more than seventy films, and during that time he helped introduce cinema verite—the art or technique of filmmaking that conveys candid realism—to the North American continent. Greaves returned to the United States in 1963. Explaining his reasons in *Sightlines*, Greaves stated: "What made me come back to America? I don't know. . . . Perhaps I felt that I had reached the limits of what Canada had to offer a creative artist. Maybe it was a decision to contribute to the redesign of the American psyche through the social engineering agency of film and television. Maybe it was Martin Luther King and the march on Washington and the hope that it held for America. . . . Maybe I was just plain homesick."

Whatever the reason, Greaves quickly established himself as a first-rate filmmaker, focusing primarily on the many facets of black experience. He made several feature and documentary films for the United Nations and the United States Information Agency, including the award-winning "Still a Brother: Inside the Negro Middle Class." In 1964 he set up his own company, William Greaves Productions, and over the next several years produced dozens of films and won numerous awards. In 1970 alone, as James P. Murray noted in *To Find an Image,* "he won ten major awards for film and television productions about the black man's problems, ambitions, and future in America." Greaves became increasingly well known and highly regarded for his innovation and independence as a filmmaker.

In 1968 William Greaves began a three-year period as scriptwriter and co-host of the original "Black Journal," National Educational Television's news show that, according to *Ebony,* "claims to be 'of, by, about and primarily for the black community.'" The program's basic purpose was to improve consciousness and pride within the Afro-American population—it aired for one hour once a month. Shortly after he began Greaves was asked to take over as executive producer, while remaining the program's co-host and writer. Consequently, "Black Journal" became the only black controlled network show in television and under Greaves's leadership earned a reputation for its exceptional quality as well as for its radical and militant approach. In 1970 the National Academy of Television Arts and Sciences paid tribute to the show's excellence and presented Greaves an Emmy Award as best executive producer.

Discussing the success of black filmmakers in an interview for Murray's *To Find an Image,* Greaves commented, "As far as I'm concerned, all the films we've done . . . have been successful, and I don't think we've had any difficulty in communicating our intentions to either the black community or the white community." He believes, moreover, that the future for black films and black film producers is a promising one. He told Murray: "I think it will be something like the same thing that has happened with black music. Our music, our speech, our behavior, and general life styles have been unique, but accepted and absorbed into society. Just like there is a steady growth and acceptance of new black publications, I feel the same will happen with black films."

AVOCATIONAL INTERESTS: Afro-American history and culture.

BIOGRAPHICAL/CRITICAL SOURCES:

BOOKS

Murray, James P., *To Find an Image: Black Films From Uncle Tom to Super Fly,* Bobbs-Merrill, 1973.

PERIODICALS

Ebony, September, 1969.
Film News, fall, 1980.
Jet, December 31, 1970.
Sightlines, September-October, 1969.

*   *   *

GREEN, Jerome Frederic   1928-
(Jerry Green)

PERSONAL: Born April 15, 1928, in New York, N.Y.; son of Frank Charles and Sylvia K. Green; married Nancy Jane Hamilton (a museum worker), December 18, 1961; children: Jennifer Elizabeth. *Education:* Brown University, A.B., 1950; Boston University, M.S., 1952.

ADDRESSES: Home—Grosse Pointe Woods, Mich. *Office*—*Detroit News,* 615 Lafayette Blvd., Detroit, Mich. 48231.

CAREER: New York Journal-American, New York, N.Y., reporter, 1952; reporter for *Star-Journal,* 1956; Associated Press, Detroit, Mich., Michigan sports editor, 1956-63; *Detroit News,* Detroit, sportswriter, 1963-73, sports columnist, 1973—. *Military service:* U.S. Navy, 1953-56; became lieutenant junior grade.

AWARDS, HONORS: Named Michigan Sportswriter of the Year, 1972, 1979, 1980, 1981, and 1982; Sportswriting Award from Michigan Associated Press, 1973 and 1979; Michigan Sportswriting Award from United Press International, 1981, 1982, 1983, and 1984; Pulitzer Prize nomination, 1982.

WRITINGS:

UNDER NAME JERRY GREEN

Year of the Tiger: The Diary of Detroit's World Champions, Coward, 1969.
Detroit Lions: Best Years, Best Teams, Macmillan, 1973.

Work represented in anthologies, including *Best Sports Stories,* 1982-87. Contributor of articles and reviews to magazines, including *Sports Illustrated* and *Sporting News.*

* * *

GREEN, Jerry
See GREEN, Jerome Frederic

* * *

GREEN, Lewis 1946-

PERSONAL: Born June 3, 1946, in Amesbury, Mass.; son of Herman W. and C. Dolly (Tiadore) Green; married Kay E. Kuechenmeister (a graphic designer), July 29, 1974. *Education:* Oakloosa-Walton Junior College, A.A., 1973; University of Florida, B.S., 1975; Marian College of Fond du Lac, certificate of education, 1978; graduate study at National College of Education.

ADDRESSES: Home and Office—737 10th Ave. E., Seattle, Wash. 98102.

CAREER: Gainesville Sun, Gainesville, Fla., sportswriter, 1975; substitute teacher in elementary schools in Gainesville, and Lake Villa, Ill., 1978-82; Scott, Foresman and Co., Glenview, Ill., editor/writer, 1982-83; founder and co-publisher of New Horizons Publishers, 1983-87. Guest on radio and television programs. *Military service:* U.S. Air Force, 1965-72; became staff sergeant; received Air Force Commendation Medal.

WRITINGS:

Bed and Breakfast Washington, New Horizons Publishers, 1984.
Fairs and Festivals of the Pacific Northwest, New Horizons Publishers, 1985.
Classic Resorts and Romantic Retreats, New Horizons Publishers, 1986.
The Bed and Breakfast Traveler: Touring the West Coast, Pacific Search, 1987.

Contributor to magazines and newspapers, including *Innsider, Country Inns, Northwest,* and *Pacific Northwest.*

SIDELIGHTS: Lewis Green told *CA:* "I look at travel writing primarily as entertainment. In an age of so much despair, I am hopeful that my writings bring a little joy into people's lives. I try to accentuate the positive, writing about places of quality and leaving the negatives for the critics. My works are subjective, however, for I discard the unworthy destinations during my research phase, so that my books and articles are filled with valuable and useful information for both the frequent and the armchair traveler. The research phase for each of my books is ongoing. I am always seeking to update and expand the information. The first three books, which were self-published, are out of print; however, much of the research that went into those titles was useful in creating *The Bed and Breakfast Traveler.*"

* * *

GREEN, Thomas Andrew 1940-

PERSONAL: Born March 18, 1940, in New York, N.Y.; son of Alan B. (in advertising; an author) and Gladys (a literary agent; maiden name, Blun) Green; married Ruth Brownell (an artist), December 21, 1968. *Education:* Columbia University, A.B., 1961; Harvard University, Ph.D., 1970, J.D., 1972.

ADDRESSES: Home—1100 Berkshire, Ann Arbor, Mich. 48104. *Office*—Law School, 304 Hutchins Hall, University of Michigan, 621 State St., Ann Arbor, Mich. 48109.

CAREER: Bard College, Annandale-on-Hudson, N.Y., assistant professor of history, 1967-69; University of Michigan, Ann Arbor, assistant professor, 1972-75, associate professor, 1975-77, professor of law, 1977—, professor of history, 1980—.

MEMBER: American Historical Association, American Society of Legal History, Mediaeval Academy of America, Conference on Critical Legal Studies, Selden Society, Royal Historical Society.

WRITINGS:

(Editor with Morris S. Arnold, Sally A. Scully, and Stephen D. White) *On the Laws and Customs of England: Essays in Honor of Samuel E. Thorne,* University of North Carolina Press, 1981.
Verdict According to Conscience: Perspectives on the English Criminal Trial Jury, 1200-1800, University of Chicago Press, 1985.
(Editor with James S. Cockburn) *Twelve Good Men and True,* Princeton University Press, in press.

Editor of *Studies in Legal History.*

WORK IN PROGRESS: History of the American Criminal Trial Jury.

SIDELIGHTS: Thomas Andrew Green told *CA:* "My work on the English and American criminal trial jury focuses mainly on the phenomenon of jury nullification of rules of law. I trace this form of jury behavior in political cases and in trials raising the question of the defendant's capacity to act 'voluntarily.' I am particularly interested in the latter kind of case and in the American debate regarding the role of the jury against the background of increasing doubts about the reality of the notion of free will."

BIOGRAPHICAL/CRITICAL SOURCES:

PERIODICALS

Times Literary Supplement, January 31, 1986.

GREENE, Bert 1923-1988

OBITUARY NOTICE—See index for *CA* sketch: Born October 16, 1923, in Flushing, N.Y.; died of a heart attack, June 10, 1988, in New York, N.Y. Art director, entrepreneur, journalist, and author. Greene was best known for his six cookbooks and weekly column, "Bert Greene's Kitchen," syndicated in numerous newspapers, including the *New York Daily News*. Greene's writings include the books *Bert Greene's Kitchen Bouquets, Honest American Fare*, and *Greene on Greens* and articles contributed to such publications as *Vogue, Esquire, Cuisine, Cosmopolitan*, and *Self*. He was also founder and co-owner of The Store, in Amagansett, New York, from 1966 to 1976. Prior to his career as a food expert and author, Greene worked as an art director for Helena Rubenstein, Incorporated, I. Miller & Sons, and *Esquire* magazine.

OBITUARIES AND OTHER SOURCES:

PERIODICALS

Los Angeles Times, June 14, 1988.

* * *

GREENLEAF, Robert Kiefner 1904-

PERSONAL: Born July 14, 1904, in Terre Haute, Ind.; son of George W. and Burchie M. (Kiefner) Greenleaf; married Esther E. Hargrace, September 26, 1931; children: Newcomb, Elizabeth (Mrs. David S. Miller), Madeline (Mrs. Gregory Jaynes). *Education:* Carleton College, B.A., 1926. *Religion:* Society of Friends (Quakers).

ADDRESSES: Home—Crosslands, Apt. 77, Kennett Square, Pa. 19348.

CAREER: Director of training for Ohio Bell Telephone Co., 1926-29; engineer and staff assistant with American Telephone & Telegraph Co., 1929-64, director of management research, 1957-64. Member of faculty at Dartmouth College, 1950-58, and Salzburg Seminar in American Studies, 1968; visiting lecturer at Harvard Business School and Massachusetts Institute of Technology, 1962-63; executive in residence at Fresno University, 1968; Elis and Signe Olsson Professor of Business Administration at University of Virginia, 1973. Trustee of Russell Sage Foundation, 1957-65; consultant to Ford Foundation, R. K. Mellon Foundation, and Lilly Endowment.

MEMBER: Harvard Club of New York City.

AWARDS, HONORS: D.H.L. from Carleton College, 1969, and Alverno College, 1984.

WRITINGS:

Servant Leadership, Paulist Press, 1977.
The Teacher as Servant: A Parable, Paulist Press, 1983.

Author of pamphlets.

WORK IN PROGRESS: The Servant as Gradualist; The Servant as Chairperson; The Servant as Nurturer of the Human Spirit.

* * *

GREGORY, Jean
See URE, Jean

GROSS, Albert C. 1947-

PERSONAL: Born June 18, 1947, in New York, N.Y.; son of Maurice J. (a nuclear engineer) and Esther S. (Cizyn) Gross. *Education:* Columbia University, A.B. (American history), 1969; San Diego State University, A.B. (psychology; with distinction), 1975; University of California, San Diego, M.A., 1976. *Politics:* Democrat. *Religion:* Jewish.

ADDRESSES: Office—2111 Edinburg Ave., Cardiff, Calif. 92007. *Agent*—Richard Curtis Associates, Inc., 164 East 64th St., Suite 1, New York, N.Y. 10021.

CAREER: Pacific Coast Alternative, San Diego, Calif., publisher, 1974-75; free-lance writer, 1975-77; City of San Diego, organization development specialist, 1977-80; Foodmaker, Inc., San Diego, director of management and organization development, 1980-81; Action Research Associates, Inc., Del Mar, Calif., president, 1981-84; Spenco Medical Corp., Waco, Tex., director of public relations, 1984-85; free-lance writer and publications consultant, 1985—. Instructor at University of California, San Diego, San Diego Community College District, Chapman College, National University, San Diego State University, and Pepperdine University; consultant to IVAC Corp., California Department of Correction, and Science Development Corp. *Military service:* U.S. Navy, 1969-74; became lieutenant.

MEMBER: San Diego Publishers Group.

WRITINGS:

(Contributor) Barry Bozeman and Jeffrey Straussman, editors, *New Directions in Public Administration*, Brooks/Cole, 1983.
(With John Howard and Christian Paul) *The Cyclist's Companion*, Stephen Greene, 1984, revised edition, 1987.
(With Howard and Paul) *Multi-Fitness*, Macmillan, 1985.
Endurance, Dodd, 1986.
Henry of Navarre, Chelsea House, 1987.

Contributor of articles and photographs to magazines and newspapers, including *Scientific American, Bicycle Sport, Journal of Applied Behavioral Science, Barron's Business Weekly, Penthouse*, and *Running Times*.

SIDELIGHTS: Albert C. Gross told *CA*: "My experience and tastes are eclectic, so I write about any topic that interests me."

AVOCATIONAL INTERESTS: Participating in endurance events, including marathons, triathlons, and bicycle races.

* * *

GROSSMAN, Louis Irwin 1901-1988

OBITUARY NOTICE: Born December 16, 1901, in Teplick, Russia (now U.S.S.R.); immigrated to United States, naturalized citizen; died March 24, 1988, in Newtown, Pa. Dental surgeon, educator, editor, and author. Grossman pioneered root canal dentistry and became known as the father of endodontics. A longtime faculty member of the University of Pennsylvania School of Dental Medicine, he began his tenure in 1926 and served as chairman of the endodontics department for many years. In 1968 he was named professor emeritus of oral medicine. Grossman wrote *Endodontic Practice*, a classic text in dentistry that has been translated into several languages, reprinted more than ten times, and is still used worldwide. His other writings include *Dental Formulas and Aids to Dental*

Practice and numerous articles and papers, and he also edited *Handbook of Dental Practice.*

OBITUARIES AND OTHER SOURCES:

BOOKS

American Men and Women of Science: The Physical and Biological Sciences, 16th edition, Bowker, 1986.
Who's Who in American Jewry, Standard Who's Who, 1980.

PERIODICALS

Chicago Tribune, March 27, 1988.
Los Angeles Times, March 29, 1988.
New York Times, March 26, 1988.
Washington Post, March 28, 1988.

*   *   *

GROTH, John (August)   1908-1988

OBITUARY NOTICE—See index for *CA* sketch: Surname is pronounced "Growth"; born February 26 (one source says February 2), 1908, in Chicago, Ill.; died June 27, 1988, in New York, N.Y. Artist, illustrator, educator, journalist, and author. Groth, a contributor of illustrations to many books and magazines, was best known for his expressionistic style of drawing, particularly of battle and sports scenes. Hired by *Esquire* magazine in 1933 as its first art director, Groth drew assignments in Mexico, Russia, England, and Germany that early demonstrated his strength as a graphic journalist. In 1936 he moved to New York City, where he free-lanced as a sports cartoonist and editorial illustrator for various periodicals. During World War II, as an artist-correspondent for the *Chicago Sun,* Groth was present at several closing battles. These he documented in a 1945 book, *Studio: Europe;* his subsequent coverage of the Korean and French Indo-Chinese wars culminated in a companion volume, *Studio: Asia.*

After the World War II Groth was a frequent contributor of drawings to *Collier's, Esquire, Vogue, Saturday Evening Post, New Yorker, Fortune, Sports Illustrated,* and other periodicals. He also illustrated several classics, including Leo Tolstoy's *War and Peace,* John Steinbeck's *Grapes of Wrath,* Erich Maria Remarque's *All Quiet on the Western Front,* and Ernest Hemingway's *Men Without Women,* for which he also wrote the introduction. Groth also taught at the Art Students League of New York, the National Academy of Design, and elsewhere. His pictures are in several collections, including the Museum of Modern Art, the Library of Congress, and the Metropolitan Museum of Art.

OBITUARIES AND OTHER SOURCES:

BOOKS

Contemporary Graphic Artists, Volume 2, Gale, 1987.
Who's Who in American Art, 17th edition, Bowker, 1986.

PERIODICALS

New York Times, June 30, 1988.

*   *   *

GRUEN, Yetta Fisher

PERSONAL: Born in Birmingham, England; immigrated to the United States, naturalized citizen; daughter of Louis (a designer) and Fanny (a housewife; maiden name, Mintz) Fisher; married Bertram Gruen (died March 23, 1986); children: two. *Education:* Attended Montgomery College.

ADDRESSES: Home—7246 Greentree Rd., Bethesda, Md. 20817. *Office*—*Washington Post,* 1150 15th St. N.W., Washington, D.C. 20071. *Agent*—Ronald Goldfarb, 916 16th St., Washington, D.C. 20006.

CAREER: Washington Post, Washington, D.C., coordinator of weekly wedding and engagement page, 1967—. Affiliated with the *New York Times.*

MEMBER: Washington Independent Writers, Writer's Center, British Embassy Players.

WRITINGS:

Your Wedding: Making It Perfect, Penguin, 1986.

Contributor to magazines.

WORK IN PROGRESS: A Pity for Living Things, a novel set in Europe at the turn of the century; research on "the history of the vegetarian discipline."

SIDELIGHTS: Yetta Fisher Gruen told *CA:* "In my youth I had always experienced great joy in reading while my mind weaved all sorts of fanciful tales of its own. Because life was too vivid as a child—not only during World War II but earlier—I did not connect my dreamings with writing until a mature adult when my confidence increased. Now my free-lance work has been very rewarding. The *Washington Post* magazine section has published a couple of my short stories, which prompted a Virginia journalist to write to me saying that I should expand them into a larger piece of work—which I intend to do.

"My book, *Your Wedding: Making It Perfect,* evolved from the many questions asked of me from the inception of my work on the bridal desk at the *Washington Post.* It became apparent that the public needed a book that takes an in-depth look at the whole wedding process because the available publications dealt only with etiquette and protocol. I became fascinated with the questions, many of which had more to do with the intricacies of human relationships rather than how to plan a wedding. Though I did not intend to preach, what I hoped from the book was that in analyzing the various questions the reader would realize that there was a philosophy woven within the fabric of the answers. Apparently, from comments, I achieved my goal. When someone poses a problem as well as what they think would be a good solution, the question I most often ask is: 'What will be gained by such an action?'

"For my book I not only did extensive research going back to ancient Roman times, but over the years I had discussed weddings with anyone who knew anything about them; not necessarily professionals in the field, but couples newly married, future brides and bridegrooms, in-laws, and guests. I have answered countless questions from telephone callers both within the *Washington Post* and the general public."

*   *   *

GRUMLEY, Michael   1941-1988

OBITUARY NOTICE—See index for *CA* sketch: Born July 6, 1941, in Bettendorf, Iowa; died of complications from acquired immune deficiency syndrome (AIDS), April 28, 1988, in New York, N.Y. Artist and author. Grumley, a writer and artist by training, was the author of *There Are Giants in the Earth, Hard Corps, Night People, Life Drawing,* and *After Midnight,* which featured his sketches of people who work night shifts. He also wrote, with Robert Ferro, *Atlantis: The Autobiography of a Search.*

OBITUARIES AND OTHER SOURCES:

BOOKS

The Writers Directory, 1988-1990, St. James Press, 1988.

PERIODICALS

New York Times, April 30, 1988.

*   *   *

GUGGENHEIM, Hans Georg   1927-

PERSONAL: Born March 30, 1927, in St. Gallen, Switzerland; son of Karl (a judge) and Nelly (Zollikofer) Guggenheim; married Anne-Grete Jensen (a dental technician), February 1, 1943; children: Maria Helena. *Education:* Attended University of Zurich, University of Geneva, University of Hamburg, and University of Paris, Sorbonne. *Religion:* Protestant.

ADDRESSES: Home—F-07400 Alba-la-Romaine, Ardeche, France.

CAREER: Tour guide, travel writer, and playwright. Has worked as a salesman, woodcutter, gas serviceman, tutor, folksinger, and assistant director while traveling in various countries, including Denmark, Germany, and the United States.

WRITINGS:

Around the World in Eighty Ways (travel book), Exposition Press of Florida, 1981.

Also author of plays, including "The Last Days," "The Golden Calf," "The Invitation," and "The Other One."

Contributor to Swiss journal *Diewoche.*

*   *   *

GUILLEN (y BATISTA), Nicolas (Cristobal)   1902-

PERSONAL: Surname pronounced "gee-*yane,*" with a hard *g* as in geese; born July 10, 1902, in Camaguey, Cuba; son of Nicolas (a silversmith, newspaper editor, and politician) and Argelia (Batista) Guillen. *Education:* Graduated from Camaguey Institute (high school), 1920; attended University of Havana, 1920-21.

ADDRESSES: Home—Calle O, No. 2, Edificio Someillan, Vedado, Havana, Cuba. *Office*—Union Nacional de Escritores y Artistas Cubanos, Calle 17, No. 351, Vedado, Havana, Cuba.

CAREER: Poet, 1922—. Founder and editor of *Lis* literary magazine in the early 1920s; contributor to Cuban newspapers and magazines, including *Diario de la marina,* c. 1922-37; correspondent in Spain for *Mediodia* magazine, 1937-38; candidate for political offices in Cuba on Popular Socialist (later Communist) ticket in the 1940s; lecturer and correspondent in Latin America and Europe in the 1940s and 1950s; president of Cuban National Union of Writers and Artists (UNEAC), 1961—; served as editor in chief of *La Gaceta de Cuba* (official cultural publication of UNEAC) and as Cuban ambassador.

AWARDS, HONORS: Lenin Peace Prize from the Soviet Union, 1954; Cuban Order of Jose Marti from the Republic of Cuba, 1981; Order of Merit from the Republic of Haiti; Order of Cyril and Methodius (first class) from the People's Republic of Bulgaria.

WRITINGS:

POETRY

Motivos de son (title means "Motifs of Sound"), 1930, special fiftieth anniversary edition, with music by Amadeo Roldan, Editorial Letras Cubanas, 1980.

Songoro cosongo, 1931, published as *Songoro cosongo: Poemas mulatos,* Presencia Latinoamericana, 1981.

West Indies Ltd.: Poemas, Imprenta Ucar, Garcia, 1934.

Cantos para soldados y sones para turistas (title means "Songs for Soldiers and Sones for Tourists"), Editorial Masas, 1937, published as *El son entero: Cantos para soldados y sones para turistas,* Editorial Losada, 1952.

Espana: Poema en cuatro angustias y una esperanza (title means "Spain: A Poem in Four Anguishes and a Hope"), Editorial Mexico Nuevo, 1937.

El son entero: Suma poetica, 1929-1946 (title means "The Entire Son"; with a letter by Miguel de Unamuno and musical notation by various composers), Editorial Pleamar, 1947, Premia Editora, 1982.

La paloma de vuelo popular (title means "The Dove of Popular Flight"), 1958, also published, in a single volume, with *Elegias* (title means "Elegies"), Editorial Losada, 1959.

Puedes? (title means "Can You?"; with drawings by the author), Libreria La Tertulia, 1961.

Elegia a Jesus Menendez, Imprenta Nacional de Cuba, 1962.

La rueda dentada (title means "The Serrated Wheel"), UNEAC, 1962.

Tengo (title means "I Have"), prologue by Jose Antonio Portuondo, Editora del Consejo Nacional de Universidades, 1964, translation by Richard J. Carr published as *Tengo,* Broadside Press, 1974.

Poemas de amor (title means "Love Poems"), Ediciones La Tertulia, 1964.

Nadie (title means "Nobody"), Sol y Piedra, 1966.

El gran zoo, Instituto del Libro, 1967, translation by Robert Marquez published as *Patria o muerte! The Great Zoo and Other Poems,* Monthly Review Press, 1972.

El diario que a diario, UNEAC, 1972.

Poemas Manuables, UNEAC, 1975.

El corazon con que vivo (title means "The Heart With Which I Live"), UNEAC, 1975.

Por que imperialismo?: Poemas (title means "Why Imperialism?: Poems"), Ediciones Calarca, 1976.

Elegias, edited by Jose Martinez Matos, illustrations by Dario Mora, UNEAC, 1977.

Coplas de Juan Descalzo (title means "The Ballad of John Barefoot"), Editorial Letras Cubanas, 1979.

Musica de camara (title means "Chamber Music"), UNEAC, 1979.

Sputnik 57, [Cuba], 1980.

Also author of *Poemas para el Che* (title means "Poems for Che"), *Buenos Dias, Fidel,* for Grafica Horizonte, and *Por el Mar de las Antillas anda un barco de papel: Poemas para ninos mayores de edad* (title means "Going Through the Antilles Sea in a Boat of Paper: Poems for Older Children"), with illustrations by Rapi Diego, for UNEAC.

POETRY COLLECTIONS

Cuba Libre, translated from the Spanish by Langston Hughes and Ben Frederic Carruthers, Anderson & Ritchie, 1948.

Songoro cosongo, Motivos de Son, West Indies Ltd., Espana: Poema en cuatro angustias y una esperanza, Editorial Losada, 1952.

Nicolas Guillen: Sus mejores poemas, Organizacion de los Festivales del Libro, 1959.

Los mejores versos de Nicolas Guillen, Editorial Nuestra America, 1961.

Antologia mayor: El son entero y otros poemas, UNEAC, 1964.

Antologia mayor, Instituto del Libro, 1969.

Antologia clave, prologue by Luis Inigo Madrigal, Editorial Nascimento, 1971.

Man-Making Words: Selected Poems of Nicolas Guillen, translated from the Spanish by Robert Marquez and David Arthur McMurray, University of Massachusetts Press, 1972.

Cuba, amor y revolucion: Poemas, Editorial Causachun, 1972.

Obra poetica, 1920-1972 (two volumes), edited by Angel Augier with illustrations by the author, Editorial de Arte y Literatura, 1974.

Latinamericason, Quatro Editores, 1974.

Nueva antologia mayor, edited by Augier, Editorial Letras Cubanas, 1979.

Paginas vueltas: Seleccion de poemas y apuntes autobiograficos (title means "Turned Pages: Selected Poems and Autobiographical Notes"), Grupo Editor de Buenos Aires, 1980.

Paginas vueltas: Memorias, UNEAC, 1982.

OTHER

Claudio Jose Domingo Brindis de Salas, el rey de las octavas (title means "Claudio Jose Domingo Brindis de Salas, King of the Octaves"; prose), Municipio de La Habana, 1935.

Prosa de prisa, cronicas (title means "Hasty Prose, Chronicles"; selection of journalistic articles published from 1938 to 1961), Universidad Central de las Villas, 1962, expanded edition published as *Prosa de prisa, 1929-1972* (three volumes), edited with introduction by Augier, Editorial Arte y Literatura, 1975.

El libro de las decimas, UNEAC, 1980.

El libro de los sones, Editorial Letras Cubanas, 1982.

Sol de domingo, UNEAC, 1982.

Cronista en tres epocas (title means "Journalist in Three Epochs"; selection of journalistic articles edited by Maria Julia Guerra Avila and Pedro Rodriguez Gutierrez), Editorial Politica, 1984.

Tengo was made into a sound recording in the 1970s and released by Consejo Nacional de Cultura.

Works represented in anthologies, including *Some Modern Cuban Poems by Nicolas Guillen and Others,* translated from the Spanish by Manish Nandy, Satyabrata Pal, 1968.

SIDELIGHTS: Nicolas Guillen, considered a master of the so-called "Afro-Cuban" style, is one of Cuba's best known and most respected poets. A mulatto from the provincial middle class, Guillen began his career as a newspaper journalist while writing poetry in his spare time. A 1930 visit to Cuba by the black American poet Langston Hughes, a leading figure in the black cultural movement known as the Harlem Renaissance, inspired Guillen to write and publish his first verse collection the same year, *Motivos de son* ("Motifs of Sound"). A group of eight poems structured rhythmically like the *son,* a popular Cuban song-and-dance arrangement with strong African elements, this work drew on a new international interest in primitive art and African culture and became identified with the Afro-Caribbean movement in Hispanic poetry that began in the mid-1920s. Like earlier white Afro-Caribbean poets in Cuba

and Puerto Rico, Guillen treated local lower-class black life as his major theme and combined onomatopoeia—the use of words whose sounds imply their sense—and African rhythms as major stylistic devices, but he went further in both style and substance than his predecessors, who tended toward somewhat stereotypical depictions of a joyful, sensual, happy-go-lucky folk. Guillen instead wrote "from within"—as G. R. Coulthard noted in *Race and Colour in Caribbean Literature*—and subtly gave poetic voice to the lives of poverty and pathos behind the picturesque facade of Havana's black slum dwellers. Guillen was also credited with capturing the genuine dialect and speech patterns of Cuban blacks, which he blended with Yoruba African words to create a unique language that relied as much on sound and rhythm as on word sense for its meaning.

Guillen further refined his Afro-Cuban poetry in *Songoro cosongo,* a 1931 verse collection that quickly earned him a worldwide reputation and became widely regarded as the poet's masterwork. Published with Guillen's lottery winnings that year, this work evinces a deeper social consciousness and still bolder style in seeking to express the tragedy, passion, and vigor of black life in Cuba. The poet moves from an implicit criticism of slum life to direct denunciations of racism and an affirmation of the roles of black men and women in building Cuban and American culture and society. According to Guillen, he sought to create a "mulatto poetry" that would reflect Cuba's true history and racial composition.

Stylistically, Guillen's occasional use of the ballad form and reliance on naive, "nonsensical" imagery in *Songoro cosongo* shows the influence of the internationally acclaimed Spanish poet Federico Garcia Lorca, whom Guillen met in Cuba as Garcia Lorca was returning to Europe from the United States. The Cuban poet's extraordinary synthesis of traditional Spanish metric forms with Afro-Cuban words, rhythms, and folkloric symbols uniquely captures the cultural flavor of the Spanish-speaking Caribbean, critics have noted. Other poems in *Songoro cosongo* rely almost entirely on onomatopoeic effects and rhythm, becoming, in a sense, abstract word-paintings with no direct representational value at all—the title itself has no meaning other than its rhythmic and symbolic suggestions. Though seemingly spontaneous, these verses are in fact carefully crafted, with rigorous attention to rhyme, meter, and tonal nuances. Often recited publicly to a drum accompaniment, Guillen's Afro-Cuban verse has also been set to music by the Spanish composer Xavier Montsalvatge and sung by the American mezzo-soprano Marilyn Horne, among others.

The current of social protest running through *Songoro cosongo* turns deeper and swifter in *West Indies Ltd.,* published just after the 1933 revolution that deposed Cuban dictator Antonio Machado. In verse that is by turns satirical and bitter, Guillen depicts the often cruel and exploitative history of slavery, colonialism, and imperialism (particularly in its contemporary American form) in the Antilles islands of the West Indies. The poet's commitment to social change grew when he traveled to Spain in 1937 to cover the civil war for *Mediodia* magazine and participate in the anti-fascist Second International Congress of Writers for the Defense of Culture. That year he joined the Cuban Communist party (then called Popular Socialist) and wrote a long, elegiac ode to the Spanish Republic titled *Espana: Poema en cuatro angustias y una esperanza* ("Spain: A Poem in Four Anguishes and a Hope") that voiced his hope for humanity's communist future. Guillen also devoted most of his 1937 verse collection, *Cantos para soldados y sones para turistas* ("Songs for Soldiers and Sones for Tourists"), to social and political themes.

Guillen spent much of the next two decades outside of Cuba, traveling around Europe and Latin America as a lecturer and correspondent for several Cuban journals. In 1962 he published a selection of these articles under the title *Prosa de prisa* ("Hasty Prose"). Guillen's poetic output during these years was somewhat reduced, although he published a major collection titled *El son entero* ("The Entire Son") in 1947 and his first English-language selection, *Cuba-Libre* (co-edited and translated by Langston Hughes), that following year. Denied permission to return to Cuba by the Fulgencio Batista dictatorship in the 1950s, Guillen spent several years in unhappy exile in Paris, France, where he wrote *La paloma de vuelo popular* ("The Dove of Popular Flight") and *Elegias* ("Elegies"), published together in one volume in 1958. These two works complement each other thematically and stylistically. The first consists mainly of broadly political—and often witty and ironical—protest poems against the Cuban dictatorship and American imperialism, while *Elegias* mourns the loss of friends and other victims of political repression in somber, lyrical tones.

The triumph of the Cuban revolution in early 1959 immediately brought Guillen back to his homeland, where he enthusiastically embraced the revolutionary cause. Already recognized as the country's greatest living poet, Guillen readily took on the role of poet laureate of the revolution. His 1964 verse collection *Tengo* ("I Have") is a joyful celebration of the revolutionary victory that reads somewhat like a historical epic, praising the insurgent heroes and depicting major battles against Batista, the dictator's flight, and the Cuban victory over the American-backed invasion at the Bay of Pigs. As the title suggests, Guillen also explores the new feelings of empowerment, possession, and comradeship that the revolution inspired in many poor Cubans.

The theme of social liberation is present as well in Guillen's 1967 collection, *El gran zoo*. Hailed as one of Guillen's outstanding later works, *El gran zoo* marked a major stylistic shift for a poet usually identified with the Afro-Cuban style. While still showing a crystalline attention to craft, these poems rely less on rhyme and strict meter than Guillen's past work and approach free verse with spare wording and fractured images. The volume is structured thematically as a visit to a metaphorical zoo, where some of the world's curious and beautiful social, natural, and metaphysical phenomena are catalogued in individual poems. Guillen's usually direct language is more allusive and enigmatic here, and his subjects range from critical jabs at imperialism to taut musings on love, the forces of nature, and the ineffable mystery of being.

Both *Tengo* and *El gran zoo*, along with another collection published in 1972, *Man-Making Words: Selected Poems of Nicolas Guillen*, are available in English translation. Guillen's poems have also been translated into many other languages, including French, German, Russian, and Hebrew. Awarded the Cuban Order of Jose Marti, the country's highest honor, in 1981, Guillen has served for many years as president of the National Union of Cuban Writers and Artists.

BIOGRAPHICAL/CRITICAL SOURCES:

BOOKS

Augier, Angel, *Nicolas Guillen: Notas para un estudio biografico-critico* (two volumes), Universidad de las Villas, 1963-64.

Coulthard, R. G., *Race and Colour in Caribbean Literature*, Oxford University Press, 1962.
Ellis, Keith, *Cuba's Nicolas Guillen: Poetry and Ideology*, University of Toronto Press, 1983.
Guillen, Nicolas, *Paginas vueltas: Memorias*, UNEAC, 1982.
Martinez Estrada, Ezequiel, *La Poesia de Nicolas Guillen*, Calicanto Editorial, c. 1977.
Sardinha, Dennis, *The Poetry of Nicolas Guillen: An Introduction*, New Beacon, 1976.

PERIODICALS

Black Scholar, July/August, 1985.
Hispania, October 25, 1942.
Latin America Research Review, Volume 17, number 1, 1982.
Opportunity, January, 1946.*

—*Sketch by Curtis Skinner*

*   *   *

GURR, David 1936-

BRIEF ENTRY: Born February 5, 1936, in London, England. Naval officer, systems analyst, house designer and builder, and author. Since the late 1970s Gurr has written a series of novels that range from spy thriller to political allegory. His first novel, *Troika* (Methuen, 1979), depicts the tensions of the Cold War by focusing on a love triangle comprised of two Russian intelligence agents—one who works for the British, one for the Soviets—and the American woman they both love. His novel *The Ringmaster* (Atheneum, 1987), which was hailed for its literary and intellectual complexity, views the rise of fascism in Germany as the acting-out of a Wagnerian opera.

After graduating from the Canadian Naval College in 1956, Gurr was a career naval officer until 1970, when he retired with the rank of lieutenant. He was a systems analyst at Computing Devices of Canada for the next two years, and then he designed and built houses from 1972 to 1978. Since 1978 Gurr has been a full-time writer. His other novels include *A Woman Called Scylla* (Viking, 1981), *An American Spystory* (McClelland & Stewart, 1984), and *The Action of the Tiger* (Seal Books, 1984). Gurr also wrote the stage play "Leonora" (1982) and worked on two screenplays with director George Cosmatos. *Addresses: Home*—P.O. Box 400, Saanichton, British Columbia, Canada V0S 1M0.

BIOGRAPHICAL/CRITICAL SOURCES:

BOOKS

Who's Who in Canadian Literature, 1985-1986, Reference Press, 1985.

PERIODICALS

Globe and Mail (Toronto), November 14, 1987.
Maclean's, October 29, 1979.
Publishers Weekly, August 20, 1979.

*   *   *

GUSTAFSON, James 1949-
(Jim Gustafson)

PERSONAL: Born November 21, 1949, in Pontiac, Mich.; son of Leslie Clifford (a businessman) and Carolyn (a training instructor; maiden name, Polasek) Gustafson. *Education:* Attended University of Michigan; Wayne State University, B.A., 1971. *Politics:* "Populist/Liberal." *Religion:* Roman Catholic.

ADDRESSES: Home—411 Pleasant, Birmingham, Mich. 48099. *Office*—615 West Lafayette, Detroit, Mich. 48231. *Agent*—Carol Mann, 174 Pacific St., Brooklyn, N.Y. 11201.

CAREER: Wayne State University, Detroit, Mich., director of Miles Modern Poetry Committee and editor of *Wayne Review,* 1970-71; singer and keyboard player for Dynaflow Blues Band, London, England, 1971-73; bartender in Bolinas, Calif., 1974-75; Left Coast Press, San Francisco, Calif., editor, 1977-78; worked for Heinold Commodies, Chicago, Ill., 1980-81; University of California, Irvine, instructor in English, 1982; freelance writer, 1982—. Director of consulting firm Artswing; creative consultant to Access Productions.

MEMBER: Detroit Blues Adventure Society (president).

WRITINGS:

POETRY

(Under name Jim Gustafson) *Tales of Virtue and Transformation,* Big Sky, 1974.
(Under name Jim Gustafson) *Bright Eyes Talks Crazy to Rembrandt,* Hanging Loose, 1975.
(Under name Jim Gustafson) *Shameless,* Tombouctou, 1979.
Virtue and Annilation, Alternative Press, 1987.

UNPUBLISHED NOVELS

The Million Dollar Punk.
Strategies for a New Universe.
Discount City.
No Money in Art.
Alive in the World.

PLAYS

"The Blues Trilogy."
"Leap of Faith Blues."
"The Broke Dick Dog Blues Band."
"Thanks for the Use of the Hall."

SCREENPLAYS

"Snuff Van."
"The Whole Enchillada."
"Astonish Me."
"The Lost Weekend" (adaptation).
"Blood on the Kitchen Floor."

OTHER

Author of video tapes "No Money in Art," for San Francisco State University, and "The Unholy Saga of Jumpcity James," for NRX Productions. Author of weekly column and feature articles in *Detroit News.* Contributor of stories and poems to *Paris Review* and *Transatlantic Review.*

WORK IN PROGRESS: Leave Here Running, a novel; *Maniac Memories,* short stories; *Rage and Rebirth,* poems; *Impulse,* essays on the creative process.

SIDELIGHTS: James Gustafson told *CA:* "I consider the human condition to be vital. The main gist of my work is to try to decipher some of its mysteries. I'm interested in everything—as an all-around information addict—with special interests in the areas of the arts, painting, all genres of writing, music, and dance. I've lived in virtually every major American city, including Detroit, New York, Los Angeles, San Francisco, Albuquerque, Baltimore, New Orleans, Miami, and Chicago, as well as London, Madrid, and Tangiers. I'm fairly adequate in Spanish, French, Swedish, Slovakian, and I can speak a bit of Tagalog."

BIOGRAPHICAL/CRITICAL SOURCES:

PERIODICALS

San Francisco Review of Books, December, 1978.

*   *   *

GUSTAFSON, Jim
   See GUSTAFSON, James

H

HAAS, Charles A. 1947-

PERSONAL: Born July 21, 1947, in St. Albans, N.Y.; son of Charles A. (an electrical engineer) and Beatrice (a homemaker; maiden name, Schmidt) Haas. *Education:* Rider College, B.A., 1969; graduate study at the University of Nebraska at Lincoln, 1970, Wroxton College, 1978, Jersey City State College, 1979, College of New Rochelle, 1980, Montclair State College, 1980, and Monmouth College, 1981.

ADDRESSES: Home—320 Dover-Chester Rd., Randolph, N.J. 07869. *Office*—Randolph High School, Millbrook Ave., Randolph, N.J. 07869.

CAREER: Randolph High School, Randolph, N.J., teacher of English and journalism, 1969—. Historical consultant to National Geographic Society, 1985-88; technical adviser to Sueddeutscher Rundfunk, Stuttgart, West Germany, 1983; coordinator of convention for the Titanic Historical Society, 1982; panel member of the Ocean Liner Museum's *Titanic* Symposium, 1985, historical consultant to Campbell Group in Sydney, Australia, for *Titanic* exhibition opening in 1989.

MEMBER: National Education Association, Steamship Historical Society of America, Titanic Historical Society (member of advisory board, 1977; vice-president, 1979; president, 1980, 1982, and 1985), New Jersey Education Association, Morris County Council of Education Associations, Randolph Education Association.

WRITINGS:

(And compiler) *White Star Calendar for 1982*, Titanic Historical Society, 1981.
(Editor with John P. Eaton) *Romance of the Sea*, National Geographic Society, 1981.
(Editor with John P. Eaton) *Roster of Valor: The "Titanic"-Halifax Legacy*, 7C's Press, 1985.
(With John P. Eaton) *"Titanic": Triumph and Tragedy*, Norton, 1986.
(With John P. Eaton) *"Titanic": Destination Disaster*, Norton, 1987.
(With John P. Eaton) *Falling Star*, Norton, 1988.

Also contributor of several articles to *"Titanic" Commutator*.

SIDELIGHTS: Charles A. Haas told *CA:* "My interest in the *Titanic* began as a teenager when I read Walter Lord's classic account, *A Night to Remember*. Once my interest was piqued, the subject of the *Titanic* and its people became a continuing source of fascination that, for me, has lasted almost three decades. It is a subject which continues to pose challenges and questions needing resolution, despite the passage of more than seventy-five years.

"It is particularly important, I feel, that those engaged in historical research share their findings with as wide an audience as possible. By doing so, public misconceptions and media hype can be dispelled, and the innate drama of an event such as the *Titanic*'s loss can be recognized. The recent plundering of the *Titanic* and her artifacts before historians could explore and catalogue them is a source of great frustration to those who have studied the ship. I hope our books will help to dispel the misinformation presented to the public as fact. Like my co-author John P. Eaton, I particularly enjoy finding and sharing what we call 'nuggets,' hitherto unknown details that flesh out the story in all its varied dimensions.

"As a teacher of journalism and English, I like to relate my experiences as an author to my students. They can see that their instructor practices what he teaches and can observe the tangible results of in-depth research; motivating them becomes a simpler task. What has, until now, been my avocation thus has become an important and useful tool in my profession."

BIOGRAPHICAL/CRITICAL SOURCES:

PERIODICALS

New York Times, May 30, 1987.

*   *   *

HACKER, Jeffrey H. 1954-

PERSONAL: Born June 5, 1954, in Newark, N.J.; son of Jack C. (a community development construction manager) and Charlotte (a cosmetician; maiden name, Strasser) Hacker. *Education:* Yale University, B.A., 1976; attended University of Connecticut, 1976-77; Fairfield University, M.A., 1981.

ADDRESSES: Home and office—114 Old Bridge Lane, Danbury, Conn. 06811.

CAREER: Institute of Living, Hartford, Conn., editor, 1976-78; Grolier, Inc., Danbury, Conn., editor, 1978-83; free-lance writer and editor, 1983—.

WRITINGS:

Government Subsidy to Industry (juvenile), F. Watts, 1982.
(Editor and contributor) *Markets in Flux: Box Office, Broadcast, and New Electronic Media; Trends and Forecasts, 1983-1987,* Knowledge Industry Publications, 1983.
Franklin D. Roosevelt (juvenile), F. Watts, 1983.
Carl Sandburg (juvenile), F. Watts, 1984.
Consumer Magazines: Industry and Market Trends, 1985-1988, Knowledge Industry Publications, 1985.
Publishing Books for Consumers: Market Trends and Forecasts, 1985-1988, Knowledge Industry Publications, 1985.
The New China (juvenile), F. Watts, 1986.

Contributing editor of *Americana Annual,* Grolier, 1979-87. Contributor to *New Book of Knowledge Annual.* Contributing editor of *Digest of Neurology and Psychiatry,* 1976-78.

SIDELIGHTS: Jeffrey H. Hacker told *CA:* "The hard, solitary, pressured work of a free-lance writer and the curious inverse relationship between creative challenge and financial remuneration are far outweighed (usually) by the opportunity to delve into diverse fields of interest; by the chance to test one's skills in various media for varied audiences; by having ultimate responsibility for the success or failure of every assignment; and, most of all, by the gratification of communicating facts and ideas—the sheer act of putting words on paper and getting them right. I have been personally enriched and professionally motivated by associations with a handful of editors and publishers who have given much and, thankfully, expected much."

* * *

HAESSLER, Herbert A(lfred)   1926-

PERSONAL: Born March 20, 1926, in Milwaukee, Wis.; son of Ferdinand Herbert and Bertha (Torchiani) Haessler; married Diane Emley Fiske, August 15, 1959; children: Ingrid, Eric, Karen, Sarah. *Education:* University of Wisconsin—Madison, B.S., 1950; graduate study at Columbia University, 1952; Marquette University, M.D., 1957.

ADDRESSES: Home—Stonehenge Rd., Lincoln, Mass. 01773. *Office*—Morton Hospital, 88 Washington St., Taunton, Mass. 02780.

CAREER: New England Medical Center, Boston, Mass., intern, 1957-58; Massachusetts General Hospital, Boston, resident in pediatrics, 1958-60, research fellow, 1960-62; Science and Engineering Inc., Waltham, Mass., senior member of staff, 1963-67, director of research, 1968; Searle Medidata, Inc., Lexington, Mass., medical director, 1968, vice-president, 1969-75; Shriver Center, Waltham, project director, 1975-81; Morton Hospital, Taunton, Mass., director of emergency medicine, 1981—. Harvard Medical School, instructor, 1962-68, assistant clinical professor of pediatrics, 1969—. *Military service:* U.S. Marine Corps Reserve, active duty, 1944-46.

MEMBER: International Health Evaluation Association, Society for Pediatric Research, Society for Advanced Medical Systems (director, 1971—), Association for the Advancement of Medical Instrumentation, Alpha Omega Alpha.

WRITINGS:

(With Raymond Harris) *Bodyworkbook,* Avon, 1981.
(With Christine Harris and Raymond Harris) *How to Make Sure Your Baby Is Well and Stays That Way: The First Guide to Over Four Hundred Medical Tests and Treat-*

ments You Can Do at Home to Check Your Baby's Daily Health and Growth, Rawson Associates, 1984.

Contributor to medical journals.

* * *

HAGUE, (Susan) Kathleen   1949-

PERSONAL: Born March 6, 1949, in Ventura, Calif.; daughter of John W. (an engineer and technical writer) and Sue (a landscaper; maiden name, Waggoner) Burdick; married Michael Hague (an author and illustrator), December 5, 1970; children: Meghan, Brittany Devon. *Education:* Art Center College of Design, B.F.A. (with honors), 1971.

ADDRESSES: Home—Colorado Springs, Colo.

CAREER: Artist. Author of children's books, 1979—.

AWARDS, HONORS: The Man Who Kept House was named one of International Reading Association's Children's Choices, 1982; *The Legend of the Veery Bird* was selected one of Child Study Association of America's Children's Books of the Year, and was exhibited at Bologna International Children's Book Fair, both 1985.

WRITINGS:

CHILDREN'S BOOKS

(With husband, Michael Hague) *East of the Sun and West of the Moon,* Harcourt, 1980.
(With M. Hague) *The Man Who Kept House,* Harcourt, 1981.
Alphabears: An ABC Book, Holt, 1984.
The Legend of the Veery Bird, Harcourt, 1985.
Numbears: A Counting Book, Holt, 1986.
Out of the Nursery, Into the Night, Holt, 1986.

AVOCATIONAL INTERESTS: Photography.*

* * *

**HALE, Jade
    See HYATT, Betty H(ale)**

* * *

HALE, William   1940-

PERSONAL: Born November 17, 1940, in Reading, England; son of Matthew Blagden and Suzanne Mary (Wilson) Hale; married Kathleen O'Donoghue, 1966; children: Sabina, Julia. *Education:* Oxford University, B.A., 1962, M.A., 1963; Australian National University, Ph.D., 1966.

ADDRESSES: Home—6 Albert St., Durham DH1 4RL, England. *Office*—Department of Politics, University of Durham, Durham, England.

CAREER: Foreign and Commonwealth Office, London, England, research assistant, 1966-67; member of staff of University of Durham, Durham, England.

MEMBER: British Society for Middle Eastern Studies.

WRITINGS:

(Editor and contributor) *Aspects of Modern Turkey,* Bowker, 1976.
The Political and Economic Development of Modern Turkey, St. Martin's, 1981.

(Editor with Ali Ihsan Bagis, and contributor) *Four Centuries of Turco-British Relations,* Eothen Press, 1984.

Also author of *Politics and the Military in Turkey,* Croom Helm.

SIDELIGHTS: William Hale's book, *The Political and Economic Development of Modern Turkey,* was welcomed by *Times Literary Supplement* critic C. H. Dodd, who wrote: "It is both unusual and refreshing to find a book on economic history ending by expressing the view that the most serious economic problem is at heart political." Hale provides an outline of Turkey's economic development from 1923, when most developing nations had not even considered economic planning, to 1960. His treatment of the years since 1960 is much more comprehensive. The author analyzes Turkey's economic problems in a fashion that his reviewer considered thorough, yet readable, and, Dodd wrote, the book "has the added merit of examining Turkey's economic history against the background of the author's extensive knowledge of Turkish politics."

BIOGRAPHICAL/CRITICAL SOURCES:

PERIODICALS

Times Literary Supplement, January 8, 1982.

*   *   *

HALL, David D(risko)   1936-

PERSONAL: Born July 8, 1936, in Washington, D.C.; married, 1960; children: three. *Education:* Harvard University, B.A., 1958; Yale University, Ph.D., 1964.

ADDRESSES: Office—Department of History, Boston University, 226 Bay State Rd., Boston, Mass. 02215.

CAREER: Yale University, New Haven, Conn., began as instructor, became associate professor of history and American studies, 1962-70; Boston University, Boston, Mass., associate professor, 1970-73, professor of history, 1973—. Research fellow at Charles Warren Center, 1973-74.

MEMBER: American Studies Association.

AWARDS, HONORS: Fellow of National Endowment for the Humanities, 1977-78.

WRITINGS:

(Editor and author of introduction and notes) *The Antinomian Controversy, 1636-1638: A Documentary History,* Wesleyan University Press, 1968.
(Editor) *Puritanism in Seventeenth-Century Massachusetts,* Holt, 1968.
The Faithful Shepherd: A History of the New England Ministry in the Seventeenth Century, University of North Carolina Press, 1972.
(With William L. Joyce) *Printing and Society in Early America,* American Antiquarian Society, 1983.
(Editor with David Grayson Allen) *Seventeenth-Century New England,* Colonial Society of Massachusetts, 1984.
(Editor with John M. Murrin and Thad W. Tate, and contributor) *Saints and Revolutionaries: Essays on Early American History,* Norton, 1984.
On Native Ground: From the History of Printing to the History of the Book, American Antiquarian Society, 1984.
(Editor with John B. Hench) *Needs and Opportunities in the History of the Book: America, 1639-1876,* American Antiquarian Society, 1987.

Contributor to *The State of American History* and to periodicals.

BIOGRAPHICAL/CRITICAL SOURCES:

PERIODICALS

American Historical Review, February, 1969, October, 1973.
History, October, 1985.
Journal of American History, June, 1986.
New England Quarterly, December, 1985.
Times Literary Supplement, June 14, 1985.
Virginia Quarterly Review, February, 1969, October, 1973.*

*   *   *

HAMBRICK-STOWE, Charles E(dwin)   1948-

PERSONAL: Born February 4, 1948, in Worcester, Mass.; son of Edwin G. (a minister) and Florence (a housewife; maiden name, Millington) Hambrick; married Elizabeth Anne Stowe (an attorney and minister), September 11, 1972; children: Anne P., Thomas W., Charles G. *Education:* Hamilton College, B.A., 1970; Pacific School of Religion, M.A., 1973, M.Div., 1973; Boston University, Ph.D., 1981. *Politics:* Democrat.

ADDRESSES: Home—1101 Davis Dr., Lancaster, Pa. 17603. *Office*—Church of the Apostles, 1850 Marietta Ave., Lancaster, Pa. 17603.

CAREER: Ordained minister of United Church of Christ, 1973; pastor of United Church of Christ in Westminster, Md., 1979-85; Church of the Apostles, Lancaster, Pa., minister of worship and stewardship, 1985—. Adjunct associate professor at Lancaster Theological Seminary, 1985—; member of Central Atlantic and Penn Central Conferences of the United Church of Christ.

MEMBER: American Society of Church History, American Historical Association, American Academy of Religion.

AWARDS, HONORS: Jamestown Manuscript Prize from Institute of Early American History and Culture, 1980, for *The Practice of Piety.*

WRITINGS:

The Practice of Piety: Puritan Devotional Disciplines in Seventeenth-Century New England, University of North Carolina Press, 1982.
Early New England Meditative Poetry: Anne Bradstreet and Edward Taylor, Paulist Press, 1988.
(Editor) *One Spirit, Many Visions: Theological Movements in the United Church of Christ,* Pilgrim Press (New York, N.Y.), 1988.

Contributor to historical and religious journals.

WORK IN PROGRESS: Research on seventeenth-century popular religion, Puritan spiritual practices, and early modern church history.

SIDELIGHTS: Charles E. Hambrick-Stowe told *CA:* "I have been drawn to the seventeenth century since college. This is a special age for America—our link with the medieval world. While the worldview of colonial New Englanders is in so many ways different from our own, I am impressed with the depth and vitality of their religious experience. Because of a certain universal quality in their spiritual quest, modern society may learn much from their example. Puritanism, of course, was also a foundational culture in the emergence of the American people. My interests do not only lie in learning from the past;

as an active pastor and scholar in the contemporary church, I seek to interpret spiritual and theological renewal today. This renewal includes liturgical developments, liberation and feminist theology, and a new emphasis on confessionalism and the nature of the church.''

*   *   *

HAMILTON, (Charles) Denis   1918-1988

OBITUARY NOTICE—See index for *CA* sketch: Born December 6, 1918, in South Shields, England; died after a long illness, April 7, 1988, in London, England. News executive, journalist, editor, and author. Hamilton, editor in chief of Times Newspapers from 1967 to 1981 and chairman of Reuters news agency from 1979 to 1985, was a leading figure in the British newspaper industry. Among other innovations, he was credited with introducing to British journalism the color magazine supplement, now a feature of weekly newspapers throughout England. He was also the first president of the International Press Institute, an organization of some two hundred editors and publishers, and the recipient of knighthood in 1976. His writings include *Who Is to Own the British Press?* and *Kemsley Manual of Journalism.*

OBITUARIES AND OTHER SOURCES:

BOOKS

Who's Who, 140th edition, St. Martin's, 1988.

PERIODICALS

Los Angeles Times, April 8, 1988.
New York Times, April 8, 1988.
Times (London), April 8, 1988.
Washington Post, April 9, 1988.

*   *   *

HAMILTON, Hamish   1900-1988

OBITUARY NOTICE: Given name originally James; name legally changed; born November 15, 1900, in Indianapolis, Ind.; died after a long illness, May 24, 1988, in London, England. Diplomat, publisher, editor, and author. Hamilton founded the London publishing house Hamish Hamilton Limited, which became known for its list of famous British, American, and European authors, including James Thurber, J. D. Salinger, Raymond Chandler, E. B. White, Jean-Paul Sartre, John Kenneth Galbraith, Truman Capote, and John F. Kennedy. Hamilton began his career in London as an apprentice with the Jonathan Cape publishing firm and served as manager of the London office of New York publisher Harper & Brothers beginning in 1926. In 1931 he founded his own firm, serving as chairman even after the company's 1965 sale to Thomson Publications Limited. Hamish Hamilton Limited was acquired by the Viking-Penguin publishing house in 1985, four years after Hamilton's resignation. Hamilton edited anthologies such as *Decade* and *Majority* and contributed articles on publication to periodicals. He was also a qualified lawyer, although he never practiced, and at one time served as an honorary attache in the British embassy in Washington.

OBITUARIES AND OTHER SOURCES:

BOOKS

The International Who's Who, 51st edition, Europa, 1987.
Who's Who, 140th edition, St. Martin's, 1988.

PERIODICALS

Chicago Tribune, May 28, 1988.
Los Angeles Times, May 27, 1988.
New York Times, May 28, 1988.
Publishers Weekly, June 10, 1988.
Times (London), May 26, 1988.
Washington Post, May 27, 1988.

*   *   *

HAMM, Glenn B(ruce)   1936-1980

OBITUARY NOTICE—See index for *CA* sketch: Born May 30, 1936, in Dayton, Ohio; died in 1980. Artist, educator, and author. During his more than twenty years as a teacher of arts and crafts Hamm shared his expertise with students of all ages. He also served as a juror in art shows and a participant in workshops and art exhibits in Virginia and Pennsylvania. His work is represented in private collections throughout the United States. Hamm was the author of *Painting the Nude* and a contributor of articles and reviews to *Leonardo: International Journal of the Contemporary Artist.*

OBITUARIES AND OTHER SOURCES:

Date of death provided by wife, Monica M. Hamm.

BOOKS

International Authors and Writers Who's Who, 8th edition, Melrose, 1977.

*   *   *

HAN, Henry H.   1932-

PERSONAL: Born August 3, 1932, in Korea (now North Korea); children: Daniel H., Erica H., Rebecca H. *Education:* California State University, Sacramento, B.A., 1957, M.S., 1958; Columbia University, Ph.D., 1967. *Religion:* Episcopal.

ADDRESSES: Home—P.O. Box 461, Mount Pleasant, Mich. 48858. *Office*—Central Michigan University, Mount Pleasant, Mich. 48859.

CAREER: Hospital for Special Surgery, New York, N.Y., administrative analyst, 1961-64; Central Michigan University, Mount Pleasant, professor of international law and relations, 1965—. Director of Conferences on United Nations Affairs, sponsored jointly by Central Michigan University and American Society of International Law, 1967—.

MEMBER: International Studies Association, American Society of International Law, U.S. Air Force Association, National Geographic Society, Aircraft Owners and Pilots Association.

AWARDS, HONORS: Commendations for leadership in international education from President Jimmy Carter, the U.S. Department of State, and Michigan Council on International Education.

WRITINGS:

International Legislation by the United Nations: Legal Provisions, Practice, and Prospects, Exposition, 1971.
Human Rights, Development, and World Order, University Press of America, 1979.
Terrorism, Political Violence, and World Order, University Press of America, 1984.

Problems and Prospects of the Organization of American States: Perceptions of the Member States' Leaders, Peter Lang, 1986.

Contributor to scholarly journals.

WORK IN PROGRESS: International Relations: An Analytical Framework.

*   *   *

HANIGAN, James Patrick   1938-

PERSONAL: Born April 16, 1938, in New York, N.Y.; son of Francis F. (a safety warden) and Loretta A. (a teacher; maiden name, O'Raw) Hanigan; married Elizabeth Coulbourn (a church worker), June 5, 1976. *Education:* Fordham University, A.B., 1961, M.A., 1965; Woodstock College, M.Div., 1968; Duke University, Ph.D., 1973.

ADDRESSES: Home—1146 North Negley Ave., Pittsburgh, Pa. 15206. *Office*—Department of Theology, Duquesne University, Pittsburgh, Pa. 15282.

CAREER: LeMoyne College, Syracuse, N.Y., assistant professor of philosophy, 1971-72; Marquette University, Milwaukee, Wis., assistant professor of theology, 1973-75; Villa Marie College, Erie, Pa., assistant professor of religion and philosophy, 1975-79; Duquesne University, Pittsburgh, Pa., assistant professor, 1979-82, associate professor, 1982-87, professor of theology, 1987—.

MEMBER: Catholic Theological Society of America, American Academy of Religion, Society of Christian Ethics, College Theology Society.

WRITINGS:

What Are They Saying About Sexual Morality? Paulist/Newman, 1982.
Martin Luther King, Jr.: The Foundations of Nonviolence, University Press of America, 1984.
As I Have Loved You: The Challenge of Christian Ethics, Paulist Press, 1986.
Homosexuality: The Test Case for Christian Sexual Ethics, Paulist Press, 1988.

Contributor to theology and philosophy journals.

WORK IN PROGRESS: The Meaning and the Extent of Social Responsibility, publication by Paulist Press expected in 1990; *The Ethical Issues of Life and Death,* publication by Paulist Press expected in 1991.

SIDELIGHTS: James Patrick Hanigan told *CA:* "Human freedom and the human capacity for both responsibility and self-deception remain constant sources of wonder, hope, and pain. Faith in a loving God motivates me to try to understand human possibilities for constructing a liveable and compassionate social order.

"I began writing about sexual morality almost by chance. I was teaching courses on the subject, and, when Paulist Press was looking for a book on the subject to fit their 'What Are They Saying About?' series, I decided to give it a try. My major interest and concern remains the social dimension of human existence, but it grows increasingly clear that American culture has privatized the meaning of human sexuality to the point where we have become almost oblivious to the social consequences of what we do sexually. It is remotely possible that the AIDS (Acquired Immune Deficiency Syndrome) crisis will change this, but I doubt it.

"Consequently, all my research and writing is attentive to the social dimension of human life, and that is why I want to do a more systematic, theoretical explanation of the nature and extent of human social responsibility. Whatever social responsibility means and however far it extends, it is something other than the false and corrosive notion of collective guilt, and it is a direct refutation of the Ayn Rand version of objective egoism, which is culturally more prevalent than it is healthy."

*   *   *

HANSON, Eric O.   1942-

PERSONAL: Born March 5, 1942, in San Francisco, Calif.; son of Donald O. (a businessman) and Jean (a homemaker; maiden name, Francis) Hanson; married Kathleen Hennessy (a professor), June 18, 1972; children: Erin, Kara. *Education:* Gonzaga University, B.A., 1966, M.A., 1967; Stanford University, M.A., 1972, Ph.D., 1976. *Politics:* Democrat. *Religion:* Roman Catholic.

ADDRESSES: Office—Department of Political Science, University of Santa Clara, Santa Clara, Calif. 95053.

CAREER: University of Santa Clara, Santa Clara, Calif., assistant professor, 1976-82, associate professor of political science, 1982—. Member of Stanford University's Center for International Security and Arms Control.

AWARDS, HONORS: Award from Chicago Institute of Theology and Culture, 1980, for *Catholic Politics in China and Korea.*

WRITINGS:

Catholic Politics in China and Korea, Orbis, 1980.
The Catholic Church in World Politics, Princeton University Press, 1987.

WORK IN PROGRESS: The Internationalization of East Asia: Church, Corporation, and State Security Policy.

SIDELIGHTS: Eric O. Hanson "demonstrated great competence" in his first book, *Catholic Politics in China and Korea,* where he "traced the interplay among historical, organizational and ideological factors in response to the changeable demands of political flux," asserted Michael Czerny in the Toronto *Globe and Mail.* Czerny explained that in his "scholarly" second book, *The Catholic Church in World Politics,* Hanson "tries to account for the role of the Catholic Church in national and international politics," a topic the reviewer described as "fascinating."

Hanson told *CA:* "It is no accident that historically the worst political years for the Catholic Church coincided with the heyday of the sovereign nation state in the West. As the nineteenth-century international system dissolved into the chaos of two world wars, the Vatican again began to exercise influence in global affairs."

BIOGRAPHICAL/CRITICAL SOURCES:

PERIODICALS

Globe and Mail (Toronto), July 25, 1987.
New York Times Book Review, June 7, 1987.

*   *   *

HARDING, Neil   1942-

PERSONAL: Born March 14, 1942, in Pontypridd, Wales;

married Deanna Elizabeth Wilkey (a physiotherapist); children: Alexander, Gareth, Daniel, Benjamin, Thomas. *Education:* University of Wales, University College, Swansea, B.A. (with honors), 1963; London School of Economics and Political Science, London, M.Sc., 1965.

ADDRESSES: Home—2 Overland Rd., Mumbles, Swansea SA3 4LS, Wales. *Office*—Department of Politics, University College, University of Wales, Swansea, Wales.

CAREER: University of Wales, University College, Swansea, reader in politics, 1963—.

AWARDS, HONORS: Isaac Deutscher Memorial Prize, 1981-82, for *Lenin's Political Thought.*

WRITINGS:

Lenin's Political Thought, Macmillan, Volume I, 1977, Volume II, 1981.
(Editor) *Marxism in Russia: Key Documents, 1879-1906,* Cambridge University Press, 1983.
(Editor) *The State in Socialist Society,* State University of New York Press, 1983.

Scriptwriter for British Broadcasting Corporation Overseas Service. Contributor to political studies journals.

WORK IN PROGRESS: Theory of the Soviet State; The Soviet Political Tradition.

SIDELIGHTS: Neil Harding told *CA:* "I am something of a francophile with Celtic roots. I am fairly proficient in French and Russian; in English I cultivate the arcane. I've been influenced by the Beatles, Rolling Stones, and Status Quo rock groups and in other directions by Rees, Mill, Marx, Fourier, and guild socialism. I have no heroes, but poet-artist William Morris comes close."

AVOCATIONAL INTERESTS: Rugby, tending his vineyard, theater, and restoring a large, old house.

*   *   *

HAREWOOD, George Henry Hubert Lascelles 1923-

PERSONAL: Surname is pronounced "*Har*-wood"; born February 7, 1923, in London, England; son of Henry George Charles (6th Earl of Harewood) and Princess Mary (Victoria Alexandra Alice Mary) Lascelles; married Maria Donata, 1949 (divorced, 1967); married Patricia Elizabeth Tuckwell, 1967; children: (first marriage) David Henry George (Viscount Lascelles), James Edward, Jeremy Hugh; (second marriage) Mark Hubert, one stepson. *Education:* Received M.A. from King's College, Cambridge.

ADDRESSES: Home—Harewood House, Leeds LS17 9LG, England; and 22 Bloomfield Rd., London W9 1AD, England.

CAREER: Succeeded his father as 7th Earl of Harewood, 1947; president of British Board of Film Classification, 1985-86. British Broadcasting Corp., member of general advisory council, 1969-77, governor, 1985-87; artistic director of 1988 Adelaide Festival, 1986—; affiliated with English National Opera as managing director, 1972-85, and as chairman, 1986—; member of Arts Council of Great Britain, 1966-72. *Military service:* British Army, Grenadier Guards, 1939-45, prisoner of war, 1944-45; became captain.

MEMBER: English Football Association (president, 1963-72), Leeds United Football Club.

AWARDS, HONORS: Austrian Great Silver Medal of Honour, 1959; LL.D. from University of Leeds, 1959, and University of Aberdeen, 1966; D.Mus. from University of Hull, 1962; Lebanese Order of the Cedar, 1970; Janacek Medal, 1978; D.Univ. from University of York, 1982; Knight Commander of Order of the British Empire, 1986.

WRITINGS:

(Editor) *Kobbe's Complete Opera Book,* Bodley Head, 1953, third edition, 1987.
The Tongs and the Bones, Weidenfeld & Nicolson, 1981.

*   *   *

HARNACK, William J. 1953-

PERSONAL: Born February 21, 1953, in Milwaukee, Wis. *Education:* State University of New York at Buffalo, B.A. (cum laude), 1975.

ADDRESSES: Home—124 Highland Ave., Buffalo, N.Y. 14222. *Office*—*Humanist,* 7 Harwood Dr., Amherst, N.Y. 14226.

CAREER: American Humanist Association, Amherst, N.Y., copy editor and assistant editor of *Humanist,* 1980—. Assistant copy editor of *Moody Street Irregulars: A Jack Kerouac Newsletter,* 1980—.

MEMBER: Sigma Delta Chi.

WRITINGS:

Links of the Chain (stories), Textile Bridge Press, 1983.

Contributor of articles and reviews to magazines, including *Pierian Spring* and *Country Rambler,* and newspapers.

BIOGRAPHICAL/CRITICAL SOURCES:

PERIODICALS

Milwaukee Journal, June 12, 1983.

*   *   *

HARPER, F. E. W.
See HARPER, Frances Ellen Watkins

*   *   *

HARPER, Frances E. W.
See HARPER, Frances Ellen Watkins

*   *   *

HARPER, Frances E. Watkins
See HARPER, Frances Ellen Watkins

*   *   *

HARPER, Frances Ellen
See HARPER, Frances Ellen Watkins

HARPER, Frances Ellen Watkins   1825-1911
(F. E. W. Harper, Frances Ellen Harper, Frances E. W. Harper, Frances E. Watkins Harper, Mrs. F. E. W. Harper, Frances Ellen Watkins; Effie Afton, a pseudonym)

PERSONAL: Born September 24, 1825, in Baltimore, Md.; died of heart failure, February 22, 1911, in Philadelphia, Pa.; buried at Eden Cemetery in Philadelphia; married Fenton Harper (a farmer), November 22, 1860 (died, May, 1864); children: Mary. *Education:* Educated in Baltimore, Md., and in Pennsylvania and Ohio. *Religion:* Unitarian.

CAREER: Writer, social reformer, and public lecturer. Worked as a nursemaid and domestic; Union Seminary, Columbus, Ohio, sewing teacher, 1850-52; elementary school teacher in Little York, Pa., 1852-53; Underground Railroad worker in Little York, 1853-54; lecturer for Maine Anti-Slavery Society, 1854-56, and other organizations, 1856-60, and reader of antislavery verse; lecturer and poetry reader advocating freedmen's rights, Christian temperance, and women's suffrage, 1864-1911. Organizer and assistant superintendent of Young Men's Christian Association (YMCA) Sabbath School, 1872; director of American Association of Education of Colored Youth, 1894. Associated with American Woman Suffrage Association conventions, 1875 and 1887; speaker at International Council of Women in Washington, 1888, National Council of Women, 1891, and World Congress of Representative Women at Columbian Exposition in Chicago, 1893.

MEMBER: National Council of Women in the United States, National Association of Colored Women (founding member, 1886; vice-president, 1897), National Women's Christian Temperance Union (executive committee member; superintendent of Philadelphia and Pennsylvania chapters of Colored Branch, 1875-82; head of northern U.S. division, 1883-93), American Equal Rights Association.

WRITINGS:

(Under name Frances Ellen Watkins) *Forest Leaves* (also referred to as *Autumn Leaves;* poems and prose), privately printed (Baltimore, Md.), c. 1845.

(Under name Frances Ellen Watkins) *Poems on Miscellaneous Subjects* (poems and essays), preface by William Lloyd Garrison, J. B. Yerrinton & Son (Boston, Mass.), 1854, reprinted, Kraus, 1971, enlarged edition, [Philadelphia, Pa.], 1855, 2nd enlarged edition, Merrihew & Thompson (Philadelphia), 1857, reprinted with new introduction by Maxwell Whiteman, Rhistoric Publications, 1969, 20th edition, enlarged, Merrihew & Son (Philadelphia), 1871.

(Under pseudonym Effie Afton) *Eventide* (poems and tales), Ferridge & Co. (Boston), 1854.

(Under name Mrs. F. E. W. Harper) *Moses: A Story of the Nile* (poems and essay), 2nd edition, Merrihew, 1869, 3rd edition, 1870, enlarged edition, privately printed (Philadelphia), 1889.

(Under name Frances E. Watkins Harper) *Poems,* Merrihew & Son, 1871, reprinted, AMS Press, 1975.

(Under name Frances E. Watkins Harper) *Sketches of Southern Life* (poems), George S. Ferguson (Philadelphia), 1891.

(Under name Frances E. W. Harper) *Iola Leroy; or, Shadows Uplifted* (novel), Garrigues Bros. (Philadelphia), 1892, 2nd edition, with introduction by William Still, James H. Earle, 1893, McGrath, 1969, AMS Press, 1971.

(Under name Frances Ellen Harper) *Atlanta Offering: Poems* (contains *The Sparrow's Fall and Other Poems* and *The

Martyr of Alabama and Other Poems), George S. Ferguson, 1895, reprinted, Mnemosyne, 1969.

(Under name Frances E. Watkins Harper) *Poems,* George S. Ferguson, 1895, Books for Libraries, 1970, enlarged edition, privately printed (Philadelphia), 1898, 2nd enlarged edition, privately printed (Philadelphia), 1900.

(Under name F. E. W. Harper) *Idylls of the Bible* (contains *Moses*), privately printed (Philadelphia), 1901, reprinted, AMS Press, 1975.

(Annotator) John Bartram, *Diary of a Journey Through the Carolina, Georgia, and Florida, July 1, 1775—April 10, 1776,* Philosophical Society (Philadelphia), 1942.

The Poems of Frances E. W. Harper, Books for Libraries, 1970.

Also author of poem collections *The Sparrow's Fall and Other Poems,* c. 1890, *The Martyr of Alabama and Other Poems,* c. 1894, and *Light Beyond Darkness,* Donohue & Henneberry (Chicago, Ill.). Poems and essays represented in anthologies and sociological/historical studies, including *The Black Man: His Antecedents, His Genius, and His Achievements,* edited by William Wells Brown, Hamilton/Wallcut, 1863; *The Negro Caravan,* edited by Sterling A. Brown, Arthur Davis, and Ulysses Lee, Dryden, 1941; *In Their Own Words: A History of the American Negro, 1619-1865,* edited by Milton Meltzer, Crowell, 1964; and *Kaleidoscope: Poems by American Negro Poets,* edited by Robert Hayden, Harcourt, 1967. Contributor to periodicals, including *African Methodist Episcopal Church Review, Anglo-African Magazine, Crisis, Englishwoman's Review, Frederick Douglass's Paper, Liberator,* and *National Anti-Slavery Standard.*

SIDELIGHTS: Afro-American Frances Ellen Watkins Harper captivated black and white audiences alike with dramatic recitations of her antislavery and social reform verse. Conventional lyric poetry with familiar themes and imagery, Harper's verse gained much—according to a contemporary, Phebe A. Hanaford in her *Daughters of America; or, Women of the Century*—from the orator/poet's "clear, plaintive, melodious voice" and "the flow of her musical speech." A social lecturer whose long life was devoted to abolition, freedmen's rights, Christian temperance, and women's suffrage, Harper used prose and poetry to enhance her message and stir audience emotions. "Mrs. Harper's verse is frankly propagandist, a metrical extension of her life dedicated to the welfare of others," Joan R. Sherman decided in *Invisible Poets: Afro-Americans of the Nineteenth Century.* "She believed in art for humanity's sake."

Born of free parents in the slave state of Maryland, Harper was raised by an aunt and uncle after her parents' early deaths and educated at her uncle's school for free blacks. Her first job at thirteen was caring for the children of a bookseller; there she began writing, composing poems, and reading the popular literature of the period. Intent on living in a free state, Harper moved to Ohio, where she worked as a teacher. A subsequent move to Little York, Pennsylvania, acquainted her with the workings of the Underground Railroad and she decided to become actively involved in the antislavery movement. Her first abolitionist speech was a marked success; preaching social and political reform and moral betterment, Harper spent the next several years lecturing for antislavery societies throughout the North and included readings from her *Poems on Miscellaneous Subjects.* The poet's most popular book, the collection sold several thousand copies and saw at least twenty editions. Containing her most-acclaimed abolitionist poem, "Bury Me in a Free Land," it firmly established Harper's literary reputation.

Thought to resemble the poetry of Henry Wadsworth Longfellow, John Greenleaf Whittier, and Felicia Dorothea Hemans, Harper's largely narrative verse uses rhymed tetrameter and the ballad stanza, both "well suited to some of her material" and creating "an excellent elocutionary pattern," commented J. Saunders Redding in *To Make a Poet Black*. Emotionally charged and frequently didactic (with authorial intrusions), the poems mirrored the conventions of the day and were tailored to Harper's social intent and to audience expectations. Varying little in form, language, or technique, the verse is simple, direct, and lyrical. Writing in *Drumvoices: The Mission of Afro-American Poetry*, Eugene B. Redmond observed: "Up until the Civil War, Mrs. Harper's favorite themes were slavery, its harshness, and the hypocrisies of America. She is careful to place graphic details where they will get the greatest result, especially when the poems are read aloud." He continued: "Critics generally agree that Mrs. Harper's poetry is not original or brilliant. But she is exciting and comes through with powerful flashes of imagery and statement."

Married to a farmer when she was thirty-five, Harper retired from public life and bore a child but soon returned to lecturing when she was widowed. Following the Civil War she traveled south for the first time and was appalled by the unfair treatment of freed blacks; she saw flagrant voting rights violations, meager educational opportunities, and overt physical abuse. Particularly stirred by the plight of black women—whose subjugation had not only continued, but had grown worse with emancipation—the poet determined that "a free people could be a moral people only when the women were respected," according to Larsen Scruggs, quoted in an article in *Black American Literature Forum*, and Harper appealed to sisters of all colors to work towards social equality. For the remaining decades of her life, Harper spoke and wrote for social and reform organizations that supported her ideals of racial justice, women's rights, and Christian humanism; her notable posts included director of the American Association of Education of Colored Youth, executive member of the National Women's Christian Temperance Union, and founding member and vice-president of the National Association of Colored Women.

Redding maintained that by addressing a spectrum of social ills in her writings Harper broke free of the "willful (and perhaps necessary) monopticism" that had confined other black authors. "If our talents are to be recognized we must write less of issues that are particular and more of feelings that are general," the poet once acknowledged to an editor acquaintance, Redding related. "We are blessed with hearts and brains that compass more than ourselves in our present plight." Sherman, too, saw Harper as an innovator who combined race issues with national and universal concerns, inspiring succeeding black writers. Like the majority of critics, Sherman also proclaimed Harper's post-Civil War verse "more objective and intellectual" and informed with a strong optimism.

The poet breaks with conventional meter and sentiment, creating a correspondence between subject and technique, in *Moses: A Story of the Nile*, considered her best work. This volume is an extended blank-verse biblical allegory without overt racial references; recounting the life of the Hebrew patriarch and focusing on his leadership and self-sacrifice, Harper urges similar leadership and sacrifice among blacks. "The poem's elevated diction, concrete imagery, and formal meter harmoniously blend to magnify the noble adventure of Moses' life and the mysterious grandeur of his death," related Sherman, discussing the work's artistic merits. "Mrs. Harper maintains the pace of her long narrative and its tone of reverent admiration

with scarcely a pause for moralizing. *Moses* is Mrs. Harper's most original poem and one of considerable power."

Referring to a second critically praised Harper work, Sherman added that the poet "shows a similar talent for matching technique and subject in the charming series of poems which make up most of *Sketches of Southern Life*." Narrated by politically aware ex-slaves Aunt Chloe and Uncle Jacob, the poems provide a commentary on the concerns of southern blacks: family, education, religion, slavery, and Reconstruction. Admired for their wit and irony, the narratives are written in Afro-American vernacular speech—"a new idiom in black poetry," Sherman elaborated, "which ripens into the dialect verse of [James Edwin] Campbell, [Daniel Webster] Davis, and [Paul Laurence] Dunbar in the last decades of the century." "Serious issues sketched with a light touch are rare in Mrs. Harper's work," the critic added, "and it is unfortunate that Aunt Chloe's fresh and lively observations were not enlarged."

A writer of prose as well as poetry, Harper produced essays, articles, short stories, and a novel. "Her prose is frankly propagandic," remarked Redding, joining the consensus that the writer's prose is "less commendable" than her poetry. Harper's reform essays and articles appeared frequently in journals and periodicals, however, and her short story "The Two Offers" was the first to be published by a black American. In addition, her novel *Iola Leroy; or, Shadows Uplifted* pleased contemporary readers and critics, although current assessments consider it a contrived and sentimental piece unable to transcend the conventions of its age. The story of light-skinned Negroes who reject "passing" as whites in order to work and live among their people, *Iola Leroy* expresses its author's belief that sacrifice is essential to black progress. Considered a transitional novel because it treats both antebellum and postbellum periods, the story is particularly significant for featuring educated, socially committed black characters. Redding concluded that "as a writer of prose [Harper] is to be remembered rather for what she attempted than for what she accomplished."

A figure of more historic than artistic importance, Harper has sparked renewed interest among latter twentieth-century scholars. Described variously as an early feminist, one of the first Afro-American protest poets, and—in the words of *Black American Literature Forum* writer Patricia Liggins Hill—"a major healer and race-builder of nineteenth-century America," Harper nonetheless made aesthetic contributions of pioneer significance. In a *Crisis* editorial following the poet's death, W.E.B. Du Bois reflected: "It is, however, for her attempts to forward literature among colored people that Frances Harper deserves most to be remembered. She was not a great singer, but she had some sense of song; she was not a great writer, but she wrote much worth reading. She was, above all, sincere. She took her writing soberly and earnestly; she gave her life to it."

BIOGRAPHICAL/CRITICAL SOURCES:

BOOKS

Barksdale, Richard and Keneth Kinnamon, *Black Writers of America: A Comprehensive Anthology*, Macmillan, 1972.
Bell, Roseann P. and others, editors, *Sturdy Black Bridges: Visions of Black Women in Literature*, Anchor Books, 1979.
Bone, Robert, *The Negro Novel in America*, revised edition, Yale University Press, 1965.

Brawley, Benjamin, *The Negro in Literature and Art in the United States,* Duffield, 1929.

Brown, Hallie Q., *Homespun Heroines and Other Women of Distinction,* Aldine, 1926, reprinted, Books for Libraries, 1971.

Christian, Barbara, *Black Women Novelists: The Development of a Tradition, 1892-1976,* Greenwood Press, 1980.

Christian, Barbara, *Black Feminist Criticism: Perspectives of Black Women Writers,* Pergamon, 1985.

Dannett, Sylvia G.L., *Profiles of Negro Womanhood:* Volume I: *1619-1900,* M. W. Lads, 1964.

Dictionary of Literary Biography, Volume 50: *Afro-American Writers Before the Harlem Renaissance,* Gale, 1986.

Giddings, Paula, *When and Where I Enter: The Impact of Black Women on Race and Sex in America,* Morrow, 1984.

Gloster, Hugh M., *Negro Voices in American Fiction,* University of North Carolina Press, 1948, Russell, 1968.

Goldstein, Rhoda L., *Black Life and Culture in the United States,* Crowell, 1971.

Hanaford, Phebe A., *Daughters of America; or, Women of the Century,* B. B. Russell, 1882.

Kerlin, Robert T., *Negro Poets and Their Poems,* Associated Publishers, 1923, revised third edition, 1935.

Loewenberg, Bert James and Ruth Bogin, *Black Women in Nineteenth-Century American Life: Their Words, Their Thoughts, Their Feelings,* Pennsylvania State University Press, 1976.

Loggins, Vernon, *The Negro Author: His Development in America,* Columbia University Press, 1931, reprinted, Kennikat, 1969.

Majors, M. A., *Noted Negro Women: Their Triumphs and Activities,* Donohue & Henneberry, 1893.

Montgomery, Janey Weinhold, *A Comparative Analysis of the Rhetoric of Two Negro Women Orators: Sojourner Truth and Frances E. Watkins Harper,* Fort Hays Kansas State College, 1968.

O'Connor, Lillian, *Pioneer Women Orators,* Columbia University Press, 1954.

Redding, J. Saunders, *To Make a Poet Black,* University of North Carolina Press, 1939, McGrath, 1968.

Redmond, Eugene B., *Drumvoices: The Mission of Afro-American Poetry, A Critical History,* Anchor/Doubleday, 1976.

Richings, G. F., *Evidences of Progress Among Colored People,* George S. Ferguson, 1896, AFRO-AM Press, 1969.

Robinson, William H., Jr., editor, *Early Black American Poets: Selections With Biographical and Critical Introductions,* W. C. Brown, 1969.

Sherman, Joan R., *Invisible Poets: Afro-Americans of the Nineteenth Century,* University of Illinois Press, 1974.

Sillen, Samuel, *Women Against Slavery,* Masses & Mainstream, 1955.

Still, William Grant, *The Underground Railroad,* Porter & Coates, 1872, reprinted, Arno/New York Times, 1968.

Twentieth-Century Literary Criticism, Volume 14, Gale, 1984.

Wagner, Jean, *Black Poets of the United States From Paul Laurence Dunbar to Langston Hughes,* translation by Kenneth Douglas, University of Illinois Press, 1973.

Whiteman, Maxwell, *A Century of Fiction by American Negroes, 1853-1952: A Descriptive Bibliography,* Albert Saifer, 1955.

Williams, Kenny J., *They Also Spoke: An Essay on Negro Literature in America, 1787-1930,* Townsend, 1970.

Woodson, Carter G. and Charles H. Wesley, *The Negro in Our History,* Associated Publishers, 1922.

PERIODICALS

African Methodist Episcopal Church Review, April, 1892.
Anglo-Saxon Magazine, May, 1859.
Black American Literature Forum, summer, 1981.
Black World, December, 1972.
Crisis, April, 1911.
Jet, February 23, 1961, February 24, 1966.
Journal of Negro History, October, 1917.
Massachusetts Review, winter/spring, 1972.
Messenger, February, 1927.
Nation, February, 1893.
Negro History Bulletin, December, 1938, January, 1942.

OTHER

Daniel, Theodora Williams, "The Poems of Frances E.W. Harper" (masters thesis), Howard University, 1937.

Graham, Maryemma, "The Threefold Cord: Blackness, Womanness, and Art; A Study of the Life and Work of Frances Ellen Watkins Harper" (masters thesis), Cornell University, 1973.*

—*Sketch by Nancy Pear*

* * *

HARPER, Mrs. F. E. W.
See HARPER, Frances Ellen Watkins

* * *

HARRIS, Michael (Terry) 1948-

PERSONAL: Born March 11, 1948, in Toronto, Ontario, Canada; son of Charles Arthur and Audrey Eleanor (Tilley) Harris; married Lynda Smith (a researcher), August 31, 1970; children: Sarah Peyton, Emily Kathleen. *Education:* York University, Toronto, B.A. (with honors), 1971; attended University College, Dublin, Ireland, 1972.

ADDRESSES: Home—c/o General Delivery, Topsail, Newfoundland, Canada A0A 3Y0. *Office*—c/o *Sunday Express,* 40 O'Leary Ave., St. John's, Newfoundland, Canada, A1B 2C7. *Agent*—Colbert Agency, 303 Davenport Rd., Toronto, Ontario, Canada M5R 1K5.

CAREER: Canadian Broadcasting Corporation, Ottawa, Ontario, host of "The Harris Report," in St. John's, Newfoundland, 1979-80, host of "The Harris/Lorimer Report" in Halifax, Nova Scotia, 1980-81; *Globe and Mail,* Toronto, Ontario, bureau chief in Halifax, 1981-85, parliamentary correspondent in Ottawa, 1985-86; *Sunday Express,* St. John's, publisher and editor in chief, 1987—.

AWARDS, HONORS: Woodrow Wilson scholarship; Radio and Television News Directors award; Michener Award for Journalism, merit citation.

WRITINGS:

Justice Denied: The Law Versus Donald Marshall (nonfiction), Macmillan (Toronto), 1986.
The Crosbies (history), Penguin Books, 1988.
Fast and Loose (biography), Macmillan (Toronto), in press.

Also author of television scripts. Contributor to periodicals, including *Atlantic Insight* and *Maclean's.*

WORK IN PROGRESS: Four novels, *At Last a Mother's Son, The Hound, Death-Footage,* and *The Bigger Game,* which will all have an investigational theme.

SIDELIGHTS: Michael Harris's best-selling *Justice Denied* is the true account of Donald Marshall, a seventeen-year-old Micmac Indian who was sentenced to life imprisonment for a murder he did not commit. He served eleven years before a successful appeal resulted in acquittal. According to Clayton Ruby, a criminal lawyer reviewing for the Toronto *Globe and Mail, Justice Denied* is a "marvellous and gripping book, full of gritty detail, on the case; but it is also a lot more—it is the story of a criminal justice system defending itself from criticism." Ruby declared that the story "leaves anyone who cares for our system of justice with a cold, burning rage."

Harris told *CA:* "I plan to write four novels, *At Last a Mother's Son, The Hound, Death-Footage,* and *The Bigger Game.* I have been circling around the themes for these works for eight years. Each is sufficiently ambitious in scope to rule out writing them part time. As a journalist, my specialty has been getting at the truth through complex investigations into the world of politics and big business, crime and the justice system. In a phrase, journalists look for truth and come up with facts about other people and events; the characters of my planned novels will either seek truth or be driven by it all the way to revelations about themselves and the terms of their existence."

BIOGRAPHICAL/CRITICAL SOURCES:

PERIODICALS

Globe and Mail (Toronto), September 6, 1986.

*   *   *

HARRIS, Thomas Harold   1933-

PERSONAL: Born September 28, 1933, in Taber, Alberta, Canada; immigrated to United States, 1961, naturalized citizen, 1966; son of Harold Joseph and Yvonne (Bernier) Harris; married Glenda Bullock, November 1, 1952; children: Darrell Vance, Valorie Linn, Lynette Renee. *Education:* Attended high school in Provo, Utah. *Politics:* Republican. *Religion:* Church of Jesus Christ of Latter-day Saints (Mormons).

ADDRESSES: Office—Sacramento Bee, 21st and Q Sts., Sacramento, Calif. 95852.

CAREER: Tri City Herald, Kennewick, Wash., reporter, 1961-63; *Hayward Daily Review,* Hayward, Calif., reporter, 1963-65; *Fremont Argus,* Fremont, Calif., editor, 1965-68; *San Jose Mercury News,* San Jose, Calif., environmental writer, 1968-84; *Sacramento Bee,* Sacramento, Calif., environmental writer, 1984—. Part-time teacher and lecturer in environmental journalism and environmental enforcement at schools, including San Jose State University, University of California at Berkeley, and the American Press Institute at Columbia University.

AWARDS, HONORS: Energy fellow at Stanford University, 1973; Fred Garretson Award from San Francisco Press Club, 1983, for "Water: California's Liquid Gold"; investigative reporting award from Associated Press and George S. Polk Award from Long Island University, both 1985, for series "Uncle Sam's Hidden Poisons"; Fred Garretson Award from San Francisco Press Club, 1986, for "Selenium: A Conspiracy of Silence."

WRITINGS:

Down the Wild Rivers, Chronicle Books, 1972.

WORK IN PROGRESS: Paradise Lost: Dwindling Natural Resources and Vanishing Species in the Nation's Most Populous State, "a hard look at the early years of the next century."

SIDELIGHTS: Thomas Harold Harris told *CA:* "I have specialized in environmental reporting in California for nearly twenty years with special projects (in reprint form) ranging from native American fishing disputes on the salmon rivers of northern California, the energy crisis of the 1970s, and the state's record drought of 1976 and 1977. Additionally, I've covered issues such as the preservation of San Francisco Bay and establishment of its wildlife refuge, California's continuing water wars, hazardous waste, and—more recently—the contaminated irrigation drainage that deformed and killed thousands of birds, fish, and other wildlife at Kesterson National Wildlife Refuge (featured as 'Selenium: A Conspiracy of Silence').

"My environmental bent is an outgrowth of a life in the outdoors of Canada, where I spent years as a fish and game columnist in the provinces of Alberta—including work there for the *Edmonton Journal*—and Saskatchewan. My environmental speciality evolved from writing about air and water pollution issues in the late 1960s and remained a full-time assignment thereafter.

"My book, *Down the Wild Rivers,* combines the adventures of canoeing with my wife, son, two daughters, and pet poodle with a beginner's guide to canoeing in California. The book sold out both printings of five thousand copies each and led to experiences such as my serving as an expert witness in a court case involving navigability issues and as a consultant to the Army Corps of Engineers in determining the recreational and historic navigability of three main river systems. It was the first work of its kind in the nation."

*   *   *

HARRISON, Paul Carter   1936-
(Paul Carter-Harrison)

PERSONAL: Born March 1, 1936, in New York, N.Y. *Education:* Attended New York University, 1953; Indiana University, B.A., 1957; graduate study at Ohio University, summers, 1959 and 1960; New School for Social Research, M.A., 1962.

*ADDRESSES: Home—*P.O. Box 143, Leeds, Mass. 01053. *Office—*Department of Theater/Music, Columbia College, 600 South Michigan Ave., Chicago, Ill. 60605.

CAREER: Howard University, Washington, D.C., assistant professor of theater arts, 1968-70; Kent State University, Kent, Ohio, associate professor of Afro-American literature, 1969; California State University, Sacramento, professor of theater arts, 1970-72; University of Massachusetts at Amherst, professor of theater arts and Afro-American studies, 1972-76; Columbia College, Chicago, Ill., artistic producer and chairman of theater/music department, 1976-80, writer in residence, 1980—. Visiting artist in residence at State University of New York at Buffalo, summer, 1965; Institute of Pan-African Culture, resident fellow at the University of Massachusetts at Amherst, consultant to the New England Regional Committee in Lagos, Nigeria, 1973-74; adjunct professor of theater communications at University of Illinois at Chicago Circle, 1978-82; visiting professor of Afro-American studies at Smith College and Wesleyan University, spring, 1984. Dramaturgical consultant to the Mickery Theater, Loenesloat, Netherlands; resource adviser to Colloquium on Black Education, Pajaro Dunes, Calif., 1970-71; touring symposium member of the African Continuum Forum, 1970-72; literary adviser to Lincoln Center Repertory Company, 1972-73; consultant to Theater Communications Group, 1972-74; theater panelist of Illinois Arts Council, 1976-79. Associate producer of the Association for the Advancement of Creative Musicians concert series, Columbia College, 1983-85.

Director of plays, including "Junebug Graduates Tonight," 1967, "Tabernacle," 1969, "Ain't Supposed to Die a Natural Death," 1970, "Tophat," 1971, "Homecookin'," 1971, "Lady Day: A Musical Tragedy," 1972, "Ceremonies in Dark Old Men," 1979, "The Owl Answers," 1980, "In an Upstate Motel," 1981, "My Sister, My Sister," 1981, "No Place to Be Somebody," 1983, "The River Niger," 1987, and "Anchorman," 1988. Producer of plays, including "Black Recollections," 1972; artistic producer of new American plays at Columbia College Performance Company, 1976-80. Developer and associate producer of television film "Leave 'Em Laughin'," Columbia Broadcasting System (CBS-TV), 1981.

MEMBER: American Theater Association, Dramatists Guild, Society for Directors and Choreographers, Actors Studio (playwrights and directors units).

AWARDS, HONORS: National Science Foundation fellowship; Obie Award for Best Play from the *Village Voice,* 1974, for "The Great MacDaddy"; Audelco (Audience Development Committee) Recognition Award for outstanding musical creator, 1981, for "Tabernacle"; Humanitas Prize from the Human Family Educational and Cultural Institute, 1981, for 'Leave 'Em Laughin'"; Illinois Art Council grant for playwriting, 1984; Rockefeller Foundation fellowship for American playwriting, 1985-86.

WRITINGS:

(Editor, under name Paul Carter-Harrison) *Voetnoten bij modern toneel* (essays; title means "The Modern Drama Footnote"), Bezige, 1965.
Dialog van het verzet (essays; title means "Dialogue From the Opposition"), Bezige, 1966.
(Under name Paul Carter-Harrison) *The Drama of Nommo: Black Theater in the African Continuum* (essays), Grove, 1972.
(Editor, contributor, and author of introduction) *Kuntu Drama: Plays of the African Continuum,* preface by Oliver Jackson, Grove, 1974 (also see *PLAYS*).
(With Charles Stewart) *Chuck Stewart's Jazz Files* (photo documentary), New York Graphic Society/Little, Brown, 1985.
(Editor, contributor, and author of introduction) *Totem Voices* (plays), Grove, 1988.

PLAYS

"The Postclerks" (one-act), first produced in New York at Actor's Studio, 1963.
"Pavane for a Dead-Pan Minstrel" (one-act; first produced in New York at Actor's Studio, 1964), published in *Podium* (Amsterdam), November, 1965.
"Tophat" (one-act), first produced at Buffalo University Summer Theater, 1965; produced in New York by Negro Ensemble Co., 1972.
"Pawns" (one-act), first produced in New York by 2nd Story Players, 1966.
"The Experimental Leader" (one-act; first produced in New York by Dore Co., 1968), published in *Podium,* 1965.
"Folly for Two" (one-act; first produced in New York at Actor's Studio, 1968), published in *Podium,* 1967, revised as "Interface."
"Tabernacle" (first produced in Washington, D.C., at Howard University, 1969; produced in New York at Afro-

American Studio, 1976), published in *New Black Playwrights,* Avon, 1970.
"Ain't Supposed to Die a Natural Death" (adapted from Melvin Van Peebles's *Ain't Supposed to Die a Natural Death;* first produced at University of California, Sacramento, 1970).
"The Great MacDaddy" (first produced at University of California, Sacramento, 1972; produced in New York at St. Mark's Playhouse, February 12, 1974), published in *Kuntu Drama: Plays of the African Continuum,* Grove, 1974.
"Dr. Jazz" (two-act), first produced on Broadway, 1975.
"The Death of Boogie Woogie" (two-act; first produced in Northampton, Mass., at Smith Collge, 1976; produced in New York at Richard Allen Center, 1979), published in *Callaloo,* 1985.
"Ameri/cain Gothic" (two-act), first produced in Chicago at Columbia College, 1980; produced in New York at New Federal Theater, 1985.
"Abercrombie Apocalypse" (two-act), first produced in Chicago at Columbia College, 1981; produced Off-Broadway at Westside Arts Theater, June 22, 1982.

Also author of "Adding Machine" and adapter of Van Peebles's "Brer Soul."

SCREENPLAYS

"Impressions of American Negro Society," VPRO-TV (Hilversum, Netherlands), c. 1963.
"Stranger on a Square," VPRO-TV, 1964.
"Intrusion," [Belgium], 1965.
"Lord Shango," Bryanstone Pictures, 1974.
"Youngblood," Aion, 1978.
"Gettin' to Know Me," Children's Television International, 1980.

OTHER

(With Julius Hemphill) "Anchorman" (two-act operetta; with music by Hemphill), first produced in Chicago at Columbia College, 1982; produced in New York at Theater Four, 1988.

Contributor to American and Dutch periodicals, including *American Rag, Black Review, Black World, Choice, Nummo,* and *Players.* Critical consultant to *Choice,* 1973—; theater and contributing editor to *Elan,* 1981-83.

WORK IN PROGRESS: "Kanaan," a folk opera; "Happy Hour," a play.

SIDELIGHTS: The playwright Paul Carter Harrison, best known for integrating modern American thought and African tradition in his works, sums up his theories on drama and the philosophy behind his play writing in his 1972 collection of critical essays, *The Drama of Nommo.* In this book, as in his plays, Harrison stresses the importance of combining traditional African values, rituals, and philosophy—including the belief in a holistic universe, where all elements are connected—with contemporary American points of view to reflect the total black experience on stage. The author feels that the theater should attempt to free blacks' spiritual energy by providing virtually ceremonial interaction between the actors and audience. Furthermore, Harrison maintains, a play should utilize black linguistic idiom, character, music, literature, and folklore, which will show the audience the traditional mythologies at work in contemporary black experience. Critics deemed *The Drama of Nommo* valuable and thought-provoking, praising Harrison for stimulating African culture, for advancing black dramatic criticism, and for establishing black drama as an entity separate from the conventional body of writing for the theater.

Harrison graduated from Indiana University and then the New School for Social Research before setting out for Europe in 1961. He eventually settled in Amsterdam, Netherlands, and lived there for seven years, staging readings by black poets and writing and producing television programs and plays for the theater. He began composing one-act plays during this period, with characters ranging from blue-collar workers unhappy with their lives to a Jew living in Nazi Germany unsure of his future. Harrison also experimented with reversing traditional roles based on gender or race. For example, "Tophat" features a female dominating a submissive male, and in "Pavane for a Dead-Pan Minstrel" a white man and black man switch identities by marking their faces with clown-white and minstrel cork and assuming the other's behavior.

While visiting the United States in 1964 Harrison witnessed the Harlem riots. When he returned to Europe he began writing his first full-length play, "Tabernacle," about the events leading up to the racial unrest. The main character, the Reverend, has been compared to an African ceremonial leader as he conducts his congregation (the audience) in a church service commemorating the victimization of black youths by the police. Throughout the play Harrison mixes jazz and African music—thereby symbolically integrating American innovation with African tradition—and uses a number of devices to remove the barrier between actor and audience, such as giving the audience an active role in the drama. Although Harrison completed the play in 1965, he felt that because of its content "Tabernacle" should be performed only by Afro-Americans, so it was not presented until 1969 at Howard University in Washington, D.C., where he directed the production.

Harrison also utilized techniques to lessen the distance between actor and audience in his adaptation of work by Melvin Van Peebles. He saw Van Peebles's work as an exploration of city life, so he created an urban atmosphere in the theater, filling it—on stage and in the audience—with actors playing derelicts, drunks, prostitutes, and other lowlife, who interacted with the theatergoers. Because the productions of "Ain't Supposed to Die" were improvisational, with Van Peebles's works acting only as the tying thread, each of the performances presented at California State University in Sacramento in November, 1970, provoked a unique audience response.

Four years later Harrison won an Obie Award for the Off-Broadway production of his play "The Great MacDaddy." In a review for the *New York Times* Clayton Riley declared the play a "brilliant ritual drama" and admired its "metaphorical richness and visual imagery." "The Great MacDaddy" features mythic figures from black American folklore, all of whom MacDaddy encounters on his spiritual trek across Depression-era America in search of, according to Riley, "the knowledge needed for blacks to retain their soul in the soulless technology of America." This play, in which many of Harrison's dramatic principles are winningly combined, is considered his masterpiece. In it the playwright introduced African cultural elements in an American setting, placed emphasis on the Afro-American's spirituality and place in society, and utilized black street slang and dialect and African rhythmic music in the drama. Harrison published "The Great MacDaddy" in a collection of critically acclaimed works that he edited, *Kuntu Drama: Plays of the African Continuum.* The anthology contains plays by black writers—including Aime Cesaire, Amiri Baraka, Adrienne Kennedy, and Lennox Brown—who agreed with Har-

rison's dramatic tenets and drew extensively on African speech rhythms, rituals, traditions, values, and myths in their works featured.

Harrison has also written on black themes for television and film. During the early 1960s he penned and produced two films for television in the Netherlands, "Impressions of American Negro Poetry" and "Stranger on a Square." His writing for American television includes four segments of a children's folklore series produced in 1980, "Gettin' to Know Me." In addition, Harrison wrote the screenplays for an Americn short feature filmed in Belgium and for the motion picture "Youngblood," an American commercial release about a teenager who joins a ghetto street gang.

CA INTERVIEW

CA interviewed Paul Carter Harrison by telephone on May 19, 1986, at Columbia College in Chicago.

CA: As writer, director, scholar, and teacher, you've been involved in theater for a good twenty-five years, at a very important time for black theater. How would you assess the gains in black theater during those years?

HARRISON: I think the most important thing the last twenty-five years have revealed is a literature for black theater. The opportunity for production is not always there, but certainly the last twenty-five years have produced an enormous amount of new writing for the theater, and a lot of *good* new writing—not just fledgling works but very developed works. That's the best result of the period, the new literature that has emerged from it. The second thing is a peculiarly unique kind of aesthetic sensibility inside of that work so that it very often suggests an alternative approach to performing or writing for theater than the traditional American approach.

CA: Along the lines of what you've tried to do and what you've written about, especially in The Drama of Nommo?

HARRISON: Exactly. Very much of what I've been talking about for several years is starting to appear in a lot of the new works particularly. I'm not really saying that it's a question of copying my work; rather, it's a matter of empathizing with a process. Having identified the process, a lot of people are perhaps more willing to execute plays with some of my devices in mind. In other words, they were doing it anyway without necessarily knowing that there was a formal approach to what they were doing. It is simply a question of articulating what is the process at this point. So new works are not accidentally being conceived along those lines; they are very deliberately being structured from an Afrocentric point of view.

CA: So you think The Drama of Nommo *has had a very direct influence on some writers, at least?*

HARRISON: Yes. I would say quite a few, as a matter of fact. But I have also found it to be not only black writers who have been paying attention to it, but a lot of white writers as well, white writers who are trying to move into more ritual styles of work. It might seem paradoxical, but most of the people who have responded to that book have been linguists as opposed to theater people. There's an enormous number of white scholars who are involved in that particular research—linguists and anthropologists. I've been contacted about the work by several white writers or people who were writing in, or concerned about, ritual styles. It's not that the blacks are not paying attention, but rather that we very often take for granted that ritual is part of the ethos influencing the work that we do, and thus, do not necessarily make any additional inquiry about it. Not directly. Indirectly it will show up in our work.

CA: I'm not surprised that linguists have noticed the book. You wrote a great deal about black speech and the confusion it has caused among scholars. Has important work been done on the spoken language since The Drama of Nommo *was published that bears out some of your points?*

HARRISON: A lot of work has been done on it. Thomas Kochman, particularly, of the University of Illinois, refers in almost all of his books to the discussions in *The Drama of Nommo.*

CA: How did you come to choose playwriting and directing as a focus in your career? Was drama an early interest?

HARRISON: Yes, the theater was an early interest when I was a liberal arts student. One first comes to it through poetry, not as a writer but simply listening to poetry and listening to language; listening to poets in Greenwich Village in New York as a kid, and being fascinated with the language of the new poets of that time, the Beat Generation Poets: LeRoi Jones, Ted Jones, Frank O'Hara, [Allen] Ginsberg, and that crowd. They were sort of peers, though they were slightly older than I and they were much more active in that period than I was. Another factor was becoming very acquainted with the Off-Broadway theater and the European works that came through. My first active interest in the theater was through European theater, the more avant-garde works in the 1950s as opposed to the American plays. I was never very much concerned with American theater literature. I was never particularly interested in Tennessee Williams, for example, and only marginally interested in [Eugene] O'Neill. Even now I still don't have a great affection for the American theater works. I shouldn't say that I dislike it; I just don't have a great affection for it. It seems a little bit too personal, private, and melodramatic. It doesn't seem to have a collective world view that I can identify with.

CA: Did you have a strong background in classical drama?

HARRISON: No, I just had a strong background in European philosophy. I came to theater through workshops in New York. My graduate studies were in psychology. When I was doing my graduate work, I became more active as a writer. I would say that writing papers in phenomenology at the New School for Social Research helped me more with understanding how to deal with character development than anything else I've ever done, that is, understanding how people perceive themselves in the world. And writing papers on phenomenology helped me focus the question of personality which led me to Gestalt psychology. Out of that I discovered African philosophy and realized that I was doing African philosophy all the time. When I discovered the African philosophies and the cosmology of African logic, then I saw that what I was trying to do in the theater had nothing to do with the rituals of classical theater. Nor was it avant-garde. Rather, I was trying to organize a ritual mode, or what you would call a force field if you were looking at it in a scientific way. In a cosmological sense, if you understand the world to be made up of forces, then your characters must all be forces as opposed to being personalized, individualized characters. They have to be archetypes, in my sense.

CA: Does the cosmological approach to drama that you discussed in The Drama of Nommo *have connections to other disciplines besides Gestalt psychology?*

HARRISON: If you were to read some Chinese or Japanese works, you'd probably find something quite akin to it. If you examine much of what's done in new music, the musical philosophy of people like [Alban] Berg, [Karlheinz] Stockhausen, and Pierre Boulez, even going back to how the serial music or twelve-tone music is formulated, you'll find that kind of abstraction of ideas somewhat akin to what I'm talking about as well. Further, you can look at what is happening in jazz, and I think the very crux of what I'm dealing with in Afro-American ideograms emerges from blues and jazz and their evolvement into contemporary black music forms of today. I'm not talking about pop music, but music in the so-called jazz mode. The kind of organization of its musical ideas is exactly what I'm doing now. Such orchestrated sounds clearly define the logic I've described in *The Drama of Nommo.* It's still African cosmological sensibility that's informing that work. Somebody else might say, "The Gestaltists were saying the same thing." Well, it's somewhat like that. That's how I came to it. I didn't study theater formally; I came to it secondarily and finally had to make a decision. I left graduate school and went to live in Europe, and my work evolved out of living abroad. But African logic is the greatest influence on my work.

CA: How did you happen to choose Holland? Was there some special opportunity there?

HARRISON: It was just fortuitous. I was living in Spain for about a year. Then I went up to Amsterdam to visit a friend, and I ended up staying there. It was quite wonderful. What was productive about Amsterdam was, first, that it had a youthful core, a youthful attitude. The social and artistic climate of Amsterdam at that time, the early 1960s, seemed to be centered around young people. Some of my peers at the time I was there are major forces in arts and letters in Holland today—like Peter Schat, who is one of the major composers, and Lodewijk de Boerr, who is one of the major playwrights of the country. I was young, in my mid-twenties, and I found opportunities there as a young man that I could not have found in the States: opportunities to direct, to produce plays, to produce film, to have my work published. Those opportunities normally come later in America. There I was in Amsterdam and all of my peers were active in the center of the city's artistic, social, and political life. I was able to take advantage of that. It's the same way in Amsterdam today. Young people set the tone.

CA: "The Great MacDaddy" had productions in California and in Washington before its Obie-winning run by the Negro Ensemble Company at the St. Marks Playhouse that began in February, 1974. Did it go through many changes before it went to New York?

HARRISON: There were some things that had to be changed for the New York production. That really was a question of the director's judgment at that time, his feeling that some changes were needed for the commercial production. The first productions were not commercial ones. In fact, the first emerged out of the process of conceptualizing it, and I directed it at the University of California at Sacramento, where I had already developed Melvin Van Peebles's *Ain't Supposed to Die a Natural Death.* I was using the workshop there as a kind of a laboratory to develop works. The production went very well.

Then I had it performed at the Black Arts West at Seattle, and then it was selected for the Governor's Festival in Olympia. By the time it got to Seattle, it was quite refined. Of course, I had to make an additional refinement of the script when it came to New York. There it was directed by Douglas Turner Ward of the Negro Ensemble Company [NEC].

"The Great MacDaddy" was revived once. I had the wonderful pleasure of seeing it under two sets of circumstances. The 1974 production was at the small theater at the St. Marks Playhouse. I won an award for it, and it was very gratifying. But when they, the NEC, took the play to Saint Croix in the Caribbean in 1978 for a revival, and mounted it down there on a huge stage, it was as if the play was levitating on the stage, absolutely magical. It was extraordinary to see it down there under such conditions.

CA: Perhaps the music needed that kind of space?

HARRISON: The music, and also the aura that was being created inside of the play. The particular kind of magical aura that was being created needed a lot more breadth on the stage. The piece sort of levitated; that's the beauty of it down there. Then we came back to the Theatre de Lys, which has a small proscenium stage. The magic was gone; the internal energy was vitiated by the constraint of the proscenium, and thus lost its visual impact. It was interesting to see the difference between what happens to a play like that on a large, open stage as opposed to the proscenium stage.

CA: There are so many variable factors in any production, and in the life of any play, that it must be pretty hard to hit a good combination.

HARRISON: It's something that one has to be concerned with. You do the best that you can. There are a lot of new plays being written, and not always the opportunity for production. One of the reasons is simply that sometimes the scale of the production is larger than the potential to mount it. Most black plays are not being mounted commercially. They simply do not generate enough of a theater-going audience. They must clearly count on the black population seeing these plays, but that's not enough. It's harder to sustain them without the whites coming to see them. Whites will come to see the better plays, of course. *A Soldier's Play*, by Charles Fuller, for example; whites came out to see that in great numbers. But that's not always the case. And with plays that require large numbers of characters, large stages, producers are not willing to commit themselves, especially if it's a black play. They're afraid of not being able to develop the audience for it. It's unfortunate but true. So many of these plays are seen in the provinces, in community theaters and/or the university theaters, but might not necessarily get back to New York or to the mainstream public or be witnessed by mainstream critics. Thus they aren't given the kind of attention they should receive.

CA: Should regional theater be doing more than it is to produce black theater?

HARRISON: I think it is imperative that they do more, but they *don't* do more. Regional theaters have regionalisms, you might say. They seem to be locked into their constituency without bringing their constituency any novel ideas or new samplings of theater. They usually do reasonably traditional stuff. People who work in what we call the black theater— that is, plays of black authorship and with a focus on the black

experience—very often bring something quite novel and interesting and intriguing and informative beyond simply the interest of the black community. The plays are there to inform the black community, but at the same time they can reveal quite a bit to the white audience as well, much like viewing a play from another culture such as the Japanese Kabuki theater. But a lot of people are not willing to test that reality, largely because they feel they are already intimately informed about blacks and need not be more curious than their local newspaper stories.

CA: But in theater across the board, regional or New York, most of the decisions finally seem to come down to economics. It's very costly to produce a play.

HARRISON: Yes, it is very expensive to mount plays. I have plays that I finished a few years ago and am only now getting around to doing because they have been with the Negro Ensemble Company. The Negro Ensemble Company can only do four or five plays a year, and they have at least a dozen writers that they consider to be their career-writers, I included. We all can't get to have a play performed every year, so that means I have to wait. The play I did last year, "Ameri/cain Gothic," had been around about five years without anybody dealing with it. I performed it finally with the New Federal Theater last year, under Woody King's direction, because it had been sitting around for a long time and I thought it was time to put it out there. In 1988 I'll be directing my blues operetta, "Anchorman," with the American Folk Theatre. That's been sitting around for three years with the NEC. This is not a complaint, obviously. It's simply to say that no one else is asking for the piece, so one had to wait until they had time to do it. If the play is not successful, people will simply say, "Well, it's a miss." But if it's as successful as we think it will be, everybody will jump on the bandwagon and say, "Where has that play been? Why haven't we had an opportunity to look at it, to do something with it?"

CA: Do you prefer directing your own plays to having them directed by someone else?

HARRISON: No. Next fall will be the first time I will have directed my own play in a commercial theater. I usually direct my own plays in a community theater or university theater, and I do that so I can continue to refine the work. If it goes into a commercial production in New York or regional theater, then I always distance myself from it. I don't involve myself in it directly because I don't think it's a good idea to wear that many hats. But in the case of "Anchorman," since the music that I have put with it is so intimately tied to the style of the production and to how the characters are conceived, and having had a hand in shaping Julius Hemphill's music, and manipulating the environment to create a certain kind of impact on the dramatic action, it's very difficult for me to turn it over to a director. Any director who would touch this particular piece would come to it as an auteur and begin to manipulate the devices in a way that accommodates his or her sense of directorial authorship, as it were. It's hard for me to turn loose of the total concept, and for that reason I will direct this production at the Negro Ensemble Company myself. Otherwise I wouldn't do it. But once I've done it to establish how I think it should work, then anybody can do it after that.

CA: Race memory is a concept crucial to everything you write about. How do you think it can be kept more alive in young black people?

HARRISON: Race memory is more than simply having a holiday once a year for Dr. Martin Luther King, who certainly should be celebrated. Race memory is more than singing the black national anthem, which is truly a glorious song. Race memory, I think, has to do with a feeling, a sustained interest in our cultural manifestations, the social styles of black American people. A person coming to the city from a rural or Southern community should not feel that he or she is socially backward. There are certain adjustments you must make when coming to the city, but you must also bring with you those things from your background which have been culturally sound, and then transmit those things to your children. What happens is that, very often, as we become more and more acculturated in American society, we tend just like any other immigrants to leave behind us those things which belong to the old culture. The more we become acculturated, the less definition we have as a people inside the cultural artifacts we produce in the new experience.

I have a young black student here, a very good writer, who doesn't want to write black characters. He only wants to write plays with white characters. I asked him why, and he said it's because he wants to be able to get the plays or the films produced. It sounds like a cynical notion, but he's not really being cynical about it; he feels it is the practical way for him to earn his living as a writer. My main statement to him was, "The country does not need you to write white characters. We have enough white writers to write white characters. I don't think you can inform anybody about white characters that another white writer can't do. There must be, in the heart of your plays, a *life*, something that produces a pulse we can feel. If you cannot bring a pulse to these characters, your play will have no resonance. It will be a hollow experience." The young man's plays are great as far as the writing is concerned, technically speaking, but there's no pulse in them. The only way you can have that pulse is by having at least one black character that you recognize and identify with.

It would be a pity if we're not able to maintain a contact with our cultural resources. I'm not talking about the refinements of European culture, but the kinds of experiences that have refined our sensibilities as black people, that are embedded in our culture—the sacred systems, the social systems. We understand the accountability, let's say, between child and mother, between elders and young people. But that understanding is eroding away from us. We're becoming a little bit too open-minded, too closely intimate with American society. We, who are of course much more vulnerable than most whites to the conceits and deceits of this country, can't afford to lose contact with those values that have sustained us all these years. This is not about being isolationist. Of course we function inside American society. But we must function with a sense of who we are, where we are coming from, and where we are going.

CA: It must be very hard for young people, especially, to maintain a balance required to hold to the cultural heritage while functioning in the larger society.

HARRISON: It's very difficult. When I see what young people are preoccupied in today, I feel it's self-defeating. When those particular preoccupations fall apart, and they're out there on their own without a sense of who they are, they'll be in desperate need of something but it will be too difficult for them to recover. They'll be stranded, because they did not pay attention to those values that are vitally important to informing a particular way of being. Oddly enough, black women writers

today are beginning to show an enormous amount of cultural resonance inside their work, in the style of their writing as well as in the consciousness of themselves as women, and particularly black women. Alice Walker's work may have a caustic response to her experience as a black woman vis-a-vis black men, but that doesn't matter. The point in fact is that, inside of what she's talking about, there's clearly that ethos, which is inextricable from a certain kind of cultural information.

BIOGRAPHICAL/CRITICAL SOURCES:

BOOKS

Arata, Esther Spring, *More Black American Playwrights*, Scarecrow Press, 1978.
Dictionary of Literary Biography, Volume 38: *Afro-American Writers After 1955: Dramatists and Prose Writers*, Gale, 1985.
Fabre, Genevieve, *Drumbeats, Masks, and Metaphors: Contemporary Afro-American Theater*, translated by Melvin Dixon, Harvard University Press, 1983.
Hill, Errol, editor, *The Theater of Black Americans*, two volumes, Prentice-Hall, 1980.

PERIODICALS

Los Angeles Times Book Review, January 5, 1986.
New York Times, March 3, 1974, May 25, 1978, June 27, 1982.

—Sketch by Carol Lynn DeKane
—Interview by Jean W. Ross

*   *   *

HART, Jon
  See HARVEY, John (Barton)

*   *   *

HART, Matthew   1945-

PERSONAL: Born April 14, 1945, in Ottawa, Ontario, Canada; son of John Garton (an executive) and Theresa (Turner) Hart; married Sylvia Alden Morley (a businesswoman), March 28, 1985.

ADDRESSES: Agent—Colbert Agency, 303 Davenport Rd., Toronto, Ontario, Canada M5R 1K5.

CAREER: Affiliated with *Ottawa Citizen*, Ottawa, Ontario; affiliated with *Montreal Star*, Montreal, Quebec; affiliated with Canadian Broadcasting Corp.; affiliated with *Maclean's*.

WRITINGS:

Death Train, New American Library of Canada, 1981.
Golden Giant: Hemlo and the Rush for Canada's Gold, Douglas & McIntyre, 1985.
A Viewer's Guide to Halley's Comet, Simon & Schuster, 1985.

BIOGRAPHICAL/CRITICAL SOURCES:

PERIODICALS

Globe and Mail (Toronto), June 1, 1985.

*   *   *

HARTMAN, Geoffrey H.   1929-

PERSONAL: Born August 11, 1929, in Frankfurt-am-Main, Germany (now West Germany); immigrated to United States,

1946; naturalized U. S. citizen, 1946; son of Albert and Agnes (Heumann) Hartman; married Renee Gross, October 21, 1956; children: David, Elizabeth. *Education:* Queens College of the City of New York (now Queens College of the City University of New York), B. A., 1949; attended University of Dijon, 1951-52; Yale University, Ph.D., 1953.

ADDRESSES: Home—260 Everit St., New Haven, Conn. 06511. *Office*—Department of Comparative Literature, Yale University, New Haven, Conn. 06520.

CAREER: Yale University, New Haven, Conn., instructor, 1955-60, assistant professor of English, 1961-62; University of Iowa, Iowa City, associate professor, 1962-64, professor of English, 1964-65; Cornell University, Ithaca, N. Y., professor of English, 1965-67; Yale University, professor, 1967-74, Karl Young Professor of English and Comparative Literature, 1974—, faculty adviser to Video Archive of Holocaust Testimonies. Visiting professor at institutions such as University of Chicago, Princeton University, New York University, Hebrew University, and University of Zuerich. Christian Gauss Lecturer at Princeton University, 1970; Clark Lecturer at Trinity College, Cambridge, 1983; Tamblyn Lecturer at University of Western Ontario, 1983. Director and senior fellow of School of Theory and Criticism, 1982-87. *Military service:* U. S. Army, 1953-55.

MEMBER: Modern Language Association of America, American Academy of Arts and Sciences.

AWARDS, HONORS: Fulbright fellowship, 1951-52; fellowship from American Council of Learned Societies, 1963; Christian Gauss Award from Phi Beta Kappa, 1965, for *Wordsworth's Poetry, 1787-1814;* Guggenheim fellowships, 1969 and 1986; Distinguished Alumni Award from Queens College of the City University of New York, 1971; fellowship from National Endowment for the Humanities, 1975.

WRITINGS:

The Unmediated Vision: An Interpretation of Wordsworth, Hopkins, Rilke, and Valery, Yale University Press, 1954.
Andre Malraux, Hilary House, 1960.
Wordsworth's Poetry, 1787-1814, Yale University Press, 1964, revised edition, 1971, reprinted, Harvard University Press, 1988.
(Editor) *Hopkins: A Collection of Critical Essays,* Prentice-Hall, 1966.
(Editor) *Selected Poetry and Prose of William Wordsworth,* New American Library, 1970.
Beyond Formalism: Literary Essays, 1958-1970, Yale University Press, 1970.
(Editor with David Thorburn) *Romanticism: Vistas, Instances, Continuities,* Cornell University Press, 1973.
The Fate of Reading, and Other Essays, University of Chicago Press, 1975.
Akiba's Children (poetry), Iron Mountain Press, 1978.
(Editor) *Psychoanalysis and the Question of the Text,* Johns Hopkins University Press, 1978.
Criticism in the Wilderness: The Study of Literature Today, Yale University Press, 1980.
(Contributor) Lawrence Lipking, editor, *High Romantic Argument: Essays for M. H. Abrams,* Cornell University Press, 1981.
Saving the Text: Literature/Derrida/Philosophy, John Hopkins University Press, 1981.
Easy Pieces, Columbia University Press, 1985.

(Editor with Patricia Barker) *Shakespeare and the Question of Theory,* Methuen, 1985.
(Editor) *Bitburg in Moral and Political Perspective,* Indiana University Press, 1986.
(Editor with Sanford Budick) *Midrash and Literature,* Yale University Press, 1986.
The Unremarkable Wordsworth, University of Minnesota Press, 1987.
(Editor) *Holocaust and Memory,* Blackwell, in press.

Contributor to periodicals, including *Critical Inquiry* and *New Republic.*

WORK IN PROGRESS: Theory and Critical Style, publication by Harvard University Press expected in 1990.

SIDELIGHTS: Geoffrey H. Hartman is a prominent literary theorist who has distinguished himself by exploring the nature of the creative imagaination and the implications of theoretical criticism. He has probably gained greatest recognition for his works on deconstruction, philologist-philosopher Jacques Derrida's controversial analytic strategy which traces underlying principles in language and literature. For Hartman, literature is inevitably indirect or oblique, and this obliquity is its underlying strength. Like Derrida, Hartman rejects formalism, which presupposes absolute meaning, and he perceives texts as elusive and stratified instead of as objectively knowable. He also complicates the notion that books enrich readers, arguing that readers also enrich texts through various, and even contradictory, reactions and responses. Thus for Hartman, criticism "has its own dignity," one at times equal with fiction. The greatest writing, he believes, is that which is endlessly interpretable.

In his own writings Hartman evidences many of the same qualities—contradiction, equivocation, and indeterminacy—that he prizes in Derrida and critic-theorists such as Harold Bloom and Paul de Man. Detractors of Hartman dismiss him as a confused, self-aggrandizing obscurantist, but supporters of his often radical work respect him as an innovative and engaging thinker. Among those critics who admire his work are *Nation's* Terrence Des Pres, who praised Hartman as "one of our smartest scholars" and declared, "His method is playful, for reasons he clearly sets forth, but his message is deeply in earnest."

Hartman began his writing career in 1954 with *The Unmediated Vision,* a relatively straightforward, though unconventional, analysis of the creative imagination. Abjuring then-prevalent formalism, he discussed various poems as "pure representations" of consciousness and approached creativity as an inevitably solipsistic endeavor. Hartman, as a phenomenologist, disputed the notion of objective perception, and like poet Wallace Stevens he considered poetry ultimately self-reflexive. Hartman wrote that poetry served as a mediation between readers and reality, and poets thus served as a medium. He admired poets for living free of mediation and for enduring direct experience. "Great poetry," Hartman contended, "is written by men who have chosen to stay bound by experience, who would not—or could not—free themselves by an act of knowledge from the immediacy of good and evil."

In *The Unmediated Vision,* Hartman analyzed poetry as the poet's conscious rendering of reality, and in *Wordsworth's Poetry, 1787-1814,* he traced romantic poet William Wordsworth's artistic crisis in creating that rendering. According to Hartman, at the turn of the eighteenth century Wordsworth became increasingly aware of his imagination as independent of perceivable reality. This awareness led Wordsworth—who considered himself a poet of nature—to accord greater recognition to that autonomy. "The poet's later strength," Hartman contended, "has its origin in experiences that intimate (negatively) a death of nature and (positively) a faculty whose power is independent of nature." Christopher Ricks, writing in the *New York Review of Books,* commended *Wordsworth's Poetry, 1787-1814* as an "important, various, and stimulating book." Similarly, a reviewer for the *Times Literary Supplement,* while questioning some of Hartman's observations, conceded that the work was provocative and added that "his detailed criticism can be very good."

Both *The Unmediated Vision* and *Wordsworth's Poetry, 1787-1814* proved unconventional as critical inquiries in a field dominated by formalism's objectifying approach. But these works were nonetheless relatively direct in analyzing the complex relationship between the creative imagination and reality. In his next book, the essay collection *Beyond Formalism,* Hartman commenced a more radical inquiry into critical analysis. Chiefly, he attacked formalism and the notion of absolute meaning as both illusory and contradictory to the nature of poetry. Poetry's esotericism demands critical elucidation, Hartman declared, but that same esotericism should not be compromised in a futile attempt to establish absolute meaning. Thus for Hartman, formalist criticism is reductive and potentially counterproductive. A true criticism, he affirmed, respects poetry's complex endings and concedes the possibility of countless, varied interpretations.

Consistent with this notion, Hartman resisted drawing easy conclusions in his arguments, and he shaped *Beyond Formalism* with what Joseph N. Riddel, writing in the journal *Comparative Literature,* called "an indirectness and a sense of the problematic." In his review, Riddel hailed *Beyond Formalism* as a "major critical statement" and added that, despite the seeming arbitrariness of Hartman's analysis, the twenty-one essays comprised "a single consciousness exploring the problematic of consciousness, questioning itself, seeking, and holding final answers at a distance." Laurence Lerner, however, was undone by Hartman's method, writing in *Encounter* that it was "suggestive but maddeningly elusive." Lerner complained that many of the essays were "totally opaque" and stated, "I read [Hartman] with a kind of bemused admiration, but to learn anything from a critic I need to understand a rather larger fraction of what he says."

In his next essay collection, *The Fate of Reading,* Hartman developed a more explicitly deconstructionist interpretation of literature. Among the most intriguing aspects of *The Fate of Reading* is Hartman's analysis of conventional literary history, which he condemned as unfounded and misleading. He charged that the very notion of history is "over-objectifying"; that is, its alleged objectivity only serves to indicate the biases of any given era. History, Hartman wrote, is no less susceptible to varied interpretations than is literature, and is thus no less than a form of "critical energy."

Although critics respected the intelligence and ambition of *The Fate of Reading,* few commended Hartman for what he considered to be intentional subtlety. "There are real problems here, real opportunities for literary history, which Hartman explores with a cunning elegance," observed Jonathan Culler in *Yale Review.* He added, however, that Hartman's indeterminacy undermined his own credibility. "It is sad," Culler wrote, "when so talented a critic evades problems he could treat so well." And Denis Donahue, who reviewed *The Fate of Reading* in the *Times Literary Supplement,* conceded that

Hartman "can write as lucidly as any critic" but added that "his current style [is] too self-regarding to be wholesome."

In 1980 Hartman produced what may be his best-known work, *Criticism in the Wilderness,* in which he opposed Anglo-American academia's compartmentalization of history, literature, and philosophy. Charging that the isolation of these subjects from one another resulted in dull, merely practical scholasticism, Hartman called for a more unifying perspective and claimed as his model a European tradition, one that included Hegel, the German romantics, and Derrida. Here Hartman stressed the fallacy of perceiving criticism and creative writing as separate forms, and he argued that in rectifying this misperception critics could redeem criticism from its undeserved status as a lesser literary practice.

Criticism in the Wilderness, like *The Fate of Reading,* often drew respect for its ambition and rejection for its execution. Denis Donahue, for example, wrote in the *New York Times Book Review* that Hartman's style was alternately impressive and exasperating. "In one mood, he is a vigorous, witty trenchant writer, formidably lucid and polemical," Donahue observed. "Many of the sentences make me feel: I wish I had said that. But some of them make me feel: I wonder would that be worth the labor of understanding it?" On a more general level, Gerald Graff wrote in *New Republic* that Hartman, while expressing sound criticism, steadfastly refused to sensibly articulate it. Graff wrote: "The trouble with Hartman's view lies not . . . in his conflation of the critical with the literary, or his wish to merge literature, philosophy, and history. . . . The trouble lies rather in Hartman's conception of what is 'literary,' a conception that excludes the making of statements. One assumes Hartman is not incapable of consecutive argument, but that he has decided that if it's consecutive argument you want you should have gone into electrical engineering or zero-sum accounting."

Less equivocal in their praise of *Criticism in the Wilderness* were Peter Rudnytsky, who reviewed the book in *World Literature Today,* and Terrence Des Pres, who wrote in *Nation.* Rudnytsky called Hartman's work "an unqualified triumph both of speculation and close reading," and Des Pres declared that "*Criticism in the Wilderness* may be the best, most brilliant, most broadly useful book yet written by an American about the sudden swerve from the safety of established decorum toward bravely theoretical, mainly European forms of literary criticism." Des Pres also wrote that Hartman's volume "enriches the study of literature immensely," and he stated that reading it "turns out to be great fun and cause for high intellectual excitement."

Since completing *Criticism in the Wilderness,* Hartman has published such volumes as *Saving the Text* and *Easy Pieces.* In *Saving the Text* he analyzes Derrida's *Glas,* a willfully complex and unorthodox volume that, appropriately, blurs distinctions between fiction and criticism. For Hartman, *Glas* is literature's "most deliberate and curious work" since James Joyce's *Finnegans Wake,* and in his discourse on Derrida's difficult work Hartman fashions a similarly elusive and demanding text. Writing in *World Literature Today,* Peter Rudnytsky acknowledged *Saving the Text* as a "counterstatement" to Derrida's *Glas,* and he called Hartman's work "a masterpiece."

With the essay collection *Easy Pieces* Hartman confirmed his status as a leading figure in literary theory. David Lodge, writing in the *New York Times Book Review,* noted that the book's range of subjects—from romanticism to literacy and communication—"testifies to the impressive breadth of Mr. Hartman's intellectual interests and the fervor of his commitment to the life of the mind." Similarly, David Gross wrote in *World Literature Today* that "Hartman's . . . work provides constant examples of an engaging, active thinker at work."

In addition to his critical writings, Hartman has edited volumes on writers such as William Shakespeare and Gerard Manley Hopkins. Most of Hartman's works as editor, however, are devoted to the romantic poets. Among these works are *Selected Poetry and Prose of William Wordsworth* and *Romanticism: Vistas, Instances, and Continuities*. In addition, Hartman also served as editor of *Bitburg in Moral and Political Perspective*, an essay collection examining the implications and repercussions of U. S. President Ronald Reagan's controversial visit in 1985 to a West German cemetery where Nazi soldiers had been buried. In the *Los Angeles Times Book Review*, Jonathan Kirsch wrote that "Hartman has erected a monument to the victims of the Holocaust, and a moral guidepost to the world after Auschwitz." For Kirsch, *Bitburg in Moral and Political Perspective* proved a "compelling and wholly successful effort."

Hartman told *CA* that he he holds a "historical interest in hermeneutics, including the tradition of early Rabbinic exegesis called *midrash*." He added: "The open nature yet vigor of *midrash* are more fundamental to me than contemporary movements and new polemics. I intervene in these polemics as an engaged historian, not as a willful provocateur."

BIOGRAPHICAL/CRITICAL SOURCES:

BOOKS

Arac, Jonathan, Wlad Godzich, and Wallace Martin, editors, *The Yale Critics: Deconstruction in America*, University of Minnesota Press, 1983.

Atkins, G. Douglas, *Reading Deconstruction/Deconstructive Reading*, University Press of Kentucky, 1983.

Contemporary Literary Criticism, Volume 27, Gale, 1984.

Davis, Robert Con, and Ronald Schleifer, editors, *Rhetoric and Form: Deconstruction at Yale*, University of Oklahoma Press, 1985.

Dictionary of Literary Biography, Volume 67: *Modern American Critics Since 1955*, Gale, 1988.

Moynihan, Robert, *A Recent Imagining: Interviews With Harold Bloom, Geoffrey Hartman, J. Hillis Miller, Paul de Man*, Archon Books, 1986.

O'Hara, Daniel T., *The Romance of Interpretation: Visionary Criticism From Pater to de Man*, Columbia University Press, 1985.

Salusinszky, Imre, *Criticism in Society: Interviews With Jacques Derrida, Northrop Frye, Harold Bloom, Geoffrey Hartman, Frank Kermode, Edward Said, Barbara Johnson, Frank Lentricchia, J. Hilis Miller*, Methuen, 1987.

PERIODICALS

Commonweal, January 22, 1965.
Encounter, June-July, 1982.
Harper's, August, 1981.
Los Angeles Times Book Review, November 2, 1980, July 13, 1986.
Nation, November 8, 1980.
New Republic, November 1, 1980.
New Yorker, October 14, 1974, May 3, 1982.
New York Review of Books, April 20, 1975, November 9, 1980, May 12, 1985, August 31, 1986.

New York Times Book Review, April 20, 1975, November 9, 1980, May 12, 1985, August 31, 1986.
Times Literary Supplement, April 29, 1965, August 22, 1975, November 22, 1985, September 12, 1986.
World Literature Today, summer, 1981, winter, 1982, winter, 1986.
Yale Review, June, 1965, June, 1971, autumn, 1975, autumn, 1981.

—*Sketch by Les Stone*

*   *   *

HARTY, (Fredric) Russell   1934-1988

OBITUARY NOTICE: Born September 5, 1934, in Blackburn, Lancashire, England; died of hepatitis, June 8, 1988. Educator, producer, broadcaster, and columnist. A well-known television personality in Great Britain, Harty became a successful talk show host after working many years behind the camera as a producer. Harty began his broadcasting career in 1967 after ten years of teaching high school English and drama in England and lecturing in 1964 at the City University of New York. As a radio producer for the British Broadcasting Corporation (BBC), he worked on programs pertaining to arts and books then joined the London Weekend Television (LWT) staff in 1969. Harty helped develop LWT's "Aquarius" arts series and received an Emmy Award for a program about Spanish painter Salvador Dali; in 1972 he became host of his own show and won the Pye Award for outstanding new personality of the year. Rejoining the BBC in 1980, Harty continued as a talk show host and made documentaries; seven years later he began hosting a radio talk show, "Start the Week." In addition to broadcasting, he wrote the weekly column "Notebook" for the London *Sunday Times*.

OBITUARIES AND OTHER SOURCES:

PERIODICALS

Times (London), June 9, 1988.

*   *   *

HARVEY, John (Barton)   1938-
(John B. Harvey; pseudonyms: Jon Barton, William S. Brady, L. J. Coburn, Jon Hart, William M. James, Terry Lennox, John J. McLaglen, Thom Ryder, J. D. Sandon; J. B. Dancer and James Mann, joint pseudonyms)

PERSONAL: Born December 21, 1938, in London, England. *Education:* Goldsmith's College, London, teaching certificate, 1963; Hatfield Polytechnic, B.A., 1974; University of Nottingham, M.A., 1979.

ADDRESSES: Home—Flat 4, Arundel House, 1 Park Valley, The Park, Nottingham NG7 1BS, England. *Agent*—Blake Friedmann, 37-41 Gower St., London WC1E 6HH, England.

CAREER: Writer. English and drama teacher in England, at schools in various cities such as Heanor, Andover, and Stevenage, 1963-74; *Slow Dancer* (poetry magazine), Nottingham, England, editor and publisher, 1977—. Part-time film and literature teacher in American Studies Department at University of Nottingham, Nottingham, 1979-86.

WRITINGS:

NOVELS

(Under pseudonym Thom Ryder) *Avenging Angel*, New English Library, 1975.
(Under Ryder pseudonym) *Angel Alone*, New English Library, 1975.
Amphetamines and Pearls, Sphere, 1976.
The Geranium Kiss, Sphere, 1976.
One of Our Dinosaurs Is Missing (novelization of screenplay), New English Library, 1976.
(Under pseudonym Jon Barton) *Kill Hitler*, Corgi, 1976.
(Under Barton pseudonym) *Forest of Death*, Corgi, 1977.
(Under Barton pseudonym) *Lightning Strikes*, Corgi, 1977.
Junkyard Angel, Sphere, 1977.
Neon Madman, Sphere, 1977.
(Under pseudonym L. J. Coburn) *The Raiders* (western), Sphere, 1977.
(Under pseudonym J. B. Dancer) *Evil Breed* (western), Coronet, 1977.
(Under Dancer pseudonym) *Judgement Day* (western), Coronet, 1978.
Herbie Goes to Monte Carlo (novelization of screenplay), illustrations by Tony Masero, New English Library, 1978.
(Under Coburn pseudonym) *Bloody Shiloh* (western), Sphere, 1978.
(Under Dancer pseudonym) *The Hanged Man* (western), Coronet, 1979.
Frame, Methuen, 1979.
Blind, Methuen, 1981.
(With Laurence James, under joint pseudonym James Mann) *Endgame*, New English Library, 1982.
(Under pseudonym Terry Lennox) *Dancer Draws a Wild Card*, R. Hale, 1985.

JUVENILE

What About It, Sharon? Penguin, 1979.
Reel Love, Scholastic Press, 1982.
Sundae Date, Scholastic Press, 1983.
What Game Are You Playing? Scholastic Press, 1983.
Footwork, Scholastic Press, 1984.
Wild Love, Pan, 1986.
Last Summer, First Love, Pan, 1986.
Kidnap! Beaver, 1987.
Daylight Robbery! Beaver, 1987.
Hot Property! Beaver, 1987.

SCRIPTS

"Just Another Little Blues Song" (television drama), British Broadcasting Corporation (BBC-TV), 1984.
"Anna of the Five Towns" (dramatic television adaptation), BBC-TV, 1985.
"Ivy Who?" (radio drama), BBC-Radio, 1987.
"Hard Cases" (dramatic television series), Central Television, 1987-88.
"The Old Wives' Tale" (dramatic television adaptation), BBC-TV, 1987-88.

OTHER

Provence (poetry), Priapus Press, 1978.
The Old Postcard Trick (poetry), Slow Dancer Press, 1985.
Duty Free (adaptation of television series), Ravette, 1986.
More Duty Free (adaptation of television series), Ravette, 1986.
Neil Sedaka Lied (poetry), Smith: Doorstop Press, 1987.

Contributor of short stories to periodicals, including *Western*.

WESTERN NOVELS UNDER PSEUDONYM WILLIAM S. BRADY

Blood Money, Fontana, 1979.
Killing Time, Fontana, 1980.
Blood Kin, Fontana, 1980.
Desperadoes, Fontana, 1981.
Whiplash, Fontana, 1981.
Dead Man's Hand, Fontana, 1981.
Sierra Gold, Fontana, 1982.
Death and Jack Shade, Fontana, 1982.
War Party, Fontana, 1983.
Border War, Fontana, 1983.
Killer! Fontana, 1983.
The Lost, Fontana, 1984.

NOVELS UNDER PSEUDONYM JON HART; "MERCENARIES" SERIES

Black Blood, Mayflower, 1977.
High Slaughter, Mayflower, 1977.
Triangle of Death, Mayflower, 1977.
Guerilla Attack! Mayflower, 1977.
Death Raid, Mayflower, 1978.

WESTERN NOVELS UNDER NAME JOHN B. HARVEY; "HART THE REGULATOR" SERIES

Cherokee Outlet, Pan, 1980.
Blood Trail, Pan, 1980.
Tago, Pan, 1980.
The Silver Lie, Pan, 1980.
Blood on the Border, Pan, 1981.
Ride the Wide Country, Pan, 1981.
Arkansas Breakout, Pan, 1982.
John Wesley Hardin, Pan, 1982.
The Skinning Place, R. Hale, 1983.
California Bloodlines, R. Hale, 1983.

WESTERN NOVELS UNDER PSEUDONYM WILLIAM M. JAMES; "APACHE" SERIES

Blood Rising, Pinnacle, 1979.
Blood Brother, Pinnacle, 1980.
Death Dragon, Pinnacle, 1981.
Death Ride, Pinnacle, 1983.
The Hanging, Pinnacle, 1983.

WESTERN NOVELS UNDER PSEUDONYM JOHN J. McLAGLEN; "HERNE THE HUNTER" SERIES

River of Blood, Corgi, 1976.
Shadow of the Vulture, Corgi, 1977.
Death in Gold, Corgi, 1977.
Cross-Draw, Corgi, 1978.
Vigilante! Corgi, 1979.
Sun Dance, Corgi, 1980.
Billy the Kid, Corgi, 1980.
Till Death . . ., Corgi, 1980.
Dying Ways, Corgi, 1982.
Hearts of Gold, Corgi, 1982.
Wild Blood, Corgi, 1983.

WESTERN NOVELS UNDER PSEUDONYM J. D. SANDON; "GRINGOS" SERIES

Cannons in the Rain, Mayflower, 1979.
Border Affair, Mayflower, 1979.
Mazatlan, Mayflower, 1980.
Wheels of Thunder, Mayflower, 1981.

WORK IN PROGRESS: *Lonely Hearts*, a police thriller featuring a detective named Resnick; more police thrillers featuring character Resnick; a thriller series for BBC-TV; "possibly a second series of 'Hard Cases' for Central Television"; some juvenile thrillers, for Beaver; a new collection of poetry.

SIDELIGHTS: John Harvey told *CA:* "I am trying now to write in the areas of both television and fiction, probably keeping my fiction to the areas of juvenile novels and adult thrillers, while letting my television work take up more 'personal' themes, as well as allowing scope for dramatizations—a fascinating and difficult task, but well worth it. At the back of all this lies my love of film: most of my writing has film not far from its style and execution as well as subject matter. The move into television has made this even more so."

*   *   *

HARVEY, John B.
See HARVEY, John (Barton)

*   *   *

HASSINGER, Edward W(esley)   1925-

PERSONAL: Born November 20, 1925, in Morton, Minn.; son of Harold L. (a locomotive engineer) and Wilma M. (a homemaker; maiden name, Munsell) Hassinger; married Isabelle E. Cabaniss (a homemaker), August 12, 1960; children: Edward Wesley, Jr., James Harold, Louise Marie, Diane Elizabeth. *Education:* University of Minnesota—Twin Cities, B.S., 1948, M.A., 1951, Ph.D., 1956. *Religion:* Christian (Disciples of Christ).

ADDRESSES: Home—4115 Defoe Dr., Columbia, Mo. 65203. *Office*—Department of Rural Sociology, University of Missouri—Columbia, Columbia, Mo. 65211.

CAREER: University of Missouri—Columbia, instructor, 1953-56, assistant professor, 1956-62, associate professor, 1962-68, professor of rural sociology, 1968—.

MEMBER: American Sociological Association, Rural Sociology Society, American Public Health Association, National Rural Health Association.

WRITINGS:

Rural Health Organization: Social Networks and Regionalization, Iowa State University Press, 1982.
(With James Pinkerton) *The Human Community,* Macmillan, 1986.

WORK IN PROGRESS: The Rural Church: Learning From Three Decades of Change, with John S. Holik and J. Kenneth Benson; a study of rural hospitals.

SIDELIGHTS: Edward W. Hassinger told *CA:* "The questions that concern me are the adaptations of rural institutions in a changing rural society. The issue is, how can rural communities maintain some degree of social control while participating actively in an increasingly urban society?"

*   *   *

HATHAWAY, Richard Dean   1927-

PERSONAL: Born August 8, 1927, in Chillicothe, Ohio; son of Dale M. and Edith (Hart) Hathaway; married Shirley Cornwell (marriage ended); married Viola Hale (a writer), April 16, 1978; children: Linda Hathaway Ellis, Bruce. *Education:* Oberlin College, A.B. (summa cum laude), 1949; Harvard

University, A.M., 1952; Case Western Reserve University, Ph.D., 1964. *Religion:* Society of Friends (Quakers).

ADDRESSES: Home—11 Crescent Lane, New Paltz, N.Y. 12561. *Office*—Department of English, State University of New York College at New Paltz, New Paltz, N.Y. 12562.

CAREER: Maritime College of the State University of New York, Bronx, instructor in English, 1955; Rensselaer Polytechnic Institute, Troy, N.Y., instructor in English, 1957-62; State University of New York College at New Paltz, assistant professor, 1962-65, associate professor, 1966-70, professor of English, 1970—. Danforth associate, 1960—; associate professor at Millsaps College, 1965-66. *Military service:* U.S. Naval Reserve, 1945-47.

MEMBER: Modern Language Association of America, American Studies Association, Phi Beta Kappa.

WRITINGS:

Sylvester Judd's New England, Pennsylvania State University Press, 1981.

Co-author with John Langan of a series of computer programs for composition instruction, including "Sentence Skills" and "Reading and Study Skills," for McGraw, 1988.

SIDELIGHTS: Richard Dean Hathaway told *CA:* "My book, *Sylvester Judd's New England,* is a critical biography of the one author associated with both transcendentalism and New England regionalist fiction. As a convert from Calvinism to Unitarianism, Judd is also of interest to the cultural historian."

*   *   *

HATTERAS, Amelia
See MENCKEN, H(enry) L(ouis)

*   *   *

HATTERAS, Owen
See MENCKEN, H(enry) L(ouis)
and NATHAN, George Jean

*   *   *

HAVELOCK, Eric A(lfred)   1903-1988

OBITUARY NOTICE—See index for CA sketch: Born June 3, 1903, in London, England; naturalized U.S. citizen; died April 4, 1988, in Poughkeepsie, N.Y. Educator and author. Havelock, a leading scholar of ancient Greek culture, was professor of classics and chairman of the classics department at Yale University from 1963 until his retirement as professor emeritus in 1971. Earlier he had taught at Acadia University in Wolfville, Nova Scotia, Victoria College in Toronto, Ontario, and—from 1946 to 1963—at Harvard University, where he served as professor of Greek and Latin and chairman of the classics department. His writings include *The Liberal Temper in Greek Politics, Preface to Plato, The Greek Concept of Justice, The Literate Revolution in Greece and Its Cultural Consequences,* and articles contributed to professional journals.

OBITUARIES AND OTHER SOURCES:

BOOKS

Directory of American Scholars, Volume III: *Foreign Languages, Linguistics, and Philology,* 8th edition, Bowker, 1982.

PERIODICALS

New York Times, April 7, 1988.

*   *   *

HAYTER, Stanley William   1901-1988

OBITUARY NOTICE: Born December 27, 1901, in London (one source says Hackney), England; died of cardiac arrest, May 4, 1988, in Paris, France. Chemist, geologist, educator, artist, and author. Regarded as one of the most influential graphic artists of his generation, Hayter developed engraving techniques that revolutionized the art of printmaking in the twentieth century. After receiving degrees in geology and chemistry from Kings College, Hayter worked in the oil fields of Iran during the early 1920s, painting landscapes and portraits in his spare time. When he returned to England in 1926 he exhibited some of his paintings in London, and later that year he moved to Paris to study printmaking at the Academie Julian, where he became a master of line engraving. In 1927 he founded Atelier 17, his famous Paris art studio and workshop, where he taught printmaking techniques to such artists as Jackson Pollock, Salvador Dali, Alexander Calder, Marc Chagall, Joan Miro, and Pablo Picasso. Hayter was also an accomplished painter, and many of his works have been displayed in art exhibitions and museums worldwide. His works of the 1930s are considered surrealistic while those of later periods are described as European abstract impressionist. He discussed his innovative printmaking techniques in two books, *New Ways of Gravure* and *About Prints*, which are considered required reading for printmakers.

OBITUARIES AND OTHER SOURCES:

BOOKS

Current Biography, H. W. Wilson, 1945, June, 1988.
Who's Who, 140th edition, St. Martin's, 1988.
Who's Who in Art, 22nd edition, Art Trade Press, 1986.

PERIODICALS

Los Angeles Times, May 7, 1988.
New York Times, May 6, 1988.
Times (London), May 7, 1988.
Washington Post, May 6, 1988.

*   *   *

HEADLEY, Gwyn   1946-

PERSONAL: Born July 17, 1946, in England; son of Lewis Victor (a minister) and Elaine (Young) Headley. *Education:* Attended secondary school in Westminster, England. *Religion:* Anglican.

ADDRESSES: Office—HPR Publicity, 22 Mount View Rd., London N4 4HX, England. *Agent*—John Farquharson Ltd., 162-168 Regent St., London W1R 5TB, England.

CAREER: HPR Publicity, London, England, managing director, 1976—.

MEMBER: Folly Society (founder), British Mah-Jong Association (founder and chairman).

WRITINGS:

(With Yvonne Seeley) *Mah-Jong*, A. and C. Black, 1978.
(With Wim Meulenkamp) *Follies: A National Trust Guide*, J. Cape, 1986.

Hidden Treasure, J. Cape, 1989.
The Savoy Food and Drink Book, Octopus, 1989.
Cat Lovers, Genesis, in press.

Author of "Follies," first broadcast by BBC-TV, February, 1988, and "Monstrous Erections," first broadcast by London Weekend Television, 1988.

SIDELIGHTS: Gwyn Headley told *CA:* "I write not because I enjoy the act of writing but in order to express my lively sense of wonder in what surrounds us. If critics are kind enough to express their pleasure, then that's a bonus.

"*Hidden Treasure* is an exploration of the secret troves to be found in Britain's lesser-known museums. I wrote to 1500 museums in the United Kingdom to discover what they were proudest of."

*   *   *

HEALY, George W(illiam), Jr.   1905-1980

OBITUARY NOTICE—See index for *CA* sketch: Born September 22, 1905, in Natchez, Miss.; died November 2, 1980. Editor and author. During his nearly fifty-year association with the *New Orleans Times-Picayune*, Healy served successively as reporter, city editor, managing editor, and editor. He was also director of the Times-Picayune Publishing Corporation during much of that time. The author of an autobiography, *A Lifetime on Deadline: Self-Portrait of a Southern Journalist*, Healy contributed to *The Iron Gate*, *Do You Belong in Journalism?*, and *William Faulkner of Oxford*. He also served as editor of *Scream* during the 1920s and contributing editor of *Collier's* during the 1930s.

OBITUARIES AND OTHER SOURCES:

BOOKS

The International Year Book and Statesmen's Who's Who, Thomas Skinner Directories, 1982.
Who Was Who in America, With World Notables, Volume VII: *1977-1981*, Marquis, 1981.

*   *   *

HEARNE, John (Edgar Caulwell)   1926-
(John Morris, a joint pseudonym)

PERSONAL: Born February 4, 1926, in Montreal, Quebec, Canada; son of Maurice Vincent and Doris (May) Hearne; married Joyce Veitch, September 3, 1947 (divorced); married Leeta Mary Hopkinson (a teacher), April 12, 1955; children: two. *Education:* Attended Jamaica College; Edinburgh University, M.A., 1950; University of London, teaching diploma, 1950. *Religion:* Christian.

ADDRESSES: Home—P.O. Box 335, Kingston 8, Jamaica. *Office*—Creative Arts Centre, University of the West Indies, Kingston 7, Jamaica. *Agent*—Claire Smith, Harold Ober Associates, Inc., 40 East 49th St., New York, N.Y. 10017.

CAREER: Teacher at schools in London, England, and in Jamaica, 1950-59; information officer, Government of Jamaica, 1962; University of the West Indies, Kingston, Jamaica, resident tutor in extramural studies, 1962-67, head of Creative Arts Centre, 1968—. Visiting Gregory Fellow in Commonwealth Literature at University of Leeds, England, 1967; Colgate University, New York, visiting O'Connor Professor in Literature, 1969-70, and visiting professor in literature, 1973. *Military service:* Royal Air Force, air gunner, 1943-46.

MEMBER: International P.E.N.

AWARDS, HONORS: John Llewelyn Rhys Memorial Prize, 1956, for *Voices Under the Window;* Silver Musgrave Medal from Institute of Jamaica, 1964.

WRITINGS:

NOVELS

Voices Under the Window, Faber, 1955, reprinted, 1985.
Stranger at the Gate, Faber, 1956.
The Faces of Love, Faber, 1957, published as *The Eye of the Storm*, Little, Brown, 1958.
The Autumn Equinox, Faber, 1959, Vanguard Press, 1961.
Land of the Living, Faber, 1961, Harper, 1962.
(With Morris Cargill, under joint pseudonym John Morris) *Fever Grass*, Putnam, 1969.
(With Cargill, under joint pseudonym John Morris) *The Candywine Development*, Collins, 1970, Lyle Stuart, 1971.
The Sure Salvation, Faber, 1981, St. Martin's, 1982.

SHORT STORIES

"The Wind in This Corner" and "At the Stelling" appear in *West Indian Stories*, edited by Andrew Salkey, Faber, 1960; "A Village Tragedy" and "The Lost Country" appear in *Stories From the Caribbean*, edited by Salkey, Elek, 1965, published as *Island Voices: Stories From the West Indies*, Liveright, 1970.

OTHER

(With Rex Nettleford) *Our Heritage*, University of the West Indies, 1963.
(Editor and author of introduction) *Carifesta Forum: An Anthology of Twenty Caribbean Voices*, Carifesta 76 (Kingston, Jamaica), 1976.
(Editor and author of introduction) *The Search for Solutions: Selections From the Speeches and Writings of Michael Manley*, Maple House Publishing Co., 1976.
(With Lawrence Coote and Lynden Facey) *Testing Democracy Through Elections: A Tale of Five Elections*, edited by Marie Gregory, Bustamante Institute of Public and International Affairs (Kingston, Jamaica), 1985.

Also author of teleplays, including "Soldiers in the Snow," with James Mitchell, 1960, and "A World Inside," 1962; author of stage play "The Golden Savage," 1965. Work represented in anthologies, including O. R. Dathorne's *Caribbean Narrative: An Anthology of West Indian Writing*, Heinemann, 1966, and Barbara Howes's *From the Green Antilles: Writings of the Caribbean*, Macmillan, 1966.

Contributor of short stories and articles to periodicals, including *Atlantic Monthly*, *New Statesman*, and the *Trinidad Guardian*.

SIDELIGHTS: A West Indian writer who sometimes collaborates with Morris Cargill as the pseudonymous John Morris, John Hearne is known for his vivid depictions of life among the West Indies and their people. In particular, several of his writings focus on Jamaica—the native land of his parents—and address complex social and moral issues affecting both individual relationships and, to a lesser extent, the cultural and political aspects of the island. Much of Hearne's fiction—including the novels *Stranger at the Gate*, *The Faces of Love*, *The Autumn Equinox*, and *Land of the Living*—also takes place on Cayuna, a mythical counterpart of Jamaica. More generally, his work relates a broad, first-hand account of the Caribbean experience and features elements of racial and social

inequities as well as recurrent themes of betrayal and disenchantment. Especially noteworthy are Hearne's acclaimed narrative skill and descriptive style, which distinguish his fiction as characteristically evocative and lifelike.

Hearne's 1981 novel, *The Sure Salvation*, takes place in the southern Atlantic Ocean aboard a sailing ship of the same name. Set in the year 1860, the story chronicles the illegal buying and selling of negroes more than fifty years after England first enacted laws prohibiting the practice commonly known as slave trade. Through a "series of deft flashbacks," observed *Times Literary Supplement* critic T. O. Treadwell, Hearne recounts individual circumstances that led to his characters' unlawful fraternity on board the *Sure Salvation*. Risking constant danger and the death penalty if they are caught, the captain and crew hope to amend their ill-fated lives with monies paid for the vessel's charge of five hundred Africans. While the "beastliness isn't played down," Treadwell noted, we come "to understand, and even sympathize with" these men and their despicable dealings due to Hearne's successful literary craftsmanship and execution. Treadwell further announced that the "author's gift for irony . . . that the slavers are no freer than" their shackled cargo, provides this "absorbing" tale with its utmost pleasures, and he concluded that *The Sure Salvation* proves the "power of the sea story . . . as potent as ever."

Hearne commented that his writing is influenced by his growing up in an island society large enough to be interesting but small enough for "characters" to be known intimately. He added: "I have been much concerned with politics (as a commentator) as Jamaica has tried to fashion itself into a newly independent society since the early 1960s."

BIOGRAPHICAL/CRITICAL SOURCES:

BOOKS

James, Louis, editor, *The Islands In Between: Essays on West Indian Literature*, Oxford University Press, 1968.
Ramchand, Kenneth, *The West Indian Novel and Its Background*, Barnes & Noble, 1970.

PERIODICALS

Times Literary Supplement, June 19, 1981.

*   *   *

HEFFERNAN, Thomas J(ohn Andrew)   1944-

PERSONAL: Born April 7, 1944, in New York, N.Y.; son of Thomas John and Anne (Cusack) Heffernan; married Judith Jennings (a social worker), October 8, 1971; children: Anne Katherine. *Education:* Manhattan College, B.A., 1968; New York University, M.A., 1970; Cambridge University, Ph.D., 1977.

ADDRESSES: Home—715 Scenic Dr., Knoxville, Tenn. 37919. *Office*—Department of English, University of Tennessee, Knoxville, Tenn. 37916.

CAREER: University of Tennessee, Knoxville, began as assistant professor, 1975, became associate professor of English.

MEMBER: Mediaeval Academy of America, South Atlantic Modern Language Association.

AWARDS, HONORS: Elliott Prize from Mediaeval Academy of America, 1977; fellow of American Philosophical Society, 1977, and National Humanities Center, 1986-87.

WRITINGS:

(Editor) *The Popular Literature of Medieval England,* University of Tennessee Press, 1985.
Sacred Biography, Oxford University Press, 1988.

Contributor to literature journals. Editor of *Studies in the Age of Chaucer.*

WORK IN PROGRESS: Cistercian Spirituality in Twelfth-Century England.

BIOGRAPHICAL/CRITICAL SOURCES:

PERIODICALS

Knoxville Journal, July 25, 1987.
Times Literary Supplement, August 14, 1987.

*　　*　　*

HEGENER, Mark Paul 1919-1988

OBITUARY NOTICE: Born April 6, 1919, in Petoskey, Mich.; died March 19, 1988, in Oak Brook, Ill. Clergyman, administrator, editor, and writer. Director of the Franciscan Herald Press for more than thirty-five years, Hegener published works on Catholic theology and numerous biographies of St. Francis of Assisi. He entered the Franciscan order in 1938 and was ordained a priest seven years later. In 1939 Hegener joined the press, became its director in 1949, and subsequently edited its *Franciscan Herald* and *Forum,* a journal for lay Franciscans. He retired in 1986. In addition to his publishing work Hegener served as provincial director of the Lay Franciscans for twenty-five years and founded three apartment complexes for the elderly. His writings include *The Poverello: St. Francis of Assisi* and *Short History of the Third Order of St. Francis.*

OBITUARIES AND OTHER SOURCES:

BOOKS

American Catholic Who's Who, Volume 23: *1980-1981,* National Catholic News Service, 1979.
Who's Who in the World, 8th edition, Marquis, 1986.

PERIODICALS

Chicago Tribune, March 25, 1988.

*　　*　　*

HEIN, Marvin Lester 1925-

PERSONAL: Born April 12, 1925, in Isabella, Okla.; son of David (a farmer) and Marie (a homemaker; maiden name, Suderman) Hein; married Mary Helen Martens (a homemaker), September 1, 1946; children: Patricia, Penelope (Mrs. David Unruh), Holly. *Education:* Tabor College, A.B., 1951; Central Baptist Theological Seminary, B.D., 1955, Th.M., 1958. *Politics:* Republican.

ADDRESSES: Home—3036 East Magill, Fresno, Calif. 93710. *Office*—North Fresno Mennonite Brethren Church, 5724 North Fresno St., Fresno, Calif. 93710.

CAREER: Ordained Mennonite minister, 1951; pastor of Congregational church in Wakefield, Kan., 1953-56; began as assistant pastor, became senior pastor of Mennonite church in Hillsboro, Kan., 1956-80; North Fresno Mennonite Brethren Church, Fresno, Calif., senior pastor, 1980—. Chairman of board of directors of Herald Publishing Co., 1974-80; member of board of directors of Mennonite Brethren Biblical Semi-

nary, 1975-87; Mennonite Brethren Church of North America, member of board of education, 1969-80, vice-chairman of Board of Christian Literature, 1987—, chairman of Pacific District Conference, chairman, vice-chairman, and member of Board of Reference and Counsel; past member of board of directors of Kansas Foundation for Private Colleges.

MEMBER: Kansas Association of Evangelicals (president, 1969-72).

WRITINGS:

The Ties That Bind, Kindred Press, 1980.
Like a Shock of Wheat: Meditations on Death, Herald Press, 1981.

Contributor to religious magazines.

SIDELIGHTS: Marvin Lester Hein told *CA:* ''*Like a Shock of Wheat: Meditations on Death* resulted from officiating at some 350 funeral services in a large congregation where more than 450 persons were over sixty-five years old. The book's perspective is different from most in that it seeks to steer clear of the old cliches, the false promises like 'he is just away,' and tries to be more direct and honest about the feelings associated with death and bereavement. *Ties That Bind* represents the first book of sermons published by a Mennonite Brethren pastor.''

*　　*　　*

HEINEMAN, Helen 1936-

PERSONAL: Born August 1, 1936, in Queens, N.Y.; daughter of Joseph (a business manager) and Margaret (a housewife; maiden name, Friedel) Kliegl; married John L. Heineman (a professor), September 30, 1961; children: John, Mike, George, Joseph. *Education:* Queens College of the City of New York (now Queens College of the City University of New York), B.A. (summa cum laude), 1958; Columbia University, M.A., 1959; Cornell University, Ph.D., 1967. *Religion:* Roman Catholic.

ADDRESSES: Home—Framingham, Mass. 01701. *Office*—Department of English, Framingham State College, 100 State St., Framingham, Mass. 01701.

CAREER: College professor, 1967-73; Framingham State College, Framingham, Mass., professor of English, 1973—.

WRITINGS:

Mrs. Trollope: The Triumphant Feminine in the Nineteenth Century, Ohio University Press, 1978.
Frances Trollope, G. K. Hall, 1984.
Restless Angels: The Friendship of Six Victorian Women, Ohio University Press, 1984.

Poems represented in *New England Poetry Engagement Book* and *The Cape Codder.* Contributor of articles to *Dictionary of Literary Biography* and to periodicals, including *American Quarterly, Radcliffe Quarterly, International Journal of Women's Studies, Harvard Magazine, Ariel, Christian Science Monitor,* and *Boston Globe.*

WORK IN PROGRESS: Two mystery novels, *Tawasentha: A Cape Cod Mystery* and *Midsummer Madness: Murder on a Literary Tour.*

SIDELIGHTS: Helen Heineman's biographical studies of several little-known Victorian women attracted critical attention and won acclaim as fascinating, perceptive, thoroughly researched, and well written. In *Restless Angels: The Friendship of Six Victorian Women* Heineman examines the lives of six nineteenth-century middle-class women who corresponded with each other during a twenty-five-year period. The circle of friends included two sets of sisters: the Wrights, Frances and Camilla, and the Garnetts, Harriett, Frances, and Julia; and Frances Trollope, who was fifteen years older than the others. Heineman chronicles the efforts of these six Victorian women to live fulfilling lives in a society that placed severe restrictions on them. In *Mrs. Trollope: The Triumphant Feminine in the Nineteenth Century,* an earlier publication, Heineman had focused on the most resolute of these six women, Frances Trollope, who coped with the loss of fortune, husband, and several children, and built a successful career as a writer. *Frances Trollope,* Heineman's 1984 book on the Victorian author, develops a critical guide to Trollope's prolific writings and argues for her significance as a pathbreaker in theme and technique for later novelists.

Among the critics admiring Heineman's biographies were *Review of English Studies* contributor A.F.T. Lurcock, who described *Mrs. Trollope: The Triumphant Feminine in the Nineteenth Century* as "a triumphant success . . . meticulous and enthusiastic" and judged it "so far superior to all other accounts of Mrs. Trollope that no comparison is worthwhile," and *Victorian Studies* reviewer Lee Chambers-Schiller, who lauded *Restless Angels: The Friendship of Six Victorian Women* for "beautifully articulat[ing] the dilemma" of a nineteenth-century feminine generation unable to decide whether happiness and fulfilment "lie in work or in the affections, in the self-actualization promised by meaningful occupation or the giving up of self to love." Similarly, Cara Chanteau, writing in *Books and Bookmen,* called *Restless Angels* a "goldmine of a correspondence, . . . full of rich seams of understanding and food for thought."

Heineman told *CA:* "I first became interested in Frances Trollope when working on my Ph.D. I soon fell in love with her. She represented what 'the triumphant feminine' meant to me when I made that phrase the subtitle of my biography. She was a woman who successfully combined a full writing career—thirty-five novels, six travel books—with a devotion to her family. For me she was both subject and inspiration, as I researched and wrote her story during the years when I had four children under the age of five.

"My biographies are scholarly and literary. Yet my hope has always been to interest what Virginia Woolf called 'the common reader' in my subjects. I am not a debunking biographer. Because I must live so long with my subjects, I must love and respect them for me to do my best. My relationship between biographer and subject resembles that between close dear friends.

"I was led to my investigation of the women in *Restless Angels* through my fortuitous friendship with Cecilia Payne-Gaposhkin, world-famed astronomer, who died in 1980, and who owned the letters upon which I based my book. I found her while researching Frances Trollope, and she generously put her family papers at my disposal. Her great-grandmother was Mrs. Trollope's best friend. Mrs. Gaposhkin encouraged me to try the composite biography and was my guide, mentor, and inspiration throughout.

"I'm now writing mystery novels and have completed two. They are 'literary' tales, mainly because my heroine—and amateur detective—is Winiefred Burren, assistant professor of English, aided by her historian husband, Mike. I've written dozens of critical articles and reviews but am longing to achieve success with these novels. Meanwhile, for fun, I read mysteries. Ruth Rendell is my favorite and, of course, P. D. James.''

AVOCATIONAL INTERESTS: Music, cross-country skiing, swimming, family life in general.

BIOGRAPHICAL/CRITICAL SOURCES:

PERIODICALS

Books and Bookmen, April, 1984.
Choice, May, 1980, January, 1985.
Review of English Studies, August, 1982.
Times Literary Supplement, December 5, 1980.

*   *   *

HEINLEIN, Robert A(nson)   1907-1988
(Anson MacDonald, Lyle Monroe, John Riverside, Caleb Saunders, Simon York)

OBITUARY NOTICE—See index for *CA* sketch: Surname rhymes with "fine line"; born July 7 (one source says October 21), 1907, in Butler, Mo.; died of heart failure, May 8 (one source says May 7), 1988, in Carmel, Calif.; cremated and ashes scattered at sea with military honors. Engineer and author. Considered one of the world's most creative and influential writers of science fiction, Heinlein authored more than forty-five books, some of which were made into motion pictures. His novels have been published in at least thirty languages and have sold more than forty million copies. Ranked with Isaac Asimov and Arthur C. Clarke as a master of the science fiction genre, Heinlein has been lauded for his ability to create entire societies in economical but convincing detail. His fictional writings have often anticipated scientific and technical advances.

Prior to turning to writing full time, Heinlein worked as an architect, real estate agent, aeronautical engineer, and electronics company official, and he owned a silver mine. He also served as an aviation engineer with the U.S. Navy during World War II, a period in which he wrote several engineering textbooks. Among Heinlein's most popular titles are *Stranger in a Strange Land, Double Star, The Green Hills of Earth, Citizen of the Galaxy, Day After Tomorrow,* and *Door Into Summer.* Heinlein was also the author of two screenplays and contributor of many short stories and articles, some under pseudonyms, to *Saturday Evening Post, Analog, Galaxy, Astounding Science Fiction,* and other publications. Among his many awards and honors were four Best Science Fiction Novel awards from the World Science Fiction Convention in 1956, 1959, 1961, and 1966; an unprecedented four Hugo awards, the "Oscars" of science fiction writing; and the first Grand Master Nebula Award, given to Heinlein in 1975 by the Science Fiction Writers of America for his lifelong contribution to the genre. Heinlein was also a guest commentator with CBS-TV reporter Walter Cronkite during the Apollo 11 space mission that put the first man on the moon.

OBITUARIES AND OTHER SOURCES:

BOOKS

Current Biography, H.W. Wilson, 1988.
Who's Who in the World, 8th edition, Marquis, 1986.

PERIODICALS

Chicago Tribune, May 11, 1988.
Detroit News, May 10, 1988.
Los Angeles Times, May 10, 1988.

New York Times, May 10, 1988.
Times (London), May 11, 1988.
Washington Post, May 10, 1988.

*   *   *

HELLER, Dawn Hansen 1932-

PERSONAL: Born August 11, 1932, in Green Bay, Wis.; daughter of Norbert and Dorothy Hansen; married Anton G. Heller. *Education:* Carleton College, A.B., 1954; Rosary College, M.A.L.S., 1966.

ADDRESSES: Home—516 South Ashland Ave., LaGrange, Ill. 60525. *Office*—P.O. Box 431, LaGrange, Ill. 60525.

CAREER: Member of editorial staff of Peterson Publishing, Chicago, Ill., 1954-57; Riverside-Brookfield School District, Riverside, Ill., high school English teacher, 1957-65, librarian, 1965-71, district media coordinator, 1971—. Co-publisher of *Library Insights: Promotion and Programs*, 1978—. Speaker and presenter for conferences and workshops. Independent video producer.

MEMBER: American Library Association, Library Administration and Management Association, American Association of School Librarians, National School Public Relations Association, Illinois Library Association (past president), Illinois Association for Media in Education (past president).

AWARDS, HONORS: Grants from Illinois Humanities Council, 1979, and Illinois State Library, 1982; Honor Award from Illinois Association for Media in Education, 1981; award from American Association of School Librarians and Encyclopaedia Britannica, 1984, for the National School Library Media Program of the Year.

WRITINGS:

(Contributor) Kathleen Rummel and Esther Perica, editors, *Persuasive Public Relations*, American Library Association, 1983.
(Contributor) Marian S. Edsall, editor, *Practical PR for School Library Media Centers*, Neal-Schuman, 1984.
(With Ann Montgomery Tuggle) *Grand Schemes and Nitty Gritty Details: Library PR That Works*, Libraries Unlimited, 1987.
Winning Ideas From Winning Schools: Recognizing Excellence, American Bibliographical Center-Clio Press, in press.

Contributor to library journals. Guest editor of *Illinois Libraries*.

SIDELIGHTS: Dawn Hansen Heller told *CA:* "Most of my 'writing' happens in my head before I sit down at the computer keyboard or pick up yellow legal pad. It is nonproductive to start the process too soon. Where am I going? How am I going to get there? When I have the route mapped, then I am ready to spell out the directions on paper, complete with scenic highlights along the way.

"It seems as though I have always written for publication, from the junior high school newspaper to press releases that helped pay college tuition, and articles for trade journals in the restaurant, hotel/motel, and hospital fields. But those were the 'quick and dirty' kinds of writing. It was a different kind of effort to complete the *Grand Schemes* book for Libraries Unlimited and to face the editor's corrections from the other side of the equation. Undoubtedly good for the soul but different nevertheless.

"More and more the focus is on public relations—sharing with others 'how to do it right and let others know about it.' Since no one is rushing to pick up the movie and television rights for our first book, Ann Tuggle and I are considering another kind—'quick and semi-dirty'—but we're not sure our life experiences qualify us for this kind of best-seller category. Perhaps the answer is to forget the writing and concentrate on the life experiences."

*   *   *

HEMINGWAY, Maggie 1946-

PERSONAL: Born March 17, 1946, in Orford, England; daughter of John (a doctor) and Elizabeth (Johnston) Hemingway; married, 1967 (divorced, 1977). *Education:* University of Edinburgh, M.A., 1967.

ADDRESSES: Home—London, England; and Kent, England. *Agent*—Curtis Brown, 162-8 Regent St., London W1R 5TA, England.

CAREER: Held production, editorial, and home and foreign rights posts in publishing trade, 1976-86; full-time writer, 1987—.

AWARDS, HONORS: The Bridge received The Royal Society of Literature Award (under the Winifred Holtby Bequest), 1987.

WRITINGS:

The Bridge (novel), Atheneum, 1986.
Stop House Blues (novel), Hamish Hamilton, 1988.

Contributor of reviews to *Times Educational Supplement*.

WORK IN PROGRESS: A third novel.

SIDELIGHTS: Maggie Hemingway, in her first novel, *The Bridge*, portrays an actual British impressionist painter, Philip Steer, whose sensual and creative art abruptly and significantly diminished in quality after 1891. Hemingway's book provides a fictional explanation for this decline. In the summer of 1887, at the seaside Suffolk village of Walberswick, England, Steer falls in love with Isobel Heatherington, the lonely wife of a London stockbroker. Due to the impropriety of their romance, the two are agonizingly separated, and their missed happiness renders the once artistically inspirational village unbearable for the painter. Although *Washington Post* critic Brigitte Weeks defined Hemingway's plot as "fragile," unable to bear the burden of a responsibility as great as ruining an artist's career, she commended the novel: "As a prose poem, in the 19th-century summer among the upper middle classes made up of evocative descriptions linked by a tenuous plot, this novel is worth reading." A "cerebral and suggestive writer," Hemingway, wrote Weeks, "knows how to evoke a scene; she can probe her characters' minds; she has a flair for detail."

Hemingway told *CA:* "If I were to be asked what preoccupies me principally in my writing, I would say that the central subject in my novels is freedom—how people handle the various freedoms they possess and those to which they have potential access. I am perpetually surprised and eternally curious, after years of observation, about the way that if people are not 'everywhere in chains,' then those without start to manufacture them, either real or imaginary. It is a subject with such infinite variations of tragedy and comedy that it could fascinate me forever."

BIOGRAPHICAL/CRITICAL SOURCES:

PERIODICALS

Washington Post, February 17, 1987.

*   *   *

HEMPTON, David   1952-

PERSONAL: Born February 19, 1952, in Belfast, Northern Ireland; son of Thomas William (a salesman) and Winnie (a housewife; maiden name, Boyd) Hempton; married Louanne McCrory (a social worker), July 7, 1979; children: Stephen Neil, Jonathan Andrew. *Education:* Received B.A. (with honors) from Queen's University, Belfast, and Ph.D. from University of St. Andrews.

ADDRESSES: Home—1 Inver Park, Holywood, County Down BT18 9NF, Northern Ireland. *Office*—Department of History, Queen's University, University Rd., Belfast BT7 1NN, Northern Ireland.

CAREER: College of Ripon and York St. John (University of Leeds), York, England, lecturer in history, 1977-79; Queen's University, Belfast, Northern Ireland, lecturer in history, 1979—.

MEMBER: Royal Historical Society, American Historical Association.

AWARDS, HONORS: Whitfield Prize from Royal Historical Society, 1984, for *Methodism and Politics in British Society, 1750-1850*.

WRITINGS:

Methodism and Politics in British Society, 1750-1850, Stanford University Press, 1984.
(Contributor) Tom Dunne, editor, *The Writer as Witness: Literature as Historical Evidence*, Cork University Press, 1987.
(Contributor) Terry Thomas, editor, *The British: Their Religious Beliefs and Practices*, Routledge & Kegan Paul, 1988.
(Contributor) Patrick Loughridge, editor, *The People of Ireland*, Appletree Press, 1988.
(Contributor) Jeremy Black, editor, *Britain in the Eighteenth Century*, Macmillan, in press.
(Contributor) Hugh McLeod and Bob Scribner, editors, *Social History of Religion in the Industrial Revolution in Britain and Ireland, 1770-1870*, Methuen, in press.
(Contributor) S. W. Gilley and W. J. Sheils, editors, *Religion in Britain: A History*, Basil Blackwell, in press.

Contributor to history and theology journals, including *Albion, Arena, Eighteenth-Century Studies, Fortnight, History, History of Education, History Today, Irish Historical Studies, Journal of Ecclesiastical History, Journal of Irish Christian Study Centre, Linen Hall Review, Northern History, Saothar, Scottish Historical Review, Themelios*, and *Third Way*.

WORK IN PROGRESS: Popular Protestantism: Culture and Society in Ulster, 1750-1900, with Myrtle Hill, publication by Hutchinson expected in 1990; a contribution to a volume in honor of W. R. Ward, edited by Keith Robbins, publication by Basil Blackwell expected in 1989; "Methodism in Nineteenth-Century Britain," to be included in a collection edited by D. G. Paz, publication expected in 1989.

SIDELIGHTS: David Hempton told *CA:* "The main themes of my writing, as is understandable for someone who grew up in Northern Ireland in the 1960s, are the complex relationships between popular religion and politics in Britain and Ireland in the modern period. More recently I have been concerned with understanding the nature of religious belief and practice (within a proper cultural context) in the British Isles. In so doing I have tried to use the widest possible range of sources and methods, including quantitative, literary, comparative, and interdisciplinary approaches. There is much yet to be done.''

*   *   *

HENDERSON, F. C.
See MENCKEN, H(enry) L(ouis)

*   *   *

HENDERSON, George Wylie   1904-

PERSONAL: Born June 14, 1904, in Warrior's Stand, Ala. *Education:* Attended Tuskegee Institute.

CAREER: Novelist and short story writer. Printing apprentice for New York *Daily News.*

WRITINGS:

NOVELS

Ollie Miss, Stokes, 1935, University of Alabama Press, 1988. *Jule*, Creative Age, 1946.

Contributor of short stories to periodicals, including New York *Daily News* and *Redbook*.

SIDELIGHTS: In the history of Afro-American literature, George Wylie Henderson's writing places the novelist between the Harlem Renaissance, a period of heightened literary activity in the 1920s, and the social protest movement of the 1940s led by author Richard Wright. Most noted for his realistic and straightforward novels portraying the poor, the ordinary, and the forgotten with humanity and dignity, Henderson derived his works both from black tradition as well as the newly intensified social consciousness of his time. His first and more successful novel, the 1935 *Ollie Miss*, outlines the struggles of an alienated eighteen-year-old girl, Ollie, in a small southern town. Finding herself pregnant and rejected by her love Jule, the heroine perseveres with strength and independence. The novel was well received by critics, who praised the work for its pastoral elegance, stunning realism, careful characterization, and, especially, Henderson's authentic use of black dialect.

His second novel, *Jule*—a sequel to *Ollie Miss*—relates the growth and social struggle of Jule, the illegitimate son of Ollie and the elder Jule. Henderson traces the boy's passage from innocence to experience, as the southerner ventures north, only to be met with racial conflict. Unlike *Ollie Miss*, *Jule* addresses the issues of social protest and attempts to make a statement on racism. Despite its bold efforts, the book was negatively received. Reviewers criticized Henderson for failing to deal with the complex, internal states of his characters, as well as for his one-dimensional portrayals of blacks and whites. After this unsuccessful second work, Henderson never wrote another novel.

BIOGRAPHICAL/CRITICAL SOURCES:

BOOKS

Bone, Robert, *The Negro Novel in America*, Yale University Press, 1965.

Dictionary of Literary Biography, Volume 51: *Afro-American Writers Before the Harlem Renaissance to 1940*, Gale, 1987.

PERIODICALS

New York Herald Tribune, February 23, 1935.
New York Times, February 24, 1935, October 13, 1946.
Weekly Book Review, October 20, 1946.*

*   *   *

HENRIES, A. Doris Banks   1913(?)-1981
(Doris Henries)

PERSONAL: Born February 11, 1913 (some sources say 1919 or 1930), in Live Oak, Fla. (some sources say Middletown, Conn., or Liberia); immigrated to Liberia, c. 1940; died of cancer, February 16, 1981, in Middletown (one source says Middleton), Conn.; married Richard Abrom Henries (a politician) in 1942 (died in April, 1980); children: two sons. *Education:* Received B.Sc. from Willimantic Normal School (now Eastern Connecticut State University); attended Connecticut State Teachers' College, Yale University, Hartford Seminary Foundation (now Hartford Seminary), and University of Besancon in France; received M.A. and Ph.D. from Columbia University. *Politics:* True Whig. *Religion:* Methodist.

ADDRESSES: Home—Middletown, Conn.

CAREER: Principal of Fuller Normal School, 1934-39; United Methodist Church of the United States, missionary in Liberia, c. 1939; director of education in Maryland County, Liberia, 1940-42; Liberia College (became University of Liberia, 1951), Monrovia, professor, 1942-59, dean of William V. S. Tubman Teachers College, 1951-55, dean, 1955-59, acting president, 1956-57 and 1958-59; government of Liberia, director of higher education and textbook research, 1959-78, acting assistant minister of education, 1978. Served in Liberia as regional director for Africa and member of executive committee of World Council for Curriculum and Instruction, chairman of Methodist board of education, president of National YMCA (Young Men's Christian Association), and vice-chairman of Opportunities Industrial Centre.

MEMBER: African Studies Association, American Academy of Social Sciences, Liberian National Teachers Organization (former president), International Alliance of Women, Zonta International, Federation of Women's Organizations (former vice-president of Liberian chapter), Liberia Authors Association (former president).

AWARDS, HONORS: Methodist Trust Fund Grant from United Methodist Church of the United States, c. 1939; honorary D.Ed. from Liberia College, 1949; Knight Official, Star of Africa, 1950, Grand Band, Humane Order of African Redemption, 1955, Dame Grand Commander, Order of Knighthood of Pioneers of Liberia, 1959, all from Liberia; Ordre des Arts et des Lettres (France), 1958; Order of the Grand Cross and Order of Merit, both from Germany in 1962.

WRITINGS:

(Under name Doris Henries; with husband, Richard Henries) *Liberia, the West African Republic*, F. R. Bruns, 1950.
Civics for Liberian Schools, Collier-Macmillan, 1953, revised edition, 1966.
The Liberian Nation: A Short History, Collier-Macmillan, 1953, revised edition, 1966.
Heroes and Heroines of Liberia (juvenile), Macmillan, 1962.

More About Heroes and Heroines of Liberia, Book II (juvenile), illustrations by Ceasar W. Harris, Liberian Information Service, 1962.
Development of Unification in Liberia, Department of Education, Monrovia, Liberia, 1963.
(Editor) *Poems of Liberia, 1836-1961*, Macmillan (London), 1963.
Presidents of the First African Republic, Macmillan (London), 1963.
The Life of Joseph Jenkins Roberts, 1809-1876, and His Inaugural Addresses, illustrations by Geoffrey Whittman, Macmillan (London), 1964.
(Editor) *Liberian Folklore: A Compilation of Ninety-nine Folktales With Some Proverbs*, Macmillan (London), 1966, St. Martin's, 1968.
(Contributor) *New Sum of Poetry From the Negro World*, Volume 57, Presence Africaine, 1966.
A Biography of President William V. S. Tubman, Macmillan (London), 1967.
Africa: Our History, Collier-Macmillan, 1969.
(Editor) *Liberia's Fulfillment: Achievements of the Republic of Liberia During Twenty-five Years Under the Administration of President William V. S. Tubman, 1944-1969*, Monrovia, 1969.
(Editor) *Liberian Literature, Grade 8*, Ministry of Education, Monrovia, 1976.
(Editor) *Liberian Literature, Grade 9*, Ministry of Education, Monrovia, 1976.

Also author of *Living Together in City and Country, Maryland Melodies*, and children's book *Liberians at Work;* co-author of *Education in Liberia* and *Fatu's Experiences.* Editor of *Education Laws of Liberia, 1926-1974.* Contributor to anthology *Liberian Writing.*

SIDELIGHTS: A. Doris Banks Henries grew up in America, but shortly after finishing her graduate education at Columbia University she immigrated to the African republic of Liberia. She became a leading educator of her adopted country, eventually serving as acting assistant minister of education, and was also one of Liberia's most prolific writers. Henries's works range from poetry, biography, and history to critical essays, anthologies, and textbooks. In April of 1980, the government of Liberia was overthrown in a coup and her husband, Richard A. Henries, who was the speaker of the House of Representatives of Liberia, was executed—one of thirteen Liberian officials killed by firing squad. One month later Henries returned to the United States.

AVOCATIONAL INTERESTS: Bridge, drama, traveling, writing.

OBITUARIES:

PERIODICALS

New York Times, February 18, 1981.*

*   *   *

HENRIES, Doris
See HENRIES, A. Doris Banks

*   *   *

HERSH, Reuben   1927-

PERSONAL: Born December 9, 1927, in New York, N.Y.; son of Philip (a merchant) and Mildred (a merchant; maiden name, Shluger) Hersh; married Phyllis Falchook (an engineer),

February 13, 1949; children: Daniel, Eva. *Education:* Harvard University, B.A., 1946; New York University, M.S., 1960, Ph.D., 1962.

ADDRESSES: Home—1423 Bryn Mawr Dr. N.E., Albuquerque, N.M. 87106. *Office*—Department of Mathematics, University of New Mexico, Albuquerque, N.M. 87131.

CAREER: Scientific American, New York, N.Y., assistant editor, 1948-52; Varityper Corp., Newark, N.J., machinist, 1955-57; Fairleigh Dickinson University, Rutherford, N.J., assistant professor of mathematics, 1962; Stanford University, Palo Alto, Calif., instructor in mathematics, 1962-64; University of New Mexico, Albuquerque, assistant professor, 1964-67, associate professor, 1967-70, professor of mathematics, 1970—. Visiting member of Courant Institute, New York University, 1970-71; visiting professor at Brown University, 1979, and University of California, Berkeley, 1979. *Military service:* U.S. Army, 1946-47.

MEMBER: American Mathematical Society, Mathematical Association of America, American Association of University Professors.

AWARDS, HONORS: Chauvenet Prize from Mathematical Association of America, 1975, for an article; American Book Award from Association of American Publishers, 1983, for *The Mathematical Experience.*

WRITINGS:

(With Philip J. Davis) *The Mathematical Experience,* introduction by Gian-Carlo Rota, Birkhauser Boston, 1981.
(With Davis) *Descartes' Dream: The World According to Mathematics,* Harcourt, 1986.

Contributor of articles to mathematical journals and *Scientific American.*

SIDELIGHTS: Reuben Hersh and Philip J. Davis have produced two books about mathematics for general readers. Their 1981 *The Mathematical Experience* explores the philosophy of mathematics and explains what professional working mathematicians do. A critical and popular success, the volume won an American Book Award. *Descartes' Dream: The World According to Mathematics* followed in 1986. Detailing the increasing mathematization of contemporary society, the authors warn against looking for the answer to human problems in the abstract realm of the mathematician; "the solution . . . lies in the cultivation of strong values that lie outside science," they insist.

Hersh told *CA: "The Mathematical Experience* was an attempt to let the world at large have a glimpse at the rather little-known and esoteric inner life of mathematics and mathematicians; and also to let mathematicians see themselves in a perspective broader and more humane than the usual technical narrow focus."

See also *DAVIS, Philip J.*

BIOGRAPHICAL/CRITICAL SOURCES:

PERIODICALS

Christian Science Monitor, May 14, 1982.
Harper's, October, 1981.
Los Angeles Times, November 11, 1986.
New Statesman, December 12, 1986.
New Yorker, March 9, 1981.
New York Review of Books, August 13, 1986.

New York Times Book Review, October 5, 1986.
Times Literary Supplement, May 14, 1982, February 13, 1987.

* * *

HERSTEIN, I(srael) N(athan)   1923-1988

OBITUARY NOTICE: Given name originally Itzhak; name legally changed; born March 28, 1923, in Lublin, Poland; immigrated to United States; naturalized citizen, 1980; died of cancer, February 9 (one source says February 8), 1988, in Chicago, Ill. Mathematician, educator, editor, and author. Professor of mathematics at the University of Chicago for more than twenty-five years, Herstein wrote two algebra textbooks that have become standards, *Topics in Algebra* and *Noncommutative Rings.* Herstein taught at the universities of Kansas and Pennsylvania and at Cornell University before joining the faculty of Chicago in 1962. He was also a visiting professor at a number of institutions worldwide, including Yale University, University of Palermo, and Hebrew University of Jerusalem, and he was a Fulbright lecturer in Brazil and in the Canary Islands. His last book, *Primer on Linear Mathematics,* was published in February, 1988, just prior to his death. Herstein also edited one book and wrote more than one hundred papers.

OBITUARIES AND OTHER SOURCES:

BOOKS

American Men and Women of Science: The Physical and Biological Sciences, 16th edition, Bowker, 1986.
Who's Who in Technology Today, Volume I: *Electronics and Computer Science,* 4th edition, J. Dick, 1984.

PERIODICALS

Chicago Tribune, February 11, 1988.
New York Times, February 10, 1988.

* * *

HERTZ, David Michael   1954-

PERSONAL: Born May 30, 1954, in Bay Shore, N.Y.; son of Joseph H. (a teacher) and Sarah (a teacher) Hertz. *Education:* Indiana University—Bloomington, B.A. (with honors), 1976, B.S. (with distinction), 1977, M.A., 1979; New York University, M.Phil., 1982, Ph.D., 1983.

ADDRESSES: Home—Bloomington, Ind. *Office*—Department of Comparative Literature, Ballantine Hall, Indiana University—Bloomington, Bloomington, Ind. 47401.

CAREER: New York University, New York, N.Y., lecturer in liberal studies and instructor in comparative literature, both 1981-83, Mellon postdoctoral fellow, 1983-84, assistant professor of comparative literature, 1984-86; Indiana University—Bloomington, visiting assistant professor of comparative literature, 1987—. Director of Eastern Comparative Literature Conference, 1985-86; pianist and composer for orchestra and string quartet.

MEMBER: Modern Language Association of America, Dramatists Guild, American Comparative Literature Association, American Society of Composers, Authors, and Publishers.

WRITINGS:

The Tuning of the Word: The Musico-Literary Poetics of the Symbolist Movement, Southern Illinois University Press, 1987.

Contributor of articles and reviews to comparative literature journals.

WORK IN PROGRESS: The Angels of Reality: Frank Lloyd Wright, Wallace Stevens, and Charles Ives, publication expected in 1989; music for an opera about China.

SIDELIGHTS: David Michael Hertz told *CA:* "My goal is to live the double life of artist and scholar. As a composer I always try to build on the great achievements of the past yet above all to be sensitive—in every sense of the word—to the sounds of *today.* From both a scholarly and artistic point of view, I believe that real originality must happen organically, from within, and must never be self-conscious.

"My first book is the logical result of my in-depth study of two art forms that have become unnecessarily distinct in the modern world—literature and music. *The Tuning of the Word* reflects, too, my continuing interest in musical poetry and poetic music. My title grew out of my gradual realization that the 'word,' as used by the poets, was literally 'tuned up' to approximate the condition of the musical note in the nineteenth century. I focused on the Symbolists because one can trace, in many important respects, the origins of modern styles in art to them.

"My present manuscript, *Angels of Reality: Frank Lloyd Wright, Wallace Stevens, and Charles Ives,* is a search for my own roots as an American artist. The title comes from a poem by Stevens in which he argues that reality is the 'necessary angel.' The work is a study of how three major American artists found unique, fresh, and distinctly un-European voices in architecture, poetry, and music, respectively. These three Americans were influenced by dominant European intellectuals. In the case of Stevens, the major presence was [French symbolist poet Stephane] Mallarme. For Ives, it was [French composer Claude] Debussy. For Wright, [French architect Eugene Emmanuel] Viollet-le-duc. Yet all three were able to find their individuality through the contemplation of ordinary American reality. For them, the reality of everyday America was the 'necessary angel' that linked imaginative ideas of the possibilities of art to the surrounding world. The celebration of everyday reality is what distinguishes Wright, Stevens, and Ives from their European predecessors."

*   *   *

HERZOG, Peter Emilius   1925-

PERSONAL: Born December 25, 1925, in Vienna, Austria; immigrated to the United States, 1950, naturalized citizen, 1955; son of Paul and Leopodine (Mannhart) Herzog; married Brigitte Ecolivet, June 29, 1970; children: Paul, Elizabeth Ann. *Education:* Attended University of Vienna, 1949-50; Hobart College, B.A., 1952; Syracuse University, LL.B. (summa cum laude), 1955; Columbia University, LL.M., 1956. *Religion:* Roman Catholic.

ADDRESSES: Home—112 Erregger Rd., Syracuse, N.Y. 13224. *Office*—College of Law, 334 E. I. White Hall, Syracuse University, Syracuse, N.Y. 13244.

CAREER: New York State Department of Law, Albany, deputy assistant attorney general, 1955-57, assistant attorney general, 1957-58; Syracuse University, Syracuse, N.Y., assistant professor, 1958-62, associate professor, 1962-66, professor of law, 1966-83, Crandall Melvin Professor, 1983—, law librarian, 1960-68. Visiting professor at University of Paris, 1976-77. Staff member of Columbia University's Project on

Inter Procedure, 1960-63; associate director of Project on European Legal Institutions, 1968—; member of staff of United Nations Commission on International Trade Law, 1968-69; research fellow in procedural aspects of international law, 1968-71; director of studies at The Hague Academy of International Law, 1969; consultant to New York State Eminent Domain Commission.

MEMBER: International Law Association, American Society of International Law, Societe de Legislation Comparee, Wissenschaftliche Gesellschaft fuer Verfahrensrecht, Phi Beta Kappa, Coif.

WRITINGS:

(With Martha Weser) *Civil Procedure in France,* Nijhoff, 1967.
(With Ivan Head and Frank Dawson) *International Law, National Tribunals, and the Rights of Aliens,* Syracuse University Press, 1971.
(With Hans Smit) *The Law of the European Economic Community: A Commentary,* six volumes, Matthew Bender, 1976, revised edition, 1988.
(Editor) *Harmonization of Laws in the European Communities,* University Press of Virginia, 1983.
(With Rudolf B. Schlesinger, Hans Baade, and Mirjan Damaska) *Comparative Law: Cases and Materials,* Foundation Press, fifth edition, 1987.

Contributor to law journals. Member of board of editors of *American Journal of Comparative Law,* 1977—.

*   *   *

HEXHAM, Irving   1943-

PERSONAL: Born April 14, 1943, in Whitehaven, Cumbria, England; son of Thomas Johnson and Elsie (Bell) Hexham; married second wife, Karla Poewe (an anthropologist), 1988; children: (first marriage) Jeremy, Janet. *Education:* University of Lancaster, B.A. (with honors), 1970; University of Bristol, M.A. (with commendation), 1972, Ph.D., 1975. *Politics:* New Democrat. *Religion:* Anglican.

ADDRESSES: Home—P.O. Box 3880, High River, Alberta, Canada T0L 1B0. *Office*—Department of Religious Studies, University of Calgary, Calgary, Alberta, Canada.

CAREER: North-Western Gas Board, Stockport, England, apprentice gas fitter, 1958-64, manager in Ashton-under-Lyne, England, 1964-65; Stretford Technical College, Stretford, England, lecturer in gas technology, 1967; Bishop Lonsdale College, Derby, England, assistant professor of religious studies, 1974-77; Regent College, Vancouver, British Columbia, assistant professor of philosophy of religion, 1977-80; University of Manitoba, Winnipeg, assistant professor of religious studies, 1980-84; University of Calgary, Calgary, Alberta, assistant professor of religious studies, 1984—. Religious broadcaster on Canadian Broadcasting Corp. weekly program "The Calgary Eyeopener."

MEMBER: Canadian Society for the Study of Religion, Evangelical Theological Society, Society for the Scientific Study of Religion, American Academy of Religion, Royal African Society, South African Institute of Race Relations.

AWARDS, HONORS: Grants from Social Science and Humanities Research Council of Canada.

WRITINGS:

The Irony of Apartheid, Edwin Mellen, 1982.

(With wife, Karla Poewe) *Understanding Cults and New Religions,* Eerdmans, 1986.
(Editor with Walter Block) *Religion, Economics, and Social Thought: Proceedings of an International Symposium,* Fraser Institute, 1987.
(Editor) *Texts on Zulu Religion: Traditional Zulu Ideas About God,* Edwin Mellen, 1988.

WORK IN PROGRESS: Debunking Cults and New Age Religions, publication expected in 1989; *Charismatic Christianity: A Cross-Cultural Perspective,* publication expected in 1990; editing the works of F. B. Welbourn; research on religion and racial reconciliation in South Africa.

SIDELIGHTS: Irving Hexham told *CA:* "I am an evangelical Christian working in the field of religious studies. My particular interests are new religious movements and religion and society in South Africa. Since 1969 I have been involved in the study of South African society and a member of the South African Institute of Race Relations, which is thoroughly opposed to apartheid. I am interested in the Afrikaners and the role of religion, especially Calvinism, in forming their social and political views.

"I became interested in South Africa as an undergraduate student because of the claim that it was the Calvinist religion of the Afrikaners which had originally created apartheid. If true, this created a major problem for my understanding of Christianity. My interest in new religious movements arose as a result of meeting 'hippies' in the late 1960s and early 1970s. Originally I intended to write my master's thesis on South Africa but Fred Welborn insisted that I had to 'get my hands dirty' by studying a religious group through participant observation and not simply from books. Therefore, he argued, I could only study the Afrikaners by going to South Africa, learning their language and living among them. As this was not feasible when I was studying for my master's degree, I had to find a local subject where I could immerse myself in the culture of the group I was studying. The result was that in my master's thesis I analysed the lifestyles and beliefs of the 'hippies' of Glastonbury, England. I then went to South Africa and spent two years in the Afrikaner Nationalist heartland where I did my archival work at the University of Potchefstroom. At the same time I made every effort to follow an anthropological approach to understanding the Afrikaners by simply living with them. Throughout my career I have believed that understanding preceeds criticism and that informed criticism of any position, whether cults or Afrikaner Nationalism, can only be made after the critic has thoroughly immersed him or herself in the beliefs and lifestyle of the peoples being studied."

BIOGRAPHICAL/CRITICAL SOURCES:

PERIODICALS

Globe and Mail (Toronto), June 6, 1987.

*   *   *

HEYER, Marilee   1942-

PERSONAL: Born May 7, 1942, in Long Beach, Calif.; daughter of Arthur Henry (a machinist) and Esther May (Orth) Heyer. *Education:* Art Center College of Design, B.A. (with honors), 1965.

ADDRESSES: Home—21100 Gary Dr., No. 313, Hayward, Calif. 94546. *Agent*—Toni Mendez, 141 56th St., New York, N.Y. 10022.

CAREER: Scene designer for children's television cartoon shows, including "The Lone Ranger," "Journey to the Center of the Earth," "The Hardy Boys," and "The Archies," 1965-70; Liberty House Department Store, San Francisco, Calif., fashion illustrator, 1970-77; Compendium Design Studio, San Francisco, illustrator, 1977-80; I. Magnin Department Store, San Francisco, fashion illustrator, 1980—. Assistant storyboard artist for "Return of the Jedi," 1982.

MEMBER: San Francisco Society of Illustrators.

WRITINGS:

The Weaving of a Dream (self-illustrated juvenile), Viking-Penguin, 1986.
The Forbidden Door (self-illustrated juvenile), Viking-Penguin, 1988.

WORK IN PROGRESS: A fairy tale, for Viking-Penguin.

*   *   *

HIGGINS, Joan   1948-

PERSONAL: Born June 15, 1948, in Yorkshire, England; daughter of Kenneth (a nurse) and Kate (a nurse) Higgins; married John Powell Martin (a professor), September 16, 1983. *Education:* Newcastle upon Tyne Polytechnic, B.A. (with honors), 1969; University of York, Diploma in Social Administration, 1971; University of Southampton, Ph.D., 1979.

ADDRESSES: Office—Department of Sociology and Social Policy, University of Southampton, Southampton, Hampshire SO9 5NH, England.

CAREER: Portsmouth Polytechnic, Portsmouth, England, research assistant, 1971-73, lecturer in social policy, 1973-74; University of Southampton, Southampton, England, lecturer, 1974-86, senior lecturer in social policy, 1986—, director of Institute for Health Policy Studies, 1987—. Chairman of Hampshire Council on Alcoholism, 1984—; member of Southampton and Southwest Hampshire District Health Authority, 1982—.

MEMBER: British Institute of Management.

WRITINGS:

The Poverty Business, Basil Blackwell, 1978.
States of Welfare, Basil Blackwell, 1981.
(With Nicholas Deakin, John Edwards, and Malcolm Wicks) *Government and Urban Policy: Inside the Policy-Making Process,* Basil Blackwell, 1983.
The Business of Medicine: Private Health Care in Britain, Macmillan, 1988.

Chairman of editorial board of *Journal of Social Policy,* 1987—.

WORK IN PROGRESS: Comparison of private health care in Britain and Hungary; writing about welfare markets.

BIOGRAPHICAL/CRITICAL SOURCES:

PERIODICALS

Annals of the American Academy of Political and Social Science, September, 1980.
Times Literary Supplement, July 15, 1983.

*   *   *

HILL, Arthur Norman   1920(?)-1988

OBITUARY NOTICE: Born c. 1920 in Sault Sainte Marie,

Mich.; died March 16, 1988, in Stoughton, Wis. Staffer at advertising agencies, columnist, and author. A devoted fan of the Detroit Tigers baseball team, Hill was best known as the author of two books on America's favorite pastime, *Don't Let Baseball Die* and *I Don't Care If I Never Come Back*. Hill worked at advertising agencies in the Detroit area before moving to Wisconsin. For a column that he wrote for a Wisconsin newspaper, Hill was named by that state's Newspaper Association best weekly columnist in 1985.

OBITUARIES AND OTHER SOURCES:

PERIODICALS

Detroit Free Press, March 18, 1988.

*   *   *

HILL, Charles William, Jr.   1940-

PERSONAL: Born September 17, 1940, in Martinsburg, W.Va.; son of Charles W. (a welder) and Fern Mae Hill; married Mary Louise Bland (a teacher), July 23, 1962; children: Charles William III, Stewart Adams. *Education:* Shepherd College, B.A., 1962; American University, M.A., 1964, Ph.D., 1969. *Politics:* "Republican moderate." *Religion:* Evangelical Lutheran.

ADDRESSES: Home—1627 Millwood Dr., Salem, Va. 24153. *Office*—Department of History and Political Science, Roanoke College, Salem, Va. 24153.

CAREER: U.S. Advisory Commission on Intergovernmental Relations, Washington, D.C., librarian, 1964; Central Economic Development Organization, Inc., Washington, D.C., research assistant, 1965-67; U.S. Department of Housing and Urban Development, Model Cities Administration, Washington, D.C., program specialist, 1967-69; Roanoke College, Salem, Va., assistant professor, 1969-76, associate professor, 1977-81, professor of political science, 1982—.

MEMBER: American Political Science Association, National Collegiate Honors Council, Southern Political Science Association, American Culture Association, Virginia Social Science Association (secretary-treasurer), Virginia Collegiate Honors Council (executive committee member).

WRITINGS:

The Political Theory of John Taylor of Caroline, Fairleigh Dickinson University Press, 1977.

WORK IN PROGRESS: A book on American political humor, with Denis Lape.

SIDELIGHTS: Charles William Hill told *CA:* "My work on John Taylor was a study of a Virginia Jeffersonian who served to link Jeffersonian agrarianism with the state sovereignty ideas that achieved prevalence in the antebellum South. Although Taylor is often considered to be a forerunner of John C. Calhoun, the South Carolina politician, I argue that the Virginian was always a unionist because of the more optimistic assumptions he made about human nature and the active influence of higher law in political affairs.

"I continue my interest in the republicanism of the U.S. founding period. There was an appreciation then for the importance of aspiring to serve the public interest, the overlap of personal and public virtue, and an active citizenship—which is largely missing from the cynical interest-group pluralism and neo-Marxist interpretation of politics today. To some extent the founders may be considered philosophic conservatives, but there are some very important differences, also, and I intend to explore these in future writings.

"In the area of American political humor, I combine my interests in art and politics by writing on the subject of political cartooning. Recent monographs have dealt with the treatment of vice-presidential candidate Geraldine Ferraro by political cartoonists and the devolution of Uncle Sam from a proud national symbol to almost a bozo character. More generally, Denis Lape and I hope to be working during a future sabbatical on a book that reviews American comic character-types in the light of the social and political events that they satirized. Our thesis is that humor has often been used as a vehicle to convey some pretty serious conclusions about politics. In our writing we will cover at least the following character-types: Yankees, frontiersmen and women; common people; fools; little people lost; and Jewish, black, and Irish character-types."

*   *   *

HILL, Lawrence   1912-1988

OBITUARY NOTICE: Born May 26, 1912, in New York, N.Y.; died of emphysema, March 14, 1988, in Norwalk, Conn. Administrator, book salesman, publisher, and editor. Involved in the publishing business for more than four decades, Hill founded Lawrence Hill publishing company in the early 1970s. The firm produces mostly books that address political and social themes, especially those concerning the third world, the Middle East, and Afro-Americans. Hill joined the sales department of the Alfred Knopf publishing house in 1942 and subsequently worked as editor and sales manager of Hill & Wang, publishers of plays and books on the theater, before establishing his own company.

OBITUARIES AND OTHER SOURCES:

BOOKS

The Biographical Encyclopedia of Who's Who of the American Theatre, James Heineman, 1966.

PERIODICALS

New York Times, March 15, 1988.
Publishers Weekly, April 1, 1988.

*   *   *

HILL, Leslie Pinckney   1880-1960

PERSONAL: Born May 14, 1880, in Lynchburg, Va.; died of a stroke, February 16 (one source says February 15), 1960, in Philadelphia, Pa.; buried in Kennett Square, Philadelphia, Pa.; son of Samuel Henry (a stationary engine operator) and Sarah Elizabeth (a laundress; maiden name, Brown) Hill; married Jane Ethel Clark, June 29, 1907; children: Eleanor Taylor (Mrs. Clifford Valentine), Hermione Clark (Mrs. Thomas S. Logan), Elaine Serena (Mrs. Frank Snowden), Natalie Dubois (Mrs. Rosamond Nelson), Mary Dorothea (Mrs. Herbert Tucker). *Education:* Harvard University, B.A. (cum laude), 1903, M.A., 1904. *Politics:* Republican.

ADDRESSES: Home—46 Lincoln Ave., Yeadon, Pa.

CAREER: Tuskegee Normal and Industrial Institute (now Tuskegee Institute), Tuskegee, Ala., English teacher and director of department of education, 1904-07; Manassas Industrial Institute, Manassas, Va., principal, 1907-13; Institute for Colored Youth (now Cheyney State College), Cheyney, Pa., principal, 1913-30, president, 1931-51, president emeritus, 1951-60; Mercy-Douglass Hospital, Philadelphia, Pa., administrator, 1953-56. Lecturing professor of general education at institutions, including University of California, Los Angeles. Member of Board of Presidents of Pennsylvania State Teachers Colleges, Pennsylvania Department of Welfare, Delaware County Board of Assistance, and Philadelphia Citizens Commission on City Policy; president of board of trustees of Manassas Industrial Institute; founder and president of Camp Hope; director of Armstrong Association of Philadelphia, Interracial Committee of Philadelphia, Delaware County Tuberculosis and Health Association, and Delaware County Health and Welfare Council.

MEMBER: National Education Association Committee on the Defense of Democracy Through Education, National Council Student Christian Associations, American Teachers Association, American Association of School Administrators, American Academy of Political and Social Science, United Service Organization, Peace Section of the American Friends Service Committee, Association of Negro Secondary and Industrial Schools (secretary-treasurer), Hoover Commission on Reorganization of Federal Government, Eastern States Association of Teachers Colleges and Professional Schools for Teachers, State Commission on Study of Urban Colored Population, Pennsylvania Education Association, Pennsylvania Association of Teachers of Colored Children (co-founder), Pennsylvania Teachers Association (founder), Pennsylvania State Negro Council (founder and president), Citizens Council of Delaware County, Visitation of Delaware County (member of board), West Chester Community Center (founder and president of board of directors), Phi Beta Kappa, Kappa Alpha Psi.

AWARDS, HONORS: Received LL.D. from Morgan State College, 1939, and Haverford College, 1951; Ed.D., Rhode Island College of Education, 1956; and Litt.D. from Lincoln University. Seltzer Award for distinguished service.

WRITINGS:

The Wings of Oppression (poems), Stratford, 1921, reprinted, Books for Libraries Press, 1971.
(Contributor) James Weldon Johnson, editor, *The Book of American Negro Poetry*, Harcourt, 1922.
(Contributor) Robert T. Kerlin, *Negro Poets and Their Poems*, Associated Publishers, 1923.
Toussaint L'Ouverture: A Dramatic History, Christopher, 1928.
(Contributor) Sterling A. Brown, Arthur P. Davis, and Ulysses Lee, editors, *The Negro Caravan*, Dryden, 1941.
(Contributor) Rayford W. Logan, editor, *What the Negro Wants*, University of North Carolina Press, 1944.
(Contributor) Langston Hughes and Arna Bontemps, editors, *The Poetry of the Negro*, Doubleday, 1949.

Also author of *Jethro*, a biblical drama, first published in 1931. Poetry represented in anthologies and in such periodicals as *Crisis, Life, Opportunity, Outlook, Phylon,* and *Teacher-Education Journal.*

SIDELIGHTS: Leslie Pinckney Hill is most known as a dedicated educator and activist poet who devoted his career and writings to the highest standards of education and equal race relations. After earning both his bachelor's and master's degrees from Harvard University, he began his teaching career at institutions in the South. Hill went on to serve at the Institute for Colored Youth in Pennsylvania (now Cheyney State College) for nearly forty years, guiding the school toward becoming a fully recognized and state-supported teachers college.

Though primarily an educator and active participant in civic organizations, the poet Hill sought to lend hope to members of his race through his writings, emphasizing the value of blacks and their contributions to America.

In his collection of sixty-nine poems, *Wings of Oppression,* Hill characterizes the black race as a group specifically chosen by God to endure suffering and as a vehicle through which God would eventually establish universal brotherhood. Additionally, the author stresses patience and calm endurance, believing that a small victory is better than none. Hill furthered his philosophy of peaceful triumphs in the 1928 five-part, blank-verse drama *Toussaint L'Ouverture,* which portrays the famed Haitian leader. In depicting L'Ouverture's successful rule, Hill praises both the Haitian's advocation of racial harmony and freedom for all as well as his condemnation of massacre and violence as a means of revolution.

Hill's views of racial relations differed markedly from the protest and black-pride writers of his time, and it is not certain whether Hill's philosophy was widely shared by American blacks. Not all of the author's writing, though, contained racial overtones; some of his educational writings and lectures promoted industry, stressed the importance of knowledge, and urged general goodwill toward all of humanity.

BIOGRAPHICAL/CRITICAL SOURCES:

BOOKS

Dictionary of Literary Biography, Volume 51: *Afro-American Writers From the Harlem Renaissance to 1940,* Gale, 1987.
Mays, Benjamin E., *The Negro's God,* Atheneum, 1969.

OBITUARIES:

PERIODICALS

Journal of Negro History, April, 1960.
New York Times, February 16, 1960.*

*   *   *

HILLER, Herbert L. 1931-

PERSONAL: Born July 14, 1931, in New York, N.Y.; son of Morris (a clothing manufacturer) and Stephanie (a homemaker; maiden name, Weiner) Hiller; married Mary Lee Ataie, 1958 (divorced, 1976); children: Nancy Rebecca, Magda Amelia. *Education:* Union College, Schenectady, N.Y., A.B., 1952; Harvard University, LL.B., 1955. *Politics:* Democrat. *Religion:* Jewish.

ADDRESSES: Home and office—3641 Park Lane, Coconut Grove, Fla. 33133.

CAREER: Norwegian Caribbean Lines, Miami, Fla., vice-president of public affairs, 1970-71; Caribbean Travel Association, New York, N.Y., executive director, 1971-73; Florida International University, Miami, assistant professor of international relations, 1973-76; travel trade consultant, 1976-80 and 1982-84; American Bicycling Association, Miami, executive director, 1980-81; Coconut Grove Chamber of Commerce, Coconut Grove, Fla., director, 1981-82; American Youth Hostels, Inc., Washington, D.C., national director, 1984—. Organizer of Caribbean Research and Development Center, Barbados, 1973, weekly Coconut Grove Farmer's Market, 1977, and Florida Bicycle Program, 1980; chairman of Florida Bicycle Council, 1984-86; tourism marketing consultant in Miami. *Military service:* U.S. Coast Guard Reserve, 1955-59; lieutenant junior grade.

MEMBER: American Youth Hostels, Partners for Livable Places.

AWARDS, HONORS: Charter honoree, Florida Governor's Physical Fitness Award, 1980.

WRITINGS:

Guide to the Small and Historic Lodgings of Florida, illustrations by Charles Greacen, Pineapple Press, 1986, 2nd edition, 1988.

Author of television script "After the Glass Box, What?" and "Sound and Light at Vizcaya," both 1982. Also author of column "Florida Wayfarer" for *Miami Today,* 1984—.

WORK IN PROGRESS: Research on the "dynamics of the small and historic lodgings sector in America."

SIDELIGHTS: Herbert L. Hiller told *CA:* "Since childhood I have been motivated by a sense of place and, generally, by the importance of heritage values in daily life. This has led me to organize projects around values which then became sources of earnings—for example, the annual Miami-Bahamas Goombay Festival that celebrates black heritage in Miami and now attracts some four hundred thousand persons for one weekend a year."

BIOGRAPHICAL/CRITICAL SOURCES:

PERIODICALS

Miami Herald, September 29, 1984.

*   *   *

HIRSH, M(ary) E(lizabeth)   1947-

PERSONAL: Born June 16, 1947, in Boston, Mass.; daughter of Edward L. (an English professor) and Margaret (a librarian; maiden name, Kelly) Hirsh; married David H. Montenegro (a writer), January 5, 1985. *Education:* Attended Boston College, 1966-68; Goddard College/Cambridge Institute, M.A. in Social Research, 1971.

ADDRESSES: Home—Boston, Mass. *Agent*—Berenice Hoffman, 215 West 75th St., New York, N.Y. 10023.

CAREER: Massachusetts Department of Public Welfare, Boston, director of public affairs, 1973-76; engaged in free-lance public affairs work in Boston, 1976—. Presidential assistant at Lower Roxbury Development Corp., Boston, 1984-86.

MEMBER: Spy Theater Company (Boston; board member).

WRITINGS:

A Low Income Housing Handbook, Commonwealth of Massachusetts, 1972.
Kabul (novel), Atheneum, 1986.

Contributor of book reviews to Boston *Phoenix* and *Los Angeles Times;* contributor to *Boston Business.*

WORK IN PROGRESS: Skylight, a novel set in contemporary America.

SIDELIGHTS: In her first novel, *Kabul,* M. E. Hirsh explores Afghanistan's political climate during the turbulent six years preceding the 1979 Soviet "Christmas Invasion." The story of a prominent Afghan family, *Kabul* describes how "the Anwari family is torn apart by personal crises even as the country is about to be ripped by . . . many political crises," *Los Angeles Times* reviewer Debra Denker revealed. "[Hirsh] skill-

fully and subtly weaves the politics of prewar Afghanistan into her narrative," continued the critic, "held together by the thread of the Anwari family's intimate involvement in their country's destiny." Writing in the *New York Times Book Review,* Wendy Smith commented that Afghan cabinet minister and family head Omar Anwari sees in his volatile, contentious children "the incoherence and despair that are destroying his country."

Smith's review, however, drew fire from such readers as Theodore L. Eliot, Jr., who served as U.S. ambassador to Afghanistan between 1973 and 1978. Objecting to the negative tone of Smith's critique and to what he characterized as her unfamiliarity with the "political complexities" of the country as represented in *Kabul,* the ambassador wrote to the *New York Times Book Review* to say that he found Hirsh's "treatment [of the period during which he served in Afghanistan] . . . impressively sensitive to the subtle forces that were in play." Eliot also commended Hirsh for a "fine job of portraying the tensions felt by younger, middle-class Afghans, torn between their sense of duty and responsibility to a traditional culture and their modern values . . . derived from their exposure to the West."

Other critical reaction to *Kabul* was generally favorable. *Kirkus Reviews,* which distinguished the novel with a starred review on the cover of its December 1, 1985, issue, called Hirsh's work an "expeditiously compressed and simplified—and quite splendidly mounted—action-and-*angst* version of the tragic and tumultuous recent history of Afghanistan." Writing in the *Washington Post,* Marjorie Williams offered similar praise, describing the novel as a "fully imagined, closely researched, energetically written story fixed in a distinctive place and time." Denker called Hirsh's "interestingly flawed Afghans . . . believable as characters." Williams concurred, noting that "it's rare to find such a large cast that numbers not a single lazily drawn character or . . . political sandwich board among its members." Williams concluded that *Kabul* "is well worth the trip . . . it's never hard to pick up, and often hard to put down . . . may it live long."

Kabul has also been published in Great Britain and Germany.

BIOGRAPHICAL/CRITICAL SOURCES:

PERIODICALS

Kirkus Reviews, December 1, 1985.
Los Angeles Times, May 8, 1986.
New York Times Book Review, February 2, 1986, March 23, 1986.
Time, February 17, 1986.
Washington Post, February 17, 1986.

*   *   *

HITCHCOCK, Henry-Russell   1903-1987

PERSONAL: Born June 3, 1903, in Boston, Mass.; died of cancer, February 19, 1987, in New York, N.Y.; son of Henry Russell, Sr. and Alice Whitworth (Davis) Hitchcock. *Education:* Harvard University, A.B., 1924, M.A., 1927.

CAREER: Vassar College, Poughkeepsie, N.Y., assistant professor of art, 1927-28; Wesleyan University, Middletown, Conn., assistant professor, 1929-41, associate professor, 1941-47, professor of art, 1947-48; Smith College, Northampton, Mass., professor, 1948-61, Sophia Smith Professor of Art, 1961-68, director of Museum of Art, 1949-55; University of

Massachusetts at Amherst, professor of art, 1968; New York University, New York, N.Y., adjunct professor at Institute of Fine Arts, beginning in 1969. Member of faculty of Connecticut College, 1934-42; lecturer at Massachusetts Institute of Technology, 1946-48, New York University, 1951, 1957, Yale University, 1951-52, 1959-60, 1970, Cambridge University, 1962, 1964, and Harvard University, 1965; Mathews Lecturer at Columbia University, 1971.

AWARDS, HONORS: Guggenheim fellow, 1945-46; grant from American Council of Learned Societies, 1961; D.F.A. from New York University, 1969; D.Litt. from University of Glasgow, 1973; award of merit from American Institute of Architects, 1978; D.H.L. from University of Pennsylvania, 1976, and Wesleyan University, Middletown, Conn., 1979; Benjamin Franklin Award from Royal Society of Arts, 1979.

WRITINGS:

Modern Architecture: Romanticism and Reintegration, Payson & Clarke, 1929, reprinted, Hacker Art Books, 1970.

(With Philip Johnson) *The International Style: Architecture Since 1922,* Norton, 1932.

The Architecture of H. H. Richardson and His Times, Museum of Modern Art, 1936, revised edition, MIT Press, 1966.

(With Catherine K. Bauer) *Modern Architecture in England,* Museum of Modern Art, 1937, reprinted, Arno, 1969.

American Architectural Books: A List of Books, Portfolios, and Pamphlets on Architecture and Related Subjects Published in America Before 1895, five volumes, privately printed, 1938-39, 4th edition, Da Capo, 1975.

Rhode Island Architecture, Rhode Island Museum Press, 1939, reprinted, Da Capo, 1968.

In the Nature of Materials, 1887-1941: The Buildings of Frank Lloyd Wright, Duell, Sloan & Pearce, 1942, reprinted, Da Capo, 1973.

Painting Toward Architecture, Duell, Sloan & Pearce, 1948.

(Editor with Arthur Drexler) *Built in USA: Post-War Architecture,* Museum of Modern Art, 1952.

Early Victorian Architecture in Britain, two volumes, Yale University Press, 1954, abridged edition, 1976.

Boston Architecture, 1637-1954, Reinhold, 1954.

Latin American Architecture Since 1945, Museum of Modern Art, 1955.

Architecture: Nineteenth and Twentieth Centuries, Penguin, 1958, 4th edition, 1977.

(Author of introduction) Ernst Danz, *Architecture of Skidmore, Owings & Merrill, 1950-1962,* Praeger, 1963.

(Author of introduction) Trewin Copplestone, editor, *World Architecture: An Illustrated History,* McGraw, 1963.

Richardson as a Victorian Architect, Smith College, 1966.

(Author of introduction) Philip Johnson, *Architecture, 1949-1965,* Thames & Hudson, 1966.

German Rococo: The Zimmermann Brothers, Penguin, 1968.

Rococo Architecture in Southern Germany, Phaidon, 1968.

(Contributor) Edgar Kaufmann, Jr., editor, *The Rise of an American Architecture,* Praeger, 1970.

Bauten und Entwuerfe—Buildings and Projects: Hentrich-Petschnigg & Partner (bilingual in German and English), Econ (Duesseldorf, West Germany), 1973.

(With William Seale) *Temples of Democracy: The State Capitols of the U.S.A.,* Harcourt, 1976.

Netherlandish Scrolled Gables of the Sixteenth and Early Seventeenth Centuries, College Art Association of America, 1978.

German Renaissance Architecture, Princeton University Press, 1981.

Editor of series "University Prints: Modern and American Architecture." Technical writer for Pratt & Whitney Aircraft, 1943-45. Contributor to journals in the United States and abroad.

SIDELIGHTS: Henry-Russell Hitchcock was highly respected as an architectural historian and educator. His prolific writings ranged widely in scope, from the field of medieval architecture to the work of such modern architects as Frank Lloyd Wright. All of his writings were based on first-hand, on-site research. In addition to his writing and teaching, Hitchcock popularized architectural history by presenting numerous exhibitions. One of his most influential was the International Style Show at the Museum of Modern Art in 1932, which focused on architectural styles that were, at the time, considered to be quite radical.

BIOGRAPHICAL/CRITICAL SOURCES:

BOOKS

Searing, Helen, editor, *In Search of Modern Architecture: A Tribute to Henry-Russell Hitchcock,* MIT Press, 1982.

PERIODICALS

New York Times, February 20, 1987.*

* * *

HOBBS, Albert Hoyt 1940-

PERSONAL: Born May 15, 1940, in Philadelphia, Pa.; son of Albert Hoyt (a college professor) and Ruth (Jasper) Hobbs; married Joy Adzigian (a free-lancer). *Education:* University of Pennsylvania, B.A., 1964; Brandeis University, M.A., 1966, Ph.D., 1968.

ADDRESSES: Office—Department of Philosophy, C.W. Post College of Long Island University, Greenvale, N.Y. 11548.

CAREER: Affiliated with philosophy department at C.W. Post College of Long Island University, Greenvale, N.Y.

WRITINGS:

(With wife, Joy Adzigian) *A Complete Guide to Egypt and the Archaeological Sites,* Morrow, 1981.

WORK IN PROGRESS: Fielding's Guide to Spain and Portugal.

* * *

HOCHSCHILD, Adam 1942-

PERSONAL: Born October 5, 1942, in New York, N.Y.; son of Harold K. (in business) and Mary (an artist; maiden name, Marquand) Hochschild; married Arlie Russell (a sociology professor), June 26, 1965; children: David, Gabriel. *Education:* Harvard University, A.B. (cum laude), 1963; graduate study at University of Geneva. *Politics:* "Non-denominational progressive." *Religion:* None.

ADDRESSES: Home—San Francisco, Calif. *Office—Mother Jones,* 2nd floor, 1663 Mission St., San Francisco, Calif. 94103. *Agent*—Georges Borchardt, Inc., 136 East 57th St., New York, N.Y. 10022.

CAREER: Free-lance writer, 1965—; *San Francisco Chronicle,* San Francisco, Calif., reporter, 1965-66; *Ramparts* magazine, San Francisco, writer and editor, 1966-68, 1973-74; *Mother Jones* magazine, San Francisco, co-founder, editor, and writer, 1976—. Presidential campaign staff member for Sen. George McGovern, 1972; commentator for National Public Radio in Washington, D.C., 1982-83; member of board of directors of *Nuclear Times* magazine, 1982—; regents lecturer at University of California at Santa Cruz, 1987; commentator for Public Interest Radio in New York, N.Y., 1987—; lecturer. *Military service:* U.S. Army Reserve, 1964-70.

MEMBER: National Writers Union, Overseas Press Club, National Book Critics Circle, Media Alliance, Foundation for National Progress (board of directors, 1976—), Campaign for Peace and Democracy/East and West, Commission on United States-Central American Relations.

AWARDS, HONORS: Certificate of Excellence from Overseas Press Club of America, 1981, for *Mother Jones* article on South Africa; Bryant Spann Memorial Prize from Eugene V. Debs Foundation, 1984, for *Mother Jones* article on El Salvador; *Half the Way Home* was named Notable Book of the Year for 1986 by the *New York Times Book Review* and the *American Library Association.*

WRITINGS:

Half the Way Home: A Memoir of Father and Son, Viking, 1986.

Contributor of articles and reviews to periodicals, including *Harper's, New Republic, Village Voice, Nation, Washington Monthly, New York Times,* and *Los Angeles Times.*

WORK IN PROGRESS: Magazine essays and reviews; several works for children.

SIDELIGHTS: A co-founder of *Mother Jones* magazine who has been its editor and who continues to write for it, and contributor to numerous publications, including *Harper's, Village Voice,* and the now-defunct *Ramparts,* Adam Hochschild has earned respect and achieved success in the world of the alternative press. It is a success different from that envisioned by his father, however, as Hochschild recounts in his 1986 autobiography, *Half the Way Home: A Memoir of Father and Son.* "By turns nostalgic and regretful, lyrical and melancholy," described Michiko Kakutani in a review of the book in *New York Times, Half the Way Home* "creates a deeply felt portrait of a man and a boy" narrated with "Proustian detail and affection." "Mr. Hochschild illuminates, with rare tact, the situations of fathers and sons," professed Mary Gordon in *New York Times Book Review,* "and he avoids the traps of sentimentality and rancor both."

Hochschild's grandfather, Berthold Hochschild, came from Germany to New York in 1886, where he was one of the founders of a company that eventually became AMAX, Inc., a worldwide mining empire. The Hochschilds rejected their Jewish heritage to better assimilate into the white Gentile majority. Clinching his acceptance into the WASP elite, Berthold's son Harold married Mary Marquand, a white Protestant with excellent social and political connections, when he was forty-nine and she was forty-one. A year later they had a son, Adam.

An only child, Adam Hochschild grew up with all the servants, fine homes, travel, and quality education wealth could provide, and also with all the expectations his anxious parents could place on him. In Gordon's words, Harold Hochschild "believed that the world was a difficult place and that his son was born to run it." Recognized for his benevolence, sound judgment, and irrefutable reason, Harold Hochschild raised his son with the same quiet reserve and emotional detachment he employed with business associates. But although such authoritative tactics worked smoothly with business executives, they came across to Harold's son as domineering, patriarchal, and

intimidating. Adam Hochschild's mother adored both her husband and son, but while young Adam was encouraged by her devotion, he also felt betrayed by her failure to intercede on his behalf. "For," as Gordon explained, "he had to believe the justice of his father's criticisms if the mother who adored him went along with them."

Hochschild's break from his father's authority and his parents' world began after a visit to mines owned by the company his father was head of, in central Africa. Concern over racial injustice there and in the United States led Hochschild as a young man to join the civil rights movement. A political activist during the 1960s, Hochschild demonstrated against the Vietnam War and joined the leftist ranks of the alternative press, eventually helping to found *Mother Jones,* named after labor organizer Mary Harris Jones. The self-proclaimed "magazine for the rest of us," *Mother Jones* brought the goals of progressive politics—disarmament, the non-involvement of the United States in the internal affairs of other countries, race and gender equality, and other ideals of social justice—to a large and diverse audience.

The differences between Adam and Harold Hochschild on the surface seem apparent, critics point out, but they are in fact difficult to define. While Adam Hochschild fairly clearly led the life of a 1960s radical, Harold Hochschild was not a stereotypical ruthless entrepreneur. The company the elder Hochschild directed had major holdings in central and southern Africa, where the mines often ran under the oppressive contract labor system, yet, like his peace-activist son, he publicly opposed the Vietnam War. Though he had many business contacts in China, he supported the Communist Revolution there. And, unlike many other corporate tycoons, as an ecologist he brought about some of the most effective environmental legislation in New York State. His fatherly disapproval, then, was not so much of his son's political and social beliefs as of his ways of expressing those beliefs. In Richard Eder's words in *Los Angeles Times Book Review,* Harold Hochschild's criticism grew "out of concern that Adam was wasting his life."

That Adam Hochschild can so readily illustrate his and his father's similarities as well as their differences adds credibility and depth to his story in critics' eyes. Gordon observed, for example, that "it would indeed have been easy [for Hochschild] to present himself as the hero of the piece and his father as the villain, but he does not."

Also adding depth, according to reviewers, is Hochschild's realistic portrayal of the relative peace he and his father attained during the last few years of the elder Hochschild's life. "*Half the Way Home* isn't only a story of flight. It's also a story of a son's reconciliation with his father," Suzanne Gordon asserted in *Washington Post Book World.* Hochschild remembers fondly that eventually his father, in the words of reviewer Kakutani, "even hands out gift subscriptions to [*Mother Jones*], as an unspoken gesture that he approves, perhaps even takes pride, in his son's vocation." Like other critics, Kakutani noted with relief that there "are no tearful reconciliation scenes between father and son—just as there were never any declarations of overt hostility." The reconciliation takes place quietly, the reviewer observed, and "by the time Harold Hochschild lies dying in a hospital bed, Adam has been able to move toward an acceptance of this difficult man, and even to acknowledge his own love."

Critics compared Hochschild's book favorably with other parent-child reminiscences; Roger W. Fromm, for example, writing in *Library Journal,* deemed the book "an honest, sensitive, fascinating portrait of a father-son relationship that is unique, yet one of universal experience.'' And *Newsday* contributor Merin Wexler praised *Half the Way Home* as ''an intriguing memoir, gently told,'' adding that Hochschild's book contains memories which are ''in themselves remarkable, but his telling makes them doubly so.''

CA INTERVIEW

CA interviewed Adam Hochschild by telephone on March 19, 1987, at his office in San Francisco.

CA: Your "magazine for the rest of us," Mother Jones, celebrated its tenth birthday in the summer of 1986. How did it all begin?

HOCHSCHILD: The idea for *Mother Jones* was actually born in 1974. It takes close to two years to get a new magazine off the ground, if you do it properly, in terms of publicity, fund-raising, assembling a staff, and making sure there's an audience there. So we started planning the magazine in early 1974 and published the first issue two years later, in early 1976. The idea was to do a magazine of progressive politics that covered a lot of issues having to do with social justice, prevention of war, keeping the U.S. out of parts of the world where it doesn't have any business, equality between men and women, equality between the races—all the classic issues of the progressive social conscience in America. But we wanted to do that magazine for a large audience; we were not interested in reaching the very small circle of already committed true believers who traditionally have read liberal or left magazines in the United States. That's one reason it took us so long to start, because we wanted to make sure there was an adequate business and promotional apparatus to go with the magazine. We also wanted it to have a format that was really good looking, on glossy paper, making good use of art and photographs; and we wanted to be sure that it would be widely distributed. Somewhat to our surprise, we succeeded.

CA: Was it an immediate and unanimous decision to have the magazine take its name from labor organizer Mary Harris Jones, or were there other contenders?

HOCHSCHILD: There were other contenders, and we actually did our first promotional mailing under the rather unexciting name of *New Dimensions*, which we'd settled on at that point. As soon as the promotional mailing reached people, we got an upset letter from an existing periodical we'd not been aware of called *New Dimensions*. These folks told us to stop using their name, and of course they were right. This forced us to look for another name, and at the last minute we came up with *Mother Jones*. I initially thought it was a terrible idea, but I was proven wrong.

CA: Are most of your articles assigned?

HOCHSCHILD: Yes. Most of them are assigned to free-lance writers, many of whom work with us pretty regularly. We sometimes publish articles based on excerpts from books, and sometimes editors or other staff members here also write pieces.

CA: What are the absolute essentials required of your writers and their work?

HOCHSCHILD: Writers for the magazine are generally people who share our point of view. I don't mean that somebody has

to subscribe to a very rigid and fixed set of beliefs in order to write for *Mother Jones,* but we want people who really have that passion for social justice which animates the magazine. We also look for people who know how to tell a good story. This matters a great deal. There are plenty of people out there who've got the right ideas and care about the right things, but can't write worth a damn because they don't know the first thing about storytelling. A magazine, and particularly a magazine that's aiming for a large audience, *has* to be well written. Otherwise, people are not going to pull it off the newsstand and read it. You're competing for people's time and attention with many other magazines. Storytelling ability and the ability to write good prose are immensely important.

CA: Your articles for Mother Jones have won several journalism awards, and some readers say you've carved out a distinctive form in these pieces. Do you think so?

HOCHSCHILD: It was only after I'd done seven or eight longer pieces for the magazine that I began to realize that most were of a particular type. I seem attracted to oppressive countries, for one thing. For *Mother Jones* I've been twice to the Soviet Union, twice to South Africa, once to East Germany, once to El Salvador. In some cases there was some very specific thing I was reporting on; in others—particularly the ones about South Africa, which I know fairly well—I was trying to give a more general impression. If there's a distinctive style to these pieces, it's mainly because my time is limited: I don't like to abandon my family for more than a few weeks, so when I go somewhere on a reporting trip I like to really pack it in. I work sixteen hours a day; I feel restless and frustrated if there are empty patches of time. As a reporter I try to avoid the cliche scenes foreign correspondents habitually report on; you have to watch for that, just as you try to avoid verbal cliches in writing. I work very hard to get into situations which I can portray in a way that will seem fresh, unexpected, moving. When I was in South Africa last year I managed to get a psychotherapist to allow me to sit in on a session where she counseled a torture victim; it was a profoundly moving experience. When your time in another place is short, you learn to keep your eyes open, to soak up all impressions, to be very aggressive in seeing the people you want to see, and to observe your own emotional reactions, which—especially if you want to evoke emotion on the part of the reader—are often an important part of the story.

CA: In your critique of Mother Jones's first ten years, "The Second Decade Begins," you noted the difficulty of publishing such a magazine in a country "whose progressive movements are weak and in disarray." Do you see that as the greatest hurdle for the next several years?

HOCHSCHILD: Yes, I do. I don't think the progressive movements have really pulled themselves together yet. And many people have made the point—it's certainly not an original one with me—that in a country where the left is scattered and disorganized, in some sense progressive media take the place of a movement. I think that's unfortunate. I would rather there was a good strong movement out there of which we could be sometimes the inspirer, sometimes the critic, sometimes the gadfly. But there really isn't at this point.

CA: You were hired by the South African anti-apartheid newspaperman Patrick Duncan for summer work while you were still in college. Had you thought before that about being a writer?

HOCHSCHILD: Vaguely so, yes. I think from the time that I was seventeen or eighteen I had always had at least a hazy idea that I wanted to do some form of journalism. This was, in a way, the first real job I had.

CA: So writing was tied into your social and political concerns from the start, rather than a separate ambition?

HOCHSCHILD: The two were pretty closely intertwined, sometimes hard to separate, sometimes not. But I do think that most of the writing I've done, with a few exceptions here and there, has been fairly closely tied to social and political issues. And I have a feeling that's going to remain the case for the rest of my writing life. And my reading life, for that matter. This spring [of 1987] I have a position they call Regents Lecturer at the University of California at Santa Cruz, in which they let you design whatever kind of course you want to teach. I'm doing a seminar on literature and politics, which will enable me to play in a different fashion with how these two interests come together.

CA: What books and writers have influenced you particularly?

HOCHSCHILD: I've always preferred writers who are concerned with interweaving personal and political issues, or who at least look outward as well as inward. To me, many of the great nineteenth-century novelists did this better than some in the twentieth century. In the classic dichotomy between lovers of [Leo] Tolstoy and lovers of [Feodor] Dostoevski, I'm with those who prefer Tolstoy. I reread just two weeks ago his wonderful short novel *Hadji Murad*, which is based on his experiences as a soldier in the Caucasus in the mid-nineteenth century. It is a great novel about colonialism and guerilla warfare and the tragedy of a superpower trying to subdue an independently minded people. Its lessons apply to the Russians in Afghanistan today and to the U.S. in Nicaragua. I admire Tolstoy a great deal, and certainly of the classics he's my favorite.

Of books in my own time, there are two groups from recent years that I would single out as special favorites. One is Doris Lessing's "Children of Violence" novels—particularly the first four volumes of that five-volume cycle, which concern her growing up in what was then Rhodesia and is now Zimbabwe. I find them wonderful books because of that sense of the social context in which her heroine was living. Lessing's character faced all the questions of personal life but also took political issues very seriously. Another group of books which means a great deal to me is Paul Scott's "Raj Quartet" novels about the final years of the British rule in India. I read those novels and wrote about them in *Mother Jones* before the television series based on them came out. Scott is one of the very few contemporary Western authors who has written seriously about imperialism, in all its dimensions.

Another contemporary writer I like a great deal is Nadine Gordimer, from South Africa. Of contemporary American books, my favorite is E. L. Doctorow's *The Book of Daniel*, loosely based on the [Ethel and Julius] Rosenberg case [in which they were convicted of espionage and executed as traitors to the United States]. It's a wonderful book, and by far his best, I think.

CA: Your own book, Half the Way Home, *is a very moving account of your difficult relationship with your father, Harold Hochschild. How soon after his death, in 1981, did you begin the book?*

HOCHSCHILD: I didn't begin it until a little after a year later. And it wasn't published until 1986.

CA: How long did it take you to write Half the Way Home?

HOCHSCHILD: My writer's block always takes the form of having a hard time getting started on something, but once I'm going I work pretty quickly. I wrote the first draft in about two and a half months. After that, I revised, cut and polished, rewriting many times—which took a lot longer. In total, I would estimate that I spent about half my work time on the book over a course of about three years. The other half of the time I was doing magazine articles, book reviews, commentaries for National Public Radio, some speaking. That worked out fine: It meant I could rewrite a draft of the book, then put it aside for a month or two when I went somewhere to do a magazine story, then come back to it with fresh eyes. It's always nice to be able to do that when you're writing something without a tight deadline.

CA: In what genre do you place Half the Way Home? *Biography? Autobiography?*

HOCHSCHILD: It seems to fall in between. In the last twenty years there've been a number of books that are neither traditional biography nor traditional memoirs, but rather biographies of a relationship. I think of Susan Cheever's *Home Before Dark*, about herself and her father, the writer John Cheever; Russell Baker's *Growing Up*, which was really about him and his mother; Geoffrey Wolff's *The Duke of Deception;* and—my favorite—Michael Arlen's *Passage to Ararat*. Why are people writing more books like this now? Difficult parents have been with us for a long time, but maybe the age of therapy has made it easier for sons and daughters to talk about them. Although, of course, they've done it before: Edmund Gosse's wonderful *Father and Son* was about such a relationship in the middle of the nineteenth century.

CA: Such a book must be the hardest kind to write. It can be like psychoanalysis in a very real way, picking at the most painful emotions. Were you ever tempted to quit?

HOCHSCHILD: No, and actually I didn't feel it was like psychoanalysis. People often ask me if I found it therapeutic to write my book. I would have to answer no. God knows we all need enough therapy in life, and sometimes we get it—or could be getting it—from friends and lovers and professional therapists and the passage of time. But I think it's a mistake to look at writing as an act of therapy. Maybe writing in a journal or diary, yes. But when you sit down to write a book or a short story or an article that's going out to the public, I think you have to have the therapeutic work largely behind you. A book written for an audience is successful only if in the act of writing it you can discipline yourself to be thinking constantly about what's going to interest the audience and what's going to be the most effective way to tell the story. Even though in my life I had to work out my relationship with my father—just as we all must come to terms with our parents—basically I was lucky enough to be able to do that before he died. As I tried to tell in the last third of *Half the Way Home*, when my father was in his eighties and I was in my late thirties, we really did reach a much more comfortable relationship than we'd had before. You have to record and evoke your feelings when you write, but I don't think the act of writing a book is a substitute for working out things in real life.

CA: What kind of response have you had from readers?

HOCHSCHILD: People have been very enthusiastic. The book is far from being a bestseller, but I've gotten hundreds of letters from people. I think when you write about something that's extremely personal, people identify with it in one way or another. Many of the letters are from friends, some from people that I haven't seen for many years, and some from complete strangers. In the letters, people almost invariably end up describing their own lives and the difficulties they've had relating to parents or, in some cases, to children.

CA: In the April, 1985, issue of Mother Jones *there was an article of yours on Patrick Duncan, with a footnote saying it was from a book in progress. Is there another book in the works?*

HOCHSCHILD: No. A much condensed version of that article was a chapter in *Half the Way Home.* I cut it down to a third or so of the length it was in the magazine and put it in the book. I also took portions from a few other pieces I had written, trying to discipline myself just to pick what was relevant to the themes of my book. But there isn't another book in progress at the moment. For the last seven months I've been back at work fulltime as the editor of *Mother Jones,* although I expect to stop that next month and resume writing.

CA: You seem to enjoy doing book reviews.

HOCHSCHILD: Yes. I think there's nothing more enjoyable than talking with people about books you've read. If you can do it in print, it's even more fun. I've done it for *Mother Jones* regularly for some years and on and off for other publications as well. To some extent I think it can be a useful discipline for a writer. If you have to pin down exactly why you like a book or why you don't like it, it can make you a better reader.

CA: Do you feel writing magazine articles, doing journalism, is in any way a lesser calling, so to speak, than writing books?

HOCHSCHILD: I think the qualities that make for good writing really are the same, whatever form you're working in. Unless you're doing very straightforward newspaper writing or investigative reporting or something like that, I think what makes for good writing of the sort I'm interested in is the ability to evoke feelings in your readers. And the ability to do that ultimately depends on all of the classic skills that the great writers have had and the rest of us try to emulate.

CA: What magazines and newspapers do you consider "must" reading on a regular basis?

HOCHSCHILD: It's dreadful for me to say this as co-founder of a magazine, but I think people shouldn't be reading magazines and newspapers; they should be reading books. I, however, am an incurable newspaper and magazine addict. I always try to reduce the amount of time I spend on them and spend more time on books. That's my ambition. But I read *Mother Jones* regularly, of course, and write parts of it. I look fairly regularly at the *Nation,* the *Progressive,* the *New Republic* (even though I rarely agree with it), the *New Yorker,* the *New York Review of Books,* the *Atlantic, Harper's.* For a while I read the *New Statesman* from England. I keep trying to kick the magazine habit, but then I get withdrawal symptoms.

CA: What are your biggest concerns now for the country—political, social, or otherwise?

HOCHSCHILD: The major one, of course, is the arms race. I don't see any indication that the people in power in this country right now realize that this is something they've got to bring under control. But it is *the* big issue. It's just insane that we're living in a world where we think we're going to be safer by having thirty thousand nuclear warheads instead of twenty thousand. I think it's an absolute tragedy that, at the moment in the history of the twentieth century when the Soviet Union at last has a government which clearly wants to make a deal on arms, on weapons testing, on reduction of troops in Europe, we've got a government that doesn't want to make a deal. What a tragedy!

Other issues that concern me are getting the U.S. untangled from Central America. We don't have business being there in a military sense. I'd like to see us get out and let that region solve its own problems. And I think the whole issue of social justice here at home is a great concern. We have massive unemployment in this country, and to a large extent it's hidden unemployment because they keep redefining the way they tabulate unemployment statistics so as to reduce the number of people classified as unemployed. But you see it everywhere. As I'm talking to you right now from my office at *Mother Jones,* I look out the window and on the other side of the street there's an office where people get tickets entitling them to meals and a place at night in a shelter for the homeless. There's always a line of people on the sidewalk there standing around waiting for this. And you can see the same thing in cities all over the country.

CA: Your father had a plan for your life that involved public service in a political capacity. Any regrets about taking your own path to service?

HOCHSCHILD: No. There isn't a whole lot that I would have done differently.

BIOGRAPHICAL/CRITICAL SOURCES:

PERIODICALS

Library Journal, May 15, 1986.
Los Angeles Times, June 21, 1987.
Los Angeles Times Book Review, June 15, 1986.
Mother Jones, July/August, 1986.
Newsday, July 6, 1986.
New York Times, June 21, 1986.
New York Times Book Review, June 15, 1986.
Village Voice, August 12, 1986.
Washington Post Book World, May 11, 1986.

—Sketch by Christa Brelin
—Interview by Jean W. Ross

*   *   *

HODGES, Devon Leigh 1950-

PERSONAL: Born February 23, 1950, in Santa Monica, Calif.; daughter of Kenneth M. Hodges (a consultant) and Shirley Wolfe (a librarian; maiden name, Davis); married Eric Swanson (an economist); children: Tristan, Cecily. *Education:* Attended Reed College, 1968-71; University of California, Berkeley, B.A., 1972; State University of New York at Buffalo, M.A., 1977, Ph.D., 1979.

ADDRESSES: Home—2015 North Lincoln St., Arlington, Va. 22207. *Office*—Department of English, George Mason University, 4400 University Dr., Fairfax, Va. 22030.

CAREER: University of Wyoming, Laramie, assistant professor, 1979-80; George Mason University, Fairfax, Va., assistant professor, 1981-86, associate professor of English and American studies, 1986—.

WRITINGS:

Renaissance Fictions of Anatomy, University of Massachusetts Press, 1985.
(With Janice Doane) *Nostalgia and Sexual Difference,* Methuen, 1987.

WORK IN PROGRESS: Research on feminist theory and the discourses of maternal propriety.

SIDELIGHTS: Devon Leigh Hodges told *CA:* "Anatomies were a fad in Renaissance England. In a wide range of texts—theological, scientific, and literary—Renaissance writers used their pens as scalpels to strip away appearances and expose the truth. In my 1985 book, *Renaissance Fictions of Anatomy,* I make use of contemporary literary theory to argue that the anatomy is a transitional form marking the shift from a metaphorical to an analytical view of the world.

"*Nostalgia and Sexual Difference,* written with Janice Doane, also uses poststructuralist theories of language to analyze representation—in this case, the rhetorical practices associated with nostalgia. In the imaginative past of nostalgic writers, men were men, women were women, and reality was real. In lamenting the 'degeneracy' of the American of the present, these writers often chose to scapegoat the women's movement, especially feminist writing. At issue are basic questions about the authority of women's writing and the power of male discourse to define reality."

*   *   *

HODGSON, John A(lfred)   1945-

PERSONAL: Born May 25, 1945, in Washington, D.C.; married wife, Elizabeth, 1970; children: Emily, Michael. *Education:* Dartmouth College, B.A., 1967; Yale University, M.A., 1968, Ph.D., 1972.

ADDRESSES: Office—Department of English, University of Georgia, Athens, Ga. 30602.

CAREER: Carleton College, Northfield, Minn., instructor in English, 1970-71; Yale University, New Haven, Conn., assistant professor, 1972-79, associate professor of English, 1979-81; University of Georgia, Athens, associate professor of English, 1981—.

MEMBER: Modern Language Association of America, Wordsworth-Coleridge Association, South Atlantic Modern Language Association.

AWARDS, HONORS: Woodrow Wilson fellow, 1967-68; Morse fellow, Yale University, 1976-77; fellow at National Humanities Center, 1981-82.

WRITINGS:

Wordsworth's Philosophical Poetry, 1797-1814, University of Nebraska Press, 1980.
(Contributor) Morton W. Bloomfield, editor, *Allegory, Myth, and Symbol,* Harvard University Press, 1981.
Coleridge, Shelley, and Transcendental Inquiry: Rhetoric, Argument, Metapsychology, University of Nebraska Press, 1989.

Contributor to literature journals.

WORK IN PROGRESS: Wordsworth's Revolutionary Poetry.

BIOGRAPHICAL/CRITICAL SOURCES:

PERIODICALS

Times Literary Supplement, February 20, 1981.

*   *   *

HOFFMAN, Mark S.   1952-

PERSONAL: Born July 5, 1952, in New York, N.Y.; son of Seymour S. (an accountant) and Janet L. (an office manager; maiden name, Winegrad) Hoffman; married Helen Katzenstein (a personnel manager), June 17, 1973; children: Paul M. *Education:* Hofstra University, B.A., 1974; New York University, M.A., 1975, doctoral study, 1976—.

ADDRESSES: Home—77-11 35th Ave., Jackson Heights, N.Y. 11372. *Office—World Almanac,* 200 Park Ave., New York, N.Y. 10166.

CAREER: Environment Information Center, New York City, managing editor, 1975-77; Engineering Information, Inc., New York City, production editor, 1978-83; *World Almanac,* New York City, managing editor, 1983-86, editor, 1986—. Adjunct professor at City College of the City University of New York, 1978—.

WRITINGS:

(Editor) *The Kids' World Alamanc,* Pharos Books, 1985.
(Editor) *The World Almanac and Book of Facts,* Newspaper Enterprise Association, 1986.
(Editor) *The Second Kids' World Almanac,* Pharos Books, 1987.

SIDELIGHTS: Mark S. Hoffman told *CA:* "After working in the technical/reference book and journal segment of the publishing industry, I was looking for something that would combine the reference book aspects of publishing with the more commercial (trade) side of the industry. When I received the offer to become the managing editor of *The World Almanac and Book of Facts,* I knew that I had, luckily, found that combination.

"To put together the annual publication of *The World Almanac,* we combine original research on a broad spectrum of topics—such as economics, technology, sports, and entertainment—with the efforts of information gatherers throughout the United States. In addition to relying on federal, state, and local government agencies and departments, including the Bureau of the Census and the Defense Department, to supply the most up-to-date data, we employ experts in various fields to supplement our in-house editorial and research team. Our experts include people such as Dr. Kenneth Franklin, former astronomer at the Hayden Planetarium, Dr. Glenn Seaborg, Nobel Prize-winning scientist, and many other well-known authorities. The process of putting together each year's publication takes an entire year. In addition to developing new features annually in order to keep up with the latest trends and concerns, we review those sections that seemingly should have no changes, such as the Declaration of Independence or the summary of U.S. and world history.

"The ideal editor for *The World Almanac* is someone who has varied interests. The editor of the large sports section is also our economics editor, for instance, and the editor for the entertainment section is also the editor of the agriculture and environment sections. The skills required include the ability to do original research, to gather and interpret data, to write in a concise, objective style, and to have an exceptionally sharp eye for detail. The job also requires a great deal of stamina and the ability to remain focused on one major project throughout the course of a year.''

* * *

HOHLWEIN, Kathryn Joyce   1930-

PERSONAL: Surname is pronounced *"Hole-*vine''; born May 18, 1930, in Salt Lake City, Utah; daughter of Warner P. (an insurance agent) and Helen (a pianist; maiden name, Yeoman) Jerrell; married Hans Hohlwein (a painter and printmaker), October 30, 1954 (deceased); children: Reinhard, Andrea, Laura. *Education:* University of Utah, B.A., 1951; Middlebury College, M.A., 1953.

ADDRESSES: Home—2230 G St., Sacramento, Calif. 95816. *Office*—Department of English, California State University, 6000 J St., Sacramento, Calif. 95819. *Agent*—Raphael Sagalyn, Inc., 2813 Bellevue Ter. N.W., Washington, D.C. 20007.

CAREER: Beirut College for Women, Beirut, Lebanon, instructor in English, 1954-57; Mount Mary College, Milwaukee, Wis., instructor in English, 1957-61; Ohio State University, Columbus, lecturer in English and comparative literature, 1961-66; California State University, Sacramento, lecturer, 1968-69, assistant professor, 1969-73, associate professor, 1973-76, professor of English, 1976—, also teaches one course per year in the humanities department. Book reviewer on public television, 1971-73. Visiting professor at Tamkang University, Taiwan, 1981-82.

MEMBER: Modern Language Association of America, American Association of University Professors.

WRITINGS:

(Editor with Mary E. Giles) *Enter the Heart of the Fire: A Collection of Mystical Poems,* California State University, 1981.
(Contributor) Mary E. Giles, editor, *The Feminist Mystic, and Other Essays on Women and Spirituality,* Crossroad Publishing, 1982.
(With Patricia Frazer Lamb) *Touchstones: Letters Between Two Women, 1953-1964,* Harper, 1983.
Aufbruch in der Mittleren Jahre (title means "Entrance Into the Middle Years''), edited by Angela Praesent, Rowoehlt Verlag, 1987.

Poetry and art editor of quarterly *Studia Mystica,* 1975-87.

WORK IN PROGRESS: The Truth at the Center of Your Life, an autobiographical novel; a second volume of *Touchstones;* poems and essays.

SIDELIGHTS: Kathryn Joyce Hohlwein and her co-author Patricia Frazer Lamb attended college together in Utah, before the social upheavals of the 1960s changed women's lives. Upon graduation, both women married and followed their husbands abroad. Hohlwein lived in Beirut and Scotland, while her friend moved to Tanganyika. For more than ten years the friends corresponded. Their letters, which reveal both the details of their personal lives and their changing attitudes about the issues of the decade, comprise the collaborative 1983 volume *Touchstones.* According to an article in the *New York Times Book Review,* the "book is as rich as the lives and minds that inspired it.''

Hohlwein commented to *CA:* "I am a happier person when I am writing. I travel extensively and invariably enjoy other lands and other people. Music and good conversation sustain me. In 1985 the Arthur and Elizabeth Schlesinger Library of American Women asked me and Lamb to submit all our original letters to the archives at Radcliffe College.''

BIOGRAPHICAL/CRITICAL SOURCES:

PERIODICALS

New York Times Book Review, March 20, 1983.

* * *

HOLLIS, C(harles) Carroll   1911-

PERSONAL: Born October 27, 1911, in Needham, Mass.; son of Stanley Meredith and Agnes (Carroll) Hollis; married Alice Willard (a librarian), September 19, 1936; children: Charles C., Joseph W., Michael S. *Education:* Marquette University, Ph.B., 1935; University of Wisconsin—Madison, M.A., 1937; graduate study at St. Louis University, 1937-38; University of Michigan, Ph.D., 1954. *Politics:* Democrat. *Religion:* Roman Catholic.

ADDRESSES: Office—104 Glendale Dr., Chapel Hill, N.C. 27514.

CAREER: University of Detroit, Detroit, Mich., instructor, 1938-41, assistant professor, 1941-46, associate professor, 1946-57, professor of English, 1957-61, chairman of department, 1959-61; Library of Congress, Washington, D.C., manuscript specialist in American cultural history, 1961-63; University of North Carolina at Chapel Hill, professor of American literature, 1963-77, chairman of department of English, 1966-71, chairman of Humanities Division, 1971-74. Member of editorial board of University of Detroit Press, 1959-61. Supervisor of Detroit Department of Parks and Recreation, summers, 1945-55.

WRITINGS:

(Contributor) Harold Gardiner, editor, *Fifty Years of American Fiction,* Scribner, 1951.
(Contributor) Harold Gardiner, editor, *The Great Books: A Christian Appraisal,* Devin-Adair, 1952.
(Contributor) Herbert Petit, editor, *Essays and Studies in Language and Literature,* Duquesne University Press, 1964.
(Contributor) Leonard Gilhooley, editor, *No Divided Allegiance,* Fordham University Press, 1980.
Language and Style in Leaves of Grass, Louisiana State University Press, 1983.
(Contributor) Beverly Taylor and Robert Bain, editors, *The Cast of Consciousness,* Greenwood Press, 1987.

Contributor of articles and reviews to periodicals. Member of editorial board of *Fresco,* 1957-61.

WORK IN PROGRESS: Continuing research on Walt Whitman, with a book expected to result.

* * *

HOLMES, John Clellon   1926-1988

OBITUARY NOTICE—See index for *CA* sketch: Born March 12, 1926, in Holyoke, Mass.; died of cancer, March 30, 1988, in Old Saybrook, Conn. Educator and author. Holmes, author of novels, short stories, essays, and poems, is best known as a chronicler of the ideology and lifestyle of the literary bohemians of post-World War II America known as "beat generation writers." Though Holmes never achieved the fame of his contemporaries Jack Kerouac and Allen Ginsberg, his works excel at illuminating the people and aspirations of that postwar movement. Among them are his novels *Go, The Horn,* and *Get Home Free;* a volume of reminiscences titled *Visitor: Jack Kerouac in Old Saybrook; Nothing More to Declare,* containing character sketches of his literary peers and autobiographical pieces covering two decades of his writing career, and *Displaced Persons: The Travel Essays of John Clellon Holmes,* published just before his death. Holmes was also the author of two volumes of poetry, *The Bowling Green Poems* and *Death Drag: Selected Poems 1948-1979.* He contributed poems, articles, and stories to *Holiday, Esquire, New York Times Magazine, Harper's, Partisan Review,* and other literary magazines and periodicals. In addition, Holmes taught at several universities during the 1960s and 1970s, capping his academic career as professor of English at the University of Arkansas.

OBITUARIES AND OTHER SOURCES:

BOOKS

Contemporary Novelists, 4th edition, St. Martin's, 1986.
Dictionary of Literary Biography, Volume 16: *The Beats: Literary Bohemians in Postwar America,* Gale, 1983.
Who's Who in America, 44th edition, Marquis, 1986.

PERIODICALS

Los Angeles Times, April 1, 1988.
Times (London), April 2, 1988.

*　　*　　*　　**

HOPKINS, (Hector) Kenneth　1914-1988
(Christopher Adams, Anton Burney, Warwick Mannon, Paul Marsh, Edmund Marshall, Arnold Meredith)

OBITUARY NOTICE—See index for *CA* sketch: Born December 7, 1914, in Bournemouth, Hampshire, England; died April 1, 1988, in Norwich, England. Educator, publisher, editor, and author. Hopkins is credited with writing some sixty books and pamphlets, including detective stories and children's books, often under pseudonyms, and with editing, publishing, and contributing to many more. Among his more notable works are the critical studies *The Poets Laureate* and *Portraits in Satire;* a biographical tribute to the Powys brothers, John Cowper, Llewelyn, and Theodore; many poetry collections, including *Love and Elizabeth,* lyric poems addressed to his wife; and an autobiography, *The Corruption of a Poet.* Hopkins was for many years a regular reviewer for the *Eastern Daily Press* and served as literary editor of *Everybody's* following World War II. Furthermore, he operated his own publishing house and taught English literature and creative writing at several American universities.

OBITUARIES AND OTHER SOURCES:

PERIODICALS

Guardian (London), April 12, 1988.
Times (London), April 7, 1988.

HORNE, Frank (Smith)　1899-1974
(Xavier I)

PERSONAL: Born August 18, 1899, in Brooklyn, N.Y.; died of arteriosclerosis, September 7, 1974, in New York, N.Y.; son of Edwin Fletcher and Cora (Calhoun) Horne; married Frankye Priestly (one source says Frankie Bunn), August 19, 1930 (died c. 1940); married Mercedes Christopher Rector, August 15, 1950; children: two stepchildren. *Education:* College of the City of New York (now City College of the City University of New York), B.S. (one source says B.A.), 1921; received degree from Northern Illinois College of Optometry (now Illinois College of Optometry), c. 1922; University of Southern California, A.M., c. 1932.

CAREER: Private practice of optometry in Chicago, Ill., and New York, N.Y., 1922-26; Fort Valley High and Industrial School (renamed Fort Valley Normal and Industrial School, 1932-39; now Fort Valley State College), Fort Valley, Ga., c. 1926-36, began as teacher, became dean and acting president; National Youth Administration, Washington, D.C., assistant director of Negro Affairs division c. 1936-38; worked in various administrative capacities for agencies of U.S. Housing Authority, including Housing and Home Finance Agency and Office of Race Relations, Washington, D.C., and later New York City c. 1938-55; New York City Commission on Intergroup Relations, New York City, executive director c. 1956-62; New York City Housing Redevelopment Board, New York City, consultant on human relations c. 1962-74; poet. Founder of National Committee Against Discrimination in Housing.

MEMBER: American Civil Liberties Union (past board member), National Association for the Advancement of Colored People (NAACP), National Association of Housing Officials, National Association of Intergroup Relations Officials, National Housing Conference, Phelps-Stokes Fund (past secretary), Hudson Guild (past board member), Omega Psi Phi.

AWARDS, HONORS: Received second prize for poetry in *Crisis* Amy Spingarn Contest, 1925, for composite poem "Letters Found Near a Suicide"; recipient of James J. and Jane Hoey Award for Inter-Racial Justice from Catholic Inter-Racial Council of New York, Inc.

WRITINGS:

POETRY

Haverstraw (collection; contains "Haverstraw," "Walk," "Mamma!," "Patience," "Hubbard Tank," "Communion," "Symphony," and composite "Letters Found Near a Suicide" [also see below]), Breman, 1963.

Also author of "On Seeing Two Brown Boys in a Catholic Church," "To a Persistent Phantom," "Kid Stuff," "Toast," "More Letters Found Near a Suicide," "'Balm in Gilead': A Christmas Jingle," "He Won't Stay Put: A Carol for All Seasons," "Nigger, A Chant for Children," and others.

"Letters Found Near a Suicide" was originally published in *Crisis,* under the pseudonym Xavier I.

Work represented in numerous anthologies, including *Caroling Dusk: An Anthology of Verse by Negro Poets,* edited by Countee Cullen, Harper, 1927; *The Poetry of the Negro, 1746-1949,* edited by Langston Hughes and Arna Bontemps, Doubleday, 1949; and *American Negro Poetry,* edited by Bontemps, Hill & Wang, 1963.

OTHER

Author of pamphlet *I Never Saw Him Before: A Mississippi Folk Song*, published by Breman in 1962.

Contributor of poetry, short stories, essays, and articles—such as "Black Verse," "I Am Initiated Into the Negro Race," "Harlem," "The Man Who Wanted To Be Red: A Story," "The Epic of Fort Valley," "Running Fools: Athletics in a Colored School," "Concerning White People," "Providing New Housing for Negroes," and "Dog House Education"—to periodicals, including *Crisis* and *Opportunity*.

SIDELIGHTS: As a poet and public administrator on race relations who wrote about prevailing prejudices and oppression experienced by blacks, Frank Horne qualifies as "an important minor voice of the Harlem Renaissance," according to Sarah M. Washington in *Dictionary of Literary Biography*. He especially took issue with inequitable housing practices and with discrimination on the basis of color. To a greater extent, however, Horne's poetry focuses on personal concerns rather than on emerging issues of the "New Negro" espoused by younger writers of the period. Much of his work features such somber themes as death and infirmity as well as "a crisis of faith" that Washington further observed as prevalent among many early twentieth-century writers.

Horne's literary reputation derives mainly from his award-winning 1925 "Letters Found Near a Suicide," published in *Crisis*. A composite work that was pseudonymously submitted under the name Xavier I, it contains eleven poems individually addressing people who had an impact on the speaker's life. With the exception of "To Chick," which recalls a rewarding friendship with a fellow football player, the letters express mainly negative feelings and a general disappointment with life and the world. By 1929 Horne added seven new poems that were also published in *Crisis* as "More Letters Found Near a Suicide." These subsequently appeared along with the original eleven letters as the first section of Horne's 1963 collection, *Haverstraw*.

A portion of Horne's poetry also reflects a preoccupation with ill health. Reportedly the victim of a disease that impaired his ability to walk and required him to move to a warmer climate, he imbued his poems with frequent references to dysfunctional legs and the accompanying physical pain. In particular, the tone of "To James" (contained in "More Letters Found Near a Suicide") suggests Horne's lamentation over his handicap and envy for those more physically fit, as the poem's speaker encourages a boy to *run* to victory.

Other writings prove variously influenced by political and religious themes, and some Horne intended as a means of instruction. His poem "Nigger, A Chant for Children," for instance, serves as a history lesson that teaches black children to be proud of their race and heritage. Through repeated emphasis on the term "nigger" and an effective "juxtaposition of children's songs and shouts of the bigot," explained Washington, Horne manages to transcend the negative connotation traditionally attributed to the word. In a similar fashion, the story "The Man Who Wanted To Be Red" illustrates what Horne perceived as the absurdities of discrimination purely on the basis of skin color.

In 1936 Horne embarked upon a career in public service, specializing in problems of public housing. His administrative involvement precipitated various related publications, including "Providing New Housing for Negroes," and virtually eclipsed his creative output. Nonetheless, Horne continued producing a sporadic number of poems, and this—coupled with his earlier poetry—seems to validate further discussion and reading of his work.

BIOGRAPHICAL/CRITICAL SOURCES:

BOOKS

Bontemps, Arna, editor, *The Harlem Renaissance Remembered*, Dodd, 1972.

Brown, Sterling, *Negro Poetry and Drama*, Associates in Negro Folk Education, 1937.

Dictionary of Literary Biography, Volume 51: *Afro-American Writers From the Harlem Renaissance to 1940*, Gale, 1987.

Kerlin, Robert T., *Negro Poets and Their Poems*, 2nd edition, Associated Publishers, 1935.

OBITUARIES:

PERIODICALS

New York Times, September 8, 1974.*

*   *   *

HOROWITZ, Helen Lefkowitz   1942-

PERSONAL: Born January 31, 1942, in Shreveport, La.; daughter of David (a rabbi) and Leona (Atlas) Lefkowitz; married Daniel Horowitz (a historian), August 18, 1963; children: Benjamin, Sarah Esther. *Education:* Wellesley College, B.A., 1963; Harvard University, M.A., 1965, Ph.D., 1969.

ADDRESSES: Office—Program for the Study of Women and Men in Society, Taper Hall, University of Southern California, Los Angeles, Calif. 90089.

CAREER: Massachusetts Institute of Technology, Cambridge, instructor in humanities, 1969-70; Union College, Schenectady, N.Y., visiting assistant professor of history, 1970-72; Scripps College, Claremont, Calif., assistant professor, 1973-80, associate professor of American history, 1980-86; University of Southern California, Los Angeles, professor of history and chair of program for the study of women and men in society, 1986—. Visiting professor at Carleton College, 1980, and University of Michigan, 1983-84.

MEMBER: American Historical Association, American Studies Association (council member), Organization of American Historians, Society of Architectural Historians, Berkshire Conference in Women's History, Phi Beta Kappa.

AWARDS, HONORS: Fellow of Smithsonian Institution, 1972-73, and American Council of Learned Societies, 1977-78; Rockefeller Foundation humanities fellowship and National Humanities Center fellowship, both 1984-85.

WRITINGS:

Culture and the City: Cultural Philanthropy in Chicago From the 1880s to 1918, University Press of Kentucky, 1976.

Alma Mater: Design and Experience in the Women's Colleges From Their Nineteenth-Century Beginnings to the 1930s, Knopf, 1984.

Campus Life: Undergraduate Cultures From the End of the Eighteenth Century to the Present, Knopf, 1987.

Contributor to periodicals, including *New York History*, *Journal of American History*, *Reviews in American History*, *Chicago History*, and *Landscape*. Member of editorial board of *History of Education Quarterly*, 1980-83.

WORK IN PROGRESS: A biography of educator M. Carey Thomas, for Knopf.

SIDELIGHTS: In *Alma Mater: Design and Experience in the Women's Colleges From Their Nineteenth-Century Beginnings to the 1930s* Helen Lefkowitz Horowitz presents a socio-architectural history of ten leading American women's colleges, examining how their physical forms reflected the way women were perceived by men and the way members came to perceive themselves. Originally conceived as protective seminaries furthering femininity and domesticity, the institutions gradually assumed—in architecture and curriculum—standards indistinguishable from traditional male universities. "As Helen Lefkowitz Horowitz makes clear in her instructive history . . . the intentions of those who planned and built colleges for women were often at odds with the institutions that actually came to life," observed Diane Ravitch in the *New York Times Book Review.* "Ironically, notes Mrs. Horowitz, 'buildings designed to protect femininity became places where women learned to act like men.'"

Deeming Horowitz's "densely researched" study "intriguing" and "absorbing," Anne Chamberlin stated in a *Washington Post Book World* critique, "Presenting the design of colleges as an embodiment of their purpose gives a fresh and provocative slant on their history." Reviewing the book for the *Los Angeles Times,* Elaine Kendall determined that "within strictly circumscribed boundaries, 'Alma Mater' is a useful adjunct to the still small body of literature on women's education in America. . . . [Horowitz] investigat[es] her particular territory conscientiously while arousing our curiosity about other aspects of a dramatic experiment." And, admiring the author's "keen understanding of esthetics and design," Ravitch advanced a similar evaluation: "Helen Lefkowitz Horowitz has written a history that will inform those interested in women's history and in the history of higher education. Some readers may wish that she had provided greater detail about curriculum and social issues and less about architecture, but she has done a splendid service in capturing the interrelationships among the nation's premier women's colleges in their formative years."

Horowitz continues to survey the history of college education in *Campus Life: Undergraduate Cultures From the End of the Eighteenth Century to the Present.* As Ann Japenga reported in the *Los Angeles Times,* Horowitz believes that "throughout history . . . [college] students have sorted themselves into mini-cultures." These subgroups include the aggressively sociable "college men" often seen in fraternities, the more studious "outsiders," who come to college driven by a respect for knowledge or a desire to overcome poverty and discrimination, and the "rebels," concerned with social issues within and outside of the university. To portray these various student cultures, noted Japenga, "Horowitz undertook an exhaustive historical search" through autobiographies, fiction, interviews, and the writings of academics. *Christian Science Monitor* contributor Robert Marquand said that "the story Horowitz tells is detailed and fascinating." He concluded, "overall, this is an important book at a time of renewed debate about the role and purpose of college in America."

Horowitz told *CA:* "It is difficult to summarize the nature of my work as a cultural historian. I have attempted in various ways to probe the nature of American culture. In *Alma Mater* I tried to look at the relation between the forms and spaces of buildings and attitudes toward women in our society. In my most recent study of undergraduate life, I have explored the way that traditions created early in American collegiate history

have continued to inform the way students think and act. In my current research on life in the women's colleges I am looking at the complex process by which young women matured in college. In each of these works I have had to turn to other disciplines. In *Alma Mater* I drew on my recently acquired training in architecture and planning as well as on the broad field of women's studies. In the work on collegiate cultures I turned to social psychology, sociology, and anthropology for their detailed studies of college students. Presently I am drawn to psychology and anthropology to understand what happened to college women."

BIOGRAPHICAL/CRITICAL SOURCES:

PERIODICALS

Christian Science Monitor, May 11, 1987.
Los Angeles Times, November 1, 1984, April 20, 1987.
Los Angeles Times Book Review, June 21, 1987.
New York Times Book Review, October 28, 1984, August 9, 1987.
Washington Post Book World, January 27, 1985, May 31, 1987.

*   *   *

HOUSE, Karen Elliott   1947-

BRIEF ENTRY: Born December 7, 1947, in Matador, Tex. American journalist. Winner of the 1984 Pulitzer Prize for international reporting, House began her career as a reporter for the *Dallas Morning News* in 1970 and has worked at the *Wall Street Journal* since 1974. Starting as the *Journal*'s regulatory correspondent, she subsequently became energy and agriculture correspondent in 1975, diplomatic correspondent in 1978, and foreign editor in 1984. House's additional honors include the 1980-81 Edward Weintal Award for diplomatic reporting from Georgetown University, the 1982 Edwin Hood Award for diplomatic reporting from the National Press Club, and the 1984 Bob Considine Award from the Overseas Press Club. *Addresses: Home*—47 Westcott Rd., Princeton, N.J. 08540. *Office*—Wall Street Journal, 200 Liberty St., New York, N.Y. 10281.

BIOGRAPHICAL/CRITICAL SOURCES:

BOOKS

Who's Who in America, 44th edition, Marquis, 1986.

*   *   *

HOUSMAN, A(lfred) E(dward)   1859-1936 (Tristram)

PERSONAL: Born March 26, 1859, in Fockbury, Worcestershire, England; died April 30 (some sources say May 1; one source says October 30), 1936, in Cambridge, England. Son of Edward (a solicitor) and Sarah Jane (Williams) Housman. *Education:* St. John's College, Oxford, pass degree, 1882; received M.A. *Politics:* Tory.

CAREER: Her Majesty's Patent Office, London, England, civil servant, 1882-92; University College, University of London, London, professor of Latin, 1892-1911; Trinity College, Cambridge University, Cambridge, England, Kennedy Professor of Latin, 1911-36.

WRITINGS:

POETRY

A Shropshire Lad, Kegan Paul, 1896, J. Lane, 1900, reprinted, with notes and biography by Carl J. Weber, Greenwood Press, 1980.

Last Poems, Holt, 1922.

More Poems, edited by brother, Laurence Housman, Knopf, 1936.

The Collected Poems of A. E. Housman, J. Cape, 1939, Holt, 1940, revised edition published as *Collected Poems,* Penguin Books, 1956, Holt, 1965.

Manuscript Poems: Eight Hundred Lines of Hitherto Uncollected Verse From the Author's Notebooks, edited by Tom Burns Haber, University of Minnesota Press, 1955 (published in England as *The Manuscript Poems of A. E. Housman: Eight Hundred Lines of Hitherto Uncollected Verse From the Author's Notebooks,* Oxford University Press, 1955).

Complete Poems: Centennial Edition, introduction by Basil Davenport, commentary by Tom Burns Haber, Holt, 1959.

EDITOR

(With others) *M. Manilii Astronomica,* five volumes, Grant Richards, 1903-30, published as *Astronomicon,* Georg Olms, 1972.

D. Junii Juvenalis Saturae, Grant Richards, 1905, revised edition, Cambridge University Press, 1931, published as *Saturae,* Greenwood Press, 1969.

M. Annaei Lucani Belli civilis libri decem, Basil Blackwell, 1926, Harvard University Press, 1950.

LECTURES

Introductory Lecture, Delivered Before the Faculties of Arts and Laws and of Science in University College, London, October 3, 1892, Cambridge University Press, 1892, Macmillan, 1937.

The Name and Nature of Poetry, Macmillan, 1933.

The Confines of Criticism: The Cambridge Inaugural, 1911, notes by John Carter, Cambridge University Press, 1969.

LETTERS

Thirty Housman Letters to Witter Bynner, edited by Tom Burns Haber, Knopf, 1957.

A. E. Housman to Joseph Ishill: Five Unpublished Letters, edited by William White, Oriole Press, 1959.

The Letters of A. E. Housman, edited by Henry Maas, Harvard University Press, 1971.

Sir James G. Frazer and A. E. Housman: A Relationship in Letters, Duke University Press, 1974.

Fifteen Letters to Walter Ashburner, introduction and notes by Alan S. Bell, Tragara Press, c. 1976.

COLLECTIONS

A Centennial Memento, commentary by William White, Oriole Press, 1959.

A. E. Housman: Selected Prose, edited by John Carter, Cambridge University Press, 1961.

Poetry and Prose: A Selection, edited by F. C. Horwood, Hutchinson, 1971.

The Classical Papers of A. E. Housman, three volumes, collected and edited by J. Diggle and F.R.D. Goodyear, Cambridge University Press, 1972.

Collected Poems and Selected Prose, edited by Christopher Ricks, Allen Lane, 1988.

OTHER

Co-founder, with A. W. Pollard, of undergraduate periodical *Ye Rounde Table.* Contributor of more than one hundred articles to scholarly journals, including *Classical Review* and *Journal of Philology;* contributor, under pseudonym Tristram, to *Ye Rounde Table.*

SIDELIGHTS: At first glance nothing seems more unlikely than that the poet of the enormously popular *A Shropshire Lad* should be the classical scholar A. E. Housman. This Cambridge University professor of Latin left no doubt as to his priorities: the emendation of classical texts was both an intellectual search for the truth and his life's work; poetry was an emotional and physiological experience that began with a sensation in the pit of the stomach. The apparent discrepancies in this man who became both a first-rate scholar and a celebrated poet should be a reminder that, whatever else poetry does, it also records the interior life, a life that has its roots well beneath the academic gown or the business suit. Furthermore, in Housman's case, though he did aspire to be a great scholar first, scrutiny of his life and work reveals that he valued poetry more highly than he often admitted and that many of the presumed conflicts between the classical scholar and the romantic poet dissolve in the personality of the man.

Born in the village of Bromsgrove in Worcestershire, the county east of Shropshire, Alfred Edward Housman grew up in a typically large middle-class Victorian family. He was extremely close to his mother but gradually came to see his father's shortcomings through family difficulties that resulted from the senior Housman's pennilessness. Being the oldest of seven children, Alfred took upon himself part of the task of educating his siblings. One brother, Laurence, later a writer of some note himself, preserved in his memoir *My Brother, A. E. Housman* the literary character of many of these activities initiated by Alfred: "We all wrote poems, even the unpoetic ones [children]: lyrics, ballads, sonnets, narrative poems, nonsense rhymes, and compositions to which each contributed a verse (not always in the same metre) occupied a large part of our playtime."

In 1870 Housman entered the reputable Bromsgrove School, where he received a solid grounding in the classics. Though quiet and shy at Bromsgrove, Housman thrived on the rigorous academic regimen and took such honors as the Lord Lyttleton Prize for Latin Verse, the honorarium for Greek verse, and the prize for composition in English verse, the latter awarded for "The Death of Socrates," a conventional poem in heroic couplets. While Housman was at Bromsgrove, his mother died after a painful illness. As Laurence Housman remarked, "Her death had a profound effect upon him for there had been between them a deep bond of affection and understanding." This death severely shook his Christian faith, and a year later, as Richard Perceval Graves reported in *A. E. Housman: The Scholar-Poet,* "he learned to think of himself as a Deist, believing that there was a God but no more than that." The indifference of God to man's suffering became an important theme in most of Housman's mature poetry.

Housman received a scholarship to attend St. John's College, Oxford, in 1877. His correspondence at this time reveals the confidence he had developed in himself as a scholar, touched with the irreverence of youth. In *A. E. Housman: A Critical Biography* Norman Page summed up his subject's initial reactions to Oxford: "This particular eighteen-year-old firmly declined to be impressed by the solemn traditions of the ancient university, noting that its statutes forbid him, among other things, 'to trundle a hoop,' and that the document recording his admission was written in 'what passes at Oxford for Latin.'" Nor was he much impressed with the single lecture he attended by the great classical scholar, Benjamin Jowett.

Housman's Oxford days clearly influenced his later intellectual life. While he enjoyed much academic success at the university, even taking a first in the intermediate exam in 1879, he failed miserably in his culminating exam two years later. Thus all the promise of the early years ended in what Housman and others considered abject disgrace. He did, in 1882, complete a "pass" degree, but this achievement was small consolation for a student with his classical background and talents. Housman's initial academic failure no doubt motivated him during the next decade to become a great scholar through his tireless, solitary work in the British Museum after a day's work at a menial job. His rude rejection by the Oxford world of classical scholarship just as surely contributed to the lifelong acrimonious debates with other scholars for which he became notorious.

Furthermore, the Oxford years had great importance in the development of Housman's emotional life. He became friends with such fellow students as Andrew S. F. Gow and Alfred Pollard, who later became successful scholars, and a relationship with a young scientist and athlete, Moses Jackson, became the deepest attachment of his life. According to Graves, Housman recalled in old age that "Oxford had not much effect on me, except that I there met my greatest friend"; moreover, the poet responded to an inquiry about a portrait over his fireplace, "That was my friend Jackson, the man who had more influence on my life than anybody else." Modern commentators such as Graves and Page have been candid about the homosexual nature of this relationship. Housman suffered rejection, however, when Moses Jackson married in 1889, shortly after he had accepted a position as principal of a college in Karachi, India. Housman and Jackson continued regular correspondence until Jackson's death in 1923 in Vancouver, British Columbia, but clearly this sort of connection never satisfied Housman's depth of feeling for his friend. There cannot be much doubt that the dual frustrations in academic pursuits and in love were the sparks igniting the creative effort that produced Housman's best poetry, beginning with *A Shropshire Lad* in 1896. Speaking of the popular poem "When I Was One-and-Twenty," Tom Burns Haber in *A. E. Housman* said that "in this poem, and very frequently elsewhere, Housman speaks of his Oxford crisis: the full surrender of his affections, the reflex of guilt and the unbearable loneliness that came with it, the impulse of suicide."

While the flowering of Housman's genius in scholarship and poetry did not come until much later, the Oxford years show him plying his trade in both areas. Instead of studying the ancient philosophy that would have prepared him for his final examination, he spent considerable time on textual criticism of the Latin poet Prospertius. This work was never published but proved invaluable for the development of scholarly principles that later made him what W. H. Auden in his poem "A. E. Housman" called "The Latin Scholar of his generation." Nor was he idle in the area of original composition. With A. W. Pollard, he founded an undergraduate periodical called *Ye Rounde Table*, for which he became the most prolific contributor, writing under the pen name "Tristram." In *A. E. Housman*, Haber commented on the young writer's penchant for parody and satire in such works as "Tennyson in the Moated Grange," "Varsity Ballads"—the first ballad being a satirical barb at the university proctor—and "The Eleventh Eclogue," showing his scorn of Oxford scholarship: "So it may be fairly said that the arrogant scholar Housman later became, whose devastating critiques made the leading Classicists of Europe pale when they unwrapped their literary journals, was coming to life in the jibing, idol-shattering 'Tristram' of *Ye Rounde Table*."

After Housman left Oxford in disgrace in 1881, he took the civil service examination and secured a position in the Patent Office in London. While he frequently criticized the hierarchy of this bureaucracy, he seems to have been successful at the kind of detailed scrutiny it required and adept at official correspondence. During these eleven years before he obtained a professorship at University College, London, the outcast scholar developed his textual skills. Although this is the least documented period of his personal life—no Housman letters from 1880 to 1885 exist—the record of his scholarship during this time is extraordinary. As Page observed, by 1892 when he assumed the Latin professorship at University College, "this Civil Service clerk who had never held an academic post had a list of twenty-five papers to his credit—more than many dons could show in a lifetime."

Though the modern student is usually more interested in Housman's poetry than his textual criticism, some survey of his scholarship is important for an appreciation of his overall contribution and of the cast of mind that could be so devoted—and so imperious—in the search for truth. From his early work on Propertius at Oxford University through his professorship at University College, London, and culminating in his office as Kennedy Professor of Latin at Cambridge University, Housman was not interested in the intepretation of the works of the classical writers he treated. Instead, he was solely involved in the establishment of reliable texts of their works. This process usually required the peeling away of centuries of error made by previous editors, whom Housman frequently treated with unmitigated scorn. In "The Application of Thought to Textual Criticism," a paper presented to the Classical Association at Cambridge in 1921 and collected in John Carter's 1961 edition of the writer's prose, Housman described textual criticism as both a science and an art, requiring reason and common sense. As a science, however, it was not exact, he declared: "A textual critic engaged upon his business is not at all like Newton investigating the motion of the planets: he is much more like a dog hunting for fleas." Housman railed against the prevailing practice of accepting earlier manuscripts as better manuscripts or of accepting all readings—however inane—within a manuscript simply because of the authority of the whole. In this regard he criticized scholars for being lazy, and this tone of moral rectitude permeated the entire paper. Many scholars, he said, are stupid, lazy, vain—or all three. His last sentence put a cap on it: "Knowledge is good, method is good, but one thing beyond all others is necessary; and that is to have a head, not a pumpkin, on your shoulders, and brains, not pudding, in your head."

Concerning Housman's own reputation as a classical scholar, D. R. Shackleton Bailey in a 1959 *Listener* article said that he was "beyond serious dispute, among the greatest of all time." Bailey spoke of the scholar's "passionate zeal to see each one of the innumerable problems in his text not as others had presented it or as he might have preferred it to appear but exactly as it was." Housman's greatest single textual work was his five-volume edition of the *Astronomica* of Manilius, a first century A.D. Latin poet. The first volume of this work was published in 1903 and the last in 1930. That Housman chose Manilius, a second-rate poet, over Propertius or any of the other better writers with whom he was familiar reveals his desire to establish for himself an unassailable reputation, for as Andrew S. F. Gow declared in *A. E. Housman,* the scholar realized that the *Astronomica* of Manilius provided him the greatest opportunity "of approaching finality in the solution of the problems presented." Housman also edited the works of Juvenal and Lucan and published over one hundred articles in classical journals. During his early career he published as much on Greek writers as he did on Roman, but while at University College he decided that he could not do justice to both literatures and thus concentrated on the Romans.

In a letter to Housman's biographer Graves, G. P. Goold, a later holder of the Latin chair at University College, summed up the scholar's accomplishments: "The legacy of Housman's scholarship is a thing of permanent value; and that value consists less in obvious results, the establishment of general propositions about Latin and the removal of scribal mistakes, than in the shining example he provides of a wonderful mind at work.... He was and may remain the last great textual critic.... And if we accord [Richard] Bentley the honour of being England's greatest Latinist, it will be largely because Housman declined to claim the title for himself."

It was at University College that Housman experienced his most sustained period of poetry composition, and the main fruit of this period was the publication of *A Shropshire Lad* in 1896. In a 1933 letter Housman declared: "I did not begin to write poetry in earnest until the really emotional part of my life was over; and my poetry, so far as I could make out, sprang chiefly from physical conditions, such as a relaxed sore throat during my most prolific period, the first months of 1895." Many readers have assumed from this statement that Housman engaged in a frenzied period of composition early in 1895, writing all or most of *A Shropshire Lad* at this time. Graves has noted, however, that while Housman was a clerk at the Patent Office he filled eighty pages of a notebook with drafts of poems; Tom Burns Haber, in his collection of Housman's *Manuscript Poems,* has suggested that about one-third of the volume belongs to the period before 1895, another third to the early months of 1895, and the final third to the latter months, with August, 1895, as the most fruitful time of all.

Commentators have considered why Housman's composition, while fairly steady over the years, should pick up at this time and why he would consider publishing a volume of the poetry that hitherto had seemed only a diverting product of a scholar's leisure time. Graves concluded that the death of Housman's father in November, 1894, was one important reason for the poet's creative activity in 1895, not because the two were close but because the senior Housman's death was a kind of liberating factor for his son; it was, as Housman's sister Katharine Symons said in *Alfred Edward Housman: Recollections,* the removal of a "burden and a distress." Another contribution to the creative activity and desire to publish, according to Graves, was Housman's decision to use a persona, the rural Shropshire peasant Terence Hearsay, as subject of many of the poems. This device provided some distance between the poetry and the professor of Latin.

The third major impetus to publish at this time came from a combination of two events, both indirectly related to Housman's homosexuality. In May, 1895, Oscar Wilde, the famous novelist, dramatist, and symbolic representative of the aesthetic movement of the 1890s, was sentenced to two years of hard labor for homosexuality. In a poem published posthumously with his brother's memoir, Housman wrote movingly about a man imprisoned "for the colour of his hair." The

Wilde trial, along with the suicide of a homosexual naval cadet at Woolwich, which Laurence Housman said deeply disturbed his brother, seems to have stirred his creative urges. The cadet appears in a *Shropshire Lad* poem: "Shot? so quick, so clean an ending? / Oh that was right, lad, that was brave: / Yours was not an ill for mending, / 'Twas best to take it to the grave." George I. Watson, who was in *A. E. Housman: A Divided Life* the first writer to assess fully the effects of Housman's homosexuality on his poetry, has summed up the dual incidents of the trial and the suicide: "In contemplating the wilful death of a young man likewise afflicted, but so mercifully rendered 'clear of danger, clean of guilt' by one courageous act of violence, Housman could not resist this appeal to his innermost feelings, and in the train of thoughts induced by the penitential agonies of Oscar Wilde, he was filled with a new urgency to relieve his oppressed conscience."

First offered to Macmillan Company in 1896 under the title "Poems by Terence Hearsay," *A Shropshire Lad* was rejected by that publisher; it was subsequently brought out in the same year by Kegan Paul, with the change in the title suggested by Housman's friend Pollard. The book was published at the author's own expense, and he insisted that he receive no royalties. There wouldn't have been many anyway, since Kegan Paul printed only five hundred copies, and, as Maude M. Hawkins noted in *A. E. Housman: Man Behind a Mask,* the book "sold so slowly that Laurence Housman at the end of two years bought up the last few copies." Though the volume was better appreciated in the United States than in England, Hawkins called most of the critical reviews "lukewarm or adverse." *A Shropshire Lad* did not sell well until it was republished by Grant Richards, a man with whom Housman became lifelong friends. Richards's first edition was five hundred copies in 1897, which sold out; he then printed one thousand copies in 1900 followed by two thousand in 1902. Hawkins summed up the volume's early public reception: "After the slow stream of Housman readers from 1896 to 1903, the momentum of popularity increased rapidly. During this period *A Shropshire Lad* had been reviewed in thirty-three periodicals with both praise and condemnation."

During the twentieth century *A Shropshire Lad* has been more of a popular than a critical success. Looking back to the heyday of the book's success, George Orwell remarked in *Inside the Whale and Other Essays:* "Among people who were adolescent in the years 1910-25, Housman had an influence which was enormous and is now [1957] not at all easy to understand. In 1920, when I was about seventeen, I probably knew the whole of *A Shropshire Lad* by heart." In accounting for this popularity, Orwell spoke of certain elements in the poetry: a snobbism about belonging to the country; the adolescent themes of murder, suicide, unhappy love, and early death; and a "bitter, defiant paganism, a conviction that life is short and the gods are against you, which exactly fitted the prevailing mood of the young."

Christopher Ricks, in the introduction to his *A. E. Housman: A Collection of Critical Essays,* has noted that other influential critics—such as R. P. Blackmur, Conrad Aiken, W. H. Auden, and Hugh Kenner—have tended to use the word "adolescent" in describing Housman's poetry. Usually carrying an at least mildly pejorative meaning, the word assumes a different connotation in the interpretation offered by W. H. Auden and quoted by Ricks: "It has often been said that Housman is a poet of adolescence, and this is fair enough as long as this judgment is not meant to imply, as it usually is, that nobody over the age of twenty-one can or should enjoy reading him.

To grow up does not mean to outgrow either childhood or adolescence but to make use of them in an adult way.''

Most critics discuss Housman's poetry as a whole, without much regard for the separateness of volumes. During his lifetime he published only two volumes, *A Shropshire Lad* and *Last Poems*. After Housman's death, his brother Laurence edited *More Poems*, which appeared in 1936, and in the following year he published eighteen additional poems along with his memoir of his brother. While valid points can be made concerning the separate structural unity of *A Shropshire Lad*— and B. J. Leggett was the first to do so in *Housman's Land of Lost Content*—the poetry can also be usefully examined as a whole for two reasons. First, there is little development either in idea or style between the poems Housman wrote in 1895 and earlier for *A Shropshire Lad* and the new poems he produced for *Last Poems* in 1922. Second, many of the works in the later volumes were actually written early but were held back from publication, often because of their personal nature.

In his poetry, Housman continually returns to certain favorite themes. The predominant theme, discussed by Cleanth Brooks in the Ricks collection of essays, is that of time and the inevitability of death. As Brooks said, "Time is, with Housman, always the enemy." In the first poem of *A Shropshire Lad,* "1887," one of the few to be titled, the conventional patriotism of the Queen's jubilee is shot through with the irony that God can only save the Queen with the help of those who have died for her sake: "The saviours come not home tonight: / Themselves they could not save." Housman frequently deals with the plight of the young soldier, and he is usually able to maintain sympathy both for the youth who is the victim of war and for the patriotic cause of the nation. Robert B. Pearsall suggested in a 1967 *PMLA* essay that Housman dealt frequently with soldiers because "the uniform tended to cure isolation and unpopularity, and soldiers characteristically bask in mutual affection."

It is not only war but nature, too, that brings on thoughts of death in Housman's poetry. In the famous *Shropshire Lad* lyric beginning "Loveliest of trees, the cherry now," the speaker says that since life is all too short, he will go out "To see the cherry hung with snow," an obvious suggestion of death. In a well-known verse from *Last Poems,* a particularly wet and cold spring causes the speaker to move from a description of nature—"The chestnut casts his flambeaux, and the flowers / Stream from the hawthorn on the wind away"—to a sense that this lost spring brings one closer to the grave, which, in turn, occasions a splenetic remark about the deity: "Whatever brute and blackguard made the world." To his credit, Housman often does not merely wallow in such pessimistic feelings but counsels a kind of stoical endurance as the proper response: "Shoulder the sky, my lad, and drink your ale." When the sky cannot be shouldered, a type of Roman suicide may be appropriate, as in "Shot? so quick, so clean an ending?" or in another *Shropshire Lad* poem, which ends with the lines: "But play the man, stand up and end you, / When your sickness is your soul.''

Another frequent theme in Housman's poetry, one that is related to the death motif, is the attitude that the universe is cruel and hostile, created by a God who has abandoned it. In the poem "Epitaph on an Army of Mercenaries" in *Last Poems,* mercenaries must take up the slack for an uncaring deity: "What God abandoned, these defended, / And saved the sum of things for pay." In such a world where "malt does more than Milton can / To justify God's ways to man," as the lyricist wrote in

A Shropshire Lad, poetry can serve the purpose of inuring one to the harshness of reality. R. Kowalczyk, in a 1967 *Cithara* essay, summed up this prevalent theme: "Housman's poetic characters fail to find divine love in the universe. They confront the enormity of space and realize that they are victims of Nature's blind forces. A number of Housman's lyrics scrutinize with cool, detached irony the impersonal universe, the vicious world in which man was placed to endure his fated existence.''

Within such a universe, the pastoral theme of the preciousness of youth and youthful beauty is everywhere to be found. In "To an Athlete Dying Young," the youth is praised for leaving a world with his accomplishments intact. Like the young girl Lucy in romantic poet William Wordsworth's lyrics, Housman's youths sometimes die into nature and become part of the natural surroundings: "By brooks too broad for leaping / The lightfoot boys are laid; / The rose-lipt girls are sleeping / In fields where roses fade." But as Cleanth Brooks declared, as recorded in Ricks's collection of essays, Housman's nature cannot be the same as Wordsworth's after the century's achievement in science: "Housman's view of nature looks forward to our time rather than back to that of Wordsworth. If nature is lovely and offers man delight, she does not offer him solace or sustain him as Wordsworth was solaced and sustained. For between Wordsworth and Housman there interpose themselves Darwin and Huxley and Tindall—the whole achievement of Victorian science.''

Furthermore, society sometimes intrudes into Housman's world of nature, and when it does, the rustic youth frequently comes in conflict with it. As Oliver Robinson noted in *Angry Dust: The Poetry of A. E. Housman,* "Housman is especially sympathetic with the man who is at odds with society, the man who cannot keep 'these foreign laws of God and man.'" In one poem from *A Shropshire Lad,* the speaker pities the condemned man in Shrewsbury jail whom he calls "a better lad, if things went right, / Than most that sleep outside.''

These themes in Housman's poetry reveal the influence of ballad literature on his work. In a letter to the Frenchman Maurice Pollet, Housman spoke of the sources of his poetry as being in "Shakespeare's songs, the Scottish border ballads and [German poet Heinrich] Heine." The ballads also had a strong effect on his style. In his *A. E. Housman* Tom Burns Haber wrote of Housman's lyrics that "although they exhibit numerous variants in line length and line number, with patterns of rhyme and accent of several different kinds, a glance into his *Complete Poems* shows that the typical ballad stanza predominates." Norman Marlow in *A. E. Housman: Scholar and Poet* explained why the writer invariably cast his verse into balladic measure and form: "Probably it is because a man under the influence of an immediate, overmastering emotion finds that these short lines come naturally to his lips; they are, so to speak, the natural language of the heart.''

The themes of his poetry and his emotional handling of them mark Housman as an extension of the romantic movement that flourished in England in the early part of the nineteenth century and had a resurgence in the aesthetic movement of the 1890s. The critical evaluation of Housman's work in the two decades after his death in 1936 is tinged with the anti-romanticism of the period. The directness and simplicity of much of Housman's poetry were viewed as faults. In *A. E. Housman and W. B. Yeats* Richard Aldington reported a rumor that circulated about Cambridge University to the effect that when influential critic I. A. Richards left Housman's Cambridge inaugural lecture he was heard to say: "This had put us back ten years." And Cyril Connolly, in a 1936 *New Statesman* article reprinted in Ricks's collection, said that Housman's poems "are of a triteness of technique equalled only by the banality of thought." He also talked about the limitations of the poet's themes of man's mortality and rebellion against his lot.

But Housman has also had some surprising defenders—critics whose theories would lead one to expect outright denunciation. Such distinguished figures as William Empson and Cleanth Brooks set the precedent for much subsequent modern criticism of Housman. While Brooks found a serious problem of tone—a slipping into sentimentality—in much of the poetry, he carefully selected for his approval what he regarded as a wealth of irony. From the time of the appearance of *A Shropshire Lad*, readers perceived the cruel ironies of Housman's universe; but Brooks and others detected a modern aesthetic in Housman in terms of ironic technique.

Such a technique was treated in a *Victorian Poetry* article by B. J. Leggett, who cautioned readers that the rustic speaker is not the poet. Leggett went so far as to say, in fact, that "the persona thus becomes a kind of Yeatsian mask or anti-self, the opposite of all that the poet represents in his private life." Christopher Ricks, in the essay in his collection on Housman, made much the same point about irony but focused more on style than on Housman's distance from his speaker. He noted that "everyone seems to take it for granted that Housman's poems unwaveringly endorse the pessimistic beliefs which they assert. To me his poems are remarkable for the ways in which rhythm and style temper or mitigate or criticize what in bald paraphrase the poem would be saying."

To see irony in Housman's poetic technique is to mitigate some of what would otherwise be considered faults: the adolescent nature of some of the thought and the sentimental handling of it. Not all critics, however, think Housman's work needs to be rescued by irony. In a 1983 *Victorian Poetry* essay Brian Rosebury found Housman's effectiveness as a poet to reside in his "visual decorum—the fitness of image to mood," and declared that "the tone of his better poems is in harmony with, not ironically (or apologetically) at odds with, the feeling implicit in the meaning."

Regardless of whether one finds irony in the poetic technique, it is true that Housman tried to place some distance between himself and his work. Referring to *A Shropshire Lad* in a letter written in 1933, Housman stated that "very little in the book is biographical" and said that his view of the world was "owing to my observation of the world, not to personal circumstances." As to the county of Shropshire itself, Housman admitted in a letter to Maurice Pollet: "I was born in Worcestershire, not Shropshire, where I have never spent much time."

Housman's growing fame as a poet in the early twentieth century did not divert his attention from his primary interest in classical scholarship. In 1910 he left his position at University College for the more prestigious professorship of Latin at Cambridge. His teaching duties there were much less onerous than at University College, and thus he had more time to devote to his continued task of editing the *Astronomica* of Manilius. It was there that he completed the last three volumes of the work—the third in 1916, the fourth in 1920, and the final volume, after much delay, in 1930, six years before his death.

Always a solitary man, Housman's reputation for aloofness grew beyond all bounds during his years at Cambridge. He took long daily walks around the town until almost the time of his death, and he became notorious for his unwillingness to acknowledge—much less speak to—anyone he encountered along the way. Tom Burns Haber in *A. E. Housman* reported the story of an unfortunate man who introduced himself to Housman as a friend of his brother Laurence, only to receive the curt reply: "Knowing my brother is no introduction to *me*." He did maintain a small group of intimate friends—mainly Grant Richards, his publisher; Percy Withers, a physician; and the author Arthur Benson—but most of his time was spent in his small rooms at Trinity College poring over his classical texts.

One diversion he did allow himself was an annual vacation to the continent, in later years almost exclusively to Paris. Earlier he included Venice on his itinerary, and his biographer Graves recorded the details of a homosexual affair he had there with a gondolier. Graves summed up the appeal Paris had for Housman: "Not only was it the gastronomic capital of the world, but if offered a rich diet of sexual adventures." While Housman also lived the life of the gastronome in England, he seems there to have been the model of discretion in his sexual life.

One of Housman's duties at Cambridge was the presentation of public lectures, and the most famous of these was the "Leslie Stephen Lecture," delivered in 1933. This speech was subsequently published as *The Name and Nature of Poetry* and later included in Carter's *Selected Prose*. Housman's only major attempt at literary criticism, the lecture was reluctantly undertaken when his health was beginning to fail. Norman Page recorded Housman's own evaluation of his product: "I do not think highly of my lecture, which I wrote against the grain and almost under compulsion."

As B. J. Leggett said in his essay in *Modern Language Quarterly*, "The Leslie Stephen Lecture . . . seemed to confirm what Housman's verse also suggested: he was hopelessly out of touch with the kind of poetry which [Ezra] Pound was then championing and with the kind of scientific criticism for which [I. A.] Richards is now well known." The lecture is a throwback to Wordsworth's preface to his and Samuel Taylor Coleridge's *Lyrical Ballads*, in the vein of this earlier work's "spontaneous overflow of powerful feelings." In fact, Housman not only placed feelings above thought but also emphasized the physiological origins of poetry. He said, for example, that he seldom wrote poetry unless he was "rather out of health."

In the lecture Housman judged the poetry of the eighteenth century to be inferior primarily because the poets attempted to write with the intellect and that involved—and here he quoted Matthew Arnold—"some repressing and silencing of poetry," "some touch of frost to the imaginative life of the soul." He also lashed out at the literary critics of his own day, saying they believed criticism imparts truth and knowledge, whereas it is only "personal opinions."

It may be true, as Norman Page said, that Housman took up "an extreme position partly for the delight of startling an audience, and partly for the intellectual exercise of defending it." But it is also possible that the critic in this lecture was approaching poetry from the poet's point of view, telling his Cambridge audience not what they wanted to hear but what he had experienced in writing his own poetry. It was this integrity in the man that spanned his different lives as classical scholar and romantic poet.

Bailey spoke of the integrity in the classical scholar as a zeal to see the text "not as others had presented it or as he might have preferred it to appear but exactly as it was." The integrity in the poet may have relegated him to a rank below that of the major poets of his age. His poetry, based as it is on emotion, never goes beyond what he could verify with his own feelings. As Edmund Wilson said in an essay appearing in the Ricks collection, "His world has no opening horizons; it is a prison that one can only endure. One can only come the same painful cropper over and over again and draw from it the same bitter moral." But few writers have expressed this dark if limited vision with more poignancy and clarity than Housman.

BIOGRAPHICAL/CRITICAL SOURCES:

BOOKS

Aldington, Richard, *A. E. Housman and W. B. Yeats,* Peacock Press, 1955.
Carter, John, editor, *A. E. Housman: Selected Prose,* Cambridge University Press, 1961.
Dictionary of Literary Biography, Volume 19: British Poets, 1840-1914, Gale, 1983.
Empson, William, *Some Versions of Pastoral,* New Directions, 1960.
Gow, Andrew S. F., *A. E. Housman,* Macmillan, 1936.
Graves, Richard Perceval, *A. E. Housman: The Scholar-Poet,* Scribner, 1979.
Haber, Tom Burns, *Manuscript Poems: Eight Hundred Lines of Hitherto Uncollected Verse From the Author's Notebooks,* University of Minnesota Press, 1955.
Haber, Tom Burns, editor, *The Making of "A Shropshire Lad": A Manuscript Variorum,* University of Washington Press, 1966.
Haber, Tom Burns, *A. E. Housman,* Twayne, 1967.
Hawkins, Maude M., *A. E. Housman: Man Behind a Mask,* Henry Regnery, 1958.
Housman, A. E., *A Shropshire Lad,* Kegan Paul, 1896.
Housman, A. E., *Last Poems,* Holt, 1922.
Housman, A. E., *More Poems,* edited by Laurence Housman, Knopf, 1936.
Housman, Laurence, *My Brother, A. E. Housman,* Scribner, 1938.
Leggett, B. J., *Housman's Land of Lost Content: A Critical Study of "A Shropshire Lad,"* University of Tennessee Press, 1970.
Leggett, B. J., *The Poetic Art of A. E. Housman: Theory and Practice,* University of Nebraska Press, 1978.
Marlow, Norman, *A. E. Housman: Scholar and Poet,* Routledge & Kegan Paul, 1958.
Orwell, George, *Inside the Whale and Other Essays,* Penguin Books, 1957.
Page, Norman, *A. E. Housman: A Critical Biography,* Schocken, 1983.
Richards, Grant, *Housman, 1897-1936,* Oxford University Press, 1942.
Ricks, Christopher, editor, *A. E. Housman: A Collection of Critical Essays,* Prentice-Hall, 1968.
Robinson, Oliver, *Angry Dust: The Poetry of A. E. Housman,* Bruce Humphries, 1950.
Scott-Kilvert, Ian, *A. E. Housman,* Longman, 1955.
Sparrow, John, *Controversial Essays,* Chilmark House, 1966.
Symons, Katharine E. and others, *Alfred Edward Housman: Recollections,* Holt, 1937.
Twentieth-Century Literary Criticism, Gale, Volume 1, 1978, Volume 10, 1983.
Wallace-Hadrill, F., editor, *Alfred Edward Housman,* Holt, 1937.

Watson, George I., *A. E. Housman: A Divided Life,* Richard Hart, 1957.
Withers, Percy, *A Buried Life,* J. Cape, 1940.

PERIODICALS

Cithara, Volume 6, number 2, 1967.
Listener, Volume 61, 1959.
Modern Language Quarterly, June, 1963, March, 1971.
PMLA, June, 1945, March, 1967.
Victorian Poetry, spring, 1972, summer, 1972, autumn, 1976, winter, 1976, autumn, 1983.*

—*Sidelights by David G. Holborn*

*   *   *

HOWARD, J. Grant   1929-

PERSONAL: Born April 19, 1929, in Prescott, Ariz.; son of J. Grant and Orean Archer Howard; married Audrey J. Rudes, August 18, 1951; children: Jim, Beth, Jeanne, Juli. *Education:* Attended University of Arizona, 1947-49; Wheaton College, Wheaton, Ill., B.A., 1951; Dallas Theological Seminary, Th.M., 1959, Th.D., 1967.

ADDRESSES: Office—Department of Pastoral Theology, Western Conservative Baptist Seminary, 5511 Southeast Hawthorne Blvd., Portland, Ore. 97215.

CAREER: Ordained Baptist minister, 1957; youth minister at Baptist church in Dallas, Tex., 1959-60; pastor of Bible church in Phoenix, Ariz., 1962-71; Western Conservative Baptist Seminary, Portland, Ore., professor of pastoral theology, 1971—. Visiting professor at Asian Theological Seminary, Manila, Philippines, 1979-80, 1983-84, 1987-88, and Columbia Bible College and Graduate School, 1985. Worked with missionaries, nationals, and American military personnel in Hong Kong, Singapore, Indonesia, Pakistan, Kenya, Zaire, Greece, Italy, Spain, Portugal, Austria, Germany, and France, 1980-84, 1987-88.

MEMBER: Evangelical Theological Society.

WRITINGS:

Knowing God's Will—and Doing It! Zondervan, 1976.
The Trauma of Transparency, Multnomah, 1979.
Balancing Life's Demands, Multnomah, 1983.
Creativity in Preaching, Zondervan, 1987.

SIDELIGHTS: J. Grant Howard told *CA:* "When I write, it is eight hours a day, five days a week, for six to eight weeks. All of the research and development has come before that. I need to teach and preach a subject at least five years before I am ready to write about it. Then I write through my fingers on the keyboard of the computer. I work hard and long on the first draft; very little rewriting is necessary on the final manuscript.

"My books are popular and practical in nature. The latest, though, *Creativity in Preaching,* is aimed more at the professional teacher or preacher. This is a new venture for me, writing for a limited audience.

"I have been around the world three times in the last nine years, concentrating attention on teaching and training in schools and churches in third world countries—primarily in the Philippines. Overseas work has made me more deeply conscious of the significance of culture—mine and everybody else's!"

HOWARTH, T(homas) E(dward) B(rodie) 1914-1988(?)

OBITUARY NOTICE: Born October 21, 1914, in Rutherglen, Scotland; died c. 1988. Educator, editor, and author. As personal liaison officer to Field Marshal Bernard Montgomery during World War II, Howarth arranged for the surrender of the German Army of Occupation in Denmark. After the war he taught at various institutions and was eventually named headmaster at King Edward's School in Birmingham. In 1952 he took the position of second master of Winchester College, where he remained for ten years, after which he was appointed high master of St. Paul's School in London. Howarth subsequently joined Magdalene College of Cambridge University as a fellow, and upon his retirement in 1980 he became headmaster at Campion School in Athens, Greece, for two years. Howarth's writings include a biography of King Louis Philippe of France, *The Citizen King; Cambridge Between Two Wars,* his view of the social atmosphere at the university between World War I and World War II; *Prospect and Reality: Great Britain, 1945-1955,* a sociopolitical history; and *Culture, Anarchy, and the Public Schools.* Howarth also edited *Monty at Close Quarters,* a biography of Montgomery consisting of twelve essays by people who knew him personally.

OBITUARIES AND OTHER SOURCES:

BOOKS

Who's Who, 136th edition, St. Martin's, 1984.

PERIODICALS

Spectator, May 27, 1978, May 11, 1985, August 24, 1985.
Times (London), May 9, 1985, May 11, 1988.
Times Literary Supplement, July 10, 1969, May 26, 1978, June 21, 1985.

*   *   *

HUAN Yue
See SHEN Congwen

*   *   *

HULL, Suzanne W(hite) 1921-

PERSONAL: Born August 24, 1921, in Orange, N.J.; daughter of Gordon Stowe (a motion picture association executive) and Lillian (an institutional administrator; maiden name, Siegling) White; married George I. Hull (an attorney), February 20, 1943; children: George Gordon, James Rutledge, Anne Hull Cabello. *Education:* Swarthmore College, B.A. (with honors), 1943; University of Southern California, M.S. in L.S., 1967.

ADDRESSES: Home—1465 El Mirador Dr., Pasadena, Calif. 91103. *Office*—1151 Oxford Rd., San Marino, Calif. 91108.

CAREER: Lumbermen's Insurance Co., New York, N.Y., director of personnel, 1944-45; Save the Children Federation, New York, secretary to director, 1946-47; *Los Angeles Times,* Los Angeles, Calif., news stringer, 1953-55; homemaker, 1955-67; Los Angeles public library system, Los Angeles, substitute librarian, 1967-69; Huntington Library, Art Gallery, and Botanical Gardens, San Marino, Calif., staff member, 1969-86, officer, 1972-86, director of administration and public services, 1974-86, reader, 1986—. President of Children's Service League, Los Angeles, 1963-64, and Los Angeles Young Women's Christian Association (YWCA), 1967-69; member of board of directors of Welfare Planning Council, San Fer-

nando Valley, 1963-68, Los Angeles YWCA, 1963-69 and 1970-73, United Service Organizations (USO), Los Angeles and Hollywood, Calif., 1967-70, Recreation and Youth Services Planning Council, Los Angeles, 1968-69, Friends of Los Angeles YWCA, 1968-72 (also co-founder), and Pasadena Planned Parenthood Association, 1978—; member of Swarthmore Alumni Council, 1959-62, 1983—, and Community Advisory Council of Los Angeles Job Corps Center for Women, 1972-78; member of advisory board, Hagley Museum and Library, 1983-86; founder and member of Huntington Library Women's Studies Seminar, 1983—.

MEMBER: Renaissance Society of America, British Studies Conference, Western Association of Women Historians, Monumental Brass Society (Britain), California Congress of Parents and Teachers (honorary life member), Beta Phi Mu.

WRITINGS:

Chaste, Silent, and Obedient: English Books for Women, 1475-1640, Huntington Library, 1982.

Also author of *The State of the Art in Women's Studies.* Contributor to periodicals, including *School Press Review* and *Calendar;* editor and public relations writer for community organizations.

WORK IN PROGRESS: Women According to Men, an annotated anthology of instructions written by men for sixteenth- and seventeenth-century women.

SIDELIGHTS: Suzanne W. Hull's *Chaste, Silent, and Obedient* is a historical study of English books written for women between 1475 and 1640. Examining practical, recreational, polemic, and devotional literature, Hull concludes that the feminine virtues advocated in Tudor and Stuart times—appropriate to a subordinate—contrast markedly with those valued in our own enlightened age. Yet in the *Times Literary Supplement* Julia Briggs pointed out that "Green, Shakespeare and Middleton were all commercial writers whose lively and forceful heroines were always chaste, not always obedient, and seldom silent." She added: "Curiously, the contrast here implied is considerably less evident in the reading-matter itself which . . . strongly recalls the typical contents of our own women's magazines."

While Briggs felt that "a more searching account of the material might have been possible had the author sifted through the contents of her selection in finer detail," the critic nonetheless determined, "[Hull's] booklist provides a fascinating and valuable guide to the feminine tastes of the age." Writing as a sixteenth-century representative "of that faire but weake sexe," *Los Angeles Times* reviewer Elizabeth Wheeler offered a similar opinion. "Tho theyre all things I would have done in divers ways," stated the fictional yoretime critic, "I must say that she has written a good Booke, & one interesting for ladies as rare in hir day as it was in mine."

Hull told *CA:* "With one foot in sixteeenth-century books for a female audience and a few toes in twentieth-century business and cultural activities, I am constantly being made aware of the changes in women's lives that have taken place since the sixteenth century—and how far women still have to go to achieve opportunities and recognition, equal with men. The more I learn about the past, the more I am concerned about the present. I still have a perhaps naive faith that writing can be a major contributor to progress and understanding in this field—as in others."

BIOGRAPHICAL/CRITICAL SOURCES:

PERIODICALS

Los Angeles Times, April 23, 1982.
Times Literary Supplement, November 19, 1982.

*   *   *

HULME, Keri   1947-

PERSONAL: Born March 9, 1947, in Christchurch, New Zealand; daughter of John W. (a carpenter and businessman) and Mere (a credit manager; maiden name, Miller) Hulme. *Education:* Attended University of Canterbury, 1967-68. *Politics:* None. *Religion:* "No formal religion."

ADDRESSES: Home—Okarito Private Bag, Westland, New Zealand.

CAREER: Writer. Worked as fisher, television director, and cook. Writer in residence at Otago University, Dunedin, New Zealand, 1978, and University of Canterbury, Christchurch, New Zealand, 1985.

MEMBER: New Zealand Literary Fund (advisory committee), New Zealand Indecent Publications Tribunal.

AWARDS, HONORS: New Zealand Book Award for fiction and Pegasus Award for Maori literature from Mobil Oil, both 1984, and Booker McConnell Prize, 1985, all for *The Bone People.*

WRITINGS:

The Silence Between: Moeraki Conversations (poetry), Victoria University Press, 1982.
The Bone People (novel), Spiral, 1984, Louisiana University Press, 1985.
Lost Possessions, Victoria University Press, 1985.
Te Kaihau/The Windeater (short stories), Victoria University Press, 1986, Braziller, 1987.
Strands (poetry), Auckland University Press, 1988.

WORK IN PROGRESS: A novel, tentatively entitled *Bait,* and a short story collection.

SIDELIGHTS: Keri Hulme is a celebrated New Zealander writer best known for *The Bone People,* her highly acclaimed first novel about the stormy relationship of three social outcasts. The central character is Kerewin Holmes, a woman who is, like Hulme, one-eighth Maori. Coarse, yet clever, and engaging, though essentially aloof, Kerewin lives in voluntary isolation in a seaside tower. Living nearby is Joe Gillayley, a temperamental factory worker who had earlier attended divinity school. Completing the triumverate is Simon, a mute child who washed ashore near the tower and is fostered by Joe.

Kerewin is nonplussed by most human contact, but she does enjoy Joe's company at her extravagant tea parties and free-wheeling drinking sessions. She casually invites Joe and Simon to join her on a fishing expedition at her family's beach dwelling. Before they embark, however, Kerewin discovers that Joe has been venting his frustration and anger on Simon by thrashing him. Upon securing Joe's assurances that he will control his temper, Kerewin continues with the fishing plans.

Faced with the unavoidable presence of the silent Simon, whom she had found merely tolerable—and not particularly likeable—Kerewin grows increasingly fond of the boy. Their relationship, though, is disrupted when Joe once again beats the child and is consequently imprisoned and deprived of the boy's custody. Having barely survived the vicious thrashing, Simon is sent to a Catholic orphanage. Kerewin returns to the tower and dismantles the top four levels.

Separately, each of the three characters then experiences a personal crisis. Joe, after serving three months imprisonment, attempts suicide, fails, and finally finds a focus for his life by accepting his own Maori heritage. Simon, deafened from the nearly fatal beating, escapes from the orphanage and desperately tries to reunite with Joe. Kerewin, meanwhile, comes to a new understanding of a previously disturbing family conflict—one that had driven her into her present seclusion—and, after a mystical experience cures her of cancer, she unites with Simon and, eventually, Joe.

Plot synopsis, while revealing themes, affords little understanding of *The Bone People*'s scope and unique sense of language. In the novel, Hulme has fashioned a dazzling literary style similar to that of such writers as Laurence Sterne and James Joyce. The work abounds in wordplay and incorporates both the vernacular and archaic, the poetic and the prosaic. Verses are regularly included, as are unique words and phrases that have reminded some readers of Joyce's similar feats in *Finnegan's Wake.* As such, *The Bone People* has been acknowledged as an innovative work deriving force from its consummate fusion of style and content.

The Bone People was an immense success upon publication in New Zealand in 1984, enjoying consistently high praise from critics there and impressive sales with the public. Its success continued the following year when it appeared in England and won that country's prestigious Booker McConnell Prize. Among the many commendations *The Bone People* received from British critics was one from Antony Beevor, who wrote in the *Times Literary Supplement* that the novel was "remarkable" and that the characterization of Kerewin Holmes constituted a particularly "sensitive and convincing psychological portrait."

Still more praise came to *The Bone People* when it was published in the United States in late 1985. Claudia Tate, writing in the *New York Times Book Review,* described the novel as "unforgettably rich and pungent" and noted that the work "summons power with words, as in a conjurer's spell." Elizabeth Ward, who reviewed *The Bone People* in the *Washington Post Book World,* called it "a work of immense literary and intellectual ambition" and "an original, overwhelming . . . work of literature." And even the *New York Times*'s Michiko Kakutani, who expressed reservations about the work's "uneven" writing and its imposing length, nonetheless acknowledged that the work's culminating passages, in which the characters experience spiritual rejuvenation, "testify to [Hulme's] considerable . . . gifts as a writer."

Many American reviewers were especially impressed by Hulme's ability to convey both psychological and spiritual tension and provide insight into Maori culture and sensibility. Ursula Hegi, for instance, wrote in the *Los Angeles Times* that Hulme "writes with great insight about the culture of the Maori, reflecting their battle between destruction and hope." A *New Yorker* critic also noted Hulme's Maori perspective and observed that "a collective, Jungian spirit of the Maori people is invoked in a moving, lyrical conclusion." Similarly, *Village Voice* reviewer Diane Jacobs deemed *The Bone People* "a spiritual quest, a meditation on racial identity, and a celebration of social identity" and added that it is "an affirmation of the larger families we are born into."

Aside from *The Bone People,* Hulme has produced such works as *The Silences Between,* a volume of verse, and *Te Kaihau/*

The Windeater, a collection of short stories. The latter work was published in the United States in 1987, and though it received less attention than did *The Bone People,* it received recommendations as a notable collection. Among those reviewers who praised *Te Kaihau/The Windeater* was Elizabeth Ward, who wrote in the *Washington Post* that the volume, though uneven and not entirely comprehensible to non-New Zealanders, was full of "Hulme's irrepressible narrative energy." Ward added that "the variety and vitality of Hulme's imagination will ensure that those who were captivated by [*The Bone People*] will find much to treasure here also."

CA INTERVIEW

Keri Hulme granted *CA* a written interview in March, 1987.

CA: The remarkable success of The Bone People *includes Mobil Oil's Pegasus Prize and the New Zealand Book Award, both in 1984, and England's Booker McConnell Prize in 1985. This success has meant major publicity and increased travel for you and has resulted in a life that seems the opposite of the type you were leading before the book's publication. Has being in the public eye changed the nature of your life as a writer? Can you go back to the quietness?*

HULME: The last part of that question should read, "*Have you gone back to the quietness,*" to which the answer is "yes."

Nothing much has changed with the way I live—except I have a lot more money, my family group has a lot more money. Not enough to cause problems (except maybe with our Inland Revenue Department!), enough to solve them, enough to ease our collective way considerably. Being in the public eye is a very temporary phenomenon in New Zealand, and while I'd probably cause ripples if, say, I was caught drunk in charge or announced that I was entering a Carmelite monastery, all the hoha has died away. I avoid occasions to resurface to the public gaze, whether they be invitations to talk to conferences or poetry readings. I'm not a lecturer, I'm not trained to speak in public, and I'm not comfortable when I do.

I live in a fairly remote area of New Zealand—to get to Okarito you've got to traverse ten kilometers of dirt road after driving a good way through New Zealand's most unpopulated province. The population of our village is currently fourteen, and most of them are very helpful, almost protective. If people come looking for me (and more than one or two have), the locals are likely to direct them down the road to Okuru or say, "O, she's shifted to Stewart Island," or (my favorite) "Keri who?"

Living the quiet life isn't a gimmick or a publicity stunt as far as I am concerned. It is a necessity. It is my *life.*

CA: Although you are only one-eighth Maori, you identify with the Maori, and The Bone People *has a great deal to do with Maori myth and legend. Was the Maori influence a strong part of your growing up?*

HULME: That's difficult to answer shortly. It was . . . and it wasn't.

Kai Tahu, my mother's people, my tribe, *the* South Island tribe—we're renowned for being a humble people (little bit of New Zealand humor there)—were the first Maori to encounter Europeans, the first to interbreed with Europeans. In the early part of the nineteenth century, we were devastated by visita-

tions of influenza and measles, decimated by a disastrous family feud (called "kai huaka," which means "eat relations"), and walloped in a series of battles with an invading North Island tribe, Kati Toa, under the formidable generalship of Te Rauparaha. Actually, we were fighting back (having got European firearms at last) and winning when the missionaries and Christianity intervened and ruined it all.

Okay, Kai Tahu aren't slow. We saw that fighting Europeans could wipe us out. There was another effly-alternative that we had been practicing since the 1780s. Let's do that, thought our olds; it's more pleasurable, more profitable, and we persist as a people, albeit diluted.

And that is why I say the Maori influence was, and was not, a strong part of my growing up. The Maori influence was my mother's family. She is very fair (what is called "urukehu")—in fact, in her youth, she had glorious auburn hair, cream-white skin, and green eyes! (Her brother, Bill, is dark and has brown skin, black hair when he was young, and dark brown eyes, yet curiously he has the Pakeha features, and my mother's are very Maori. Heigh-ho for the jokes of genetics.) Her father was born Tommy Rakakino Mira, transforming to Thomas R. Miller, elder of the Presbyterian Church, very responsible Railway Union worker (he shoveled coal, which eventually gave him cancer of the throat and a miserable lingering death); and the gentle, strong husband of Mary Ann Yorston Matches, an Orkney woman; and the father of my mother and her brothers. (One of their abiding memories is of the fact that, in an era when children could be brought up very roughly indeed, without any kind of social or legal censure, he never laid a hand on anyone. He didn't believe in physical punishment. He believed good people—and naturally his family was good—eventually felt enough shame to right themselves.)

At Oamaru and Moeraki and Purakanui, we ate mutton birds and mussels, heard a kind of pidgin Maori, were told much more interesting stories and family gossip, and—this is for me, personally—found a hell of a lot more tolerant and understanding breed of adult. Some of them were very visibly different to my father's Christchurch relations too—it is both a family joke and a family legend that the first time I was introduced to my great-uncle Dave Miller (who was very black. Or very brown. I'm uneasy about this labeling of every other-than-white people as "black." I follow the lead of one of my kuia, who said to angry young Maori radical, "Don't you go calling me black! I'm not mangu, I'm brown and proud of it!")—he could be a grave and formal man, and with one of his favorite niece's children, two-year-old me, he decided to be courtly and shake me by the hand. I shook his hand formally (I am told) and then ruined it all by looking at my own hand and looking back at his. Ah, hell, it doesn't rub off.

Sorry, very long answer—which could go on for several books' length (indeed has, and will).

In short, the Maori influence was my family influence—immediate extended family influence. My whanau. While I started collecting Maori words (made a dictionary of them for the rest of the benighted outside world!) at seven, while I loved my mother's relations for the acceptance and tolerance and love I found there, I didn't realize we were any way Maori while I was a child.

We won't go into my adolescence and young adulthood, when I learned a bloody sight more, because that involves land courts and my father's death and growing up at Moeraki and my discovery of myself and a few other small but potent matters.

CA: Are the rhythms of the prose often based on those of the Maori language?

HULME: Of my prose? A lot of them, yes.

There are at least four kinds of Maori, each with their own especial rhythms and melodies: classical, that you'll find in the collections of waiata and hear from the paramount orators on today's marae; colloquial, the everyday chat people use day-to-day; pidgin, which was what my child ears heard when I heard Maori at all; and Maori-English: "Key that door and we go, eh?"

I heard colloquial Maori at Motueka in 1965 when I left home for the first time to pick tobacco. I could understand bits. I couldn't understand enough. (That was also the first time I learned North Island Maori weren't just in stories; hell, they still existed!) I read classical Maori after long painstakingly acquired lessons. What you put your brain's sweat into stays with you, affects what you do.

CA: So often the prose is very close to poetry, and your first published book, The Silences Between, *is poetry. Was poetry your first writing?*

HULME: No. The first thing I recall writing down was that dictionary I mentioned. I won what were called "essay prizes" at both primary and secondary school. I might mention that I've never actually been sure where the boundary line is between poetry and prose (which will probably delight some critics to no end. "Yah, we knew it! Ignorant slob!").

Maori is a very positional and metaphoric language. Words take color and strength from where they are, from the intensives by them—indeed, from the circumstances and surroundings where they are spoken. A very simple sentence in Maori can sound poetic: "Kua taki te kaka" ("The forest parrot has cried out."), or bathetic: ("Geddup."). Both are legitimate translations of a Kai Tahu phrase.

Incidentally, the first time I can remember consciously being critical, or analytical, was with a phrase I wrote while biking to school my first year at high school in 1960. It was part of a poem that began, "The sky is full of skudding clouds," which sounded okay to twelve-year-old me (my birthday isn't until March, and New Zealand high school/secondary schools start the year in February), but what the hell did "skudding" mean? Why should it fit so well, sound so right, if it didn't actually have a dictionary meaning?

CA: In "Tara Diptych," the foreword to Te Kaihau/The Windeater, *there's a "you" and an "I." It ends, "You'd be a brave human who would say where all the influences come from, but I think the word sets the whole thing up...." Are you writing about the influences on your work?*

HULME: Yes, inasmuch as words are things that I love. Words are real. They have power. They can make you easy, make you ache, give you strength, hurt or heal others. That would be the major influence on whatever work I do. (A word *can* set the whole thing up—the story "Hooks & Feelers" came from a phrase I found in Eric Partridge's *A Dictionary of Slang and Unconventional English.* I wrote it with the help of a box of twenty-five King Edward cigars and a half-gallon of white wine in a three-day weekend because I desperately needed

money at the time and there was this short story competition going, with a deadline Monday, that had a three-hundred-dollar first prize. Go for it, Hulme.) Other influences are everything I read (I'm a reader primarily, a writer secondarily) and a wee obscure need to pass on thoughts and feelings I have.

CA: The Bone People began, you said in its preface, as a *short story written when you were eighteen, and the characters "wouldn't go away." Did its growth into a novel follow a rather steady path, or were there many changes and re-writings?*

HULME: No steady path, no way. That first short story stopped in a drawer for a couple of years. I played with some characters in paintings, in words. The story bent and climbed and went into weird areas. (For instance, at one time Simon Peter was a cave-dweller; at another, he only appeared in other characters' dreams—you never knew whether he was real or imaginary—and in one story, scrapped very quickly, he died midway through the book. Similar transmogrifications happened to everyone in what eventually became *The Bone People.*) There were at least seven re-writings of the settled manuscript.

May I emphasize that up until last year I considered myself an apprentice? The poetry book, slender and all as it is, is my first book of poetry. *The Bone People* is my first novel. *Te Kaihau/The Windeater* is my first collection of stories—written, incidentally, over nearly a fourteen-year period. Between twenty-five and thirty-nine a lot can happen to a human.

CA: You've said that The Bone People *was about yourself "cunningly disguised as a Kerewin Holmes." Did you have any qualms along the way about revealing so much of yourself?*

HULME: How much have I revealed?

Kerewin was my touchstone character, and I gave her attributes of myself. I didn't give her ALL the attributes of myself. Besides, that book was for New Zealanders, and I thought (hoped hugely) for about six hundred, seven hundred, migod maybe a thousand New Zealand readers.

If I had any inkling that *The Bone People* was eventually to be published overseas in the way it has been, Kerewin would've been, umm, rather more herself, rather less me. Too bloody late, eh?

CA: You're an artist as well as a writer, and usually you draw or paint the characters to get them straight in your mind. Also I noticed, in The Bone People, *where descriptions of paintings were set to poetry. How much do the art and writing intertwine?*

HULME: All the way through.

Aside from anything, my imagination—theater of the head—is wholly visual. I dream in color. I illustrate with words.

A pertinent sidenote: Most Maori I know who are actively involved in "The Arts" are multi-talented, not because we're whakahihi, but because, truly, one thing leads to another, which is part of the third and the thirty-third and the first. Hari Williams is a photographer and painter and writer; Katerina Mataira is a writer and painter (and teacher); Patricia Grace does many things, not least write superbly; and Witi Ihimaera, as well as being our consul in New York and the first (many would say foremost) Maori writer to be published in English, is also a musician and lyricist. I write, I paint, I sing bad winesongs. Okay, so what's new?

CA: Does the writing leave much time for painting now? Does much the same kind of energy go into each activity?

HULME: Well, this year it's more a matter of, "Does the painting leave much time for writing?" Answer, I'm not sure. Because I've spent so much time with writing-related matters these past three years, drawing and painting hasn't got much of a look-in. Last year, I bought a 1979 Ford Transit van, grossly in need of doing up (but it has a good 2999 c.c. Ford Capri engine in it, which won my heart). This Hoonmobile will shortly be taking to the roads, complete with hoon-Hulme driving, on a kind of painting safari round the South Island. Next year: the North!

Does much the same kind of energy go into each activity? Exactly the same, far as I know. Your gut tingles in the same way if you've done something right, drawing it, writing it, singing it, fishing it, saying it, being it.

CA: The Bone People and some of the short stories in Te Kaihau/The Windeater *seem to be very much about families. Do you think of the family as a conscious concern in your writing?*

HULME: My family is the *the* THE most important thing in my life.

I better define family, what that word means for me, before I go any further. "Family" is the group of people I was born into, my whanau. Mother, father, siblings, parents' parents, parents' siblings, in-laws, relations, everybody on your bloodline, and quite a few others besides. Those who "marry" in (many sexual relationships, while long-lasting, are informal); those who are adopted in (the whangai are a big part of my family group, to the latest generation); those who, through long and trusted support and partaking of the family group, come to have the status of relations.

I can meet someone and think, What a shit, and then learn that they are whanauka and immediately—well, not necessarily revise my opinion of them, but add to it, Well, they're a *family* shit. It truly makes a difference to me to know that you are Kai Tahu, of my hapu KatiRakiamoa or KaiRuahikihiki— or that you're a Hulme, from Lancashire. Or a Matches or Rendall from Mainland, Orkney.

Now, given all that, given the vital love and security I have from my family group, the respect we have for one another, the dignity we give each other, it distresses me to see the many many people in New Zealand who are bereft of their families— who have either never had them, or who have lost their family groups. I think that is bereavement, that is loss, that is a primary wound.

Incidentally, lest I seem to be allied with certain fundamentalist Christian groups in my concern with families, may I emphasize that their kind of family and my kind of family are diametrically opposed? I come from a working class, unmonied class, a striving mongrel kind of class of people who basically are not Christian (as far as I know, none of my whanau are practicing Christians, and many of us are actively non-Christian), but who hold to the belief in family as continuum.

"We carry our ghosts on our shoulders: we are never alone." (You can't ever be alone: the air you breathe is full of other people, other beings—and all their breathing—and you yourself are a knit and weaving of a thousand generations.) I write about what I love—or what I perceive New Zealanders need to take a closer look at. Or just to entertain us, talking about

what we already think we know. (That's a course that is always good for surprises, laughs, and tears.)

CA: Do you think of The Bone People *as a feminist novel, as some of the critics have done?*

HULME: Can I answer this in circuitous fashion?

Yes it is, because I am a female (sexually, though I think my gender is neuter), and I am a stroppy, feminally-biased female, and all that I write is, on one way, quite deliberately meant to emphasize the strengths and superiorities of females. No it's not, because I am a fringe-dweller and have never joined wholeheartedly with any feminist group or consciously ever ordered anything but my language in a politically acceptable fashion.

I have, inborn, a self-deflating sense of humor. I have been trained by my family and by my societies at large to be whaka-itiiti (a word which means, roughly, "self-consciously but naturally humble"—do you start to see where New Zealanders, but particularly Maori New Zealanders, get their peculiar sense of humor from?).

What that ultimately means is, I can't ever be a fanatic about anything. And I can't be committed absolutely to anything (except, she said with a sly grin, to self a family—possibly).

I'm a feminist because I'm female.

I don't write feminist tracts.

Hate me.

I'll care only if you happen to be whanauka.

CA: Have you found New Zealand's critics to be harder on The Bone People *than reviewers in other English-speaking countries?*

HULME: Critics in New Zealand for the first few editions of *The Bone People* were uniformly supportive and laudatory. Hell o dear, that's an understatement: I think some critics used up their lifetimes' supply of congratulatory and praise words, and I shudder to imagine what's going to be said about the next equivalent to *The Bone People*. Do you know that *The Bone People* had sold over twenty-five thousand copies in New Zealand before the Booker McConnell Award? That in New Zealand, ten thousand to twelve thousand copies of a book of fiction by a *well-established* author (say McAuley, Stead, or Frame) is a runaway best-seller? (In 1985 I certainly was NOT a well-established New Zealand author.) That it has now sold over eighty thousand copies—and no other serious work in New Zealand has ever sold anything like that? (Sir Keith Sinclair's *A History of New Zealand* has sold over seventy-five thousand copies—over a twenty-five-year period.)

Forgive this rave. That was a bit whakahihi.

There *has* been adverse comment on *The Bone People* within New Zealand (I would mention particularly criticism by C. K. Stead, a very well respected professor of English at Auckland University Press, himself an extraordinarily good New Zealand fiction writer, his works including *Smith's Dream*, a seminal work, and *All Visitors Ashore*, a rather wicked piece of satire) and a rather "snitchy-bitchy" second-time-round review that appeared in the Christchurch press by a hitherto unknown book reviewer. ("Snitchy-bitchy" is a term coined by the late and lamented Denis Glover, a loved New Zealand poet who coined the phrase that every New Zealander knows:

"Quardle oodle ardle wardle doodle,

The magpies said."

You don't have magpies in your land?

Oh.)

The most negative criticisms have come from England, where, I think, many people took it as a personal affront that a book from an erstwhile colony could snea/grab/steal/purloin/be-given-as-a-political-gesture—anything but win—their premier literary prize. (It was made worse by the fact that, in everybody's minds, an Aussie was runner-up!) On the other hand—and this is called "choppin the tall poppies" in New Zealand—when the collection of short stories came out, most critics had a bone to pick.

CA: Do the characters live beyond the book in your mind? Do their stories continue?

HULME: Yes, they do.

I was tempted to stop right there. (Being, as many people have pointed out, a verbose person, however—o sheeit, I continue.)

I was curious, after a painting I did in '85, to find out what things could be like three years after. I wrote a very long short story, nearly forty thousand words, a novella, and found out. Trouble is, you do these things, and then you don't know what to do with them. My drawers are fat with such self-indulgences. They complain. Tough.

Sooo, I've followed Kerewin, and Joe, and Himi, three years on. I took a wee additional look at Luce Mihi Tainui, because he aggravated me as a character. I finally and thoroughly buried the kaumatua (who has my great-grandfather's name, by the way, and whom I tangi'ed over in the book).

There isn't any sequel, but one of these days when I get rash, I might have a go at publishing "The Reef in Winter" (which is the novella/long story/thingy I wrote). Without paintings, I think.

CA: Kerewin Holmes first lives in a tower and later designs herself a spiral house patterned on a seashell. There are other homes in The Bone People, *some of them temporary. The concept of home and how it is expressed seems very important to you.*

HULME: O gawd. Yeah it is, but how do I express it without going on at boring length?

Home is, initially and most importantly, the land (or for some, the sea) you're on. Papatuanuku. (Or Takaroa.)

Sometimes, you may wander an inordinate length of days and never find the land you're supposed to settle on. Maybe you aren't meant to settle. Sometimes, the land, the island, calls you quickly, and there you are, happily bedded on it.

After you've found the land you're part of, then there is the matter of your shelter.

For some people, this can be anything.

For me, and for pretty well every person in my family, it has got to be especially *something*. We spent most of our lives making homes. Ape-nests. Dwellings. Host-places. Welcomes. We're good at it. Talking about it seems irrelevant and onerous, so may I escape by saying these three things: Wharenui (also called whare-rununga, and whare-puni, and whare-whakairo) are ancestors—their ribs arch over you, their arms greet you, you dwell within them. I have a kaitiaki outside my house—he guards it, protects it, so no one unwanted gets in. Home is where the fire is.

CA: You built yourself an eight-sided house to live in. How did you learn to build?

HULME: By happenstance, through necessity.

My father was a carpenter (and painter and decorator; he'd served his trades in both) so I wasn't unfamiliar with tools.

In 1970 I shifted to the West Coast (from Christchurch, where I'd been working as a postie in Sockburn). In 1972, when I decided to retire and become a writer, I bought a house in Cobden, Greymouth. The previous tenants had pulled up one of the floors and installed a car engine in the middle of the wreckage and chopped down the verandah for firewood. The place was a shambles. (The old bloke who'd been the landlord was feeling ill and wanted to get shot of it—it really was a wreck. He sold me the heap and an acre and a half of land, for $650, and that, in New Zealand at that time, was bloody cheap. A bargain.)

CA: The Spiral Collective formed to publish The Bone People. *Are they still going strong?*

HULME: Spiral Collective Number Five was actually formed to publish *three* novels. To wit, *A Figurehead, A Face,* by Heather McPherson. (Heather is a radical lesbian feminist, a neat woman, an excellent poet. She had been mucked round with by another publisher and had waited years for this collection of her poems to be published. Heather is Pakeha.) *The House of the Talking Cat,* by J. C. Sturm. Jacqui was the wife of one of New Zealand's most famous poets. She had considerable difficulty in getting this, her first collection of short stories, published. (People kept insinuating that her husband, James K. Baxter, must have had a hand in writing them—despite the fact that Jacqui was one of the first Maori ever to have stories published in English in New Zealand.) *The Bone People,* by Keri Hulme. (Well, there was this stupid mongrel who believed that what she wrote held *something*, and despite its undoubted deficiencies, her sprawl of a novel should be left to stand as it was, lest that something escape.)

The women of Spiral Collective Number Five are Miriama Evans, Maori (part Kai Tahu), mother of three, holds first class honors degree in Classical Maori, currently lecturing at Victoria University, and involved in a high position in the Ministry of Women's Affairs; Marian Evans, Pakeha (and no relation!), mother of three, university educated, and currently a free-lance editor. (Our dream-facilitator—she really does have that rare gift of making dreams come true. A radical feminist, with all the human virtues.) Irihapeti Ramsden, Kai Tahu, mother of two, Ngati Irakehu, toku whanauka—having fought the public health system to a standstill, attempting to instill Maori virtue into it, she has resigned her position as a public health nurse and is currently tutoring in nursing.

The collective had no other reason for being other than to publish those three books. Having done so, Spiral Collective Number Five destructed (except as a legal fiction to distribute funds garnered from the three above-mentioned books). Other Spiral Collectives continue in New Zealand—I think we're up to Number Nine now.

CA: You've been a member of the New Zealand Fund Advisory Committee and the recipient of grants for writing. How much patronage is there for literary pursuits in New Zealand?

HULME: I continue as a member of the New Zealand Literary Fund Advisory Committee, an ad hoc body which has just celebrated its fortieth birthday. Other than governmental patronage, there is very little support for New Zealand literature indeed. The Mobil Corporation's sponsorship of the Pegasus Prize for Maori Literature was a one-off. There is the Choysa Bursary for children's literature (part-sponsored by Quality Packers) and the ICI co-sponsorship (with the New Zealand Literary Fund) of the New Zealand Writing Bursary. There're four short story awards and some very minor prizes organized by writers' bodies, and the year-long fellowships partly funded by the four main universities (Canterbury, Otago, Auckland, and Victoria). And that's about it.

Total funding for the New Zealand Literary Fund amounted to a bit over a quarter of a million dollars (from vote and from special grants by the New Zealand Lotteries Board). Private patronage totalled less than a tenth of $250,000.

There is pathetically little support for literary pursuits here—but, then again, we're not a rich country, we have other priorities, and literature has always been regarded as a rather frivolous indulgence, pursued by the eccentric few.

CA: How much do you feel New Zealand's geographical situation affects its literature?

HULME: Affects? Or affected?

You see, there is a strong feeling among most writers working here today of: "Read what we write if you want. If you don't want, or you don't understand it, tough. We're writing for us, for New Zealanders."

Doubtless because this is a middle phase in the evolution of New Zealand literature (the initial phase was a rebellion against received ideas of English and European superiority, a conscious and self-conscious start to "speaking with our own tongues"), and because it does reflect a burgeoning national confidence in ourselves, it will change. But for now, we know who we are and *where we are*—and we don't perceive ourselves as an isolated island group at the end of the world anymore. That feeling *was* a significant factor in the writing of the earliest generations of Pakeha settlers, but I think it had gone before I was born.

There are other facets of your question that I'm carefully ignoring (proximity to the larger and stronger nation of Australia, a kind of Canada-U.S.A. situation in miniature; how living along the faultline of the Indo-Austral tectonic plate can affect the country's feelings of security; what it is to be an *island* nation, and how the continuous sound of the sea can alter your speech and the way you think).

There are also the facts that while New Zealand is not only very closely tied to the rest of the world through communications and trade and political links, it also has an extraordinarily mobile population. We're inveterate travelers and always have been. Many of us still look on these islands as one more step in a continuing heke, another springboard to elsewhere. Most of the writers are stay-at-homes, however.

CA: The business card you use in your position as cultural ambassador lists your professions as writer, painter, and per-

son who fishes, according to Nancy Ramsey's article about you in the New York Times Book Review. *Do you think of yourself primarily as a writer now?*

HULME: No. I think of myself primarily as Keri Hulme, Mary's daughter, the eldest sibling, a Kai Tahu woman, a citizen of Aotearoa/New Zealander, a chauvinistic South Islander who loves to be able to paint and write and fish and build and play jokes and games. And who is in the happy, and lucky, position of being able to please herself doing that. I enjoy calling myself a writer—but it is, "The craft is part of my life," not, "My life is part of the craft."

CA: You describe yourself as a creature of small ambitions. Are there goals you've set for the writing, books you feel you must do?

HULME: If I live long enough I want to do this: complete the novel *Bait* (working title only) and another collection of short stories and a second book of poetry (which also has a working title, *Singing Ghosts and Pauashell Gods*). That'll be the journeyman stage finished with then, and if I don't consider, readers and critics don't consider, it's a proper improvement on the apprentice lot, I'll stop writing for publication right there. (I won't stop writing for my own delight: I've always done that and shall do that until I die.) I will have told the most pressing stories I want to tell by then, anyway.

I'd dearly love, however, to continue and produce, if not masterworks, at least a lasting threesome to cap things off. I'm a creature who delights in offbeat symmetries and patterns, and that would make a good ordering of part of my life.

There are two things that could inhibit such a pattern. My father's side of the family has a disconcerting habit of dropping suddenly dead from heart attacks and CVAs, and I have inherited his high blood pressure. (I am emphatically not a workaholic, as he was, however.) Annnd, I have a hobby in a drawer that could take over. I jam heavy things on top of it and spread barbed wire against it in my dreams, but there is, pullulating and throbbing and hummin away to itself, a vast set of notes and scribbled drawings and outlines and gamesplans. It's an entertainment, a personal entertainment, that has the cheek to call itself an embryo trilogy. I play with it when I am feeling particulary deft and carefree, but I don't want to get seriously involved with it for a good while yet because, migod!, could it take over!

Incidentally, does any other writer out there truly detest talking about work you plan to do? Talking about it in any revealing fashion seems, to me, to expose it prematurely, and kill it thereby.

CA: Do you see yourself as being part of mainstream New Zealand literature? You have talked about writing in your country as being "gutless," and you said that you wanted to offer readers "something meaty, something they can get their teeth into."

HULME: How words come back to haunt you! I said that in the course of a Radio New Zealand interview, in an inebriated state from a hotel room in Salt Lake City, just after the announcement of the Booker McConnell Award. Blame it on the champagne bubbles. A lot of New Zealand writing *has* been lacking in spirit and verve, as well as guts. To quote from a *New Zealand Listener* review, "By and large, writing in New Zealand has been, and still is, quite like that—orderly, accessible, sober and highminded.'' And rather boring. To my mind, our literature had been in the hands of academic practitioners for far too long.

Things change. Things change even as you say them. Books published here over the last two years are exciting and meaty enough for anybody.

If anybody is interested in what happens up here at the top of the world, try reading the following anthologies: *New Zealand Writing Since 1945*, chosen by Jackson and O'Sullivan; *Into the World of Light*, edited by Long and Ihimaera; *The Penguin Book of New Zealand Verse*, edited by Wedde and McQueen; and *Women's Work*, a collection of contemporary short stories by New Zealand women, chosen by McLeod and Weavers.

And having waded through their combined 1700-odd pages, you'll be ready to enjoy the new and growing wave of fiction, like Ian Wedde's *Symme's Hole;* Patricia Grace's *Potiki;* Janet Frame's three-volumed variation on autobiography; Sue McAuley's *Then Again;* Maurice Shadbolt's *The Season of the Jew;* Witi Ihimaera's *The Matriarch*—o the goodies are many, the feast is rich.

Do I see me as being a part of mainstream New Zealand literature?

Now I do. At least, as much as painting-intrigued word-obsessed whitebaiter can be.

AVOCATIONAL INTERESTS: Painting, fishing, drinking.

BIOGRAPHICAL/CRITICAL SOURCES:

BOOKS

Contemporary Literary Criticism, Volume 39, Gale, 1986.

PERIODICALS

Ariel, October, 1985.
Chicago Tribune, November 17, 1985.
Commonweal, March 28, 1986.
Economist, October 26, 1985.
Globe and Mail (Toronto), January 4, 1986.
London Review of Books, December 19, 1985, January 23, 1986.
Los Angeles Times, November 18, 1985.
New Yorker, February 3, 1986.
New York Review of Books, February 27, 1986.
New York Times, November 13, 1985.
New York Times Book Review, November 17, 1985.
Times Literary Supplement, October 25, 1986.
Village Voice, December 24, 1985.
Washington Post, February 27, 1987.
Washington Post Book World, December 1, 1985.
World Literature Today, spring, 1986.

—*Sketch by Les Stone*

—*Interview by Jean W. Ross*

*   *   *

HUME, Stephen   1947-

PERSONAL: Born January 1, 1947, in Blackpool, Lancashire, England; son of James (a journalist) and Joyce (a nurse; maiden name, Potter) Hume; married Susan Winifred Mayse (a novelist and dramatist), July 29, 1970. *Education:* University of Victoria, B.A., 1971; attended University of Alberta, 1975-77, and Banff School of Advanced Management, 1980. *Politics:* "Nonpartisan." *Religion:* "Nondenominational."

ADDRESSES: Office—*Edmonton Journal*, Box 2421, Edmonton, Alberta, Canada T5J 2S6.

CAREER: Edmonton Journal, Edmonton, Alberta, arctic correspondent from Yellowknife Northwest Territories, 1971-73, city editor, 1975-77, weekend editor, 1977-78, news editor, 1978-81, editor, 1981-87, general manager, 1987—. Member of journalism advisory committee at Grant MacEwan Community College, 1980-87, and literary arts advisory committee at Lakeland College, 1987—. Member of board of directors, Edmonton Downtown Development Corp. and Edmonton Downtown Business Association, both 1987—.

WRITINGS:

Signs Against an Empty Sky (poems), Quadrant Editions, 1980.
And the House Sank Like a Ship in the Long Prairie Grass (poems), Cormorant Books, 1987.

Work represented in anthologies, including *Alberta Jubilee Anthology*, 1980; *Inside Poetry*, Academic Press, 1984; and *If I Were Prime Minister*, Hurtig, 1987. Contributor to magazines, including *Time, Life,* and *Canadian Forum,* and to newspapers in Canada, the United States, and Europe.

Editor of *The Martlet*, 1967-68; co-editor of *Junction 21*, 1967-68, and of *Absolute Cannon Review*, 1969-70.

WORK IN PROGRESS: A poetry cycle that explores the destruction of aboriginal culture in Canada, from early times to the present; a collection of essays on the Canadian experience.

SIDELIGHTS: Stephen Hume told *CA:* "Our concept of the past is a map we make of the landscape of experience. We journey through it, navigating only by those reference points that lie behind us. Where we are going is determined by where we have been. Writing is our notation of landmarks.

"Much of my work has been a response to the vastness and power of the natural world and the forces that drive it. Traveling alone in the immensity of the Canadian Arctic, with its purity of form and austerity of content, I found the vantage point of my perceptions had been forever altered.

"How we internalize the landscape through which we travel, the meaning of the past and how we take direction from the signs we find in it, how we translate them into our own expressive symbology—these are the problems that occupy my present work."

AVOCATIONAL INTERESTS: Rugby, basketball, gardening, fly fishing.

BIOGRAPHICAL/CRITICAL SOURCES:

PERIODICALS

Books in Canada, Volume 17, number 1, 1988.
Edmonton Journal, December 13, 1980, December 5, 1987.

*   *   *

HUNTER, Jane (Harlow)   1949-

PERSONAL: Born January 31, 1949 in Hanover, N.H.; daughter of Ralph William (a physician) and Ann (a homemaker; maiden name, Wilkinson) Hunter; married Joel Charles Bernard (a historian), July 14, 1980; children: Eliza Jacqueline. *Education:* Yale University, B.A., 1971, Ph.D., 1981.

ADDRESSES: Home—18 Dalton St., Waterville, Me. 04901.

Office—History Department, Colby College, Waterville, Me. 04901.

CAREER: Colby College, Waterville, Me., assistant professor of history, 1980—. Radcliffe Research Scholar at the Henry A. Murray Center of Radcliffe College, 1984-85; visiting scholar at Radcliffe College, 1986-87.

AWARDS, HONORS: George Washington Egleston Award from Yale University history department, 1981, for best essay in American history; Governors Award from Yale University Press for *The Gospel of Gentility*.

WRITINGS:

The Gospel of Gentility: American Women Missionaries in Turn-of-the-Century China, Yale University Press, 1984.

WORK IN PROGRESS: The Changing Experience of American Girlhood, 1860-1930.

SIDELIGHTS: Jane Hunter's *The Gospel of Gentility* examines the women evangelists and educators who went to China as the apostles of American evangelism in the late nineteenth and early twentieth centuries. Drawing upon the diaries and letters of the women themselves, and upon the archives of the sponsoring Congregational and Methodist mission boards, Hunter explores the lifestyles of these volunteers.

Hunter's book won the attention and praise of several critics. Professor and religious scholar Martin E. Marty, writing in *Reviews in American History*, lauded *The Gospel of Gentility*'s "remarkable photographs" that provide "telling images" of these missionaries' exportation of Victorian American concepts of domesticity and judged the book "an important and often entertaining work that never quite decides whether it is mainly about China missions or about American ideals of womanhood in the period." A *Christian Century* contributor pronounced that "Jane Hunter writes better than most novelists, and she has a topic more demanding and rewarding than the subjects many novelists deal with." Jonathan Spencer, writing in the *New York Review of Books*, concurred, calling *The Gospel of Gentility* a "fine study of an aspect of the mission world in China that never before received such probing, affectionate, detailed treatment." Similarly, Richard Harris of the *Times Literary Supplement* described Hunter's work as a "well-researched" study that "concentrates on the ideas, the expectations, the emotions, the trials of the women missionaries, single and married; of how they adapted to life in China, what they wore, ate and how they lived." In addition, he found *The Gospel of Gentility* "generous in its appreciation of a now distant era," when the American missionary movement was thriving, and female missionaries in China outnumbered their male counterparts.

BIOGRAPHICAL/CRITICAL SOURCES:

PERIODICALS

American Quarterly, winter, 1985.
Arizona Daily Star, June 9, 1984.
Christian Century, May 9, 1984, November 14, 1984.
Journal of American History, December, 1984.
Los Angeles Times, March 15, 1984.
Louisville Courier-Journal, April 1, 1984.
New York Review of Books, September 27, 1984.
Reviews in American History, September, 1986.
Times Literary Supplement, August 3, 1984.
Village Voice, May 29, 1984.

HURKOS, Peter   1911-1988

OBITUARY NOTICE: Name originally Pieter Van Der Hurk; born May 21, 1911, in Dordrecht, Netherlands; came to United States, 1956; naturalized citizen, 1959; died of heart failure, June 1, 1988, in Los Angeles, Calif. Psychic, actor, house painter, and author. Hurkos is best known as the "telepathic detective" who cooperated with police departments on the Boston Strangler case in 1964, the Charles Manson mass murders five years later, and the Ann Arbor, Michigan, co-ed murders. Working as a painter in 1941, Hurkos fell four stories from a ladder and sustained a brain injury. When he regained consciousness four days later he claimed to have psychic powers enabling him to see into the future and track down missing persons. Unable to work full time because he found his psychic faculty distracting, Hurkos made numerous television and radio appearances and helped investigators solve cases. He also acted in the motion pictures "The Boston Strangler," "The Amazing World of Psychic Phenomena," and "Now I Lay Me Down to Sleep." Hurkos's autobiographical works include *Psychic: The Story of Peter Hurkos, The Psychic World of Peter Hurkos*, and *Peter Hurkos: I Have Many Lives*.

OBITUARIES AND OTHER SOURCES:

BOOKS

Christopher, Milbourne, *Mediums, Mystics, and the Occult*, Crowell, 1975.
Encyclopedia of Occultism and Parapsychology, 2nd edition, Gale, 1984-85.
Puharich, Andrija, *Beyond Telepathy*, Doubleday, 1962.
Who's Who in the West, 20th edition, Marquis, 1985.

PERIODICALS

Los Angeles Times, June 2, 1988.
New York Times, June 3, 1988.
Times (London), June 3, 1988.

*   *   *

HURT, Ray Douglas   1946-

PERSONAL: Born July 11, 1946, in Hays, Kan.; son of Ray Kent (a laborer) and Margaret Jane (a secretary; maiden name, Miller) Hurt; married Mary Ellen Cox (a housewife), August 20, 1980; children: Adlai Andrew, John Austin. *Education:* Fort Hays Kansas State College (now Fort Hays State University), B.A., 1969, M.A., 1971; Kansas State University, Ph.D., 1975.

ADDRESSES: Home—505 Maplewood, Columbia, Mo. 65203. *Office*—State Historical Society of Missouri, 1020 Lowry, Columbia, Mo. 65201.

CAREER: University of Mid-America, Lincoln, Neb., researcher in Great Plains history, 1975-76; Smithsonian Institution, Washington, D.C., fellow in history of science and technology, 1976-77; Texas Tech University, Lubbock, visiting assistant professor of American history, 1977-78; Ohio Historical Society, Columbus, curator of agricultural history, 1978-86; State Historical Society of Missouri, Columbia, associate director, 1986—. Associate editor of *Timeline*; adjunct professor of history at Ohio State University.

MEMBER: Organization of American Historians, Agricultural History Society, Western History Association.

WRITINGS:

The Dust Bowl: An Agricultural and Social History, Nelson-Hall, 1981.

American Farm Tools: From Hand Power to Steam Power, Sunflower University Press, 1982.

Indian Agriculture in America: Prehistory to the Present, University Press of Kansas, 1988.

The Department of Agriculture, Chelsea House, 1988.

(Editor) *Thomas Hart Benton,* State Historical Society of Missouri, in press.

Contributor to history journals, including *American Heritage.*

WORK IN PROGRESS: American Agriculture: A Short History, for University Press of Kansas; *Rural Life in Little Dixie, 1820-1860.*

SIDELIGHTS: Ray Douglas Hurt told *CA:* "As a boy I hauled hay, plowed, and seeded crops for farmers near my home town. I thoroughly enjoyed the work. During my undergraduate years I became fascinated with the populist movement that swept the Great Plains during the late nineteenth century. The study of agricultural history seemed to be an excellent way to combine two things that I loved—farming and history.

"I have a compulsive need to know how things have come to be as they are. The study of agricultural history helps me satisfy that need. For me, agricultural history is the story of innovation, adaptation, and perseverance combined with science, technology, economics, politics, and the art of daily living. It is an incredibly diverse and exciting field of study."

*   *   *

HUTT, W(illiam) H(arold)   1899-1988

OBITUARY NOTICE—See index for *CA* sketch: Born August 3, 1899, in London, England; died of complications from a stroke, June 19, 1988, in Irving, Tex. Economist, educator, and author. Hutt, an economist who championed free enterprise and challenged the South African government's policy of racial separation known as apartheid, taught from 1926 to 1965 at the University of Cape Town. In 1965 he came to the United States, where he continued to teach at a number of American universities until his 1981 retirement from the University of Dallas as professor emeritus. Hutt was the author of twelve books and a contributor of numerous articles to economic journals. His 1964 publication, *The Economics of the Colour Bar,* is considered a classic in the field of economics and race relations. Other titles include *The Theory of Collective Bargaining, The Theory of Idle Resources, Keynesianism: Retrospect and Prospect,* and *The Keynesian Episode.*

OBITUARIES AND OTHER SOURCES:

BOOKS

Who's Who, 140th edition, St. Martin's, 1988.

PERIODICALS

Chicago Tribune, June 22, 1988.
New York Times, June 21, 1988.
Times (London), June 25, 1988.

*   *   *

HYATT, Betty H(ale)   1927-
(Jade Hale)

PERSONAL: Born January 4, 1927, in Texas; daughter of Floyd P. (a stone mason) and Velma Lucinda (a housewife) Hale; married Richard Hyatt, November 5, 1949 (divorced December, 1973); married Theodore F. Pfeffer (a geologist), December 15, 1985; children: (first marriage) David, Judith, James, Priscilla. *Education:* Attended University of New Mexico.

ADDRESSES: Home—5327 Montgomery N.E., No. 41, Albuquerque, N.M. 87109. *Agent*—Harvey Klinger, Inc., 301 West 53rd St., New York, N.Y. 10019.

CAREER: Free-lance writer.

MEMBER: National League of American Pen Women, Southwest Romance Writers of America, Southwest Writers Workshop.

WRITINGS:

ROMANCE NOVELS

Ivy Halls, Arcadia House, 1967.
The Vesper Bells, Arcadia House, 1967.
Heiress of Wainscote, Dell, 1972.
Friory's Dor, Dell, 1973.
Chantilly, Dell, 1973.
Scarlet Hills, Dell, 1973.
The Castle of Kudara, Dell, 1974.
The Mistress of Priory Manor, Dell, 1974.
The Golden Falcon, Dell, 1975.
Portrait of Errin, Dell, 1976.
The Brigand's Bride, Dell, 1976.
The Gallant Spy, Dell, 1976.
Pandora's Box, Dell, 1977.
Love's Untold Secrets, Dell, 1978.
The Chevalier's Lady, Dell, 1979.
The Jade Pagoda, Doubleday, 1980.
Anna's Story, Playboy Paperbacks, 1980.
Linnet's Story, Playboy Paperbacks, 1980.
Fandora's Story, Playboy Paperbacks, 1981.
Shalimar Pavilion, Doubleday, 1982.
The Sapphire Lotus, Doubleday, 1983.

Author of "The House of Lancien" series for Playboy Paperbacks.

WORK IN PROGRESS: Green Shadows, a Victorian romantic suspense novel; *Shadows on the Sand,* a Victorian suspense novel.

SIDELIGHTS: Betty H. Hyatt, who sometimes uses the pseudonym Jade Hale, told *CA* that she spent twelve years traveling around the world in search of settings for her books. She has lived in India, Nepal, Kashmir, China, Taiwan, Hong Kong, Japan, and all of Europe. In addition to her previous study in Japanese and Mandarin Chinese, Hyatt intends to further these studies.

*   *   *

HYATT, Daniel
See JAMES, Daniel (Lewis)

*   *   *

HYMAN, B(arbara) D(avis)   1947-

PERSONAL: Born May 1, 1947, in California; daughter of William Grant Sherry (an artist) and Ruth Elizabeth Davis (an actress); married Jeremy A. Hyman (a film executive and writer),

January 4, 1964; children: J. Ashley, Justin Roger (sons). *Education:* Studied at private schools and under tutors. *Politics:* Conservative. *Religion:* Pentacostal Christian.

ADDRESSES: Home and office—P.O. Box F-3403, Freeport, Grand Bahama, Bahamas.

CAREER: Homemaker in New York, Connecticut, and Pennsylvania, 1964-83; writer and illustrator. Volunteer worker for civic and community organizations.

MEMBER: Freeport Garden Club.

WRITINGS:

My Mother's Keeper, Morrow, 1985.
(With husband, Jeremy Hyman) *Narrow Is the Way,* Morrow, 1987.

WORK IN PROGRESS: Writing and illustrating *Guardian's Secret: Randolph Goes Fishing,* the first volume of the Guardian series (books for eight- to twelve-year-olds about a group of forest creatures learning to be happier through knowing and loving Jesus), with Jeremy Hyman.

SIDELIGHTS: In *My Mother's Keeper* B. D. Hyman, the only natural child of actress Bette Davis, describes what life was like growing up with the legendary film star. Portraying the performer as an abusive, domineering mother with a serious drinking problem, Hyman recounts that even after she left home Davis's invasive behavior continued: the actress tried repeatedly to ruin her daughter's marriage and terrorized her grandsons. "Regard this, Mother, as my cry in the wilderness, to prepare the way and make straight your path," wrote born-again Christian Hyman in her book, explaining the motivation behind the memoir. "Hyman claims that the only way to reach her mother, and to establish a normal relationship," elaborated Faiga Levine in the *Washington Post Book World,* "is by the one method her mother understands and appreciates—fighting back."

Proving a bestseller, *My Mother's Keeper* drew a mix of critical response. Reviewing the book for Toronto's *Globe and Mail,* Joy Fielding objected to Hyman's scrupulous recall of "every wrong move her mother ever made, every ill-chosen word, every ill-conceived utterance." The reviewer remarked: "No parent is everything the child would have him or her be. . . . Most of the population would sound vaguely crazed when held up to such intense, unforgiving scrutiny." *Times Literary Supplement* critic Patrice Chaplin, too, felt that—for Hollywood—Davis's imperfect parenting efforts were at least well-intentioned; "in such a climate the minor domestic games complained of by Hyman, seem unimportant and uninteresting," decided the reviewer. And in a critique for the *New York Times Book Review* Janice Eidus questioned the author's professed purpose in writing the volume, contending that "a book exposing [Davis] to the public as pathetic is not going to help her very much." Still, the critic was moved by Hyman's story and wished mother and daughter resolution.

Writing that "hurt cries out from almost every page," Levine, likewise, found *My Mother's Keeper* compelling. "Though most of the conversations are, no doubt, reconstructed and filtered through many layers of memory," related the critic, "many do have the shock and immediacy of truth." Chaplin offered a similar assessment; while wishing that Hyman had included her mother's working life in the memoir, the reviewer nonetheless determined: "Her anecdotes about Davis are entertaining, and the dialogue . . . seems authentic. It includes sharp and witty observations. . . . The ambivalence that the daughter feels toward her legendary and demanding mother is well and often touchingly expressed." And maintaining that "there is something moving in the spectacle of their clashes, near misses, and rare moments of genuine rapport," Daphne Merkin contemplated the attraction of the familial tell-all in an article for *Film Comment.* "It is every wounded child's (and which of us has not been wounded) dream come true: spilling the beans on Daddy and Mommy dearest," she reflected. "How [one] interpret[s] the grievances marshalled in *My Mother's Keeper*—as evidence against the accused parent or as an indictment of the daughter who accumulated them—depends ultimately on . . . one's feelings, on the directions of one's sympathies. . . . Naively well-meant or crassly gossip-mongering . . . I suspect the truth is somewhere in between."

In collaboration with husband Jeremy Hyman, B. D. Hyman wrote *Narrow Is the Way*—a sequel to *My Mother's Keeper* that recounts the couple's rediscovery of and commitment to Jesus Christ during the preparation of the Hollywood memoir. Revealing B. D.'s search for the right church, book tour experiences, and altered vision as a born-again Christian, the volume was judged "meandering, prosy and all-too-personal" by Hanna Rubin in the *New York Times Book Review.*

B. D. Hyman told *CA:* "My first book was a self-explanatory portrait of my mother and myself, motivated by the need to resolve an impossible relationship with her and to stop the damage she was doing to my children. Subsequently, my husband and I found a relationship with Jesus Christ and became born again. Since we are all searching for solutions to the troubles life hands us, my husband and I wanted to share the miraculous answer God had for us in *Narrow Is the Way.* We believe that this book offers hope and joy to all who are willing to hear. We have already received mail from people who were profoundly touched by what Jesus did and continues to do in our lives; as a result, their own lives have been changed. This is our desire for *Narrow Is the Way.* If readers relate to my experiences in either book—even if their agonies are of a different kind—the Lord's love applies to all.

"I am continuing to write with my husband, Jeremy, in the Christian field; the children's books are only one of the projects we hope to accomplish. I am also illustrating the Guardian series—which is a joy—as I've enjoyed painting all my life."

AVOCATIONAL INTERESTS: Riding horses, skin diving, painting.

BIOGRAPHICAL/CRITICAL SOURCES:

BOOKS

Hyman, B. D., *My Mother's Keeper,* Morrow, 1985.
Hyman, B. D. and Jeremy Hyman, *Narrow Is the Way,* Morrow, 1987.

PERIODICALS

Detroit Free Press, May 4, 1986.
Film Comment, December, 1985.
Globe and Mail (Toronto), July 13, 1985.
New York Times Book Review, June 9, 1985, April 26, 1987.
Time, August 19, 1985.
Times Literary Supplement, November 22, 1985.
Washington Post Book World, June 2, 1985.

*   *   *

HYMAN, Jeremy (A.)

PERSONAL: Married Barbara Davis Sherry (a homemaker,

writer, and illustrator), January 4, 1964; children: J. Ashley, Justin Roger (sons). *Religion:* Pentacostal Christian.

ADDRESSES: Home—P.O. Box F-3403, Freeport, Grand Bahama, Bahamas.

CAREER: Film executive and writer.

WRITINGS:

(With wife, B. D. Hyman) *Narrow Is the Way*, Morrow, 1987.

WORK IN PROGRESS: Guardian's Secret: Randolph Goes Fishing, the first volume of the Guardian series (books for eight- to twelve-year-olds about a group of forest creatures learning to be happier through knowing and living for Jesus), with B. D. Hyman.

SIDELIGHTS: British film executive Jeremy Hyman married Barbara Davis Sherry, the only natural child of actress Bette Davis, in 1964. After his wife produced the 1985 best-selling *My Mother's Keeper,* an unflattering account of life growing up with the legendary Hollywood star, the Hymans collaborated on *Narrow Is the Way.* The autobiographical sequel describes the couple's new relationship with Jesus Christ as Pentacostal born-again Christians.

See also *HYMAN, B(arbara) D(avis).*

BIOGRAPHICAL/CRITICAL SOURCES:

BOOKS

Hyman, B. D. and Jeremy Hyman, *Narrow Is the Way,* Morrow, 1987.

PERIODICALS

New York Times Book Review, April 26, 1987.*

I

IACOCCA, Lee
See IACOCCA, Lido Anthony

* * *

IACOCCA, Lido Anthony 1924-
(Lee Iacocca)

PERSONAL: Best known as Lee Iacocca; born October 15, 1924, in Allentown, Pa.; son of Nicola (in business) and Antoinette (Perrotto) Iacocca; married Mary McLeary (a receptionist), September 29, 1956 (died May 15, 1983); second marriage ended in divorce; children: (first marriage) Kathryn Lisa Hentz, Lia Antoinette Nagy. *Education:* Lehigh University, B.S., 1945; Princeton University, M.E., 1946.

ADDRESSES: Office—Chrysler Corporation, 12000 Chrysler Dr., Highland Park, Mich. 48288.

CAREER: Ford Motor Co., Dearborn, Mich., engineer in Dearborn and in Edgewater, N.J., 1946, member of sales and marketing staff of Eastern district, headquartered in Chester, Pa., 1947-56, district sales manager in Washington, D.C., 1956, returned to Dearborn as truck marketing manager of Ford division, 1956-57, car marketing manager, 1957-60, vehicle marketing manager, 1960, vice-president of company and general manager of Ford division, 1960-65, vice-president of car and truck group, 1965-67, headed Ford North American automotive operations as executive vice-president, 1967-68, and as president, 1969-70, president of company, 1970-78; Chrysler Corp., Highland Park, Mich., president and chief operating officer, 1978-79, chairman of board and chief executive officer, 1979—, chairman of corporate executive committee. Former chairman of Statue of Liberty-Ellis Island Centennial Commission and Statue of Liberty-Ellis Island Foundation; co-chairman of Governor of Michigan's Commission on Jobs and Economic Development. Chairman of Iacocca Foundation, and committee for corporate support of Joslin Diabetes Foundation; Lehigh University, honorary trustee, chairman of Asa Packer Society, and leader of fundraising campaign; honorary chairman of centennial campaign of Catholic University of America; member of board of Detroit Symphony Orchestra.

MEMBER: National Academy of Engineering, The Conference Board, Society of Automotive Engineers, Detroit Press Club Foundation, Economic Club of Detroit, Founders Society of Detroit Institute of Arts, New Detroit, Inc.

AWARDS, HONORS: Ralph Coats Roe Medal from American Society of Mechanical Engineers, 1984; honorary doctorates from numerous colleges and universities, including Alma College, Babson Institute, Duke University, George Washington University, Hillsdale College, LaSalle University, Lawrence Institute of Technology, Lehigh University, Massachusetts Institute of Technology, Muhlenberg College, University of Michigan, and University of Southern California.

WRITINGS:

UNDER NAME LEE IACOCCA

(With William Novak) *Iacocca: An Autobiography* (excerpts first published in *Newsweek,* October 8, 1984), Bantam, 1984, adaptation for cassette recording, read by Iacocca, Bantam Audio Cassette, c. 1986.
(With Sonny Kleinfield) *Talking Straight* (Book-of-the-Month Club selection; excerpts first published in *People,* May 30, 1988), Bantam, 1988.

Contributor of articles to Los Angeles Times Syndicate and to periodicals, including *Fortune, Newsweek, Saturday Evening Post,* and *U.S. News and World Report.*

SIDELIGHTS: When Lee Iacocca became president of Chrysler Corporation in 1978, the company—long the weakest of Detroit's three major automakers—was on the verge of bankruptcy. A few years later Chrysler posted record profits and, according to Martin Gottlieb of the *New York Times,* Iacocca was being hailed as America's "first corporate folk hero" for his role in reversing the firm's fortunes. Sought out by the publishers of Bantam Books, he worked on his memoirs with professional writer William Novak. The resulting book, *Iacocca: An Autobiography,* sold more than two million copies within a year of publication and set a sales record for general interest nonfiction in hardcover. The author's widespread popularity, Gottlieb averred, rests on his image as "the streetsmart scrapper who takes his lumps but triumphs over an aloof establishment."

Iacocca suggests in his autobiography that he learned how to be resilient during his youth. Born in 1924 of Italian immigrants, he regularly endured taunts about his ethnic background while growing up in Allentown, Pennsylvania; his father, a highly successful entrepreneur, lost all his money at the onset of the Great Depression of the 1930s and then supported the family by running a restaurant. Iacocca trained as an engineer at Lehigh and Princeton universities, and in 1945 he got his first job at Ford Motor Company in that field. Soon disappointed with the nature of his work, he joined the sales and marketing staff of Ford's Eastern district, headquartered in suburban Philadelphia. To improve sluggish car sales in 1956, Iacocca developed an easy-payment plan that rocketed sales in the Philadelphia division from last to first place in the country. His success drew the notice of senior Ford executives, and he was brought to company headquarters the same year as a national marketing manager.

Iacocca quickly rose through the executive ranks, and in the mid-1960s, as a corporate vice-president, he played a major role in developing one of Ford's most successful automobiles, the Mustang. This model combined the practicality of a four-seat family car with the styling of a sports car, and it was highly popular with the emerging market of young adult consumers. Iacocca became known as a protege of company chairman Henry Ford II, who in 1970 raised him to second-in-command as company president.

Surprisingly, Iacocca soon entered the most difficult period of his career. As depicted in the author's autobiography, Henry Ford II was a capricious, authoritarian boss who found it difficult to accept the advice of his executives and often felt threatened by their successes. Iacocca contends that Ford soon decided to fire his president as he had several predecessors, and that in the mid-1970s Ford ordered a massive, secret investigation of Iacocca's professional and private life. Unable to find any scandal, Ford finally fired Iacocca in 1978 because, as the author quotes him, "sometimes you just don't like somebody."

Exiled to a shabby warehouse office to conclude his business affairs, Iacocca filled with rage and despair. "It was enough to make me want to kill," he recalls—"I wasn't quite sure who, Henry Ford or myself. . . . I really felt I was coming apart at the seams." He soon accepted an offer to take charge of financially troubled Chrysler, although he later wrote that the firm's condition was far worse than he realized. Plagued by mismanagement, massive debts, and an uncompetitive product, Chrysler needed a broad and complex reorganization in order to become solvent again. Iacocca convinced Chrysler's creditors to voluntarily accept delayed payment of its debts. Rebuilding the company required an infusion of additional money, and since banks considered Chrysler a bad risk Iacocca lobbied the U. S. Congress to guarantee repayment of the loans with public funds. Opponents branded the move a violation of America's free-enterprise system, contending that a company that had exercised bad judgment should be allowed to fail. Nevertheless Congress approved the guarantees, spurred by concern that the failure of Chrysler would create widespread unemployment.

Many of Iacocca's actions anticipated the retrenchment measures that became common in American business in the 1980s. He fired dozens of senior executives, closed factories considered outdated or inefficient, and laid off thousands of assembly-line workers, many permanently. He convinced labor unions to accept substantial pay cuts in order to save the company. To build a new public image for Chrysler, he broke with usual auto-industry practice and became a high-profile spokesman for the company, appearing regularly in television commercials to promote what he called "The New Chrysler Corpo-

ration." (As Iacocca tells readers of his autobiography, he owes his fame to the commercials as much as to his accomplishments in business.)

In the 1980s Chrysler rebounded dramatically. The company increased its share of the car market, repaid its loans well ahead of schedule, and saw the price of its stock soar. Many Americans agreed with William Serrin of the *New York Times* that Iacocca had accomplished "one of the most brilliant turnarounds in American business history." At the request of President Ronald Reagan he led efforts to restore the Statue of Liberty and the historic immigration facilities at Ellis Island. And as the Democratic party sought to improve its political fortunes, speculation persisted that Iacocca might be convinced to seek the party's nomination for president. No longer simply an important businessman, Iacocca was becoming a prominent figure in American life.

In his autobiography Iacocca briefly recounts his childhood, describes at length his years at Ford and Chrysler, and then sketches his program for improving the American economy. The book is based on extensive conversations that he had with co-author Novak, and both men strove to give the resulting manuscript an entertaining, spontaneous style. Consequently, as Patrick Boyle said in the *Los Angeles Times Book Review,* "much of the book reads the way Iacocca talks to his audiences—a combination of dramatic monologue and half-time pep talk."

Many reviewers agreed with Mark Dowie of the *Times Literary Supplement* that "the Ford chapters are really the heart" of the book because of the vivid portrayal of Henry Ford II. As Bernard A. Weisberger observed in *Washington Post Book World,* "Iacocca plainly has a wonderful time in these pages depicting his former boss as a heavy-drinking, jet-setting playboy who doesn't know his axle from a hole in the hood." The author calls Henry Ford "a real bastard" who "was a sucker for appearances" and "behave[d] like a spoiled brat," and he supports these epithets with numerous personal anecdotes. Ford, Iacocca recalls, was a man who openly berated his executives for racial insensitivity and then privately expressed disgust and fear when blacks drove by his suburban mansion. But Iacocca's recollections depict more than the clash of two powerful people, as economist John Kenneth Galbraith stressed in *New York Review of Books:* when the author discusses working life at Ford and Chrysler, he provides a valuable insider's view of the American corporation.

Reviewers noted that Iacocca was reluctant to describe his personal life, although "as autobiographies by celebrities go," Robert Lekachman noted in *Nation,* "this is an unusually candid book." "The value of the book is not in learning something new about Lee Iacocca," averred Patrick Boyle in the *Los Angeles Times Book Review,* "but in having some of Iacocca's incredible fire and enthusiasm perhaps rub off on the people who will read it. His career making and selling cars has helped him become a salesman of ideas."

Iacocca's observations, on subjects that range from management style to international trade policies, are sprinkled throughout his narrative. He calls decisiveness the most important quality in a manager and stresses that "despite what the textbooks say, most important decisions in corporate life are made by individuals, not by committees," because only an individual can make a decision promptly. "My policy has always been to be democratic all the way to the point of decision," he states. "Then I become the ruthless commander." He also recalls, however, that many promising executives have failed to win promotions because in their egotism they never learned to work harmoniously with others.

In the closing chapters of the book Iacocca turns from autobiography to discuss the broader topic of revitalizing America's economy. He criticizes both labor and management, upbraiding unions for unrealistic contract demands and disparaging those businessmen who prefer to make money through financial manipulation rather than by fostering productive companies. He acknowledges that Japan has boosted its economy through many unfair trade practices, but he argues that the key to Japanese success is its national industrial policy, in which broad government planning assists economic growth. America needs such planning as well, Iacocca says, in order to save its basic industries—the country can no longer expect "to be great by accident." "Some people say that an industrial policy is nothing more than lemon socialism," he admits, but he retorts that "if it is, I'll take a crateful—because unless we act fast, our industrial heartland is going to turn into an industrial wasteland." Noting the author's "crisp, straight-talking, hard-headed" persona, Weisberger spoke for many reviewers when he said that *Iacocca* was "strong, illuminating, and a rousing read."

In 1988 Iacocca produced *Talking Straight*, a second book about his life and views that he wrote with Sonny Kleinfield of the *New York Times*. "Readers will get another mouthful," promised *People* magazine, "some cutting, some heartfelt, much of it plainly sensible." Iacocca expands briefly on his personal life, including a fond appreciation of his daughters and his late wife, Mary. He says he was tempted to run for the presidency but decided that for a "hands-on" manager such as himself the burden of office would be too great. And in an admission that made headlines, he writes that in 1987 some prominent businessmen encouraged him to make a take-over bid for General Motors, an auto company vastly larger than Chrysler that was increasingly plagued by financial difficulties during the 1980s.

Most of *Talking Straight*, however, consists of Iacocca's observations and opinions about politics and business, in a style reminiscent of his first book. While working on the Statue of Liberty project, for instance, Iacocca met at length with President Reagan and his advisers. Reagan impressed the author as a man of great personal warmth, considerate of his guests, phoning to express sympathy when Iacocca's wife died. But "nice as he was," Iacocca observes, Reagan "was totally incapable of focusing in on any issue. Anytime you talked to him about something, he would drift off into an anecdote." Iacocca does not share the widespread admiration for Reagan's management style, which basically involved a willingness to delegate responsibility. Executives usually share their power, Iacocca suggests, but "Reagan delegated to a bunch of stooges and then went off and rode horses."

Noting the enthusiastic letters he received about the management tips in his first book, Iacocca codifies eight common-sense "commandments of management." He also tells managers to meet privately with personnel well below them in rank in order to remain aware of the potential talent in their organizations. Turning to politics, he names an ideal presidential cabinet—for someone else—and advocates a mandatory year of public service for the nation's young people. "It's the [national] spirit I'm worried about," he explains, advising America's youth that "you can't have the material things and the quality of life you'd like without investing a little." In *Talking*

Straight, wrote Janice Castro in *Time*, Iacocca "dispenses the folk wisdom his fans were asking for."

BIOGRAPHICAL/CRITICAL SOURCES:

BOOKS

Abodaher, David J., *Iacocca*, Macmillan, 1982.
Gordon, Maynard M., *The Iacocca Management Technique: A Profile of the Chrysler Chairman's Unique Key to Business Success*, Dodd, 1985.
Iacocca, Lee, and William Novak, *Iacocca: An Autobiography*, Bantam, 1984.
Iacocca, Lee, and Sonny Kleinfield, *Talking Straight*, Bantam, 1988.
Lacey, Robert, *Ford: The Men and the Machine*, Little, Brown, 1986.
Moritz, Michael, and Barrett Seaman, *Going for Broke: Lee Iacocca's Battle to Save Chrysler*, Anchor, 1984.
Wyden, Peter, *The Unknown Iacocca*, Morrow, 1987.

PERIODICALS

American Spectator, May, 1985.
Chicago Tribune, May 5, 1985.
Chicago Tribune Book World, November 11, 1984.
Commentary, May, 1985.
Detroit Free Press, October 1, 1984, June 1, 1988, June 2, 1988, June 3, 1988, June 4, 1988, June 5, 1988.
Detroit News, October 2, 1984.
Globe and Mail (Toronto), November 24, 1984.
Los Angeles Times, November 18, 1984.
Nation, November 17, 1984.
New Republic, May 13, 1985.
Newsweek, October 8, 1984, June 13, 1988.
New York Review of Books, April 10, 1986.
New York Times, May 16, 1983, December 23, 1984, August 26, 1985, October 31, 1985, February 13, 1986, July 3, 1986.
New York Times Book Review, November 11, 1984, September 13, 1987, July 17, 1988.
Observer (London), February 10, 1985.
People, May 5, 1986, May 30, 1988.
Publishers Weekly, September 28, 1984, October 19, 1984.
Time, June 13, 1988.
Times Literary Supplement, March 29, 1985.
Washington Post, March 14, 1985, December 13, 1987.
Washington Post Book World, October 28, 1984.

(Sketch verified by John E. Guiniven, director of corporate public relations at Chrysler Corporation.)

—*Sketch by Thomas Kozikowski*

*   *   *

IRISH, Jerry

PERSONAL: Education—Cornell University, B.A., 1958; Southern Methodist University, B.D., 1964; Yale University, Ph.D., 1967.

ADDRESSES: Office—201 Sumner Hall, Pomona College, Claremont, Calif. 91711.

CAREER: Affiliated with Wichita State University, Wichita, Kan.; Pomona College, Claremont, Calif., professor of religion and vice-president and dean of college, 1986—.

WRITINGS:

A Boy Thirteen, Westminster, 1975.

The Religious Thought of H. Richard Niebuhr, John Knox Press, 1983.

*   *   *

ISMAEL, Tareq Y.

PERSONAL: Education—Baghdad University, B.A. (with first class honors), 1958; Indiana University—Bloomington, M.A., 1961; George Washington University, Ph.D., 1967.

ADDRESSES: Office—Department of Political Science, University of Calgary, 2920 24th Ave. N.W., Calgary, Alberta, Canada T2N 1N4.

CAREER: University of Calgary, Calgary, Alberta, professor of political science, 1967—.

MEMBER: International Association of Middle Eastern Studies (president, 1980—).

WRITINGS:

Governments and Politics of the Contemporary Middle East, Dorsey, 1970.
The UAR in Africa: Egypt's Policy Under Nasser, Northwestern University Press, 1971.
The Middle East in World Politics: A Study in Contemporary International Relations, Syracuse University Press, 1974.
The Arab Left, Syracuse University Press, 1976.
(Editor with Peyton B. Lyon) *Canada and the Third World*, Macmillan, 1976.
Iraq and Iran: Roots of Conflict, Syracuse University Press, 1982.
Canadian-Arab Relations: Policy and Perspectives, Jerusalem International Publishing House, 1984, 2nd edition, 1984.
(With Jacqueline S. Ismael) *Government and Politics in Islam*, St. Martin's, 1985.
Canada and the Arab World, University of Alberta Press, 1985.
The International Relations of the Contemporary Middle East: A Study in World Politics, Syracuse University Press, 1986.
(With Jacqueline S. Ismael) *PDR Yemen: The Politics of Socialist Transformation*, Frances Pinter, 1986.

CONTRIBUTOR

N. Aryri, editor, *The Palestinian Resistance to Israeli Occupation*, Medina University Press, 1970.
H. Desfosos and J. Levesque, editors, *Socialism in the Third World*, Praeger, 1975.
R. El-Droubie, editor, *Arabic and Islamic Themes*, Islamic Cultural Centre, 1977.
B. Szajkowski, editor, *Marxist Governments: A World Survey*, Macmillan, 1981.
S. Taher-Khali and N. Ayobi, editors, *The Gulf War*, Foreign Policy Institute [Philadelphia, Pa.], 1983.
M. Mzali, editor, *Les Provinces Arabes*, Centre d'Etudes et de Recherches sur les Provinces Arabes a l'Epoque Ottomane, 1984.
Peter St. John, editor, *MacKenzie King to Philosopher King: Canadian Foreign Policy in the Modern Age*, University of Manitoba, 1985.

William F. Dowdy and Russell B. Trood, editors, *The Indian Ocean: Perspectives on a Strategic Arena*, Duke University Press, 1985.

Also contributor to *The Arab World and Black Africa* and *The Diversification of Communism*. Contributor of more than twenty articles to scholarly journals.

OTHER

Guest editor of *Middle East Forum*, 1971-73.

BIOGRAPHICAL/CRITICAL SOURCES:

PERIODICALS

Annals of the American Academy of Political and Social Science, May, 1972.

*   *   *

ITULE, Bruce D.   1947-

PERSONAL: Surname is pronounced "It-*too*-lee"; born November 2, 1947, in Tucson, Ariz.; son of Joseph J. (in business) and Tamaan (in sales) Itule; married Priscilla Lee, May 17, 1969; children: Dena Lee, Justin M. *Education:* University of Arizona, B.A., 1969; University of Colorado, M.A., 1970.

ADDRESSES: Home—2006 East Pebble Beach, Tempe, Ariz. 85282. *Office*—Office of Student Publications, Arizona State University, Tempe, Ariz. 85287-1502.

CAREER: Arizona Daily Star, Tucson, feature writer and photographer, 1967-69; *Denver Post*, Denver, Colo., copy editor, 1969-70; *Phoenix Gazette*, Phoenix, Ariz., copy editor, 1970-74; New Mexico State University, Las Cruces, assistant professor of journalism, 1974-75; Arizona State University, Tempe, assistant professor, 1975-80, associate professor of journalism, 1980; *Chicago Tribune*, Chicago, Ill., night city editor, 1980-85; Arizona State University, director of student publications, 1985—.

MEMBER: Society of Professional Journalists, Sigma Delta Chi (member of board of directors, 1985—).

WRITINGS:

Joseph Clum's Tombstone Epitaph, Tombstone Epitaph, 1969.
(With Douglas Anderson) *Contemporary News Reporting*, Random House, 1984.
(With Anderson) *News Writing and Reporting for Today's Media*, Random House, 1987.
(With Anderson) *Writing the News*, Random House, 1988.

Contributor of articles and photographs to periodicals.

WORK IN PROGRESS: Visual Editing for Newspapers, with Howard I. Finberg, publication by Wadsworth expected in 1990.

J

JACKSON, MacDonald P. 1938-

PERSONAL: Born October 13, 1938, in Auckland, New Zealand; son of Donald Leslie (a teacher) and Margaret (a housewife; maiden name, Pairman) Jackson; married Nicole Philippa Lovett (a medical research assistant), September 2, 1964; children: Cameron, Anna, Juliet. Education: University of Auckland, B.A., 1959, M.A., 1960; Merton College, Oxford, B.Litt., 1963.

ADDRESSES: Home—21 Te Kowhai Pl., Rumera, Auckland 5, New Zealand. Office—Department of English, University of Auckland, Private Bag, Auckland, New Zealand.

CAREER: University of Auckland, Auckland, New Zealand, junior lecturer, 1960-61, lecturer, 1964-68, senior lecturer, 1969-77, associate professor of English, 1978—.

WRITINGS:

(Editor) Poetry Australia: New Zealand Issue, South Head Press, 1966.
Studies in Attribution: Middleton and Shakespeare, University of Salzburg, 1979.
(Editor) "The Revenger's Tragedy," Attributed to Thomas Middleton: A Facsimile of the 1607/8 Quarto, Associated University Presses, 1983.
(Editor with Vincent O'Sullivan) The Oxford Book of New Zealand Writing Since 1945, Oxford University Press, 1983.
(Editor with Michael Neill) The Selected Plays of John Marston, Cambridge University Press, 1986.

CONTRIBUTOR

Ian Wards, editor, Thirteen Facets, New Zealand Government Printer, 1978.
Gary Taylor and Michael B. Warren, editors, The Division of the Kingdoms: The Two Texts of "King Lear," Oxford University Press, 1983.
Stanley Wells, editor, The Cambridge Companion to Shakespeare Studies, Cambridge University Press, 1986.
Wells and Taylor, editors, William Shakespeare, The Complete Works, Oxford University Press, 1986.

Contributor of more than seventy articles and reviews to academic journals.

WORK IN PROGRESS: Editing William Shakespeare's Pericles, The Complete Works of Thomas Middleton, and The Selected Poems of A.R.D. Fairburn, all for Oxford University Press; a chapter on New Zealand poetry, to be included in The Oxford History of New Zealand Literature, for Oxford University Press.

* * *

JACKSON, Michael P. 1947-

PERSONAL: Born January 7, 1947, in Oldham, England; son of Herbert (a clerk) and Norma (a clerk; maiden name, Peart) Jackson; married wife, Sylvia (a teacher), August 15, 1970; children: Karen, Callum. Education: University of Hull, B.A., 1968, M.A., 1970.

ADDRESSES: Home—Thordewe, Perth Rd., Dunblane, Scotland. Office—Department of Sociology, University of Stirling, Stirling, Scotland.

CAREER: University of Stirling, Stirling, Scotland, lecturer, 1970-79, senior lecturer in sociology, 1979—. Chairman of Social Security Appeal Tribunal.

WRITINGS:

Labour Relations on the Docks, Lexington Books, 1973.
The Price of Coal, Verry, 1974.
Industrial Relations, Croom Helm, 1977, 3rd edition, 1985.
(With B. M. Valencia) Financial Aid Through Social Work, Routledge & Kegan Paul, 1979.
(With Victor J. B. Hanby) Work Creation: International Experiences, Saxon House, 1979.
Trade Unions, Longman, 1982.
(With Victor J. B. Hanby) British Work Creation Programs, Gower Publishing, 1982.
Youth Unemployment, Croom Helm, 1985.
Strikes in the U.S.A., Australia, and the United Kingdom, Wheatsheaf Books, 1987.

Contributor to professional journals.

* * *

JACKSON, Richard A(rlen) 1937-

PERSONAL: Born May 9, 1937, in Minneapolis, Minn.; son

of Albert R. (a farmer) and Louise (Craig) Jackson; married Virginia Smith (a teacher), March 7, 1986. *Education:* Attended Free University of Berlin, 1958-59; University of Minnesota, B.A., 1960, M.A., 1963, Ph.D., 1967.

ADDRESSES: Office—Department of History, University of Houston, Houston, Tex. 77004.

CAREER: University of Houston, Houston, Tex., instructor, 1965-67, assistant professor, 1967-71, associate professor of history, 1971—. Visiting professor at University of Strasbourg, 1979-83.

MEMBER: Majestas.

AWARDS, HONORS: Grants from American Philosophical Society, 1969-74, and National Endowment for the Humanities, 1985; fellow of American Council of Learned Societies, 1970-71; honorary visiting fellow at Institute for Research in the Humanities, University of Wisconsin—Madison, 1970-71; honorary doctorate in letters and human sciences from University of Reims, 1975.

WRITINGS:

Vive le Roi! A History of the French Coronation From Charles V to Charles X, University of North Carolina Press, 1984.

Author of computer software manuals. Contributor to history and political science journals in France, Germany, Belgium, and the United States.

WORK IN PROGRESS: Critical editions of medieval French coronation texts.

SIDELIGHTS: Some of Richard A. Jackson's works—including his computer software—have been written and published in French and German.

BIOGRAPHICAL/CRITICAL SOURCES:

PERIODICALS

Times Literary Supplement, January 25, 1985.

*   *   *

JACOBS, Renee   1962-

PERSONAL: Born January 1, 1962, in Philadelphia, Pa.; daughter of Michael (a sales representative) and Sondra (a homemaker; maiden name, Moss) Jacobs. *Education:* Pennsylvania State University, B.A., 1983.

ADDRESSES: Home and office—2027 Wisteria Lane, Lafayette Hill, Pa. 19444.

CAREER: Free-lance photographer, 1983—. Photography instructor at Pennsylvania State University, 1984.

AWARDS, HONORS: Robert F. Kennedy Journalism Award from Robert F. Kennedy Memorial, 1982, for "Cynthia's Case"; natural resources fellow at Northwestern School of Law, Lewis and Clark College, 1987.

WRITINGS:

(Contributor) Mark Levey, *Thinking in the Photographic Idiom*, Prentice-Hall, 1984.
Slow Burn: A Photodocument of Centralia, Pennsylvania, University of Pennsylvania Press, 1986.

Contributor of photographs to periodicals, including *Boston Phoenix, New York Times*, and *Philadelphia Inquirer*.

WORK IN PROGRESS: "Photodocuments with oral histories of the coal region, environmental issues and law, and feminist themes."

SIDELIGHTS: In the early 1960s a fire began in the abandoned coal mines beneath Centralia, Pennsylvania, burning uncontrollably for more than twenty years. Poisonous fumes filled homes of residents, many of whom had to be evacuated, smog choked the air, and water ran hot from cold faucets. In *Slow Burn: A Photodocument of Centralia, Pennsylvania*, Renee Jacobs depicts the community with what *New York Times Book Review* writer Ben A. Franklin praised as "stark Works Progress Administration-style photographs." One picture shows a resident at home near a machine monitoring carbon monoxide levels; another presents a Brownie troop parading past a tall pipe venting steam and smoke from underground. According to Franklin, the book "portrays with poignancy a . . . community . . . poised in stubborn bewilderment."

BIOGRAPHICAL/CRITICAL SOURCES:

PERIODICALS

New York Times Book Review, January 4, 1987.

*   *   *

JAFFE, Aniela   1903-

PERSONAL: Born February 20, 1903, in Berlin, Germany. *Education:* Attended University of Hamburg, 1931-33.

ADDRESSES: Home—Zurich, Switzerland. *Agent*—Dr. Robert Hinshaw, Daimon Verlag, Am Klosterplatz, CH-8840 Einsiedeln, Switzerland.

CAREER: C. G. Jung Institute, Zurich, Switzerland, secretary, 1947-55, personal secretary to Dr. C. G. Jung, 1955-61. Analyst, 1955—. Worked with children prior to coming to Zurich, and later with elderly people in retirement homes.

MEMBER: Swiss Society for Practical Psychology, Swiss Parapsychology Society, Swiss Society for Analytical Psychology, International Society for Analytical Psychology, Zurich Society of Arts.

WRITINGS:

(With Gretel Vettiger and Alban Vogt) *Alte Menschen im Altersheim: Soziologische, Psychologische, und Medizinische* (title means "Old People in the Retirement Home"), Schwabe, 1951.
Geistererscheinungen und Vorzeichen: Eine Psychologische Deutung (foreword by C. G. Jung), Rascher, 1958, with indexes, Walter, 1978, translation published as *Apparitions: An Archetypal Approach to Death, Dreams, and Ghosts*, Spring Publications, 1979.
(Editor) C. G. Jung, *Erinnerungen, Traume, Gedanken*, Rascher, 1962, translation by Richard and Clara Winston published as *Memories, Dreams, Reflections*, Pantheon, 1963.
Apparitions and Precognition: A Study From the Point of View of C. G. Jung's Analytical Psychology (foreword by C. G. Jung), University Books, 1963.
Der Mythus vom Sinn im Werk von C. G. Jung, Rascher, 1967, translation by R.F.C. Hull published as *The Myth of Meaning*, C. G. Jung Foundation, 1971, new edition, Daimon Press, 1984.
Aus Leben und Werkstatt von C. G. Jung, Rascher, 1968, translation by R.F.C. Hull published as *From the Life*

and Work of C. G. Jung, Harper, 1971, translation by Hull and Murray Stein, with new last chapter, published as *Jung's Last Years and Other Essays,* Spring Publications, 1984.

(Contributor) Ian McPhail, editor, *Alchemy and the Occult,* Yale University Press, 1968.

Jung Over Parapsychologie en Alchemie: Jungs Laatste Jaren (title means "Jung on Parapsychology and Alchemy: Jung's Last Years"), Lemniscaat, 1969.

(Editor with Gerhard Adler) *C. G. Jung: Briefe,* Walter, 1972, translation by R.F.C. Hull published as *C. G. Jung: Letters,* Volume I: *1906-1950,* Volume II: *1951-1961,* Princeton University Press, 1973.

(Editor) *C. G. Jung, Hundert Briefe* (title means "One Hundred Letters"), Walter, 1975.

(Editor) *C. G. Jung: Bild und Wort,* Walter, 1977, translation by R.F.C. Hull and others published as *C. G. Jung: Word and Image,* Princeton University Press, 1979.

Bilder und Symbole aus E.T.A. Hoffmanns Marchen "Der Goldne Topf" (title means "Images and Symbols in E.T.A. Hoffmann's Tale, 'The Golden Pot'"), Gerstenberg Verlag, 1978.

Aus C. G. Jungs Welt: Gedanken und Politik; Vier Ausatze (title means "Out of C. G. Jung's World: Thoughts and Politics; Four Essays"), W. Classen, 1979, new edition published as *Parapsychologie, Individuation, Nationalsocialismus: Themen bei C. G. Jung* (title means "Themes Related to C. G. Jung: Parapsychology, Individuation, National Socialism"), Daimon Verlag, 1985.

(With Liliane Frey-Rohn and Marie-Louise von Franz) *Im Unkreis des Todes* (title means "Concerning Death"), Daimon Verlag, 1980.

Religoser Wahn und schwarze Magie: Das tragische Leben der Anna Kingsford (title means "Religious Delusion and Black Magic: The Tragic Life of Anna Kingsford"), Bonz Verlag, 1980.

Aufsatze zur Psychologie C. G. Jungs (title means "Essays on the Psychology of C. G. Jung"), Daimon Verlag, 1982.

(Editor with Gerhard Adler) *Selected Letters of C. G. Jung, 1909-1961,* Princeton University Press, 1984.

Also contributor to academic journals.

WORK IN PROGRESS: Collection of essays in German; essays in English on C. G. Jung and his analytical psychology: both for Daimon Verlag.

SIDELIGHTS: Aniela Jaffe, C. G. Jung's personal secretary as well as a practicing analyst, wrote and edited many of the definitive volumes on Jung and analytical psychology in cooperation with the doctor himself. *C. G. Jung: Word and Image* contains reproductions of more than two hundred photographs and paintings, including some of Jung's own paintings and stone carvings, as well as letters and selections from his writings, some never before published. A reviewer for *Choice* remarked that "no book better suggests the 'feel' of Jung." In *New Republic* Joyce Carol Oates called *Word and Image* "fascinating" and praised the color illustrations of the stone carvings Jung did at Bollingen in his old age.

Jaffe recorded and edited *Memories, Dreams, Reflections* in consultation with Jung, but it was not actually completed until shortly after Jung's death. At first reluctant to approve a biography of himself, Jung finally agreed to have Jaffe edit the book and eventually became occupied with ensuring its comprehensiveness and accuracy. Jaffe said in the introduction to the book that Jung, in the latter part of 1957 when the project was under way, wrote: "I shall fend off other obligations long enough to take up the very first beginnings of my life and consider them in an objective fashion. This task has proved so difficult and singular that in order to go ahead with it, I have had to promise myself that the results would not be published in my lifetime. Such a promise seems to me essential in order to assure for myself the necessary detachment and calm. It became clear that all the memories which have remained vivid to me had to do with emotional experiences that arouse uneasiness and passion in the mind—scarcely the best condition for an objective account." Because the biography was not a "scientific account," wrote Jaffe, Jung specifically requested that the book should not be made a part of his "Collected Works."

"The chapters are rapidly moving beams of light that only fleetingly illuminate the outward events of Jung's life and work," Jaffe wrote in the foreword to *Memories, Dreams, Reflections.* "In recompense, they transmit the atmosphere of his intellectual world and the experience of a man to whom the psyche was a profound reality. I often asked Jung for specific data on outward happenings, but I asked in vain. Only the spiritual essence of his life's experience remained in his memory, and this alone seemed to him worth the effort of telling."

AVOCATIONAL INTERESTS: "I am interested in music and literature and loved mountaineering."

BIOGRAPHICAL/CRITICAL SOURCES:

BOOKS

Encyclopedia of Occultism and Parapsychology, 2nd edition, Gale, 1984.

PERIODICALS

Contemporary Psychology, Volume 24, number 12, 1979.
Library Journal, July, 1979.
New Republic, August 4, 1979.

*   *   *

JAMES, C(yril) L(ionel) R(obert) 1901-
(J. R. Johnson)

PERSONAL: Born January 4, 1901, in Chaguanas, Trinidad; son of a schoolteacher; married first wife (divorced); married Selma Weinstein, 1955; children (first marriage): one. *Education:* Queen's Royal College secondary school (Port of Spain), graduated, 1918.

ADDRESSES: c/o Allison & Busby, 6-A Noel St., London WIV 3RB, England. *Home*—Brixton, London, England.

CAREER: Writer, c. 1920—; member of the Maple cricket team, Port of Spain, Trinidad; *Trinidad* (literary magazine), Port of Spain, editor, 1929-30; teacher at Queen's Royal College, Port of Spain, until 1932; *Manchester Guardian,* London, England, correspondent, 1932-38; editor of *Fight* (later *Workers' Fight;* Marxist publication), London, until 1938; trade union organizer and political activist in the United States, 1938-53; West Indian Federal Labor Party, Port of Spain, secretary, 1958-60; *The Nation,* Port of Spain, editor, 1958-60. Lecturer at colleges and universities, including Federal City College, Washington, D.C.; commentator for the British Broadcasting Company (BBC); cricket columnist for *Race Today.*

WRITINGS:

The Life of Captain Cipriani: An Account of British Government in the West Indies, Nelson, Lancashire, Coulton, 1932, abridged edition published as *The Case for West-Indian Self-Government,* Hogarth, 1933, University Place Book Shop, 1967.

(With L. R. Constantine) *Cricket and I,* Allan, 1933.

Minty Alley (novel), Secker & Warburg, 1936, New Beacon, 1971.

Toussaint L'Ouverture (play; first produced in London, 1936; revised version titled *The Black Jacobins* and produced in Ibadan, Nigeria, 1967), published in *A Time and a Season: Eight Caribbean Plays,* edited by Errol Hill, University of the West Indies (Port of Spain), 1976.

World Revolution 1917-1936: The Rise and Fall of the Communist International, Pioneer, 1937, Hyperion Press, 1973.

A History of Negro Revolt, Fact, 1938, Haskell House, 1967, revised and expanded edition published as *A History of Pan-African Revolt,* Drum and Spear Press, 1969.

The Black Jacobins: Toussaint L'Ouverture and the San Domingo Revolution, Dial, 1938, Random House, 1963.

(Translator from the French) Boris Souvarine, *Stalin: A Critical Survey of Socialism,* Longman, 1939.

State Capitalism and World Revolution (published anonymously), privately printed, 1950, Facing Reality, 1969.

Mariners, Renegades, and Castaways: The Story of Herman Melville and the World We Live In, privately printed, 1953, Bewick Editions, 1978.

Modern Politics (lectures), PNM (Port of Spain), 1960.

Beyond a Boundary, Hutchinson, 1963, Pantheon, 1984.

The Hegelian Dialectic and Modern Politics, Facing Reality, 1970, revised edition published as *Notes on Dialectics: Hegel, Marx, Lenin,* Lawrence Hill, 1980.

Nkrumah and the Ghana Revolution, Lawrence Hill, 1977, revised edition, Allison & Busby, 1982.

The Future in the Present: Selected Writings of C. L. R. James, Lawrence Hill, 1977.

(With Tony Bogues and Kim Gordon) *Black Nationalism and Socialism,* Socialists Unlimited, 1979.

(With George Breitman, Edgar Keemer, and others) *Fighting Racism in World War II,* Monad, 1980.

Spheres of Existence: Selected Writings, Lawrence Hill, 1981.

Eightieth Birthday Lectures, Race Today, 1983.

At the Rendezvous of Victory: Selected Writings, Lawrence Hill, 1985.

Cricket, Allison & Busby, 1986.

Contributor of short stories to the collections *The Best Short Stories of 1928,* Cape, 1928, and *Island Voices,* Liveright, 1970; author, sometimes under pseudonym J. R. Johnson, of numerous political pamphlets; contributor of articles to newspapers and magazines.

WORK IN PROGRESS: An autobiography.

SIDELIGHTS: C. L. R. James is a leading Trinidadian political and literary figure whose interests and values were profoundly shaped by his experience growing up in the British West Indian colony at the beginning of the century. The son of a schoolteacher father, James was raised in the capital of Port of Spain in a highly respectable—indeed, rather puritanical—middle-class black family suffused in British manners and culture. The James family home faced the back of a cricket field, and young Cyril developed a lifelong passion for the baseball-like sport watching matches from his living room window. The boy also grew up with an intense love for English

literature—at age ten he had memorized long passages of William Makepeace Thackeray's *Vanity Fair*—and both his reading and his cricket-playing often distracted him from his studies at the elite Queen's Royal College in Port of Spain. Dashing his parents' hopes that he would pursue a political career with the colonial administration, James chose instead to play professional cricket and teach at the Queen's Royal College in the 1920s. At the same time, he set about chronicling the lives of the Trinidadian lower class in a series of naturalistic short stories that shocked his peers and foreshadowed his future Marxism. James's first-hand study of the Port of Spain slums also furnished background for his only novel, *Minty Alley,* an affecting but unsentimental look at the complex personal relationships and humble aspirations of the denizens of a rundown boarding house.

In 1932, chafing under the placid routines of a life in a colonial backwater, James accepted an invitation to go to London to help the great black Trinidadian cricketer Learie Constantine write his autobiography. With Constantine's help, James secured a job as a cricket correspondent with the *Manchester Guardian* and published his first nonfiction book, *The Life of Captain Cipriani: An Account of British Government in the West Indies* (later abridged and published as *The Case for West-Indian Self-Government*). This influential treatise—one of the first to urge full self-determination for West Indians—introduced James to leading figures in the two political movements that were to profoundly shape his thinking in the years to come: Pan Africanism and Marxism.

James first developed his Pan Africanist ideas in Trinidadian leftist activist George Padmore's London-based African Bureau, where he joined future African independence leaders Jomo Kenyatta and Kwame Nkrumah as a political propogandist in the mid-1930s. James emphasized the importance of West Indians' coming to terms with their African heritage in order to help forge a sense of national identity in their racially and culturally polyglot society. He also came to regard the struggle to liberate and politically unify colonial Africa as a way of inspiring and mobilizing oppressed people of color around the world to seize control of their destinies. James later examined Pan Africanist theory and practice in two historical works, *A History of Negro Revolt* (later revised and published as *History of Pan-African Revolt*), which surveys nearly two centuries of the black liberation struggle against European colonialism, and *Nkrumah and the Ghana Revolution,* an analysis of the first successful independence movement in modern Africa.

While participating in the vanguard of the African liberation movement, James also became a committed Marxist during his sojourn in London in the 1930s. He took the Trotskyist position in the great dispute over Stalinism that split the world communist movement during those years and wrote a history from that perspective in 1937 titled *World Revolution, 1917-1936: The Rise and Fall of the Communist International.* James's Marxism also informed his 1938 historical study *The Black Jacobins: Toussaint L'Ouverture and the San Domingo Revolution.* In this book, generally regarded as his masterwork, James analyzes the socioeconomic roots and leading personalities of the Haitian revolution of 1791 to 1804, the first and only slave revolt to achieve political independence in world history.

At the center of the revolution and the book stands Toussaint L'Ouverture. The self-taught black slave turned charismatic political leader and redoubtable military commander organized and led a disciplined army of former slaves, who defeated crack French and British expeditionary forces mustered to crush the insurgency. Of particular interest in *The Black Jacobins,* critics noted, is the author's success in relating the Haitian events to the course of the French Revolution, whose ideals inspired Toussaint even as he fought first Maximilien Robespierre and then Napoleon Bonaparte to free France's most important Caribbean sugar colony, then known as Saint Domingue. The democratic ideals of the Haitian revolution, which culminated in full political independence a year after Toussaint's death in 1803, touched off a wave of slave revolts throughout the Caribbean and helped inspire anti-slavery forces in the southern United States. *New York Herald Tribune Books* reviewer Clara Gruening Stillman judged *The Black Jacobins* as gripping as the events it recounted: "Brilliantly conceived and executed, throwing upon the historical screen a mass of dramatic figures, lurid scenes, fantastic happenings, the absorbing narrative never departs from its rigid faithfulness to method and documentation."

Shortly after publishing *The Black Jacobins* James moved to the United States, where he joined the Trotskyist Socialist Workers Party (SWP) and became a full-time political activist, organizing auto workers in Detroit, Michigan, and tenant farmers in the South. He broke with the SWP in the late 1940s over the question of the nature of the Soviet Union, which he dubbed "state capitalist," and co-founded a new Detroit-based Trotskyist political organization with Leon Trotsky's former secretary Raya Dunayevskaya. James's political activities eventually provoked the wrath of the McCarthy-era U.S. government, which denied him American citizenship and deported him to Great Britain in 1953. While awaiting his expulsion on Ellis Island, the ever-resourceful James managed to write a short study of Herman Melville titled *Mariners, Renegades, and Castaways* that drew a parallel between Ahab's pursuit of the great white whale in Melville's classic, *Moby Dick,* and left-wing intellectuals' infatuation with Soviet political leader Joseph Stalin.

After five years in London, James returned to Trinidad in 1958 to join the movement for political independence there. In Port of Spain he edited *The Nation* magazine and served as secretary of the West Indian Federal Labor Party, whose leader, Dr. Eric Williams, became Trinidad's first premier in 1960. Like the United States authorities, however, Williams found James's outspoken Marxism politically threatening and soon compelled James, who had once been Williams's schoolmaster, to go back to England. James left Trinidad aggrieved that the emerging Caribbean nations had failed to achieve a lasting formula for political federation, which he believed necessary to further their social and economic development.

Back in London, James returned to political writing and lecturing, particularly on the Pan Africanist movement, West Indian politics, and the black question in the United States. He also rekindled his passion for cricket after leading a successful campaign to have the Trinidadian Frank Worrell named the first black captain of the West Indian international cricket team. Worrell's spectacular playing at the Australian championship competition in 1961 galvanized a sense of national pride and identity among the emerging West Indian nations and partly inspired James to write *Beyond a Boundary,* his much-praised 1963 survey of cricket's social and cultural significance in Great Britain and the Caribbean. The book's title refers both to the game's objective of driving a ball beyond a marked boundary and James's novel thesis that this gentlemen's sport can help overcome certain false cultural, racial, and political boundaries within society. On a purely aesthetic level, James

argues, cricket has "the perfect flow of motion" that defines the essence of all great art; he holds that a good cricket match is the visual and dramatic equivalent of so-called "high art" and that the sport should be recognized as a genuinely democratic art form. Cricket's high standards of fairness and sportsmanship, on the other hand, illustrate "all the decencies required for a culture" and even played a historic role by showing West Indian blacks that they could excel in a forum where the rules were equal for everyone. The integrated Caribbean cricket teams, James believes, helped forge a new black self-confidence that carried the West Indian colonies to independence. The author renders these observations in a lively, anecdotal style that includes both biographical sketches of great cricketers and personal reminiscences from his own lifelong love affair with the sport. "*Beyond a Boundary* is one of the finest and most finished books to come out of the West Indies," remarked Trinidadian novelist V. S. Naipaul in *Encounter.* "There is no more eloquent brief for the cultural and artistic importance of sport," added *Newsweek*'s Jim Miller.

In recent years, James has published two well-received collections of essays and articles that display his broad literary, cultural, and political interests. *The Future in the Present* contains that author's short story "Triumph," about women tenants in a Port of Spain slum, along with essays ranging from critical interpretations of Pablo Picasso's painting "Guernica" and Melville's *Moby Dick* to a political analysis of workers' councils in Hungary and a personal account of organizing a sharecroppers' strike in Missouri in 1942. "The writings are profound, sometimes; cranky, occasionally; stimulating, always," remarked *Village Voice* critic Paul Berman, and *Times Literary Supplement* reviewer Thomas Hodgkin found the book "a mine of richness and variety." *At the Rendezvous of Victory,* whose title James took from a verse by the great West Indian poet Aime Cesaire, includes an essay on the Solidarity union movement in Poland and critical discussions of the work of black American novelists Toni Morrison and Alice Walker. The more than eighty-year-old James "shows no diminution of his intellectual energies," wrote Alastair Niven in his review of the collection for *British Books News.* "Throughout this book James's elegant but unmannered style, witty and relaxed when lecturing, reflective and analytical when writing for publication, always conveys a sense of his own robust, humane, and giving personality. Was there ever a less polemical or more persuasive radical?"

BIOGRAPHICAL/CRITICAL SOURCES:

BOOKS

James, C. L. R., *Beyond a Boundary,* Pantheon, 1984.
James, C. L. R., *The Future in the Present: Selected Writings of C. L. R. James,* Lawrence Hill, 1977.
Mackenzie, Alan, and Paul Gilroy, *Visions of History,* Pantheon, 1983.

PERIODICALS

American Scholar, summer, 1985.
British Book News, May, 1984.
CLA Journal, December, 1977.
Encounter, September, 1963.
Nation, May 4, 1985.
Newsweek, March 26, 1984.
New Yorker, June 25, 1984.
New York Herald Tribune Books, November 27, 1938.
New York Times Book Review, March 25, 1984.
Radical America, May, 1970.

Times Literary Supplement, December 2, 1977, January 20, 1978, September 25, 1987.
Village Voice, February 11, 1981, July 10, 1984.
Washington Post Book World, April 22, 1984.

—*Sketch by Curtis Skinner*

*   *   *

JAMES, Daniel (Lewis)   1911-1988
(Daniel Hyatt, Danny Santiago)

OBITUARY NOTICE: Born in 1911 in Kansas City, Mo.; died May 18, 1988, in Monterey, Calif. Volunteer social worker, screenwriter, playwright, and author. James caused a controversy in the literary world when it was revealed he was the author of the prize-winning *Famous All Over Town,* a novel exploring Mexican-American society in an east Los Angeles neighborhood. Writing under the Hispanic pseudonym Danny Santiago, James was lauded for portraying an authentic and colorful view of ethnic life. He received the prestigious Richard and Hinda Rosenthal Foundation Award for fiction from the American Academy and Institute of Arts and Letters in 1984 and the P.E.N. President's Award in 1985.

The son of a wealthy Kansas City businessman, James and his wife worked for more than twenty years as volunteer social workers in the Los Angeles neighborhood portrayed in *Famous All Over Town.* James first wrote stories set in the predominately Mexican-American area in the 1950s that were published in such popular American and Hispanic magazines as *Redbook, Playboy,* and *Nuestro.* James assumed the Santiago pseudonym when submitting these stories because he was afraid they would not be published; he had been called before the House Committee on Un-American Activities (HUAC) in 1951 for his previous association with the Communist Party and could no longer find work writing for the stage or screen under his own name. Previously James wrote the screenplay for "The Great Dictator" with Charlie Chaplin; with his wife Lilith he penned the libretto for the hit Broadway musical "Bloomer Girl"; and after he testified before the HUAC he created the screenplays for "The Giant Behemoth" and "Gorgo" under the pseudonym Daniel Hyatt. Also, under his own name, he edited and authored the introduction of *The Complete Bolivian Diary of Che Guevara and Other Captured Documents,* the journal of Argentinean leader Ernesto "Che" Guevara, and wrote a biography of the revolutionary, *Che Guevara.*

OBITUARIES AND OTHER SOURCES:

PERIODICALS

Commonweal, May 20, 1983.
Los Angeles Times, July 22, 1984, May 13, 1985, May 21, 1988, June 19, 1988.
New Statesman, December 4, 1970.
New York Review of Books, August 16, 1984.
New York Times, July 22, 1984, May 21, 1988.
New York Times Book Review, August 25, 1968, April 24, 1983.
Partisan Review, winter, 1969.
Punch, October 7, 1970.
Washington Post, October 29, 1969, January 30, 1970, May 23, 1988.

*   *   *

JAMES, Paul   1921-

PERSONAL: Born August 22, 1921, in Singapore; married; children: four. *Education:* Polytechnic of Central London, diploma in architecture (with honors), 1949. *Religion:* Roman Catholic.

ADDRESSES: Home—Lawnside, 3 Hungershall Park, Tunbridge Wells, Kent, England.

CAREER: Hospital Design Partnership, London, England, partner and chairman, 1966-82. Lecturer in health facility planning at Medical Architecture Research Unit, Polytechnic of North London, 1966-80.

MEMBER: Royal Institute of British Architects (fellow).

WRITINGS:

Alcohol and Drug Dependence: Treatment Facilities, King Edward's Hospital Fund, 1972.
(With William Tatton-Brown) *Hospitals: Design and Development,* Architectural Press, 1986, Van Nostrand, 1987.

Contributor to health service and architecture journals.

WORK IN PROGRESS: The Life and Works of George Basevi, F.R.I.B.A. (1794-1845); research on neoclassical architecture, mainly in London, 1825-45.

*   *   *

JAMES, William M.
See HARVEY, John (Barton)

*   *   *

JANGER, Kathleen N.   1940-

PERSONAL: Born January 21, 1940, in Davenport, Iowa; daughter of Leo J. and Eileen (Martens) Nugent; married Stephen A. Janger (a foundation president), March 8, 1970; children: Margaret Michelle, Jay Adam, Andrea Lee. *Education:* Attended William Smith College.

ADDRESSES: Home—1502 Mintwood Dr., McLean, Va. 22101. *Office*—Young Writer's Contest Foundation, P.O. Box 6092, McLean, Va. 22106.

CAREER: AIMS-International, Washington, D.C., co-founder and administrative assistant, 1966-70; Close Up Foundation, Arlington, Va., co-founder and administrative coordinator, 1970-75; free-lance writer and editor, 1975-84; Young Writer's Contest Foundation, McLean, Va., co-founder and executive director, 1984—.

WRITINGS:

(With Michael Korenblit) *Until We Meet Again,* Putnam, 1983.
(With Joan Korenblit) *Knowing Beans About Coffee,* WRC Publishing, 1985.
(Editor) *Rainbow Collection: Stories and Poetry by Young People,* Young Writer's Contest Foundation, 1985 edition, 1985, 1986 edition, 1986, 1987 edition, 1987, 1988 edition, 1988.

Editor of computer software programs. Contributor to newspapers.

WORK IN PROGRESS: Quest for the Perfect Hairdo—and Other Dead Ends; a collection of essays.

SIDELIGHTS: Kathleen N. Janger told *CA:* "*Until We Meet Again* is a true story that takes place during World War II. It is about my co-author's parents as teenagers in Poland and their separation. After internment in thirteen concentration camps between them, they found each other after the war. While we were writing the book, our research led us on a trail that resulted in the discovery of my co-author's uncle (long thought dead) alive and well in Newcastle, England. Writing the book was an extraordinary experience—a very personal one. When we began, we thought we had one miracle; we ended up with two miracles. We wrote it to record two people's experiences under the Nazis and to offer testimony to refute the *Historical Review* people's claims that the Holocaust never took place. The book is written from the view of the two main characters; there is no discussion of military offensives or the like because the characters were not aware of such information. They know only what was happening to themselves.

"While I continue to write for and about myself, most of my attention is focused on the Young Writer's Contest Foundation, a national writing competition for first through eighth graders. Through this activity, we hope to encourage youngsters to care about their native tongue and to use it to express themselves, not only creatively, but also in a manner suitable to practical applications."

*   *   *

JEFFERSON, Janet
  See MENCKEN, H(enry) L(ouis)

*   *   *

JHA, Lakshmi Kant   1913-1988

OBITUARY NOTICE: Some sources spell given name Lakshimi; born November 22, 1913, in Bhagalpur, India; died of a cardiac arrest, January 16, 1988, in Poona, India. Economist, politician, and author. A major force behind India's economic policy, Jha worked in various capacities since joining the Indian civil service in 1936. He served as chief controller of imports and exports, secretary of the department of economic affairs of the Ministry of Finance, secretary to Prime Minister Lal Bahadur Shastri, and director of the reserve and state banks of India. In addition, he was alternate governor of the World Bank for four years, Indian ambassador to the United States from 1970 to 1973, governor of the state of Jammu and Kashmir from 1973 until 1981, and at the time of his death he was Prime Minister Rajiv Gandhi's adviser on administrative reforms. Jha, who studied at Trinity College of Cambridge University under the distinguished economist John Maynard Keynes, wrote numerous books, including *Price Policy in a Developing Economy, The International Monetary Scene and the Human Factor in Economic Development, Shortages and High Prices: The Way Out,* and *Economic Strategy for the Eighties.*

OBITUARIES AND OTHER SOURCES:

BOOKS

The International Who's Who, 51st edition, Europa, 1987.
The International Year Book and Statesmen's Who's Who,
  Thomas Skinner Directories, 1982.

PERIODICALS

Los Angeles Times, January 17, 1988.

*   *   *

JOHN, Angela V.   1948-

PERSONAL: Born September 24, 1948, in Neath, Wales; daughter of Ivor and Peggy (Scott) John. *Education:* University of Birmingham, B.A., 1969; University of Wales, University College of Swansea, M.A., 1971; Victoria University of Manchester, Ph.D., 1976. *Politics:* Labour.

ADDRESSES: Office—Thames Polytechnic, Wellington St., Woolwich, London S.E.18, London.

CAREER: Dartford College of Education, Kent, England, lecturer, 1974-78; Thomas Polytechnic, London, England, lecturer, 1978-82, senior lecturer in history, 1982—.

MEMBER: Society for the Study of Welsh Labour History (member of executive committee).

AWARDS, HONORS: Children's literature award, 1985, for *Coalmining Women.*

WRITINGS:

By the Sweat of Their Brow, Croom Helm, 1980.
Coalmining Women (juvenile), Cambridge University Press, 1984.
(Author of introduction) Florence Bell, *At the Works,* Virgo, 1984.
(Editor) *Unequal Opportunities: Women's Employment in Nineteenth-Century England,* Basil Blackwell, 1986.
"An Unsuitable Job for a Woman?" (play), first broadcast by BBC-Radio, June 10, 1986.
(With Revel Guest) *Lady Charlotte,* Weidenfeld & Nicolson, 1988.

SIDELIGHTS: Angela V. John commented: "My idea of sheer luxury is to be able to sit by the typewriter in my stone cottage in Wales and work on my latest book. Once teaching has finished for the term, I am lucky enough to indulge myself. I have recently discovered the joys and frustrations of writing historical biography, and this is the direction in which I want to move.

"For the past few years I have been working on a biography of Lady Charlotte Guest/Schreiber (1812-1895). She was a translator, collector, traveler, industrialist, and educator. In addition to all this (and having ten children) she kept a daily journal. This she began at the age of nine and continued until she was seventy-nine. It is a wonderful way of looking at the nineteenth century as it spans the period 1822-1891, and Lady Charlotte had the knack of usually being in the right place at the right time."

*   *   *

JOHNSON, Charles S(purgeon)   1893-1956

PERSONAL: Born July 24, 1893, in Bristol, Va.; died following a heart attack, October 27, 1956, in Louisville, Ky.; son of Charles Henry (a minister) and Winifred (Branch) Johnson; married Marie Antoinette Burgette, November 6, 1920; children: Charles, Jr., Robert Burgette, Jeh Vincent, Patricia Marie Clifford. *Education:* Virginia Union University, B.A., 1916; University of Chicago, Ph.B., 1918. *Politics:* Democrat. *Religion:* Congregationalist.

ADDRESSES: Home—1611 Meharry Blvd., Nashville, Tenn. *Office*—c/o Fisk University, Nashville, Tenn.

CAREER: Director of Department of Research and Investigations for Chicago Urban League, 1917-19; associate executive secretary for Chicago Commission on Race Relations, 1919-21; National Urban League, New York, N. Y., director of Department of Research and Investigations, 1921-28; Fisk

University, Nashville, Tenn., professor of sociology and chairman of department of social sciences, beginning in 1928, president of the university, 1946-56. Delegate to United Nations Educational, Scientific, and Cultural Organization (UNESCO) conferences in Paris in 1946 and in Mexico City in 1947. Delegate to World Council of Churches in Amsterdam in 1948 and to Conference on Indian-American Relations in New Delhi in 1949. Member of numerous government committees on sociological matters, including the commission appointed by the League of Nations to investigate forced labor in Liberia in 1930, the commission sent to Japan in 1946 by the State Department to organize the Japanese educational system, and the commission established by the Eisenhower administration in 1952 to study the health needs of the nation. Participant in several private organizations, including director in 1933 and co-director from 1934 to 1938 of the Institute of Race Relations at Swarthmore College, co-director of the race relations program and a member of the board of trustees from 1943 to 1948 of the Julius Rosenwald Fund, and a director from 1944 to 1950 of the Race Relations Division of the American Missionary Association of the Congregational and Christian Churches of America. *Military service:* U. S. Army, 1918-19, served as a sergeant with the 893d Pioneer Infantry.

AWARDS, HONORS: Recipient of many awards and honors, including the William E. Harmon Gold Medal from the Harmon Foundation, 1930, for his achievements in the field of social science, the Anisfield-Wolf Award from *Saturday Review,* 1938, for his book *The Negro College Graduate,* the Russwurm Award for Public Service from the Negro Newspaper Publishers' Association, and the Social Action Churchmanship Award of the General Council of the Congregational Christian Churches. Honorary Litt.D. degrees conferred by Virginia Union University in 1938 and Columbia University in 1947, an honorary L.H.D. degree by Howard University in 1941, and honorary LL.D. degrees by Harvard University in 1948, the University of Glasgow, Scotland, in 1952, Lincoln University in 1955, and Central State College, Xenia, Ohio, in 1956.

WRITINGS:

(Editor) *Ebony and Topaz: A Collectanea,* Urban League, 1927, reprinted, Books for Libraries, 1971.
The Negro in American Civilization: A Study of Negro Life and Race Relations in the Light of Social Research, Holt, 1930, reprinted, Johnson, 1970.
Negro Housing: Report of the Committee on Negro Housing, edited by John M. Gries and James Ford, President's Conference on Home Building and Home Ownership (Washington, D. C.), 1932, reprinted, Negro Universities Press, 1969.
The Economic Status of Negroes: Summary and Analysis of the Materials Presented at the Conference on the Economic Status of the Negro, Held in Washington, D.C., May 11-13, 1933, Under the Sponsorship of the Julius Rosenwald Fund, Fisk University Press, 1933, reprinted, New York Public Library, 1974.
Shadow of the Plantation, University of Chicago Press, 1934, reprinted, 1966.
(With Willis Duke Weatherford) *Race Relations: Adjustment of Whites and Negroes in the United States,* Heath, 1934, reprinted, Negro Universities Press, 1969.
(With Edwin R. Embree and W.W. Alexander) *The Collapse of Cotton Tenancy: Summary of Field Studies and Statistical Surveys, 1933-1935,* University of North Carolina Press, 1935, reprinted, Books for Libraries, 1972.

A Preface to Racial Understanding, Friendship, 1936.
The Negro College Graduate, University of North Carolina Press, 1938, reprinted, Negro Universities Press, 1969.
Growing Up in the Black Belt: Negro Youth in the Rural South, with an introduction by St. Clair Drake, American Council on Education, 1941, reprinted, Schocken, 1967.
(Co-author) *Statistical Atlas of Southern Counties: Listing and Analysis of Socio-Economic Indices of 1,104 Southern Counties,* University of North Carolina Press, 1941.
Patterns of Negro Segregation, Harper, 1943, reprinted as *Backgrounds to Patterns of Negro Segregation,* Crowell, 1970.
(Co-author) *To Stem This Tide: A Survey of Racial Tension Areas in the United States,* Pilgrim Press, 1943, reprinted, AMS Press, 1969.
(Editor) *Education and the Cultural Process: Papers Presented at Symposium Commemorating the Seventy-fifth Anniversary of the Founding of Fisk University, April 29-May 4, 1941,* University of Chicago Press, 1943, reprinted, Negro Universities Press, 1970.
(With Herman H. Long) *People Versus Property: Race Restrictive Covenants in Housing,* Fisk University Press, 1947.
(Co-author) *Into the Main Stream: A Survey of Best Practices in Race Relations in the South,* University of North Carolina Press, 1947, reprinted, 1967.
Bitter Canaan: The Story of the Negro Republic, with an introduction by John Stanfield, Transaction Books, 1987.

Contributor to *Recent Gains in American Civilization,* edited by Kirby Page, Harcourt, 1928. Contributor of articles to periodicals, including *Opportunity, Journal of Negro History,* and *New York Times.*

SIDELIGHTS: For four decades Charles S. Johnson worked quietly but steadfastly in his efforts to improve race relations between blacks and whites in the United States. As the chief black sociologist of his period Johnson wrote the scholarly books that documented the causes of race riots, the effects of racism on the personalities of black youths, and the necessity for blacks to become a part of the mainstream of American life. As the first black president of Fisk University Johnson was the driving force behind the establishment of Fisk as a first-rate institution the rival of Booker T. Washington's Tuskegee Institute. And, most of all, as founder and editor of the National Urban League's *Opportunity: A Journal of Negro Life,* Johnson helped generate one of the most impressive cultural movements in American history, the Harlem Renaissance of the 1920s.

It was in 1923 that, in addition to his duties as director of the National Urban League's Department of Research and Investigations, Johnson assumed the task of editing the league's new magazine, *Opportunity.* Eugene Kinckle Jones, executive secretary of the league, set the tone of *Opportunity* when in the first issue he wrote that it would "depict Negro life as it is with no exaggerations. We shall try to set down interestingly but without sugar-coating or generalization the findings of careful scientific surveys and the facts gathered from research." Johnson, while supporting Jones's position, noted an additional dimension that *Opportunity* would report, when in the next issue he wrote: "There are aspects of the cultural side of Negro life that have been long neglected." Very quickly *Opportunity* became more than a house organ of the Urban League.

Like W.E.B. Du Bois's *Crisis* magazine, *Opportunity* provided an outlet for publication to young black writers and scholars whose work was not acceptable to other established media. Although *Crisis* was older and had a larger circulation than *Opportunity,* the orientation of its editor, W.E.B. Du Bois, was more political than Johnson's. *Opportunity* did not neglect political issues: it too reported on scientific surveys of discrimination and conditions in the black community in housing, health, employment, and other economical and sociological areas. *Opportunity,* however, made its most enduring contribution in reporting black culture in the United States and the world at large. In the May, 1924, issue, for instance, black scholars Alain Locke, Albert C. Barnes, and Paul Guillaume all contributed articles to a special issue on African art. And in the November, 1926, issue, *Opportunity* presented a special "Caribbean issue." Among other features it included poems by Claude McKay, an article on West Indian composers and musicians, and W.A. Domingo's "The West Indies."

It was in the popular *Opportunity* dinners and contests, however, that Johnson was most successful in promoting the new awakening of black culture. An early observer of the creative genius of the many black artists of the 1920s, Johnson, along with the Urban League administration, moved deliberately to bring the white publishers and the black writers together. The dinners, which gathered together white editors and black artists, served to showcase black literary and artistic talent and to secure patronage for the Renaissance movement from white publishers. The contests, which awarded first, second, and third prizes for short stories, poems, plays, and essays as well as a guarantee of publication, were open not only to black contributors but also to nonblacks on topics about blacks. Many of the contest winners, for the most part unknown to white publishers, were well known within black literary circles. Among them were short-story writers John F. Matheus, Zora Neale Hurston, and Eric D. Walrond, poets Langston Hughes and Countee Cullen, essayists E. Franklin Frazier, Sterling A. Brown, and Laura D. Wheatley, and playwright Warren A. MacDonald.

The first *Opportunity* dinners and contests were the most successful. In subsequent years there were more contestants, but the submissions were of a lesser quality, causing Johnson's enthusiasm to wane. In 1927, the year before he left the Urban League, Johnson gathered what he judged to be the best of the work published in *Opportunity* and collected it in *Ebony and Topaz, A Collectanea.* A diverse sampling of Johnson's conception of Afro-American artistic pursuits in the 1920s, the volume contained poetry, short fiction, drama, essays, translations, paintings, and drawings. Represented are the best known artists and writers of the Harlem Renaissance, including Gwendolyn Bennett, Arna Bontemps, Sterling A. Brown, Countee Cullen, Langston Hughes, Zora Neale Hurston, and Helene Johnson.

Years later Johnson had occasion in "The Negro Renaissance and Its Significance," a speech given at Howard University and later assembled by Fisk University Library into a special collection, to look back at the Harlem Renaissance. Even though more than a quarter of a century had passed since its heyday, Johnson seemed more convinced than ever of its success. He said of the 1920s: "It was a period, not only of the quivering search for freedom but of a cultural, if not a social and racial emancipation. It was unabashedly self-conscious and race conscious. But it was race consciousness with an extraordinary facet in that it had virtues that could be incorporated into the cultural bloodstream of the nation."

BIOGRAPHICAL/CRITICAL SOURCES:

BOOKS

Anderson, Jervis, *This Was Harlem: A Cultural Portrait, 1900-1950,* Farrar, Straus, 1981.
Blackwell, James E. and Morris Janowitz, editors, *Black Sociologists: Historical and Contemporary Perspectives,* University of Chicago Press, 1974.
Bone, Robert A., *The Negro Novel in America,* Yale University Press, 1958.
Bontemps, Arna, editor, *The Harlem Renaissance Remembered,* Dodd, 1972.
Clarke, John Henrik, editor, *Harlem: A Community in Transition,* Citadel, 1964.
Cruse, Harold, *The Crisis of the Negro Intellectual,* Apollo, 1968.
Current Biography, H.W. Wilson, 1946, January, 1957.
Dictionary of Literary Biography, Volume 51: *Afro-American Writers From the Harlem Renaissance to 1940,* Gale, 1987.
Embree, Edwin R., *Thirteen Against the Odds,* Viking, 1945.
Huggins, Nathan I., *Harlem Renaissance,* Oxford University Press, 1971.
Lewis, David Levering, *When Harlem Was in Vogue,* Knopf, 1981.
Locke, Alain, *The New Negro,* Atheneum, 1969.
Meier, August, *Negro Thought in America, 1880-1915,* University of Michigan Press, 1963.
Richardson, Joe M., *A History of Fisk University, 1865-1946,* University of Alabama Press, 1980.

PERIODICALS

Black World, November, 1970.
Ebony, February, 1957.
Massachusetts Review, autumn, 1979.
Negro History Bulletin, April, 1968.
Opportunity, Volume I, number 1, January, 1923; Volume I, number 2, February, 1923.
Phylon, Volume 17, fourth quarter, 1956.

OBITUARIES:

PERIODICALS

New York Times, October 28, 1956.*

—Sketch by Joanne M. Peters

* * *

JOHNSON, Edgar 1901-1972

OBITUARY NOTICE—See index for *CA* sketch: Born December 1, 1901, in Brooklyn, N.Y.; died in August, 1972. Educator, editor, and author. Johnson is best known for his monumental biographies *Charles Dickens: His Tragedy and Triumph* and *Sir Walter Scott: The Great Unknown,* the latter of which won the American Heritage biography prize in 1969. A specialist in nineteenth-century literature, Johnson taught at City College of the City University of New York for more than four decades, advancing from tutor to professor and chairman of the English department and retiring as distinguished professor emeritus in 1972. Johnson was also a visiting lecturer at a number of other universities, including Vassar College, University of Hawaii, University of Chicago, Princeton University, and Vanderbilt University. Among his other writings are the novels *Unweave a Rainbow* and *The Praying Mantis;* two anthologies, *A Treasury of Biography* and *A Treasury of*

Satire, which he edited; and critical articles and reviews contributed to magazines and newspapers.

OBITUARIES AND OTHER SOURCES:

BOOKS

The Blue Book: Leaders of the English-Speaking World, St. Martin's, 1976.
Contemporary Science Fiction Authors, Arno, 1975.
Directory of American Scholars, Volume I: *History,* 6th edition, Bowker, 1974.
Who's Who in America, 39th edition, Marquis, 1976.

PERIODICALS

New York Times, December 21, 1977.

*   *   *

JOHNSON, Georgia Douglas (Camp)   1886-1966

PERSONAL: Born September 10, 1886, in Atlanta, Ga.; died May 14, 1966, in Washington, D.C.; daughter of George and Laura (Jackson) Camp; married Henry Lincoln Johnson (a lawyer and politician) in 1903 (husband died, 1925); children: Henry Lincoln, Jr., Peter Douglas. *Education:* Attended Atlanta University, Howard University, and Oberlin College. *Politics:* Republican.

CAREER: Writer. Taught school in Alabama. Served various U.S. government agencies in Washington, D.C., including as commissioner of conciliation in Department of Labor, 1925-34.

MEMBER: League of Neighbors, League for Abolition of Capital Punishment.

AWARDS, HONORS: First prize in drama contest sponsored by *Opportunity* magazine, 1927, for *Plumes;* received honorary doctorate in literature from Atlanta University, 1965.

WRITINGS:

POETRY

The Heart of a Woman, and Other Poems, introduction by William Stanley Braithwaite, Cornhill, 1918, AMS Press, 1975.
Bronze: A Book of Verse, introduction by W. E. B. DuBois, B. J. Brimmer, 1922, AMS Press, 1975.
An Autumn Love Cycle, introduction by Alain Locke, H. Vinal, 1928, Books for Libraries Press, 1971.
Share My World: A Book of Poems, privately printed in Washington, D.C., 1962.

Poetry represented in anthologies, including *An Anthology of Revolutionary Poetry,* edited by Graham Marcus; *Black and White: An Anthology of Washington Verse,* edited by Joseph Cloyd Byars; *The Book of American Negro Poetry,* edited by James Weldon Johnson; *The Poetry of Black America,* edited by Arnold Adoff; *The Poetry of the Negro, 1746-1970,* edited by Langston Hughes and Arna Wendell Bontemps; and *Voice of the Negro, 1919,* edited by Robert T. Kerlin.

PLAYS

Blue Blood (first produced in New York City in 1927), Appleton, 1927.
Plumes: A Play in One Act (first produced in Brooklyn at Central YMCA, February 28, 1928), Samuel French, 1927.
"Frederick Douglass Leaves for Freedom," first produced in Los Angeles at the New Negro Theatre, 1940, published

in *Negro History in Thirteen Plays,* edited by Willis Richardson and May Miller, Associated (Washington, D.C.), 1935.

Also author of "William and Ellen Craft," "A Sunday Morning in the South: A One-Act Play," "Blue-Eyed Black Boy," and "Safe."

Plays represented in anthologies, including *An Anthology of American Negro Literature,* edited by Victor Francis Calverton; *Black Theatre, U.S.A.: Forty-five Plays by Black American Playwrights, 1847-1974,* edited by James V. Hatch and Ted Shine; *Fifty More Contemporary One-Act Plays,* edited by Frank Shay; and *Plays of Negro Life,* edited by Alain Locke and Montgomery Gregory.

OTHER

Also author of songs and short stories.

Contributor to periodicals, including *Crisis, Journal of Negro History, Liberator, Opportunity, Phylon, Voice of the Negro,* and *Worker's Monthly.*

WORK IN PROGRESS: Rainbow Silhouettes, a collection of short stories; *The Life and Times of Henry Lincoln Johnson,* a book about Georgia Douglas Johnson's husband; *The Torch,* a collection of works by various authors.

SIDELIGHTS: Georgia Douglas Johnson was one of the first black female poets to achieve prominence in America and is considered one of the finest writers of her time. Her four volumes of verse, published between 1918 and 1962, contain more that two hundred poems, and her poems and plays have been published in numerous anthologies of black literature. A resident of Washington, D.C., since 1909, Johnson took part in literary activities there and hosted regular meetings with Harlem Renaissance writers and other artists, including Countee Cullen, Langston Hughes, Alain Locke, May Miller, and Jean Toomer. In addition to writing, Johnson worked for U.S. government agencies and actively supported women's and minorities' rights.

Johnson's first volume of poetry, *The Heart of a Woman, and Other Poems,* contains short, introspective verses describing emotions—such as "Sympathy," "Isolation," and "Despair"—that the author felt dwell within "the heart of a woman." The poet's second collection, *Bronze,* addresses the issue of race as well as that of gender; in contrast to the subtle, placid tone of Johnson's first work, observed Winona Fletcher in *Dictionary of Literary Biography, Bronze* "gives evidence of a new strength in Johnson's feelings of protest against injustice and racism." Through her verse, Fletcher noted, Johnson "reached out to the people who had blazed the trail from slavery through Reconstruction to the modern world of segregation and racism."

An Autumn Love Cycle, Johnson's third collection of poetry, expresses mature acceptance of life's conditions instead of impetuous outrage at civil inequality. "It [reflects] more of the earlier, romantic poet" depicted in *The Heart of a Woman,* ventured Fletcher, "and less of the voice of social protest" in *Bronze.* Divided into five sections, "*An Autumn Love Cycle* focuses upon the various states of love, from enraptured initial engagement to disillusionment with the loss of love," the reviewer explained. Johnson's final collection of verse, *Share My World,* was printed privately in 1962.

In addition to her poetry, Johnson wrote several plays. Two were published in 1927: *Blue Blood* and *Plumes,* which was named best play by *Opportunity* magazine in its 1927 drama contest. Through many of her plays, Johnson expressed the moral outrage she withheld from her poetry. "A Sunday Morning in the South," "Blue-Eyed Black Boy," and "Safe," for example, protested the brutal and unreasonable lynchings of blacks by white mobs. Despite the respect the plays have gained since their publication in various anthologies, producers during Johnson's lifetime refused to stage the plays because, as Fletcher explained, "they were all aghast at [Johnson's] notion that a lynching could take place for no obvious 'good reason' and impugned the playwright for suggesting this in her drama."

In 1965 the poet and playwright accepted an honorary doctorate in literature from Atlanta University. At the time of her death the following year, Johnson left uncompleted three manuscripts: *The Torch,* a collection of works by various authors; *The Life and Times of Henry Lincoln Johnson,* about the author's husband; and *Rainbow Silhouettes,* a collection of Johnson's short stories.

BIOGRAPHICAL/CRITICAL SOURCES:

BOOKS

Dictionary of Literary Biography, Volume 51: *Afro-American Writers From the Harlem Renaissance to 1940,* Gale, 1987.

PERIODICALS

Atlanta University Bulletin, July, 1953, July, 1963.
Crisis, number 25, 1923, number 36, 1929, December, 1952.
Ebony, February, 1949.
Opportunity, December, 1923, April, 1929.*

*　　*　　*

JOHNSON, J. R.
   See JAMES, C(yril) L(ionel) R(obert)

*　　*　　*

JOHNSON, James Weldon   1871-1938

PERSONAL: Born June 17, 1871, in Jacksonville, Fla.; died following an automobile accident, June 26, 1938, in Wiscasset, Me.; buried in Brooklyn, N.Y.; son of James (a restaurant headwaiter) and Helen Louise (a musician and schoolteacher; maiden name, Dillette) Johnson; married Grace Nail, February 3, 1910. *Education:* Atlanta University, A.B., 1894, A.M., 1904; graduate study at Columbia University, c. 1902-05.

ADDRESSES: Home—Nashville, Tenn.

CAREER: Poet, novelist, songwriter, editor, historian, civil rights leader, diplomat, lawyer, and educator. Stanton Central Grammar School for Negroes, Jacksonville, Fla., teacher, later principal, 1894-1901; *Daily American* (newspaper), Jacksonville, founder and co-editor, 1895-96; admitted to the Bar of the State of Florida, 1898; private law practice, Jacksonville, 1898-1901; songwriter for the musical theater in partnership with brother, J. Rosamond Johnson, and Bob Cole, New York City, 1901-06; United States Consul to Puerto Cabello, Venezuela, 1906-09, and to Corinto, Nicaragua, 1909-13; *New York Age* (newspaper), New York City, editorial writer, 1914-24; National Association for the Advancement of Colored People (NAACP), New York City, field secretary, 1916-20, executive secretary, 1920-30; Fisk University, Nashville, Tenn., professor of creative literature and writing, 1931-38.

Elected treasurer of the Colored Republican Club, New York City, and participated in Theodore Roosevelt's presidential campaign, both in 1904; lectured on literature and black culture at numerous colleges and universities during the 1930s, including New York, Northwestern, and Yale universities, Oberlin and Swarthmore colleges, and the universities of North Carolina and Chicago. Served as director of the American Fund for Public Service and as trustee of Atlanta University.

MEMBER: American Society of Composers, Authors, and Publishers (charter member), Academy of Political Science, Ethical Society, Civic Club (New York City).

AWARDS, HONORS: Spingarn Medal from NAACP, 1925, for outstanding achievement by an American Negro; Harmon Gold Award for *God's Trombones;* Julius Rosenwald Fund grant, 1929; W.E.B. Du Bois Prize for Negro Literature, 1933; named first incumbent of Spence Chair of Creative Literature at Fisk University; honorary doctorates from Talladega College and Howard University.

WRITINGS:

The Autobiography of an Ex-Coloured Man (novel), Sherman, French, 1912, Arden Library, 1978.
(Translator) Fernando Periquet, *Goyescas; or, The Rival Lovers* (opera libretto), G. Schirmer, 1915.
Fifty Years and Other Poems, Cornhill, 1917, AMS Press, 1975.
(Editor) *The Book of American Negro Poetry,* Harcourt, 1922, revised edition (publisher unknown), 1969.
(Editor) *The Book of American Negro Spirituals,* Viking, 1925.
(Editor) *The Second Book of Negro Spirituals,* Viking, 1926.
(Editor) *The Books of American Negro Spirituals* (contains *The Book of American Negro Spirituals* and *The Second Book of Negro Spirituals*), Viking, 1940, reprinted, 1964.
God's Trombones: Seven Negro Sermons in Verse (poetry), illustrations by Aaron Douglas, Viking, 1927, Penguin, 1976.
Black Manhattan (nonfiction), Knopf, 1930, Arno, 1968.
Along This Way: The Autobiography of James Weldon Johnson, Viking, 1933, Da Capo, 1973.
Negro Americans, What Now? (nonfiction), Viking, 1934, Da Capo, 1973.
Saint Peter Relates an Incident: Selected Poems, Viking, 1935, AMS Press, 1974.
The Great Awakening, Revell, 1938.

Also author of *Selected Poems,* 1936.

Contributor of articles and poems to numerous newspapers and magazines, including the *Chicago Defender, Times-Union* (Jacksonville, Fla.), *New York Age, New York Times, Pittsburgh Courier, Savannah Tribune, The Century, The Crisis, The Nation, The Independent, Harper's, The Bookman, Forum,* and *Scholastic;* poetry represented in many anthologies; songs published by Joseph W. Stern & Co., Edward B. Marks Music Corp., and others; author of numerous pamphlets on current events published by the NAACP, *The Nation, The Century,* and others.

SIDELIGHTS: James Weldon Johnson distinguished himself equally as a man of letters and as a civil rights leader in the early decades of the twentieth century. A talented poet and novelist, Johnson is credited with bringing a new standard of artistry and realism to black literature in such works as *The Autobiography of an Ex-Coloured Man* and *God's Trombones.* His pioneering studies of black poetry, music, and theater in the 1920s also helped introduce many white Americans to the genuine Afro-American creative spirit, hithterto known mainly through the distortions of the minstrel show and dialect poetry. Meanwhile, as head of the National Association for the Advancement of Colored People (NAACP) during the 1920s, Johnson led determined civil rights campaigns in an effort to remove the legal, political, and social obstacles hindering black achievement. Johnson's multi-faceted career, which also included stints as a diplomat in Latin America and a successful Tin Pan Alley songwriter, testified to his intellectual breadth, self-confidence, and deep-rooted belief that the future held unlimited new opportunities for black Americans.

Johnson was born in Jacksonville, Florida, in 1871, and his upbringing in this relatively tolerant Southern town may help explain his later political moderation. Both his father, a resort hotel headwaiter, and his mother, a schoolteacher, had lived in the North and had never been enslaved, and James and his brother John Rosamond grew up in broadly cultured and economically secure surroundings that were unusual among Southern black families at the time. Johnson's mother stimulated his early interests in reading, drawing, and music, and he attended the segregated Stanton School, where she taught, until the eighth grade. Since high schools were closed to blacks in Jacksonville, Johnson left home to attend both secondary school and college at Atlanta University, where he took his bachelor's degree in 1894. It was during his college years, as Johnson recalled in his autobiography, *Along This Way,* that he first became aware of the depth of the racial problem in the United States. Race questions were vigorously debated on campus, and Johnson's experience teaching black schoolchildren in a poor district of rural Georgia during two summers deeply impressed him with the need to improve the lives of his people. The struggles and aspirations of American blacks form a central theme in the thirty or so poems that Johnson wrote as a student.

Returning to Jacksonville in 1894, Johnson was appointed a teacher and principal of the Stanton School and managed to expand the curriculum to include high school-level classes. He also became an active local spokesman on black social and political issues and in 1895 founded the *Daily American,* the first black-oriented daily newspaper in the United States. During its brief life, the newspaper became a voice against racial injustice and served to encourage black advancement through individual effort—a "self-help" position that echoed the more conservative civil rights leadership of the day. Although the newspaper folded for lack of readership the following year, Johnson's ambitious publishing effort attracted the attention of such prominent black leaders as W.E.B. Du Bois and Booker T. Washington.

Meanwhile Johnson read law with the help of a local white lawyer, and in 1898 he became the first black lawyer admitted to the Florida Bar since Reconstruction. Johnson practiced law in Jacksonville for several years in partnership with a former Atlanta University classmate while continuing to serve as the Stanton School's principal. He also continued to write poetry and discovered his gift for songwriting in collaboration with his brother Rosamond, a talented composer. Among other songs in a spiritual-influenced popular idiom, Johnson penned the lyrics to "Lift Every Voice and Sing," a tribute to black endurance, hope, and religious faith that was later adopted by the NAACP and dubbed "the Negro National Anthem."

In 1901, bored by Jacksonville's provincialism and disturbed by mounting incidents of racism there, the Johnson brothers set out for New York City to seek their fortune writing songs for the musical theater. In partnership with Bob Cole they secured a publishing contract paying a monthly stipend and over the next five years composed some two hundred songs for Broadway and other musical productions, including such hit numbers as "Under the Bamboo Tree," "The Old Flag Never Touched the Ground," and "Didn't He Ramble." The trio, who soon became known as "Those Ebony Offenbachs," avoided writing for racially exploitative minstrel shows but often found themselves obliged to present simplified and stereotyped images of rural black life to suit white audiences. But the Johnsons and Cole also produced works like the six-song suite titled "The Evolution of Ragtime" that helped document and expose important black musical idioms.

During this time James Weldon Johnson also studied creative literature formally for three years at Columbia University and became active in Republican party politics. He served as treasurer of New York's Colored Republican Club in 1904 and helped write two songs for Republican candidate Theodore Roosevelt's successful presidential campaign that year. When the national black civil rights leadership split into conservative and radical factions—headed by Booker T. Washington and W.E.B. Du Bois, respectively—Johnson backed Washington, who in turn played an important role in getting the Roosevelt Administration to appoint Johnson as United States consul in Puerto Cabello, Venezuela, in 1906. With few official duties, Johnson was able to devote much of his time in that sleepy tropical port to writing poetry, including the acclaimed sonnet "Mother Night" that was published in *The Century* magazine and later included in Johnson's verse collection *Fifty Years and Other Poems.*

The consul also completed his only novel, *The Autobiography of an Ex-Coloured Man,* during his three years in Venezuela. Published anonymously in 1912, the novel attracted little attention until it was reissued under Johnson's own name more than a decade later. Even then, the book tended to draw more comment as a sociological document than as a work of fiction. (So many readers believed it to be truly autobiographical that Johnson eventually wrote his real life story, *Along This Way,* to avoid confusion.)

The Autobiography of an Ex-Coloured Man bears a superficial resemblance to other "tragic mulatto" narratives of the day that depicted, often in sentimental terms, the travails of mixed-race protagonists unable to fit into either racial culture. In Johnson's novel, the unnamed narrator is light-skinned enough to pass for white but identifies emotionally with his beloved mother's black race. In his youth, he aspires to become a great black American musical composer, but he fearfully renounces that ambition after watching a mob of whites set fire to a black man in the rural South. Though horrified and repulsed by the whites' attack, the narrator feels an even deeper shame and humiliation for himself as a black man and he subsequently allows circumstances to guide him along the easier path of "passing" as a middle-class white businessman. The protagonist finds success in this role but ends up a failure in his own terms, plagued with ambivalence over his true identity, moral values, and emotional loyalties.

Early criticism of *The Autobiography of an Ex-Coloured Man* tended to emphasize Johnson's frank and realistic look at black society and race relations more than his skill as a novelist. Carl Van Vechten, for example, found the novel "an invaluable source-book for the study of Negro psychology," and the *New Republic*'s Edmund Wilson judged the book "an excellent, honest piece of work" as "a human and sociological document'' but flawed as a work of literature. In the 1950s and 1960s, however, something of a critical reappraisal of the *Autobiography* occurred that led to a new appreciation of Johnson as a crafter of fiction. In his critical study *The Negro Novel in America,* Robert A. Bone called Johnson "the only true artist among the early Negro novelists," who succeeded in "subordinating racial protest to artistic considerations." Johnson's subtle theme of moral cowardice, Bone noted, set the novel far above "the typical propaganda tract of the day." In a 1971 essay, Robert E. Fleming drew attention to Johnson's deliberate use of an unreliable narrative voice, remarking that *The Autobiography of an Ex-Coloured Man* "is not so much a panoramic novel presenting race relations throughout America as it is a deeply ironic character study of a marginal man." Johnson's psychological depth and concern with aesthetic coherence anticipated the great black literary movement of the 1920s known as the Harlem School, according to these and other critics.

In 1909, before the *Autobiography* had been published, Johnson was promoted to the consular post in Corinto, Nicaragua, a position that proved considerably more demanding than his Venezuelan job and left him little time for writing. His three-year term of service occurred during a period of intense political turmoil in Nicaragua, which culminated in the landing of U.S. troops at Corinto in 1912. In 1913, seeing little future for himself under President Woodrow Wilson's Democratic administration, Johnson resigned from the foreign service and returned to New York to become an editorial writer for the *New York Age,* the city's oldest and most distinguished black newspaper. The articles Johnson produced over the next ten years tended toward the conservative side, combining a strong sense of racial pride with a deep-rooted belief that blacks could individually improve their lot by means of self-education and hard work even before discriminatory barriers had been removed. This stress on individual effort and economic independence put Johnson closer to the position of black educator Booker T. Washington than that of the politically militant writer and scholar W.E.B. Du Bois in the great leadership dispute on how to improve the status of black Americans, but Johnson generally avoided criticizing either man by name and managed to maintain good relations with both leaders.

During this period Johnson continued to indulge his literary love. Having mastered the Spanish language in the diplomatic service, he translated Fernando Periquet's grand opera *Goyescas* into English and the Metropolitan Opera produced his libretto version in 1915. In 1917, Johnson published his first verse collection, *Fifty Years and Other Poems,* a selection from twenty years' work that drew mixed reviews. "Fifty Years," a sonorous poem commemorating the half-century since the Emancipation Proclamation, was generally singled out for praise, but critics differed on the merits of Johnson's dialect verse written after the manner of the great black dialect poet Paul Laurence Dunbar. The dialect style was highly popular at the time, but has since been criticized for pandering to sentimental white stereotypes of rural black life. In addition to his dialect work, Johnson's collection also included such powerful racial protest poems as "Brothers," about a lynching, and delicate lyrical verse on non-racial topics in the traditional style.

In 1916, at the urging of W.E.B. Du Bois, Johnson accepted the newly created post of national field secretary for the NAACP, which had grown to become the country's premier black rights advocacy and defense organization since its founding in 1910. Johnson's duties included investigating racial incidents and

organizing new NAACP branches around the country, and he succeeded in significantly raising the organization's visibility and membership through the years following World War I. In 1917, Johnson organized and led a well-publicized silent march through the streets of New York City to protest lynchings, and his on-site investigation of abuses committed by American marines against black citizens of Haiti during the U.S. occupation of that Caribbean nation in 1920 captured healines and helped launch a congressional probe into the matter. Johnson's in-depth report, which was published by the *Nation* magazine in a four-part series titled "Self-Determining Haiti," also had an impact on the presidential race that year, helping to shift public sentiment from the interventionist policies associated with the Wilson Democrats toward the more isolationist position of the Republican victor, Warren Harding.

Johnson's successes as field secretary led to his appointment as NAACP executive secretary in 1920, a position he was to hold for the next ten years. This decade marked a critical turning point for the black rights movement as the NAACP and other civil rights organizations sought to defend and expand the social and economic gains blacks had achieved during the war years, when large numbers of blacks migrated to the northern cities and found industrial and manufacturing jobs. These black gains triggered a racist backlash in the early years of the decade that found virulent expression in a sharp rise in lynchings and the rapid growth of the white supremacist Ku Klux Klan terror organization in the North as well as the South. Despite this violent reaction, Johnson was credited with substantially increasing the NAACP's membership strength and political influence during this period, although his strenuous efforts to get a federal anti-lynching bill passed proved unsuccessful.

Johnson's personal politics also underwent change during the postwar years of heightened black expectations. Disappointed with the neglectful minority rights policies of Republican presidents Harding and Calvin Coolidge, Johnson broke with the Republican party in the early 1920s and briefly supported Robert LaFollette's Progressive party. LaFollette also lost the NAACP leader's backing, however, when he refused to include black demands in the Progressives' 1924 campaign platform. Though frustrated in his political objectives, Johnson opposed Marcus Garvey's separatist "Back to Africa" movement and instead urged the new black communities in the northern cities to use their potentially powerful voting strength to force racial concessions from the country's political establishment.

Even with the heavy demands of his NAACP office, the 1920s were a period of great literary productivity for Johnson. He earned critical acclaim in 1922 for editing a seminal collection of black verse, titled *The Book of American Negro Poetry.* Johnson's critical introduction to this volume provided new insights into an often ignored or denigrated genre and is now considered a classic analysis of early black contributions to American literature. Johnson went on to compile and interpret outstanding examples of the black religious song form known as the spiritual in his pioneering *The Book of American Negro Spirituals* and *The Second Book of Negro Spirituals.* These renditions of black voices formed the background for *God's Trombones,* a set of verse versions of rural black folk sermons that many critics regard as Johnson's finest poetic work. Based on the poet's recollections of the fiery preachers he had heard while growing up in Florida and Georgia, Johnson's seven sermon-poems about life and death and good and evil were deemed a triumph in overcoming the thematic and technical limitations of the dialect style while capturing, according to critics, a full resonant timbre. In *The Book of American Negro Poetry*, Johnson had compared the traditional Dunbar-style dialect verse to an organ having only two stops, one of humor and one of pathos, and he sought with *God's Trombones* to create a more flexible and dignified medium for expressing the black religious spirit. Casting out rhyme and the dialect style's buffoonish misspellings and mispronunciations, Johnson's clear and simple verses succeeded in rendering the musical rhythms, word structure, and vocabulary of the unschooled black orator in standard English. Critics also credited the poet with capturing the oratorical tricks and flourishes that a skilled preacher would use to sway his congregation, including hyperbole, repetition, abrupt mood juxtapositions, an expert sense of timing, and the ability to translate biblical imagery into the colorful, concrete terms of everyday life. "The sensitive reader cannot fail to hear the rantings of the fire-and-brimstone preacher; the extremely sensitive reader may even hear the unwritten 'Amens' of the congregation," declared Eugenia W. Collier in a 1960 essay for *Phylon*.

Johnson's efforts to preserve and win recognition for black cultural traditions drew praise from such prominent literary figures as H. L. Mencken and Mark Van Doren and contributed to the spirit of racial pride and self-confidence that marked the efflorescence of black music, art, and literature in the 1920s known as the Harlem Renaissance. This period of intense creative innovation forms the central subject of *Black Manhattan*, Johnson's informal survey of black contributions to New York's cultural life beginning as far back as the seventeenth century. The critically well-received volume focuses especially on blacks in the theater but also surveys the development of the ragtime and jazz musical idioms and discusses the earthy writings of Harlem Renaissance poets Langston Hughes, Countee Cullen, and Claude McKay. "*Black Manhattan* is a document of the 1920's—a celebration, with reservations, of both the artistic renaissance of the era and the dream of a black metropolis," noted critic Allan H. Spear in his preface to the 1968 edition of Johnson's book.

In December 1930, fatigued by the demands of his job and wanting more time to write, Johnson resigned from the NAACP and accepted a part-time teaching post in creative literature at Fisk University in Nashville, Tennessee. In 1933, he published his much-admired autobiography *Along This Way,* which discusses his personal career in the context of the larger social, political, and cultural movements of the times. Johnson remained active in the civil rights movement while teaching at Fisk, and in 1934 he published a book-length argument in favor of racial integration titled *Negro Americans, What Now?* The civil rights struggle also figures in the title poem of Johnson's last major verse collection, *Saint Peter Relates an Incident: Selected Poems.* Inspired by an outrageous act of public discrimination by the federal government against the mothers of black soldiers killed in action, Johnson's satirical narrative poem describes a gathering of veterans' groups to witness the Resurrection Day opening of the Tomb of the Unknown Soldier. When this famous war casualty is finally revealed, he turns out to be black, a circumstance that provokes bewilderment and consternation among the assembled patriots. Despite this original conceit, the poem is generally regarded as one of Johnson's lesser efforts, hampered by structural flaws and somewhat bland writing.

Johnson died tragically in June 1938 after a train struck the car he was riding in at an unguarded rail crossing in Wiscasset, Maine. The poet and civil rights leader was widely eulogized

and more than two thousand mourners attended his Harlem funeral. Known throughout his career as a generous and invariably courteous man, Johnson once summed up his personal credo as a black American in a pamphlet published by the NAACP: "I will not allow one prejudiced person or one million or one hundred million to blight my life. I will not let prejudice or any of its attendant humiliations and injustices bear me down to spiritual defeat. My inner life is mine, and I shall defend and maintain its integrity against all the powers of hell." Johnson was buried in Brooklyn's Greenwood Cemetery dressed in his favorite lounging robe and holding a copy of *God's Trombones* in his hand.

MEDIA ADAPTATIONS:

"God's Trombones" (sound recording with biographical notes by Walter White, and texts of the poems), read by Bryce Bond, music by William Martin, Folkways Records, 1965.

"Reading Poetry: The Creation" (motion picture with study guide), read by Raymond St. Jacques and Margaret O'Brien, Oxford Films, 1972.

"James Weldon Johnson" (motion picture), includes an adaptation of "The Creation" read by Raymond St. Jacques, Oxford Films, 1972.

BIOGRAPHICAL/CRITICAL SOURCES:

BOOKS

Bone, Robert A., *The Negro Novel in America,* Yale University Press, 1958.

Fleming, Robert E., *James Weldon Johnson and Arna Wendell Bontemps: A Reference Guide,* G. K. Hall, 1978.

Johnson, James Weldon, *Along This Way: The Autobiography of James Weldon Johnson,* Viking, 1933, Da Capo, 1973.

Levy, Eugene, *James Weldon Johnson: Black Leader, Black Voice,* Chicago University Press, 1973.

Twentieth-Century Literary Criticism, Volume 19, Gale, 1986.

Wagner, Jean, *Les Poetes negres des Etats Unis,* Librairie Istra, 1962, translation by Kenneth Doublas published as *Black Poets of the United States: From Paul Laurence Dunbar to Langston Hughes,* University of Illinois Press, 1973.

PERIODICALS

American Literature, March, 1971.
Crisis, June, 1971.
Journal of Popular Culture, Spring, 1968.
Nation, July 2, 1938.
New Republic, February 1, 1928, February 21, 1934.
Newsweek, July 4, 1938.
Phylon, December, 1960, Winter, 1971.
Time, July 4, 1938.*

—*Sketch by Curtis Skinner*

*   *   *

JOHNSON, Joyce 1935-
(Joyce Glassman)

BRIEF ENTRY: Born September 27, 1935, in New York, N.Y. American editor and author. A contributing editor at *Vanity Fair* magazine beginning in 1987, Johnson has worked since 1965 for a number of publishing houses in New York City, including Dial Press, McGraw-Hill, and Atlantic Monthly Press. During her career she has edited numerous books, some by such well-known authors as LeRoi Jones, Abby Hoffman, and Ann Moody. In 1983 Johnson's critically acclaimed *Minor*

Characters (Houghton) was published and won the National Book Critics Circle Award in the biography/autobiography category for that year. A candid but unromanticized memoir of her involvement with prominent members of the Beat Generation during the late 1950s, the book chronicles Johnson's love affair with novelist Jack Kerouac and touches upon the lives of poet Allen Ginsberg, fiction writer William Burroughs, and various Greenwich Village literati. Among her other writings are three novels, *Bad Connections* (Putnam, 1978), *In the Night Cafe* (Dutton, 1988), and *Come and Join the Dance* (Atheneum, 1962)—which was written under the name Joyce Glassman. Johnson also wrote "The Children's Wing," a short story for which she shared the 1987 O. Henry Award. *Addresses: Home*—595 West End Ave., New York, N.Y. 10024. *Office*—*Vanity Fair*, 350 Madison Ave., New York, N.Y. 10024. *Agent*—Berenice Hoffman Literary Agency, 215 West 75th St., New York, N.Y. 10023.

BIOGRAPHICAL/CRITICAL SOURCES:

BOOKS

Dictionary of Literary Biography, Volume 16: *The Beats: Literary Bohemians in Postwar America*, Gale, 1983.
Who's Who in America, 44th edition, Marquis, 1986.

PERIODICALS

Harper's, August, 1978.
Los Angeles Times, January 31, 1983.
New York Times Book Review, January 16, 1983.
Publishers Weekly, January 14, 1983.
Voice Literary Supplement, April, 1983.

*   *   *

JOHNSON, Nancy E(dith)   1941-

PERSONAL: Born June 9, 1941, in Washington, D.C.; stepdaughter of Guy A. (a historian and diplomat) and daughter of Freda J. (a housewife) Lee. *Education:* Oberlin College, A.B., 1963; Oxford University, B.A., 1967, M.A. and D.Phil., both 1971.

ADDRESSES: Home—Washington, D.C. *Office*—U.S. Department of State, Washington, D.C. 20520.

CAREER: University of Reading, Reading, England, research fellow, 1974-77; U.S. Department of State, Washington, D.C., contract historian at Office of the Historian, 1979; U.S. Environmental Protection Agency, Washington, D.C., writer and editor, 1980-82; U.S. State Department, foreign service officer, 1982—.

WRITINGS:

(Editor) *Diary of Gathorne Hardy, Later Lord Cranbrook, 1866-1892: Political Selections*, Oxford University Press, 1981.

SIDELIGHTS: Nancy E. Johnson told *CA:* "I became a foreign service officer when I could not find a permanent teaching job; happily, the foreign service was always the 'other thing' I wanted to do. Now my pen is entirely at Uncle Sam's disposal.

"I am in a two-year program learning Arabic prior to serving in the Middle East."

*   *   *

JOHNSTON, Wayne   1958-

PERSONAL: Born May 22, 1958, in St. John's, Newfound-land, Canada; son of Arthur Reginald (a civil servant) and Genevieve (a secretary; maiden name, Everard) Johnston; married Rosemarie Patricia Langhout (a professor of history). *Education:* Memorial University of Newfoundland, B.A., 1978; University of New Brunswick, M.A., 1984.

ADDRESSES: Home—1A Howley Ave., St. John's, Newfoundland, Canada A1C 2T1.

CAREER: St. John's Daily News, St. John's, Newfoundland, reporter, 1979-81; free-lance writer, 1981—.

AWARDS, HONORS: W. H. Smith/Books in Canada First Novel Award, 1985, for *The Story of Bobby O'Malley*.

WRITINGS:

The Story of Bobby O'Malley (novel), Oberon, 1985.
The Time of Their Lives (novel), Oberon, 1987.

Contributor of poems and stories to magazines. Poetry editor of *Fiddlehead*, 1984-86.

WORK IN PROGRESS: A novel dealing with contemporary Newfoundland.

SIDELIGHTS: Wayne Johnston wrote: "I have greatly admired the Russian novelists and may have been influenced by them. I believe that the best writing in Canada has come from the 'regions,' not from the cities."

Set in the author's native Newfoundland, *The Story of Bobby O'Malley* is the fictional reminiscence of a boy who was raised in a community near St. John's. "Johnston's hero," wrote William French in the *Globe and Mail*, "must overcome not only the pains of growing up, but the added stresses of growing up in a closed society, away from the mainland and the mainstream." Bobby's father is an eccentric television weatherman, and his mother is an intensely devout Catholic. The humor that the author injects into his characterizations endears Bobby and his family to the reader and allows, according to French, "a glimpse of a fairly hermetic society at a time of transition, [which] enables us to see Newfoundlanders in a new way." The reviewer considered Johnston's novel to be "an honorable addition" to the province's already distinguished literary tradition.

Also taking place in an isolated Newfoundland village outside of St. John's, Johnston's second novel, *The Time of Their Lives*, is much bleaker than the comic *The Story of Bobby O'Malley*. In a review of *The Time of Their Lives* for the *Globe and Mail*, French asserted that the tale of three generations of a Newfoundland family "is claustrophobic, but Johnston clearly intended it to be. He wants us to share the suffocatingly small universe of his characters, and he succeeds too well; reading it isn't a comfortable experience." Ever-present tension among kin is exacerbated when a son who moved to Ontario returns to his hometown with a wife and children. The relatives reject them, prejudiced against the wife because she is not a Newfoundland native. Unable to make peace with his father, the husband and his family return to Ontario. "Despite our resistance to the characters' unappealing natures and unfortunate circumstances," French ventured, "Johnson portrays these characters with great skill, and the story grips us with its power."

BIOGRAPHICAL/CRITICAL SOURCES:

PERIODICALS

Globe and Mail (Toronto), February 15, 1986, January 9, 1988.

JONAS, Norman N. 1931-1988

OBITUARY NOTICE: Born in 1931 in New York, N.Y.; died after a heart attack, March 27, 1988, in Brooklyn, N.Y. Editor and journalist. Economics editor of *Business Week* beginning in 1985 and its former Washington, D.C., senior economics correspondent for twelve years, Jonas began his journalism career as a copy editor for the *Wall Street Journal.* He subsequently worked as a reporter for the *New York Journal-American,* and as a copy editor, first for the *New York Times,* and then for *Business Week,* beginning in 1966. He became contributing editor three years later, then associate economics editor, and in 1973 was named the magazine's senior economics correspondent.

OBITUARIES AND OTHER SOURCES:

PERIODICALS

Washington Post, March 31, 1988.

* * *

JONES, Annabel
See LEWIS, Mary (Christianna)

* * *

JONES, Cheslyn Peter Montague 1918-1987(?)

OBITUARY NOTICE: Born July 4, 1918; died c. 1987. Clergyman, educator, editor, and author. Ordained a priest in 1942, Jones was curate of two parishes before entering the monastic life at Nashdom Abbey in England. He left the monastery to be chaplain at Wells Theological College and subsequently at Christ Church Cathedral in Oxford, and then became a librarian at Pusey House in Oxford. From 1956 until 1969 he served as principal of Chichester Theological College and as chancellor of its cathedral. He was eventually named principal of Pusey House, where he remained from 1971 until 1981, when he resigned to become a parish priest in Northamptonshire. In addition, he was affiliated with the faculties of Cambridge University and the University of Sheffield, edited numerous collections on theology, including *A Manual for Holy Week,* and was contributing editor of such works as *For Better For Worse, The Study of Liturgy,* and *The Study of Spirituality.*

OBITUARIES AND OTHER SOURCES:

BOOKS

Who's Who, 140th edition, St. Martin's, 1988.

PERIODICALS

Times (London), November 4, 1987.

* * *

JONES, David Richard 1942-

PERSONAL: Born March 20, 1942, in Charles City, Iowa; son of William J. (a banker) and Marjorie B. (Graaf) Jones; married Susan Jane Fry (a teacher), 1966; children: William Mortin, Samuel C. *Education:* Northwestern University, B.A. (magna cum laude), 1964; Princeton University, M.A., 1966, Ph.D., 1968.

ADDRESSES: Home—1611 Sunset Garden Rd. S.W., Albuquerque, N.M. 87105. *Office*—Department of English, University of New Mexico, Albuquerque, N.M. 87131.

CAREER: University of Chicago, Chicago, Ill., assistant professor of English and humanities, 1968-71; University of New Mexico, Albuquerque, associate professor of English, 1971—. Artistic director of Vortex Theatre, Albuquerque, 1976-78; literary manager of New Mexico Repertory Theatre, 1985-87.

MEMBER: Literary Managers and Dramaturges of America, Phi Beta Kappa.

AWARDS, HONORS: Woodrow Wilson fellow, 1964-65, 1967-68.

WRITINGS:

Great Directors at Work: Stanislavsky, Brecht, Kazan, Brook, University of California Press, 1986.
(Editor) *New Mexico Plays,* University of New Mexico Press, in press.

WORK IN PROGRESS: The Theatre of David Mamet; American Theatre in the 1920s.

BIOGRAPHICAL/CRITICAL SOURCES:

PERIODICALS

New York Times Book Review, July 27, 1986.
Times Literary Supplement, March 20, 1987.

* * *

JONES, Don 1924-

PERSONAL: Born August 21, 1924, in Norwood, Ohio; son of Don Edgar (a tool and die maker) and Loretta G. (a housewife; maiden name, Kendall) Jones; married Mickey Venora, 1950 (divorced, 1975); married Margriet Spier (a travel agent), February 14, 1984; children: (first marriage) Douglas. *Education:* Attended University of Toledo, 1946-49.

ADDRESSES: Home—5700 Etiwanda Ave., No. 217, Tarzana, Calif. 91356. *Office*—11000 Wilshire Blvd., No. C-200, Los Angeles, Calif. 90024.

CAREER: United Press, Los Angeles, Calif., journalist, 1950-55; National Broadcasting Co., Burbank, Calif., publicist, 1955-63; U.S. Information Agency, Washington, D.C., foreign service officer, 1963—. *Military service:* U.S. Marine Corps, 1942-45; served in Pacific theater; received Purple Heart.

MEMBER: Marine Corps Combat Correspondents Association.

AWARDS, HONORS: U.S. Information Agency Superior Service Award, 1968, Meritorious Service Award, 1974.

WRITINGS:

Oba, the Last Samurai (nonfiction), Presidio Press, 1986, translation by A. Nakamura from original English manuscript published as *Tapotchau,* [Japan], 1982.

Author of screenplay based on the book *Oba.* Contributor to magazines and newspapers.

WORK IN PROGRESS: Audio and video lesson in basic spoken Japanese.

SIDELIGHTS: Don Jones told *CA:* "During World War II, I was a Marine corporal serving as a battalion-level interpreter on the island of Saipan. The standing orders of my unit, the Second Marine Division, were to capture or eliminate Captain Sakae Oba, a Japanese soldier who organized and led a resistance force that continued to fight a guerilla-type warfare after American forces had taken the island. Between the island's capture in July, 1944, and the war's end, I engaged in several firefights with the wily captain and his 350-person (there were women, too) band, and I became intrigued by the resourcefulness of the man. Oba actually, if not officially, ended World War II when he surrendered himself and his remaining 36 men on December 1, 1945—the last organized unit of Japanese resistance to lay down its arms.

"At one point, in early 1945, I seriously considered a plan to leave a note in the jungle saying I wanted to meet with Captain Oba and promising to be at that spot the next day, unarmed. Twenty years later I asked Oba what would have happened if I had shown up alone with no weapon. 'My men probably would have killed you,' he replied. So much for valor.

"In 1965, while posted to Japan, I obtained Oba's telephone number. When I dialed, a man answered. 'Is this Captain Oba?' I asked. There was a long silence—no one had called him 'captain' in twenty years—then he replied with a question in his voice, 'Yes?'

"'You don't know me, Captain, but I know a lot about you,' I said, then proceeded to tell him of our mutual experiences. Two days later he and his wife traveled from their home near Nagoya to ours in Niigata and spent a four-day weekend with us.

"His story was one I carried within me since 1945. But it wasn't until 1979 that I decided to write it.

"All nations except Japan have war heroes. 'Put the war behind you,' General MacArthur told the Japanese in 1945. And they did. As I discovered through questioning some 75 young Japanese, there is no recognition or appreciation of the sacrifices made by their fathers, grandfathers, and uncles during World War II. To young people today, the war almost is something that didn't happen. Japan, I decided, had been denied a legacy: the right to at least be aware of its heroes.

"And since I knew of one honest-to-God hero, I decided to write a book about him, hoping it would prompt Japanese writers to produce stories of others. This way, I reasoned, the total information accumulated in these stories could fill in the still-blank pages of Japanese history books.

"During the first forty-five days after the book's publication in Japan, in 1982, we sold an encouraging 45,000 copies through such promotional activities as taking Oba and 19 of his final 36 men back to Saipan for three days . . . with 26 media people. It was an emotional trip. Sales of the English version of the book have been moderate. Oba and his wife made their first trip to the United States in 1986 to accompany me on a nationwide promotion tour, then returned to Japan where Oba is a retired city councilman in the town of Gamagori, Aichi Prefecture."

BIOGRAPHICAL/CRITICAL SOURCES:

PERIODICALS

Chicago Tribune, September 15, 1986.

*   *   *

JONES, Tad
    See JONES, Thaddeus B.

JONES, Thaddeus B.   1952-
    (Tad Jones)

PERSONAL: Born September 19, 1952, in New Orleans, La.; son of C. Palmer (an engineer) and Phyllis (a housewife; maiden name, Bunel) Jones. *Education:* Loyola University, New Orleans, La., B.A., 1975; attended Belmont College, 1977-79. *Religion:* Roman Catholic.

ADDRESSES: Home—4124 Prytania St., New Orleans, La. 70115.

CAREER: WWOM-FM Radio, New Orleans, La., disc jockey, 1971; WLDC-Radio, New Orleans, music director, 1972-74; WWL-AM Radio, New Orleans, producer of the "Bob Ruby Show," 1975-77; television production assistant and historical consultant, 1979-83; McGlinchey, Stafford, Mintz, Cellini & Lang, New Orleans, paralegal, 1983-85; Herman, Herman, Katz & Cotlar, New Orleans, paralegal, 1985-87; writer, 1987—. Instructor at University of New Orleans, 1985-87. WWOZ-FM Radio, member of volunteer staff, 1980-86, member of programming committee, 1985-86; editor of record album *New Orleans Blues,* Volume I, released by Delmark Records in 1982; producer of music concerts. Member of board of directors of Summa 2-4-U Corp.

MEMBER: New Orleans Paralegal Association.

AWARDS, HONORS: Spotlight Award, and grants from Jean Lafitte National Park and National Endowment for the Humanities, all 1981.

WRITINGS:

UNDER NAME TAD JONES

(Contributor) Richard Wootton, editor, *Honky Tonkin': A Guide to Music U.S.A.,* BBC Publications, 1977.
(Author of appendix) John Broven, *Walkin' to New Orleans,* Pelican Press, 1978.
(With Jason Berry and Jonathan Foose) *Up From the Cradle of Jazz: New Orleans Music Since World War II,* University of Georgia Press, 1986.

Contributor to magazines in the United States and abroad, including *Blues Unlimited, Crazy Music, Golden Memories, Ragtimes, Blues,* and *Wavelength.* Editor of *Living Blues,* 1977-82.

BIOGRAPHICAL/CRITICAL SOURCES:

PERIODICALS

Los Angeles Times Book Review, December 21, 1986.
New Orleans Times-Picayune, September 6, 1985.

*   *   *

JORGENSON, Lloyd P.   1912-

PERSONAL: Born May 27, 1912, in Valley City, N.D.; son of Olof M. (a clergyman) and Marie (a housewife; maiden name, Lorentzen) Jorgenson; married Virginia Olson (a housewife), April 5, 1942; children: Ann M. Jorgenson Denney, Charles M. *Education:* Sioux Falls College, B.A., 1934; University of Wisconsin—Madison, M.A., 1946, Ph.D., 1949. *Religion:* Protestant.

ADDRESSES: Home—304 East Burnam Rd., Columbia, Mo. 65203. *Office*—403 South Sixth St., Columbia, Mo. 65211.

CAREER: High school history teacher at public schools in Forest River, N.D., 1934-37, and Madison, Wis., 1937-52;

University of Oklahoma, Norman, associate professor of educational history, 1952-57; University of Missouri—Columbia, professor of educational history, 1957-80, co-founder and co-director of semester abroad program, 1963-80. *Military service:* U.S. Army, Field Artillery, 1942-46; served in European theater; became captain; received Bronze Star.

MEMBER: American Association of University Professors (chapter president, 1970-71), History of Education Society (president, 1960-61), Comparative Education Society.

WRITINGS:

The Founding of Public Education in Wisconsin, State Historical Society of Wisconsin, 1956.
The State and the Non-Public School, 1825-1925, University of Missouri Press, 1987.

Contributor to history and education journals.

SIDELIGHTS: Lloyd P. Jorgenson told *CA:* "Hostility to non-public schools was an integral part of the outlook of the leaders of the Common School Movement (1830-1860). On further examination, it becomes clear that this hostility was rooted in anti-Catholicism. Spurred on by the agitations of the Know-Nothings, prohibition of public financial aid to nonpublic schools and the inclusion of religious observances in the public schools were firmly established policies in most states by 1860. The former became an enduring policy, much later to be elevated to constitutional status by the U.S. Supreme Court. The latter policy began to disintegrate later in the century, giving way to a secularism abhorrent to many Protestants and Catholics alike. The study reveals the difficulties of maintaining the balance between majority rule and minority rights."

*   *   *

JUGENHEIMER, Donald W(ayne) 1943-

PERSONAL: Surname is pronounced "*You*-gen-high-mer"; born September 22, 1943, in Manhattan, Kan.; son of Robert William (a professor) and Mabel Clara (a housewife; maiden name, Hobert) Jugenheimer; married Bonnie Jeanne Scamehorn, August 30, 1970 (died, 1983); married Kaleen Brown (a marketing executive), July 25, 1987; children: (first marriage) Beth Carrie. *Education:* University of Illinois at Urbana-Champaign, B.S., 1965, M.S., 1968, Ph.D., 1972. *Religion:* Presbyterian.

ADDRESSES: Home—59 Flaming Arrow Rd., Mahwah, N.J. 07430. *Office*— Department of Communications, Fairleigh Dickinson University, Teaneck, N.J. 07666.

CAREER: Fillman and Associates, Champaign, Ill., advertising copywriter, 1963-64; Leo Burnett Co., Chicago, Ill., media buyer, 1965-66; Fillman and Associates, advertising copywriter, 1966; University of Kansas, Lawrence, assistant professor, 1971-75, associate professor, 1975-80, professor of

journalism, 1980-85, chairman of advertising, 1974-78; Louisiana State University, Baton Rouge, Manship Professor of Journalism, 1985-87; Fairleigh Dickinson University, Teaneck, N.J., professor of journalism and chairman of department of communications, 1987—. *Journal of Advertising*, subscription manager, 1971-74, business manager, 1974-79. President of Lawrence School-Community Relations Council, 1974-75. Consultant to U.S. Army and Louisiana Dairy Promotion Board. *Military service:* U.S. Air Force, 1961-67; became captain.

MEMBER: American Academy of Advertising (president, 1985-87), Association for Education in Journalism (head of Advertising Division, 1977-78), American Association of University Professors, Kappa Tau Alpha, Alpha Delta Sigma.

AWARDS, HONORS: Kellogg national fellow of W. K. Kellogg Foundation, 1984-87.

WRITINGS:

(With Arnold Barban and Peter B. Turk) *Advertising Media Sourcebook and Workbook*, NTC Business Books, 1975, 3rd edition, 1988.
(With Ronald D. Michman) *Strategic Advertising Decisions*, Grid Publishing, 1976.
(With Gordon E. White) *Basic Advertising*, Southwestern Publishing, 1979, 2nd edition, 1988.
(With Turk) *Advertising Media*, Wiley, 1980.
(With Alan D. Fletcher) *Problems and Practices in Advertising Research: Readings and Workbook*, Wiley, 1982.
(Editor) *Proceedings of the Convention of the American Academy of Advertising*, American Academy of Advertising, 1983.

Contributor to scholarly journals. Member of board of editors of *Journal of Advertising*, 1985—.

WORK IN PROGRESS: Intimidation: How to Use It and How to Escape It; How to Succeed in College.

SIDELIGHTS: Donald W. Jugenheimer told *CA:* "Because the teaching of advertising has grown drastically in the past decade, the number of available textbooks has not kept pace. There are many texts for the introductory level, but few for the specific and advanced courses. I have tried to fill in some of these gaps with specialized materials. Because of this shortage of texts, some of our books have been adopted for teaching courses for which they were not originally intended: research courses using advertising media texts and campaign courses using basic anthologies.

"As the discipline grows and matures, I hope that the quality of books will improve in content and that the advertising industry will cooperate in this effort."

K

KABBANI, Rana 1958-

PERSONAL: Born January 14, 1958, in Damascus, Syria; daughter of Sabah (a diplomat) and Maha (Naamani) Kabbani; married Mahmoud Darweesh, December 16, 1976 (divorced, 1982); married Patrick Seale (a writer), October 26, 1985; children: one son. *Education:* Georgetown University, B.A., 1977; American University of Beirut, M.A., 1979; Jesus College, Cambridge, Ph.D., 1984.

ADDRESSES: Home—2 Motcomb St., London SW1X 8JU, England. *Agent*—Ann McDermid, Curtis Brown Ltd., 162-168 Regent St., London W1R 5TA, England.

CAREER: American University of Beirut, Beirut, Lebanon, university fellow and lecturer in English, 1977-79; Quartet Books, London, England, editor, 1984-86; free-lance journalist and literary commentator, 1986—.

MEMBER: International P.E.N., Oxford and Cambridge University Club.

AWARDS, HONORS: Prize from Sotheby's International Poetry Competition, 1981, for poem "Family Tree."

WRITINGS:

Europe's Myths of Orient: Devise and Rule, Macmillan, 1986.
(Translator from Arabic) Mahmoud Darweesh, *Sand and Other Poems,* Routledge & Kegan Paul, 1986.
(Editor) *The Passionate Nomad: Diaries of Isabelle Eberhardt,* Virago Press, 1987.

WORK IN PROGRESS: A novel, publication by Methuen expected in 1990.

SIDELIGHTS: Rana Kabbani told *CA:* "My interests are cross-cultural exchange, the ways in which racial and sexual stereotypes emerge historically, and what can be done to dismantle them. I am a committed feminist."

AVOCATIONAL INTERESTS: International travel.

BIOGRAPHICAL/CRITICAL SOURCES:

PERIODICALS

Los Angeles Times Book Review, December 20, 1987.
New York Times Book Review, January 4, 1987.

KANE, L. A.
See MANNETTI, Lisa

*   *   *

KAPEL, David E(dward) 1932-

PERSONAL: Born July 11, 1932, in Wilmington, Del.; son of Edward Martin and Adele Marion Kapel; married Marilyn M. Brown, August 27, 1955; children: Michael, Larry, Amy. *Education:* Temple University, B.S., 1955, M.Ed., 1957, Ed.D., 1964. *Politics:* Democrat. *Religion:* Jewish.

ADDRESSES: Home—1501 Chimney Wood Lane, New Orleans, La. 70126. *Office*—College of Education, University of New Orleans, New Orleans, La. 70148.

CAREER: Teacher of social studies and mathematics at schools in Philadelphia, Pa., 1955-64; Glassboro State College, Glassboro, N.J., professor of education, 1964-69; Temple University, Philadelphia, professor of education, 1969-76; University of Nebraska, Omaha, professor of education and associate dean of College of Education, 1976-80; University of Louisville, Louisville, Ky., professor of education and associate dean of School of Education, 1980-85; University of New Orleans, New Orleans, La., professor of education and dean of College of Education, 1985—. *Military service:* U.S. Air Force, 1951-52.

MEMBER: American Academy of Political and Social Science, American Educational Research Association, Association for Supervision and Curriculum Development, National Council for Measurement in Education, Association of Teacher Educators, Phi Delta Kappa.

AWARDS, HONORS: Gold Medal from Phi Delta Kappa, 1964; postdoctoral fellow of U.S. Office of Education at American Institutes for Research in the Behavioral Sciences, 1966-67; *American Educators' Encyclopedia* was named the outstanding reference source of 1982 by the American Library Association.

WRITINGS:

An Assessment of the Impact of Vocational Education, American Management, 1972.
(With Ann McPherson Wilderman and Harold S. Resnick) *Metric Measurement Simplified,* Prindle, Weber & Schmidt, 1974.

(Editor with Edward L. Dejnozka) *American Educators' Encyclopedia*, Greenwood Press, 1982, revised edition, with wife, Marilyn Kapel and C. Gifford, 1988.

(With M. Kapel) *The Preparation of Teachers for the Urban Schools*, Educational Resources Information Center Clearinghouse on Urban Education, 1982.

Contributor to education journals. Editor of *Urban Review,* 1976—.

WORK IN PROGRESS: A national study of the psychological, social, and emotional fitness of teacher education candidates.

SIDELIGHTS: David E. Kapel told *CA:* "Much is discussed in education about the psychological, social, and emotional fitness of teachers, but little is done about measuring or assessing such fitness. It appears that public institutions are more concerned with 'due process' related to fitness, while private institutions are not as concerned.

"*American Educators' Encyclopedia* is for educational professionals, parents, and others who need a reference for terms, events, and so forth that are educationally related. More than eighteen hundred terms are defined and/or described in the text."

*   *   *

KAPLAN, Andrew (Gary)   1941-

PERSONAL: Born May 18, 1941, in Brooklyn, N.Y.; son of Joseph (an ironworker) and Rose (a housewife; maiden name, Berman) Kaplan; married Anne M. McClure (a school psychologist), July 19, 1980; children: Justin Spencer. *Education:* Attended Ben-Gurion University of the Negev, 1967-68; Tel-Aviv University, B.A., 1970; Oregon State University, M.B.A., 1972.

ADDRESSES: Home—Los Angeles, Calif. *Agent*—June Hall, June Hall Agency, 19 College Cross, London N1 1PT, England.

CAREER: Free-lance writer, 1961-75; Computer Sciences Corp., El Segundo, Calif., senior marketing specialist and writer, 1975-78; free-lance writer and consultant in marketing and technical documentation to the computer industry, 1978-82; Amdahl Corp., Marina Del Rey, Calif., manager of technical publications, 1982-83; Protocol Computers, Inc., Los Angeles, Calif., director of corporate communications, 1983-84; writer, 1984—. *Military service:* U.S. Army Reserve, 1960-66. Israel Defense Force, 1967-70; served in Six-Day War; became first lieutenant.

MEMBER: International P.E.N., Authors Guild, Mystery Writers of America.

WRITINGS:

Hour of the Assassins (novel), Dell, 1980, revised edition, Warner Books, 1987.
Scorpion (novel), Macmillan, 1986.
Dragonfire (novel), Warner Books, 1987.

WORK IN PROGRESS: A spy thriller set in Latin America, publication by Warner Books expected in 1989.

SIDELIGHTS: Andrew Kaplan told *CA:* "I knew early in life that I wanted to be a writer. Like others of the Beat Generation, I traveled, first throughout the United States, then around the world. I learned twelve languages and sought experience, often in places that were off the beaten tracks, like the Sahara desert, the Amazon jungle, and the Middle East during the Six-Day War.

"After failing to publish my early novels, I became interested in writing spy thrillers in order to break through to a wider, more popular audience. John le Carre had shown that one could write a serious novel within the boundaries of the genre: that instead of an adult cartoon, you could have an existential hero in an environment of moral ambiguity; in other words, the real world. Then, too, I had some background in this area. I had worked as a free-lance journalist in various hot spots around the world and within Israeli military intelligence. The CIA had even tried to recruit me on several occasions. I once went through the whole process, almost to the point of joining the CIA's Career Training Program.

"I consider myself not so much a writer of thrillers as a serious novelist who happens to be working in the spy thriller genre. In my work I try to accomplish two things: to keep the reader turning the pages (the writer's primary job) and to write authentic and serious work within the framework of the genre."

*   *   *

KARLOWICH, Robert A.   1927-

PERSONAL: Born April 24, 1927, in Branford, Conn.; son of Anthony J. and Mabel (Wester) Karlowich; married Dorothy Anne Warner (an art therapist), April 7, 1981. *Education:* New York University, B.A., 1954; Columbia University, M.S., 1960, D.L.S., 1981; graduate study at Leningrad Library School, 1962.

ADDRESSES: Home—P.O. Box 473, Buckingham, Pa. 18912. *Office*—School of Computing, Information, and Library Sciences, Pratt Institute, 215 Ryerson St., Brooklyn, N.Y. 11205.

CAREER: University of Illinois at Urbana-Champaign, Urbana, head of Slavic acquisitions, 1960-64; Columbia University, New York, N.Y., head of Slavic acquisitions, 1964-68; Pratt Institute, Brooklyn, N.Y., assistant professor at graduate school of library and information science, 1971-81, associate professor, 1981-85, associate professor of computing, information, and library sciences, 1985—. *Military service:* U.S. Navy, 1944-46.

MEMBER: American Association for the Advancement of Slavic Studies, American Library Association.

AWARDS, HONORS: Grant for study at Leningrad Library School from Interuniversity Travel Grants for Study in the U.S.S.R. (now International Research and Exchanges Board for the U.S.S.R.), 1962.

WRITINGS:

Young Defector (juvenile), Messner, 1983.
Rise Up in Anger: Latin America Today (juvenile), Messner, 1985.
(With Edward Kasinec) *A History of Russian and Soviet Book Culture: The Book, Libraries, and Bibliography From the Beginning of Writing to the End of World War II*, M. E. Sharpe, 1988.
The Russian-Language Periodical Press in New York City, 1889-1914, Scarecrow Press, in press.

WORK IN PROGRESS: Compiling *Scholarly Resources for the Study of the Russian Empire and the Soviet Union in the New York Metropolitan Area: A Preliminary Guide.*

SIDELIGHTS: Robert A. Karlowich told *CA:* "While my main work is in library science, with special emphasis on the Russian and Soviet area, I enjoy writing for children and young adults. Writing for young people is both challenging and satisfying: challenging in that one must present complex subjects in a form that young people can understand; satisfying in that one can reach out to the young generation with ideas that are controversial and, one hopes, inspire debate. *Young Defector* is a true story about Walter Polovchak, who refused to return to the Soviet Union with his parents. *Rise Up in Anger* concerns the struggles of the people of Latin America to find their own road to freedom and dignity, and the gigantic stumbling blocks, both national and international, that have been placed in their path.

"My study *The Russian-Language Periodical Press in New York City* tells one part of the history of the great influx of immigrants who came to America in the period from 1881 to 1914. It has close ties with the Jewish community in New York, the revolutionary movement in Russia and Europe, and reflects the efforts of its editors and readers to find a new life here without abandoning previous cultural values and intellectual beliefs. On the Jewish side, elements of this history have already been described; on the Russian side, there has never been a clear exposition of the people and publications as well as their importance to this part of American history. My compilation *Scholarly Resources for the Study of the Russian Empire* is the first attempt to bring together the many institutions and individuals in the New York area that own collections in this field. The New York area is one of the richest centers for such study outside the Soviet Union.

"For *A History of Russian and Soviet Book Culture*, I wrote the section on the Soviet period. The book world in all its ramifications was part of the great cultural changes that Russia experienced after 1917. Part of my task was to sort out and make clear the individual and group influences in this world and to show how they evolved as the initial revolutionary fervor and debate were gradually suppressed by Soviet ruler Joseph Stalin. Soviet sources do not always provide unbiased reports on this evolution."

*   *   *

KASSIS, Hanna (Emmanuel) 1932-

PERSONAL: Born April 5, 1932, in Gaza, Palestine; son of Ibrahim and Martha (el-Haj) Kassis; married Anne Christine; children: Norman, Magdalena, Omar. *Education:* American University of Beirut, B.A., 1959; Harvard University, Ph.D., 1965. *Religion:* Christian.

ADDRESSES: Office—Department of Religious Studies, University of British Columbia, Vancouver, British Columbia, Canada V6T 1W5.

CAREER: University of British Columbia, Vancouver, assistant professor, 1964-68, associate professor, 1968-85, professor of religious studies, 1985—.

MEMBER: American Oriental Society, Archaeological Institute of America, American Numismatic Society (fellow), Oriental Numismatic Society, Middle East Studies Association.

AWARDS, HONORS: Grants from Canada Council and Social Science and Humanities Research Council of Canada; Killam fellow, 1987-88.

WRITINGS:

A Concordance to the Qur'an, University of California Press, 1983.

(With Karl I. Kobbervig) *Las Concordancies del Coran*, Instituto Hispano-arabe de Cultura (Madrid), 1987.
(Editor and author of introduction) *The Mozarabs: Christians, Muslims, and Jews in Medieval Spain; A Symposium*, AMS Press, 1988.

Contributor to Oriental and Islamic studies journals. Member of editorial board of *Maghreb Review*.

WORK IN PROGRESS: A Numismatic History of the Almoravids of the eleventh and twelfth centuries; *The Muslim-Christian Confrontation in Medieval Spain Prior to the Crusades.*

SIDELIGHTS: Hanna Kassis told *CA:* "The confrontation between Middle Eastern and Islamic societies on one hand and the West on the other has its roots in religion and in the failure of the West to comprehend Islam. Such negativism and its consequences began with the rise and spread of Islam beginning in the seventh century. It was further exacerbated by the manner in which each of the two religious polities reacted to its respective crises. From the outset Islam's reaction to its many internal social or political crises was to re-affirm the faith that converted warring and factious groups into a solid and viable community. One witnesses this phenomenon as much in the Middle Ages as in the twentieth century.

"The inability of the secularized West to match this ideological renewel has incessantly generated an attitude of hostility towards Islam and Muslim societies. As a member of a Christian minority in a Muslim environment I came to comprehend the Muslim attitude of tolerance toward such minorities as well as the minority's attempt to avoid total cultural absorption by Islam to preserve its particular identity, which in itself inevitably leads to confrontation.

"I believe that a deeper awareness of what separates human beings may lead to their being drawn closer to one another. In the sphere of Muslim-Christian confrontation, a respectful understanding of Islam (its scriptures, prophet, and institutions, all of which have been systematically repudiated in the past) might reduce the tension that has kept the two communities apart for the past fourteen centuries. Such may never be fully accomplished in our lifetime; but this is no reason why what has already been started by many authors (a Catholic, Norman Daniel; a Calvinist, Bruno Etienne; a secularized Christian, Edward Said; or a Marxist Jew, Maxime Robinson, among many others) should not be nurtured. Such achievement is not the monopoly of authors or intellectuals. Rather, it stems from the simple recognition that there is an 'other' whose religious or political beliefs, way of life, color of skin, eating habits, or language, are different from the 'norm'—and that this 'otherness' is enriching to one's own life. I say that this recognition is not the monopoly of intellectuals because I learned it first from simple men and women, Muslim and Christian, in the land of my birth and upbringing."

*   *   *

KATES, Gary (Richard) 1952-

PERSONAL: Born November 9, 1952, in Los Angeles, Calif.; son of Harvey (a businessman) and Joyce (a housewife; maiden name, Goldberg) Kates; married Lynne Diamond (a physician), March 1, 1978; children: Emily, Max. *Education:* Pitzer College, B.A., 1974; University of Chicago, M.A., 1975, Ph.D., 1978. *Politics:* Liberal. *Religion:* Jewish.

ADDRESSES: Office—Department of History, Trinity University, San Antonio, Tex. 78284.

CAREER: Trinity University, San Antonio, Tex., assistant professor, 1980-86, associate professor of history, 1986—. Member of board of directors of Jewish Federation of San Antonio.

MEMBER: American Historical Association, Society for French Historical Studies.

WRITINGS:

The Cercle Social, the Girondins, and the French Revolution, Princeton University Press, 1985.

WORK IN PROGRESS: Thomas Paine and the French Revolution.

SIDELIGHTS: Gary Kates told *CA:* "I am interested in the political behavior of intellectuals and writers during political crises. My book *The Cercle Social, the Girondins, and the French Revolution* is a study of a group of writers who got into politics during the French Revolution. They ran for office, started political journals, and dominated an important political party, the Girondins. My book shows how intellectuals often fail to become good politicians because in the end they write little more than propaganda, and their participation is used by others. Thomas Paine and the Marquis de Condorcet are two writers featured in my book."

*   *   *

KAUFFMANN, C. Michael   1931-

PERSONAL: Born February 5, 1931, in Frankfurt, Germany; son of Arthur (an art dealer) and Tamara (a physician) Kauffmann; married Dorothea Hill, 1954; children: Francis, Martin. *Education:* Merton College, Oxford, M.A., 1953; Warburg Institute, London, Ph.D., 1956.

ADDRESSES: Home—53 Twyford Ave., London W3 9PZ, England. *Office*—Courtauld Institute of Art, University of London, 20 Portman Sq., London W1H 0BE, England.

CAREER: University of London, Warburg Institute, London, England, assistant curator of photographic collection, 1957-58; Manchester City Art Gallery, Manchester, England, keeper, 1958-60; Victoria and Albert Museum, London, assistant keeper, 1960-75, assistant to director, 1963-66, keeper of department of prints, drawings, and paintings, 1975-85; University of London, director and professor of the history of art at the Courtauld Institute of Art, 1985—. Visiting associate professor at University of Chicago, 1969.

MEMBER: British Academy (fellow), Museums Association (fellow).

WRITINGS:

The Baths of Pozzuoli: Medieval Illuminations of Peter of Eboli's Poem, Cassirer, 1959.
An Altar-Piece of the Apocalypse, H.M.S.O., 1968.
Victoria and Albert Museum: Catalogue of Foreign Paintings, H.M.S.O., 1973.
British Romanesque Manuscripts, 1066-1190: A Survey of Manuscripts Illuminated in the British Isles, Harvey Miller, 1975.
Sketches by John Constable in the Victoria and Albert Museum, H.M.S.O., 1981.
Catalogue of Paintings in the Wellington Museum, H.M.S.O., 1982.

John Varley, 1778-1842, Batsford, 1985.

Contributor to art history journals.

BIOGRAPHICAL/CRITICAL SOURCES:

PERIODICALS

Times Literary Supplement, August 22, 1975, April 26, 1985.

*   *   *

KAUFFMANN, (Franklin) Lane   1922(?)-1988

OBITUARY NOTICE: Born c. 1922 in Washington, D.C.; died of emphysema, May 24, 1988, in Towson, Md. Author. Winner of an Edgar Allan Poe Award for his novel *The Perfectionist,* Kauffmann also penned *Another Helen* and *An Honorable Estate.*

OBITUARIES AND OTHER SOURCES:

PERIODICALS

Washington Post, May 25, 1988.

*   *   *

KAVANAGH, Dan(iel)   1946-
(Basil Seal)

PERSONAL: Born January 20, 1946, in Sligo, Ireland; son of Paddy (a carpenter) and Betty (Corrinder) Kavanagh. *Education:* Attended secondary school in Sligo, Ireland. *Politics:* None. *Religion:* "Cradle Catholic."

ADDRESSES: Agent—A. D. Peters and Co. Ltd., 10 Buckingham St., London WC2N 6BU, England.

CAREER: Writer. Worked as deckhand, waiter, bouncer, baggage handler, and pilot.

AWARDS, HONORS: Silver Truncheon Award from London Metropolitan Police, 1981, for *Duffy.*

WRITINGS:

Duffy (crime novel), J. Cape, 1980.
Fiddle City (crime novel), J. Cape, 1981.
Putting the Boot In (crime novel), J. Cape, 1985.
Going to the Dogs (crime novel), Viking, 1987.

Worked as journalist, under pseudonym Basil Seal.

WORK IN PROGRESS: Research on another crime novel.

SIDELIGHTS: Dan Kavanagh told *CA:* "I believe that the traditional novel, as practiced in England and Ireland, is an exhausted genre. True creativity lies in those hitherto despised domains of 'sub-literature'—the ballad, the folk poem, the thriller—just as the true energy of a nation comes, not from its soft capital city, but from its extremities, from its despised and downtrodden citizens."

Kavanagh's crime novels feature a bisexual ex-cop named Duffy who pursues his "civilian" investigations in some of the seamier parts of London. Critics have called the books, which depict Soho and Heathrow as accurately as a guided tour, lively and inventive entertainment. The author has been recognized as a skillful, well-paced storyteller who takes the reader on a colorful romp through the London underworld, commenting without moralizing on crime and the police, justice and revenge, and urban corruption.

BIOGRAPHICAL/CRITICAL SOURCES:

PERIODICALS

London Review of Books, May 26, 1983.
Times Literary Supplement, July 4, 1980, October 30, 1981, February 28, 1982.

* * *

KAYMOR, Patrice Maguilene
See SENGHOR, Leopold Sedar

* * *

KAZAN, Frances 1946-

PERSONAL: Born November 18, 1946, in Brighton, England; daughter of Joseph Charles (an accountant) and Rita Doris (a social service worker) Wright; married Peter David Rudge (a manager), April 5, 1969 (divorced); married Elia Kazan (a writer), June 28, 1982; children: (first marriage) Joseph Daniel, Charlotte. *Education:* Hockerill Teachers College, Teaching Degree, 1968; attended New York University, 1980-81. *Religion:* Church of England.

ADDRESSES: Agent—Stein & Day, Scarborough House, Briarcliff Manor, N.Y. 10510.

CAREER: Schoolteacher in London, England, 1968-72; housewife, 1972-80; writer, 1980—.

WRITINGS:

Good Night, Little Sister, Stein & Day, 1986.

Contributor to *Self.*

WORK IN PROGRESS: A novel.

SIDELIGHTS: Frances Kazan told *CA:* "I travel between New York, the Bahamas, and England, where my family still lives. Living on two continents has, I hope, given my work a broader perspective."

* * *

KEEFE, Terry 1940-

PERSONAL: Born February 1, 1940, in Birmingham, England; son of Wilfrid (a die turner) and Laura (Mitchell) Keefe; married Sheila Parkin (a teacher), June, 1962; children: Simon, Rosanna. *Education:* University of Leicester, B.A. (French), 1962, M.A., 1968; University of London, B.A. (philosophy), 1966.

ADDRESSES: Home—33 Granville Ave., Oadby, Leicester LE2 5FL, England. *Office*—Department of French, University of Leicester, University Rd., Leicester, England.

CAREER: Schoolmaster (French teacher) in Lincoln, England, 1963-65; University of Leicester, Leicester, England, lecturer, 1965-80, senior lecturer in French, 1980—, head of department, 1982—, dean of Faculty of Arts, 1985—.

MEMBER: Society for French Studies.

WRITINGS:

Simone de Beauvoir: A Study of Her Writings, Barnes & Noble, 1983.
French Existentialist Fiction: Changing Moral Perspectives, Barnes & Noble, 1986.

Contributor to language journals and newspapers.

WORK IN PROGRESS: A monograph on Beauvoir's *Le Deuxieme Sexe,* publication by Grant & Cutler expected in 1990.

SIDELIGHTS: Terry Keefe told *CA:* "Many of my publications center on the moral thought of Jean-Paul Sartre and Simone de Beauvoir. *French Existentialist Fiction* tries to show how their ethical preoccupations (and Albert Camus's) changed markedly with the outbreak of World War II and again in the immediate postwar years. I continue to be intrigued by the impact and influence of these writers in the moral and social sphere when the theoretical foundations of their ethics are visibly weak."

BIOGRAPHICAL/CRITICAL SOURCES:

PERIODICALS

Times Literary Supplement, March 16, 1984.

* * *

KEENAN, Desmond (Joseph) 1933-

PERSONAL: Born November 28, 1933, in Newry, Northern Ireland; son of Joseph (a railway employee) and Christina (a teacher) Keenan. *Education:* Mellifont Abbey Seminary, Certificate for Ordination, 1960; Pontifical University of St. Thomas, Rome, Italy, S.T.L., 1961; Pontifical Biblical Institute, Rome, L.S.S. (cum laude), 1963; Queen's University, Belfast, B.S.Sc., 1974, Ph.D., 1979. *Religion:* Roman Catholic.

ADDRESSES: Home—129 Bluebird Walk, Chalk Hill Rd., Wembley Park, Middlesex NA9 9YF, England.

CAREER: Mellifont Abbey, Collon, Republic of Ireland, lecturer in biblical studies and head of department, 1963-70; writer and researcher, 1979—. Sociology tutor at Northern Ireland Polytechnic, Jordanstown, 1974-75.

WRITINGS:

The Catholic Church in Nineteenth Century Ireland: A Sociological Study, Barnes & Noble, 1983.

WORK IN PROGRESS: The Struggle for Catholic Emancipation in Ireland, 1793-1829; The History of Ireland, 1800-1850: A Re-Interpretation; The New Testament and the Creed.

SIDELIGHTS: Desmond Keenan told *CA* that his goal is "to express Roman Catholic doctrine in modern language, taking into account the language of the New Testament, the traditional formulations, the contemporary ideas." The author also indicated a concern "for the problem of Northern Ireland as a result of false emphases and wrong directions in the writing of past history. I want to see the application of modern methods and ideas to the writing of Irish history.

"Over the past five years I have been much concerned with the question as to how a history of Ireland, and a history of Catholicism in Ireland, which is a very different thing, should be written. Speaking in general, one can say that no satisfactory approach to a general history has ever been devised. (I am not referring to monographs on particular limited historical subjects which can at times be excellent.) A brief survey of historiography in Ireland will make this clear.

"In Ireland, in the Middle Ages, as in most other European countries, there were the monastic annalists, but these did not attempt to provide ordered narratives. In the two centuries following the Reformation, history in Ireland, as elsewhere in

Europe, consisted of highly colored accounts of the wickedness of those on the other side of the sectarian divide. As late as 1798 this form of sectarian propaganda was evident. About the middle of the eighteenth century various amateur antiquarians tried to provide a history of ancient Ireland based on the study of 'antiquities.' Ireland was provided with a glorious past. The antiquarian selected some famous people of antiquity, Etruscans, Babylonians, or Phoenicians, according to fancy. He then connected the ancient Irish with this people by means of selected antiquities—bits of inscriptions, bits of helmets, or bits of carvings. The development of the science of archaeology in the nineteenth century ended this phase.

"About the middle of the last century the phase was replaced by the theory of romantic nationalism, an offshoot of the romantic movement in literature and art. In this version of history, many countries passed through three stages. The first stage was that of freedom under their own kings, a happy time. Kings were just, men brave, women chaste, children respectful, and harvests bountiful. The second stage was that of subjection to the invader or foreigner. The people were downtrodden and subjected to endless extortions and punishments. Many times they rose in arms to try to expel the harsh and unjust foreigners but were always defeated. The third stage was that of the great national struggle. Brave, honest, and totally disinterested leaders rose up to rally the people and to lead them in an armed struggle against the oppressor until finally the goal of national independence was achieved. This schema of history writing originated in Germany in the early years of the nineteenth century and was enthusiastically adopted by nationalist writers in Ireland for propaganda purposes. It is superfluous to say that it has little connection with reality at any point. The picture it presents is not one that Irish Unionists, those Irish Protestants and Catholics who considered a permanent fixed union with Great Britain a better option for Ireland, would recognize. For Nationalists, all social evils in Ireland were attributed to a single cause: foreign rule. Remove the cause of the evils and all the evils would disappear. Unionists were therefore guilty of a grave crime in trying to maintain foreign rule. The Unionists, not without reason, considered, and still consider, Nationalists as being out of their minds.

"The problem has been stated necessarily at some length. A satisfactory solution is not obvious. The approach I have adopted is taken in a general way from sociology, in particular from general systems theory. The various groups and subgroups in a society are identified and described. Second, the process of their interactions over the period of fifty years is related. Nationalism was virtually nonexistent in Ireland in the first half of the nineteenth century, so Nationalist writers rarely wrote about the period. It was the absence of serious research on the period that first attracted me to it."

* * *

KEEPING, Charles (William James)   1924-1988

OBITUARY NOTICE—See index for *CA* sketch: Born September 22, 1924, in Lambeth, London, England; died May 16, 1988. Educator, artist, illustrator, and author. Widely regarded as the most brilliant and original British children's illustrator of his generation, Keeping also attracted considerable criticism for the often morbid quality of his pictures and for his routine rejection of conventional narrative. Leaving school at age fourteen, Keeping became a printer's apprentice, then served as a naval wireless operator in World War II. After the war he became a student at Regent Street Polytechnic, working in

drawing, etching, engraving, and lithography. His lithographs have been exhibited in several countries, and a number of museums and galleries own his work.

Keeping began work as an illustrator in 1956, commissioned by the Oxford University Press to illustrate stories by children's book author Rosemary Sutcliff. Among Keeping's illustrations and drawings for the work of other authors are two retellings of the Greek myths by Leon Garfield and Edward Blishen, *The God Beneath the Sea* and *The Golden Shadow;* Alfred Noyes's poem *The Highwayman,* which won Keeping the 1982 Kate Greenaway Medal from the American Library Association (his second); and the Folio Society's *Complete Dickens,* which Keeping began illustrating in 1981. His own picture books began to appear in the mid-1960s. Titles include *Charley, Charlotte and the Golden Canary,* for which Keeping received the 1968 Kate Greenaway Medal, *Joseph's Yard, Through the Window, The Spider's Web, The Railway Passage,* and *Willie's Fire Engine*—all closely based on the experiences of his own city childhood. Besides illustrating books, Keeping was a visiting lecturer at several British art schools; created advertising art, wall murals, posters, comic strips, and book jackets; and worked on children's films for television. He was also runner-up for the 1974 Hans Christian Andersen International Children's Book Medal, awarded biennially for the most distinguished contribution to international children's literature.

OBITUARIES AND OTHER SOURCES:

BOOKS

Who's Who, 139th edition, St. Martin's, 1987.

PERIODICALS

Times (London), May 20, 1988.

* * *

KEETON, Kathy   1939-

PERSONAL: Born February 17, 1939, in South Africa; daughter of Keith and Queenie Keeton. *Education:* Attended Royal Ballet School, London.

ADDRESSES: Office—Omni Magazine, 1965 Broadway, New York, N.Y. 10023.

CAREER: Penthouse International, New York, N.Y., vice-chairperson, beginning in 1969; associate publisher and editor of *Viva* (magazine), New York City; *Omni* (magazine), New York City, president, 1978—.

MEMBER: American Institute of Aeronautics and Astronautics, American Space Foundation, Space Studies Institute, Space Generation Foundation (trustee), L-5 Society (member of board of directors), Robotics International of SME (senior member), Amateur Astronomers Association of New York City, National Coalition Against Censorship, New York Veteran Police Association, Fund for the Aging, Junior Achievement.

AWARDS, HONORS: Named outstanding woman in publishing by the March of Dimes; publisher-of-the-year citation from Periodical and Book Association of America.

WRITINGS:

(With Yvonne Baskin) *Woman of Tomorrow,* St. Martin's, 1985.

Creator of *Omni* magazine. Executive producer of *OMNI: Visions of Tomorrow* and *OMNI: The New Frontier.*

SIDELIGHTS: Kathy Keeton, creator and president of the popular science and science fiction magazine *Omni*, forsees many scientific and technological advances in the twenty-first century that will enhance the lives of women, such as improved fertilization and contraceptive techniques, improved health care, and home computers and robots that perform household duties. She explains her views in *Woman of Tomorrow*, reporting with co-author Yvonne Baskin possible case studies of future women's lives "in a technological Utopia, full of wondrous productive people," described Roselle M. Lewis in the *Los Angeles Times*. In an excerpt from her book in the *Chicago Tribune*, for example, Keeton suggests that future women "won't have to spend their spare time writing checks, keeping track of household expenses, planning meals, making lists or shopping for anything. . . . The computers will do these chores." In addition, the author adds, "women of tomorrow are going to use electronics to reassign household responsibilities and help make all family members more competent, self-sufficient and less dependent on mother. . . . A woman of tomorrow will be the best biochemist or chairman of the board she can be during the day, spend time with her partner in the evening, indulge in her hobbies, and . . . play games with her children if that's the way she enjoys spending her time."

In *Woman of Tomorrow* Keeton "is unfailingly optimistic" in her assertion of women's abilities and their future achievements, observed Alex Raksin in the *Los Angeles Times Book Review*. "This book underscores women's strengths, imparting a human dimension to technological facts," he noted. "Though Keeton's view is visionary," Lewis reflected, "her methodology is statistical," for the author's assertions are based on recent surveys conducted on the aspirations of women around the world. "A superb book of imagination and information," the reviewer assessed, *Woman of Tomorrow* "posits the future most entertainingly."

Keeton told *CA:* "I admire achievement in science and technology most of all. Today's biochemists, genetic engineers, and aerospace researchers are part of a team that is shaping our future. From their ranks will emerge tomorrow's leaders and heroes. My dream, and the impetus for *Woman of Tomorrow*, is that women will make up a significant percentage of these heroes. Not that she will become like man, but that she will influence the forces of change—scientific and technological—with her own unique vision, understanding, and sensitivity."

BIOGRAPHICAL/CRITICAL SOURCES:

BOOKS

Authors in the News, Volume 2, Gale, 1976.

PERIODICALS

Chicago Tribune, March 30, 1986, August 8, 1986.
Los Angeles Times, December 26, 1985.
Los Angeles Times Book Review, October 5, 1986.
Miami Herald, December 7, 1975.
Omni, December, 1985, June, 1987.

* * *

KEIGER, John F(rederick) V(ictor)   1952-

PERSONAL: Born December 7, 1952, in Wembley, Middlesex, England; son of F.G.M. and A.I.C. Keiger. *Education:* Universite d'Aix-Marseille III, diplome de l'Institut d'Etudes Politiques, 1974; attended Sorbonne, University of Paris, 1976-77; Corpus Christi College, Cambridge, Ph.D. 1980.

ADDRESSES: Home—1 Brooklands Ave., Withington, Manchester M2O 8JE, England. *Office*—Department of Modern Languages, University of Salford, Salford M5 4WT, England.

CAREER: University of Salford, Salford, England, lecturer in sociological and political studies, 1979-81, lecturer in French history and politics, 1979—. Visiting professor of history of international relations at Institut d'Etudes Politiques, Universite d'Aix-Marseille, 1985.

WRITINGS:

France and the Origins of the First World War, Macmillan, 1983.
(Contributor) Kenneth Bourne and D. Cameron Watt, editors, *British Documents on Foreign Affairs: Reports and Papers From the Foreign Office Confidential Print*, Volumes 1-19, University Publications of America, 1987-88.

Contributor to history journals.

WORK IN PROGRESS: Raymond Poincare: A Political Life, publication by Allen & Unwin.

SIDELIGHTS: According to critic D. R. Watson, John F. V. Keiger began his research in the 1970s, after the French archives first opened its doors to scholars and historians. The author's access to original and previously unavailable French documents allowed him to present in his book *France and the Origins of the First World War* a perspective on the origins of World War I that differed greatly from traditional historical interpretations. Keiger focused on the role of Raymond Poincare, who served as the president of France before and during the first world war. His research suggested that Poincare played a much more dominant and competent role as a political leader and decision maker than earlier historical accounts would allow. Watson wrote in the *Times Literary Supplement* that Keiger has "broadened his scope to provide a clear and authoritative analysis of French policy. . . . The evidence here presented allows us to reject interpretations of Poincare's conduct of French foreign policy that have been too widely accepted." He regarded Keiger's book as a reliable and noteworthy addition to the history of World War I.

BIOGRAPHICAL/CRITICAL SOURCES:

PERIODICALS

New York Review of Books, March 29, 1984.
Times Literary Supplement, April 27, 1984.

* * *

KEITH, Lee
See SUNNERS, William

* * *

KELLEHER, Catherine McArdle   1939-
(Catherine McArdle)

PERSONAL: Born January 19, 1939, in Boston, Mass.; daughter of Francis X. and Catherine (Roche) McArdle; married James J. Kelleher, 1966; children: Michael, Diane. *Education:* Mount Holyoke College, A.B., 1960; attended Free University of Berlin, 1960-61; Massachusetts Institute of Technology, Ph.D., 1967.

ADDRESSES: Office—Center for International Security Studies, School of Public Affairs, University of Maryland at College Park, College Park, Md. 20742.

CAREER: Columbia University, Barnard College, New York, N.Y., assistant professor of political science, 1967-69; University of Illinois at Chicago Circle, Chicago, assistant professor, 1969-71, associate professor of political science, 1972-73; University of Michigan, Ann Arbor, associate professor of political science, 1973-78; University of Denver, Denver, Colo., professor of international studies, 1978-82; National War College, Washington, D.C., professor of military strategy, 1980-82; University of Maryland at College Park, professor of public policy and director of Center for International Security Studies, 1982—. Fellow of International Institute for Strategic Studies, London, England, 1975-76; member of staff of National Security Council, 1977-78; member of research council of Centre d'Etudes et Recherches sur l'Armee, of the Committee for International Security and Arms Control, and of the advisory board of National Security Archives, WGBH Nuclear Era Project, Institute for Peace at Notre Dame University; director of Maryland International Security Project. Consultant to National Defense University, National Security Council, Office of Secretary of Defense, Arms Control and Disarmament Agency, U.S. Information Agency, Brookings Institution, Ford Foundation, and the MacArthur Foundation.

MEMBER: Inter-University Seminar on Armed Forces and Society (executive committee member; national conference chairman, 1972-73), Institute for the Study of World Politics (council member, 1976—), Council on Foreign Relations (international affairs fellow, 1976-77), Academy of Arts and Science (member of European Security Study, 1982-85, and Committee on International Security Studies, 1985—), International Peace and Security Studies, National Academy of Sciences (member of panel on the Contributions of the Behavioral and Social Sciences to the Prevention of Nuclear War, 1985—), International Studies Association (vice-president, 1987-88), American Political Science Association, Committee for National Security, American Council of Germany, Phi Beta Kappa.

AWARDS, HONORS: Fulbright fellow, 1960-61; Ford Foreign Area Fellowship, 1961-67; fellow at Institute for War and Peace Studies, Columbia University, 1967-69, and Center for West European Studies, Harvard University, 1969-70; D.Litt. from Mount Holyoke College, 1980; Ford Foundation grant, 1981-85; diploma from National War College, 1981; fellow of German Marshall Fund, 1976-77, and North Atlantic Treaty Organization (NATO), 1982-84; National Defense Education Act Fellowship.

WRITINGS:

(With Norman Padelford) *The Financing of Future Peace and Security Operations Under the United Nations,* Center for International Studies, Massachusetts Institute of Technology, 1962.
(Under name Catherine McArdle) *The Role of Military Assistance in the Problems of Arms Control: The Middle East, Latin America, and Africa,* Center for International Studies, Massachusetts Institute of Technology, 1963, revised edition, 1964.
The Nature of Political-Military Gaming, Deutsche Gesellschaft fuer Auswaertige Politik, 1965.
(With Warren R. Schilling and others) *American Arms and a Changing Europe,* Columbia University Press, 1973.
Germany and the Politics of Nuclear Weapons, Columbia University Press, 1975.
Germany, Nuclear Weapons, and Alliance Relations, 1954-1966, Columbia University Press, 1975.

(With William K. Domke and Richard C. Eichenberg) *Wealth, Welfare, and Western Security,* Macmillan, in press.

EDITOR

Political-Military Systems: Comparative Perspectives, Sage Publications, 1974.
(With Wolf Dieter Eberwein; also contributor) *Sicherheit: Zum welchem Preis?* (title means ''Security: At What Price?''), Olzog Verlag, 1983.
(With Frank Kerr and George Quester) *Nuclear Deterrence: New Risks, New Opportunities,* Pergamon-Brassey, 1986.
(With Gale A. Mattox) *Evolving European Defense Policies,* Heath, 1987.

CONTRIBUTOR

Warner R. Schilling and William T. R. Fox, editors, *European Security and an Atlantic System,* Columbia University Press, 1975.
Kenneth Booth and Peter Wright, editors, *American Thinking on Peace and War,* Harvester, 1978.
Viola Drath, editor, *Germany in World Politics,* Gycro Press, 1978.
Wolfram Hanrieder, editor, *West German Foreign Policy,* Westview, 1980.
Sam C. Sarkesian, editor, *Non-Nuclear Conflicts in the Nuclear Age,* Praeger, 1980.
Edwin Feder, editor, *Defense Politics of the Atlantic Alliance,* Praeger, 1980.
Todd Sandler, editor, *The Theory and Structures of International Political Economy,* Westview, 1981.
Richard K. Betts, editor, *Cruise Missiles: Technology Strategy and Politics,* Brookings Institution, 1981.
Douglas Murray and Paul Viotti, editors, *The Defense Policies of Nations,* Johns Hopkins University Press, 1982.
Lawrence Freedman, editor, *The Troubled Alliance,* Heinemann, 1983.
William Staudenmaier and Keith Dunn, editors, *Military Strategy in Transition,* Westview, 1984.
R. G. Livingston, editor, *The Federal Republic in the 1980s,* German Information Center, 1984.
Robert Hunter, editor, *NATO: The Next Generation,* Westview, 1984.
George E. Thibault, editor, *The Art and Practice of Military Strategy,* National Defense University Press, 1984.
Robert Art, Vince Davis, and Samuel Huntington, editors, *Reorganizing America's Defenses: Leadership in War and Peace,* Pergamon-Brassey, 1985.
Geoffrey Till, editor, *The Futures of British Seapower,* Macmillan, 1985.
Peter C. Sederberg, editor, *Nuclear Winter, Deterrence, and the Prevention of Nuclear War,* Praeger, 1986.
Terry Deibel and John Gaddis, editors, *Containment,* National Defense University Press, 1986.
Ashton B. Carter, John D. Steinbruner, and Charles A. Zrakat, editors, *Managing Nuclear Operations,* Brookings Institution, 1987.

Also contributor to *The Future of European Navies,* Royal Netherlands Naval College, 1980, and to political science and international studies journals. Member of editorial board of *Armed Forces and Society,* 1974—, *International Security,* 1979—, and *Information Studies Quarterly,* 1984—.

WORK IN PROGRESS: A nuclear history project; an alliance relations project; a Bundeswehr project.

KELLER, Evelyn Fox 1936-

PERSONAL: Born March 20, 1936, in New York, N.Y.; daughter of Albert and Rachel Fox; children: Jeffrey and Sarah. *Education:* Brandeis University, B.A. (magna cum laude), 1957; Radcliffe College, M.A., 1959; Harvard University, Ph.D., 1963.

ADDRESSES: Office—University of California, Berkeley, Department of Rhetoric, Women's Studies, and History of Science, Berkeley, Calif. 94720; and Institute for Advanced Study, Princeton, N.J. 08540.

CAREER: New York University, New York, N.Y., instructor in physics, 1962-63, assistant research scientist, 1963-66; Cornell University Medical College, New York City, assistant professor, 1963-69; New York University, New York City, associate professor of mathematical biology, 1970-72; State University of New York College at Purchase, Purchase, N.Y., associate professor in division of natural science, 1972-82, chair of mathematics board of study, 1972-74; Northeastern University, Boston, Mass., professor of humanities and mathematics, beginning in 1982; University of California, Berkeley, professor of rhetoric, women's studies, and history of science, 1988—. Special lecturer in mathematical biology at University of Maryland, 1974; Massachusetts Institute of Technology Program in Science, Technology, and Society, visiting fellow, 1979-80, visiting scholar, 1980-84, visiting professor, 1985-86; visiting professor at Northeastern University, 1981-82, Northwestern University, 1985; member of Institute for Advanced Study, Princeton, 1987-88. Gordon Conference on Theoretical Biology, vice-chairman, 1973, chairman, 1974; organizer and coordinator of Boston Area Colloquium on Feminist Theory, 1982—. Guest lecturer and consultant at institutions including Rutgers University, Columbia University, Harvard University, Brandeis University, and University of California, Santa Cruz.

MEMBER: American Association for the Advancement of Science, Phi Beta Kappa, Sigma Xi.

AWARDS, HONORS: National Science Foundation, fellowship, 1957-61, visiting professorship for women, 1985; Mina Shaughnessy Scholars Award from Fund for the Improvement of Postsecondary Education, 1981-82; Mellon Fellowship from Wellesley College Center for Research on Women, 1984; Rockefeller Humanities Fellowship, 1985-86; distinguished publication award from Association for Women in Psychology, 1986; senior fellow of Society for the Humanities, Cornell University, 1986-87.

WRITINGS:

A Feeling for the Organism: The Life and Work of Barbara McClintock, W. H. Freeman, 1983.
Reflections on Gender and Science, Yale University Press, 1985.
(Editor, with Mary Jacobus and Sally Shuttleworth, and contributor) *Women, Science, and the Body,* Methuen, 1988.

Editor of "Feminist Theory" series for Northeastern University Press; adviser to Harvard University Press. American editor of *Fundamenta Scientiae;* member of editorial board of *Woman's Review of Books, Hypatia,* and *Biology and Philosophy.*

CONTRIBUTOR

Sara Ruddick and Pamela Daniels, editors, *Working It Out: Twenty-three Women Writers, Artists, Scientists, and Scholars Talk About Their Lives and Work,* Pantheon, 1977.
Sandra Harding and Merrill B. Hintikka, *Discovering Reality: Feminist Perspectives on Epistemology, Metaphysics, Methodology, and Philosophy of Science,* Reidel, 1983.
Joan Rothschild, editor, *Machine ex Dea,* Pergamon, 1983.
Everett Mendelsohn and Helga Nowotny, editors, *Nineteen Eighty-four: Science Between Utopia and Dystopia,* Reidel, 1984.
Helen Longino and Valerie Miner, editors, *Competition Among Women: A Feminist Analysis,* Feminist Press, 1987.
Animals, Humans, and Machines, Stanford University Press, 1988.
S. Messer and R. Woolfolk, editors, *Hermeneutics and Psychoanalysis,* Rutgers University Press, in press.

Contributor of numerous articles to professional journals, including *Science, Nature, Journal of Theoretical Biology, American Journal of Physics,* and *International Journal of Women's Studies,* and of reviews to periodicals, including *Change* and *New York Times Book Review.*

WORK IN PROGRESS: Editing *Keywords in Evolutionary Discourse,* with Elisabeth Lloyd.

SIDELIGHTS: "Evelyn Fox Keller's biography of Barbara McClintock is a welcome and useful addition to the growing literature on the recent history of . . . women's achievements in science," judged Margaret W. Rossiter in the *New York Times Book Review.* McClintock, recipient of the 1983 Nobel Prize for medicine and several other recent prizes and honorary degrees, was largely ignored when, in the early 1950s, she first presented her observations about the mobility or "transposition" of genes on chromosomes. In *A Feeling for the Organism: The Life and Work of Barbara McClintock,* Keller outlines several factors that may have contributed to the initial rejection of McClintock's ideas: the antifeminist nature of genetic research in that era, the unpopularity of McClintock's subject of study (maize rather than bacteria), and the incomprehension of McClintock's colleagues about her unprecedented conclusions.

Stephen Jay Gould, an acclaimed specialist in geology and evolution, described in the *New York Review of Books* the incompatibility of McClintock's early findings with the accepted notions of the time. James D. Watson and Francis Crick's 1953 discovery of the double helical structure of DNA—double "rows of beads (genes) on strings (chromosomes)," explained Gould—seemed to suggest a rigid, largely immobile structure, "subject to change only by substituting one bead for another." McClintock's model of DNA, however, suggested a structure that was "fluid and mobile, changing constantly in quality and quantity," wrote Gould. Such a model did not make sense to researchers in that era, who merely expressed "incomprehension and bewilderment" at the scientist's "revolutionary" proposals. Only in the late 1970s did "McClintock's research findings, though still controversial," related Rossiter, begin "receiving new confirmation from other scientists [who] suddenly observed phenomena very like what Miss McClintock had called 'transposition.'"

"The strength of Keller's fine book," asserted Gould, "lies in her successful attempt to . . . [provide] a rare and deep understanding of a troubling, fascinating, and general tale in the history of science—initial rejection (or, more frustratingly, simple incomprehension) of great insights." Expressing a thought echoed by other reviewers, David Graber noted in the *Los Angeles Times Book Review* that McClintock "was, one suspects, not the easiest of subjects for Keller. How does one write of a person whose whole life has been devoted to work even the specialists did not understand?'' He commended Keller, who was ''trained in the history, philosophy and psychology of science,'' as ''particularly qualified for the task of explicating Barbara McClintock.'' *A Feeling for the Organism,* he concluded, ''must of necessity be as much genetics as biography, and Keller accomplishes the dual task with intellectual power of her own.''

In her second book, *Reflections on Gender and Science,* ''Keller analyzes the pervasiveness of gender ideology, investigates how it became established and how it still shapes the course of scientific theory and experimentation, and speculates what science might be like if it were gender free,'' related Evelyn Shaw in the *New York Times Book Review.* Shaw commended Keller's use of ''a wide range of scientific and other literature to bolster her . . . arguments about how the hugely invasive precepts of gender have deformed our concepts of science, kept women from entering the disciplines and undoubtedly shaped the direction of scientific research.''

After tracing the history of women's exclusion from scientific pursuits, Keller ''pleads for a gender-free science, a pluralistic science, one in which many voices can be heard, one that integrates many visions. The methods of achieving this ideal state,'' Shaw added, ''remain illusory.'' ''Her account is more an invitation to think than a conclusion,'' observed Ian Hacking in the *New Republic,* noting that, ''in general, Keller enters a wise plea for tolerance, cooperation, mutual respect, and more sharing of resources among more competing ideas.''

BIOGRAPHICAL/CRITICAL SOURCES:

PERIODICALS

Los Angeles Times Book Review, November 6, 1983.
Nation, November 19, 1983.
New Republic, July 15 & 22, 1985.
New York Review of Books, March 29, 1984.
New York Times Book Review, October 2, 1983, April 21, 1985.

*   *   *

KELLY, George Armstrong   1932-1987

OBITUARY NOTICE: Born in 1932 in Pittsburgh, Pa.; died of a heart attack, December 23, 1987, in New York, N.Y. Educator, editor, and author. An authority on the German philosopher Georg Hegel, Kelly wrote two scholarly explorations of his work, *Idealism, Politics, and History: Sources of Hegelian Thought* and *Hegel's Retreat From Eleusis: Studies in Political Thought.* Kelly was a former faculty member of Harvard University and Brandeis University and a visiting professor of humanities at Johns Hopkins University. His works include *Lost Soldiers: The French Army and Empire in Crisis, 1947-1962* and *Politics and Religious Consciousness in America.* With Clifford W. Brown he edited *Struggles in the State: Sources and Patterns of World Revolution.*

OBITUARIES AND OTHER SOURCES:

PERIODICALS

New York Times, December 26, 1987.

*   *   *

KELLY, Ian
See KELLY, John Spence

KELLY, John Spence   1934-
(Ian Kelly)

PERSONAL: Born July 14, 1934, in Glasgow, Scotland; son of John James (an engineer) and Mary (Booth) Kelly; married Mary W. G. Cowley (a potter), July 28, 1954; children: Iain, Sharon Kelly Slaghuis, Janette Kelly Cumming, Graeme. *Education:* University of Glasgow, M.A. (geography and economics), 1954; University of Lethbridge, B.Ed. (with distinction), 1972; University of Tasmania, M.A. (urban social geography), 1981; Armidale College of Advanced Education, Graduate Diploma in Asian Studies, 1983. *Religion:* None.

ADDRESSES: Home—45 Pomona Rd., Riverside West, Tasmania 7250, Australia. *Office*—School of General Studies, Tasmanian State Institute of Technology, P.O. Box 1214, Launceston, Tasmania 7250, Australia.

CAREER: Schoolteacher in Glasgow, Scotland, 1957-59; teacher of geography, social studies, and English at high school in Launceston, Australia, 1960-62; senior social studies master at high schools in Huonville, Australia, 1963-66, and Hobart, Australia, 1967-68; high school social studies teacher in Foremost, Alberta, 1968-70; geography teacher at collegiate institute in Sarnia, Ontario, 1970-72; assistant head of department, 1972-73; teacher of French and English at high school in Launceston, 1973; Tasmanian State Institute of Technology, Launceston, lecturer in geography and Asian studies, 1974—. Member of geography committee of Schools Board of Tasmania and UNICEF National Education Committee; public speaker. *Military service:* British Army, Royal Army Education Corps, instructor, 1955-57; held rank of sergeant.

MEMBER: Union of Australian College Academics, Asian Studies Association of Australia, Institute of Australian Geographers, Australia-China Society (North Tasmanian vice-president, 1979—), Tasmanian Geography Teachers' Association (president, 1983-84; vice-president, 1985-86), Asian Studies Association of Tasmania, Academic Staff Association.

WRITINGS:

UNDER NAME IAN KELLY

(Contributor) Kenneth Marriott, editor, *Planning,* Philip & O'Neal, 1980.
(Editor with Leigh Miller, and contributor) *Living in Tasmania* (secondary school textbook), Carroll, 1986.
Hong Kong: A Political-Geographic Analysis, Macmillan, 1987.

Contributor to geography and education journals.

WORK IN PROGRESS: China Studies, publication expected in 1989; research on the Chinese in Australia.

SIDELIGHTS: Ian Kelly told *CA* that he has a continuing interest in Hong Kong and its reaction and adaptation to the Sino-British agreement. His more general concerns are peace and multicultural development education. The author has traveled in China and Indonesia, and he has some knowledge of French and Mandarin Chinese.

Kelly continued: ''The small population of Tasmania renders the island economically nonviable in the school textbook industry, and so Leigh Miller and I, with the assistance of Tasmanian Geography Teachers' Association members, produced *Living in Tasmania* for use in secondary school geography and social studies classes. Investigation of the Hong Kong circumstance was a sideline of an ongoing specialization in China studies, which commenced as part of an involvement in tertiary-level teaching about Asia. The Hong Kong study began as a social geography exercise, but during the research period spent at the University of Hong Kong, it became apparent that political-geographic perspectives were more appropriate. It is my view that Hong Kong has, as the result of the Sino-British agreement, a very substantial role to play in the future relationship between China and the rest of the world, and in the rapidly developing Asia-Pacific region—a role in which it would have been restricted as a British territory. It will, of course, depend on a continuation of the directions currently pursued by the People's Republic of China.''

AVOCATIONAL INTERESTS: Soccer, music, crossword puzzles.

*   *   *

KEMAL, Salim   1948-

PERSONAL: Born August 21, 1948, in Hyderabad, India; came to United States, 1986; son of Rahimuddin (an entrepreneur) and Asima (an educator; maiden name, Rehman) Kemal; married Jane Baston. *Education:* University of London, B.A., 1973, M.A., 1976; Cambridge University, Ph.D., 1981.

ADDRESSES: Office—Department of Philosophy, Pennsylvania State University, University Park, Pa. 16802.

CAREER: Cambridge University, Cambridge, England, elected fellow of Wolfson College, 1979; American University of Beirut, Beirut, Lebanon, assistant professor of philosophy, 1981-84; Pennsylvania State University, University Park, associate professor of philosophy, 1986—.

MEMBER: American Philosophical Association, Cambridge Society, Friends of the University of Cambridge Botanical Gardens.

AWARDS, HONORS: Grant from British Academy, 1985; research fellowship from Pennsylvania State University, 1986.

WRITINGS:

Kant and Fine Art: An Essay on Kant and the Philosophy of Fine Art and Culture, Oxford University Press, 1986.
(Contributor) Lawrence I. Conrad, editor, *The World of Ibn Tufayl: Interdisciplinary Perspectives on Hayy ibn Yaqzan,* Oxford University Press, 1988.

Contributor to *Biographical Encyclopaedia of Philosophy and Mathematics.* Contributor of articles and reviews to philosophy journals.

WORK IN PROGRESS: An Introduction to Kant's Aesthetic Theory; The "Poetics" in Islam: Reason and Community in Medieval Philosophy of Art, Oxford University Press, 1990; editor with Ivan Gaskell, *Cambridge Studies in Philosophy and the Arts,* Cambridge University Press, Volume I: *Creativity and Interpretation in the Modern Visual Arts,* 1990, Volume II: *The Language of Art History,* 1990, and future volumes, including *Explanation and Value in the Literary and Visual Arts, Authenticity and Interpretation in the Performing Arts,* and *Landscape, Natural Beauty, and the Arts.*

SIDELIGHTS: Salim Kemal told *CA:* "My interest in philosophy and in the German philosopher Immanuel Kant are easily explained. In 1955 my father published a book, *The Concept of Constitutional Law in Islam,* and explained to me the difference between a concept and the thing to which the concept

applies. Once that distinction was clear I had little choice but to study philosophy. As for my interest in Kant: my great uncle was the first to translate Kant's *Critique of Pure Reason* from German into Urdu. Combining these influences with my interest in film, novels, and pictures, I was led to Kant's aesthetic theory.

"In 1981 I joined the faculty at the American University of Beirut, where I came into contact with the profound and suggestive medieval Arabic commentaries on Aristotle's *Poetics.* It seemed that in the commentaries their authors, Al Farabi (known in Medieval Latin texts as Alpharabi), Ibn Sina (Avicenna), and Ibn Rushd (Averroes), were all engaged in raising questions about the validity of aesthetic claims and about the relation to community that aesthetic responses sustained. It seemed that their issues were similar to the ones which engaged both Kant and, at a much lesser level, myself.''

BIOGRAPHICAL/CRITICAL SOURCES:

PERIODICALS

Times Literary Supplement, April 24, 1987.

*   *   *

KENNEDY, Caroline   1944-

PERSONAL: Born April 30, 1944, in Godalming, Surrey, England; daughter of Geoffrey Farrer (a consultant engineer) and Daska (Ivanovic) Kennedy; married Benedicto Cabrera, November 3, 1969 (divorced, January, 1985); children: Elisar (son), Mayumi (daughter), Jasmine. *Education:* Attended London School of Journalism, 1961-62.

ADDRESSES: Home—9 Teignmouth Rd., London NW2 4HR, England. *Agent*—Douglas Rae Management, 28 Charing Cross Rd., London W.C.2, England.

CAREER: New York World-Telegram and Sun, New York City, journalist, 1964-65; WINS-Radio, New York City, producer, 1965-67; British Broadcasting Corp., London, researcher for television news, 1967-68; *Mirror,* Manila, Philippines, columnist, 1968-69; free-lance journalist and television researcher in London, 1974-84. Television presenter in Manila, 1968-69; researcher and writer for "Filipino Heritage."

MEMBER: International Training in Communication, St. James's Club, Chelsea Arts Club.

WRITINGS:

(With Phillip Knightley) *An Affair of State: The Profumo Case and the Framing of Stephen Ward,* Atheneum, 1987.

WORK IN PROGRESS: A historical novel set in the Philippines, publication expected in 1989; a television documentary drama about a political kidnapping in London; a television documentary drama about an English adventurer in nineteenth-century China; a suspense thriller filmscript.

SIDELIGHTS: An Affair of State is an expose of the government activities to which Caroline Kennedy and her co-author Phillip Knightley attribute the suicide of Stephen Ward. Ward was an engaging London osteopath and ladies' man. Among his companions were the prostitutes Mandy Rice-Davies and Christine Keeler and the Soviet naval attache, Yevgeny Ivanov, who was suspected by the British of being a Soviet spy. In 1962 British intelligence persuaded Ward to set a trap for Ivanov, using Keeler as bait. A scandal ensued when British war minister John Profumo also became intimate with Keeler, and Ward made the mistake of reporting the affair to his intelligence case officer. Profumo denied the charge; Ward retaliated by spreading the news as gossip.

At this point Ward became the subject of what Kennedy and Knightley believe to be systematic police harrassment, initiated by former home secretary Henry Brooke to silence the doctor's accusations. His social and business activities were investigated, his patients were identified and interrogated, and false criminal charges were created. By the time Profumo finally admitted his relationship with Keeler, Ward committed suicide. Anthony Firth wrote in the *Globe and Mail:* "If ever a book had to be written, this is it; and if ever a book will destroy some preconceived ideas and firmly held convictions, this is the book that will do it."

Kennedy told *CA:* "I was drawn to Stephen Ward during research on a proposed television drama/documentary on the Profumo scandal. In someone's attic I came across a box of old reel-to-reel tapes, letters, and an unfinished autobiography penned by Ward while in prison awaiting trial. Through the poor sixties quality of the tapes Ward's voice emerged with compelling clarity. It outlined in detail events leading up to the trial and the reasons and people behind the efforts to silence him. There was little doubt in my mind after I finished listening to him that he had been framed—all I needed to do was prove it, to get the right people to admit it. Then I started tracking down every person involved in the investigation and trial whom I established was still alive. At first they were nervous and hesitant to speak. Finally each one told his story, many for the first time. And, far from concurring with the official version of the day, they confirmed, in even more detail, Ward's own story.

"*An Affair of State* was a thrilling project to work on for me and, happily, it received a great deal of attention when published. It went straight to the top of the nonfiction best-seller list in England and, because of its conclusions, there are now moves in Parliament to re-examine the case as a miscarriage of justice. Unfortunately, there are still many who would prefer to see it sink without trace."

BIOGRAPHICAL/CRITICAL SOURCES:

PERIODICALS

Globe and Mail (Toronto), July 4, 1987.
Kirkus Review, July 1, 1987.
Newsday, September 2, 1987.
New York Times Book Review, September 20, 1987.
Spectator, June, 1987.
Times (London), May 14, 1987.
Washington Post Book World, December 20, 1987.

*   *   *

KENNEDY, Thomas C.   1937-

PERSONAL: Born September 25, 1937, in Dayton, Ohio; son of Harry Lawrence (a journalist and politician) and Mary Adlyn (a bookkeeper and housewife; maiden name, Cummins) Kennedy; married Mary Lynn Goecke (an editor), April 27, 1963; children: Maura, Padraic, Eamon, Caitlin. *Education:* University of Dayton, B.S. Ed., 1959; Arizona State University, M.A., 1964; University of South Carolina at Columbia, Ph.D., 1968. *Politics:* Democrat. *Religion:* "Believer."

ADDRESSES: Home—520 North Willow Ave., Fayetteville, Ark. 72701. *Office*—Department of History, University of Arkansas, Fayetteville, Ark. 72701.

CAREER: University of Arkansas, Fayetteville, professor of history, 1967—, chairman of department, 1986—. Junior high and high school history teacher. *Military service:* U.S. Army, 1960-62.

MEMBER: American Historical Association, Conference on British Studies, American Civil Liberties Union, Friends Historical Association, Conference on Peace Research in History, Western Conference on British Studies (president, 1984-85), Arkansas Association of College History Teachers.

AWARDS, HONORS: T. Wistar Brown fellow at Haverford College, 1983-84.

WRITINGS:

(Contributor) Solomon Wank, editor, *Doves and Diplomats,* Greenwood Press, 1978.
The Hound of Conscience, University of Arkansas Press, 1981.

Contributor of articles and reviews to history journals.

WORK IN PROGRESS: The Quaker Renaissance in British Society, 1880-1920; Southland College: The Society of Friends and Black Education in the South, 1864-1925.

AVOCATIONAL INTERESTS: Travel (especially England), traditional music (especially Celtic music and dance), soccer referee.

*   *   *

KERNAN, Julia K.   1901(?)-1988

OBITUARY NOTICE: Some sources spell given name Julie; born c. 1901 in Roanoke, Va.; died of an embolism, May 24, 1988, in Washington, D.C. Secretary, translator, editor, and author. For a decade, beginning in 1919, Kernan was an editor in the international law division of the Carnegie Endowment for International Peace in Washington, D.C. After graduation from George Washington University she earned a degree in French studies from the University of Grenoble in France, and from 1931 to 1934 Kernan was secretary of the French Book Club in Paris. When she returned to the United States she embarked on a publishing career that included posts with Longmans, Green, and Company, the David McKay publishing house, and P. J. Kennedy and Sons. Kernan retired in 1966. Her writings include *The Shadow of the Pope, Our Friend, Jacques Maritain: A Personal Memoir,* and *The Catholic Church in Action,* which she wrote with Michael Williams. Kernan also translated a number of volumes, such as *Life of Jesus* by Francois Mauriac and Raissa Maritain's *Adventures in Grace.*

OBITUARIES AND OTHER SOURCES:

BOOKS

American Catholic Who's Who, Volume 23: *1980-81,* National Catholic News Service, 1979.
The Author's and Writer's Who's Who, 6th edition, reprinted, Burke's Peerage, 1971.

PERIODICALS

Washington Post, May 25, 1988.

*   *   *

KERR, Alex A.   1922-
(Andy Kerr)

PERSONAL: Born January 11, 1922, in Sydney, Australia;

immigrated to the United States, 1932, naturalized citizen, 1938; son of Alexander (a violinist) and Gladys (a housewife; maiden name, Leary) Kerr; married Rusty Dreller, November 7, 1947 (died May 21, 1977); married Susan Jovovich (an attorney), June 21, 1979; children: (first marriage) Alex A., Jr., Laurie Dreller. *Education:* U.S. Naval Academy, B.S., 1944; George Washington University, J.D., 1954.

ADDRESSES: Home—MCCA 39184, P.O. Box 2870, Estes Park, Colo. 80517.

CAREER: U.S. Navy, career officer, 1944-68, served as officer in cruisers and submarines and as special counsel to secretaries of the navy John Connally, Fred Korth, Paul Nitze, and Paul Ignatius, retiring as captain; General Electric Co., Daytona Beach, Fla., New York, N.Y., and San Jose, Calif., corporate counsel, 1968-74, chief counsel for Nuclear Energy Group, 1974-78; writer, 1978—.

MEMBER: Coif, Seven Seas Cruising Association (commodore), Royal Hong Kong Yacht Club.

AWARDS, HONORS: Military—Legion of Merit; four commendation medals from Secretary of the Navy.

WRITINGS:

UNDER NAME ANDY KERR

A Journey Amongst the Good and the Great, Naval Institute Press, 1987.

Contributor to yachting magazines and law and navy journals.

SIDELIGHTS: Alex A. Kerr told *CA:* "Since 1978 I have lived aboard my forty-three-foot sailboat *Andiamo III.* My wife and I have sailed her from England to the Mediterranean, thence across the Atlantic and the Pacific. We have sailed an estimated fifty thousand miles in the last ten years. *Andiamo III* is berthed at the Royal Hong Kong Yacht Club while we decide on the next leg of our voyage.

"My book *A Journey Amongst the Good and the Great* gives, I believe, plausible evidence that Lee Harvey Oswald was shooting at John Connally and shot President John Kennedy by accident. It also gives insights into the Gulf of Tonkin incidents, the Bay of Pigs fiasco, and many other events of the Kennedy and Johnson years. The book is an autobiography. I was moved to write it because of the enthusiasm of the director of the navy's oral history program, who had previously recorded my reminiscences."

*   *   *

KERR, Andy
   See KERR, Alex A.

*   *   *

KESSLER, Herbert L(eon)   1941-

PERSONAL: Born July 20, 1941, in Chicago, Ill.; son of Ben and Bertha Kessler; married Johanna Zacharias (a writer and editor), April 24, 1976; children: Morisa Kessler-Zacharias. *Education:* University of Chicago, A.B., 1961; Princeton University, M.F.A., 1963, Ph.D., 1965.

ADDRESSES: Home—211 Ridgewood Rd., Baltimore, Md. 21210. *Office*—Department of Art, Johns Hopkins University, Baltimore, Md. 21218.

CAREER: University of Chicago, Chicago, Ill., assistant professor, 1965-68, associate professor, 1968-73, professor of art

history, 1973-76, chairman of department of art and university director of fine arts, 1973-76; Johns Hopkins University, Baltimore, Md., professor of art history and chairman of department, 1976—, Charlotte Bloomberg Professor of the Faculty of Arts and Sciences, 1984—.

MEMBER: College Art Association of America, Mediaeval Academy of America, Phi Beta Kappa.

AWARDS, HONORS: Woodrow Wilson fellow, 1961-62; Dumbarton Oaks, junior fellow, 1964-65, senior fellow, 1980-86; fellow of Institute of Advanced Studies, Princeton, N.J., 1969-70; Guggenheim fellow, 1972-73; fellow of American Council of Learned Societies, 1979-80 and 1988-89; fellow of American Philosophical Society, 1980; fellow at American Academy in Rome, 1984-85.

WRITINGS:

French and Flemish Illuminated Manuscripts in Chicago Collections, Newberry Library, 1969.
The Illustrated Bibles From Tours, Princeton University Press, 1977.
(With Kurt Weitzmann) *The Cotton Genesis: British Library Codex Cotton Otho B. VI,* Princeton University Press, 1986.

WORK IN PROGRESS: Frescoes of the Dura Synagogue and Christian Art, publication expected in 1989; *Old St. Peter's in Rome,* publication expected in 1990.

*   *   *

KIBBE, Pat (Hosley)

PERSONAL: Married John Kibbe (a lawyer); children: Jonathan, Kyle, Ethan, Allison, Justine. *Education:* Graduate of American Academy of Dramatic Arts.

ADDRESSES: Home—Yorktown Heights, N.Y. 10598.

CAREER: Actress and writer.

AWARDS, HONORS: Children's Choice Award from International Reading Association for *The Hocus-Pocus Dilemma.*

WRITINGS:

FOR CHILDREN

The Hocus-Pocus Dilemma, Knopf, 1979.
My Mother, the Mayor, Maybe, Knopf, 1981.
Mrs. Kiddy and the Moonbeams, Bradbury, 1983.

*   *   *

KIERMAN, Frank Algerton, Jr.   1914-

PERSONAL: Born April 19, 1914, in Boston, Mass.; son of Frank Algerton (a telephone installer) and Lily Jean (a secretary; maiden name, Fraser) Kierman; married Marilois Ditto (a musician), February 20, 1941; children: Sean Algerton, Jean Elaine Kierman Fischer. *Education:* Wesleyan University, Middletown, Conn., A.B., 1935; Reed College, M.A., 1943; University of Washington, Seattle, Ph.D., 1953. *Religion:* Episcopalian.

ADDRESSES: Home—6 Alyce Court, Lawrenceville, N.J. 08648.

CAREER: George School, Newtown, Pa., English intern, 1935-36; Harvey School, Hawthorne, N.Y., master, 1936-40; Reed College, Portland, Ore., instructor in drama and director of drama program, 1941-44; U.S. Department of State, Washington, D.C., foreign service officer in Naking, China, Hong Kong, Karachi, Pakistan, and Nairobi, Kenya, 1948-67; Princeton University, Princeton, N.J., director of research for Chinese Linguistic Project, 1967-71; Rider College, Lawrenceville, N.J., professor of history, 1971-82, chairman of department, 1973-82; writer, 1982—. Actor and singer with Lyric Opera Company, 1940. *Military service:* U.S. Marine Corps, 1944-46.

MEMBER: American Historical Association, Association for Asian Studies, American Oriental Society, Phi Beta Kappa.

WRITINGS:

(Contributor) Walt W. Rostow, editor, *The Prospects for Communist China*, MIT Press, 1954.
Four Late Warring States Biographies, Otto Harrassowitz, 1962.
(Contributor) Davis C. Buxbaum, editor, *Transition and Permanence: Chinese History and Culture*, Cathay, 1972.
(Translator) Henri Maspero, *China in Antiquity*, University of Massachusetts Press, 1978.
(Editor with John K. Fairbank; and contributor) *Chinese Ways in Warfare*, Harvard University Press, 1981.
(Translator) Henri Maspero, *Taoism and Chinese Religion*, University of Massachusetts Press, 1981.

WORK IN PROGRESS: Warfare in History.

SIDELIGHTS: Frank Algerton Kierman, Jr., told *CA:* "*Warfare in History* will analyze how warfare affects nation, peoples, and their history. It considers a series of examples: the Dani of New Guinea (a documented example of what primitive war may have been like), the Zulu of southeastern Africa (an example of a people who moved from apparently primitive to semi-organized warfare within a few decades, the last of which are documented), the Mamluks of Egypt (a peculiar but somewhat representative example of Muslim warfare), China, Japan, and 'the West': that is, the strand of civilization beginning in the Near East, the Greeks and Romans, Europe, and the Americas.

"The major emphasis is on the ways war affects nations, destroying some, bringing others to a quite different plane of existence (Rome is a prime example), affecting polities and individuals (Sparta and Japan are cases of highly militarized states, for example), and how the need for self-defense alters nations founded with aspirations that are primarily focused on other things (the United States and the U.S.S.R. both, in their disparate ways, exemplify this).''

*   *   *

KIGER, Joseph Charles 1920-

PERSONAL: Born August 19, 1920, in Kenton County, Ky.; son of Carl C. and Genevieve (Hoelscher) Kiger; married Jean Myrick Moore, March 27, 1947; children: Carl A., John J. *Education:* Birmingham-Southern College, A.B., 1943; University of Alabama, M.A., 1947; Vanderbilt University, Ph.D., 1950.

ADDRESSES: Home—Country Club Rd., Oxford, Miss. 38655. *Office*—Department of History, University of Mississippi, University, Miss. 38677.

CAREER: University of Alabama, University, instructor in history, 1950; Washington University, St. Louis, Mo., instructor in history, 1950-51; U.S. House of Representatives, Washington, D.C., director of research for Select Committee to Investigate Foundations, 1952; American Council on Education, Washington, D.C., staff associate, 1953-55; Southern Fellowships Fund, Chapel Hill, N.C., assistant director, 1955-58; University of Alabama, associate professor of history, 1958-61; University of Mississippi, University, professor of history, 1961—, chairman of department, 1969-74. *Military service:* U.S. Marine Corps Reserve, active duty, 1942-46; became captain.

MEMBER: American Historical Association, American Studies Association, Southern Historical Association (life member).

AWARDS, HONORS: Grants from Russell Sage Foundation, 1953, Rockefeller Foundation, 1961, American Philosophical Society, 1964, American Council of Learned Societies, 1980, and National Academy of Sciences, 1980; Guggenheim fellow, 1960.

WRITINGS:

Operating Principles of the Larger Foundations, Russell Sage Foundation, 1954.
(With others) *Sponsored Research Policy of Colleges and Universities*, American Council on Education, 1954.
American Learned Societies, Public Affairs Press, 1963.
(With others) *A History of Mississippi*, University Press of Mississippi, 1973.
(Editor) *Research Institutions and Learned Societies*, Greenwood Press, 1982.
(Editor with Harold M. Keele) *Foundations*, Greenwood Press, 1984.
Historiographic Review of Foundation Literature: Motivation and Perception, Foundation Center, 1987.
International Encyclopedia of Foundations, Greenwood Press, in press.

*   *   *

KILEY, Dan (Edward) 1942-

BRIEF ENTRY: Born November 10, 1942, in Pontiac, Ill. American psychologist and author. A specialist in human behavior, Kiley worked at various educational and health facilities before entering his private practice of clinical psychology in 1977. Six years later he sparked national attention with the publication of his best-selling book, *The Peter Pan Syndrome: Men Who Have Never Grown Up* (Dodd, 1983). Based on actual case studies and named after the well-known children's story featuring a boy who never achieves manhood, the popular work advises women how to deal with adult males who continue to act like children. Similar behavioral-type problems are addressed in each of Kiley's other volumes: *Nobody Said It Would Be Easy: Raising Responsible Kids—and Keeping Them Out of Trouble* (Harper, 1978; published as *Keeping Kids Out of Trouble*, Warner Books, 1984), *Keeping Parents Out of Trouble: A Modern Guide to Old-Fashioned Discipline* (Warner Books, 1981), *Dr. Dan's Prescriptions: 1001 Behavioral Hints for Solving Parenting Problems* (Coward, McCann & Geoghegan, 1982), *The Wendy Dilemma: When Women Stop Mothering Their Men* (Arbor House, 1984), and *What to Do When He Won't Change: Getting What You Need From the Man You Love* (Putnam, 1987). Widely known as Doctor Dan, Kiley is featured in a weekly broadcast on WGN-Radio in Chicago, and he has appeared on television programs such as "Phil Donahue" and "Today." *Addresses: Office*—Suite 201, 213 West Wesley St., Wheaton, Ill. 60187.

BIOGRAPHICAL/CRITICAL SOURCES:

BOOKS

Who's Who in the Midwest, 18th edition, Marquis, 1982.

PERIODICALS

Chicago Tribune, October 5, 1983.
Los Angeles Times, December 26, 1983.
New York Times Book Review, October 30, 1983, September 23, 1984.

* * *

KINCAID, Jamaica 1949-

PERSONAL: Born May 25, 1949, in St. John's, Antigua, West Indies; immigrated to United States; naturalized U.S. citizen; daughter of a carpenter and Annie Richardson; married Allen Shawn (a composer); children: one daughter. *Religion:* Methodist.

ADDRESSES: Home—284 Hudson, New York, N.Y. *Office*—*New Yorker,* 25 West 43rd St., New York, N.Y. 10036.

CAREER: Writer. Staff writer for *New Yorker* in New York, N.Y., 1976—.

AWARDS, HONORS: Morton Dauwen Zabel Award from American Academy and Institute of Arts and Letters, 1983, for *At the Bottom of the River.*

WRITINGS:

At the Bottom of the River (short stories), Farrar, Straus, 1983.
Annie John (short story cycle), Farrar, Straus, 1985.
A Small Place, Farrar, Straus, 1988.

Contributor to periodicals, including *New Yorker.*

SIDELIGHTS: Jamaica Kincaid is the acclaimed author of *At the Bottom of the River* and *Annie John.* In these books about life on the Caribbean island Antigua, where she was born, Kincaid employs a highly poetic literary style, one celebrated for its rhythms and imagery, and shows herself a master of characterization and elliptic narration. As Ike Onwordi wrote in *Times Literary Supplement:* "Jamaica Kincaid uses language that is poetic without affectation. She has a deft eye for salient detail while avoiding heavy symbolism and diverting exotica. The result captures powerfully the essence of vulnerability."

In her first book, *At the Bottom of the River,* Kincaid showed an imposing capacity for detailing life's mundane aspects. This characteristic of her writing is readily evident in the often cited tale "Girl," which consists almost entirely of a mother's orders to her daughter: "Wash the white clothes on Monday and put them on the stone heap; wash the color clothes on Tuesday and put them on the clothesline to dry; don't walk barehead in the hot sun; cook pumpkin fritters in very hot sweet oil . . . ; on Sundays try to walk like a lady, and not like the slut you are so bent on becoming." Anne Tyler, in her review for *New Republic,* declared that this passage provides "the clearest idea of the book's general tone; for Jamaica Kincaid scrutinizes various particles of our world so closely and so solemnly that they begin to take on a nearly mystical importance."

"The Letter From Home," another story from *At the Bottom of the River,* serves as further illustration of Kincaid's style of repetition and her penchant for the mundane. In this tale a character recounts her daily chores in such a manner that the entire tale resembles an incantation: "I milked the cows, I churned the butter, I stored the cheese, I baked the bread, I brewed the tea," the tale begins, and it continues in this manner for several pages before ending as one long sentence. In *Ms.,* Suzanne Freeman cited this tale as evidence that Kincaid's style "is . . . akin to hymn-singing or maybe even chanting." Freeman added that Kincaid's "singsong style" produces "images that are as sweet and mysterious as the secrets that children whisper in your ear."

Upon publication in 1983, *At the Bottom of the River* marked Kincaid's arrival as an important new voice in American fiction. Edith Milton wrote in the *New York Times Book Review* that Kincaid's tales "have all the force of illumination, and even prophetic power," and David Leavitt noted in the *Village Voice* that they move "with grace and ease from the mundane to the enormous." Leavitt also stated that "Kincaid's particular skill lies in her ability to articulate the internal workings of a potent imagination without sacrificing the rich details of the external world on which that imagination thrives." Doris Grumbach expressed similar praise in her review for the *Washington Post Book World.* She declared that the world of Kincaid's narrators "hovers between fantasy and reality" and asserted that Kincaid's prose "results not so much in stories as in states of consciousness." Grumbach also wrote that Kincaid's style, particularly its emphasis on repetition, intensifies "the feelings of poetic jubilation Kincaid has . . . for all life."

That exuberance for life is also evident in Kincaid's second book, *Annie John,* which contains interrelated stories about a girl's maturation in Antigua. In *Annie John,* the title character evolves from young girl to aspiring nurse and from innocent to realist: she experiences her first menstruation, buries a friend, gradually establishes a life independent of her mother, and overcomes a serious illness. After recovering her health Annie John decides to depart from Antigua to become a nurse in England, though this decision results in a painful, and necessary, separation from her mother. "No, I am not you," Annie John eventually informs her mother in one tale; "I am not what you made me." By book's end Annie John has left her mother to pursue a nursing career. She is ultimately torn by her pursuit of a career outside her life in Antigua, and Kincaid renders that feeling so incisively that, as Elaine Kendall noted in her review for the *Los Angeles Times,* "you can almost believe Kincaid invented ambivalence."

Like *At the Bottom of the River,* Kincaid's *Annie John* earned widespread acclaim. Susan Kenney, writing in the *New York Times Book Review,* observed that "Kincaid . . . has packed a lot of valuable insight about the complex relationship between mothers and daughters into this slender novel." Kenney noted Annie John's ambivalence about leaving behind her life in Antigua and declared that such ambivalence was "an inevitable and unavoidable result of growing up." Furthermore, Kenney stated that she couldn't "remember reading a book that illustrates this [ambivalence] more poignantly than" *Annie John.* Kendall, who called *Annie John* a "fully fledged novel," seconded Kenney's assessment and confirmed Kincaid's status as a major writer. According to Kendall, *Annie John* possessed "a timeless quality, adding substance and weight to the smallest incident and detail."

Many critics focused particular praise on Kincaid's poetic style and artistic sensitivity. An *Atlantic* reviewer noted the "cool, precise style" of *Annie John,* and *Nation* reviewer Barbara Fisher Williamson noted that the volume's first-person narrative—Annie John's "tone flat, her language modest"—"works best when it is undercut by ironic detachment or overburdened by intense feeling.'' Comparing *Annie John* favorably to the earlier *At the Bottom of the River, Washington Post* critic Susan Wood noted that the later work ''retains the shimmering, strange beauty of the earlier stories, but its poetry is grounded in detail, in the lovingly rendered life of its adolescent heroine.'' And Kendall wrote in the *Los Angeles Times* that ''Kincaid's imagery is so neon-bright that the traditional story of a young girl's passage into adolescence takes on a shimmering strangeness, the familiar outlines continually forming surprising patterns.''

With only two books, Kincaid has become a prominent figure in American literature, and even though her books are set in a foreign land, the West Indies, she credits the United States as the place where ''I did find myself and did find my voice.'' In the *New York Times Book Review*, where she made the aforementioned comment, she added: ''What I really feel about America is that it's given me a place to be myself—but myself as I was formed somewhere else.''

BIOGRAPHICAL/CRITICAL SOURCES:

BOOKS

Contemporary Literary Criticism, Volume 43, Gale, 1987.

PERIODICALS

Atlantic, May, 1985.
Boston Herald, March 31, 1985.
Christian Science Monitor, April 5, 1985.
Listener, January 10, 1985.
Los Angeles Times, April 25, 1985.
Maclean's, May 20, 1985.
Ms., January, 1984.
Nation, June 15, 1985.
New Republic, December 31, 1983.
New Statesman, September 7, 1984.
New York Times Book Review, January 15, 1984.
Times Literary Supplement, November 29, 1985.
Village Voice, January 17, 1984.
Virginia Quarterly Review, summer, 1985.
Voice Literary Supplement, April, 1985.
Washington Post, April 2, 1985.
Washington Post Book World, February 5, 1984.
World Literature Today, autumn, 1985.

—*Sketch by Les Stone*

*   *   *

KINDEM, Gorham A(nders) 1948-

PERSONAL: Born May 28, 1948, in Dickensen, N.D.; son of Ingolf Bjarne (a minister) and Bette Ann (a housewife; maiden name, Carlson) Kindem; married Nancy Houston (a teacher), June 19, 1971; children: Peter Anders, Thomas Houston, John Paul. *Education:* Lawrence University, B.A., 1970; Northwestern University, M.A., 1972, Ph.D., 1977.

ADDRESSES: Home—301 Hickory Dr., Chapel Hill, N.C. 27514. *Office*—Department of Radio, Television, and Motion Pictures, University of North Carolina at Chapel Hill, Chapel Hill, N.C. 27514.

CAREER: Allied Film Laboratory, Chicago, Ill., color timer, 1972-74; Shaw University, Raleigh, N.C., instructor in radio and television, 1976; University of North Carolina at Chapel Hill, assistant professor, 1977-82, associate professor of radio, television, and motion pictures, 1982—, department chair-

man, 1987—. Visiting professor at University of Trondheim, 1983-84; visiting associate professor at Duke University, 1987.

MEMBER: University Film and Video Association, Society for Cinema Studies.

AWARDS, HONORS: CINE Golden Eagle Award for documentary film ''Chuck Davis, Dancing Through West Africa.''

WRITINGS:

Toward a Semiotic Theory of Visual Communication in the Cinema, Arno, 1981.
(Editor) *The American Movie Industry: The Business of Motion Pictures*, Southern Illinois University Press, 1982.
The Moving Image: Production Principles and Practices, Scott, Foresman, 1986.

Associate editor of *Cinema Journal*, 1977-82, and *UFVA Journal*, 1982—. Also associated with ''Chuck Davis, Dancing Through West Africa,'' Public Broadcasting Service (PBS-TV), 1988.

WORK IN PROGRESS: Film/Video Theory and Practice, ''an anthology applying classical and contemporary theory to aspects of film and video practice—lighting, camera work, editing, etc.''

SIDELIGHTS: Gorham A. Kindem told *CA* that his goal is ''to promote film and television as areas of serious scholarly study, focusing upon institutions and audiences, as well as artists and texts.''

AVOCATIONAL INTERESTS: Basketball, skating, skiing, reading.

*   *   *

KINDLEY, Jeffrey 1945-

BRIEF ENTRY: Born June 2, 1945, in Portland, Ore. American educator, playwright, and writer for television and film. Kindley achieved critical acclaim for a number of children's television specials, several of which received multiple awards and/or nominations, such as an Emmy Award, the George Foster Peabody Award, and the Christopher Award. Most notable among them are ''The Great Love Experiment'' (''ABC Afterschool Special,'' 1983) and two collaborations, ''Family of Strangers'' (''ABC Afterschool Special,'' 1981) and ''The Electric Grandmother'' (''NBC Project Peacock Special,'' 1982). Less successful have been Kindley's theatrical productions, which include two Off-Broadway plays and the 1982 Broadway musical ''Is There Life After High School?'' Additionally, Kindley has written ''No Big Deal,'' a television movie, and ''The Beniker Gang,'' a 1985 feature film. During the 1970s Kindley taught English at Columbia College and in 1966 he published a short collection of poetry entitled *The Under-Wood* (Phoenix Book Shop). *Addresses: Home*—27 West 96th St., No. 2C, New York, N.Y. 10025. *Agent*—Gilbert Parker, William Morris Agency, 1350 Avenue of the Americas, New York, N.Y. 10019.

BIOGRAPHICAL/CRITICAL SOURCES:

BOOKS

Contemporary Theatre, Film, and Television, Volume 1, Gale, 1984.
National Playwrights Directory, 2nd edition, Eugene O'Neill Theatre Center, 1981.

PERIODICALS

Los Angeles Times, February 25, 1984.
New York Times, May 8, 1982, May 8, 1988.

*   *   *

KING, Martin Luther, Sr.   1899-1984

PERSONAL: Born December 19, 1899, in Stockbridge, Ga.; died of heart disease, November 11, 1984, in Atlanta, Ga.; son of James (a sharecropper) and Delia King; married Alberta Christine (a schoolteacher; maiden name, Williams), 1926 (murdered, 1974); children: Christine, Martin Luther, Jr. (assassinated, 1968), Alfred Daniel Williams (died, 1969), James (died, some sources say in infancy), Delia (died, some sources say in infancy). *Education:* Morehouse College, B.Theol., 1930 (some sources say 1931).

ADDRESSES: Office—Ebenezer Baptist Church, 407-413 Auburn Ave. N.E., Atlanta, Ga. 30312.

CAREER: Ordained as lay preacher, 1914; Second Baptist Church of College Park, Atlanta, Ga., founder, 1920; Ebenezer Baptist Church, Atlanta, pastor, became pastor emeritus, 1931-75 (some sources say 1932-75). Moderator, became moderator emeritus, of Atlanta Missionary Baptist Association. Board member of the Social Action Committee of the National Association for the Advancement of Colored People (NAACP). Board member emeritus of the Southern Christian Leadership Conference, Atlanta University, Citizen's Trust Co., and Carrie-Steele-Pitts Children's Home, Atlanta. Also served on the board of trustees of Morehouse College School of Religion at the Interdenominational Theological Center, Atlanta.

MEMBER: National Baptist Convention, Atlanta Negro Voters League, Inter-racial Council of Atlanta.

AWARDS, HONORS: Voted Clergyman of the Year by Georgia region of National Conference of Christians and Jews, 1972, and Council of Christians and Jews, 1973; Order of the Lion from Republic of Senegal, West Africa, 1975; named National Father of the Year in Religion, 1978; named honorary president of Martin Luther King, Jr., Center for Social Change; recipient of Distinguished Ministers Fellowship award; holder of ten honorary doctoral degrees, including D.D. from Morris Brown College, 1945, D.Letters from University of Haiti, 1968, D.D. from Morehouse College, 1969, and D.Th. from Lutheran Academy, Hungary, 1978.

WRITINGS:

(With Clayton Riley) *Daddy King: An Autobiography,* Morrow, 1980.

SIDELIGHTS: "To many, perhaps most Americans, both black and white, the civil rights movement is a part of history, embracing the years following 1954 (with the landmark Supreme Court decision of Brown vs. Board of Education) and ending in 1968 on a motel balcony in Memphis with the assassination of Martin Luther King Jr.," Valerie Shaw commented in the *Los Angeles Times Book Review.* But in the book Shaw reviewed, *Daddy King: An Autobiography,* the Reverend Martin Luther King, Sr., states that the roots of the civil rights movement extended beyond just the years of his son's brief career to form part of a powerful political movement towards racial equality that is a central part of America's evolving social history. What the autobiography does, Shaw contended, is to reveal the powerful, if not always prominent, role the elder King played in the civil rights movement for over half a century.

In many ways, the story of King's rise from a poor background in rural Georgia to his becoming a key civic leader first in Atlanta, and later throughout the country as a whole, epitomizes the very struggle for respect the thousands of black Americans he represented faced in the United States during the early twentieth century. The second of ten children born into a poor sharecropper's family in Stockbridge, Georgia, in 1899, King learned early the harsh realities of being poor and black in the southern United States. In his early teens he was beaten by a white mill owner for refusing to hand over a bucket of water he had fetched for his mother, and he witnessed the hanging of a black man by a drunken white mob. Incidents like these, compounded by a repressive social environment, at first embittered the young King. Harris Wofford recalled King's thoughts in a review of *Daddy King* for the *Washington Post Book World.* A difficult thing "to get through his head was the idea of loving his enemies. At his mother's death bed, he 'cursed whites' who had brought so much pain to her and swore he would 'hate every white face [he] saw.'" However, the lesson he learned from his mother's response stayed with him the rest of his life. "Hatred," she told him, "makes nothin' but more hatred. . . . Don't you do it." In his autobiography King frequently stresses the importance to his later life of such lessons learned from the advice of family members.

At the age of sixteen, and already an ordained lay preacher in the Stockbridge area, the young Martin Luther King left home and moved to Atlanta, where he believed he would have a better opportunity to complete his education. As Wofford noted, King greatly valued education, and "credits his elder sister for getting through his 'stubborn head' that there was nothing you could do without [it]." So, by working on the railroads by day, and attending night school, he gained his high school diploma in 1925, and that same year persuaded the president of Morehouse College, despite the objections of the registrar, to admit him to the School of Theology, passionately predicting that "I can go further, if I work at it, and I will," Charles Kaiser in *Newsweek* cited King's autobiography.

The year of his acceptance to Morehouse, King married Alberta Hunter, the daughter of the Reverend A. D. Williams, pastor of Ebenezer Baptist, a leading black church in Atlanta. The marriage was significant not only for the couple's happiness, but it enabled King to eventually extend his reputation as a preacher. When he arrived in Atlanta, he had already been ordained and quickly established himself as pastor of two small community churches. Aware of his son-in-law's energetic and popular public speaking, Williams asked King to undertake some of the preaching duties at Ebenezer Baptist. Faced with a large congregation for the first time, King was presented with an opportunity to consolidate his oratorical and clerical skills. Over a five-year period he did just that, gaining the respect and trust of the local community while building a reputation as a gifted clergyman. When Williams died in 1931, King was chosen as his successor. The move to Ebenezer Baptist proved to be critically influential to the future direction of King's career. Gradually, over a period of months, his preaching style and popularity drew more people to the church. Membership of a few hundred under Williams's leadership swelled to several thousand. The larger congregation for King's sermons became the trial audience for his messages which he directed increasingly to the needs and concerns of the black community of Atlanta. As a reviewer for *Newsweek* wrote, it was "from the Ebenezer Baptist pulpit, where he preached for 44 years, [that] 'Daddy King' helped shape the destiny of a nation."

Throughout the 1930s, King began to find many answers to the racism and civil rights issues that plagued the southern states in the messages he preached from the Bible. With the problems clear for many, especially blacks, to see, and with solutions apparently at hand, it seemed an inevitable progression for an idealistic, driven man such as King to seek to implement change through social action. Where he found support for his ideas was in the ranks of like-minded thinkers and activists who had begun rallying around the banner of civil rights. During the 1930s, King joined organizations intent on confronting social injustice such as the National Association for the Advancement of Colored People (NAACP), the Atlanta Negro Voters League, and the Inter-racial Council of Atlanta and, more and more, the leadership he displayed in his official position of pastor to a community church was carried over into a broader, civic context. In 1936, for instance, he led a black voting rights march, the first in Atlanta's history, to the city hall, later campaigned against the discriminatory hiring policy of the Ford Motor Company and for the desegregation of elevators in the Atlanta court house, and, in 1960, played a critical role in the success of John Kennedy's presidential campaign by mobilizing black support for the Kennedy cause. As King's commitment to the civil rights movement grew, so did his reputation and influence in the black community. But perhaps his greatest influence was still to be felt—that which he exerted on his family and, in particular, on his son, Martin Luther King, Jr.

Authors and critics have only speculated as to the role the elder King played in shaping his son, but what seems clear is the strength of support "Daddy King" gave him. When Martin Luther King, Jr., then on the verge of assuming a leading role in the civil rights movement, decided to return to Montgomery, Alabama, to face almost certain imprisonment for incitement during the height of that city's race riots in 1956, it was his father who, despite pleading with his son not to go, finally acceded and drove him and his wife, Coretta, from Atlanta to Montgomery, stopping in that city to pray with his son. Seven years later, King, Sr., welcomed his son on his triumphant return to Atlanta following the famous oration the younger King gave in Washington, D.C., and was even with his son, campaigning on behalf of low-paid public service workers, when Martin Luther King, Jr., was assassinated in Memphis, Tennessee, in 1968.

The death of King, Jr., began a tragic six-year period in the elder King's life that also saw his younger son, the Reverend A. D. King, mysteriously drown in a swimming pool accident in 1969, and Alberta, his wife of forty-seven years, murdered by a crazed gunman while she played the organ during a Sunday morning service at Ebenezer Baptist. The gunman later confessed that he had been aiming for King. But even in the face of such extreme personal tragedy, King's belief in nonviolence and understanding did not waiver. Wofford related that in his autobiography King described a three-hour family meeting following his wife's murder in which the younger relatives asked, "Why did God let that crazy man kill Big Mama? Why do all these terrible things happen to our family?" To which he replied that although it was difficult to understand, "God wants us to love one another. . . . Now get out of here, and remember: Don't ever stoop so low that you let anybody make you hate."

In the years following the deaths of his wife and sons, King's continued adherence to the doctrine of nonviolence and equality earned him great respect. He could regularly be heard preaching the dual messages of love and equality at Ebenezer Baptist, and it seemed natural that, in the realm of public speaking, he should assume the mantle of his assassinated son, King, Jr. Giving speeches and addresses to organizations where his son's efforts and influence had already been felt, King's own stature as a civic leader grew to a point where, in 1976, he played a critical role in the presidential campaign of former Georgia governor Jimmy Carter. Carter had made a remark about "ethnic purity" in regards to his housing policy which, if construed as racist, could have cost him the majority of the black vote—a critical portion of the total electorate. King leapt to the candidate's defense, according to an article in *The Annual Obituary 1984,* proclaiming at a rally in Atlanta that "It is wrong to jump on a man for a slip of the tongue that everyone knows does not represent his thinking," and embraced Carter in a powerful public exoneration. Carter went on to win the 1976 presidential election with an estimated 90 percent of the black vote. Acknowledging his gratitude at King's funeral, Carter announced that "the turning-point in my 1976 campaign came . . . when Daddy King held up my hand for the world to see."

In many ways, the public celebrity of the elder King came through the greater visibility afforded him by an expanding mass media in the latter portion of this century, and by his son's tragic death. Yet he became a powerful spokesman for almost four generations of Americans during an era of massive social upheaval. In his autobiography, King offers two reasons for the South's failure to solve its racial problems, as Kaiser noted: "The long-time refusal of any white Southern minister to embrace the civil-rights movement, and the perception among whites—which endured until the 1960s—that integration would mean their own public humiliation." Nevertheless King still managed to offer an optimistic message for the future. Kaiser reported that King once remarked, "How many people thought, when I was a boy, that segregation would be gone before my life was over?"

When King died, nearly three thousand mourners listened to the tributes paid him by such figures as former President Carter, Vice-President George Bush, and Jesse Jackson, who—quoted in *The Annual Obituary*—said: "This man grew from obscurity to become king in a royal household. . . . When you hear the name Judas you think of betrayal. When you hear the name Rockefeller you think of money. When you hear the name Martin Luther King you think of justice, human rights, morality, love and character."

BIOGRAPHICAL/CRITICAL SOURCES:

BOOKS

Collins, David R., *Not Only Dreamers: The Story of Martin Luther King, Sr., and Martin Luther King, Jr.,* Brethren Press, 1986.

King, Martin Luther, Sr., and Clayton Riley, *Daddy King: An Autobiography,* Morrow, 1980.

PERIODICALS

Los Angeles Times Book Review, January 4, 1981.
Newsweek, July 4, 1976, September 15, 1980.
New York Times Book Review, February 8, 1981.
Washington Post Book World, September 21, 1980.

OBITUARIES:

BOOKS

The Annual Obituary 1984, St. James Press, 1985.

PERIODICALS

Newsweek, November 26, 1984.
New York Times, November 12, 1984.
Time, November 26, 1984.*

—Sketch by Jeremy Kane

*   *   *

KING, Peter   1925-

PERSONAL: Born September 10, 1925, in London, England; son of Leslie (a manager) and Anne (Hall) King; married Deirdre McSharry (divorced); married Cherry Carroll (a paper restorer); children: Toby, Polly, Matthew. Education: Attended Jesus College, Cambridge, 1943-44, 1947-49.

ADDRESSES: Home—Nicholas Corner, Sibford Gower, Oxfordshire, England.

CAREER: Worked in the aircraft industry; director at Massey-Ferguson, London, England; writer. Military service: Royal Air Force; became flight lieutenant.

MEMBER: Royal Geographic Society (fellow), Royal Aeronautical Society (associate), Savile Club (member of governing committee).

WRITINGS:

Grand National: Anybody's Race, Quartet, 1983.
A Viceroy's India, Sidgwick & Jackson, 1984.
The Shooting Field, Quiller, 1985.
Travels With a Superior Person, Sidgwick & Jackson, 1985.
The Viceroy's Fall: How Kitchener Destroyed Curzon, Sidgwick & Jackson, 1986.
Curzon's Persia, Sidgwick & Jackson, 1986.
Green Words, Quartet, 1986.
Protect Our Planet: A History of the World Wildlife Fund, Quiller, 1986.
(Editor) Jeeves Diary, Century Hutchinson, 1986.
(With Maria Aitken) Lady Travellers, Constable, 1987.

Author of plays for BBC-Radio.

BIOGRAPHICAL/CRITICAL SOURCES:

PERIODICALS

Times Literary Supplement, June 27, 1986.

*   *   *

KING, Philip B(urke)   1903-1987

PERSONAL: Born September 24, 1903, in Richmond, Ind.; died April 25, 1987, in Mountain View, Calif.; son of Irving King (a professor of psychology and education); married wife, Helen, 1932; children: Gertrude Myrrh Reagan. Education: University of Iowa, B.A., 1924, M.S., 1927; Yale University, Ph.D., 1929.

CAREER: Marathon Oil Co., geological assistant, 1924-25; University of Texas at Austin, instructor in geology, 1925-27; University of Arizona, Tucson, instructor in geology, 1929-30; U.S. Geological Survey, assistant geologist, 1930-34, associate geologist, 1935-39, geologist, 1940-43, senior geologist, 1943-48, principal geologist, 1948-73. Member of National Research Council committee on tectonics, 1934-38, and executive committee of its Division of Geology and Geography, 1946-49. Visiting professor at University of California,

Los Angeles, 1954-56; visiting lecturer at University of Moscow, 1965.

AWARDS, HONORS: Penrose Medal from Geological Society of America, 1965; Distinguished Service Medal from U.S. Department of the Interior, 1965; Lomonosov Medal of the U.S.S.R., 1965.

WRITINGS:

An Outline of the Structural Geology of the United States, U.S. Government Printing Office, 1932.
Geology of the Marathon Region, U.S. Government Printing Office, 1938.
Geology of the Southern Guadalupe Mountains, Texas, U.S. Government Printing Office, 1948.
Geology of the Elkton Area, Virginia, U.S. Government Printing Office, 1950.
The Tectonics of Middle North America: Middle North America East of the Cordilleran System, Princeton University Press, 1951.
(With Peter T. Flawn) Geology and Mineral Deposits of Pre-Cambrian Rocks of the Van Horn Area, Texas, Bureau of Economic Geology, University of Texas at Austin, 1953.
(With Herman W. Ferguson) Geology of Northeasternmost Tennessee, U.S. Government Printing Office, 1959.
The Evolution of North America, Princeton University Press, 1959, revised edition, 1977.
(Editor) The Physical Geography of William Morris Davis, privately printed, 1962.
Geology of the Central Great Smoky Mountains, Tennessee, U.S. Government Printing Office, 1964.
(Co-author) Tectonics of the Southern Appalachians, Department of Geological Sciences, Virginia Polytechnic Institute and State University, 1964.
Geology of the Sierra Diablo Region, Texas, U.S. Government Printing Office, 1965.
The Tectonics of North America, U.S. Government Printing Office, 1969.
(With Helen M. Beikman) The Paleozoic and Mesozoic Rocks: A Discussion to Accompany the Geologic Map of the United States, U.S. Government Printing Office, 1976.
Precambrian Geology of the United States: An Explanatory Text to Accompany the Geologic Map of the United States, U.S. Government Printing Office, 1976.
(With Helen M. Beikman) The Cenozoic Rocks: A Discussion to Accompany the Geologic Map of the United States, U.S. Government Printing Office, 1978.
(Editor with Stanley A. Schumm) The Physical Geography (Geomorphology) of William Morris Davis, Geo Abstracts, 1980.

Contributor of more than one hundred articles and maps to periodicals.

BIOGRAPHICAL/CRITICAL SOURCES:

PERIODICALS

Geographical Review, July, 1960.
Journal of Geology, January, 1961.
Washington Times, April 25, 1987.*

*   *   *

KING, Robert B.   1949-

PERSONAL: Born October 17, 1949, in Iowa City, Iowa; son of Robert Boyd (a salesman and writer) and Dorothy (a nurse; maiden name, Keating) King; married Janet M. Sterk (a nurse manager), May 21, 1982. *Education:* University of Iowa, B.A., 1972. *Politics:* Democrat. *Religion:* Roman Catholic.

ADDRESSES: Home—2507 Warren, Davenport, Iowa 52804.

CAREER: Augsburg Publishing House, Los Angeles, Calif., film inspector, 1974-76; *Daily Dispatch,* Moline, Ill., circulation supervisor, 1976-87; *Leader,* Davenport, Iowa, correspondent, 1987—.

MEMBER: Open Cities Film Society (member of board of directors, 1987).

WRITINGS:

I Wasn't Like the Cautious Man: The Life of Roy C. Smith as Told to Robert B. King, Iowa State University Press, 1987.

WORK IN PROGRESS: A novel, tentatively titled *Tom Cole;* a novel, tentatively titled *City Light.*

SIDELIGHTS: Robert B. King told *CA:* "I have a lifelong interest in history. I visit historical sites across the United States, especially in the West and Midwest, whenever I have the opportunity. My main motivation for writing is my desire to give expression to voices that might otherwise be lost to history. With these voices I hope to capture in words a part of the American spirit. I love my country, and I love to criticize it. I am fascinated, not only with the rich and powerful, but with the troubled misfits and outsiders who give this country its special character.

"I first heard of Roy C. Smith when my boss told me a fascinating story about an orphan boy who was thrown off a train one night as it passed through Columbus Junction, Iowa. The boy was adopted by a local farm couple and he went on to inherit their property, building it into a huge and profitable operation. He later entered the oil business and became rich. Meanwhile he helped countless friends, neighbors, and relatives survive the darkest years of the Depression, not by giving them handouts, but by putting them to work in jobs that restored their sense of self-respect. I knew I had to try to meet this man, even though I doubted he was still alive. But to my surprise I found his name in the Davenport telephone book and went to see him the next day.

"When he began to tell me about his life, I was amazed by his candor; he never flinched from telling things about himself that others would surely try to hide. But I was disappointed that many of the things my boss had told me turned out to be untrue. Apparently Mr. Smith's life had become a source of local legend. Yet the essence of the legend, expressing a life of great accomplishment and generosity, remained true. And the real facts of his life, encompassing many of the themes found in the history of the Midwest during the transition from rural to urban life, were even more fascinating than the myth. Finally, what struck me the most was his character. He is tough and proud. He knows where he stands, saying, 'My only religion is a clear conscience.' And though he never accepted his birthright of poverty and despair, he never forgot where he came from and never put on airs.

"My novel *Tom Cole* grows out of my childhood experiences in a poor neighborhood near downtown Davenport. It was on a Friday night in 1963 that I saw the front door of a skid row tavern fly open. A drunken old man staggered out, facing the world with all the courage he could summon. He paraded down the sidewalk and I followed him while people stopped and stared. The bright lights of the city burned all around us and I tried to see them as he did, through the mists of his alcoholic dream.

"Years later a story began to emerge in my mind. I peopled it with the children who stand outside the taverns at night, waiting for their parents to come out; with the old women alone in shabby apartments, sitting by their windows and watching the sun go down; with the petty criminals who, despite their crimes, never manage to hurt anyone more than they hurt themselves. These people provide the atmosphere, but the story itself revolves around a part-time detective out on a domestic case one night, shadowing an old woman's husband. Trying to uphold a semblance of order is a policeman who works the night shift. Although he is probably the best cop in the city, he is overwhelmed by the futility of his efforts.

"These characters are based on people I once knew. Now, all of them are either dead or gone, except for one who has gone insane. But in my story, I have tried to bring them back."

*   *   *

KINKLEY, Jeffrey C(arroll)   1948-

PERSONAL: Born July 13, 1948, in Urbana, Ill.; son of Harold Vernon (an educator) and Emily Jane Kinkley; married Chuchu Kang (an econometrician). *Education:* University of Chicago, B.A., 1969; Harvard University, M.A., 1971, Ph.D., 1977.

ADDRESSES: Home—90 Ovington Ave., Edison, N.J. 08817. *Office*—Department of History, St. John's University, Grand Central and Utopia Parkway, Jamaica, N.Y. 11439.

CAREER: Harvard University, Cambridge, Mass., lecturer in history, 1977-79; St. John's University, Jamaica, N.Y., assistant professor, 1979-86, associate professor of Asian studies, 1986-87, associate professor of history, 1987—. Chair of Modern China Seminar at Columbia University, 1987-88.

MEMBER: American Historical Association, Association for Asian Studies.

AWARDS, HONORS: Fellow of Committee on Scholarly Communication With the People's Republic of China, 1980, and American Council of Learned Societies, 1982 and 1986.

WRITINGS:

(Editor) *After Mao: Chinese Literature and Society, 1978-1981,* Council on East Asian Studies, Harvard University, 1985.
The Odyssey of Shen Congwen, Stanford University Press, 1987.
(Translator with others) Zhang Xinxin and Sang Ye, *Chinese Lives: An Oral History of Contemporary China,* edited by W. J. F. Jenner and Delia Davin, Pantheon, 1987.

Editor of Chinese section of *Fiction,* 1987. Member of editorial board of *Republican China.*

WORK IN PROGRESS: Shen Congwen bixia de Zhongguo (title means "Shen Congwen's Vision of Chinese Culture and Society"), publication in China expected in 1989; editing, with Helmut Martin, a volume of autobiographical statements by twentieth-century Chinese writers on how they became interested in literature, publication expected in 1989; translating the memoirs of Xiao Qian, *Portrait of a Chinese as an Intellectual,* publication expected in 1990; a history of Chinese literary writing about the Sino-Japanese War of 1937 to 1945, publication expected in 1992.

SIDELIGHTS: Jeffrey C. Kinkley told *CA:* "My primary interest has been analyzing twentieth-century Chinese literature as a witness to history. I have also introduced contemporary Chinese authors to an American audience through translations.

"Shen Congwen, a founder of China's modern fiction, is known for his regional novels about the southwestern Chinese frontier and its ethnic minorities and for his pioneering use in China of techniques from the international modernist movement. Xiao Qian is another Chinese creative writer who was known and appreciated in the West before 1949 but fell silent after the Communist revolution. In his memoirs he describes his colorful childhood in Peking, his experiences in England and America as a student and journalist (he was a war correspondent during World War II), and the hardships he suffered as a condemned 'Rightist' until his partial rehabilitation in the 1980s."

*   *   *

KIRGIS, Frederic L(ee), Jr.   1934-

PERSONAL: Born December 29, 1934, in Washington, D.C.; son of Frederic Lee (a lawyer) and Kathryn Alice (Burrows) Kirgis; married Carol Stroud (a dance teacher), February 1, 1957; children: Julianne, Paul F. *Education:* Yale University, B.A., 1957; University of California, Berkeley, J.D., 1960. *Politics:* Democrat. *Religion:* Presbyterian.

ADDRESSES: Office—School of Law, Washington and Lee University, Lexington, Va. 24450.

CAREER: Covington & Burling, Washington, D.C., associate, 1964-67; University of Colorado, Boulder, assistant professor, 1967-68, associate professor, 1968-71, professor of law, 1971-73; University of California, Los Angeles, visiting professor, 1973-74, professor of law, 1974-78; Washington and Lee University, Lexington, Va., professor of law, 1978-83, dean of School of Law, 1983—. Visiting professor at University of Michigan, 1983. Vice-chairman of Independent Commission on Respect for International Law. *Military service:* U.S. Air Force, 1961-64; became captain.

MEMBER: International Law Association, American Law Institute, American Society of International Law (vice-president, 1985-87), Coif.

AWARDS, HONORS: Francis Deak Prize from *American Journal of International Law,* 1974, for "Technological Challenge to the Shared Environment: United States Practice."

WRITINGS:

International Organizations in Their Legal Setting, West Publishing, 1977, Supplement, 1981.
Prior Consultation in International Law: A Study of State Practice, University Press of Virginia, 1983.

Contributor to law journals. Member of board of editors of *American Journal of International Law.*

WORK IN PROGRESS: Current International Law, completion expected in 1989.

SIDELIGHTS: Frederic L. Kirgis, Jr., told *CA:* "My work in international law is motivated largely by the firm belief that international law ought to play a much more significant role than it now does in the decision-making processes of national governments. In recent years, our government has sometimes acted in disregard of established international rules. This is

rarely in our own long-term self-interest and almost never serves the interest of a peaceful world order."

*   *   *

KIRKCONNELL, Watson   1895-1977

PERSONAL: Born May 16, 1896, in Port Hope, Ontario, Canada; died February 26, 1977; son of Thomas Allison and Bertha Gertrude (Watson) Kirkconnell; married Isabel Peel, 1924 (died, 1925); married Hope Kitchener, August 6, 1930; children: (first marriage) James and Thomas (twins); (second marriage) Helen Kirkconnell Campbell, Janet, Susan Kirkconnell Colquhoun. *Education:* Queen's University, Kingston, Ontario, M.A., 1916; attended Lincoln College, Oxford, 1921-22; Debrecen University, Ph.D., 1938. *Religion:* Baptist.

CAREER: Wesley College, Winnipeg, Manitoba, lecturer, 1922, assistant professor, 1923, associate professor, 1924-30, professor of English, 1930-33; United College, Winnipeg, professor of classics, 1933-40, head of department, 1934-40; McMaster University, Hamilton, Ontario, professor of English and head of department, 1940-48; Acadia University, Wolfville, Nova Scotia, president, 1948-64, president emeritus, 1964-77, professor of English and head of department, 1948-68. Chairman of Writers War Committee for Canada, 1942-44; chairman of Humanities Research Council of Canada, 1944-47. President of Baptist Union of Western Canada, 1938-40, and Baptist Federation of Canada, 1953-56. *Military service:* Canadian Army, 1916-18; became captain.

AWARDS, HONORS: Knight of Order of Plonia Restituta, 1936; Silver Laureate of Polish Academy of Letters, 1937; Medal of Honor from P.E.N. Club of Hungary, 1938; Lorne Pierce Gold Medal from Royal Society of Canada, c. 1931; honorary degrees include LL.D. from University of Ottawa, c. 1944, and University of New Brunswick, c. 1949, Dr.Polit.Econ. from Ukrainian Free University, 1950, D.Litt. from McMaster University, c. 1953, Assumption University, 1955, and University of Manitoba, 1957, L.H.D. from Alliance College, 1958, D. es L. from Laval University, 1962, Litt.D. from Acadia University, 1964, and St. Francis Xavier University, 1966, and D.C.L. from St. Mary's University, 1964; Knight Commander of Iceland's Order of the Falcon, 1963; Hungarian Community Medal, 1963; medal from Humanities Research Council of Canada, 1964; Shevchenko Medal, 1964; Gold Medal of Freedom of Hungary, 1964; Centennial Medal of Canada, 1967; George Washington Award from American Hungarian Studies Foundation, 1967; Officer of Order of Canada, 1968.

WRITINGS:

International Aspects of Unemployment, Allen & Unwin, 1923.
European Elegies, Graphic, 1928.
The Tide of Life and Other Poems, Ariston, 1930.
The European Heritage: A Synopsis of European Cultural Achievement, Dent, 1930.
(Editor) *The North American Book of Icelandic Verse,* L. Carrier & A. Isles, 1930.
(Editor and translator) *The Magyar Muse: An Anthology of Hungarian Poetry, 1400-1932,* Kanadai Magyar Ujsag Press, 1933.
The Eternal Quest, Columbia Press (Winnipeg, Canada), 1934.
A Canadian Headmaster: A Brief Biography of Thomas Allison Kirkconnell, 1862-1934, Clarke, Irwin, 1935.
(Editor and translator) *Canadian Overtones: An Anthology of Canadian Poetry Written Originally in Icelandic, Swed-*

ish, Norwegian, Hungarian, Italian, Greek, and Ukrainian, Columbia Press, 1935.

Golden Treasury of Polish Lyrics, Polish Press (Winnipeg, Canada), 1936.

(Translator) Janos Arany, *The Death of King Buda: A Hungarian Epic Poem,* Benjamin Franklin Bibliophile Society, 1936.

Titus the Toad, illustrations by Davina Craig, Oxford University Press (Toronto), 1938.

(Editor) *The North American Book of Verse,* five volumes, H. Harrison, 1939.

Canada, Europe, and Hitler, Oxford University Press, 1939.

The Flying Bull and Other Tales, Oxford University Press, 1940, 2nd edition, 1949.

Twilight of Liberty, Oxford University Press, 1941.

Seven Pillars of Freedom, Oxford University Press, 1944, new enlarged edition, Burns & MacEachern, 1952.

(With A. S. P. Woodhouse) *The Humanities in Canada,* Humanities Research Council of Canada, 1947.

(Editor and translator) *A Little Treasury of Hungarian Verse,* American Hungarian Federation, 1947.

The Celestial Cycle: The Theme of Paradise Lost in World Literature With Translations of the Major Analogues, University of Toronto Press, 1952.

(Translator) Adam Mickiewicz, *Pan Tadeusz; or, The Last Foray in Lithuania,* University of Toronto Press, 1962, Polish Institute of Arts in America, 1981.

(Translator with C. H. Andrusyshen) *The Ukranian Poems, 1189-1962,* University of Toronto Press, 1963.

(Translator) Laszlo Mecs, *The Slaves Sing* (poems), St. Norbert Abbey Press, 1964.

(With F. E. L. Priestley) *The Humanities in Canada,* University of Toronto Press, 1964.

(Translator) Taras Hryhorovych Shevchenko, *Poetical Works,* University of Toronto Press, 1964.

The Invincible Samson: The Theme of Samson Agonistes in World Literature With Translations of the Major Analogues, University of Toronto Press, 1964.

Centennial Tales and Selected Poems, University of Toronto Press, 1965.

A Slice of Canada: Memoirs, University of Toronto Press, 1967.

(Translator with Raymond J. Conard) Laszlo Mecs, *I Graft Roses on Eglantines* (poems in Hungarian and English), Weller Publishing, 1968.

Scottish Place-Names in Canada, Canadian Institute of Onomastic Sciences and Ukrainian Free Academy of Sciences, 1970.

Awake the Courteous Echo: The Themes and Prosody of Comus, Lycidas, and Paradise Regained in World Literature With Translations of the Major Analogues, University of Toronto Press, 1973.

(Editor) *Rest, Perturbed Spirit: Being the Life of Cecil Francis Lloyd, 1884-1938,* Lancelot Press, 1974.

Climbing the Green Tree and Some Other Branches, privately printed, 1976.

The Flavour of Nova Scotia, Lancelot Press, 1976.

(With B. C. Silver) *Wolfville Historic Homes and the Streets of Wolfville, 1650-1970,* Wolfville Historical Society, 1978.

Also author of *An Outline of European Poetry,* 1927, *Canada to Iceland,* 1930, *A Primer of Hungarian,* 1938, *Lyra Sacra,* 1939, *Our Communists and the New Canadian,* 1943, *Red Foe of Faith,* 1946, *The Future of European Freedom,* 1946, *A Tale of Seven Cities,* 1948, *Stalin's Red Empire,* 1951, *The*

Mod at Grand Pre, 1955. Author of annual, *New Canadian Letters,* 1937-65.

SIDELIGHTS: A scholar of English and the humanities, Watson Kirkconnell collected and published a series of analogues to English poet John Milton's works, an endeavor *Times Literary Supplement* deemed ''impressive.'' In his research, which spanned more than two decades, Kirkconnell sought to outline the influence of traditional literary themes and forms on Milton's work and, in turn, Milton's influence on subsequent literary patterns. The author's 1952 *Celestial Cycle* concerns Milton's *Paradise Lost,* his 1964 *Invincible Samson* studies Milton's *Samson Agonistes,* and his 1973 *Awake the Courteous Echo* includes analogues of Milton's *Comus,* ''Lycidas,'' and *Paradise Regained.* In Kirkconnell's studies of the themes and structures of Milton's poetry, *Times Literary Supplement* found a ''wealth of information . . . [that] will be indispensable to any student of Milton.'' *Choice* magazine likewise praised the works as ''thorough, weighty, and of impeccable scholarship.''

Kirkconnell's research also included topics outside the literary field. Praised by *New York Times* for its ''extreme readability,'' the scholar's 1923 *International Aspects of Unemployment* links employment in the early twentieth century to the industrial revolution and the resulting expansion of urban population. *New York Times* also praised Kirkconnell's ''commendable'' 1930 work, *European Heritage,* as a ''brief but excellent synopsis of European culture.'' In his 1939 *Canada, Europe, and Hitler,* he explores Canadian and European sentiments toward World War II before and after its outbreak. *Canadian Historical Review* praised the ''fluent and compact survey of Canadian attitudes.'' According to *Times Literary Supplement,* Kirkconnell ''is exceptionally well qualified for the analysis he has undertaken. In his survey of conditions in Central and Eastern Europe his judgments are often shrewd.''

BIOGRAPHICAL/CRITICAL SOURCES:

BOOKS

Dictionary of Literary Biography, Volume 68: *Canadian Writers, 1920-1959,* Gale, 1988.

Perkin, J. R. C., editor, *The Undoing of Babel: Watson Kirkconnell, the Man and His Work,* McClelland & Stewart, 1975.

PERIODICALS

Canadian Historical Review, March, 1940.
Choice, March, 1974.
New Republic, July 15, 1940.
New York Times, August 26, 1923, November 2, 1930.
Spectator, November 15, 1923.
Times Literary Supplement, March 15, 1923, April 17, 1930, June 8, 1940, August 22, 1975.

OBITUARIES:

BOOKS

The International Who's Who, Europa, 1979.*

*   *   *

KLAIDMAN, Stephen   1938-

PERSONAL: Born May 29, 1938, in New York, N.Y.; son of Moe (a businessman) and Pauline (a homemaker; maiden name, Hinerfeld) Klaidman; married Kitty Ehrenreich (a painter), December 27, 1959; children: Elyse Suzanne, Daniel Marc.

Education: Attended City College (now of the City University of New York), 1955-59.

ADDRESSES: Office—Kennedy Institute of Ethics, Georgetown University, Washington, D.C. 20057. *Agent*—Ron Goldfarb, 918 16th St. N.W., Washington, D.C.

CAREER: New York Times, New York City, copyboy, 1959, news clerk, 1960, copy editor, 1962-65; *Diplomat,* New York City, European columnist, 1966; *New York Times,* New York City, copy editor, 1967-68; *Washington Post,* Washington, D.C., assistant foreign editor, 1969, deputy foreign editor, 1970-71 and 1973-75, reporter, 1976; *International Herald Tribune,* Paris, France, news editor, 1977-78, chief editorial writer and columnist, 1979-81; WJLA-TV, Washington, D.C., commentator, 1982; Georgetown University, Washington, D.C., senior research fellow at Kennedy Institute of Ethics, 1982—, faculty associate at Center for Strategic and International Studies, associate of Institute for Health Policy Analysis. Dean's Lecturer at Syracuse University, 1987; consultant to Radio Free Europe and Radio Liberty.

WRITINGS:

(With Tom L. Beauchamp) *The Virtuous Journalist,* Oxford University Press, 1987.

Contributor to magazines and newspapers. Editor of *Kennedy Institute Newsletter.*

WORK IN PROGRESS: Knowing When to Be Afraid, with David McCallum, for Oxford University Press; an article for *Image Ethics,* edited by Larry Gross, John Katz, and Jay Ruby.

*   *   *

KLEINMAN, Ruth 1929-

PERSONAL: Born July 23, 1929, in Berlin, Germany; daughter of Abraham I. (in business) and Frieda (Schmidt) Kleinman. *Education:* Barnard College, A.B., 1951; Columbia University, M.A., 1952, Ph.D., 1959.

ADDRESSES: Office—Department of History, Brooklyn College of the City University of New York, Bedford Ave. and Avenue H, Brooklyn, N.Y. 11210.

CAREER: Bucknell University, Lewisburg, Pa., instructor in history, 1957-58; Brooklyn College (now of the City University of New York), Brooklyn, N.Y., member of faculty, 1958-59; Connecticut College, New London, instructor in history, 1959-62; Brooklyn College of the City University of New York, began as instructor, became associate professor, 1962-75, professor of history, 1975—.

MEMBER: American Historical Association, Renaissance Society of America, Society for French Historical Studies.

AWARDS, HONORS: Fellow of National Endowment for the Humanities, 1979-80.

WRITINGS:

(Editor) *Saint Francois de Sales and the Protestants,* Droz, 1962.
Anne of Austria, Queen of France, Ohio State University Press, 1985.

Contributor to history journals.

WORK IN PROGRESS: Research on the composition of French royal households in the seventeenth century.

KLEINZAHLER, August 1949-

PERSONAL: Born December 10, 1949, in Jersey City, N.J.; son of Marvin and Isabel (Resnitzky) Kleinzahler. *Education:* Attended University of Wisconsin—Madison, 1967-70, and University of Victoria, 1973.

ADDRESSES: Home—San Francisco, Calif., and c/o P.O. Box 842, Fort Lee, N.J. 07024.

CAREER: Poet and editor. Visiting Holloway Lecturer at University of California, Berkeley, 1987.

MEMBER: Poetry Society of America.

AWARDS, HONORS: Grants from Canada Council, 1977 and 1979, Ontario Arts Council, 1978, and New Jersey State Council on the Arts, 1980 and 1985; award for younger writers from General Electric Foundation, 1983, for poems in *Sulfur* magazine; award from Bay Area Book Reviewers Association, 1985, for *Storm Over Hackensack.*

WRITINGS:

A Calendar of Airs (poems), Coach House Press, 1978.
(Editor) *News and Weather: Seven Canadian Poets,* Brick Books, 1982.
Storm Over Hackensack (poems), Moyer Bell, 1985.
On Johnny's Time (poems), Pig Press, 1988.

SIDELIGHTS: According to Geoffrey O'Brien of the *Village Voice,* August Kleinzahler writes about the small, ordinary things of life. He uses simple language in ways which have not been achieved before. *Storm Over Hackensack,* O'Brien wrote, is a collection of "handcrafted, sinuous, intensely focused poems" which indicate "both that subject matter still has its uses and that recent death announcements for the personal lyric were slightly premature." The poet's subject matter includes the urban sprawl of Jersey City and Newark, a television repair shop, debris in city streets, and strangers who wander the corridors of the Newark airport. Kleinzahler's language, the critic reported, "veers jauntily from video parlor argot to Ovidian tropes," and he "ranges in mood from the goofy to the mournful, but always what concerns him is the shape of what he makes." O'Brien concluded: "Not many writers . . . will have either the wit or the fluent technical inventiveness to follow in Kleinzahler's track."

BIOGRAPHICAL/CRITICAL SOURCES:

PERIODICALS

Village Voice, August 20, 1985.

*   *   *

KLING, Woody 1926(?)-1988

OBITUARY NOTICE: Born c. 1926; died of lung cancer, April 10, 1988, in Los Angeles, Calif. Television producer and comedy writer. During his forty-year career as a television comedy writer Kling was nominated five times for Emmy awards and won two, in 1972 and 1973, for his scripts for "The Carol Burnett Show." He began in television writing with Buddy Arnold for Milton Berle's "Texaco Star Theater" and over the years worked for such comedians as Jackie Gleason, Will Rogers, Red Buttons, and Jack Paar. Kling created and produced the cartoons "Casper, the Friendly Ghost" and "The Beatles," co-produced Gleason's and Burnett's shows, and was co-executive producer of the hit series "All in the Family."

OBITUARIES AND OTHER SOURCES:

PERIODICALS

Chicago Tribune, April 13, 1988.
Los Angeles Times, April 11, 1988.
New York Times, April 14, 1988.
Washington Post, April 11, 1988.

*   *   *

KNEALE, Matthew (Nicholas Kerr)   1960-

PERSONAL: Born November 24, 1960, in London, England; son of Nigel (a playwright) and Judith (a writer; maiden name, Kerr) Kneale. *Education:* Magdalen College, Oxford, B.A., 1982.

ADDRESSES: Home—London, England. *Agent*—Deborah Rogers Ltd., 49 Blenheim Cres., London W11 2EF, England.

CAREER: English teacher at Cosmo International Language Institute, Japan, 1982-83. Private tutor in English and history. Free-lance photographer.

MEMBER: Society of Authors.

WRITINGS:

Whore Banquets (novel), Gollancz, 1987.
Inside Rose's Kingdom (tentative title), Gollancz, in press.

SIDELIGHTS: Matthew Kneale told *CA:* "I have traveled extensively in forty-nine countries, mainly in South America, Central America, East and Southern Asia, Europe, the Soviet bloc, and the Middle East. I feel this experience has given me a thorough grounding in cultural miscomprehensions. I spent a year in Japan living in suburban Tokyo, and it was the stranger and darker side of Japanese suburban life that particularly interested me. The book that resulted is certainly critical of Japan, but also, I hope, of the West."

BIOGRAPHICAL/CRITICAL SOURCES:

PERIODICALS

Times Literary Supplement, January 30, 1987.

*   *   *

KNIGHT, Alan   1946-

PERSONAL: Born November 6, 1946, in London, England; immigrated to the United States, 1986; son of William H. (an electrical contractor) and Eva (Crandon) Knight; married Carole Jones, April 12, 1969; married Lidia Lozano, October 30, 1985; children: (first marriage) Katharine; (second marriage) Alex, Henry. *Education:* Balliol College, Oxford, B.A., 1968; Nuffield College, Ph.D., 1974.

ADDRESSES: Home—6115 Highlandale Dr., Austin, Tex. 78731. *Office*—Department of History, University of Texas at Austin, Austin, Tex. 78712.

CAREER: Oxford University, Oxford, England, research fellow at Nuffield College, 1971-73; University of Essex, Colchester, England, lecturer in history, 1973-85; University of Texas at Austin, Anabel Irion Worsham Professor of History, 1986—.

MEMBER: American Historical Association.

AWARDS, HONORS: Albert Beveridge Prize from American Historical Association, 1986, and Bolton Prize from Conference on Latin American History, both for *The Mexican Revolution*.

WRITINGS:

The Mexican Revolution, Volume I: *Porfirians, Liberals, and Peasants*, Volume II: *Counter-Revolution and Reconstruction*, Cambridge University Press, 1986.
A History of Mexico, Longman, in press.

Contributor to Latin American studies journals.

WORK IN PROGRESS: Cardenas and Cardenismo, completion expected in 1990.

SIDELIGHTS: Alan Knight told *CA:* "The British university system, by avoiding a draconian 'publish or perish' policy, made it possible for me to undertake a major first book, which might not have been possible in the United States. The Thatcher administration, by systematically running down that system (especially the humanities), motivated me to move to the United States, thus depriving the British system of whatever academic payoff it might accrue.

"*Cardenas and Cardenismo* is a history of the Cardenas presidency in Mexico, from 1934 to 1940. I see Cardenismo as the consummation of the revolutionary cycle begun in 1910: a cycle marked by extensive popular mobilization, especially by the organized peasantry and labor unions, which transformed the political economy of Mexico but whose radical objectives were ultimately disappointed."

BIOGRAPHICAL/CRITICAL SOURCES:

PERIODICALS

Times Literary Supplement, May 29, 1987.

*   *   *

KOHLBERG, Lawrence   1927-1987

PERSONAL: Born October 25, 1927, in Bronxville, N.Y.; drowned c. January 17, 1987, in Boston, Mass.; son of Alfred and Charlotte (Albrecht) Kohlberg; married Lucille Stigberg, June 12, 1955; children: David E., Steven A. *Education:* University of Chicago, A.B., 1948, Ph.D., 1958.

CAREER: Clinical psychology trainee with the Veterans Administration, 1952-53; Children's Hospital, Boston, Mass., Russell Sage Resident, 1958-59; Yale University, New Haven, Conn., assistant professor of psychology, 1959-61; Institute for Advanced Study in the Behavioral Sciences, Palo Alto, Calif., fellow, 1961-62; University of Chicago, Chicago, Ill., assistant professor, 1962-65, associate professor of psychology, 1965-68, director of Child Psychology Training Program, 1964-68; Harvard University, Cambridge, Mass., professor of education and social psychology, 1968-87.

AWARDS, HONORS: Grant from National Institute of Mental Health, 1969-74.

WRITINGS:

(Editor with E. Turiel, and contributor) *Recent Research in Moral Development*, Holt, 1973.
The Just Community Approach to Corrections: A Manual, Moral Education Research Foundation, 1974.
The Meaning and Measurement of Moral Development, Clark University Press, 1981.
The Philosophy of Moral Development: Moral Stages and the Idea of Justice, Volume I: *Essays on Moral Development*, Harper, 1981.

(With Charles Levine and Alexandra Hewer) *Moral Stages: A Current Formulation and a Response to Critics,* Karger, 1983.

The Psychology of Moral Development: The Nature and Validity of Moral Stages, Harper, 1984.

(With Thomas Lickona) *The Stages of Ethical Development: From Childhood Through Old Age,* Harper, 1986.

(With Rheta DeVries) *Programs of Early Education: The Constructivist View,* Longman, 1987.

Child Psychology and Childhood Education: A Cognitive-Developmental View, Longman, 1987.

CONTRIBUTOR

Theodore Sizer, editor, *Religion and the Public Schools,* Houghton, 1967.

R. Hess and R. Bear, editors, *The Challenge of Early Education: Reports of Theory, Research, and Action,* Aldine, 1968.

David Goslin, editor, *Handbook of Socialization Theory and Research,* Rand McNally, 1969.

Sizer, editor, *Moral Education: Five Lectures,* Harvard University Press, 1970.

T. Mischel, editor, *Genetic Epistemology,* Academic Press, 1971.

C. Beck and E. Sullivan, editors, *Moral Education,* University of Toronto Press, 1971.

G. Lesser, editor, *Psychology and Educational Practice,* Scott, Foresman, 1971.

C. Lavatelli, editor, *The Natural Curriculum,* University of Illinois Press, 1971.

Contributor to *International Encyclopedia of the Social Sciences, International Encyclopedia of Education,* and *Handbook of Child Psychotherapy.* Contributor of articles and reviews to psychology and education journals.

BIOGRAPHICAL/CRITICAL SOURCES:

BOOKS

Des Jardines, Joseph R., *A Philosophical Analysis of Lawrence Kohlberg's Theory of Moral Development,* University of Notre Dame, 1980.

PERIODICALS

Christianity Today, June 13, 1986.
Contemporary Education, spring, 1983.
Educational Theory, summer/fall, 1981.
Jewish Education, spring, 1985.
Merrill Palmer Quarterly, July, 1984.
New Republic, February 3, 1982.
New York Times, April 9, 1987.
New York Times Book Review, August 9, 1981.*

*　　*　　*

KOLB, (Gwin) Jack (II)　1946-

PERSONAL: Born October 9, 1946, in Chicago, Ill.; son of Gwin Jackson (a professor) and Ruth (an administrative assistant; maiden name, Godbold) Kolb. *Education:* University of Chicago, B.A., 1967; attended Yale University, 1967-68; University of Virginia, Ph.D., 1971. *Politics:* Democrat.

ADDRESSES: Home—Santa Monica, Calif. *Office*—Department of English, University of California, 405 Hilgard Ave., Los Angeles, Calif. 90024.

CAREER: University of California, Los Angeles, assistant professor, 1971-77, associate professor of English, 1977—.

MEMBER: Modern Language Association of America, Tennyson Society, Owl and Serpent Club.

WRITINGS:

(Editor) *The Letters of Arthur Henry Hallam,* Ohio State University Press, 1981.

(Contributor) *Dictionary of Literary Biography,* Volume 32: *Victorian Poets Before 1850,* Gale, 1984.

Contributor to language and philology journals.

WORK IN PROGRESS: Editing *The Poetry and Prose of Arthur Henry Hallam,* publication expected in 1988; a study of Tennyson's poetry through "In Memoriam."

BIOGRAPHICAL/CRITICAL SOURCES:

PERIODICALS

New Yorker, March 15, 1982.

*　　*　　*

KOLODIN, Irving　1908-1988

OBITUARY NOTICE—See index for *CA* sketch: Born February 21 (one source says February 22), 1908, in New York, N.Y.; died April 29, 1988, in New York, N.Y. Music critic, educator, and author. In a career that spanned half a century, Kolodin wrote prolifically about a range of music that stretched from classical to jazz. During his tenure as music critic for *Saturday Review* from 1947 to 1982, Kolodin was one of the most influential critics in the country. He was also one of the first musicologists to seriously review phonograph records.

Kolodin joined the staff of the *New York Sun* in 1932 and remained with the paper until 1950, eventually becoming its chief music critic. During the 1950s he wrote program notes for the New York Philharmonic Orchestra and assembled several albums for RCA Victor, including a "Critic's Choice" album and a five-record set titled "Fifty Years of Great Operatic Singing." In 1970 he selected the classical music for the first official White House music library. From 1968 to 1986 Kolodin taught music criticism at the Juilliard School of Music. His many publications include *The Metropolitan Opera, 1883-1935,* a definitive history that he later published in updated editions in 1953 and 1966; *A Guide to Recorded Music; The Continuity of Music: A History of Influence; The Interior Beethoven: A Biography of the Music; The Opera Omnibus: Four Centuries of Critical Give and Take,* and *In Quest of Music.* Kolodin also contributed articles to music reference books and to various periodicals. Historian of the Metropolitan Opera Company, he was working on a book tracing its first one hundred years when he suffered a serious stroke in 1987.

OBITUARIES AND OTHER SOURCES:

BOOKS

Current Biography, H.W. Wilson, 1988.
Who's Who in American Music: Classical, Bowker, 1983.

PERIODICALS

Chicago Tribune, May 2, 1988.
Los Angeles Times, May 4, 1988.
New York Times, April 30, 1988.
Washington Post, May 2, 1988.

KOZICKI, Richard J(oseph) 1929-

PERSONAL: Born April 5, 1929, in Chester, Pa.; divorced; children: two. *Education:* Allegheny College, B.A., 1951; Yale University, M.A., 1953; University of Pennsylvania, Ph.D., 1959.

ADDRESSES: Office—Department of Government, University of San Francisco, 2130 Fulton St., San Francisco, Calif. 94117.

CAREER: Drexel Institute of Technology (now Drexel University), Philadelphia, Pa., instructor in political science and history, 1956; Mansfield State Teachers College (now State College), Mansfield, Pa., assistant professor, 1959-60, associate professor of political science, 1961-62; Marquette University, Milwaukee, Wis., assistant professor of political science, 1962-63; University of Illinois at Urbana-Champaign, Urbana, Asian bibliographer and member of Asian study committee, 1963-64; University of Hawaii at Manoa, Honolulu, South Asia area specialist at East-West Center, 1964-68; University of California, Berkeley, assistant research political scientist at Center for South Asia Studies, Institute for International Studies, 1968-70; University of San Francisco, San Francisco, Calif., associate professor of government, 1970—, director of Institute for Asian and Pacific Studies, 1975—.

MEMBER: International Studies Association, Association for Asian Studies.

WRITINGS:

(Editor) *International Relations of South Asia, 1947 to 1980: A Guide to Information Sources,* Gale, 1981.
(Editor with Peter Ananda) *South and Southeast Asia: Doctoral Dissertations and Masters' Theses Completed at the University of California at Berkeley, 1906-1973,* revised edition, Center for South and Southeast Asia and University Press of America, 1983.*

*   *   *

KRAMER, Charles 1915-1988

OBITUARY NOTICE: Born October 27, 1915, in Brooklyn, N.Y.; died of a heart attack, March 23, 1988, in New York, N.Y. Attorney, educator, columnist, and author. A medical malpractice lawyer, Kramer established the law firm of Kramer, Dillof, Tessel, Duffy & Moore in 1949. He wrote a number of books on law and medicine, including *The Negligent Doctor: Medical Malpractice In and Out of Hospitals and What Can Be Done About It* and *Medical Aspects of Negligence Cases,* and was co-author of a monthly column in the *New York Law Journal* titled "Medical Malpractice." Kramer also taught law at Hofstra University and served as director of the New York State Trial Lawyers Association.

OBITUARIES AND OTHER SOURCES:

BOOKS

Who's Who in America, 44th edition, Marquis, 1986.

PERIODICALS

New York Times, March 25, 1988.

*   *   *

KREMENLIEV, Boris A(ngeloff) 1911-1988

OBITUARY NOTICE—See index for *CA* sketch: Born May 23, 1911, in Razlog, Bulgaria; immigrated to United States, 1929, naturalized citizen, 1944; died April 25, 1988, in Los Angeles, Calif. Musicologist, composer, educator, and author. Through his teaching and publications Kremenliev popularized the music of his native Bulgaria and other Slavic states. Kremenliev came to the United States in 1929 to study composition at DePaul University and, later, at the Eastman School of Music in Rochester, New York. During World War II he served with U.S. Military Intelligence in Europe. After the war he joined the faculty of the University of California at Los Angeles in 1947, where he remained until his retirement in 1978. Among the several songs and instrumental works he wrote are "Bulgarian Rhapsody" and "Sonata for String, Bass, and Piano." Kremenliev also composed scores for radio, television, the stage, and films. His writings include *Bulgarian-Macedonian Folk Music; Folktales of the Bulgarian People,* authored with his wife, Elva Kremenliev; *As They Say in Bulgaria,* a book of proverbs; *Bulgarian Riddles;* and criticisms and reviews in music journals. Among the honors Kremenliev received were various grants and several ASCAP awards for his contribution to American music.

OBITUARIES AND OTHER SOURCES:

BOOKS

International Who's Who in Music and Musicians' Directory, 10th edition, Melrose, 1985.

PERIODICALS

Los Angeles Times, April 29, 1988.

*   *   *

KRUISE, Carol Sue 1939-

PERSONAL: Born August 12, 1939. *Education:* Received B.A., 1961, and M.L.S., 1975.

ADDRESSES: Home—6209 West Fair Dr., Littleton, Colo. 80123. *Office*—Mark Hopkins Elementary School, 7171 South Pennsylvania, Littleton, Colo. 80123.

CAREER: Former high school teacher of French and history. Library media specialist at Mark Hopkins Elementary School, Littleton, Colo.

MEMBER: Beta Phi Mu.

WRITINGS:

Those Bloomin' Books: A Handbook for Extending Thinking Skills, illustrations by Robert B. Phillips, Libraries Unlimited, 1987.*

*   *   *

KRUKOWSKI, Lucian 1929-

PERSONAL: Born November 22, 1929, in New York, N.Y.; son of Stefan (a violinist) and Anna (a homemaker; maiden name, Belcarz) Krukowski; married Marilyn Denmark (a professor of biology), January 14, 1955; children: Samantha. *Education:* Brooklyn College (now of the City University of New York), B.A., 1952; Yale University, B.F.A., 1955; Pratt Institute, M.S., 1958; Washington University, St. Louis, Mo., Ph.D., 1977.

ADDRESSES: Home—24 Washington Terrace, St. Louis, Mo. 63112. *Office*—Department of Philosophy, Washington University, St. Louis, Mo. 63130.

CAREER: Pratt Institute, Brooklyn, N.Y., assistant professor, 1956-58, associate professor, 1958-64, professor of art and chairman of fine arts department, 1964-69; Washington University, St. Louis, Mo., dean of School of Fine Arts, 1969-77; professor of art, 1977-85; professor of philosophy, 1985—, and chairman of philosophy department, 1986—. Artwork exhibited in group and one-man shows in New York, N.Y., and St. Louis, and represented in four museum collections. *Military service:* U.S. Marines, 1952-54.

MEMBER: American Philosophical Association, American Society for Aesthetics.

WRITINGS:

Art and Concept: A Philosophical Study, University of Massachusetts Press, 1987.

Contributor to philosophy journals.

WORK IN PROGRESS: A work on art and ideology and "the relationship between expressive, celebratory, and critical functions of art," completion expected in 1990.

SIDELIGHTS: Lucian Krukowski told *CA:* "I was originally trained as a painter, taught and exhibited extensively, and still like to paint. My training as a philosopher came later and is now my principal academic activity, occupying most of my time and energy. This may change, however, after my next book. Then, again, it may not."

*   *   *

KRUPP, Sherman Roy   1926-1988

OBITUARY NOTICE—See index for *CA* sketch: Born August 20, 1926, in New York, N.Y.; died of heart failure, June 5, 1988, in New York, N.Y. Educator and author. Krupp was professor of anthropology and sociology at Queens College of the City University of New York, beginning in 1965. Prior to joining the Queens College faculty, Krupp taught at Lehigh and Florida State universities. He wrote *Pattern in Organization Analysis: A Critical Examination* and edited *Structure of Economic Science.*

OBITUARIES AND OTHER SOURCES:

BOOKS

American Men and Women of Science: The Social and Behavioral Sciences, 12th edition, Bowker, 1973.

PERIODICALS

New York Times, June 7, 1988.

*   *   *

KUNENE, Mazisi (Raymond)   1930-

PERSONAL: Born in 1930 in Durban, South Africa. *Education:* Received M.A. from Natal University; attended School of Oriental and African Studies, London, 1959.

ADDRESSES: Office—Department of African Literature and Language, University of California, Los Angeles, 405 Hilgard, Los Angeles, Calif. 90024.

CAREER: Head of department of African studies at University College at Rome, Lesotho; director of education for South African United Front; African National Congress in Europe and United States, chief representative, 1962, director of finance, 1972; visiting professor of African literature at Stanford University, Palo Alto, Calif.; began as associate professor, became professor of African literature and language at University of California, Los Angeles.

AWARDS, HONORS: Winner of Bantu Literary Competition, 1956.

WRITINGS:

(And translator from the Zulu) *Zulu Poems,* Africana, 1970.
(And translator from the Zulu) *Emperor Shaka the Great: A Zulu Epic,* Heinemann, 1979.
(And translator from the Zulu) *Anthem of the Decades: A Zulu Epic,* Heinemann, 1981.
The Ancestors and the Sacred Mountain: Poems, Heinemann, 1982.

Work represented in anthologies, including *Modern Poetry From Africa,* edited by Gerald Moore and Ulli Beier, Penguin, 1963; *African Writing Today,* edited by Ezekiel Mphahlele, Penguin, 1967. Contributor of short stories to *Drum.*

SIDELIGHTS: Drawing on the oral tradition of Zulu literature, Mazisi Kunene writes poetry expressing Zulu culture, religion, and history. He has translated much of his work, originally written in Zulu, into English. *Emperor Shaka the Great* is Kunene's verse narrative about the life and achievements of the nineteenth-century Zulu leader who unified various Zulu fiefdoms and attempted to deal diplomatically with English settlers. Deeming it "an African epic equal to *The Iliad* and *The Odyssey,*" *World Literature Today* contributor Charles R. Larson judged the poem "a monumental undertaking and achievement by any standards." *Anthem of the Decades* details the Zulu account of how death came to mankind, and Kunene's collection *The Ancestors and the Sacred Mountain,* containing more than one hundred poems, promotes humanity, appreciation of nature, ancestral wisdom, and social action.

BIOGRAPHICAL/CRITICAL SOURCES:

PERIODICALS

Times Educational Supplement, January 28, 1983.
Times Literary Supplement, May 14, 1982.
World Literature Today, summer, 1981, summer, 1983.*

*   *   *

KURYS, Diane   1949-

PERSONAL: Born in 1949; daughter of Daniel (a clothing store owner) and Lena Kurys. *Education:* Educated in France.

ADDRESSES: Office—c/o French Film Office, 745 Fifth Ave., New York, N.Y. 10151.

CAREER: Screenwriter and director of motion pictures. Actress in stage productions, including "The Miser," and motion pictures, including "Fellini's Casanova," 1976.

AWARDS, HONORS: Prix Louis Delluc, 1978, for "Diabolo menthe"; nomination for Academy Award for best foreign-language film from Academy of Motion Picture Arts and Sciences, 1983, for "Entre Nous."

WRITINGS:

SCREENPLAYS; AND DIRECTOR

"Diabolo menthe," Gaumont, 1978, released in the United States as "Peppermint Soda," New Yorker Films, 1979.
"Cocktail Molotov," Alexandre Films/Antenne 2, 1980, released in the United States by Alexandre Films, 1981.

"Coup de foudre" (title means "Thunderclap"), Ariel Zie-
toun, 1983, released in the United States as "Entre Nous"
(title means "Between Us"), United Artists Classics, 1983.
(With Oliver Schatzky) "A Man in Love," Cinecom Pictures,
1987.

SIDELIGHTS: Diane Kurys is an acclaimed screenwriter-director
whose films derive from her personal experiences. She was
born in 1949 and was only six years old when her parents—
Russian immigrants in France—separated, a break she chronicled in the 1983 film "Entre Nous." After several years in
the French public schools, where she experienced some of the
same events she recounted in 1978's "Peppermint Soda," she
traveled to Israel and worked for one year on a kibbutz. When
she returned to France she became involved in the student
activities that sparked riots and destabilized Paris in 1968. Her
activities at that time served as inspiration for her 1980 film
"Cocktail Molotov." Her enthusiasm for radical politics waned
in the 1970s, whereupon Kurys turned to acting, appearing
mostly in secondary roles. It was while touring the United
States in a production of Moliere's "The Miser" that she became interested in screenwriting, and when she returned to
France she found funding for her first work, "Peppermint
Soda."

In "Peppermint Soda" Kurys details one year in the life of
Anne Weber, a thirteen-year-old schoolgirl whose world consists of fierce friendships, flirtations, and forbidden pantyhose.
Kurys's alter ego, Anne Weber, lives in relative comfort with
her divorced mother and a slightly older sister. Anne under-
goes the usual traumas and trials of female adolescence, including her first romance and her first menstruation, and experiences her first acquaintance with the radical politics that
were so instrumental in shaping Kurys's own life. "'Peppermint Soda' was conceived when I began thinking that there
are . . . very few films about girls in high school and how
they're raised," Kurys told the *New York Times* in 1979. "I
decided to make this film out of my own memories."

"Peppermint Soda" was a substantial critical success upon its
release in 1978. In France it received the coveted Prix Louis
Delluc, and in the United States, where it was released in
1979, it earned recognition as an unexpectedly impressive
filmmaking debut. Kurys's approach to her subject was sincere
but nonjudgmental, with events ranging from the personal to
the public and political all rendered in equally low-key manner. It was Kurys's unassuming style that most enchanted
American critics such as Richard Christiansen and Judith Martin. Christiansen, writing in the *Chicago Tribune*, praised Kurys's "taste and delicacy" and declared that "Peppermint Soda"
was "shot, selected, and arranged with the loving care lav-
ished on a treasured family album." Similarly, Martin wrote
in the *Washington Post* that the life of Anne Weber—specifically, one year: from fall, 1963, to fall, 1964—was "sensitively depicted." For Kurys, the success and acclaim was rather
intimidating. "When I made 'Peppermint Soda,' I didn't know
anything," she revealed to the *New York Times* in its 1979
profile. "Now I know a little—so I'm scared."

Despite reservations about her grasp of filmmaking, Kurys
quickly followed "Peppermint Soda" with "Cocktail Molotov," which recounts the life of a seventeen-year-old—also
named Anne—during the hectic period of student unrest in
1968 Paris. Anne is a malcontent anxious to flee her dull,
repressive home life, one which seems to epitomize middle-
class values, and find a more meaningful, fulfilling existence.
She eventually travels to Venice with intentions of departing

for Israel and life on a kibbutz there. Once in Venice, however, Anne and her companions—her boyfriend and his af-
fable, goofy best friend—learn of the disturbances in Paris.
The three innocents, suddenly dedicated to radical politics,
then hitchhike back to Paris hoping to participate in the melee.

Although "Cocktail Molotov" is an insightful perspective on
French political activism in the late 1960s, it consistently balances the political with the personal and, like "Peppermint
Soda," rarely strays from focusing on its heroine. The *New
York Times*'s Vincent Canby found Kurys's style "engaging"
and called "Cocktail Molotov" an "appealing" work. He
contended, though, that her carefree handling of the film's
more comedic aspects sometimes undermined her critical depiction of bourgeois life. "The film," charged Canby, "is a
nearly perfect example of the kind of French film that apo-
theosizes middle-class values while pretending to question
them." Nonetheless, Canby praised Kurys's filmmaking and
commended her more personalized perspective on the events
of 1968 in Paris.

In 1983 Kurys completed her third film, "Entre Nous," about
her mother's friendship with another woman and how that
bond ended her parents' marriage. As the film begins, Kurys's
mother—here named Lena—awaits deportation to a German
camp for Jews during World War II. A French camp worker
becomes interested in Lena and proposes marriage, noting that
such a union would exempt her from deportation. Lena accepts
his offer, whereupon the couple embark from the camp and
trek across mountainous terrain in winter. Meanwhile the other
woman, Madeleine, is first seen married to a charismatic teacher,
but that marriage ends abruptly when he is gunned down during a partisan attack. The narrative then skips forward several
years and refocuses on Lena and her husband, now a successful
garage mechanic, living with their two daughters in a Paris
flat. At an afternoon school presentation, Lena meets Madeleine, who is now remarried to an aspiring actor.

The two women quickly become friends, and as that friendship
grows, Lena's husband, Michel, becomes increasingly resentful. Soon Lena's bond with Madeleine supersedes her marital
relationship, much to the chagrin of Michel. And as Lena
grows closer to the artistic—though weak-willed—Madeleine,
she also becomes more self-confident and independent. Michel,
well-meaning but ultimately patronizing and even inconsider-
ate, tries to tolerate his wife's bond with Madeleine, but his
efforts only exacerbate his anxiety. Tensions finally explode
when he finds the two women together at a boutique he has
financed for Lena, who is the proprietor. Having earlier forbidden his wife to see the emotionally unstable Madeleine,
Michel is incensed to find her there, and he responds by destroying the boutique. His destructive tantrum prompts a daring, but inevitable, decision from Lena, who takes her two
daughters and leaves Paris. The film ends with the tearful
Michel realizing that he has lost his family, and as he weeps
a note appears on-screen revealing the biographical nature of
the film.

With "Entre Nous" Kurys achieved her greatest artistic triumph
to date. The film proved popular both in Europe, where it won
particular acclaim from French critics, and in the United States,
where it was eventually nominated for an Academy Award for
best foreign language film. American critics generally agreed
that "Entre Nous" was a subtle, incisive exploration of the
women's friendship and its effect on their marriages. Among
the film's many supporters was Sheila Benson, who wrote in
the *Los Angeles Times* that "Entre Nous" was an "astonish-

ing'' work. Benson was perhaps most impressed with Kurys's skill in fashioning fully realized characters, and she commended the playwright for creating ''no absolute villains.'' Furthermore, Benson noted that ''Entre Nous,'' as the product of a relatively young filmmaker, was ''an extraordinary signpost of what we may look forward to.''

Similarly, the *New York Times*'s Canby declared that Kurys, on the merits of ''Entre Nous,'' had to be ranked in ''the forefront of the commercial French cinema.'' Like Benson, Canby acknowledged Kurys's impartial perspective and her ability to portray both women and men with equal candor. ''Like all serious works of narrative film, ['Entre Nous'] examines people in particular situations and makes some speculation about what it finds,'' Canby wrote. ''After that, it's for each of us to interpret according to his own circumstances.'' For Canby, ''Entre Nous'' was a ''very personal, moving . . . film.''

After completing ''Entre Nous'' Kurys was an author of and directed ''A Man in Love,'' her first film in English. It concerns the love affair of an actor and actress on the set of a movie in which they are also cast as lovers. The actor is Steve Elliott, a cold, disdainful American who shows little regard for those beneath him in the film profession. Although married—to a woman grown bitter by her husband's haphazard marital commitment—Steve falls in love with Jane Steiner, a French actress known for her stage work. The lovers meet after Steve arrogantly refuses an interview with Jane's father, an alcoholic journalist. Jane consequently berates Steve, who thus becomes intrigued with his upstart co-star. Much of ''A Man in Love'' details the folly of the affair as Steve, playing suicidal Italian writer Cesar Pavese in the film-within-the-film, manipulates his relationship with Jane to fit his needs as a creative actor. Jane, meanwhile, is also undergoing traumatic times with her mother, who may be dying. By film's end, the narrative emphasis has shifted from Steve to Jane. Neither of her key relationships—with Steve and with her mother—ends happily for Jane. When filming is done Steve returns to his wife, and Jane's mother dies. Jane then sits before her typewriter and begins writing the story that becomes, presumably, that of ''A Man in Love.''

Among American critics, ''A Man in Love'' was considered inferior to Kurys's previous films. It earned particular ire from the *New York Times*, where Janet Maslin called it ''an unaccountably bad film'' and complained that it was both unconvincing and uncompelling. Less harsh was the *Los Angeles Times*'s Michael Wilmington, who found ''A Man in Love'' flawed but admirable. He conceded that the dialogue was rather stilted and that the film's romance was ''not as dangerous or pathetic as it should be.'' But Wilmington also contended that Kurys's work contained ''passion . . . and courage and intelligence,'' and he applauded the actors' performances. ''If ['A Man in Love'] misses,'' he concluded, ''it's an honorable miss, one made with humanity and love.''

BIOGRAPHICAL/CRITICAL SOURCES:

PERIODICALS

Chicago Tribune, September 11, 1979.
Film Comment, July-August, 1983, October, 1987.
Los Angeles Times, February 16, 1984, August 14, 1987.
New York Times, August 5, 1979, April 26, 1981, October 8, 1983, January 25, 1984, January 29, 1984, July 31, 1987.
People, October 29, 1984.
Washington Post, September 21, 1979, September 12, 1987.*

—Sketch by Les Stone

L

LACARRIERE, Jacques 1925-

BRIEF ENTRY: Born December 2, 1925, in Limoges, France. French lawyer, educator, journalist, translator, and author. Lacarriere is famous for his French translations of Greek works, including Nobel Prize-winning poet George Seferis's *Poemes* (Mercure, 1963), Aesop's *Fables* (Club des Libraires de France, 1965), and Pandelis Prevelakis's *Chronique d'une cite* (Gallimard, 1960), *Le Cretois* (Gallimard, 1962), and *Le Soleil de la mort* (Gallimard, 1965). He has written several books on pre-Christian and early Christian religion such as *Les Gnostiques* (Gallimard, 1973), translated in 1975 as *The Gnostics* (Dutton, 1977); *Les Hommes ivres de Dieu* (Fayard), translated in 1963 as *The God-Possessed* (Allen & Unwin) and in 1964 as *Men Possessed by God: The Story of the Desert Monks of Ancient Christendom* (Doubleday); and *En suivant les Dieux: Le Legendaire des hommes* (P. Lebaud, 1984). His other works include the poem *L'Aurige* (Fata Morgana, 1977) and the novel *Marie d'Egypte; ou, Le Desir brute* (Lattes, 1983). Lacarriere, who has worked as a lawyer, a journalist, and a teacher of literature in France and Greece, has also written description and travel books on the Soviet cities of Moscow and Leningrad, on France, and on ancient and modern Greece.

BIOGRAPHICAL/CRITICAL SOURCES:

PERIODICALS

Choice, March, 1978.

*   *   *

LaFANTASIE, Glenn W(arren) 1949-

PERSONAL: Surname is pronounced La-*fan*-ta-sy; born July 29, 1949, in Pawtucket, R.I.; son of Warren E. (a district manager of a bakery) and Edith (a bookkeeper; maiden name, Wynaught) LaFantasie; married Ruth M. LaBrie, March 27, 1971 (divorced, 1975); married Donna A. Dignon (a military officer), December 27, 1978; children: M. Sarah; (stepchildren) Donna M. Hayes, Ryan T. Hayes. *Education:* Providence College, A.B., 1971; University of Rhode Island, A.M., 1973; doctoral study at Brown University, 1980-84.

ADDRESSES: Home—Jenkintown, Pa. *Office*—"The Papers of Albert Gallatin," Bernard M. Baruch College of the City University of New York, 17 Lexington Ave., Box 348-A, New York, N.Y. 10010.

CAREER: Rhode Island Bicentennial Commission and Foundation, Providence, publications director, 1974-76; Rhode Island Office of the Attorney General, Providence, historical expert, 1976-78; Rhode Island Historical Society, Providence, editor of publications, 1979-85; University of Pennsylvania, Wharton School, Philadelphia, senior editor of publications, 1985-86; Bernard M. Baruch College of the City University of New York, New York, N.Y., editor and director of "The Papers of Albert Gallatin," 1986—. Visiting lecturer at Providence College, 1978-79; instructor at University of Rhode Island, 1984-85. Intern at Institute in Documentary Editing, Madison, Wis., 1979; principal investigator for "The Papers of John Dickinson," Historical Society of Pennsylvania, 1985-86; consultant to Rhode Island Committee on the Humanities.

MEMBER: Association for Documentary Editing (member of executive council and director of publications, 1984-85), American Historical Association, Organization of American Historians, Institute of Early American History and Culture (associate), Society for Historians of the Early American Republic, Southern Historical Association.

WRITINGS:

(Editor) *The Correspondence of Roger Williams,* two volumes, University Press of New England, 1988.

Contributor of articles and reviews to history journals and newspapers. Editor of *Rhode Island History,* 1979-84.

WORK IN PROGRESS: Editing *The Papers of Albert Gallatin,* publication of first volume by University of Pennsylvania Press expected in 1991; research on biography and history.

SIDELIGHTS: Glenn W. LaFantasie told *CA:* "One reviewer has said that *The Correspondence of Roger Williams* will be 'the definitive edition for the next hundred years or longer.' I appreciate the compliment, but I'm not sure the volumes will stand such a long test of time. My edition of Williams's letters has been shaped according to my own picture of the man and his world. Unlike most documentary editors, I did not shy away from including my own interpretations of Williams in my annotations to his letters. It seems to me that a documentary editor has an obligation to share with his readers all that he has learned about his subject during the course of scrutinizing—and deciphering—private correspondence. As biographers know, sometimes the plain facts do not tell the whole story. Such is also the case with documents, which often tend to mask the inner contours of a writer's personality and character. In editing Williams's correspondence, I decided not to let the documents simply speak for themselves. Instead, I purposely approached Williams as a biographer would do, using techniques of research and analysis that are commonly used by biographers—and that are woefully neglected by most documentary editors. I set out not to create an edition of Williams's letters for the ages. My edition of Williams is intended to be a conscious attempt to marry documentary editing with the art of biography. As such, it very likely will not stand for all time as the last word on Roger Williams, for other scholars will see fit to agree or disagree with my portrait of the man, a portrait that consists of more than the colors contained in the documents themselves. My edition of Williams's correspondence is not a source book alone. It is a creative reflection of myself and of my perspective on the past. 'Never,' says Jean Paul Richter, 'does a man portray his own character more vividly, than in his manner of portraying another.' With this humbling thought, I trust that I have done justice to Roger Williams—and to myself.''

*   *   *

LAMIS, Alexander P.   1946-

PERSONAL: Born May 10, 1946, in Charleston, S.C.; son of Pano A. (a hat cleaner) and Olympia Lynn (a housewife and secretary; maiden name, Moses) Lamis; married Karen Aldridge (a librarian), December 28, 1968. *Education:* College of Charleston, B.A., 1968; Vanderbilt University, M.A., 1975, Ph.D., 1982; University of Maryland, Baltimore, J.D., 1984. *Politics:* Democrat. *Religion:* Greek Orthodox.

ADDRESSES: Office—Department of Political Science, Case Western Reserve University, Cleveland, Ohio 44106.

CAREER: WCSC-TV, Charleston, S.C., evening news reporter, 1966-67; *Arizona Daily Star,* Tucson, reporter, 1971-72; *Columbia Record,* Columbia, S.C., reporter, 1972; *Tennessean,* Nashville, Tenn., part-time copy editor, 1974-75; *Bergen Record,* Hackensack, N.J., assistant news editor, 1976; *Baltimore Sun,* Baltimore, Md., copy editor, 1976-81; Towson State University, Baltimore, instructor in political science, 1978-80; Brookings Institution, Washington, D.C., research assistant, 1981; University of Mississippi, Oxford, assistant professor of political science, 1981-85; University of North Florida, Jacksonville, associate professor of political science, 1985-88; Case Western Reserve University, Cleveland, Ohio, associate professor of political science, 1988—. *Military service:* U.S. Navy, supply officer, 1968-71; served in Iceland; became lieutenant junior grade.

MEMBER: American Political Science Association, Southern Political Science Association.

AWARDS, HONORS: Co-recipient of V. O. Key Book Award from Southern Political Science Association, 1985, for *The Two-Party South.*

WRITINGS:

The Two-Party South, Oxford University Press, 1984, enlarged, 1988.

Contributor to *Encyclopedia of Southern Culture.* Contributor to political science and history journals.

WORK IN PROGRESS: Research on U.S. electoral change since 1964.

SIDELIGHTS: Alexander P. Lamis told *CA:* "My interest in southern politics began in the 1960s, when as a television news reporter in Charleston, South Carolina, I observed in action many of the South's leading political figures of the day. Some of these leaders who left vivid impressions on me were George Wallace, Martin Luther King, Jr., and Strom Thurmond. After entering graduate school at Vanderbilt University, I encountered the analytical tools and instruction I needed to make sense of what I had been witnessing in the politics of my native region.''

Samuel C. Patterson in *Perspective* described *The Two-Party South* as a "gracefully written and cogently argued book'' and "a readable and timely account of the southern politics of the present day.'' The book begins with a history of southern politics, emphasizing the movement away from a traditionally solid, Democratic South. Lamis then offers an analysis of the politics of each southern state, focusing on the period that followed the waning of the civil rights movement of the 1960s. These analyses reveal the author's view that the Republican party has established itself in each southern state, providing, as Patterson explained, "an opportunity for fully seated partisan realignment in the South, but only if the Republican party capitalizes on its opportunity.''

David D. Lee told readers of the *American Historical Review* that Lamis writes "in an engaging manner that blends colorful quotations and quantitative analysis,'' adding, what is "particularly appealing is his final chapter that draws on survey research to provide some generalizations about the current status of southern politics.'' Lamis concludes that a successful coalition between blacks and whites is essential to the future of the southern Democratic party and that the foothold established by southern Republicans clearly places the south in line with the rest of the United States in the area of truly bipartisan politics.

AVOCATIONAL INTERESTS: Travel (Europe, West Africa, Mexico, Central America).

BIOGRAPHICAL/CRITICAL SOURCES:

PERIODICALS

American Historical Review, October, 1985.
Journal of Politics, volume 48, 1986.
Journal of Southern History, November, 1985.
Perspective, November-December, 1984.
Times Literary Supplement, August 30, 1985.

*   *   *

LAMMING, R. M.   1949-

PERSONAL: Born January 10, 1949, in Isle of Man, Great Britain; daughter of Robert Love (a surgeon) and Olive (a physician; maiden name, Callow) Lamming. *Education:* St. Anne's College, Oxford, M.A., 1970.

ADDRESSES: Home—37 Chatsworth Rd., London NW2 4BL, England. *Agent*—Murray Pollinger, 4 Garrick St., London WC2E 9BH, England.

CAREER: Writer since the 1970's. Has worked part time in Oxford and London in various capacities, including teacher, classic bookseller, administrator of a subscriptions department, secretary, and clerk.

AWARDS, HONORS: David Higham Award from the National Book League, 1983, for *The Notebook of Gismondo Cavalletti.*

WRITINGS:

The Notebook of Gismondo Cavalletti (novel), Cape, 1983, Atheneum, 1985.
In the Dark (novel), Cape, 1985, Atheneum, 1986.

Also author of short stories.

WORK IN PROGRESS: A satirical novel, tentatively titled *Lights.*

SIDELIGHTS: British writer R. M. Lamming's first novel, *The Notebook of Gismondo Cavalletti,* won the David Higham Award for fiction when it was published in 1983. Called "a convincing and complex account of the corrupting powers of disappointment" by Thomas Sutcliffe in the *Times Literary Supplement,* the *Notebook* is set in Renaissance Italy as seen through the eyes of the title character, who jots down the novel's events in notebook form. While Renaissance personalities such as artists Michelangelo Buonarroti and Leonardo da Vinci, religious reformer Girolamo Savonarola, and the members of the ruling Medici family are important in forming the novel's backdrop, the story centers on Gismondo Cavalletti. Sold by his natural peasant parents at the age of ten, Gismondo is bought by a childless merchant, Piero Sassoli, who is attracted by the beauty of the boy. Sassoli and his wife hope that the child will blossom into an artistic or scientific genius; however, Gismondo, nicknamed "Gismo" by his new family, is not a genius but merely sharp in mathematical skills. Gismondo's status in the Sassoli household is lowered four years later when Sassoli's wife gives birth to her own son, dying in the process. In addition to having negative feelings towards the boy who displaces him, Gismondo is further distressed by a disfiguring growth on his face that begins to develop when he is seventeen.

Gismondo's troubled relationship with Piero Sassoli's true son and heir, Gabriello, has been interpreted in varying ways by different reviewers. According to Karen Ray in the *New York Times Book Review,* Gabriello is cruel, "tak[ing] pleasure at Gismondo's expense, one Christmas giving him a fine and expensive gift, a mirror that is a constant reminder of his obvious flaw." Kenneth Atchity declared Gismondo an admirable character in the *Los Angeles Times Book Review,* writing "for this man, honesty is a constant. He is unintimidated by all he serves and all he surveys." Laurie Stone, however, reviewing the *Notebook* in the *Village Voice,* asserted that Gismondo's problems are a matter of his own perception. "He believes Sassoli's real son hates him, plots his downfall," she wrote, "while we note that the reverse is true, that Gismo rebuffs Gabriello's attempts at affection and is eaten alive by jealousy."

Most critics agreed that perception is a central issue of the *Notebook.* Pointing out Gismondo's unreliability as a narrator, Sutcliffe averred that "Cavalletti descends into a paranoia . . . and the novel allows us to lose our trust in his account of events." The author was lauded by Stone for her "subtlety" in conveying Gismondo's vision while at the same time allowing readers to see its distortion: "To justify himself, Gismo records the harsh things said about him, but these remarks, skillfully inserted by Lamming, in fact draw an accurate picture."

Atchity praised Lamming for her "artistic empathy." Labeling the *Notebook* "remarkable," he wrote of the author's critical insight into art in these terms: "Criticism in its highest form is transubstantiation; insight into art may itself result in artistic expression." The passage of the *Notebook* which elicited this applause is a scene depicting the unveiling of Michelangelo's famous sculpture of David: "The statue vetoes petty adoration. 'Didn't you know?' it says. 'This also exists quite naturally in the universe—this thing you call perfection. And men are dwarfed, not because it exists but because they are startled by it.'"

The *Notebook* was also hailed for its mood-setting descriptions of the natural world. Sutcliffe admired Lamming's use of "the timeless details of environment; seasonal changes, the fading of daylight, the stage effects of the weather, all of which are achieved with a nostalgic precision." Atchity remarked that "the book beckons, instilling the mood and atmosphere of that splendid and unbelievable city [Florence], making us taste again the pines and smell the espresso."

Lamming's second novel, *In the Dark,* was also well received. Ostensibly very different from *The Notebook of Gismondo Cavalletti, In the Dark* is the story of Arnold Lawson, a modern-day octogenarian who is for the most part a recluse dependent on his housekeeper. Emma Fisher, however, reviewing the second book for the *Times Literary Supplement,* noted a similarity between it and the *Notebook,* writing: "R. M. Lamming has the kind of imagination which thrives on impersonating a character very remote from herself. . . . This seizing of a character and living him from the inside is the main achievement of both books." Fisher then expressed the opinion that "in both, Lamming fleshes out the central figure with an almost painful clarity."

Arnold Lawson's main pastime is sitting in his library surrounded by his collection of rare books—until Moira Gelling, married and middle-aged, comes into his life. Drawn to Lawson's house by a newspaper article on his magnificent library, Moira becomes a frequent visitor, and, in the words of Janet Madden-Simpson in the San Francisco *Examiner,* Lawson "fabricates an impossible love affair." Moira brings to Lawson's seclusion everything he had been guarding himself against and unwittingly lures him into a difficult, perplexing relationship. Lawson's attentions to Moira also provoke the jealousy of his embittered housekeeper, Edith.

Lawson's involvement with Moira is selfish, plagued by the fear of rejection and the impossibility of declaring himself. He is too egocentric to recognize Moira's motivations and feelings, though these are hinted at. Autumn turns to winter; in a characteristic tirade Lawson offends her on the subject of religion. They remain aloof from one another until Christmas, when Moira invites Lawson to a family party. There, he awkwardly reveals his affection for her. Disaster results, and Lawson returns to his home only to find that jealous Edith has revenged herself by disappearing. Frighteningly alone, his wealth, his house, and his treasured library have become traps rather than defences of a willing isolation. He is forced to confront what Madden-Simpson labeled his "own private darkness of soul." *In the Dark* ends with Lawson brought to a greater dependence on Edith, though his submission to this situation is anything but graceful. As Fisher summarized, Lawson "began old and unhappy, and he ends older and unhappier."

Arnold Lawson's decline is portrayed as tragic, causing Fisher to applaud Lamming's "sympathy and insight" into the problems of the elderly. Admiring Lamming's "impressive confidence and control over her material," Nicholas Shakespeare contended in the London *Times* that *In the Dark* "works as both a warning about what happens when life is admitted too late, as well as a warts-and-all portrait of the self-revulsion and selfishness of a man on the shelf.'' Bleak though its picture of old age may be, however, the novel is apparently not without humor. Madden-Simpson claimed that it ''has a rich potential for comedy,'' and Sarah Vogan concluded in the *New York Times Book Review* that *In the Dark* is ''wickedly funny, sad and warped at the same time.''

AVOCATIONAL INTERESTS: Superstitions, lost causes, poetry, cinema.

CA INTERVIEW

CA interviewed R. M. Lamming by telephone on November 19, 1986, at her home in London.

CA: Your first novel, The Notebook of Gismondo Cavalletti, *tells a very powerful story while it portrays the intellectual ferment and daily life of Renaissance Florence. Had you done a lot of reading on the Italian Renaissance before you began planning the book?*

LAMMING: No, I hadn't. Really, I did not set out to write a historical novel, and while the story has a historical setting, its kernel, to my mind, is the theme of an individual coming to terms with his limitations and the influence that other people's expectations of his have on him—which, of course, is a theme one would set in any age.

It just so happened that this theme grew round an image from the Renaissance. I was doing some casual reading and I came across an anecdote in Vasari's *Lives of the Artists* about da Vinci—how he used to stick bits of other animals on to the backs of lizards, creating hypothetical monsters. That got lodged in my mind; it seemed to illustrate the problem of how we can be belittled and sort of perverted by having the preconceptions of others foisted on to us. Then I realized that the Renaissance was an appropriate setting for much of what I wanted to write about. It was a time of terrific opportunity for people from poorer backgrounds—one of the first times, I think, that they really did have an opportunity to make their own future. It was a time of high expectations. Consequently, I felt that the Renaissance could act as a wonderful foil to the problems of self-doubt. People could measure where they personally were against a general sense of opportunity—and amazing achievements. So, as I say, the historical setting simply turned out to be appropriate to highlight several of the themes I had in mind.

As to research, I wrote the book trusting to that kind of osmosis that goes on all our lives, particularly about the Renaissance. We are exposed to that quite a lot through paintings and drama—Shakespeare, if no one else. Once I had drafted the book, I went back over some points and read around them. I certainly didn't want the research to come looming up out of the book as if I had swotted it up and *then* written the novel. I wanted to keep the characters in the foreground. So first I wrote, and then I checked those things I had a feeling I really didn't know, such as what the clocks would be like.

CA: Did you happen to find any odd sources—anything like diaries or notebooks of the period?

LAMMING: I stuck to three or four very basic books. For the Medici history, I used Christopher Hibbert's *Rise and Fall of the House of Medici*. Then there's a wonderful book, which is a collation of letters that were found, I think, in the last century. They were written by a merchant in Prato—not Renaissance, but roughly a century-and-a-half earlier than the

period I'm writing about. I owe quite a number of household details to reading those letters. And I used a couple of memoirs of the time, [sculptor] Benvenuto Cellini's for one. But I kept the research to a minimum. I think I did more by going around art galleries looking at portraits than by reading to get the spirit, the kind of arrogance of the men and some of that icy remoteness that comes over in the portraits of the women sometimes. Certainly the visual felt more important to me.

CA: That's most interesting, because there are scenes in the book that have the force and quality of paintings. I think it's partly the way you've set them in a certain light, such as moonlight or candlelight. I wondered, reading these, if you'd had paintings in mind when you wrote them.

LAMMING: No specific paintings. I am very suspicious of hijacking too many set pieces into fiction—I mean specific, finished representations that have helped one build up the atmosphere in one's mind. What I prefer to do is get an overall impression and then allow the imagination to go to work on it. In fact, except in the case of small factual details and one or two central images, I am rather disconcerted if I can recognize specific sources behind my fiction. To me it seems dangerous; very often those parts don't quite ring true. I think you have to let verisimilitude happen through allowing your imagination to change what is actually historically correct to what feels correct now. I had no actual portraits or paintings in mind, but I did look at a lot of them.

CA: The voice of the book seems perfectly suited to the period and the story. Did it come to you easily?

LAMMING: I was fortunate in that I didn't actually have to hunt for a great while—if one *can* hunt—for a voice. Gismondo's voice just came. I did work hard, though, not to make it too parochially English and not too contemporary. The prose style was more difficult and there was a little criticism of it in England. There are certain maneuvers that one or two critics didn't think it could handle very well. Obviously, I went to no great efforts to make it correct for its period. Instead, I hoped to avoid any kind of intrusive pastiche and rely on the voice to give the style its flavor. I was fairly content with how this worked. I think there were perhaps one or two things that, if I wrote the book again, I wouldn't do. There was this problem that not only is one writing a book set in a ''now'' when it would have been written in quite a different sytle, but of course I was also writing it in English when it would have been written in Italian. I was into a double bind there. But, on the whole, I felt the compromise was a workable one. I think there is some evidence of Latin in the style and perhaps in the voice, too. I have a fairly Latin sort of education, and I think that helped.

The other important factor about the style of the book is that the man who is writing is an accountant and not at all used to writing his own thoughts. Only figures. He has no experience of putting down verbal ideas, or really of writing any kind of prose. That is why I used a notebook style, so that I could break things up. It was also helpful, I think, in giving a kind of immediacy to the book.

CA: You studied English language and literature at St. Anne's College, Oxford. Were you already writing then?

LAMMING: Yes and no. Not for publication, but I have always been a scribbler, and to some extent I found academic

English at Oxford rather difficult to reconcile with writing—which I was already stuffing away in cupboards and so on. Really, I began to publish short stories in the seventies, and right through the seventies continued to publish short story work and build up to writing a novel. I would say that I was not a born novelist; I was a natural short story teller. I think there are perhaps hints of that beginning in *The Notebook*. It was an attractive format to somebody who had come from short stories.

CA: In both The Notebook of Gismondo Cavalletti *and your second novel,* In the Dark, *you have central characters whose perception of other people's feelings is often very distorted. I think it's a difficult job to convey this to the reader while writing from such a character's point of view. Did you take it on as a deliberate challenge?*

LAMMING: I think one of my main preoccupations is perception and how we are trapped within our own perception, which is, of course, not necessarily the truth, or not necessarily the whole truth. It's quite true that both books are studies of people who have problems seeing beyond their own obsessions or neuroses or grievances to what is real, and who have circumstances or features in their makeup that distort reality for them. This is true to some extent of everybody, and I'm interested in the problem of how to imply to the reader that the insights being presented are not necessarily the objective truth. That is a linking factor between the two books; they both try to do that. But they are both, too, as someone over here remarked in a review, books about domestic terrorism. Whatever you might think of either main character, they are both men who are involved in battles of power within a household, and for both, everyday domestic occurrences feed a sense of being persecuted until their viewpoint is hopelessly distorted. I didn't think of it until the reviewer pointed it out, but I can see that it is true. Domestic warfare is a theme in my writing, the hostile presence on the staircase—that kind of thing.

CA: In the Dark is a story of a very old man whose selfishness keeps him from receiving or enjoying any sort of love from other people. Did the book begin out of an interest in aging or more as a study of a specific character?

LAMMING: It began, I think, as a little of both. The character grew out of memories of more than one rather difficult elderly person in the community when I was a teenager, and I suppose the book is in its way a sort of character study. But a lot of the bite in the book, a lot of what made me want to write it, derives from feelings I had as a teenager of revulsion at some old people's difficultness, their impatience, their intolerance of the young—plus a feeling of tremendous pity for them, a concern about how people cope when they know that they're near the end of their life. It was a fascination with age, an adolescent fascination, that I have never forgotten.

In addition, I have become, over the years, rather dismayed by the dismissive way people talk about the elderly. It's changing a little now, but I think the elderly have had a very raw deal. And although I wanted to write a book about an old man who is not cosy, not too likeable, the book is supposed to champion him to a large extent. I didn't think it was worth writing a book about a saintly, wonderful old person, not for my purpose, because sympathizing with *them* is not really the problem. The problem is that many old people are frightened, bad-tempered, and demanding. I wanted to write a book that showed life through their eyes and their fear. *In the Dark* is

intended as a cry for them. I know Arnold Lawson is not a character who inspires immediate pity, but my aim was to make the reader feel for his horrible predicament—the tragedy of going through life and not having grown sufficiently to meet the end of it, a terrible dilemma and a common one.

I don't feel that enough is done either to help or to appreciate the old—certainly not in Britain, which is the only country I really know. But I didn't want to make this single issue too prominent in the book, because the book, I think, is very precariously balanced between being one old man's story and wider implications. And there were other issues I wanted to touch upon. For example there is the question of sexual drive in old age, which has absolutely nowhere to go. That is a complete taboo. I'm not suggesting that very elderly people would want to have an extremely athletic sex life, but the taboo is such that they can hardly express any sexuality without it being, somehow, something for everybody to wince at. I feel that is a terrible thing, how we sort of shut people down in that way.

CA: Some reviewers felt the Moira Gelling character was underdeveloped. Did you have her this way specifically to show that Arnold Lawson never saw her as an individual?

LAMMING: Yes. Again, it's back to the idea of the main character's perception being unreliable. I hope the reader will pick up hints beyond the information he or she is being given through the eyes of the old man. Moira Gelling is somebody whom Lawson only sees in a very narrow way; of course people only really exist for him insofar as they affect him. Because of his selfishness, he doesn't have any ability to stand back and see a whole person. This is demonstrated again in his attitude towards his housekeeper. He can't entertain any ideas about how desperately lonely she might be; he sees only what she does for him—and to him. Then, as well as being blinded by his selfishness, there's the fact that Lawson is partially deaf. He *is* "in the dark." His whole reception of incoming information is very limited. He misses entirely the clues that Moira is ill. So, certainly Moira is a sort of half-there character. We're never allowed to see her in the full. Lawson won't let us, because he can't do it himself.

CA: Again in In the Dark, *as you'd done in your first novel, you used light and weather wonderfully well to create moods. Is this a part of the writing you especially enjoy?*

LAMMING: Yes. Light and weather are extremely important to me. I think some of this goes back to my background. I live in a city now, but I'm not really comfortable in a city. I'm rural, small town in background. I was brought up on the fringes of countryside, and I do miss that. Of course, too, both books in different ways are deeply concerned with the passage of time. One, being a notebook, must mark the passage of time, and the other is a kind of countdown to a disaster in the old man's life. Light and weather are a natural way to create that feeling of time passing. But more than that, I think they are the great mood builders; and I think they are a feature in all my writing.

CA: Did the David Higham Award for The Notebook of Gismondo Cavalletti *have immediate effects on your writing career?*

LAMMING: I think I got more publicity for my first book, both in England and America, than I would have otherwise. It's such a tough world out there, and with a first novel it's extremely difficult to get much notice. I was fortunate; I did. I'm sure that is partly to do with having good publishers, but also it must have been connected with winning the prize. It was very useful. A terrific advantage for a starter. There was a small cash prize, and, of course, when you're at the start, that is also very important.

I think it had a good effect for the second novel, too. *In the Dark* is very different from *The Notebook* and has less obvious charisma. The Renaissance is superficially a much more glamorous thing to write about than one old man in an old house in England. I think *The Notebook*'s winning a prize encouraged critics to look at *In the Dark,* whereas otherwise they might have thought, "Oh, dull subject." On the other hand, winning a prize must always be a little unnerving, because it puts a pressure on you—not exactly pressure to win a prize for the next book, but an underlying pressure to keep your standard up. Still, it was most encouraging to win, I must say.

CA: Both novels were published in the United States very soon after their publication in England, which is unusual for a new writer.

LAMMING: I am very lucky. I think Atheneum was brave to take the second book in America because it really is a very, very English novel, and not exactly packed with action. In selling terms, I thought it had so little going for it. I take my hat off to Atheneum; I didn't see myself that there could be a market for it in the United States. I was thrilled that they took it. And the critical response to it in the States has been good.

CA: Can you tell from the mail you've gotten in response to the books how your general readership compares in the two countries?

LAMMING: I haven't had a great deal of mail from anywhere, but I would say I've probably had more from the States; I've certainly had more on *The Notebook,* and about equal amounts from the States and the U.K. [United Kingdom] on the second book.

CA: You've listed your occupations since college as bookselling, journals subscription work, and part-time office work. Are you writing full-time now?

LAMMING: Bascially, I just scramble through life trying to write. For the last two or three months, I have just been writing. But generally the pattern is that I work halftime on something else. My income from writing is not big and so I have to. I don't mind what I do—library work, bookselling. My last job was in an office for half of each week. It just depends what I can get and how things fall out. I have taught, and I have done various things. I do what I can, I live on my wits and write.

CA: Have you found that it's better for the writing if the other job is something fairly unrelated?

LAMMING: That has been my experience, although I think it may depend on the stage one is at in one's career. There's no easy solution. When I was teaching, years ago, I found that I became quite upset by the idea that I was always trying to hold a little back to use in my writing, whereas I felt that the kids deserved the best I could give them. I didn't like that dilemma of either holding back or giving so much that I came home exhausted. So that was the end of teaching—after only

a term! And as to work related to writing—yes: up till now my experience has been that one is better off, as Cyril Connolly says in *Enemies of Promise,* I think, doing something that is actually not connected with writing at all. Almost anything else impinges, I find, or feels as though it's taking energy from the writing.

CA: Are you able to write every day?

LAMMING: It doesn't work out like that when I'm doing a half-time job. I find that the day after I've done office work or whatever, it's very disheartening to try to write. My mind takes a while to turn round. So then I have to wait. It's like waiting for the wave to ride on, and then off you go. You need to create space and time; that's the real problem. It's all very well waiting for the wave, but you can't wait for the wave if you know you've got this hour and no other. So it seems to me that a major thing is to rig your life so that you have time in which you can wait. That is very important, because so much of the work happens before you ever go to the typewriter. Of course, you *can* do without it, but half the work will be done for you if you can have the quiet time.

CA: You mentioned earlier not being quite at home in the city. Do you find, though, that the activity in the city somehow stimulates the writing?

LAMMING: I'm not sure. I *am* uneasy in a city. I suppose it could be argued that the uneasiness is a form of stimulation; I don't know. I'm so aware of what is missing. In a city it's so very difficult to tell what season you're living in. You can tell the spring, but by the time you get to midsummer it's all going tired and dusty. And then there's this long featureless time when it's cold and wet but unless you make an expedition to a park you're not particularly aware of things dying off or beginning to sprout. It's a kind of divorce from the earth which goes on in the city and which I dislike intensely.

The deepest impetus for my writing comes from my background, as I suppose it does for most writers. In my case, this is an island in the middle of the Irish Sea. My childhood was spent on the Isle of Man, where there's a cross-culture between Ireland and England, with just a splash of Viking. It's rather overrun by England now, but the Island's still very Celtic in folklore and temperament. It's a place of cliffs and moorlands, gorse, heather and sea, and a relationship with landscape is still, deep down, what fires my writing. Something to do with natural forces, and rather bleak ones at that.

When it comes to the city, I'm just very reluctant to acknowledge my debt to it. And yet I must have one, because I don't actually sit around writing about heather and rocks and sea all the time. People. Of course, the city's great resource is people; vast numbers of us reacting to each other, all our incomplete perceptions becoming more and more convoluted. That *is* fascinating.

BIOGRAPHICAL/CRITICAL SOURCES:

BOOKS

Lamming, R. M., *The Notebook of Gismondo Cavalletti,* Atheneum, 1985.

PERIODICALS

Examiner (San Francisco), April 19, 1986.
Los Angeles Times Book Review, January 27, 1985.

New York Times Book Review, January 6, 1985, March 9, 1986.
Times (London), June 27, 1985.
Times Literary Supplement, December 16, 1983, June 28, 1985.
Village Voice, February 19, 1985.

—*Sketch by Elizabeth Thomas*

—*Interview by Jean W. Ross*

*   *   *

L'AMOUR, Louis (Dearborn)   1908-1988
(Tex Burns, Jim Mayo)

OBITUARY NOTICE—See index for *CA* sketch: Surname originally LaMoore; born March 22, 1908, in Jamestown, N.D.; died of lung cancer, June 10, 1988, in Los Angeles, Calif. American lecturer and author. One of the most popular writers in the world, L'Amour wrote more than one hundred books, including eighty-six novels, fourteen short story collections, and one book of nonfiction—a chronicle of life on the American frontier. All of his books are in print, reflecting sales of two hundred million copies in twenty languages. L'Amour has also published hundreds of stories in at least eighty magazines in the United States and abroad.

L'Amour quit school at age fifteen and began to roam the Western United States. He worked at a number of odd jobs, among them longshoreman, lumberjack, gold prospector, coal miner, circus roustabout, fruit picker, cattle skinner, elephant handler, amateur archaeologist, and professional boxer. He also traveled throughout the world and by age twenty had lived with bandits in Tibet and worked as a crew member on an East African schooner. His first book, a volume of poetry, was published in 1939. In 1951, writing as Tex Burns, L'Amour published his first western novels. Two years later, in 1953, *Hondo,* his first novel published under his own name, appeared. *Hondo* sold more than 1.5 million copies and was made into a film starring John Wayne. In all, forty-five L'Amour novels or short stories have been made into feature films or television movies.

Following *Hondo,* L'Amour wrote a number of paperback novels, two of which were published under the pseudonym Jim Mayo, but both have since been published under the author's own name. As of 1955 L'Amour began fulfilling a contract to Bantam to write three novels a year. He followed a strict routine of writing five pages a day, every day, and once one book was completed, he immediately started the next. Other popular L'Amour titles include *How the West Was Won, Ride the Dark Trail, The Quick and the Dead, Jubal Sackett, Last of the Breed,* and *The Haunted Mesa.* L'Amour was reportedly proofreading the manuscript of his autobiography, *Education of a Wandering Man,* just hours before his death. Although L'Amour's novels never received much critical recognition, they are known for their authenticity and accuracy. L'Amour's heroes are tough, optimistic, adventuresome, respectful of Indians and of nature, and often well-versed in classic works of Western culture, such as Plutarch's *Lives* and Juvenal's *Satires.*

A popular lecturer at such campuses as the University of Southern California, the University of Oklahoma, and Baylor University, L'Amour received an honorary doctorate in 1972 from Jamestown College. Other honors include a 1983 Congressional National Gold Medal for lifetime literary achievement and the Medal of Freedom, the nation's highest civilian award, presented to L'Amour by President Ronald Reagan in 1984.

OBITUARIES AND OTHER SOURCES:

BOOKS

Contemporary Literature Criticism, Volume 25, Gale, 1983.
Current Biography, H.W. Wilson, 1988.
Who's Who in America, 44th edition, Marquis, 1986.

PERIODICALS

Chicago Tribune, June 19, 1988.
Detroit News, June 13, 1988.
Los Angeles Times, June 13, 1988.
New York Times, June 13, 1988.
Times (London), June 14, 1988.
Washington Post, June 13, 1988.

*   *   *

LAMPTON, Chris
See LAMPTON, Christopher

*   *   *

LAMPTON, Christopher
(Chris Lampton)

PERSONAL: Education—College degree in broadcast journalism.

CAREER: Writer.

WRITINGS:

(With David Bischoff) *The Seeker,* Laser Books, 1976.
(Under name Chris Lampton) *Gateway to Limbo* (science fiction novel), Doubleday, 1979.

JUVENILE; PUBLISHED BY F. WATTS

Black Holes and Other Secrets of the Universe, 1980.
Meteorology: An Introduction, 1981.
Fusion: The Eternal Flame, 1982.
Planet Earth, 1982.
The Sun, 1982.
Dinosaurs and the Age of Reptiles, 1983.
DNA and the Creation of New Life, 1983.
Prehistoric Animals, 1983.
Programming in BASIC, 1983.
Space Sciences, 1983.
Computer Languages, 1983.
Advanced BASIC, 1984.
BASIC for Beginners, 1984.
COBOL for Beginners, 1984.
FORTRAN for Beginners, 1984.
The Micro Dictionary, 1984.
Pascal for Beginners, 1984.
PILOT for Beginners, 1984.
Advanced BASIC for Beginners, 1984.
6502 Assembly-Language Programming for Apple, Commodore, and Atari Computers, 1985.
(Editor with Maury Solomon) *Forth for Beginners,* 1985.
Graphics and Animation on the Commodore 64, 1985.
Z80 Assembly-Language: Programming for Radio Shack, Timex Sinclair, Adam, and CP/M Computers, 1985.
Graphics and Animation on the TRS-80, 1985.
Flying Safe?, 1986.
Graphics and Animation on the Apple, 1986.

How to Create Adventure Games, 1986.
How to Create Computer Games, 1986.
Mass Extinctions: One Theory of Why the Dinosaurs Vanished, 1986.
Astronomy: From Copernicus to the Space Telescope, 1987.
The Space Telescope, 1987.
Star Wars, 1987.*

* * *

LANDSHOFF, Fritz Helmut 1901-1988

OBITUARY NOTICE: Born July 29, 1901, in Berlin, Germany; immigrated to United States, 1941; died of heart failure, March 30, 1988, in the Netherlands. Publishing executive. During his distinguished sixty-year career in publishing in Europe and America, Landshoff founded four publishing houses, established a literary magazine, and published works by such writers as Bertolt Brecht, Erich Maria Remarque, and Richard Wright. He acquired his first publishing company in Potsdam, Germany (now East Germany), in 1926, and produced important radical works by writers including Brecht and Heinrich Mann. He relocated to Amsterdam, Netherlands, in 1933, and founded the literary magazine *Die Sammlung* with Klaus Mann and established an important German-language publishing house with Emmanuel Querido. The journal and the company both featured works by German emigre writers such as Remarque and Alfred Doblin, who both, like Landshoff, fled when the Nazis came to power. When the German army moved into the Netherlands Landshoff escaped to the United States and founded L. B. Fischer publishing company with Gottfried Bermann-Fischer, and printed works by such American writers as Wright and Langston Hughes. He returned to Europe briefly after World War II to found a medical publishing house, Excerpta Medica, then in 1952 was asked by Harry N. Abrams to become the European representative of his fledgling New York art book publishing company. Landshoff spent more than three decades with Abrams, acquiring numerous European art books, and retired in 1985 as executive vice-president of the company.

OBITUARIES AND OTHER SOURCES:

BOOKS

Who's Who in America, 41st edition, Marquis, 1980.

PERIODICALS

Chicago Tribune, April 3, 1988.
New York Times, April 1, 1988.
Publishers Weekly, April 15, 1988.

* * *

LANE, Thomas A(lphonsus) 1906-1975

*OBITUARY NOTICE—*See index for *CA* sketch: Born November 19, 1906, in Revere, Mass.; died April 20, 1975, in Washington, D.C.; buried in U.S. Military Academy Cemetery, West Point, N.Y. Army officer, educator, editor, journalist, and author. Lane enjoyed a long and distinguished career in both military and civilian posts. From 1928 to 1962 he was a member of the U.S. Army Corps of Engineers, serving as an instructor in military history at West Point during the 1930s and advancing to major general in 1957. Following his retirement from the army, Lane devoted most of his time to writing and lecturing, mainly on U.S. military and foreign policy. His syndicated column, "Public Affairs," ran in newspapers across the country from 1962 until his death in 1975. Lane was also

the author of several books, among them *The Leadership of President Kennedy, The War for the World, Cry Peace: The Kennedy Years, America on Trial: The War for Vietnam,* and *The Breakdown of the Old Politics,* and of numerous articles contributed to periodicals. From 1962 to 1975 Lane served as editor in chief of *Strategic Review,* published by the U.S. Strategic Institute, of which he was a director. Active in professional, civic, and religious organizations, Lane was the recipient of several military and civilian honors.

OBITUARIES AND OTHER SOURCES:

BOOKS

The National Cyclopedia of American Biography, Volume 61, James White, 1982.
Who Was Who in America, With World Notables, Volume VI: *1974-1976,* Marquis, 1976.

* * *

LARSEN, Nella 1891-1964

PERSONAL: Born April 13, 1891, in Chicago, Ill.; died March 30, 1964, in New York, N.Y.; daughter of a Danish mother and a West Indian father; married Elmer S. Imes (a physicist), May 3, 1919 (divorced, 1933). *Education:* Attended Fisk University, Nashville, Tenn., 1909-10, and University of Copenhagen, 1910-12; studied nursing at Lincoln Hospital, New York, N.Y., 1912-15.

CAREER: Tuskegee Institute, Tuskegee, Ala., assistant superintendent of nurses, 1915-16; Lincoln Hospital, New York City, nurse, 1916-18; Department of Health, New York City, nurse, 1918-21; New York Public Library, Harlem branch, assistant librarian, 1922-23, children's librarian, 1924-26; worked as a night nurse and supervising nurse at hospitals on the lower east side of Manhattan, beginning in 1941; writer.

AWARDS, HONORS: Bronze medal from the Harmon Foundation, 1928, for *Quicksand;* first black woman to receive a Guggenheim fellowship, 1930.

WRITINGS:

Quicksand (novel), Knopf, 1928, reprinted, Negro Universities Press, 1969, also published with *Passing* (also see below).
Passing (novel), Knopf, 1929, reprinted, Negro Universities Press, 1969, also published with *Quicksand* (also see below).

OMNIBUS VOLUMES

Quicksand; and, Passing, edited with an introduction by Deborah E. McDowell, Rutgers University Press, 1986.

OTHER

Contributor of short stories to various periodicals.

SIDELIGHTS: Nella Larsen was a member of the coterie of black writers associated with the Harlem Renaissance, an era of outstanding achievement in black American art and literature during the 1920s and 1930s. Though not as well known as many of her contemporaries, Larsen nonetheless won recognition for her two published novels, *Quicksand* and *Passing.*

Quicksand, which appeared in 1928, is the largely autobiographical story of Helga Crane, the daughter of a black man and a Scandinavian woman, who searches in vain for sexual and racial identity. Her quest takes her from a teaching position at a small college in the South to the elite social circles of Copenhagen and New York City to a backwoods Atlanta community pastored by the illiterate preacher she marries. The marriage fulfills Helga's longing for an uncomplicated existence and for sexual gratification, but it leaves her mired in a life of rural poverty and continual pregnancies.

Quicksand won a Harmon Foundation prize and was greeted with generally enthusiastic reviews in contemporary periodicals. Some critics faulted Larsen's characterizations as shallow and underdeveloped, but most praised the novel's complexity, sophistication, and artistry. A writer for the *New York Times*, for example, called *Quicksand* "an articulate, sympathetic first novel, which tells its story and projects its heroine in a lucid, exaggerated manner." Similarly, writing in *Crisis*, W. E. B. Du Bois deemed it "the best piece of fiction that Negro America has produced since the heyday of [Charles] Chesnutt."

More than fifty years after its initial publication *Quicksand* continues to generate critical acclaim. In his volume *From the Dark Tower: Afro-American Writers, 1900 to 1960*, Arthur P. Davis described *Quicksand* as "a fascinating case study of an unhappy and unfortunate woman," calling Helga Crane a victim not so much of a racial situation as of "her own inability to make the right decisions." She is, pronounced Davis, intriguing and complex, "a superb creation," and he assessed Larsen's book "one of the better novels of the Harlem Renaissance." Margaret Perry, author of *Silence to the Drums: A Survey of the Literature of the Harlem Renaissance*, lauded Larsen for her "awareness of female sexuality," and Addison Gayle, Jr., in his *The Way of the New World: The Black Novel in America*, called *Quicksand* "almost modern in its plot and conflicts.... It seeks to broach the wider question of identity, not the loss of it, but the search for it, and to suggest that this search in a world, race mad, must produce serious psychological problems of the spirit and soul."

Passing, like *Quicksand*, examines what *Ms.* contributor Mary Helen Washington labeled "the marginal black woman of the middle class, who was both unwilling to conform to a circumscribed existence in the black world and unable to move freely in the white world." *Passing* is the story of Clare Kendry, a beautiful fair-skinned black woman who escapes likely impoverishment by passing for white. She marries a wealthy white man, who assumes that she is also white. Her passage across the color line is completely successful until "a longing for her own kind led her to take fatal risks," posited Margaret Cheney Dawson in her review of the novel for the *New York Herald Tribune*. Clare renews ties with childhood friend Irene Redfield, who has married a black physician and is living in the upper circles of Harlem. Clare finds herself attracted to Irene's husband and he to her. Perceiving Clare as a threat to her own marriage and security, Irene wills Clare's disappearance, a wish that comes true when Clare falls, jumps, or is pushed from an open window at a Harlem apartment party just as her husband appears to confront her with his discovery of her black roots.

Critics were divided in their reaction to *Passing*. Most found it less good than *Quicksand*, flawed by what a reviewer for the *New York Times Book Review* called "its sudden and utterly unconvincing close, a close that solves most of the problems ... by simply sweeping them out of existence through the engineered death of Clare Kendry, the girl who is passing." Those critics who defended the novel averred that its strengths outweighed its weaknesses. Among these was Addison Gayle, Jr., who judged *Passing* "superior" to *Quick-*

sand "in terms of character development, organization, and fidelity to language." Similarly, *Saturday Review of Literature* contributor W. B. Seabrook lauded the novel as "classically pure in outline, single in theme and in impression, and ... powerful in its catastrophe." It was, added Seabrook, "a work so fine, sensitive, and distinguished that it rises above race categories and becomes that rare object, a good novel." Furthermore, Robert Bone wrote in his *The Negro Novel in America* that "despite a false and shoddy denouement," *Passing* was "probably the best treatment of the subject in Negro fiction." Claudia Tate, contributor to *Black American Literature Forum*, concurred, describing *Passing* as "a skillfully executed and enduring work of art that did not receive the critical attention it deserved."

At the height of her popularity in 1930, Larsen was accused of plagiarism in a dispute over a short story published in *Forum* magazine. Although later exonerated, she seemed stifled by the accusation and the scandal. At the same time she experienced marital problems that led to a crudely sensationalized 1933 divorce from her physicist husband. Consequently, during the next several years Larsen gradually withdrew from her circle of literary friends on the lower east side of New York City until she broke all ties with them. She spent the last twenty years of her life working as a nurse in Manhattan hospitals.

Larsen's work is now generally viewed both as a reflection of a black world now past and as a delineation of a particular female perspective that has endured. Larsen's two novels, according to Washington, reveal a writer "who is legally black but internally identifies with both blacks and whites, who is supposed to be content as a member of the black elite, but feels suffocated by its narrowness, who is emotionally rooted in the black experience and yet wants to live in the whole world."

Several critics expressed regret that Larsen's literary career was so brief. Among them were Washington, who averred that Larsen's "perceptive inquiries speak clearly to the predicament of the middle-class black woman of our generation," and Davis, who called Larsen "a sensitive writer, with great skill in narration." Similarly, George Kent, writing in *Blackness and the Adventure of Western Culture*, mused, "Certainly one regrets that she did not write more novels and senses that she had a complexity of awareness that might have produced great works."

BIOGRAPHICAL/CRITICAL SOURCES:

BOOKS

Bone, Robert, *The Negro Novel in America*, revised edition, Yale University Press, 1965.
Bontemps, Arna, editor, *The Harlem Renaissance Remembered*, Dodd, 1972.
Brown, Sterling, *The Negro in American Fiction*, Atheneum, 1965.
Contemporary Literary Criticism, Volume 37, Gale, 1986.
Davis, Arthur P., *From the Dark Tower: Afro-American Writers, 1900 to 1960*, Howard University Press, 1974.
Dictionary of Literary Biography, Volume 51: *Afro-American Writers From the Harlem Renaissance to 1940*, Gale, 1987.
Gayle, Addison, Jr., *The Way of the New World: The Black Novel in America*, Anchor Press, 1975.
Kent, George, *Blackness and the Adventure of Western Culture*, Third World Press, 1972.

Lewis, David Levering, *When Harlem Was in Vogue*, Knopf, 1981.

Perry, Margaret, *Silence to the Drums: A Survey of the Literature of the Harlem Renaissance*, Greenwood Press, 1976.

Singh, Amritjii, *The Novels of the Harlem Renaissance: Twelve Black Writers, 1923-1933*, Pennsylvania State University, 1976.

PERIODICALS

American Literature, December, 1986.
Black American Literature Forum, winter, 1980.
Bookman, June, 1929.
CLA Journal, March, 1973, December, 1974.
Crisis, June, 1928.
Ms., December, 1980.
New York Herald Tribune Books, May 13, 1928, April 28, 1929.
New York Times Book Review, April 8, 1928, April 28, 1929.
Opportunity, August, 1929.
Resources for American Literary Study, fall, 1978.
Saturday Review of Literature, May 19, 1928, May 18, 1929.
Voice Literary Supplement, March, 1987.
Women's Review of Books, October, 1986.*

—*Sketch by Joanne M. Peters*

* * *

LARSEN, Susan C(arol) 1946-

PERSONAL: Born October 3, 1946, in Chicago, Ill.; daughter of Ingvald (a market researcher) and Esther (a homemaker) Larsen; married Lauri Robert Martin (a photographer), April 24, 1982. *Education:* Attended Knox College, 1964-66; Northwestern University, B.A., 1968, M.A., 1972, Ph.D., 1975.

ADDRESSES: Home—1108 Dodson Ave., San Pedro, Calif. 90731. *Office*—Department of Fine Arts, University of Southern California, University Park, Los Angeles, Calif. 90089.

CAREER: Carleton College, Northfield, Minn., assistant professor of art history, 1974-75; University of Southern California, Los Angeles, associate professor of art history, 1975—. Guest lecturer at Los Angeles County Museum of Art, 1977—. Member of American Art Council; member of advisory board of Archives of American Art. Secretary and treasurer of Breedfinders, Inc.

MEMBER: College Art Association of America, American Studies Association, Southern California Art Historians Association.

AWARDS, HONORS: Fellow of Graves Foundation, 1980; research and innovation grant from University of Southern California, 1983.

WRITINGS:

Folk Art of the West Coast (exhibition catalogue), Long Beach Museum of Art, 1983.
Abstract Painting and Sculpture in America, 1927-1944, Abrams, 1984.

Contributor of articles and reviews to art and architecture journals, including *Artforum* and *Architectural Digest*.

SIDELIGHTS: Susan C. Larsen told *CA:* "I am involved in research and critical commentary upon American painting and sculpture, both historical from 1900 to 1950 and contemporary."

LARSON, Gustive O(lof) 1897-1978

OBITUARY NOTICE—See index for *CA* sketch: Born August 18, 1897, in Salt Lake City, Utah; died October 22, 1978, in Provo, Utah. Administrator, educator, and author. Larson taught history and religion at Brigham Young University from 1954 to 1972, when he retired as associate professor emeritus. Prior to his affiliation with Brigham Young, Larson was principal of Latter-day Saints Seminary and president of Latter-day Saints Institute of Religion, both in Cedar City, Utah. His writings include *Prelude to the Kingdom: Mormon Desert Conquest, A Chapter in American Cooperative Experience; Outline History of Utah and the Mormons; The "Americanization" of Utah for Statehood;* and articles contributed to *Mississippi Valley Historical Review, Utah Historical Quarterly, American West,* and other periodicals.

OBITUARIES AND OTHER SOURCES:

Date of death provided by wife, Virginia B. Larson.

BOOKS

Directory of American Scholars, Volume I: *History*, 7th edition, Bowker, 1978.

* * *

LATHAM, Caroline S. 1940-

PERSONAL: Born June 12, 1940, in Ponca City, Okla.; daughter of Robert H. (an engineer) and Mary Chilton (a housewife; maiden name, Scott) Latham; married Scott Bridge, July 29, 1957 (divorced, 1969); children: Scott, Sarah. *Education:* Graduated from Oberlin College, 1960.

ADDRESSES: Home—Hudson, N.Y. *Agent*—Alice Martell, 555 Fifth Ave., New York, N.Y. 10017.

CAREER: Appleton-Century Crofts, New York City, writer, editor, and publisher in college department, 1969-73; Latham Publishing Corp., New York City, president, 1973-78; freelance writer, 1978—.

MEMBER: Authors Guild.

WRITINGS:

Katharine Hepburn: Her Film and Stage Career, Proteus Publishing, 1982.
The Best Bars of New York, Putnam, 1984.
Michael Jackson: Thrill, Zebra Books, 1984.
Audrey Hepburn, Proteus Publishing, 1984.
How to Live With a Man, New American Library, 1984.
Miami Magic, Zebra Books, 1985.
Priscilla and Elvis: The Priscilla Presley Story, New American Library, 1985.
(With Barbara Gibson) *Life With Rose Kennedy*, Warner Books, 1986.
Carol Burnett: Funny Is Beautiful, New American Library, 1986.
The David Letterman Story, F. Watts, 1987.
(With J. Sakol) *The Royals*, Contemporary Books, 1987.
The Dodges at Detroit, Harcourt, 1988.

* * *

LAWFORD, Paula Jane 1960-

PERSONAL: Born March 9, 1960, in Romford, England;

daughter of John (a charity worker abroad) and Jennifer (Fox) Lawford; married Andrew Martyr (a telecommunications engineer and writer), November 19, 1983; children: Jonathan. *Education:* Reigate School of Art, Diploma, 1981.

ADDRESSES: Home—17 Avagon Ave., Thames Ditton, Surrey KT7 0PY, England.

CAREER: General part-time work; illustrator.

WRITINGS:

SELF-ILLUSTRATED CHILDREN'S BOOKS

(With husband, Andrew Martyr) *Willisk's Tooth,* Hamish Hamilton, 1985.
(With Martyr) *Winston's Ice Cream Caper,* Hamish Hamilton, 1986.
(With Martyr) *Patch the Pirate Cat,* Hamish Hamilton, 1987.
(With Margaret Stuart Barry) *Diz and the Big Fat Burglar,* Hamish Hamilton, 1987.
(With Martyr) *Beeswax the Bad,* Hamish Hamilton, 1988.

OTHER

Illustrator of a double page spread for the comic book *Buttons.*

WORK IN PROGRESS: Writing and illustrating a picture book with Martyr, tentatively titled *Granny's Magic Medicine,* about a baby with magic hiccups; illustrating a series of about eighteen educational books for very young readers, for Ginn.

SIDELIGHTS: Paula Jane Lawford told *CA:* "I have always wanted to be an illustrator. In particular I wanted to illustrate children's books. I met my husband in 1981, just after I had left art school. He discovered he had a flair for writing children's books. Together we created *Willisk's Tooth,* our first picture book. Our most recent book is *Beeswax the Bad,* a story in rhyme. Like Patch, Beeswax is a cat. Both characters are based on our own two cats—maybe they are our main source of inspiration."

*   *   *

LEACH, (Carson) Wilford   1932(?)-1988

OBITUARY NOTICE—See index for *CA* sketch: Born August 26, 1932 (some sources say 1929 or 1934), in Petersburg, Va.; died of stomach cancer, June 18, 1988, in Rocky Point, N.Y. Educator, director, and playwright. Leach was best known for his playwriting and directing for experimental off-off Broadway theater companies and for his innovative staging of Shakespearean plays in New York City's Central Park. His work as a director earned him Tony awards for the Broadway productions "Pirates of Penzance" in 1981 and "The Mystery of Edwin Drood" in 1986. Among his other awards were two Obies and a Drama Desk Award. Leach authored or co-authored several plays, among them *In Three Zones, Gertrude, or Would She Be Pleased to Receive It?, Carmilla,* and *Demon.* He also taught theater and film at Sarah Lawrence College from 1958 to 1981.

OBITUARIES AND OTHER SOURCES:

BOOKS

Who's Who in America, 44th edition, Marquis, 1986.

PERIODICALS

Chicago Tribune, June 22, 1988.
Los Angeles Times, June 22, 1988.
New York Times, June 21, 1988.

LEAVITT, Harold J(ack)   1922-

PERSONAL: Born May 14, 1922, in Lynn, Mass.; son of Joseph and May (Lopata) Leavitt; married January 31, 1943; children: John, Emily, David. *Education:* Harvard University, B.A., 1942; Brown University, M.S., 1944; Massachusetts Institute of Technology, Ph.D., 1949.

ADDRESSES: Home—743 Cookey Lane, Stanford, Calif. 94305. *Office*—Graduate School of Business, Stanford University, Stanford, Calif. 94305.

CAREER: Rensselaer Polytechnic Institute, Troy, N.Y., assistant professor of psychology, 1949-50; Nejelski and Co., Inc., New York, N.Y., survey director, 1950-51, vice-president, 1951-53; University of Chicago, Chicago, Ill., associate professor of business, 1954-58; Carnegie Institute of Technology (now Carnegie-Mellon University), Pittsburgh, Pa., professor of industrial administration and psychology, 1958-66; Stanford University, Stanford, Calif., Walter Kilpatrick Professor of Organization Behavior and Psychology, 1966—. National Training Laboratories, member of national board of directors, 1962-64, adviser, 1970—; faculty principal of Management Analysis Center, Inc., 1971—; visiting professor at London Graduate School of Business Studies, 1971; consultant to European Productivity Agency and Ford Foundation. *Military service:* U.S. Naval Reserve, active duty personnel research officer, 1944-46; became lieutenant junior grade.

MEMBER: American Psychological Association (fellow), Institute of Management Sciences (vice-president, 1959-60).

WRITINGS:

Managerial Psychology: An Introduction to Individuals, Pairs, and Groups in Organizations, University of Chicago Press, 1958, 5th edition, 1988.
(Editor) *The Social Science of Organizations: Four Perspectives,* Prentice-Hall, 1963.
(Editor with Louis R. Pondy) *Readings in Managerial Psychology,* University of Chicago Press, 1964, 4th edition (with Pondy and David M. Boje), 1988.
(With William R. Dill and Henry B. Eyring) *The Organizational World,* Harcourt, 1973.
(Editor with Lawrence Pinfield and Eugene Webb) *Organizations of the Future: Interaction With the External Environment,* Praeger, 1974.
Corporate Pathfinders, Dow Jones-Irwin, 1986.

Contributor to journals in the social sciences. Member of editorial board of *Omega,* 1974—.

*   *   *

LECHTENBERG, Richard   1947-

PERSONAL: Born December 10, 1947, in Boston, Mass.; son of M. Sherman and B. Rebecca Lechtenberg; married twice. *Education:* Tufts University, B.A. (summa cum laude), 1969, M.D., 1973. *Politics:* "Dubious." *Religion:* "Negligible."

ADDRESSES: Office—Department of Neurology, State University of New York Downstate Medical Center, 450 Clarkson Ave., Brooklyn, N.Y. 11203.

CAREER: State University of New York Downstate Medical Center, Brooklyn, member of department of neurology, 1977—. Chief of division of neurology at Long Island College Hospital, Brooklyn, 1985—.

MEMBER: American Academy of Neurology, American Neurological Association, Phi Beta Kappa, Alpha Omega Alpha.

WRITINGS:

Disorders of the Cerebellum, F. A. Davis, 1982.
The Psychiatrist's Guide to Diseases of the Nervous System, Wiley, 1983.
Epilepsy and the Family, Harvard University Press, 1985.
The Diagnosis and Treatment of Epilepsy, Macmillan, 1986.
The Multiple Sclerosis Fact Book, F. A. Davis, 1988.
AIDS and the Nervous System, Churchill-Livingston, 1988.

WORK IN PROGRESS: Medical books.

AVOCATIONAL INTERESTS: Motorcycling, medical history.

* * *

LEE, Andrea 1953-

PERSONAL: Born in 1953 in Philadelphia, Pa.; married. *Education:* Received M.A. from Harvard University.

ADDRESSES—Office: New Yorker, 25 West 43rd St., New York, N.Y. 10036.

CAREER: Writer. Staff writer for *New Yorker* magazine in New York, N.Y.

AWARDS, HONORS: Nomination for American Book Award for general nonfiction, 1981, for *Russian Journal;* Jean Stein Award from American Academy and Institute of Arts and Letters, 1984.

WRITINGS:

Russian Journal (nonfiction), Random House, 1981.
Sarah Phillips (novel), Random House, 1984.

Contributor to periodicals, including *New Yorker, New York Times,* and *Vogue.*

SIDELIGHTS: Andrea Lee has distinguished herself as a noteworthy journalist and novelist. In her nonfiction work, *Russian Journal,* she provides an insightful perspective on contemporary Soviet life, and in her novel, *Sarah Phillips,* she recounts the reckless past of a middle-class black woman. These writings, while embracing different themes, have earned Lee praise as a keen observer and a consummate technician, one whose probing insights are inevitably rendered with concision and grace. As Susan Richards Shreve noted in the *New York Times Book Review,* "Andrea Lee's authority as a writer comes of an unstinting honesty and a style at once simple and yet luminous."

Lee's first book, *Russian Journal,* derives from a diary she kept in 1978 while in the Soviet Union, where her husband was studying for ten months on a fellowship. Relying on public transportation and a rudimentary grasp of the Russian language, Lee visited a wide variety of Soviet places, including public baths, college campuses, farmers' markets, and nightclubs. She met bureaucrats, dissidents, and even contraband sellers; encountered many cynics and youthful materialists; observed a disturbing number of public drunks; and became acquainted with some of the country's more unsettling aspects, notably surveillance. In her journal Lee wrote that, due to their circumstances, she and her husband "got a view of life in Moscow and Leningrad that was very different from that of the diplomats and journalists we knew."

Following the 1981 publication of *Russian Journal,* critics cited the book as a refreshing, if narrow, perspective on Soviet life.

Susan Jacoby, writing in the *New York Times Book Review,* called Lee's book "a subtly crafted reflection of both the bleak and golden shadings of Russian life" and added: "The subject matter of this journal is highly idiosyncratic.... What Miss Lee offers are the people, places and experiences that touched her most deeply." Like Jacoby, *Washington Post Book World* reviewer Peter Osnos cited the book's worth for "conveying a feeling of place and atmosphere" and declared: "Lee writes very well. There is a warmth and freshness about her style that makes reading [*Russian Journal*] effortless." Osnos was especially impressed with Lee's depiction of the Soviet people, particularly its younger citizens. "What is best about the book— what distinguishes it from other books about the Soviet Union published in recent years—is her accounts of friendships with young people," he contended. Similarly, *Newsweek*'s Walter Clemons praised Lee's "unassuming delicacy and exactness" asserting that "her most winning quality is her capacity for friendship." Michael Irwin, who discussed *Russian Journal* in the *London Review of Books,* also found Lee an engaging reporter. He praised her "astuteness" and called *Russian Journal* "a considerable exercise in observation, empathy and personal and literary tact."

Lee's refusal to write about being a black person in the Soviet Union caused a few reservations among critics reviewing *Russian Journal.* Susan Jacoby called this omission "regrettable" and contended that Lee's race "must have affected [her Russian friends'] perceptions (and Miss Lee's) in some way." Jacoby added, "Miss Lee's responses would surely have been as interesting as the rest of her observations, and I wish she had included them." Peter Osnos also noted Lee's reluctance to write about race. He described the omission as "slightly awkward" and observed: "Apparently, she feels that her blackness has nothing to do with her time in the Soviet Union. That is her business. But she never even says as much."

As if responding to charges that she avoided racial subjects, Lee followed *Russian Journal* with *Sarah Phillips,* an episodic novel explicitly concerned with a contemporary black woman. The work's title character is introduced as a woman grown disgusted with her boorish, racist acquaintances—and lovers— in Paris, where she has been living in self-exile. At the end of the first chapter Sarah decides to leave Paris, and in the ensuing sections she recalls events—principally from childhood and adolescence—contributing to her present circumstances. Unlike most black characters in American fiction, Sarah is an assimilated elitist whose background is middle class, and her goal is to scandalize her bourgeois parents. She even accepts tokenism when she becomes the first black student at an exclusive girls' school. Her father is a minister involved in the civil rights movement, an involvement that actually leads to her embarrassment when he is briefly imprisoned for civil disobedience. Bored with America, Sarah leaves the country after her father's death and her graduation from college. She settles in Paris, where she indulges in various interracial sexual shenanigans, including a *menage-a-quatre.* By novel's end, however, Sarah realizes the emptiness of her assimilation into white society—both European and American—and reaches a greater understanding of herself and her heritage.

With *Sarah Phillips* Lee earned further literary acclaim. In *Saturday Review,* Bruce Van Wyngarden described the novel as a "coming-of-age remembrance in which detail and insight are delightfully, and sometimes poignantly, blended." He also deemed it "an engaging and promising" first novel. Likewise, *Best Sellers* reviewer Francis Goskowski called *Sarah Phillips* an "engaging, witty" work and asserted that with it Lee emerged as a "major novelistic talent." Patricia Vigderam was one of several critics who noted the novel's breakthrough perspective on race, particularly the characterization of Sarah as an assimilated black. Critiquing the work for the *Boston Review*, Vigderman conceded that "this novel does not fit easily into the Afro-American tradition, and may even meet with some disapproval," but she nonetheless considered it "a very gracefully written book about black identity."

With *Russian Journal* and *Sarah Phillips* Lee has gained recognition as a talented writer of immense promise, and her forthcoming works are greatly anticipated. "Without a doubt," stated Francis Goskowski, "Ms. Lee will be heard from again, and she will command our attention."

BIOGRAPHICAL/CRITICAL SOURCES:

BOOKS

Contemporary Literary Criticism, Volume 36, Gale, 1986.

PERIODICALS

Best Sellers, February, 1985.
Boston Review, February, 1985.
Economist, May 29, 1982.
London Review of Books, October 6, 1982.
National Review, September 3, 1982.
New Leader, December 10, 1984.
New Republic, February 24, 1982, November 19, 1984.
Newsweek, October 19, 1981.
New York Review of Books, November 5, 1981.
New York Times, December 6, 1984.
New York Times Book Review, October 25, 1981, November 18, 1984.
People, November 23, 1981.
Spectator, June 12, 1982.
Times Literary Supplement, August 13, 1982, April 5, 1985.
Washington Post Book World, October 25, 1981.*

—*Sketch by Les Stone*

*   *   *

LEE, George W(ashington)   1894-1976

PERSONAL: Born January 4, 1894, in Indianola, Miss.; died August 1, 1976; son of George (a minister) and Hattie Lee. *Education:* Alcorn Agricultural and Mechanical College (now Alcorn State University), B.S. *Politics:* Republican.

CAREER: Worked odd jobs as an adolescent, including cotton planter and picker, grocery boy, houseboy, dray driver, and bellhop; vice-president of the Mississippi Life Insurance Co., 1922-24; affiliated with the Atlanta Life Insurance Co., beginning as district manager, 1927-76. Edited *Vision*, a journal for the Atlanta Life Insurance Co. Active in the Republican party. *Military service:* U.S. Army, 1917-19, served in France; became lieutenant.

MEMBER: National Association for the Advancement of Colored People, National Insurance Association, American Legion, Urban League, West Tennessee Civic and Political League, Omega Psi Phi, Elks.

WRITINGS:

Beale Street: Where the Blues Began (history), R. O. Ballou, 1934.
River George (novel), Macaulay, 1937, AMS Press, 1975.

Beale Street Sundown (short stories; includes "Beale Street Anyhow," "A Beale Street Treasure Hunt," "The First Blues Singer," "King of the Rousters," "She Made a Preacher Lay His Bible Down," "Passing," and "The Beale Street Blues I'm Singing"), House of Field, 1942.

Contributor of short stories and articles to periodicals, including *Negro Digest*, *World's Digest*, *Southern Literary Messenger*, *Vision*, *Tri-State Defender*, *Memphis Press Scimitar*, and *Memphis World*.

SIDELIGHTS: George W. Lee's writings immortalized the Beale Street neighborhood of Memphis, Tennessee. As a leader in business and in his community, Lee was concerned with promoting pride in black business and decided in the early 1930s to write a factual book extolling black success in the Beale Street area. The result, 1934's *Beale Street: Where the Blues Began*, "gained wide critical acclaim," according to Edward D. Clark in *Dictionary of Literary Biography*. In spite of the fact that the book was extremely profitable for him due to its appeal to both black and white readers, Lee might have ended his career as an author to concentrate on the insurance business and politics if he had not been piqued by comments that it was *Beale Street*'s subject matter and not Lee's own writing ability that made it so popular. To put doubts concerning his literary ability to rest, Lee produced a novel, *River George*, in 1937. Later, he crowned his achievements with the short story collection *Beale Street Sundown*.

Beale Street: Where the Blues Began is divided into chapters about black individuals who contributed to the history of the neighborhood. These include Robert R. Church, Sr., who after the Civil War built up a multimillion dollar estate and helped turn Beale Street into a commercial center for the black community, and other "bankers, ministers, lawyers, realtors, doctors, businesswomen, and insurance executives, all people Lee knew," reported Clark. Lee described the yellow fever epidemic of 1878 and contrasted the numerous heroic blacks who stayed in Memphis to help save the city with the many whites who escaped in fear of the disease; he also discussed Julia A. Hooks, who started an integrated music school that produced many gifted students, and composer W. C. Handy, whom he credits with "distinguished orchestral work." Though Lee's purpose in *Beale Street* was to instill pride in black accomplishment, he balanced the work by revealing the negative aspects of the community. Pimps, prostitutes, drug dealers, and the destitute who sift through garbage piles for food share pages with Lee's objects of admiration.

Lee also intended his *River George* to promote black pride. Taking the man he wrote about in *Beale Street*'s third chapter and fictionalizing his past by adding some of his own experiences to it, Lee built a novel around the character of Aaron George. George goes to Lee's alma mater, Alcorn Agricultural and Mechanical College, in order to become a lawyer, but his education is interrupted by the death of his father. He returns home and becomes a sharecropper on Beaver Dam Plantation to help support his mother. Falling in love with a woman, Ada Green, who is also involved with the white postmaster, Fred Smith, George eventually has to leave the plantation because of a confrontation with Smith over the injustices suffered by the tenant farmers; this confrontation ends in Smith's death by his own gun. George runs to Memphis for safety and takes up lodgings with a Beale Street madame. Like the author, he enters the U.S. Army and becomes a lieutenant serving in Europe. When he returns to the United States, he tries to contact his mother and Ada, but he runs into trouble in Vicksburg,

Mississippi from whites who resent his officer's uniform. Temporarily turned aside, George becomes a deckhand on the Mississippi river and wins fame for his fighting prowess. Eventually, however, he returns to the plantation only to be lynched for the postmaster's murder upon his arrival.

Though *River George* ends with George's death, its focus is on his struggles to succeed in a world of prejudice. By the time Lee published the short story collection *Beale Street Sundown*, however, his involvement with the Republican party had led him to place less importance on inspiring blacks toward achievement of their goals. Thus, in Clark's opinion, the emphasis of *Sundown* is on folklore. Lack of didactic purpose apparently gave Lee more artistic freedom; Clark declared that *Sundown* "is evidence of tremendous literary growth." The volume's stories include "Beale Street Anyhow," which concerns uproar over a possible name change to Beale Avenue, and "A Beale Street Treasure Hunt," involving an old man's plot to make money from a fraudulent treasure hunt. Also in *Sundown* are "She Made a Preacher Lay His Bible Down," about an ex-prostitute who joins a church choir to win the love of a minister, and "Passing," about a black woman passing for white in a bordello.

BIOGRAPHICAL/CRITICAL SOURCES:

BOOKS

Dictionary of Literary Biography, Volume 51: *Afro-American Writers From the Harlem Renaissance to 1940,* Gale, 1987.
Lee, George W., *Beale Street: Where the Blues Began,* R. O. Ballou, 1934.*

*   *   *

LEE, Shelton Jackson   1957(?)-
(Spike Lee)

PERSONAL: Born c. 1957 in Atlanta, Ga.; son of William (a musician and composer) and Jacqueline (a teacher; maiden name, Shelton) Lee. *Education:* Morehouse College, B.A., 1979; graduate study at New York University, 1982.

ADDRESSES: Home—Brooklyn, N.Y. *Office*—Forty Acres and a Mule Filmworks, 124 DeKalb Ave., Brooklyn, N.Y. 11217.

CAREER: Screenwriter and director of motion pictures and music videos.

AWARDS, HONORS: Student director's award from Academy of Motion Picture Arts and Sciences, 1982, for "Joe's Bed-Stuy Barber Shop: We Cut Heads"; Prix de Jeunesse from Cannes Film Festival, 1986, for "She's Gotta Have It."

WRITINGS:

UNDER NAME SPIKE LEE

(And director) "She's Gotta Have It" (screenplay), Island, 1986.
Spike Lee's Gotta Have It: Inside Guerilla Filmmaking (includes interviews and a journal), foreword by Nelson George, photographs by brother, David Lee, Simon & Schuster, 1987.
(And director) "School Daze" (screenplay), Columbia, 1988.
(With Lisa Jones) *Uplift the Race: The Construction of School Daze,* Simon & Schuster, 1988.

Also writer and director of short films, including "The Answer," 1980, and "Joe's Bed-Stuy Barbershop: We Cut Heads," 1982. Contributor of short films to "Saturday Night Live" and to Music Television (MTV) network.

WORK IN PROGRESS: Writing and directing the motion picture "Do the Right Thing," release by Universal expected in 1989.

SIDELIGHTS: Spike Lee has become one of the film world's most promising comedic talents to appear in the late 1980s, and he is among the few commercial filmmakers of his generation to address issues and themes specific to the black community. As writer and director of the critically and commercially successful "She's Gotta Have It" and the controversial "School Daze," Lee has exploited such subjects as sexism and elitism for their comedic worth while simultaneously exploring their ramifications and manifestations within black society. "My role in film, for the most part, is as an instigator," he has claimed. But that instigation, he believes, must extend beyond the black community and entertain and enrich a broader spectrum. "It has been my contention all along that an all-black film directed by a black person can still be universal, just as . . . in the other arts," he told the *New York Times.* "I mean, nobody stopped coming to see Duke Ellington's music because he had an all-black band."

Lee began his filmmaking career while a graduate student at New York University, where he wrote and directed the short film "Joe's Bed-Stuy Barbershop: We Cut Heads." That film, which concerned a Brooklyn barbershop fronting a gambling operation, fared well at a 1983 New Directors series in New York City and was subsequently featured at international film festivals. On the strength of "Joe's Bed-Stuy Barbershop" Lee met representatives of various theatrical agencies, but those representatives, as Lee later observed in the *New York Times,* "were unable to generate me any work, not even an after-school special." For Lee, the failure of the agencies confirmed his suspicion that he could only sustain a film career by creating his own projects: "I would have to go out alone and do it alone, not rely on anyone else."

In mid-1984 Lee tried to begin a film about bicycle messengers, and he eventually obtained grants from both the American Film Institute and the New York State Council on the Arts. But after eight weeks of pre-production Lee dissolved the project, claiming to *Film Comment* that "it just never really came together with all the money and stuff." Lee and his collaborators—including cinematographer Ernest Dickerson and production supervisor Monty Ross, both former classmates—then decided to film "She's Gotta Have It," a comedy he wrote about a woman and her three lovers. The American Film Institute consequently withdrew their $20,000 grant, leaving Lee with only $18,000 from the New York arts council. Still he persevered, and while Ross tirelessly solicited additional funds, Lee assembled a small cast and crew, including family members, and directed the entire work in only twelve days.

With "She's Gotta Have It," Lee managed to create an entertaining and provocative work despite formidable limitations of time and money. The film's protagonist is Nola Darling, a fun-loving, sensitive artist with a seemingly insatiable sexual appetite. Consequently, she has three lovers, and each one perceives her differently: Jamie Overstreet is an earnest romantic who sees Nola as his future wife; Greer Childs is a narcissistic pseudo-intellectual for whom Nola as an object to be shaped and molded to his liking; and Mars Blackmon (played by Lee) is a fast-talking, diminutive joker who considers the sex-addict Nola a "freak." Much of the humor in "She's

Gotta Have It'' derives from the various suitors' rivalries and their efforts to convince Nola to reject the others. Particularly funny are Mars's deadpan remarks and his monotonous plea, "Please baby please baby please baby baby baby please," when he begs for Nola's company. Nola's Thanksgiving dinner for all three lovers also provides opportunity for humor as the men berate each other. Greer calls Mars a "chain snatcher," and Mars replies that Greer is a "pseudo black man" and, even worse, a fan of the predominantly white Boston Celtics basketball team. When Jamie intercedes to diffuse hostilities, Greer asks, "What are you? Henry Kissinger?" Eventually, Nola senses that each of her lovers is trying to dominate her, whereupon she leaves all of them. "It's about control," she explains. "My body. My mind. Whose gonna own it, them or me?''

Upon release in 1986, "She's Gotta Have It" received substantial praise from critics. *Washington Post* reviewer Paul Attanasio deemed it an "impressive first feature" and added that it was "discursive, jazzy, vibrant with sex and funny as heck." Similarly, Michael Wilmington wrote in the *Los Angeles Times* that Lee's film was "a joyfully idiosyncratic little jazz-burst of a film, full of sensuous melody, witty chops and hot licks." Wilmington was particularly impressed with the film's unstereotypic perspective and characters, declaring: "'She's Gotta Have It' gives you as non-standard a peek at black American life as you'll get: engaging, seductive and happily off-kilter. There's no overlay of sentiment or cynicism here. These characters aren't the radiant winners or sad victims you usually see, and there's not a normal citizen . . . in the bunch." Furthermore, Wilmington praised Lee as a refreshing figure in American film comedy and deemed him "an impudent original with a great eye and a flair for humor and eroticism."

"She's Gotta Have It," with its depiction of Nola as forthright and independent, also earned Lee recognition as a feminist filmmaker. Jeffrey Yorke, for instance, wrote in the *Washington Post* that Lee "managed to write a feminist story through a man's eye." Lee conceded to a *New York Times* writer that the opportunity to provide a woman's perspective on promiscuity proved his major motivation in making the film: "I decided it would be a good idea to do a film about a young black woman who's really leading her life like a man, in control, with three men dangling at her fingertips." And to *Film Comment* writer Marlaine Glicksman he confided that his film was also a response to the film world's stereotype of black men as crude and brutal. He charged the film industry with conspiring to portray black men as "one-dimensional animals," and asserted that his male characters were "full-bodied" and thus a rare exception to the stereotype.

As an independently produced, low-budget film, "She's Gotta Have It" proved a surprising success with the public as well as with critics, earning more than two million dollars at American box offices within weeks of its release—and more than seven million dollars by 1987. Lee, who seemed unsurprised by the public response to "She's Gotta Have It," credited the film's success to its unique approach and its avoidance of stereotypes. "I think that there are a lot of things in 'She's Gotta Have It' we've never seen before," he told a writer for the *Chicago Tribune*, adding that his movie was a "refreshing breath of air." And in the *New York Times* Lee noted that his film served as an indication that realistic films about blacks could be commercially viable. "The whole point is that you can take an unknown, all-black cast and put them in a story that comes from a black experience, and all kinds of people

will come to see it if it's a good film," he observed. "I wish Hollywood would get that message."

The industry apparently understood, for soon after the success of "She's Gotta Have It" Lee secured approximately six million dollars from Columbia Pictures to film "School Daze," a musical comedy about rival factions at a black college. Making that film, however, proved somewhat trying despite its budget. He commenced filming in 1987 at Morehouse College, where he studied as an undergraduate, but university officials abruptly ceased cooperation, fearing adverse publicity from the film's uncompromising perspective and its inclusion of profanity. "They booted us out in the middle of shooting there," Lee declared. "The president of the school was upset because he heard we use [obscenity] in the film—and if parents heard that word they wouldn't let their sons be Morehouse men." Lee contended that his artistic intentions were legitimate and that he was not besmirching the school's integrity. "I loved going to that school," he later told an audience following a preview. "But you can still criticize the things that aren't right, can't you?"

Lee found much to criticize about black school life, but in "School Daze" he rendered that criticism within a comedic context. Set during homecoming weekend, "School Daze" concerns the rivalry between two major campus factions: the dark-skinned Jigaboos and the politically accomodating, lighter-skinned Wannabees (as in "want to be white"), many of whom belong to the elite fraternity Gamma Phi Gamma. Among the leading Jigaboos is Dap, the key figure in a campus campaign to force university divestiture from racist South Africa. Dap's rival is Gamma Phi Gamma leader Julian, an arrogant Wannabee who loathes the Jigaboos and defends the university's business practices. Other campus factions include the Gamma Rays, a band of women Wannabees devoted to pursuing the ideal of white feminine beauty—some of them even dye their hair blonde and sport blue contact lenses; the student government, apparently comprised of one ineffectual peacemaker; and the faculty, which seems more interested in the school's failing football team than in the divestiture controversy. Still another group are the non-student blacks living in the community, and one of the film's most provocative scenes is an encounter between Dap, who fancies himself sincerely pro-black, and the non-students, who sneer at his artistic posturing and remind him that when he finishes school he will become one of them. Contrasts between these and other factions afford Lee ample opportunity to explore such themes as bigotry, elitism, and sexism, thus making "School Daze" an ambitious and provocative, as well as entertaining, work.

As with "She's Gotta Have It," much of the humor in "School Daze" derives from the antics of Lee's character. Here he plays Half Pint, a Gamma Phi Gamma hopeful preoccupied with losing his virginity. Like others aspiring to the Gamma Phi Gamma fraternity, Half Pint sports a shaved scalp and a scrawled letter G on his forehead. Although he is Dap's cousin, Half Pint is a Wannabee, and he consequently courts the influential Julian's favor. This results in a particularly funny episode in which Half Pint tirelessly tours the campus trying to procure a sexual partner for the arrogant fraternity leader. Ultimately, Lee's character complicates the otherwise clear division between the Jigaboos and the Wannabees, and his behavior and values serve to indicate the negative repercussions of such schisms.

After finishing "School Daze" away from Morehouse College, Lee clashed with his Columbia producers, whose plans for distribution and promotion he found objectionable. He accused Columbia of "ghettoizing" "School Days" by suggesting that its release day be postponed because "Action Jackson," a crime drama featuring black characters, would be opening the same day and also be drawing black audiences. Incensed, Lee claimed that his fairly challenging "School Daze" would hardly appeal to the same audience as "Action Jackson," and he charged Columbia with ignoring the diverse interests and tastes of the black public. Film studios perceive blacks as "some monolithic . . . group out there," he declared, adding: "I don't see any studio worrying about having a Woody Allen movie coming out the same week as a Chuck Norris movie. It's the same blind mentality."

Released in early 1988, "School Daze" was perceived by many critics as a thematically and stylistically daring venture. *Village Voice* writer J. Hoberman called Lee's film "a spectacle of abundance" and declared that it was "so pumped up, preening, and packed with stuff that it's almost musclebound." Similarly, Michael Wilmington wrote in the *Los Angeles Times* that the work was "packed with breezy musical numbers and a brawling gang of characters, streaming through the movie in continuous eruptions of overlapping dialogue and dizzying badinage." For Wilmington, the movie's range of wildly ambitious themes and characterizations somewhat compromised its continuity and resulted in both an unsettling narrative rhythm and some unresolved themes. But he added that even with its shortcomings Lee's second film proved accomplished and admirable. "'School Daze' tries too many targets to hit them all," Wilmington observed. "The important thing is that it hits its share, with a view of black college life that's impudent, juicy and fresh."

"School Daze" earned commendations from many critics, but it also brought Lee notoriety as a provocateur within the black community. Prominent blacks protested that Lee had produced an unfavorable depiction of blacks, and others, while conceding that he offered a valid perspective, nonetheless argued that his perception of black campus life was one best withheld from a white society. Lee, however, had anticipated such criticism. "I wasn't afraid," he told students at Howard University following a preview. "I knew it would make people squirm." He acknowledged that his depiction of sexism and elitism was troubling and unsettling, but he contended that it was nonetheless valid and even invigorating. "These things are terrible," he declared, "and I think by putting this stuff on film we can view it for what it is."

With "School Daze" Lee confirmed his status as an important, provocative new filmmaker. And though he seems unimpressed with much of his acclaim, he is confident of his talent and his continuing development as an artist. He told Stuart Mieher in the *New York Times*, "I'm a very good filmmaker. . . . I think I will be making films for the rest of my life. And I'm just going to get better."

AVOCATIONAL INTERESTS: Basketball.

BIOGRAPHICAL/CRITICAL SOURCES:

BOOKS

Lee, Spike, *Spike Lee's Gotta Have It: Inside Guerilla Filmmaking,* foreword by Nelson George, photographs by brother, David Lee, Simon & Schuster, 1987.
Lee, Spike and Lisa Jones, *Uplift the Race: The Construction of School Daze,* Simon & Schuster, 1988.

PERIODICALS

American Film, September, 1986.
Chicago Tribune, August 13, 1986, August 20, 1986, October 5, 1986, February 25, 1988, March 3, 1988.
Ebony, January, 1987.
Essence, September, 1986.
Film Comment, October, 1986.
Film Quarterly, winter, 1986-87.
Los Angeles Times, August 21, 1986, February 11, 1988, February 12, 1988.
Newsweek, September 8, 1986.
New York Times, March 27, 1983, August 8, 1986, August 10, 1986, September 7, 1986, November 14, 1986, August 9, 1987.
People, October 13, 1986.
Time, October 6, 1986.
Village Voice, February 16, 1988, March 22, 1988.
Washington Post, August 22, 1986, August 24, 1986, August 29, 1986, March 20, 1987, February 19, 1988.

—Sketch by Les Stone

*   *   *

LEE, Spike
See LEE, Shelton Jackson

*   *   *

LeMASTER, Leslie Jean   1943-

PERSONAL: Born January 26, 1943, in California; daughter of Martin P. (a physician) and Goldine (a housewife; maiden name, Black) Elston; children: Kelli. *Education:* California State University, Hayward, B.A., 1969.

CAREER: Owner and operator of word processing business in Irving, Calif., 1980—.

WRITINGS:

FOR CHILDREN

Your Heart and Blood, Childrens Press, 1984.
Your Brain and Nervous System, Childrens Press, 1984.
Cells and Tissues, Childrens Press, 1985.
Bacteria and Viruses, Childrens Press, 1985.
Nutrition, Childrens Press, 1985.

SIDELIGHTS: Leslie Jean LeMaster commented to *CA:* "I have a phobia about speaking in public, so I express myself through writing and creative arts, such as drawing, painting, and ceramics."

*   *   *

LENNON, Thomas M.   1942-

PERSONAL: Born December 7, 1942, in New York, N.Y.; son of Edwin S. F. and Dorothy (McGinn) Lennon; married Madeline Pellerano, 1965. *Education:* Attended University of Paris, 1962-63; Manhattan College, B.A., 1964; Ohio State University, Ph.D., 1968.

ADDRESSES: Office—Department of Philosophy, University of Western Ontario, London, Ontario, Canada N6A 3K7.

CAREER: University of Western Ontario, London, Ontario, Canada, assistant professor of philosophy, 1968-87, dean, faculty of arts, 1986—.

MEMBER: Canadian Philosophical Association, American Philosophical Association.

AWARDS, HONORS: National Defense Education Act Fellow, 1964-67; Woodrow Wilson Dissertation Fellow, 1967-68.

WRITINGS:

(Translator with P. J. Olscamp) Nicolas Malebranche, *The Search After Truth*, Ohio State University Press, 1980.
(Translator) Nicolas Malebranche, *Elucidations of the Search After Truth*, Ohio State University Press, 1980.
Philosophical Commentary, Ohio State University Press, 1980.
(Editor with John W. Davis and John M. Nicholas) *Problems of Cartesianism: Studies in the History of Ideas*, McGill-Queen's University Press, 1983.

Contributor of more than forty articles and reviews to journals.

WORK IN PROGRESS: A book on the struggle between Gassendism and Cartesianism, 1655-1715, publication expected in 1989.

SIDELIGHTS: Thomas M. Lennon told *CA:* "*The Search After Truth* is Nicolas Malebranche's first, longest, and most important work. Despite the historical importance of the work, there was no previous complete translation of it. My own work on Malebranche demonstrates that one can recognize the importance of an author without necessarily agreeing with him. Malebranche essentially tried to reconcile science and religious faith; in my view he failed. My work on Pierre Gassendi, on the other hand, tries to show why someone with the right views does not always have a more important place in history and why Gassendi's competitor, Rene Descartes, is in fact better known."

*   *   *

LENNOX, Terry
   See HARVEY, John (Barton)

*   *   *

LEONI, Edgar (Hugh)   1925-

PERSONAL: Born May 6, 1925, in New York, N.Y.; son of Paul G. (a business executive) and Nelly (a housewife; maiden name, Duval) Leoni. *Education:* Harvard University, B.A., 1947; Columbia University, M.A., 1952.

ADDRESSES: Home—42 West 88th St., New York, N.Y. 10024.

CAREER: American International Underwriters, New York City, marine insurance claims examiner, 1951-64; Pageant Book Co., Inc., New York City, editor in chief, 1964-66; Oxford Book Co., Inc., New York City, associate editor, 1967-72; semi-retired bookdealer, 1972—. *Military service:* U.S. Army, translator, 1943-46, 1950-51; became sergeant.

WRITINGS:

Nostradamus: Life and Literature, Exposition Press, 1961, reprinted as *Nostradamus and His Prophecies*, Bell Publishing, 1982.

SIDELIGHTS: Edgar Leoni told *CA:* "The prophecies that Nostradamus alleged extended to 3797 A.D. were published, with minor exceptions, between 1555 and 1568. They consist of ten centuries—collections of one hundred rhymed quatrains, or four-line verses—to which Nostradamus gave the collective

name 'Milliade.' Due to various irregularities, though, there are somewhat less than one thousand verses. In addition to the 'Milliade' there are two long prose prefaces that include prophecies. The first, addressed to his infant son Cesar, preceded the first edition of 1555. The second, addressed to King Henry II of France and dated 1558, preceded the last three complete centuries. Outside the better-known collections are 141 four-line verses, called the 'Presages,' collected from the almanacs Nostradamus published between 1555 and 1567. Somewhat different in style from the quatrains, the verses of the 'Presages' each have a dating by year or month and year."

*   *   *

Le POULAIN, Jean   1924-1988

OBITUARY NOTICE: Born September 12, 1924, in Marseilles, France; died of a heart attack, March 1, 1988. Administrator, actor, director, and author. One of France's most popular and versatile performers, Le Poulain acted in or directed more than one hundred plays by such writers as William Shakespeare, Moliere, Bertolt Brecht, and Jean Cocteau during his forty-year career. He graduated from National Conservatory of Theater Arts in Paris in 1949 and established his own theater troupe three years later. He also performed with France's national theater and in television and motion pictures. He stopped acting and directing in 1986 when he was named administrative director of the Comedie-Francaise theater organization. Le Poulain's writings include *I Will Have the Last Laugh.*

OBITUARIES AND OTHER SOURCES:

BOOKS

Who's Who in France, 18th edition, Lafitte, 1985.

PERIODICALS

New York Times, March 3, 1988.

*   *   *

LESTER, Alison   1952-

PERSONAL: Born November 17, 1952, in Foster, Australia; daughter of Donald Robert (a grazier) and Jean Rosalind (a nurse; maiden name, Billings) Lester; married Edwin Hume (a solicitor), January 22, 1977; children: Will, Clair, Lachlan. *Education:* Melbourne State College, Higher Diploma of Teaching, 1975.

ADDRESSES: Home—Dore Rd., Nar Nar Goon North, Victoria, Australia.

CAREER: Victorian Education Department, high school art teacher in Alexandra, Australia, 1976-77, high school art teacher at correspondence school in Melbourne, Australia, 1977-78; writer and illustrator, 1978—.

AWARDS, HONORS: Received medal for best children's picture book of the year from Australian Children's Book Council, 1983, for illustrating *Thing;* commendation from Australian Children's Book Council, 1986, for *Clive Eats Alligators.*

WRITINGS:

Clive Eats Alligators (juvenile), self-illustrated, Oxford University Press, 1985.
Ruby (juvenile), self-illustrated, Oxford University Press, 1987.
The Willow Creek Show (juvenile), self-illustrated, Oxford University Press, 1988.

"Australian Baby Books" (series of four picture books), Penguin, 1988.

ILLUSTRATOR

June Epstein, "Big Dipper" (series), Oxford University Press, 1980-84.
Robin Klein, *Thing*, Oxford University Press, 1982.
R. Klein, *Thingnapped*, Oxford University Press, 1984.
R. Klein, *Ratbags and Rascals*, Dent, 1985.
Morris Lune, *Night Night*, Oxford University Press, 1986.
June Factor, *Summer*, Penguin, 1987.

WORK IN PROGRESS: A sequel to *Clive Eats Alligators*, publication expected in 1988.

SIDELIGHTS: "After a happy childhood on my parents' farm," Alison Lester told CA, "I finished my secondary education and, like many of my contemporaries, had no ambition other than to have a good time. Years of traveling, hiking, riding, and partying ensued. After I married Edwin, we traveled in South America for a year. I've also traveled in Australia and Southeast Asia.

"The birth of our first child woke me up with a start, and I began illustrating then. Anything was preferable to being stuck at home with the housework! As I get more confident about my own writing, though, I find it difficult to illustrate for other people.

"As my imagination increases, I can't think of any work I would rather be doing, unless it is droving cattle. Still, I'm not sure that I'll keep writing children's books forever. I'm full of ideas about fabric design, toys, gardens, et cetera, and I may choose to follow one of these follies. It is hard to find time to work on all these creative things.

"My own children and my childhood memories are my greatest sources of inspiration. I'm a country girl and still live in the bush, so the horses, dogs, cats, and garden also inspire me. I love to see the funny side of things. Kids are very funny and sharp, but it is difficult to communicate humor to them without being patronizing. I also love the exotic and strange."

AVOCATIONAL INTERESTS: Horses, basketball, the beach, gardening, photography, shopping for clothes.

*   *   *

LEUCI, Bob
See LEUCI, Robert

*   *   *

LEUCI, Robert 1940-
(Bob Leuci)

PERSONAL: Born February 28, 1940, in New York, N.Y.; son of James (a pipe-factory foreman and union organizer) and Lucy (an office worker, telephone operator, and sewing-machine plant laborer; maiden name, Tuccitto) Leuci; married Regina Manarin (an insurance administrator), May 11, 1963; children: Anthony James, Santina. *Education:* Attended Baker University, 1957-58; Fordham University, 1979-80, and New School for Social Research. *Politics:* "A small step left." *Religion:* Roman Catholic; humanist.

ADDRESSES: Agent—Esther Newberg, International Creative Management, 40 West 57th St., New York, N.Y. 10019.

CAREER: New York Police Department, New York, N.Y., police officer, 1961-63, detective in Special Investigations Unit of Narcotics Division, 1963-72, detective in First Deputy Commissioner's Special Force, 1972-76, internal affairs officer, 1976-80, Civil Complaint Review Board officer, 1980-81, retired, 1981; writer. Adjunct at Western Connecticut State University, 1983-84. Resident and lecturer at universities, law schools, and police departments nationwide.

MEMBER: Amnesty International (anti-capital punishment coordinator for Danbury, Conn., group), International Association of Crime Writers, Mystery Writers of America, Authors Guild.

WRITINGS:

UNDER NAME BOB LEUCI

Doyle's Disciples (crime novel), Freundlich Books, 1984.
Odessa Beach (crime novel), Freundlich Books, 1985.
Captain Butterfly (crime novel), New American Library, 1988.

WORK IN PROGRESS: Writing the screenplay for a motion picture adaptation of *Captain Butterfly*, for Lorimar Productions; adapting *Doyle's Disciples* as a television series; a novel, tentatively titled *Marimbero;* a play, tentatively titled "Slapper."

SIDELIGHTS: Bob Leuci, the author of three crime novels, draws much of his subject matter from his experience as a detective in a special narcotics investigating unit of the New York City Police Department during the 1960s and early 1970s. A choice, self-directed group whose independence and city-wide jurisdiction earned its members the label "princes of the city," the unit also reflected the corruption present in the police department at the time. To investigate the rumors of drug dealing and other illegal activities in the police department, a special commission was formed, headed by Whitman Knapp. At that time, Leuci believed that "the concept of the Knapp Commission was outrageous," he told CA, "[because it] was focusing only on the police." He recalled telling a counsel for the commission "that I could, if I wanted, expose corruption in lawyers, judges, district attorneys, bailbondsmen, organized crime types, and a slew of others, none of whom were policemen." The counsel asked him to prove it, Leuci said, and "it was then that I realized that I'd told him too much."

Leuci agreed to work undercover for a federal team investigating the New York City criminal justice system. "Ultimately, I was convinced that I had to tell the truth about my own involvement in corruption," he told CA, but this act had unfortunate repercussions: "In admitting my own misdeeds I implicated several men who had been close friends." This act led some colleagues and observers to consider the detective a hero and others to call him a traitor, and it necessitated the protection of Leuci and his family, for a time, by armed guards. He refused the government's offer of a new identity and relocation, however, because "to run away or change my identity . . . would be to admit to myself that I was worthless," as he told Tom Zito in the *Washington Post*. "What I set out to do was not hypocritical," he explained to CA, "but really a noble ambition that unraveled and turned tragic."

Leuci's story was retold by Robert Daley in the well-received book *Prince of the City* and in director Sidney Lumet's motion picture of the same title. The former policeman reflected: "'Prince of the City' is truly a sad and tragic story. Looked at in its broadest sense, it is simply the tale of a group of basically good and decent men that lost sight of who they were and what they were about, as people and as policemen. The setting is the police world, but what is true for those described in that story is also true for anyone who loses sight of what is best in them.''

Leuci turned to writing after retiring from the police force in 1981. His first novel, *Doyle's Disciples,* echoed his own story and acted as ''a bit of a catharsis,'' Leuci was quoted as saying in the *Los Angeles Times.* Protagonist Bobby Porterfield is a New York City detective who uncovers a bloody payoff scandal that involves top police officials; the officer grapples with whether to expose department criminality or to accept the workings of a pervasively errant system. ''The resulting climax threatens his profession, his marriage, his friendships and his self-respect, as well as his life,'' described Carl Sessions Stepp in the *Washington Post.* ''Unlike the author, Leuci's fictional hero recoils from his magic opportunity to combat police corruption.''

Inspiring encouraging reviews, *Doyle's Disciples* was praised for its potent realism. ''The backgrounds and police routines are meticulously depicted,'' wrote *New York Times Book Review* critic Newgate Callendar. ''Mr. Leuci knows his way around the city, the court, [and] the precinct houses.'' As for his protagonist's moral dilemma, the critic continued, ''it will be up to the reader to decide if he has solved it.'' Stepp commended Leuci's ''skill in pacing the action and in penetrating those gritty inner-city subcultures and nerve-jangling street terrors police face daily,'' and he called the novel's theme ''provocative and disturbing—a disheartening testament to the fruitlessness of reform and the fragility of relationships.'' While deciding that ''the novel does draw its authority more from who Leuci is and where he has been than from how he writes,'' Stepp concluded, ''Leuci seems to have deeper possibilities within.''

Realizing those possibilities, Leuci scored high marks a year later with *Odessa Beach,* a thriller concerning a Russian black marketeer and New York's Mafia. Callendar observed: ''Mr. Leuci is a very good technician. . . . Everything rings true.'' Judging it ''a fascinating yarn told vulgarly, yet compellingly,'' Nick B. Williams, Sr., in the *Los Angeles Times Book Review,* placed the novel ''among the most exciting that I've read this year.''

Leuci told *CA:* ''The pleasure of my work comes from giving readers the opportunity to see the world through the eyes of street people and the police. This is the arena I know best: law officers and street people—the disenfranchised, the set upon, the predators. We live in a violent world. Why? That's the question that interests me most.

''I have been a fan all my conscious life of a certain crew of writers. Each of them has something to say, and it's in the way they say it that makes you jump off the tracks. No one here has mastered a formula, few have best-sellers. They are not self-conscious or tedious; they are simply wonderful writers of prose whose words are fine poetry. Most rely on dialogue to disclose character, and all dramatize the various ways individuals and nations sin. For me this is writing, this is what I strive to do.''

BIOGRAPHICAL/CRITICAL SOURCES:

BOOKS

Daley, Robert, *Prince of the City: The True Story of a Cop Who Knew Too Much,* Houghton, 1979.

PERIODICALS

Chicago Tribune, October 9, 1984.

Los Angeles Times, November 23, 1984.
Los Angeles Times Book Review, August 19, 1984, February 16, 1986.
New York Times Book Review, January 6, 1985, January 4, 1987.
Washington Post, January 17, 1979, August 24, 1984.

*   *   *

LEUTHNER, Stuart   1939-

PERSONAL: Born June 5, 1939, in Buffalo, N.Y.; son of Carl F. (an engineer) and Mary (a nurse; maiden name, Grant) Leuthner; married Susan Attaway (divorced); married Henrietta Cowney (divorced); married Carolyn M. Jensen (a personnel supervisor), September 25, 1984; children: Melissa Sweet, Amy Douglas. *Education:* University of Buffalo (now State University of New York at Buffalo), B.S., 1961; Rochester Institute of Technology, M.F.A., 1964; attended School of the Visual Arts.

ADDRESSES: Home—421 Hudson, New York, N.Y. 10014. *Agent*—Robert Parke, St. Mary's Church Rd., Bedford, N.Y.

CAREER: Fuchs-Leuthner, New York City, partner, 1978-83; *Ads,* New York City, creative director, 1983-86; *Credits,* New York City, creative director, 1986-87.

WRITINGS:

The Railroaders, Random House, 1983.

WORK IN PROGRESS: High Honor, on World War II aviation; *Blood and Guts,* about football in the 1950s, for Doubleday; *Edgework,* on people ''with risky jobs.''

*   *   *

LEVESQUE, Rene   1922-1987

OBITUARY NOTICE: Born August 24, 1922, in New Carlisle, Quebec, Canada; died of a heart attack, November 1, 1987, in Montreal, Quebec, Canada. Politician, administrator, radio commentator, and journalist. The former premier of Quebec who advocated the separation of that province from the rest of Canada, Levesque entered politics in the midst of a distinguished career as a radio commentator and as head of the French-language radio and television news service of the Canadian Broadcasting Corporation. A member of Quebec's Liberal Party, Levesque was elected to the legislature in 1960 and was named Minister of Natural Resources. He broke away from the Liberals in 1967 to form his own organization, the Parti Quebecois, that sought secession from Canada so that French culture would thrive in Quebec. In 1976 he was elected premier of that province, and for the next four years his party made gains to keep the French culture alive: French was made Quebec's sole official language and ''French-only'' laws were applied to education, in the work place, and on public signs, prompting an exodus of English-speaking people from the province. Nonetheless, in a referendum in 1980 the citizens of Quebec rejected autonomy; yet Levesque, still popular, was reelected the following year. In 1985 the premier resigned from his post because the Parti Quebecois was losing popular backing and because of tensions in his administration. He returned to journalism and radio commentating and wrote his *Memoirs,* translated into English by Philip Stratford.

OBITUARIES AND OTHER SOURCES:

BOOKS

Who's Who, 138th edition, St. Martin's, 1986.

PERIODICALS

Chicago Tribune, November 3, 1987.
Globe and Mail (Toronto), October 18, 1986.
Los Angeles Times, November 2, 1987.
New York Times, November 3, 1987.
Time, November 16, 1987.
Times (London), November 3, 1987.

*   *   *

LEVINE, Israel 1893(?)-1988(?)

OBITUARY NOTICE: Educator and author. Levine was a well-respected instructor at Oxford University's Exeter College who impressed upon his students that philosophy does not have to be academic and abstract. Levine's numerous writings include *Francis Bacon, Faithful Rebels, The Unconscious: A Study in Freudian Psychology,* and *Reason and Morals.*

OBITUARIES AND OTHER SOURCES:

PERIODICALS

Times (London), May 28, 1988.

*   *   *

LEVINE, Sarah 1970-

PERSONAL: Born March 9, 1970, in Pittsburgh, Pa.; daughter of Jonathan (a human relations executive) and Abby (an editor and writer; maiden name, Bernstein) Levine. *Education:* Attended junior high school in Evanston, Ill.

ADDRESSES: Home—9509 Ridgeway Ave., Evanston, Ill. 60203.

CAREER: Writer.

WRITINGS:

(With mother, Abby Levine) *Sometimes I Wish I Were Mindy* (juvenile), Albert Whitman, 1986.

*   *   *

LEVY, Faye 1951-

PERSONAL: Born May 23, 1951, in Washington, D.C.; daughter of Louis (a businessman) and Pauline (a secretary; maiden name, Dobry) Kahn; married Yakir Levy (a writer), September 28, 1970. *Education:* Attended Hebrew University of Jerusalem, 1969-70; Tel Aviv University, B.A. (magna cum laude), 1973; La Varenne Cooking School, Paris, Grand Diplome, 1977.

ADDRESSES: Home and office—835 Fourth St., Santa Monica, Calif. 90403. *Agent*—Maureen Lasher Agency, 1210 Tellem Dr., Pacific Palisades, Calif. 90272.

CAREER: Editorial assistant in Tel Aviv, Israel, 1974-76; La Varenne Cooking School, Paris, France, recipe and cookbook editor, 1976-82; certified cooking teacher and writer, 1982—. Cookbook editor, 1982-84.

MEMBER: International Association of Cooking Professionals, American Institute of Wine and Food, Newspaper Food Editors and Writers Association, Southern California Culinary Guild.

AWARDS, HONORS: Faye Levy's Chocolate Sensations was named one of the best books of 1986 by *Publishers Weekly.*

WRITINGS:

La Varenne Tour Book, Peanut Butter Publishing, 1980.
(With Fernand Chambrette) *La Cuisine du Poisson* (title means "Fish Cookery"), Flammarion, 1984.
Sefer Hakinuhim: Mivhar Matkonei Tsarfat (title means "The Book of Desserts: The Best Recipes of France"), R. Sirkis, 1984.
Sefer Haoogot: Mivhar Matkonei Tsarfat (title means "The Book of Cakes: The Best Recipes of France"), R. Sirkis, 1984.
Aruhot Halaviot: Mivhar Matkonei Tsarfat (title means "Meatless Meals: The Best Recipes of France"), R. Sirkis, 1985.
Faye Levy's Chocolate Sensations, HP Books, 1986.
Classic Cooking Techniques, Ortho Books, 1986.
Fresh From France: Vegetable Creations, Dutton, 1987.

Contributor to *French Regional Cooking, The La Varenne Cooking Course,* and *Basic French Cookery.* Work represented in anthologies, including *The Best of Gourmet* and *More of the Best From Bon Appetit.* Author of "Basics," a column in *Bon Appetit,* 1982—. Contributor to magazines and newspapers.

WORK IN PROGRESS: Writing about main courses and desserts.

SIDELIGHTS: Faye Levy told *CA:* "I first went to Israel when I was seventeen on a six-week summer camp program. I fell in love with the land and the people, in more ways than one—it was on that trip that I met my future husband, Yakir Levy. My interest in cooking came about a year later, when Yakir and I decided to get married. My future mother-in-law was not at all happy with her son's choice, because I did not know how to cook. I decided I had better learn, and I did so by reading cookbooks and following the recipes. I was happy with the results and with the fact that a person like me, who had almost no previous knowledge of cooking, could follow a recipe and produce such delicious food.

"Over the next few years I became more and more intrigued with cooking and with cookbooks, and I decided to try to follow a career in this direction. I contacted Ruth Sirkis, the Julia Child of Israel, and asked to work as her assistant. She hired me and I learned how to write recipes from her. Later my husband and I decided to move to the United States and to visit Europe en route. Since it was clear that many of the best cookbook writers had studied in Paris, I thought it would be a fascinating thing to do. I enrolled in a six-week course at a new Parisian cooking school called La Varenne and soon after worked in exchange for the remaining courses in the program and earned the Grand Diplome of the first graduating class. I took extensive notes on everything the chefs said and how they cooked. On the basis of these notebooks, I became the school's recipe editor and then the cookbook editor. I authored the school's first cookbook and had a major part in researching and writing the school's award-winning cookbooks, *French Regional Cooking, The La Varenne Cooking Course,* and *Basic French Cookery.*"

AVOCATIONAL INTERESTS: Travel.

BIOGRAPHICAL/CRITICAL SOURCES:

BOOKS

Burns, Jim, *Women Chefs,* Aris Books, 1987.

PERIODICALS

Los Angeles Herald Examiner, June 18, 1987.
New York Times, November 11, 1987.

*   *   *

LEWIS, Mary (Christianna) 1907(?)-1988
(Mary Ann Ashe, Christianna Brand, Annabel Jones, Mary Roland, China Thompson)

OBITUARY NOTICE—See index for *CA* sketch: Born December 17, 1907 (one source says 1909), in Malaya; died March 11, 1988. Author. Best known for her detective stories featuring Inspector Cockrill of the Kent County Police, Lewis wrote, under various pseudonyms, a number of mystery and suspense stories and novels. Titles include *Death in High Heels, Heads You Lose, Green for Danger, Cat and Mouse,* and *The Three-Cornered Halo.* She also wrote several children's books, notably a "Nurse Matilda" series of comic tales about a nanny; *The Brides of Aberdar,* a ghost story; and *Heaven Knows Who,* a nonfictional account of a nineteenth-century murder in Scotland. Furthermore, Lewis contributed to the anthology *Best Police Stories* and to various periodicals, including *Chicago Tribune, Saturday Evening Post,* and *Ellery Queen's Mystery Magazine.* Two of her stories won awards from the Mystery Writers of America. Prior to writing full time, Lewis worked at a number of odd jobs, among them governess, receptionist, dancer, model, sales clerk, and secretary.

OBITUARIES AND OTHER SOURCES:

BOOKS

Twentieth-Century Crime and Mystery Writers, 2nd edition, St. Martin's, 1985.

PERIODICALS

Times (London), March 14, 1988.

*   *   *

LEWIS, Mervyn K(eith) 1941-

PERSONAL: Born June 20, 1941, in Adelaide, Australia; son of Norman Malcolm (a proofreader) and Valerie (a homemaker; maiden name, Way) Lewis; married Kay Judith Wiesner (a teacher), November 24, 1962; children: Stephanie Jane, Miranda Kay, Alexandra Kim, Antonia Louise. *Education:* University of Adelaide, B.Ec. (with first class honors), 1964, Ph.D., 1978. *Religion:* Church of England.

ADDRESSES: Home—Sarum Chase, 13 Rostrevor Rd., Stirling, South Australia 5152. *Office*—Department of Economics, University of Nottingham, University Park, Nottingham NG7 2RD, England.

CAREER: Elder Smith and Co. Ltd. (stock agents), Adelaide, Australia, clerk, 1957-58; Commonwealth Trading Bank of Australia, Adelaide, clerk, 1959-64; University of Adelaide, Adelaide, temporary lecturer, 1967, lecturer, 1967-73, senior lecturer, 1973-80, reader in economics, 1980-84; University of Nottingham, Nottingham, England, Midland Bank Professor of Money and Banking, 1985—, co-director of Nottingham Institute of Financial Studies, 1985—. Visiting scholar at Bank of England, 1979-80; visiting professor at Flinders University and Cambridge University. Kingston College of Advanced Education, chairman of finance committee, 1976-79, president of council and chairman of Working Party on Finance, 1978-79; member of joint interim committee of Kingston and Murray Park Colleges of Advanced Education.

MEMBER: Royal Economic Society, Academy of Social Sciences in Australia (fellow), American Economic Association, American Finance Association.

AWARDS, HONORS: Essay prize from Australian Institute of Bankers, 1963, for article "The Case for Flexible Bank Interest Rates."

WRITINGS:

(With K. T. Davis) *Monetary Policy in Australia,* Longman Cheshire, 1980.
(Editor with Davis) *Australian Monetary Economics,* Longman Cheshire, 1981.
(With M. J. Artis) *Monetary Control in the United Kingdom,* Philip Allan, 1981.
(With Davis and John Foster) *A Member's Guide to Monetarism and Keynesianism,* Legislative Research Service, Parliament of the Commonwealth of Australia, 1983.
(Editor with R. H. Wallace, and contributor) *Australia's Financial Institutions and Markets,* Longman Cheshire, 1985.
(With R. L. Carter and Brian Chiplin) *Personal Financial Markets: An Examination of the Evolving Markets for Personal Savings and Financing in the United Kingdom and the United States,* Philip Allan, 1986.
(With Davis) *Domestic and International Banking,* MIT Press, 1987.
(With Artis) *Monetary Control in the United Kingdom,* Philip Allan, in press.

Co-editor of *Australian Economics Papers,* 1975-84.

CONTRIBUTOR

R. R. Hirst and R. H. Wallace, editors, *The Australian Capital Market,* Cheshire, 1974.
M. G. Porter, editor, *The Australian Monetary System in the 1970s,* Monash University, 1978.
F. H. Gruen, editor, *Surveys of Australian Economics,* Volume I, Allen & Unwin, 1978.
J. W. Nevile, editor, *Policies Against Stagflation,* Longman Cheshire, 1981.
Australian Financial System Inquiry: Commissioned Studies and Selected Papers, Part I, Australian Government Publishing Service, 1982.
Victor Argy and J. W. Nevile, editors, *Inflation and Unemployment: Theory, Experience, and Policymaking,* Allen & Unwin, 1985.
C. A. E. Goodhart, David Currie, and D. T. Llewellyn, editors, *The Operation and Regulation of Financial Markets,* Macmillan, 1987.
J. Creedy, editor, *Major Concepts of Economics,* Basil Blackwell, in press.

Contributor to economic and marketing journals.

SIDELIGHTS: Mervyn K. Lewis told *CA:* "Financial market developments in the United States during the 1980s—often called the 'financial services revolution'—are most often portrayed by American authors as purely indigenous phenomena. Yet developments in the United Kingdom, Australia, and many other countries are strikingly similar. My recent books explore these parallel trends in terms of the impact of inflation and high interest rates, innovations in financial technology, and the growth of international banking. Working in both the United Kingdom and Australia, along with visits to the United States, helps me to keep abreast of worldwide trends."

LEWIS, Theophilus 1891-1974

PERSONAL: Born March 4, 1891, in Baltimore, Md.; died September 3, 1974; son of Thomas and Anne Lewis; married, January 17, 1933; children: Selma Marie, Alfred Charles, Lowell Francis. *Education:* Attended public schools in Baltimore, Md., and New York, N.Y.

CAREER/WRITINGS: Manual laborer before World War I; worked for post office in New York, N.Y., beginning c. 1922. *Messenger* (periodical), drama critic, 1923-27, contributor of short stories, and co-author with George S. Schuyler of column "Shafts and Darts"; contributor of articles and drama and book reviews to numerous periodicals, including *America, Catholic World, Commonweal, Ebony and Topaz, Interracial Review, Inter-State Tattler, New York Amsterdam Star-News, Ohio Express, Opportunity, People's Voice, Pittsburgh Courier,* and *Sign.* Founding member of New York City Commission on Human Rights during 1950s. *Military service:* Served in American Expeditionary Force during World War I.

SIDELIGHTS: Theophilus Lewis wrote for numerous black and Catholic periodicals over the course of about fifty years. With no more than a high school education, he taught himself about the theater and became a well-regarded drama critic during the Harlem Renaissance, a period of heightened literary activity during the 1920s. As Theodore Kornweibel, Jr., observed in an article for *The Harlem Renaissance Remembered,* Lewis felt that theater served a vital social purpose—in Kornweibel's words, that "serious drama was the repository of a society's (or race's) collective spiritual life, culture, and character." As a drama critic for the periodical *Messenger* from 1923 to 1927, Lewis tried to encourage theater in New York City that would embody the values of black culture and eventually result in drama that would attract black audiences nationwide.

In his column for the *Messenger* Lewis repeatedly expressed disappointment with the black theater of his day, which relied heavily on comedy skits and lines of attractive female dancers to please its audience. While acknowledging the liveliness and entertainment value of such spectacles, he felt that they detracted from the higher goals of serious drama. Lewis saw black actors of great talent wasted in minor productions because they lacked substantial works to perform, and he laid part of the blame on black audiences and playwrights, both of whom, he felt, were given to low standards. But he also blasted the owners of major "black" theaters—often whites—whose background, he charged, was in circuses and carnivals rather than in culture. Such entrepreneurs were unwilling to use the profits of their light entertainment to offset the financial losses involved in promoting serious drama.

Accordingly, Lewis generally looked beyond the most popular and commercial black productions to find fit subjects for his praise. Surprisingly, some of the "black" dramas he liked were written by whites—including Eugene O'Neill's *The Emperor Jones* and *All God's Chillun Got Wings.* Lewis valued a play, regardless of its source, if it offered a realistic portrayal of black life and solid dramatic roles with which black actors could develop their talents. Furthermore, Lewis had high hopes for small, independent, nonprofit companies—often called "little theaters"—made up of black actors and playwrights. Such companies, he believed, if supported by small but appreciative audiences, could provide the basis for a dramatic community of the future that would be welcomed by black people through-

out the country. As Kornweibel observed, Lewis accented the positive in his reviews of little-theater productions, overlooking technical flaws out of respect for the company's aspirations.

Lewis's dedication to his work brought him the respect of his fellow writers of the Harlem Renaissance. "Other 'critics' rarely displayed any discrimination and did little more than promote any show that promised to be successful," Kornweibel wrote. "The word was circulated among young artists and writers that Lewis was the only drama critic they could take seriously."

Lewis was unable to earn a living as a writer, however, remaining a post office worker from the 1920s until he reached retirement age years later. He continued to be published in periodicals throughout his life, and he explored other genres besides the drama review—for the *Messenger,* for instance, he wrote several short stories and collaborated with satirist George S. Schuyler on the column "Shafts and Darts." A convert to Catholicism in 1939, Lewis contributed to a number of Catholic magazines, including *Catholic World, Commonweal,* and *America,* in which his drama reviews appeared until a few years before he died.

BIOGRAPHICAL/CRITICAL SOURCES:

BOOKS

Bontemps, Arna, editor, *The Harlem Renaissance Remembered,* Dodd, 1972.
Scally, Sister Mary Anthony, *Negro Catholic Writers, 1900-1943,* Walter Romig, 1945.*

(Date of death provided by Brother Frank Turnbull, S.J., of the office of the editor in chief of *America* magazine.)

* * *

LICHTEN, Joseph I. 1906(?)-1987

OBITUARY NOTICE: Born c. 1906 in Poland; came to United States, 1941; naturalized citizen; died December 14, 1987, in Rome, Italy. Administrator, diplomat, and author. Lichten was affiliated with the Anti-Defamation League of B'nai B'rith for more than forty years. Joining the League in 1945 as director of the Department of Intercultural Affairs, Lichten was its representative at the Second Vatican Council in the mid-1960s when the Roman Catholic hierarchy formally denounced anti-Semitism. He subsequently acted as head of the League's liaison office to the Vatican from 1971 until his retirement in 1986—the year he was honored by Pope John Paul II for his efforts to promote understanding between Catholics and Jews. Lichten served as a diplomat with the Polish Government before World War II and was attached to the embassy of the Polish Government in Exile in Washington, D.C., from 1941 until 1945. He remained in America after the war. Lichten's writings include *A Question of Judgment: Pope Pius XII and the Jews,* and he contributed to books and periodicals.

OBITUARIES AND OTHER SOURCES:

PERIODICALS

New York Times, December 17, 1987.

* * *

LIEBERT, Robert S. 1930-1988

OBITUARY NOTICE: Born January 14, 1930, in New York, N.Y.; died March 9, 1988, in New York, N.Y. Psychiatrist, educator, and author. Trained as a Freudian psychoanalyst, Liebert was a clinical professor of psychiatry at Columbia University's College of Physicians and Surgeons beginning in 1964 and served as a training and supervising psychoanalyst at that institution's Psychoanalytic Center. In addition Liebert taught art history at Columbia, and applied psychoanalytic theory to art with his 1983 book, *Michelangelo: A Psychoanalytic Study of His Life and Images.* In *Radical and Militant Youth: A Psychoanalytic Inquiry* he psychoanalyzed the motives of student rioters at Columbia in 1968, who, he attests, were only responding to deep-seated problems in society. Liebert was also an adjunct professor of psychiatry at Cornell University's medical college and contributed to scholarly and popular journals.

OBITUARIES AND OTHER SOURCES:

BOOKS

Biographical Directory of the Fellows and Members of the American Psychiatric Association, Bowker, 1977.

PERIODICALS

New York Times, March 11, 1988.

*   *   *

LINDGREN, Ethel John
  See LINDGREN-UTSI, E(thel) J(ohn)

*   *   *

LINDGREN-UTSI, E(thel) J(ohn)   1905-1988
  (Ethel John Lindgren)

OBITUARY NOTICE: Born January 1, 1905, in Evanstown, Ill.; immigrated to England; naturalized citizen, 1940; died March 23, 1988, in Aviemore, Cairngorm Mountains, Scotland. Anthropologist, reindeer breeder, educator, editor, and author. A prominent anthropologist and breeder of reindeer, Lindgren-Utsi—who wrote and edited under her name Ethel John Lindgren—was a council member of the Royal Anthropological Institute for twenty-eight years and was vice-president and honorary editor of its *Journal* for nearly a decade. She was also a founding fellow of Lucy Cavendish College of Cambridge University and lectured in social anthropology at Cambridge. While a doctoral student at Newnham College of Cambridge University Lindgren-Utsi lived in Manchuria for four years to study the Tungus reindeer, the subject of her dissertation, which, at the time of her death, was being prepared for publication by one of her students. At Newnham she also edited *The Study of Society: Methods and Problems,* and during World War II she was editor in chief of the *Wartime Social Survey.* In addition Lindgren-Utsi contributed chapters to books and articles to scholarly journals.

OBITUARIES AND OTHER SOURCES:

BOOKS

Fifth International Directory of Anthropologists, University of Chicago Press, 1975.
International Authors and Writers Who's Who, 8th edition, Melrose, 1977.

PERIODICALS

Times (London), March 28, 1988.

LININGTON, (Barbara) Elizabeth   1921-1988
  (Anne Blaisdell, Lesley Egan, Egan O'Neill, Dell Shannon)

OBITUARY NOTICE—See index for *CA* sketch: Born March 11, 1921, in Aurora, Ill.; died April 5, 1988, in Arroyo Grande, Calif. Author. Linington was a prolific writer in the genres of historical fiction and crime detection. Her historical novels, some of which involve people and events in Irish history, include *The Proud Man, The Anglophile* (written under the pseudonym Egan O'Neill), and *Greenmask!* (published in England under the pseudonym Anne Blaisdell). As Lesley Egan she published such crime novels as *Against the Evidence* and *The Wine of Life,* and as Dell Shannon she produced crime fiction such as *Coffin Corner* and *Blood Count.* Many works under the Shannon pseudonym feature police officer Luis Mendoza.

OBITUARIES AND OTHER SOURCES:

Date of death provided by Anthony F. Cambra.

*   *   *

LIN Mao
  See SHEN Congwen

*   *   *

LINNEMAN, William R(ichard)   1926-

PERSONAL: Born October 13, 1926, in Bloomington, Ill.; married in 1957; children: two. *Education:* Park College, A.B., 1950; University of Illinois at Urbana-Champaign, M.A., 1954, Ph.D., 1960.

ADDRESSES: Office—Department of English, Illinois State University, Normal, Ill. 61761.

CAREER: Florida Southern College, Lakeland, assistant professor of English, 1960-64; Illinois State University, Normal, associate professor, 1964-75, professor of English, 1975—, chairman of department, 1973-75.

MEMBER: Modern Language Association of America, National Council of Teachers of English, Conference on College Composition and Communication.

WRITINGS:

Richard Hovey, Twayne, 1976.

Contributor to literature journals.*

*   *   *

LISTER, Eric   1926(?)-1988(?)

OBITUARY NOTICE: Art gallery owner, jazz musician, and author. One of Lister's many adventures during his colorful lifetime was driving the route of the 1912 Paris-to-Peking auto race in a vintage car, with American humor writer S. J. Perelman. Lister wrote about this journey and many of his other exploits in works such as *Don't Mention the Marx Brothers.* He was interested in primitive and fantasy art—he was part owner of the Portal Gallery—and wrote with Sheldon Williams *Twentieth-Century British Naive and Primitive Painters.* In addition, Lister was known as an accomplished jazz musician who played the clarinet and sang.

OBITUARIES AND OTHER SOURCES:

PERIODICALS

Times (London), April 27, 1988.

*   *   *

LITTLE, Malcolm   1925-1965
(El-Hajj Malik El-Shabazz, Malcolm X)

PERSONAL: Born May 19, 1925, in Omaha, Neb.; assassinated February 21, 1965, in New York, N.Y.; son of Earl (a minister and activist) and Louise Little; married wife, Betty (a student nurse), 1958; children: six daughters. *Religion:* Muslim.

CAREER: Activist. Worker in Lost-Found Nation of Islam (Black Muslims) religious sect, 1952-64, began as assistant minister of mosque in Detroit, Mich., then organized mosque in Philadelphia, Pa., became national minister, 1963; established Muslim Mosque, Inc., 1964; lecturer and writer. Founded Organization of Afro-American Unity in New York City, 1964.

WRITINGS:

UNDER NAME MALCOLM X

(With Alex Haley) *The Autobiography of Malcolm X,* introduction by M. S. Handler, epilogue by Haley, Grove, 1965.

Malcolm X Speaks: Selected Speeches and Statements, edited and with prefatory notes by George Breitman, Merit Publishers, 1965.

Malcolm X on Afro-American History, Merit Pubilshers, 1967, expanded edition, Pathfinder Press, 1970.

The Speeches of Malcolm X at Harvard, edited and with an introductory essay by Archie Epps, Morrow, 1968.

Malcolm X Talks to Young People, Young Socialist Alliance, 1969.

Malcolm X and the Negro Revolution: The Speeches of Malcolm X, edited and with an introductory essay by Archie Epps, Owen, 1969.

Two Speeches by Malcolm X, Merit Publishers, 1969.

By Any Means Necessary: Speeches, Interviews, and a Letter by Malcolm X, edited by George Breitman, Pathfinder Press, 1970.

The End of White World Supremacy: Four Speeches, edited and with an introduction by Benjamin Goodman, Merlin House, 1971.

Work represented in anthologies, including *100 and More Quotes by Garvey, Lumumba, and Malcolm X,* compiled by Shawna Maglangbayan, Third World Press, 1975.

Also speaker, with Bayard Rustin, on recording *A Choice of Two Roads,* Pacifica Archives.

SIDELIGHTS: Malcolm Little was a religious and sociopolitical activist who rose to prominence, and notoriety, in the mid-1950s under the name Malcolm X. A staunch, outspoken advocate of black separatism, he inspired many with his efforts on behalf of Elijah Muhammad's Black Muslim religion, which characterizes the black race as superior and the white race as inherently evil. For Malcolm X, the Western black's sole response to racism was total withdrawal from Western culture and society. These radical contentions, while uniting a portion of the American black community, alienated other members, including civil rights activists and pacifists. Eventually Malcolm X became disillusioned with Elijah Muhammad's antag-

onistic religion and left to start his own Muslim organization. This action, in turn, offended Elijah Muhammad and his followers, and in early 1965, while preparing to speak in a Harlem ballroom, Malcolm X was gunned down by men believed sympathetic to the Black Muslims.

As I. F. Stone noted in the *New York Review of Books,* "Malcolm X was born into Black Nationalism." Earl Little, Malcolm's father, was a Baptist minister who strongly supported separatist Marcus Garvey's back-to-Africa movement in the 1920s. For his actions on behalf of Garvey, Earl Little soon found himself the target of hostility while living in Omaha, Nebraska, where members of the racist Ku Klux Klan organization threatened his family because he was sparking dissension among the normally cooperative blacks. The Littles consequently left Omaha, but during the next few years they failed to find a hospitable community and thus moved often. In his autobiography, Malcolm X recalled a particularly harrowing experience in Lansing, Michigan, where his family home was torched by members of the Black Legion, an oddly named band of white supremacists. Shortly afterwards the corpse of Earl Little was found horribly butchered.

Following Earl Little's death, Louise Little and her eight children subsisted on welfare. Eventually, however, the severe strain overwhelmed her and she succumbed to mental illness. Louise Little was then placed in a mental institution and her children were sent separately to various foster homes. Despite this continued adversity and emotional hardship, Malcolm still held aspirations of assimilation in America's predominantly white society. But even those hopes faded after he confided to his high-school English teacher that he hoped to someday become a lawyer, whereupon the teacher urged him towards a vocation instead of a profession and told him to be "realistic about being a nigger."

A distinguished student, Malcolm was shattered by his teacher's racist counseling, and soon afterward he quit high school. Living with a sister in Boston, Malcolm found menial work and began associating with low-lifes and criminals. He became involved with illegal gambling, managed his own prostitution ring, and consorted with drug dealers. Eventually he also sold narcotics, to which he swiftly became addicted, and turned to robbery to sustain his drug habit. He developed a formidable reputation as an enterprising, quick-thinking hustler, becoming notorious in the Boston ghetto as "Detroit Red." With that notoriety, however, came increasing attention from the police, and in early 1946 Malcolm was arrested and charged with robbery. That February—three months before his twenty-first birthday—he was sentenced to ten years imprisonment.

In the penitentiary Malcolm continued his reckless ways, using drugs and presenting such an unsavory demeanor that his fellow inmates referred to him as "Satan." Because of his vicious behavior he was often held in solitary confinement. But he did manage to befriend another convicted burglar, Bimbi, who introduced him to the prison's extensive library. Through the library Malcolm broadened his education and familiarized himself with subjects ranging from philosophy to politics. He also began studying the tenets of the Black Muslims' Lost-Found Nation of Islam, a religion that extolled the superiority of the black race and denounced the white as evil and doomed to destruction. The Black Muslims' founder and leader, Elijah Muhammad, proclaimed himself divine messenger of the Muslim deity, Allah, and—like Marcus Garvey—he counseled his followers to abjure white America in favor of an autonomous black society. Elijah Muhammad's doctrine of black pride exerted considerable appeal to Malcolm, who denounced his allegedly enslaving Christian surname and adopted the name Malcolm X.

While still in prison Malcolm X corresponded with Elijah Muhammad, who lived comfortably at Black Muslim headquarters in Chicago, and after obtaining freedom in 1952 he traveled there and commenced a brief tutelage under the Muslim leader. He then served briefly as an assistant minister at a Detroit mosque before becoming minister at Harlem's Mosque Number Seven. It was in Harlem that Malcolm X achieved impressive status as an articulate, mercurial spokesperson for the radical black perspective. From street corners, church pulpits, and college podiums he railed against racism and championed separatism and faith in Allah as the salvation of blacks. He claimed that civil rights, equal opportunity, and integration were all futile within a society that was determinedly racist. Even Christianity was reviled as a method of enslavement and was denounced as a historical distortion—Christ having been, according to Malcolm X, a black. He advised blacks to reject white society and unite under Elijah Muhammad and the Black Muslim faith, which held the true way to dignity for blacks.

Malcolm X proved an impressive representative for Elijah Muhammad, and as he enthusiastically proselytized for the Black Muslims their membership increased significantly. Elijah Muhammad, acknowledging the impressive effectiveness of his acolyte, named him the religion's first national minister. As Malcolm X rose in status, however, he became increasingly critical of Elijah Muhammad's materialism, particularly his many expensive cars and business suits and his lavishly furnished estate in Chicago. In addition, he was dismayed when former secretaries claimed that Elijah Muhammad had seduced them and sired their children, thus violating the sect's tenet on sexual promiscuity. Elijah Muhammad, in turn, reportedly grew resentful of Malcolm X's growing prominence across the nation and thus his formidable influence within the Black Muslim organization.

Rivalry between the two men peaked in 1963 when Malcolm X violated Elijah Muhammad's commandment of silence regarding the November 22nd assassination of President Kennedy and termed it a case of "the chicken coming home to roost." Malcolm X, who later explained that his comment was meant to indicate that "the hate in white men . . . finally had struck down the President," was reprimanded by Elijah Muhammad for the potentially incendiary remark. "That was a very bad statement," Elijah Muhammad told him. "The country loved this man." He ordered Malcolm X to refrain from public comment for ninety days, and Malcolm complied.

Within days, however, Malcolm X learned that members of his sect were plotting his demise. His dissatisfaction with the Black Muslims mounted, and he decided to tour Mecca, birthplace of the Muslim prophet Muhammad. Once there, Malcolm X experienced a powerful conversion, one which left him with greater compassion for people of all races and nationalities. He renamed himself El-Hajj Malik El-Shabazz and vowed to promote greater harmony among all blacks, including non-Muslims and civil rights activists he had alienated earlier with his uncompromising positions. Once back in the United States he founded his own Muslim association, the Organization of Afro-American Unity, and began actively working to unite blacks throughout the world.

Once he began operating outside the Black Muslim sect, Malcolm X was apparently perceived as a threat to the organization. "Now I'm out," he stated. "And there's the fear [that]

if my image isn't shattered, the Muslims in the movement will leave." He was informed that members within the organization were plotting to end his life, and in mid-February he told the *New York Times* that he was a "marked man." Around that time his home was firebombed. But he was undaunted and continued to speak on behalf of black unity and harmony. On February 21, 1965, he stepped to the podium in a Harlem ballroom and greeted the audience of four hundred that had gathered to hear him speak. Within seconds at least three men rose from their seats and began firing at Malcolm X with shotguns and pistols. Seven shots slammed him backwards while spectators scrambled for cover. As gunfire continued—more than thirty shots were reportedly heard—daring witnesses attacked and subdued the assassins. Three men—Talmadge Hayer and Black Muslims Norman 3X Butler and Thomas 15X Johnson—were eventually convicted of the killing, and it is widely believed the assassins intended to intimidate Malcolm X's followers into remaining within the Black Muslim fold.

In the years since his death Malcolm X has come to be recognized as a leading figure in the black struggle for recognition and equality. *The Autobiography of Malcolm X,* published the same year as his death, is highly regarded as a moving account of his own experiences with racism, his criminal past, and his years as an activist for both the Black Muslims and his own Afro-American organization. During the remaining years of the 1960s Malcolm X's speeches and comments were collected and published in volumes such as *Malcolm X Speaks, Malcolm X on Afro-American History,* and *Malcolm X and the Negro Revolution.* Together with the autobiography, these books offer numerous insights into America's social climate from the mid-1950s to the mid-60s and articulate the concerns of a significant portion of the black community in those years. Additionally, they serve as an imposing indication of Malcolm X's beliefs, his achievements, and his potential, which—like that of President Kennedy, Reverend Martin Luther King, Jr., and Senator Robert Kennedy—were violently rendered unrealized. As I. F. Stone noted in his essay-review for the *New York Review of Books:* "There are few places on earth where whites have not grown rich robbing [blacks]. It was Malcolm's great contribution to help make us aware of this." Stone called Malcolm X's murder "a loss to the country as well as to his race."

MEDIA ADAPTATIONS: James Baldwin adapted portions of *The Autobiography of Malcolm X* as *One Day, When I Was Lost: A Scenario,* Dial, 1973.

BIOGRAPHICAL/CRITICAL SOURCES:

BOOKS

Alexander, Rae Pace, *Young and Black in America,* Random House, 1973.

Breitman, George, *The Last Year of Malcolm X: The Evolution of a Revolutionary,* Merit Publications, 1967.

Clarke, John Henrik, editor and author of introduction, *Malcolm X: The Man and His Times,* Macmillan, 1969.

Curtis, Richard, *Life of Malcolm X,* Macrae Smith, 1971.

Darling, Edward, *When Sparks Fly Upward,* Washburn, 1970.

Goldman, Peter Louis, *Death and Life of Malcolm X,* University of Illinois Press, 1979.

Haskins, James, *Revolutionaries,* Lippincott, 1971.

Jamal, Hakin A., *From the Dead Level: Malcolm X and Me,* Random House, 1972.

Lomax, Louise E., *To Kill a Black Man,* Holloway House, 1968.

McKinley, James, *Assassination in America*, Harper, 1977.
Miah, Malik, editor and author of introduction, *Assassination of Malcolm X*, Pathfinder Press, 1976.
Paris, Peter J., *Black Leaders in Conflict: Joseph H. Jackson, Martin Luther King, Jr., Malcolm X, Adam Clayton Powell, Jr.*, Pilgrim Press, 1978.
Parks, Gordon, *Born Black*, Lippincott, 1971.
Playboy Interviews, Playboy Press, 1967.
Wolfenstein, Eugene Victor, *Victims of Democracy: Malcolm X and the Black Revolution*, University of California Press, 1981.

PERIODICALS

Catholic World, September, 1967.
Christian Century, April 7, 1965.
Ebony, October, 1965, June, 1969.
Encounter, September, 1973.
Harper's, June, 1964.
Life, March 20, 1964.
Journal of Black Studies, December, 1981.
Nation, March 8, 1965, November 8, 1965.
Negro Education Review, January, 1979.
New Statesman, June 12, 1964.
Newsweek, December 16, 1963, November 15, 1965, March 3, 1969, January 8, 1973, May 7, 1979.
New York Review of Books, November 11, 1965.
New York Times Book Review, September 11, 1966, April 13, 1969, May 16, 1971.
Saturday Review, November 20, 1965, July 30, 1966.
Spectator, February 26, 1965.
Time, March 5, 1965, February 23, 1970, June 12, 1972.
Times Literary Supplement, June 9, 1966, May 28, 1971.
Yale Review, December, 1966.

OBITUARIES:

PERIODICALS

New York Times, February 22, 1965.*

—Sketch by Les Stone

*   *   *

LLANO, George A(lbert) 1911-

PERSONAL: Born November 22, 1911, in Havana, Cuba; immigrated to the United States, naturalized citizen; married; children: three. *Education:* Cornell University, B.S., 1935; Columbia University, M.A., 1939; further graduate study at Harvard University, 1941-43, and University of Uppsala, 1946-47; Washington University, St. Louis, Mo., Ph.D., 1949.

CAREER: Biologist for U.S. Department of Agriculture, Soil Conservation Service in New York, 1935-37; instructor in biology and embryology at Pennsylvania Military College, 1940; Harvard University, Cambridge, Mass., instructor in biology and embryology, 1943; Washington University, St. Louis, Mo., microtechnician, 1946-48; Smithsonian Institution, Washington, D.C., associate curator of Division of Cryptogamia, 1948-51; Air University, Maxwell Air Force Base, Mobile, Ala., associate professor of botany, 1951-57; botanist for International Geophysical Year, U.S. National Committee, 1957-58; coordinator of biology and medical science program for Arctic Institute of North America, 1958-59; Library of Congress, Washington, D.C., scientific specialist in reference department of Scientific and Technical Division, 1960-61; National Science Foundation, Washington, D.C., director of Antarctic biology for Office of Antarctic Programs, Division of Envi-

ronmental Science, 1962-71, program manager of polar biology and medicine, Office of Polar Programs, National and International Programs, beginning in 1971. Research and education specialist at Arctic, Desert, and Tropic Information Center's Research Studies Institute, 1951-57; representative of U.S. Antarctic Research Program on USNS *Eltanin*, 1962-63, 1966-67, USCGC *Eastwind*, 1965-66, and *Glacier*, 1969. *Military service:* U.S. Army Air Forces, 1944-46. U.S. Air Force Reserve, 1946—; present rank, lieutenant colonel.

MEMBER: Arctic Institute of North America, American Bryological and Lichenological Society, American Geophysical Union, American Institute of Biological Sciences, American Polar Society, Lund Botanical Society.

AWARDS, HONORS: Fellow of Arctic Institute of North America at Arctic Laboratory in Point Barrow, Alaska, 1949-51.

WRITINGS:

A Monograph of the Lichen Family Umbilicariacene in the Western Hemisphere, Office of Naval Research, U.S. Department of the Navy, 1950.
Airmen Against the Sea: An Analysis of Sea Survival Experiences, Research Studies Institute, Arctic, Desert, and Tropic Information Center, c. 1955.
(Editor) *Biology of the Antarctic Seas*, American Geophysical Union, Volume II, 1965, Volume III (with Waldo Lasalle Schmitt), 1967, Volume IV (with I. Eugene Wallen), 1971.
(Editor) *Antarctic Terrestrial Biology*, American Geophysical Union, 1972.
Sharks: Attacks on Man, Grosset, 1976.
(Editor) *Adaptations Within Antarctic Ecosystems*, Gulf Publishing, 1977.

Editor of "Antarctic Research" series, American Geophysical Union, 1967.

*   *   *

LODDER, Christina (Anne) 1948-

PERSONAL: Born February 21, 1948, in Colchester, Essex, England; daughter of Reginald James (a civil servant) and Beatrice May Victoria Lodder; married Martin Anthony Hammer (an art historian), December 13, 1985. *Education:* University of York, B.A. (with honors), 1970; University of Sussex, M.A., 1971, D.Phil., 1980.

ADDRESSES: Office—University of St. Andrews, St. Andrews, Fife KY16 9AL, Scotland.

CAREER: Sotheby & Co. (art auction house), London, England, cataloguer and researcher, 1976-77; Polytechnic of North London, London, part-time instructor in Russian language and Soviet literature and politics, 1976-79; Architectural Association, London, visiting lectuer, 1978; Cambridge University, Cambridge, England, visiting lecturer associated with Department of Architecture, 1979; University of St. Andrews, St. Andrews, Scotland, lecturer in art history, 1979—. Consultant and supervisor for the Russian component of the Open University television series "Modern Art and Modernism" of the British Broadcasting Corporation, 1982-83; member of exhibitions committee of Scottish Arts Council, 1985—. Active in professional conferences and art exhibitions.

MEMBER: Association of Art Historians of Great Britain.

AWARDS, HONORS: Research scholarship from British Council for work in Department of Russian and Soviet Art History at University of Moscow, 1973-74 and 1977.

WRITINGS:

Russian Constructivism, Yale University Press, 1983.
(Contributor) S. Nash and J. Merker, editors, *Naum Gabo: Sixty Years of Constructivism,* Dallas Museum of Art, 1985.

Contributor of articles to periodicals, including *Architectural Association Quarterly, Architectural Design, Art Monthly,* and *Scottish Slavonic Review.* Scriptwriter and translator of course materials for Open University television series ''Modern Art and Modernism'' on British Broadcasting Corporation.

WORK IN PROGRESS: Catalog for exhibition of Soviet posters at Art Gallery of Ontario in Toronto, and research on sculptor Naum Gabo.

SIDELIGHTS: Russian Constructivism by Christina Lodder chronicles a movement in art that grew and flourished in Russia during the few years surrounding the Revolution of 1917, a time when a diverse group of artists and writers, known collectively as the Russian avant-garde, experimented with new styles of artistic expression. The constructivists in Russia tried to combine the abstract visual style of Western artistic movements such as cubism with a Marxist emphasis on making art relevant to the everyday lives of workers. Accordingly, the artists used materials and designs from modern industry in their work, and some sought employment as designers in factories. Writing in the *New York Review of Books,* John E. Bowlt predicted that Lodder's analysis of the constructivist movement ''will long serve as an essential reference book on the development of the Russian avant-garde during the 1920s.''

Lodder's account discusses individual constructivist artists, the social setting in which they worked, and their accomplishments. Along with providing short biographies of the artists involved, Lodder describes the relationship of constructivism to the fledgling Soviet bureaucracy, which fostered the movement in the first few years after the Revolution by providing official encouragement and funds for artistic projects.

Separate chapters of her book explore the critical theories behind constructivism and describe the art instruction given by participants in the movement. Not only does the author examine constructivist sculpture and painting, but also the artists' efforts to apply their ideas to the design of furniture, textiles, and stage sets. Bowlt found Lodder's survey of such practical applications ''of particular interest,'' pointing out that ''it was through such disciplines that the Constructivists tried to put their often utopian ideas into practice.'' Lodder also discusses the favorable attention constructivism gained in the West, as at the Russian Exhibition of 1922 in Berlin.

Both Jamey Gambrell in *Art in America* and Bowlt were impressed by the extensive scholarly research reflected in *Russian Constructivism.* Gambrell observed that the book ''is clearly written, convincingly argued and supported by extensive, meticulous documentation from Soviet state and private archives.''

BIOGRAPHICAL/CRITICAL SOURCES:

PERIODICALS

Art in America, February, 1984.
New York Review of Books, February 16, 1984.

LOFTHOUSE, Jessica   1916-1988

OBITUARY NOTICE—See index for *CA* sketch: Born November 9, 1916, in Clitheroe, Lancashire, England; died March 31, 1988. Educator, journalist, and author. Lofthouse was known for her travel books on England. She worked as a schoolmistress from 1937 to 1959 and wrote for various periodicals. Among her works are *The Rediscovery of the North: Exploration on Foot and by Car, Off to the Lakes: A Lakeland Walking Year, The Curious Traveller Through Lakeland, Countrygoer in the Dales,* and *North Wales for the Countrygoer.* She was also a longtime contributor to such publications as the *Blackburn Times* and *Lancashire Life.*

OBITUARIES AND OTHER SOURCES:

PERIODICALS

Times (London), April 5, 1988.

*   *   *

LONG, Steven   1944-

PERSONAL: Born July 17, 1944, in Galveston, Tex.; son of Jacob Hayward (a farmer) and Edna (a homemaker; maiden name, Earle) Long; married Jo L. Mihovil, 1966 (marriage ended, 1977); married Peggy A. Caddell, 1979 (marriage ended, 1988); children: (first marriage) Michelle Bernadette, Mary Monique. *Education:* Attended Texas Lutheran College, 1962, Sam Houston State University, 1963, and Alvin Junior College, 1964-68. *Politics:* Democrat. *Religion:* Catholic.

ADDRESSES: Home—3007 Avenue O½, Galveston, Tex. 77550. *Agent*—Edward J. Acton Inc., 928 Broadway, New York, N.Y. 10010.

CAREER: National promotion director for Horizon Records Corporation, 1968-70; studio manager for Andrus Recording Studio, 1970; partner in Blomstrom, Long & Associates, 1974-77; *In Between,* Galveston and Houston, Tex., publisher and editor, 1977—; free-lance writer for magazines, 1980—.

MEMBER: Press Club of Galveston County.

AWARDS, HONORS: ''Trouble in Paradise'' named best feature, 1985, and ''We Mourn'' named best editorial, 1986, both by Press Club of Galveston County; Gavel award from the State Bar of Texas, 1987, for *Death Without Dignity: The Story of the First Nursing Home Corporation Indicted for Murder.*

WRITINGS:

Death Without Dignity: The Story of the First Nursing Home Corporation Indicted for Murder, Texas Monthly Press, 1987.
Perot: America's Most Flamboyant Businessman (biography), McGraw, 1988.

Contributor of articles to periodicals, including *Texas Observer, Houston City Magazine, Houston Style,* and *Houston Business Journal.*

SIDELIGHTS: Steven Long told *CA:* ''My writing often reflects the dark side of contemporary American life such as nursing home abuse and neglect, as in *Death Without Dignity,* and teenage suicide, as in 'Trouble in Paradise.' Yet I am generally a happy, sunny person who enjoys life. I have an insatiable curiosity about almost everything—that's what makes me a journalist.

"My favorite authors are Thomas Thompson, Gary Cartwright, Larry McMurtry, Luigi Barzini, and Umberto Eco. These writers display a wide range of style, and my writing style is a reflection of their influences. I feel that writing a book is just like running a marathon—you do it alone—and at the end the emotions are the same—you cry."

AVOCATIONAL INTERESTS: Traveling in Italy, the Italian language, international politics, European and American contemporary history, business, health care for the elderly, classical music, water sports.

*   *   *

LORIS, Joseph James   1943-1987

OBITUARY NOTICE: Born March 19, 1943, in Philadelphia, Pa.; died of a heart attack, June 29, 1987, in Philadelphia, Pa. Business executive and publisher. In 1976 Loris founded a national trade magazine for the recording industry, *Impact*, and served as its president and publisher. The weekly, which is circulated among record companies, radio stations, and magazines, is considered the authoritative journal on black popular music.

OBITUARIES AND OTHER SOURCES:

BOOKS

Who's Who Among Black Americans, 4th edition, Who's Who Among Black Americans, 1985.

PERIODICALS

Chicago Tribune, July 5, 1987.
Washington Post, July 6, 1987.

*   *   *

LOTH, David   1899-1988

OBITUARY NOTICE—See index for *CA* sketch: Born December 7, 1899, in St. Louis, Mo.; died May 29, 1988, in Boulder, Colo. Information director, publisher, journalist, and author. Loth wrote many volumes of nonfiction. During the 1920s and 1930s he worked for newspapers, reporting for Australia's *Daily Guardian* and both editing and publishing Spain's *Majorca Sun*. He subsequently worked as a copy editor for the *New York Times* and as managing editor of Press Research. From the mid-1940s to the mid-1960s Loth was director of information for various organizations and educational institutions, including Columbia University and Finch College. His books include *The Brownings: A Victorian Idyll; Charles II, Ruler and Rake; The Columbia Bicentennial; The Erotic in Literature;* and *Crime in the Suburbs*.

OBITUARIES AND OTHER SOURCES:

BOOKS

Who's Who, 140th edition, St. Martin's, 1988.

PERIODICALS

New York Times, June 3, 1988.

*   *   *

LOURIE, Richard   1940-

BRIEF ENTRY: American translator, literary critic, and novelist. Recipient of the 1971 Joseph Henry Jackson Award for fiction, Lourie is the author of three novels, *Sagittarius in*

Warsaw (Vanguard Press, 1973), *First Loyalty* (Harcourt, 1985), and *Zero Gravity* (Harcourt, 1987). The first book is an absurdist tale about an American's bizarre experiences aboard a train in Poland. *First Loyalty*, blending philosophical discussion with suspenseful action, concerns a Soviet agent posing as a dissenting poet who defects to the United States, later to denounce the West. In Lourie's spoof thriller *Zero Gravity*, the Soviet Union and the United States vie to send the first poet to the moon, eventually agreeing to pursue the endeavor jointly. The author's extensive critical analysis of Russian dissenter Andrei Sinyavsky, who published fiction under the pseudonym Abram Tertz, was published in 1975 as *Letters to the Future: An Approach to Sinyavsky-Tertz* (Cornell University Press). Lourie is also a prolific translator of Russian and Polish texts, among them Soviet writer Vladimir Voinovich's *The Life and Extraordinary Adventures of Private Ivan Chonkin* (Farrar, Straus, 1976), *The Anti-Soviet Soviet Union* (Harcourt, 1986), and *Moscow Two Thousand Forty-two* (Harcourt, 1987); Polish Nobel Prize-winning poet Czeslaw Milosz's *Visions From San Francisco Bay* (Farrar, Straus, 1982); and *The Liberation of One: The Autobiography of Romuald Spasowski, Polish Ambassador to the United States* (Harcourt, 1986). *Addresses: Home*—Newton, Mass.

BIOGRAPHICAL/CRITICAL SOURCES:

PERIODICALS

Los Angeles Times Book Review, September 13, 1987.
Newsweek, August 26, 1985.
New York Times, October 12, 1987.
New York Times Book Review, August 4, 1985, August 31, 1986, August 30, 1987, October 18, 1987.
Times Literary Supplement, July 26, 1974.

*   *   *

LOW, Rachael   1923-

PERSONAL: Born July 6, 1923, in London, England; daughter of David (a cartoonist) and Madeline (Kenning) Low; married Michael Clement Whear, August 30, 1948; children: Madeline Watt, Nicholas Whear. *Education:* London School of Economics and Political Science, B.Sc., 1944, Ph.D., 1950.

ADDRESSES: Home—Cambridge, England.

CAREER: British Film Institute, London, England, researcher, 1945-48; writer. Lucy Cavendish College, Cambridge, Gubelkian research fellow, 1968-71.

WRITINGS:

(With Roger Manvell) *The History of the British Film*, Allen & Unwin, Volume I (covering years 1896-1906), 1948; Volume II (covering years 1906-1914), 1949; Volume III (covering years 1914-1918), 1950; Volume IV (covering years 1918-1929), 1971; Volume V: *Films of Comment and Persuasion of the 1930s*, 1979; Volume VI: *Documentary and Educational Films of the 1930s*, 1979; Volume VII: *Film Making in 1930s Britain*, 1985.

*   *   *

LOWE, Carl   1949-

PERSONAL: Born June 23, 1949, in New York, N.Y. *Education:* Yale University, B.A., 1971.

ADDRESSES: Office—Rebus, Inc., 632 Broadway, New York, N.Y. 10012.

CAREER: Rebus, Inc., New York, N.Y., senior nutrition editor of Time-Life Books series "Fitness, Health, Nutrition," 1987-88.

WRITINGS:

Television and American Culture, H. W. Wilson, 1982.
Whole Body Healing, Rodale Press, 1983.
The Complete Book of Vitamins, Rodale Press, 1984.
Reaganomics, H. W. Wilson, 1984.

WORK IN PROGRESS: A novel; short stories.

*   *   *

LUBIN, Leonard
See LUBIN, Leonard B.

*   *   *

LUBIN, Leonard B.   1943-
(Leonard Lubin)

PERSONAL: Born November 27, 1943, in Detroit, Mich.; son of Arnold and Annette (Wexler) Lubin. *Education:* Received diploma from John Herron School of Art, 1965.

ADDRESSES: Home—367 6th St., Brooklyn, N.Y. 11215. *Agent*—Dilys Evans, 1123 Broadway, New York, N.Y. 10010.

CAREER: Artist, author and illustrator of books mainly for children. Worked in various positions, including antique shop owner, free-lance artist, window dresser, and bookstore salesman, 1965-75; illustrator and writer, 1975—.

AWARDS, HONORS: The Pig-Tale obtained a Lewis Carroll Shelf Award, and *New York Times* listing as one of the year's best-illustrated books, both 1975, and was selected for the Children's Book Showcase, 1976; *The Little Swineherd, and Other Tales* was included in the American Institute of Graphic Arts Book Show, 1979; *The Birthday of the Infanta* won an American Book Award for illustration, 1980, and was chosen by *School Library Journal* as one of the year's best books, 1981.

WRITINGS:

(Illustrator) Lewis Carroll, *The Pig-Tale,* Little, Brown, 1975.
(Illustrator) Veronica S. Hutchinson, reteller, *Henny Penny* (juvenile), Little, Brown, 1976.
(Illustrator) Stephen Schwartz, *The Perfect Peach: A Story* (juvenile), Little, Brown, 1977.
(Adapter and illustrator) Madame d'Aulnoy, *The White Cat* (juvenile), Little, Brown, 1978.
This Little Pig: A Mother Goose Favorite (juvenile), self-illustrated, Lothrop, 1985.
Sing a Song of Sixpence: A Favorite Mother Goose Rhyme (juvenile), self-illustrated, Lothrop, 1987.

UNDER NAME LEONARD LUBIN

(Illustrator) Paula Fox, *The Little Swineherd, and Other Tales* (juvenile), Dutton, 1978.
(Illustrator) Oscar Wilde, *The Birthday of the Infanta,* Viking, 1979.
The Elegant Beast, self-illustrated, Viking, 1981.
(Illustrator) W. S. Gilbert, *Gilbert Without Sullivan* (libretti selection; contains "H.M.S. Pinafore," "The Pirates of Penzance," "The Mikado," and "The Gondoliers"), Viking, 1981.

(Adapter and illustrator) *Aladdin and His Wonderful Lamp* (juvenile), translation from the Arabic by Richard F. Burton, Delacorte, 1982.
(Illustrator) Isabelle Holland, *Kevin's Hat* (juvenile), Lothrop, 1984.
(Illustrator) Jane Leslie Conly, *Racso and the Rats of NIMH* (juvenile) Harper, 1986.*

*   *   *

LUCAS, Stephen E.   1946-

PERSONAL: Born October 5, 1946, in White Plains, N.Y.; son of Henry Edward (an air force officer) and Inez (a bookkeeper; maiden name, Brown) Lucas; married Patricia Jean Vore (a reading specialist), June 14, 1969; children: Jeffrey, Ryan. *Education:* University of California, Santa Barbara, B.A., 1968; Pennsylvania State University, M.A., 1970, Ph.D., 1972.

ADDRESSES: Home—Madison, Wis. *Office*—Department of Communication Arts, University of Wisconsin—Madison, Madison, Wis. 53706.

CAREER: University of Wisconsin—Madison, assistant professor, 1972-76, associate professor, 1976-82, professor of communication arts, 1982—. Radio and television consultant on American political oratory.

MEMBER: International Society for the History of Rhetoric, Organization of American Historians, Society of Eighteenth-Century Studies, Institute of Early American History and Culture, Speech Communication Association, Central States Speech Communication Association.

AWARDS, HONORS: Pulitzer Prize nomination, 1976, and Golden Anniversary Award from the Speech Communication Association, 1977, both for *Portents of Rebellion.*

WRITINGS:

Portents of Rebellion: Rhetoric and Revolution in Philadelphia, 1765-1776, Temple University Press, 1976.
The Art of Public Speaking, Random House, 1983, 3rd edition, in press.

Contributor of articles and reviews to speech, communication, and history journals. Member of editorial board of *Communication Monographs* and *Quarterly Journal of Speech.*

WORK IN PROGRESS: A monograph on the Declaration of Independence as a rhetorical work; a monograph on George Washington and the art of oratory.

SIDELIGHTS: Stephen E. Lucas told *CA: "The Art of Public Speaking* is one of the most successful textbooks of its kind in the history of college publishing. Revising it from edition to edition to keep the material current and well-geared to the needs of today's students is a constant challenge—especially in combination with the demands of also writing scholarly books and articles. Yet it is extremely rewarding to know that one is having an impact on the teaching of public speaking and the education of students all across the country. No teacher could ask for more."

BIOGRAPHICAL/CRITICAL SOURCES:

PERIODICALS

American Historical Review, February, 1978.
Journalism History, summer, 1977.
Quarterly Journal of Speech, February, 1977.

LYNN, (Dorcas) Joanne (Harley) 1951-

PERSONAL: Born July 2, 1951, in Oakland, Md.; daughter of John B. (a physician) and Mary Dorcas (a physician; maiden name, Clark) Harley; married Barry W. Lynn (an attorney), June 6, 1970; children: Christina, Nicholas. *Education:* Dickinson College, B.S., 1970; Boston University, M.D., 1974; George Washington University, M.A., 1982.

ADDRESSES: Home—11711 Amkin Dr., Clifton, Va. 22024. *Office*—ICU Research, George Washington University, 2300 K St. N.W., Washington, D.C. 20037.

CAREER: Private practice in Clinton, Maryland, 1979; George Washington University, Washington, D.C., faculty associate for medicine and humanities in Division of Experimental Programs, 1978-81, associate professor of health care sciences and medicine in Division of Geriatric Medicine, 1979—, co-director of Division of ICU Research, 1986—. Medical director of Washington Home and Hospice of Washington. Assistant director of medical studies for President's Commission for the Study of Ethical Problems in Medicine and Biomedical and Behavioral Research, 1981-83.

MEMBER: American Association for the Advancement of Science, American Bar Association Commission on Legal Problems of the Elderly, American College of Physicians (fellow, 1987), American Geriatrics Society (committee on public policy, 1983—), American Medical Director's Association, Concern for Dying (board of directors, 1985—), Hastings Institute (fellow, 1984, vice-president, 1987), International Hospice Institute (physician's advisory committee, 1984—), Medical and Chirurgical Faculty of the State of Maryland, Medical Society of the District of Columbia (legislative affairs committee, 1985—), Society for Health and Human Values, Society for Research and Education in Primary Care Internal Medicine.

AWARDS, HONORS: Grand Prize overall and in veterinary medicine from International Science Fair, 1967; Robert Wood Johnson Clinical Scholar, 1976-78.

WRITINGS:

(Editor and contributor) *By No Extraordinary Means: The Choice to Forego Life-Sustaining Food and Water*, Indiana University Press, 1986.

CONTRIBUTOR

C. Cassel and J. R. Walsh, editors, *Geriatric Medicine: Principles and Practice*, Springer-Verlag, 1984.

R. E. Cranford and A. E. Doudera, editors, *Institutional Ethics Committees and Health Care Decision-Making*, University of Michigan Health Administration Press, with American Society of Law and Medicine, 1984.

P. Torrens, editor, *Hospice Programs and Public Policy*, American Hospital Association, 1985.

L. Paradis, editor, *Hospice Handbook: A Guide for Managers and Planners*, Aspen Systems, 1985.

E. Doudera, M. B. Kapp, and H. E. Pies, editors, *Legal and Ethical Aspects of Health Care for the Elderly*, Health Administration Press, 1985.

J. Walton and P. B. Beeson, editors, *The Oxford Companion to Medicine*, Oxford University Press, 1986.

K. V. Iserson, A. B. Sanders, D. R. Mathieu, and A. E. Buchman, *Ethics in Emergency Medicine*, Williams & Wilkins, 1986.

J. E. Hamner III and B. J. S. Jacobs, editors, *Life and Death Issues*, University of Tennessee Press, 1986.

Contributor of numerous articles to professional journals, including *Journal of Medical Education, Medical Ethics for the Physician*, and *New England Journal of Medicine*.

WORK IN PROGRESS: Research on prognosis and decision-making for critically ill, hospitalized adults; development of guidelines for the care of dying persons in health care facilities.

SIDELIGHTS: Joanne Lynn told *CA:* "*By No Extraordinary Means: The Choice to Forego Life-Sustaining Food and Water* grew out of a very rewarding conference sponsored by the Society for Health and Human Values. It addresses what is probably the most commonly identified problem in nursing homes: whether or not patients must be artificially fed.

"While I have resolved some aspects of the issue, on others I am quite uncertain. There are people whose lives are rendered miserable or meaningless by being force-fed and we should learn to abstain from causing that. However, what we should do in regard to permanently unconscious or severely demented persons is more troubling.

"Since publication of the book, there have been a large number of court cases, legislative actions, and publications on the issue. We do seem, as a society, to be moving toward intelligent discussion of the issues and possibly toward resolution of the range of options that will be open to patients."

M

MABIE, Margot C(auldwell) J(ones) 1944-

PERSONAL: Born November 9, 1944, in Utica, N.Y.; daughter of Vincent Starbuck (a newspaper editor) and Nancy vanDyke (a housewife; maiden name, Parsons) Jones; married James Tucker Mabie (an assistant headmaster), June 26, 1971; children: Jocelyn Naizing. *Education:* Mills College, B.A., 1966.

ADDRESSES: Home—13 Oval Ave., Riverside, Conn. 06878.

CAREER: Harcourt Brace Jovanovich, Inc., New York, N.Y., sales correspondent in college department, 1967-68, art editor, 1968-70, copy editor, 1970-71; art teacher at school in Sheffield, Mass., 1971-74; Harcourt Brace Jovanovich, Inc., copy editor in trade department, 1974-78, associate editor, 1978-81; free-lance writer and editor, 1981—.

WRITINGS:

Vietnam There and Here (young adult), Holt, 1985.
The Constitution: Reflection of a Changing Nation (young adult), Holt, 1987.

Contributor to local magazines and newspapers.

*   *   *

MACARTNEY, (Carlile) Aylmer 1895-1978

OBITUARY NOTICE—See index for *CA* sketch: Born January 24, 1895, in Kent, England; died June 18, 1978. Government official, intelligence worker, historian, educator, broadcaster, editor, and author. Macartney was an authority on European history. During the early 1920s he worked as British vice-consul in Vienna, and in 1928 he began eight years of service with the intelligence department of the League of Nations Union. From 1936 to 1965 Macartney was a research fellow at Oxford University's All Souls College, and from 1949 to 1956 he was also Montagu Burton Professor of International Relations at the University of Edinburgh. In addition, he worked in Munich as a broadcaster for Radio Free Europe. Among Macartney's writings are *The Social Revolution in Austria; Studies in the Earliest Hungarian Historical Sources; A History of Hungary, 1929-1944;* and *The Hapsburg Empire, 1790-1918.* He also edited the volume *Hapsburg and Hohenzollern Dynasties in the Seventeenth and Eighteenth Centuries.*

OBITUARIES AND OTHER SOURCES:

BOOKS

Who Was Who, Volume VII: *1971-1980,* A. & C. Black, 1981.

*   *   *

MacCULLOCH, Diarmaid 1951-

PERSONAL: Given name is pronounced "*Der*-mid"; born October 31, 1951, in Folkestone, England; son of Nigel (an Anglican priest) and Jennie (a housewife; maiden name, Chappell) MacCulloch. *Education:* Cambridge University, M.A., 1972, Ph.D., 1976; University of Liverpool, Diploma in Archive Administration, 1973; Oxford University, Diploma in Theology, 1987. *Politics:* Socialist.

ADDRESSES: Home—Wesley College, Henbury Rd., Bristol BS10 7QD, England.

CAREER: Ordained priest of Church of England, 1988; Cambridge University, Cambridge, England, junior research fellow of Churchill College, 1976-78; University of Bristol, Bristol, England, lecturer in history, 1978—. Tutor at Wesley College, 1978—; corresponding fellow of University of East Anglia, 1986—.

MEMBER: Royal Historical Society (fellow), Society of Antiquaries of London (fellow).

AWARDS, HONORS: Whitfield Prize from Royal Historical Society, 1986, for *Suffolk and the Tudors.*

WRITINGS:

(Editor) *The Chorography of Suffolk,* Suffolk Records Society, 1976.
Suffolk and the Tudors: Politics and Religion in an English County, 1500-1600, Clarendon Press, 1986.
Groundwork of Christian History, Epworth, 1987.
(With J. Comby) *How to Read Church History,* Volume II, SCM Press, 1988.
Society and Religion in England, 1547-1603, Macmillan, in press.

Contributor to history magazines.

WORK IN PROGRESS: Thomas Ganmer, publication by Basil Blackwell expected in 1995.

BIOGRAPHICAL/CRITICAL SOURCES:

PERIODICALS

History Today, July, 1987.
Times Literary Supplement, February 6, 1987.

*   *   *

MacDONALD, Anson
See HEINLEIN, Robert A(nson)

*   *   *

MacDONALD, Suse   1940-

PERSONAL: Given name rhymes with "news"; born March 3,1940, in Evanston, Ill.; daughter of Stewart Y. (a professor) and Constance R. McMullen; married Stuart G. MacDonald (an owner of a construction company), July 14, 1962; children: Alison Heath, Ripley Graeme. *Education:* Attended Chatham College, 1958-60; University of Iowa, B.A., 1962; also attended Radcliffe College, Art Institute, and New England School of Art and Design.

ADDRESSES: Home—Box 86, Weston, Vt. 05161. *Studio*—Box 25, South Londonderry, Vt. 05155. *Agent*—Phyllis Wender, 3 East 48th St., New York, N.Y. 10017.

CAREER: United Press International, New York City, executive secretary to the picture editor, 1964; Caru Studios, New York City, textbook illustrator, 1964-69; MacDonald & Swan Construction, South Londonderry, Vt., architectural designer, 1969-76; author and illustrator, 1976—. Co-founder, past president, and co-director of Little School Nursery and Day Care Center.

MEMBER: Society of Children's Book Writers, Authors Guild.

AWARDS, HONORS: Alphabatics was the "editor's choice" of *Book List,* 1986; it was also on the *School Library Journal*'s "best books of the year" list and the American Booksellers Association "pick of the lists," 1986; Golden Kite Award from Society of Children's Book Writers and Caldecott Honor Award from American Library Association, 1987, also for *Alphabatics.*

WRITINGS:

Alphabatics (children's picture book; Junior Literary Guild selection), Bradbury, 1986.
(With Bill Oakes) *Numblers* (children's picture book), Dial, 1988.

WORK IN PROGRESS: "Bill Oakes and I are planning to do a number of books together. As with *Alphabatics* and *Numblers,* they will encourage children to use their imaginations; to develop the ability to make spontaneous connections between unrelated objects; and to look at the world in new ways."

SIDELIGHTS: Suse MacDonald told *CA:* "After college I married, and my husband and I settled in New York City. I wanted to get a job using my artistic talents, but several years passed before I landed a position at Caru Studios, where I made illustrations for textbooks. I stayed there for five years.

"Then my husband and I moved back to the family farm in Weston, Vermont, and took over a construction company. We worked together in the construction business for ten years and raised two children. While both kids were young, we spent a lot of time at the farm pond, and I found myself searching, as I had when I was a child, among the reeds and beneath the surface to find out what lived there. I began making drawings and thinking once again about illustrating books.

"When our second child entered first grade, I decided to pursue that interest. I quit my job and went back to school. I drove back and forth between Vermont and Boston for four years, attending classes at Radcliffe, the Art Institute, the New England School of Art and Design, and other schools in the city. I took courses in all sorts of things, including illustration, silkscreening, paper making, sketching, drawing, design, topography, and writing. It is hard to pinpoint the time when I decided that children's book illustration was the field in which I wanted to concentrate my energies. My interests just seemed to lean in that direction.

"Eventually I enrolled in Marion Perry's classes in children's book writing and illustration at Radcliffe. It was then that I really became involved in children's books. I wrote and illustrated several stories, including 'Matt the Fat Cat,' a tale which my young son had written.

"After completing my studies, I bought an old house in South Londonderry, Vermont, in partnership with two other artists. We spent six months renovating the building and setting up six artist's studios, one for each of us and three which we rent. I put together a portfolio and began to look for work, in both advertising and the children's book field. My first assignments were paper sculpture for advertising. These kept me going financially as I began to make the rounds of the publishers.

"*Alphabatics* is the result of an idea which I had for a long time. The idea emerged from the wealth of information which I gathered while taking topography in art school. In that course, we worked exclusively with letter forms, shrinking and expanding them and manipulating their shapes in various ways. I was intrigued by the process and felt there were possibilities in it for a book. It was several years, however, before I put my ideas down on paper. Once I did, the first publisher I showed it to liked the idea, and I was on my way.

"Selling this book, which is my first, has been very exciting. I love the picture book format and feel it offers challenging opportunities for creative illustration."

*   *   *

MACY, Joanna Rogers   1929-

PERSONAL: Born May 2, 1929, in Los Angeles, Calif.; daughter of Hartley (a stockbroker) and Margaret (a housewife and office manager; maiden name, Kinsey) Rogers; married Francis Underhill Macy (an educator), May 30, 1953; children: Christopher, John, Margaret. *Education:* Wellesley College, B.A., 1950; graduate study at the University of Bordeaux; Syracuse University, Ph.D., 1978.

ADDRESSES: Home—1306 Bay View Pl., Berkeley, Calif. 94708. *Office*—California Institute of Integral Studies, 765 Ashbury St., San Francisco, Calif. 94117.

CAREER: Syracuse University, Syracuse, N.Y., lecturer in religion, 1976-77; American University, Washington, D.C., lecturer in religion, 1978-79; writer and researcher, 1980-86; professor at California Institute of Integral Studies, San Francisco, 1987—. Staff associate of Shalem Institute for Spiritual Formation, 1979—; co-director of Interhelp, 1980—; member of board of directors of Sarvodaya International, 1981—; associate of Center for Cooperative Global Development, 1981—.

MEMBER: Society for Values in Higher Education, Society for General Systems Research, American Academy of Religion, Buddhist Peace Fellowship.

AWARDS, HONORS: Fulbright scholarship, Ford Foundation grant, 1979-80.

WRITINGS:

Dharma and Development, Kumarian Press, 1982, revised edition, 1985.
Despair and Personal Power in the Nuclear Age, New Society Publications, 1983.

Contributor of articles on Buddhist metaphysics and ethics to philosophy journals.

WORK IN PROGRESS: Research on Buddhism as a resource for social action; research on the theory and practice of "deep ecology."

SIDELIGHTS: Joanna Rogers Macy told *CA:* "I am active as a speaker, trainer, and workshop leader within the context of citizen action for justice, peace, and ecological survival. My teaching at the California Institute of Integral Studies focuses on general systems theory, Buddhism, and nonviolence."

BIOGRAPHICAL/CRITICAL SOURCES:

PERIODICALS

Yoga Journal, January/February, 1985.

* * *

MAGNIN, Cyril I(saac) 1899-1988

OBITUARY NOTICE—See index for *CA* sketch: Born July 6, 1899, in San Francisco, Calif.; died of cardiac failure, June 8, 1988, in San Francisco, Calif. Retail trade executive, philanthropist, and author of an autobiography. Magnin was known for his business success, his charity work, and his tireless endeavors on behalf of San Francisco. As head of a chain of thirty-six department stores, he pioneered the development of junior fashions. He also became known as an avid promoter of San Francisco, often assisting city officials by entertaining important visitors. Through his enthusiasm and ready services Magnin gained the nickname Mr. San Francisco and the title of official protocol chief. In addition, he used his fund-raising skills in assisting various charities, including the March of Dimes and the American Cancer Society. Magnin's autobiography, *Call Me Cyril,* was published in 1981.

OBITUARIES AND OTHER SOURCES:

BOOKS

Who's Who in America, 43rd edition, Marquis, 1984.

PERIODICALS

Los Angeles Times, June 9, 1988.
New York Times, June 9, 1988.

* * *

MAINLAND, William Faulkner 1905-1988(?)

OBITUARY NOTICE: Born May 31, 1905; died c. 1988. Educator, translator, editor, and author. A professor of German at England's University of Sheffield for seventeen years,

Mainland was an authority on the German poet, playwright, and critic Johann Schiller. He wrote a collection of essays on the writer's poetic philosophy, *Schiller and the Changing Past,* and edited at least two of his works, *Jungfrau Versus Orleans,* with E. J. Engel, and *Wilhelm Tell.* Mainland also wrote *German for Students of Medicine* and, with August Closs, *German Lyrics of the Seventeenth Century;* he translated *Wilhelm Tell* and edited E. T. A. Hoffmann's *Der goldene Topf.* Prior to joining the faculty at Sheffield, Mainland taught at the University of Manitoba and at University College, King's College, and Birkbeck College of the University of London.

OBITUARIES AND OTHER SOURCES:

BOOKS

International Authors and Writers Who's Who, 8th edition, Melrose, 1977.
Who's Who, 140th edition, St. Martin's, 1988.

PERIODICALS

Times (London), May 27, 1988.

* * *

MALAMUD, Phyllis Carole 1938-

PERSONAL: Born September 15, 1938, in Brooklyn, N.Y.; daughter of Louis (a cantor) and Hannah (a housewife; maiden name, Unterman) Malamud; married Matthew A. Clark, Jr. (a medical writer), November 9, 1986. *Education:* City College of the City University of New York, B.A., 1960; graduate study at Washington University, St. Louis, Mo., 1968-69.

ADDRESSES: Office—*Newsweek,* 444 Madison Ave., New York, N.Y. 10022.

CAREER/WRITINGS: Newsweek, New York, N.Y., publicity assistant, 1960-62, researcher, 1962-64, feature reporter, 1964-74, New York political reporter, 1975-77, chief of New England bureau in Boston, Mass., 1977—, editor of column "My Turn," 1983—.

MEMBER: Coffee House.

AWARDS, HONORS: Gavel Award from American Bar Association, 1968; award from American Psychological Association, 1975; award from New York Newspaper Guild, 1977.

* * *

MALCOLM X
See LITTLE, Malcolm

* * *

MANDELA, Nelson R(olihlahla) 1918-

PERSONAL: Born 1918 in Umtata, Transkei, South Africa; son of Henry (a Tembu tribal chief) Mandela; married Edith Ntoko (a nurse; divorced); married Nomzamo Winnie Madikileza (a social worker and political activist), June 14, 1958; children: (first marriage) two sons (one deceased) and one daughter, Makaziwe Phumla Mandela; (second marriage) Zenani (married to Prince Thumbumuzi Dhlamini of Swaziland), Zindziswa. *Education:* Attended University College of Fort Hare and Witwatersrand University; University of South Africa, law degree, 1942.

ADDRESSES: Pollsmoor Prison, Cape Town, South Africa; c/o African National Congress of South Africa, 801 Second Avenue, New York, N.Y. 10017.

CAREER: Mandela and Tambo law firm, Johannesburg, South Africa, partner, 1952- c. 1960; political organizer and leader of the African National Congress (ANC), Johannesburg, South Africa, 1944—, held successive posts as secretary and president of the Congress Youth League, deputy national president of the ANC, and commander of the Umkonto we Sizwe ("Spear of the Nation") paramilitary organization; sentenced to five years in prison for inciting Africans to strike and for leaving South Africa without a valid travel document, 1962; sentenced to life imprisonment for sabotage and treason, 1964; incarcerated in various penal institutions, including Robben Island and Pollsmoor prisons, South Africa, 1962—.

AWARDS, HONORS: Honorary doctor of laws degrees from the National University of Lesotho, 1979, and City College of the City University of New York, 1983; Jawaharlal Nehru Award for International Understanding from the government of India, 1980; Bruno Kreisky Prize for Human Rights from the government of Austria, 1981; named honorary citizen of Glasgow, 1981, and Rome, 1983; Simon Bolivar International Prize from UNESCO, 1983; nominated for 1987 Nobel Peace Prize.

WRITINGS:

No Easy Walk to Freedom (nonfiction), Basic Books, 1965.
Nelson Mandela Speaks (nonfiction), African National Congress Publicity and Information Bureau (London), c. 1970.
The Struggle Is My Life (nonfiction), International Defence and Aid Fund (London), 1978, revised and updated edition published by Pathfinder Press, 1986.

Contributor of articles to the South African political journal *Liberation*, 1953-59.

SIDELIGHTS: Nelson and Winnie Mandela have been called "the first family of South Africa's freedom fight." Through their charismatic leadership and great personal sacrifices, the husband-and-wife team have come to symbolize the struggle against apartheid, the system of enforced racial inequality that denies political rights to the country's black majority. Nelson Mandela, a leader of the banned African National Congress (ANC) insurgent movement, has been jailed by white governments for the past quarter of a century for his efforts to enfranchise his fellow blacks. His incarceration has raised his political prestige to almost messianic proportions in the eyes of his oppressed countrymen, and public opinion polls show that he would easily be elected South Africa's first black prime minister if democratic elections were held today. Many political observers believe that the nationalist leader represents the last hope for achieving a negotiated solution between blacks and whites in the current South African climate of rising violence and racial polarization, but the governing authorities have resisted a worldwide campaign to free him. During the course of her husband's long confinement, Winnie Mandela has carried his political torch with distinction, enduring repeated jailings, banishment, and house arrest to emerge as a redoubtable leader in her own right and the most visible and outspoken antagonist of white minority government in South Africa today.

Both Nelson and Winnie Mandela are descended from Xhosa-speaking tribal chieftains from the Transkei region of South Africa. Because of their eighteen-year age difference, Nelson Mandela had already become a well-known political figure

while his future wife was still a schoolgirl. As Winnie was to do some years later, Nelson left his ancestral home at a young age to avoid an arranged marriage and pursue a professional career in the commercial capital of Johannesburg. He was soon drawn to the struggle for black social and political rights being waged by the ANC and decided to study law to prepare for a political career. Obtaining his law degree from the University of South Africa in 1942, Nelson Mandela joined the ANC two years later at the age of twenty-six and helped found the Congress Youth League (CYL) with Walter Sisulu, Oliver Tambo, and others. With Mandela as its secretary, the CYL urged its parent organization (the ANC) to abandon the strictly constitutional approach to reform that it had fruitlessly pursued with successive white minority governments since its founding in 1912 and to pursue a more militant and confrontational strategy. Under strong youth pressure, the ANC adopted a new program of action in 1949 that recognized such nonviolent but sometimes illegal tactics as electoral boycotts, "stay-at-homes" (general strikes), student demonstrations, and civil disobedience as legitimate weapons in the struggle to win black rights.

In June, 1952, Nelson Mandela mounted the first major test of the new ANC program by organizing the Defiance Against Unjust Laws campaign, a coordinated civil disobedience of six selected apartheid laws by a multiracial group of some eighty-six hundred volunteers. The legal and social code known as apartheid (meaning "apartness" in the Afrikaans language) denied South African blacks—who make up three-quarters of the country's population—the right to vote or run for national public office. It also restricted them to low-paying occupations, prevented them from choosing freely where to live, travel, and work, and kept them rigidly segregated from whites in all public facilities. The government's heavy-handed response of beatings and jailings to the Defiance Campaign generated a backlash of popular support for the ANC that helped thrust Nelson Mandela into national prominence. It also brought him a nine-month suspended jail sentence, a two-year government "banning" order that confined him to Johannesburg and prohibited him from attending public gatherings, and an order to resign his ANC leadership posts as deputy president of the national organization, president of the Transvaal branch, and president of the CYL. Mandela refused to do so, but he was obliged to conduct most of his political organizing work under the cover of his Johannesburg law partnership with Oliver Tambo and to limit his public profile to writing articles for the pro-ANC journal *Liberation*.

In December, 1956, following a year of ANC-led mass protests against the Nationalists' proposal to create seven tiny tribal "homelands" in which to segregate South Africa's black population, the government brought charges against Nelson Mandela and 155 other antiapartheid leaders under anti-Communist and treason statutes. During most of the four-and-one-half years that the so-called Treason Trial lasted, Mandela remained free on bail and continued to work at his law office during the evenings and discreetly engage in political activities within the limitations of a new five-year banning order leveled on him in February, 1956. In early 1960, however, the ANC and a more militantly black nationalist offshoot, the Pan-Africanist Congress (PAC), began organizing street demonstrations against the so-called pass laws that required black South Africans to carry government identification documents showing their assigned residence and employment at all times. In a notorious action that marked a historical watershed in the peaceful struggle for black rights in South Africa, the police turned their weapons on a group of unarmed pass protesters in the Johannesburg suburb of Sharpeville in March of that year, killing sixty-nine people. The massacre sparked a wave of angry new protests and public pass-book burnings, to which the government responded by declaring a state of national emergency, banning the ANC and PAC, and detaining some eighteen hundred political activists without charges, including Nelson Mandela and the other Treason Trial defendants. This crackdown prompted the trial lawyers to withdraw from the case, declaring that the emergency restrictions prevented them from mounting an effective defense, and left Mandela, Duma Nokwe, Walter Sisulu, and several others to represent their sizable group of ANC leaders.

As an advocate, Nelson Mandela distinguished himself with his legal ability and eloquent statements of the ANC's political and social philosophy. He stoutly defended the 1949 Programme of Action and the Defiance Campaign as necessary disruptive tactics when the government was indifferent to legal pressure, and he sought to assuage white fears of a black political takeover by insisting that the ANC's form of nationalism recognized the right of all South African racial groups to enjoy political freedom and nondiscrimination together in the same country. In a unique legal victory for South African black activists, the trial judge acquitted all the defendants for insufficient evidence in March, 1961, finding that the ANC did not have a policy of violence. Nelson Mandela's impressive defense at the widely publicized Treason Trial brought him international recognition and the respect of many South Africans of all races.

Among those anxiously awaiting the verdict was Nomzamo Winnie Madikileza, who had married Nelson Mandela during the early stages of the trial in June, 1958. A graduate of the Jan Hofmeyr School of Social Work in Johannesburg, Winnie Mandela had taken a job as South Africa's first black medical social worker at Baragwaneth Hospital in the sprawling black satellite city of Soweto. Her political life as a leader of the ANC's Women's League and her status as the wife of Nelson Mandela soon overshadowed her professional career, however. In 1958, after taking part in an antipass protest, Winnie Mandela was jailed for two weeks and then fired from her hospital job, the first of many professional posts she was to lose in the years to come because of her antiapartheid activism. After much difficulty, she subsequently found a similar position with the privately run Child Welfare Society in Johannesburg that allowed her to continue with her political work.

The government's ban of the ANC meant an end to any normal home life for the Mandelas, however. Immediately after his release, Nelson Mandela went underground to avoid new government banning orders. He surfaced in late March to deliver the keynote speech at the All-In African Conference held in Pietermaritzburg, which had been organized by the ANC and other opposition political organizations to address the Nationalists' plan to declare a racialist South African republic in May of that year. The All-In Conference opposed this proposal with a demand that the government hold elections for a fully representative national convention empowered to draft a new and democratic constitution for all South Africans. Meeting no response to the assembly's demands from the H. F. Verwoerd government, Mandela helped organize a three-day general strike for the end of May to press for the convention. Verwoerd's security forces mobilized heavily against the strike by suspending civil liberties, making massive preemptive arrests, and deploying heavy military equipment, which succeeded in limiting public support for the action, although hundreds of thousands of Africans nationwide still stayed away from work.

Facing arrest, Nelson Mandela once again disappeared underground, this time for seventeen months, and assumed numerous disguises in a cat-and-mouse game with the police during which he became popularly known as the "Black Pimpernel." Remarkably, Winnie managed to elude near-constant police surveillance and meet with her fugitive husband on numerous occasions during this period. The ANC leader was finally captured disguised as a chauffeur in the province of Natal by police acting on an informer's tip in August, 1962. Brought to trial in October on charges of inciting Africans to strike and on leaving the country without a valid travel document, Mandela turned his defense into a ringing indictment of the apartheid system. In an eloquent statement to the presiding judge, the ANC leader rejected the right of the court to hear the case on the grounds that—as a black man—he could not be given a fair trial under a judicial system intended to enforce white domination, and furthermore, he considered himself neither legally nor morally bound to obey laws created by a parliament in which he had no representation. Mandela vigorously cross-examined prosecution witnesses on the inequities of apartheid and delivered a stirring pre-sentencing statement in which he described his personal career and political education, and explained why he felt justified in having taken "extra-legal" (as opposed to illegal) action. Despite his bravura courtroom performance, Mandela was convicted of both charges and sentenced to five years in prison.

Unknown to the authorities at the time of his trial, Nelson Mandela and other ANC leaders had also reluctantly decided to launch an underground paramilitary movement in 1961 for the first time in the ANC's history. Among the principal factors prompting this decision were the Sharpeville massacre and the government's repressive response to the May, 1961, general strike, which seemed to close the door on avenues for peaceful change. Mandela also believed that the black townships were about to explode into spontaneous violence, and that this violence would either be channeled into a conscious political movement or degenerate into anarchic terrorism and race war. Accordingly, in November of 1961, he helped organize and assumed command of the Umkonto we Sizwe ("Spear of the Nation") guerrilla organization and began planning a sabotage campaign directed against government installations, other symbols of apartheid, and economic infrastructure. Umkonto's first military action occurred on December 16, 1961, when the organization simultaneously attacked government buildings in Johannesburg, Port Elizabeth, and Durban. The group went on to engage in many more acts of sabotage over the next year while Mandela traveled surreptitiously to England, Ethiopia, Algeria, and other African countries to meet political leaders, seek arms for the movement, and undergo military training.

Mandela's role in leading Umkonto came to light in June, 1963, when police raided the ANC's underground headquarters in the Johannesburg suburb of Rivonia and discovered documents relating to the armed movement. Nine top ANC leaders were arrested, including Walter Sisulu, Govan Mbeki, and Dennis Goldberg, and brought to trial with Mandela in early 1964 on charges of committing sabotage and conspiring to overthrow the government by revolution and with the help of foreign troops. Mandela once again conducted his own vigorous defense, using the courtroom as a platform to explain and justify the ANC's turn to armed struggle and to condemn the apartheid regime. "Peace in our country must be considered already broken when a minority Government maintains its authority over the majority by force and violence," Mandela had earlier declared in a speech before the 1961 Pan-Africanist Conference in Ethiopia, and, he added at the trial, "it would be unrealistic and wrong for African leaders to continue preaching peace and non-violence at a time when the Government met our peaceful demands with force." He fully acknowledged helping to found Umkonto and planning acts of sabotage, but denied the government's contention that the ANC and Umkonto intended to subject the antiapartheid struggle to revolutionary control, either foreign or domestic.

Mandela specifically addressed at some length the government's often-stated claim that he, and the ANC as a whole, were manipulated and controlled by the South African Communist Party. The ANC leader acknowledged longstanding ties and significantly overlapping memberships between the two organizations, but insisted that their alliance was a practical one relating to their shared objective of ending apartheid and achieving black majority rule. Mandela counterposed the Communists' declared long-term objective of alleviating class struggle, overthrowing capitalism, and undertaking an economic revolution to the ANC's African nationalism, which sought to harmonize class distinctions under conditions of majority rule. While he acknowledged being strongly influenced by Marxist thought, Mandela denied ever having been a member of the Communist party, insisting rather that he held a deep and abiding admiration for Western legal and political institutions and wished to "borrow the best from both East and West" to reshape South African society. As elaborated in the ANC's Freedom Charter, a 1955 manifesto that Mandela helped to draft that remains the basic statement of the group's political purpose, the ANC looked forward to a democratic, pluralist society with certain mildly socialistic reforms—including land redistribution, nationalization of the country's mines, and a progressive tax and incomes policy—intended to dilute the economic power of the white race and raise the country's majority out of poverty. In recent interviews, the ANC leader has reiterated that his basic political objectives remain a unified South Africa with no artificial homelands, black representation along with all other races in a central parliament, and one-man, one-vote democracy in a multi-party system. The ANC leader also asserted that his organization would be prepared to immediately suspend the armed struggle once the minority government agrees to legalize the ANC and other black political parties, to release all political prisoners, and to start negotiations to dismantle the apartheid system.

Nelson Mandela's trial ended in June, 1964, when he and eight other defendants were convicted of sabotage and treason and sentenced to life imprisonment. Confined to the notorious Robben Island fortress for political prisoners seven miles offshore from Cape Town, the ANC leaders were kept rigidly isolated from the outside world. They were denied access to radio, television, and newspapers and prohibited from publishing articles, giving public interviews, or even discussing politics with visitors. All Mandela's past speeches and published work were banned, and merely possessing his writings in South Africa was made a criminal offense. Despite these restrictions, two book-length collections of Mandela's best-known political statements were published abroad and have since circulated widely among South African antiapartheid activists. *No Easy Walk to Freedom,* published in 1965, includes Mandela's 1953 presidential address to the Transvaal province ANC, in which he discusses the Defiance Campaign, his speech at the 1961 All-In African Conference, and excerpts from his testimony at his three political trials. A second collection, *The Struggle Is My Life,* was published by Pathfinder Press in 1986

and contains material from 1944 to 1985, including four prison statements from Mandela.

Nelson Mandela's political views and leadership were also tirelessly promoted by his wife, Winnie, who endured near-constant government harassment in the 1960s and 1970s to emerge as a formidable black leader in her own right. Shortly after Nelson's 1962 conviction, Winnie Mandela received her first government banning order restricting her to Johannesburg and preventing her from attending public or private meetings of any kind. In 1965 the government forced her out of her job with the Child Welfare Society by further restricting her to her home township of Orlando West and preventing her from engaging in essential fieldwork elsewhere in the Soweto district. She was then fired from a succession of low-paying jobs in the white commercial district after the security police pressured her employers, and she finally found herself reduced to supporting her two young daughters on the charity of friends and political associates.

Despite this hardship, Winnie Mandela continued to work surreptitiously with the ANC in the 1960s by helping produce banned political pamphlets and newsletters in her home. The suspicious police ransacked the Mandela house repeatedly during this period, arresting Winnie so often that she began keeping a suitcase permanently packed with her prison necessities, but prosecutors could never find enough evidence to bring a court case against her. In May, 1969, however, Winnie Mandela was arrested with other suspected ANC sympathizers under a new law that allowed the government to detain "terrorist" suspects indefinitely without charges. Taken to Pretoria Prison, she was interrogated virtually nonstop for five days and nights about her supposed links to ANC saboteurs. She was then jailed without charges for seventeen months, spending the first two hundred days of this period incommunicado and in solitary confinement. Deprived of any reading, recreational, or work materials, she later described spending days taking apart and reweaving her blanket and scouring her cell for an ant or fly in her desperation to see another living creature. Her diet consisted mainly of gruel and she received a one-liter bottle of water per day to satisfy all of her drinking and bathing needs. Finally, under pressure from Nelson Mandela's lawyers, the authorities improved Winnie's confinement conditions and brought her to trial on twenty-one political charges in September, 1970. The trial judge dismissed the case against her and all but one of her co-defendants for insufficient evidence, and Winnie Mandela was released that month.

Though freed from prison, Winnie Mandela was still subjected to close police vigilance in the early 1970s as South Africa's white minority government reacted to new challenges from a growing world antiapartheid movement and the anticolonial wars in nearby Mozambique and Angola. Immediately upon her release, she was placed under a new five-year banning order that confined her to her home during the evenings and on weekends. She was subjected to frequent police home searches in ensuing years and was arrested and sentenced to six months in prison for talking to another banned person in 1974. Remarkably, though, the authorities allowed her banning order to expire in October, 1975, and over the next ten months she was able to enjoy the rights of free association and movement for the first time in many years.

This period of relative freedom for Winnie Mandela coincided with the birth of a militant "Black Consciousness" youth movement led by Stephen Biko and other students in Soweto. Inspired in part by the recent nationalist victories in Angola and Mozambique, the student revolt had as its immediate aim the annulment of the Bantu Education Act, which consigned blacks to inferior education and obliged them to learn Afrikaans, the language of South African whites of Dutch descent, instead of English. When police shot down a number of unarmed demonstrators in Soweto in June, 1976, however, the township's youth erupted in a fury of uncontrolled rioting and clashes with the security forces that left at least six hundred people dead. Many of those participants in the Soweto uprising who escaped being killed or imprisoned fled the country and made contact with ANC exile headquarters in Lusaka, Zambia. This militant young cadre helped to radicalize the Congress and substantially strengthen its military wing, allowing the ANC to reestablish both a political and military presence inside South Africa by the end of the decade.

As a leader of the Black Parents' Association in Soweto, Winnie Mandela had sought to mediate the conflict between the student leaders and the authorities and prevent the rebellion from degenerating into indiscriminate rioting. The security police, however, suspected her of having incited the uprising and detained her again for five months, along with the other Parents' Association leaders. She was released to house arrest in January, 1977, but in May of that year the police made yet another midnight raid on her home and informed her that she was being banished immediately to the remote town of Brandfort in conservative Orange Free State. As government trucks carted off their possessions, she and her daughter Zindziswa (nicknamed Zinzi) were taken that very night to their new home—a tiny, three-room house in the black ghetto, with no electricity, sewage, or running water. To further isolate her, the authorities kept Winnie Mandela under a banning order that confined her to her home during evenings and weekends, prevented her from meeting with more than one person at a time, and prohibited her from having her remarks published or quoted in South Africa. Despite these restrictions, she still managed to subvert the rigid rural segregation system during her seven years of exile in Brandfort by ignoring "whites only" signs in public places, which inspired other blacks to do the same. Winnie Mandela also put her social worker's skills to use improving conditions in the wretchedly impoverished ghetto and attempting to empower its meek and humble inhabitants. With outside donations, she managed to open a medical clinic and a soup kitchen in her home, and she trained groups of local women to start sewing and baking enterprises. Instead of isolating her as the regime had hoped, Winnie Mandela's exile only increased international interest in her as a symbol of the antiapartheid movement, and she received visits from a steady stream of journalists and diplomats who reported her views abroad.

The ebb in the popular struggle after the Soweto uprising lasted until 1984, when the townships exploded again over the adoption of a new South African constitution that year that gave parliamentary representation to "Coloureds" and Indians but none to blacks. The townships remained in a state of near-continuous political turmoil in succeeding years as antigovernment youth clashed violently with the security forces and other blacks accused of collaborating with the regime. But unlike the situation a decade earlier, when the township civilians stood unorganized and alone against the might of the apartheid state, a number of powerful social and political forces joined the fray in the mid-1980s to mount the greatest challenge to white minority rule in South African history. The United Democratic Front (UDF), a coalition of some 680 antiapartheid organizations that supports the political line of the

ANC, organized large street demonstrations and protests by township squatters facing eviction that were harshly repressed by the government in 1985. Meanwhile, the ANC itself stepped up its guerrilla campaign in South Africa and began targeting white residential areas and causing civilian casualties for the first time. The Nationalist government of P. W. Botha also came under mounting attack from abroad as the United States and other Western countries imposed limited trade and investment sanctions on South Africa in a bid to force reform. Finally, the one-million-strong black trade union movement began to flex its powerful muscles in 1987 with strikes by workers in the strategic transport and mining sectors.

Winnie and Nelson Mandela continue to play central roles in this many-sided campaign against white minority rule. A common demand voiced by all the diverse forces seeking to change the apartheid system is that Nelson Mandela, South Africa's foremost black leader, be released immediately. In 1985, Winnie Mandela managed to break the government restrictions on her and return to Soweto to join the fight for her husband's freedom. This remarkable turn of events occurred after her Brandfort house was firebombed and burned to the ground in August of that year while she was in Johannesburg for medical treatment. Accusing the security police of the attack and saying that she feared for her life, Winnie Mandela insisted on moving back to her Soweto house, and amid much local and international publicity, the Botha government permitted her to do so. She subsequently turned down an offer of $10,000 from the U.S. Government to rebuild her Brandfort house in protest of the Reagan Administration's aquiescent policy of "constructive engagement" with the apartheid regime, but she later accepted a $100,000 donation from the United Nations diplomatic community. In succeeding months Winnie Mandela took advantage of the government's weakened position and openly flouted her banning orders by giving press interviews and speaking out militantly at public demonstrations and at the funerals of young township victims of government repression. Speaking at a funeral on a return visit to Brandfort in April, 1986, for example, Winnie Mandela denounced the authorities as "terrorists" and called on blacks to take "direct action" against the government to free the imprisoned nationalist leaders. "The time has come where we must show that we are disciplined and trained warriors," she added in what some observers interpreted as a call to insurrection. Astonishingly, the Botha regime chose not to prosecute her but instead lifted all banning restrictions on Winnie Mandela in July, 1986, in a bid to improve its international image and deflect criticism of a new state of emergency it had imposed the previous month. Among Winnie Mandela's first public actions once her right to free speech had been restored was to call for international economic sanctions against the apartheid government.

Winnie Mandela discusses her personal and political past and her hopes for the future in her 1985 autobiography, *Part of My Soul Went With Him.* The book is based on a series of tape-recorded interviews that the black leader gave to South African journalist Anne Benjamin and also includes personal sketches of Winnie by friends and colleagues and copies of her recent correspondence with Nelson Mandela. In her political comments, Winnie Mandela affirms the multiracial goals of the ANC but rejects the idea of special minority rights in a transitional government, as proposed by some South African liberals, insisting rather that the only topic worthy of political discussion concerns the mechanics of handing over power directly to the country's black majority. She also describes in some detail the tribulations of her Brandfort exile and the happier time of her courtship and early years of marriage with Nelson. In a particularly poignant passage, the author recounts a visit to her imprisoned husband in May, 1984, when the couple was permitted to embrace for the first time in twenty-two years. *Part of My Soul Went With Him* "is both a moving personal story of courage and dignity and a powerful indictment of apartheid in South Africa," opined Toronto *Globe and Mail* reviewer Norman Richmond.

The future for the Mandelas and South Africa remains unsettled. Thus far, the Botha government has met the current crisis with a "divide and rule" strategy combining harsh repression and isolated reforms that do not fundamentally alter the structure of apartheid. While repealing such egregious symbols of apartheid as the pass laws and long-standing bans on interracial sex and marriage, the government has violently crushed the township uprisings and detained tens of thousands of antiapartheid protestors without trial under sweeping state-of-emergency powers. In late 1987 the Botha regime began hinting of the possibility that it might finally release Nelson Mandela unconditionally in an attempt to mollify domestic and international public opinion. The advisability of releasing the ANC leader in terms of domestic politics has reportedly stimulated a hot debate in the Botha cabinet, with those in favor of the move arguing that Mandela is now more conservative than much of the current ANC leadership and could effect a split in the organization. Detractors contend that freeing South Africa's best-known political prisoner could further alienate hard-line whites and possibly stimulate a black insurrection. Reform-minded South Africans, on the other hand, believe Mandela may now be the only political leader prestigious enough to win the confidence of both liberal whites and the increasingly alienated black township youth, thereby delivering the country from the specter of race war. Fearing the popular reaction if Mandela were to die in prison, previous South African governments had sought to find a face-saving way to free him at least as early as 1973, but the confined ANC leader had always rejected conditions that he accept exile abroad or in the Transkei "homeland" and that he renounce violence by the insurgent organization. In November, 1987, the authorities unconditionally freed Mandela's long-time comrade-in-arms Govan Mbeki, a top ANC and South African Communist party leader who was convicted at the Rivonia Trial and served twenty-four years on Robben Island, as a way of testing the political waters for Mandela's possible release.

While this debate goes on, Winnie Mandela has been allowed to continue her public political work with only occasional harassment. In January, 1987, she and Zinzi were detained by the police for several hours without explanation and in November the police raided her Soweto home and arrested several of her young bodyguards. Nelson Mandela endures his incarceration at Pollsmoor Prison near Cape Town, having been transferred to the more modern facility from Robben Island in 1982. The conditions of his confinement have improved markedly in recent years, and he is now allowed to receive weekly family visits and give occasional interviews for publication. Nelson Mandela shares a relatively spacious, sunlit cell with four other ANC leaders and spends his time studying (economics and history are favorite subjects) and tending a rooftop vegetable garden. Although he is still denied access to current news sources, visitors describe the black leader as remarkably well-informed about current affairs in South Africa and abroad.

The sixty-nine-year-old Mandela is said to be still the healthy, commanding, and charismatic leader of old, completely unbroken by his long years of confinement and possessed by the firm conviction that he will one day be free to help his people achieve their social and political emancipation. Winnie Mandela firmly shares this belief. "I am like a battery—I go down there to be recharged," she remarked to *New York Times* correspondent John F. Burns of her visits to her imprisoned husband. "You see, he is liberated already! With his attitude, he is already free!"

BIOGRAPHICAL/CRITICAL SOURCES:

BOOKS

Benson, Mary, *Nelson Mandela: The Man and the Movement,* Norton, 1986.
Harrison, Nancy, *Winnie Mandela* (biography), Braziller, 1986.
Mandela, Nelson R., *No Easy Walk to Freedom,* Basic Books, 1965.
Mandela, Nelson R., *The Struggle Is My Life,* Pathfinder Press, 1986.
Mandela, Winnie, *Part of My Soul Went With Him* (autobiography), edited by Anne Benjamin and Mary Benson, Norton, 1985.

PERIODICALS

Crisis, February, 1983.
Ebony, December, 1985, September, 1986.
Globe and Mail (Toronto), December 14, 1985.
Ms., November, 1985, January, 1987.
New Statesman, June 7, 1985.
Newsweek, September 9, 1985, February 24, 1986.
New York Review of Books, May 8, 1986.
New York Times, July 19, 1978, July 7, 1985, July 29, 1986.
New York Times Book Review, December 8, 1985.
Time, January 5, 1987.*

—Sketch by Curtis Skinner

*   *   *

MANDELA, (Nomzamo) Winnie (Madikileza)   1936-

PERSONAL: Born September, 1936, in Pondoland, Transkei, South Africa; daughter of Columbus (a schoolteacher and Pondo tribal chief; later minister of agriculture and forestry in Transkei Bantustan) and Gertrude (a schoolteacher and homemaker) Madikileza; married Nelson Mandela (an attorney and political activist), June 15, 1958; children: Zenani (married to Prince Thumbumuzi Dhlamini of Swaziland), Zindziswa. *Education:* Jan Hofmeyr School of Social Work, diploma, 1956. *Religion:* Anglican.

ADDRESSES: 8115 Orlando West, Soweto, South Africa; c/o African National Congress of South Africa, 801 Second Avenue, New York, N.Y. 10017.

CAREER: Baragwaneth General Hospital, Soweto, South Africa, medical social worker, 1956-58; Child Welfare Society, Johannesburg, South Africa, social worker, c. 1960-65; worked briefly in Johannesburg at a furniture store, correspondence college, shoe shop, dry cleaners, and office; employed at Frank and Hirsch, Johannesburg, 1975-78. Joined Women's League of the African National Congress in 1957, later became branch chairman; executive member of the Federation of South African Women; under government banning orders restricting her employment and civil liberties, 1962-86; incarcerated seventeen months in Pretoria Prison, 1969-70; leader of the Black Parents' Association in Soweto, 1976; banished to Brandfort, Orange Free State, 1977-85; returned to political activism in Soweto in 1986.

AWARDS, HONORS: Honorary doctor of laws degree from Haverford Quaker College; Freedom Prize from newspapers *Politiken* (Denmark) and *Dagens Nyheter* (Sweden); Robert F. Kennedy Human Rights Award from Georgetown University, 1985; first International Simone de Beauvoir Award from *Ms.*, 1986.

WRITINGS:

Part of My Soul Went With Him (autobiography), edited by Anne Benjamin and Mary Benson, Norton, 1985.

See also *MANDELA, Nelson R(olihlahla)*.

BIOGRAPHICAL/CRITICAL SOURCES:

BOOKS

Harrison, Nancy, *Winnie Mandela* (biography), Braziller, 1986.
Mandela, Winnie, *Part of My Soul Went With Him* (autobiography), edited by Anne Benjamin and Mary Benson, Norton, 1985.

PERIODICALS

Detroit Free Press, December 17, 1985.
Ebony, December, 1985.
Globe and Mail (Toronto), December 14, 1985.
Insight, February 24, 1986.
Ms., November, 1985, January, 1987.
New York Review of Books, May 8, 1986.
New York Times, December 6, 1985, January 14, 1986, April 6, 1986, July 8, 1986, January 26, 1987, January 27, 1987.
New York Times Book Review, December 8, 1985, April 27, 1986.
Time, January 25, 1982, January 5, 1987, May 4, 1987.*

*   *   *

MANHEIM, Emanuel   1897-1988

OBITUARY NOTICE: One source spells given name Emmanuel; professionally known as Mannie Manheim; born November 13, 1897, in Syracuse, N.Y.; died June 26, 1988, in Santa Monica, Calif. Television producer and radio and television comedy writer for such entertainers as Jackie Gleason, Bob Hope and Bing Crosby, Frank Sinatra, Rudy Vallee, and Al Jolson. Manheim began his career as a comedy writer in the mid-1930s, when he was hired to write radio scripts for Groucho Marx. Manheim made the transition from radio to television with Marx to write for the comedian's program "You Bet Your Life"; Marx attributed his successful television career to Manheim's sketch writing. Manheim was also the head writer for Milton Berle's radio show, and during the four decades that he spent writing for television he scripted and produced "The George Jessel Show" and wrote for numerous programs, including "People Are Funny," "The Donna Reed Show," "The Real McCoys," and "My Three Sons."

OBITUARIES AND OTHER SOURCES:

BOOKS

International Motion Picture Almanac, Quigley, 1982.

PERIODICALS

Los Angeles Times, July 9, 1988.
New York Times, July 13, 1988.

MANN, James
    See HARVEY, John (Barton)

*   *   *

MANNETTI, Lisa   1953-
    (L. A. Kane)

PERSONAL: Born January 9, 1953, in White Plains, N.Y.; daughter of Armand J. (in sales) and Anne (a public health director; maiden name, Luongo) Mannetti; married Terence L. Kane (an engineer), September 9, 1978. *Education:* Fairfield University, B.A., 1975; Fordham University, M.A., 1981, doctoral study, 1983-84.

ADDRESSES: Home—Wappingers Falls, N.Y. 12590.

CAREER: New York, New York City, editorial assistant, 1975-76; *More*, New York City, editorial assistant, 1976-77; Walter Panas High School, Shrub Oak, N.Y., substitute English teacher, 1977-81; writer.

MEMBER: National Writers Union.

WRITINGS:

Equality (juvenile), F. Watts, 1985.
Iran and Iraq: Nations at War (juvenile), F. Watts, 1986.

WORK IN PROGRESS: Fiction.

AVOCATIONAL INTERESTS: Theatre, sculpting.

*   *   *

MANNING, Peter J.   1942-

PERSONAL: Born September 27, 1942, in New York, N.Y. *Education:* Harvard University, B.A., 1963; Yale University, M.A., 1965, Ph.D., 1968.

ADDRESSES: Office—Department of English, University of Southern California, Los Angeles, Calif. 90089.

CAREER: University of California, Berkeley, assistant professor of English, 1967-75; University of Southern California, Los Angeles, 1975—, began as assistant professor, became professor of English and chair of department.

MEMBER: Modern Language Association of America, Byron Society, Keats-Shelley Association, Wordsworth-Coleridge Association.

AWARDS, HONORS: Guggenheim fellow, 1981-82.

WRITINGS:

Byron and His Fictions, Wayne State University Press, 1978.
(Contributor) James Hogg and E. A. Stuerzl, editors, *Byron: Poetry and Politics*, Humanities, 1981.
(Contributor) Jerome McGann, editor, *Textual Studies and Literary Interpretation*, University of Chicago Press, 1985.

Contributor to literature journals.

WORK IN PROGRESS: A continuing study of Wordsworth.

SIDELIGHTS: Peter J. Manning told *CA:* "I am interested in the intersection of psychoanalytic perspectives with political and social forces: what in their lives and historical moment influences the romantic poets."

MANNON, Warwick
See HOPKINS, (Hector) Kenneth

*   *   *

MANSFIELD, Harvey C(laflin)   1905-1988

OBITUARY NOTICE—See index for *CA* sketch: Born March 3, 1905, in Cambridge, Mass.; died of stomach cancer, May 4, 1988, in New York, N. Y. Political scientist, educator, government executive, monetary consultant, editor, and author. Mansfield taught at Columbia University from 1965 to 1973, when he retired as Ruggles Professor of Public Law and Government. During the 1940s he worked as an executive and division director for the Federal Office of Price Administration in Washington, D. C., and he later worked for the U.S. Government as a consultant on banking and currency. He wrote such works as *Lake Cargo Coal Rate Controversy, The Comptroller General,* and *A Short History of OPA,* and he collaborated on other volumes. In addition, Mansfield was managing editor of *American Political Scientist Review* from 1956 to 1965.

OBITUARIES AND OTHER SOURCES:

BOOKS

American Men and Women of Science: The Social and Behavioral Sciences, 13th edition, Bowker, 1978.

PERIODICALS

New York Times, May 10, 1988.

*   *   *

MANTEL, Hilary (Mary)   1952-

PERSONAL: Born July 6, 1952, in Derbyshire, England; married Gerald McEwen (a geologist), September 23, 1972. *Education:* Attended London School of Economics and Political Science, 1970; University of Sheffield, Jur.B., 1973.

ADDRESSES: Agent—A. M. Heath & Co., Ltd., 79 St. Martin's Ln., London W.C.1, England.

CAREER: Writer. Worked in a variety of jobs, including saleswoman, social worker in a geriatric hospital, and secondary school English teacher, until 1986; lived and worked in Botswana, southern Africa, 1977-82, and Jeddah, Saudi Arabia, 1983-86. Full-time writer in United Kingdom, 1986—.

MEMBER: Society of Authors.

AWARDS, HONORS: Shiva Naipaul Memorial prize for travel writing, 1987.

WRITINGS:

Every Day Is Mother's Day (novel), Chatto & Windus, 1985.
Vacant Possession (novel), Chatto & Windus, 1986.
(Contributor) *Best Short Stories of 1987,* Heinemann, 1987.
Eight Months on Ghazzah Street, Viking, 1988.

Film critic for *Spectator,* 1987—. Contributor of short stories and reviews to periodicals, including *London Magazine, London Review of Books, Literary Review,* and *Encounter.*

WORK IN PROGRESS: Fludd, a novel, for Viking.

SIDELIGHTS: In her first book, *Every Day Is Mother's Day,* which *London Magazine* reviewer John Mellors called "an accomplished novel of striking originality," Hilary Mantel

"extracts comedy from the lives of misfits and the mentally disordered." Mantel depicts Colin Sidney, a history teacher who, while taking night classes in order to get away from his wife and children, meets and carries on an affair with Isabel Field, a young and unsatisfied social worker. Isabel meanwhile has been assigned the case of Muriel Axon—a mentally retarded woman living with her insane mother, Evelyn—who happens to live next door to Colin's sister. In portraying its characters' miserable, mad, and eccentric lives, the novel "starts as simple black comedy," explained *Daily Mail* columnist Auberon Waugh, "and then slips into a savage satire on the social services." Waugh proclaimed *Mother's Day* "one of the bleakest commentaries on contemporary English life I have ever read." And heralding Mantel as a "major new talent," Waugh commended the author for her "beautifully constructed" plot, her "vivid imagination," and "the pert, surreal precision of her characters' dialogue."

The same characters, setting, and style appear in Mantel's second book, *Vacant Possession,* a sequel to *Mother's Day.* This "exceptional novel," asserted *New Statesman* reviewer Bill Greenwell, is "filled with fiendish glee, all of it held in hysterical check by the writer's wry style. . . . It has a wittily nasty plot, but never gloats over its victims." The welfare services are again the object of Mantel's derision, but Greenwell noted that the author's satire "is finely tempered by the rampant ironies of the narrative." Mantel adds continuing crisis and excessive coincidence to her novel of "interlocking complexity and crafty irony," commented Greenwell. In *Vacant Possession* Muriel Axon had been institutionalized and, having just been released, proceeds to wreak revenge, for various reasons, upon a number of targets: Colin Sidney's family, including his wife, mother, and sister; Isabel Field, who had institutionalized her; and Isabel's father, who had sexually abused Muriel in the past.

Although the story is complicated, *Times Literary Supplement* reviewer Christopher Hawtree applauded Mantel's handling of plot in *Vacant Possession,* as her "succession of neatly juxtaposed scenes leaves one torn between horror and delight at the unfolding, malevolent design." Greenwell further praised Mantel's style, noting that the author's "violently observant" passages play "both . . . dangerously and brilliantly with the reader's sensibility." Enthusiastic about Mantel's first two works, the reviewer concluded: "If you read only one book—I mean two, of course—this year, make sure that Hilary Mantel wrote it (them)."

Mantel told *CA:* "In *Every Day Is Mother's Day* and its sequel, *Vacant Possession,* I wrote about the nature of time, prisons, ghosts, family life, marital discord, and social policy. Both novels were set in the north of England, but I wrote them while I was living abroad, and I think that factor made my perception of home sharper than it would have been otherwise. Distance makes things funny as well—when you move around a lot you are not obliged to take any society seriously. With those two books, I wanted to make people laugh; to make some points about social work theory and practice; and to give a picture of the state of England as I saw it.

"When I wrote *Every Day Is Mother's Day* I was interested in Bruno Bettleheim's work on autism and his accounts of the victims of concentration camps; I had my social worker tell a story from one of his books. All my characters had created prisons for themselves, and the more they tried to break out, the more securely they found themselves confined. The ultimate prison is lack of imagination; the characters are so tightly sealed into their own worlds that they are oblivious to the dire events laying waste to everything around them.

"*Vacant Possession* is a much more exuberant book—with, however, a higher mortality rate among the characters. The starting point was the policy decision to close long-term hospitals for the mentally ill and mentally retarded, and release their former inmates into 'the community'—a community which on the whole did not want them and had done nothing to prepare for them. This policy frees Muriel Axon to take revenge on the people whom she believes have injured her. Though it is hard to imagine how the events of *Vacant Possession* could take place in real life, I hope that in the book they have a threatening logic of their own. Some people read it as a rather left-wing book, but one magazine called it 'Thatcherite.' I am quite happy for this uncertainty to continue.

"Recently I have begun to draw material from periods spent living abroad—five years in Africa and three-and-one-half years in Saudi Arabia. *Eight Months on Ghazzah Street* is based on my experiences in Jeddah, Saudi Arabia, but it is certainly not a disguised autobiography. It is about Frances Shore, a young Englishwoman living in that city; her circle of British and American friends; and her involvement—which turns out to be a rather dangerous involvement—in the affairs of her Muslim neighbors."

BIOGRAPHICAL/CRITICAL SOURCES:

PERIODICALS

Daily Mail, March 28, 1985.
London Magazine, March, 1985.
New Statesman, May 30, 1986.
Times Literary Supplement, June 20, 1986.

*   *   *

MARAN, Rene   1887-1960

PERSONAL: Born November 5 (some sources say November 15), 1887, in Fort-de-France, Martinique, West Indies; immigrated to France, c. 1891; died May 8, 1960, in Paris, France. *Education:* Graduated from Lycee de Talance, in Bordeaux, France, 1909.

CAREER: Served as an officer for the colonial civil service in French Equatorial Africa, 1909-23; poet, novelist, biographer, and essayist.

AWARDS, HONORS: Goncourt Prize from Goncourt Academy, 1922, for *Batouala;* Grand Prix Broguette-Gonin from l'Academie francaise, 1942; Grand Prix de la Societe des Gens de lettres, 1949; Prix de la Mer et de l'Outre-Mer, 1950; Prix de Poesie from l'Academie francaise, 1959.

WRITINGS:

NOVELS

Batouala: Veritable Roman negre, Albin, 1921, translation by Adele Szold Seltzer published as *Batouala*, T. Seltzer, 1922 (published in England as *Batouala: A Negro Novel From the French*, Cape, 1922), reprinted, Kennikat, 1969, translation by Alvah C. Bessie published as *Batouala: A Novel*, illustrations by Miguel Covarrubias, Limited Editions Club, 1932, *Batouala: Veritable Roman negre*, author's definitive edition (contains *Youmba, la mangouste;* also see below), Albin, 1938, reprinted, 1982, translation from the author's definitive edition by Barbara Beck and Alexandre Mboukou published as *Batouala: A True Black*

Novel, introduction by Donald Herdeck, Black Orpheus, 1972, published as *Batouala: An African Love Story*, Black Orpheus, 1973.
Djouma, chien de brousse, Albin, 1927.
Le Coeur serre, Albin, 1931.
Le Livre de la brousse, Albin, 1934.
Betes de la brousse, Albin, 1941.
Un Homme pareil aux autres, Arc-un-Ciel, 1947.
Bacouya, le cynocephale, Albin, 1953.

POETRY

Le Visage calme, 7th edition, Aux Editions du Monde Nouveau, 1922.
Les Belles Images, Delmas, 1935.
Le Livre du souvenir, Presence Africaine, 1958.

Also author of *La Maison du bonheur* and *La Vie interieure*.

OTHER

"Le Petit Roi de Chimerie" (short story), preface by Leon Bocquet, Albin, 1924.
Livingston et l'exploration de l'Afrique, Gallimard, 1938.
Brazza et la fondation de l'A.E.F., Gallimard, 1941.
Mbala, l'elephant, illustrations by Andre Collot, Arc-en-Ciel, 1943.
Les Pionniers de l'empire, three volumes, Albin, 1943-55.
Savorgnan de Brazza, Dauphin, 1951.
Felix Eboue, grand commis et loyal serviteur, 1885-1944, Editions Parisiennes, 1957.
Bertrand du Guesclin, l'epee du roi, Albin, 1960.
Djogoni: Eaux-fortes, Presence Africaine, c. 1966.
Voyages de decouverte au Canada entre les annees 1534 et 1542, Anthropos, 1968.

Also author of *Le Tchad de sable et d'or*, 1931, and *Peines de coeur*, 1944. Contributor of novellas, including *Bokorro, Boum et Dog, Deux amis, L'Homme qui attend, Legendes et coutumes negres de l'Oubanqui-Chari: Choses vues*, and *Youmba, la mangouste*, to a monthly Paris periodical, *Les Oeuvres libres*, between 1921 and 1937. Also contributor of essays to periodicals, including *Le Monde illustre* and *Candide*.

SIDELIGHTS: Acclaimed by some critics for writing a "masterpiece" of black literature, Rene Maran gained recognition as the first black author to authentically record African tribal life under colonial French rule during World War I in his 1921 novel *Batouala: Veritable Roman negre* (translated as *Batouala: A True Black Novel*). For this work Maran received the prestigious Goncourt Prize in 1922; he was the first black writer to be so honored. The novel was subsequently translated into fifty languages.

Born in Martinique in 1887 and educated in Bordeaux, France, Maran, by the age of sixteen, had begun writing and already had some of his poetry published. In 1909 he joined the French colonial service in Africa, where he spent six years in the Congo. After writing *Batouala*, Maran returned permanently to France in 1923, where he was a prolific poet, biographer, essayist, and novelist. *Batouala*, however, is the only one of his works to have been translated from French. And its success, asserted *Nation*'s reviewer Charles R. Larson, is due to "Maran's genius" in rendering tribal life "so fully and objectively."

In *Batouala* Maran "presents us with the cycle of traditional African life from birth to death," observed Larson. The story is told mainly through the eyes of the aging African chief, Batouala, who finds his authority challenged by a younger man. Batouala and his small tribe of Bandas live under "oppressive French colonial rule," explained Michael Olmert of the *New York Times Book Review,* and are "resigned to the new lifestyle that clashes so stridently with the one that had done so well for their ancestors." But it is not so much the plot that makes *Batouala* impressive, but rather, stated Olmert, the fact that "the tale is a framework for what can almost be considered a compendium of Banda folklore and tribal life." The reader is able to experience the intimate aspects of Batouala's life as the book is, as Larson described, "alive with the sounds and smells of an African village." Olmert further praised the book: "Maran has done a perfect job of weaving the details of eating, shelter, rites of passage, lore, and art into his novel. Nothing escapes him."

Despite the novel's acclaim, *Batouala,* upon its first publication, met with controversy. Protest came from members of the French literary establishment who objected to *Batouala*'s preface, which is an attack on the French colonial service. With his novel, though, Maran only "wanted to be objective in his recording of African life as it was, as he knew it. 'It doesn't show indignation: it records,'" Larson quoted the author. But with this objective outlook—and contrary to the notion that this was a piece of black protest fiction—the novel's intimate and unromanticized portrayal of tribal rites and rituals paradoxically served to reinforce some readers' theories of black inferiority. Larson, nevertheless, deemed *Batouala* a "seminal piece of African literature," concluding that "Maran's novel deserves recognition as one of the most imaginative pieces of black writing of all times."

BIOGRAPHICAL/CRITICAL SOURCES:

PERIODICALS

Freeman, November 29, 1922.
Literary Review, September 9, 1922.
Nation, September 20, 1922, March 26, 1973.
New York Times, August 20, 1922.
New York Times Book Review, January 28, 1973.
Times Literary Supplement, January 8, 1922.*

*   *   *

MARCHANT, John H.   1951-

PERSONAL: Born June 12, 1951, in Gosport, Hampshire, England; son of Leslie Frank (a lecturer in botany) and Jean (Kirkpatrick) Marchant; married Jane Frances Ruth Murray (an ornithologist), April 9, 1983; children: Katharine Frances. *Education:* Sidney Sussex College, Cambridge, B.A. (with honors), 1972, M.A., 1975.

ADDRESSES: Home—17 Church View, Long Marston, Tring, Hertfordshire HP23 4QB, England. *Office*—British Trust for Ornithology, Beech Grove, Tring, Hertfordshire HP23 5NR, England.

CAREER: British Trust for Ornithology, Tring, England, research officer, 1973—. Buckinghamshire county bird recorder, 1982—; member of Rarities Committee of *British Birds,* 1985—.

MEMBER: Buckinghamshire Bird Club.

AWARDS, HONORS: British Birds named *Shorebirds* the best bird book of 1986.

WRITINGS:

(With A. J. Prater and Juhani Vuorinen) *Guide to the Identification and Ageing of Holarctic Waders,* British Trust for Ornithology, 1977.
(With P. J. Hayman and A. J. Prater) *Shorebirds: An Identification Guide to the Waders of the World,* Croom Helm, 1986, revised edition, Christopher Helm, 1987.
(With S. P. Carter and P. A. Whittington) *Population Trends of Common Birds,* British Trust for Ornithology, in press.

Contributor to *The Birdwatcher's Yearbook and Diary* and *The Atlas of Wintering Birds in Britain and Ireland.* Contributor of about seventy articles to ornithology journals. .

SIDELIGHTS: John H. Marchant told *CA:* "My main goal as an author has been to acquire and disseminate information about birds for the benefit of people who enjoy watching and studying them. I am glad that some of my work, particularly *Shorebirds,* may be useful in the effort toward conservation of birds and their habitats. I regard usefulness and accuracy to be the prime considerations for writings in my field, and I trust that most of what I do scores well on both counts."

*   *   *

MARGOLIES, Alan   1933-

PERSONAL: Born October 12, 1933, in New York, N.Y.; son of William B. (a postal supervisor) and Helen (Kraus) Margolies. *Education:* City College (now of the City University of New York), B.A., 1954; New York University, M.A., 1960, Ph.D., 1969. *Politics:* Democrat. *Religion:* Jewish.

ADDRESSES: Home—201 East 25th St., New York, N.Y. 10010. *Office*—John Jay College of Criminal Justice of the City University of New York, 445 West 59th St., New York, N.Y. 10010.

CAREER: Pratt Institute, Brooklyn, N.Y., part-time instructor in English, 1960-63; City University of New York, lecturer in English at Brooklyn College, 1961-68, lecturer in English at City College, 1969-70, assistant professor at John Jay College of Criminal Justice, 1970-75, associate professor, 1976-80, professor of English, 1980—. *Military service:* U.S. Army, 1954-56.

MEMBER: Bibliographical Society of America, Modern Language Association of America, Hemingway Society, Association for Documentary Editing, Association for Computers and the Humanities, Northeast Association for Computers and the Humanities (president, 1983-85), Northeast Modern Language Association (president, 1986-87).

AWARDS, HONORS: Faculty Research Award from City University of New York, 1971-74, 1980, 1983; American Council of Learned Societies grant-in-aid, 1972; National Endowment for the Humanities grant, 1979-81; Award for Outstanding Academic Achievement from City University of New York, 1985.

WRITINGS:

(Compiler with others) J. Albert Robbins, editor, *American Literary Manuscripts: A Checklist in Academic, Historical, and Public Libraries, Museums, and Authors' Homes in the United States,* 2nd edition, University of Georgia Press, 1977.
(Editor) *F. Scott Fitzgerald's St. Paul Plays: 1911-1914,* Princeton University Library Press, 1978.

(Contributor) *Fitzgerald/Hemingway Annual: 1978*, Gale, 1978.
(Contributor) Jackson R. Bryer, editor, *The Short Stories of F. Scott Fitzgerald*, University of Wisconsin Press, 1982.
(Contributor) Saul N. Brody and Harold Schechter, editors, *City University of New York, CUNY English Forum*, Volume 1, AMS Press, 1985.
(Contributing editor) *Contemporary Authors*, Volume 123, Gale, 1988.

Contributor to *Fitzgerald/Hemingway Annual*, Microcard Editions, 1970-72, 1974. Also contributor to periodicals, including *Papers of the Bibliographical Society of America* and *Journal of Modern Literature*.

WORK IN PROGRESS: A Catalogue of F. Scott Fitzgerald's Library; A Catalogue of F. Scott Fitzgerald's Papers.

*   *   *

MARKER, Gary 1948-

PERSONAL: Born October 1, 1948, in Philadelphia, Pa.; married Ann S. Brody, August 23, 1970; children: Joshua Brody. *Education:* University of Pennsylvania, B.A., 1969; graduate study at University of Illinois at Urbana-Champaign, 1969-70; University of California, Berkeley, M.A., 1971, Ph.D., 1977.

ADDRESSES: Home—101 Bleeker St., Port Jefferson, N.Y. 11777. *Office*—Department of History, State University of New York at Stony Brook, Stony Brook, N.Y. 11794.

CAREER: Oberlin College, Oberlin, Ohio, assistant professor of history, 1977-78; University of California, Berkeley, lecturer in history, 1978-79; State University of New York at Stony Brook, assistant professor, 1979-85, associate professor of history, 1985—.

MEMBER: American Historical Association, American Association for the Advancement of Slavic Studies.

WRITINGS:

Publishing, Printing, and the Origins of Intellectual Life in Russia, 1700-1800, Princeton University Press, 1986.

WORK IN PROGRESS: Readers and Reading in Russia, 1650-1800, completion expected in 1989.

BIOGRAPHICAL/CRITICAL SOURCES:

PERIODICALS

American Historical Review, April, 1986.
Times Literary Supplement, March 7, 1986.
Virginia Quarterly Review, winter, 1986.

*   *   *

MARSH, Paul
See HOPKINS, (Hector) Kenneth

*   *   *

MARSHALL, Edmund
See HOPKINS, (Hector) Kenneth

*   *   *

MARSHALL, Richard (D.) 1947-

PERSONAL: Born May 5, 1947, in Los Angeles, Calif. *Education:* California State University, Long Beach, B.A., 1969,

graduate study, 1972-73; attended University of California, Irvine, 1969-70.

ADDRESSES: Office—Whitney Museum of American Art, 945 Madison Ave., New York, N.Y. 10021.

CAREER: Whitney Museum of American Art, New York City, assistant curator, 1974-77, associate curator of exhibitions, 1978—. Consultant to Museum of Modern Art.

WRITINGS:

(With Jean Lipman) *Art About Art*, Dutton, 1978.
New Image Painting, Whitney Museum of American Art, 1978.
Developments in Recent Sculpture, Whitney Museum of American Art, 1981.
(With Suzanne Foley) *Ceramic Sculpture: Six Artists*, University of Washington Press, 1981.
(With Richard Armstrong) *Five Painters in New York*, Whitney Museum of American Art, 1984.
American Art Since 1970, Whitney Museum of American Art, 1984.
(With Mark Rosenthal) *Jonathan Borofsky*, Abrams, 1984.
Fifty New York Artists, Chronicle Books, 1986.
Alex Katz, Rizzoli International, 1986.

Also editor of *Paris Review*, 1978—.

*   *   *

MARSTON, David W(eese) 1942-

PERSONAL: Born July 17, 1942, in Knoxville, Tenn.; son of David S. (a writer and editor) and Ruth (a housewife; maiden name Weese) Marston; married Linda Zacherle (a government administrator), June 11, 1966; children: Karen, David, Michael. *Education:* Maryville College, B.A. (honors), 1964; Harvard Law School, LL.B., 1967.

ADDRESSES: Home—584 Bryn Mawr Ave., Bryn Mawr, Pa. 19010. *Office*—Buchanan Ingersoll, 1101 Market St., Suite 1450, Philadelphia, Pa. 19107. *Agent*—Gerald F. McCauley, Inc., P.O. Box AE, Katonah, N.Y. 10536.

CAREER: Admitted to the Bar of Pennsylvania, 1967; Montgomery, McCracken, Walker & Rhoads (law firm), Philadelphia, Pa., attorney, 1967-73; U.S. Capitol, Washington, D.C., legislative aide to senator Richard S. Schweiker, 1973-76; U.S. Department of Justice, Washington, D.C., U.S. attorney for Eastern District of Pennsylvania, 1976-78; Republican candidate for mayor of Philadelphia, 1979; lawyer in private practice and writer, 1980-85; Buchanan Ingersoll (law firm), Philadelphia, partner, 1985—. Teacher of criminal constitutional law at the National Institute for the Administration of Justice at Temple University, 1970-73. Chairman of board of Northeast Commuter Services Corporation (NCSC), 1982; representative on the Southeastern Pennsylvania Transportation Authority (SEPTA) board, 1983-86. Free-lance writer, 1967—. *Military service:* U.S. Navy, 1967-69; served as gunnery officer in Persian Gulf; became lieutenant junior grade.

AWARDS, HONORS: Honored by the Chapel of Four Chaplains for public service, 1978.

WRITINGS:

(With Neil J. Welch) *Inside Hoover's FBI: The Top Field Chief Reports*, Doubleday, 1984.

Contributor of articles to periodicals, including *Fortune*.

WORK IN PROGRESS: A book about the legal profession, for Morrow.

SIDELIGHTS: In *Inside Hoover's FBI: The Top Field Chief Reports,* David W. Marston and co-author Neil J. Welch relate what Gene Lyons of *Newsweek* called an "episodic account" of Welch's career as an agent for the Federal Bureau of Investigation, which was run by J. Edgar Hoover for almost fifty years. Although Lyons claimed that the book "adds little to the vast record of the bureau's triumphs and follies," *Washington Post*'s Edwin M. Yoder, Jr., commended the book as "entertaining and informative . . . full of fascinating anecdotes, and for the most part wittily told."

It is as the U.S. attorney for Pennsylvania who was fired by the Carter administration in 1978, however, that Marston is most known. A graduate of Harvard Law School who served as an attorney for a prestigious law firm in Philadelphia and then as an aide to Senator Richard S. Schweiker in Washington, D.C., Marston was appointed by Republican President Gerald Ford in 1976 to serve as a U.S. attorney for Pennsylvania. When Democratic President Jimmy Carter took office the following year, it seemed likely that the Republican Marston would be replaced by a Democrat. Carter, however, was obliged to retain Marston because of a campaign statement he had made: "All federal judges and prosecutors should be appointed strictly on the basis of merit without any consideration of political aspects or influence." Remaining a federal prosecutor, Marston seemed to prove his merit; he had "built himself a generally deserved reputation as a dogged attacker of misdeeds in high places," said *Time.* What is more, reported the newsmagazine, "Marston [had] endeared himself to Philadelphians by being the first prosecutor in recent years to hit political corruption hard."

In his fight against corruption, Marston was subsequently accused of political bias by Democrats such as House Speaker Tip O'Neill, who, according to *Time,* called the Republican attorney a "political animal" whose goal was "to get Democrats." Refuting that accusation, though, was Marston's record for indicting both Republicans and Democrats during his eighteen months as a U.S. prosecutor.

In September of 1976, Marston's office convicted a former Chester County commissioner, Republican Theodore Rubino, of extortion. In June, 1977, Marston helped to convict the former speaker of the Pennsylvania house of representatives, Democrat Herbert Fineman, for accepting more than $50,000 in bribes. And Marston's most important conviction came on December 30, 1977, when he prosecuted one of the most powerful members of the Pennsylvania State Senate, Democrat Henry Cianfrani. Cianfrani was found guilty on four charges of income tax evasion amounting to $62,282 as well as 106 other counts, including mail fraud and accepting $52,500 in bribes. He was sentenced to serve five years in prison.

Soon after the Cianfrani conviction, Marston was fired by the Carter administration, a move that Sheldon M. Smith of *National Review* called "an act of thundering political ineptitude. . . . A bunch of scoundrels were being brought to justice, and . . . the man who had been responsible for the prosecutions was being canned."

The manner in which Marston was fired was highly criticized not only for its seeming political bias but for its alleged illegality, as high ranking officials were accused of obstruction of justice in the events that preceeded the removal: Pennsylvania Democratic Congressman Joshua Eilberg and another

prominent Pennsylvania Democrat, Congressman Daniel Flood, were being investigated by Marston's office for irregularities concerning the way in which Eilberg's law firm obtained federal funds for the construction of a new Philadelphia hospital, while also accepting unusually high legal fees. On November 4th, 1977, Marston began an investigation of Eilberg's law firm. That same day, Eilberg called President Carter urging him to fire Marston. (Eilberg, however, later denied knowing that he was being investigated by Marston at the time he made the call to the president.) Reportedly, Eilberg did not give Carter a reason for wanting Marston removed, and Carter did not ask; "the System was at work," commented a writer for *Time.* The newsmagazine added that the president phoned Griffin Bell a few days later; "Carter's message: there was local Democratic pressure to get rid of that Republican Marston in Philly. See to it."

In a January 12, 1978 press conference, Carter denied that he had been involved in any procedures leading to Marston's removal. Investigative reporting and the release of affidavits by the Justice Department, however, ultimately revealed evidence of the president's direct role in the process to have Marston fired. His handling of the Marston affair subsequently found Carter caught in what *Time* called a "skein of presidential lies," as well as guilty of breaking a campaign promise by giving in to Democratic party pressure. "The President was getting into trouble because he felt guilty about having to admit he used patronage as every President before him had done," commented writer William Safire in *New York Times Magazine.* Consequently, according to *Newsweek*'s Don Holt, Carter "lost some credibility" with the American public.

More serious than breaking a campaign promise, though, was the possibility that Carter had broken the law: "If Eilberg knew that Marston was after him and made the call to Carter to take the heat off himself," explained Safire, "that could be a crime, and the Presidency the weapon used to impede justice." The Justice Department ultimately announced, however, that Carter was not guilty of obstruction of justice, because, related Safire, he "had 'no guilty knowledge,' of the Eilberg investigation at the time of the call on [November] 4." Nevertheless, many still criticize the practice of political patronage, as Safire commented: "The great weakness in the patronage system is that it might be used on occasion by a politician trying to save his skin. That is precisely what has happened here, profoundly embarrassing the President and his men." And "thanks to the Administration's ineptness" in enacting this system, summarized *Time,* "a martyr's image has been created for Marston."

BIOGRAPHICAL/CRITICAL SOURCES:

PERIODICALS

National Review, March 17, 1978.
New Republic, March 18, 1978.
Newsweek, January 30, 1978, October 1, 1984.
New York Times Biographical Service, January, 1978.
New York Times Magazine, February 19, 1978.
Time, January 23, 1978, February 6, 1978.
Washington Post, December 10, 1984.

—*Sketch by Janice E. Drane*

*   *   *

MARTEL, Leon C. 1933-

PERSONAL: Born June 14, 1933, in Providence, R.I.; son of

Leon Charles and Irene (Brouillette) Martel; married Marilee Norling (a filing systems consultant), January 12, 1956; children: Christopher, Jonathan. *Education:* Dartmouth College, B.A., 1955; Columbia University, M.A. and Certificate from Russian Institute (now Harriman Institute), 1957, Ph.D., 1965. *Religion:* Roman Catholic.

ADDRESSES: Home and office—600 West 111th St., New York, N.Y. 10025. *Agent*—Esther Newberg, International Creative Management, 40 West 57th St., New York, N.Y. 10019.

CAREER: Hofstra University, Hempstead, N.Y., faculty member, 1965-72, tenured faculty member in political science, 1972-74; Hudson Institute, Croton, N.Y., member of professional staff, 1974-76, deputy to director Herman Kahn, 1976-77, executive vice-president and director of Research Management Council, 1977-80, acting president, 1979-80; freelance writer and lecturer, 1981—. *Military service:* U.S. Naval Reserve, 1958—, active duty as Russian interpreter and translator in charge of Russian and East European Desk of European Intelligence Center, 1958-64, operations coordinator for intelligence debriefing of prisoners of war returning from Vietnam, 1973; present rank, captain; received Secretary of the Navy Medal for Achievement.

MEMBER: World Future Society, American Political Science Association, Naval Reserve Association, Ends of the Earth Club.

AWARDS, HONORS: Mastering Change was named one of the year's ten outstanding business books by *Best of Business Quarterly* in 1986.

WRITINGS:

(With Herman Kahn and William Brown) *The Next Two Hundred Years: A Scenario for America and the World,* Morrow, 1976.
Lend-Lease, Loans, and the Coming of the Cold War: A Study in the Implementation of Foreign Policy, Westview, 1979.
Mastering Change, Simon & Schuster, 1986.

Contributor to magazines, including *Futures.*

WORK IN PROGRESS: Research on the emerging global economy and the responses that businesses in America and abroad must make in product development, financing, and marketing.

SIDELIGHTS: Leon C. Martel told *CA:* "I arrived at Hudson Institute in July, 1974, on a one-year leave from Hofstra University as a Soviet military analyst to work on the institute's contracts with the Pentagon. Very soon, however, I came under the study of the institute's founder and director, Herman Kahn, who literally soaked up newly minted Ph.D.'s. By then Herman, as everyone who knew him called him, had published *The Year 2000* and turned his all-encompassing attention to the whole world and all of its history, past and to come. Awed by his towering intellect, convinced of his evidence opposing *The Limits to Growth* and other doom and gloom prophecies, and smitten with the notion of trying to comprehend all of the trends—technological, economic, political, social—shaping the world's future, I resigned from the university, collaborated with Herman on *The Next Two Hundred Years,* and set out on my own career as a futurist.

"Most futurists and most authors who give advice for preparing for the future make knowledge of the present the starting point of their forecasts or the foundation of their advice. This is true, for example, of influential works like *The Global 2000 Report* and *Megatrends.* In sharp contrast, my new book, *Mastering Change,* argues that the future will be different, that it will be changed from the present. Thus, it insists that the best way to prepare for the future is to understand change. *Mastering Change* further shows that this can be done because changes have patterns, with dimensions that can be seen and measured—some more readily than others, but all to some degree. These patterns indicate that all changes fall into two categories, structural (permanent, irreversible) and cyclical (temporary, reversible). The examination of these two categories provides an optimistic outlook for the future, reinforcing the view set forth by Herman and others in our studies at Hudson, for it is the structural changes (slowing population growth rates, rising agricultural productivity, spreading economic development, increasing literacy and communications, etc.) that mean achievement and progress, while it is the cyclical changes (rises and falls in economic growth, upswings and downswings in violence, crime, divorce rates, etc.) that cause problems. But because the changes of this second category are cyclical, they are positive as often as they are negative, and as we experience further structural changes we will continue to improve the human condition, enhancing all the while our ability to dampen the negative phases of the cyclical changes.''

BIOGRAPHICAL/CRITICAL SOURCES:

PERIODICALS

American Historical Review, February, 1983.
Zelo, Volume I, number 2, 1986.

*   *   *

MARTELLI, Leonard J.   1938(?)-1988

OBITUARY NOTICE: Born c. 1938 in Beverly, Mass.; died of complications resulting from acquired immune deficiency syndrome (AIDS), February 7, 1988, in Brooklyn, N.Y. Publishing executive, editor, and author. Martelli was editorial director of the elementary and high school book division of McGraw-Hill publishing company for more than a decade. An author of numerous elementary school social studies textbooks, he also wrote, with Fran D. Peltz and William Messina, *When Someone You Know Has AIDS: A Practical Guide.*

OBITUARIES AND OTHER SOURCES:

PERIODICALS

New York Times, February 12, 1988.

*   *   *

MARTIN, James Kirby   1943-

PERSONAL: Born May 26, 1943, in Akron, Ohio; son of Paul E. (in business) and Dorothy (a housewife; maiden name, Garrett) Martin; married Karen Wierwille (a book editor), August 7, 1965; children: Darcy Elizabeth, Sarah Marie, Joelle Kathryn Garrett. *Education:* Hiram College, B.A. (summa cum laude), 1965; University of Wisconsin—Madison, M.A., 1967, Ph.D., 1969.

ADDRESSES: Home—Houston, Tex. *Office*—Department of History, University of Houston, 4800 Calhoun Rd., Houston, Tex. 77004-3785. *Agent*—Gerard W. McCauley, Gerard McCauley Agency, Inc., P.O. Box AE, Katonah, N.Y. 10536.

CAREER: Rutgers University, New Brunswick, N.J., assistant professor, 1969-73, associate professor, 1973-79, professor of history, 1979-80, assistant provost for administration, 1972-74, vice-president for academic affairs, 1977-79; University of Houston, Houston, Tex., professor of history, 1980—, chairman of department, 1980-83. Visiting associate professor and professor of alcohol studies at Rutgers Center of Alcohol Studies, 1978—. Scholar in residence at David Library of the American Revolution and research fellow at Philadelphia Center for Early American Studies, University of Pennsylvania, winter, 1988.

MEMBER: American Historical Association, Organization of American Historians, Society for Historians of the Early American Republic, Southern Historical Association, Texas State Historical Association, Texas Association for the Advancement of History (vice-president), New Jersey Historical Society, Phi Beta Kappa, Phi Kappa Phi, Phi Alpha Theta, Pi Gamma Mu, Omicron Delta Kappa.

AWARDS, HONORS: Respectable Army appeared on the U.S. Army's "Contemporary Military Reading List" in 1982; R. P. McCormick Prize from New Jersey Historical Commission, 1984, for *Citizen-Soldier.*

WRITINGS:

Men in Rebellion: Higher Governmental Leaders and the Coming of the American Revolution, Rutgers University Press, 1973.

(Editor) *Interpreting Colonial America: Selected Readings,* Dodd, 1973, 2nd edition, Harper, 1978.

The Human Dimensions of Nation Making: Essays on Colonial and Revolutionary America, Wisconsin State Historical Society, 1976.

(Editor with K. R. Stubaus) *The American Revolution: Whose Revolution?,* Robert E. Krieger, 1977, revised edition, 1981.

In the Course of Human Events: An Interpretive Exploration of the American Revolution, Harlan Davidson, 1979.

(With Mark Edward Lender) *A Respectable Army: The Military Origins of the Republic, 1763-1789,* Harlan Davidson, 1982.

(Editor with Mark Edward Lender) *Citizen-Soldier: The Revolutionary War Journal of Joseph Bloomfield,* New Jersey Historical Society, 1982.

(With Mark Edward Lender) *Drinking in America: A History, 1620-1980,* Free Press, 1982, revised and expanded edition, 1987.

(Co-author) "Drinking in America" (film), released by Gary Whiteaker Co., 1984.

(With Randy Roberts, Steven Mintz, and others) *America and Its People,* Scott, Foresman, in press.

General editor of series "American Social Experience," New York University Press. Member of editorial board of *New Jersey* and *Houston Review;* past member of editorial board of "Papers of William Livingston" and "Papers of Thomas Edison."

WORK IN PROGRESS: With Robert S. Rutter, *The Newburgh Conspiracy: A Novel,* publication expected in 1990; *Benedict Arnold: Revolutionary Hero,* publication by Knopf expected in 1991; a study of Peggy Shippen, "temptress of the Revolution"; a study of David Peterman, a Civil War soldier.

SIDELIGHTS: James Kirby Martin's book *Drinking in America* was hailed as a "brilliant social history" by Anatole Broyard of the *New York Times.* The history begins in colonial times, when Americans consumed more than six gallons of alcoholic beverages per person per year. These Americans regarded ordinary water with suspicion, and they believed their cider and beer would not only protect them from the cold and disease, but strengthen their constitutions and improve their general health. In 1784 Dr. Benjamin Rush, a signer of the Declaration of Independence, tried to promulgate the idea that alcoholism was a disease, but his advice was little heeded and Americans steadily increased their per capita consumption to more than seven gallons over the next thirty years.

Temperance movements were established as early as 1808, but they lost their influence during the crisis of the Civil War. When Prohibition was finally approved in 1919, many people hoped that only "hard liquor" would be affected by the new law. The severity of the legislation that was enacted outraged Americans who might have accepted a milder version of the law. In addition, according to Martin and co-author Mark Edward Lender, the coming of the Depression required the federal government to increase its tax revenues, and Prohibition was doomed.

Over the years, drinking was not considered to be a national or even a social problem, but rather a personal, individual, and relatively infrequent one. It was not until the 1950s that the American Medical Association declared that alcoholism was a physical disease. Since then drinking has become as much a part of daily life as it once was in the colonies, and scores of government agencies and private organizations like Alcoholics Anonymous have dedicated their work to eradicating the disease.

Such is the story that Martin and Lender relate in their scholarly book. In Broyard's opinion: "Besides being highly readable and filled with witty and interesting asides, 'Drinking in America' is almost amazingly free of prejudice or special pleading. It's the best kind of social history." Similarly, Ben Irwin wrote in the *Los Angeles Times,* "This is a scholarly, informative book," adding that it "covers an astonishing amount of ground; one does not need to be an alcoholic . . . to appreciate its scholarship and dedication."

Martin told *CA:* "Pursuing the craft of history can be both frustrating and rewarding. The well-trained historian understands that there are never enough documents to comprehend past events. Writing good history, from my point of view, involves unleashing one's creative energy in prose after carefully assembling the data. Despite what some historians assert, the past does not interpret itself.

"In my own career as an academic historian, I have been influenced by a number of outstanding professors who taught me the value of mastering the art of critical analysis and interpretation. The production of good history, one of my professors argued, will always depend upon ongoing reasearch in the archives and the creative act of interpretation.

"Getting at the sources is the first step, and the second is to assess the behavior of past generations of human actors. Too often—in the rush to identify and define forces, trends, concepts, and ideologies—historians forget that human beings of all types and kinds, ordinary as well as extraordinary, initiate and direct movements and events. Thus in my own history, people are at the center. Further, the sources demonstrate that these actors rarely operate in some sort of celestial harmony. Rather, human conflict gives form to the past and drives it forward toward a meaningful present. Those who frame their history in terms of human consensus miss the fundamental reality of what provokes change over time.

"In my own writing, human conflict has been a persistent theme. Studying such grand events as the American Revolution, or looking at such persistent reform efforts as temperance and Prohibition, it is impossible to ignore conflict as the formative ingredient of the past. The analysis of human conflict allows the historian to bring perspective to the present.

"In recent years my work has stretched beyond my initial specialization in early American history with a primary focus on the American Revolution. Too often, from my point of view, academically trained historians keep digging into smaller and smaller topics. My decision had been to go the other way, to reach into new fields, including U.S. military history and the social history of alcohol and drug use. Further, some of my future work will have much more of a biographical orientation, featuring ordinary as well as extraordinary lives. If this is fleeing from overspecialization, so let it be. As an old beer commercial once stated, 'we only go around once,' so why not take some chances along the way."

BIOGRAPHICAL/CRITICAL SOURCES:

PERIODICALS

American Historical Review, December, 1984.
Annals of the American Academy of Political and Social Science, March, 1984.
Los Angeles Times, November 16, 1982.
New York Times, January 8, 1983.
New York Times Book Review, January 9, 1983.

*   *   *

MARTIN, (Roy) Peter   1931-
(James Melville)

PERSONAL: Professionally known as James Melville; born January 5, 1931, in London, England; son of Walter (a postal worker) and Annie Mabel (a dressmaker; maiden name, Cook) Martin; married Marjorie Peacock in 1951 (divorced in 1960); married Joan Drumwright in 1960 (divorced in 1977); married Catherine Sydee (a textile artist), April 11, 1978; children: (second marriage) Adam Melville, James Peter. *Education:* University of London, B.A. (honors), 1953, M.A., 1956; graduate study at University of Tuebingen, 1958-59.

ADDRESSES: Home—Barn Cottage, Hatfield, Leominster, Herefordshire HR6 0SF, England. *Agent*—Curtis Brown, Curtis Brown Ltd., 162-168 Regent St., London W1R 5TB, England.

CAREER: London County Council, London, England, local government officer, 1948-49 and 1951-54; teacher in London, 1954-56; Royal Festival Hall, London, deputy publicity officer, 1956-60; British Council officer in England, Indonesia, Japan, and Hungary, 1960-83, director of British Cultural Institute, Kyoto, Japan, 1963-70, cultural attache at British Embassy in Budapest, Hungary, 1972-73, cultural counselor at British Embassy in Tokyo, Japan, 1979-83; writer, lecturer, and critic. *Military service:* Royal Air Force, Education, 1949-51; became sergeant instructor.

MEMBER: British Academy of Film and Television Arts, Mystery Writers of America, Crime Writers Association, Detection Club, Travellers' Club.

AWARDS, HONORS: Member of the Order of the British Empire (MBE), 1970.

WRITINGS:

(With wife, Joan Martin) *Japanese Cooking,* foreword by John Pilcher, illustrations by Clifton Karhu, Bobbs-Merrill, 1970.

UNDER PSEUDONYM JAMES MELVILLE

The Wages of Zen (crime novel), Secker & Warburg, 1979, Methuen, 1981.
The Chrysanthemum Chain (crime novel), Secker & Warburg, 1980, St. Martin's, 1982.
A Sort of Samurai (crime novel), St. Martin's, 1981.
The Ninth Netsuke (crime novel), St. Martin's, 1982.
Sayonara, Sweet Amaryllis (crime novel), St. Martin's, c. 1983.
Death of a Daimyo (crime novel), St. Martin's, 1984.
The Death Ceremony (crime novel), St. Martin's, 1985.
Go Gently, Gaijin (crime novel), St. Martin's, 1986.
The Imperial Way (historical novel), Deutsch, 1986, Fawcett, 1988.
Kimono for a Corpse (crime novel), Secker & Warburg, 1987.
The Reluctant Ronin (crime novel), Scribner, 1988.

WORK IN PROGRESS: Two historical novels, *A Tarnished Phoenix,* publication expected in 1989, and *The Last Samurai,* publication expected in 1990; another crime novel, *A Haiku for Hanae,* publication expected in 1989.

SIDELIGHTS: In his popular crime novels featuring the Japanese police superintendent Tetsuo Otani, his wife Hanae, and inspectors Jiro Kimura and Ninja Noguchi, James Melville combines intrigue and mystery with detailed observations of Japanese culture. Often involving non-Japanese victims or suspects, his plots provide ample opportunity to examine the differing viewpoints of Japanese and foreigners. According to Jean M. White of the *Washington Post Book World,* Melville creates an "absorbing interplay of two cultures" in his writing, weaving "the subtleties of Japanese manners and the stylized protocol of diplomatic life with delicious irony" into his second Otani novel, *The Chrysanthemum Chain.* His insight into Japan, along with his appealing characters, draws frequent praise from reviewers. Writing for the *Los Angeles Times,* Elaine Kendall noted that, "while crucial to the plot" of *The Death Ceremony,* "the murder is almost incidental to Melville's meticulous exploration of Japanese manners and psychology." Kendall assessed the novels as being "to the usual thriller what sushi is to steak—an acquired taste with a loyal and enthusiastic following . . . elegant, restrained and in the best possible taste."

AVOCATIONAL INTERESTS: Music, Japan.

CA INTERVIEW

CA interviewed James Melville by telephone on January 30, 1987, at his home in Leominster, Herefordshire, England.

CA: Before you became a full-time writer, you had a career in the diplomatic service from 1960 to 1983. Tell me a bit about that.

MELVILLE: I was not a regular diplomat in the sense of doing general diplomatic duties; I was always concerned with cultural affairs. During my second period in Japan, from 1979 to 1983, I was directly attached to the [British] Embassy as cultural counselor. But when I was in Japan from 1963 to 1970, I was director of the British Cultural Institute in Kyoto. I suppose the easiest way for an American to understand the setup would be to think of it as a little like what used to be called the United States Information Agency.

CA: How did you happen to fall in love with Japan rather than Indonesia or Hungary, the other countries where you worked?

MELVILLE: I enjoyed my first three years in Indonesia well enough, though it was a difficult time politically for British people. But somehow, although I took an interest in the culture around me, it didn't hit me in quite the way Japan did when I first went there. I was very fortunate because I was sent for seven whole years to the city of Kyoto, the cultural center of Japan and the actual capital for over a thousand years until the middle of the nineteenth century. I first became interested in Japanese food and cooking. As a matter of fact, my first published book was about Japanese cooking.

By the time I went to Hungary in 1972, I was already hopelessly committed to Japan. As for Indonesia, I think I was too young, too inexperienced. My job was much more tricky there, and I had too little time to become absorbed in Indonesian history. In Japan I found a situation where not only was there every facility for both amateur and more far-reaching research, but also people with not too many political anxieties and preoccupations, people who were ready to discuss Japanese culture. I became totally hooked on it. Within a matter of weeks of arriving in Kyoto in 1963, I was waking up in the morning and thinking I ought to pinch myself, wondering if I was really being paid to live in such a fascinating place.

CA: Japanese Cooking *was published in England in 1970 and in the United States in 1971. Then there was a lapse of almost ten years before* The Wages of Zen *was published, to begin your series of crime and mystery novels. Were you doing some form of writing during those years along with the other work?*

MELVILLE: I did a little occasional amateur journalism; from time to time I put together essays and articles on this and that, usually concerned with Japan in some way. I didn't write anything of book length until *The Wages of Zen.* But that book germinated over quite a long time. I was working in London, in fact, in the mid-seventies when I first started to write it—or to think I might be able to write a mystery.

CA: How did you happen to choose the form of the crime novel?

MELVILLE: I had been a murder mystery buff for a long time—in fact, throughout my adult life I'd always enjoyed reading them, particularly the classic kind, the Golden Age books published in Britain and the great work of [Dashiell] Hammett, [Raymond] Chandler, and so on. When I found myself on the fringes of a real-life murder in Kyoto, naturally the format suggested itself. Because I'd enjoyed that form myself, I wanted first and foremost to entertain readers rather than to be earnestly informative. So I thought I would have a shot at writing in the genre which I had enjoyed myself for so many years.

CA: And how did you come to write the novels under the pseudonym James Melville?

MELVILLE: When I was lucky enough to have *The Wages of Zen* accepted, it so worked out that it was going to be published in the early summer of 1979. It was precisely then that

I was due to arrive back in Japan as a senior member of the British Embassy. Because I was dealing with low life in high places, as it were, I thought, and so did my then superiors, that it might be wise if I used a nom de plume. It struck me as a sensible precaution, just in case the Japanese with whom I would have to deal officially took offense.

As to the choice of the name, although it has echoes of Henry James and Herman Melville, in fact it's made up of the names of my two sons; one is called James and the other has the middle name Melville. My cover remained fairly waterproof for a couple of years, and then it was blown in the *Sunday Times.* To my surprise and pleasure, my Japanese friends weren't upset at all; they were rather tickled. It caused no problems whatever when it was discovered that there I was sitting in the British Embassy writing books about Japanese gangsters and murders.

CA: Your characters Superintendent Otani and his wife and Inspectors Kimura and Noguchi wear very well on the reader. Were those characters a long time developing in your mind before you put them on paper?

MELVILLE: Yes, they were. Although *The Wages of Zen* was the first of my books to be published, a very incompetent and unsatisfactory version of *The Chrysanthemum Chain,* which is number two in the series, was the first book of that kind that I actually wrote. Otani just sort of walks onto the page as a relatively minor character in that first draft, simply because I needed a senior Japanese policeman. But I didn't at that time think I was going to write a book about a Japanese detective; I was writing a book about something else entirely.

Otani soon became much more important to me, and I tried deliberately to make things difficult for myself by making him a rather old-fashioned, conservative Japanese, and above all by making him unable to speak English. That made it absolutely vital that he should have at least one close associate who was a fluent English-speaker. And because that person obviously represented one type of modern Japanese, the Westernized, fashionable, trendy go-getter, unconsciously I must have felt that I needed a tough, street-wise cop to balance the setup. So Inspector Noguchi made his appearance.

Although I have subsequently met Japanese who resemble in some particulars all three of my types, I'm happy that I can truthfully say none of them is based on any specific Japanese whom I've met. In fact, the character of Noguchi, strangely enough, probably owes a lot to my own late father—who had nothing to do with Japan—in his personality, his mixture of gruffness and sentimentality.

CA: One of the very interesting things brought out in your books is how the class system is still very prevalent in Japanese society. Does it seem to be diminishing at all?

MELVILLE: No. If anything, slightly the reverse. Most public-opinion polls carried out among Japanese come up with the slightly surprising conclusion that the overwhelming majority of Japanese consider themselves to be middle-class. They used, of course, to have a system of nobility—titles and so on—just as we do in England still. It was fairly short-lived; it was instituted after the Meiji Restoration in 1868, and it survived until the end of World War II. Now the only titles in Japan are those belonging to the Emperor and his immediate family. Even there, the Emperor has three daughters who are married to ordinary Japanese, people with no titles, and they are just

Mrs. Shimizu, Mrs. This, Mrs. That. They are no longer princesses. But the Emperor's sons and their wives have titles, and so do their children.

I was talking to a very well informed Japanese friend not too long ago who said that now that Japan is so affluent there is even a feeling it wouldn't be bad to bring back the old system. In the meantime, although they don't have an aristocracy as such, they revel in titles. The Japanese is a little like a German in this respect: he usually refers to other people by their status—company president, professor, department director or whatever. He doesn't call someone Mr. Takemoto; he calls him Mr. Director or Mr. Section Head. People are very sensitive about those titles. So I think the Japanese are not so much class-conscious in the social sense as status-conscious.

CA: It was a shocker to read that most murders in Japan are committed by women.

MELVILLE: Most murders in most places in the world are committed by people who know the victim. They are what you might call family murders. In Japan, to be more accurate, most murders which are not the result of gangster warfare are committed by women and are within the family.

CA: Does the device of using alternating narratives in the writing—the Japanese characters doing something, and then a breakaway to the English characters doing something else—make it necessary to outline your plot in advance of the actual writing?

MELVILLE: Cutting from one to the other isn't a plotting device as such. I do it to underline the contrasting approaches of Japanese and non-Japanese, mostly Westerners. One of the things which absorb me very much is the fact that although in many ways Japanese are no different from any other human beings anywhere else in the world, in other ways they are. They have a special way of thinking about things which is broadly different from people brought up in the Western cultural tradition. Although I don't like to be too heavy about this and write a kind of solemn, academic-type study of the phenomenon, I do like to draw attention, not only in serious ways but in humorous ways, to the possibilities of misunderstanding, sometimes quite comical, between Japanese and Westerners. So in a sense it has become a kind of habit for me to adopt this technique, which tends to keep the story moving and to say that here we are, talking (usually, in my books) about Westerners living in Japan and coming into collision sometimes as well as into contact with these very distinctively Japanese ways of doing things. Sometimes I produce an outline plot in advance, but more often I let a book develop organically from a basic idea.

CA: The Otanis' visit to England in Death of a Daimyo *sheds some light on the difficulties of Japanese tourists. They have the reputation of being rather intense and humorless. Is this a response to the cultural differences and the language barrier rather than a reflection of Japanese traits?*

MELVILLE: I'm sure it is very much that. I think you have to distinguish fairly sharply between Japanese who have chosen or who have been directed as a result of their jobs to live in other countries and Japanese who go visiting as tourists. I think that any tourist, provided no disaster happens, is likely to come away with a fairly glowing impression of the place visited—it was picturesque, it was fun, etc. People who have

to make their living and do their jobs in that kind of alien environment very soon find that it isn't all cafes and restaurants and sightseeing.

I do sympathize very much with any involuntary expatriate, anyone who has trouble in adjusting to a different way of doing things. Japanese are in any case much more clubbable people, to use the English idiom, than the English tend to be. They like to do things in groups. They like the sense of mutual support which comes from being a member of a group. So the Japanese business community in London, for example, is very closely knit—just as English people abroad, I know from personal experience in various places in the Far East particularly, tend to cling to each other. They have their clubs and societies, and they like to remind themselves of what it's like back home. I think such people are not worried about the language barrier, on the whole. They have all the resources of their companies or the organizations for which they work to help take care of the practicalities of life. But they have a sort of nostalgia for their own ways of doing things, and they're more comfortable with their own people, having perhaps been grappling with some rather difficult locals.

The tourist is in a different position entirely. The tourist, especially the Japanese tourist, does like to have everything meticulously organized, likes to be cosseted and protected, to be shepherded around so that there's no possibility of anything going amiss. And the language barrier is for the Japanese tourist a real obstacle to going it alone, just as it is for the Western visitor to Japan.

CA: How is it to be in England writing about Japan as opposed to being in Japan writing about Japan?

MELVILLE: I think some of my Japanese friends would say—in fact they have said, in almost these words—that distance lends enchantment to the view. My view of Japan is perhaps a little too rosy, a little too sentimentalized, because of the distance. On the other hand, I find it can help me to put my own Japanese experiences into better sort of proportion to be distanced from the country. But I would always feel that I must return to Japan at fairly regular intervals to bring myself up to date with the smells and the colors and the tastes and the textures and so on. In fact I was there just a few months ago, and I would like to think that, if all goes well, I shall revisit Japan for a month or so every year or every eighteen months. Of course I read the Japanese newspapers. I have a great many friends in the world of Japanese studies in Britain, though I'm not myself an academic. So I keep in touch with things Japanese, and I refresh my feelings about the atmosphere by going back.

On the other hand, I think, paradoxically, I would find it rather difficult to sit down in Japan and write a novel about Japan. I like to go and take extensive notes and absorb a lot, and then come home to this quiet village in England and think about it and digest it. Then it comes out in a form which I think is more satisfactory.

CA: The Imperial Way, *published in 1986, is a different kind of book, based on a historical event, a political uprising in Japan in 1936. Did you do a great deal of research for it?*

MELVILLE: Yes. As soon as I began studying Japanese history as an amateur, I became absolutely fascinated not only by this particular historical incident itself but what it revealed to me about Japanese ways of thinking and doing things. I had long wanted to write a serious novel about an aspect of Japan. I am now fifty-six, and I was just a little child at the time the events I describe happened, so I have no personal recollection. But at least I can think about the thirties in a fairly realistic way, whereas if I were writing a novel set in the seventeenth century, I would have very few points of reference.

I went to Japan, and I spent a long time researching in newspapers and magazines of the period to make quite sure that I got absolutely every detail right, from the women's hairstyles and fashions to what was showing at the movies. That was a major research effort of a quite different kind from what I—perhaps immodestly—call my research for the Otani books.

CA: Does The Imperial Way *signal a new direction in your work? Will you do more books of that kind?*

MELVILLE: I'm already workng on another historical novel. I would like to feel it's not a change of direction, it's an additional direction. I have no present plans to give up the Otani series, though I have a problem now that Otani's getting older, of course; he really ought to retire. The Otani I'm working on now, which will come out in about two years' time, is a flashback which takes an episode of his earlier career. I think I might do one or two more young Otanis, as it were. But I shall certainly go on writing crime fiction. On the other hand, now that I am a full-time writer, I have more time and energy to devote to my work, and I am tremendously interested in Japanese history of a personal kind, the history of people rather than the history of political events. So I plan to write a more substantial novel like *The Imperial Way* perhaps every two or three years while keeping up the annual Otani book.

CA: You've said elsewhere that you want primarily to entertain your readers.

MELVILLE: Yes. I very much hope that, as a result of reading my books, people will get a somewhat more accurate impression of what daily life for ordinary people is actually like in Japan without losing the stimulus of the exotic flower of it. But that is not my primary purpose. My primary purpose is simply to entertain in the Otani books. I think my ambitions are pitched a little bit more seriously in *The Imperial Way* and will be in any other historical novel I subsequently write. But basically I would like for people to be beguiled, perhaps for a couple of hours on a plane journey, and come away having enjoyed the story as such, and the characterization, which is more important to me than the plot, actually. If they come away with a feeling of having learned something interesting about Japan, that's lovely.

CA: Do you have a large Japanese readership?

MELVILLE: Surprisingly so. I think that is due to the fact that some of my books are actually translated into Japanese, and those are mass paperbacks and presumably are read by a lot of people. I think this is something that is a little unusual in the sense that Japanese are perhaps unique in feeling rather flattered when a foreigner writes books about them. They like to read them. I don't think the same thing would apply in reverse. If a Japanese crime writer were to invent a typical English village cozy kind of thing, I don't think it would sell at all in this country because people wouldn't be interested to know what a Japanese thought about English social life. But it doesn't work that way, oddly enough, with the Japanese. I've had quite a lot of press coverage in Japan, TV interviews

and one thing and another. And people regard me as something of a freak, because so far as I know, I'm the only *British* crime writer, at least, who's writing murder mysteries set in Japan and involving Japanese people in the most important roles.

CA: We get your books rather quickly here after they're published in England. Are you happy with their U.S. reception by both readers and reviewers?

MELVILLE: Yes, I am. American reviewers have been extremely kind to me, and what I get in the way of fan mail—which is not, I must admit, by the sackful—is predominantly from Americans. I get far more letters from nice people in America who write to say they've enjoyed my books than I do from anywhere else. And I'm particularly happy now that, in the past year or so, my books have started coming out in Fawcett paperback, because people don't on the whole buy hardback fiction unless it's by the blockbusters. One tends to get a very discerning audience as a hardback writer, but a much wider audience in purely quantitative terms when one's books are available in paperback, as five, maybe six, of mine now are. Fawcett is going to be publishing *The Imperial Way* too, some time soon.

CA: Mysteries are enjoying great popularity in this country now. Do you feel it's the same in England?

MELVILLE: Not quite as successful here, but yes, it's a very popular genre, certainly. I was in the United States in October last, and I had a very brief visit, just a week, which took me from coast to coast. I was in Los Angeles and Chicago and New York. On each occasion I was attending signing sessions and meeting mystery fans. I was really astonished and touched by the reception I got, because I'm quite realistic; I know I'm not a household name in crime writing by any means.

What also interested me very much was the way so many people in the United States actually study the genre. You have these fanzines and so forth which come up with some remarkably scholarly articles. I was very pleased and flattered and a little daunted when, a few months ago, in the journal of the Mystery Readers of America, there was an article written by a person I'd never met in my life, a very complicated analysis of the Otanis accompanied by little diagrams showing where they lived and where Otani's father was a teacher and conjecturing about the date they must have got married and all the rest of it. I keep this by me now as a reference, because I didn't know half of these things!

I think that, as in so many other contexts, the American zest and enthusiasm, the characteristic spirit of vigor, does extend not only to crime writing but to crime readers too. I suppose one's readership here in England is almost certainly mainly among middle-aged people, whereas I get the impression it's much more across the board in the United States. That kind of studious interest in mysteries here has been in a rather specific context: that is, concerned with Sherlock Holmes and to all intents and purposes only Sherlock Holmes. There's always been an apparatus of jokey scholarship connected with [Arthur] Conan Doyle's books, although, so far as I know, no other writer has been given that sort of treatment in Britain until recently. But it's beginning here too now.

BIOGRAPHICAL/CRITICAL SOURCES:

PERIODICALS

Los Angeles Times, January 17, 1986.

Washington Post Book World, August 22, 1982.

—*Interview by Jean W. Ross*

*   *   *

MARTIN, Taffy 1945-

PERSONAL: Born May 27, 1945, in Philadelphia, Pa.; daughter of Alfred W. and Anne (Wynne) Martin; married Jean Pierre Pouzol (a poet, editor, and bookseller), September 17, 1949. *Education:* Gwynedd Mercy College, B.A., 1967; Georgetown University, M.A., 1969; Temple University, Ph.D., 1979.

ADDRESSES: Home—Sireyjol-Gignac, 46600 Martel, France.

CAREER: Educator and writer.

WRITINGS:

Marianne Moore, Subversive Modernist, University of Texas Press, 1986.

Contributor to literary and artistic journals.

WORK IN PROGRESS: A manuscript on "La France Profonde"; literary translation; literary research.

*   *   *

MASON, Joseph B(igsbee) 1903-

PERSONAL: Born May 13, 1903, in Niagara, Wis.; son of Joseph Treadway (owner of a country store) and Emma A. (a writer; maiden name, Yeager) Mason; married Harriet Smith, 1927 (marriage ended, 1979); married Helen Ann Winstone, 1980; children: Leslie Ann Mason Ray, Susan Elizabeth Mason Callegari. *Education:* University of Wisconsin—Madison, Ph.B., 1926.

ADDRESSES: Home—643-B Heritage Village, Southbury, Conn. 06488.

CAREER: Associated Press, Chicago, Ill., reporter on night city desk, beginning in 1926; *Building Age,* Chicago, assistant editor, 1928, editor in chief, 1929; *American Builder,* Chicago, managing editor, beginning in 1930, editor in chief, beginning in 1940; *Good Housekeeping,* New York, N.Y., building and architectural editor, beginning in 1946; *Professional Builder,* Des Plaines, Ill., senior editor, 1970-87.

MEMBER: Overseas Press Club of America, Sigma Delta Chi.

AWARDS, HONORS: Citation from Federal Housing Administration, 1958; Presidential Citation from National Association of Home Builders, 1968; inducted into National Housing Hall of Fame, 1979.

WRITINGS:

History of Housing in the U.S., 1930-1980, Gulf Publishing, 1982.

SIDELIGHTS: Joseph B. Mason told *CA:* "My family circle was a literate oasis in a backwoods community. It was natural that I decided to go to the University of Wisconsin at Madison. I reached Madison in 1921, by means of hitchhiking, pickup trucks, and a brief and frightening ride on the cowcatcher of a freight train. I arrived with few funds, but great expectations, and quickly got three jobs—one as an assistant on the copy desk of the local Associated Press service, another as a dishwasher, and a third as a waiter.

"In journalism and English literature I found my niche. I graduated happily and went to work for the Associated Press in Chicago. Before long my interest in home building surfaced, and I landed a dream job as the assistant editor of *Building Age,* an old and respected New York journal. I became the editor in chief of the magazine in 1928 at the age of twenty-five.

"I was in my new office on Fifth Avenue on that night in October of 1929 when the headlines read 'Stocks Collapse—16 Million Shares Sold.' Thus I witnessed the 1929 stock market crash and lived through the subsequent collapse of housing and the nation's mortgage finance structure—the worst economic debacle in U.S. history.

"My subsequent career spanned a tumultuous fifty-year period in U.S. housing history. I remained in active contact with architects, builders, financial interests, and the new breed of community developers who changed the face of U.S. home development and environmental planning.

"In 1982 I published a detailed record of the progress and growth of the industry from 1930 to 1980. My book *History of Housing in the U.S.* was unique, because it covered an industry of hundreds of thousands of small builders and entrepreneurs, and it chronicled for the first time the details of their problems, failures, and successes. I wanted to show the remarkable record achieved by the builders of America. They built more homes and better ones than any other nation, and the work was done by thousands of small-volume builders, working largely under an unfettered private enterprise system, contrary to the disastrous systems of many other countries to provide public housing through government entities. It was a tumultuous but amazingly productive and creative era for American home building. New concepts in land planning, architectural design, building techniques, financial systems, and basic research transformed the industry and changed the face of America.

"My personalized account traces the decade-by-decade evaluation and advancement of all these aspects of the housing industry. It covers the establishment of a national home financing system (the FHA), in which I participated, the Federal Home Loan Bank Board, the Home Owner's Loan Corporation, which rescued a million foreclosed homes between 1933 and 1940, the Federal National Mortgage Association, the Government National Mortgage Association, and later federal agencies that vastly expanded the availability of mortgage financing for the private sector of housing.

"In the seventies, large-volume, corporate entities became active in building and brought new concepts of community planning. There was a veritable revolution in management, marketing, and design. The end of this period may have marked the peak of a golden era which provided fifty-three million new homes in fifty years. The houses were generally well-built and equipped, and they provided a new, high standard of living for Americans.

"The housing slowdown of the early eighties was the result of high interest and financing costs and a variety of environmental, zoning, and building code restraints. I conclude, however, that the enterprise and spirit of achievement will return once more and will enable the builders of the nation to achieve the American dream of a decent home for every American."

MASSENGALE, John (Edward) Montague 1951-

PERSONAL: Born September 25, 1951, in New York, N.Y.; son of John E. III (an attorney) and Jean (an art historian; maiden name, Montague) Massengale. *Education:* Harvard University, A.B., 1974; University of Pennsylvania, M.Arch., 1978. *Politics:* Democrat. *Religion:* Episcopalian.

ADDRESSES: Home—125 East 63rd St., New York, N.Y. 10021; Rural Route 2, Bedford, N.Y. 10506. *Office*—Pier Fine Associates, 18 East 16th St., New York, N.Y. 10003.

CAREER: Associated with Voorsanger & Mills Architects, New York City, 1979-80; associated with Robert A. M. Stern Architects, New York City, 1979-83; associated with Braunfels & Partner, Munich, West Germany, 1983-84; associated with Bradford Perkins & Associates, New York City, 1984-85; partner with Pier Fine Associates, New York City. 1986—. Director of Center for American Architectural Research (CAAR).

MEMBERSHIPS: New York Racquet and Tennis Club.

WRITINGS:

(With Robert A. M. Stern) *The Anglo-American Suburb,* Academy Editions, 1980.
(With Stern and Gregory Gilmartin) *New York 1900: Metropolitan Architecture and Urbanism, 1890-1915,* Rizzoli International, 1984.

Contributor to *Skyline, Contemporanea,* and *Spy.*

WORK IN PROGRESS: Building in the Tradition: American Regionalism Today, to be published in 1988.

SIDELIGHTS: In *New York 1900: Metropolitan Architecture and Urbanism, 1890-1915* architects Robert A. M. Stern, Gregory Gilmartin, and John Montague Massengale provide a comprehensive look at urban growth in turn-of-the-century New York. An average early nineteenth-century commercial port that burgeoned into the nation's leading metropolis by 1900, New York City was the site of bold new buildings and building types (like the skyscraper, modern hotel, and luxury apartment) that reflected an optimistic society bent on progress. "What these authors . . . have attempted is something more than architectural history, something less than social and political history," described Paul Goldberger, critiquing the study for the *New York Times Book Review.* "They have tried to use architecture as a lens through which to bring the entire picture of New York in this era into focus."

Writing in the *Voice Literary Supplement,* Jeff Weinstein felt that the authors of *New York 1900* "approach their subject with too little theory, unacknowledged theory, or no theory at all." The critic admitted, however, that the book's "cornucopian details . . . satisfy the way details do: encyclopedically, anecdotally"; "the poetry of old photographs is unavoidable," Weinstein added. Golberger, likewise, had difficulty with the authors' urban theorizing ("teases at being general while really having its heart in architecture"), maintaining that "urban history should not be considered primarily a tale of esthetic ambitions." Still, the reviewer praised the study's thorough discussions of building types and neighborhood development and its more than five hundred rare period photographs. "'New York 1900' is a monumental achievement of assemblage," concluded Goldberger. "Rarely does this kind of project yield anything as lavish, celebratory and, for all its shortcomings, so truly appealing."

BIOGRAPHICAL/CRITICAL SOURCES:

PERIODICALS

New York Times Book Review, March 18, 1984.
Voice Literary Supplement, April, 1984.

* * *

MATHABANE, Mark 1960-

PERSONAL: First name originally Johannes; name changed, 1976; born in Alexandra, South Africa; son of Jackson (a laborer) and Magdelene (a washerwoman; maiden name, Mabaso) Mathabane; married Gail Ernsberger (a writer), in 1987. *Education:* Attended Limestone College, 1978, St. Louis University, 1979, and Quincy College, 1981; Dowling College, B.A., 1983; attended Columbia University, 1984. *Religion:* "Believes in God."

ADDRESSES: Home—341 Barrington Park Ln., Kernersville, N.C. 27284.

CAREER: Free-lance lecturer and writer, 1985—.

MEMBER: Authors Guild.

AWARDS, HONORS: Christopher Award, 1986.

WRITINGS:

Kaffir Boy: The True Story of a Black Youth's Coming of Age in Apartheid South Africa, Macmillan, 1986, published as *Kaffir Boy: Growing out of Apartheid,* Bodley Head, 1987.

WORK IN PROGRESS: A sequel to *Kaffir Boy.*

SIDELIGHTS: "What television newscasts did to expose the horrors of the Vietnam War in the 1960s, books like 'Kaffir Boy' may well do for the horrors of apartheid in the '80s," Diane Manuel determined in a *Chicago Tribune Book World* review of Mark Mathabane's first novel. In his 1986 *Kaffir Boy: The True Story of a Black Youths' Coming of Age in Apartheid South Africa,* Mathabane recounts his life in the squalid black township of Alexandra, outside of Johannesburg, where he lived in dire poverty and constant fear until he seemingly miraculously received a scholarship to play tennis at an American college. *Washington Post Book World* critic Charles R. Larson called *Kaffir Boy* "violent and hard-hitting," while Peter Dreyer in the *Los Angeles Times Book Review* found Mathabane's autobiography "a book full of a young man's clumsy pride and sorrow, full of rage at the hideousness of circumstances, the unending destruction of human beings, [and] the systematic degradation of an entire society (and not only black South African society) in the name of a fantastic idea."

The Alexandra of *Kaffir Boy* is one of overwhelming poverty and deprivation, of incessant hunger, of horrific crimes committed by the government and citizen gangs, and of fear and humiliation. It is a township where one either spends hours at garbage dumps in search of scraps of food discarded by Johannesburg whites or prostitutes himself for a meal, and where "children grow up accepting violence and death as the norm," reflected Larson. One of Mathabane's childhood memories is of his being startled from sleep, terrified to find police breaking into his family's shanty in search of persons who emigrated illegally, as his parents had, from the "homelands," or tribal reserves. His father was imprisoned following one of these raids, and was repeatedly jailed after that. Mathabane recalls in *Kaffir Boy* that his parents "lived the lives of perpetual fugitives, fleeing by day and fleeing by night, making sure that they were never caught together under the same roof as husband and wife'' because they lacked the paperwork that allowed them to live with their lawful spouses. His father was also imprisoned—at one time for more than a year with no contact with his family—for being unemployed, losing jobs as a laborer because he once again lacked the proper documents.

''Born and bred in a tribal reserve and nearly twice my mother's age,'' Mathabane wrote in his memoir, ''my father existed under the illusion, formed as much by a strange innate pride as by a blindness to everything but his own will, that someday all white people would disappear from South Africa, and black people would revert to their old ways of living.'' Mathabane's father, who impressed upon his son tribal laws and customs, was constantly at odds with his wife, who was determined to see her son get an education. Mathabane's mother waited in lines at government offices for a year in order to obtain his birth certificate so that he could attend school, then worked as a washerwoman for a family of seventeen so that he could continue to study and, with luck, escape the hardships of life in Alexandra. The father burned his son's schoolbooks and ferociously beat his wife in response to her efforts, claiming that an education would only teach Mathabane to be subservient.

Yet those living in the urban ghettos near Johannesburg are more fortunate than people in the outlying ''homelands,'' where black Africans are sent to resettle. ''Nothing is more pathetic in this book than the author's description of a trip he takes with his father to the tribal reserve, ostensibly so that the boy will identify with the homelands,'' judged Larson. ''The son, however, sees the land for what it really is—barren, burned out, empty of any meaning for his generation.'' In Kaffir Boy Mathabane depicts the desolation of the Venda tribal reserve as ''mountainous, rugged and bone-dry, like a wasteland. . . . Everywhere I went nothing grew except near lavatories. . . . Occasionally I sighted a handful of scrawny cattle, goats and pigs grazing on the stubbles of dry brush. The scrawny animals, it turned out, were seldom slaughtered for food because they were being held as the people's wealth. Malnutrition was rampant, especially among the children.'' Larson continued to note that ''the episode backfires. The boy is determined to give up his father's tribal ways and acquire the white man's education.''

Although Mathabane had the opportunity to get at least a primary education, he still contemplated suicide when he was only ten years old. ''I found the burden of living in a ghetto, poverty-stricken and without hope, too heavy to shoulder,'' he confesses in his memoir. ''I was weary of being hungry all the time, weary of being beaten all the time: at school, at home and in the streets. . . . I felt that life could never, would never, change from how it was for me.'' But his first encounter with apartheid sparked his determination to overcome the adversities.

His grandmother was a gardener for an English-speaking liberal white family, the Smiths, in an affluent suburb of Johannesburg. One day she took her grandson to work, where he met Clyde Smith, an eleven-year-old schoolboy. ''My teachers tell us that Kaffirs [blacks] can't read, speak or write English like white people because they have smaller brains, which are already full of tribal things,'' Smith told Mathabane, the author recalled in his autobiography. ''My teachers say you're not people like us, because you belong to a jungle civilization. That's why you can't live or go to school with us, but can only be our servants.'' He resolved to excel in school, and

even taught himself English—blacks were allowed to learn only tribal languages at the time—through the comic books that his grandmother brought home from the Smith household. ''I had to believe in myself and not allow apartheid to define my humanity,'' Mathabane points out.

Mrs. Smith also gave Mathabane an old wooden tennis racket. He taught himself to play then obtained coaching. As he improved and fared well at tournaments he gained recognition as a promising young athlete. In 1973 Mathabane attended a tennis tournament in South Africa where the American tennis pro Arthur Ashe publicly condemned apartheid. Ashe became Mathabane's hero, ''because he was the first free black man I had ever seen,'' the author later was cited in the New York Times. After watching the pro play, he strove to do as well as Ashe. Mathabane eventually became one of the best players in his country and made contacts with influential white tennis players who did not support apartheid. Stan Smith, another American tennis professional, befriended Mathabane, and urged him to apply for tennis scholarships to American schools. Mathabane won one, and Kaffir Boy ends with the author boarding a plane headed for South Carolina.

Lillian Thomas in the New York Times Book Review asserted that ''it is evident that [Mathabane] wrestled with the decision whether to fight or flee the system'' in South Africa. The author participated in the 1976 uprisings in Soweto, another black township near Johannesburg, after more than six hundred people were killed there when police opened fire on a peaceful student protest. Yet Mathabane continued to be friends with whites whom he had met at his athletic club. He also was the only black in a segregated tournament that was boycotted by the Black Tennis Association, but he participated believing that he would meet people who could help him leave South Africa. Afterward he was attacked by a gang of blacks who resented his association with whites and only escaped because he outran them.

David Papineau in the Times Literary Supplement does not find fault with Mathabane for leaving South Africa. The critic contended that Mathabane ''does make clear the limited choices facing black youths in South Africa today. One option is political activity, with the attendant risk of detention or being forced underground. . . . Alternatively you can keep your head down and hope for a steady job. With luck and qualifications you might even end up as a white-collar supervisor with a half-way respectable salary.''

''For me to deny my anger and bitterness would be to deny the reality of apartheid,'' Mathabane told David Grogan in People. The author resides in the United States and maintains that he would be jailed for speaking out against apartheid if he returned to South Africa. ''If I can turn that anger into something positive, I really am in a very good position to go on with my life,'' he said to the New York Times. Now he lectures, taking the memoir of his early life ''as a springboard to talk about apartheid in human terms.'' But he does want to return to South Africa, with the hopes of inspiring ''other boys and girls into believing that you can still grow up to be as much of an individual as you have the capacity to be,'' Mathabane was quoted in another article in the New York Times. ''That is my dream.''

BIOGRAPHICAL/CRITICAL SOURCES:

BOOKS

Mathabane, Mark, Kaffir Boy, Macmillan, 1986.

PERIODICALS

Chicago Tribune Book World, April 13, 1986.
Christian Science Monitor, May 2, 1986.
Los Angeles Times Book Review, March 30, 1986.
New York Times, March 2, 1987, September 24, 1987.
New York Times Book Review, April 27, 1986.
People, July 7, 1986.
Times Literary Supplement, August 21, 1987.
Washington Post Book World, April 20, 1986.

—*Sketch by Carol Lynn DeKane*

*   *   *

MATHIEU, Joe
See MATHIEU, Joseph P.

*   *   *

MATHIEU, Joseph P.   1949-
(Joe Mathieu)

PERSONAL: Born January 23, 1949, in Springfield, Vt.; son of Joseph A. (a car dealer) and Patricia (a housewife; maiden name, Biner) Mathieu; married Melanie Gerardi, September 7, 1970; children: Kristen, Joey. *Education:* Rhode Island School of Design, B.F.A., 1971.

ADDRESSES: Home—258 Pheasant Lane, Brooklyn, Conn. 06234.

CAREER: Author and illustrator of books for children. Designer of album covers for Stomp Off records.

AWARDS, HONORS: The Magic Word Book, Starring Marko the Magician! was named one of the fifty best books by the American Institute of Graphic Arts, 1973; *Ernie's Big Mess* was selected as a Children's Choice by the International Reading Association, 1982.

WRITINGS:

SELF-ILLUSTRATED PICTURE BOOKS FOR CHILDREN; UNDER NAME JOE MATHIEU

The Amazing Adventures of Silent "e" Man, Random House, 1973.
The Magic Word Book, Starring Marko the Magician! Random House, 1973.
Big Joe's Trailer Truck, Random House, 1974.
I Am a Monster, Golden Press, 1976.
The Grover Sticker Book, Western Publishing, 1976.
The Count's Coloring Book, Western Publishing, 1976.
The Sesame Street Mix or Match Storybook: Over Two Hundred Thousand Funny Combinations, Random House, 1977.
Who's Who on Sesame Street, Western Publishing, 1977.
Busy City (nonfiction), Random House, 1978.
The Olden Days (nonfiction), Random House, 1981.
Bathtime on Sesame Street, edited by Janet Schulman, Random House, 1983.
Big Bird Visits the Dodos, Random House, 1985.

ILLUSTRATOR; UNDER NAME JOE MATHIEU

Ossie Davis, *Purlie Victorious*, Houghton, 1973.
Scott Corbett, *Dr. Merlin's Magic Shop*, Little, Brown, 1973.
Genevieve Gray, *Casey's Camper*, McGraw, 1973.
Byron Preiss, *The Electric Company: The Silent "e's" From Outer Space*, Western Publishing, 1973.
Corbett, *The Great Custard Pie Panic*, Little, Brown, 1974.

Suzanne W. Bladow, *The Midnight Flight of Moose, Mops, and Marvin*, McGraw, 1975.
Howard Liss, *The Giant Book of Strange but True Sports Stories*, Random House, 1976.
Hedda Nussbaum, *Plants Do Amazing Things* (nonfiction), Random House, 1977.
Katy Hall and Lisa Eisenberg, *A Gallery of Monsters*, Random House, 1981.
Cindy West, *The Superkids and the Singing Dog*, Random House, 1982.
Harold Woods and Geraldine Woods, *The Book of the Unknown* (nonfiction), Random House, 1982.
Liss, *The Giant Book of More Strange but True Sports Stories*, Random House, 1983.

Also illustrator of numerous books in the "Sesame Street" series, including Sarah Roberts's *Ernie's Big Mess*, Random House, 1981.

AVOCATIONAL INTERESTS: Bicycling (especially touring the New England states), jazz and ragtime.*

*   *   *

MATOSSIAN, Mary Kilbourne   1930-

PERSONAL: Born July 9, 1930, in Los Angeles, Calif.; daughter of Norman and Katharine (Hillix) Kilbourne; married Garo Matossian, July 9, 1954 (divorced, 1980); children: Lou Ann, Michele, Viken, Mark. *Education:* Stanford University, B.A., 1951, Ph.D., 1955; University of Beirut, M.A., 1952.

ADDRESSES: Office—Department of History, University of Maryland at College Park, College Park, Md. 20742.

CAREER: Columbia University, New York, N.Y., research associate in Soviet history, 1955-56; Harvard University, Cambridge, Mass., research fellow at Center for Mid Eastern Studies, 1957-58; State University of New York College at Buffalo, assistant professor of history, 1960-62; University of Maryland at College Park, lecturer, 1963-67, assistant professor, 1967-72, associate professor of history, 1973—.

AWARDS, HONORS: National Academy of Sciences grant for study in U.S.S.R., 1984.

MEMBER: American Association for the Advancement of Slavic Studies, American Association for the History of Medicine.

WRITINGS:

The Impact of Soviet Politics in Armenia, E. J. Brill, 1957.
(Contributor) *The Russian Peasant in the Nineteenth Century*, Stanford University Press, 1968.
Village Life in Armenia, Wayne State University Press, 1982.
(With Susie Hoogasian Villa) *Armenian Village Life Before 1914*, Wayne State University Press, 1982.
Ergot, Molds, and History, Yale University Press, in press.

Contributor to history and Slavic studies journals.

*   *   *

MATTISON, Christopher   1949-

PERSONAL: Born July 25, 1949, in Southampton, Hampshire, England; son of Ronald (a printer) and Rosina (Lewis) Mattison; divorced; children: Victoria, James. *Education:* Attended grammar school in Southampton, England; additional study at University of Sheffield, 1986—.

ADDRESSES: Home—138 Dalewood Rd., Sheffield S8 0EF, England.

CAREER: University of Southampton, Southampton, England, zoology technician, 1967-75; Southampton General Hospital, Southampton, laboratory technician, 1975-77; University of Sheffield, Sheffield, England, zoology technician, 1977-86.

WRITINGS:

The Care of Reptiles and Amphibians in Captivity, illustrated with own photographs, Blandford, 1982, revised edition, 1987.
Snakes of the World, illustrated with own photographs, Facts on File, 1986.
Frogs and Toads of the World, illustrated with own photographs, Facts on File, 1987.

Contributor of articles and photographs to wildlife and zoology journals.

WORK IN PROGRESS: Keeping and Breeding Snakes; Lizards of the World.

SIDELIGHTS: Christopher Mattison told *CA:* ''My outside interests are photography and travel, during which I obtain photographic material and information. In this connection, I have made several research trips to southern Europe, as well as Trinidad and Tobago, Malaysia, Sumatra, Ecuador, and the United States.

''Over the years, I have become more and more interested in the interactions of all living things with each other and with their environment. I see myself as an observer and communicator, and I attempt to convey my fascination with the diversity and variety of nature through my books and photographs and through talks given to natural history societies.''

BIOGRAPHICAL/CRITICAL SOURCES:

PERIODICALS

Times Literary Supplement, July 4, 1986.

*   *   *

MAUPIN, Armistead   1944-

BRIEF ENTRY: Surname is pronounced ''Maw-pin''; born May 13, 1944, in Washington, D.C. American journalist and author. Maupin became known to readers of the *San Francisco Chronicle* in 1976 when the columnist began a series of fictional articles characterizing residents of that city. At the suggestion of Harvey Ginsberg, senior editor for Harper & Row Publishers, the stories were collected in 1978 and published in novel form by Harper as *Tales of the City.* After the success of this first book, later columns were also collected and published by Harper as *More Tales of the City* (1980), *Further Tales of the City* (1982), *Babycakes* (1984), and, after Maupin's move to the San Francisco *Examiner* in 1986, *Significant Others* (1987). His writings have been praised for their blend of humor and drama, their careful characterization, and their maturity in dealing with topics such as acquired immune deficiency syndrome (AIDS) in both heterosexual and homosexual contexts. Before joining the *San Francisco Chronicle* in 1976, Maupin worked as a reporter for the Charleston *News and Courier* and the Associated Press, a columnist for the San Francisco *Pacific Sun,* and a publicist for the San Francisco Opera. He also served San Francisco's KRON-TV as a commentator in 1979. *Addresses: Home*—San Francisco, Calif.

Agent—Jed Mattes, International Creative Management, 40 West 57th St., New York, N.Y. 10019.

BIOGRAPHICAL/CRITICAL SOURCES:

PERIODICALS

Chicago Tribune, April 28, 1983.
Hudson Review, spring, 1980.
Los Angeles Times Book Review, July 19, 1987.
New York Times Book Review, November 18, 1984.
Publishers Weekly, March 20, 1987.

*   *   *

MAX
See DIOP, Birago (Ismael)

*   *   *

MAYO, Jim
See L'AMOUR, Louis (Dearborn)

*   *   *

MAYOUX, Jean-Jacques   1901(?)-1987(?)

OBITUARY NOTICE: Born c. 1901; died c. 1987 in Paris, France. Educator, administrator, translator, and author. Author of numerous critical studies of literature and painting, Mayoux was a longtime professor of Anglo-American studies at the University of Paris, Sorbonne. Though a liberal, he resisted the application of Marxist theory to criticism, valuing British and American authors for their individuality and contending that English art is characterized by its imaginative qualities. Early in his career Mayoux was a lecturer in French at Liverpool University, and in the aftermath of World War II he held a junior ministerial post in the French Government of Charles de Gaulle. His writings include *L'Humour et l'absurde: Attitudes anglo-saxonnes, attitudes francaises; La Peinture anglaise: De Hogarth aux preraphaelites* (translation published as *English Painting: From Hogarth to the Pre-Raphaelites*); and book-length studies of Herman Melville, James Joyce, and Samuel Beckett. Mayoux translated William Shakespeare's play *As You Like It* into French.

OBITUARIES AND OTHER SOURCES:

PERIODICALS

Times (London), January 1, 1988.

*   *   *

MAZUMDAR, Maxim   1952(?)-1988

OBITUARY NOTICE: Born c. 1952 (one source says c. 1949), in Bombay, India; immigrated to Canada, 1969; naturalized Canadian citizen; died following a long illness, April 28, 1988, in Halifax, Nova Scotia, Canada. Actor, director, administrator, and playwright. Artistic director of Newfoundland's popular Stephenville Festival, which he founded in 1979, Mazumdar also established Montreal's Phoenix Theatre, Theatre Newfoundland and Labrador, and the arts program of New Brunswick's Memramcook Institute. He wrote three one-man shows, ''Oscar Remembered,'' ''Rimbaud,'' and ''Dance for Gods,'' which he performed in Canada, New York, and London. His directing credits include ''Evita'' and ''Godspell.'' Mazumdar also wrote the plays ''Invitation to the Dance,'' ''Tennessee and Me,'' and ''Journeys.''

OBITUARIES AND OTHER SOURCES:

PERIODICALS

Globe and Mail (Toronto), April 30, 1988.
Times (London), May 6, 1988.

* * *

McARDLE, Catherine
See KELLEHER, Catherine McArdle

* * *

McCLELLAN, George Marion   1860-1934

PERSONAL: Born September 29, 1860, in Belfast, Tenn.; died May 17, 1934; son of George Fielding and Eliza (Leonard) McClellan; married Mariah Augusta Rabb, October 4, 1988; children: Marion S. (one source says Lochiel), Theodore R. *Education:* Fisk University, B.A., 1885, M.A., 1890; Hartford Theological Seminary, B.D., 1891; attended University of California at Los Angeles. *Religion:* Congregationalist. *Politics:* Republican.

ADDRESSES: Home—1123 West Hill St., Louisville, Ky.

CAREER: Poet and short story writer. Congregationalist minister in Louisville, Ky., c. 1887-90; Fisk University, Nashville, Tenn., financial agent, 1892-94; State Normal School, Normal, Alabama, teacher and chaplain, 1894-96; pastor for Congregationalist church in Memphis, Tenn., 1897-99; Central Colored High School, Louisville, teacher of Latin and English, 1899-1911; Dunbar Public School, Louisville, principal, 1911-19. Solicited funds for an anti-tubercular sanatorium for black people in Los Angeles, Calif.

WRITINGS:

Poems, A.M.E. Church Sunday School Union, 1895, reprinted, Books for Libraries Press, 1970.
Songs of a Southerner (poems), Press of Rockwell & Churchill, 1896.
(Contributor) Daniel Wallace Culp, editor, *Twentieth Century Negro Literature; or, A Cyclopedia of Thought on the Vital Topics Relating to the American Negro,* J. L. Nichols, 1902.
Old Greenbottom Inn and Other Stories, privately printed, 1906, reprinted, AMS Press, 1975.
The Path of Dreams (poems), J. P. Morton, 1916, reprinted, Books for Libraries Press, 1970.

SIDELIGHTS: George Marion McClellan, who wrote poetry and short stories during the late nineteenth and early twentieth centuries, was known for his sentimental and conservative works. In the 1890s McClellan's poetry "was based mainly on the kinds of themes and images that were staples in the popular, genteel verse of the period," noted Dickson D. Bruce, Jr., in *Dictionary of Literary Biography.* This type of sentimentalism was characteristic among black writers of that decade who, in hopes of making race insignificant, used literature to portray a sophisticated, middle-class black world that could be readily assimilated into white mainstream society. But at the beginning of the century many black writers turned to the unique history and experience of blacks in the United States, demonstrating in their works a strong race-consciousness and concern for racial identity. McClellan, however, held fast to the conservative assimilationist philosophy during this time, hence distinguishing himself from other black writers.

"The strength of his views indicates, above all," commented Bruce, "the depth of his commitment to the American literary and cultural mainstream, a commitment which, however unusual, would remain a constant in his literary career."

Exemplary of McClellan's conservative, mainstream style is his 1895 *Poems,* a collection of sentimental works about nature, love, and religion. The poetry shows no awareness of the rising concern for a distinctive black literature, and in the book's introduction McClellan, explained Bruce, "actually, if tacitly, denied the validity of these new directions in black literary thought." Departing slightly from his sentimentalist approach, McClellan gives a general overview of black literature in a 1902 essay, "The Negro as a Writer," appearing in *Twentieth Century Negro Literature.* The author shows an interest in ideas of racial pride but, tied to his conservative views of black literature, focuses only on black writers who had significant white readership and works focusing on genteel heroes and heroines.

By 1906, though, McClellan came to a point in his writing where he was prepared to produce literature based on the unique aspects of black life in America. Illustrating his view that the struggle of blacks against society in the South contains the elements of classic tragedy is McClellan's short story collection *Old Greenbottom Inn.* The stories relate such scenarios as interracial love, folk tradition, seduction, and violence. "Uniting all the stories in the volume," related Bruce, "is a sense that blacks were caught up in a world not of their making and powerfully out of control." Bruce qualified, however, that McClellan still clung to an essentially white literary tradition, for he modeled his characters not after figures exclusive to black culture and history but, rather, after literary figures drawn from a larger Western tradition, such as those found in the tragic dramas of Aeschylus and William Shakespeare. Furthermore, continued Bruce, McClellan never actually departed from his assimilationist ideals: "Viewing the black experience as, most profoundly, the stuff of tragedy, [the author] saw the origins of tragedy in racism's indifferent hostility to black aspirations, which he conceived of as, above all, making a place in the American mainstream."

All but one of the stories in *Old Greenbottom Inn,* along with poetry previously appearing in *Poems,* were reprinted in McClellan's 1916 *The Path of Dreams,* which featured an additional story also dealing with the tragic theme of race relations. Summing up the author's work, Bruce wrote: "As he focused his attention on the tragedies of black American life, he wrote in ways that presented a consistent vision of the emotional and psychological realities of racism, helping to illuminate the impact of prejudice on human lives." Placing the author in the context of black American literary figures, Bruce concluded that, although McClellan was not a major writer during his lifetime, his work is "significant . . . because of its conservatism," while it provides "an important perspective on the development of black thought and culture at the turn of the century."

BIOGRAPHICAL/CRITICAL SOURCES:

BOOKS

Culp, Daniel Wallace, *American Negro: His History and Literature,* Arno Press, 1969.
Dictionary of Literary Biography, Volume 50: *Afro-American Writers Before the Harlem Renaissance,* Gale, 1986.
Kerlin, Robert T., *Negro Poets and Their Poems,* revised and enlarged edition, Associated Publishers, 1935.

Long, Richard A. and Eugenia W. Collier, *Afro-American Writing: An Anthology of Prose and Poetry,* Volume 1, New York University Press, 1972.

Sherman, Joan R., *Invisible Poets: Afro-Americans of the Nineteenth Century,* University of Illinois Press, 1974.

White, Newman Ivey and Walter Clinton Jackson, *An Anthology of Verse by American Negroes,* Trinity College Press, 1924.*

*   *   *

McCONNELL, James Douglas Rutherford   1915-1988
(Douglas Rutherford; Paul Temple, a joint pseudonym)

OBITUARY NOTICE—See index for *CA* sketch: Born October 14, 1915, in Kilkenny, Ireland; died April 29, 1988. Educator, editor, and author. McConnell was a longtime Eton College teacher and writer of instructional books, war stories, and many crime novels. Under the name Douglas Rutherford he published most of his crime fiction, including *Gunshot Grand Prix, Killer on the Track,* and *Rally to the Death.* He also collaborated with Francis Durbridge on crime novels such as *The Pig-Tail Murder, A Game of Murder,* and—under the joint pseudonym Paul Temple—*The Tyler Mystery.*

OBITUARIES AND OTHER SOURCES:

PERIODICALS

Times (London), May 5, 1988.

*   *   *

McCORMICK, James P(atton)   1911-1988

OBITUARY NOTICE: Born March 1, 1911, in Chicago, Ill.; died February 3, 1988, in Tucson, Ariz.; cremated and ashes buried in Valley View Cemetery, Ticonderoga, N.Y. Educator, administrator, and author. McCormick taught English at Wayne State University beginning in 1938, becoming assistant to the vice-president for academic administration in 1957, secretary to the board of governors in 1960, and vice-president in 1965. He transferred to Detroit Edison Company as vice-president for educational affairs in 1968. He later worked as an adjunct professor at the University of Arizona and a visiting professor at universities in England, Taiwan, Iran, and New Zealand. McCormick's books include *As a Flame Springs,* a biography of Robert and Elizabeth Barrett Browning; *Rah for the Engineers! A Century of Change; Patterns in Recent American Literature;* and a collaboration with Walker Lee Cisler on the latter's reminiscences, *A Measurable Difference.*

OBITUARIES AND OTHER SOURCES:

BOOKS

Directory of American Scholars, Volume II: *English, Speech, and Drama,* 6th edition, Bowker, 1974.

PERIODICALS

Detroit Free Press, February 6, 1988.

*   *   *

McCULLOCH, Sarah
See URE, Jean

McCULLOUGH, Dale Richard   1933-

PERSONAL: Born December 5, 1933, in Sioux Falls, S.D.; son of Guy (a farmer) and Rose (a homemaker; maiden name, Bies) McCullough; married Karen Thomas, 1958 (divorced, 1970); married Yvette Blazzard (a teacher), July 3, 1974; children: (first marriage) Kevin, Mark, Lissa; (second marriage) Brent, Cheryl. *Education:* South Dakota State University, B.S., 1957; Oregon State University, M.S., 1960; University of California, Berkeley, Ph.D., 1966.

ADDRESSES: Home—249 Stanford Ave., Kensington, Calif. 94708. *Office*—Department of Forestry-Resource Management, University of California, 2120 Oxford St., Berkeley, Calif. 94720.

CAREER: University of Michigan, Ann Arbor, assistant professor of wildlife management, 1966-69, associate professor of wildlife and fisheries, 1969-74, professor of natural resources, 1974-80, chairman of resource ecology program, 1971-74; University of California, Berkeley, professor of wildlife biology and management, 1980—. *Military service:* U.S. Army, 1953-55.

MEMBER: American Society of Mammalogists, Ecological Society of America, Wildlife Society.

AWARDS, HONORS: The Tule Elk: Its History, Behavior, and Ecology was named outstanding academic book by *Choice* magazine, 1971; *The George Reserve Deer Herd: Population Ecology of a K-Selected Species* was chosen the outstanding book of the year by the Wildlife Society, 1981.

WRITINGS:

The Tule Elk: Its History, Behavior, and Ecology, University of California Press, 1971.
The George Reserve Deer Herd: Population Ecology of a K-Selected Species, University of Michigan Press, 1979.

Contributor of numerous articles to professional journals.

WORK IN PROGRESS: Research on the population dynamics of deer and the ecology of kangaroos.

SIDELIGHTS: Dale Richard McCullough told *CA:* "I am interested in conservation and management of wildlife in general and large mammals in particular. I have done research on threatened animals such as the grizzly bear in Yellowstone National Park and the tule elk in California. I want to protect and conserve natural habitats of wild animals on a global scale in order to manage and preserve wild species in the face of increasing human populations."

*   *   *

McDERMOTT, Catherine   1952-

PERSONAL: Born December 14, 1952, in Rochdale, Lancashire, England; daughter of William (a confection and tobacco dealer) and Ethel (Mills) McDermott. *Education:* University of Leeds, B.A. (with honors), 1975; Barber Institute of Fine Arts, M.A., 1977.

ADDRESSES: Home—2 Elms Rd., Clapham SW4 9EU, England. *Office*—Department of Design History, Kingston Polytechnic, Kingston upon Thames, Surrey, England. *Agent*—David Higham Associates Ltd., 5-8 Lower John St., Golden Sq., London W1R 4HA, England.

CAREER: Teesside Polytechnic, Middlesbrough, Cleveland, England, lecturer in design history, 1977-79; City of London

Polytechnic, London, senior lecturer in design history, 1979-81; Kingston Polytechnic, Kingston upon Thames, England, senior lecturer in design history, 1981—.

MEMBER: British Design History Society (chairperson, 1980-84).

WRITINGS:

Street Style: British Design in the 80s, Rizzoli International, 1987 (first published by Design Council, 1987).

Contributor to magazines, including *Creative Review, Building Design, Crafts, Typographic,* and *Design Week.*

WORK IN PROGRESS: A book of essays on contemporary design, for Architectural Press; organizing a major exhibition of British design at a museum in Holland.

SIDELIGHTS: Catherine McDermott told *CA:* "I teach theoretical studies at one of England's best-known design schools. In addition, I work as a free-lance design writer. My interest is contemporary design, and I have lectured widely on the subject.

"In the late 1970s England was pioneering the new subject of design history. A group of writers and teachers formed the Design History Society in 1977, and I became a committee member. Working hard to stimulate interest in this new subject, I developed new courses on design—specifically on that of the postwar period. In 1985 the Design Council approached me to write an account of contemporary British design. During the 1980s a great deal of international interest focused on a new spirit behind British style, particularly the so-called street style fashion design of Vivienne Westwood. These areas of popular fashion and graphics are closely allied with another uniquely British phenomenon—youth culture. My book, *Street Style: British Design in the 80s,* charts the influence of ideas such as punk. Since its publication, the volume has received a great deal of publicity, and there is an indication that U.S. interest in things very British is very strong at the present time."

BIOGRAPHICAL/CRITICAL SOURCES:

PERIODICALS

Times (London), March 25, 1987.

*   *   *

McDONALD, David J(ohn) 1902-1979

OBITUARY NOTICE—See index for *CA* sketch: Born November 22, 1902, in Pittsburgh, Pa.; died August 8, 1979, in Palm Springs, Calif. Labor leader and author. McDonald was a prominent labor union official. In 1923 he was named private secretary to Philip Murray, who was then vice-president of the United Mine Workers. When Murray became president of the steelworker's union, McDonald accompanied him and served as secretary-treasurer of that organization until 1953, when he succeeded Murray as president. McDonald secured impressive wage increases for steelworkers in the 1950s but presided over a devastating strike in the winter of 1959-60. By the early 1960s, his authority within the union had been undermined by sluggish economic conditions, and his reputation had been compromised by his relatively opulent standard of living. In 1964 he lost the union presidency to his own deputy, I. W. Abel, in close voting. McDonald spent his later years in Palm Springs. Among his writings are *Coal and Unionism* and an autobiography, *Union Man: The Life of a Labor Statesman.*

OBITUARIES AND OTHER SOURCES:

BOOKS

Current Biography, H. W. Wilson, 1953, October, 1980.
Who Was Who in America, With World Notables, Volume VII: 1977-1981, Marquis, 1981.

PERIODICALS

Newsweek, August 20, 1979.
New York Times, August 10, 1979.
Time, August 20, 1979.

*   *   *

McDONOUGH, Jack 1944-

PERSONAL: Born August 10, 1944, in Scranton, Pa. *Education:* King's College, Wilkes-Barre, Pa., B.A., 1966; University of North Carolina at Chapel Hill, M.A., 1968.

CAREER: Wake Forest University, Winston-Salem, N.C., instructor in English, 1968-70; free-lance writer, 1970—. Chairman of San Rafael Redevelopment Agency citizens' advisory committee, 1984-85.

MEMBER: American Society of Composers, Authors, and Publishers.

WRITINGS:

San Francisco Rock: The Illustrated History, 1965-1985, Chronicle Books, 1985.

Correspondent for *Billboard.* Contributor of several hundred articles to national and local magazines.

WORK IN PROGRESS: Slider, a baseball novel; *The Katyn Legacy,* a nuclear espionage novel.

*   *   *

McKEOWN, Thomas 1912-1988

OBITUARY NOTICE: Born November 2, 1912, in Portadown, Ireland (now Northern Ireland); died June 13, 1988. Physician, educator, editor, and author. A specialist in the field of public health, McKeown was professor of social medicine at the University of Birmingham from 1945 until he retired in 1977. He contended that environment and behavior were more important to improved human health than technical advances in medicine. McKeown wrote *Medicine in Modern Society, The Modern Rise of Population,* and *The Role of Medicine: Dream, Mirage, or Neurosis?,* and he helped edit *Screening in Medical Care* and *Medical History and Medical Care.* He was joint editor of the *British Journal of Preventive and Social Medicine* from 1950 to 1958.

OBITUARIES AND OTHER SOURCES:

BOOKS

Who's Who, 140th edition, St. Martin's, 1988.
Who's Who in the World, 8th edition, Marquis, 1986.

PERIODICALS

Times (London), June 20, 1988.

*   *   *

McLAGLEN, John J.
See HARVEY, John (Barton)

McLOUGHLIN, R. B.
See MENCKEN, H(enry) L(ouis)

*   *   *

McMANUS, Jason 1934-

PERSONAL: Born March 3, 1934, in Mission, Kan.; son of John Alan and Stella Frances (Gosney) McManus; married Patricia Ann Paulson, October 18, 1958 (divorced February, 1966); married Deborah Hall Murphy (an architect), December 2, 1973; children: (first marriage) John Alan; (second marriage) Sophie Eleanor, Mage Caroline. *Education:* Davidson College, B.A., 1956; Princeton University, M.P.A., 1958; attended Oxford University, 1958-59.

ADDRESSES: Office—Time Inc., Time and Life Building, Rockefeller Center, New York, N.Y. 10020.

CAREER: Time Inc., New York, N.Y., staff writer for *Time*, 1959-62, chief of Common Market bureau in Paris, France, 1962-64, associate editor, 1964-68, senior editor, 1968-76, assistant managing editor, 1976-78, executive editor, 1978-83, corporate editor, 1984-85, managing editor of *Time*, 1985-87, editor in chief, 1987—. Member of presidential advisory committee of International Educational Exchange, 1982-85. Director of Hastings Center; member of board of governors, Columbia University Seminars on Media and Society; trustee of Nightingale-Bamford School; member of Council on Foreign Relations.

MEMBER: Century Association.

AWARDS, HONORS: Rhodes scholar, 1958-59; Litt.D. from Davidson College, 1979.

WRITINGS:

Introduction: Stories by New Writers, Faber, 1960.

*   *   *

McMEEKIN, Dorothy 1932-

PERSONAL: Born February 24, 1932, in Boston, Mass.; daughter of Thomas LeRoy (a biochemist) and Vera (a secretary; maiden name, Crockatt) McMeekin. *Education:* Wilson College, B.A., 1953; Wellesley College, M.A., 1955; Cornell University, Ph.D., 1959.

ADDRESSES: Home—1055 Marigold St., East Lansing, Mich. 48823. *Office*—Department of Natural Science, 335 North Kedzie, Michigan State University, East Lansing, Mich. 48823.

CAREER: Upsala College, East Orange, N.J., assistant professor of biology, 1959-64; Bowling Green State University, Bowling Green, Ohio, assistant professor of biology, 1964-66; Michigan State University, East Lansing, assistant professor, 1966-69, associate professor, 1969-75, professor of natural science, 1975—.

MEMBER: American Phytopathological Society, Mycological Society of America, Botanical Society of America, National Science Teachers Association, American Civil Liberties Union (member of board of directors of Lansing chapter, 1982—), Michigan Women's Studies Association, Michigan Botanical Club (member of board of directors, 1986—), Sigma Xi, Phi Kappa Phi.

WRITINGS:

Diego Rivera: Science and Creativity in the Detroit Murals, Michigan State University Press, 1985.

Contributor to scientific journals.

WORK IN PROGRESS: Writing and editing a television program on Diego Rivera and science in his Detroit murals; research on the representation of science in the Rivera murals in Mexico; research on botanical images in pre-Columbian Mesoamerican designs and on factors influencing the growth of the obligately parasitic fungus *Peronospora parasitica* on crucifers.

SIDELIGHTS: Dorothy McMeekin told *CA:* "The professional survival of many women scientists who graduated in the 1950s was linked, because of sex discrimination, to diversification and not specialization. My career reflects that reality. I have taught both basic biology and specialized botany classes. Currently I instruct non-science majors in general education science, which includes information on atoms, molecules, cells, genetics, evolution, geology, and ecology. It is this science background, atypical of art historians, that has enabled me to understand and appreciate the scientific aptitude of the Mexican muralist Diego Rivera.

"In 1986 I participated in a People-to-People delegation to China, where I visited universities and research stations. I have also traveled in Europe, and in the Americas from Ellesmere Island in the Arctic to the Andes Mountains in Peru."

AVOCATIONAL INTERESTS: Gardening, home decoration, sewing, carpentry.

*   *   *

McNAMEE, Thomas 1947-

PERSONAL: Born July 31, 1947, in Memphis, Tenn.; son of Charles T. (in business) and Gladys (a homemaker; maiden name, Runyon) McNamee; married Louise Rossett (an advertising agency president), May 27, 1970. *Education:* Yale University, B.A., 1969.

ADDRESSES: 121 Washington Pl., New York, N.Y. 10014. *Agent*—Jeanne Drewsen, 14635 Sutton St., Sherman Oaks, Calif. 91403.

CAREER: Affiliated with CBS Records, New York, N.Y., 1969-76; free-lance writer, 1976—.

WRITINGS:

The Grizzly Bear (nonfiction), Knopf, 1984.

Contributor of poetry to numerous periodicals, including *New Yorker*, *Poetry Review*, and *New England Review*. Also author of essays published in *Audubon*, *Life*, *London Times*, and *Washington Post*.

WORK IN PROGRESS: Two novels, *A Story of Deep Delight* and *Desire*.

SIDELIGHTS: Years of investigation, both in the field and in the library, went in to Thomas McNamee's *Grizzly Bear*. The book examines the natural history of this endangered species and the controversies surrounding its management in U.S. national parks in the West. Preservationists, who consider any industrial developments near the bear's habitat a death sentence for the animal, face opposition from business interests and some area residents who feel the depressed local economy must take precedence over the animal's welfare. Others fear for the safety of park visitors who are sometimes attacked by the bears for no apparent reason. According to Tim Cahill of the *New York Times Book Review,* "Mr. McNamee does a good job of reporting the conflicts among the various parties, as well as their legitimate concerns." Although he numbers the author among the preservationists, Cahill credits McNamee with producing a "balanced, comprehensible work" and one that is "lyrical, lucid, evocative, sometimes funny and always stylishly written."

BIOGRAPHICAL/CRITICAL SOURCES:

PERIODICALS

Los Angeles Times Book Review, January 13, 1985.
New York Times Book Review, August 25, 1985.

*   *   *

MEADOW, Barry 1947-

PERSONAL: Born January 29, 1947, in Brooklyn, N.Y.; son of Morton and Myrtle (Rothstein) Meadow; married Cora Miranda, December 5, 1970; children: Scott. *Education:* Attended State University of New York at Binghamton, 1963-65.

ADDRESSES: Home—527 South Sonya St., Anaheim, Calif. 92802.

CAREER: National Armstrong Daily, New York, N.Y., columnist and racing handicapper, 1970; *American Turf Monthly,* New York City, editor, 1971; Kutshers Country Club, Monticello, N.Y., tennis director, 1972-78; free-lance writer, 1979—. *Military service:* U.S. Navy, 1966-70.

MEMBER: Writers Guild of America West, American Society of Journalists and Authors.

WRITINGS:

Success at the Harness Races, Citadel, 1967.
Professional Harness Betting, TR Publishing, 1987.
Money Secrets at the Racetrack, TR Publishing, 1988.

Writer for television series, including "What's Happening," "Carter Country," and "One in a Million." Columnist for *Gambling Times.*

SIDELIGHTS: Barry Meadow told *CA:* "Writers of material about horse-race handicapping have generally enjoyed a reputation somewhere between vermin and slime. And much of this has been deserved. In recent years, though, there's been a trend toward treating horse-race handicapping as a legitimate subject worthy of intellectual investigation. As a horseplayer who writes, and as a writer who bets on horses, I've tried to tell the truth about racetrack betting as I know it from thousands of occasionally happy hours spent pouring money through mutuel machines from coast to coast.

"My books have attempted to help the reader learn how to analyze and bet races so that he'll have an edge over his competition, the other fans. They don't promise a million dollars in a week or a fleet of yachts just beyond the horizon. Making money at racetrack betting is hard work, a job like any other, requiring ability and perseverance. This news may come as a disappointment to those seeking instant enlightenment and a Rolls Royce by Friday."

MEKETA, Jacqueline
See MEKETA, Jacqueline Dorgan

*   *   *

MEKETA, Jacqueline Dorgan 1926-
(Jacqueline Meketa)

PERSONAL: Surname is pronounced *"Mah-key-tah";* born July 28, 1926, in Ancon, Panama Canal Zone; daughter of William James (an electrician) and Elsie (a homemaker; maiden name, Schetler) Dorgan; married Charles Edward Meketa (an engineering designer), October 31, 1946; children: James E., Michael C., Richard A., Anthony S., Robert W., Thomas P., Rebecca Meketa-May. *Education:* University of New Mexico, B.A. (magna cum laude), 1977. *Politics:* Democrat. *Religion:* Roman Catholic.

ADDRESSES: Home and office—Star Route, Box 1163, Corrales, N.M. 87048.

CAREER: JDM Ventures (marketing research firm), Albuquerque, N.M., owner, 1962-67; Los Alamos Scientific Laboratory, Los Alamos, N.M., public information clerk, 1967-74; Zia Research, Albuquerque, N.M., manager of marketing, 1980-84; free-lance writer and historian, 1980—. Guest lecturer at universities and for historical and fraternal groups. Volunteer librarian; volunteer at Young Children's Health Center.

MEMBER: Westerners International, Western Writers of America, Order of the Indian Wars, Council on America's Military Past—U.S.A., New Mexico Historical Society, Sandoval County Historical Society.

WRITINGS:

(Under name Jacqueline Meketa; with husband, Charles Meketa) *One Blanket and Ten Days Rations,* Southwest Parks and Monuments Association, 1980.
Louis Felsenthal, Citizen-Soldier of Territorial New Mexico, University of New Mexico Press, 1982.
(Editor) *Legacy of Honor, The Life of Rafael Chacon,* University of New Mexico Press, 1986.

Contributor of articles to *New Mexico Historical Review.*

WORK IN PROGRESS: Research on military activity in New Mexico, both during the Mexican-American War period and the Civil War era; writing a series of articles on the lesser-known New Mexicans of the territorial period that may be incorporated into a book; contemporary and historical articles for magazines and newspapers.

SIDELIGHTS: Jacqueline Dorgan Meketa told *CA:* "I was born and raised of American parents in the Panama Canal Zone. I moved to New Mexico, a tri-cultural state (Indian, Hispanic, Anglo), thirty-six years ago.

"I empathize with native Hispanics who have been exploited, particularly in the last century in New Mexico, and have been trying to 'correct' unfair and unflattering history, particularly military, written about the Hispanics here by Anglos."

AVOCATIONAL INTERESTS: "I am always happy to share my knowledge of life in the Southwest during the territorial period, especially when I can 'humanize' it for my listeners."

MELONEY, Franken
    See FRANKEN, Rose (Dorothy)

*   *   *

MELVILLE, James
    See MARTIN, (Roy) Peter

*   *   *

MENCKEN, H(enry) L(ouis)   1880-1956
    (Herbert Winslow Archer, Pierre d'Aubigny,
    W. L. D. Bell, Atwood C. Bellamy, James
    Drayham, William Fink, J. D. Gilray, Amelia
    Hatteras, F. C. Henderson, Janet Jefferson,
    R. B. McLoughlin, Harriet Morgan, George
    Weems Peregoy, James P. Ratcliffe, The
    Ringmaster, Francis Clegg Thompson, Raoul della
    Torre, W. H. Trimball, Marie de Verdi, Irving S.
    Watson, James Wharton, Robert W. Woodruff,
    pseudonyms; C. Farley Anderson, Owen Hatteras,
    joint pseudonyms)

PERSONAL: Born September 12, 1880, in Baltimore, Md.;
died of heart failure, January 29, 1956, in Baltimore, Md.;
son of August (a cigar manufacturer) and Anna (Abhau)
Mencken; married Sara Powell Haardt (a writer), August 27,
1930 (died, 1935). *Education:* Attended Baltimore Polytechnic Institute, 1892-96.

ADDRESSES: Home and office—1524 Hollins St., Baltimore,
Md. 21223.

CAREER: Herald, Baltimore, Md., reporter, 1899-1901, Sunday editor, 1901-03, city editor, 1903-05, editor in chief, 1906;
Evening News, Baltimore, Md., news editor, 1906; *Sunpapers,* Baltimore, Md., Sunday editor, 1906-10, editor and columnist, 1910-16; *Evening Mail,* New York, N.Y., columnist,
1917-18; *Sunpapers,* Baltimore, Md., editor, columnist, and
political correspondent, 1919-41, political correspondent, 1948.
Co-editor of *The Smart Set: A Magazine of Cleverness,* 1914-
23; creator and co-editor of *Parisienne,* 1915, *Saucy Stories,*
1916, and *Black Mask,* 1920; founder and editor of *The American Mercury: A Monthly Review,* 1924-33.

MEMBER: Saturday Night Club (Baltimore).

AWARDS, HONORS: Gold medal from National Institute and
American Academy of Arts and Letters, 1950, for essays and
criticism; "H. L. Mencken Writing Award" established in
author's memory by the *Sunpapers,* given annually "to the
newspaper columnist who most exemplifies the spirit and social commentary of H. L. Mencken."

WRITINGS:

*Ventures into Verse: Being Various Ballads, Ballades, Ron-
    deaux, Triolets, Songs, Quatrains, Odes, and Roundels,
    All Rescued From the Potter's Field of the Old Files and
    Here Given Decent Burial (Peace to Their Ashes) by Henry
    Louis Mencken, with Illustrations & Other Things by
    Charles S. Gordon & John Siegel,* Marshall, Beck & Gor-
    don, 1903.
George Bernard Shaw: His Plays, Luce, 1905, Haskell House,
    1976.
The Philosophy of Friedrich Nietzsche, Luce, 1908, R. West,
    1978.

(Editor and author of introduction) Henrik Ibsen, *A Doll's
    House,* Luce, 1909.
(Editor and author of introduction) Ibsen, *Little Eyolf,* Luce,
    1909.
(With Leonard Keene Hirshberg) *What You Ought To Know
    About Your Baby,* Butterick, 1910.
(Editor) *The Gist of Nietzsche,* Luce, 1910, Norwood Editions,
    1977.
*Men Versus the Man: A Correspondence Between Rives La
    Monte, Socialist, and H. L. Mencken, Individualist,* Holt,
    1910, Arno Press, 1972.
The Artist: A Drama Without Words (also see below), Luce,
    1912, Folcroft Library, 1973.
(With George Jean Nathan and Willard Huntington Wright)
    Europe After 8:15, illustrations by Thomas H. Benton,
    John Lane, 1914.
A Book of Burlesques (includes *The Artist: A Drama Without
    Words*), John Lane, 1916, revised edition, Knopf, 1920,
    reprinted, Scholarly Press, 1971.
A Little Book in C Major (Opus 11), John Lane, 1916.
(With Nathan, under joint pseudonym Owen Hatteras) *Pistols
    for Two,* Knopf, 1917, Folcroft Library, 1977.
A Book of Prefaces (Opus 13), Knopf, 1917, Octagon, 1977.
(Author of introduction) Ibsen, *The Master Builder* [and] *Pil-
    lars of Society* [and] *Hedda Gabler,* Boni & Liveright,
    1917.
Damn! A Book of Calumny, Philip Goodman, 1918, repub-
    lished as *A Book of Calumny,* Knopf, 1918.
In Defense of Women, Philip Goodman, 1918, revised edition,
    Knopf, 1922, reprinted, Octagon, 1977.
*The American Language: A Preliminary Inquiry Into the De-
    velopment of English in the United States,* Knopf, 1919,
    4th edition, revised, corrected, and enlarged (Book-of-
    the-Month Club selection), 1936, reprinted, 1974, *Sup-
    plement I,* 1945, reprinted, 1975, *Supplement II,* 1948,
    reprinted, 1975.
Prejudices: First Series, Knopf, 1919, Octagon, 1977.
Prejudices: Second Series, Knopf, 1920, Octagon, 1977.
(Editor and author of introduction) Edwin Muir, *We Moderns:
    Enigmas and Guesses,* Knopf, 1920.
(Editor and author of introduction) Friedrich Wilhelm Nietzsche,
    The Antichrist, Knopf, 1920.
(With Nathan) *The American Credo: A Contribution Toward
    the Interpretation of the National Mind,* Knopf, 1920,
    Octagon, 1977.
(With Nathan) *Heliogabalus: A Buffoonery in Three Acts,*
    Knopf, 1920.
Prejudices: Third Series, Knopf, 1922, Octagon, 1977.
Prejudices: Fourth Series, Knopf, 1924, Octagon, 1977.
Prejudices, J. Cape, 1925.
(Editor) *Americana,* Knopf, 1925.
Notes on Democracy, Knopf, 1926, Octagon, 1977.
Prejudices: Fifth Series, Knopf, 1926, Octagon, 1977.
James Branch Cabell (also see below), McBride, 1927.
Prejudices: Sixth Series, Knopf, 1927, Octagon, 1977.
Selected Prejudices, Knopf, 1927.
Selected Prejudices: Second Series, J. Cape, 1927.
(Editor with Sara Powell Haardt) *Menckeniana: A Schimpflex-
    ikon,* Knopf, 1928, Octagon, 1977.
Treatise on the Gods, Knopf, 1930, 2nd revised edition, 1946,
    reprinted, Random House, 1963.
Making a President: A Footnote to the Saga of Democracy,
    Knopf, 1932.
Treatise on Right and Wrong, Knopf, 1934, Octagon, 1977.

(Editor and author of preface) Sara Powell Haardt, *Southern Album*, Doubleday, 1936.

(Editor and contributor) *The Sunpapers of Baltimore, 1837-1937*, Knopf, 1937.

Happy Days, 1880-1892 (also see below), Knopf, 1940.

Newspaper Days, 1899-1906 (also see below), Knopf, 1941.

(Editor) *A New Dictionary of Quotations on Historical Principles From Ancient and Modern Sources*, Knopf, 1942.

Heathen Days, 1890-1936 (also see below), Knopf, 1943.

Christmas Story, illustrations by Bill Crawford, Knopf, 1946.

(Author of introduction) Theodore Dreiser, *An American Tragedy*, World, 1946.

The Days of H. L. Mencken: Happy Days, Newspaper Days, Heathen Days, Knopf, 1947.

(Contributor) *Literary History of the United States*, Macmillan, 1948.

A Mencken Chrestomathy, Knopf, 1949, Franklin Library, 1980.

Alistair Cooke, editor, *The Vintage Mencken*, Vintage Books, 1955.

Malcolm Moos, editor, *A Carnival of Buncombe*, Johns Hopkins Press, 1956, reprinted, University of Chicago Press, 1984.

Minority Report: H. L. Mencken's Notebooks, Knopf, 1956.

Robert McHugh, editor, *A Bathtub Hoax and Other Blasts & Bravos From the Chicago Tribune*, Knopf, 1958, Octagon, 1977.

Prejudices; A Selection Made by James T. Farrell, and with an Introduction by Him, Vintage Books, 1958.

H. L. Mencken on Music: A Selection by Louis Cheslock, Knopf, 1961.

Guy J. Forgue, editor, *Letters of H. L. Mencken*, Knopf, 1961.

Huntington Cairns, editor, *The American Scene: A Reader*, Knopf, 1965.

William H. Nolte, editor, *H. L. Mencken's "Smart Set" Criticism*, Cornell University Press, 1968.

(Contributor) *James Branch Cabell: Three Essays in Criticism*, Kennikot, 1971.

Carl Bode, editor, *The Young Mencken: The Best of His Work*, Dial Press, 1973.

C. Merton Babcock, editor, *The Mating Game—And How to Play It*, illustrations by Charles Saxon, Hallmark, 1974.

John Dorsey, editor, *Mencken's Baltimore*, Sunpapers, 1974.

Fenwick Anderson, editor, *Quotations From Chairman Mencken; or, Poor Henry's Almanac*, University of Illinois Press, 1974.

Theo Lippman, Jr., editor, *A Gang of Pecksniffs: And Other Comments on Newspaper Publishers, Editors, and Writers*, Arlington House, 1975.

Bode, editor, *The New Mencken Letters*, Dial Press, 1976.

Joseph C. Goulden, editor, *Mencken's Last Campaign: H. L. Mencken on the 1948 Election*, New Republic Book Company, 1976.

Edward L. Galligan, editor, *A Choice of Days* (contains excerpts from *Happy Days, Newspaper Days*, and *Heathen Days*), Knopf, 1980.

John Dorsey, editor, *On Mencken*, Knopf, 1980.

P. E. Cleator, editor, *Letters From Baltimore: The Mencken-Cleator Correspondence*, Associated University Presses, 1982.

Thomas P. Riggio, editor, *Dreiser-Mencken Letters: The Correspondence of Theodore Dreiser and H. L. Mencken, 1907-1945*, University of Pennsylvania Press, 1986.

Marion Elizabeth Rodgers, editor, *Mencken & Sara: A Life in Letters*, McGraw-Hill, 1987.

Jon Winokur, editor, *The Portable Curmudgeon*, New American Library, 1987.

Peter W. Dowell, editor, *"Ich Kuss die Hand": The Letters of H. L. Mencken to Gretchen Hood*, University of Alabama Press, 1987.

Bode, editor, *The Editor, the Bluenose, and the Prostitute: H. L. Mencken's History of the "Hatrack" Censorship Case*, Roberts Rinehart, 1988.

Charles Fecher, editor, *The Diary of H. L. Mencken*, Knopf, 1989.

Contributor of essays and literary criticism, sometimes under various pseudonyms, to numerous periodicals, including *The Smart Set, Chicago Sunday Tribune, Atlantic Monthly, Bookman, Criterion, World Review, Vanity Fair, New Yorker, Nation, New Republic, Cosmopolitan, Virginia Quarterly Review, Yale Review, Esquire, Reader's Digest, Encore, Harper's*, and *Saturday Review*. Contributor of fiction to *Short Stories* and *The Bohemian*.

SIDELIGHTS: Journalist and critic H. L. Mencken exercised an enormous influence on life and letters in early twentieth-century America. Described by William Henry Chamberlain in a 1956 issue of *New Leader* as the "scourge of the boobs," Mencken lambasted such sacred national institutions as religion, marriage, democracy, popular literature, and mass movements; according to *Dictionary of Literary Biography* contributor Elton Miles, the jolly attacks "yanked the garment of delusion off mankind to expose naked pretension, quackery, and stupidity." During the height of his notoriety in the 1920s, Mencken was called "the most powerful private citizen in the United States" in a *New York Times* editorial, and fellow journalist Walter Lippman deemed him "the most powerful personal influence on this whole generation of educated people." Mencken's singular voice rose from the pages of numerous nonfiction books, from magazines such as *The Smart Set* and *The American Mercury*, and from his hometown newspaper, the Baltimore *Sun*. As William Manchester noted in *Disturber of the Peace: The Life of H. L. Mencken*, the author's stinging prose "rolled across the nation and broke with a tremendous roar, sending the self-appointed policemen of our moral and political standards scampering about to see what was the matter." In a 1987 issue of *Reason*, correspondent Thomas W. Hazlett observed that even after more than three decades following his death, Mencken rests "alone at the top among the epoch's essayists and satirists. Mencken's pen savaged all that was Great and Bogus in America: the cads in Washington, the Babbitts on main street, the archmorons in the pulpits. . . . Mencken was charming *and* correct, a combination virtually unheard of in the annals of American Thought. Hence, his life was a gem."

"Mencken took aim upon politicians, bishops, Holy Rollers, Christian Scientists, Methodists, Baptists, Presbyterians, and evangelicals of high and low degree," wrote James J. Kilpatrick in *Menckeniana*. "He belabored [censors], chiropractors, prohibitionists, . . . charity mongers, drive managers, YMCA secretaries, executive secretaries, town boomers, Rotarians, Kiwanians, Boomers, and Elks. He scorned bank presidents, tin roofers, delicatessen dealers, retired bookkeepers, nose and throat specialists, railroad purchasing agents, and the National Association of Teachers of English. More broadly, the Mencken blunderbuss sprayed powder and shot upon fools, yokels, half-wits, ignoramuses, dunderheads, scoundrels, lunatics, morons, rogues, charlatans, mountebanks, imbeciles, barbarians, vagabonds, clowns, fanatics, idiots, bunglers, hacks, quacks, and wowsers." Mencken was neither willing nor able to ignore the foolish antics of many of his fellow Americans. A born individualist, he took a dim view of mass tastes and of any laws—civic or religious—that threatened the growth of a free personality. Hence, the era of the Ku Klux Klan, Prohibition, book censorship, and literal interpretation of the Bible found in Mencken its harshest and most unrelenting critic. In *H. L. Mencken: Iconoclast From Baltimore,* Douglas C. Stenerson claimed that the author "was moved to indignation by the discrepancy between the realities he observed about him and his vision of the kind of art, ethics, and personal behavior a society composed exclusively of truth-seekers and artists would produce." Mencken fought the prevailing American standards in a personal crusade of penned polemic, and in the process he helped to elevate the aims of American thought and literature and the quality of American prose.

Mencken's attacks on what he called the "booboisie" were given added emphasis because, as Kilpatrick put it, he "wrote with a twinkle in his eye." Whether he was reviewing a novel or covering a political convention, Mencken strove first to entertain his audience. In a biography entitled *Mencken,* Carl Bode declared that the critic's prose style "was one of the striking creations of his era, far more dynamic than his solidly conservative ideas. His genius for seizing the unexpected and amusing word, for making the irreverent comparison, and for creating a tone that was not acid but alkaline helped to make him the most readable of American essayists." A humorist in the tradition of Mark Twain and the frontier journalists of the nineteenth century, Mencken played on his readers' emotions by employing a prodigious and colorful vocabulary—and by stating his opinions bluntly. *New World Writing: Sixth Mentor Selection* contributor James T. Farrell contended that as a voice of the Roaring Twenties, Mencken "made revolt and protest fun. He was a great satirist and humorist. He lambasted right, left, and center, and everything fell before his original onslaught of words. Some of this is interesting today only because it is so well-written. . . . But practically everything he wrote is remarkable for its style. You will always come upon a neologism, a vivid phrase, a sharp sentence, a tirade of words which pour out and reveal an amazing capacity to handle the American language."

Henry Louis Mencken was born on September 12, 1880, in Baltimore, Maryland. His father and uncle jointly owned a cigar factory, so the family was prosperous enough to afford a comfortable rowhouse just outside the central business district. When Mencken was three, his parents moved to this home at 1524 Hollins Street, and there Mencken grew up, the oldest of four children. Education was stressed in the Mencken household—throughout the seventeenth and eighteenth centuries, Mencken ancestors had been noted scholars and theologians—so young Henry was sent to Professor Friedrich Knapp's Institute, a private school for children of German descent. He then attended Baltimore Polytechnic Institute, a public secondary school, and graduated at the top of his class when he was only sixteen. Mencken was expected to take a position in his father's business, and he did so reluctantly after high school. For many years he had been fascinated with writing, literature, and newspapers, and he wanted more than anything to be a reporter. While his father lived, however, he had to content himself with correspondence courses and a program of independent reading. In 1899, his father died suddenly of an acute kidney infection. Henry, free to make his own decisions at last, announced that he was going to seek newspaper work.

Although he was a year shy of twenty and had no prior journalistic experience, Mencken presented himself at the offices of the Baltimore *Herald* and asked for a job. He was promptly turned down, but the editor, sensing the youth's enthusiasm, invited him to drop in from time to time in case some opening should occur. Mencken did drop in—every night. His persistence amused the staff. Finally, on a snowy evening, he was sent to the suburbs to report on a stolen horse. A few days later he was asked to rewrite some obituaries. For several months he worked for free, taking assignments as they came, and by summer he had earned a staff job with a salary of seven dollars per week. According to Philip Wagner in his pamphlet *H. L. Mencken,* the young reporter "soon demonstrated his ability and moved swiftly through every job in the office: police reporter, drama critic, Sunday editor, city editor, and by 1906 at the age of twenty-five actually the editor of the paper." Mencken worked eighteen hours a day and loved every minute of it. In his memoir *Newspaper Days, 1899-1906,* he wrote that the life of a cub reporter "was the maddest, gladdest, damndest existence ever enjoyed by mortal youth. At a time when the respectable bourgeois youngsters of my generation were college freshmen, oppressed by simian sophomores and affronted with balderdash daily and hourly by chalky pedagogues, I was at large in a wicked seaport of half a million people, with a front seat at every public show, as free of the night as of the day, and getting earfuls and eyefuls of instruction in a hundred giddy arcana, none of them taught in schools."

In 1906 the *Herald* folded, and its exuberant editor was hired by the Baltimore *Sun.* By that time Mencken was recognized as "in no way a common talent," to quote William H. Nolte in the *Dictionary of Literary Biography.* Wagner noted that the *Sun* "provided the real launching pad for [Mencken's] career as a national figure and in turn gained immeasurably from the relationship." There Mencken wrote theater reviews and anonymous editorials, chiefly for the Sunday edition. He also found time to write and publish the books *George Bernard Shaw: His Plays* and *The Philosophy of Friedrich Nietzsche.* Both were the first full-length treatments of Shaw and Nietzsche to appear in America; critics feel that their lasting value lies more in the way they demonstrate Mencken's developing mindset than in the way they explore the topics at hand. Neither book had much impact on the reading public, but they did draw the attention of the editor of *The Smart Set,* a magazine based in New York City. In 1908 Mencken agreed to write a monthly book review column for *The Smart Set* in addition to his duties at the *Sun.* At the *Smart Set* offices, Mencken met George Jean Nathan, the magazine's new theater critic. The two men struck up a friendship that eventually led to a partnership; though they came from different backgrounds they were united in their cynical view that American art had all the quality and lasting power of a carnival sideshow.

Shortly after Mencken's thirtieth birthday, the editors of the *Sun* approached him about writing a bylined column. Manchester described the assignment: "It might deal with any subject whatever, so long as it remain irresponsible and readable. It was a significant order. It marked Mencken's final departure from the world of anonymous opinion. . . . He had left, and for good, the army of unidentified writers who present a newspaper's daily information and commentary and had become a public personality, free to exploit his own name." Mencken called his column "The Free Lance," and his pieces "swiftly became the sort of thing that no one of consequence in Baltimore dared not to read," according to Wagner. With rollicking good humor, Mencken opposed everything respectable, defended prostitution, alcohol, and war, and attacked every example of city boosterism, political hypocrisy, and public posturing. Manchester suggested that these "lethal and highly subversive ideas were couched in a language designed to inflame the greatest possible number of readers." While the editors of the *Sun* ground their teeth, Mencken was denounced from pulpits and from City Hall, but many ordinary readers seemed to appreciate his irreverent tone. "The Free Lance" ran from 1911 until 1915 and was canceled because Mencken openly favored Germany in the escalating World War I. Manchester concluded, however, that long before "The Free Lance" was at last discontinued, "it had developed Mencken as one of the foremost polemical writers of his day. . . . It had, however, done more than that. In its columns of fine body type lay the blueprint of all his future books."

Mencken's penchant for "stirring up the animals" was not confined to Baltimore. Through the pages of *The Smart Set*, first as book critic and then, in 1914, as co-editor, he became one of the country's most influential literary critics. Wagner wrote that the flood of Mencken's criticism, published in *The Smart Set* and reprinted in his books, "swept away the deadening literary standards, and the deadly standard-bearers, of our early twentieth century and cleared the way for a tremendous flowering of new writing." In scathing essays such as "Puritanism as a Literary Force," published in *A Book of Prefaces*, Mencken took issue with the Puritan stress on morality in literature and art. American fiction, he felt, was being stifled by religious censorship; he called for an art that could question accepted axioms and standards and for writing that portrayed the cold realities of life. *New Republic* contributor Alfred Kazin called Mencken "the last literary critic in this country to inspire novelists more than professors." Indeed, Mencken was instrumental in discovering or promoting numerous acclaimed authors, including Theodore Dreiser, Sinclair Lewis, F. Scott Fitzgerald, James Joyce, and Eugene O'Neill. Nolte remarked: "H. L. Mencken is not generally remembered for his criticism of belles lettres. Still, the fact is that Mencken, more than any other writer, helped to create a sophisticated reading public and thereby pave the way for the literature that came into being in the years just before, during, and after World War I."

The years of that war were difficult ones for Mencken. The *Sun* closed its doors to him because of his pro-German sympathies, and *The Smart Set* offered little salary as he and George Jean Nathan struggled to edit and publish it on a shoestring budget. Bode noted, however, that the lack of a forum during the war "did nothing to reduce [Mencken's] vitality as a writer. It simply channeled that vitality into his books." Mencken finally found time to produce a work on the subject that fascinated him the most—the American language and its hardy independent evolution from its parent tongue, European English. In 1919, Mencken published *The American Language: A Preliminary Inquiry Into the Development of English in the United States*. Mencken and his publisher Alfred A. Knopf were both surprised and delighted by the interest in the lengthy volume. Its first printing sold out rapidly; Wagner contended that the impression it made "on the new college generation especially, by its style, its humor and its lightly worn scholarship, was tremendous." In *On Mencken*, Alistair Cooke described *The American Language* as "a prolonged demonstration of the fact that the Americans, in a three-hundred-year experience of a new language, new crops, new climates, a new society, and the melding of many immigrant languages and ways of life, had developed institutions, foods, habits, relationships that coined thousands of new nouns, adjectives, and—in their speech—even new syntactical forms. It was, in

fact, a new dialect." The first edition of *The American Language* was hardly on the bookstore shelves before Mencken began to work on an expanded version. Throughout the rest of his life, he returned to this linguistic work regularly, constantly updating and revising his book. Bode concluded of *The American Language:* "The scholarship would become more and more specific, more and more monumental. . . . The acclaim of the work would grow with its size. . . . It would end as a classic, something few foresaw when it appeared in 1919."

Reception of the first edition of *The American Language* was a harbinger of things to come. In the 1920s, a new generation of disillusioned war veterans and sophisticated college students began to see Mencken, in Wagner's words, as "what the times needed: a clearinghouse for the cynicism and discontents of the postwar years and a lash for their excesses wielded with alternating scorn and high good humor." Gradually Mencken drifted away from literary criticism and became instead a critic of the mundane American scene. He found much to criticize: bungling politicians like Warren G. Harding, Bible-thumping zealots like William Jennings Bryan, unscrupulous businessmen, Southerners, censor boards, the Ku Klux Klan, and especially Prohibition. Wagner related: "The object was to make his victim a butt of ridicule. . . . By inference, his readers could never be identified with the bores, shams, and neanderthals whom he delighted to take apart. . . . Before going into battles, Mencken always saw to it that the cheering section—his reader—was in good heart and ready to back him. He was a master of this sort of rhetorical sleight of hand." In *On Native Grounds: An Interpretation of Modern American Prose Literature,* Kazin observed: "By prodigious skill [Mencken] managed to insult everyone except his readers. He flattered them by kindling a sense of disgust; his ferocious attacks on Babbitry implied that his readers were all Superior Citizens; his very recklessness was intoxicating." ("Babbitry" refers to American scholar and critic Irving Babbit who, with Paul Elmer More, founded the New Humanism Movement, which called for literary moderation and restraint in the manner of classical literature and traditions.)

Mencken felt no need to present a balanced argument in his essays. He was content to express his opinion, with the humor serving as a warning not to take him too seriously. When he was serious, it was generally in defense of individual rights or intellectual freedom, as Farrell explained. "The key to Mencken's thought is to be found in his libertarianism," Farrell wrote. "He believed in complete liberty. . . . He saw encroachments on the liberty of the individual from all sides. The institutions of society in general, and of democracy in particular, were threatening the liberty of the individual. And liberty meant, more than anything else, liberty of thought." Mencken also held that all people were *not* equal—especially intellectually—and that democracy, "the worship of jackals by jackasses," merely legislated the lowest mass tastes. Religion, as Mencken saw it, was just another tool used to bamboozle and manipulate the credulous masses, but it too served to stifle freedom through censorship and blue laws. Farrell concluded that Mencken "took the privilege of . . . liberty in his own writings. Like or dislike them, agree or disagree with them, one cannot fail but be struck by their honesty and vigor."

"Much of Mencken's genius lay in the drive and dexterity that allowed him to be a newspaperman at the same time that he was an author and editor," noted Bode. "One role is enough for an ordinary person. Mencken played all three to the hilt. He became, certainly during the 1920s, the most influential magazine editor in the country. And, within the sphere of the subjects he chose, he became the best-known writer." Mencken still considered himself first and foremost a newspaperman, and he began writing for the *Sun* again in 1920. In addition to covering such spectacles as political conventions and the 1924 Scopes trial in Dayton, Tennessee, that challenged the teaching of evolution, Mencken wrote weekly "Monday Articles" for the *Sun*'s editorial page. These "imprinted his particular brand of commentary on the psyche of America," according to *Dictionary of Literary Biography* contributor J. James McElveen. Bode likewise observed that the general record of the Monday Articles "was magnificent. Over a span of eighteen years, from 1920 to 1938, Mencken published more good writing, through these columns, than any other newspaperman of his era. The Free Lance made him famous locally but the Monday Articles helped to establish his national renown."

Simultaneously, Mencken and Nathan were becoming celebrities through their magazine work. Having kept *The Smart Set* afloat during the war—sometimes by writing most of the issue themselves under an array of pseudonyms—they watched as circulation rose steadily in the first years of the 1920s. Neither editor was entirely satisfied with *The Smart Set*, however, so in 1924 they founded a new magazine, *The American Mercury*. Within the year, Mencken became sole editor of *The American Mercury,* and as Manchester related, "it became a product of the peculiar maelstrom which he had created, and in which he now lived." McElveen described Mencken's product: "With its Paris-green cover, the magazine was simply designed by standards of later decades but was a superb typographical specimen in its day. It was not only a status symbol but a voice of critical significance during the wild, unabashed decade of prosperity and Prohibition. . . . Mencken was an imaginative editor, and his special writing style, along with his keen insight and trenchant wit, gave the *American Mercury* a lively and intellectually stimulating quality that appealed to sophisticated and perceptive readers." Manchester remarked that Mencken's "stupendous gift for invective had now reached heights so incredible, so breathtaking, so awe-inspiring, so terrible, that in its indictment of the national culture it wrung monthly gasps from sixty thousand readers and porcupined the hair of intellectuals, Army officers, bond salesmen, and garage mechanics in St. Paul, St. Louis, St. Joseph, and St. Cloud. How could so violent a hymn of hate be sung so jubilantly?" Bode concluded that *The American Mercury* "was more than a breath of fresh air; it was a gust that once or twice grew into a gale."

Mencken's literary output during the 1920s was prodigious. Corollary to his regular journalism, his collected articles appeared in a series of volumes entitled *Prejudices,* and his thoughts on politics appeared in *Notes on Democracy.* His work attracted praise from other writers and critics, as well as from the college students who so admired him. "In so far as [Mencken] has influenced the tone of public controversy he has elevated it," Lippman wrote in *Men of Destiny. New Republic* essayist Edmund Wilson likewise contended that Mencken "is the civilized consciousness of modern America, its learning, its intelligence and its taste, realizing the grossness of its manners and mind and crying out in horror and chagrin." According to Joseph Wood Krutch in *If You Don't Mind My Saying So . . . Essays on Man and Nature,* Mencken's was "the best prose written in America during the twentieth century. Those who deny that fact had better confine themselves to direct attack. They will be hard put to find a rival claimant." In *Bookman* F. Scott Fitzgerald concluded simply that Mencken "has done more for the national letters than any man alive."

Mencken's detractors were equally passionate. Many colorful diatribes against him emanated from the hinterland; Manchester quotes one of these, from a Reverend Doctor Charles E. Jones in *Gospel Call:* "If a buzzard had laid an egg in a dunghill and the sun had hatched a thing like Mencken, the buzzard would have been justly ashamed of its offspring." Other more objective critics also found fault with Mencken. "The total effect of his writing is nearer to intellectual vaudeville than to serious criticism," observed Irving Babbitt in *Modern Writers at Work,* encapsulating a commonly held belief that Mencken sacrificed discrimination for bombast. Stenerson wrote: "Despite the changes which transformed America during Mencken's lifetime, his basic attitudes remained much the same in his maturity as they had been in his youth. His wide-ranging interests, the soundness of his information on many issues, and the common sense with which he treated them, were offset, to a considerable extent, by his failure to see any need for modifying his premises. . . . His prejudices were the themes of his art, not the building blocks of a coherent system of thought." This was to be Mencken's downfall, as Upton Sinclair predicted in *The Bookman:* "The darling and idol of the young intelligenzia has no message to give them, except that they are free to do what they please—which they interpret to mean that they are to get drunk, and read elegant pornography, and mock at the stupidities and blunders of people with less expensive educations. . . . For the present, that is all that is required; that is the mood of the time. But some day the time spirit will change; America will realize that its problems really have to be solved."

The spirit did change, almost overnight, with the 1929 stock market crash. As Hilton Kramer noted in the *New York Times Book Review,* the "carnival atmosphere that had supported Mencken's outrageous rhetoric was, after all, the coefficient of a false prosperity, and the collapse of that prosperity left him stranded in a style remote from the needs of a new social reality." Mencken's humorous attacks on "Homo boobiens" no longer seemed funny as the depression deepened. Moreover, Mencken, the great individualist, opposed the New Deal programs and discounted the seriousness of Hitler's rise to power in Germany. "What were jesting matters for him were serious or painful for most, and he lost his audience," states Galbraith in the *Washington Post Book World.* Though he caused a stir by marrying writer Sara Powell Haardt in 1930, Mencken witnessed a precipitous decline in his popularity over the next several years. Two books for which he had high hopes, *Treatise on the Gods* and *Treatise on Right and Wrong* sold few copies and earned lackluster reviews. The power he continued to wield became more and more localized in Baltimore, where his Monday Articles still appeared in the *Sun.* "Ten years before," claims Manchester, "[Mencken] had ridden in on a wave of disillusion and irresponsibility, the surprised beneficiary of a changed society. Now that society had changed again and he was riding out, as helplessly the victim of the public whim as he had once been its darling. . . . There was no room for a writer with nothing to say about the crisis gripping the world. There was no room for H. L. Mencken."

In one particular arena, however—political convention coverage—Mencken continued to dominate throughout the 1930s. "Mencken's political specialty . . . was the national conventions, occasions which accorded him not only the greatest scope for his talent but much personal pleasure as well," Galbraith contended in the *Washington Post Book World.* "And here he was ahead of his time; before anyone, he saw them as a triumph of banality over content. . . . Mencken, a full 40 years ago, learned what all but the television people now know: the convention is our greatest non-event." Through Mencken's cynical eye, the colorful conventions were quickly reduced to absurdities punctuated by vacuous speeches and the antics of hero-worshipping hayseeds. According to Joe Conason in the *Village Voice,* Mencken "could enliven the deadliest bore in politics—Coolidge, Hoover, Landon—long enough to elicit a hearty laugh, and dismiss him when the guffaws subsided. His comic view of politics enabled him to see its absurdity with a clarity that seems contemporary 60 years later." From 1920 to 1948, with the sole exception of 1944, Mencken covered every convention, Democratic, Republican, and third party. Even as his energies waned and the *Sun*'s deadlines grew tighter, he never tired of the quadrennial political spectacles.

In 1935, Mencken's wife Sara died. The era's most notorious confirmed bachelor had enjoyed his brief marriage, and he mourned his wife's loss for many years thereafter. Mencken was unable to face life alone in the apartment he and Sara had shared, so he returned to the home that had been his base almost his whole life—1524 Hollins Street. From there, beginning in the late 1930s, he began to write anecdotal essays about his childhood for the *New Yorker* magazine. Wagner noted of these stories: "Absolutely and literally true they certainly were not. . . . They were better than that: they caught and preserved the smells and flavor and temper of an era." The essays accumulated: Mencken's youth on Hollins Street, his cub reporter days at the *Herald,* his recollection of the Great Baltimore Fire of 1904, his early travels to New York. Eventually these were published in three popular volumes, *Happy Days, 1880-1892; Newspaper Days, 1899-1906,* and *Heathen Days, 1890-1936.* Bode declared that the tales "were too extended to be called anecdotes. They were too actual to be local-color fiction. They were too exuberant and personal to qualify as social history. Perhaps the best way to put it is that they constituted the human comedy of young Mencken in old Baltimore. The writing was supple and deft, avoiding quaintness, condescension, and sentimentality. And above all it had the apparent artlessness which concealed the skills and resources he drew on." Bode concluded that "the result was classic." The *Days* books introduced Mencken to a new generation of readers and revived his national reputation. Wagner felt these works to be "what he gave to our literature which time is least likely to tarnish or erode."

Mencken's last productive year was 1948. He spent it in characteristic ways—covering the political conventions, attacking segregation laws as "relics of Ku Kluxery," and defending civil rights and civil liberties. His last article for the *Sun* lambasted a rule that would not allow blacks and whites to play tennis together on a local court. Several days later he suffered a severe stroke, the lasting legacy of which was an inability to read, write, or speak clearly. William Manchester was one of the few people Mencken continued to see after the stroke; in *Disturber of the Peace* Manchester described Mencken's condition: "The great tragedy of his situation was that everything which had given life meaning for him was gone. Since his boyhood days the pattern of his life had built around the reading of the written word and the expression of his reflections. For sixty years . . . the cultivation of that expression had been the moving purpose of his life, and he had developed it to an art unmatched in his time. Now that was impossible, and he was left to vegetate back to a robust physical health with the purposes of his very being withdrawn. It was a terrible blow, and he was the first to recognize its magnitude." Attended by his brother and visited only by his secretary and a few close friends, Mencken lived eight more years in his Hollins Street home. He died there, in his sleep, on January 29, 1956.

Most critics agree that Mencken's influence has survived his death. "If Mencken had never lived," Kazin observed in *On Native Grounds,* "it would have taken a whole army of assorted philosophers, monologists, editors, and patrons of the new writing to make up for him. As it was, he not only rallied all the young writers together and imposed his skepticism upon the new generation, but also brought a new and uproarious gift for high comedy into a literature that had never been too quick to laugh." Nor has time dimmed the pertinence of Mencken's message, according to McElveen. "Mencken's dissent—his way of demolishing society's hypocrisy, of smashing the idols of human folly—set him apart from other writers of his day," wrote McElveen. "His thought embraced the whole range of the twentieth century; and his writings have not aged, because mankind is subject to the same shortcomings and foibles that prevailed in his day." Indeed, much of Mencken's work remains in print, new volumes of collected correspondence are still appearing, and a thriving Mencken Society, based in Baltimore, keeps his memory alive. "Mencken's basic attitude at all times, disrespect for the powers of this earth, for everything seeking to make us more righteous and obedient at all costs, will always lead people back to his work," Kazin stated in the *New York Review of Books.* Ben Hecht, commenting on Mencken in *A Child of the Century,* concluded that the work penned by the famous "Sage of Baltimore" is "proof that brave words can still lift the soul of man."

In a note published in *The Letters of H. L. Mencken,* the author himself summed up his philosophy. "My notion is that all the larger human problems are insoluble, and that life is quite meaningless—a spectacle without purpose or moral," he wrote. "I detest all efforts to read a moral into it. I do not write because I want to make converts. . . . I write because the business amuses me. It is the best of sports."

MEDIA ADAPTATIONS: A character based on Mencken appears in the play *Inherit the Wind,* by Jerome Lawrence and Robert E. Lee; an Off-Broadway one-man show entitled "An Evening With H. L. Mencken" was performed at the Cherry Lane Theater in 1975.

AVOCATIONAL INTERESTS: Music, especially piano.

BIOGRAPHICAL/CRITICAL SOURCES:

BOOKS

Adler, Betty, *H. L. M.: The Mencken Bibliography,* Johns Hopkins Press, 1961, *Ten-Year Supplement, 1962-1971,* Enoch Pratt Free Library, 1971.

Angoff, Charles, *H. L. Mencken: A Portrait From Memory,* Thomas Yoseloff, 1956.

Babbitt, Irving, *Modern Writers at Work,* Macmillan, 1930.

Bode, Carl, *Mencken,* Southern Illinois University Press, 1969, Johns Hopkins University Press, 1986.

Bode, Carl, editor, *The New Mencken Letters,* Dial Press, 1976.

Boyd, Ernest, *H. L. Mencken,* McBride, 1925.

Brooks, Van Wyck, *The Confident Years: 1885-1915,* Dutton, 1952.

Cabell, James Branch, *Some of Us: An Essay in Epitaphs,* McBride, 1930.

Cooke, Alistair, editor, *The Vintage Mencken,* Vintage Books, 1955.

Cooke, Alistair, *Six Men*, Knopf, 1977.

DeCasseres, Benjamin, *Mencken and Shaw: The Anatomy of America's Voltaire and England's Other John Bull*, Silas Newton, 1930.

Dictionary of Literary Biography, Gale, Volume 11: *American Humorists, 1800-1950*, 1982, Volume 25: *American Newspaper Journalists, 1901-1925*, 1984, Volume 63: *Modern American Critics, 1920-1955*, 1988.

Dolmetsch, Carl R., *The "Smart Set," a History and Anthology*, Dial Press, 1966.

Dorsey, John, editor, *On Mencken*, Knopf, 1980.

Douglas, George H., *H. L. Mencken: Critic of American Life*, Archon Books, 1978.

Farrell, James T., *New World Writing: Sixth Mentor Selection*, New American Library, 1954.

Farrell, James T., *Reflections at Fifty and Other Essays*, Vanguard, 1954.

Fecher, Charles A., *Mencken: A Study of His Thought*, Knopf, 1978.

Fecher, Charles A., editor, *The Diary of H. L. Mencken*, Knopf, 1989.

Fitzpatrick, Vincent, *H. L. M.: The Mencken Bibliography, Second Ten-Year Supplement*, Enoch Pratt Free Library, 1986.

Geismar, Maxwell, *The Last of the Provincials: The American Novel, 1915-1925*, Secker & Warburg, 1947.

Gingrich, Arnold and L. Rust Hills, editors, *The Armchair "Esquire,"* Putnam, 1958.

Goldberg, Isaac, *The Man Mencken: A Biographical and Critical Survey*, Simon & Schuster, 1925.

Hecht, Ben, *A Child of the Century*, D. I. Fine, 1985.

Hobson, Fred C., *Serpent in Eden: H. L. Mencken and the South*, Louisiana State University Press, 1974.

Kazin, Alfred, *On Native Grounds: An Interpretation of Modern American Prose Literature*, Reynal & Hitchcock, 1942.

Kemler, Edgar, *The Irreverent Mr. Mencken*, Little, Brown, 1950.

Krutch, Joseph Wood, *If You Don't Mind My Saying So . . . Essays on Man and Nature*, Sloane, 1964.

Lewis, Wyndham, *Paleface: The Philosophy of the "Melting Pot,"* Chatto & Windus, 1929.

Lippmann, Walter, *Men of Destiny*, Macmillan, 1927.

Manchester, William, *Disturber of the Peace: The Life of H. L. Mencken*, Harper, 1950, 2nd edition, University of Massachusetts Press, 1986.

Martin, Edward A., *H. L. Mencken and the Debunkers*, University of Georgia Press, 1984.

Mayfield, Sara, *The Constant Circle: H. L. Mencken and His Friends*, Delacorte, 1968.

Mencken, H. L. and Sara Powell Haardt, editors, *Menckeniana: A Schimpflexikon*, Knopf, 1928, Octagon, 1977.

Mencken, H. L., *Happy Days, 1889-1892*, Knopf, 1940.

Mencken, H. L., *Newspaper Days, 1899-1906*, Knopf, 1941.

Mencken, H. L., *Heathen Days, 1890-1936*, Knopf, 1943.

Nathan, George Jean, *The Borzoi 1920: Being a Sort of Record of Five Years' Publishing*, Knopf, 1920.

Nathan, George Jean, *The World of George Jean Nathan*, Knopf, 1952.

Nolte, William H., *H. L. Mencken, Literary Critic*, Wesleyan University Press, 1966.

Riggio, Thomas P., editor, *Dreiser-Mencken Letters: The Correspondence of Theodore Dreiser and H. L. Mencken, 1907-1945*, University of Pennsylvania Press, 1986.

Rodgers, Marion Elizabeth, editor, *Mencken & Sara: A Life in Letters*, McGraw, 1987.

Scruggs, Charles, *The Sage in Harlem: H. L. Mencken and the Black Writers of the 1920s*, Johns Hopkins University Press, 1984.

Shivers, Frank R., *Maryland Wits & Baltimore Bards: A Literary History With Notes on Washington Writers*, Maclay & Associates, 1985.

Singleton, M. K., *H. L. Mencken and the "American Mercury" Adventure*, Duke University Press, 1962.

Smith, H. Allen, *The Best of H. Allen Smith*, Trident, 1972.

Stenerson, Douglas C., *H. L. Mencken: Iconoclast from Baltimore*, University of Chicago Press, 1971.

Twentieth-Century Literary Criticism, Volume 13, Gale, 1984.

Wagner, Philip, *H. L. Mencken*, University of Minnesota Press, 1966.

Williams, W. H. L., *H. L. Mencken*, Twayne, 1977.

Wright, Richard, *Black Boy: A Record of Childhood and Youth*, Harper, 1964.

PERIODICALS

Americana, September-October, 1980.

American Literature, May, 1965.

Atlantic, January, 1946, May, 1956.

Bookman, March, 1921, November, 1927.

Commentary, April, 1977.

Comparative Literature Studies, March, 1970.

Harper's, July, 1950, August, 1950.

Life, August 5, 1946.

Menckeniana, fall, 1981.

Nation, May 13, 1950, September 12, 1953, September 16, 1961, May 24, 1965.

New Leader, March 19, 1956.

New Republic, June 1, 1921, March 8, 1943, September 13, 1954, May 21, 1956, April 17, 1965, September 14, 1968, January 12, 1972, December 27, 1975, March 12, 1977, October 22, 1984.

Newsweek, April 5, 1948, September 18, 1961.

New Yorker, May 31, 1969.

New York Herald Tribune Books, April 30, 1930.

New York Review of Books, June 11, 1981, February 26, 1987.

New York Times, February 10, 1987.

New York Times Book Review, August 19, 1973, December 19, 1976, September 7, 1980, November 9, 1986.

Philadelphia Inquirer, February 27, 1987.

Reason, December, 1987.

Saturday Review, December 11, 1926, August 6, 1949, September 10, 1955, September 7, 1968.

Sewanee Review, summer, 1966.

South Atlantic Quarterly, spring, 1964.

Spectator, September 4, 1982.

Sun Magazine (Baltimore), September 7, 1980.

Times Literary Supplement, March 13, 1969, September 27, 1985, July 17, 1987.

Village Voice, November 6, 1984.

Washington Post, June 9, 1984, October 5, 1985.

Washington Post Book World, August 15, 1976, September 14, 1980, January 25, 1987.

OTHER

"Henry L. Mencken, Interviewed by Donald Howe Kirkley, Sr." (sound recording), Library of Congress Recording Library, 1948.

Mencken's collected papers and books are stored at the Enoch Pratt Free Library in Baltimore, Maryland. Collections of Mencken's correspondence can be found at numerous libraries and universities, including New York Public Library, Dartmouth College, Goucher College, and Harvard, Princeton, and Yale universities.

OBITUARIES:

PERIODICALS

Life, February 20, 1956.
New Leader, February 13, 1956.
Newsweek, February 6, 1956, February 20, 1956.
New York Times, January 30, 1956, January 31, 1956, February 1, 1956.
New York Times Book Review, March 11, 1956.
Saturday Review, February 11, 1956.*

—*Sketch by Anne Janette Johnson*

*   *   *

MENDELSOHN, Robert S(aul)   1926-1988

OBITUARY NOTICE: Born July 13, 1926, in Chicago, Ill.; died of acute cardiac arrest, April 5, 1988, in Evanston, Ill. Physician, educator, administrator, and author. A medical doctor who specialized in health care for children, Mendelsohn gained national attention for a skeptical attitude toward his profession. He argued that medical procedures, including many operations and vaccinations, were often either harmful or unnecessary. Mendelsohn worked for the federal government's Head Start program for child welfare in the 1960s, advancing from director for Cook County, Illinois, to national director of the medical consultation service. He was forced to resign in 1969 after he testified before the U.S. Congress that inferior public schools were undermining many of Head Start's benefits. Mendelsohn joined the faculty of the University of Illinois College of Medicine that year, serving as associate professor of preventive medicine and community health until 1980. He began writing a syndicated column, "The People's Doctor," in 1976 and published several books that questioned contemporary medicine: *Confessions of a Medical Heretic, Male Practice: How Doctors Manipulate Women,* and *How to Raise a Healthy Child in Spite of Your Doctor.*

OBITUARIES AND OTHER SOURCES:

BOOKS

Who's Who in America, 44th edition, Marquis, 1986.

PERIODICALS

Chicago Tribune, April 7, 1988.
Los Angeles Times, April 14, 1988.
New York Times, April 16, 1988.
Washington Post, April 14, 1988.

*   *   *

MEREDITH, Arnold
See HOPKINS, (Hector) Kenneth

*   *   *

MERRICK, Gordon   1916-1988

OBITUARY NOTICE—See index for *CA* sketch: Born August 3, 1916, in Cynwyd, Pa.; died of lung cancer, March 27, 1988, in Colombo, Sri Lanka. Actor, journalist, and author. Merrick was an actor who turned to writing for newspapers in the early 1940s. He subsequently produced several novels, including *The Strumpet Wind, The Hot Season, The Lord Won't Mind, The Quirk,* and *Perfect Freedom.*

OBITUARIES AND OTHER SOURCES:

BOOKS

The Writers Directory, 1988-1990, St. James Press, 1988.

PERIODICALS

New York Times, April 23, 1988.

*   *   *

MILANO, Paolo   1904-1988

OBITUARY NOTICE: Born in 1904 in Rome, Italy; died of Parkinson's disease, April 2, 1988, in Rome, Italy. Literary critic, educator, translator, editor, and author. Milano was a prominent literary critic in Italy and the United States. A contributor to Italian literary and theatrical journals during the 1930s, he was drama critic of "Italia Letteraria" from 1931 to 1935 and editor of "Scenario" from 1932 to 1938. Milano was Jewish and he fled Italian fascism in 1938, residing first in France and then, beginning in 1940, in the United States. There he taught at the New School for Social Research and was professor of romance languages and comparative literature at Queens College. By the late 1950s Milano had settled once more in Italy, where he was literary critic of *L'Espresso* from 1957 to 1986. He edited *The Portable Dante,* wrote *Henry James: The Voluntary Exile,* and contributed to such periodicals as *Nation, Partisan Review,* and *Politics.* In addition, he translated *La morte a Venezia: Le confessioni di un cavaliere d'industria,* by German author Thomas Mann, into Italian. A selection of Milano's writings was published in the collection *Il lettore di professione.*

OBITUARIES AND OTHER SOURCES:

PERIODICALS

Chicago Tribune, April 5, 1988.
Los Angeles Times, April 5, 1988.
Washington Post, April 5, 1988.

*   *   *

MILLER, Arthur S(elwyn)   1917-1988

OBITUARY NOTICE—See index for *CA* sketch: Born March 4, 1917, in Oregon; died of a brain tumor, May 13, 1988, in Key West, Fla. Educator, law scholar, consultant, and author. Miller was professor of law at George Washington University from 1961 to 1978. He was particularly knowledgeable on constitutional law, a subject on which he consulted to various congressional committees and to the chairman of the Senate committee that investigated the Watergate incident of 1972. Miller wrote such books as *The Supreme Court and the Living Constitution, Social Change and Fundamental Law, The Emergent Constitution of Control,* and *The Political Role of the Supreme Court.*

OBITUARIES AND OTHER SOURCES:

PERIODICALS

New York Times, May 16, 1988.
Washington Post, May 14, 1988.

*   *   *

MILLER, Darlis A(nn)   1939-

PERSONAL: Born June 6, 1939, in Chariton, Iowa; daughter

of Joseph E. (a construction foreman) and Helen (a housewife; maiden name, Krutsinger) Miller; married August Miller (a physicist), December 23, 1964. *Education:* Colorado State College (now University of Northern Colorado), B.A., 1961; New Mexico State University, M.A., 1970; University of New Mexico, Ph.D., 1977.

ADDRESSES: Home—P.O. Box 3512, Las Cruces, N.M. 88003. *Office*—Department of History, New Mexico State University, Las Cruces, N.M. 88003.

CAREER: New Mexico State University, Las Cruces, instructor, 1975-77, assistant professor, 1977-81, associate professor, 1981-86, professor of history, 1986—.

MEMBER: American Historical Association, Organization of American Historians, Coordinating Committee of Women in the Historical Profession, Western History Association.

AWARDS, HONORS: Woodrow Wilson fellow, 1961-62; Ray A. Billington Award from Western History Association, 1980, for article "The Gentle Tamers Revisited: New Approaches to the History of Women in the American West"; Zia Award from New Mexico Press Women, 1986, for *New Mexico Women;* Dorothy Woodward Award from Historical Society of New Mexico, 1986.

WRITINGS:

The Frontier Army in the Far West, Forum Press, 1979.
The California Column in New Mexico, University of New Mexico Press, 1982.
(Editor with Joan Mary Jensen) *New Mexico Women: Intercultural Perspectives,* University of New Mexico Press, 1986.

Contributor to history journals.

WORK IN PROGRESS: Soldiers and Settlers: Military Supply in the Southwest, a study of the frontier army's economic impact in the Southwest, 1861-1885.

SIDELIGHTS: Darlis A. Miller told *CA:* "My major goal has been to document the life of ordinary citizens who helped settle the American West. This, in addition to a fascination with the Civil War, led to my study of the California volunteers and their social, political, and economic contributions to post-Civil War New Mexico. In conducting research for this study, I discovered that military records abound with information about civilians—men and women alike. Thus, based on material gleaned from military records, I have written and published articles on women in New Mexico. My forthcoming book, a study of the economic impact of the frontier army on New Mexico, Arizona, west Texas, and southern Colorado, focuses on men and women who supplied goods and services to the army."

BIOGRAPHICAL/CRITICAL SOURCES:

PERIODICALS

American Historical Review, October, 1983.

*   *   *

MISHLER, William (Thomas Earle II)   1947-

PERSONAL: Born October 14, 1947, in Miami, Fla.; son of William Thomas Earle (in business) and Marie (a housewife; maiden name, Schmitz) Mishler; married Catherine Tanner (a librarian), August 5, 1972. *Education:* Stetson University, B.A.

(magna cum laude), 1969; Duke University, M.A., 1971, Ph.D., 1973.

ADDRESSES: Home—Route 2, Box 301 AB, Columbia, S.C. 29212. *Office*—Department of Government and International Studies, University of South Carolina at Columbia, Columbia, S.C. 29208.

CAREER: Duke University, Durham, N.C., assistant professor of political science, 1972-78; State University of New York at Buffalo, associate professor, 1978-83, professor of political science and chairman of department, 1983-86; University of South Carolina at Columbia, professor of government and chairman of department of government and international studies, 1986—. Visiting professor at University of Strathclyde, 1976-77; director of National Science Foundation's Political Science Program, 1982-84. *Military service:* U.S. Army Reserve, 1969-77; became captain.

MEMBER: International Political Science Association, International Studies Association, American Political Science Association, Southern Political Science Association, Midwestern Political Science Association, Phi Beta Kappa.

AWARDS, HONORS: Woodrow Wilson fellowship, 1969-70.

WRITINGS:

(With Allan Kornberg) *Influence in Parliament: Canada,* Duke University Press, 1976.
Political Participation in Canada, Macmillan of Canada, 1979.
(With Kornberg and Harold Clarke) *Representative Democracy in the Canadian Provinces,* Prentice-Hall of Canada, 1982.
(Editor with Kornberg and Barry Cooper) *The Resurgence of Conservatism in Anglo-American Democracies,* Duke University Press, 1987.

WORK IN PROGRESS: Political Performance: Empirical Theory and Cross-National Analysis.

*   *   *

MITCHELL, Broadus   1892-1988

OBITUARY NOTICE—See index for *CA* sketch: Born December 27, 1892, in Georgetown, Ky.; died April 28, 1988, in Tarrytown, N.Y. Historian, educator, and author. Mitchell was an authority on the economic history of the American South. He taught at several institutions, retiring in 1958 after eleven years as professor of economics at Rutgers University. Among his writings are *The Industrial Revolution in the South, Economists in Their Times, Postscripts to Economic History,* and *The Price of Independence.* In addition, he published works on Alexander Hamilton, including a two-volume biography, and wrote economics textbooks.

OBITUARIES AND OTHER SOURCES:

BOOKS

The International Who's Who, 51st edition, Europa, 1987.

PERIODICALS

Chicago Tribune, May 1, 1988.
New York Times, April 30, 1988.
Washington Post, May 2, 1988.

MITCHELL, Margaret (Munnerlyn)   1900-1949
(Peggy Mitchell, Margaret Mitchell Upshaw;
Elizabeth Bennett, a pseudonym)

PERSONAL: Born November 8, 1900, in Atlanta, Ga.; died from brain injuries sustained when struck by an automobile, August 16, 1949, in Atlanta, Ga.; buried in Oakland Cemetery, Atlanta, Ga.; daughter of Eugene Muse (an attorney) and Maybelle (a women's suffrage activist; maiden name, Stephens) Mitchell; married Berrien Kinnard Upshaw, September 2, 1922 (annulled, October 16, 1924; died January 10, 1949); married John Robert Marsh (in public relations), July 4, 1925 (died May 5, 1952). *Education:* Attended Smith College, 1918-19.

ADDRESSES: Home—1268 Piedmont Ave., Atlanta, Ga.

CAREER: Atlanta Journal, Atlanta, Ga., feature writer, 1922-26, free-lance columnist, 1926; novelist, 1926-36; homemaker, 1936-49. Volunteer selling war bonds during World War II; volunteer for the American Red Cross in the 1940s.

AWARDS, HONORS: Pulitzer Prize from Columbia University Graduate School of Journalism, 1937, for *Gone With the Wind;* M.A. from Smith College, 1939; named honorary citizen of Vimoutiers, France, 1949, for helping the city obtain American aid after World War II.

WRITINGS:

Gone With the Wind, Macmillan, 1936, two-volume edition, Macmillan, 1939, motion picture edition, Macmillan, 1939, anniversary edition illustrated by Ben Stahl, Macmillan, 1961, two-volume edition illustrated by John Groth, with introduction by Henry Steele Commager, Heritage Press, 1968, anniversary edition with introduction by James A. Michener, Macmillan, 1975, illustrated by Robert Reid, Franklin Library, 1976, limited edition illustrated by Ken Dallison, Franklin Library, 1978, fiftieth anniversary facsimile edition, Macmillan, 1986.

Margaret Mitchell's "Gone With the Wind" Letters, edited by Richard Harwell, Macmillan, c. 1976, recent edition, Collier Books, 1986.

A Dynamo Going to Waste: Letters to Allen Edee, 1919-1921, edited by Jane Bonner Peacock, Peachtree Publications, 1985.

Also author, under names Peggy Mitchell and Margaret Mitchell Upshaw, of numerous feature stories, and author, under pseudonym Elizabeth Bennett, of column "Elizabeth Bennett's Gossip," all for the *Atlanta Journal.* Author of unpublished short stories, plays, and the unpublished novella "'Ropa Carmagin."

SIDELIGHTS: In 1936 Margaret Mitchell completed what was to become a lasting part of American culture—her novel, *Gone With the Wind.* After selling a record-breaking one million copies in six months, *Gone With the Wind* went on to become the largest-selling book in history with the exception of the Bible. By 1976 the work had been translated into twenty-seven languages in thirty-seven countries, and as Anne Edwards reported in her biography of Mitchell, *Road to Tara,* by 1983 the novel had "sold six million hardcover copies in the United States; one million copies in England; and nine million copies in foreign translation." Approximately 250,000 paperback copies of the book are sold annually in the United States.

Gone With the Wind's sales, however, are only a partial measure of Mitchell's importance as an author. Through her novel

and the 1939 film of the same title, Mitchell's characters, especially Scarlett O'Hara and Rhett Butler, have become household names. As Edwards put it, "who can now think of the South before, during, and after the Civil War without images drawn from the pages of *Gone With the Wind?* Scarlett seated under the shade of a huge oak, surrounded by beaus at the Wilkeses' barbecue . . . [and] defying convention and dancing in her widow's weeds with the dashing scoundrel, Rhett Butler; the hundreds of wounded lying in the pitiless sun, . . . the burning of Atlanta, . . . the moment when Scarlett claws the earth to take from it a radish root to stave her hunger, . . . Prissy during the birth of Melanie's baby; and—oh, yes— Scarlett O'Hara crying 'What shall I do?'. . . and Rhett's reply, 'My dear, I don't give a damn.'"

The woman who created these scenes was born into a middle-class Atlanta family in 1900. As a small child she heard stories of the Civil War told by relatives who had experienced the conflict, and her maternal grandmother, Annie Fitzgerald Stephens, showed her where Confederate forces had dug trenches in her backyard. Mitchell would tell the stories she heard, and stories she had herself made up, to her brother, Stephens, and his friends. She grew up knowing almost everything there was to know about the Civil War—except that the South had lost. This fact she finally learned at the age of ten from the black field workers of a relative's farm where she was spending a summer.

History was not the only thing Mitchell learned during childhood that would appear in her famous novel. From witnessing the different levels of prosperity apparent less than fifty years after the Civil War, she learned that some people were able to rebuild after the conflict's devastation but others were not, the difference being a matter of character and intelligence. From one of her great aunts she received the buckwheat analogy that Grandma Fontaine uses in *Gone With the Wind* to comfort Scarlett: "We're not wheat, we're buckwheat! When a storm comes along it flattens ripe wheat because it's dry and can't bend with the wind. But ripe buckwheat's got sap in it and it bends. And when the wind has passed, it springs up almost as straight and strong as before."

Mitchell's mother, Maybelle, who was active in the women's suffrage movement, used a more literal example to instill values in her daughter. According to Edwards, when Mitchell came home from school one day complaining that "she hated arithmetic and did not want to go back," her mother first spanked her and then took her in their horse-drawn carriage southward towards Jonesboro. The mother pointed out derelict plantations to her daughter, telling her that the people who had inhabited them had once been "fine and wealthy." Maybelle explained to Mitchell that some of the houses had been destroyed by Northern troops when U.S. General William Tecumseh Sherman made his famous "March to the Sea," but that others had decayed more gradually as their owners grew increasingly poorer during Reconstruction. Some houses were still well-tended, however, and Maybelle reportedly told her daughter, "Now, those folk stood as staunchly as their houses did. . . . The world those people lived in was a secure world, just like yours is now. But theirs exploded right from underneath them. Your world will do that to you one day, too, and God help you, child, if you don't have some weapon to meet that new world. Education! . . . For all you're going to be left with after your world upends will be what you do with your hands and what you have in your head." Mitchell's mother concluded her lecture by telling the girl that she would go back to school the next day and "conquer arithmetic." In addition to determination, Scarlett is able to save herself and her family from starvation because of her "good head for figures."

When Mitchell was eleven years old her family moved from the Jackson Hill area of Atlanta to the more prestigious Peachtree Street. Her mother's work for the women's movement and her Catholicism had a tendency to separate Mitchell from the rest of the neighborhood children, whose parents were generally conservative and Protestant. Her tomboyish early childhood did not help either; as Edwards observed, "Margaret was not accepted by the young residents of Peachtree Street, who had been learning the social niceties of Southern society while she had been sliding into first, second, or third base." Meanwhile, her brother had turned seventeen and was too old to let his young sister follow him around. Increasingly, then, Mitchell turned to writing to fill her hours. She continued penning adventures, mostly in the form of plays, filling notebooks with titles like "Phil Kelly: Detective," "A Darktown Tragedy," and "The Fall of Roger Rover." When she wasn't writing the pieces themselves, she was making plans for them, as evidenced by a notebook page cited by Edwards with the heading "Locations" followed by a list of exotic places, including Africa, China, Egypt, Russia, Turkey, and Hades.

Mitchell's writing continued through her years at Washington Seminary, a private girls' school near her home which she began attending at the age of fourteen. Though she was unhappy with being expected to act like a lady by her peers as well as by her teachers of manners and deportment, she preferred Washington to the alternative—being sent to a convent school as the women on her mother's side of the family traditionally were. Mitchell did find encouragement for her writing at the school, however. A sympathetic English teacher, Eva Paisley, commented extensively on her papers, helping her towards the goals of unity, coherence, and simplicity. Paisley often read Mitchell's papers aloud in class, and it was during the year that she was Paisley's pupil that Mitchell made her first attempt at a novel. Titled "The Big Four," it concerned four friends in a girls' boarding school. The heroine was named Margaret and engaged in valiant exploits such as leading her classmates through a fire and destroying incriminating documents that would have ruined a friend's family. Though she managed to finish the story, which amounted to fourteen chapters and four hundred copybook pages in cursive writing, she was not pleased with it after rereading it. According to Edwards, Mitchell inscribed on the inside of its back cover: "There are authors and authors but a *true* writer is born and not made. Born writers make their characters real, living people, while 'made writers' have merely stuffed figures who dance when the strings are pulled—that's how I know I'm a 'made' writer." Though she considered herself a failure as a novelist, she continued to write shorter pieces of fiction.

In the spring of 1917 the United States entered World War I, and Mitchell's brother, Stephens, was drafted soon afterwards. During her summer vacation from Washington she and her family entertained soldiers who were stationed in Atlanta. The following summer was similar, except that Mitchell was nearly eighteen and had graduated from Washington Seminary. She planned to enter Smith College in the fall, and told her family that she would eventually become a doctor. She had read Freud, and thought she might specialize in psychiatry. Maybelle Mitchell, in keeping with her suffragette activities, encouraged her daughter to be more than a housewife.

Mitchell also confided her ambitions to one of the soldiers stationed in Atlanta that summer, Lieutenant Clifford Henry.

She met him at a party, and she was attracted to his knowledge of literature, his seriousness, and his fair good looks. In spite of what Edwards labeled "his homosexual tendencies," Henry was attracted to Mitchell as well. When he learned in August that he would be transferred to the European front, they became engaged and corresponded frequently by letters. Rather than being declarative of passion, Mitchell's letters were full of hopes for her academic and professional future. Henry's were filled with his feelings of disillusionment about the war.

At Smith College Mitchell was not nearly as successful as she wanted to be. In most of her classes she barely met the average standard. Though she admitted her doubts to no one, it became increasingly clear that she would be unable to become a psychiatrist. In one subject, however, she excelled—English composition. According to Edwards, her professor declared Mitchell "a youthful genius." But this praise did not buoy her spirits. She felt that the piece that led her instructor to make the pronouncement was bad, and that he lacked the discernment of her high school teacher, Paisley.

Mitchell still felt some of the social awkwardness that she had experienced at Washington Seminary in her new surroundings at Smith College. At the prestigious New England school, the young woman was encircled by others who were for the most part wealthier and better educated than she was. In addition, few of her peers were Southerners. Nevertheless, she fared better making friends in college than she had previously. She got along well with her fellow house members at Ten Henshaw Street, nicknamed Ten Hen by the students. Mitchell's roommate, Virginia Morris, described in *Photoplay* how the author was regarded by the other residents: "[We] were awed by the bulk of her overseas mail and enslaved by her Irish sense of humor which was considerably broader than you'd expect to find in a frail flower of the south. Moreover, we respected her scorn for campus rules and her smoking skill—when to be found with cigarettes was a shortcut to being expelled.

"In the evenings, no one ever thought of studying. Instead there was usually S[tanding] R[oom] O[nly] in our rooms listening to [Mitchell] talk. When topics took more serious turns you could pretty safely depend that [she] would get around to the Civil War.... She felt about [Southern general] Robert E. Lee pretty much as if he was the current film idol."

In September of 1918 Mitchell's fiance was seriously wounded at the battle of Saint-Mihiel in France. Henry died of his wounds in mid-October. Mitchell was said to grieve deeply, and she later declared that Henry had been the one great love in her life. This statement, along with the evidence of Henry's character traits, led Edwards to conjecture that he was the model for Ashley Wilkes, the idealistic but weak married man whom Scarlett O'Hara pursues throughout *Gone With the Wind*. Mitchell faced another emotional setback the following January when her mother fell desperately ill, a victim of the influenza epidemic that had swept the nation. Her father had been stricken by the flu earlier but had already convalesced. Maybelle also developed pneumonia in one lung, and by the time Mitchell arrived home, summoned by the news that her mother had slipped into a coma, she was dead. Mitchell was also shocked to find that her father was unable to accept Maybelle's death. According to Edwards, Eugene Mitchell often repeated "Your mother's not well," to his children. Though he regained contact with reality as he watched his wife's burial, he occasionally returned to a state of confusion in the weeks following the funeral, and Mitchell feared her father was going insane. He did recover, however, and urged Margaret to go back to Smith. The experience stayed with her and manifests itself in *Gone With the Wind*, as Edwards points out. "The similarities between Gerald O'Hara's grief over his wife's death and Eugene Mitchell's breakdown when Maybelle died are too striking to be dismissed."

With her mother dead, Mitchell's motivation to do well at Smith and become a psychiatrist failed her. After she finished her first year she returned to Atlanta to run the household for her father and brother. Having been away for a time, and never having had many friends in her home town, her social life was virtually nonexistent. Fearing his daughter might become a lonely spinster if left to her own devices, Eugene Mitchell urged her to apply for membership in Atlanta's prestigious Debutante Club. Mitchell acquiesced, and by January of 1920 she was approved for membership. At one of the many gatherings she was invited to as a result of this formal declaration of social status, she met Berrien Kinnard Upshaw, nicknamed Red by his friends. Though her family and debutante friends felt that Red was rough, rude, and thoroughly unsuitable for Mitchell, Edwards reported that "there was a certain mystery surrounding Upshaw that intrigued [her]; he had an aura of glamour that made him a topic of discussion among her peers and their families. It was known that he was the eldest son of a respectable old Georgia family now living in North Carolina, but there were also whisperings of scandal—although no one seemed to know any of the details."

After causing a minor scene by doing a sensual Apache dance in a suggestively slitted costume for a debutante charity function, Mitchell did not receive an invitation to become a member of Atlanta's Junior League, the expected next step for debutantes. Mitchell was hurt and angry, but she was now also free of all restraints on her behavior except those imposed by her family. Her relationship with Upshaw deepened, and in his company she joined the Peachtree Yacht Club—in Edwards's words, "a drinking club that had nothing at all to do with boats." With the club members, Mitchell could indulge her taste for liquor, cigarettes, and risque jokes without censure. She wrote short humorous plays to entertain her new friends; these were performed at the family house until her disapproving father put a stop to them. At this time she also became friends with Red Upshaw's roommate, John Marsh. Totally opposite in personality to Upshaw, Marsh discussed literature with Mitchell and critiqued her short stories. Eventually both men declared their love for her. Though her father and brother showed a decided preference for Marsh as a more stable and respectable man, Mitchell was excited by Upshaw, who, according to Edwards, "claimed to have played a secret, dashing role in [World War I], something to do with espionage and being behind enemy lines," and was a liquor bootlegger during the days of Prohibition when alcoholic beverages were illegal. Noting similarities between Red Upshaw and Mitchell's fictional creation Rhett Butler, Edwards asserted: "Both were 'masterful,' 'scoundrelly,' and of 'low morals,' and both had been expelled from service academies—Rhett, from West Point; Red, from Annapolis. Both had been profiteers, Rhett using the war for profit; Red, Prohibition. . . . and both were Southerners, but not Atlantans. But it was the volatile spirits of the two men that were most synonymous—the inner violence, the strong passions, the brilliant minds always so self-serving, and the animal magnetism."

On September 2, 1922, Mitchell married Upshaw, with John Marsh serving as best man. By the following December the couple had separated, Upshaw leaving Atlanta for Asheville, North Carolina. Reportedly he told Mitchell she could get a

divorce if she wished because he was never going to return. He did, however, in July of 1923 after Mitchell had been persuaded by Marsh to obtain a job as a feature writer for the *Atlanta Journal*. Mitchell asked him to come into the family house; no one else but the maid was there. In a deposition for their subsequent divorce, Edwards reported, Mitchell testified that Upshaw attempted to rape her. She struggled to get away, and her screams brought the family servant to investigate just as Upshaw decided to flee. He had beaten Mitchell so severely that she had to be hospitalized, and she was badly bruised. According to Edwards, Mitchell later "conceded that she never should have discussed her romantic feelings for Clifford Henry" during her honeymoon with Upshaw, "nor sent [Henry's parents] a postcard."

By October of 1924 Mitchell was granted an annulment of her marriage to Upshaw, and on July 4, 1925, she married John Marsh, on whom she had come to depend during her trials with Red. Throughout these changes in her personal life, Mitchell continued as a feature writer for the *Atlanta Journal*. She had her first byline feature printed in the paper, a story about an Atlanta plant expert, in early January, 1923. By the time she left the paper's employment, Edwards reported, Mitchell had written "139 by-lined features and 85 news stories, assisted in the writing of a personal advice column and a film column, and wrote a chapter for one of the *Journal*'s weekly serials when parts of a manuscript were lost." Her earlier assignments, however, usually dealt with light and humorous subjects. Dissatisfied with these topics, she requested that she be allowed to develop a more serious set of articles on eminent women in Georgia history. Though her editors had misgivings, Mitchell won permission to do a four-part series. Her first feature discussed four women: Rebecca Latimer Felton, who became the first woman United States senator though appointed to the post upon the death of her husband rather than elected; Lucy Mathilde Kenney, who disguised herself as a man to fight alongside her husband in the Civil War; Mary Musgrove, a Native American woman who was named the empress of the Creek tribe despite having had three white husbands; and Nancy Hart, who took prisoner an entire troop of British soldiers when they attempted to gain entrance to her kitchen during the American Revolution. As Edwards pointed out, "the only one who fitted the ladylike stereotype of the Southern heroine was Rebecca Latimer Felton," and the article drew a large amount of negative response from the paper's readership. Because Mitchell had favorably depicted strong women who did not fit contemporary standards for femininity, "she [was] accused of everything from defaming Georgian womanhood to bastardizing history in order to sell newspapers." The rest of the series was cancelled, and Mitchell, deeply hurt by the criticism she had received, limited herself to mostly lighter features such as an interview with film star Rudolph Valentino and articles which asked questions like "Should Husbands Spank Their Wives?"

A few months after marrying Marsh, however, Mitchell was asked to do a series of articles for the *Atlanta Journal* on the five Confederate generals selected to represent Georgia on the Stone Mountain Memorial, on which construction would soon begin. Because of her enthusiasm for Confederate history, Mitchell put much energy into the research and writing of the first article, which discussed generals John B. Gordon and Pierce M. Butler Young. Readers were so pleased with the feature that Mitchell's editor decided to stretch the series over the next three weeks so that she could compose an article about each of the remaining generals. These, too, were well received, but their importance went beyond their immediate reception. As Mitchell examined sources for her piece on General Henry Benning, "she found herself almost more caught up in the story of his wife," noted Edwards. Benning's wife had heroically struggled during the Civil War to keep the family plantation in operation, cared for her elderly parents and for her brother's widow, and nursed wounded Confederate soldiers. Edwards conjectured that Mitchell's interest in this woman's experiences and her desire to write the features on prominent women in Georgia foreshadowed her portrayal of the Civil War from the point of view of the women left behind by the men who went to battle in *Gone With the Wind*.

When Mitchell's husband, who was never completely happy about her working outside the home, received a raise in salary from the public relations department of the Georgia Power and Light Company in 1926, he urged her to leave her post at the *Atlanta Journal*. She did so, though she continued to write a free-lance column for the *Journal* called "Elizabeth Bennett's Gossip," which was more a compilation of historical anecdotes than of gossip, until she injured her ankle in an automobile accident and could not sit at the typewriter. By the time Mitchell had completely given up newspaper work, however, she had already ceased to find it sufficiently challenging to her as a writer. With Marsh's encouragement she began working on her fiction again. Mitchell started a Jazz Age novel with a heroine named Pansy Hamilton. As Edwards asserted, "the young men and women in Pansy's circle all bore a strong resemblance to the group that belonged to the [Peachtree] Yacht Club," and the hero "closely resembled Red Upshaw." Mitchell apparently found the similarity between truth and fiction too unpleasant to continue with her story after the first thirty pages. She next attempted a novel set during the 1880s in Georgia's Clayton county, where her ancestors once owned a plantation. It became the unpublished novella "'Ropa Carmagin," the tale of the daughter of a once great antebellum plantation family now declining and her mulatto lover, the son of one of the family's slaves. A tragedy, the story ends with the hero being killed and 'Ropa being driven from her ancestral home by hostile neighbors. Though she finished it, Mitchell put it aside because her husband did not like it. Later, however, it was mistakenly given to Harold Latham, her editor at Macmillan Publishing Company, along with the manuscript of *Gone With the Wind*. When he returned the novella to her he wrote, in a letter dated August 15, 1935, quoted by Edwards: "I have read this with a great deal of interest and very genuine admiration. It seems to me a splendid piece of work, expertly done. . . . It confirms my very high opinion of you as a writer—if that needed confirmation—and shows you can handle more than one type of material and character." Latham advised Mitchell to save the novella until after the publication of *Gone With the Wind*, and then seek to publish it in a magazine. She never did, and the manuscript of "'Ropa Carmagin" was eventually destroyed.

Mitchell's late 1926 accident and ankle injury required her to spend three weeks in a cast and then several more weeks in bed. During her convalescence Marsh brought her many books from the library to read. As Edwards reported, "The day [Mitchell] graduated to crutches, early in 1927, [Marsh] came home from work with a stack of copy paper and told her that there was hardly a book left in the library that she would enjoy." Her husband informed her that she would have to write a book herself if she was to have anything to read. Feeling as though she had been challenged, the next day she sat down at her typewriter and began the best selling novel in

history. She started with the last chapter, but afterward worked more or less in chronological order. Visitors to her apartment began to notice huge stacks of manila envelopes piling up in the area of her sewing table, but whenever acquaintances appeared, recalled Mitchell's friend Lois Cole in a *New York Times Book Review* article, "she threw a bath towel over the table." Finis Farr avowed in his 1965 biography *Margaret Mitchell of Atlanta: The Author of "Gone With the Wind"* that "by the end of 1928, one stack of envelopes was solid enough to sit on—and some callers did. . . . For a while she used two or three envelopes as a prop under the leg of an ailing sofa. On others she jotted notes that had nothing to do with the work in progress, using the manuscript-fat envelopes as memorandum pads for telephone numbers, recipes, grocery lists and dinner invitations."

Mitchell spent long hours in the basement of the Atlanta public library poring over old Atlanta newspapers to check the accuracy of her novel's historical details. As she worked on the Civil War epic, Mitchell called it "Tomorrow Is Another Day," taken from Scarlett's famous last lines after Rhett's departure: "I'll think of it all tomorrow, at Tara. I can stand it then. Tomorrow, I'll think of some way to get him back. After all, tomorrow is another day." Also, throughout the process of writing the novel, the heroine's name was Pansy rather than Scarlett, while the name of the O'Hara plantation was initially Fontenoy Hall rather than Tara.

Pointing out the fact that Pansy was also the name of the heroine in Mitchell's aborted Jazz Age novel, Edwards noted the many similarities between Pansy (later Scarlett) O'Hara and her creator: "Both were mavericks, constantly flouting convention and society, and both suffered identity problems caused by strong, righteous, Catholic mothers. Both had to care for their fathers after their mothers' deaths. Both were flirts and teases. . . . Both turned their backs on the Catholic church. Both were women who drank in a society that frowned on such 'unladylike' behavior, and both had set society against them. Both had had romanticized, unfulfilled first loves, [and] a violent marriage." Edwards also revealed, however, the correspondences between Pansy and Mitchell's maternal grandmother: "The O'Hara family had much in common with the Fitzgeralds, and had settled in Clayton County at about the same time. And, like Pansy O'Hara, Annie Fitzgerald Stephens had remained in Atlanta until the fire, had nursed the injured soldiers who had fallen or been brought there, had taken her firstborn infant back to Jonesboro alone just after the fire, and had remained there, fighting starvation and carpetbaggers, until the men returned from the war. Also, like Pansy, Annie was just a few years younger than the city of Atlanta." This likeness between Pansy and her grandmother, coupled with the resemblances between Rhett Butler and Red Upshaw, and Ashley Wilkes and Clifford Henry, made Mitchell hesitant about ever submitting the novel for publication.

Despite her hesitation, Mitchell worked fairly steadily on the novel from 1926 to 1934 except for a few periods of discouragement. The first of these came in the spring of 1927, when, Edwards reported, Mitchell read author James Boyd's Civil War novel, *Marching On*. She was apparently intimidated by the superiority of Boyd's writing. Edwards observed: "She [felt that she] did not write with the intellectual power of Boyd, nor did she understand the Confederate strategy or the Union aims as well as he did. She was writing a book about the great war without taking any of her characters into battle, and she was convinced that it was cowardly for her to avoid such scenes, that it only proved how inadequate she was for the job she was attempting.'' Mitchell did not touch her manuscript for three months. Another three-month break in the writing came after Mitchell read Stephen Vincent Benet's epic poem on the Civil War, *John Brown's Body*. She had much of the novel on paper, however, though disorganized and in a rough state, when another automobile accident in 1934 forced her to wear a brace that made composing at the typewriter difficult. Again, she stopped work on the book.

According to Edwards, Mitchell had just been told she would be able to do without the brace in a week's time when Macmillan acquisitions editor Harold Latham arrived in Atlanta looking for publishable manuscripts in April, 1935. Mitchell was enlisted by one of her former newspaper colleagues to entertain the visiting editor and help him in his search. Though she mentioned various friends and acquaintances who were working on novels, she did not tell him of her own project. Mitchell's friend Lois Cole worked for Macmillan, however, and though she had by that time moved to their New York offices, she remembered that Mitchell was writing a book and mentioned it to Latham. Latham, entranced by Mitchell's storytelling ability as she showed him the sights of her native city, inquired about her novel, but she denied she was writing one.

The night before Latham was to return to New York, however, Mitchell appeared at his hotel room accompanied by huge piles of manila envelopes. Apparently, derisive remarks from a friend about her lack of ambition and talent made her angry enough to show her manuscript to the Macmillan editor. On the train home, Latham examined what Mitchell had brought him and was nearly discouraged by what Edwards termed ''the worst-looking manuscript he had ever been given in his long career in publishing.'' But when he started reading, in Edwards's words, ''like all future readers of this book, whose numbers were to be in the millions, Harold Latham was hooked.'' Despite the fact that there was no real first chapter, several versions of other chapters, and missing bridges between the various incidents in the novel, Latham sent Mitchell a telegram saying that her book had great potential.

Eventually Macmillan purchased the book, and after an extensive revision, a name change for the heroine—Pansy became Scarlett because ''pansy'' was a slang term for a male homosexual in the North and Latham wished to avoid any negative connotations—and a search for a new title (because, as Cole explained, ''there were thirteen books in print with titles beginning [with] 'Tomorrow. . .'''), it became the 1,037-page opus, *Gone With the Wind*. The story's time ranges from just before the advent of the Civil War to the days when the South began to recover from the handicaps placed on it by Reconstruction. Though Scarlett O'Hara is much battered and bruised by the historical events of the period, she continues throughout in her selfish personal pursuits. Undaunted by the fact that the man she loves, Ashley Wilkes, is engaged to his angelic cousin Melanie Hamilton at the novel's beginning, she tells him of her passion, unaware until Ashley rejects her and leaves the room that they have been overheard by the mysterious visitor from Charleston, Rhett Butler. To spite Ashley, Scarlett turns her charms on Melanie's brother Charles, flirting with him until he is smitten enough to marry her when news is received of the declaration of war. Charles enlists, only to meet a quick end in the conflict, though his demise is the result of pneumonia and measles rather than a Northern bullet. He did, however, live long enough to impregnate his young wife, who gives birth to a son, Wade. Scarlett, still enamored of Ashley, as indeed she is throughout most of the novel, is sent to visit

her sister-in-law and rival Melanie in Atlanta. Spending most of the war there, she tends wounded soldiers not from any loyalty to the Southern cause but because it is expected of her. Scarlett also comes into further contact with Rhett, who is now, as a blockade runner for the Confederacy, seen by Atlanta as a dashing hero. Scarlett doesn't like Rhett and feels threatened by him, but because he witnessed her shameful scene with Ashley she must be at least somewhat polite to him.

When Ashley returns on furlough at Christmastime, he begs Scarlett to promise that she will take care of the fragile, innocent Melanie while he is away. She does, and thus she must stay in Atlanta through the hot summer while the Yankee troops draw nearer because Melanie, now pregnant, is too frail to risk a journey south. On the day Melanie goes into labor, Scarlett discovers they are two of the very few people left in town. The doctor is too busy nursing the wounded and dying soldiers pouring into the city from the battlefield to assist in the delivery, and Scarlett must do it herself with only the extremely lazy and ignorant slave Prissy to aid her. As the Confederate troops rush through Atlanta in retreat before the forces of Union General Sherman, the baby is born. Fortunately, Rhett Butler is still in town—he has several Northern friends, and he does not fear the advancing Union Army. Scarlett sends Prissy to summon Rhett, and he steals a broken-winded horse and a rickety wagon to take them out of Atlanta. After guiding Scarlett and her son Wade, Prissy, and an unconscious Melanie lying in the back of the wagon with her baby out of the burning city, Rhett abandons them to join up with the Confederate Army that he has scorned for so long. Cursing Rhett's timing in becoming a Southern patriot, Scarlett drives on to her plantation home, Tara, managing to evade the retreating Confederate soldiers who would confiscate her horse and wagon for the army's use.

When Scarlett arrives at Tara, she finds that the comfort and protection she sought are nowhere to be found. Only the fact that the conquering Union forces used the house as a temporary headquarters prevented it from being burned down like the neighboring homes, including Ashley's once stately Twelve Oaks. Scarlett's mother is dead from typhoid and her two younger sisters are still weak with the disease; her father has become mentally incompetent, refusing to accept the reality of his wife's death. The Yankees have taken the plantation's store of food with them, and starvation is a distinct possibility. The Northern troops also freed the O'Hara's field slaves, leaving only the loyal but relatively useless house servants. Despite these hardships Scarlett struggles to keep her family fed and to maintain Tara as a working plantation. She finds an unlikely ally in Melanie, who loyally aids her in trials which include shooting and burying a looting Union deserter and putting out a fire that threatens Tara. Scarlett, though annoyed by Melanie's charitable insistence on sharing their hard-won food with the Confederate soldiers who pass through the area, gains a grudging respect for her sister-in-law which does not, however, prevent her from being in love with Melanie's husband.

The war, ending in defeat for the South, finally comes to a close, and Ashley, long feared dead by Scarlett and Melanie, makes his slow way home. He attempts to adjust to life at Tara, but his genteel background has not made him suitable for splitting rails and other plantation chores. Scarlett, meanwhile, has more pressing problems than her frustrated love for another woman's husband. The O'Hara's former overseer, a Northerner who was fired for moral indiscretions, is now involved in Reconstruction politics and has raised the taxes on

Tara in order to force Scarlett to sell it to him. Despairing without the money, Scarlett privately begs Ashley to run away with her to Mexico. Though Ashley cannot resist falling into a passionate embrace with Scarlett, he refuses to leave Melanie, and in his guilt at wanting Scarlett declares his intent to leave Tara. This shakes Scarlett into a firmer control of her emotions, and she tells Ashley, ''You need not go. . . . I won't have you all starve, simply because I've thrown myself at your head. It will never happen again.'' Her failure to win Ashley away from Melanie makes her more determined than ever to save Tara, and she remembers all the money Rhett Butler made profiteering during the war. Because Rhett has never kept secret his desire for Scarlett, she at first thinks that if she visits him in Atlanta she can get him to marry her. When married he would have to give her the money to save Tara. But Scarlett also recalls his teasing, ''I am not a marrying man,'' and realizes that she may have to consent to be his mistress to get the money for the taxes. She resolves to save Tara at any cost.

Upon her arrival in Atlanta, armored in a new dress made from her mother's green velvet drapes, Scarlett learns that Rhett has been imprisoned, ostensibly for the murder of a black man. He informs her that he cannot give her any money because the Yankees, now in complete control of the conquered South, suspect him of hoarding some of the Confederate treasury and would confiscate any money he tried to draw. Rhett does not make this admission, however, until he has gotten Scarlett to offer sex as ''collateral.'' Feeling humiliated, ashamed, and still not knowing where she will get the wherewithal to save her home, Scarlett exits Rhett's jail cell only to encounter Frank Kennedy, her sister Suellen's fiance. Kennedy shows her his store, which has been profitable; Scarlett lies and tells him Suellen has engaged herself to another man, and gets him to marry her.

Though Tara is saved, Scarlett must live with Frank near his store in Atlanta. Eventually, Scarlett gains enough money of her own to buy a lumber mill and offers Ashley a partnership to get him to come to Atlanta rather than take a job in a bank in New York. Ashley refuses until Scarlett's tears make Melanie beg him to reconsider: ''Ashley, how could you refuse her? And after all she's done for us! How ungrateful you make us appear!''

In the course of running her mill—which she enjoys, despite the fact that her genteel Atlanta neighbors criticize her active involvement in business as unfeminine—Scarlett travels through a dangerous part of town alone in her carriage and is attacked by one of the newly freed slaves who live in shacks there. The incident causes some of Atlanta's men, including Frank and Ashley, to make a Ku Klux Klan raid on Shantytown; the Union troops, in Atlanta to enforce Reconstruction, are prepared for them, however, and only Rhett Butler's skillfully drawn alibi that the men were with him in Belle Watling's bordello prevents their arrest and hanging. Rhett's rescue is not complete, though; Frank was shot and killed during the raid.

With Scarlett a widow once more and feeling guiltily responsible for her husband's death, Rhett wastes no time in proposing marriage to her. He explains his change of heart about marriage: ''I always intended having you, one way or another. But as you and Frank have made a little money, I know you'll never be driven to me again with any interesting propositions of loans and collaterals. So I see I'll have to marry you.'' Scarlett accepts, partially because Rhett proceeds to kiss her into submission but mostly because he has enough money to

take away her anxieties about returning to poverty and somehow losing Tara.

Scarlett and Rhett's marriage is almost a happy one initially; Scarlett bears her third child (her second was a daughter with Frank Kennedy), a girl nicknamed Bonnie, preferred to her half-siblings by her mother and adored by Rhett. Scarlett still loves Ashley, however, and after Bonnie's birth decides that any further babies will damage her figure and cause Ashley to lose his attraction to her. She banishes Rhett from her bedroom; hurt, he complies with her request though he tells her, ''If I wanted you, no lock would keep me out.'' This state of affairs continues, with Rhett finding gratification at Belle Watling's, until the day of Ashley's surprise birthday party. Sent to the mill to distract Ashley while Melanie prepares the house for the party, Scarlett is caught in his arms by his sister India, and soon all of Atlanta has heard the story, including Rhett. Ironically, though Scarlett and Ashley have been guilty on other occasions, what India mistakes for a passionate embrace is only two friends sharing a comforting hug after being saddened by too much reminiscing about the days before the war.

Rhett forces Scarlett to attend Melanie's party alone and face the many people who think her an adulteress. Melanie, not believing a word of wrong about Scarlett and Ashley, stands by her staunchly throughout the party so that other guests do not dare shun her. Afterwards, Rhett, angrily declaring, ''By God, this is one night when there are only going to be two in my bed,'' carries Scarlett up to the room from which he has been long prohibited. The next morning, Scarlett almost comes to the realization that it is really Rhett who she loves rather than Ashley, but she and Rhett slide back into exchanging sarcastic remarks despite mutual good intentions, and Rhett announces he is taking Bonnie and going on a trip for an indefinite period. When he returns three months later, Scarlett tells him she is pregnant again. Though both intend to be kind to each other, they revert to insults; Scarlett is so angered that she falls down the stairs trying to assault Rhett and suffers a miscarriage.

Scarlett and Rhett continue throughout the rest of *Gone With the Wind* at cross-purposes. Scarlett wants Rhett desperately while enduring the loss of her unborn child but is too afraid of rejection to call for him; Rhett fears for her life but will not go to her unless he is asked for, attributing Scarlett's reticence as anger at him for his treatment of her. They sustain another loss when Bonnie is killed in a riding accident, but instead of being drawn together by this tragedy they are pushed further apart, Scarlett blaming Rhett for their daughter's death. Rhett becomes temporarily insane and refuses to give up Bonnie's body for burial; only Melanie's patient kindness and persuasion return him to reason.

Not long after Bonnie's death, Melanie, having never fully recovered from the birth of her first child, suffers a miscarriage. Scarlett rushes to her bedside, and as Melanie dies, realizes how much she has come to love and appreciate her once-hated rival. In the ensuing chaos of Melanie's family's grief, Scarlett also comes to realize that not only has Ashley loved Melanie all along, but that she herself never loved Ashley: ''He never really existed at all, except in my imagination,'' Scarlett confesses to herself. ''I loved something I made up, something that's just as dead as Melly is, I made a pretty suit of clothes and fell in love with it. And when Ashley came riding along, so handsome, so different, I put that suit on him and made him wear it whether it fitted him or not. And I wouldn't see what he really was. I kept on loving the pretty clothes—and not him at all.''

Scarlett also realizes that she loves Rhett, and dashes from the Wilkeses' home to her own to tell her husband of her discoveries. But she is too late—Rhett's love for Scarlett has died; he asks her: "Did it ever occur to you that even the most deathless love could wear out?" Since she does not wish for the scandal of a divorce, Rhett assures her that he will return to her often enough to prevent gossip, but he is, in effect, leaving her. To Scarlett's pleading objections and questions Rhett delivers the immortal line, "My dear, I don't give a damn," and makes his exit. Though the novel ends with Scarlett's hopeful resolution to win him back after recovering at Tara, readers are offered no real clue as to whether she succeeds, and Mitchell remained firm throughout her life in her refusal to speculate on the subject.

Gone With the Wind was an immediate success. Before it was even published it was chosen as a Book-of-the-Month Club main selection; shortly after the novel's publication the motion picture rights had been purchased for fifty thousand dollars—a high sum in 1936—by Selznick-International Pictures. Even at the price of three dollars a copy, exorbitant for the Great Depression, Mitchell's book was quickly on its way to becoming the best-selling work of fiction of all time. Indeed, Farr credited Mitchell with doing a great deal for the ailing American economy. "Benefits flowed through The Macmillan Company from top to bottom," he reported. "In December, Christmas bonuses appeared for the first time in recent memory." This prosperity spread throughout the bookselling industry as well. "The million copies of *Gone With the Wind* the public bought by Christmas of 1936 caused $3,000,000 to go through the retailers' cash registers," Farr added. Mitchell became an overnight celebrity, receiving countless pieces of fan mail, most of which she felt it her duty to answer personally. Her phone, which remained listed in the Atlanta directory, rang constantly; as Edwards revealed, one of the early callers was Red Upshaw. He reportedly told Mitchell that he figured she still loved him, because "Rhett Butler is obviously modeled after [him]." When Mitchell asked him what he wanted, he said he would "tell her someday in person" and hung up.

Hearing from Upshaw, coupled with her sudden phenomenal fame, made Mitchell fear that much of her private life would be exposed. But she was also flattered by the attention her book received, though she was baffled by it. In a letter to Herschel Brickell, one of *Gone With the Wind*'s early reviewers, dated October 9, 1936, Mitchell described her lack of ability to understand her novel's popularity. "I sit down and pull the story apart in my mind and try to figure it all out," she wrote. "Despite its length and many details it is basically just a simple yarn of fairly simple people. There's no fine writing, there are no grandiose thoughts, there are no hidden meanings, no symbolism, nothing sensational—nothing, nothing at all." Nevertheless, as she told Brickell, "the bench and bar like it, judges write me letters about it. The medical profession . . . like it. . . . The psychiatrists especially like it. . . . File clerks, elevator operators, sales girls in department stores, telephone operators, stenographers, garage mechanics, clerks in Helpsy-Selfsy stores, school teachers—oh, Heavens, I could go on and on!—like it. What is more puzzling, they buy copies. . . . The Sons of Confederate Veterans crashed through with a grand endorsement. . . . The debutantes and dowagers read it. Catholic nuns like it." Critics, though, were not as mystified as the author, generally explaining the novel's suc-

cess by linking Scarlett's struggle to overcome poverty and Reconstruction to the struggles of the average American during the Great Depression—Scarlett's determination made her a character a reader could admire and identify with in spite of her negative qualities.

Mitchell became so famous, even winning the 1937 Pulitzer Prize for *Gone With the Wind*, that women began impersonating her for their own ends. Edwards reported that "impostors were appearing in California, Mexico, and New York who claimed to be Margaret Mitchell, gave statements to the press and, in one case, tried to use her name to establish financial credit." Farr observed that "Margaret found it distressing to hear that a woman habitually rode the club car of the Congressional Limited between Washington [D.C.] and New York [City], striking up acquaintance with men, accepting drinks, and proclaiming that she was Margaret Mitchell. Another imposter caused a disturbance at the Miami Airport, ordering officials to bring out an airplane immediately for a chartered flight to the Caribbean. This woman appeared to be drunk, which heightened the embarrassment, but also caused the airline people to have certain doubts, and telephone Atlanta." Mitchell was also plagued by false rumors which circulated about her, including, according to Farr and Edwards, ones which claimed she was insane, that she had a wooden leg, that her husband John had really written *Gone With the Wind*, that she had paid author Sinclair Lewis to write the book *for* her, that she was dying of leukemia, and that she was going blind.

More serious but equally ludicrous was the lawsuit brought against Mitchell by Susan Lawrence Davis, author of *An Authentic History of the Ku Klux Klan, 1865-1877*. Davis sued Mitchell for $6,500,000,000, claiming that the latter had plagiarized her work. As Farr explained, "Miss Davis submitted a 461-page brief pointing out, among other suspicious circumstances, that both books were in Confederate gray binding; that both used the phrase 'Fiery Cross'; that Miss Davis spoke of 'ghosts from the nearby battlefields' and Miss Mitchell called a character 'wraithlike'; that Miss Davis mentioned Fort Sumter, and so did Miss Mitchell; Miss Davis wrote 'Charleston,' Miss Mitchell, 'Charlestonians'; Miss Mitchell used the words 'practically destitute,' infringing on Miss Davis's 'utterly impoverished'; [General] Stonewall Jackson, [Colonel] Wade Hampton, and [Confederate President] Jefferson Davis were in Miss Davis' book, and also in Miss Mitchell's; Miss Davis had described a Southern home as having 'mirrors above the mantel,' while on page 868 of *Gone With the Wind*, Margaret Mitchell wrote of 'gilt frame mirrors and long pier glasses'; and so on." The suit was eventually dismissed. Mitchell brought her own suit, however, against entertainment entrepreneur Billy Rose, who included a satire of *Gone With the Wind* in one of his theatrical extravaganzas without her permission. She was also very much involved in legal disputes over commercial tie-ins based on her characters and foreign copyright problems.

Critics discussed *Gone With the Wind* almost as avidly as the rest of the American public. Most were unanimous in their praise of its ability to hold a reader's attention; author Stephen Vincent Benet, reviewing the novel in the *Saturday Review of Literature*, avowed that "in spite of its length, the book moves swiftly and smoothly—a three-decker with all sails set." The best-seller's literary merit was less easily decided upon. Poet John Peale Bishop dismissed *Gone With the Wind* in the *New Republic* as "one of those thousand-page novels, competent but neither very good nor very sound"; critic Bernard DeVoto in the *Saturday Review of Literature* labeled Mitchell's work "wish-fulfillment literature" and complained that "its sentiments'' were ''commonplace and frequently cheap.'' On the other hand, reviewer Malcolm Cowley asserted that *Gone With the Wind* ''has a simple-minded courage that suggests the great novelists of the past.'' Belle Rosenbaum, critiquing in *Scribner's Magazine,* pointed out that ''Scarlett O'Hara and Rhett Butler retained a touch of [authors James] Joyce, [Ernest] Hemingway, [and F. Scott] Fitzgerald, and the aftermath of the Civil War was interpreted in modern terms with Scarlett O'Hara emerging as the modern prototype of [author William Makepeace] Thackeray's immortal [character] Becky Sharp.'' And, though Mitchell was criticized for her glorification of a society that practiced slavery, she was also lauded for her careful attention to historical detail.

Critical debate over *Gone With the Wind* continues through to the arguments of contemporary scholars. In a 1958 *Georgia Review* article, critic Robert Y. Drake, Jr., defended the novel as an epic comparable to ancient Roman author Virgil's *Aeneid.* ''It dramatically demonstrates, as the *Aeneid* did before it, that you cannot destroy a traditional society simply by destroying its machinery,'' Drake asserted. He concluded, ''I know of no other Civil War novel with as much 'breadth' in conception as *Gone With the Wind.*'' W. J. Stuckey, however, in his 1966 *The Pulitzer Prize Novels: A Critical Backward Look,* reaffirmed DeVoto's stance by opining that ''Miss Mitchell's art most noisily proclaims its indebtedness to the literature of wish fulfillment—the bosomy and sub-pornographic historical romance, the sentimental novel, and the Hollywood extravaganza.'' Similarly, citing the book's prudery, sentimentality, and ''anti-Negro racism,'' critic Floyd C. Watkins condemned *Gone With the Wind* in a 1970 *Southern Literary Journal* article as ''false to the human heart'' and a ''bad novel.'' By contrast, Dawson Gaillard saw the novel as a positive feminist example of a *bildungsroman* (story of personal development) in a 1974 issue of the *Georgia Review.* ''To me it seems that Margaret Mitchell wanted to write a success story,'' Gaillard explained, ''about a woman who was successful in breaking away from the life of self-effacement her mother had lived, in working counter to the existing patriarchal system as she matures from a young, frivolous girl to a twenty-eight-year-old serious-minded woman.'' Other conflicting opinions range from Leslie A. Fielder's view of *Gone With the Wind* as an exercise in sadomasochism in his 1979 *The Inadvertent Epic: From ''Uncle Tom's Cabin'' to ''Roots,''* to Elizabeth Fox-Genovese's depiction of the work as an allegory for the United States' development as a country in a 1981 *American Quarterly* article.

Even during the first rush of fame that met Mitchell after the publication of *Gone With the Wind,* speculation was rampant as to how the film version of the work would be cast. Though Mitchell firmly refused to take an active roll in the filming of her novel, the public pleaded with her to give her opinions on the subject. Popular consensus was almost unanimous in demanding actor Clark Gable for the role of Rhett, but divided on who should portray Scarlett. Producer David O. Selznick was in favor of casting a relatively unknown actress in the role, and initiated talent auditions. In addition to that of Scarlett, acting hopefuls were encouraged to try out for minor parts. When these auditions were held in Atlanta, Mitchell was besieged by people who accosted her and forced her to watch them perform, not comprehending that the author had no influence on the film's casting. In one such incident, Edwards reported, ''a mother with her small girl done up as a prospective Bonnie, in tight curls and wearing a riding habit, appeared at [Mitchell's] hairdresser's and pulled the dryer from

[the author's] head so that the child's recitation of a Confederate poem could be heard.''

Despite several changes of screenwriters, a change of directors, and casting difficulties, the film version of *Gone With the Wind* won ten Academy Awards, including one for best picture. Starring Gable as Rhett, British actress Vivien Leigh as Scarlett, Leslie Howard as Ashley, and Olivia De Havilland as Melanie, the film finally premiered in Mitchell's hometown Atlanta in December, 1939. The premiere was a huge event, with Mitchell and most of the film's major stars in attendance at Atlanta's Loew's Grand Theatre. After the film, nearly four hours in length, was shown and had received a standing ovation, Mitchell addressed the crowd. Edwards concluded: ''It seemed doubtful that anything further could occur in her life that would equal the sense of accomplishment she had felt as she stepped out of the Selznick limousine before the Loew's Grand Theatre, unless it had been the moment when she had stood alone, front and center of the Grand's stage, waiting for the ovation that was being given her to subside.''

After the release of ''Gone With the Wind,'' most of the publicity Mitchell had been receiving died down. Her best-selling novel had changed her life irrevocably, however; she spent the rest of her life answering fan letters, and most critics assume that she was too intimidated by the amazing success of her first published work to ever seriously attempt another novel, though she sometimes joked about writing a sequel to be given the title ''Back With the Breeze.'' With the entrance of the United States into World War II, Mitchell busied herself in the war effort, serving as a volunteer in the American Red Cross, selling war bonds, corresponding with American servicemen overseas, and even christening the ill-fated cruiser the U.S.S. *Atlanta,* later sunk in battle. After the war she sent packages of food and supplies to Europe, eventually being named an honorary citizen of Vimoutiers, France, for her relief efforts. According to Edwards, Mitchell seemed proud of the fact that *Gone With the Wind* had been banned in Nazi-occupied Europe during the war and black market copies had sold for high prices among the rebellious citizens of occupied France, who identified heavily with her portrayal of the conquered but unbowed Southerners. Though she had been accused of racism by many of her novel's reviewers, she involved herself in a charitable campaign to build a paying hospital for blacks in Atlanta, who at that time were segregated to charity hospitals whose facilities were often inferior. Also, many of Mitchell's black acquaintances had complained to her of their shame at having to take charity in order to receive medical care.

Mitchell was troubled at this time, however, by worries about her husband John's health (he suffered a heart attack in December, 1945, which left him a semi-invalid), and by premonitions that she would die a violent death. In a 1945 letter to friend and reviewer Edwin Granberry, Edwards reported, she wrote: ''I'm going to die in a car-crash. I feel very certain of this.'' Also, in January, 1949, Mitchell's personal secretary brought her an obituary clipping stating that her first husband, Red Upshaw, had died in a fall from the fifth-story fire escape of a Galveston, Texas, hotel; his death had been ruled a suicide.

On August 11, 1949, Mitchell and her husband decided to view a film at a local theater. As Mitchell helped John across the street, a speeding car came at them from around a corner. Mitchell panicked, released her husband's arm, and started running back to the curb. The car, having initially swerved to avoid the couple, hit her; the driver, Hugh D. Gravitt, was intoxicated. Mitchell died of brain injuries five days later.

While she lay unconscious many calls about her condition were made to the hospital, including one from U.S. President Harry S. Truman. So many people wished to attend Mitchell's funeral that tickets had to be distributed. Farr quoted from Mitchell's brother Stephens's account of her burial in Atlanta's Oakland Cemetery: "There was a crowd there for two or three days. She had said something to her people and they had answered."

Long after Mitchell's death she and her famous book have continued to make news. As of 1988 a debate over whether to preserve the Atlanta apartment in which she wrote *Gone With the Wind* or destroy it to facilitate urban development still raged. Because of *Gone With the Wind*'s unresolved ending, readers have long demanded a sequel, and, according to Claudia Glenn Dowling in *Life* magazine, they will have one by 1990. With the approval of the Mitchell estate, author Alexandra Ripley has been enlisted for the undertaking. Ripley acknowledged to Dowling the difficulty of continuing one of the best loved stories of all time, but optimistically observed: "Thank God for Mitchell's plot. She left a lot of tantalizing tidbits."

MEDIA ADAPTATIONS: A film version of *Gone With the Wind* was released, starring Clark Gable, Vivien Leigh, Leslie Howard, and Olivia De Havilland, by Metro-Goldwyn-Mayer in 1939.

BIOGRAPHICAL/CRITICAL SOURCES:

BOOKS

Dictionary of Literary Biography, Volume 9: *American Novelists, 1910-1945*, Gale, 1981.
Edwards, Anne, *Road to Tara: The Life of Margaret Mitchell*, Ticknor & Fields, 1983.
Farr, Finis, *Margaret Mitchell of Atlanta: The Author of "Gone With the Wind*," Morrow, 1965.
Fiedler, Leslie A., *The Inadvertent Epic: From "Uncle Tom's Cabin" to "Roots,"* Simon & Schuster, 1979.
Mitchell, Margaret, *Gone With the Wind*, Macmillan, 1936.
Mitchell, *Margaret Mitchell's "Gone With the Wind" Letters*, edited by Richard Harwell, Macmillan, c. 1976.
Stuckey, W. J., *The Pulitzer Prize Novels: A Critical Backward Look*, University of Oklahoma Press, 1966.
Twentieth-Century Literary Criticism, Volume 11, Gale, 1983.

PERIODICALS

American Quarterly, fall, 1981.
Chicago Tribune, June 26, 1986, February 7, 1988.
Detroit Free Press, May 19, 1988.
Georgia Review, summer, 1958, spring, 1974.
Life, May, 1988.
Los Angeles Times, April 21, 1988.
New Republic, July 15, 1936, September 16, 1936.
Newsweek, June 30, 1986.
New York Times, June 24, 1986, July 3, 1986, July 6, 1986, April 26, 1988.
New York Times Book Review, June 25, 1961.
Photoplay, March, 1938.
Saturday Review of Literature, July 4, 1936, January 8, 1938.
Scribner's Magazine, August, 1937.
Southern Literary Journal, spring, 1970, fall, 1980.
Washington Post, December 28, 1987.
Washington Post Book World, June 29, 1986.*

—*Sketch by Elizabeth Thomas*

MITCHELL, Peggy
See MITCHELL, Margaret (Munnerlyn)

*   *   *

MONKMAN, Leslie
See MONKMAN, Leslie G.

*   *   *

MONKMAN, Leslie G.   1946-
(Leslie Monkman)

PERSONAL: Born August 13, 1946, in Owen Sound, Ontario, Canada; son of Gordon Emerson and Islay Annie (Sinclair) Monkman; married Marni Isobel Lockington, December 19, 1975; children: Lindsay Alexandra, Fraser Douglas. *Education:* University of Western Ontario, B.A., 1968; University of Toronto, M.A., 1969; York University, Ph.D., 1975.

ADDRESSES: Home—599 Union St. W., Kingston, Ontario, Canada K7M 2H7. *Office*—Department of English, Queen's University, Kingston, Ontario, Canada K7L 3N6.

CAREER: University of Guelph, Guelph, Ontario, lecturer, 1969-71, 1973-76, assistant professor, 1976-80, associate professor of English, 1980-84; Queen's University, Kingston, Ontario, associate professor of English, 1984—.

MEMBER: Association for Commonwealth Language and Literature Studies (vice-chairman, 1980-83), Association of Canadian University Teachers of English, Humanities Association of Canada, Association for Canadian and Quebec Literatures.

WRITINGS:

(Editor with Douglas M. Daymond) *Towards a Canadian Literature: Essays, Editorials, and Manifestos*, Tecumseh Press, Volume I: *1752-1940*, Volume II: *1940-1983*, 1984-85.
(Editor with Daymond) *On Middle Ground* (novellas), Methuen, 1987.

UNDER NAME LESLIE MONKMAN

(Editor with Daymond) *Literature in Canada*, Volumes I-II, Gage Publishing, 1978.
(Editor with Daymond) *Stories of Quebec*, Oberon Press, 1980.
(Editor with Daymond) *Canadian Novelists and the Novel*, Borealis Press, 1981.
A Native Heritage: Images of the Indian in English-Canadian Literature, University of Toronto Press, 1981.

Contributor of essays to *Canadian Literature, Journal of Canadian Fiction, Etudes Canadiennes, African Literature Today, Essays on Canadian Writing*, and *Profiles in Canadian Literature*. Associate editor of *World Literature Written in English*.

WORK IN PROGRESS: Research on Canadian, New Zealand, and Australian fiction, and on "genre theory in relation to postcolonial literatures."

SIDELIGHTS: In his 1981 book, *A Native Heritage: Images of the Indian in English-Canadian Literature*, Leslie G. Monkman dispells "conclusively a prevalent idea that the Indian has always been . . . a minor figure" in the literature of Canada, wrote Alfred G. Bailey in *Canadian Poetry*. Exploring how these native Americans are variously depicted in some 250 English-language works, the author discusses an array of genres and writers. The study covers an "impressive range of material," wrote Carole Gerson in *Canadian Literature*. "Especially interesting are Monkman's ventures into some of the narrower byways of [Canada's] cultural history." Commending the topical rather than historical arrangement of Monkman's investigation, Bailey noted that the author provides "coherent accounts of diverse themes and with a degree of illumination not . . . obtainable" in volumes that adhere to a strictly historical framework. Also noteworthy is Monkman's "lengthy examination" of the Indian mythology and legend revealed in the numerous writings. According to Bailey, questions "of authenticity" are raised concerning physical and anthropological attributes, which many of the authors employed as literary devices to describe the native Americans. "From Monkman's study emerges the irony that . . . writers have presented simultaneously conflicting stereotypes of Canada's native peoples," observed Gerson. Native Americans have been presented as both vicious savages and children of nature, "a group without a history" that has "supplied identity-hungry white writers with indigenous historical heroes." Asserting that Monkman makes "consistently just interpretations of the intent of many authors," Bailey determined that *A Native Heritage* stands as "a major contribution to the growing body of critical studies" addressing Canadian literature.

BIOGRAPHICAL/CRITICAL SOURCES:

PERIODICALS

Books in Canada, December, 1985.
Canadian Literature, autumn, 1982.
Canadian Poetry, spring/summer, 1982.
Globe and Mail (Toronto), September 7, 1985.

*   *   *

MONROE, Lyle
See HEINLEIN, Robert A(nson)

*   *   *

MOON, Warren G.   1946-

PERSONAL: Born March 2, 1946, in Westfield, Mass. *Education:* Tufts University, M.A., 1967; University of Chicago, A.M., 1968, Ph.D., 1974.

ADDRESSES: Home—5806 Baskerville Walk, Middleton, Wis. 53562. *Office*—316 Elvehjem Museum of Art, University of Wisconsin—Madison, 800 University Ave., Madison, Wis. 53706.

CAREER: University of Wisconsin—Madison, instructor, 1970-73, assistant professor, 1973-75, associate professor, 1975-80, professor of ancient art and classics, 1980—, visiting fellow at Institute for Research in the Humanities, 1975-76, member of executive committee of the institute, 1980-83. President of the appraising firm of W. G. Moon and Associates. Visiting research curator at Art Institute of Chicago, 1975-80; visiting professor at University of Michigan-University of Wisconsin Program in Florence, Italy, 1985. Chairman of board of directors of Art Place/Center Gallery, 1982-83; member of board of directors of Creative Arts Over Sixty, 1982—, and Madison Art Center, 1984—; expert witness on art authentication and art fraud; consultant to J. Paul Getty Museum and Minneapolis Institute of Art.

MEMBER: American Philological Association, Archaeological Institute of America (president of Madison society, 1978—),

College Art Association of America, American Numismatic Association, Societe Suisse de Numismatique (corresponding fellow), Vereinigung der Freunde Antike Kunst (corresponding fellow), Midwest Art History Society, Classical Association of the Midwest and South, Phi Beta Kappa, University Club (member of board of directors, 1981-85).

AWARDS, HONORS: Ford Foundation travel fellow, 1968; Ryerson fellow at American School of Classical Studies in Athens, 1969-70; fellow of National Endowment for the Arts, 1979-80; fellow of National Endowment for the Humanities, 1988.

WRITINGS:

Greek Vases in Midwestern Collections, Art Institute of Chicago, 1980.
Ancient Greek Art and Iconography, University of Wisconsin Press, 1983.
(With A. K. Narain) *Greece, Rome, and India: A Comparative Iconographic Study*, University of Wisconsin Press, in press.

Co-general editor of "Wisconsin Studies in Classics," published by University of Wisconsin Press. Contributor to *World Book Encyclopedia*. Contributor to art and archaeology journals. Book review editor of *American Journal of Archaeology*, 1982-86; member of editorial board of *Wisconsin Academy Review*, 1982—.

WORK IN PROGRESS: Corpus Vasorum Antiquorum: State of Wisconsin, two volumes, publication expected in 1989; research on the silk route and the legacy of Alexander the Great.

SIDELIGHTS: Warren G. Moon told *CA:* "I have degrees both in Latin and Greek language and literature and in art history and classical archaeology; iconography, mythology and legend in artistic representation, is an exciting meeting ground between these disciplines. My current research area deals with the images on Hellenistic and Roman coins, hoards of which have been excavated along the silk route between Turkey and western China. These Greek images, signs, and symbols seem to have provided artistic inspiration in certain Jewish synagogues, such as the famous one in eastern Syria at Dura Europas, and similarly may have influenced some artistic programs at the other end of the silk route, in Buddhist art, at Ghandara and elsewhere.

"*Corpus Vasorum Antiquorum* is an international series of scholarly treatises that describe and commit to record ancient Greek vases in the museums of the world. Six museums in the state of Wisconsin have exceptional holdings in this medium of ancient art, and two volumes in this series will shortly present them to the scholarly community. Some of these works of ancient painting are particularly interesting for their iconographic programs."

Moon added: "I have been asked to orchestrate a major international symposium on ancient Greek sculpture for the Minneapolis Institute of Arts to be held there in October, 1989. The three-day event with fifteen major scholars presenting recent research is entitled 'Polykleitos and His Times, the Doryphoros and Its Influence.'"

BIOGRAPHICAL/CRITICAL SOURCES:

PERIODICALS

Times Literary Supplement, August 24, 1984.

MOREAU, Daniel 1949-

PERSONAL: Born September 16, 1949, in Lockport, N.Y.; son of Arthur W. (an artist) and Doris N. (a nurse; maiden name, Lewton) Moreau; married Jean Martin (a developer), December 26, 1983. Education: Buffalo State College, B.A., 1976; Harvard University, M.A., 1982.

ADDRESSES: Home—403 Elm Ave., Takoma Park, Md. 20912. Office—1729 H St. N.W., Washington, D.C. 20006. Agent—Meg Ruley, Jane Rotrosen Agency, 318 East 51st St., New York, N.Y. 10022.

CAREER: Times-Union, Rochester, N.Y., reporter, 1977-78; Richmond Times-Dispatch, Richmond, Va., reporter, 1978-81; Changing Times, Washington, D.C., writer, 1983—. Military service: U.S. Army, 1968-70, served as medic; became sergeant.

MEMBER: National Press Club.

WRITINGS:

Death Without Honor (novel), Pocket Books, 1987.
Ploughshares (novel), Pocket Books, 1988.

WORK IN PROGRESS: Wilson's Fudge, a novel.

SIDELIGHTS: Daniel Moreau told CA: "I enjoy the prospects of an ordinary person thrust into extraordinary circumstances. I wrote my first novel, Death Without Honor, from an outline. I 'assembled' complete chapters in my head before I wrote and little revision was necessary. My second novel, Ploughshares, was written under less organized circumstances and included an eighty-page false start. Nevertheless, I liked the naturalness of the structure. My third novel, in progress, was to have been well outlined in advance when it was conceived several years ago. Now, however, I am letting much of it run where it will."

AVOCATIONAL INTERESTS: Tennis, sailing, trout fishing.

* * *

MORGAN, Ann Lee 1941-

PERSONAL: Born January 12, 1941, in Minneapolis, Minn.; daughter of Joe Warner (a journalist) and Jeanne (a teacher; maiden name, Murray) Morgan; divorced from first husband, 1968; married Charles William Gear (a professor of computer science), November 19, 1976; stepchildren: (second marriage) Jodi (daughter), Christopher. Education: Knox College, B.A. (magna cum laude), 1962; Florida State University, M.A., 1963; University of Iowa, Ph.D., 1973.

ADDRESSES: Home—899 South Plymouth Court, Apt. 1709, Chicago, Ill. 60605; and 3302 Lakeshore Dr., Champaign, Ill. 61821.

CAREER: University of Illinois at Urbana-Champaign, Urbana, instructor, 1968-73, assistant professor of art history, 1973-78; New Art Examiner, Chicago, Ill., assistant editor, 1979-81, books editor, 1980-82, Chicago/Midwest editor, 1981-82; St. James Press, Chicago, editor of art reference books, 1982-85; University of Illinois at Chicago Circle, Chicago, visiting assistant professor of art history, 1985-86; free-lance writer and editor, 1986—. Guest lecturer at University of Grenoble and University of Lyon, 1978; lecturer at University of Illinois at Chicago Circle, 1981, Columbia College, Chicago, 1981-82, and School of the Art Institute of Chicago, 1985-86.

MEMBER: College Art Association of America, American Studies Association, Society of Architectural Historians, Phi Beta Kappa.

AWARDS, HONORS: Travel grant for France from U.S. Information Service, 1978.

WRITINGS:

(Editor) Contemporary Designers, Gale, 1984.
Arthur Dove: Life and Work, With a Catalogue Raisonne, University of Delaware Press, 1984.
(Editor) International Contemporary Arts Directory, St. James Press, 1985.
Dear Stieglitz, Dear Dove, University of Delaware Press, 1987.

Chicago correspondent for Art International, 1981-82. Contributor to World Book Encyclopedia and Encyclopaedia Britannica. Contributor of articles and reviews to art journals. Contributing editor of New Art Examiner, 1982—.

WORK IN PROGRESS: Research on the history of art in Chicago.

* * *

MORGAN, Harriet
See MENCKEN, H(enry) L(ouis)

* * *

MORRIS, John
See HEARNE, John (Edgar Caulwell)

* * *

MOSLEY, J(ohn) Brooke (Jr.) 1915-1988

OBITUARY NOTICE: Born October 18, 1915, in Philadelphia, Pa.; died of a heart attack, March 4, 1988, in New York, N.Y. Clergyman, administrator, and author. A liberal Episcopal priest who was ordained in 1941, Mosley served as a pastor in a slum neighborhood in Cincinnati and as dean of St. John's Cathedral in Wilmington, Delaware, before he became bishop of Delaware, a post he held from 1955 to 1968. During those years he was both an outspoken advocate of civil rights and an opponent of the war in Vietnam. Mosley gained national attention in 1970 when he was named head of the prominent Union Theological Seminary. At that time the school was torn by disputes between traditionalists who sought to preserve its academic excellence and younger seminarians who advocated its greater involvement in social issues. Four years after taking office Mosley was forced to resign amid further controversy about minority admissions and budget deficits. He went to the diocese of Pennsylvania, where he was assistant bishop until he retired in 1982. Mosley wrote Christians in the Technical and Social Revolutions of Our Time: Suggestions for Study and Action.

OBITUARIES AND OTHER SOURCES:

BOOKS

Current Biography, H. W. Wilson, 1970, April, 1988.

PERIODICALS

New York Times, March 6, 1988.
Washington Post, March 10, 1988.

MURFIN, Ross C. 1948-

PERSONAL: Born November 14, 1948, in Richmond, Ind., son of Mark (a professor) and Elizabeth (a teacher; maiden name, Crawford) Murfin; married Pamela Martin (a teacher), January 23, 1971; children: Audrey Dean, Justin Riley. *Education:* Princeton University, A.B. (with honors), 1971; University of Virginia, M.A., 1972, Ph.D. (with distinction), 1974.

ADDRESSES: Home—4550 Alhambra Circle, Coral Gables, Fla. 33146. *Office*—Department of English, University of Miami, University Station, Coral Gables, Fla. 33124.

CAREER: Yale University, New Haven, Conn., assistant professor, 1974-80, associate professor, 1980-81; University of Miami, Coral Gables, Fla., professor of English and associate dean of College of Arts and Sciences, 1981—, master of Honors Residential College, 1984-87.

MEMBER: Modern Language Association of America, South Atlantic Modern Language Association, Victorians Institute.

WRITINGS:

Swinburne, Hardy, Lawrence, and the Burden of Belief, University of Chicago Press, 1978.
The Poetry of D. H. Lawrence: Texts and Contexts, University of Nebraska Press, 1983.
(Editor) *Conrad Revisited: Essays for the Eighties,* University of Alabama Press, 1985.
Sons and Lovers: A Novel of Division and Desire, G. K. Hall, 1987.
(Editor) *Heart of Darkness: A Theoretical Edition,* Bedford Books, 1988.

WORK IN PROGRESS: A study of Joseph Conrad's *Lord Jim,* publication by G. K. Hall expected in 1990; researching a book on politics and the English novel, 1832-1885.

SIDELIGHTS: Ross C. Murfin told *CA:* "My interest in the relationship between political representation and the representation of reality in fiction led me, during my sabbatical year from 1987 to 1988, to London, where I conducted research into nineteenth-century novels and parliamentary reform at the British Library. An earlier sabbatical from Yale University, from 1978 to 1979, was spent in Florence, Italy, where I wrote my book on D. H. Lawrence's poetry."

*   *   *

MURPHY, N(orman) T. P. 1933-

PERSONAL: Born May 20, 1933, in Croydon, Surrey, England; son of Thomas (a doctor) and Norma (a teacher; maiden name, Blewitt) Murphy; married Charlotte Archibald (a copy editor), January 7, 1961; children: Timothy John Alexander, Helen Virginia Clare. *Education:* Oxford University, M.A., 1956.

ADDRESSES: Home—Gosforth, Cumbria CA20 1AJ, England.

CAREER: British Army, 1952-84, commissioned in Green Howards, National Service, 1952-53, Territorial Army, 1953-59, attended Army Staff College, Camberley, England, 1966, held logistic staff appointments in the Middle East and Germany and with the Ministry of Defence, retired as lieutenant colonel, 1984. Schoolteacher in Oxford, England, 1956-57; salesman for International Business Machines Co., Middlesbrough, England, 1957-59.

WRITINGS:

In Search of Blandings, privately printed, 1981, reprinted, Secker & Warburg, 1986.

Contributor to periodicals, including *Punch, Blackwood's,* and *Country Life.*

WORK IN PROGRESS: A history of London streets, publication by Century Hutchinson expected in 1989; a review "of certain Victorians, whose energy and enthusiasm led them to lives that seem unbelievably eccentric today."

SIDELIGHTS: N. T. P. Murphy told *CA:* "I have spent most of my life trying to combine curiosity with the discipline of earning a living. I attribute any success I have had to a sense of enthusiasm coupled with a fly-paper memory. I am grateful to the Jesuits for teaching me that there are two sides to every question, to Oxford for teaching me to examine the factors on either side, and to the Army for teaching me to decide what action is necessary.

"A P. G. Wodehouse enthusiast all my life, I noticed certain coincidences between the author's own life and the settings of the Wodehouse novels. Since I was then working at the Ministry of Defence at Whitehall, I used the libraries and other reference sources of London to find a basis for the fictional aunts that bedevil so many of the young men in the Wodehouse novels. As coincidence after coincidence came to light, I realized that beneath the superb language of P. G. Wodehouse lay a basis of fact. My book caused a stir in the literary world because, although several collections and listings had been made of Wodehouse's fictional characters, no one had ever dreamed that they could be based on reality.

"I still admire P. G. Wodehouse as one of the best writers in the English language. I am proud that my amateur researches have done nothing to diminish the skill, hard work, and humor that have made his novels beloved throughout the English-speaking world.

"I believe firmly that the important thing in writing is for the author to say what he wants but to do so in a way that his readers will accept. 'It isn't what you say, it's the way you say it' is a rule I learned while working in Whitehall and with my colleagues at NATO."

BIOGRAPHICAL/CRITICAL SOURCES:

PERIODICALS

Punch, April 16, 1986.

*   *   *

MURRAY, Henry A(lexander) 1893-1988

OBITUARY NOTICE: Born May 13, 1893, in New York, N.Y.; died of pneumonia, June 23, 1988, in Cambridge, Mass. Psychiatrist, educator, editor, and author. A teacher of psychology at Harvard University from 1926 until he retired in 1962, Murray was considered a pioneer in the study of human personality. He was one of the first American practitioners of psychoanalysis, undergoing the procedure himself with the renowned Carl Jung and helping to found the Boston Psychoanalytic Society. In 1926 Murray helped establish the Harvard Psychological Clinic, which combined research and psychotherapy, and he directed the clinic from 1928 to 1937. A developer of the Thematic Aperception Test, used to diagnose personality traits, Murray was called on by the U.S. Office of Strategic Services during World War II to employ psychology as an aid in determining the fitness of secret agents. His writings include *Explorations in Personality: A Clinical and Experimental Study of Fifty Men of College Age; A Clinical Study of Sentiments; Assessment of Men;* and *Endeavors in Psychology: Selections From the Personology of Henry A. Murray.* Murray edited the Herman Melville novel *Pierre; or, The Ambiguities,* and when he died was at work on a book tentatively titled *A Melville Mosaic: Morsels From the Unpublished Biography.*

OBITUARIES AND OTHER SOURCES:

BOOKS

Maddi, Salvatore R., *Humanism in Personology: Allport, Maslow, and Murray,* Aldine, 1972.
Thinkers of the Twentieth Century, 2nd edition, St. James Press, 1987.

PERIODICALS

New York Times, June 24, 1988.

*   *   *

MURRAY, (Anna) Pauli(ne) 1910-1985

PERSONAL: Born November 20, 1910, in Baltimore, Md. (one source says Durham, N.C.); died of cancer, July 1, 1985, in Pittsburgh, Pa.; daughter of William Henry (a school principal) and Agnes Georgianna (a nurse; maiden name, Fitzgerald) Murray; divorced. *Education:* Hunter College (now of the City University of New York), A.B., 1933; Howard University, LL.B. (cum laude), 1944; University of California (now University of California, Berkeley), LL.M., 1945; Yale University, J.S.D., 1965; General Theological Seminary, M.Div. (cum laude), 1976.

ADDRESSES: Home—Pittsburgh, Pa.

CAREER: Worked at a number of odd jobs, including four years in U.S. Government work relief program Work Projects Administration. Admitted to the Bar of California State, 1945, the Bar of New York State, 1948, and the Bar of the U.S. Supreme Court, 1960; deputy attorney general of California, 1946; American Jewish Congress, New York, N.Y., attorney for commission on law and social action, 1946-47; worked for a time at private practice of law in New York City; Paul, Weiss, Rifkind, Wharton & Garrison (law firm), New York City, associate attorney in litigation department, 1956-60. University of Ghana, near Accra, senior lecturer, 1960-61; Benedict College, Columbia, S.C., vice-president, 1967-68, also served as professor of political science; Brandeis University, Waltham, Mass., professor of American studies, 1968-73, Louis Stulberg Professor of Law and Politics, 1972-73; Boston University, Boston, Mass., lecturer at school of law, 1972. Ordained Episcopal priest, 1977, served churches in Washington, D.C., Baltimore, Md., and Pittsburgh, Pa., retired in 1984.

Co-founder and member of National Organization for Women, 1970-84; director of Beacon Press, 1968-69. Consultant to fourth assembly of World Council of Churches in Uppsala, Sweden, 1968; member of Commission on Ordained and Licensed Ministries, 1969-70. Affiliated with a number of government agencies and civil rights groups, including Presidential Commission on the Status of Women, 1962-63; American Civil Liberties Union, 1965-73; Equal Employment Opportunity Commission, 1966-67; and Martin Luther King, Jr., Center for Non-Violent Social Change, 1970-84.

MEMBER: National Bar Association, American Bar Association (vice-chairperson of committee on women's rights, 1971-73), National Association for the Advancement of Colored People (NAACP; life member), National Association of Women Lawyers, National Council of Negro Women, New York County Bar Association, Hunter College Alumni Association.

AWARDS, HONORS: Recipient of honorary degrees, including LL.D. from Dartmouth College, 1976, D.H.L. from Radcliffe College, 1978, and D.D. from Yale University, 1979; named Woman of the Year by National Council of Negro Women, 1946, and by *Mademoiselle* magazine, 1947; alumni award for distinguished postgraduate achievement in law and public service from Howard University, 1970; Eleanor Roosevelt award from Professional Women's Caucus, 1971; recipient of first Whitney M. Young, Jr., Memorial Award, 1972; named to Hunter College Hall of Fame, 1973; award for "Exemplary Christian Ministry" from National Institute for Women of Color, 1982; Robert F. Kennedy Book Award and Christopher Award, both 1988, for *Song in a Weary Throat: An American Pilgrimage;* among others.

WRITINGS:

(Editor) *States' Laws on Race and Color,* Woman's Division of Christian Service, Board of Missions and Church Extension, Methodist Church, 1951, supplement (with Verge Lake), 1955.
Proud Shoes: The Story of an American Family (biography), Harper, 1956, new edition, 1978.
(With Leslie Rubin) *The Constitution and Government of Ghana,* Sweet & Maxwell, 1961, 2nd edition, 1964.
Human Rights U.S.A., 1948-1966, Service Center, Board of Missions, Methodist Church, 1967.
Dark Testament, and Other Poems (collection), Silvermine, 1970.
(Contributor) Mary Lou Thompson, editor, *Voices of the New Feminism,* Beacon Press, 1970.
Song in a Weary Throat: An American Pilgrimage (autobiography), Harper, 1987.

Also author of speeches and addresses, including *The Negro Woman in the Quest for Equality,* 1964.

Contributor to journals and other publications, including *Crisis* magazine.

Poetry represented in anthologies, including *The Poetry of Black America,* edited by Arnold Adoff, Macmillan, 1968; *The Poetry of the Negro, 1746-1970,* edited by Langston Hughes and Arna Bontemps, Doubleday, 1970; and *A Rock Against the Wind: Black Love Poems,* edited by Lindsay Patterson, Dodd, 1973.

SIDELIGHTS: For her pioneering efforts in a number of different areas, Pauli Murray is remembered as a woman ahead of her time. As an activist for the civil rights and feminist movements, beginning in the late 1930s, she became a forerunner in the subsequent struggle for racial and sexual equality in the United States. During a period when blacks and women were still restricted from certain educational and professional opportunities, she achieved consecutive goals as an attorney and educator, and in 1977 Murray became the first black woman to be ordained an Episcopal priest. An aspiring writer, she also published a number of books on law as well as a collection of poetry, *Dark Testament, and Other Poems,* and two critically acclaimed personal histories, *Proud Shoes* and *Song in a Weary Throat.* Described as a versatile and determined woman, Murray allegedly maintained that her successive careers followed a logical progression toward eliminating racial and sexist discrimination. Along the way, Murray earned a dual reputation as a "freedom fighter" and a "firebrand." Each of her prodigious achievements "represented a calculated attack on some boundary—of sex, of race—that society had placed in her way," remarked Pat Williams in the *New York Times Book Review*. Similarly, *Detroit News* writer Frances A. Koestler commented that Murray's diverse accomplishments "were dictated by a burning sense that social inequities had to be challenged and overcome."

To some extent Murray's childhood both shaped her character and influenced her ambitions as an adult. Orphaned at the age of three, when her mother died and her father subsequently entered a mental hospital, she grew up in the care of her mother's relatives in Durham, North Carolina. Though sources disagree on whether it was Murray's maternal grandparents or aunts who actually reared her, there is a general consensus of opinion attributing Murray's independent nature and strong sense of pride to that of her appointed guardians. From them she learned of her heterogeneous ancestry that included not only blacks and whites, slaves and slave owners, but Cherokee Indians as well. Like most black Americans of her day who descended from a blend of cultures and races, Murray experienced alienation—feelings of not belonging to any specific group of people. Her mulatto background both prevented her from identifying solely with her African heritage and excluded her from white society. Though proud of her individuality, Murray—who preferred the term "Negro" to the word "black"—sought to discover the origins of her being and thus establish her roots.

In an attempt to recreate her past, Murray wrote *Proud Shoes: The Story of an American Family*. Due to a general lack of interest in its subject matter, however, the book "sank with scarcely a trace" after its initial publication in 1956, reflected *Los Angeles Times* reviewer Robert Kirsch. But with the appearance of an expanded edition in 1978, Murray's biography captured public attention and critical acclaim, eliciting comparisons to Alex Haley's best-selling novel *Roots*. Despite some similarities between the two works, Kirsch observed that Murray's "marvelous and moving family memoir . . . is a very different story." Describing what he thought distinguished Murray's story from Haley's, Jack Hicks wrote in *Nation* that "*Proud Shoes* traps the beast of American slavery" while *Roots* "dwells on African continuations in the black American family." Essentially, Murray's book focuses on the multiple conflicts affecting the progeny of interracial unions, those "unwilling agents of love and animosity" who were trapped between black and white, Hicks commented. According to Nellie McKay in the *Dictionary of Literary Biography*, Murray's *Proud Shoes* represents more than an individual's search for identity; it "embodies the most important elements in the evolution of the contemporary black family" and serves as a microcosm of the total black experience in white America. As such, *Proud Shoes* also qualifies as a slice of U.S. history.

During the course of her personal search for identity, Murray was confronted by questions of equality on the basis of sex and skin color. In particular, she "was awakened to the universal dimensions of the struggle for human dignity by sustained contact with the labor movement," reported Sherley Anne Williams in the *Los Angeles Times Book Review*. With characteristic defiance she challenged various institutions of government, business, education, and finally religion, opposing practices of discrimination and segregation that historically excluded blacks and women. In 1938, for example, Murray

"waged a highly publicized battle for admission to" the University of North Carolina at Chapel Hill, related Susan McHenry in *Ms*. Though school officials rejected her application, her efforts forged the path leading to a federal court ruling that ordered the school's integration in 1951. Similarly, Murray was jailed for refusing to sit in the back of a Virginia bus in 1940. She also organized and/or participated in a number of rallies and demonstrations, among them a series of sit-ins aimed at desegregating restaurants and other public places in Washington, D.C. Murray's activism recurrently led to confrontations with the law. In view of this fact, she chose to become an attorney, convinced "that the law was the fastest route to racial equality," wrote Koestler.

Murray's ongoing crusade against racial and sexual barriers eventually took issue with the U.S. Supreme Court and later with the Episcopal church. Though she proved unsuccessful in her appeal to fill the traditionally male-occupied position of Supreme Court Justice, Murray's initiative again prepared the way for others of her sex. Amid controversy she resolved in 1974 to enter the priesthood, a station the Episcopal church hitherto reserved only for men. In an article for the *New York Times*, Eleanor Blau quoted Murray on her objective: "'I want to be a positive force for reconciliation both in terms of race and . . . sex.'" Three years later Murray became the first woman ordained an Episcopal priest.

Dark Testament, and Other Poems, Murray's 1970 collection, serves as a reflection of her personal and professional encounters. In the words of McKay, the volume is "a poetic mirror of Murray's life and career, and a testament to" the broad expanse of her personal interests. Utilizing her imagination and an array of intense emotion, Murray features a melange of topics that range from philosophic musings and the concerns of racial oppression to themes of love and friendship. Especially noteworthy is the title poem, in which Murray uses symbolism to address specific characteristics of the human mind and will.

Like her volume of poetry, Murray's posthumously published autobiography, *Song in a Weary Throat: An American Pilgrimage*, documents her multifaceted career and exists as a testament to her lifelong quest for personal identity. Even more, it "distinctively recounts the kind of sustained commitment and often unheralded effort that fed into the great civil rights victories," asserted McHenry. Generally, critics viewed Murray's highly acclaimed book as a unique, eloquent, and inspiring piece of work. Reviewing in *Washington Post Book World*, Jonathan Yardley added that *Song in a Weary Throat* is "a splendid book . . . smoothly written, good-humored, passionate, thoughtful. . . . One comes to its powerfully moving final pages utterly convinced that Murray was one of the great Americans of her time."

BIOGRAPHICAL/CRITICAL SOURCES:

BOOKS

Diamonstein, Barbaralee, *Open Secrets: Ninety-four Women in Touch With Our Time*, Viking, 1972.
Dictionary of Literary Biography, Volume 41, *Afro-American Poets Since 1955*, Gale, 1985.

PERIODICALS

Detroit News, April 26, 1987.
Los Angeles Times Book Review, October 6, 1978, May 24, 1987.
Ms., May, 1987.

Nation, December 16, 1978, May 23, 1987.
New York Times, February 11, 1974.
New York Times Book Review, March 29, 1987.
Washington Post Book World, April 5, 1987.

OBITUARIES:

PERIODICALS

New York Times, July 4, 1985.
Washington Post, July 4, 1985.*

                                        —*Sketch by Barbara A. Cicchetti*

*   *   *

MYLONAS, George Emmanuel   1898-1988

OBITUARY NOTICE: Born December 9, 1898, in Smyrna, Ottoman Empire (now Izmir, Turkey); immigrated to United States, 1928, naturalized citizen, 1937; died of a heart attack, April 15, 1988, in Athens, Greece; buried at Mycenae, Greece. Archaeologist, educator, administrator, and author. A specialist in the ancient history of Greece, Mylonas led archaeological excavations in that country at Mycenae, Eleusis, and Aghios Kosmas. In 1933 he joined the faculty of Washington University in St. Louis, where he was professor of art and archaeology from 1936 to 1969. Mylonas, who served as de-

partment head for many years, retired from the university as Rosa May Distinguished University Emeritus Professor of the Humanities. He taught intermittently at the American School for Classical Studies in Athens, the University of Athens, and the University of Illinois and was an honorary lecturer at several universities. From 1980 until his death Mylonas was secretary-general of the Archaeological Society of Athens, supervising government grants for further excavations. His numerous writings include *Ancient Mycenae: The Capital City of Agamemnon, Mycenae and the Mycenaen Age, Eleusis and the Eleusinian Mysteries, The Hymn to Demeter and Her Sanctuary at Eleusis,* and *Aghios Kosmas: An Early Bronze Age Settlement and Cemetery in Attica.*

OBITUARIES AND OTHER SOURCES:

BOOKS

Directory of American Scholars, Volume I: *History,* 6th edition, Bowker, 1974.
Who's Who in America, 42nd edition, Marquis, 1982.

PERIODICALS

Chicago Tribune, May 4, 1988.
New York Times, May 3, 1988.
Times (London), April 18, 1988.

N

NAGATSUKA, Ryuji   1924-

BRIEF ENTRY: Born April 20, 1924, in Nagoya, Japan. Japanese educator, journalist, translator, and author. Nagatsuka, who during his career has written for a daily newspaper and taught at Toyko's Nihon University, is the author of *I Was a Kamikaze* (Macmillan, 1973), an account of his experience as a World War II Japanese Army airman assigned to make suicide attacks on American ships. The book, which chronicles airmen's reactions to suicide missions as well as the brutality of Japan's military training, was described by a *Times Literary Supplement* reviewer as "eloquent." Nagatsuka, a longtime devotee of French culture, has also authored and translated books about prominent French political and literary figures. *Addresses: Home*—282-4, Oizumigakuen-Cho, Nerima-ku, Tokyo, Japan.

BIOGRAPHICAL/CRITICAL SOURCES:

PERIODICALS

Best Sellers, April 15, 1974.
Observer, August 12, 1973.
Times Literary Supplement, August 3, 1973.

*　　*　　*

NEGLEY, Glenn (Robert)   1907-1988

OBITUARY NOTICE—See index for *CA* sketch: Born November 5, 1907, in Indianapolis, Ind.; died May 15, 1981. Educator and author. Negley was professor of philosophy at Duke University from 1946 to 1975. He wrote *The Organization of Knowledge* and *Political Authority and Moral Judgment,* and he collaborated on *Democracy vs. Dictatorship* and *The Quest for Utopia.* He also contributed to various volumes and professional journals.

OBITUARIES AND OTHER SOURCES:

Date of death provided by David H. Sanford.

*　　*　　*

NELSON, Randy F(ranklin)   1948-

PERSONAL: Born May 20, 1948, in Charlotte, N.C.; son of W. H. and Nadine (Nance) Nelson; married Susan Diane Linker, December 28, 1968; children: three. *Education:* North Caro-lina State University, B.A., 1970, M.A., 1972; Princeton University, M.A., 1975, Ph.D., 1976.

ADDRESSES: Office—Department of English, Davidson College, Davidson, N.C. 28036.

CAREER: University of Louisville, Louisville, Ky., assistant professor of English, 1976-77; Davidson College, Davidson, N.C., assistant professor, 1977-84, associate professor of English, 1984—.

MEMBER: Modern Language Association of America, Thoreau Society, Mark Twain Society, Poe Society, Southern Writers Conference.

WRITINGS:

Almanac of American Letters, William Kaufman, 1981.
The Martial Arts: An Annotated Bibliography, Garland Publishing, 1988.

Editor of textual research for series "Writings of Henry David Thoreau," Princeton University Press, 1976—.

BIOGRAPHICAL/CRITICAL SOURCES:

PERIODICALS

Los Angeles Times Book Review, October 18, 1981.

*　　*　　*

NEVELSON, Louise   1900(?)-1988

OBITUARY NOTICE—See index for *CA* sketch: Born September 23, 1900 (some sources say 1899), in Kiev, Russia (now U.S.S.R.); immigrated to United States, 1905; died April 17, 1988, in New York, N.Y. Artist and author. Nevelson, a renowned sculptor, was best known for her large outdoor works comprised of various objects and materials. She also devised massive steel structures and wall sculptings, most of which were executed in black and shared similarities with architectural concepts. Her works are featured in many major museums and have been represented in such exhibition catalogs as *Nevelson: Wood Sculptures* and *Louise Nevelson: The Fourth Dimension.* She collaborated on the autobiographical *Dawns and Dusks: Taped Conversations With Diana MacKown.*

OBITUARIES AND OTHER SOURCES:

BOOKS

Current Biography, H. W. Wilson, 1967, May, 1988.
Who's Who in American Art, 17th edition, Bowker, 1986.

PERIODICALS

Chicago Tribune, April 19, 1988.
Los Angeles Times, April 19, 1988.
New York Times, April 19, 1988.
Times (London), April 19, 1988.
Washington Post, April 19, 1988.

*   *   *

NEWBORN, Jud   1952-

PERSONAL: Born November 8, 1952, in New York, N.Y.;
son of Solomon (a public official) and Rita (an actress and
singer; maiden name, Cohen) Newborn. *Education:* New York
University, B.A. (magna cum laude), 1974; graduate study at
Clare Hall, Cambridge, 1974-75; University of Chicago, M.A.,
1977, further graduate study, 1977—. *Politics:* "Left-lib-
eral." *Religion:* Jewish.

ADDRESSES: Home—Plainview, N.Y. *Office*—Museum of
Jewish Heritage, Suite 717, 342 Madison Ave., New York,
N.Y. 10017. *Agent*—Elaine Markson, Elaine Markson Liter-
ary Agency, Inc., 44 Greenwich Ave., New York, N.Y. 10011.

CAREER: Nassau County Museum of Natural History, Gar-
vies Point Museum, Glen Cove, N.Y., museum technician and
assistant crew chief, 1971-72; archaeological researcher in Po-
lolu Valley, Hawaii, 1973; Oxford University Press, New York,
N.Y., trade copywriter and publicist, 1975-76; anthropological researcher on Nazi Germany in Munich, West Germany,
1978-79 and 1980-83; free-lance writer, 1983-86; New York
Holocaust Memorial Commission, Museum of Jewish Heritage, New York, N.Y., senior researcher, writer, and design
team member, 1986—. Fellow at Clare Hall, Cambridge, 1978;
lecturer, free-lance writer, translator, and consultant.

MEMBER: American Anthropological Association, Authors
Guild, Phi Beta Kappa.

AWARDS, HONORS: Fellowship from Memorial Foundation
for Jewish Culture, 1978-79; Fulbright fellowship, 1980-82;
grant from Wenner-Gren Foundation for Anthropological Research, 1984; Newcombe fellowship from Woodrow Wilson
National Fellowship Foundation, 1984-85.

WRITINGS:

(With Annette E. Dumbach) *Shattering the German Night: The
Story of the White Rose,* Little, Brown, 1986.

Contributor of articles and book reviews to *Journal of Asian
Studies, Journal of Modern History, Newsday, New York Times,*
and *Philadelphia Inquirer,* and of poetry and fiction to *Little
Magazine* and *Nation.*

*WORK IN PROGRESS: Work Makes Free: The German Cul-
tural Bases of Nazi Genocide and the Death Camps;* a book
on Jewish resistance in Nazi-occupied Europe.

SIDELIGHTS: In *Shattering the German Night: The Story of
the White Rose,* Jud Newborn and Annette E. Dumbach describe the lives and activities of a group of young German
students who called themselves the White Rose and dared to
defy Adolf Hitler during World War II. Deemed "a stirring

story, well-told," by *Chicago Tribune* reviewer Patrick Reardon, the book "pieces together the fragmentary evidence of
the group's secret life and places it within the context of the
social, political and intellectual currents of German history."
Observed Reardon, "The result is a powerful, yet restrained,
narrative."

The White Rose consisted largely of idealistic upper middle-
class students at the University of Munich, many of them former members of the Hitler Youth. Troubled by the nihilism
they came to recognize in Nazism, they began to write and
distribute leaflets condemning Nazi atrocities and advocating
resistance to the Nazi war effort. To keep the distribution secret they addressed the leaflets to names randomly chosen from
phone books and dropped them in mailboxes in other cities.
Between 1942 and 1943 the group produced only a handful of
issues, but they had "a unique importance," wrote Richard
Eder in the *Los Angeles Times.* "To some Germans inside the
country and to many abroad, the White Rose meant that there
was a remnant of their youth that had not been corrupted and
destroyed, that there was a moral future for Germany." Lauded
Hans Knight, writing in the *Philadelphia Inquirer,* "By whatever definition one chooses to celebrate courage, it has seldom
resided in greater measure and purer form than in the White
Rose."

Disclosing at its beginning that the youths ultimately were
caught and that many were executed, *Shattering the German
Night* "commands our attention," asserted Andrew Nagorski
in *Newsweek.* "It also raises broader issues about man and his
relationship to this century's totalitarian regimes." While some
critics faulted the work for occasional overwriting, fragmen-
tation, and a wavering between novelistic and expository style,
most agreed that it is compelling and well researched. "Not
a word is wasted in this tightly woven tale," remarked Katherine Ullmer in the *Dayton Daily News.* "It all rings true."

Newborn told *CA:* "My aim is to communicate—in particular
I am deeply involved in seeking answers to the seeming in-
comprehensibility of the Holocaust, in scholarly, popular, and
museum form. I've spent a great deal of my time and energy
working both as a cultural anthropologist and as a writer, trying
to help explain Nazi genocide and the form of the death camps.
Along the way I've done a good deal of free-lance writing and
public speaking on the subject of German opposition to Hitler
(especially that of the youthful White Rose) and the Kurt
Waldheim affair, and have tried to help correct some frustrating misconceptions about Jewish responses to Nazi oppression, particularly by bringing out the remarkable scope and
significance of Jewish resistance. I also consult for the national
media, for filmmakers, and for museums on Nazi Germany as
a whole as well as on the particulars of the Holocaust. And
yet, large as this subject is, my writing interests go beyond it
to issues of politics, nature and the environment, anthropology, and film."

BIOGRAPHICAL/CRITICAL SOURCES:

PERIODICALS

Chicago Tribune, August 28, 1986.
Dayton Daily News, July 27, 1986.
Hyde Park Herald, August 20, 1986.
Los Angeles Reader, March 20, 1987.
Los Angeles Times, July 9, 1986.
Mother Jones, July-August, 1986.
Newsweek, September 29, 1986.
New York Times, May 15, 1986, October 12, 1986.

New York Times Book Review, August 17, 1986.
Philadelphia Inquirer, August 24, 1986.
Washington Jewish Week, October 30, 1986.

*   *   *

NIENHAUSER, William H., Jr. 1943-

PERSONAL: Born December 10, 1943, in St. Louis, Mo.; son of William H. (in sales) and Nancy (a housewife; maiden name, Brown) Nienhauser; married Judith Brockway (a teacher), 1961; children: Daniel, Susan. *Education:* Indiana University—Bloomington, A.B. (summa cum laude), 1966, A.M., 1968, Ph.D., 1972.

ADDRESSES: Office—Department of East Asian Languages, 1208 Van Hise Hall, University of Wisconsin—Madison, Madison, Wis. 53706.

CAREER: Indiana University—Bloomington, visiting assistant professor of German, 1972-73; University of Wisconsin—Madison, assistant professor, 1973-79, associate professor, 1979-82, professor of Chinese language and literature, 1983—. Professor at National Taiwan University, 1983 and 1985-87. *Military service:* U.S. Army, 1962-65.

MEMBER: Chinese Language Teachers Association, American Oriental Society, Association for Asian Studies, Modern Language Association of America, American Comparative Literature Association, Phi Beta Kappa.

AWARDS, HONORS: Best Book Award from *Choice,* 1986, for *The Indiana Companion to Traditional Chinese Literature.*

WRITINGS:

(With William Crawford) *Liu Tsung-yuan,* Twayne, 1973.
(Editor) *Critical Essays on Chinese Literature,* Chinese University of Hong Kong, 1976.
P'i Jih-hsui, Twayne, 1979.
(Editor) *The Indiana Companion to Traditional Chinese Literature,* Indiana University Press, 1986.

Contributor to Asian studies journals. Editor of *Chinese Literature: Essays, Articles, Reviews,* 1979—.

WORK IN PROGRESS: A survey of early Chinese narrative, publication by E. J. Brill expected in 1989.

BIOGRAPHICAL/CRITICAL SOURCES:

PERIODICALS

Los Angeles Times Book Review, April 27, 1986.
Times Literary Supplement, May 9, 1986.

*   *   *

NILES, John D(eWitt) 1945-

PERSONAL: Born August 4, 1945, in St. Louis, Mo.; son of Walter W. (a banker) and Helen (an artist; maiden name, Beccard) Niles; married Joyce Chagi, 1971 (divorced, 1981); married Carole E. Newlands (a professor), August 14, 1982; children: Daniel, Margaret, Alan, Emily. *Education:* University of California, Berkeley, B.A., 1967, M.A., 1969, Ph.D., 1972.

ADDRESSES: Office—Department of English, University of California, Berkeley, Calif. 94720.

CAREER: Brandeis University, Waltham, Mass., assistant professor of English, 1972-76; University of California,

Berkeley, assistant professor, 1976-86, associate professor of English, 1986—.

MEMBER: Modern Language Association of America, Mediaeval Academy of America, American Folklore Society.

WRITINGS:

(Translator and author of introduction) *Seven Songs of Guilhem IX: First of the Known Troubadours,* University of Arizona Press, 1978.
(Editor, translator, and author of introduction and notes) *Guilhem IX: The Songs,* Ross-Erikson, 1978.
(Editor) *Old English Literature in Context,* D. S. Brewer, 1981.
Beowulf, Harvard University Press, 1983.
(Co-editor) *Anglo-Scandinavian England,* University Press of America, 1988.

Contributor to literature, language, and folklore journals.

WORK IN PROGRESS: Editing a collection of songs and stories gathered in Scotland; a book on the classic English-language ballads.

SIDELIGHTS: John D. Niles told *CA:* "I am interested in oral, traditional literature in all its forms and in the interplay between oral and literate traditions, whether in the ancient world, in medieval Europe, or in current society. My book on *Beowulf* is my chief attempt to date to lay bare how a major literary work emerged from oral antecedents. I am in the midst of a fieldwork project focusing on the singing and storytelling traditions of the traveling people of Scotland, and I plan to make use of this research in a book on English-language ballading, as well as in future studies of medieval literature."

*   *   *

NOVAK, Matt 1962-

PERSONAL: Born October 23, 1962, in Trenton, N.J.; son of Theresa (a factory worker; maiden name, Belfiore) Novak. *Education:* Attended Kutztown State University, 1980-81; School of Visual Arts, New York, N.Y., B.F.A., 1985.

ADDRESSES: Home and office—P.O. Box 686, Hoboken, N.J. 07030.

CAREER: Pegasus Players, Sheppton, Pa., puppeteer, 1979-83; Walt Disney World, Orlando, Fla., animator, 1983; St. Benedict's Preparatory School, Newark, N.J., art teacher, 1986—. Instructor at Parsons School of Design, 1986—.

MEMBER: Society of Children's Book Writers.

WRITINGS:

Rolling (juvenile), self-illustrated, Bradbury Press, 1986.
Claude and Sun (juvenile), self-illustrated, Bradbury Press, 1987.

SIDELIGHTS: Matt Novak told *CA:* "My work deals primarily with nature. I want to impart my amazement at nature's beauty to children so that they may gain a sense of the importance of all of it. I grew up in a small town, surrounded by fields and woodland, so these things are important to me. A lot of children don't have the opportunity to experience living in such an environment. I write and illustrate books I would want to buy myself. That's how I judge my own work."

NOYES, Crosby S(tuart)   1921-1988

OBITUARY NOTICE: Born March 2, 1921, in Washington, D.C.; died of a heart attack, April 7, 1988, in Washington, D.C. Journalist. Noyes was born into the family that co-owned the now defunct *Washington Star* newspaper, where he spent his journalistic career. He began as a reporter in 1947, specializing in foreign affairs. In 1954 he opened the paper's Paris bureau, remaining there as European correspondent until 1964, except for an interlude from 1956 to 1958 when he was national editor in Washington, D.C. Noyes was foreign editor and columnist in the U.S. capital from 1964 until the mid-1970s, when his family and other owners of the *Star* sold the failing paper to outside interests. Noyes was a member of the French Legion of Honor and a recipient of a 1958 National Headliner Club award for a series of articles on Charles de Gaulle's accession to the presidency of France.

OBITUARIES AND OTHER SOURCES:

BOOKS

Who's Who in America, 40th edition, Marquis, 1978.

PERIODICALS

New York Times, April 10, 1988.
Washington Post, April 8, 1988.

*   *   *

NUGENT, Bruce
See NUGENT, Richard Bruce

*   *   *

NUGENT, Richard Bruce   1906(?)-
(Richard Bruce, Bruce Nugent)

PERSONAL: Born July 2, 1906 (one source says 1905), in Washington, D.C.; son of Richard Henry and Pauline Minerva (Bruce) Nugent; married wife, Grace.

ADDRESSES: Home—Hoboken, N.J.

CAREER: Artist, writer, and actor. Associated with Work Projects Administration, Federal Arts Project, and Federal Theater. Founder of Harlem Cultural Council. Work exhibited in shows at the Harmon Foundation, 1931 and 1936; work exhibited in collections, including the National Archives. Appeared on stage in "Porgy," and in documentary film "Before Stonewall," 1984.

WRITINGS:

(Under pseudonym Richard Bruce) "Sadhji, an African Ballet" (one-act; first produced in Rochester, N.Y., at the Eastman School of Music, 1932), published in *Plays of Negro Life: A Source-Book of Native American Drama,* Harper, 1927.
Lighting Fire!!, Fire!! Press (Metuchen, N.J.), 1982.

Works represented in anthologies, sometimes under the name Richard Bruce or Bruce Nugent, including *The New Negro: An Interpretation,* edited by Alain Locke, A. & C. Boni, 1925, and *Caroling Dusk: An Anthology of Verse by Negro Poets,* edited by Countee Cullen, Harper, 1927. Contributor of illustrations, poetry, and short stories to periodicals, including *Challenge, Crisis, Dance, Ebony, Fire!!, Harlem: A Forum of Negro Life, New Challenge, Opportunity, Palms, Topaz,* and *Trend.* Contributor to the "Negroes of New York," Federal Writers' Project.

SIDELIGHTS: Described as the "ultimate bohemian" by Eric Garber in an article in the *Dictionary of Literary Biography,* Richard Bruce Nugent was the basis for the character of Paul Arbian—a talented but undisciplined artist and author—in Wallace Thurman's 1932 novel *Infants of the Spring.* Although he was not a prolific illustrator and writer, Nugent secured his position as an integral figure in New York literary circles during the 1920s by his association with some of the outstanding authors of the Harlem Renaissance.

First introduced to the black literati of New York at a party in 1925, Nugent emerged as a regular on the Harlem social scene. He was notorious for his liberal sexual escapades and carousing—he took the pseudonym Richard Bruce at this time not to upset his mother—as well as for what Thurman labeled the "bizarre and erotic" subjects of the drawings and writings he was producing. Nugent penned a first-person narrative about a nineteen-year-old unemployed artist who was struggling with his sexuality, "Smoke, Lilies, and Jade," which critics contended was loosely autobiographical. This short piece and two of his brush-and-ink illustrations appeared in *Fire!!,* the literary periodical Thurman edited, and Nugent's first published story, "Sadhji," focusing on an ill-fated love triangle set in historic Africa, was anthologized by Alain Locke and Montgomery Gregory in *Plays of Negro Life: A Source-Book of Native American Drama* after Nugent had rewritten it as a drama.

Although Nugent publishes literary works in anthologies and periodicals, he is primarily an artist. According to Thomas H. Wirth in the *Black American Literature Forum,* through innovative use of color and technique Nugent's creations—whether on the walls of nightclubs or in popular journals—are "highly stylized and instantly recognizable." Eroticism permeates Nugent's drawings, oil paintings, and pastel works, prompting Thurman to describe Arbian/Nugent's illustrations as "nothing but highly colored phalli." Wirth saw more, however, maintaining that the artist's "unexpected juxtapositions of colors, strongly idiosyncratic stylistic elements, and unconventional composition emphasizing the borders rather than the center combine to stunning effect."

BIOGRAPHICAL/CRITICAL SOURCES:

BOOKS

Dictionary of Literary Biography, Volume 51: *Afro-American Writers From the Harlem Renaissance to 1940,* Gale, 1987.
Thurman, Wallace, *Infants of the Spring,* Macauley, 1932.

PERIODICALS

Black American Literature Forum, spring, 1985.*

*   *   *

NYERERE, Julius K(ambarage)   1922-

PERSONAL: Born in March, 1922, in Butiama-Musoma, Tanganyika (now Tanzania); son of Mtemi Nyerere Burito and Mugaya Nyang'ombe; married Maria Magige (a shopkeeper), 1953; children: five sons, two daughters. *Education:* Makerere University, teacher's diploma, 1945; received M.A., Edinburgh University. *Religion:* Roman Catholic.

ADDRESSES: Office—P.O. Box 9120, Dar es Salaam, Tanzania.

CAREER: St. Mary's Roman Catholic School, Tabora, Tanganyika, teacher, 1946-49; St. Francis's Roman Catholic College, Pugu, Tanganyika, teacher, 1953-55; Tanganyika Government, member of legislative council, 1957, leader of Elected Members Organization, 1958-60, member for Easter Province, 1958, member for Dar es Salaam, 1960; Republic of Tanganyika (now Tanzania), Dar es Salaam, chief minister, 1960-61, prime minister, 1961-62, president, 1962-64, minister of external affairs, 1962-63; United Republic of Tanzania, Dar es Salaam, president, 1964-85, minister of external affairs, 1965-72, commander in chief of the armed forces, beginning in 1973, founder and chairman of Chama Cha Mapinduzi (Revolutionary Party), beginning in 1977, chairman of Defense and Security Committee of Tanzania. Chancellor of University of East Africa, 1963-70, and of University of Dar es Salaam, 1970-85. President of Pan-African Freedom Movement of Eastern and Central Africa.

MEMBER: Organization for African Unity (chairman, 1984-85), African Association of Dar es Salaam (president, 1953), Tanganyika African Association (now Tanganyika African National Union; president, 1953-77).

AWARDS, HONORS: Third World Award, 1981; LL.D. from Edinburgh University and Duquesne University.

WRITINGS:

(Translator into Swahili) William Shakespeare, *Julius Caesar*, Oxford University Press, 1963.

(With Joshua Nkomo) *Rhodesia: The Case for Majority Rule*, Indian Council for Africa, 1966.

Freedom and Unity—Uhuru na Umoja: A Selection From Writings and Speeches, 1952-1965, Oxford University Press, 1967.

Freedom and Socialism—Uhuru na Ujamaa: A Selection From Writings and Speeches, 1965-1967, Oxford University Press, 1968.

Ujamaa: Essays on Socialism, Oxford University Press, 1968.

Nyerere on Socialism, Oxford University Press, 1969.

(Translator into Swahili) Shakespeare, *A Merchant of Venice*, Oxford University Press, 1969.

Quotations From President Julius K. Nyerere, Collected From Speeches and Writings, edited and published by Morogoro College of National Education, 1970.

Tanzania Ten Years After Independence: Report, Ministry of Information and Broadcasting, 1971.

Freedom and Development—Uhuru na Maendeleo: A Selection From Writings and Speeches, 1968-1973, Oxford University Press, 1973.

Moyo kabla ya silaha, EAPH, 1973.

Man and Development—Binadamu na Maendeleo, Oxford University Press, 1974.

The Arusha Declaration Ten Years After, Government Printer, 1977.

Wafanyakazi na ujamaa Tanzania, Makao Makuu ya NUTA, 1977.

Crusade for Liberation, Oxford University Press, 1978.

(With Samir Amin and Daniel Perren) *Le Dialogue inegal: Ecueils du nouvel ordre economique international*, Centre Europe-Tiers Monde, 1979.

Also author of booklet "Barriers to Democracy."

SIDELIGHTS: When the African nation of Tanganyika became independent in 1961, after decades of foreign rule, Julius K. Nyerere was its first prime minister. After the 1964 union of Tanganyika and Zanzibar under the name Tanzania, Nyerere governed the new country as well. Rising out of a tribal background to become teacher, political leader, and writer, he is "the father of homespun African socialism" and "one of the Third World's most prominent statesmen," according to *Time* writer Hunter R. Clark. Assessed John Darnton in the *New York Times*, "No other African head of state has set such high standards for his countrymen, for Africa or, for that matter, for all mankind as the intense, scholarly . . . President of Tanzania."

Originally a teacher, Nyerere turned increasingly to politics in the early 1950s, ultimately giving up academia to lead his country to independence and improved socioeconomic conditions. As president he socialized farming and industry—although 85 percent of the farmers returned to subsistence farming as a result of inefficient pricing and distribution—and promoted national pride, a national language, and improved health care and education. Noted Clark, "Although he has failed . . . to create the prosperous, egalitarian society that he once envisioned, his policies will continue to shape the country—and the continent—for decades." Several of his policies were at least partially successful: Tanzania has achieved 83 percent literacy and enjoys "perhaps the lowest level of tribal strife of any country on the continent," observed Clark, and it has demonstrated concern for civil and human rights—helping to overthrow neighboring Uganda's brutal dictator Idi Amin in 1979.

Nyerere's numerous speeches, essays, and other writings detail his policies and viewpoints, emphasizing central themes such as the importance of human beings and of allowing a country to develop in its own way, considering useful ideas from without and within. *Freedom and Socialism—Uhuru na Ujamaa: A Selection From Writings and Speeches, 1965-1967* "sets out guidelines for new policies which are among the most exciting, and encouraging, in Africa," judged a *Times Literary Supplement* reviewer, who considered Nyerere's prescription "entirely realistic and rational." The author highlights racial equality and African unity in *Freedom and Unity—Uhuru na Umoja: A Selection From Writings and Speeches, 1952-1965*.

Throughout his political career, asserted a *Times Literary Supplement* critic, "Tanzania's President has dwelt on the deep underlying principles of statecraft." He has earned a reputation for consistency and integrity, for supporting human rights and democratic institutions such as free elections and independent courts of law. In 1976 U.S. Secretary of State Henry Kissinger "made it clear that he regards Mr. Nyerere as the prime link to black Africa," remarked Darnton. Upon Nyerere's resignation in 1985 a political opponent, quoted in *Time*, characterized the former president as "a real man of the people."

AVOCATIONAL INTERESTS: Reading.

BIOGRAPHICAL/CRITICAL SOURCES:

BOOKS

Hatch, John, *Two African Statesmen: Kaunda of Zambia and Nyerere of Tanzania*, Regnery, 1976.

PERIODICALS

New York Times, September 16, 1976.
Time, November 4, 1985.
Times Literary Supplement, March 30, 1967, August 28, 1969.

O

O'HARA, Charles E.   1912-1984

*OBITUARY NOTICE—*See index for *CA* sketch: Born August 6, 1912, in New York, N.Y.; died December 10, 1984; buried in Calverton National Cemetery. Criminologist, educator, and author. O'Hara worked for the New York Police Department from 1940 to 1962, and he later served as director of the National Criminological Research Institute in New York City. Prior to entering law enforcement, he taught physics at St. Peter's College in New Jersey. Among O'Hara's writings are *An Introduction to Criminalistics*, which he wrote with James W. Osterburg, *Fundamentals of Criminal Investigation*, and *Photography in Law Enforcement*.

OBITUARIES AND OTHER SOURCES:

Date of death provided by son, Gregory Leo O'Hara.

*   *   *

O'NEIL, Paul E.   1909(?)-1988

OBITUARY NOTICE: Born c. 1909; died of complications resulting from surgery for a brain tumor, June 12, 1988, in Port Chester, N.Y. Journalist and author. O'Neil spent most of his career with Time Inc., first as a stringer in Seattle, Washington, in the 1930s, and then as a staff writer for *Time* magazine beginning in 1944. He joined the company's *Sports Illustrated* in 1954, transferred to *Life* in 1957, and also wrote for Time-Life Books, where his work included *Barnstormers and Speed Kings, The Frontiersmen,* and *The Rivermen.*

OBITUARIES AND OTHER SOURCES:

PERIODICALS

New York Times, June 16, 1988.

*   *   *

O'NEILL, Egan
See LININGTON, (Barbara) Elizabeth

*   *   *

ONYEAMA, (Charles) Dillibe   1951-

PERSONAL: Born January 6, 1951, in Enugu, Nigeria; immigrated to England, 1959; son of Charles Dadi (a judge) and Susannah (a homemaker; maiden name, Ogwudu) Onyeama; married Ethel Ekwueme (a teacher), December 18, 1982; children: three. *Education:* Attended schools in Nigeria and England. *Politics:* "Free enterprise."

*ADDRESSES: Home—*8B Byron Onyeama Close, P.O. Box 1172, Enugu, Anambra State, Nigeria. *Office—*Delta Publications (Nigeria) Ltd., 172 Ogui Rd., Enugu, Nigeria. *Agent—*Elspeth Cochrane Agency, 11/13 Orlando Rd., London SW4, England.

CAREER: Drum Publications, London, England, subeditor, 1974-75; *West Africa* magazine, London, journalist, 1979; Delta Publications (Nigeria) Ltd., Nigeria, managing director, 1988—; free-lance writer and author. Former editor for Satellite Books.

WRITINGS:

Nigger at Eton, Frewin Publishers, 1972, revised edition, Delta, 1982.
John Bull's Nigger, Frewin Publishers, 1974.
(Compiler) *The Book of Black Man's Humour,* Satellite Books, 1975.
(Compiler of text, with John Walters) *I'm the Greatest! The Wit and Humour of Muhammad Ali,* Frewin Publishers, 1975.
Sex Is a Nigger's Game (novel), Satellite Books, 1976.
Ju Ju: A Novel, Satellite Books, 1977, Archer Editions, 1980.
Secret Society: A Novel, Satellite Books, 1978.
The Return: Homecoming of a Negro From Eton, Satellite Books, 1978.
Female Target: A Novel, Satellite Books, 1979.
Revenge of the Medicine Man, Sphere, 1980.
Rules of the Game: Nigeria's Constitution, Foulsham, 1981.
Chief Onyeama: The Story of an African God (biography), Delta, 1982.
Night Demon, Sphere, 1982.
Modern Messiah: The Jim Nwobodo Story, foreword by Nnamdi Azikiwe, Delta, 1983.
Godfathers of Voodoo: A Novel, Delta, 1985.
African Legend: The Incredible Story of Francis Arthur Nzeribe (biography), Delta, 1985.
Correct English, Foulsham, 1986.
Notes of a So-Called Afro-Saxon, Delta, 1988.

SIDELIGHTS: A one-time subeditor for Drum Publications in England and full-time journalist and author, Dillibe Onyeama has written various biographies and a number of controversial novels. In particular, his writing addresses racial and political issues, ranging from his personal experiences to those of his native country of Nigeria.

Onyeama told *CA:* "Words hold for me the same beauty and fascination as well-arranged flowers."

AVOCATIONAL INTERESTS: Reading, occult matters.

BIOGRAPHICAL/CRITICAL SOURCES:

PERIODICALS

Spectator, August 17, 1974.
Times Literary Supplement, July 14, 1972, April 19, 1985.

*   *   *

OSBORN, Paul   1901-1988

OBITUARY NOTICE—See index for *CA* sketch: Born September 4, 1901, in Evansville, Ind.; died in 1988. Educator and author of many plays and film scripts. Osborn began his playwriting career in the 1920s after teaching at the University of Michigan and Yale University. He first enjoyed success in the 1930s with original works such as "The Vinegar Tree" and "Mornings at Seven," but by the 1940s he was writing adaptations such as "A Bell for Adano," which he derived from the novel by John Hersey, and "The World of Suzie Wong," based on the novel by Richard Mason. Osborn also adapted many works for film, including John Steinbeck's *East of Eden* and James A. Michener's *Sayonara*. Although Osborn's last play was produced in 1965 and his last screenplay was filmed even earlier, the writer gained renewed prominence in 1980 when "Mornings at Seven" was revived to great acclaim in the United States and received a Tony Award.

OBITUARIES AND OTHER SOURCES:

BOOKS

Who's Who in America, Supplement to 44th edition, Marquis, 1987.

PERIODICALS

Times (London), May 17, 1988.

*   *   *

OSBORN, Stella Brunt
See OSBORN, Stellanova

*   *   *

OSBORN, Stellanova   1894-1988
(Stella Brunt Osborn)

OBITUARY NOTICE: Name originally Stella Brunt; later known as Stella Brunt Osborn; name legally changed to Stellanova Osborn; born July 31, 1894, in Hamilton, Ontario, Canada; died in Sault Sainte Marie, Mich., in March, 1988. International policy activist, secretary, editor, and author. Osborn began her career with a succession of editorial positions, including associate editor of *Whimsies* and editor of the official publications of the University of Michigan. During the 1920s she began to achieve some notoriety as the personal secretary and companion of a former Michigan governor, Chase S. Osborn, who was separated from his wife but unable to remarry. Chase Osborn legally adopted Stellanova in 1931 but annulled the adoption and married her only two days before his death

in 1949. Osborn then became highly active in one of the former governor's favorite causes—a union of democratic nations that would span the Atlantic. To that end she helped lead such groups as Atlantic Union Committee, International Movement for Atlantic Union, and Federal Union, and she edited such publications as *Atlantic Union Herald* and *Freedom and Union*. The Osborns wrote several books together, including *Northwoods Sketches* and *The Conquest of a Continent*. Stellanova Osborn was sole author of *A Tale of Possum Poke in Possum Lane* and the poetry volume *Polly Cadotte: A Tale of Duck Island in Verse*.

OBITUARIES AND OTHER SOURCES:

BOOKS

The Canadian Who's Who, Volume XXII, University of Toronto Press, 1987.
Who's Who in the World, 6th edition, Marquis, 1982.

PERIODICALS

Detroit Free Press, March 20, 1988.

*   *   *

OSBORNE, (Reginald) Arthur   1906-1970

OBITUARY NOTICE—See index for *CA* sketch: Born September 25, 1906, in London, England; died May 8, 1970. Educator, editor, and author. Osborn worked and lived in the Far East and India. He taught English at Chulalongkorn University in Bangkok during World War II. Among Osborne's writings are *Ramana Arunachala, Ramana Maharshi and the Path of Self-Knowledge, The Incredible Sai Baba, Buddhism and Christianity in the Light of Hinduism,* and *The Question of Progress*. In addition, he was editor of the South India quarterly *Mountain Path*.

OBITUARIES AND OTHER SOURCES:

Date of death provided by wife, Lucia Osborne.

*   *   *

OSLEY, A(rthur) S(idney)   1917-1987

PERSONAL: Born January 21, 1917; died March 19, 1987; married Betty Laird (marriage ended); married Sheila Branigan; children: (first marriage) two sons. *Education:* University of London, graduated (with first class honors).

CAREER: British Admiralty, member of administrative staff, 1940-66; Ministry of Defence, civil servant, 1966-78, undersecretary of Price Commission, 1978; Council of Engineering Institutions, member of staff, 1978-83. Founder and publisher of Glade Press, 1969; printer and bookbinder; consultant to Engineering Council.

WRITINGS:

(Editor) *Calligraphy and Palaeography: Essays Presented to Alfred Fairbank on His Seventieth Birthday*, Faber, 1965, October House, 1966.
(Editor, translator, and author of introduction) Giovanni Francesco Cresci, *Essemplare di piu sorti lettere*, Nattali & Maurice, 1968.
Mercator: A Monograph on the Lettering of Maps, Etc., in the Sixteenth Century Netherlands, With a Facsimile and Translation of His Treatise on the Italic Hand and a Translation of Ghim's "Vita Mercatoris," Watson-Guptill, 1969.

Luminario: An Introduction to the Italian Writing-Books of the Sixteenth and Seventeenth Centuries, Miland, 1972.

(Editor, translator, and author of introduction) *Scribes and Sources: Handbook of the Chancery Hand in the Sixteenth Century; Texts From the Writing-Masters,* David Godine, 1980.

Berthold Wolpe Retrospective Survey, Faber, 1984.

BIOGRAPHICAL/CRITICAL SOURCES:

PERIODICALS

Times (London), March 26, 1987.
Times Literary Supplement, February 24, 1966, February 5, 1970, April 6, 1973, May 16, 1980.
Virginia Quarterly Review, winter, 1981.*

*   *   *

OUSMANE, Sembene   1923-

PERSONAL: Name cited in some sources as Ousmane Sembene; born January 8, 1923, in Ziguinchor, Casamance, Senegal. *Education:* Attended technical school; studied at Gorki Film Studios in early 1960s.

ADDRESSES: Home—c/o P.O. Box 8087 YOFF, Dakar, Senegal.

CAREER: Worked as fisherman in Casamance, Senegal, and as plumber, mechanic's aid, and bricklayer in Dakar, Senegal, before World War II; worked as docker and stevedore in Marseilles, France, in late 1940s; became union leader. Writer and filmmaker. *Military service:* Served in French Army during World War II.

AWARDS, HONORS: Literature prize from Dakar Festival of Negro Arts, 1966, for *Vehi-Ciosane ou Blanche-genese, suivi du Mandat;* prize from Cannes Film Festival, 1967, for "Le Noire de . . ."; special prize from Venice Film Festival, 1968, and award for best foreign film from Atlanta Film Festival, 1970, both for "Mandabi."

WRITINGS:

Le Docker noir (novel; title means "The Black Docker"), Nouvelles Editions Debresse, 1956.
Oh Pays, mon beau peuple! (novel; title means "Oh My Country, My Beautiful People"), Le Livre Contemporain, 1957.
Les Bouts de bois de Dieu (novel), Amiot-Dumont, 1960, translation by Francis Price published as *God's Bits of Wood,* Doubleday, 1962.
Voltaieque (short stories), Presence Africaine, 1962, translation by Len Ortzen published as *Tribal Scars, and Other Stories,* INSCAPE, 1974.
Vehi-Ciosane; ou, Blanche-genese, suivi du Mandat (two novellas), Presence Africaine, 1965, translation by Clive Wake published as *The Money Order, With White Genesis,* Heinemann, 1971.
Xala (novel; title means "Impotence"), Presence Africaine, 1973, translation by Clive Wake published as *Xala,* Lawrence Hill, 1976.
Dernier de l'empire (novel), Harmattan, 1981, translation by Adrian Adams published as *The Last of the Empire,* Heinemann, 1983.

Also author of the novel *Fat Ndiay Diop,* 1976.

OTHER PUBLISHED FICTION

"La Noire de . . ." (short story), published in *Presence africaine* in 1961, translation by Ellen Conroy Kennedy pub-

lished as "Black Girl" in *African Short Stories,* edited by Charles R. Larson, Macmillan, 1970.
Referendum (novel; first novel in *L'Harmattan* trilogy), published in *Presence africaine* in 1964.

SCREENPLAYS; AND DIRECTOR

"La Noire de . . ." (adapted from Ousmane's story; also see above), Actualities Francais/Films Domirev of Dakar, 1966 (released in the United States as "Black Girl," New Yorker Films, 1969).
"Mandabi" (adapted from Ousmane's novella *The Money Order;* also see above), Jean Maumy, 1968 (released in the United States by Grove Press, 1969).
"Emitai," Paulin Soumanou Vieya, 1971 (released in the United States by New Yorker Films, 1973).
"Xala" (title means "Impotence"), Societe Nationale Cinematographique/Films Domirev, 1974 (released in the United States by New Yorker Films, 1975).
"Ceddo," released in the United States by New Yorker Films, 1978 (first released in 1977).

Also screenwriter and director of "Borom Sarret," 1964; "Niaye," 1964; "Tauw," 1970; and the unreleased film "Songhays," 1963.

OTHER

Contributor to periodicals, including *Presence africaine.* Founding editor of periodical *Kaddu.*

SIDELIGHTS: Sembene Ousmane is a respected Senegalese artist who has distinguished himself in both literature and film. He was born in 1923 in the Casamance region and attended school only briefly before working as a fisherman. After moving to Senegal's capital, Dakar, Ousmane found various jobs in manual labor. He worked in Dakar during the late 1930s, but when World War II began he was drafted by the colonial French into their armed forces, and he eventually participated in the Allied invasion of Italy. When the war ended Ousmane returned home to the Casamance area and resumed his early life as a fisherman. After a short period, however, he traveled back to France, where he found work as a stevedore on the Marseilles docks.

Ousmane's experiences as a dockworker provided background for his first novel, *Le Docker noir* ("The Black Docker"). In this work Ousmane wrote of a black stevedore who writes a novel but is robbed of the manuscript by a white woman. Much of the novel delineates the ensuing consequences of that incident. Although *Le Docker noir* proved somewhat flawed, it nonetheless represented an alternative career for Ousmane after a back injury rendered him unfit for dock work.

With *Le Docker noir* Ousmane sought to express the plight of many minorities—including Spaniards and Arabs as well as blacks—exploited and abused at the French dockyards. But while he specified afterwards that his perspective was that of the minority, and thus contrary to that of whites, Ousmane was quick to add that he was not advocating *negritude,* a black-pride movement that he dismissed as sentimental and narrow-minded in its emphasis. He remained, however, a champion of black rights in Africa.

Ousmane's concern over conflicting philosophies within Africa's black community is evident in his second novel, *O Pays, mon beau peuple!* ("O My Country, My Beautiful People"), which concerns the failings of an ambitious Senegalese farmer returning home after a long absence. Accompanied by his white wife, the farmer alienates himself from both whites and blacks, for both groups resent his interracial marriage and his efforts to modernize the community's farming system. Eventually the farmer's behavior becomes intolerable to the villagers, and he is killed.

Like *Le Docker noir, O Pays, mon beau peuple!* was written in French, but unlike the earlier novel, Ousmane's second work fared well throughout much of Europe and was even published in Japan. After completing *O Pays, mon beau peuple!* Ousmane spent a few years traveling in many of the countries where the novel was earning acclaim. He eventually left Europe, however, and visited Cuba, China, and even the Soviet Union, where he studied filmmaking at a leading studio.

In 1960 Ousmane published his third novel, *Les Bouts de bois de Dieu* (*God's Bits of Wood*), which became his first work to gain significant attention from English readers. *God's Bits of Wood* is a fictionalized account of a railroad workers' strike that stalled transportation from Dakar to Niger in late 1947 and early 1948. Much more ambitious than Ousmane's previous works, the third novel is a sweeping, epic-style account featuring several characters and spanning Senegal's political and social extremes. In 1970, when the novel appeared in English translation, *Times Literary Supplement*'s reviewer T. M. Aluko wrote that Ousmane's work was a vivid rendering of the strike and the strikers. Aluko also cited Ousmane's particular skills as a novelist, declaring that he possessed "the ability to control a wide social panorama, without once losing sight of, or compassion for, the complexity and suffering of individuals."

Ousmane followed *God's Bits of Wood* with a short story collection, *Voltaieque* (*Tribal Scars*), and *Referendum*, the first part of a trilogy entitled *L'Harmattan* ("The Storm"). He then completed *Vehi-Ciosane; ou, Blanche-genese, suivi du Mandat* (*The Money Order, With White Genesis*), a volume comprised of two novellas. The book was an immense critical success, earning Ousmane the literature prize from the 1966 Dakar Festival of Negro Arts.

By the mid-1960s Ousmane was also working in film. In 1964 he completed his first notable work in that medium, the sociological study "Borom Sarret," and three years later he wrote and directed "Le Noire de . . ." ("Black Girl"), which detailed the degrading circumstances endured by an African servant in a French household. These films were shown together in New York City in 1969, and A. H. Weiler writing in the *New York Times* called both works insightful and provocative. Weiler also wrote that Ousmane's films derived from "the quiet distinctions of simplicity, sincerity and subdued anger toward the freed black man's new burdens." In addition, Weiler contended that the works "put a sharp, bright focus on an emerging, once dark African area."

Ousmane enjoyed even greater acclaim as a filmmaker with "Mandabi," his adaptation of his own novella *The Money Order*. "Mandabi" is a comedy about a middle-aged fool, Dieng, who receives a considerable financial sum from a nephew in Paris. Much of the humor in "Mandabi" derives from Dieng's vain, foolhardy efforts to secure identification papers necessary for cashing the money order. In the course of his efforts Dieng is swindled, robbed, thrashed, and publicly humiliated by his greedy family and fellow citizens. Adding further to the humor is the actual behavior of Dieng, an arrogant dimwit who smugly parades about his village oblivious of the animosity he provokes. In the *New York Times,* Roger Greenspun noted as much when he wrote that because Dieng "is such a pompous fool, so blithely superior to his two wives, so glut-

tonous with his food and confident in his walk, his troubles seem deserved and funny." Greenspun described Ousmane's directorial style as "spare, laconic, slightly ironic" and added that he "displays a reticence towards his characters that grants him freedom from explicit moral judgment."

Humor did not figure in Ousmane's next film, "Emitai," which he completed in 1971. In this work he chronicles a conflict between Senegalese natives and French colonialists at the beginning of World War II. The conflict centers on the natives' opposition to French troops sent into the Senegalese village to commandeer several tons of rice. Neither faction particularly cherishes the rice: For the villagers it is intended for use in religious ceremonies; for the French, it is rendered unnecessary by a change in military tactics. Nonetheless, neither side concedes to the other, and the conflict is resolved with futile violence. In his *New York Times* review, Roger Greenspun found "Emitai" a refreshing, if sobering, counterpoint to the Hollywood adventure films of the 1930s and 1940s, observing that "the absolute ineffectiveness of massed spears against a few well-placed rifles should lay to rest the memories of a good many delicious terrors during Saturday afternoons at the movies." Greenspun also commended Ousmane's directorial reserve and subtlety and declared that the filmmaker's relatively detached style resulted in a film "that keeps surprising you with its ironic sophistication."

Ousmane's next filmmaking venture, "Xala," marked his return to comedy. In "Xala" he lampoons the increasing Westernization of African politics and business. The protagonist of "Xala" is El Hadji, a corrupt bureaucrat who also serves his community as an importer of fairly exotic goods, including whiskey, yogurt, and perfume. Like his Western counterparts, El Hadji wears costly European business suits, totes a briefcase, and continually confers with advisers and fellow bureaucrats. His corrupt ways, while causing no good to his community, have contributed greatly to his considerable prosperity. That prosperity, however, is undermined when El Hadji takes a third wife and discovers that he is suddenly impotent. Apparently the victim of a curse, El Hadji consults witch doctors, including one fellow who sports an expensive business suit while squatting in his hut. That witch doctor fails to cure El Hadji, but for a substantial sum another doctor is able to restore the bureaucrat's sexuality. Unfortunately, troubles continue to plague El Hadji when he is implicated in a corrupt business action and is dismissed, by equally corrupt fellow bureaucrats, from the community's chamber of commerce. More marital problems then ensue, for El Hadji fails to pay his witch doctor and is thus once again impotent. Another cure is then attempted, one in which El Hadji must remove his clothing and allow several cripples to spit on him. He complies, but a much greater catastrophe awaits him.

"Xala" was released in 1974, only months after Ousmane had published his novel of the same title. When the film was shown in the United States in 1975, it was commended in the *New York Times* as "an instructive delight" and as "cutting, radiant and hilarious." *Time*'s reviewer, Richard Eder, added that Ousmane's film was George Orwell's novel *Animal Farm* "applied to African independence." Similarly, Ousmane's novel *Xala* was cited by *Nation* reviewer Eve Ottenberg as a witty portrait of "the destruction of tribal values." She wrote that the themes of *Xala* allowed Ousmane "to show people at their most flawed, eccentric, energetic and comic."

Ousmane continued to probe cultural discontinuity in "Ceddo," his 1977 film about religious conflict in an unspecified African kingdom. This conflict is triggered when a Catholic king converts to Islam and brings a Moslem teacher into his band of advisers. The king's associates then convert to Islam, too, leaving only the common villagers outside the Islamic faith. Resentful of the king's changing policies, the villagers kidnap the king's daughter and thus force him to negotiate. During meetings between factions, the opportunistic Islamic teacher intercedes and precipitates the slaughter of all the non-Moslems. Vincent Canby, in his review for the *New York Times*, noted that the manner of "Ceddo" was "reserved, cool, almost stately." He confirmed that the obviously anti-Moslem film had been banned in Senegal, but Canby observed that the banning was prompted by a seemingly trivial aspect: Ousmane refused to render the spelling of the film's title to be consistent with his government's own spelling.

Ousmane's stature as an African artist has risen steadily since he published his first work in 1956. In the ensuing years he has used his art to protest injustice against blacks and to decry the increasing disintegration of black Africa's heritages. He has also established himself as a formidable filmmaker in a medium where commercial considerations are usually dominant over the artistic, and the critical acclaim accorded his films in the United States testifies to his wide appeal and considerable achievements. Ousmane's works thus transcend cultural specifics and assure him recognition as a leading artist of his time.

BIOGRAPHICAL/CRITICAL SOURCES:

BOOKS

Brench, A. C., *The Novelists' Inheritance in French Africa: Writing From Senegal to Cameroon*, Oxford University Press, 1967.
Dathorne, O. R., *African Literature in the Twentieth Century*, Heinemann Educational, 1976.
Silver, Helene and Hans M. Zell, editors, *A Reader's Guide to African Literature*, Africana Publishing, 1971.

PERIODICALS

Africa Report, February, 1963.
American Cinematographer, November, 1972.
Black Orpheus, November, 1959.
Cineaste, Volume 6, number 1, 1973.
Cinema Quebec, March/April, 1973.
Film Quarterly, spring, 1973.
Nation, April 9, 1977.
New Yorker, May 16, 1977.
New York Times, January 13, 1969, September 30, 1969, November 9, 1969, February 10, 1973, October 1, 1975, January 27, 1978.
New York Times Book Review, November 28, 1976.
Quarterly Review of Film Studies, spring, 1979.
Times Literary Supplement, October 16, 1970.
World Literature Today, winter, 1978.*

—*Sketch by Les Stone*

*　　*　　*

OUSTON, Philip (Anfield)   1924(?)-1988(?)

OBITUARY NOTICE: Born c. 1924; died c. 1988. Educator and author. A professor at King's College, London, beginning in 1975, Ouston held the chair of French language and literature when he left the institution in 1983. Previously he was on the staffs of the universities of Dundee, St. Andrews, and British Columbia. Ouston wrote *France in the Twentieth Century* and *The Imagination of Maurice Barres*.

OBITUARIES AND OTHER SOURCES:

PERIODICALS

Times (London), July 2, 1988.

P

PACHECO, C.
See PESSOA, Fernando (Antonio Nogueira)

*   *   *

PACK, S(tanley) W(alter) C(roucher)   1904-1977

OBITUARY NOTICE—See index for *CA* sketch: Born December 14, 1904, in Portsmouth, England; died December 7, 1977. Military officer, meteorologist, educator, and author. Pack served in Britain's Royal Navy for thirty-three years, retiring in 1960 as captain. In the navy he was involved in weather research, and in the early 1950s he was deputy director of the Naval Weather Service. Earlier, he had taught at the Royal Naval College. Pack's writings include *Weather Forecasting, Admiral Lord Anson, Windward of the Caribbean, Night Action Off Cape Matapan*, and *The Battle of Sirte.*

OBITUARIES AND OTHER SOURCES:

BOOKS

Who Was Who, Volume VII: *1971-1980*, A. & C. Black, 1981.

*   *   *

PAISH, F(rank) W(alter)   1898-1988

OBITUARY NOTICE—See index for *CA* sketch: Born January 15, 1898, in Croydon, England; died May 23, 1988. Banker, administrator, economist, educator, editor, and author. Paish is probably best known for advocating federally controlled unemployment as a means of stabilizing inflation. This notion, so daring—and unpopular—when Paish introduced it in the 1960s, is now acceptable to many economists. Paish worked in banking and, during World War II, as deputy director of the British Ministry of Aircraft Production. He spent most of his career, however, as a teacher at the London School of Economics and Political Science, from which he retired in 1965 after sixteen years as professor. He wrote such works as *The Post-War Financial Problem, Business Finance, Long-Term and Short-Term Interest Rates in the United Kingdom, Rise and Fall of Incomes Policy*, and *How the Economy Works, and Other Essays.* In addition, he edited some volumes of *Benham's Economics.*

OBITUARIES AND OTHER SOURCES:

BOOKS

Who's Who, 140th edition, St. Martin's, 1988.

PERIODICALS

Times (London), May 26, 1988.

*   *   *

PARETSKY, Sara   1947-

BRIEF ENTRY: Born June 8, 1947, in Ames, Iowa. American insurance company executive and author. Regarded as one of America's current leading women detective writers, Paretsky is the author of four highly successful novels featuring V. I. Warshawski, a witty and attractive Chicago private eye who is particularly adept at exposing financial scams and solving murders and who, according to *Chicago Tribune* contributor Mary T. Schmich, "stands out like a nun in a Marine Corps drill." Paretsky's titles include *Indemnity Only* (Dial, 1982), *Deadlock* (Dial, 1984), *Killing Orders* (Morrow, 1985), *Bitter Medicine* (Morrow, 1987), and the forthcoming *Toxic Shock.*

Before turning to writing detective fiction full time, Paretsky worked in the marketing department of the Continental National America insurance companies. Her writing then was limited to a few short stories, some business publications, and speeches for corporate executives. Paretsky was named one of *Ms.* magazine's 1987 women of the year "for bringing a woman detective and feminist themes to murder mysteries, and for championing women writers in this mostly male genre." *Addresses: Agent*—Dominick Abel, 498 West End Ave., New York, N.Y. 10024.

BIOGRAPHICAL/CRITICAL SOURCES:

PERIODICALS

Chicago Tribune, July 16, 1987.
Chicago Tribune Book World, January 31, 1982, March 4, 1984, June 2, 1985.
Ms., October, 1987, January, 1988.
Newsweek, July 13, 1987.
New York Times Book Review, April 25, 1982, March 18, 1984, September 15, 1985, August 2, 1987.

PATON, Alan (Stewart) 1903-1988

OBITUARY NOTICE—See index for *CA* sketch: Born January 11, 1903, in Pietermaritzburg, South Africa; died of throat cancer, April 12, 1988, in Botha's Hill (near Durban), Natal, South Africa. Political and social activist, educator, academic administrator, and author. Paton was probably best known for his 1948 novel, *Cry, the Beloved Country,* in which he vividly portrayed the horrors of South Africa's racist apartheid system. Paton worked as a high-school teacher in the 1920s and 1930s and as a reformatory principal from 1935 to 1948. He began writing *Cry, the Beloved Country* in 1947 while touring European and American prisons and reformatories. The novel concerns a black minister's loss of religious faith as he searches for his son, a suspected murderer, in the vast Johannesburg ghetto. Though some critics found *Cry, the Beloved Country* pretentious and occasionally awkward, the book proved enormously successful, and Paton was soon perceived as a figurehead for South Africa's antiapartheid movement.

In the early 1950s, Paton founded the Liberal party of South Africa and increased his opposition to his country's racist policies. His actions prompted retaliation from the South African Government in the 1960s, when it effectively banned the Liberal party and revoked Paton's passport. Paton, however, continued to oppose apartheid, though in his later years he was sometimes perceived as a conservative for his protests against foreign sanctions and disinvestment. Among his other writings are the novel *Too Late the Phalarope,* the short story collection *Tales From a Troubled Land,* and the autobiographical works *Towards the Mountain* and the posthumously published *Journey Continued* (title listed in one source as *Journey's End*).

OBITUARIES AND OTHER SOURCES:

BOOKS

Current Biography, H. W. Wilson, 1952, May, 1988.

PERIODICALS

Chicago Tribune, April 13, 1988.
Los Angeles Times, April 12, 1988.
New York Times, April 13, 1988.
Times (London), April 13, 1988.

*   *   *

PAUL, David (Tyler) 1934-1988

OBITUARY NOTICE: Born November 18, 1934, in New York, N.Y.; died of lung cancer, March 28, 1988, in Willow Grove, Pa. Publishing executive, producer, editor, and author. An account supervisor at Meridien Gravure Company from 1959 to 1960, Paul then worked successively as an art or design director for Macmillan Company, *Popular Boating* magazine, Parents Magazine Press, and Random House until 1969. He subsequently served as vice-president and managing editor, then president, of Abelard-Schuman and Criterion Books from 1969 to 1971; publisher of Drake Publications from 1973 to 1974; and co-founder and editor of *Fire Islander* magazine from 1975 to 1977. Between 1976 and 1981 he was managing editor successively of *Northeastern Industrial World* magazine and of Cambridge Book Company, for which he was also executive editor for video and audiovisual. Thereafter he was an independent television producer. Paul was also director of Photo-Media Limited and proprietor of Graphics Consultations

by D. T. Paul. An author of children's books, he wrote *Harbor Tug* and *Tugboat Adventure.*

OBITUARIES AND OTHER SOURCES:

BOOKS

Who's Who in America, Supplement to 44th edition, Marquis, 1987.

PERIODICALS

New York Times, March 31, 1988.

*   *   *

PAYNE, A. J.
See PAYNE, Anthony

*   *   *

PAYNE, Anthony 1952-
(A. J. Payne)

PERSONAL: Born May 22, 1952, in Northampton, England; son of David Gordon (an engineer) and Lenna (Botterill) Payne; married Jill Caves (a secretary), September 15, 1973; children: Nicholas James, Christopher John. *Education:* Churchill College, Cambridge, B.A. (with honors), 1973, M.A., 1977; Victoria University of Manchester, Ph.D., 1978.

ADDRESSES: Home—13 Shawfield Ave., Holmfirth, West Yorkshire HD7 1L2, England. *Office*—Department of Politics, University of Sheffield, Sheffield S10 2TN, England.

CAREER: Teacher of politics at school in Somerset, England, 1977-78; Huddersfield Polytechnic, Huddersfield, England, lecturer, 1979-81, senior lecturer in politics, 1981-85; University of Sheffield, Sheffield, England, lecturer in politics, 1985—. Specialist adviser to House of Commons Foreign Affairs Committee, 1981-82.

MEMBER: Royal Institute of International Affairs, Political Studies Association of Great Britain, Society of Caribbean Studies, Caribbean Studies Association, Society of Latin American Studies.

WRITINGS:

(Under name A. J. Payne) *The Politics of the Caribbean Community, 1961-1979: Regional Integration Among New States,* St. Martin's, 1980.
Change in the Commonwealth Caribbean, Royal Institute of International Affairs, 1981.
(Editor with Paul K. Sutton) *Dependency Under Challenge: The Political Economy of the Commonwealth Caribbean,* Manchester University Press, 1984.
The International Crisis in the Caribbean, Johns Hopkins University Press, 1984.
(With Paul K. Sutton and Tony E. Thorndike) *Grenada: Revolution and Invasion,* St. Martin's, 1984.
(Editor with Colin G. Clarke) *Politics, Security, and Development in Small States,* Allen & Unwin, 1987.
Politics in Jamaica, Christopher Hurst, 1988.
Universities and Politics in the Third World, Routledge & Kegan Paul, in press.

Contributor to political science journals.

WORK IN PROGRESS: Research on international politics in the Caribbean and on democracy and development.

SIDELIGHTS: Anthony Payne told *CA:* "I am simply a professional political analyst, employed as an academic in a British university. I enjoy the mixture of teaching, research, administration, and travel the job provides. My field is the Third World and international politics, and I have thus far specialized in the area of the Caribbean. I am fond of the region and never miss an opportunity to go there. I value its tradition of democracy and sympathize with its development plight.

"I first went to the Caribbean in 1974 as a research student. In those days the department of government at Manchester and at the University of the West Indies in Jamaica had a thriving exchange scheme at the postgraduate level, founded by the later-Universities council. Many West Indian political scientists came to Manchester to train; I was one of the few to go to the Caribbean. I simply fell in love with Jamaica as a country and Jamaicans as a people. Indeed, my book on Jamaica I see as a repayment of a debt: a critical connecting of the politics of post-independence Jamaica by someone who is fond of all things Jamaican. In writing about the Caribbean I have always tried to take advantage of my position as an outsider to offer hard-headed, realistic political options, tempered by a belief in compromise and the values of what in Britain we would call social democracy. It is obvious, however, that the future of the region is increasingly bound up with the policy of the United States, and I find my research moving more and more in the direction of U.S. foreign policy."

*   *   *

PEACOCK, Daniel J.   1919-

PERSONAL: Born October 3, 1919, in Amityville, N.Y.; son of Daniel L. (a teacher) and Elsa (a nurse; maiden name, Wortman) Peacock; married Shirley Green (a secretary), September 12, 1946; children: Karen M., Paula Peacock Bertolin, Daniel L. *Education:* Earlham College, B.A., 1948; graduate study at University of Pennsylvania, 1952; Drexel Institute of Technology (now Drexel University), M.S. in L.S., 1959. *Religion:* Society of Friends (Quakers).

ADDRESSES: Home—500 University Ave., Honolulu, Hawaii 96826.

CAREER: Young Men's Christian Association (Y.M.C.A.), North Philadelphia, Pa., youth work secretary, 1949-53; teacher, trainer of teachers, and district director of education in Palau District, Trust Territory, Pacific Islands, 1953-58; Pacific Islands Central School, Ponape, Caroline Islands, teacher and librarian, 1959-66; Trust Territory Headquarters, Saipan, Mariana Islands, supervisor of library services, 1966-80; writer, 1980—.

WRITINGS:

(With Paul Woodhead) *Lee Boo: A Prince in Rotherhithe* (pamphlet), Rotherside Books, 1984.
Lee Boo: A Prince in London, University of Hawaii Press, 1987.

Contributor to newspapers.

WORK IN PROGRESS: Research and writing projects related to Micronesia and the author's experience in the Trust Territory of the Pacific Islands.

SIDELIGHTS: Daniel J. Peacock told *CA:* "I am one of those people to whom it is said, 'you write the most interesting letters.' Most of them, however, were written as a civil servant working for the Department of the Interior at some of its most distant outposts in the Trust Territory of the Pacific Islands. Now retired, I am trying to write my way out of the captivity of twenty-seven years of experiences in Micronesia.

"My first book was historical and biographical. Prince Lee Boo, of whom I wrote, was the first Micronesian student to study abroad (in London, as it happens, where I spent more than a year tracing his footsteps). Since Lee Boo's time a very substantial number of Micronesians have left their islands to further their education. It is inevitable that they should do so, and it is natural that they would seek out colleges they first learned of through their American teachers. In so doing they often find themselves trying to understand how a nation that held their islands in trust for some forty years could have so little knowledge of Micronesians and their islands.

"Although a very great deal has been written about Micronesia, no one has as yet written and published a personalized account of a career in those islands. I am now two hundred pages into such an account. My own career, however, was atypical, having stayed in the islands much longer than most. Fortunately I kept notes, which are now piled on my desk. Once entirely through them I do not know what the outcome will be. I do not perceive the task as one for the memoirist. I am more inclined to relate that which reflects the common experiences of those who knew the islanders as outsiders no matter how long they may have been on the inside. In so doing I hope I can help Micronesian scholars of the future to better understand who we were, where we came from, and what made us tick."

*   *   *

PELISSIER, Anthony   1912-1988

OBITUARY NOTICE: Born in 1912; died in Eastbourne, England, April 2, 1988. Actor, producer, director, and screenwriter. Though he began as an actor in London, England, Pelissier became better known as a director of plays and films. He also produced plays. His screenplays include "The History of Mr. Polly," adapted from an H. G. Wells novel, and "The Rocking Horse Winner," adapted from a short story by D. H. Lawrence.

OBITUARIES AND OTHER SOURCES:

BOOKS

Halliwell's Filmgoer's Companion, 7th edition, Granada, 1980.

PERIODICALS

Los Angeles Times, April 7, 1988.
New York Times, April 7, 1988.

*   *   *

PEREGOY, George Weems
See MENCKEN, H(enry) L(ouis)

*   *   *

PEREZ GALDOS, Benito   1843-1920

BRIEF ENTRY: Born May 10, 1843, in Las Palmas, Canary Islands; died January 4, 1920, in Madrid, Spain. Spanish political figure, journalist, and author. Perez Galdos is widely considered Spain's greatest writer since Miguel de Cervantes. He began his writing career by contributing articles to leftist publications in Las Palmas, and he continued his political writing after coming to Madrid in 1862. In 1868 he published two historical novels, the success of which led him to create *Episodios nacionales* (''National Episodes''), a series of tales recounting Spanish history. During the next decade Perez Galdos wrote twenty volumes of *Episodios nacionales* and established himself as contemporary Spain's master novelist. Although these works were highly popular, they failed to meet his own artistic standards, and in 1879 he abandoned the series to commence a new one entitled *Novelas espanolas contemporaneas* (''Contemporary Spanish Novels''), in which he sought to depict all aspects of human existence.

In the next nine years Perez Galdos completed twenty works in the *Novelas espanolas contemporaneas* series. He also stayed active in Spanish politics, and in 1886 he gained election to the Spanish Parliament. Unfortunately, the *Novelas espanolas contemporaneas,* though now considered his greatest achievement, were not as popular as the *Episodios nacionales,* and by the end of the 1890s Perez Galdos was compelled by monetary circumstances to revive the earlier series. But subsequent volumes failed to restore his popularity. Then his health declined: In 1905 he suffered a debilitating stroke, and in 1912 he became blind. Eight years later he died.

Perez Galdos wrote more than seventy novels. Among the forty-six works in the *Episodios nacionales* series are *La corte de Carlos IV* (1873; translation published as *The Court of Charles IV* in 1888) and *La batalla de los Arapiles* (translation published as *The Battle of Salamanca* in 1895). The twenty-four volume *Novelas espanolas contemporaneas* includes *Tormento* (1884; translation published as *Torment* in 1952), the four-part *Fortunata y Jacinta* (1886-87; translation published as *Fortunata and Jacinta* in 1973), *Tristana* (1892; translation published under the same title in 1961), and *Misericordia* (1897; translation published as *Compassion* in 1962). In addition, he wrote plays.

BIOGRAPHICAL/CRITICAL SOURCES:

BOOKS

Berkowitz, H. Chonon, *Perez Galdos: Spanish Liberal Crusader,* University of Wisconsin Press, 1948.
Eoff, Sherman, *The Novels of Perez Galdos: The Concept of Life as Dynamic Process,* Washington University Studies, 1954.
Gilman, Stephen, *Galdos and the Art of the European Novel: 1867-1887,* Princeton University Press, 1981.
Pattison, Walter P., *Benito Perez Galdos,* Twayne, 1975.
Twentieth-Century Literary Criticism, Volume 27, Gale, 1988.

*   *   *

PESSOA, Fernando (Antonio Nogueira)   1888-1935
(Charles Robert Anon, Baron de Teive, Alberto
Caeiro, Alvaro de Campos, C. Pacheco, Ricardo
Reis, Alexander Search, Bernardo Soares)

BRIEF ENTRY: Born June 13, 1888, in Lisbon, Portugal; died November 30, 1935, in Lisbon, Portugal. Business correspondent, publisher, translator, and author. Pessoa is probably twentieth-century Portugal's greatest poet. He received his early education in South Africa at an English school, and by age fifteen he showed impressive talent for writing sonnets like those of William Shakespeare. He returned to Portugal in 1905 and within two years found lifelong employment as a business correspondent. At that time Pessoa favored the works of En-

glish masters—notably Shakespeare and John Milton—and he produced more Shakespearean sonnets, attributing them to the pseudonymous Alexander Search. In 1909 Pessoa began writing in Portuguese and studying Portuguese literature, and by 1915 he had generated a significant body of Portuguese poetry. His work from this period reflects his mastery of wide-ranging styles and his interest in various literary movements.

Around 1917 Pessoa began curtailing his activities within the Portuguese literary community and began concentrating on producing works by writers of his own creation, supplying them with extensive biographical—and even astrological—backgrounds. Most notable among these alter egos—referred to by Pessoa as ''heteronyms''—is Alberto Caeiro, a naive realist whose occasionally mundane poems explicate his perspective; Ricardo Reis, a classicist whose work recalls that of ancient Rome's great poet Horace; and Alvaro de Campos, an existentialist whose passionate verse bears similarities to that of Walt Whitman. Other heteronyms include Charles Robert Anon, C. Pacheco, Bernardo Soares, and Baron de Teive. Pessoa died in 1935 after years of alcohol abuse. Most of his work appeared posthumously. Collections in English translation include *Selected Poems* (1971), *Sixty Portuguese Poems* (1971), and *Fernando Pessoa: Selected Poems* (1974).

BIOGRAPHICAL/CRITICAL SOURCES:

BOOKS

Encyclopedia of World Literature in the Twentieth Century, Volume III, revised edition, Ungar, 1983.
Monteiro, George, editor, *The Man Who Never Was: Essays on Fernando Pessoa,* Gavea-Brown, 1982.
Twentieth-Century Literary Criticism, Volume 27, Gale, 1988.

PERIODICALS

New Republic, September 7, 1987.
New York Review of Books, September 21, 1972.
New York Times Book Review, December 13, 1987.

*   *   *

PHILBY, Harold Adrian Russell   1912-1988
(Kim Philby)

OBITUARY NOTICE: Born January 1, 1912, in Ambala, India; died May 11, 1988, in Moscow, U.S.S.R.; buried in a military cemetery in Moscow, U.S.S.R. Intelligence agent, journalist, and author. Dubbed ''the most remarkable spy in the history of espionage'' by the London *Times,* Philby was a high-ranking officer in British intelligence who stunned the West when he defected to the Soviet Union in 1963, approximately thirty years after he and fellow Cambridge students Guy Burgess and Donald Maclean were secretly recruited by the Soviets.

Philby began working for British intelligence in 1940, and within four years he was placed in charge of British intelligence efforts against the Soviet Union, a major coup for a Soviet double agent. He also served as liaison between British and American spy agencies and was being groomed for even more important posts. In 1951, however, Philby was accused of warning Burgess and Maclean, then officials in the British Foreign Office, that they were suspected of espionage and were about to be interrogated, thus allowing them to escape to the Soviet Union. The British investigated the allegation, but the evidence against Philby was circumstantial and seemed insufficient to prosecute him for treason.

Surprisingly, Philby continued to work for British intelligence as a field agent, but he then turned to journalism, reporting from Beirut, Lebanon, for the *Economist* and the London *Observer*. In 1963, when the British finally uncovered conclusive evidence of his guilt, Philby defected to the Soviet Union and his treasonous activities became generally known. Sources say that he remained active in Soviet intelligence activities until his death. He defended his actions in the 1968 book *My Silent War: The Soviet Master Spy's Own Story*, written under his nickname, Kim Philby.

OBITUARIES AND OTHER SOURCES:

BOOKS

The Historical Encyclopedia of World War II, Facts on File, 1980.
Philby, Kim, *My Silent War: The Soviet Master Spy's Own Story*, Grove Press, 1968.
Seth, Ronald, *Encyclopedia of Espionage*, new edition, New English Library, 1975.

PERIODICALS

Chicago Tribune, May 13, 1988.
Los Angeles Times, May 12, 1988.
New York Times, May 12, 1988.
Times (London), May 12, 1988, May 14, 1988.
Washington Post, May 12, 1988.

*   *   *

PHILBY, Kim
See PHILBY, Harold Adrian Russell

*   *   *

PHILIPS, Michael 1942-

PERSONAL: Born April 2, 1942, in Los Angeles, Calif.; son of Seymour M. (an attorney) and Mary Lee (an executive; maiden name, Kleiman) Philips; married Marion Kovach (a reporter), July 16, 1974. *Education:* University of California, Riverside, B.A. (with high honors), 1964; Johns Hopkins University, Ph.D., 1968.

ADDRESSES: Office—Department of Philosophy, Portland State University, Box 751, Portland, Ore. 97207.

CAREER: Portland State University, Portland, Ore., assistant professor, 1968-80, associate professor, 1980-84, professor of philosophy, 1984—, chairperson of department of philosophy, 1974-75, faculty senate alternate, 1974, 1977, member of College of Arts and Letters division board, 1974, member of University speakers committee, 1974, 1980, member of department of philosophy pay, promotion, and tenure committee, 1972-74, 1977, and curriculum committee, 1974, 1980. Visiting assistant professor at University of Hawaii at Manoa, 1979-80, visiting associate professor at University of Miami, 1983-84; consultant on business and medical ethics. Playwright and actor, 1974-77.

MEMBER: American Association of University Professors, American Philosophical Association, Society for the Study of Business and Professional Ethics.

AWARDS, HONORS: National Endowment for the Humanities summer seminar fellowships, 1980 and 1984; Oregon Committee for the Humanities fellowship, 1983.

WRITINGS:

(Editor) *Philosophy and Science Fiction*, Prometheus Books, 1984.
(Contributor) Patricia Werhane and Kendall D'Andrade, editors, *Profit and Responsibility: Issues in Business and Professional Ethics*, Mellen, Edwin, 1985.

UNPUBLISHED PLAYS

"Bye, Bye American Sky" (for radio), first broadcast in Portland, Ore., by Radio Station KBOO, 1974.
"The Birthday," first produced in Portland by the Family Circus Theater, 1976.
"La Lucha de Juan y Maria," first produced in Portland by Concerned Actors Ensemble, 1976.
"The American Screw," first produced in Portland by Family Circus Theater, 1977.
"The Queen's Blood," first produced in Portland by Storefront Theater, 1977.

OTHER

Contributor of articles to professional journals, including *Canadian Journal of Philosophy*, *Ethics*, *Journal of Business Ethics*, *Journal of Value Inquiry*, *Law and Philosophy*, *Law and Society Review*, *Nous*, and *Philosophical Studies*. Also contributor to the *New York Times*.

WORK IN PROGRESS: A book on moral theory, the purpose of which "is to enable us to understand the nature of moral disagreements and the possibilities for resolving them."

SIDELIGHTS: Michael Philips told *CA:* "During the Vietnam War I gave up philosophy for political activism. Philosophy seemed much too ethereal, especially academic philosophy. Both professional philosophy and I have changed since the early 1970s. By the mid-1970s it was possible to address important moral questions in philosophy without loss of reputation, but I did not take advantage of the opportunity until 1981 or so. In the interim I wrote and acted in plays produced by local theater companies in Portland.

"When I visited the University of Hawaii from 1979 to 1980, however, my interest in philosophy was rekindled, and I began to write for a professional audience again. I have published a good deal since then, and I am now passionately involved with my work on moral theory. Although I plan to address all the important traditional questions, my aim is to produce a work that will help all thoughtful people better to understand their moral differences and similarities to others. My book will succeed if a thoughtful encounter with it enriches the moral resources of the reader."

BIOGRAPHICAL/CRITICAL SOURCES:

PERIODICALS

Los Angeles Times Book Review, August 8, 1984.

*   *   *

PIELMEIER, John 1949-

BRIEF ENTRY: Born February 23, 1949, in Altoona, Pa. American playwright and screenwriter. Pielmeier wrote the acclaimed play *Agnes of God* (New American Library, 1985; first produced in 1978), about a psychiatrist's efforts to determine whether a young nun is mentally fit to stand trial for the murder of her newborn baby. The play shared top honors at the 1980 Festival of New American Plays and eventually played on Broadway for seventeen months. In 1985 Pielmeier adapted "Agnes of God" for film (released by Columbia). Among Pielmeier's other plays are "Sleight of Hand" (first produced in 1978), a thriller about a nasty magician; "Courage" (first produced in 1980), a monodrama about *Peter Pan* author J. M. Barrie; and "The Boys of Winter" (first produced in 1985), a drama concerning several soldiers preparing for a suicidal mission in Vietnam. *Addresses:* Jeannine Edmunds, J. Michael Bloom Ltd., 400 Madison Ave., New York, N. Y. 10017.

BIOGRAPHICAL/CRITICAL SOURCES:

BOOKS

Contemporary Theatre, Film, and Television, Volume 1, Gale, 1984.
Who's Who in America, 43rd edition, Marquis, 1984.

PERIODICALS

Los Angeles Times, February 14, 1984.
New York Times, March 31, 1982, May 14, 1984, December 2, 1985, May 4, 1987.
Time, August 26, 1985.

*   *   *

PIKE, E(dgar) Royston   1896-1980

OBITUARY NOTICE—See index for *CA* sketch: Born April 9, 1896, in Enfield, Middlesex, England; died June 6, 1980. Editor and author. Pike worked for Amalgamated Press as an associate editor from 1932 to 1944 and as editor of its *World Digest* throughout the 1950s. He wrote such works as *The Story of the Crusades: A Popular Account, Temple Bells; or, The Faiths of Many Lands, Slayers of Superstition, Round the Year With the World's Religions,* and *Encyclopaedia of Religion and Religions.*

OBITUARIES AND OTHER SOURCES:

Date of death provided by wife, Winifred Pike.

*   *   *

PINERO, Miguel (Antonio Gomez)   1946-1988

OBITUARY NOTICE—See index for *CA* sketch: Born December 12 (some sources say December 19), 1946, in Gurabo, Puerto Rico; died of cirrhosis of the liver, June 16 (some sources say June 17), 1988, in New York, N. Y. Actor, editor, and author. Pinero wrote "Short Eyes," a prison drama that won an Obie Award from the *Village Voice* and was declared 1976's best American play by the New York Drama Critics Circle. Prior to playwriting, Pinero lived a life of crime, hustling in pool halls and stealing from vending machines. When he developed a drug addiction, he turned to dealing in narcotics and committing robberies. He was serving a prison sentence when he wrote the first draft of "Short Eyes," a drama about the prison killing of a recently convicted child rapist. Upon his release, Pinero continued to work on the play, which was first staged in 1974 with a theatre workshop called The Family. Later that year, "Short Eyes" was produced Off-Broadway to great success, and in 1976 it was adapted by Pinero for film. He appeared in the motion picture version, and in subsequent years he found more work as an actor in films such as "Fort Apache, the Bronx," "Times Square," and "Alphabet City." His other writings include the plays "The Sun Always Shines for the Cool," "Straight From the Ghetto," "A Midnight Moon at the Greasy Spoon," and "Eu-

logy for a Small-Time Thief." He co-edited the volume *Nuyorican Poetry: An Anthology of Puerto Rican Words and Feelings.*

OBITUARIES AND OTHER SOURCES:

BOOKS

Contemporary Dramatists, 4th edition, St. James Press, 1988.
Current Biography, H. W. Wilson, 1983.

PERIODICALS

Chicago Tribune, June 19, 1988.
Los Angeles Times, June 18, 1988.
New York Times, June 18, 1988.
Times (London), June 21, 1988.
Washington Post, June 19, 1988.

*   *   *

PISERCHIA, Doris (Elaine)   1928-
(Curt Selby)

PERSONAL: Born October 11, 1928, in Fairmont, W.Va.; daughter of Dewey Leslie and Viola (Crihfield) Summers; married Joseph John Piserchia, August 25, 1953; children: Linda Elizabeth, John Joseph, James Anthony, Dewey Leslie, Patricia Jane. *Education:* Fairmont State College, A.B., 1950; graduate study at University of Utah, 1963-65.

ADDRESSES: Agent—E. J. Carnell Literary Agency, Rowneybury Bungalow, Sawbridgeworth, near Old Harlow, Essex CM20 2EX, England.

CAREER: Homemaker, 1954—; writer, 1966—. *Military service:* U.S. Navy, 1950-54; became lieutenant.

WRITINGS:

Mister Justice, Ace Books, 1973.
Star Rider, Bantam, 1974.
A Billion Days of Earth, Bantam, 1976.
Earthchild, DAW, 1977.
Spaceling, Doubleday, 1978.
The Spinner, Doubleday, 1980.
The Fluger, DAW, 1980.
Earth in Twilight, DAW, 1981.
Doomtime, DAW, 1981.
(Under pseudonym Curt Selby) *Blood County*, DAW, 1981.
(Under Selby pseudonym) *I, Zombie*, DAW, 1982.
The Dimensioneers, DAW, 1982.
The Deadly Sky, DAW, 1983.

Work represented in anthologies, including *The Best Science Fiction for 1972*, edited by Frederik Pohl, Ace Books, 1972; *Orbit 12* and *Orbit 13*, edited by Damon Knight, Putnam, 1973 and 1974; *Orbit 15* and *Orbit 16*, edited by Knight, Harper, 1974 and 1975; *Crisis*, edited by Roger Elwood, Nelson, 1974; *The Best From Galaxy 2*, Award, 1974; *Best SF 1974*, edited by Harry Harrison and Brian Aldiss, Bobbs-Merrill, 1975; and *Science Fiction Discoveries*, edited by F. Pohl and Carol Pohl, Bantam, 1976. Contributor of stories to periodicals, including *Fantastic, Galaxy,* and *If.*

SIDELIGHTS: Upon the 1973 publication of her first science fiction novel, *Mister Justice*, Doris Piserchia was praised by Harlan Ellison in the *Magazine of Fantasy and Science Fiction* as "easily one of the most interesting new writers to come down the pike." Depicting a vigilante who overcomes criminals by traveling through time, the book "is written in a strange and almost surrealistic manner,'' noted Ellison. ''The plot is complex, the writing graceful and yet forceful, every page crammed with originality or ideas and . . . verve for the craft of writing.'' Piserchia's characters drew further praise from the critic, who judged the book ''splendid.''

In later books, such as *Star Rider*, Piserchia focuses on interstellar, intergalactic, and interdimensional travel, and many stories explore Earth's future. *Earth Child*, for instance, postulates an Earth covered with eons of garbage, in which two shape-changing creatures fight to control the planet, with Reee, the last human living there, caught in the middle. According to Gerald Jonas, writing in the *New York Times Book Review*, Piserchia's ''enormously energetic style . . . ensnares the reader in the first paragraph.'' Jonas expressed disappointment that the energy ''seems to flag'' near the end, but he found the author's prose memorable and characterized the book as ''a paean to life.''

AVOCATIONAL INTERESTS: Swimming, diving, horseback riding, coin collecting.

BIOGRAPHICAL/CRITICAL SOURCES:

PERIODICALS

Analog Science Fiction/Science Fact, March 30, 1981.
Los Angeles Times Book Review, December 20, 1981, July 18, 1982, October 10, 1982.
Magazine of Fantasy and Science Fiction, January, 1974.
New York Times Book Review, August 28, 1977.
Spectator, April 1, 1978.
Times Literary Supplement, June 16, 1978.*

*   *   *

POLITE, Frank (C.)   1936-

PERSONAL: Born September 18, 1936, in Youngstown, Ohio; son of Jacob (a city employee) and Nancy (a housewife; maiden name, Zarella) Polite; married Dorothea L. Bailik, September 18, 1983; children: Khepri (son). *Education:* Youngstown University (now State University), B.A., 1960; University of Iowa, M.F.A., 1968.

ADDRESSES: Home—113 Madison Ave., Youngstown, Ohio 44505.

CAREER: University of Minnesota—Duluth, instructor in writing and literature, 1960-62; Vitro Aerospace Corp., Silver Spring, Md., technical editor, 1962-63; Youngstown State University, Youngstown, Ohio, instructor in writing and literature, 1963-69; U.S. Forces in Europe, education counselor and director of Education Center in Cakmakli, Turkey, 1970-72; Ohio Bureau of Vocational Rehabilitation, Toledo, counselor, 1972-75; University of Maryland at College Park, European Division, lecturer in English and literature in Turkey and Germany, 1983-87. *Military service:* U.S. Navy, hospital corpsman, 1954-57; served in the Pacific and Far East.

AWARDS, HONORS: Artist in residence at Yaddo Colony, 1965, and MacDowell Colony, 1968; individual artist award of $5,000 from Ohio Arts Council, 1979; Pulitzer Prize nomination, 1979, for *Letters of Transit*.

WRITINGS:

Letters of Transit (poetry), City Miner Books, 1979, 2nd edition, 1981.

The Pool of Midnight (poetry), Pangborn Books, 1983.
Longissima Via, Pangborn Books, 1988.

Work represented in anthologies, including *New Yorker Book of Poems*, 1969; *A Geography of Poets*, 1979; and *Up Late: American Poetry Since 1970*, 1987. Contributor to magazines, including *New Yorker*, *Nation*, *Harper's*, *Carleton Miscellany*, *North American Review*, and *Poetry*, and to newspapers.

WORK IN PROGRESS: Considering the Source, publication expected in 1989.

*   *   *

POLLOCK, Thomas Clark   1902-1988

OBITUARY NOTICE—See index for *CA* sketch: Born March 31, 1902, in Monmouth, Ill.; died of pneumonia, May 12, 1988, in Durham, N. C. Educator, academic administrator, editor, and author. Pollock was professor of English at New York University from 1944 to 1970 and was dean of the school's Washington Square College from 1947 to 1962. He wrote *The Philadelphia Theatre in the Eighteenth Century, The Nature of Literature*, and—with Oscar Cargill—*Thomas Wolfe at Washington Square*. In addition, he co-edited the volume *Correspondence of Thomas Wolfe and Homer Andrew Watt*.

OBITUARIES AND OTHER SOURCES:

PERIODICALS

New York Times, May 13, 1988.

*   *   *

POSENER, Georges (Henri)   1906-1988

OBITUARY NOTICE: Born September 12, 1906, in Paris, France; died May 16, 1988, in Paris, France. Archaeologist, educator, administrator, and author. A renowned specialist in the study of ancient Egypt, Posener was director of studies at the Ecole Pratique des Hautes Etudes from 1935 to 1961 and professor of Egyptian philology and archaeology at the College de France from 1961 to 1972. As a postgraduate student in Egypt in the early 1930s, he worked with the Institut Francais d'Archeologie Orientale, which uncovered numerous limestone tablets inscribed in ink. Posener spent much of his professional career translating these hieroglyphics and publishing his findings. His books include *Litterature et politique dans l'Egypte de la XIIe dynastie; De la divinite du pharaon;* and, with Serge Sauneron and Jean Yoyotte, *Dictionnaire de la civilisation egyptienne* (translation published as *Dictionary of Egyptian Civilization*).

OBITUARIES AND OTHER SOURCES:

BOOKS

Who's Who in France, 18th edition, Lafitte, 1985.
Who's Who in the World, 2nd edition, Marquis, 1973.

PERIODICALS

Times (London), May 19, 1988.

*   *   *

POSTON, Ted
See POSTON, Theodore Roosevelt Augustus Major

POSTON, Theodore Roosevelt Augustus Major
1906-1974
(Ted Poston)

PERSONAL: Known professionally as Ted Poston; born July 4, 1906, in Hopkinsville, Ky.; died after a long illness, January 11, 1974, in Brooklyn, N.Y.; son of Ephraim (a newspaper publisher) and Mollie (Cox) Poston; married Miriam Rivers, 1935 (divorced); married Marie Byrd Jackson, 1941 (divorced, 1955); married Ersa Hines, August 21, 1957. *Education:* Tennessee Agricultural and Industrial College (now Tennessee State University), A.B., 1928; attended New York University.

ADDRESSES: Home—101 Chauncey St., Brooklyn, N.Y.

CAREER: Contender, Hopkinsville, Ky., copy clerk, beginning in 1922; writer for Alfred E. Smith presidential campaign, New York, N.Y., 1928; dining car waiter for Pennsylvania Railroad and columnist for *Pittsburgh Courier,* c. 1928-29; *Amsterdam News,* New York City, reporter, 1929-34, city editor, 1934-c. 1936; writer for Works Progress Administration, c. 1936; *New York Post,* New York City, reporter, c. 1937-72. Traveled to U.S.S.R. as extra for unproduced film "Black and White," 1932. *Wartime service:* Worked in Washington, D.C., from 1940 to 1945 as public relations consultant for National Advisory Defense Commission, Office of Production Management, War Production Board, and War Manpower Commission, and as chief of Negro News Desk in news bureau of Office of War Information.

MEMBER: Newspaper Guild (Washington chapter), Omega Psi Phi.

AWARDS, HONORS: Heywood Broun Memorial Award from American Newspaper Guild, 1950, for coverage of racial discrimination in a trial in Tavares, Fla.; George Polk Award from Long Island University, 1950, for coverage of racial discrimination in Florida; award from Irving Geist Foundation, 1950, for coverage of antiblack rioting in Groveland, Fla.; award from Newspaper Guild of New York, 1950, and Unity Award from Beta Delta Mu, 1951, both for promoting interracial tolerance; award from Black Perspective, 1972; distinguished service medal from City of New York; distinguished service plaques from boroughs of Brooklyn, Bronx, and Queens.

WRITINGS:

SHORT STORIES

"A Matter of Record," published in *New Republic,* February 26, 1940.
"You Go South," published in *New Republic,* September 9, 1940.
"Law and Order in Norfolk," published in *New Republic,* October 7, 1940.
"The Making of Mamma Harris," published in *New Republic,* November 4, 1940.
"The Revolt of the Evil Fairies," published in *New Republic,* April 6, 1942.

Contributor of additional stories to periodicals. Work represented in anthologies, including *The Negro Caravan,* edited by Sterling A. Brown, Arthur P. Davis, and Ulysses Lee, Arno, 1970; *Black Joy,* edited by Jay David, Cowles, 1971; and *The Best Short Stories by Negro Writers: An Anthology From 1899 to the Present,* edited by Langston Hughes, Little, Brown, 1967.

OTHER

(Contributor) Paul L. Fisher and Ralph Lowenstein, editors, *Race and the News Media,* Praeger, 1967.

Contributor of articles and reviews to periodicals, including *Ebony, Nation, Negro Digest, New Republic, Saturday Review, Survey.*

SIDELIGHTS: A reporter for the *New York Post* from the late 1930s until he retired in 1972, Ted Poston was one of the first black journalists to work full time for a white-owned daily newspaper. He grew up in Hopkinsville, Kentucky, and as a teenager he helped out at his family's weekly, the *Contender,* until the paper became so controversial that it was moved out of town. After earning a bachelor's degree at Tennessee Agricultural and Industrial College in 1928, Poston joined the staff of a prominent black weekly in New York City, the *Amsterdam News.* He advanced to city editor in 1934, but after he helped lead a strike to unionize the *News,* its owners fired him.

A few years later Poston applied for a job at the *Post*—a difficult move, since only two black journalists had ever worked for a white-owned daily in the city. He was promised work if he could find a front-page story for the next day's paper. Doubtful of his prospects Poston took the subway back toward his home in Harlem, and as he left the train he saw a white man pursued by a group of angry blacks. Curiosity aroused, Poston discovered that the white was trying to serve notice of a lawsuit on Father Divine, a charismatic black preacher whose followers often called him an incarnation of God. The angry crowd represented some of Divine's protectors, known as his "angels." Poston had his story and his reporter's job.

The *Post* assigned him to cover New York City Hall, and as he later told *Editor and Publisher,* journalists there "would look at me as if to say I had a hell of a nerve coming into that white man's province. Whenever there was a breaking story, [they] would go into another room to compare notes." Finally, Poston said, "I got tired of it and began to scoop them on stories. That broke the ice."

Poston stressed that his reporting was not limited to events involving race, and in addition to the city hall beat he was known for exclusive interviews with two of the best-known politicians of his day: Huey Long, controversial political boss of Louisiana, and Wendell Willkie, 1940 Republican nominee for president. But Poston's most dramatic—and dangerous—work often concerned race relations in the South.

While employed by the *News* he went to Alabama to cover the Scottsboro case, in which a group of young black men was falsely accused of raping two white women. Poston was afraid to appear openly as a black reporter from the North, so he dressed in shabby clothes and attended the trial as an itinerant preacher. When a group of suspicious whites caught him mailing a report to New York City, he calmed them down by producing some false identification that showed he was a minister. (He later recounted the incident in an article for *Negro Digest* titled "My Most Humiliating Jim Crow Experience.") After Poston attended a similar rape trial in Florida for the *Post* in 1949, a gang of whites chased him out of town; when he covered the 1955 bus boycotts in Montgomery, Alabama, his boss asked him to call New York every night to show he was still alive. Such assignments earned Poston several awards in the 1950s, including the Heywood Broun Award of the American Newspaper Guild.

Over the course of Poston's life at least twenty of his short stories appeared in magazines and anthologies, and in *New Republic* he gained a national audience for several narratives about the plight of black Americans. In "A Matter of Record," for example, a decrepit boxer clings to a press clipping of his past glory; in "The Making of Mamma Harris" a woman leads a strike to unionize a tobacco factory; and in "You Go South" a New Yorker prepares himself for the racial humiliations he will face when he travels to the South.

Many of Poston's short stories are autobiographical accounts of life in Hopkinsville at the Booker T. Washington Colored Grammar School. "Revolt of the Evil Fairies," which appeared in *New Republic* and a number of anthologies, illustrates racial barriers in the South by depicting a school play in which roles are assigned on the basis of skin color. According to the narrator, Good Fairies tend to be children "with straight hair and white folks' features," and Prince Charming and Sleeping Beauty are "*always* light-skinned." "And therein lay my personal tragedy," the narrator continues. "I made the best grades in my class, I was the leading debater, and the scion of a respected family in the community. But I could never be Prince Charming, because I was black." Humiliated by his role as leader of the Evil Fairies, the narrator rebels in the middle of a performance by punching Prince Charming, and the dark- and light-skinned children are soon in open combat. "They wouldn't let me appear in the grand dramatic offering at all next year," the narrator concludes. "But I didn't care. I couldn't have been Prince Charming anyway."

Poston knew that his job on a white-owned daily was an opportunity that few blacks had been allowed to share. He actively encouraged more minorities to follow his lead, and when the *Post* hired minority trainees he monitored their progress and lobbied the paper's publisher to keep them on the staff. When Poston retired in 1972, the journalistic organization Black Perspective honored him both for professional excellence and for his efforts on behalf of other blacks in his field. Poston said he hoped to return to Hopkinsville and write more short stories about his youth, but his health failed and he died in 1974.

Shortly after his death Poston was lauded in the *Washington Post* by Joel Dreyfuss, a younger black reporter who had worked with him in New York. Dreyfuss praised Poston's "flowing graceful prose" and skill as a rewrite man, and reminded readers of the inner strength Poston must have possessed to endure the "constant pressure," "isolation," and humiliation of his difficult role. The headline on Dreyfuss's story read: "The Loneliness of Being First."

BIOGRAPHICAL/CRITICAL SOURCES:

BOOKS

Dictionary of Literary Biography, Volume 51: *Afro-American Writers From the Harlem Renaissance to 1940,* Gale, 1987.

PERIODICALS

Black Perspective, spring, 1972.
Editor and Publisher, April 29, 1972.
Negro Digest, April, 1944, December, 1949.
Newsweek, April 11, 1949.

OBITUARIES:

PERIODICALS

New York Times, January 12, 1974.

Time, January 21, 1974.
Washington Post, January 19, 1974.*

—*Sketch by Thomas Kozikowski*

*   *   *

POTTER, Philip   1907-1988

OBITUARY NOTICE: Born November 14, 1907, in Minneapolis, Minn.; died of an apparent stroke, April 27, 1988, in Sonoma, Calif. Journalist. After joining the Baltimore *Sun* in the early 1940s, Potter became city editor, then covered the last months of World War II in Southeast Asia, remaining to report on the military occupation of Japan and Korea. After the war he divided his time between covering national politics in Washington, D.C., and overseas assignments, which included reporting on the civil war in Greece, the 1948 battles for Israeli independence, the American airlift of supplies to West Berlin, and the Korean War. He was bureau chief in New Delhi, India, from 1961 to 1962, in Washington, D.C., from 1964 to 1972, and in London from 1972 until 1974, when he retired. Early in his career Potter worked for the Associated Press, and he was managing editor of the *Rapid City Daily Journal* from 1936 to 1941. He contributed to a book titled *The Candidates.*

OBITUARIES AND OTHER SOURCES:

BOOKS

Who's Who in the World, 2nd edition, Marquis, 1973.

PERIODICALS

Washington Post, April 29, 1988.

*   *   *

PRICE, Archibald Grenfell   1892-1977

OBITUARY NOTICE—See index for *CA* sketch: Born January 28, 1892, in Adelaide, South Australia; died July 20, 1977, in Adelaide, South Australia. Geologist, educator, academic administrator, government official, editor, and author. Price is respected for his studies of South Australia's history and geography. He was associated with the University of Adelaide from 1925 to 1962, during which time he taught geography and presided as master of the school's St. Mark's College. During the early 1940s, he also served as a Liberal member of the Federal House of Representatives. Price was knighted in 1963. His writings include *What of Our Aborigines?; Australia Comes of Age: A Study of Growth to Nationhood and of External Relations; The Western Invasions of the Pacific and Its Continents: A Study of Moving Frontiers and Changing Landscapes, 1513-1958; The Importance of Disease in History;* and *The Challenge of New Guinea: Australian Aid to Papuan Progress.* Price also edited the volume *The Humanities in Australia: A Survey With Special Reference to the Universities.*

OBITUARIES AND OTHER SOURCES:

BOOKS

Geographers: Bibliographical Studies, Volume 9, Mansell, 1985.
Kerr, Colin, *Archie: The Biography of Sir Archibald Grenfell Price,* Macmillan, 1983.

PRICE, E(dgar) Hoffmann (Trooper)   1898-1988

OBITUARY NOTICE—See index for *CA* sketch: Born July 3, 1898, in Fowler, Calif.; died June 18, 1988, in Redwood City, Calif. Factory supervisor, technician, and author of fantasies, westerns, war adventures, and spy stories. Price turned to full-time writing in the early 1930s after working as a plant superintendent for Union Carbide. His first stories appeared in periodicals such as *Weird Tales* and *Oriental Tales,* and by the early 1950s his tales were also published in *Argosy* and *Adventure.* Price's first books are the fantasies *Strange Gateways* and *Far Lands, Other Days.* Subsequent writings include *Grubstake, The Devil Wives of Li Fong, The Jade Enchantress,* and *Operation Long Life.*

OBITUARIES AND OTHER SOURCES:

BOOKS

International Authors and Writers Who's Who, 10th edition, International Biographical Centre, 1986.

PERIODICALS

Los Angeles Times, July 2, 1988.

*   *   *

PROVIST, d'Alain
See DIOP, Birago (Ismael)

Q-R

QUADE, E(dward) S(chaumberg) 1908-1988

OBITUARY NOTICE: Born June 28, 1908, in Jacksonville, Fla.; died after a stroke, June 4, 1988, in Laguna Hills, Calif. Mathematician, educator, administrator, editor, and author. Quade taught mathematics at the University of Florida for nearly twenty years before joining the RAND Corporation in 1948 as a mathematician and administrator. Quade, who helped develop systems analysis, a rational approach to decision-making, retired from RAND in 1973. He wrote *Analysis for Public Decisions,* as well as numerous short studies for the RAND Corporation. In addition, he was editor of *Analysis for Military Decisions* and, with W. I. Boucher, of *Systems Analysis and Policy Planning: Applications in Defense.*

OBITUARIES AND OTHER SOURCES:

BOOKS

American Men and Women of Science: The Physical and Biological Sciences, 13th edition, Bowker, 1976.

PERIODICALS

Washington Post, June 8, 1988.

*   *   *

QUINAN, Jack
See QUINAN, John F.

*   *   *

QUINAN, John F. 1939-
(Jack Quinan)

PERSONAL: Born November 28, 1939, in Somerville, Mass.; son of John F. and Dorothy (a writer; maiden name, Cheney) Quinan; divorced; children: John F., Jr. *Education:* Dartmouth College, B.A., 1962; received M.A., Brown University, Ph.D., 1973.

ADDRESSES: Office—Department of Art History, 611 Clemens Hall, North Campus, State University of New York at Buffalo, Buffalo, N.Y. 14206.

CAREER: State University of New York at Buffalo, associate professor of art history, 1979—.

WRITINGS:

(Under name Jack Quinan) *Frank Lloyd Wright's Larkin Building: The Myths and the Facts,* MIT Press, 1987.

Contributor to periodicals, including *Antiques* and *Journal of the Society of Architectural Historians.*

WORK IN PROGRESS: Frank Lloyd Wright and Darwin D. Martin: An Architect-Client Relationship.

SIDELIGHTS: John F. Quinan told *CA:* "I feel that architectural history has been too long oriented toward the building as object. It needs more emphasis upon context, especially socio-cultural considerations. This should make the discipline of interest to a wider audience."

*   *   *

RABI, I(sidor) I(saac) 1898-1988

OBITUARY NOTICE: Surname is pronounced "*Rah*-bee"; born July 29, 1898, in Rymanow, Austro-Hungarian Empire (now Poland); died after a long illness, January 11, 1988, in New York, N.Y. Physicist and author. Rabi received the Nobel Prize in physics in 1944 for his work on measuring the spin of subatomic particles. He spent most of his career teaching physics at Columbia University, beginning as a lecturer in 1929 and ultimately retiring as University Professor Emeritus in 1967. During World War II Rabi was granted leave to work as associate director of the radiation laboratory at the Massachusetts Institute of Technology, where he helped to perfect radar and advised developers of the atomic bomb. Disturbed, however, by the destruction potential of atomic weaponry, the scientist subsequently joined with fellow physicists Robert Oppenheimer and Enrico Fermi in efforts to limit the nuclear arms race. He became vice-president of the International Conference on the Peaceful Uses of Atomic Energy and of a similarly named United Nations body. Rabi was also a member of the general advisory committee of the Atomic Energy Commission from 1946 to 1956, chairing the group from 1952 to 1956, and a member of what became known as the President's Science Advisory Committee from 1952 to 1968. Rabi's writings include *My Life and Times as a Physicist, Man and Science,* and *Science: The Center of Culture.*

OBITUARIES AND OTHER SOURCES:

BOOKS

Current Biography, H. W. Wilson, 1948, March, 1988.
The International Who's Who, 51st edition, Europa, 1987.
Who's Who, 136th edition, St. Martin's, 1984.

PERIODICALS

New York Times, January 12, 1988.

*   *   *

RAELIN, Joseph A(lan) 1948-

PERSONAL: Born April 10, 1948, in Cambridge, Mass.; son
of Julius (a family physician) and Doris (Goodman) Raelin;
married Abby Dolin (a school psychologist), September 5,
1974; children: Jonathan, Jeremy. *Education:* University of
Paris, certificat, 1969; Tufts University, B.A. (magna cum
laude), 1970, Ed.M., 1971; Boston University, certificate of
advanced graduate study, 1974; State University of New York
at Buffalo, Ph.D., 1977.

ADDRESSES: Office—Department of Administrative Science,
Boston College, 140 Commonwealth Ave., Chestnut Hill, Mass.
02167.

CAREER: State University of New York at Buffalo, research
associate at Human Resource Institute, 1974-77; Boston College, Chestnut Hill, Mass., assistant professor, 1977-82, associate professor, 1982-87, professor of administrative sciences, 1987—. President of own consulting firm.

MEMBER: Academy of Management, Industrial Relations Research Association, New England Human Resource Planning
Society (past member of board of directors).

AWARDS, HONORS: Grants from Alfred P. Sloan Foundation, 1978-79, Charles F. Kettering Foundation, 1979, W. E.
Upjohn Institute for Employment Research, 1979-80, and National Science Foundation, 1980-82.

WRITINGS:

Building a Career, W. E. Upjohn Institute for Employment
   Research, 1980.
The Salaried Professional, Praeger, 1984.
The Clash of Cultures: Managers and Professionals, Harvard
   Business School Press, 1986.

Contributor of about forty articles to professional journals.

SIDELIGHTS: Joseph A. Raelin told *CA* that his writing and
research reflect his desire "to explore all avenues of managing
professionals in organizations," to consider the conflict between the professional's demand for autonomy and the manager's need for control, and to examine "the ethical consciousness of professionals, cohort effects (in the sixties
generation) on professional behavior, career concerns of
professionals, professionals and unions, and professionalism
in the international arena."

In his most recent book, *The Clash of Cultures,* the author
considers the conflict between traditional managers and America's increasing numbers of professionals. Raelin describes today's professionals as highly educated employees, who "don't
like being told what to do, who don't trust The Company, who
want more than the satisfactions of money and title and who,
deep down, though they haven't said so recently, want to contribute something to society," according to Robert Krulwich

in the *New York Times Book Review.* Raelin's strategies for
satisfying this new generation of professionals include provisions for lateral as well as upward mobility, management by
objectives, job security, the availability of creative, in-house
challenges, and adherence to ethical standards.

BIOGRAPHICAL/CRITICAL SOURCES:

BOOKS

Bennett, S. J. and M. H. Snell, *Executive Chess,* New American Library, 1987.

PERIODICALS

Globe and Mail (Toronto), July 4, 1987.
New York Times Book Review, December 14, 1986.

*   *   *

RALEIGH, Donald J(oseph) 1949-

PERSONAL: Born November 17, 1949, in Chicago, Ill.; son
of William L. and Lorraine (Plaziak) Raleigh; married Karen
Sanders (a banker), December 31, 1971; children: Adam Sanders. *Education:* Knox College, B.A., 1971; Indiana University—Bloomington, M.A., 1972, Ph.D., 1978.

ADDRESSES: Home—60 North Beretania, Apt. 3102, Honolulu, Hawaii 96817. *Office*—Department of History, University of Hawaii at Manoa, Honolulu, Hawaii 96822.

CAREER: American Historical Review, Bloomington, Ind.,
editorial assistant, 1976-77; Council for the International Exchange of Scholars, Washington, D.C., Fulbright program officer, 1977-78; University of Hawaii at Manoa, Honolulu, assistant professor, 1979-85, associate professor of history,
1985—.

MEMBER: American Historical Association, American Association for the Advancement of Slavic Studies, Western Slavic
Association, Study Group on the Russian Revolution.

WRITINGS:

Revolution on the Volga: 1917 in Saratov, Cornell University
   Press, 1986.
*Russia's Second Revolution: The February 1917 Uprising in
   Petrograd,* Indiana University Press, 1987.
*A Russian Civil War Diary: Alexis V. Babine in Saratov, 1917-
   1922,* Duke University Press, 1988.

Contributor to history and Slavic studies journals. Editor of
Soviet Studies in History, 1979—.

SIDELIGHTS: With *Revolution on the Volga,* asserted reviewer Tsuyoshi Hasegawa in *American Historical Review,*
"[Donald J.] Raleigh has written a major work that should be
considered one of the classics on the Russian Revolution."
Most previous studies of the revolution concentrated on major
urban areas, such as Petrograd, but Raleigh chose to consider
the provincial Volga River town of Saratov. In 1917 Saratov
was a market town, a significant agricultural administrative
center, and a site of military stations. Crowded with refugees
from war and tormented by the same shortages that crippled
the rest of the country, Saratov provided a ripe atmosphere for
political revolution. "Raleigh clearly demonstrates," averred
Hasegawa, "that the revolutionary process in Saratov was not
a mere echo of the events in Petrograd but rather a violent
revolutionary process of its own, which . . . followed the logic
of local conditions." Praising the author's research, critic John
Keep wrote in the *Times Literary Supplement,* "Raleigh's ex-

emplarily thorough study of . . . published material—he was denied access to Soviet archives—does cast fresh light on the Russian Revolution from an unfamiliar angle, and is welcome for that reason.'' Hasegawa agreed, adding that ''Raleigh's work should thus encourage specialists outside the Soviet Union.''

BIOGRAPHICAL/CRITICAL SOURCES:

PERIODICALS

American Historical Review, February, 1987.
Times Literary Supplement, September 12, 1986.

* * *

RAMENOFSKY, Ann F. 1942-

PERSONAL: Born October 21, 1942, in Wichita Falls, Tex.; daughter of Abraham I. (a physician) and Elizabeth (a housewife; maiden name, Lantin) Ramenofsky; married Thomas M. Wood (a teacher), December 21, 1978; children: Benjamin, Katherine. *Education:* Attended University of California, Berkeley, 1960-63; Arizona State University, B.A. (cum laude), 1965, M.A., 1968; University of Washington, Seattle, Ph.D., 1982.

ADDRESSES: Home—865 Magnolia Wood, Baton Rouge, La. 70808. *Office*—Department of Geography and Anthropology, 216 Geology Annex, Louisiana State University, Baton Rouge, La. 70803.

CAREER: U.S. National Park Service, Washington, D.C., park ranger and archaeologist at Bandelier National Monument, 1965-66; Merritt Community College, Oakland, Calif., instructor in anthropology, 1968-69; Laney Community College, Oakland, instructor in anthropology, 1969-75; University of Washington, Seattle, instructor in archaeology, 1980 and 1982; Louisiana State University, Baton Rouge, assistant professor of archaeology, 1983—.

MEMBER: American Anthropological Association, Society for American Archaeology, American Association for the Advancement of Science, American Society of Ethnohistory, Southeastern Archaeological Conference, Eastern States Archaeological Federation, Louisiana Archaeological Society, Missouri Archaeology Society, Paleopathology Association, Archaeological Conservancy, Sigma Xi.

WRITINGS:

Vectors of Death: The Archaeology of European Contact, University of New Mexico Press, 1987.

Contributor to *Environmental Science and Technology,* 1988, and *Studies in Archaeological Method and Theory,* edited by M. B. Schiffer.

WORK IN PROGRESS: One chapter on the sixteenth-century Zuni contact record, and another, co-authored by E. Richard Hart, on Zuni population trends from the eighteenth through twentieth centuries, to be included in *Zuni Through Time,* edited by Roger Leonard and Roger Anyon, publication expected in 1990.

SIDELIGHTS: Ann F. Ramenofsky told *CA:* ''My interest in Native Americans stems, I think, from my childhood years in Arizona. I was surrounded by Native Americans and their antiquities. As I grew older, I became fascinated with the question of contact and its frequently disastrous consequences to native peoples. Archaeology seemed to be the best way to

explore this problem. There is a very important story to be told here, and I hope I have opened up new avenues of research for that task.

''I am currently working on several projects. My interest in European contact is now directed toward a long-term archaeological field study of the contact period in Louisiana. I am also trying to mount a conference (in light of the Columbian Quincentenary) that would bring archaeologists, ethnologists, historians, and epidemiologists together to discuss the sixteenth and seventeenth centuries in the Americas. If successful, there will be an edited volume on this important topic.

''More recently I have become interested in archaeological chemistry, diffusion or transportation of elements in soil, and the diagenesis of buried bone. This research has a practical application. Because time is incorporated in the archaeological record, we can calculate the rate of movement of certain metal species. Engineers can use this information to estimate movement of similar metal species in landfills and other hazardous waste dump sites.''

AVOCATIONAL INTERESTS: Hiking, backpacking, cooking, ''and—not so avocational—being a mother of two small children.''

* * *

RAMEY, Mary Ann 1947-

PERSONAL: Born June 7, 1947, in Evanston, Ill.; daughter of Sherman Thomas and Anne (Zebroski) Ramey. *Education:* University of Pittsburgh, B.A. (summa cum laude), 1967, M.L.S., 1976; Columbia University, M.A. (with high honors), 1970; law student at Georgia State University, 1984—.

ADDRESSES: Home—1706 McLendon Ave. N.E., Apt. 4, Atlanta, Ga. 30307. *Office*—Reference Department, Pullen Library, Georgia State University, Atlanta, Ga. 30303.

CAREER: West Virginia University, Morgantown, reference librarian, 1976-78; National Clearinghouse for Alcohol Information, Rockville, Md., library manager, 1978-79; Georgia State University, Atlanta, reference librarian at Pullen Library and assistant professor, 1980—. Presents workshops.

MEMBER: American Library Association, American Bar Association, Georgia Library Association, Atlanta Area Bibliographic Instruction Group (president, 1984-85), Metropolitan Atlanta Library Association, Beta Phi Mu, Outer Barristers Guild, Phi Beta Kappa.

AWARDS, HONORS: Fulbright fellow at University of York, 1967-68; American Jurisprudence Award in criminal law.

WRITINGS:

Library Skills Reference Book, Contemporary Publishing, 1986.
(Editor with Mary Reichel) *Conceptual Frameworks for Bibliographic Education: Theory Into Practice,* Libraries Unlimited, 1987.

Contributor to *Research Strategies.* Notes and comments editor of *Georgia State University Law Review,* 1987-88.

WORK IN PROGRESS: Research on legal liability of librarians and other information providers; linear thinking in library instruction.

SIDELIGHTS: Mary Ann Ramey told *CA:* ''I have been happy to spend part of my career with librarians and their professional theories. Both the philosophy and people who have a place in real librarianship have a unique, nonjudgmental respect for the ideas and needs of those served by libraries. I have tried to reflect this respect in my writing on library instruction."

* * *

RAMSDELL, Kristin (Romeis) 1940-

PERSONAL: Born June 3, 1940, in Fresno, Calif.; daughter of Robert S. and L. Haldene (Oller) Romeis; married Jerald R. Ramsdell, August 21, 1965; children: Jennifer Haldene, Jacob Brooks, Jonathan Richard. *Education:* Carthage College, B.A., 1962; California State University, Sacramento, M.A., 1969; University of California, Los Angeles, M.L.S., 1983.

ADDRESSES: Home—16611 Rolando Ave., San Leandro, Calif. 94578. *Office*—University Library, Reference Department, California State University, Hayward, Calif. 94542.

CAREER: Teacher of various subjects at high school in Los Angeles, Calif., 1978-83; Los Angeles County Public Library, Claremont Public Library, Claremont, Calif., librarian, 1983-84; Stanford University, Stanford, Calif., undergraduate reference librarian at Meyer Library, 1984-87; California State University, Hayward, reference and bibliographic instruction librarian, 1987—.

MEMBER: American Library Association, American College and Research Librarians, Library Instruction Round Table, California Library Association, California Clearinghouse on Library Instruction, California Academic and Research Librarians.

WRITINGS:

Happily Ever After: A Guide to Reading Interests in Romance Fiction, Libraries Unlimited, 1987.

Author of educational materials for Parish Life Press, 1975—. Contributor of articles and reviews to library journals.

SIDELIGHTS: Kristin Ramsdell told *CA:* "My interest in popular fiction and reading is of long standing. As an avid and omnivorous reader from childhood, a teacher of English (among other things), and a librarian, I have enjoyed not only reading and recommending all types of fiction but also studying why people enjoy reading what they do and how this relates to contemporary social and cultural conditions. Romance fiction intrigues me in particular because, although it is and has been throughout much of our literary history a genre that is extremely popular with the reading public, it has been all but ignored in the current reference, research, and scholarly literature. This, incidentally, is in sharp contrast to some of the other genres, in particular, mystery/thriller and science fiction.

"*Happily Ever After: A Guide to Reading Interests in Romance Fiction* is a product of this interest and was written primarily to provide librarians involved in readers' advisory service with a basic background in romance fiction. *Happily Ever After* functions as a guide to the literature, providing definitions, histories, readers' advisory suggestions, research sources, and selected bibliographies for a variety of romance fiction subgenres, including historical, contemporary, romantic mystery, young adult, inspirational, gay, and the saga.

"My other literary interests include a love of children's literature and a fascination with the science fiction and fantasy genres. My professional library interests focus on bibliographic instruction and a commitment to teaching people effective and creative ways of doing library research."

RAMSEY, (Arthur) Michael 1904-1988

OBITUARY NOTICE—See index for *CA* sketch: Born November 14, 1904, in Cambridge, England; died April 23, 1988, in Oxford, England. Clergyman, educator, and author. Ramsey was a leading figure in the Church of England, serving as archbishop of Canterbury from 1961 to 1974. He was ordained to the priesthood in 1929 and thereafter filled many church posts. He also held titled academic posts, including Van Mildert Professor of Divinity at the University of Durham throughout the 1940s. Ramsey's writings include *The Gospel and the Catholic Church, The Resurrection of Christ, Introducing the Christian Faith, Beyond Religion?, Sacred and Secular: A Study in the Other Worldly and This Worldly Aspects of Christianity,* and *Jesus and the Living Past.*

OBITUARIES AND OTHER SOURCES:

BOOKS

Current Biography, H. W. Wilson, 1960, June, 1988.
The Writers Directory: 1988-1990, St. James Press, 1988.

* * *

RANDOLPH, A(sa) Philip 1889-1979

PERSONAL: Born April 15, 1889, in Crescent City (one source says Jacksonville), Fla.; died May 16, 1979, in New York, N.Y.; son of James William (a minister) and Elizabeth (Robinson) Randolph; married wife, Lucille E. (a beauty parlor operator), 1914 (one source says 1915). *Education:* Attended College of the City of New York (now City College of the City University of New York). *Politics:* Socialist. *Religion:* Methodist.

ADDRESSES: Home—230 West 150th Street, New York, N.Y. *Office*—Brotherhood of Sleeping Car Porters, 217 West 125th Street, New York, N.Y.

CAREER: The Messenger, New York, N.Y., editor, 1917-25; instructor at Rand School of Social Science, c. 1920; founder and president of International Brotherhood of Sleeping Car Porters, 1925-68, and Negro American Labor Council; president of National Negro Congress; founder of League for Nonviolent Civil Disobedience Against Military Segregation, 1947; vice-president of the American Federation of Labor-Congress of Industrial Organizations (AFL-CIO). Member of New York Mayor Fiorello La Guardia's Commission on Race, 1935, and of New York Housing Authority, 1942.

MEMBER: Elks, Masons.

AWARDS, HONORS: LL.D. from Howard University, 1941; Spingarn Medal from the National Association for the Advancement of Colored People, 1942, for leadership in labor; David L. Clendenin award from Workers' Defense League, 1944, for distinguished service to labor's rights; named honorary vice-chairman of Liberal party, 1946; Presidential Medal of Freedom, 1964.

WRITINGS:

The Negro Freedom Movement, Lincoln University, American Studies Institute, 1968.

Contributor to periodicals, including *Opportunity* and *Survey Graphic.*

SIDELIGHTS: "With a rich baritone voice that seemed destined to command, an imperturbability under fire, a refusal to bend with the times or the fashions, A. Philip Randolph overcame opposition simply by being himself," began a *Time* magazine tribute to one of the most successful black American labor organizers and civil rights activists. Courteous yet determined, Randolph attacked social and economic injustices in government and industry for more than six decades. He organized the first all-black union that was chartered by the American Federation of Labor (AFL); he campaigned for the desegregation of the defense industry, the military, and the civil service; and he was an early and highly visible leader of the civil rights movement of the 1960s. "[Randolph] confronted the establishment [and was] prepared to shake it to its foundations," asserted Nathan Irvin Huggins in the *New York Times Book Review,* "but always with the aplomb and dignity of a gentleman."

"What was your class at Harvard, Phil?" President Franklin D. Roosevelt jokingly asked Randolph, remarking on the union leader's eloquence and graceful manner. In fact, Randolph had dreamed of becoming a Shakespearean actor but his plan was vetoed by his more realistic parents. Instead he took night classes in economics and political science at the College of the City of New York after traveling north from his home in Florida. Through his studies he learned German philosopher Karl Marx's theory that forms of economic inequality are based on race, and from his father, a Jacksonville minister, he learned of the power of united blacks. Once when a Negro accused of a crime was taken to a county jail, Randolph's father called the men of his parish together to stand guard outside the prison to protect the man from a group of angry whites. Through seeing the organized parishioners save a man from lynching and his readings on racial injustice, Randolph realized that economic and political wrongs could be remedied by cooperation among laborers and unity within racial groups. "From the beginning," stated Huggins, "[Randolph] insisted that blacks would get only what they could take and keep only what they could hold. And the power to take and to keep awaited blacks' willingness to organize themselves with purpose and discipline, for group-interest over self-interest, toward the radical transformation of the American economic system."

In 1917 Randolph and Chandler Owen established *The Messenger: The Only Radical Negro Magazine in America,* a black-oriented monthly. In his editorials he urged black men not to fight in the armed forces during World War I because they would be defending a country that denied them civil rights. In response to Randolph's call, the U.S. Justice Department named *The Messenger* one of the most subversive publications in the nation and Randolph "the most dangerous Negro in America." Previously Randolph had been arrested in Cleveland, Ohio, because of his open opposition to blacks participating in World War I, but he was released after spending two days in the city jail. "He contended," explained writer and poet Langston Hughes in *Famous American Negroes,* "that he was simply agitating for fulfillment of Constitutional guarantees for *all* citizens and protection of law for everybody," not just for black equity.

Randolph stressed that workers, regardless of race, could advance economically and socially through unionizing. He helped organize motion picture operators and garment trade workers, and founded a union of elevator operators. Then in 1925 five members of the fledgling Brotherhood of Sleeping Car Porters (BSCP) asked Randolph to help them organize. Notoriously overworked and underpaid, "the porter has always been poor and menial," observed Murray Kempton in a *New Republic* article. "Segregation created his job; the Pullman Company hired Negroes as porters because Negroes were inexpensive." Although he was not a porter, Randolph was elected president of the union, whose members were earning only $67.50 for three hundred to four hundred hours of work a month. At first membership in the union grew slowly because Pullman Palace Car Company strongly opposed the Brotherhood and fired workers who were active in the union. Nonetheless, by 1928 more than one-half of the railroad maids and porters were members of the BSCP and ready to strike if the railroad company refused to consider their demands for higher pay and shorter working hours. The workers' boycott was canceled due to lack of support from other railroad unions, but the struggle between Pullman and the Brotherhood, which also received little support from the Negro religious community and newspapers, raged for ten years.

Finally in 1934 the amended Railway Labor Act created a national mediation board, composed of railroad management and union representatives, to hear grievances. The membership of the porter's union increased. Three years later Pullman signed a contract with the BSCP giving the employees two million dollars in pay increases and guaranteeing them shorter hours and pay for overtime. By September, 1950, due to union pressure, the eighteen thousand members of the BSCP worked a monthly average of 205 hours for which they were paid a minimum of nearly $240. Randolph used the Brotherhood as an example of what could be attained through cooperation among laborers, and as a stronghold against discrimination within the workers' movement. Yet Huggins maintained that "the Union's ultimate victory was to make Randolph one of the most respected and influential black men since Booker T. Washington."

Randolph emphasized that blacks must organize their own groups, choose their own leaders, and raise their own funds, because only with financial independence could an organization control its direction. With the BSCP he made money by sponsoring picnics, parties, and sporting events rather than accepting the financial patronage of well-intentioned white unions. In 1929, when the BSCP joined the American Federation of Labor (AFL), it was the first all-black union to receive an international charter by that organization. Randolph's critics claimed he compromised the position of the Brotherhood by joining the white-run AFL, but he countered by saying that united laborers would have more bargaining power with industries than an isolated union would. When the AFL merged with the Congress of Industrial Organizations (CIO) in 1955, Randolph was named its first vice-president and he undertook a campaign against prejudice in the unions. Demanding that all chapters—black and white—be desegregated, he insisted that blacks had no more right than whites to exclude a prospective member because of race. George Meany and Lane Kirkland, the former president and former secretary-treasurer of the AFL-CIO, commended Randolph for his even-handedness in the desegregation of the organization. They were quoted in the *New York Times:* "Even in the darkest days, Phil never lost sight of the goals, the needs, the aspirations of workers—both white and black, male and female."

Believing that organized labor was in a position to make economic demands on businesses that held government contracts, Randolph entered the political arena. With the approach of World War II Randolph took the opportunity to fight discrimination in the industries producing armaments. Defense companies were not hiring blacks to work in the factories, and after Randolph met with a number of government leaders to no avail, he threatened to lead 50,000 Negroes to Washington, D.C., in protest against the injustice. President Franklin D. Roosevelt called Randolph to the White House immediately. After a standoff with the union leader, the president signed Executive Order 8802 on June 25, 1941, which established the Fair Employment Practices Committee, banning discrimination in the government and defense industries.

As tensions increased between the United States and the Soviet Union in the late 1940s, President Harry S. Truman called for the first peace-time draft in American history. Randolph, again by threatening a massive protest and Negroes' resistence to military service, pressured Truman into desegregating the armed forces. Huggins related that Randolph told Truman on March 22, 1948: "The mood among Negroes of this country is that they will never bear arms again until all forms of bias and discrimination are abolished." Truman uttered in response, "I wish you hadn't said that, Mr. Randolph. I didn't like it at all." The following month Randolph testified before the Senate Armed Services Committee, maintaining, "Negroes have reached the limit of their endurance when it comes to going into another Jim Crow Army to fight another war for democracy—a democracy they have never gotten." As with Roosevelt, Randolph pressured Truman into issuing an executive order, this one officially banning racial segregation in the armed services.

Randolph finally did march on Washington in August, 1963. Originally he announced that he would call 100,000 Negroes to the capital in October, 1963, to demonstrate against unemployment, but in the late spring of that year President John F. Kennedy introduced his civil rights bill in Congress. Randolph rescheduled the protest for August so that it would include demonstrating for personal liberties. "There was suddenly the surprising prospect that Congress would debate these bills with thousands of Negroes standing outside," recounted Kempton.

Today Randolph's "March on Washington for Jobs and Freedom in 1963" is better remembered as the massive civil rights demonstration where Martin Luther King, Jr., gave his famous "I Have a Dream" speech before more than 200,000 people. Randolph's star has been eclipsed by more famous leaders of the civil rights movement, especially King. "It's so sad because there are so many young people today for whom that name means very little," observed Benjamin L. Hooks, former director of the National Association for the Advancement of Colored People in the *New York Times,* upon hearing of Randolph's death in 1979. "And yet, for more than forty years, he was a tower and beacon of strength and hope for the entire black community." Kempton concurred, commenting on Randolph's program of passive resistance: "He is a pacifist in a native American tradition; before most members of King's non-violent army were born, he was reminding the Negro of Thoreau's prescription to cast the total vote with feet and voice along with the ballot."

Even Malcolm X, a leader of the Lost-Found Nation of Islam, the Black Muslims, respected Randolph's accomplishments. Randolph invited the advocate of black separatism from white Western society to join a committee that the union leader was organizing on Harlem's financial problems. Kempton related that when Randolph met with Malcolm X he explained his disagreement with the militant's separatist viewpoint, claiming that blacks and whites had to work together for socioeconomic harmony. He commended the Black Muslims, however, for their fight against drugs and liquor, calling it "the greatest

contribution any of us have ever made." Later Malcolm X stated that although all leaders of black communities are muddled, Randolph is the least confused. In the spring of 1963 the Black Muslims put a picture of the pacifist Randolph on the cover of their weekly journal, *Muhammad Speaks.*

A. H. Raskin in *New Leader* also paid tribute to the union organizer and activist, maintaining that "Randolph's triumph paralleled that of Mahatma M. K. Gandhi in India, and it stemmed from the same ability to prevail by dint of an unshakeable combination of gentleness and conviction over the entrenched forces of obstructionism." Randolph's strength came from his belief in the inevitability of a reformed society, where all laborers enjoyed equal rights. He often stressed that "we never separated the liberation of the white workingman from the liberation of the black workingman," related a reporter for *Time.* Nonetheless, when Randolph died on the eve of the twenty-fifth anniversary of the Supreme Court's historic decision outlawing segregation in public schools, Americans remembered his role as an agitator for civil rights as well as for his labor organizing. "As an elder statesman, he was a guiding light for a new generation of civil-rights advocates," Dennis A. Williams of *Newsweek* commented. Former U.S. President Jimmy Carter, quoted in the *New York Times,* spoke of Randolph: "His dignity and integrity, his eloquence, his devotion to nonviolence and his unshakeable commitment to justice all helped shape the ideals and spirit of the civil rights movement."

AVOCATIONAL INTERESTS: Reading (especially William Shakespeare and George Bernard Shaw), baseball, basketball, football, tennis.

BIOGRAPHICAL/CRITICAL SOURCES:

BOOKS

Adams, Russell L., *Great Negroes, Past and Present,* Afro-American Publishing, 1963.
Anderson, Jervis, *A. Philip Randolph: A Biographical Portrait,* Harcourt, 1973.
Bontemps, Arna Wendell, *One Hundred Years of Negro Freedom,* Dodd, 1961.
Cook, Roy, *Leaders of Labor,* Lippincott, 1966.
Davis, Daniel S., *Mr. Black Labor: The Story of A. Philip Randolph, Father of the Civil Rights Movement,* Dutton, 1972.
Flynn, James J., *Negroes of Achievement in Modern America,* Dodd, 1970.
Hughes, Langston, *Famous American Negroes,* Dodd, 1954.
Quarles, Benjamin, *Black Leaders of the Twentieth Century,* University of Illinois Press, 1982.
Redding, Jay Saunders, *The Lonesome Road: The Story of the Negro's Part in America,* Doubleday, 1958.
Richardson, Ben, *Great American Negroes,* Crowell, 1945, 2nd revised edition, with W. A. Fahey, published as *Great Black Americans,* Crowell, 1976.

PERIODICALS

Crisis, August/September, 1979.
Dissent, fall, 1979.
Ebony, May, 1969.
Journal of Negro History, fall, 1979.
Negro History Bulletin, December, 1964, December, 1971.
New Leader, June 4, 1979.
New Republic, July 6, 1963.
Newsweek, September 30, 1940, June 7, 1948, May 28, 1979.

New Yorker, December 2, 1972, December 9, 1972, December 16, 1972.
New York Times, April 29, 1940, September 15, 1940.
New York Times Book Review, May 27, 1973.
Time, September 20, 1937, May 28, 1979.

OBITUARIES:

PERIODICALS

New York Times, May 18, 1979.
Washington Post, May 18, 1979.*

—*Sketch by Carol Lynn DeKane*

*　　*　　*

RATCLIFFE, F(rederick) W(illiam)   1927-

PERSONAL: Born May 28, 1927; son of Sydney and Dora (Smith) Ratcliffe; married Joyce Brierley (a college lecturer), August 20, 1952; children: Richard George, Helen Laura Ratcliffe Wareham, Robert John. *Education:* Victoria University of Manchester, B.A. (with honors), 1951, M.A., 1952; Ph.D., 1954; Cambridge University, M.A., 1980. *Religion:* Church of England.

ADDRESSES: Home—Light Alders Farm, Light Alders Lane, Disley, Cheshire SK12 2LW, England. *Office*—Library, Cambridge University, West Rd., Cambridge CB3 9DR, England.

CAREER: Victoria University of Manchester, Manchester, England, began as assistant cataloger at university library, became cataloger, 1954-62; University of Glasgow, Glasgow, Scotland, sub-librarian, 1962-63; University of Newcastle upon Tyne, Newcastle upon Tyne, England, deputy librarian, 1963-65; Victoria University of Manchester, university librarian, 1965-80, director of John Rylands University Library, 1972-80, honorary lecturer in historical bibliography, 1970-80; Cambridge University, Cambridge, England, university librarian and fellow of Corpus Christi College, 1980—. Visiting professor at Loughborough University of Technology, 1981—. Chairman of advisory committee of National Preservation Office of British Library; trustee of St. Deiniol's Library, Hawarden, England, 1975—. Justice of the peace of Stockport, 1972-80, and Cambridge, 1981. *Military service:* British Army, North Staffordshire Regiment, 1945-48.

MEMBER: Bibliographical Society, Royal Society for the Encouragement of the Arts.

WRITINGS:

The Psalm Translation of Heinrich von Muegeln, John Rylands University Library, Victoria University of Manchester, 1961.
(With D. Patterson) *Preservation Policies and Conservation in British Libraries: Report of the Cambridge University Library Conservation Project*, British Library, 1984.

Contributor to library, German, and literary journals.

WORK IN PROGRESS: Editing the psalm translations of Heinrich von Muegeln; *University Library Management and Organisation.*

BIOGRAPHICAL/CRITICAL SOURCES:

PERIODICALS

Times Literary Supplement, October 5, 1984.

RATCLIFFE, James P.
See MENCKEN, H(enry) L(ouis)

*　　*　　*

RAZ, Joseph   1939-

PERSONAL: Surname originally Zaltsman; legally changed, 1963; born March 21, 1939, in Haifa, Palestine (now Israel); son of Shmuel (an electrician) and Sonya (a nurse; maiden name, Alterkovsky) Zaltsman; married Yael Rappeport, September 20, 1963 (divorced, 1981); children: Noam. *Education:* Hebrew University of Jerusalem, M.J., 1963; Oxford University, D.Phil., 1967.

ADDRESSES: Office—Balliol College, Oxford University, Oxford OX1 3BJ, England.

CAREER: Hebrew University of Jerusalem, Jerusalem, Israel, lecturer in law and philosophy, 1967-70; Oxford University, Oxford, England, research fellow at Nuffield College, 1970-72, tutorial fellow at Balliol College, 1972-85, professor of philosophy of law, 1985—. *Military service:* Israel Army, 1957-59; became sergeant.

MEMBER: British Academy (fellow).

AWARDS, HONORS: W. J. M. Mackenzie book prize from England's Political Science Association, and Elaine and David Spitz prize for best book in democratic or liberal theory from the Conference for the Study of Political Thought, both 1986, both for *The Morality of Freedom.*

WRITINGS:

The Concept of a Legal System, Oxford University Press, 1970, 2nd edition, 1980.
Practical Reason and Norms, Hutchinson, 1975.
(Editor with P. M. H. Hacker) *Law, Morality, and Society: Essays in Honour of H. L. A. Hart*, Oxford University Press, 1977.
(Editor) *Practical Reasoning*, Oxford University Press, 1978.
The Authority of Law, Oxford University Press, 1979.
The Morality of Freedom, Oxford University Press, 1986.

Co-editor of "Clarendon Law Series," Oxford University Press. Member of editorial board of *Law and Philosophy* and *Ratio Juris.*

BIOGRAPHICAL/CRITICAL SOURCES:

PERIODICALS

Times Literary Supplement, June 5, 1987.

*　　*　　*

REAMER, Judy   1940-

PERSONAL: Born August 7, 1940, in Baltimore, Md.; daughter of Oscar (a lawyer and judge) and Rena (Frieman) Zenitz; married Bernard Reamer (an investor), April 5, 1962; children: Mark, Johnny, Jeff, Jill. *Education:* University of Maryland at College Park, B.A., 1962.

ADDRESSES: Home—6405 Lake Charlene Dr., Pensacola, Fla. 32506.

CAREER: Art teacher at public schools in Baltimore, Md.; writer and public speaker.

WRITINGS:

(With Donna Arthur) *Feelings Women Rarely Share,* Whitaker House, 1987.

SIDELIGHTS: Judy Reamer told *CA:* "My book, *Feelings Women Rarely Share,* boldly confronts an issue that is often avoided by Christians: sexual temptation."

* * *

REED, John 1909-

PERSONAL: Born May 30, 1909, in Aldershot, England; son of Joseph William and Annie Elizabeth Reed; married Edith Marion Hampton, October 30, 1936; children: two sons, two daughters. *Education:* University of London, B.A. (with honors), 1935.

ADDRESSES: Home—130 Fog Lane, Didsbury, Manchester M20 0SW, England.

CAREER: Schoolmaster, 1935-46; British Broadcasting Corp., London and Manchester, England, affiliated with educational and administrative services, 1946-68; writer, 1968—. Director of Manchester Camerata.

MEMBER: Royal Musical Association, Victorian Society, Halle Society.

AWARDS, HONORS: Vincent H. Duckles Award from American Music Library Association, 1985, for *The Schubert Song Companion.*

WRITINGS:

Schubert: The Final Years, Faber, 1972.
The Schubert Song Companion, Manchester University Press, 1985.
Schubert, Dent, 1987.

Contributor to music journals.

SIDELIGHTS: John Reed's second book, *The Schubert Song Companion,* is a detailed study of some six hundred songs composed by Franz Peter Schubert during his short life. The text of each song is present in English translation by Norma Deane and Celia Larner and is accompanied by the author's critical analysis. Reed also included brief commentaries on each of Schubert's more than one hundred poems. Paul Hamburger wrote in the *Times Literary Supplement* that "the author wears his impressive scholarship so lightly, and condenses his lengthy research into such plain-sounding statements that, whether interested or not, the reader is won over." He commented: "This is a most welcome book for the scholar, singer and music-lover."

Schubert is a critical biography of the prolific composer, who died in 1828 at the age of thirty-one. Reed covered not only Schubert's life, but also his circle of friends, the society in which he functioned, and the composer's philosophical framework. To Eric Sams, a *Times Literary Supplement* reviewer, Reed's book is one of the most valuable studies of Schubert that has been published in the last forty years. Sams wrote: "The authentic flavour of a whole epoch is conveyed by lively extracts judiciously selected from tedious documents, and illuminating excerpts from unfamiliar works." The critic concluded by saying that the biography of the composer, "an essential vade-mecum for all Schubertians, is sure of a second edition."

BIOGRAPHICAL/CRITICAL SOURCES:

PERIODICALS

Saturday Review, January 30, 1973.
Times Literary Supplement, October 27, 1972, September 6, 1985, July 17, 1987.

* * *

REICHEL, Mary 1946-

PERSONAL: Born July 14, 1946, in Kansas City, Mo.; daughter of George Paul, Jr., and Dorothy (Lahl) Reichel; married Rao Aluri; children: Krishna Paul. *Education:* Grinnell College, B.A., 1968; University of Wales, University College of Wales, Aberystwyth, M.Sc.Econ., 1972; University of Denver, M.A., 1972; doctoral study at Georgia State University, 1983—.

ADDRESSES: Home—1520 South Avenida Los Reyes, Tucson, Ariz. 85748. *Office*—Main Library, University of Arizona, Tucson, Ariz. 85721.

CAREER: University of Nebraska at Omaha, educational specialist and social science reference librarian, 1974-76; State University of New York at Buffalo, Amherst, senior reference librarian, 1976-80; Georgia State University, Atlanta, head of reference department, 1980-86; University of Arizona, Tucson, assistant university librarian for central services, 1986—.

MEMBER: American Library Association, Association of College and Research Libraries (Bibliographic Instruction Section, member of executive committee, 1980-82, chairperson, 1985-86), Georgia Library Association.

WRITINGS:

(Contributor) Carolyn A. Kirkendall, editor, *Bibliographic Instruction and the Learning Process: Theory, Style, and Motivation,* Pierian, 1984.
(Contributor) Alice S. Clark and Kay F. Jones, editors, *Teaching Librarians to Teach,* Scarecrow, 1986.
(Editor with Mary Ann Ramey) *Conceptual Frameworks for Bibliographic Education: Theory Into Practice,* Libraries Unlimited, 1987.

Contributor to library journals.

WORK IN PROGRESS: Work on reference service evaluation.

SIDELIGHTS: Mary Reichel told *CA:* "Bibliographic education is the discipline of teaching students about finding and critically evaluating information. A comment often heard from professional librarians is that they wished they had known about library resources and the research process when they pursued their own undergraduate degrees. To remedy this situation, librarians are concentrating on teaching students how to find the previously published literature on their subjects, as well as trying to instill in students an independence of thinking and of love of learning.

"My own work has focused on teaching the most important concepts from library and information science to students in a manner that is relevant to the rest of their academic work. By focusing on principles—not details—I hope that the students are motivated and stimulated.

"*Conceptual Frameworks for Bibliographic Education* resulted from a desire to share the exciting conceptual approaches that many different librarians are using to teach the information search process. Mary Ann Ramey and I hope the chapters in this book will lead to even more sophisticated and challenging approaches. It was exciting to edit the book because we were involved in identifying and promoting some of the best work in our field.

"In my present position at the University of Arizona, I am one of the assistant directors of a major research library with a collection of more than five million items and a staff of 250 serving an academic community of 35,000 faculty, staff, and students. My work is administrative—dealing with personnel and budgetary issues, policies, procedures, and effective communication. But like any library administrator, I may lose the ability to focus on the intellectual life that brought me to libraries and higher education in the first place. Writing and research brings me back to the core of what academic libraries are all about."

*   *   *

REID, Daniel P. (Jr.)   1948-
(Lee Daniel)

PERSONAL: Born December 2, 1948, in San Francisco, Calif.; son of Daniel P. (an airline executive) and Heidi M. (Blume) Reid. *Education:* Attended Occidental College, 1966, and Columbia University, 1967; University of California, Berkeley, B.A., 1970; Monterey Institute of International Studies, M.A. (with high honors), 1973. *Politics:* "Absolutely none."*Religion:* Buddhist/Taoist.

ADDRESSES: Home—Taipei, Taiwan. *Office*—Center for Traditional Chinese Studies, P.O. Box 1-145, Taipei, Taiwan. *Agent*—Robert I. Ducas, 9 West 29th St., New York, N.Y. 10001.

CAREER: Hilton International Hotels, Taipei, Taiwan, assistant manager, 1973-74; American Club in China, Taipei, food and beverage manager, 1974-76; free-lance writer, 1978—. Member of Price-Pottenger Nutrition Foundation and Center for Traditional Chinese Studies; consultant to Taiwan's Tourism Bureau.

WRITINGS:

Complete Guide to China, CFW Publications, 1982.
Complete Chinese Cookbook, Lansdowne, 1982.
Insight Guide Taiwan, APA Productions, 1983.
Images of Taiwan, Hong Kong Publishing, 1984.
(Under pseudonym Lee Daniel) *Dragon Mountain* (novel), [New York, N.Y.], 1984.
Chinese Herbal Medicine, Shambhala, 1987.
Perspectives on Taiwan, Hilit Publishing, 1987.
Reflections of Taiwan, R. Ian Lloyd Productions, 1987.
Korea Guide, Asia Guide Series, 1987.
The Tao of Health, Sex, and Longevity, Simon & Schuster, 1988.

Contributor to magazines and newspapers, including *Discovery, Horizon, Winds,* and *Sawasdee.*

WORK IN PROGRESS: In the Footsteps of the Buddha, publication expected in 1989; "Tau: The Harmony of Heaven, Earth, and Humanity," a series of six titles "on various practical aspects of Tau, such as meditation, exercise, geomancy, and spiritual matters," publication expected in 1989.

SIDELIGHTS: Daniel P. Reid told *CA:* "I was born in 1948 in San Francisco, and at the age of four I moved with my family to Addis Ababa, Ethiopia, where I lived for nine years. I graduated from the University of California at Berkeley with

a bachelor of arts degree in East Asian studies. Then I completed a master of arts degree at the Monterey Institute of International Studies, for which I wrote a thesis in Chinese on the tenth-century lyrical poet Lee Yu.

"Since 1973 I have been living in Peitou, Taiwan, where I have worked in the hotel, restaurant, and club business. In 1978 I commenced a career as a free-lance writer, specializing in traditional Chinese culture and contemporary Asian travel.

"I regard health to be the most vital subject for writing in this day and age. Without basic physical health, all else is in vain. Traditional Chinese Taoism is my greatest inspiration as a total way of life, while Buddhism provides the most insightful and scientific teachings about the human mind, spirit, and afterlife. Among my favorite writers on subjects dear to my heart is John Blofeld, whom I met and got to know in Bangkok only two months before his death in June, 1987. Travel is another major influence on my writing and philosophy of life. As a form of people-to-people diplomacy, it is a major force for peace and understanding in the world today. Travel and culture in the Orient are therefore my major writing topics."

*   *   *

REILLY, Paul   1912-

PERSONAL: Born May 29, 1912, in Liverpool, England; son of Charles Herbert (an architect and educator) and Dorothy Gladys (Pratt) Reilly; married Pamela Wentworth Foster, 1939 (marriage ended); married Annette Rose Stockwell, September 25, 1952; children: (first marriage) Victoria Wentworth Reilly Spicka. *Education:* Hertford College, Oxford, M.A., 1933; graduate study at London School of Economics and Political Science, London, 1933-34. *Politics:* Independent. *Religion:* Church of England.

ADDRESSES: Home—3 Alexander Pl., London SW7 2SG, England.

CAREER: Venesta Ltd., London, England, salesman and sales manager, 1934-36; *News Chronicle,* London, editor of Leader Page and features editor, 1936-40; *Modern Plastics,* New York, N.Y., member of editorial staff, 1946; Design Council, London, chief information officer, 1948-54, deputy director, 1954-60, director, 1960-77. Director of Conran Design Group and Building Trades Exhibition Ltd.; chairman of trustees of Building Conservation Trust, 1977-82; chairman of Conran Foundation, 1981-86. Member of council of British Tourist Authority, 1960-70, and Royal College of Art, 1963-81; member of British Broadcasting Corp. General Advisory Council, 1964-70, British National Export Council, 1966-70, British Railways Board Design Panel, 1966—, and Environment Panel, 1977-84; member of Greater London Council Historic Buildings Committee, 1967-82, Post Office Stamp Advisory Committee, 1967—, and Design Advisory Committee, 1970-84; member of British Telecommunications Design Committee, 1981-83, British Council Fine Arts Advisory Committee, 1970-80, and French Conseil Superieur de la Creation Esthetique Industrielle, 1971-73; member of Advisory Council of Science Policy Foundation, 1971—, British Crafts Centre Board, 1972-77, National Theatre Design Advisory Committee, 1974—, Royal Fine Art Commission, 1976-81, and Crafts Advisory Committee, 1977-81 (chief executive, 1971-77); vice-president of Institute of Contemporary Arts, 1979—. Governor of Hammersmith College of Art and Building, 1948-67, Central School of Art and Design, 1967-77, Camberwell School of Art and Design, 1967-77, and City of Birmingham Polytechnic, 1970-77; member of court of governors of London School of Economics and Political Science, London, 1975-80. *Military service:* British Army, Royal Armoured Corps, 1940; Royal Naval Volunteer Reserve, 1941-45.

MEMBER: International Council of Societies of Industrial Design (vice-president, 1963-67), World Crafts Council (president, 1978-80), Royal Society of Arts (member of council, 1959-62, 1963-70), Society of Designer-Craftsmen (president, 1976-84), Association of Art Institutions (president, 1977-80), Society of Industrial Artists (honorary member), Royal Institute of British Architects (honorary fellow), Modular Society (vice-president, 1968-77), Svenskasloejdforeningen (honorary corresponding member), London Society (vice-president, 1977—), Rye Conservation Society (vice-president, 1980—), Arts Club.

AWARDS, HONORS: Honorary member of Art Workers Guild, 1961; commander of Royal Order of Vasa of Sweden, 1961; bicentennial medal from Royal Society of Arts, 1963; honorary associate of Manchester College of Art, 1963; knighted, 1967; Royal College of Art, senior fellow, 1972, honorary doctorate, 1978; D.Sc. from Loughborough University of Technology, 1977, and University of Aston in Birmingham, 1981; created baron (life peer) of Brompton, 1978; honorary liveryman of Furniture Makers Company, 1980; honorary commissioner of Japan Design Foundation, 1983.

WRITINGS:

(Co-editor) *British Plastics Encyclopaedia,* National Trade Press, 1947.
An Introduction to Regency Architecture, Art and Technics, 1948.
An Eye on Design (autobiography), Max Reinhardt, 1987.

Contributor to journals.

SIDELIGHTS: Paul Reilley told *CA* that the highlight of his career was staying with the Queen at Windsor Castle. He loves to travel and believes that "design is all-important to industry."

*　　　*　　　*

REINHART, Theodore R(ussell) 1938-

PERSONAL: Born January 24, 1938, in Sellersville, Pa.; son of Russell William and Arlene (Greene) Reinhart; married Joy Baxter, August 10, 1958; children: Steven Theodore, Brian Chester. *Education:* Pennsylvania State University, B.A. (with distinction), 1961; George Washington University, M.A., 1964; University of New Mexico, Ph.D., 1968.

ADDRESSES: Home—938 Jamestown Rd., Williamsburg, Va. 23185. *Office*—Department of Anthropology, College of William and Mary, Williamsburg, Va. 23185.

CAREER: College of William and Mary, Williamsburg, Va., assistant professor, 1968-73, associate professor, 1973-86, professor of anthropology, 1986—. *Military service:* U.S. Army, 1955-58.

MEMBER: American Anthropological Association, Society for Historical Archaeology, Society for American Archaeology, Archaeological Society of Virginia (president, 1987-88), Sigma Xi.

WRITINGS:

(Editor) *The Archaeology of Shirley Plantation,* University Press of Virginia, 1984.

Material Culture, Social Relations, and Spatial Organization on a Colonial Frontier: The Pope Site (44SN180), Southampton County, Virginia, College of William and Mary, 1987.

Contributor to anthropology journals.

SIDELIGHTS: Theodore R. Reinhart told *CA:* "Writing is an expected activity of an archaeologist; excavation destroys archaeological sites, and data not reported are lost forever. Our fieldwork at Shirley Plantation, a Virginia plantation settled in the seventeenth century and still operating today, provides a good example of what both archaeologists and historians can learn from archaeology. Most of the early records pertaining to the plantation were lost in the Civil War. Archaeology, however, has been able to reconstruct many aspects of life at the plantation during the seventeenth and eighteenth centuries. My second book, *Material Culture, Social Relations, and Spatial Organization on a Colonial Frontier,* provides a glimpse of colonial life on a small frontier farmstead in southern Virginia during the eighteenth century. Although the farm is mentioned in surviving county records, archaeology has provided the details of everyday life there."

*　　　*　　　*

REIS, Ricardo
See PESSOA, Fernando (Antonio Nogueira)

*　　　*　　　*

REMIZOV, A. M.
See REMIZOV, Alexey (Mikhailovich)

*　　　*　　　*

REMIZOV, Alexey (Mikhailovich) 1877-1957
(A. M. Remizov)

BRIEF ENTRY: Some sources transliterate first name as Aleksiei, Aleksei, or Aleksey and middle name as Mikhaylovich; born June 7 (one source says June 24), 1877, in Moscow, Russia (now U.S.S.R.); died November 26 (one source says November 28), 1957, in Paris, France. Russian critic, folklorist, novelist, short story writer, dramatist, and memoirist. Remizov was one of the most prolific, versatile, and original of Russian writers in the decade before the Bolshevik Revolution of 1917. Best remembered for his ornate prose style, which influenced a generation of Soviet writers, Remizov was the author of a diverse body of work that included folk tales, parables, and legends, four plays, numerous novels and short stories, literary criticism, and a unique memoir genre that combined a chronicle of postrevolutionary Russia, reminiscences, autobiography, biographical sketches, fantasy, and essays on life and literature. His lifelong fascination with the world of dreams culminated in an original collection describing his own dreams, *Martyn Zadeka* (1954), and is evident as well in a penetrating critical commentary on Russian writers, *Ogon veschei* (title means "The Fire of Things," 1954).

Disillusioned with life under the Soviet regime, Remizov and his wife left Russia in 1921 and settled in Paris, where they remained for the rest of their lives. Remizov's other works include the novels *Prud* (title means "The Pond," 1908) and *Piataia iazva* (1912; translated as *The Fifth Pestilence,* 1927) and an autobiography, *Podstrizhennymi glazami* (1951).

BIOGRAPHICAL/CRITICAL SOURCES:

BOOKS

Columbia Dictionary of Modern European Literature, 2nd revised edition, Columbia University Press, 1980.
Encyclopedia of World Literature in the Twentieth Century, Volume IV, revised edition, Ungar, 1984.
Twentieth-Century Authors: A Biographical Dictionary of Modern Literature, lst Supplement, H. W. Wilson, 1955.
Twentieth-Century Culture: A Biographical Companion, Harper, 1983.
Twentieth-Century Literary Criticism, Volume 27, Gale, 1988.

* * *

RENO, Dawn E. 1953-

PERSONAL: Born April 15, 1953, in Waltham, Mass.; daughter of Donald Earle (a driver) and Elaine (Gordon) Brander; married Richard Tutela, April 29, 1972 (divorced, 1974); married Robert Gene Reno (a builder), February 25, 1978; children: (second marriage) Jennifer April. *Education:* Bunker Hill Community College, A.A., 1976. *Politics:* Independent. *Religion:* Agnostic.

ADDRESSES: Home—R.R.1, Box 500, Montgomery Center, Vt. 05471. *Agent*— Helen McGrath, 1406 Idaho Court, Concord, Calif.

CAREER: Reno's Antiques, Montgomery Center, Vt., antiques dealer, 1978—. Training supervisor for Transitional Employment Enterprises, Boston, Mass., 1978-79; administrative assistant at U.S. Trust (bank), Boston, 1979-81; public relations director of Reno Public Relations, 1985-87; legal assistant, 1987—. Member of National Trust for Historic Preservation and Smithsonian Institution.

MEMBER: International P.E.N., National Writers Union, Society of Children's Book Writers, National Geographic Society, Jacques Cousteau Society, Vermont Literary Association.

AWARDS, HONORS: Certificate of Merit from *Writer's Digest* competition, 1987.

WRITINGS:

Jenny's First Friend (juvenile), Delair, 1978.
Jenny Moves (juvenile), Delair, 1978.
Collecting Black Americana, Crown, 1986.
American Indian Collectibles, Ballantine, 1988.

Contributor of nearly two hundred articles to magazines and newspapers, including *New England Antiques Journal, Antique Trader Weekly, Vermont Life, Vermont Woman, House Beautiful,* and *Black Family.* Editor of and columnist for *Black Ethnic Collectibles.*

WORK IN PROGRESS: Amaryllis, a novel; *Don't Drink the Water,* a novel; "Clorinda," a children's book series.

SIDELIGHTS: Dawn E. Reno told *CA:* "Currently my career focuses on writing about areas of antique collecting which have not yet been discussed completely. Ethnic collectibles interest me because of their history, and I try to intersperse historical information with the other material in my books. *Collecting Black Americana* was the first book published on that subject."

Reno added that she is studying photography so that she will be able to illustrate her own writings with photographs. Eventually, however, the author intends to concentrate more heavily on fiction than her present commitments permit.

AVOCATIONAL INTERESTS: Travel, gardening, classical music and ballet, long-distance bicycling.

* * *

REYNOLDS, Paul R(evere) 1904-1988

OBITUARY NOTICE—See index for *CA* sketch: Born July 21, 1904, in New York, N.Y.; died June 10, 1988, in Waterbury, Conn. Literary agent and author. A successful literary agent for more than fifty years—including sixteen as president of his own company—Reynolds represented such important writers as Richard Wright, William Shirer, Irving Wallace, and Howard Fast. In addition, he wrote several instructional books, including *The Writer and His Markets, The Writing and Selling of Nonfiction, The Writing and Selling of Fiction, A Professional Guide to Marketing Manuscripts,* and *The Nonfiction Book.* He also wrote an autobiography, *The Middle Man: The Adventures of a Literary Agent.*

OBITUARIES AND OTHER SOURCES:

PERIODICALS

Chicago Tribune, June 12, 1988.
New York Times, June 11, 1988.
Publishers Weekly, June 24, 1988.

* * *

RICHARDS, Walter Alden (Jr.) 1907-1988

OBITUARY NOTICE: Born March 11, 1907, in Springfield, Ill.; died May 23, 1988, in Burbank, Calif. Business executive, producer, and scriptwriter. Richards was a producer and administrator at several radio stations in the Midwest until World War II, when he became head of the U.S. Marine Corps Radio Unit. He then worked as an editor and writer for NBC-Radio's "Cavalcade of America" for two years before becoming president of R-Star Productions in Burbank, California. Richards also served as president of Micro Products Corporation beginning in 1956 and as a consultant to Marshall Field Communications during the 1960s. He wrote scripts for radio shows such as "Lux Radio Theater" and for television programs. One of his most popular scripts was published as a children's book, *Santa's Own Story of the First Christmas: The Gift of the Little Shepherd.*

OBITUARIES AND OTHER SOURCES:

BOOKS

Who's Who in the West, 17th edition, Marquis, 1980.

PERIODICALS

Chicago Tribune, June 2, 1988.
Los Angeles Times, June 3, 1988.
New York Times, May 31, 1988.

* * *

RICHARDSON, J. G.
See RICHARDSON, Jacques (Gabriel)

RICHARDSON, Jacques (Gabriel) 1924-
(J. G. Richardson)

PERSONAL: Born January 20, 1924, in Baltimore, Md.; son of John Benjamin and Adrienne Marguerite (Bit) Richardson; married Erika Buggert (a television film and radio producer); children: Pamela A., Michelle D. *Education:* Attended Concordia University, 1940-42, and Trinity College, 1942; University of Michigan, B.A., 1947; graduate study at Georgetown University, 1951-52.

ADDRESSES: Home—78 avenue de Suffren, 75015 Paris, France. *Office*—Cidex 400 Authon la Plaine, 91410 Dourdan, France.

CAREER: Guide Publications, Inc., Baltimore, Md., associate editor, 1948-49; U.S. Information Agency, Washington, D.C., regional editor, 1950-54; Department of the Army, Washington, D.C., civilian technical editor in office of the quartermaster general, 1955-60, senior technical editor in office of the chief of staff, 1960-61; Conover-Mast Publications, Inc., New York, N.Y., European correspondent in New York and Paris, France, 1962-68; Technology Communication, Inc., Paris, European director, 1969-70; *La Recherche,* Paris, associate publisher, 1971-72; UNESCO, Paris, journal editor and head of Science and Society Section, 1972-85; writer, correspondent, and consultant in technical communication, 1985—; Words and Publications Ltd., Oxford, England, French-based partner, 1987—. Lecturer at Seikei Gakuin University, 1955-60. Member of corporation of American Hospital in France, 1970—; member of Democrats in France, 1978—, and French section of Pugwash Conferences on Science and World Affairs; consultant to International Council of Scientific Unions. *Military service:* U.S. Army, 1943-48; became first lieutenant; received Bronze Star.

MEMBER: International Union of Technical Associations (member of board of directors), International Science Writers Association, American Association for the Advancement of Science, American Club of Paris, Association des Journalistes Scientifiques de la Presse d'Information, New York Academy of Science, Club of Vienna (a professional association concerned with the Third World).

AWARDS, HONORS: Ordre du Merite Social de Belgique, 1975; certificate from Technical Writers Institute, 1962.

WRITINGS:

(With Adrieno Buzatti-Traverso) *La Sfida della Scienza,* Mondadori, 1976, translation published as *The Scientific Enterprise,* UNESCO, 1978.
(With J. R. Baker and J. P. Green) *Julian Huxley: Scientist and World Citizen,* UNESCO, 1978.
(Editor) *Integrated Technology Transfer,* Lomond, 1979, 2nd edition, 1982.
(Editor with Colette M. Kinnon and A. N. Kholodilin; under name J. G. Richardson) *The Impact of Modern Scientific Ideas on Society: In Commemoration of Einstein,* D. Reidel, 1981.
(Editor) *Models of Reality: Shaping Thought and Action,* Lomond, 1984, 2nd edition, Lomond, 1986.
(Editor with Alexandra Kornhauser) *Teaching and Popularizing Science and Technology as Aids to Development,* Edvard Kardelj University Press, 1984.
(Editor) *Managing the Ocean: Resources, Research, Law,* Lomond, 1985, 2nd edition, 1987.
Windows on Creativity and Invention, Lomond, 1988.

Contributor to technical journals. Editor in chief of *Impact of Science and Society,* 1972-85.

WORK IN PROGRESS: The Sources of Creation and Innovation, completion expected in 1991.

SIDELIGHTS: Jacques Richardson told *CA:* "My special interest is the development of the relationships between the natural sciences, engineering, economics, and culture. I have a continuing fascination in the creative process, with belief in genius receding by the year, and a growing appreciation for the random processes of opportunity and luck."

* * *

RIGHTER, Carroll (Burch) 1900-1988

OBITUARY NOTICE—See index for *CA* sketch: Born February 2, 1900, in Salem, N.J.; died from complications of aging, May 1 (some sources say April 30), 1988, in Santa Monica, Calif. Astrologer, columnist, and author. Righter was astrologer to numerous celebrities, including Marlene Dietrich, Tyrone Power, Rhonda Fleming, Grace Kelly, and Ronald Reagan. Righter's astrology column, which he began writing in 1950, appeared in three hundred newspapers around the world. Among Righter's books are *Astrology and You, Astrological Guide to Marriage and Family Relations, Astrological Guide to Health and Diet,* and *Dollar Signs.*

OBITUARIES AND OTHER SOURCES:

Current Biography, H. W. Wilson, 1972, June, 1988.
Who's Who in the World, 8th edition, Marquis, 1986.

PERIODICALS

Chicago Tribune, May 5, 1988.
Los Angeles Times, May 3, 1988.
New York Times, May 4, 1988.

* * *

RINGMASTER, The
See MENCKEN, H(enry) L(ouis)

* * *

RINK, Oliver A(lbert) 1947-

PERSONAL: Born December 12, 1947, in Monohans, Tex.; son of Oliver Albert (a machinist) and Virginia M. (a homemaker; maiden name, Griffin) Rink; married Marsha A. Townsend, June 8, 1971 (divorced January 9, 1988); children: Diane M., David O., Gary W. *Education:* University of Southern California, B.A. (magna cum laude), 1970, M.A., 1973, Ph.D., 1976.

ADDRESSES: Home—Bakersfield, Calif. *Office*—Department of History, California State College, 9001 Stockdale Highway, Bakersfield, Calif. 93309.

CAREER: University of Southern California, Los Angeles, instructor in history, 1974-75; California State College, Bakersfield, assistant professor, 1975-79, associate professor, 1979-83, professor of history, 1983—, chairman of department, 1983—. Instructor at Santa Ana College, summer, 1975.

MEMBER: American Historical Association, Organization of American Historians, Phi Beta Kappa, Phi Alpha Theta, Phi Kappa Phi.

AWARDS, HONORS: Manuscript prize from New York State Historical Association, 1984, and Andrew Hendricks Award, 1987, both for *Holland on the Hudson.*

WRITINGS:

Holland on the Hudson: An Economic and Social History of Dutch New York, Cornell University Press, 1986.

Contributor of articles and reviews to history and genealogy magazines.

WORK IN PROGRESS: With Charles Gehring, a biography of Peter Stuyvesant, the last governor of Dutch New York, publication expected in 1990.

SIDELIGHTS: Oliver A. Rink told *CA:* "The motivation for researching and writing *Holland on the Hudson* came from a desire to know more about the non-English inhabitants of colonial America and to understand on a personal level the history of my own Dutch ancestry. My goals as a historian include the study of the process of ethnic assimilation in the eighteenth century. It is this prelude to the age of the 'melting pot' which determined the unique American response to diversity, and it is this age which produced the classic responses of racism, anti-Catholicism, anti-Semitism, and xenophobia."

*   *   *

RIVERSIDE, John
See HEINLEIN, Robert A(nson)

*   *   *

ROBINSON, Daniel Sommer   1888-1977

OBITUARY NOTICE—See index for *CA* sketch: Born October 19, 1888, in North Salem, Ind.; died November 29, 1977, in Los Angeles, Calif. Clergyman, philosopher, educator, academic administrator, editor, translator, and author. Robinson was a proponent of philosophical idealism. After working as a Congregational minister, he began his teaching career in 1919 at the University of Wisconsin. He taught at various schools for the next thirty-five years, retiring from the University of Southern California in 1954 after eight years as professor of philosophy and director of the School of Philosophy. Robinson wrote such works as *The Principles of Reasoning, The God of the Liberal Christian, An Introduction to Living Philosophy, Political Ethics,* and *Critical Issues in Philosophy.* He also translated works by Georg Wobbermin and edited such volumes as *An Anthology of Recent Philosophy.*

OBITUARIES AND OTHER SOURCES:

BOOKS

The National Cyclopedia of American Biography, Volume 60, James White, 1981.

*   *   *

ROCKWELL, Harlow   1910-1988

OBITUARY NOTICE—See index for *CA* sketch: Born in 1910; died after a long illness, April 7, 1988. Illustrator and author. Rockwell wrote and illustrated many children's books, including *ABC Book, My Doctor, My Nursery School, My Dentist,* and *Our Garage Sale.* He also collaborated with his wife, Anne Rockwell, on writing and illustrating many other books for children.

OBITUARIES AND OTHER SOURCES:

PERIODICALS

Publishers Weekly, May 20, 1988.

*   *   *

RODNEY, Walter   1942-1980

PERSONAL: Born in 1942 in British Guiana (now Guyana); died in a car-bomb explosion, June 13, 1980, in Georgetown, Guyana.

CAREER: Historian, educator, political activist, author. Taught at University College of the West Indies at Mona, Jamaica, until 1968; taught history at University of Dar es Salaam, Tanzania, 1969-72; leader of Working People's Alliance in Guyana, 1979-1980.

WRITINGS:

West Africa and the Atlantic Slave Trade, East African Publishing House, 1967.
The Groundings With My Brothers (collection of lectures), introduction by Richard Small, Bogle-l'Ouverture Publications, 1969, reprinted with introduction by Omawale, 1975.
A History of the Upper Guinea Coast: 1545-1800, Clarendon Press, 1970, Monthly Review Press, 1980.
How Europe Underdeveloped Africa, Bogle-l'Ouverture Publications, 1972, reprinted with postscript by A. M. Babu, Howard University Press, 1974, reprinted with introduction by Vincent Harding, Robert Hill, and William Strickland, Howard University Press, 1981.
The Pan-Africanist Struggle in Africa (recording), Institute of the Black World (Atlanta), 1974.
(Editor and author of introduction) *Guyanese Sugar Plantations in the Late Nineteenth Century: A Contemporary Description From the "Argosy,"* Release Publishers (Georgetown, Guyana), 1979.
A History of the Guyanese Working People: 1881-1905, foreword by George Lamming, Johns Hopkins University Press, 1981.
Signs of the Times: Rodney's Last Speech, 6/6/80, tributes by Rupert Roopnaraine, Eusi Kwayana, and Horace Campbell, Working People's Alliance, 1981.
(With Kapepwa Tambila and Laurent Sago) *Migrant Labour in Tanzania During the Colonial Period: Case Studies of Recruitment and Conditions of Labour in the Sisal Industry,* Institut fuer Afrika-Kunde im Verbund der Stiftung Deutsches Oersee-Institut, 1983.

SIDELIGHTS: Walter Rodney was a Guyanese historian who championed the rights of black people throughout the world. He directed his Marxist writings, which denounced capitalism and imperialism for the destruction they brought to black societies, toward both the uneducated and the educated, believing that only an informed public could bring about positive social change. For Rodney, wrote Richard Gray in *History Today,* there was "no division between scholarship and the problems of daily life. His discoveries were valid for him only if he could communicate them to his less-learned, less-privileged brothers."

As a college instructor in Jamaica during the 1960s, Rodney urged his students to interpret Caribbean history in the context of African history, colonialism, and slavery; to recognize and oppose racial segregation in contemporary Caribbean society; and to provoke the masses into revolutionary action against the racist elite. Six of his Jamaican lectures are collected in *The Groundings With My Brothers*, a volume that, according to Basil A. Ince's 1971 review in *Afro-American Studies*, "provides a useful insight into West Indian society and the current new left revolution that is taking hold in these islands." Because of the radical nature of his lectures, Rodney was deemed subversive by the government and ordered to leave Jamaica in 1968—an action that caused riots in Jamaica's capital and similarly affected the rest of the Caribbean.

After teaching history at the University of Dar es Salaam in Tanzania for three years, Rodney returned to his native Guyana in 1974 to accept an appointment as professor and chairman of history at the University of Guyana. The appointment, however, was revoked, apparently because of governmental pressure. A few years later Rodney became a leader of the Working People's Alliance, a group established in 1979 in opposition to Guyana's prime minister, Forbes Burnham, and his regime, which had been in power for more than twenty years. On June 13, 1980, Rodney died in a car-bomb explosion, suspected to be the work of Burnham's party.

"Only 38 years old at the time of his death," observed Sidney Mintz in *New York Times Book Review*, "[Rodney] had already earned an international reputation as one of the West Indies' brightest young historians." Most of his studies concerned European colonialism and its effects on black societies around the world. In his *History of the Upper Guinea Coast: 1545-1800*, Rodney focuses on the coastal region in West Africa that is now called Guinea—a region that, according to Philip D. Curtin in the *Journal of African History*, "contributed more than any other to the sixteenth-century slave trade" and contains numerous records that "make it possible to trace developments over several centuries." P. E. H. Hair of *History* praised Rodney's treatment of the Portuguese period—the era from the mid-sixteenth to the mid-seventeenth centuries when the Portuguese dominated trade in Guinea—as "scholarly and stimulating, [for it] contains a mass of useful information drawn from printed as well as manuscript sources." Although some critics maintained that Rodney's study was incomplete because it relied too heavily on archaic sources and ignored current findings, most agreed with Gray's assessment that the author's "research raised a whole set of fresh questions concerning the nature of African social institutions in the Upper Guinea coast in the sixteenth century and of the impact of the Atlantic slave trade."

Reviewing Rodney's next book, *How Europe Underdeveloped Africa*, in *Interchange*, Gerald L. Caplan declared: "Rodney has put together the most important book we now have on the history of Africa," asserting that the historian "knows why modern Africa is in its present shabby state, and his title says it all." Examining the problem from a Marxist viewpoint, Rodney blames Africa's underdevelopment on European colonialism and its present-day repercussions. Even today, he writes, when European rulers no longer directly control African nations, "political puppets" compromise African interests in favor of European interests by agreeing to unfair trade bargains. The way to end the exploitation, Rodney claims, is to make a "radical break with the international capitalist system, which has been the principal agency of the underdevelopment of Africa over the last five centuries." While pointing out the destructive effects of European imperialism, however, he warns Africans against the temptation to place all blame for their underdevelopment on other nations. "None of these remarks are intended to remove the ultimate responsibility for development from the shoulders of Africans," Rodney stresses.

"Every African has a responsibility to understand the [imperialist] system and work for its overthrow."

Opoku Agyeman, writing in *Africa Today*, praised *How Europe Underdeveloped Africa* as "a remarkable feat, the secret of its success being that its author conducted his analysis from an African perspective, untrammeled by any servility to the bourgeois world-view. It portrays black academic maturity and independence at its best." Martin A. Klein of the *International Journal of African Historical Studies* likewise deemed the book "brilliantly conceived," adding that "it provides a passionate and angry vision which directs that anger into the quest for revolutionary change." And Hashim Gibrill in *Monthly Review* called the work "an inspiration to all of us concerned to understand our past and to fashion a meaningful future."

Rodney again examines the past to interpret the present and future in probably his most highly regarded work, *A History of the Guyanese Working People: 1881-1905*, which was published a year after he died. Intended as the first of two volumes exploring Guyanese history, the work demonstrates the growing importance of the working class during an era beginning "some two centuries after the introduction of slave labor [in Guyana] and about fifty years after the formal emancipation," according to George Lamming in his foreword to the book. Rodney explains that when the black slaves were freed in 1838, their former owners—the planters—feared that higher labor costs would soon result. To assure themselves of a constant supply of cheap labor, the planters began importing workers, mainly from India, to flood the labor market. By encouraging prejudice between the Africans and Indians, the planters slowed the advent of worker solidarity. Nevertheless, Rodney writes, the working class did manage to unite in opposition to the planters: "It was through political struggle that the working class (and the middle class) clarified their identity and tested their relationship with other classes and strata."

Monica Schuler lauded Rodney's work in *Americas* as "an excellent analysis of the conjunction of labor competition and ethnic diversity in Guyana. . . . [*A History of the Guyanese Working People*] stands as a primer of themes and theses for future students of Guyana's past to explore in greater detail." Mintz, in his *New York Times Book Review* critique, commended Rodney's ability to reach a diverse audience through *A History of the Guyanese Working People* and other works by addressing the uneducated as well as the educated: "He consciously de-intellectualized history as he wrote it, in a bold effort to make his ideas—and indeed the very practice of history—entirely intelligible to the people about whom, and for whom, he wrote."

BIOGRAPHICAL/CRITICAL SOURCES:

BOOKS

Alpers, Edward A. and Pierre-Michel Fontaine, editors, *Walter Rodney, Revolutionary and Scholar: A Tribute*, Center for Afro-American Studies and African Studies Center, University of California, Los Angeles, 1982.

Contemporary Issues Criticism, Volume 2, Gale, 1984.

Rodney, Walter, *How Europe Underdeveloped Africa*, Howard University Press, 1974.

Rodney, Walter, *A History of the Guyanese Working People: 1881-1905*, foreword by George Lamming, Johns Hopkins University Press, 1981.

PERIODICALS

Africa Today, summer, 1973.

Afro-American Studies, June, 1971.
Americas, January, 1983.
History, June, 1971.
History Today, September, 1980.
Interchange, Volume IV, number 4, 1973.
International Journal of African Historical Studies, Volume VII, number 2, 1974.
Journal of African History, Volume XI, number 3, 1970.
Monthly Review, October, 1980.
New York Times Book Review, January 17, 1982.*

—*Sketch by Christa Brelin*

*   *   *

ROGOWSKI, Ronald (Lynn) 1944-

PERSONAL: Born May 16, 1944, in Alliance, Neb.; son of Lindall R. (a farmer) and Iola (a housewife; maiden name, Langston) Rogowski; married Katherine A. Bertram (a secretary), August 5, 1972. *Education:* University of Nebraska, B.A., 1964; Princeton University, Ph.D., 1970.

ADDRESSES: Home—Los Angeles, Calif. *Office*—Department of Political Science, 4289 Bunche Hall, University of California, 405 Hilgard Ave., Los Angeles, Calif. 90024.

CAREER: Princeton University, Princeton, N.J., research assistant in comparative politics at Center for International Studies, 1968-69, faculty associate and lecturer, 1969-70, assistant professor of political science, 1970-75; Duke University, Durham, N.C., associate professor, 1975-80, professor of political science, 1980-81; University of California, Los Angeles, professor of political science, 1980—, chairman of department, 1987—. Research fellow at Center for West European Studies, Harvard University, 1970-71, and Center for European Studies, 1975; fellow at Center for Advanced Study in the Behavioral Sciences, Palo Alto, 1983-84.

MEMBER: American Political Science Association.

WRITINGS:

Rational Legitimacy, Princeton University Press, 1974.
(Editor with Edward A. Tiryakian) *New Nationalisms of the Developed West,* Allen & Unwin, 1986.

WORK IN PROGRESS: Trade and Political Cleavages.

SIDELIGHTS: Ronald Rogowski told *CA:* "I am interested in comparative politics generally, with a focus on Western Europe; other interests include modern political theory and formal theory."

AVOCATIONAL INTERESTS: Bicycling, judo, gardening, baroque music, nineteenth-century novels.

*   *   *

ROLAND, Mary
See LEWIS, Mary (Christianna)

*   *   *

ROMER, Stephen 1957-

PERSONAL: Born August 20, 1957, in Bishops Stortford, England; son of Mark Lemon (a lawyer) and Philippa (a portrait painter; maiden name, Tomson) Romer; married Bridget Strevens (a painter and translator), July 17, 1982; children: Thomas. *Education:* Graduated with first class honors from

Trinity Hall, Cambridge, 1978, Ph.D., 1985; graduate study at Harvard University, 1978-79.

ADDRESSES: Home—6 rue de Verneuil, 75007 Paris, France.

CAREER: British Institute in Paris, Paris, France, lecturer in English literature, 1983—. Lecturer at American College in Paris, 1987—.

AWARDS, HONORS: Eric Gregory Trust Award for young poets from Society of Authors, 1986, for *Idols.*

WRITINGS:

(Translator) Jacques Dupin, *The Growing Dark* (poems), Twofold, 1981.
Idols (poems), Oxford University Press, 1986.

Contributor of poems, translations, and reviews to magazines, including *PN Review.* Editor of *Twofold,* 1980-84, and *Smale Fowls,* 1987—.

WORK IN PROGRESS: T. S. Eliot, Post-Symbolist.

SIDELIGHTS: Stephen Romer told *CA:* "The poet T. S. Eliot, in *Four Quartets,* makes clear that the poem elapsing in time is also the life of the poet elapsing in time. Eliot is 'post-symbolist' because of his open struggle with language and with meaning; he believed that the vision beyond the poetry is what matters. French poets today do battle with or abdicate in front of the scientists of language. But there is a return to the world outside of language, or even prior to language, which I find fascinating. My own poetry aims to remain intimately bound to life in time (one's overriding experience) and must entail an awareness of death and the value it confers on that life."

*   *   *

ROMTVEDT, David 1950-

PERSONAL: Born June 7, 1950, in Portland, Ore.; son of Arthur W. Young (a carpenter) and Borgny Romtvedt (a schoolteacher). *Education:* Attended University of Arizona, 1968-69; Reed College, B.A., 1972; University of Iowa, M.F.A., 1975. *Politics:* Democratic Socialists of America.

ADDRESSES: Home—P.O. Box 484, Port Townsend, Wash. 98368.

CAREER: Writer-in-residence for state arts commissions of Alaska, Washington, Nevada, and Montana, 1979—. Visiting writer at Mississippi County College, Blytheville, Ark., 1984. Writing consultant for National Endowment for the Humanities "All My Somedays" program, 1982-83. Associated with Ground Zero Center for Nonviolent Action.

MEMBER: Port Townsend Peace Coalition.

AWARDS, HONORS: National Endowment for the Arts writer-in-residence fellowship, 1979; honorable mention from Academy of American Poets, 1974; King County (Seattle) Arts Commission publication project award, 1983.

WRITINGS:

(Contributor of translations and assistant editor) *Writing From the World,* University of Iowa Press, 1976.
Moon (poems), Bieler, 1982.
"Loaf of Bread and a Bus Ticket Home" (play), first produced in Tacoma, Wash., at Tacoma Actors' Guild, 1982.
Free and Compulsory for All (stories), Graywolf, 1984.

Also translator of *Rincon Poetico,* Pacific Island Press, 1975. Contributor to literary magazines, including *Paris Review* and *American Poetry Review.*

WORK IN PROGRESS: All My Lovely Swimmers.

SIDELIGHTS: In *Free and Compulsory for All* David Romtvedt presents an assortment of short stories about high school that marry the commonplace with the unexpected. Familiar secondary school characters and situations slide into the ironic or fantastic: a heretofore heterosexual gym teacher wrongly accused of lesbianism, for instance, eventually takes her female replacement as a lover; a student at odds with her constantly changing body awakes one morning to find her head a metronome. Reviewing the collection for the *Village Voice Literary Supplement,* Polly Shulman determined: "[Romtvedt] has no lessons to teach; he does not want us to come to any particular conclusions, only to think about what he tells us. He expects us to be puzzled by what he says; he is puzzled himself." The critic pointed out that "occasionally Romtvedt's conscientious ambiguity and quiet style can be patronizing, like a teacher refusing to settle a dispute or give away an answer," but decided, "Usually the stories are honestly and provocatively elusive."

Romtvedt told *CA:* "My work has been most influenced by the assistance of several women writers and editors, most notably Sandra McPherson and Kathleen Fraser. I am a student of Cajun music and it has influenced me. Languages spoken include French and Spanish; I travel extensively in Central and East Africa, France, Spain, England, Mexico, and North America. In my work I try to combine the secret personal life of a speaker with the larger social/political currents that surround that speaker."

BIOGRAPHICAL/CRITICAL SOURCES:

PERIODICALS

Village Voice Literary Supplement, October, 1984.

*   *   *

ROSEN, Leonard   1954-

PERSONAL: Born January 7, 1954, in Baltimore, Md.; son of Sidney (an engineer) and Esther (Renbaum) Rosen; married Linda Cohen (an engineer), March 3, 1983; children: Jonathan Lipman. *Education:* Trinity College, Hartford, Conn., B.A., 1975; American University, Ph.D., 1981.

ADDRESSES: Home—199 Babcock St., Brookline, Mass. 02146. *Office*—Department of English, Bentley College, Beaver and Forest Sts., Waltham, Mass. 02254. *Agent*—Mark Kramer, 20 Bluewater Hill, Westport, Conn. 06880.

CAREER: Bentley College, Waltham, Mass., assistant professor of English, 1982—. Consultant to Digital Equipment Organization.

WRITINGS:

The Everyday English Handbook, Doubleday, 1985.
(With Larry Behrens) *Writing and Reading Across the Curriculum,* Little, Brown, 1985, revised edition, 1987.
(With Larry Behrens) *Reading for College Writers,* Little, Brown, 1987.
(With Larry Behrens) *Theme and Variations: The Impact of Great Ideas,* Little, Brown, 1988.

WORK IN PROGRESS: Moonwalking, a novel.

ROSEN, Ruth (E.)   1945-

PERSONAL: Born July 25, 1945, in Manhattan, N.Y.; daughter of Herman (a lawyer) and Ida (a housewife; maiden name, Ginsberg) Rosen. *Education:* University of Rochester, B.A. (with highest honors), 1967; University of California, Berkeley, M.A., 1969, Ph.D., 1976. *Religion:* Jewish.

ADDRESSES: Office—Department of History, University of California, Davis, Calif. 95616. *Agent*—Sandra Dijkstra, Sandra Dijkstra Literary Agency, 1237 Camino del Mar, Del Mar, Calif. 92014.

CAREER: University of California, Davis, professor of history, 1974—.

AWARDS, HONORS: Social Science Research Council fellow from 1972-73; Rockefeller Humanities fellowships, 1978-79 and 1988; Distinguished Teaching Award from University of California, 1983; Rockefeller Foundation Gender Roles fellow, 1988.

WRITINGS:

(Editor, with Sue Davidson) *The Maimie Papers,* Feminist Press, 1978.
The Lost Sisterhood: Prostitution in America, 1900-1918, Johns Hopkins University Press, 1982.
(Contributor) Todd Gitlin, editor, *Watching Television,* Pantheon, 1987.

WORK IN PROGRESS: A book about the origins and transformation of American feminism.

SIDELIGHTS: With *The Lost Sisterhood: Prostitution in America, 1900-1918,* historian Ruth Rosen "has broken entirely new ground in what will surely remain the definitive study of urban prostitution in America for many years to come," asserted Betty Wood in the *Times Literary Supplement.* Relying on extensive research and objective, discriminating analysis, the author examines the relationship between economics and prostitution and explores the attitudes of middle-class reformers toward the profession. Remarked Frederika Randall in the *New York Times Book Review,* Rosen "shows that the early 20th-century campaign against prostitution absorbed a broad array of middle-class social and political concerns in a society where class structure and relations between the sexes were rapidly changing."

According to Rosen, many prostitutes did not see themselves the way reformers saw them—as "helpless or hapless victims in need of rescue," recounted Wood. Prostitutes, in fact, often judged their profession a "less demanding . . . more lucrative, and no more demeaning" alternative to factory labor, noted *Washington Post Book World* critic Jonathan Yardley. Perceiving prostitution as a social evil, symbolic of declining morals and exploitation, reformers ignored such economic and physical considerations. Moreover, observed Yardley, "consciously or unconsciously, their attack on prostitution represented an attack on a male-dominated society." As Rosen convincingly argues, however, the crusade only drove prostitution underground, making it more dangerous and more closely affiliated with organized crime. Putting the issue in historical perspective, Rosen's "sophisticated analysis" provides "considerable food for thought," assessed Wood. "In Ruth Rosen," the reviewer concluded, "these women . . . have at last found their historian, and a most perceptive historian at that."

Rosen told *CA:* "Since 1968, my life project has been to understand how gender shapes and is shaped by human culture. All my educational efforts, research, and writings are directed to that end. My abiding political concerns are to foster human rights, support anti-interventionist efforts, and work for the peace and health of the planet and its people."

BIOGRAPHICAL/CRITICAL SOURCES:

PERIODICALS

New York Times Book Review, February 27, 1983.
Times Literary Supplement, July 29, 1983.
Washington Post Book World, December 12, 1982.

*   *   *

ROSS, Kenneth Lynn   1940-

PERSONAL: Born May 3, 1940, in Howell, Mich.; son of Clifford Eldon and Iva Pearl (Boardman) Ross; married Geraldine Kay DeLong, August 24, 1963; children: Eric, Michael. *Education:* Michigan State University, B.A., 1962; University of Michigan, M.A., 1963. *Religion:* Congregationalist.

ADDRESSES: Office—c/o *Detroit News,* 615 West Lafayette Blvd., Detroit, Mich. 48231.

CAREER/WRITINGS: Chicago Tribune, Chicago, Ill., writer and editor, 1963-77; University of Missouri—Columbia, associate professor, 1977-78; *Detroit News,* Detroit, Mich., business editor, 1979-84; *Hartford Courant,* Hartford, Conn., business editor, 1984-87; *Detroit News,* Detroit, business columnist, 1987—. Contributor to *Northeast* magazine.

MEMBER: Society of American Business Editors and Writers.

WORK IN PROGRESS: Developing a media awareness program for use in business schools.

*   *   *

ROSSANT, Murray J(oseph)   1923-1988

OBITUARY NOTICE: Born June 9, 1923, in New York, N.Y.; died of stomach cancer, June 28, 1988, in New York, N.Y. Educator, administrator, and journalist. Known for his financial reporting, Rossant began working for *Time* magazine as contributing editor during the 1940s and for *Business Week* in the early 1950s, serving as senior editor in charge of financial coverage. He then joined the *New York Times,* where he was a financial columnist and editorial writer before he left in 1967 to become director of the Twentieth Century Fund, a think tank on public policy issues. Rossant was New York correspondent for the *Economist* from 1970 until his death, and he contributed financially oriented articles to such publications as *Esquire, Fortune, Harper's, Reporter, Financial Times,* and *Spectator.* He taught at the University of Wisconsin's school of banking for about ten years, beginning in 1958.

OBITUARIES AND OTHER SOURCES:

BOOKS

Who's Who in the World, 2nd edition, Marquis, 1973.

PERIODICALS

Chicago Tribune, July 3, 1988.
New York Times, June 29, 1988.

ROUMAIN, Jacques (Jean Baptiste)   1907-1944

PERSONAL: Born June 4, 1907, in Port-au-Prince, Haiti; died of a heart attack, August 18, 1944, in Port-au-Prince, Haiti; married; children: one son. *Education:* Attended schools in Haiti, Switzerland, Germany, Spain, Belgium, France, and the United States, including University of Paris, Musee de l'Homme, Paris, c. 1938, and Columbia University, c. 1939.

CAREER: Political leader, ethnologist, and writer. Co-founder of journals *La Trouee: Revue d'interet general* and *La Revue indigene: Les Arts et la vie,* 1927-28; co-founder and president of Ligue de la jeunesse patriote haitien; chief of Haitian Department of Interior, beginning in 1930; founder of Haitian Communist Party, 1934; journalist in Cuba, c. 1940; co-founder of Bureau d'Ethnologie, Haiti, 1941; Haitian charge d'affaires to Mexico, beginning in 1942.

WRITINGS:

La Proie et l'ombre (short stories; title means "The Prey and the Darkness"; contains "La Veste," "Fragment d'une confession," "Preface a la vie d'un bureaucrate," and "Propos sans suite"), preface by Antonio Vieux, Editions La Press, 1930, reprinted, Ateliers Fardin, 1977.
Les Fantoches (novel; title means "The Puppets"), Imprimerie de l'Etat, 1931.
La Montagne ensorcelee (novel; title means "The Enchanted Mountain"), preface by Jean Price-Mars, Imprimerie E. Chassaing, 1931, reprinted, Editions Fardin, 1976.
Gouveneurs de la rosee (novel), Imprimerie de l'Etat, 1944; translation by Langston Hughes and Mercer Cook published as *Masters of the Dew,* Reynal & Hitchcock, 1947, reprinted with introduction by J. Michael Dash, Heinemann Educational, 1978, 2nd edition, introduction by Cook, Collier Books, 1971.
Bois d'ebene (poems), Imprimerie Henri Deschamps, 1945; translation by Sidney Shapiro published as *Ebony Wood* (includes French text; contains "Ebony Wood," "Love and Death," "New Negro Sermon," and "Dirty Negroes"), Interworld Press, 1972.
Oeuvres choisies (title means "Selected Works"), preface by Jacques-Stephen Alexis, study by Eugenie Galperina, Editions du Progress (Moscow), 1964.
La Montagne ensorcelee (collection; contains *La Proie et l'ombre, La Montagne ensorcelee,* essay "Griefs de l'homme noir," and poems), preface by Jacques-Stephen Alexis, Editeurs Francais Reunis, 1972.

Also author of ethnological monographs. Poems represented in anthologies, including *An Anthology of Contemporary Latin-American Poetry,* edited by Dudley Fitts, New Directions, 1942; *The Poetry of the Negro, 1746-1949,* edited by Langston Hughes and Arna Bontemps, Doubleday, 1949; and *Black Poets in French,* edited by Marie Collins, Scribner, 1972. Contributor of essays, articles, and fiction to periodicals, including *Bulletin du Bureau d'Ethnologie, Haiti-Journal, Le Nouvelliste, Le Petit Impartial, La Press, La Revue indigene,* and *La Trouee.*

SIDELIGHTS: During the late 1920s and 1930s Jacques Roumain was the leader of young Haitian intellectuals seeking an end to America's military occupation of Haiti. Riding a wave of nationalistic fervor, the youths demanded a new aesthetic as well—one that stirred national pride by focusing on native Haitian culture. Responding with writings about the intricacies of class, politics, and religion in his native land, Roumain also explored Haiti's African roots and the similar pasts of blacks in other countries of the Caribbean, Latin America, and the United States. Disenchantment, however, with the ineffectual nationalist government that replaced U.S. occupational forces —and with the myopic excesses of Africanists—eventually turned the writer to Marxism, where color and class are viewed not in moral terms, but as resultant economic phenomena. Roumain came "to consider the Haitian situation in non-parochial terms . . . in the context of an international system of exploitation," wrote J. Michael Dash in his *Literature and Ideology in Haiti, 1915-1961,* pointing out the "shift from the exclusively personal or national concerns of [Roumain's] early work to the broader vision of his last works." Discussing *Masters of the Dew,* the writer's final and most acclaimed piece, *Renaissance of Haitian Poetry* author Naomi M. Garret made a similar comment: "Here, [Roumain] changes his perspective and alters the aim of his art. A Comitern inspired view of the uniting of the working classes of all nations into a revolutionary international force supersedes his desire for the joining together of the forces of all Haitians into a power for the progress of his country and his race." And in *Anthologie negro-africaine* editor Lilyan Kesteloot observed, "What constitutes Roumain's greatness . . . is precisely the fact that he was able to give breadth to his humanism."

Son of a wealthy mulatto landowner (and grandson of Haitian president Tancrede Auguste), Roumain received much of his education abroad. Familiar with the great literatures of Europe and the Americas and with the art and philosophy of the Near East (as well as engineering and agronomy), the cosmopolite returned to Haiti in 1927, drawn by pro-nationalism activities. With other young Haitian intellectuals he founded the journals *La Trouee* and *La Revue indigene,* designed to inform and rouse the Haitian populace; the latter proved most successful, publishing the poetry and fiction of Haitian contributors. Roumain also wrote for the leftist newspaper *Le Petit Impartial* and, with George Petit, founded the Ligue de la jeunesse patriote haitien, a coalition of youths from Haiti's fractured social strata. An article in *La Petit Impartial* criticizing the French clergy led to a seven-month imprisonment for the pair; it was to be the first of several political arrests for Roumain during his lifetime.

Already recognized as a nationalist leader by the age of twenty-three, Roumain was among Haitian representatives who determined that country's new provisional president at a U.S.-Haitian conference in 1930. President Eugene Roy appointed Roumain head of the Department of the Interior, a post he held again under Haiti's first elected president, Stenio Vincent. By mid-decade, however, the writer was unhappy with the nationalist government's inability to improve the economic and social conditions besetting the peasants and laborers with whom he so strongly sympathized. Gleaning a solution in the teachings of Marx and Engels, Roumain founded the Haitian Communist Party in 1934, and leftist political activities—real and imagined—resulted in charges of conspiracy and a three-year prison sentence.

Because communism was banned in Haiti in 1936, Roumain fled to Europe with his wife and child following release from prison. During a five-year exile he wrote articles and fiction for European journals; for a short time he worked as a journalist in Cuba. Roumain also pursued his keen interest in ethnology, studying at Paris's Musee de l'Homme and attending anthropology classes at Columbia University in New York City. When a new Haitian government offered amnesty to political exiles the writer returned to his homeland, establishing the Bureau d'Ethnologie for the study and preservation of Haiti's indigenous culture. Appointed charge d'affaires to Mexico in 1942 ("a kind of honorary banishment that would at least keep him out of prison and provide leisure for writing," explained Langston Hughes and Mercer Cook in the introduction to their translation of *Masters of the Dew*), Roumain died two years later of a heart attack. While the quantity of his writings was limited by political activities, incarceration, and exile, the impact of his life and works was profound in his native country. *Saturday Review of Literature* critic Linton Wells related, "Jacques Roumain['s] . . . sympathy for the underdog and . . . death . . . at thirty-eight, after years of imprisonment and exile, are said to have inspired the revolution which succeeded in overthrowing the dictatorial Lescot regime."

Roumain began to write poetry in his student days, initially exhibiting the influence of the French romantics, using traditional themes, forms, and imagery. Elements of nature reflected the human psyche; for Roumain this internal landscape was often melancholic—the speaker/poet unable to apprehend the meaning of existence, despairing over futile attempts to know and shape his destiny. The writer's early prose expressed similar themes and motifs, with the short story collection *La Proie et l'ombre* and novel *Les Fantoches* showing the aimlessness and despair that paralyzed many of his generation. The works feature young bourgeois intellectuals haunted by the pettiness and monotony of existence who turn to sordid diversions in the shadows of Port-au-Prince after dark. "The hero now, in the early prose, becomes a spokesman for a kind of Lost Generation, unable to find fulfillment in the old values and unable to find any new ones, and so existing in a vacuum," noted Carolyn Fowler in her Roumain literary biography *A Knot in the Thread.* "It is not the vacuum which ultimately destroys these heroes, but their lucidity about their condition."

Fowler also commented that in *La Proie et l'ombre,* published in 1930, "the storyteller implicit in the novelist vies still with the impressionmaker implicit in the poet." A year later in *Les Fantoches,* however, "the storyteller comes more clearly into his own, creating more fully developed characters, who move in a better delineated environment and who exteriorize their feelings to a much greater extent through conversation." Still, this tale of three young men—their attempts at love, public success, meaningful existence—"is not yet a fully developed novel," decided Fowler, "due to the sparseness of plot." She added that Roumain's contemporaries nevertheless embraced his formative prose, finding in it "a kind of solace . . . an esthetization of an inner life which they could recognize as their own." Literary critic Edmund Wilson, unimpressed by Roumain's later peasant novels, expressed admiration for *Les Fantoches* in his *Red, Black, Blond and Olive: Studies in Four Civilizations:* "It is quite evident that Jacques Roumain did not know the black peasants well. But he did know the Mulatto bourgeoisie, to which he himself belonged, and . . . *Les Fantoches,* . . . which deals with the elite of Port-au-Prince, throws so much light on its subject that one regrets it should not have been projected on a more extensive scale."

A rural counterpoint to Roumain's urban studies, *La Montagne ensorcelee* also explores the tension between passivity and action, this time in a Haitian peasant community. Relating how village inhabitants respond to a series of calamities with voodoocraft, the novel neither condemns nor sensationalizes the traditional practice; the author sees the religion as an important part of Haitian culture, reflecting and reinforcing feelings of powerlessness springing from restrictive attitudes about color and class. Concerned with indigenous cultural detail, *La Mon-*

tagne ensorcelee evokes the idioms of Haiti, with subtle shifts from French to Creole to patois, or slang. Of particular significance to Haitian letters as that country's first peasant novel, it is the work of a more assured storyteller. "Jacques Roumain already seems in full possession of his artistic abilities," wrote Roger Gaillard, discussing *La Montagne ensorcelee* in *L'Univers romanesque de Jacques Roumain*. "What strikes one first in this tale is its extraordinary precision: a simple story, related without digressions, with a deliberate intention to be brief; a clear, spare language that only approaches lyricism by accident; the avoidance of any complicity with negative characters in the story or pity for the victims. Let me say the word that comes to my mind as a description of his novel—classical. Classical because of the clarity of its construction; classical because of the inflexible detachment that the author imposes upon himself; classical because of the moderation of its style."

Roumain sought to evoke Haitian idioms in his later poetry as well, looking to other black poets, like America's Langston Hughes, for ways to transform indigenous musical forms and folk material into verse. Thematic content, however, was the primary focus of these later poems; in the collection *Ebony Wood*, produced while Roumain was in exile and published after his death, the poet angrily speaks for the world's downtrodden (but particularly for Africa's displaced), decrying slavery, exile, forced labor, lynching, segregation, and colonial oppression. Written in free verse, "the poems are unified by their utopian impulse," according to Dash, "and the Marxist imprecations they convey."

Dash further remarked that during the last four years of Roumain's life the writer forsook "the early iconoclasm" and pronouncements for "idealistic revolt," becoming "more capable of compromise." *Masters of the Dew*—considered the best work of fiction to come out of Haiti—was written during that time; unlike earlier Roumain protagonists incapable of action, its hero, Manuel, rallies feuding villagers to work together and irrigate their drought-stricken land. Although eventually killed by a jealous rival, the leader refuses to name the murderer as he dies, safeguarding the peasants' fledgling unity. Touching on a number of themes important to Roumain (nationalism, communism, romantic love, effective leadership, agricultural reform, and true friendship), *Masters of the Dew* is admired for its masterful synthesis of indigenous Haitian language, music, and folklore. "The novel is a beautiful, exact and tender rendering of Haitian life, of the African heritage, of the simple, impulsive, gravely formal folk, of the poetry and homely bite of their speech, of Congo dances, tropical luxuriance, the love of a land and its people," stated B. D. Wolfe in a critique for the *New York Herald Tribune Weekly Review*.

While manifestly a communist novel ("You have the struggle against the bourgeoisie, the summons of the exploited to class solidarity, the martyr who dies for the cause," enumerated Wilson), *Masters of the Dew* transcends its political parameters. Writing in *L'Esprit createur*, Beverly Ormerod remarked that "strong elements of myth and ritual . . . underpin the novel. . . . Earth and *coumbite*, dew and water, dust and drought are the recurrent symbols through which the hero's adventure is invested with a legendary quality." Allusions to Manuel as a Christ-figure are frequent, and to pagan vegetation gods Tammuz, Attis, and Adonis. Roumain scholar Jacques-Stephen Alexis called such writing "symbolic realism." "In theme and outline 'Masters of the Dew' is a fairly conventional proletarian novel; in style, imagination, observed detail it is a work of unusual freshness and beauty," judged R. G. Davis

in the *New York Times*. Calling the work "charming, vivid, and original," a *New Yorker* critic concurred that it is "a routine, almost commonplace story, . . . but one that is so freshly told and has so highly colored a background that it achieves the glowing effect of a tropical blossom."

BIOGRAPHICAL/CRITICAL SOURCES:

BOOKS

Cobb, Martha, *Harlem, Haiti, and Havana: A Comparative Critical Study of Langston Hughes, Jacques Roumain, Nicolas Guillen*, Three Continents Press, 1979.

Cook, Mercer, editor, *An Introduction to Haiti*, Pan American Union (Washington, D.C.), 1951.

Coulthard, George Robert, *Race and Colour in Caribbean Literature*, Oxford University Press, 1962.

Dash, J. Michael, *Literature and Ideology in Haiti, 1915-1961*, Barnes & Noble, 1981.

Fisher, Dexter, and Robert B. Stepto, editors, *Afro-American Literature: The Reconstruction of Instruction*, Modern Language Association of America, 1979.

Fowler, Carolyn, *A Knot in the Thread: The Life and Work of Jacques Roumain*, Howard University Press, 1980.

Galliard, Roger, *L'Univers romanesque de Jacques Roumain*, Henri Deschamps (Port-au-Prince, Haiti), 1965.

Garret, Naomi M., *The Renaissance of Haitian Poetry*, 1954, reprinted, Presence Africaine, 1963.

Janheinz, Jan, *Neo-African Literature*, translation by Oliver Coburn and Ursula Lehrburger, Grove, 1968.

Kesteloot, Lilyan, editor, *Anthologie negro-africaine*, Gerard (Verviers, Belgium), 1967.

Twentieth-Century Literary Criticism, Volume 19, Gale, 1986.

Wilson, Edmund, *Red, Black, Blond, and Olive: Studies in Four Civilizations, Zuni, Haiti, Soviet Russia, Israel*, Oxford University Press, 1956.

PERIODICALS

African Literature Today, number 9, 1978.
Black Images, spring, 1973.
College Language Association Journal, September, 1974, December, 1974.
Europe, January, 1971.
French Review, May, 1946.
Journal of Negro History, April, 1947.
Left Review, October, 1937.
L'Esprit Createur, summer, 1977.
Massachusetts Review, winter, 1977.
New Masses, May 22, 1945.
New Republic, March 27, 1937.
New Yorker, June 28, 1947.
New York Herald Tribune Weekly Review, August 3, 1947.
New York Times, June 15, 1947.
Opportunity, May, 1935.
Phylon, Volume XVII, number 3, 1956.
Saturday Review of Literature, July 5, 1947.
Virginia Quarterly Review, spring, 1973.*

—*Sketch by Nancy Pear*

*   *   *

ROWAN, Dan (Hale)   1922-1987

OBITUARY NOTICE: Born July 2, 1922, in Beggs, Okla.; died of lymphatic cancer, September 22, 1987, in Englewood, Fla. Comedian, producer, salesman, and author. Together with Dick Martin, Rowan was the host of NBC's "Rowan and

Martin's Laugh-In,'' a highly popular television comedy series that ran from 1968 to 1973 and won several Emmy Awards. With George Schlatter, Rowan and Martin also produced the show, which was known for a fast pace emphasizing short skits and one-liner jokes and which gave national exposure to such emerging comic talents as Lily Tomlin and Goldie Hawn.

Rowan worked briefly as a junior writer at Paramount Studios before serving in the U.S. Army Air Forces during World War II. After the war he sold cars until he met Martin in the early 1950s, and the two formed a nightclub comedy act. In their routines Rowan was the "straight man," providing a calm, self-assured contrast to Martin's clowning. NBC offered them the "Laugh-In" spot after they appeared as guest-hosts of Dean Martin's program in 1966. Rowan largely retired from show business after "Laugh-In" left the air. His book, *A Friendship*, consists of letters between himself and novelist John D. McDonald, author of the Travis McGee detective stories. Rowan's own novel, a spy thriller, remained unpublished at his death.

OBITUARIES AND OTHER SOURCES:

BOOKS

Current Biography, H. W. Wilson, 1969, November, 1987.

PERIODICALS

Chicago Tribune, September 24, 1987.
Los Angeles Times, September 23, 1987.
Newsweek, October 5, 1987.
New York Times, September 23, 1987.
Time, October 5, 1987.
Times (London), September 23, 1987.
Washington Post, September 23, 1987.

*   *   *

RUBEL, Nicole 1953-

PERSONAL: Born April 29, 1953, in Miami, Fla.; daughter of Theodore (an importer) and Janice (an importer; maiden name, Berman) Rubel; married Richard Langsen (a family therapist), May 25, 1987. *Education:* Tufts University and Boston Museum School of Fine Arts, B.S. (joint degree), 1975.

CAREER: Painter, illustrator, and writer. Designer of toys and greeting cards.

AWARDS, HONORS: Children's Books Showcase Award for Outstanding Graphic Design, 1976, for illustrating *Rotten Ralph;* award from American Book Association, and award from American Institute of Graphic Arts, both 1979; *Rotten Ralph* was included in *American Bookseller*'s "pick of the lists," 1984.

WRITINGS:

(And illustrator) *Getting Married*, St. Martin's, 1988.

SELF-ILLUSTRATED CHILDREN'S BOOKS

Sam and Violet Are Twins, Avon, 1981.
Sam and Violet Go Camping, Avon, 1981.
Sam and Violet's Christmas Story, Avon, 1981.
Sam and Violet's Birthday Book, Avon, 1982.
Bruno Brontosaurus, Avon, 1983.
Me and My Kitty, Macmillan, 1983.
I Can Get Dressed, Macmillan, 1984.
Bernie the Bulldog, Scholastic Inc., 1984.
Sam and Violet's Get Well Story, Avon, 1985.
Sam and Violet's Bedtime Mystery, Avon, 1985.

Pirate Jupiter and the Moondogs, Dial, 1985.
Uncle Henry and Aunt Henrietta's Honeymoon, Dial, 1986.
It Came From the Swamp, Dial, in press.
Goldie, Harper, in press.
Goldie's Nap, Harper, in press.

ILLUSTRATOR

Jack Gantos, *Rotten Ralph*, Houghton, 1975.
Jack Gantos, *Sleepy Ronald*, Houghton, 1976.
Jack Gantos, *Fairweather Friends*, Houghton, 1977.
Jack Gantos, *Aunt Bernice*, Houghton, 1978.
Jack Gantos, *Worse Than Rotten Ralph*, Houghton, 1979.
Steven Kroll, *Woof! Woof!*, Dial, 1982.
Jack Gantos, *Rotten Ralph's Rotten Christmas*, Houghton, 1984.
Michaela Muntean, *The House That Bear Built*, Dial, 1984.
Michaela Muntean, *Alligator's Garden*, Dial, 1984.
Michaela Muntean, *Little Lamb Bakes a Cake*, Dial, 1984.
Michaela Muntean, *Monkey's Marching Band*, Dial, 1984.
Patty Wolcott, *This Is Weird*, Scholastic Inc., 1986.

Also illustrator of *Willy's Raiders*, Parents Magazine Press, 1978; *The Perfect Pal*, Houghton, 1979; *Greedy Greeny*, Doubleday, 1979; *The Werewolf Family*, Houghton, 1980; and *Swamp Alligator*, Simon & Schuster, 1980. Contributor of illustrations to periodicals including *Boston*, *Instructor*, and *Scholastic Pre-K*.

AVOCATIONAL INTERESTS: Raising tropical plants, orchids, "and my Siamese cat, Cougar."

*   *   *

RUDENSKY, Morris "Red"
See FRIEDMAN, Max Motel

*   *   *

RUDOFSKY, Bernard 1905-1988

*OBITUARY NOTICE—*See index for *CA* sketch: Born April 13, 1905, in Vienna, Austria; died of cancer, March 12, 1988, in New York, N.Y. Architect, designer, museum exhibition director, photographer, educator, editor, and author. Rudofsky gained recognition during the 1940s for his exhibitions at New York City's Museum of Modern Art, where he worked intermittently from 1941 to 1965. His first display, adapted in 1947 as the book *Are Clothes Modern?*, and later exhibits and writings such as *The Unfashionable Human Body* examine the absurdities of various clothing styles. *Architecture Without Architects*, which began as a museum display of the author's own photographs, describes what Rudofsky considers practical and unpretentious building plans. Also a designer of posters, billboards, housewares, wallpaper, and other items, Rudofsky studied architecture and engineering in his native Vienna, Austria, and during the 1930s was self-employed as an architect in Italy and Brazil. In 1957 and 1958 he served as chief architect for the U.S. government's exhibitions at the Universal Exposition in Brussels, Belgium. Rudofsky, who received Fulbright, Guggenheim, and Rockefeller Foundation fellowships, lectured at the Massachusetts Institute of Technology, Yale University, Copenhagen's Royal Academy of Fine Arts, and Tokyo's Waseda University. He served as associate editor of *New Pencil Points* (now *Progressive Architecture*) and editorial director of *Interiors*. The architect's additional works include *Behind the Picture Window*, *The Kimono Mind*, *Streets for People: A Primer for Americans*, *The Prodigious Builders*, and *Now I Lay Me Down to Eat: Notes and Footnotes on the*

Lost Art of Living, his 1980 critique of social customs among various cultures.

OBITUARIES AND OTHER SOURCES:

BOOKS

McGraw-Hill Dictionary of Art, McGraw, 1969.

PERIODICALS

Chicago Tribune, March 17, 1988.
Los Angeles Times, March 19, 1988.
New York Times, March 14, 1988.
Times (London), March 21, 1988.

*   *   *

RUSBRIDGER, Alan   1953-

PERSONAL: Born December 29, 1953, in Lusaka, Northern Rhodesia (now Zambia); son of G. H. and B. E. (Wickham) Rusbridger; married Lindsay Mackie (a journalist) in 1982; children: Isabella, Elizabeth. *Education:* Magdalene College, Cambridge, M.A., 1976.

ADDRESSES: Agent—Anthony Sheil, 43 Doughty St., London WC1N 2LF, England.

CAREER: Cambridge Evening News, Cambridge, England, reporter and feature writer, 1976-79; *Guardian,* London, England, reporter and columnist, 1979-86; *Observer,* London, columnist, 1986-87; *London Daily News,* London, Washington correspondent, 1987—. Broadcaster for British Broadcasting Corporation (BBC-Radio).

WRITINGS:

A Concise History of the Sex Manual, 1886-1986, illustrations by Posy Simmonds, Faber, 1986.

Contributor of articles to *Spectator, London Review of Books,* and *Tatler.*

SIDELIGHTS: In *A Concise History of the Sex Manual, 1886-1986* Alan Rusbridger chronicles the fallacious—and often ludicrous—notions espoused in sex manuals during the last one hundred years. Excluding major sexology figures (like Kinsey or Masters and Johnson) and classic texts, the author surveys what *Spectator* critic David Sexton described as "the outpourings of an odd assortment of clerics, doctors, scoutmasters, feminists, opportunists and plain dirty old men" whose authoritarian pronouncements commonly veiled personal preferences and private fantasies. "Most varieties of sex were, until recently," commented John Mortimer in a review for the *Times Literary Supplement,* "thought to have dire and fatal consequences."

Noting that *A Concise History of the Sex Manual* is "not . . . a consecutive history of the subject," Sexton related: "[Rusbridger] claims to be working on behalf of those oppressed by incompetent authorities. . . . [He] has cheerfully served up all these absurdities, without attempting any analysis of the material [or] . . . serious argument." The reviewer added that manuals addressing human behaviors are frequently laughable because they "necessarily treat the body as a standard product." Mortimer, likewise, found the survey "entertaining because sex manuals are funny, but not consciously so." The critic wondered if readers ever seriously took such directives to heart. "Do couples, overcome with passion, really go to sex manuals for advice," he contemplated, "or are millions of copies a year simply bought for laughs?"

BIOGRAPHICAL/CRITICAL SOURCES:

PERIODICALS

Spectator, May 10, 1986.
Times Literary Supplement, June 20, 1986.

*   *   *

RUSSELL, Dora (Winifred Black)   1894-1986

PERSONAL: Born in 1894; died following a series of strokes, May 31, 1986, in Porthcurno, Cornwall, England; daughter of Frederick Black (a civil servant); married Bertrand Arthur William Russell (a philosopher), 1921 (divorced, 1935); married Pat Grace, 1940; children: (first marriage) John Conrad, Katharine Jane Tait; (with Griffin Barry) one son and one daughter. *Education:* Girton College, Cambridge, received first class degree; attended Peking University, 1921.

CAREER: Secretary to father, Frederick Black, chairman of the British Mission, in New York City, beginning in 1917; founded Workers' Birth Control Group, 1924; founded and directed Beacon Hill School, Sussex, England, with husband, Bertrand Russell, 1927-1943 (one source says 1927-1939); participated in Campaign for Nuclear Disarmament during 1950s; helped organize Women's Caravan of Peace throughout Europe, 1958. Unsuccessful Labour Party candidate for Parliament. *Wartime service:* Worked for British Ministry of Information, chiefly in Soviet Relations Division, during World War II.

MEMBER: National Council for Civil Liberties (founding member).

WRITINGS:

(With first husband, Bertrand Russell), *The Prospects of Industrial Civilization,* Century, 1923, 2nd edition, Allen & Unwin, 1959.
Hypatia; or, Woman and Knowledge, Dutton, 1925, reprinted, Folcroft, 1976.
The Right to Be Happy, Harper, 1927.
In Defence of Children, H. Hamilton, 1932, published as *Children: Why Do We Have Them?,* Harper, 1933.
The Tamarisk Tree (autobiography), Volume I: *My Quest for Liberty and Love,* Putnam, 1975, Volume II: *My School and the Years of War,* Virago, 1980, Volume III: *Challenge to the Cold War,* Virago, 1985.
The Religion of the Machine Age, Routledge & Kegan Paul, 1983, Methuen, 1985.
The Dora Russell Reader: Fifty-seven Years of Writing and Journalism, 1925-1982 (includes *Hypatia; or, Woman and Knowledge* and excerpts from *The Right to Be Happy* and *In Defence of Children*), foreword by Dale Spender, Pandora Press, 1983, published as *The Dora Russell Reader: Fifty Years in Writing and Journalism, 1925-1982,* Methuen, 1985.

Science correspondent for fantasy publication *British Ally.* Contributor to anarchistic and humanist periodicals.

SIDELIGHTS: Dora Russell was an active campaigner for feminist and social causes in England throughout the twentieth century. She is especially remembered for co-founding and directing the progressive Beacon Hill School in Sussex with her first husband, Nobel Prize-winning philosopher Bertrand Russell, during the late 1920s and 1930s. The school was considered remarkable in its day for its permissive approach toward discipline and for its controversial topics of instruction. Dora Russell was an early advocate of birth control—she founded the Workers' Birth Control Group in 1924—and she participated in campaigns for peace and nuclear disarmament during the 1950s. Beginning in the 1920s, the activist wrote several essays and books on social issues, including *Hypatia; or, Woman and Knowledge,* which espouses women's rights, *The Right to Be Happy,* which advocates sexual freedom, and, in 1983, *The Religion of the Machine Age,* which deplores the unrestricted development of industry, technology, and mass warfare. During the 1970s and 1980s she wrote her three-volume autobiography, *The Tamarisk Tree.* Russell died in 1986, a year after the third volume was published.

The first volume of *The Tamarisk Tree,* subtitled *My Quest for Liberty and Love,* focuses primarily on Dora Russell's relationship with Bertrand Russell. "When Dora . . . first encountered the distinguished middle-aged philosopher" around 1919, recounted Rosemary Dinnage in the *Times Literary Supplement,* "the conversation had turned to free love, of which she was an earnest supporter. When she answered his question about the fate of the children of such unions by announcing that they were solely the mother's concern, Russell laughed and said that whoever he had children by, it certainly would not be her." Dinnage added, "Their first child was born a year or two later." As lovers, the two traveled together to the Soviet Union and China, and it was after a year at Peking University that Dora first became pregnant. Bertrand proposed in 1921 that they marry after he divorced his first wife, but Dora objected to legalized matrimony and "felt doubts about tying herself down for life." She soon relented, however, and they were married that year. "Soon after," reported Michael Rosenthal in the *New York Times Book Review,* "Dora learned that, however radical [Bertrand's] rhetoric about women's rights might be, he really wanted a wife who would serve his needs without asking much in return."

To exercise their theories of free love and sexual equality, Dora and Bertrand Russell agreed to have an open marriage, and both had extra-marital affairs. For a while, Dinnage noted, Bertrand Russell, "impotent at the time with [Dora], had stood by their progressive principles by all but encouraging her to have another child, while he too pursued affairs of his own. Their marriage, they had both believed, was independent of convention and too genuine to be shaken by such details as the paternity of the children." But when Dora did have two children by a lover, in addition to the two she had by her husband, Bertrand "waged an unsuccessful struggle against his jealousy . . . and he found a still younger woman, Patricia Spence, who pleased him better," recounted W. Warren Wagar in *Saturday Review.* Dora and Bertrand Russell divorced, after reportedly vicious legal disputes, in 1935.

In 1927 Dora and Bertrand Russell had founded Beacon Hill School, where they attempted to instruct children in a non-authoritarian manner on subjects the two felt were valuable. Dora Russell managed the school alone from the time of her divorce until around 1940, when she remarried. The second volume of her autobiography, subtitled *My School and the Years of War,* "is a sane and straightforward account" of the teachers' and students' daily activities and the philosophy behind the school, described Nicolas Walter in the *Spectator.*

"Today, of course, it is hard to see what all the fuss was about. . . . Sensible clothing and food, factual information about sex and society, open teaching about politics and religion, the emphasis on doing rather than reading and on thinking rather than learning—what was fantasy a century ago is now orthodox," Walter observed. In addition, Stuart Sutherland noted in the *Times Literary Supplement,* "the teachers laid down no rules and there were no punishments. There was a democratic 'school council' consisting of all the children gathered in conclave" that made and enforced rules solely by popular opinion. "Nevertheless," Sutherland added, "Dora Russell does admit to having insisted on daily showers and the use of a toothbrush. On being told to have recourse to the latter, one child scornfully but perceptively remarked: 'Call this a free school?'"

Sutherland complained in his review that Dora Russell "provides only a superficial account of the school's activities. . . . She makes no systematic effort to evaluate the school's success," while Bertrand Russell is highly critical of the school in his own brief autobiographical account, surmising "in retrospect that he and Dora had not provided enough 'routine and order' and that there was 'a pretence at more freedom than in fact existed.'" Walter, however, allowed for the differences of opinion and interpretation by remarking: "Dora Russell tends to be sentimental about it, whereas Bertrand Russell tended to be cynical about it. . . . No doubt the balance lies somewhere in between." The reviewer concluded: "Dora Russell at Beacon Hill did something to bring education to children rather than the other way round. Looking at the educated world, who is to say she was wrong?"

The third volume of Russell's autobiography, *Challenge to the Cold War,* "is more general, more ruminative," than the previous two volumes, judged Fiona MacCarthy in her London *Times* review. "[It is] the more leisurely and stately culmination of a trilogy which as a document of our feminist lives and times is totally unrivalled." In the book, Russell reflects on the social and political issues for which she campaigned—such as maternity leave, nuclear disarmament, and an end to media censorship and government propaganda in England—and also on the struggles within her own family. "There was much that was tragic in her family life," recounted Anne Smith in her *New Statesman* review. Russell's older son, diagnosed as schizophrenic, was dependent on her; the younger son was paralyzed in a mining accident; and a granddaughter, reported Smith, "committed suicide in the Far East by setting herself alight in a protest." As MacCarthy observed, "For someone so dedicated to world peace-making Dora Russell's progress, both within the women's movement and in her domestic life, has been astonishingly, breathtakingly, turbulent. . . . Vast and endless dramas of revenge, insanity, self-immolation, are played out within the pages of these memoirs."

MacCarthy admitted, however, that "as Dora Russell aficionados know, you do not read this writer for her scintillating prose style." Noting that "this book has many longueurs," MacCarthy nevertheless called the autobiography "irresistible in its portrayal of formidable female personality, of doggedness combined with that element of craziness which seems inseparable from the lives and loves of ladies of the extremist left." The *New Statesman*'s Smith, similarly, found in *Challenge to the Cold War* "the honest story of one highly intelligent, compassionate woman, who has committed her whole life to making the world a better place." And Jose Harris, reviewing the book in the *Times Literary Supplement,* predicted that *The Tamarisk Tree: Challenge to the Cold War* "will survive as a major primary source on mid-twentieth-century feminism, peace movements, advanced radicalism and the politics of applied science.''

BIOGRAPHICAL/CRITICAL SOURCES:

BOOKS

Russell, Bertrand, *The Autobiography of Bertrand Russell*, Simon & Schuster, c. 1967-1969.
Russell, Dora, *The Tamarisk Tree*, Volume I: *My Quest for Liberty and Love*, Putnam, 1975, Volume II: *My School and the Years of War*, Virago, 1980, Volume III: *Challenge to the Cold War*, Virago, 1985.

PERIODICALS

New Statesman, September 6, 1985.
New York Times Book Review, February 15, 1986.
Saturday Review, January 10, 1976.
Spectator, April 19, 1980.
Times (London), August 8, 1985.
Times Educational Supplement, May 25, 1984.

Times Literary Supplement, August 1, 1975, April 4, 1980, December 9, 1983, October 11, 1985.

OBITUARIES:

PERIODICALS

Chicago Tribune, June 3, 1986.
Detroit Free Press, June 3, 1986.
New York Times, June 2, 1986.*

—*Sketch by Christa Brelin*

*   *   *

RUTHERFORD, Douglas
    See McCONNELL, James Douglas Rutherford

*   *   *

RYDER, Thom
    See HARVEY, John (Barton)

S

SALBER, Eva J. 1916-

PERSONAL: Born January 5, 1916, in Cape Town, South Africa; immigrated to United States, 1956, naturalized citizen, 1961; daughter of Moses (a partner in wholesale meat company) and Fanny (a housewife; maiden name, Srolowitz) Salber; married Harry T. Phillips (a physician and professor), November 1, 1939; children: David, Mark, Rosalie, Philip. *Education:* University of Cape Town, M.B., Ch.B., 1938, D.P.H., 1945, M.D., 1955. *Politics:* Democrat. *Religion:* Jewish.

ADDRESSES: Home—1308 Arboretum Dr., Chapel Hill, N.C. 27514.

CAREER: Provincial Hospital, Port Elizabeth, South Africa, 1939; Queen Elizabeth Hospital for Children, London, England, 1940; Sir Henry Elliott Hospital, Umtata, South Africa, 1940-41; Cape Town Free Dispensary, Cape Town, South Africa, 1941-42; Institute of Family and Community Health, Durban, South Africa, family physician, 1945-54; University of Cape Town, Cape Town, medical officer, 1954-55; Children's Hospital Medical Center, Boston, Mass., fellow in medicine, 1957-58, assistant physician, 1958-67; Martha M. Eliot Family Health Center, Boston, chief, 1967-69; Harvard Center for Community Health and Medical Care, Boston, Mass., senior associate, 1969-70; Duke University, Durham, N.C., assistant professor, 1971-72, professor of community and family medicine and director of Community Health Models, 1972-82, professor emeritus, 1982—.

Harvard School of Public Health, Milton Research Associate in Maternal and Child Health, 1957-58, research associate in epidemiology, 1959-61, senior research associate, 1961-66; lecturer at Harvard Medical School, 1967-70; University of North Carolina at Chapel Hill, lecturer in maternal and child health, 1972-78, research associate at Health Services Research Center, 1975—. Member of board of directors of Edgemont Community Clinic, 1971-75, Center for Consumer Health Education, Vienna, Va., 1979-82, and Orange, Person, Chatham Area Mental Health Center, 1981-83; member of advisory board of North Carolina Student Rural Health Coalition, 1978—; member of health advisory committee of Chapel Hill-Carrboro Interfaith Council for Social Services, 1984—; consultant to World Health Organization, Massachusetts Interagency Council on Smoking and Health, and Boston Association for Childbirth Education.

MEMBER: International Epidemiological Association, American Public Health Association (fellow), American Gerontological Society.

AWARDS, HONORS: Senior bursar of South African Council for Scientific and Industrial Research, 1950-53 and 1955; Milton research associate in maternal and child health for Harvard School of Public Health, 1957-58; Radcliffe Institute for Independent Study, scholar, 1966-67, Macy fellow, 1969-70; senior international fellow of Fogarty International Center, 1980.

WRITINGS:

(Contributor) E. F. Bargatta and R. R. Evans, editors, *Smoking, Health, and Behavior,* Aldine, 1968.
(Contributor) H. T. Phillips and R. S. Parkinson, editors, *Enhancing the Role of the Consumer in Comprehensive Health Planning,* American Association for Comprehensive Health Planning, 1974.
Caring and Curing: Community Participation in Health Services, Neale Watson Academic Publications, 1975.
(With Connie Service) *Community Health Education: The Lay Advisor Approach,* Duke University Press, 1983.
Don't Send Me Flowers When I'm Dead: Voices of the Rural Elderly, Duke University Press, 1983.

Contributor of nearly a hundred articles to medical journals. Member of editorial board of *Journal of Health Politics, Policy, and Law,* 1978-80.

WORK IN PROGRESS: The Mind Is Not the Heart: Recollections of a Woman Physician, for Duke University Press.

SIDELIGHTS: Eva J. Salber told *CA:* "I write in an attempt to show people what life is like for the poor, the neglected, the elderly, and the sick. I have published two books of this kind based on tape-recorded, unstructured interviews. In the first of these, *Caring and Curing: Community Participation in Health Services,* I interviewed people of low income who lived in an inner-city housing project in Boston, where I set up services for mothers and children. In the second book, *Don't Send Me Flowers When I'm Dead: Voices of the Rural Elderly,* I interviewed rural elderly people living alone in North Carolina.

"A third book of this kind, *The Mind Is Not the Heart: Recollections of a Woman Physician,* is in essence a self-interview. Here I describe my experiences as a working mother and doctor in South Africa; Boston, Massachusetts; and North Carolina.

"I wrote these books because I felt that scientific writing, important as it is, is not the medium for conveying the flavor of society's neglected people. My journal articles could not express the feel of hunger or despair, or the loneliness of bereavement. Nor could my journal articles expose my own emotions about apartheid and its consequences in South Africa—the country of my birth—or about poverty and discrimination even in our rich United States—my adopted country. In addition, my scientific articles couldn't show the conflicts between loyalty to my family and to the communities I served as a doctor.

"In large part these three books are about the 'ordinary' people I knew in South Africa and the United States and the effect they had on me. As a community physician—and a protagonist of social medicine—I came in contact with people that I might not have met if I had followed a different profession. In the preface to this third book I say: 'Accepting the beauty and the burden of their trust enlarged my own humanity and shaped me as a person and a doctor.'"

*   *   *

SALZMAN, Paul   1953-

PERSONAL: Born November 17, 1953, in Melbourne, Australia; son of Mark (a businessman) and Leah (Kliman) Salzman; married Susan Lesley Bye (a teacher), January 8, 1987. *Education:* Monash University, B.A. (with honors), 1975; Pembroke College, Cambridge, Ph.D., 1979.

ADDRESSES: Office—Department of English, La Trobe University, Bundoora, Victoria, Australia.

CAREER: University of Adelaide, Adelaide, Australia, research fellow, 1980-82; University of Melbourne, Parkville, Australia, tutor in English, 1982-85; La Trobe University, Bundoora, Australia, lecturer in English, 1985—.

WRITINGS:

English Prose Fiction, 1558-1700: A Critical History, Clarendon Press, 1985.
(Editor) *An Anthology of Elizabethan Fiction,* Oxford University Press, 1987.

Contributor to periodicals, including *Restoration, Southern Review,* and *Meridian.*

WORK IN PROGRESS: An anthology of seventeenth-century fiction; a book on Australian fiction (with Kenneth Gelder) for Penguin, publication expected in 1989.

SIDELIGHTS: Prose Fiction, 1558-1700 "will do much to stimulate interest in the rather neglected field of sixteenth and seventeenth-century fiction," H. R. Woudhuysen told readers of the *Times Literary Supplement.* The book covers a wide variety of fictions, many of which have been almost forgotten. The author does not neglect the role of women in the world of literature, particularly in the seventeenth century. "His appetite," wrote Woudhuysen, "is astonishing: his interest rarely flags and he has a very sharp eye for illustrative quotations." Salzman's prose, he continued, "is free from modern critical jargon and easy to follow."

BIOGRAPHICAL/CRITICAL SOURCES:

PERIODICALS

Times Literary Supplement, March 6, 1987.

*   *   *

SAMKANGE, S. J. T.
See SAMKANGE, Stanlake (John Thompson)

*   *   *

SAMKANGE, Stanlake (John Thompson)   1922-1988
(S. J. T. Samkange)

OBITUARY NOTICE—See index for *CA* sketch: Born March 11, 1922, in Mariga, Rhodesia (now Zimbabwe); died of heart and lung ailments, March 6, 1988, in Harare, Zimbabwe. Political activist, businessman, educator, publisher, and author. Beginning in the 1950s, Samkange campaigned actively for the independence of British-ruled Rhodesia, which became the independent republic of Zimbabwe in 1979. He held important positions in the political parties of activists Joshua Nkomo and Bishop Abel Muzorewa during that time, in addition to directing various companies in Salisbury, Rhodesia, from 1958 to 1965. He then taught history at Northeastern University for twelve years and lectured at Fisk University and Harvard University, returning to Africa in 1977 to serve as Muzorewa's political adviser. Two years later he opened a publishing house in Zimbabwe. Samkange wrote several books, including *The Chief's Daughter Who Would Not Laugh, Origins of Rhodesia, Christ's Skin Colour: Was He a White or Black Man?, Among Them Yanks,* and, under the name S. J. T. Samkange, *What Rhodes Really Said About Africans* and *The Origin of African Nationalism.*

OBITUARIES AND OTHER SOURCES:

BOOKS

In Black and White, 3rd edition, Gale, 1980.

PERIODICALS

New York Times, March 9, 1988.
Times (London), March 8, 1988.
Washington Post, March 10, 1988.

*   *   *

SANDERS, Gladys (Shultz)   1919(?)-1988

OBITUARY NOTICE: Born c. 1919; died of cancer, May 29, 1988, in Greenwich, Conn. Public relations consultant, copywriter, and author. Formerly a copywriter for Young & Rubicam, Sanders worked for Carl Byoir & Associates public relations firm from 1970 to 1986. An author of books about fashion and a contributor to magazines and newspapers, she wrote *The Independent Woman* with Rae Wisely.

OBITUARIES AND OTHER SOURCES:

PERIODICALS

New York Times, June 1, 1988.

*   *   *

SANDON, J. D.
See HARVEY, John (Barton)

SANTIAGO, Danny
See JAMES, Daniel (Lewis)

* * *

SARGENT, Alice G(oldstein) 1939-1988

OBITUARY NOTICE—See index for *CA* sketch: Born February 5, 1939, in Cincinnati, Ohio; died of cancer, June 5, 1988, in Indio, Calif. Management consultant, educator, editor, and author. Beginning in the late 1970s Sargent served as an independent management consultant to numerous government agencies and private corporations, including the Federal Executive Institute, the Securities Exchange Commission, E. I. duPont de Nemours, and Proctor & Gamble. She also conducted management work conferences for the National Training Laboratories (NTL) Institute in Washington, D.C., and in the mid-1970s was project coordinator for a national study on women in education for the U.S. Department of Health, Education, and Welfare (now Department of Health and Human Services). Sargent taught management courses at various institutions, including San Diego State University, Trinity College, University of Southern California, and the Australian Institute of Management, and for nine years she was dean and director of staff training at University of Massachusetts. Sargent wrote *The Androgynous Manager*, edited *Beyond Sex Roles*, and co-edited, with Roger A. Ritvo, *The NTL Managers' Handbook*.

OBITUARIES AND OTHER SOURCES:

BOOKS

Who's Who of American Women, 15th edition, Marquis, 1986.

PERIODICALS

Washington Post, June 14, 1988.

* * *

SARTOR, Margaret 1959-

PERSONAL: Born August 12, 1959, in Monroe, La.; daughter of Fred Williams (a surgeon) and Tommie Sue (a painter; maiden name, Eaves) Sartor; married Alex Harris (a photographer and professor), December 18, 1982. *Education:* Attended Trinity University, 1977-78, and Southern Methodist University, Paris, France, 1979; University of North Carolina at Chapel Hill, B.A., 1981; graduate study at North Carolina State University, 1983-85.

ADDRESSES: Home—4604 Erwin Rd., Durham, N.C. 27705.

CAREER: University of North Carolina Press, Chapel Hill, paste-up artist, 1981-82; John Ulmstead Hospital, Butner, N.C., special education teacher at Children's Psychiatric Institute, 1982-83; free-lance photographer, 1984-85; Carnegie Corp. of New York, New York, N.Y., graphic designer, 1985-86; North Carolina State University, Raleigh, lecturer in photography, 1987—. Graphic designer for Duke University, 1982—; guest curator of International Center of Photography, 1983, 1986.

WRITINGS:

(Editor with husband, Alex Harris) *Gertrude Blom: Bearing Witness*, University of North Carolina Press, 1983.

Contributor of articles, poems, and photographs to magazines, including *Carolina Quarterly*, *Windhover*, and *Cellar Door*.

WORK IN PROGRESS: The Heart of the Matter, a photographic documentary of Monroe, Louisiana.

SIDELIGHTS: Margaret Sartor told *CA:* "I work primarily in the field of documentary photography as a teacher, editor, photographer, and designer. In all these roles I feel my work is an attempt to define and refine the concepts and ideas one uses to describe the documentary approach."

* * *

SASSON, Sarah Diane Hyde 1946-

PERSONAL: Born August 27, 1946, in Asheville, N.C.; daughter of Arnold (a social worker) and Dorothy (a homemaker; maiden name, Roberts) Hyde; married Jack M. Sasson (a professor), June 29, 1969; children: David, Noah, Daniel. *Education:* University of North Carolina at Chapel Hill, B.A., 1968, Ph.D., 1980; University of Illinois at Urbana-Champaign, M.A., 1971.

ADDRESSES: Home—1505 Halifax Rd., Chapel Hill, N.C. 27514. *Office*—120 Allen, Duke University, Durham, N.C. 27706.

CAREER: University of North Carolina at Chapel Hill, instructor, 1980-81, lecturer, 1981-82, American Council of Learned Societies fellow in Shaker literature, 1982-83, coordinator of program in the humanities, 1984-87, and director of research project on church, state, and the First Amendment, 1984-87; Duke University, Durham, N.C., teacher of American studies and director of master of arts in liberal studies program, 1987—.

MEMBER: American Folklore Society, American Studies Association, Modern Language Association of America, National Continuing Education Association, Association of Graduate Liberal Studies.

AWARDS, HONORS: Grant from National Endowment for the Humanities, 1984-87.

WRITINGS:

The Shaker Spiritual Narrative, University of Tennessee Press, 1983.
(Editor) *Religion, Education, and the First Amendment*, University of North Carolina at Chapel Hill, 1987.

SIDELIGHTS: Sarah Diane Hyde Sasson told *CA:* "My interest in Shakers originally grew out of an interest in American autobiography. Many Shakers were inveterate scribblers, and a large body of fascinating materials are extant in manuscript and virtually unknown. My early work, then, concentrated on how Shakers told stories about their lives and how they adapted the materials of their own experience to the patterns expected by the Shaker community.

"More recently I have been exploring how Shaker culture both challenged and reflected the values of the larger American culture. Creating a community based on the common good and eschewing private property, the Shakers and other communal societies challenged the individualistic spirit of the age. At the same time, their belief in the power of spiritual experience, particularly during the 1840s, encouraged individual visionary experiences, which at times contested the authority of the community hierarchy."

* * *

SATTELMEYER, Robert 1946-

PERSONAL: Born September 21, 1946, in Cleveland, Ohio;

son of Robert D. (an engineer) and Marilyn (Sanders) Sattelmeyer; married Suzanne Shames (an economist), December 14, 1974; children: Sarah, Daniel. *Education:* Indiana University—Bloomington, A.B., 1968; University of New Mexico, M.A., 1972, Ph.D., 1975.

ADDRESSES: Home—2002 Sunborough, Columbia, Mo. 65203. *Office*—Department of English, University of Missouri—Columbia, Columbia, Mo. 65211.

CAREER: University of Missouri—Columbia, assistant professor, 1975-81, associate professor, 1981-85, professor of English, 1985—.

MEMBER: Modern Language Association of America.

AWARDS, HONORS: Fellow of National Endowment for the Humanities, 1979, and Huntington Library, 1984.

WRITINGS:

(Editor) Henry David Thoreau, *Journal,* Princeton University Press, Volume I (with Elizabeth Hall Witherell, William L. Howarth, and Thomas Blanding): *1837-1844,* 1981, Volume II: *1842-1848,* 1984.
(Editor with J. Donald Crowley) *One Hundred Years of Huckleberry Finn: The Boy, His Book, and American Culture,* University of Missouri Press, 1985.
Thoreau's Reading, Princeton University Press, 1988.

Member of editorial board of "Writings of Henry D. Thoreau," Princeton University Press/University of Missouri Press. Essays editor of *Missouri Review.*

WORK IN PROGRESS: Research on Mark Twain's years as a steamboat pilot.

SIDELIGHTS: Robert Sattelmeyer told *CA:* "I have been interested in and fascinated by Henry David Thoreau since I read an excerpt from his book *Walden* in my high school anthology of American literature twenty-five years ago. After I finished my dissertation on Thoreau I worked at the files of the 'Thoreau Edition' at Princeton University, and eventually I began working on the editing of his journals for that edition. What attracted me to the project was the opportunity to help put in print the many passages and sections from his journals that had not been published before, especially some notebooks and parts of notebooks dating from his stay at Walden Pond from 1845 to 1847.

"The collection on Mark Twain's *Huckleberry Finn* grew out of an idea that the University of Missouri ought to mark the centennial of that famous novel by the state's most celebrated writer. The collection turned out to be an especially satisfying project. It demonstrated, to my mind, the perennial freshness of that book and its seminal position in our culture as an expression both of our deepest longings for freedom and of the shameful reality of our culture's participation in the freedom-denying forms of slavery and other versions of domination.

"Currently I am interested in Mark Twain's steamboat pilot years because it occurs to me that we—literary critics, biographers, and literary historians—have always unconsciously relied upon Twain's own highly colored and even fictional accounts of these years in his autobiographical writings, and that in fact relatively little is actually known about his life during these years. Using material unearthed by other scholars and material I turn up myself in the archives of Mississippi Valley newspapers from this period, I hope to build a picture of the author's life to set alongside the one most readers are most familiar with, and to begin to judge the ways in which his experiences during these years were transformed in his fictional treatments of this world in his most famous books."

*   *   *

SATTERLY, Weston
    See SUNNERS, William

*   *   *

SAUNDERS, Caleb
    See HEINLEIN, Robert A(nson)

*   *   *

SAUNDERS, Sally Love   1940-

PERSONAL: Born January 15, 1940, in Bryn Mawr, Pa.; daughter of Lawrence and Dorothy (Love) Saunders. *Education:* Attended Temple University, 1962-63; George Williams College, B.S., 1965. *Religion:* Episcopalian.

ADDRESSES: Home—Academy House, 1420 Locust St., No. 36C, Philadelphia, Pa. 19102. *Office*—639 Timber Lane, Devon, Pa. 19333.

CAREER: Margaret Fuller Settlement House, Cambridge, Mass., teacher, summers, 1958-61; poetry teacher at about a dozen public schools in eastern Pennsylvania, 1962-71; Institute of Pennsylvania Hospital, Philadelphia, poetry therapist, 1969-74; lecturer, teacher, and workshop and seminar conductor, 1974—. Teacher at Navajo reservation in Fort Defiance, Ariz., 1963, and Young Men's Jewish Center, Chicago, Ill., 1964-65; guest on radio and television programs; public speaker.

MEMBER: Academy of American Poets, Association for Humanistic Psychology, Poets and Writers Guild, Poetry Society of America, Poetry Therapy Association (former vice-president), National Writers Club, Free Women's School, Pennsylvania Poetry Society, Press Club of San Francisco, Pen and Brush Club, Ina Coolbrith Circle, Bay Area Poets' Coalition.

AWARDS, HONORS: Grants from City of Philadelphia, Pennsylvania State Department, and Philadelphia Foundation; finalist in Wilory Farm Poetry contest, 1981, with "Grandpop John's Funeral"; book award from Nutmegger; Poetry Day Book Award from Spearman Publishers; winner of National League of American Pen Women contest; award from Pennsylvania Poetry Society; third place finalist from Bay Area Poets' Choice, 1988, with "Kicking Stones."

WRITINGS:

POETRY COLLECTIONS

Past the Near Meadows, Saunders, 1961.
Pauses, Golden Quill, 1978.
Fresh Bread, Golden Quill, 1982.
Poetic Symphony: Music From the Heart, Fine Arts Press, 1986.
Rainbows and Rhapsodies: Poetry of the Eighties, Fine Arts Press, 1987.

Work represented in anthologies, including *Mirrors of the Wistful Dreamer,* New Worlds, 1980; *Poets Anonymous,* Skills Unlimited; *Gate Becomes Bridge,* Ben Lomand Center. Contributor of poems and articles to magazines, including *Hoofstrikes, Wormwood Review, Seventeen, Mark Twain Journal,*

Z Miscellaneous, Quaker Life, and *New Athenaeum,* and to newspapers.

WORK IN PROGRESS: A manuscript on "poetry as therapy, poetry as healer, and my years as a poetry therapist."

SIDELIGHTS: Sally Love Saunders told *CA:* "I began writing poetry at a very early age. Realizing a childhood dream of becoming a poetry therapist, I have shared my love of poetry by working in libraries, schools, and mental institutions, bringing comfort and peace to others. A grant enabled me to initiate a poetry therapy program at the Institute of Pennsylvania Hospital in Philadelphia, where my work prompted Dr. Lance Wright to characterize me as 'the obstetrician of my patients' poems.' I hope my poetry will have a 'Johnny Appleseed' effect, planting seeds that will take root and grow. I believe that everyone is a potential poet and through my art I hope to enable people to get in touch with their own feelings."

*   *   *

SAX, Richard   1949-

PERSONAL: Born May 5, 1949, in Passaic, N.J.; son of Sander (a certified public accountant) and Frances (Mandell) Sax. *Education:* Attended University of Pennsylvania, 1966-68; Northwestern University, B.S., 1970; attended Culinary Institute and New York City Community College (now New York City Technical College), 1975, and Le Cordon Bleu, 1977. *Religion:* Jewish.

ADDRESSES: Home—718 Broadway, No. 8D, New York, N.Y. 10003. *Agent*—Susan Lescher, Lescher & Lescher, 67 Irving Pl., New York, N.Y. 10003.

CAREER: High school drama teacher in Illinois, 1970-71; taught and directed theater and ran catering service in Union County, N.J., 1971-75; American Express Co., New York, N.Y., chef, 1976; Hotel Plaza Athenee, Paris, France, apprentice, 1977; ran restaurant in Martha's Vineyard, Mass., 1977-78; chef-director of test kitchen and columnist for *Food and Wine* magazine, 1978-80; Time-Life Books, London, England, cookbook consultant, 1980-81; free-lance writer, interviewer, cooking teacher, lecturer, and restaurant and product consultant, 1981—.

MEMBER: International Association of Cooking Professionals, American Institute of Wine and Food, New York Association of Cooking Teachers, James Beard Foundation, Authors Guild.

WRITINGS:

(With David Ricketts) *Cooking Great Meals Every Day,* Random House, 1982.
Old-Fashioned Desserts, Irena Chalmers, 1983.
New York's Master Chefs, Knapp Press, 1984.
The Cookie Lover's Cookie Book, Harper, 1986.
(With Sandra Gluck) *From the Farmers' Market,* Harper, 1986.

Co-author of "Cooking Healthy," a monthly column in *Bon Appetit;* author of book review column in *Cuisine,* 1982-84. Contributor to magazines, including *Food and Wine, Gourmet, Yankee,* and *Elle.*

WORK IN PROGRESS: Research on old-fashioned desserts and home cooking from around the world, using an oral history approach that emphasizes people as well as their food; research on cheese.

SIDELIGHTS: Richard Sax told *CA:* "My interest in food exploded not long after college. I soon wanted to write about it, feeling I had an unsnobbish approach and a gut, instinctual sense of the things that I could convey to the reader with immediacy. But since I resent a dilletantish approach to food ('experts' who have no training or can't cook), I went 'through the kitchen,' working as a caterer and training as a chef, so I'd know what I was talking about myself. Little by little, I veered off into the writing, and I have not worked in restaurants for several years.

"I still cook everything I publish, and I cook like a fiend in my own kitchen. But I have the luxury of serving two per night in the comfort of my own home, not dozens in a restaurant. And the more I work with food, the simpler my tastes become.

"Two chefs I respect: Seppi Renggli of New York's Four Seasons, Jean-Louis Palladin of Jean-Louis in Washington, D.C. (an unstoppable mad genius). I love visiting Alsace, France, and Hungary for great food, as well as roaming our country, where things are currently very exciting.

"By old-fashioned desserts, I mean simple, home-cooked things like rice puddings, warm fruit desserts like cobblers and crisps, home-baked pies and cakes. I concentrate on them because, first, they evoke an immediate response in people that goes beyond good taste (i.e., 'Oh, that reminds me of something my grandmother would make every Thanksgiving'). Plain, unfancy, unstudied desserts. And because they are irresistible to eat. And because these kinds of home-cooked dishes are a fragile legacy—recipes that sometimes aren't written down, and should be preserved.

"I don't see my preferences as 'retro' or nostalgia, by the way, but as enjoying foods with basic appeal. In the world of food, some things (e.g., bread, cheese, wine) are fundamental."

BIOGRAPHICAL/CRITICAL SOURCES:

PERIODICALS

Gourmet, March, 1983.

*   *   *

SCANLON, James Edward   1940-

PERSONAL: Born May 20, 1940, in Steubenville, Ohio; son of John L. and Sarah (a registered nurse; maiden name, Bennett) Scanlon. *Education:* Georgetown University, A.B. (cum laude), 1962; University of Wisconsin—Madison, M.A., 1965; University of Virginia, 1969. *Politics:* Democrat.

ADDRESSES: Home—Sereday, Route 1, Box 237-S, Ruther Glen, Va. 22546. *Office*—Department of History, Randolph-Macon College, Ashland, Va. 23005.

CAREER: Randolph-Macon College, Ashland, Va., assistant professor, 1968-72, associate professor, 1972-79, professor of history, 1980—, chairman of department, 1981-85. Lay lector and eucharistic minister at St. Ann's Roman Catholic Church. Chairman of numerous faculty committees.

MEMBER: Organization of American Historians, American Association of University Professors, Virginia Historical Society, Packard Club, Walter P. Chrysler Club.

AWARDS, HONORS: Gray Distinguished Professor Award, 1984.

WRITINGS:

Randolph-Macon College: A Southern History, 1825-1967, University Press of Virginia, 1983.

Contributor to history journals.

WORK IN PROGRESS: Research on Thomas Jefferson and the physiocrats.

SIDELIGHTS: James E. Scanlon told *CA:* "*Randolph-Macon College: A Southern History, 1925-1967* celebrates the sesquicentennial of that institution by treating its history as connected to the society that sustained and shaped it. A small college invites considerable participation in its life, and the committee work gives insights into the operations of a school that are invaluable in writing its history.

"The physiocrats were a school of agrarian and libertarian philosophers in eighteenth-century France whose principles ought to have formed a major source for Jefferson's thought. Curiously, despite living in Paris for four years, Jefferson did not incorporate their economic models."

AVOCATIONAL INTERESTS: Travel (Canada and Central Europe), haiku, calligraphy, hunting, automobiles.

*　　*　　*

SCANNELL, Francis P.　1915-1988
(Frank Scannell)

OBITUARY NOTICE: Born in 1915; died January 10, 1988, in Royal Oak, Mich. Screenwriter and novelist. Scannell wrote his first novel, *In Line of Duty,* while serving in the U.S. Army as a cryptographer stationed in the South Pacific during World War II. He began his affiliation with MGM Studios in Hollywood after the war, writing scripts for series, including "The Lone Ranger." In 1955 Scannell moved to Michigan to work on automotive accounts for the Jam Handy organization. His second book, *Ready or Not,* published under the name Frank Scannell, deals with life in the corporate world. At the time of his death the author was working on several manuscripts.

OBITUARIES AND OTHER SOURCES:

PERIODICALS

Detroit Free Press, January 14, 1988.

*　　*　　*

SCANNELL, Frank
See SCANNELL, Francis P.

*　　*　　*

SCHATZ, Ronald W.　1949-

PERSONAL: Born June 20, 1949, in Chicago, Ill.; son of Norman H. and Eleanor (Brodsky) Schatz; married Cynthia A. Wells (an editor), 1978; children: Lily. *Education:* University of Wisconsin—Madison, B.A., 1971; Harvard University, M.A.T., 1972; University of Pittsburgh, Ph.D., 1977.

ADDRESSES: Office—Department of History, Wesleyan University, Middletown, Conn. 06457.

CAREER: Stanford University, Stanford, Calif., Mellon fellow in history, 1977-79; Wesleyan University, Middletown, Conn., assistant professor, 1979-85, associate professor of history, 1985—.

AWARDS, HONORS: Fellow of National Endowment for the Humanities, 1980-81; Yale-Mellon fellowship from Yale University, 1987-88.

WRITINGS:

The Electrical Workers: A History of Labor at General Electric and Westinghouse, University of Illinois Press, 1983.

WORK IN PROGRESS: A history of the industrial relations profession from the 1890s to the present.

*　　*　　*

SCHILZ, Thomas F.　1950-

PERSONAL: Born November 28, 1950, in Saginaw, Mich.; son of Frank L. (a business executive) and Jewel (a homemaker; maiden name, Crawford) Schilz; married Jodye Lynn Dickson (a college professor), August 22, 1981. *Education:* University of Houston, B.A., 1973, M.Ed., 1975; Texas Christian University, M.A., 1982, Ph.D., 1983. *Religion:* Episcopalian.

ADDRESSES: Home—819 South Minnesota, St. Peter, Minn. 56082. *Office*—American Indian Studies Program, Minority Groups Studies Center, Mankato State University, Box 61/MGSC, Mankato, Minn. 56001.

CAREER: Austin College, Sherman, Tex., adjunct professor of history, 1982, 1983; New Mexico State University, Las Cruces, assistant professor of history, 1984; Texas Christian University, Fort Worth, assistant professor of history, 1984-85; Mankato State University, Mankato, Minn., assistant professor of history and coordinator of American Indian Studies Program, 1985—. Consultant to Texas Committee for the Humanities and Minnesota Historical Society.

MEMBER: American Historical Association, Western History Association, Western Social Science Association, Arizona Historical Society, Oklahoma Historical Society.

WRITINGS:

The Lipan Apaches in Texas, Texas Western Press, 1987.
(Editor) *Red, Black, Brown, and Yellow: A Multicultural/Multiethnic Handbook,* Mankato State University and Minnesota State University, 1987.
(Contributor) Alvin Bailey and L. T. Cummins, editors, *A Guide to the History of Texas,* Greenwood Press, 1987.
Buffalo Hump and the Penateka Chiefs (biography), Texas Western Press, in press.

Contributor to history journals.

WORK IN PROGRESS: The Tonkawa Indians, a history of a "frequently ignored but significant Texas tribe"; a history of the Wild West Show, co-authored with wife, Jodye Lynn Dickson-Schilz; a contribution to *The Handbook of Texas,* edited by Thomas Cutrer, publication by Texas State Historical Association expected in 1992.

SIDELIGHTS: Thomas F. Schilz told *CA:* "I think the writing of Indian history is important for overcoming stereotypes and developing an ethnohistorical philosophy for the study of pre-industrial and tribal peoples. One important aspect I have begun to explore is the field of comparative ethnohistory. Through this discipline we can develop respect for the spectrum of heritages of our global village.

"The significance of the Tonkawas—whom I will examine in a forthcoming book—lies in their role as allies of the United

States in its conflicts with other southern plains Indians. In the end, the Tonkawas were treated no differently from the other tribes—a lesson, perhaps, for other small nations that have sought the protection of superpowers.

"The Wild West shows are significant for providing the first opportunity for reservation Indians to encounter their white contemporaries and learn about white culture. Further, the stereotyping of Indians in these shows fed the American thirst for stereotypical 'savages' that was carried on in later motion pictures."

* * *

SCHMIDT, Alexander 1956-

PERSONAL: Born June 2, 1956, in Kalamazoo, Mich.; son of William Douglas (an engineer) and Janet Anna (a music teacher; maiden name, Renson) Schmidt; married Elaine White (an artist), May 23, 1981; children: Jordan White, Kate Frances. *Education:* Bowling Green State University, B.A., 1978, M.A., 1980; apprentice to a carpenter, 1980-83. *Religion:* Protestant. *Politics:* "Very liberal."

ADDRESSES: Home—8330 Lochdale, Dearborn Heights, Mich. 48217.

CAREER: Writer, 1980—; licensed carpenter, 1983—. Worked as a free-lance journalist in Michigan and Ohio and as a house painter.

MEMBER: Woodworkers' Association of Southeastern Michigan.

WRITINGS:

Wild Blue Triangles (poetry), Driftwood Press, 1979.
Green House Effects (poetry), Cold Water Publications, 1984.
Lines From a Carpenter Poet (poetry), Downriver Press, 1987.

WORK IN PROGRESS: A book on furniture restoration, publication by Downriver Press expected in 1989.

SIDELIGHTS: Alexander Schmidt told *CA:* "Too much poetry being written and published today has lost touch with real life, with people in everyday situations. It's abstract and isolationist. The purpose of poetry is to enlighten, to discover and convey the grace of mundane situations and the simple ties that define our daily lives. This is art: empathy and connection. It is not the clever manipulation of line-breaks or vague postulations passing for artistic philosophy.

"There really is no great connection between carpentry and poetry. I am a carpenter because of the tangibility of the work, and because I like it. The wood simply feels good in my hand. My grandfather was a woodworker. I learned from him the pleasure of working hard and being fair to that work."

* * *

SCHMIDT, Margaret Fox 1925-1979

OBITUARY NOTICE—See index for *CA* sketch: Born February 10, 1925, in Frankell, Tex.; died of cancer, August 19, 1979. Air-traffic controller, gallery owner, journalist, and author. Schmidt began her journalistic career as a reporter for the *Albuquerque Tribune* in 1944, later serving the *Fort Worth Press* as reporter and feature writer for fourteen years. Schmidt also spent one year as an air-traffic controller for the Civil Aeronautics Administration, and from 1962 to 1965 she owned an art gallery in San Miguel de Allende, Mexico. Her book

Passion's Child: The Extraordinary Life of Jane Digby, a Literary Guild selection, was published in 1976. With her husband, James Norman Schmidt, she also wrote *A Shopper's Guide to Mexico: Where, What, and How to Buy.*

OBITUARIES AND OTHER SOURCES:

Date of death provided by husband, James Norman Schmidt.

* * *

SCHMITTROTH, John 1924-1988

OBITUARY NOTICE—See index for *CA* sketch: Born June 29, 1924; died of cancer, June 29, 1988, in Southfield, Mich. Educator, producer, and editor. Schmittroth taught English at the University of Detroit from 1951 to 1981 and later taught part time at Macomb Community College. He was co-editor, with John Mahoney, of *The Insistent Present; New Poets, New Music;* and *New Fiction, Non-Fiction.* The professor also produced a musical revue about a French poet and musician, titled "Jacques Brel Is Alive and Well and Living in Paris," which premiered in 1973.

OBITUARIES AND OTHER SOURCES:

PERIODICALS

Detroit Free Press, July 4, 1988.

* * *

SCHOENBRUN, David (Franz) 1915-1988

OBITUARY NOTICE—See index for *CA* sketch: Born March 15, 1915, in New York, N.Y.; died after a heart attack following prostate surgery, May 23, 1988, in New York, N.Y. Educator, labor relations adjustor, journalist, and author. The first broadcast journalist to report from Vietnam and one of the first commentators on the "Voice of America" overseas radio program, Schoenbrun received several awards for distinguished reporting, including an Emmy Award and an Overseas Press Club award, both in 1958, and the Alfred I. duPont Best Commentator of the Year award in 1959. After serving with U.S. Army Intelligence as a correspondent and commentator during World War II, then acting as Paris bureau chief for the Overseas News Agency for two years, the journalist was recruited to Columbia Broadcasting System (CBS) by broadcast news pioneer Edward R. Murrow. Schoenbrun was chief of CBS's Paris bureau from 1947 to 1960 and chief of the network's Washington, D.C., bureau from 1960 to 1963. After leaving CBS Schoenbrun worked as a news commentator and analyst for various radio and television networks, and he lectured at Columbia University and the New School for Social Research. Prior to becoming a journalist Schoenbrun worked in New York City as a high school French and Spanish teacher and as a labor relations adjustor for the Dress Manufacturers Association. His books include *As France Goes; The Three Lives of Charles de Gaulle; Viet Nam: How We Got In, How to Get Out; The New Israelis; Soldiers of the Night: The Story of the French Resistance;* and *America Inside Out: At Home and Abroad From Roosevelt to Reagan.*

OBITUARIES AND OTHER SOURCES:

BOOKS

Current Biography, H. W. Wilson, 1960, July, 1988.
International Authors and Writers Who's Who, 10th edition, International Biographical Centre, 1986.

PERIODICALS

Chicago Tribune, May 25, 1988.
Los Angeles Times, May 25, 1988.
New York Times, May 24, 1988.
Washington Post, May 25, 1988.

*   *   *

SCHULZE, Franz   1927-

PERSONAL: Born January 30, 1927, in Uniontown, Pa.; son of Franz (an engineer) and Anna (a housewife; maiden name, Krimmel) Schulze; married Marianne Gaw (a psychological counselor), June 24, 1961 (divorced, 1975); children: Franz Clement Matthew, Lukas Andreas. *Education:* University of Chicago, Ph.B., 1945; School of the Art Institute of Chicago, B.F.A., 1949, M.F.A., 1950. *Politics:* Liberal Democrat. *Religion:* "No formal religion."

ADDRESSES: Home—872 Northmoor Rd., Lake Forest, Ill. 60045. *Office*—Department of Art, Lake Forest College, Lake Forest, Ill. 60045. *Agent*—Maxine Groffsky Literary Agency, 2 Fifth Ave., New York, N.Y. 10011.

CAREER: Purdue University, West Lafayette, Ind., instructor in art, 1950-52; University of Chicago, Chicago, Ill., lecturer in art, 1952-53; Lake Forest College, Lake Forest, Ill., assistant professor, 1953-55, associate professor, 1955-62, professor of art, 1962—, Hollender Professor of Art, 1975—, chairman of department of fine arts, 1952-64, artist-in-residence, 1958-62. Colorado College, visiting professor of art during summer sessions, 1966-75, critic-in-residence during summer sessions, 1966-67.

MEMBER: American Association of University Professors, College Art Association of America (member of board of directors, 1982-85), Society of Architectural Historians.

AWARDS, HONORS: Adenaur fellowship in painting from Federal Republic of Germany, 1956-57; Ford Foundation traveling fellowship for critics, 1964-65; college teaching fellowship from National Endowment for the Humanities, 1981 and 1982; award for best biography from Society of Midland Authors of College Art Association of America, Best Non-Fiction Book award from Friends of Literature (Chicago), and honorable mention from Alice Davis Hitchcock Book Award Committee of Society of Architectural Historians, all 1986, all for *Mies van der Rohe.*

WRITINGS:

Art, Architecture, and Civilization, Scott, Foresman, 1968.
Fantastic Images: Chicago Art Since 1945, Follett, 1972.
(With Oswald Grube and Peter C. Pran) *One Hundred Years of Architecture in Chicago: Continuity of Structure and Form,* J. Philip O'Hara, 1976.
Mies van der Rohe: A Critical Biography, University of Chicago Press, 1985.
(Contributor of introductory notes) Arthur Drexler, editor, *The Mies van der Rohe Archive,* four volumes, Garland Publishing, 1986.

Also author of scripts for documentaries about Mies van der Rohe.

Chicago art correspondent for *Art News,* 1958-64 and 1972—, *Christian Science Monitor,* 1958-62, and *Art International,* 1966-67. Art critic for *Chicago Daily News,* 1962-78, *Chicagoan,* 1973-74, and *Chicago Sun-Times,* 1978-85. Contributing editor to *Art in America,* 1965—, and *Inland Architect,* 1975—.

WORK IN PROGRESS: Editing a book of essays by Stanford Anderson, James Ingo Freed, Fritz Neumeyer, Richard Pommer, and Wolf Tegethoff on Mies van der Rohe, publication by the Museum of Modern Art expected in 1988; editing and writing text for catalog of Mies van der Rohe's American drawings, publication by Garland Publishing expected in 1988 or 1989; research on a biography, tentatively titled *Philip Johnson: Life and Work,* publication by Knopf expected in 1991; editing a revised edition of *Chicago's Famous Buildings,* for University of Chicago Press.

SIDELIGHTS: Franz Schulze devoted six years to the complex research that resulted in his critical biography *Mies van der Rohe,* about "the 20th Century's most influential architect," according to architecture critic Paul Gapp in *Chicago Tribune Book World.* In 1977 Schulze was approached by the Museum of Modern Art to collaborate on the project, and he eventually became the sole author. He made three trips to Europe to gather information on van der Rohe's early life and work, and his job was complicated by the refusal of the East German government to cooperate in the endeavor. Undaunted, Schulze interviewed hundreds of architects, family members, and friends of Mies van der Rohe, and he spent weeks immersed in the van der Rohe archives of the Museum of Modern Art and the Library of Congress.

The result of Schulze's work is, according to Paul Gapp, "the most comprehensive book ever written about the master designer and, by any measure, the best." The author neither neglected nor sensationalized the architect's personal faults, Gapp noted, adding that in an era which has become critical of van der Rohe's style, Schulze provided careful, insightful appraisals of the architect's major works, both in the United States and Germany. Gapp wrote: "In Schulze's hands, the facts about Mies, the man, and Mies, the architect, comprise an almost seamless fabric—even as they did in life." The critic found the book to be "a finely structured prose composition good enough to be called literature." He concluded: "This is a genuinely *readable* book."

Schulze told *CA:* "My interest in Mies van der Rohe stems from his period of residence and activity in Chicago. He was the great figure of the visual arts in this city during the 1950s and 1960s. My views about him gradually changed. Mies became more complex in my mind; moreover, he emerged far more as a unique artist than as an architect with a theory that could easily be learned by others.

"The Germans knew less about Mies than the Americans did. He had, after all, left his native country in 1938. Nonetheless, I learned a great deal about the environment he grew up in, both in his native Aachen and his adopted Berlin. The East German authorities, bogged down in bureaucracy, helped me not at all. Their West German counterparts were far more flexible and eminently cooperative. I became acquainted with some first rate architectural scholars there, some of them doing very good and original work on Mies.

"Philip Johnson was early on a disciple of Mies and I interviewed him several times for the Mies book. After that biography was published, it seemed attractive to write another about Johnson, who has been a major architect, critic, and all-around cultural presence in America for nearly sixty years. Johnson is a colorful personality who has always been on the cutting edge of architectural ideas."

BIOGRAPHICAL/CRITICAL SOURCES:

PERIODICALS

Chicago Tribune Book World, October 27, 1985.

*　　*　　*

SCHUMM, Ruth Frances   1921-1988

OBITUARY NOTICE: Born December 7, 1921, in Dallas, Tex.; died of cancer, June 25, 1988, in Washington, D.C. Entrepreneur and journalist. Schumm began her career in journalism in 1945 as a reporter for the Washington, D.C., bureau of the *Philadelphia Record* and, later, worked for the *Dallas News.* For four years beginning in 1959, she served as public affairs assistant to Senate majority leader Lyndon Baines Johnson, who became vice-president of the United States in 1961. Schumm owned and operated a real estate investment firm for more than twenty years after she retired from journalism in the 1960s.

OBITUARIES AND OTHER SOURCES:

BOOKS

Who's Who of American Women, 7th edition, Marquis, 1972.

PERIODICALS

Chicago Tribune, July 3, 1988.

*　　*　　*

SCHWARTZ, Al(bert)   1911(?)-1988

OBITUARY NOTICE: Born c. 1911; died of emphysema, March 26, 1988, in Los Angeles, Calif. Radio and television scriptwriter. A member of the original writing team for "The Bob Hope Show" when it made its radio debut on September 27, 1938, Schwartz went on to write scripts for numerous radio and television shows. He began work in television in 1955 with "The Milton Berle Show" and "December Bride" and later wrote for other comedy programs, including "Here's Lucy," "Gilligan's Island," "Petticoat Junction," "Chico and the Man," "Good Times," and "The Brady Bunch." Schwartz shared a 1961 Emmy Award for his work on "The Red Skelton Show."

OBITUARIES AND OTHER SOURCES:

PERIODICALS

Los Angeles Times, March 29, 1988.
Washington Post, March 31, 1988.

*　　*　　*

SCHWARTZ, Anna J(acobson)   1915-

PERSONAL: Born November 11, 1915, in New York, N.Y.; daughter of Hillel Joseph (a rabbi) and Pauline (a housewife; maiden name, Shainmark) Jacobson; married Isaac Schwartz (a businessman), October 18, 1936; children: Jonathan, Paula, Naomi, Joel. *Education:* Barnard College, A.B., 1934; Columbia University, A.M., 1935, Ph.D., 1964.

ADDRESSES: Home—490 West End Ave., New York, N.Y. 10024. *Office*—269 Mercer St., New York, N.Y. 10003.

CAREER: Columbia University, New York City, research associate of Social Science Research Council, 1936-41; National Bureau of Economic Research, New York City, member of

senior research staff, 1941—. Adjunct professor of economics at New York University, 1969-70, and Graduate Center of the City University of New York, 1986—; honorary visiting professor at City University Business School, London, England, 1984-89. Staff director of U.S. Gold Commission, 1987-88.

MEMBER: American Economic Association, National Economists Club, Shadow Open Market Committee, Western Economic Association (president, 1987-88), Phi Beta Kappa.

AWARDS, HONORS: George Welwood Murray fellow, 1934-35; fellow of Committee on Research in Economic History, 1945; H.D.L. from University of Florida, 1987.

WRITINGS:

(With A. D. Gayer and W. W. Rostow) *The Growth and Fluctuation of the British Economy, 1790-1850,* two volumes, Clarendon Press, 1953, reprinted, Harvester Press, 1975.
(With Milton Friedman) *A Monetary History of the United States, 1867-1960,* Princeton University Press, 1963.
(With Friedman) *Monetary Statistics of the United States: Estimates, Sources, Methods,* National Bureau of Economic Research, 1970.
(With Friedman) *Monetary Trends in the United States and United Kingdom: Their Relation to Income, Prices, and Interest Rates, 1867-1975,* University of Chicago Press, 1982.
(Editor with Michael D. Bordo) *Retrospective on the Classical Gold Standard, 1821-1931,* University of Chicago Press, 1984.
Money in Historical Perspective, University of Chicago Press, 1987.
(Contributor) William S. Haraf, editor, *Restructuring the Financial System,* American Enterprise Institute for Public Policy Research, 1988.

Member of board of editors of *American Economic Review,* 1972-78, *Journal of Money, Credit, and Banking,* 1974-75 and 1984—, and *Journal of Monetary Economics,* 1975—.

*　　*　　*

SCHWARTZ, Selwyn S.   1907(?)-1988
(Shloime Schwartz)

OBITUARY NOTICE: Born in 1907 (one source says 1910) in Poland; immigrated to United States; died March 20, 1988, in Chicago, Ill. Sales director, educator, and poet. An internationally acclaimed poet, Schwartz wrote four volumes of verse in English and six volumes in Yiddish. Although he was director of sales for a photographic supply company for nineteen years, he regarded writing as his main vocation. According to the *Chicago Tribune,* poet and editor John Ciardi considered Schwartz "as volatile as boiling ether, a poet with an amazing gift of language." Schwartz also lectured at the University of Chicago and Northwestern University. The author's works in English include *Horn in the Dust, Preface to Maturity, The Poet in Blue Minor,* and *Letter to My Unborn Son.* His Yiddish poetry volumes were published under the name Shloime Schwartz.

OBITUARIES AND OTHER SOURCES:

PERIODICALS

Chicago Tribune, March 23, 1988.

SCHWARTZ, Shloime
See SCHWARTZ, Selwyn S.

*   *   *

SCOTT, Sally (Elisabeth)   1948-

PERSONAL: Born May 30, 1948, in London, England; daughter of Paul Mark (a writer) and Elisabeth (a writer; maiden name, Avery) Scott; divorced. *Education:* University of York, B.A., 1970.

ADDRESSES: Home—London, England. *Agent*—Bruce Hunter, David Higham Associates Ltd., 5-8 Lower John St., London W.1., England.

CAREER: Illustrator and writer.

MEMBER: Society of Authors.

WRITINGS:

FOR CHILDREN

(Illustrator) Paul Scott, *After the Funeral,* Whittington/Heinemann, 1980.
The Elf King's Bride; or, How Prince Armandel Prevailed Against the Twilight, self-illustrated, MacRae, 1981.
(Illustrator) Ruskin Bond, *Tales and Legends From India,* F. Watts, 1982.
The Magic Horse, self-illustrated, MacRae, 1985, Greenwillow, 1986.
The Three Wonderful Beggars, self-illustrated, MacRae, 1987, Greenwillow, 1988.

Also author of two historical novels for adults, under a pseudonym.

WORK IN PROGRESS: A new picture book.

AVOCATIONAL INTERESTS: Music, reading, drama for screen, radio, and stage.

*   *   *

SEAGRAVE, Sterling   1937-

BRIEF ENTRY: Born April 15, 1937, in Columbus, Ohio. American television producer, journalist, and author. Seagrave is known for his writings on Asian political and military events. Though born in the United States, he spent much of his early childhood in Burma and India. During the Burmese civil war, he returned with his mother to the United States, where he eventually attended the University of Miami. Seagrave also studied at universities in Latin America during the late 1950s, and in the latter months of the Cuban Revolution he was arrested by government troops and held in the dungeons of El Principe Fortress for three days. After obtaining his freedom, Seagrave joined with Fidel Castro's rebel army and documented the final months of the Communist leader's revolutionary activities. He subsequently worked as a reporter for *Time* and the *Washington Post.*

In 1965 Seagrave returned to Burma. During the revolution there, he resigned from the *Post* and for ten years served as an independent foreign correspondent for such periodicals as *Atlantic Monthly, Life,* and *Saturday Evening Post.* At that time he also wrote and produced television documentaries for the American Broadcasting Companies and edited *Bangkok Magazine.* In the mid-1970s Seagrave joined Time-Life Books. Among his publications are *Yellow Rain: A Journey Through*

the Terror of Chemical Warfare (Evans, 1981), documenting illegal warfare conducted in Laos; *Soldiers of Fortune* (Time-Life, 1981), concerning mercenary pilots in the twentieth century, and part of the Time-Life series "Epic of Flight"; *The Bush Pilots* (Time-Life, 1983), another "Epic of Flight" book; *The Soong Dynasty* (Harper, 1985), about the clan that influenced Chinese politics in the first half of the twentieth century; and *The Marcos Dynasty: The Incredible Inside Story Behind the Rise of Imelda and Ferdinand Marcos and the Roles Played by American Business, Organized Crime, the CIA, and the White House* (Harper, 1987). *Addresses: Home*—Kent Island, Md. *Agent*—Robert Gottlieb, William Morris Agency, 1350 Avenue of the Americas, New York, N. Y. 10019.

BIOGRAPHICAL/CRITICAL SOURCES:

PERIODICALS

Los Angeles Times Book Review, January 3, 1982, May 19, 1985.
New York Times Book Review, October 18, 1981, March 17, 1985.
People, October 5, 1981.
Tribune Books, August 2, 1987.
Village Voice, October 28, 1981.

*   *   *

SEAL, Basil
See KAVANAGH, Dan(iel)

*   *   *

SEARCH, Alexander
See PESSOA, Fernando (Antonio Nogueira)

*   *   *

SEIDMANN, Ginette
See SPANIER, Ginette

*   *   *

SEIFERHELD, Alfredo M.   1950-1988

OBITUARY NOTICE: Born in 1950; died of cancer, June 3, 1988, in Paraguay. Historian, journalist, and author. A correspondent for *Time* magazine and the Associated Press in Asuncion, Paraguay, Seiferheld also wrote for the controversial Asuncion newspaper *ABC Color* until 1984; at that time the publication was closed down by Paraguayan President Alfredo Stroessner for printing allegedly subversive articles. Seiferheld is the author of several books in Spanish on political and historical subjects, whose titles, in English, include *The Asylum of Peron, The Fall of Federico Chavez, Jews in Paraguay,* and *Political-Military Conversations.*

OBITUARIES AND OTHER SOURCES:

PERIODICALS

Los Angeles Times, June 4, 1988.

*   *   *

SELBY, Curt
See PISERCHIA, Doris (Elaine)

SEMBENE, Ousmane
See OUSMANE, Sembene

*   *   *

SEMLER, H. Eric   1965-

PERSONAL: Born January 20, 1965, in Portland, Ore.; son of Herbert Joseph (a physician) and Shirley (an interior decorator; maiden name, Lesman) Semler. *Education:* Dartmouth College, B.A. (magna cum laude), 1987.

ADDRESSES: Home—6215 Southwest Hamilton, Portland, Ore. 97221.

CAREER: News clerk for *New York Times,* 1987—. U.S. State Department, Washington, D.C., delegate to conference on confidence and security-building measures and disarmament, 1986.

MEMBER: Phi Beta Kappa.

WRITINGS:

(With James Benjamin and Adam Gross) *The Language of Nuclear War: An Intelligent Citizen's Dictionary,* Harper, 1987.

Contributor to periodicals.

WORK IN PROGRESS: The Nuclear (In)Difference: A Historical Look at Arms Control, 1815-1987.

SIDELIGHTS: H. Eric Semler told *CA:* "I got the idea for *The Language of Nuclear War* from reading the newspaper and feeling frustrated by my own inability to understand nuclear jargon. To my surprise, I found that no one had written a nuclear dictionary for the layman. The nuclear issue is the one issue where complex language helps to inhibit public participation in the debate. People see words they don't understand and figure the issue is beyond their control and comprehension. Thus, *The Language of Nuclear War* was an effort to simplify nuclear jargon for the ordinary person.

"My current work on the history of arms control attempts to show that the way people negotiated over weapons before the nuclear era (all the way back to 1815 and the Rush-Bagot Convention between the United States and Canada) is not much different from the way people have negotiated over nuclear weapons since 1945. This may suggest that we haven't treated nuclear weapons much differently from other weapons and thus may explain why we've continued to get many of the same patterns and results in arms control over the last two hundred years.

"I feel that it is vital to increase public awareness of the nuclear issue because the nuclear question is the one question whose outcome has the potential to devastate *every* single human being."

*   *   *

SEMPLE, Lorenzo, Jr.

BRIEF ENTRY: American writer for television and screen. In 1966 Semple was writing episodes for the popular television program "Batman." According to some critics he produced much of his best work as the "Bat-Bard" of that series. Since then, Semple has authored or co-authored several screenplays, including the critically acclaimed "Pretty Poison," which captured a New York Film Critics Award for best screenplay in

1968, and the not-so-successful remakes of three film classics: "King Kong" (1976), "Hurricane" (1979), and "Flash Gordon" (1980). Among his other movie credits are "The Parallax View," "Three Days of the Condor," and "Never Say Never Again," a James Bond adventure. In addition to television work and screenwriting, Semple wrote a Broadway play called "The Golden Fleecing," which was published in 1960 and subsequently adapted for film as "The Honeymoon Machine," starring the late Steve McQueen. *Addresses: Agent*—Creative Artists Agency, 1888 Century Park E., Suite 1400, Los Angeles, Calif. 90067.

BIOGRAPHICAL/CRITICAL SOURCES:

BOOKS

Contemporary Theatre, Film, and Television, Volume 5, Gale, 1988.
The International Dictionary of Film and Filmmakers, Volume IV: *Writers and Production Artists,* St. James Press, 1987.

PERIODICALS

Chicago Tribune, April 16, 1979, December 8, 1980, October 7, 1983.
New York Times, April 12, 1979, October 7, 1983.
Washington Post, April 12, 1979, October 6, 1983.

*   *   *

SENGHOR, Leopold Sedar   1906-
(Silmang Diamano, Patrice Maguilene Kaymor)

PERSONAL: Born October 9, 1906, in Joal, Senegal (part of French West Africa; now Republic of Senegal); son of Basile Digoye (a cattle breeder and groundnut planter and exporter) and Nyilane (Bakoume) Senghor; married Ginette Eboue, September, 1946 (divorced, 1956); married Collette Hubert, October 18, 1957; children: (first marriage) Francis-Aphang, Guy-Waly (deceased); (second marriage) Philippe-Maguilen (deceased). *Education:* Baccalaureat degree from Lycee of Dakar, 1928; Sorbonne, University of Paris, agregation de grammaire, 1933, studied African languages at Ecole des Hautes Etudes, Paris, 1929-32.

ADDRESSES: Home—Corniche Ouest, Dakar, Senegal Republic; 1 square de Tocqueville, 75017 Paris, France. *Office*—c/o Presidence de la Republique, Dakar, Senegal Republic.

CAREER: Lycee Descartes, Tours, France, instructor in Greek and Latin classics, 1935-38; Lycee Marcelin Berthelot, St. Maur-des-Fosses, France, instructor in literature and African culture, 1938-40, 1943-44; Ecole Nationale de la France d'Outre Mer, professor, 1945; French National Assembly, Paris, France, and General Council of Senegal, Dakar, Senegal, elected representative, beginning 1946; Bloc Democratique Senegalais, Dakar, founder, 1948; French Government, Paris, delegate to United Nations General Assembly in New York, New York, 1950-51, Secretary of State for scientific research, and representative to UNESCO conferences, 1955-56, member of consultative assembly, 1958, minister-counsellor to Ministry of Cultural Affairs, Education, and Justice, 1959-60, advisory minister beginning 1960; City of Thies, Senegal, mayor, beginning 1956; Senegalese Territorial Assembly, elected representative, beginning 1957; founder and head of Union Progressiste Senegalaise, beginning 1958; Mali Federation of Senegal and Sudan, president of Federal Assembly, 1959-60; Republic of Senegal, President of the Republic, 1960-80, Minister of Defense, 1968-69; Socialist Inter-African, chairman of executive bureau, 1981—; Haut Conseil de la Francophonie, vice-president, 1985—. Co-founder, with Lamine Gueye, of Bloc Africain, 1945; representative for Senegal to French Constituent Assemblies, 1945, 1946; official grammarian for writing of French Fourth Republic's new constitution, 1946; sponsor of First World Festival of Negro Arts, Dakar, 1966; chairman of Organisation Commune Africaine et Malgache, 1972-74; established West African Economic Community, 1974; chairman of ECONAS, 1978-79. *Military service:* French Army, infantry, 1934-35; served in infantry battalion of colonial troops, 1939; prisoner of war, 1940-42; participated in French Resistance, 1942-45; received serviceman's cross, 1939-45.

MEMBER: Comite National des Ecrivains, Societe des Gens de Lettres, Societe Linguistique de France.

AWARDS, HONORS: Numerous awards, including corresponding membership in Bavarian Academy, 1961; International French Friendship Prize, 1961; French Language Prize (gold medal), 1963; International Grand Prize for Poetry, 1963; Dag Hammarskjoeld International Prize—Gold Medal for Poetic Merit, 1963; Marie Noel Poetry Prize, 1965; Red and Green International Literature Grand Prix, 1966, German Book Trade's Peace Prize, 1968; associate membership in French Academy of Moral and Political Sciences, 1969; Knokke Biennial International Poetry Grand Prix, 1970; membership in Academy of Overseas Sciences, 1971; membership in Black Academy of Arts and Sciences, 1971; Grenoble Gold Medal, 1972; Haile Selassie African Research Prize, 1973; Cravat of Commander of Order of French Arts and Letters, 1973; Apollinaire Prize for Poetry, 1974; Prince Pierre of Monaco's Literature Prize, 1977; Prix Eurafrique, 1978; Alfred de Vigny Prize, 1981; Aasan World Prize, 1981; election to Academie Francaise, 1983; Jawaharlal Nehru Award, 1984; Athinai Prize, 1985; also Grand Cross of French Legion of Honor, Commander of Academic Palms, Franco-Allied Medal of Recognition, membership in Agegres de Grammaire and American Academy of Arts and Letters. Numerous honorary doctorates, including those from Fordham University, 1961; University of Paris, 1962; Catholic University of Louvain (Belgium), 1965; Lebanese University of Beirut, 1966; Howard University, 1966; Laval University (Quebec), 1966; Harvard University, 1971; Oxford University, 1973; and from the universities of Ibadan (Nigeria), 1964; Bahia (Brazil), 1965; Strasbourg (France), 1965; Al-Azan (Cairo, Egypt), 1967; Algiers (Algeria), 1967; Bordeaux-Talence (France), 1967; Vermont, 1971; California at Los Angeles, 1971; Ethiopia—Haile Selassie I, 1971; Abidjan (Ivory Coast), 1971; and Lagos (Nigeria), 1972.

WRITINGS:

POETRY

Chants d'ombre (title means "Songs of Shadow"; includes "Femme noire" and "Joal"), Seuil, 1945; also see below.
Hosties noires (title means "Black Sacrifices"; includes "Au Gouverneur Eboue," "Mediterranee," "Aux Soldats Negro-Americains," "Tyaroye," and "Priere de paix"), Seuil, 1948; also see below.
Chants pour Naeett (title means "Songs for Naeett"), Seghers, 1949; also see below.
Chants d'ombre [suivi de] *Hosties noires* (see above; title means "Songs of Shadow" [followed by] "Black Sacrifices"), Seuil, 1956.
Ethiopiques (includes "Chaka," poetic adaptation of Thomas Mofolo's historical novel *Chaka;* "A New York"; and "Congo"), Seuil, 1956, critical edition with commentary

by Papa Gueye N'Diaye published as *Ethiopiques: Poemes,* Nouvelles Editions Africaines, 1974.
Nocturnes (includes *Chants pour Naeett* [see above], "Elegie de minuit," and "Elegie a Aynina Fall: Poeme dramatique a plusieurs voix" [title means "Elegy for Aynina Fall: Dramatic Poem for Many Voices"]), Seuil, 1961, translation by John Reed and Clive Wake published as *Nocturnes,* Heinemann Educational, 1969, with introduction by Paulette J. Trout, Third Press, 1971.
Elegie des Alizes, original lithographs by Marc Chagall, Seuil, 1969.
Lettres d'hivernage, illustrations by Marc Chagall, Seuil, 1973.
Paroles, Nouvelles Editions Africaines, 1975.

Poems published in periodicals such as *Chantiers, Les Cahiers du Sud, Les Lettres Francaises, Les Temps Modernes, Le Temp de la Poesie, La Revue Socialiste, Presence Africaine,* and *Prevue.*

CRITICAL AND POLITICAL PROSE

(With Robert Lemaignen and Prince Sisowath Youtevong) *La Communaute imperiale francaise* (includes "Views on Africa; or, Assimilate, Don't Be Assimilated"), Editions Alsatia, 1945.
(With Gaston Monnerville and Aime Cesaire) *Commemoration du centenaire de l'abolition de l'esclavage,* introduction by Edouard Depreux, Presses Universitaires de France, 1948.
(Contributor) *La Nation en construction,* [Dakar], 1959.
Rapport sur la doctrine et le programme du parti, Presence Africaine, 1959, translation published as *Report on the Principles and Programme of the Party,* Presence Africaine, 1959, abridged edition edited and translated by Mercer Cook published as *African Socialism: A Report to the Constitutive Congress of the Party of African Federation,* American Society of African Culture, 1959.
Rapport sur la politique generale, [Senegal], 1960.
Nation et voie africaine du socialisme, Presence Africaine, 1961, new edition published as *Liberte II: Nation et voie africaine du socialisme,* Seuil, 1971, translation by Mercer Cook published as *Nationhood and the African Road to Socialism,* Presence Africaine, 1962, abridged as *On African Socialism,* translation and introduction by Cook, Praeger, 1964.
(Contributor) *Cultures de l'Afrique noire et de l'Occident,* Societe Europeenne de Culture, 1961.
Rapport sur la doctrine et la politique generale; ou, Socialisme, unite africaine, construction nationale, [Dakar], 1962.
(With Pierre Teilhard de Chardin) *Pierre Teilhard de Chardin et la politique africaine* [and] *Sauvons l'humanite* [and] *L'Art dans la ligne de l'energie humaine* (the first by Senghor, the latter two by Teilhard de Chardin), Seuil, 1962.
(With others) *Le Racisme dans le monde,* Julliard, 1964.
Theorie et pratique du socialisme senegalais, [Dakar], 1964.
Liberte I: Negritude et humanisme, Seuil, 1964, selections translated and introduced by Wendell A. Jeanpierre published as *Freedom I: Negritude and Humanism,* [Providence, R.I.], 1974.
(In Portuguese, French, and Spanish) *Latinite et negritude,* Centre de Hautes Etudes Afro-Ibero-Americaines de l'Universite de Dakar, 1966.
Negritude, arabisme, et francite: Reflexions sur le probleme de la culture (title means "Negritude, Arabism, and Frenchness: Reflections on the Problem of Culture"), preface

by Jean Rous, Editions Dar al-Kitab Allubmani (Beirut), 1967, republished as *Les Fondements de l'Africanite; ou, Negritude et arabite,* Presence Africaine, 1967, translation by Mercer Cook published as *The Foundations of "Africanite"; or, "Negritude" and "Arabite,"* Presence Africaine, 1971.

Politique, nation, et developpement moderne: Rapport de politique generale, Imprimerie Nationale (Rufisque), 1968.

Le Plan du decollage economique; ou, La Participation responsable comme moteur de developpement, Grande Imprimerie Africaine (Dakar), 1970.

Pourquoi une ideologie negro-africaine? (lecture), Universite d'Abidjan, 1971.

La Parole chez Paul Claudel et chez les Negro-Africains, Nouvelles Editions Africaines, 1973.

(With others) *Litteratures ultramarines de langue francaise, genese et jeunesse: Actes du colloque de l'Universite du Vermont,* compiled by Thomas H. Geno and Roy Julow, Naaman (Quebec), 1974.

Paroles (addresses), Nouvelles Editions Africaines, 1975.

(Contributor) *La Senegal au Colloque sur le liberalisme planifie et les voies africaines vers le socialisme, Tunis, 1-6 juillet 1975* (includes *Pour une relecture africaine de Marx et d'Engels;* also see below), Grand Imprimerie Africaine (Dakar), 1975.

Pour une relecture africaine de Marx et d'Engels (see above; includes "Le socialisme africain et la voie senegalaise"), Nouvelles Editions Africaines, 1976.

Pour une societe senegalaise socialiste et democratique: Rapport sur la politique generale, Nouvelles Editions Africaines, 1976.

Liberte III: Negritude et civilisation de l'universel (title means "Freedom III: Negritude and the Civilization of the Universal"), Seuil, 1977.

(With Mohamed Aziza) *La Poesie de l'action: Conversations avec Mohamed Aziza* (interviews), Stock (Paris), 1980.

Ce que je crois: Negritude, francite, et la civilisation de l'universel, Grosset, 1988.

Also author of *L'Apport de la poesie negre,* 1953; *Langage et poesie negro-africaine,* 1954; *Esthetique negro-africain,* 1956; and *Liberte IV: Socialisme et planification,* 1983. Author of four technical works on Wolof grammar.

Author of lectures and addresses published in pamphlet or booklet form, including *The Mission of the Poet,* 1966; *Negritude et germanisme,* 1968; *Problemes de developpement dans les pays sous-developpes,* 1975; *Negritude et civilisations mediterraneennes,* 1976; and *Pour une lecture negro-africaine de Mallarme,* 1981.

Contributor, sometimes under the pseudonyms Silmang Diamano or Patrice Maguilene Kaymor, of critical, linguistic, sociological, and political writings to periodicals and journals, including *Journal de la Societe des Africanists, Presence Africaine,* and *L'Esprit.*

OTHER

(Editor) *Anthologie de la nouvelle poesie negre et malgache de langue francaise* [precede de] *Orphee noir, par Jean-Paul Sartre* (poetry anthology; title means "Anthology of the New Negro and Malagasy Poetry in French [preceded by] *Black Orpheus,* by Jean-Paul Sartre"), introduction by Sartre, Presses Universitaires de France, 1948, 4th edition, 1977.

(With Abdoulaye Sadji) *La Belle Histoire de Leuk-le-Lievre* (elementary school text; title means "The Clever Story of Leuk-the-Hare"), Hachette, 1953, reprinted as *La Belle Histoire de Leuk-le-Lievre: Cours elementaire des ecoles d'Afrique noir,* illustrations by Marcel Jeanjean, Hachette, 1961, British edition (in French) edited by J. M. Winch, illustrations by Jeanjean, Harrap, 1965, adaptation published as *Les Aventures de Leuk-le-Lievre,* illustrations by G. Lorofi, Nouvelles Editions Africaines, 1975.

(Author of introductory essay) *Anthologie des poetes du seizieme siecle* (anthology), Editions de la Bibliotheque Mondiale, 1956.

(Contributor of selected texts) *Afrique Africaine* (photography), photographs by Michel Huet, Clairfontaine, 1963.

(Contributor) *Terre promise d'Afrique: Symphonie en noir et or* (poetry anthology), lithographs by Hans Erni, Andre et Pierre Gonin (Lausanne), 1966.

(Contributor of selected texts) *African Sojourn* (photography), photographs by Uwe Ommer, Arpel Graphics, 1987.

Author of prose tale "Mandabi" (title means "The Money Order").

Translator of poetry by Mariane N'Diaye.

Founder of journals, including *Condition Humaine;* with Aime Cesaire and Leon Gontran Damas, *L'Etudiant Noir;* and, with Alioune Diop, *Presence Africaine.*

OMNIBUS VOLUMES

Leopold Sedar Senghor (collection of prose and poems; with biographical-critical introduction and bibliography), edited by Armand Guibert, Seghers, 1961, reprinted as *Leopold Sedar Senghor: Une Etude d'Armand Guibert, avec un choix de poemes* [et] *une chronologie bibliographique, "Leopold Sedar Senghor et son temps,"* Seghers, 1969.

(In English translation) John Reed and Clive Wake, editors and translators, *Selected Poems,* introduction by Reed and Wake, Atheneum, 1964.

Poemes (includes *Chants d'ombre, Hosties noires, Ethiopiques, Nocturnes,* and "poemes divers"), Seuil, 1964, 4th edition, 1969, reprinted 1974, new edition, 1984.

L. S. Senghor: Poete senegalais, commentary by Roger Mercier, Monique Battestini, and Simon Battestini, F. Nathan, 1965, reprinted, 1978.

(In English translation) *Prose and Poetry,* selected and translated by Reed and Wake, Oxford University Press, 1965, Heinemann Educational, 1976.

(In French with English translations) *Selected Poems = Poesies choisies,* English-language introduction by Craig Williamson, Collings, 1976.

(In French) *Selected Poems of Leopold Sedar Senghor,* edited, with English-language preface and notes, by Abiola Irele, Cambridge University Press, 1977.

Elegies majeures [suivi de] *Dialogue sur la poesie francophone,* Seuil, 1979.

(In English translation) *Poems of a Black Orpheus,* translated by William Oxley, Menard, 1981.

SIDELIGHTS: President of the Republic of Senegal from the proclamation of that country's independence in 1960 until he stepped down in 1980, Leopold Sedar Senghor is considered, according to *Time,* "one of Africa's most respected elder statesmen." Yet until 1960 Senghor's political career was conducted primarily in France rather than in Africa. He is a product of the nineteenth-century French educational system, a scholar of Greek and Latin, and a member of the elite Academie Francaise, but he is best known for developing "negritude," a wide-ranging movement that influenced black culture worldwide. As the chief proponent of negritude, Senghor is credited with contributing to Africa's progress toward independence from colonial rule and, according to Jacques Louis Hymans in his *Leopold Sedar Senghor: An Intellectual Biography,* with "setting in motion a whole series of African ideological movements." Senghor first gained widespread recognition, however, when his first collection of poetry was published in 1945; he followed that volume with a highly esteemed body of verse that has accumulated numerous prestigious honors, most notably consideration for the Nobel Prize in Literature. Senghor, thus, seems to be, as Hymans suggests, "the living symbol of the possible synthesis of what appears irreconcilable: he is as African as he is European, as much a poet as a politician, . . . as much a revolutionary as a traditionalist."

From the outset, disparate elements comprised Senghor's life. He was born in 1906 in Joal, a predominantly Moslem community established by Portuguese settlers on the Atlantic coast south of Dakar, a major Senegalese port and capital of what was then known as French West Africa. Senghor's mother was a Roman Catholic, and through maternal or paternal lines Senghor was related to the Fulani ethnic group, the Mandingo tribe, and the Serer ethnic group—said to provide a connection between Senghor and Serer royalty. His early childhood afforded contact with traditional customs and beliefs, with indigenous poetry, and with the surrounding natural setting. These contacts, critics note, strongly influenced Senghor's later life. As Sebastian Okechukwu Mezu explained in his 1973 study, *The Poetry of Leopold Sedar Senghor:* "This early childhood gave Senghor the material for his lyric poems. . . . Despite the splendours of political life, perhaps because of the excess of its paraphernalia, [Senghor] comes back to these memories of childhood . . . in his poems, events evoked several times in his public speeches and television interviews, images that have become a kind of obsession, romanticized during the years of his absence from Senegal, and because of this process of nostalgic remembrance, taken to be reality itself. Poetic life for Senghor as a result of this becomes a continual quest for the kingdom of childhood, a recovery, a recapture of this idyllic situation."

As a child Senghor demonstrated a lively intelligence and an early ambition to become a priest or a teacher, and was accordingly enrolled in a Catholic elementary school in 1913. The following year he began living in a boarding house four miles from Joal at N'Gasobil, where he attended the Catholic mission school operated by the Fathers of the Holy Spirit. There Senghor was encouraged to disparage his ancestral culture while he learned Latin and studied European civilization as part of a typical nineteenth-century French teaching program. In 1922 he entered Libermann Junior Seminary in Dakar. In his four years there Senghor acquired a sound knowledge of Greek and Latin classics. Obliged to leave the seminary when he was deemed ill-suited to the priesthood, Senghor, disappointed, entered public secondary school at a French-style lycee in Dakar. There he earned numerous scholastic prizes and distinction for having bested white pupils in academic performance. Senghor obtained his secondary school degree with honors in 1928 and was awarded a half scholarship for continued study in France.

In Paris Senghor boarded at the Lycee Louis-le-Grand, where top-ranking French students study for entrance exams to France's elite higher education programs. One of Senghor's classmates was Georges Pompidou, later prime minister and, eventually, president of France. Pompidou exposed Senghor to the works of French literary masters Marcel Proust, Andre Gide, and Charles Baudelaire. During this time Senghor was also influenced by the writings of Paul Claudel, Arthur Rimbaud, and Maurice Barres. Senghor's lycee education in Paris emphasized methodology for rigorous thought and instilled habits of intellectual discipline, skills that Senghor embraced. He meanwhile continued to observe Roman Catholicism and expressed support for a restoration of the French government to monarchy. According to Hymans, Senghor in his student days was considered fully assimilated into Paris's intellectual milieu, which began including political and social liberation movements such as socialism, rationalism, humanism, and Marxism.

Europe was also reassessing African cultural traditions. European writers, artists, and musicians were exploring Africa's cultural wealth and incorporating what they discovered into their own creations. Paris of the late 1920s was permeated with Europe's new cultural appreciation of Africa, and in this atmosphere an exciting period of discovery began for Senghor. He began meeting with black students from the United States, Africa, and the Caribbean, and soon a friendship grew between Senghor and Aime Cesaire, a writer from the French West Indian territory of Martinique. Another of Senghor's acquaintances was Paulette Nardal, a West Indian and the editor of a journal, *La Revue du Monde Noir.* Published in French and English, the journal was intended to provide a forum for black intellectuals writing literary and scientific works, to celebrate black civilization, and to increase unity among blacks worldwide. Through its editor Nardal, Senghor met West Indian writers Etienne Lero and Rene Maran and read the poetry of black Americans.

In *The New Negro,* an anthology published in 1925, Senghor encountered the works of prominent writers such as Paul Laurence Dunbar, W. E. B. Du Bois, Countee Cullen, Langston Hughes, Claude McKay, Zora Neale Hurston, James Weldon Johnson, and Jean Toomer. The anthology's editor, Alain Locke, was a professor of philosophy at Harvard University and a contributor to *La Revue du Monde Noir;* Senghor met him through Nardal as well. When Senghor, Cesaire, and Leon Gontran Damas, a student from French Guiana, sought a name for the growing Francophone interest in African culture, they borrowed from the title of Locke's anthology and dubbed the movement "neo-negre" or "negre-nouveau." These labels were later replaced by "negritude," a term coined by Cesaire. Senghor credits Jamaican poet and novelist Claude McKay with having supplied the values espoused by the new movement: to seek out the roots of black culture and build on its foundations, to draw upon the wealth of African history and anthropology, and to rehabilitate black culture in the eyes of the world. With Cesaire and Damas, Senghor launched *L'Etudiant Noir,* a cultural journal.

In exalting black culture and values, Senghor emphasized what he perceived as differences between the races. He portrayed blacks as artistic geniuses less gifted in the areas of scientific thought, attributing emotion to blacks and reason to whites. Europe was seen as alien, dehumanized, and dying, while Africa was considered vital, nourishing, and thriving. As racism and fascism swept through Europe in the 1930s, Senghor's attitudes were affected. For a brief period he became disillusioned with Europe in general and abandoned his religious faith. "By Senghor's own admission," Hymans revealed, "the same Romantic anti-rationalism that fathered racism among the Fascists of the 1930s underlay his early reaction against the West." But Senghor observed the increasing turmoil in Europe caused by Fascist regimes in Italy and Germany and understood the dangers of racism. Accordingly he modified his position.

Senghor nevertheless continued to cite what he considered to be differences between the races, such as an intuitive African way of understanding reality. But more importantly, as negritude evolved, he emphasized racial pride as a way of valuing black culture's role in a universal civilization. In this vein, he published an essay in 1939 titled "What the Negro Contributes." Themes that Senghor introduced to negritude at this time included a humanism based on the solidarity of all races, a moderate position that gave primacy to culture and maintained respect for other values. As Senghor told an audience he addressed in Dakar in 1937: "Assimilate, don't be assimilated." He later developed negritude further, however, by working to insure not only that African cultural identity became accessible to blacks worldwide, but that the unique aspects of African life were accorded status in the cultural community of society as a whole. Once African modes of thought and artistic expression are restored to their proper place among the world's cultures, Senghor proposed, then a sort of cultural cross-breeding can occur. This mixing of the races, according to Mezu, was conceived as "a symbiotic union where blacks will bring to the rendezvous of the races their special . . . talents." Hymans examined this development of negritude since its inception in the 1930s and quoted Senghor's retrospective assessment of the movement: "Like life, the concept of negritude has become historical and dialectical. It has evolved."

Much of what later informed negritude had yet to be developed when in 1933 Senghor became the first African to obtain the coveted agregation degree. This distinction led to his first teaching position, at the Lycee Descartes in Tours, France. Senghor's new appreciation for Africa, coupled with his estrangement from his homeland, created an internal conflict that found resolution when he began writing poetry. Influenced by the works of Andre Breton and other surrealist writers, Senghor drew on surrealist techniques for his poetic style. Surrealism, with its emphasis on the irrational, depended on a creative process that tapped latent energies and subconscious sources of imagination without drawing a distinction between the fantastic and the real. Senghor found this process similar to traditional African modes of thought and employed it in his poetry. "By adopting the surrealist techniques," Mezu explained, "he was at the same time modern and African: educated and modernist from the white European viewpoint, traditional and faithful to the motherland from the African viewpoint. This dualism, or rather ambivalence, is ever present in Senghor's theories, poetry and actions." Nevertheless, Mezu noted, "there is a difference between the surrealist norm and the Senghorian philosophy. The difference is basically one of degree. For the surrealists, their effort, and an effort only, was to discover the point where reality and dream merge into one. For Senghor . . . this principle is already possessed, already a part of the ancestral culture."

The poems Senghor wrote in the late 1930s were later published in the collection *Chants d'ombre*. For the most part, these poems express Senghor's nostalgia for Africa, his sense of exile, estrangement, and cultural alienation, and his attempt to recover an idealized past. In a style based on musical rhythms, the poet evokes the beauty of the African landscape and peoples, the richness of Africa's past and the protecting presence of the dead, and the innocence and dignity inherent in his native culture. These poems, critics note, celebrate an Africa Senghor knew as a child, one transformed by nostalgia into a paradise-like simplicity. In some of the volume's other poems Senghor

laments the destruction of the continent's culture and the suffering of its people under colonial rule. One of the collection's frequently cited pieces, "Femme noir," employs sensual yet worshipful language intended to glorify all black women. In "Joal" Senghor returns to his native village, revisiting places and inhabitants he had once known very well; it is, according to Mezu, "easily one of the most beautiful poems created by Senghor." When *Chants d'ombre* was published in 1945 it was well received in Paris and brought Senghor to public attention as a voice of black Africa. "In recreating the distant continent by verse," Hymans observed, "Senghor helped blaze the trail that led to the phenomenon of negritude."

World War II intervened between the writing of the poems collected in *Chants d'ombre* and their eventual publication. Germany invaded Poland in September, 1939, and Senghor was immediately called to active duty to protect France at the German border. While the holder of a high academic degree is usually made a commissioned officer, Senghor as a black man was made a second-class soldier in the Colonial Infantry. France fell to the German assault in June, 1940, the same month Senghor was captured and interned in a German prison camp. At the time of his capture he was almost shot along with some other Senegalese prisoners, but a French officer interceded on his behalf. While in prison Senghor met African peasants who had been recruited into the French Army, and began to identify with their plight. He wrote a number of poems that he sent by letter to his old classmate and friend Georges Pompidou; they were hand-delivered by a German guard who had been a professor of Chinese at the University of Vienna before the war. These poems later formed the core of Senghor's second published collection, *Hosties noires,* which appeared in 1948.

Hosties noires documents Senghor's realization that he was not alone in his exile from Africa, explores his increasing sense of unity with blacks as an exploited race, and elucidates the positive meaning Senghor finds in the sacrifices blacks have made. In poems such as "Au Gouveneur Eboue," which treats a black man's willingness to die for the salvation of the white world, Senghor memorializes blacks fighting for Europe. Elsewhere in *Hosties noires,* Senghor protests the exploitation of black soldiers and attacks western sources of power and violence. In other poems, such as "Mediterranee" and "Aux Soldats Negro-Americains," he rejoices in the common bonds formed with fellow soldiers and with American blacks. And with "Priere de paix" and "Tyaroye" Senghor hopes for unity and peace; while denouncing colonialism, he calls for an end to hatred and welcomes the new life that succeeds death. The collection, according to Mezu, is "the most homogeneous volume of Senghor's poetry, from the point of view not only of theme but also of language and sentiment."

Through the influence of West Indian colleagues Senghor was released from prison in June, 1942, and resumed teaching at the lycee in suburban Paris where he had earlier served as instructor of literature and African culture. He joined a Resistance group and also participated in activities involving colonial students. During the war, negritude had gained momentum, and when *Chants d'ombre* appeared in 1945, a new group of black intellectuals eagerly embraced Senghor's poetry and cultural theories. That year he published the influential essay "Views on Africa; or, Assimilate, Don't Be Assimilated." While in the 1930s Senghor concentrated on cultural rather than political issues, after the war he was encouraged by colonial reforms extended to French West Africans. He decided to run for election as one of Senegal's representatives in the French

National Assembly. With Lamine Gueye, Senghor formed the Bloc Africain to involve Senegalese in their political fate. France was forming a new constitution, and in recognition of his linguistic expertise, France's provisional government appointed Senghor the document's official grammarian. Senghor founded the Bloc Democratique Senegalais (BDS) in 1948; throughout the 1950s the BDS dominated Senegalese politics.

Senghor's literary activities also continued. In 1947 he founded, with Alioune Diop, the cultural journal *Presence Africaine*. Along with a publishing house of the same name, *Presence Africaine* under Diop's direction became a powerful vehicle for black writing worldwide. As editor of *Anthologie de la nouvelle poesie noire et malgache de langue francaise*, published in 1948, Senghor brought together contemporary poetry written by francophone blacks. An essay titled "Orphee noir" ("Black Orpheus"), by French philosopher and writer Jean-Paul Sartre, introduced the anthology. Sartre's essay outlined the cultural aims of black peoples striving to recapture their heritage. In the process Sartre defined and gained notoriety for the philosophy of negritude, portraying negritude as a step toward a united society without racial distinction. Many consider "Black Orpheus" to be the most important document of the negritude movement.

After 1948 Senghor became increasingly active politically, serving as France's delegate to the 1949 Council of Europe and as a French delegate to the United Nations General Assembly in 1950 and 1951; he won resounding reelection to the French National Assembly in 1951 as well. In 1955 and 1956 Senghor served in the cabinet of French president Edgar Faure as secretary of state for scientific research and attended UNESCO conferences as a representative of France. While some French-held territories sought independence from colonial rule, often with accompanying violence, Senghor pushed for an arrangement giving French overseas territories equal status in a federation relationship facilitating economic development. He constantly modified his stance while avoiding violence and making small gains. In Dakar in 1953, according to Hymans, Senghor defined politics as "the art of using a method which, by approximations that are constantly corrected, would permit the greatest number to lead a more complete and happy life."

A collection of poems Senghor had been working on since 1948 was published as *Ethiopiques* in 1956. These poems reflect Senghor's growing political involvement and his struggle to reconcile European and African allegiances through crossbreeding, both figurative and literal. The year *Ethiopiques* was published Senghor divorced his African wife to marry one of her friends, a white Frenchwoman; critics have suggested that Senghor's views on cross-breeding represent an attempt to resolve his personal conflict by eliminating the divisive social elements that divided his loyalties. One of *Ethiopique*'s poems, "Chaka," is a dramatic adaptation of Thomas Mofolo's novel about a Zulu hero who forged and ruled a vast domain in the early nineteenth century. Mezu called "Chaka" Senghor's "most ambitious piece." Others have drawn parallels between Senghor's life and the poem's attempt to combine in the character of Chaka both the poet and politician. In "Chaka" Senghor applied his theories about the combination of music, dance, and poetry found in native African art forms. As Mezu noted, "Senghor aimed to illustrate what he considered an indigenous form of art where music, painting, theatre, poetry, religion, faith, love, and politics are all intertwined." In addition to musical and rhythmic elements, native plants and animals also figure prominently in *Ethiopiques*, whose other poems include "A New York," and "Congo."

When France's Fourth Republic collapsed in 1958 and France began to form a new constitution—along with new African policies—Senghor joined the advocates of independence for African territories. The French government, under Charles de Gaulle, appointed Senghor to the consultative assembly that would formulate the new constitution and policies. De Gaulle's proposed constitution, which was adopted in late 1958, accorded French West African territories autonomy within the French Community. At the same time De Gaulle warned Senghor that complete independence for West Africa would mean a cessation of technical and financial aid. In 1959 Senghor countered with the Mali Federation, linking Senegal and the Sudan (now Mali). The Mali Federation proclaimed its independence in June, 1960, but two months later Senegal withdrew and reproclaimed its independence. A Senegalese constitution was drawn up in August, 1960, and the following month Senghor was elected to a seven-year term as president of the new Republic of Senegal. Almost twenty-five years later Senghor told *Time,* "The colonizing powers did not prepare us for independence."

Poems Senghor wrote during the tumultuous years leading up to his election as president of Senegal were published in the 1961 collection *Nocturnes,* which featured a group of love poems previously published as *Chants pour Naeett* in 1949. In *Nocturnes* Senghor ponders the nature of poetry and examines the poetic process. Critics have noted that in this volume, particularly in poems such as "Elegie de minuit," Senghor reveals his regret for time spent in the empty pomp of political power, his nostalgia for his youth, and his reconciliation with death. Mezu called "Elegie de minuit" the poet's "'last' poem."

After 1960, Senghor wrote mainly political and critical prose, tied closely to the goals, activities, and demands of his political life. During this time he survived an attempted coup d'etat staged in 1962 by Senegal's prime minister, Mamadou Dia. The following year Senghor authorized the Senegalese National Assembly to draw up a new constitution that gave more power to the president, elected to five-year terms. Known for his ability to hold factions together, he remained in power, reelected in 1968 and 1973, despite more coup attempts, an assassination plot in 1967, and civil unrest in the late 1960s. Much of Senghor's writing from this era outlines the course he feels Africa must hold to, despite upheavals. Commenting on the instability suffered after African nations achieved independence, Senghor told *Time:* "The frequency of coups in Africa is the result of the backwardness in civilization that colonization represented. . . . What we should all be fighting for is democratic socialism. And the first task of socialism is not to create social justice. It is to establish working democracies."

According to Hymans, Senghor's brand of socialism, often called the African Road to Socialism, maps out a middle position between individualism and collectivism, between capitalism and communism. Senghor sees socialism as a way of eliminating the exploitation of individuals that prevents universal humanism. Some of Senghor's writings on this topic were translated by Mercer Cook and published in 1964 as *On African Socialism*. Appraising *On African Socialism* for *Saturday Review,* Charles Miller called its selections "exquisitely intellectual tours de force." Senghor's important political writings include *Liberte I: Negritude et humanisme,* of which portions are available in translation; a work translated by Cook as *The Foundations of "Africanite": or, "Negritude" and "Arabite"; Politique, nation, et developpement moderne; Li-*

berte III: Negritude et civilization de l'universel; and *Liberte IV: Socialisme et planification.* In a collection of interviews with Mohamed Aziza published in 1980, Senghor discussed poetry and both his politics and his life. Senghor "comes across in these interviews as a brilliant, sincere, and steadfast leader who has yet managed to retain a sense of humility," wrote Eric Sellin, reviewing the collection for *World Literature Today.* Sellin continued: "His unswerving fidelity to personal and national programs is more readily understandable in light of his autobiographical introspections about his youth and education." Published as *La Poesie de l'action,* the volume, Sellin concluded, is "an important and interesting book." Later in 1980, Senghor stepped down from Senegal's presidency when his protege, Prime Minister Abdou Diouf, took office.

Senghor is revered throughout the world for his political and literary accomplishments and a life of achievement that spans nearly six decades. He was widely thought to have been under consideration in 1962 for the Nobel Prize in Literature in recognition of his poetic output. When a major English-translation volume devoted to Senghor's body of poetry appeared in 1964, *Saturday Review* likened Senghor to American poet Walt Whitman and determined that the poems represented were "written by a gifted, civilized man of good will celebrating the ordinary hopes and feelings of mankind." The *Times Literary Supplement* called Senghor "one of the best poets now writing in [French]" and marveled at his "astonishing achievement to have combined so creative a life with his vigorous and successful political activities." Senghor was elected to one of the world's most prestigious and elite intellectual groups, the Academie Francaise, in 1983.

When a new collected edition of Senghor's poetry appeared in 1984, Robert P. Smith, Jr., writing in *World Literature Today* identified Senghor as a "great poet of Africa and the universe." Praising the masterly imagery, symbolism, and versification of the poetry, Smith expressed particular admiration for Senghor's "constant creation of a poetry which builds up, makes inquiries, and expands into universal dimensions," and cited an elegy Senghor wrote for his deceased son as "one of the most beautiful in modern poetry." Critics characterize Senghor's poetic style as serenely and resonantly rhetorical. While some readers detect a lack of tension in his poetry, most admire its lush sensuality and uplifting attitude. Offered as a means of uniting African peoples in an appreciation of their cultural worth, Senghor's poetry, most agree, extends across the chasm that negritude, at least in its early form, seemed to have created in emphasizing the differences between races. "It is difficult to predict whether Senghor's poetry will excite the same approbation when the prestige of the President and that of the idealist no longer colour people's view of the man," Mezu acknowledged. "The Senegalese poet will certainly survive in the history of the Black Renaissance as the ideologist and theoretician of negritude."

Senghor's negritude in its more evolved form refuses to choose between Africa and Europe in its quest for worldwide national, cultural, and religious integration. Himself a synthesis of disparate elements, Senghor, in his role as reconciler of differences, holds to negritude as a median between nationalism and cultural assimilation. "Politically, philosophically, Senghor has been a middle-of-the-roader, a man of conciliation and mediation," Mezu declared, adding: "Negritude should . . . be seen as a stage in the evolution of the literature of the black man. . . . The contemporary trend in African poetry seems to be away from the negritude movement as the racism and colonialism that inspired this literature dies out or becomes less

barefaced." Senghor's life, according to Hymans, "might be summarized as an effort to restore to Africa an equilibrium destroyed by the clash with Europe." For those who see contradictions in Senghor's effort over more than five decades, Hymans observed that "one constant in his thought appears to surmount the contradictions it contains: universal reconciliation is his only goal and Africa's only salvation."

MEDIA ADAPTATIONS: Senghor's prose tale "Mandabi" was adapted for film by Ousmane Sembene.

BIOGRAPHICAL/CRITICAL SOURCES:

BOOKS

Blair, Dorothy S., *African Literature in French,* Cambridge University Press, 1976.
Bureau de Documentation de la Presidence de la Republique, *Leopold Sedar Senghor: Bibliographie,* 2nd edition, Fondation Leopold Sedar Senghor, 1982.
Crowder, Michael, *Senegal: A Study in French Assimilation Policy,* Oxford University Press, 1962.
Guibert, Armand, *Leopold Sedar Senghor: L'Homme et l'oeuvre,* Presence Africaine, 1962.
Hymans, Jacques Louis, *Leopold Sedar Senghor: An Intellectual Biography,* Univeristy Press, Edinburgh, 1971.
Markovitz, Irving Leonard, *Leopold Sedar Senghor and the Politics of Negritude,* Atheneum, 1969.
Mezu, Sebastian Okechuwu, *The Poetry of Leopold Sedar Senghor,* Fairleigh Dickinson University Press, 1973.
Moore, Gerald, *Seven African Writers,* Oxford University Press, 1962.
Neikirk, Barend van Dyk Van, *The African Image (Negritude) in the Work of Leopold Sedar Senghor,* A. A. Balkema, 1970.
Rous, Jean, *Leopold Sedar Senghor,* J. Didier, 1968.

PERIODICALS

Black World, August 14, 1978.
Ebony, August, 1972.
Essence, September, 1987.
French Review, May, 1982.
Saturday Review, January 2, 1965.
Time, June 9, 1978, January 16, 1984.
Times Literary Supplement, June 11, 1964.
World Literature Today, Spring, 1965, Autumn, 1978, Summer, 1981, Winter, 1985.

—*Sketch by Diane L. Dupuis*

*   *   *

SHAARA, Michael (Joseph, Jr.) 1929-1988

OBITUARY NOTICE—See index for *CA* sketch: Born June 23, 1929, in Jersey City, N.J.; died of a heart attack, May 5, 1988, in Tallahassee, Fla. Paratrooper, sailor, police officer, professional boxer, educator, and author. Shaara won the 1975 Pulitzer Prize for fiction for his Civil War novel *The Killer Angels,* which is often consulted as a factual source because of its historical accuracy. Shaara wrote three other novels, *The Broken Place, The Herald,* and *Soldier Boy,* and he wrote numerous short stories, some of which he published in his *Collected Short Stories.* During the 1940s and 1950s the author worked variously as a U.S. Army paratrooper, a merchant seaman, a police officer, and a prizefighter. He was an associate professor of English at Florida State University from 1961 to 1973.

OBITUARIES AND OTHER SOURCES:

BOOKS

Authors in the News, Volume 1, Gale, 1976.
Contemporary Literary Criticism, Volume 15, Gale, 1980.
Dictionary of Literary Biography Yearbook: 1983, Gale, 1984.
Who's Who in America, 44th edition, Marquis, 1986.

PERIODICALS

Los Angeles Times, May 7, 1988.
New York Times, May 9, 1988.
Washington Post, May 7, 1988.

*   *   *

SHANNON, Dell
See LININGTON, (Barbara) Elizabeth

*   *   *

SHAPIRO, Alan 1952-

PERSONAL: Born February 18, 1952, in Boston, Mass.; son of Harold (a salesman) and Marilyn (a secretary; maiden name, Katz) Shapiro; married Della Pollock (a professor), September 7, 1984. *Education:* Brandeis University, B.A., 1974.

ADDRESSES: Office—Department of English, Northwestern University, Evanston, Ill. 60201.

CAREER: Stanford University, Stanford, Calif., Stegner fellow in poetry, 1975, lecturer in creative writing, 1976-79; Northwestern University, Evanston, Ill., lecturer, 1979-85, associate professor of English, 1985—.

AWARDS, HONORS: Fellow of National Endowment for the Arts, 1984; Guggenheim fellow, 1986; received nomination for National Book Critics Circle award, 1987, for *Happy Hour*.

WRITINGS:

POETRY

After the Digging, Elpenor Books, 1981.
The Courtesy, University of Chicago Press, 1983.
Happy Hour, University of Chicago Press, 1987.

SIDELIGHTS: Alan Shapiro told *CA:* "When I was writing the poems in my first two books, *After the Digging* and *The Courtesy*, most American poetry was committed to free verse lyric of some kind, and most poets and critics of poetry assumed that formal verse was old-fashioned and mechanical, incapable of responding to the urgencies of the contemporary world. Poets as different as Allen Ginsberg, Robert Duncan, Galway Kinnell, and Adrienne Rich claimed that only free verse and its improvised rhythms could render faithfully the contours of immediate experience, and that the business of the poet was not to traffic in ideas or statements but to present and juxtapose images and feelings with as much concreteness and intensity as possible. There was, moreover, almost exclusive attention to the poem as self-expression, and to form as the transparent medium of personality. Although my first two books differ greatly in style and subject, they share the ambition to go against the grain of many of these assumptions and tendencies and to attempt to win back some of the territory given up to prose.

"*After the Digging* comprises two suites of historical narratives, one devoted to the potato famine in Ireland in the mid-nineteenth century, and the other to the seventeenth-century American Puritans. My intention was to enter into lives foreign to my own as imaginatively and accurately as I could, so as to better understand the historical and cultural circumstances out of which arose the Irish famine on the one hand, and the Salem witch trials on the other.

"*The Courtesy* deals with more contemporary experience: the problems of familial and religious continuities in a secular and mobile culture, and the tensions between desire and circumstance in the context of love. Most of these poems are in rhyme and meter, yet the style is plain and idiomatic. Although *The Courtesy* is primarily a book of lyric poems concerned with personal experience, I am less interested in autobiography or confessional self-exposure than in distilling from personal experience some sort of understanding that can clarify, if not resolve, emotional and psychological complexity.

"In a way my most recent book, *Happy Hour*, attempts to combine the best qualities of *After the Digging* and *The Courtesy*. All these poems are grounded in contemporary life, yet most of them are narrative, not lyrics, and are therefore only indirectly personal. I am still working in a plain style but there is greater attention to circumstance and detail, not quite so much exposition, and there is also a wider range of forms—a variety of free verse lines as well as some traditional measures. The concerns of *Happy Hour* are similar to those of *The Courtesy*, but in the best poems they are treated more inclusively, more dramatically.

"It is difficult to say exactly where my new work is going. One proceeds intuitively, from line to line, and poem to poem, and it is only in retrospect that one can see how the work developed. What I hope is that the poems I am writing now continue to cultivate the same inclusive tendency begun in *Happy Hour*. I want to write poems that can speak to individual experience without restricting themselves to private mood and feeling, the staples of the lyric mode.

"During the late 1970s and early 1980s I began to write essays and reviews on contemporary poetry, and since then criticism has become a vital aspect of my intellectual and artistic life. The criticism, however, is very much a poet's, not a scholar's. It is highly polemical, preoccupied with principles of judgment and evaluation, and eager to challenge the assumptions many poets of my generation have uncritically accepted, assumptions that I believe have a limiting effect on the practise and understanding of the art. Perhaps a less fancy way of putting this would be to say that like all poet-critics, I write criticism to create an audience for the poetry I am struggling to write and the poetry by others I admire. I want to stress, too, that the criticism follows from the poetry, not the other way around. My conception of what poetry is or can be changes as my own work develops and evolves. Thus, just as I find it difficult to forecast the poems I may go on to write, so also I find it difficult to say what direction my criticism will take in the future."

*   *   *

SHAPLEN, Robert (Modell) 1917-1988

OBITUARY NOTICE—See index for *CA* sketch: Born March 22, 1917, in Philadelphia, Pa.; died of cancer, May 15, 1988, in New York, N.Y. Journalist and author. Shaplen, the recipient of five Overseas Press Club awards, specialized in Asian and Pacific topics during his thirty-six year career as a *New Yorker* correspondent. Before joining the magazine's staff in 1952, he worked for the now-defunct *New York Herald Tri-*

bune and for *Collier's, Fortune,* and *Newsweek* magazines. In the course of his reporting career, Shaplen flew over Nagasaki, Japan, hours after its destruction by an atomic bomb in 1945, and he observed the fall of Saigon in Vietnam in 1973. He wrote two books of fiction, *A Corner of the World* and *A Forest of Tigers,* and several nonfiction works, including *Kreuger: Genius and Swindler, The Lost Revolution: The U.S. in Vietnam, Time Out of Hand: Revolution and Reaction in Southeast Asia, A Turning Wheel,* and *Bitter Victory.*

OBITUARIES AND OTHER SOURCES:

BOOKS

International Authors and Writers Who's Who, 9th edition, [and] *International Who's Who in Poetry,* 6th edition, Melrose, 1982.
Who's Who in America, 44th edition, Marquis, 1986.

PERIODICALS

Los Angeles Times, May 18, 1988.
New York Times, May 16, 1988.
Times (London), May 18, 1988.
Washington Post, May 17, 1988.

*   *   *

SHARKAWI, A(bdel)-R(ahman)   1920-1987

OBITUARY NOTICE: Some sources cite given names without hyphen and surname as el-Sharkawy or El-Sharkawi; born November 11, 1920; died of a heart attack, November 10 (one source says November 11), 1987, in Cairo, Egypt. Political activist, journalist, poet, playwright, and novelist. Though active in Egyptian politics, serving as secretary-general of the Afro-Asian Peoples' Solidarity Organization beginning in 1985, Sharkawi was known primarily for his writings. Recipient of Egypt's highest literary honor, the state prize for literature, he first captured international attention in the 1950s with his poem "From an Egyptian Father to President Truman." Sharkawi achieved further recognition for his first book, *The Land,* a novel concerned with the suffering of peasants under feudalism; his many other works include *Egyptian Earth* and *Abu Bakr al-Sedik.* Several of his poems, plays, and novels, which often feature religious, heroic, and political themes, are required reading in Egyptian universities. Sharkawi, who served as secretary-general of the Supreme Arts Council and was a member of Egypt's National Assembly and Supreme Press Council, wrote a column for the newspaper *Al Ahram* and once chaired the political weekly *Rose al-Youssef.*

OBITUARIES AND OTHER SOURCES:

PERIODICALS

Los Angeles Times, November 12, 1987.
New York Times, November 11, 1987.
Times (London), November 17, 1987.
Washington Post, November 13, 1987.

*   *   *

SHEARER, John   1947-

PERSONAL: Born in 1947 in New York, N.Y.; son of Ted (a cartoonist and illustrator) and Phyllis (a social services deputy commissioner; maiden name, Wildman) Shearer. *Education:* Attended Rochester Institute of Technology and School of Visual Arts.

ADDRESSES: Home—Tatomuck Rd., Pound Ridge, N.Y. 10576. *Office*—School of Journalism, Columbia University, Broadway and West 116th St., New York, N.Y. 10027.

CAREER: Photographer and writer. Staff photographer for magazines *Look,* 1970—, and *Life,* 1971-73; Columbia University School of Journalism, New York, N.Y., teacher of photojournalism, 1975—. Shearer Visuals, White Plains, N.Y., president, 1980-84. Producer of films for "Sesame Street," featuring his series characters Billy Jo Jive and Susie Sunset. Photographic work represented in exhibits, including "Harlem on My Mind" at Metropolitan Museum of Art, and in shows at Grand Central Station and IBM Galleries, all New York City.

AWARDS, HONORS: Recipient of more than twenty national awards, including Ceba Award for communications, and for animated film "Billy Jo Jive Super Private Eye: The Case of the Missing Ten Speed Bike," both 1978.

WRITINGS

"*BILLY JO JIVE*" FICTION SERIES, FOR CHILDREN

Billy Jo Jive Super Private Eye: The Case of the Missing Ten Speed Bike, illustrations by father, Ted Shearer, Delacorte, 1976.
The Case of the Sneaker Snatcher, illustrations by T. Shearer, Delacorte, 1977.
Billy Jo Jive and the Case of the Missing Pigeons, illustrations by T. Shearer, Delacorte, 1978.
Billy Jo Jive and the Walkie Talkie Caper, illustrations by T. Shearer, Delacorte, 1981.
Billy Jo Jive and the Case of the Midnight Voices, illustrations by T. Shearer, Delacorte, 1982.

NONFICTION, FOR CHILDREN

I Wish I Had an Afro, self-illustrated with photographs, Cowles Book, 1970.
Little Man in the Family, self-illustrated with photographs, design by Don Mendell, foreword by Gordon Parks, Delacorte, 1972.

OTHER

Contributor of photographs to magazines, including *Popular Photography, Look,* and *Infinity.*

WORK IN PROGRESS: A semi-autobiographical novel.

MEDIA ADAPTATIONS: Billy Jo Jive Super Private Eye: The Case of the Missing Ten Speed Bike was adapted as an animated film of the same title, Shearer Visuals, 1978.*

*   *   *

SHEN Congwen   1902-1988
(Bi Shang-guan, Chen Jia, Huan Yue, Lin Mao)

OBITUARY NOTICE: Some sources transliterate name as Shen Ts'ung-wen; name originally Shen Yuehuan; born December 28, 1902, in Hunan, China; died of a heart attack, May 10, 1988, in Beijing (Peking), China. Author. One of the most widely translated and anthologized modern Chinese writers, Shen is best known for his lyrical short stories which evoke the beauty and simplicity of rural life in his native Hunan. His first major work was the psychological novel *Fengzi,* which was published in 1932; critics, however, consider *Long River,* his 1943 publication, his greatest work of fiction. His writings, which reflect a belief in literary and intellectual independence, were burned by mainland publishing houses after the Communist takeover of China in 1949, and they were banned in Nationalist Taiwan as well. Criticized as a reactionary, Shen tried to commit suicide by drinking kerosene and slitting his throat and wrists. He was subsequently forced by Communist authorities to attend political indoctrination seminars, agree to self-criticism, and work at menial jobs. By the 1970s he was considered partially rehabilitated. Though he was permitted to write whatever he wished beginning in 1978, Shen devoted the remainder of his life to academic research on Chinese history and culture.

OBITUARIES AND OTHER SOURCES:

PERIODICALS

Chicago Tribune, May 15, 1988.
Los Angeles Times, May 14, 1988.
New York Times, May 13, 1988
Times (London), May 14, 1988.
Washington Post, May 14, 1988.

*   *   *

SHIPLEY, Joseph T(wadell)   1893-1988
  (Roy Goliard)

OBITUARY NOTICE—See index for *CA* sketch: Born August 19, 1893, in Brooklyn, N.Y.; died of a stroke, May 11, 1988, in London, England. Educator, drama critic, editor, and author. Shipley began his lengthy reviewing career in 1918 with *The Call,* which later changed its name to the *New Leader,* where he remained as theater critic for forty-four years. His radio program "First Nights" was broadcast by New York station WEVD from 1940 to 1982. He served for two years as president and sixteen years as secretary of the New York Drama Critics Circle. Shipley had a long career in education as well, teaching English at Stuyvesant High School from 1914 to 1957. Concurrently, he helped found New York City's Yeshiva College (now University) in 1926, where he soon became head of the English department and taught until 1944. During that time he also lectured for ten years at City College (now City College of the City University of New York) and for eight years at Brooklyn College (now Brooklyn College of the City University of New York), and he conducted seminars for playwrights. Shipley wrote and edited numerous books, including *The Art of Eugene O'Neill, The Crown Guide to the World's Great Plays: From Ancient Greece to Modern Times, In Praise of English, Encyclopedia of Literature, The Origins of English Words: A Discursive Dictionary of Indo-European Roots,* and, under the pseudonym Roy Goliard, *A Scholar's Glossary of Sex.*

OBITUARIES AND OTHER SOURCES:

BOOKS

International Authors and Writers Who's Who, 10th edition, International Biographical Centre, 1986.
Who's Who in America, 44th edition, Marquis, 1986.

PERIODICALS

New York Times, May 14, 1988.
Times (London), June 24, 1988.

SICKMAN, Laurence C(halfant) S(tevens)   1906-1988

OBITUARY NOTICE—See index for *CA* sketch: Born August 27, 1906, in Denver, Colo.; died May 7, 1988, in Kansas City, Mo. Art collector, museum director, editor, and author. Sickman was an expert on traditional paintings of China and is renowned for gathering one of the finest collections of Chinese art in the world. He began collecting art works while traveling throughout China in the early 1930s. In 1935 he became curator of Oriental art at the William Rockhill Nelson Gallery of the Atkins Museum of Fine Arts in Kansas City, Missouri, where the collection is displayed. He became vice-director of the museum in 1946 and from 1953 to 1977 served as director. Sickman lectured on Oriental art at Harvard University from 1937 to 1939. He wrote and edited, under various forms of his name, several books in his field, including *The University Prints, Early Chinese Art, The Art and Architecture of China,* and *Chinese Calligraphy and Painting in the Collection of John M. Crawford, Jr.* He also edited the *Archives* for the Chinese Art Society of America.

OBITUARIES AND OTHER SOURCES:

BOOKS

Who's Who in American Art, 17th edition, Bowker, 1986.

PERIODICALS

New York Times, May 11, 1988.
Times (London), May 13, 1988.

*   *   *

SIEGEL, Irving H(erbert)   1914-1988

OBITUARY NOTICE—See index for *CA* sketch: Born February 1, 1914, in New York, N.Y.; died of cardiac arrest, May 18, 1988, in Bethesda, Md. Economist, educator, editor, and author. Siegel served as economic adviser to numerous governmental and private organizations, including the U.S. Department of Commerce and, from 1953 to 1961, President Dwight D. Eisenhower's Council of Economic Advisers. During the 1940s and 1950s Siegel was associated with the U.S. Bureau of Labor Statistics, the U.S. Veterans Administration, and Twentieth Century Fund. In the following decade he served as an economist for the Research Analysis Corporation and for the W. E. Upjohn Institute for Employment Research, and from 1972 to 1979 he was economic adviser to the U.S. Department of Commerce. He lectured in political economy for three years at Johns Hopkins University, where he also directed a study of Soviet productivity for the Operations Research Office. Throughout his career he was a consultant for various organizations, including George Washington University's Patent, Trademark, and Copyright Research Institute, the International Business Machines Corporation, and the American Chemical Society. Siegel wrote numerous books in his field, including *Concepts and Measurement of Production and Productivity, Strengthening Washington's Technical-Resource Base, Productivity Measurement: An Evolving Art, Fuller Employment With Less Inflation,* and *Productivity Measurement in Organizations: Private Firms and Public Agencies,* and he edited *Manpower Tomorrow: Prospects and Priorities.*

OBITUARIES AND OTHER SOURCES:

BOOKS

The Writers Directory: 1988-1990, St. James Press, 1988.

PERIODICALS

Washington Post, May 21, 1988.

*   *   *

SIMAK, Clifford D(onald)   1904-1988

*OBITUARY NOTICE—*See index for *CA* sketch: Born August 3, 1904, in Millville, Wis.; died April 25, 1988, in Minneapolis, Minn. Educator, journalist, and author. Simak, who was inducted into the Science Fiction Hall of Fame in 1973, was a prolific writer of science fiction novels and short stories. The recipient of three Hugo awards, two Nebula Awards, and a Grand Master Award for his lifetime contribution to science fiction, Simak is best known for his books *City, Way Station,* and *The Visitors,* and for his collection *Skirmish: The Great Short Fiction of Clifford D. Simak.* The writer taught school and worked for several Michigan newspapers in his early career, then joined the *Minneapolis Star and Tribune* in 1939. He eventually became news editor and science editor of that publication, retiring in 1976. Simak's other works include the novels *The Creator, Special Deliverance,* and *Highway of Eternity,* the story collections *Strangers in the Universe* and *The Worlds of Clifford Simak,* and the nonfiction works *The Solar System: Our New Front Yard* and *Trilobite, Dinosaur, and Man: The Earth's Story.*

OBITUARIES AND OTHER SOURCES:

BOOKS

Contemporary Literary Criticism, Volume 1, Gale, 1973.
Dictionary of Literary Biography, Volume 8: *Twentieth-Century American Science Fiction Writers,* Gale, 1981.
The Writers Directory, 1988-1990, St. James Press, 1988.

PERIODICALS

Los Angeles Times, April 29, 1988.
New York Times, April 28, 1988.
Times (London), April 29, 1988.
Washington Post, April 30, 1988.

*   *   *

SIMPSON, Norman T.   1919(?)-1988

OBITUARY NOTICE: Born in 1919 (one source says 1918); died of complications from the flu, April 5, 1988, in Stockbridge, Mass. Publisher and author. Creator and author of the travel guide series *Country Inns and Back Roads,* Simpson started his own publishing company, Berkshire Traveller Press, in 1966 to distribute the book. Each new edition in the series offers an updated comprehensive listing of small hotels and bed-and-breakfast accommodations. Harper & Row currently publishes American, British, and European editions of the *Country Inn* volumes, as well as *Bed and Breakfast, American Style,* which Simpson also researched and wrote.

OBITUARIES AND OTHER SOURCES:

PERIODICALS

New York Times, April 21, 1988.
Publishers Weekly, April 29, 1988.

*   *   *

SKLAR, George   1908-1988

*OBITUARY NOTICE—*See index for *CA* sketch: Born June 1, 1908, in Meriden, Conn.; died of cardiac arrest, May 16, 1988, in Los Angeles, Calif. Playwright, screenwriter, and novelist. Sklar is remembered for the protest plays he wrote for the Federal Theater Project during the Great Depression, most notably "Stevedore," which concerned racism and unionism. His other plays include "Merry Go Round," which he co-authored with Albert Maltz, "Peace on Earth," "Life and Death of An American," "And People All Around," and "Brown Pelican." Sklar wrote screenplays during the 1940s but, blacklisted by Hollywood during the mid-twentieth century because of his socialist politics, he turned to writing novels. His books include *The Two Worlds of Johnny Truro*—a best-seller that was made into a movie—*The Promising Young Men, The Housewarming,* and *The Identity of Dr. Frazier.*

OBITUARIES AND OTHER SOURCES:

BOOKS

International Authors and Writers Who's Who, 9th edition, [and] *International Who's Who in Poetry,* 6th edition, Melrose, 1982.
Who's Who in America, 44th edition, Marquis, 1986.

PERIODICALS

Los Angeles Times, May 18, 1988.
New York Times, May 18, 1988.

*   *   *

SMITH, Harold L(ester)   1942-

PERSONAL: Born November 25, 1942, in Ottumwa, Iowa; son of Harvey William and Lela Gwen (McCreery) Smith; divorced. *Education:* State College of Iowa (now University of Northern Iowa), B.S., 1965; University of Iowa, M.A., 1967, Ph.D., 1971; postdoctoral study at University of California, Los Angeles, 1977, and Christ Church, Oxford, 1985.

ADDRESSES: Home—211 Avalon, Victoria, Tex. 77901. *Office*—Department of History, Victoria Campus, University of Houston, 2302-C Red River, Victoria, Tex. 77901.

CAREER: University of Missouri—Kansas City, Kansas City, visiting assistant professor of history, 1971; University of Montana, Missoula, visiting assistant professor of history, 1972-73; Augustana College, lecturer, 1974; University of Iowa, Iowa City, visiting assistant professor of history, 1975-76; University of Houston, Victoria Campus, Victoria, Tex., visiting assistant professor, 1976-78, assistant professor, 1978-80, associate professor, 1980-85, professor of history, 1985—.

MEMBER: Western Conference on British Studies (president, 1987-88).

AWARDS, HONORS: Fellow of National Endowment for the Humanities, 1977, American Philosophical Society, 1979 and 1985, and National Science Foundation, 1982.

WRITINGS:

(Contributor) Justin Wintle, editor, *The Makers of Nineteenth Century Culture,* Routledge & Kegan Paul, 1982.
(Editor) *War and Social Change: British Society in the Second World War,* Manchester University Press, 1986.
(Contributor) Frank N. Magill, editor, *Great Lives From History: American Series,* Salem Press, 1987.
(Contributor) Gerald Jordan, editor, *British Military History: A Guide to the Recent Literature,* Garland Publishing, 1988.

British Feminism in the Twentieth Century, Edward Elgar, in press.

Contributor to *Magill's Literary Annual.* Contributor to professional journals, including *Societas, Journal of Modern History, Historian,* and *Historical Journal.* Editorial consultant to Salem Press, 1987.

WORK IN PROGRESS: The "Equal Pay for Equal Work" Issue in Great Britain, 1888-1975, publication expected in 1990; *Women in Britain: A Social History Since 1850,* publication by Longman expected in 1992.

SIDELIGHTS: Harold L. Smith told *CA:* "My interest in writing British women's history developed early in the 1970s when I was teaching courses comparing the American women's movement with similar developments in Britain. I found it a frustrating experience because, apart from the suffrage campaign, very little had been published on British women. I went to London in the summer of 1976 to gather materials for my course, and I found several issues so compelling that I began to write about them. My articles on the equal pay controversy were published in 1978 in *Societas* and in 1981 in the *Journal of Modern History.* My interest in the relationship between socialism and feminism led to an article on 'Sex vs. Class' in *Historian.* Current discussions about the difficulty that feminist groups have experienced in securing equal employment opportunities for women resulted in my *Historical Journal* article, which addresses the efforts by British feminists to achieve this objective during World War II. My preoccupation with the problem of how change has come about on gender issues—or, more precisely, why there has been so little change—has culminated with book-length studies underway on the equal pay issue, British feminism since 1900, and British women since 1850."

BIOGRAPHICAL/CRITICAL SOURCES:

PERIODICALS

Times Literary Supplement, May 15, 1987.

*   *   *

SMULLYAN, Raymond
See SMULLYAN, Raymond M(errill)

*   *   *

SMULLYAN, Raymond M(errill)   1919-
(Raymond Smullyan)

PERSONAL: Born May 25, 1919, in Far Rockaway, N.Y.; married wife, Blanche. *Education:* Attended Pacific University, 1938, Reed College, 1939, University of Wisconsin at Madison, 1943, University of Chicago, 1952; studied piano privately in San Francisco, Calif., 1939; University of Chicago, B.S., 1955; Princeton University, Ph.D., 1959.

ADDRESSES: Office—Department of Philosophy, Indiana University—Bloomington, Sycamore Hill 026, Bloomington, Ind. 47405.

CAREER: Roosevelt College of Chicago (now Roosevelt University), Chicago, Ill., instructor in music, 1945; magician in New York City, 1950, and Chicago, 1951-54; Dartmouth College, Hanover, N.H., instructor in mathematics, 1954-56; Princeton University, Princeton, N.J., instructor, 1956-59, lecturer in mathematics, 1959-61; Yeshiva University, New York City, assistant professor, 1961-63, asociate professor

of mathematics, 1963-68; City University of New York, New York City, professor of mathematics at Lehman College and graduate division, 1968-76, professor of philosophy at graduate center, 1976-81; Indiana University—Bloomington, Visiting Oscar Ewing Professor of Philosophy, 1981-82, Oscar Ewing Professor of Philosophy, 1982—.

MEMBER: American Mathematical Society, American Mathematical Association, Association for Symbolic Logic.

WRITINGS:

Theory of Formal Systems (monograph), Princeton University Press, 1961.
First-Order Logic, Springer-Verlag, 1968.
The Tao Is Silent, Harper, 1977.
What Is the Name of This Book?: The Riddle of Dracula and Other Logical Puzzles, Prentice-Hall, 1978.
(Under name Raymond Smullyan) *The Chess Mysteries of Sherlock Holmes,* Knopf, 1979.
This Book Needs No Title: A Budget of Living Paradoxes, Prentice-Hall, 1980.
(Under name Raymond Smullyan) *The Chess Mysteries of the Arabian Knights,* Knopf, 1981.
(Under name Raymond Smullyan) *The Lady or the Tiger?: And Other Logic Puzzles, Including a Mathematical Novel That Features Goedel's Great Discovery,* Knopf, 1982.
Alice in Puzzle-Land: A Carrollian Tale for Children Under Eighty, Morrow, 1982.
(Under name Raymond Smullyan) *5000 B.C. and Other Philosophical Fantasies,* St. Martin's, 1983.
To Mock a Mockingbird, Knopf, 1985.
(Under name Raymond Smullyan) *Forever Undecided: A Puzzle Guide to Goedel,* Knopf, 1987.
Incompleteness and Undecidability, Oxford University Press, in press.

Contributor of numerous articles to mathematics and philosophy journals. Contributor of puzzles to *Scientific American* and *Manchester Guardian.*

WORK IN PROGRESS: Diagonalization and Self-Reference, a monograph; articles on mathematics and philosophy.

SIDELIGHTS: Known for a series of distinctive works on philosophy, chess, logic, and mathematics, Raymond M. Smullyan is a man "whose mind," as Hugh Kenner said in *Harper's,* "seems to have been largely his own invention." Smullyan told *Smithsonian*'s Ira Mothner that he was "a bit of a prodigy" as a child, dropping out of high school "because no one there would teach me what I wanted to learn." Admitted to college on the strength of what he had taught himself, Smullyan attended a series of schools and supported himself along the way as a nightclub magician under the name "Five-Ace Merrill." He became a professor at Dartmouth College after Rudolf P. Carnap, who had taught him philosophy at the University of Chicago, recommended him for the post even though Smullyan had not yet earned his bachelor's degree. Dartmouth hired him, and the next year Chicago gave him a B.S. based on proven competence. Smullyan soon went on to Princeton University for his Ph.D. and turned his thesis, "Theory of Formal Systems," into his first book. Martin Gardner in *New Leader* called the work "an elegant treatise that has had enormous influence on mathematicians studying recursive functions, proof theory and artificial intelligence."

In the late 1970s Smullyan began to write books for a more general audience, and while his concerns have ranged from Oriental mysticism to chess to esoteric principles of mathematics, reviewers have consistently found the works inventive, entertaining, and intellectually rewarding. "Professor Smullyan is uninhibited," remarked Pulitzer Prize-winning author Douglas Hofstadter in the *New York Times Book Review,* calling him "a free spirit who has no fear of mixing serious ideas with the most outrageous humor in a casual, spontaneous style." In the same publication George Johnson called him "a master at translating difficult ideas into stories and puzzles that require no formal background, only patience and a passion to learn."

Smullyan's first book for general readers, *The Tao Is Silent,* concerns the ancient Chinese philosophy of Taoism, which Smullyan refers to as "a Delightful Paradox," according to Gardner. Taoism promotes such principles as action through inaction, and although it emphasizes that all humanity is only an insignificant part of a vast universal system, believers find this a cause for self-assured laughter rather than despair. To convey the nature of Taoism to his readers, Smullyan uses both essays and a literary genre that Kenner said he calls "philosophical fiction." A form of the genre was used by the ancient Greek philosopher Plato, Kenner noted, explaining that "it's a fiction with an easy narrative line and lots of conversation, but with ideas instead of characters." For instance, the book ends with a discussion among characters with names such as Moralist, Practical Man, and Mystic, who debate the future of philosophy. In *Washington Post Book World,* Hofstadter praised the author's "magnificent repartee."

Smullyan continues to use philosophical fiction in his second work, *The Chess Mysteries of Sherlock Holmes.* Reviving the main characters of Arthur Conan Doyle's popular detective stories, Smullyan allows Holmes, an investigator known for his brilliant deductions, to explain chess problems to the inquisitive Dr. Watson. The problems are highly unusual because they require "retrograde analysis"—while most chess writers display a partly finished game and ask the reader to complete it, Smullyan asks his audience what moves have already happened. Hailing the author's "genial expertise" as a puzzle-maker, Peter Jay of the *Times Literary Supplement* called the work "unusually entertaining." When Smullyan wrote another retrograde-analysis book, *The Chess Mysteries of the Arabian Knights,* Neal Johnston stated in the *New York Times Book Review* that the puzzles could inspire "fury, rage, mortification and a compulsive need to stay up another 30 minutes to see if this next one can't be cracked."

Smullyan has gone on to write several books of logic puzzles, and the works have been repeatedly praised for their uniqueness and creativity. Mothner noted that Martin Gardner, himself a famed puzzle-master, said that Smullyan's "output of brand-new problems is absolutely fantastic." Using a framework such as the adventures of the fictional Inspector Craig of Scotland Yard, the author introduces readers to knights and vampires who either do or do not tell the truth, or asks them to deduce which of nine doors hides a beautiful woman, while the other doors may hide nothing or a ferocious tiger—and along the way, readers must exercise their skills with the science of logic. "A page of Mr. Smullyan," George Johnson averred, "requires a great deal of thinking."

Moreover, Smullyan confronts his audience with the limitations of logic, inspired by the mathematician Kurt Goedel's Incompleteness Theorem, which shows that any sufficiently strong system of reasoning must rest on statements it cannot prove. Many of Smullyan's books use a story with a sequence of logic puzzles to take nonprofessionals through the steps of Goedel's proof and help them to appreciate its paradoxical assertion that logic is inextricably linked to faith. As Hofstadter observed, "members of the Smullyan fan club" are likely to be "people who savor contradictions, who don't shove them under the rug but feel them alive in themselves." He continued, "Such people *inevitably* have to confront Zen and other Eastern views (as Professor Smullyan did in hs stimulating book 'The Tao Is Silent'), because there they recognize an undeniably kindred spirit." Praising the author for his intellectual complexity, Kenner asserted that "to be offered a handle on what you thought you'd never understand, that's a heady experience."

CA INTERVIEW

CA interviewed Raymond Smullyan by telephone on December 19, 1986, while he was on holiday from Indiana University.

CA: Among your many puzzle fans are some young children, one of whom provided, at the age of nine-and-a-half, a better solution then your own to a puzzle in What Is the Name of This Book? *Do you think we all start out loving puzzles?*

SMULLYAN: Most kids love them, yes.

CA: Why do some of us lose interest?

SMULLYAN: I don't know. I think it's possibly the educational system. Kids are usually taught in a very dull way, so their curiosity is stifled.

CA: Let's say I'd like to enjoy puzzles but, whenever I pick up a book like To Mock a Mockingbird *and start reading, I begin to feel intimidated and perhaps slightly stupid. How do I begin to enjoy puzzles, assuming that's possible?*

SMULLYAN: Don't think of a puzzle in terms of whether you can solve it or not, but just think in terms of whether it's a nice puzzle. You can enjoy them for their own sake, as works of art, rather than a challenge to you, whether you can personally solve them.

CA: How do you think up puzzles? Is there a moment of inspiration?

SMULLYAN: Usually, yes.

CA: Can you tell me something about the process of creating them?

SMULLYAN: Impossible! Utterly indescribable, unfortunately.

CA: Do you ever have an answer and then work out the question, as with the chess problems you've invented?

SMULLYAN: Yes. Sometimes I say, Can I create a situation that will do such-and-such? Then I investigate to see if I can create such a situation. And sometimes I do it in reverse.

CA: Are computers greatly increasing the possibilities for puzzles?

SMULLYAN: Computers have been programmed to try and solve some of my puzzles. In *To Mock a Mockingbird,* there's a computer line called Arbnet, and you must ask it any problem and the computer will solve it. It solves all the puzzles in the book. On the other hand, people have written Ph.D. theses trying to find an automatic way of solving my chess puzzles. So far, no one has been successful. They're much harder. Conventional chess problems, like White to play and mate in so many moves, yes. But these are retrograde puzzles. Computers cannot yet handle them.

CA: They require more human intelligence to solve?

SMULLYAN: Yes, they seem to. One day they may have computers that can do it, but as of now they do not.

CA: Was your inclination toward math and logic apparent when you were very young?

SMULLYAN: In my grade school days, I was interested in chemistry. I had my own chemical laboratory and I read my brother's high school and college chemistry books. I had very much the image in my mind of the mad Hollywood scientist; I wanted to be a mad, eccentric scientist like Frankenstein and create a monster when I grew up. I disliked arithmetic very much in grade school. I disliked first-year algebra intensely when I got to that in high school. It was just like a cookbook recipe. But when I saw geometry, I knew that was it. For the first time I really saw a logical reason that it should be taught.

CA: So that was the door to all the following interest in math and logic?

SMULLYAN: Absolutely. Actually, modern algebra is a great field. If I hadn't gone into logic, I would have gone into modern algebra. That's really deductive.

CA: One of the very interesting things I've read about you is that you dropped out of high school and three or four colleges before you got your Ph.D. Was there a lack of intellectual stimulation in the schools?

SMULLYAN: I was just interested in other things that I wanted to study on my own. That was my main motivation. I drifted back—I don't know exactly how. And after I'd been away for a while, before I got my bachelor's degree, I suddenly got a job teaching math at Dartmouth College. It was very, very funny. Finally the University of Chicago was sensible: they gave me a degree based on courses I taught, which I had never had—like freshman calculus.

CA: Before you became a teacher, you earned a living for a while by doing magic shows in nightclubs. Is it too farfetched to suspect that the two endeavors have a lot in common?

SMULLYAN: Oh, I think they do. It's not farfetched at all.

CA: How do you go about putting some spice in your teaching?

SMULLYAN: I like to turn people on with whatever I do, whether it's magic or teaching or writing or anything else. I guess I'm just what's called a ham by nature, as my family would say.

CA: Probably not a bad quality for teaching.

SMULLYAN: I think so, though some teachers are excellent without that. It's just different styles.

CA: If I were starting one of your classes in logic, say, what could I expect to happen the first day? Would you do some-

thing special to get me and the other students interested in the course?

SMULLYAN: I'd give you a puzzle. Shall I give you the puzzle to think about?

CA: Please do.

SMULLYAN: Suppose I put a dollar bill and a million-dollar bill on the table. I tell you to make a statement. If the statement is true, I promise to give you one of the two bills. If the statement is false, you won't get either bill. If you say two plus two is four, for example, I will either give you the dollar or the million dollars. But if you say two plus two is five, you get nothing. What statement could you make that would force me to give you the million-dollar bill? There *is* one. A puzzle like this usually gets people interested right away, because anybody is interested in how to win a million dollars.

CA: I may have just failed your course. Let me change the subject quickly, back to magic. Looked at one way, magic and logic might seem to be antithetical. Do they have strong connections, in fact?

SMULLYAN: I don't see anything antithetical about them. They're not the same thing. But the way I do logic is a little bit magical, I've been told. I like to have surprises; I like to do proofs that have the air of a magic trick.

CA: Most of us, I believe, think of students of mathematics and logic as a special breed. Do they really have a kind of intellectual ability that other people lack?

SMULLYAN: I don't really know. I don't know how much of it is hereditary and how much environmental.

CA: Do you think people who think they're bad at those disciplines actually are just intimidated by them early?

SMULLYAN: Yes, definitely.

CA: And how can they get over their fear or anxiety?

SMULLYAN: That's a big psychological problem. A lot of studies have been done on how to overcome math anxiety. I know how to eliminate math anxiety. It's very simple: stop giving examinations. That will do it.

CA: Do you see a lot of students in your classes overcome math anxiety?

SMULLYAN: Yes. It's one of my main functions to try and help them do that, certainly. I try to get them to be interested in the problems for their own sake and forget themselves altogether. As one of my students once told me—it's very interesting—"We know you're an easy grader, you demand nothing from us, you don't insist we do homework, and yet I've never had to work so hard at any course as this one."

CA: So you're motivating students to provide their own challenge?

SMULLYAN: Exactly.

CA: Do you find many students who promise to become good logicians?

SMULLYAN: A few.

CA: What is the real business of a philosopher now? What should he or she be concerned with?

SMULLYAN: I don't think there's any answer to that question. Different philosophers are concerned with very different things.

CA: But you don't feel that modern philosophy has lost relevance in our world?

SMULLYAN: It's so highly technical that there's not much interest in the people not practicing it. Yet those who do it, such as those who practice the philosophy of language, claim that it is relevant to the issues which most people are concerned with. I just don't know how to evaluate that claim.

CA: How do you feel for yourself? Do you do your work because you enjoy it rather than because you feel it has some great social relevance?

SMULLYAN: I do it because I enjoy it, absolutely. If it has social relevance, so much the better, but that's not why I do it. Very few mathematicians work that way.

CA: Hugh Kenner said in Harper's *that you were "currently the hottest property on the flourishing pop-math circuit." If there is such a thing as pop math, what does it encompass, and what makes it* pop *math as opposed to some other kind of math?*

SMULLYAN: I don't know of any such *field* as pop math. All Kenner meant, I think, is trying to give an exposition of mathematical things that most people could understand.

CA: Is there a specific point at which math and philosophy merge?

SMULLYAN: They merge in the field of mathematical logic somewhat. Mathematical logic is taught in both math and philosophy departments, and often these days in computer science as well.

CA: Are you involved in computer science at all?

SMULLYAN: It's very strange. My best audience is computer scientists. Those are the ones who like my puzzle books the most, other than children. Many things I've done have had all sorts of applications for computer science, but I don't know a thing about computer science, so I have no idea just how they're applied.

CA: What kind of mail response do your books elicit?

SMULLYAN: All sorts—a whole bunch of delightful correspondence. There was one marvelous letter from a Scotsman who was in London at the time. He had just read my book on Eastern philosophy called *The Tao Is Silent.* And he said, "I've very much enjoyed your book. I'm even thinking of buying a copy." I'm very bad at answering correspondence, by the way. I should be better. But I wouldn't get any work done if I were.

CA: Do you get many puzzles through the mail?

SMULLYAN: Not many. I had a fellow graduate student at Princeton thirty years ago who recently bought my puzzle book.

His son sent me a variant of a puzzle, which is delightful; it gave me an idea for a whole chapter. (He was only nine-and-a-half years old, the same as the little girl I mentioned in the preface to *What Is the Name of This Book?*) So I called up. I hadn't spoken to the father for about thirty years. But before I spoke to the little boy, the father said to me in a very soft conspiratorial tone, "Listen. He loves your book. But don't let him know that it's math, because he hates math." That's typical.

CA: Two of your puzzle books center on chess: The Chess Mysteries of Sherlock Holmes *and* The Chess Mysteries of the Arabian Knights. *Is chess an ongoing hobby for you?*

SMULLYAN: Yes, though I don't play much at all. I'm only a moderate player. It takes an entirely different ability to play chess than to invent chess puzzles; thye're completely different. Can I try another puzzle on you?

CA: Sure.

SMULLYAN: OK. This is a little game. I'm going to make a statement. If the statement is true, all you have to do is promise to give me your autograph. It doesn't have to be on a check, you know; it can be on a blank piece of paper. If the statement is false, you don't give me your autograph. You agree? All right; here's the statement: You will give me neither your autograph nor a kiss. Now, let's analyze this very carefully. If the statement were true, you'd have to give me your autograph as agreed. But that would make the statement false, wouldn't it? Because, if you gave me your autograph, it would be *false* that you gave me neither one. Therefore, the statement can't be true. It must be false. Since the statement is false, it's not the case that you'll give me neither your autograph nor a kiss, so you'll have to give me *either* your autograph or a kiss. But you can't give me your autograph for a false statement, so you owe me a kiss!

CA: Do you read puzzle books for pleasure or other kinds of books, maybe fiction?

SMULLYAN: I don't read puzzle books or fiction much. My reading is mainly in the area of mysticism and religion. My favorite book is still *Cosmic Consciousness* by Richard Bucke, written about 1900.

CA: How long have you been interested in Taoism?

SMULLYAN: About fifteen years. That I'm very fond of.

CA: Are you generally working on a book, or do you take long breaks from the writing between books?

SMULLYAN: I have a technical book coming out from Oxford University Press—its present working title is *Incompleteness and Undecidability*—and I'm working on a second one. Also, I've been writing a whole bunch of essays about Christian fundamentalism. They may possibly become a book; I don't know yet. The first question I like to ask ministers is whether, in their judgment, God is unwilling or unable to save people from hell. It's an interesting question, because I get very different responses. Some say unwilling, against God's justice; others say unable.

CA: Which blows the theory that God is all-powerful.

SMULLYAN: Exactly. There's another question I like to ask. Suppose that when you get to heaven, God says to the saved assembly, "Look, I know there's been much controversy in Christianity as to whether hell is a good thing or a bad thing. I have my own ideas on the subject, but I want you all to be happy, so I'm going to let you vote on it. How would you vote—for or against?" That's another interesting pyschological question.

CA: Are you at work now on new torments for your readers, new puzzles?

SMULLYAN: I will be soon again, I hope.

BIOGRAPHICAL/CRITICAL SOURCES:

PERIODICALS

Discover, October, 1982.
Harper's, March, 1983.
Los Angeles Times Book Review, October 24, 1982.
New Leader, May 23, 1977.
New York Times Book Review, May 28, 1978, August 10, 1980, November 15, 1981, June 21, 1987.
Smithsonian, June, 1982.
Times Literary Supplement, February 29, 1980, March 8, 1985.
Washington Post Book World, December 2, 1979, May 15, 1983.

—*Sketch by Thomas Kozikowski*

—*Interview by Jean W. Ross*

*   *   *

SNOKE, Albert W(aldo)   1907-

PERSONAL: Born July 19, 1907, in Steilacoom, Wash.; son of John Waldo and Helene (Nielsen) Snoke; married Parnie Hamilton Storey (a physician); children: Albert Thomas, John Arthur, Michael David. *Education:* University of Washington, Seattle, B.S. (magna cum laude), 1928; Stanford University, M.D., 1933.

ADDRESSES: Home—100 Santa Fe Ave., Hamden, Conn. 06517. *Office*—Department of Public Health, Yale University, New Haven, Conn. 06520.

CAREER: Stanford University, Stanford, Calif., intern at university hospital, 1932-33, assistant resident in medicine and pathology, 1933-34, assistant resident in pediatrics, 1934-35, resident in pediatrics, 1935-36; Strong Memorial Hospital, Rochester, N.Y., associate resident in pediatrics, 1936-37, assistant director of hospital, 1937-46; Yale University, New Haven, Conn., professor of epidemiology and public health (hospital administration), 1946-68, lecturer in epidemiology and public health, 1968—, executive director of Yale-New Haven Hospital, 1965-68, consultant to hospital board, 1968—.

Fellow of American Board of Pediatrics, 1937, and American Board of Preventive Medicine and Public Health, 1949; American College of Hospital Administrators, fellow, 1953, regent, 1957-60; director of Grace-New Haven Hospital, 1946-65. Coordinator of health services for the state of Illinois, 1969-73; acting executive director of Illinois Comprehensive State Health Planning Agency, 1970-73; chairman of Connecticut Regional Visiting Nurse Agency, 1978-79; chairman of board of Connecticut-Quinnipiac Valley Health District, 1978-80. Chairman of Connecticut governor's Hospital Planning Committee, 1960-62; chairman of Veterans Administration Hospital Construction Advisory Council, 1963-69; chairman of medical advisory committee of Connecticut State Department of Welfare, 1968-69. U.S. Public Health Service, member of federal council, 1951-58, member of Medical Care Advisory Committee, 1956, and Advisory Committee on Hospitals and Clinics, 1962-65; member of Joint Commission for Improvement of Care of the Patient, 1952-59, and Joint Commission on Accreditation of Hospitals, 1955-64; member of National Advisory Health Council committee on clinical research centers, 1960; member of Civil Service Commission advisory committee on federal employees health insurance, 1961-63; member of medical advisory committee of U.S. Vocational Rehabilitation Administration, 1963-68; member of National Commission on Public General Hospitals, 1975-79; consultant to Connecticut Regional Medical Program. Member of board of directors of Carrier Corp., 1962-79.

MEMBER: American Association of Hospital Consultants, American Hospital Association (life member; chairman of Council on Hospital Planning and Plant Operations, 1945-47; chairman of Council on Prepayment Plans and Hospital Reimbursement, 1950-51; chairman of Council on Professional Practice, 1951-55; president, 1956-57; member of House of Delegates, 1960-63), American Medical Association, American Public Health Association (fellow), Association of American Medical Colleges (chairman of Medical School Teaching Hospital Section, 1960-61), Connecticut Association of Human Services, Connecticut Hospital Association (life member; president, 1954-55; chairman of Council on Government Relations, 1959-61), New York Academy of Medicine, New Haven County Medical Society, Phi Beta Kappa, Sigma Xi, Alpha Omega Alpha.

AWARDS, HONORS: Distinguished Service Award from American Hospital Association, 1965; Gold Medal from American College of Hospital Administrators, 1966; honorary doctorate from Chicago College of Osteopathy, 1972; Distinguished Service Medal from Connecticut Hospital Association, 1972.

WRITINGS:

Hospitals, Health, People, Yale University Press, 1987.

WORK IN PROGRESS: A short book on the problems of caring for people in the future, publication by Yale University Press expected in 1989.

SIDELIGHTS: Albert W. Snoke told *CA:* "I wrote my book *Hospitals, Health, People* at the suggestion of the editor of the Yale University Press. He was aware of what I had been doing in health and hospital administration over the past fifty years, and he thought that it might be worth a book. It is essentially the story of how a cocky, young doctor, over a period of forty to fifty years, gradually stopped looking at people as a collection of symptoms and signs of disease but as overall human beings. Along with this, it addresses what I did in the way of trying to affect the organized and disorganized health system to take care of people, rather than patients.

"Costs for health services alone in the United States are increasing virtually exponentially. Competition and the dollar sign are becoming the major factors in today's health and human services priorities. I am not aware of an adequate national health and human services system. Our present approach is primarily an individual one—that of raising more money to meet the increased costs, competition, co-insurance, and deductibles—or going without. Our present system is duplicative, fragmented, and inefficient. We should realize that basic human services of good quality are a right, not a privilege, and we should organize human services locally or regionally and around a continuum of care.

"Public dissatisfaction with our present system—or non-system—and the dissatisfaction of my colleagues in medicine and hospitals are growing. But I fear that increased emphasis upon governmental health services would be as bad or worse. I would urge a public-private partnership, with the care of the patient predominating over the dollar and the politics."

*   *   *

SOARES, Bernardo
See PESSOA, Fernando (Antonio Nogueira)

*   *   *

SOTO, Gary   1952-

PERSONAL: Born April 12, 1952, in Fresno, Calif.; son of Manuel and Angie (Trevino) Soto; married Carolyn Oda, 1975; children: Mariko. *Education:* California State University, Fresno, B.A., 1974; University of California, Irvine, M.F.A., 1976.

ADDRESSES: Home—1020 Santa Fe, Albany, Calif. 94108. *Office*—Department of English-Chicano Studies, University of California, Berkeley, Calif. 94720.

CAREER: University of California, Berkeley, associate professor, 1985—.

MEMBER: Coordinating Council of Literary Magazines (member of board).

AWARDS, HONORS: Academy of American Poets Prize, 1975; award from *Nation,* 1975, for "The Discovery"; United States Award from International Poetry Forum, 1976, for *The Elements of San Joaquin;* Bess Hokin Prize from *Poetry,* 1978; Guggenheim fellowship, 1980; creative writing fellowship from National Education Association, 1982; Levinson Award from *Poetry,* 1984; American Book Award from Before Columbus Foundation, 1985, for *Living up the Street.*

WRITINGS:

The Elements of San Joaquin (poems), University of Pittsburgh Press, 1977.
The Tale of Sunlight (poems), University of Pittsburgh Press, 1978.
Father Is a Pillow Tied to a Broom (poems), Slow Loris Press, 1980.
Where Sparrows Work Hard (poems), University of Pittsburgh Press, 1981.
Black Hair (poems), University of Pittsburgh Press, 1985.
Living up the Street: Narrative Recollections (prose memoirs), Strawberry Hill Press, 1985.
Small Faces (prose memoirs), Arte Publico, 1986.
Lesser Evils: Ten Quartets (essays), Arte Publico, 1988.
(Editor) *California Childhood: Recollections and Stories of the Golden State,* Creative Arts Book Company, 1988.

Contributor of poetry to periodicals, including *Antaeus, Nation, New Republic, North American Review, Poetry,* and *Revista Chicano-Riquena.* Contributor of articles to *Bloomsbury Review, Image, MELUS, Parnassus,* and *San Francisco Review of Books.*

WORK IN PROGRESS: Where We Left Off, poems.

SIDELIGHTS: Gary Soto is an American poet and prose writer influenced by his working-class Mexican-American background. Born in Fresno, California, in the center of the agricultural San Joaquin Valley, he worked as a migrant laborer during his childhood. In his writing, as Raymund Paredes noted in the *Rocky Mountain Review,* "Soto establishes his acute sense of ethnicity and, simultaneously, his belief that certain emotions, values, and experiences transcend ethnic boundaries and allegiances." Many critics have echoed the assessment of Patricia De La Fuente in *Revista Chicano-Requena* that Soto displays an "exceptionally high level of linguistic sophistication."

In his first volume of poetry, *The Elements of San Joaquin,* Soto offers a grim portrait of the lives of Mexican-Americans. His poems depict the violence of urban life, the exhausting labor of rural life, and the futility of trying to recapture the innocence of childhood. In the book *Chicano Poetry* Bruce-Novoa repeatedly likened Soto's poetic vision to T.S. Eliot's bleak portrait of the modern world, *The Waste Land.* Soto uses wind-swept dust as a dominant image, and he also introduces such elements as rapes, unflushed toilets, a drowned baby, and, as Bruce-Novoa quotes him, "men / Whose arms / Were bracelets / Of burns." Soto's skill with the figurative language of poetry has been noted by reviewers throughout his career, and in *Western American Literature* Jerry Bradley praised the metaphors in *San Joaquin* as "evocative, enlightening, and haunting." Though unsettled by the negativism of the collection, Bruce-Novoa felt the work "convinces because of its well-wrought structure, the craft, the coherence of its totality." Moreover, he thought, because it brings such a vivid portrait of poverty to the reading public, *San Joaquin* is "a social as well as a literary achievement."

Soto's social concerns and aspects of his poetry style have led several critics to compare him to poet Philip Levine, who taught Soto at the Fresno campus of California State University. Levine's poetry focuses on the degraded lives of American working people, and, as Vicki Armour-Hileman noted in *Denver Quarterly,* its plain language and short, run-on lines are similar to Soto's work. When Soto spoke to *CA,* he acknowledged Levine's influence but stressed his familiarity with other poets too.

Many critics have also observed that Soto's writing transcends social commentary. Bruce-Novoa said that one reason why the author's work has "great significance within Chicano literature" is because it represents "a definite shift toward a more personal, less politically motivated poetry." As Alan Williamson suggested in *Poetry,* Soto avoids either idealizing the poor for their oppression or encouraging their violent defiance. Instead, he focuses on the human suffering that poverty engenders. When Peter Cooley reviewed Soto's second volume of poetry, *The Tale of Sunlight,* in *Parnassus,* he praised the author's ability to temper the bleakness of *San Joaquin* with "imaginative expansiveness." The poems in *Sunlight,* many of which focus on a child named Molina or on the owner of a Hispanic bar, display both the frustrations of poverty and what Williamson called "a vein of consolatory fantasy which passes beyond escapism into a pure imaginative generosity toward life." Williamson cited as an example "the poem in which an uncle's gray hair is seen as a visitation of magical butterflies."

When Soto discusses American racial tensions in the prose collections *Living up the Street* and *Small Faces,* he uses vignettes drawn from his own childhood. One vignette shows the anger the author felt upon realizing that his brown-skinned brother would never be considered an attractive child by conventional American standards. Another shows Soto's surprise at discovering that, contrary to his family's advice to marry a Mexican, he was falling in love with a woman of Japanese ancestry. In these deliberately small-scale recollections, as Paredes noted, "it is a measure of Soto's skill that he so effectively invigorates and sharpens our understanding of the commonplace."

In *Black Hair*, Soto focuses on his friends and family. He portrays fondly the times he shared with his buddies as an adolescent and the more recent moments he has spent with his young daughter. Some critics, such as David Wojahn in *Poetry*, felt that Soto was thus moving away from his strengths as a writer. While acknowledging that "by limiting his responses to a naive aplomb, Soto enables himself to write with a freshness that is at times arresting," Wojahn considered the work "a disappointment." He praised *San Joaquin* and *Tale of Sunlight* as "thematically urgent . . . and ambitious in their scope" and said that "compared to them, *Black Hair* is a distinctly minor achievement." Others, such as Ellen Lesser in *Voice Literary Supplement*, were charmed by Soto's poetic tone, "the quality of the voice, the immediate, human presence that breathes through the lines." Lesser contended that Soto's celebration of innocence and sentiment is shaded with a knowledge of "the larger, often threatening world." In the *Christian Science Monitor*, Tom D'Evelyn hailed Soto's ability to go beyond the circumstances of his own life and write of "something higher," concluding, "Somehow Gary Soto has become not an important Chicano poet but an important American poet. More power to him."

CA INTERVIEW

CA interviewed Gary Soto by telephone on November 21, 1986, at his home in San Francisco.

CA: The hard growing up you've described in your autobiographical writing, especially in the prose memoir Living up the Street, *would seem the least likely breeding ground for a poet. Where do you think the desire to write poetry came from?*

SOTO: I went to a city college, and my intention was to major in geography, but then I gravitated toward literature. I know the day the change began, because it was when I discovered in the library a collection of poems edited by Donald Allen called *The New American Poetry*. I discovered this poetry and thought, This is terrific; I'd like to do something like this. So I proceeded to write my own poetry, first alone, with no one's help, and then moving on to take classes at Fresno State [now California State University, Fresno] and meeting other writers. I don't think I had any literary aspirations when I was a kid. In fact, we were pretty much an illiterate family. We didn't have books, and no one encouraged us to read. So my wanting to write poetry was a sort of fluke.

CA: After you discovered the Donald Allen anthology, did you find specific poets and other writers that you could consider models in some way?

SOTO: In my very, very young years, when I discovered that first book, there were people like Gregory Corso, Edward Field, Kenneth Koch—very rambunctious, lively, irreverent writers. I liked that. The hippy movement had already dissipated a little (this was 1972), but there were still remnants of the rebellious feeling. Those writers had it, and I wanted to be something like them. Later on there were other poets who were more sophisticated, poets like Weldon Kees, Theodore Roethke, W. S. Merwin. Their work had an impact on my life as writing.

CA: Critics like to associate you with the "Fresno school" of poets and the influence of Philip Levine. How do you feel about that?

SOTO: The Fresno poets are remarkable in that most of the writers were born in Fresno. They're not like the Iowa poets, who gravitate to [the University of] Iowa on the rumor that there's great instruction. We grew up in Fresno and were very humble students, not full of ourselves. We just took classes and listened and were critiqued and went on to do our thing. There is, I guess, a Fresno school of poetry. In fact, my wife and I are publishing a new book of Fresno poets, called *Piecework: Nineteen Fresno Poets*. But the name is just a catchall. People may say the Fresno poets all write the same thing, but on a closer inspection it's obvious that they really vary in style.

Levine did have an influence on me, I think, but so did other writers. I think he has an influence on all his students, and that's not necessarily a bad thing. I haven't seen him in about five years; we're not close at all. And that's true of a lot of the writers. We're not having beers at his house or anything like that.

CA: Reviewing Black Hair *in the* Christian Science Monitor, *Tom D'Evelyn wrote, "Somehow Gary Soto has become not an important Chicano poet but an important American poet." What are your feelings about the Chicano poet label?*

SOTO: One of the things I would like to do is make that leap from being a Chicano writer to being simply a writer. I think the label can be very damaging to the individual, though not in sales: it can mean that libraries will look at the writer's book and feel they should have it for their collections *because* of the label. But the fact of the matter is that, except for two books, mine are not heavily concerned with Mexican themes. *Living up the Street* is, but not the poetry after *The Tale of Sunlight*. I got a radio review from Jascha Kessler in which he lamented my leaving the barrio to live this cosmopolitan life, or some such silly thing. Some critics want to keep Mexicans in the barrio and, once they get out of there, they point the finger and say, Shame, shame. I think it's a matter of maturity. The initial books may be very, very painful books. The ones that follow, at least for me, are less painful. I don't think there's anything wrong with that. I like to do different things, and each book is slightly different from the others.

CA: The child's imagination is often strong in your poetry. What part does it play in the conception of a poem? Is it always there?

SOTO: I think I'm very childlike, and I often write youthful poems. It's sort of a silly act, writing itself. I don't know why anyone would pay attention to these half-schooled, half-literate poets. But when I write I like the youth in my poetry, sort of a craziness. For me that's really important. I don't want to take a dreary look at the world and then start writing. I left that somewhere along the line.

CA: Is there something you do consciously to keep the child's imagination alive?

SOTO: One thing I do is not take things too seriously. I think a lot of writers do—their own careers, themselves. I can write a poem a day, and if I can do that, I figure it can't be that good! You've got to take it at that. I like writing. I'm fairly prolific; it's a daily activity for me. And that keeps the youth and the imagination going. If I were to stop, I would be in serious trouble.

CA: How do poems usually begin in your mind, if there is a usual way?

SOTO: It depends on what I'm doing. If I'm writing a book, as opposed to working on a collection of miscellany, I like to think in terms of the overall structure of the book. I get up and write from about nine to twelve daily, and I will think about an area that I want to delve into. One could be, say, marriage. I sit there and just mull it over. When I've been thinking about this for some time, I will start to write, and the words will come out on the theme of marriage, whatever that may mean on that given day. But I don't know until I sit down to write. I may have a slight suspicion that it's going to be on marriage, or it's going to be a childhood piece, or it's going to be on a friend, or a place. But I don't know exactly what the ultimate subject will be until I start writing.

CA: With fiction, it's necessary for the writer to put a kind of distance between himself and the actual personal experience in order to create something new out of that experience. To what extent do you find that's true with poetry?

SOTO: It may be partly true. Fiction is one thing, and poetry is another. I think that impressions are often important in the making of a poem. That's less true in fiction writing, where you have a plan that you have to stick with. In poetry you have lyric, and lyrics are not necessarily logical progressions, not even of time or character or space. In fiction writing, I think you have to have that logical progression of time and space and character. In poetry, I don't think that exists—unless it's a narrative poem, and even then I don't think you have characters who deepen and develop; they simply happen.

CA: So there's not the danger in poetry of writing something so autobiographical that it doesn't reach out to the reader?

SOTO: No.

CA: Tell me something about the voice of Molina in The Tale of Sunlight.

SOTO: There was a Molina family where we grew up, a very whimsical family of about nine kids, and dirt-poor. But they had the gift of being simple; they were absolutely wonderful people. The voice in the Molina poems is almost like my alter ego, that character I'd like to be, that person inside me. In many ways that part of the book is like a section of instruction; my alter ego is telling me to do this, do that. That's part of the scheme, I think. But it's funny—I haven't read those poems for a long time.

CA: In Living up the Street *you went from poetry to prose. How did that feel?*

SOTO: I think it felt a little awkward at first, because I'd never considered myself a prose writer. And to this day, some other people don't consider me a prose writer! But I wanted to do something different, and I'm glad I did. It was a testing ground to see if I could write prose. I didn't tire of poetry, but I wanted to move on into a thicker forest.

CA: Somebody obviously likes your prose; you won an American Book Award for Living up the Street.

SOTO: That's true. And it's done well in sales and reviews; people do tend to like it. I am pretty happy with it. Some people have commented that the progression between the childhood pieces and the jump to college isn't all that smooth, but they're individual pieces, after all; it's not an autobiographical novel. I liked writing that book. I also have the book called *Small Faces,* a collection of little essays, three or four pages each. I like that book quite a lot too. That was doing something slightly different from *Living up the Street.*

CA: Will there be more prose?

SOTO: Yes. In fact, I have a novel, but I haven't gotten anyone interested in it yet. It's actually a children's novel, about a dog and a young boy.

CA: Do you have a hypothetical reader or readership in mind when you're writing the poems?

SOTO: I don't see the reader behind what I'm doing. What I see is the great tradition of literature. I don't think I can compete with characters like [William] Shakespeare or [John] Donne or [Geoffrey] Chaucer, but you think of writing in terms of the great writers, and you want to compete with them. I try to write poetry of high literary value, to do the best job that I can. I'm also competing with my peers. It's very competitive. It's not that I wish them evil, that I wish their reviews will be horrible and their books will flop, but I'm a very competitive person. I don't think I'm a social climber in this literary world, but I like to do well. And I think often of my peers as my readers, which is the case more often than not. Few people buy poetry.

CA: You've indicated that your Spanish isn't as strong as your English. Do you think the Spanish has influenced the rhythms of your writing in any way?

SOTO: I don't think the Spanish language has anything to do with my rhythms. As I recall, there are very few good writers who work in two languages. Carlos Fuentes works in Spanish, though I think he has written only one novel in English. But he's a rare breed. Samuel Beckett worked in French and English, no? But most writers stay with one language that they feel comfortable with. I think the sources are what's important in my work, my themes. They're what I'm interested in.

CA: When your daughter was born, she seemed to give the poems a new turn, a new object.

SOTO: Yes. I think it just has to do with the fact that there's another life in the world and you're marveling at this life. You produce a child and you see your end in this child who's more or less your replacement. There are a lot of mixed emotions involved in raising a kid. It's another life. It's like falling in love. *That,* for me, was a great inspiration and actually a turning point in my poetry.

CA: Has publishing with small presses given you more control over your material and maybe even a voice in the design of the books?

SOTO: I think a writer has to separate himself from things like book design. Otherwise books would be extremely ugly, because some of the writers I've known have terrible taste. With *Small Faces* I asked the publisher, Arte Publico, to use a photograph. They did it in such a way that it was very attractive and pleasing for me. With [University of] Pittsburgh Press, it's a hit-or-miss proposition. I've seen some really horrible books from them. In fact, *The Tale of Sunlight* was awful. But *The Elements of San Joaquin* was attractive. *Black Hair* was fine, and *Where Sparrows Work Hard* was fine also.

I've had some feuds with editors about the writing itself. I think writers sometimes can't see their own imperfections. I assume I'm doing a good job, and sometimes when I see editorial changes I'm kind of irked. I take of a lot of criticism from my peer poets, my friends, and then when it goes out elsewhere to editors, I just think they're not as smart. They simply can't understand what I'm doing. This may be ego, but there's some truth to it. Editors want to play around with other people's work. That's very natural. The publisher-writer relationship often just isn't the best sort of relationship. It's happened to everyone, this situation where the writer doesn't like the publisher and the publisher doesn't like the writer. That's part of the process.

CA: Is your wife an early sounding board for the work?

SOTO: She is most certainly a sounding board. She has a good eye, and she will suggest things—especially with my prose. She is by training an editor, so she can look at my prose and see if it stinks. With the poetry, we play a game of rate this poem on a scale of one to ten. She'll say eight, or seven, or three. It's an intuitive thing for her with the poetry, and more often than not she's right about it. With the prose, though, she takes a careful look at things like sentence structure and word choice.

CA: Are you still teaching Chicano studies?

SOTO: Yes, and English.

CA: How do you feel about the combination of teaching and writing? Do the two activities mesh well for you?

SOTO: I think they should. You should take whatever sensitivity you have in writing and carry it over into teaching. However, poems don't talk back and students do. I have some real wars with my students. For example, I had a student who told me her mother had died of cancer. She was missing classes and owed me some papers, and I forgave her. I was very moved by this experience. Later on, during the summer, I found out that her mother was alive. There's a lot of this sort of thing. But I hope that whatever sensitivity I have toward the writing can be carried over into the teaching. It should be, because you're trying to spread the gospel of literature and make students interested in writing and what it takes to be a writer.

CA: The field of Chicano studies is very new as an academic discipline. Does that affect the way it has to be taught?

SOTO: It certainly affects what is being taught. I use the same texts over and over. I have a high sense of literature, and some of the things that are being published by Chicanos aren't really good. There are a lot of Chicano writers who are *going* to be good, but the first collection and the second collection are not

so startling. I use the same three or four books that I've been using over the years. I cannot use weak literature. It's too difficult for me to pretend that something is really good. In the last couple of years I've been using other ethnic literature that is a lot richer. Black literature is so superb, there's no comparison between it and Chicano literature. We don't have a James Baldwin or a Richard Wright or a John A. Williams. These are really high-caliber figures. Or comparing Chicano literature with Jewish-American literature, we don't have a Bernard Malamud or a Philip Roth. Those are truly good writers.

CA: What do you stress in presenting literature to the students?

SOTO: I stress mechanics—how a piece is put together, characterization, dialogue, pace, symbolism—so that students can take what they've learned from reading one novel and apply it to other literature to see how it works and to deepen their understanding of writing. I show them how to spot cliches, for example where Mexicans are stereotyped, and things that are too contrived to be believable. I want them to be able to go on from this to appreciate other things and to understand how a writer puts things together, to see that it's not simply a mishmash of feelings.

CA: Are there other books finished besides the children's novel?

SOTO: I have a new book of essays finished. They're very similar to the ones in *Small Faces;* this one is called *Lesser Evils.* It's more or less about being an evil man, but with lesser evils, things that are not horrible. I'm not bombing people, for example, like this country does. It's more about basic male treachery—lustful ways and so on. Then I have a new book of poems done, called *Where We Left Off.* I haven't planned beyond that. I've just finished these two books, and I'm so tired. I was writing every day for a very long time. Now I'm going to rest for a bit.

BIOGRAPHICAL/CRITICAL SOURCES:

BOOKS

Bruce-Novoa, *Chicano Poetry: A Response to Chaos,* University of Texas Press, 1982.
Contemporary Literary Criticism, Volume 32, Gale, 1985.

PERIODICALS

American Book Review, July-August, 1982.
Christian Science Monitor, March 6, 1985.
Denver Quarterly, summer, 1982.
Parnassus, fall-winter, 1979.
Poetry, March, 1980, June, 1985.
Revista Chicano-Riquena, summer, 1983.
Rocky Mountain Review, Volume 41, Numbers 1-2, 1987.
San Francisco Review of Books, summer, 1986.
Voice Literary Supplement, September, 1985.
Western American Literature, spring, 1979.

—*Sketch by Thomas Kozikowski*

—*Interview by Jean W. Ross*

*   *   *

SPANIER, Ginette   1904-1987
(Ginette Seidmann)

OBITUARY NOTICE: Born in 1904 in Paris, France; died April 18, 1988. Couture executive and author. As the director of the prestigious House of Balmain beginning in 1947, Spanier set the trends in Paris fashion for almost three decades. She largely influenced French designer Pierre Balmain's polished "jolie madame" look, and she dressed numerous celebrities, including Katharine Hepburn, Marlene Dietrich, Sophia Loren, and Queen Sirikit of Thailand. During the occupation of France by the Germans in World War II, Spanier and her husband, who were Jews, were forced to flee to the south of France and live under false papers. Later, she was instrumental in gathering an international group of interpreters to assist in the Allied trials of German war criminals at Nuremberg, West Germany. Spanier wrote three memoirs, entitled *It Isn't All Mink, And Now It's Sables,* and *The Long Road to Freedom.*

OBITUARIES AND OTHER SOURCES:

BOOKS

The Author's and Writer's Who's Who, 6th edition, reprinted, Burke's Peerage, 1971.

PERIODICALS

Times (London), April 22, 1988.

*   *   *

SPECK, Ross V(ictor)   1927-

PERSONAL: Born October 22, 1927, in St. Catharines, Ontario, Canada; immigrated to United States, 1951, naturalized citizen, 1957; son of Victor Earl and Evelyn Clara (Fritshaw) Speck; married Joan Lincoln Kendig Gill. *Education:* University of Toronto, M.D., 1951; postdoctoral study at University of Michigan, 1955-56, and Philadelphia Psychoanalytic Institute, 1959-69.

ADDRESSES: Home—120 Kenilworth St., Philadelphia, Pa. 19147.

CAREER: Albany Medical Center Hospital, Albany, N.Y., intern, 1951-52; State Hospital, Poughkeepsie, N.Y., resident in psychiatry, 1952-54; Philadelphia General Hospital, Philadelphia, Pa., resident in psychiatry, 1954-55; University of Michigan, Ann Arbor, senior clinical instructor in psychoanalysis, 1955-56; Eastern Pennsylvania Psychiatric Institute, Philadelphia, director of adult outpatient department, 1958-60, clinical director, 1960-64; Jewish Family Service, New York, N.Y., clinical director of Family Mental Health Clinics, 1965-67; served at Family Institute of Philadelphia. Private practice of psychiatry, 1970—; Hahnemann Medical College, senior instructor, 1959-61, assistant professor, 1961-64, associate professor and head of social psychiatry, 1964-70; research associate at Philadelphia Psychiatric Center, beginning in 1958; fellow at Center for the Study of Social Change, 1970-75; clinical professor in department of psychiatry and human behavior at Jefferson Medical College, 1980—. *Military service:* U.S. Army, Medical Corps, chief of psychiatric consultation service at Brooke Army Hospital, 1956-58; became captain.

MEMBER: American Psychiatric Association (fellow), Canadian Psychiatric Association, Royal College of Psychiatrists (fellow), American Society of Psychoanalytic Physicians (fellow), American Family Therapy Association, American Association of Marriage and Family Therapists (fellow).

WRITINGS:

(With A. S. Friedman, I. Nagy, J. E. Jungreis, G. Lincoln, H. E. Mitchell, J. C. Sonne, and G. Spivack) *Psychotherapy for the Whole Family,* Springer Publishing, 1965.

(With Friedman, Sonne, J. P. Barr, Nagy, G. Cohen, Jungreis, Lincoln, G. Spark, and O. R. Weiner) *Therapy With Families of Sexually Acting-Out Girls,* Springer Publishing, 1970.
(With Barr, R. Eisenman, E. Foulks, A. Goldman, and J. Lincoln) *The New Families: Youth, Communes, and the Politics of Drugs,* Basic Books, 1972.
(With Carolyn L. Attneave) *Family Networks,* Pantheon, 1973.
(With Uri Rueveni and Joan L. Speck) *Therapeutic Intervention: Healing Strategies for Human Systems,* Human Sciences, 1982.

BIOGRAPHICAL/CRITICAL SOURCES:

PERIODICALS

Annals of the American Academy of Political and Social Science, March, 1973.
New York Times Book Review, September 23, 1973.

*   *   *

SPENDER, Dale   1943-

PERSONAL: Born September 22, 1943, in Newcastle, New South Wales, Australia; daughter of Frank Henry (an accountant) and Ivy (an accountant; maiden name, Davis) Spender; divorced. *Education:* University of Sydney, received B.A. and Dip.Ed.; University of New South Wales, M.A., 1972; University of New England, B.Litt., 1975; University of London, Ph.D., 1981. *Politics:* "Feminist."

ADDRESSES: Home—New South Wales, Australia. *Agent*—Tessa Sayle, Literary and Dramatic Agency, 11 Jubilee Place, Chelsea, London SW3 3TE, England.

CAREER: Schoolteacher in New South Wales, Australia, 1960-72; James Cook University, Townsville, Queensland, Australia, lecturer in English education, 1973-74; Institute of Education, University of London, London, England, lecturer in English, 1976-78; full-time writer, 1978—.

MEMBER: Fawcett Society of Fawcett Library (London; executive member and honorary librarian).

WRITINGS:

(With Garth Boomer) *The Spitting Image: Reflections on Language, Education, and Social Class,* Boynton Cook, 1976.
(Editor with Elizabeth Sarah) *Learning to Lose: Sexism and Education,* Women's Press, 1980.
Man Made Language, Routledge & Kegan Paul, 1980.
(Editor) *Men's Studies Modified: The Impact of Feminism on the Academic Disciplines,* Pergamon, 1981.
Invisible Women: The Schooling Scandal, Writers & Readers, 1982.
Women of Ideas and What Men Have Done to Them: From Aphra Behn to Adrienne Rich, Routledge & Kegal Paul, 1982.
(Editor) *Feminist Theorists: Three Centuries of Key Women Thinkers,* introduction by Ellen Carol DuBois, Pantheon, 1983 (published in England as *Feminist Theorists: Three Centuries of Women's Intellectual Traditions,* Women's Press, 1983).
There's Always Been a Women's Movement in This Century, Pandora Press, 1983.
(Editor with sister, Lynne Spender) *Gatekeeping: The Denial, Dismissal, and Distortion of Women,* Pergamon, 1983.
(With Lynne Spender) *Scribbling Sisters,* R. Hale, 1984, Camden House, 1985

Time and Tide Wait for No Man, Pandora Press, 1984.
For the Record: The Making and Meaning of Feminist Knowledge, Women's Press, 1985.
(Editor with Carole Hayman) *How the Vote Was Won, and Other Suffragette Plays*, Methuen, 1985.
Mothers of the Novel: One Hundred Good Women Writers Before Jane Austen, Pandora Press, 1986.
(With Sally Cline) *Reflecting Men at Twice Their Natural Size*, cartoons by Rianca Duncan, Seaver, c. 1987.
(Editor) *The Education Papers: Women's Quest for Equality in Britain, 1850-1912*, Routledge & Kegan Paul, 1987.
Writing a New World: Two Centuries of Australian Women Writers, Pandora Press, 1988.
(Editor) *Anthology of Australian Women's Writing*, Penguin Books, 1988.
(Editor with Janet Todd) *Anthology of British Women Writers*, Pandora Press, in press.
The Writing or the Sex: The Judgement of Literary Men, Pergamon, in press.
Mrs. Pepys's Diary (tentative title), Grafton Books, in press.

Editor of *Women's Studies International Forum*, Pergamon.

WORK IN PROGRESS: History of Women's Writing, for Pandora Press; *The Knowledge Explosion*, with Cheris Kramarae, for Pergamon; *Novel Knowledge*, a guide to the women's novel of the nineteenth century, for Pandora Press.

SIDELIGHTS: Dale Spender, a prolific writer of feminist literature, has earned respect for her celebration of women's achievements. With books such as *Invisible Women: The Schooling Scandal, Women of Ideas and What Men Have Done to Them, Feminist Theorists: Three Centuries of Key Women Thinkers*, and *Mothers of the Novel: One Hundred Good Women Writers Before Jane Austen*, Spender attempts to correct society's historic disregard for women and their accomplishments.

In *Invisible Women: The Schooling Scandal*, Spender, a former teacher, points out the disadvantages girls suffer in coeducational schools, such as receiving only a third of their teachers' attention and consistently being seated in the back of the classroom, and she suggests that sex-segregated schools would be more beneficial to them. "Coeducation, [Spender] charges, is grossly unjust, intellectually nullifying and sexually abusive to girls," explained Ann Snitow in her *Nation* review. Helen Baehr, writing for the *New Statesman*, noted Spender's particular criticism of "the male educational establishment for emphasising the so-called 'social advantages' of co-education, when they have known all along that the price has been a drop in girls' academic performance." Although the shortcomings of coeducation are well known, the author maintains, little has been done to solve the problem. "It is amazing," Snitow lamented, "that the obvious [inequity] has not *been* obvious, that gross oppression remains invisible oppression. Coeducational schools pretend to a gender neutrality so far from girls' actual experience that the discrepancy is breathtaking." The reviewer added: "We can't simply add some positive images of women to the textbooks and give girls seats in metalworking class to even things up."

Spender argues that girls must learn and grow in an environment where they, like boys, can feel important and autonomous. "In single-sex schools," Snitow quoted her as saying, "girls are protected from the daily messages supplied by boys that the girls are unworthy." Recognizing, however, that modern schools will not likely revert from coeducation to sex-segregation, Spender also offers alternative solutions. "Her practical suggestions," Snitow summarized, "include en-

claves within schools; . . . independent feminist institutions of research and learning; and even direct feminist action in mixed classrooms."

Another point Spender makes in *Invisible Women*, according to critic Catherine Jones in the *Times Educational Supplement*, is that "our system of knowledge—and hence our system of education—is man-made and reflects, therefore, an exclusively male view of what counts in our past and in our present." As Baehr put it: "Men have the monopoly in defining what constitutes human knowledge." Although Jones agreed with that premise, she declared that Spender's proposed solution—a rewriting of history from a non-masculine perspective—"displays either a breath-taking naivete about the scale of the task in hand or . . . a lack of serious interest in the quality of the end product." While acknowledging the need to lessen the struggle of women in man-made society, Jones insisted that "it seems . . . unrealistic to suggest that a quick re-writing of the rules in women's favour might do the trick." Baehr, however, applauded Spender's goal of reinterpreting history and reworking teaching methods: "Dale Spender's insights into classroom sexual politics should be a lesson to us all."

In *Women of Ideas and What Men Have Done to Them*, reported Phyllis Willmott in the *Times Literary Supplement*, Spender "collected a mass of shocking evidence of what men did to keep women under their yoke for so long." In the book, comprised of 150 biographical essays, the author cites numerous historic examples of oppression, such as the denial of women's rights to vote, own property, work for adequate pay, or receive a thorough education. *Women of Ideas* "is no mere string of biographies," asserted Harriett Gilbert in *New Statesman*. "It is a holistic history of feminist political theory from the middle of the 17th century to today."

Several critics felt that Spender's caustic writing style detracted from her message. Paddy Kitchen in the *Times Educational Supplement*, for example, declared that although "the scope of Dale Spender's book is exciting and admirable," the work's "opinionatry leads to inaccuracy." Likewise, Willmott criticized *Women of Ideas* as "flawed . . . by much hostile polemic" and "presented with too much impassioned acrimony." For these reasons, T. C. Holyoke ventured in *Antioch Review*, "this potentially valuable book will please radical feminists only to be ignored by . . . those to whom its message might well be addressed." Gilbert, on the other hand, affirmed the value of Spender's work, which "gives to the post-'60s feminist a strengthened confidence that neither her sense of oppression, nor her analysis of its causes, are the frivolous, merely-fashionable things that men would have her believe."

Feminist Theorists: Three Centuries of Key Women Thinkers is a "readable, eclectic series of portraits of feminists," according to Lindsy Van Gelder, writing in *Ms.* The book documents the lives and accomplishments of twenty-one women—such as Simone de Beauvoir, Emma Goldman, and Christabel Pankhurst—who interpreted and advanced feminism in different ways. "What they share," observed Gilbert in *New Statesman*, "is an awareness of women's oppression, and the joint belief that they should, and could, do something to help remove it." *There's Always Been a Women's Movement in This Century*, similarly, is a "collection of interviews with five feminist activists . . . [who] differ widely in their views," described Jill Burrows in the *Times Educational Supplement*. The women—Dora Russell and Rebecca West among them—are alike, however, in that they "all share a far from resigned humour in the face of the mechanisms of male privilege and a considerable, out-going wisdom.''

Female authors, who wrote the majority of novels in the eighteenth century, are the subject of *Mothers of the Novel: One Hundred Good Women Writers Before Jane Austen.* ''Spender sets out in this book to unmask what she sees as a conspiracy,'' critic John Gross determined in the *Observer,* ''a conspiracy of silence, for the most part, though one in which condescension and denigration have played their part as well.'' The ''conspiracy'' was that of ignoring or unjustly criticizing the myriad of books written by women during the eighteenth century, while recognizing and praising men's novels. ''More important,'' suggested John Bayley in his *Times Literary Supplement* review, ''is the general point that women novelists tended to remain in an area of indeterminacy, unshaped and unconcluded by a sustaining [literary] tradition.'' He added, ''The sadness is . . . how frequently promising women writers were blown off course,'' through faulty advice or belittlement, ''because they allowed their gifts to be channelled in the wrong direction.'' Though Gross conceded that ''the whole tradition of women's fiction before Jane Austen hasn't yet been given its due,'' he also proposed that many of the writers probably did not deserve much attention and that Spender's work thus reflected ''strident overstatement.'' He remarked, however, that the biographical material in *Mothers of the Novel* ''provide[s] a good deal of hard-to-come-by information about figures who ought to be much better known.''

One of Spender's later works is *Mrs. Pepys's Diary,* a diversion from her usual form of writing. Samuel Pepys, a seventeenth-century British Navy officer, is known for his unique and revealing diary. In a fabricated journal based on research about Mr. and Mrs. Pepys, the author offers a ''fictional alternative to Mr. Pepys's authoritative documentation of British history,'' Spender told *CA.*

With each of her books, Spender attempts to speak for the women who, until recently, have been unable to record their own ideas or celebrate their own accomplishments. ''With so little access to education, money, power, or the printing presses, women have had less chance than men to bequeath their ideas to posterity,'' noted Gilbert in her critique of *Women of Ideas.* ''From as far back as Spender has been able to reach, women have been protesting against their subservience to men. . . . By exposing this continuum, Spender performs an invaluable service.'' Snitow's observation about *Invisible Women*—that it ''is a small book on a large subject''—may apply equally well to the small but growing field of women's literature. According to Gilbert, Spender's writings contribute significantly to that field by documenting women's struggle for—and partial attainment of—recognition and authority: ''The balance of power is shifting and . . . the information that Spender has unearthed will help to shift it even further.''

CA INTERVIEW

CA interviewed Dale Spender by telephone on February 26, 1987, at her home near Sydney, Australia.

CA: You've given your family credit for great support in your work. Your parents, you said in the acknowledgments for Man Made Language, *provided ''an example of living cooperation and sharing, long before we heard the term feminism.'' In what ways did they do this?*

SPENDER: I think my parents were products of dual spheres. They each did their own thing, but they couldn't have survived without the other. They're honorable people, compassionate, caring people who are concerned not only that their family has a good quality of living but that the world around them is all right.

CA: Did your household set a kind of standard, then, for your later feminism?

SPENDER: It wasn't a feminist household that I lived in at all, just a compassionate one, which means that there's no enormous prejudice to women. It was still incredibly sexist by our standards. My mother worked a lot harder than my father in so many ways, and I suppose I always thought that was unfair. From the day I first went to school I was aware that girls are treated differently from boys, and I couldn't really work out why. I think feminism in lots of ways was simply a name for the sense of injustice I had. The good thing about feminism is that the injustice is just the first step. After that there's an awful lot of work to do, and there's a great celebration. As a feminist you've got to strike a balance between being deeply distressed at the inhumanity of this world and deeply delighted at the celebration of women's culture.

CA: I suspect you became a serious reader rather early on. How much of a part did books play in shaping your feminist consciousness?

SPENDER: They couldn't have played a very great part in a direct way until twenty years ago, because there were no feminist books that I read earlier than that. One of the reasons I write books is that they're ones I want to read. But the habit of reading, of wanting to read books and spending a lot of time on my own ruminating about the world and what you can do, is well and deeply ingrained. I believe that novels, which I've read an enormous number of, have been the source of women's wisdom. They are the repository of women's ideas. They are where women have controlled the world and said ''What if?'' and explored relationships. Women invented the novel to tell each other about women's lives. In fact, what I'd really like to be is a professor of novels. I think until there's a professor of novels in all universities, there's something lacking in the world.

CA: One thinks of Australia as conservative in some ways but possibly rather open in others because of its history and geography. When you were growing up there, did you have any sense of how the situation for women compared with that in England and the United States?

SPENDER: I don't think so. As an Australian, I did a lot of British history and very little Australian history. In some ways Australia is a bit like the States: It is the New World, open to all sorts of possibilities. There have been frontiers here, and women have lived extremely hard lives; there's been no time when women haven't had to work. I think that's a very important part of my Australian background. And I suppose in lots of ways the stories about Britain made it seem to me a sort of fairy land.

CA: One of the points you've emphasized in your writing is that, in the words of feminist Mary Stott that gave you the title for one of your books, ''There's always been a women's movement in this century!'' And there was a women's movement long before this century. Do you think women's studies are bringing about an increased awareness of this fact?

SPENDER: There are so many different sorts of women's studies. Of course, as soon as you've got a conscious women's studies discipline, you get a lot more interest, a lot more publishing, a lot more activity in the area. But I think it's producing a hundred different sorts of values because of the research that's going on. And I hope it would be producing a lot of history. It's also producing a lot of contemporary sociology and such things.

CA: The number of women's studies departments in colleges and universities seems to be increasing quite rapidly, at least in the United States. Do you have any sense of how good a teaching job they're doing overall?

SPENDER: I've lectured in some of the universities in the States. It's changed enormously. Initially, the people who started women's studies courses were making their own knowledge, actually forging the sorts of meanings that were required. Now those meanings have been codified. The field was about women sharing their experiences, but then those experiences got written down and passed on, and now it's not enough to have your own experience. Now it's becoming like another discipline, a body of knowledge to be transmitted instead of created. That, of course, is quite good, because you want more than your own experience. But it's different, and I think it creates some problems. The thing that worries me sometimes is the notion that you could fail women's studies.

CA: Are there strong women's studies programs in other countries you're familiar with?

SPENDER: Australia's is very similar to the States', but Britain's is a little bit different; there it's polarized. I think there's probably more interest in Britain in continuing and adult education, workers' education classes, women's part-time education. In those areas there are all sorts of courses going on for women. But in the universities themselves, there are not a lot of courses concerned with women. There's a kind of compulsory, token reference to women in any nineteenth-century history course, for example, or to women in science. But basically there are no departments of women's studies—or not as many as there are in the United States. There are only about three British universities where you can get a degree in women's studies. I did my Ph.D. at the University of London on man-made language. That was about as feminist as you could get. There was no department, no support for doing that.

CA: You were a schoolteacher for nine years. Was teaching your first ambition?

SPENDER: There was no ambition; I just didn't know what else to do but be a wife and mother. There was no other model available to me. Teaching seemed to be "a good job for a girl"; my mother said you could always go back to it after you had your children. I came out of the fifties—I started university in 1960—and that was the dark ages. It wasn't considered acceptable then to say, "I want to work." Every female I knew said, "I want to get married, but I wouldn't mind doing something beforehand." I didn't like the idea that happiness was having your own kitchen, that you should go off and get married and have four children before you could say Jack Robinson. But there didn't seem to be much else you could do. And certainly when I got married it was basically

because I was at a loss about what else to do with my life. All my friends said I *would* be until I got married; then I'd be really happy. Well, I got married and I wasn't. That's when it all started. I woke up the day after I got married thinking, "Now I should be happy." Oh, God.

CA: In Invisible Women: The Schooling Scandal *you argued for single-sex schools because of the bias toward males in the coeducational system. On the other side of the coin, how well are female students of all-girl schools equipped to compete in a sexually integrated society when they have to take that step?*

SPENDER: There isn't any simple answer. As I've said, the problem with single-sex schools is that you have to have single-sex jobs and single-sex marriages if you're going to preserve the value of them. As soon as you do put girls and boys together, boys can override girls, no matter what the background. But by the same token, if I were a mother I would have a very different notion of protecting girls until they could acquire some of the resources to deal with it. I think, sadly, that if you're in mixed-sex classes from a very early age, often you never acquire those resources.

I also think it's not as simple as single-sex schools. It is much more about the curriculum and about giving girls a sense of confidence. There's not a debate at all about whether we should or shouldn't give girls confidence; most people these days think that's important. But the huge issue is, how do you do it? I'd desperately love to know how you take young women who feel, quite rightly, that the world is against them, that the odds aren't as good for them, that there are all sorts of contingency plans they must make—it depends on whom they marry, how many children they have, where they're going to live—and give them confidence to cope with the world. I live with a man; I've lived with him for thirteen years and it's a very, very pleasant relationship in so many ways. I do not want to see all men hanged, drawn, and quartered. But it is difficult for them to understand that women have as much right to the world as they do.

CA: What women have managed to do under the circumstances seems a demonstration of great strength.

SPENDER: I think so. I think women have got enormous resources, and a lot of those resources come from each other. A lot of them come from women's knowledge, which society still doesn't value. A lot of it is the knowledge of survival, of relationships, of nurturing, of knowing what society needs in order to keep going and trying to do that for others as well as for one's self.

CA: One of the finest achievements of the most recent push of the women's movement, I think, is that we've become each other's friends. That didn't seem to be largely true in the fifties.

SPENDER: In the fifties I had no notion that you could be very good friends with women. I'm sure I would have been terribly embarrassed then to go into a restaurant with a group of women. I can remember a night before someone was getting married. The males went off together and the women said, "We're not going to sit at home again; let's all meet." We were so self-conscious we didn't know what to do, because we'd never met as a group before in a public place. Now women go in and out of restaurants. It's great to see women enjoying each other's company. I think that's been the revolution, women recognizing other women.

CA: For many years now women have been urged to take up "networking," an activity that men are said to practice quite routinely and naturally. How well do you think we're doing it?

SPENDER: Look at the male competitive society. Men are at each other's throats competing. They have to have a literature about bonding and networks and believe in it or they'd kill each other. Women have always networked; it's just been called something different. Women have always had bonding relationships: mother-daughter relationships, sisterhood, looking after each other's children. The webs among women have been amazing. I think it's hilarious that our society has produced a literature which says that women don't like each other and that men bond and get on well with each other. It's almost the other way around. I've just been doing some work on literary partnerships. There are a lot of women who've combined to write books, and there are occasional partnerships between women and men. But you almost never find two men. They can't do that sort of cooperative thing, whereas women have learned to work together closely. Their egos don't get in the way.

What women *haven't* done in the past is try to advance each other's careers through a sort of patronage system. I think we're still bad at being mentors, at bringing in younger women and sharing our knowledge with them and pushing them on their way. It's partly because women often don't think they've got valuable knowledge to pass on, so it doesn't occur to them to do it. We've got to start valuing our knowledge and our understanding.

CA: Would you comment on the Fawcett Society's importance in women's studies and specifically in your work?

SPENDER: You can't measure the value of the Fawcett Society and the Fawcett Library. There've been trends about women being in fashion. There were the fifties, when women receded into the woodwork. In the sixties they bloomed a little again. Whether women are in or out of fashion, the library is there. It was incredibly good for me to go to Britain and find this huge reservoir of women's meanings. It had almost gone defunct at one stage for lack of support, during the forties and fifties. A couple of devoted women preserved it. So when I turned up in London in the seventies, here was this one-hundred-year-old library that was just fantastic. I think it's vitally important to ensure that this time next century, whether women are in or out of fashion, someone can go into the Fawcett Library and find out about all of this.

CA: You've given something back in service as an executive member of the Fawcett Society and an honorary librarian.

SPENDER: It's not hard work. People say to me sometimes about being a writer, "Goodness, you must be well disciplined." But it's not really discipline if it's what you want to do with your life. Discipline to me is doing something I *don't* want to do. I've never felt I've done anything more than celebrate the Fawcett Library or enjoy being a writer.

CA: Are there still many untapped areas in women's studies for young scholars to explore? Is it a good field to go into?

SPENDER: If I had a hundred Ph.D. students, I could give each of them three topics. There's that much I want to know, and life's going to be too short for me to find it out. I read now at least two novels a day, and I'll be dead before I finish the pile I've got. There's so much to do, so much to understand. It's like trying in the space of twenty years to catch up on all the literature and history and psychology that men have been preserving and debating for the last three hundred. Women have done as much as men.

This is why I get upset when people say that we've "got a book on women's history." We've got five hundred books on men's history; the issue there is the debate that goes on about why this one is better than that one, what another one leaves out. It's not *a* book on women's history or *a* book on women's novels; it's the intricacy of all the discussion that can go on. I think it's vitally important that if the next generation wants to understand what women's cumulative wisdom is about, they can go and look it up. You can't teach people things they don't want to know, and I've never been a missionary; I've no desire in the world to go around trying to make people see things my way. But what I do want to ensure is that if people ask questions, the information is there to help answer them. That's what I didn't have.

CA: Do you see a backlash among younger women, a kind of complacency about the rights we have gained?

SPENDER: A lot of my friends in their forties have teenage daughters who are frightfully embarrassed by their feminism. But I think it's the usual pattern that you get one generation who thinks it's all OK and the next generation thinks it's dreadful and fights for change. The pendulum goes back and forth. I think grandmothers and granddaughters often have more in common than mothers and daughters. I sometimes think if I'm the product of a sexist society and the lack of options of the fifties, maybe it's a good thing. It's made me do something with my life. The younger generation has been told equality is all theirs, and they do different things with it. Human beings are perverse, you know.

CA: As a full-time writer, do you find it hard to strike a good balance between the solitary work of writing and the necessary social and professional contact with other people?

SPENDER: I think a lot depends on what I'm doing. When I was doing *Mothers of the Novel*, which involved me reading about five hundred novels that nobody else I knew had read, that felt terrible. All these things I wanted to talk about, and nobody to talk about them with. But a lot of the time I don't want social contacts. I find them quite intrusive. I tend to go and write a book and then take a month off and sit in the sun and go out to dinner. The thing I'm in real danger of when I'm writing is starving to death, because I won't cook! It seems a terrible waste of time to have to go out and buy food, or go out and eat. So I could be found in a little heap one day. But back here in Australia my mother and my sisters are superb about looking out for me; in fact, I think I've put on weight, they've been so good. All I need is emotional support and someone to give me a cuddle. I'd rather, once I start writing, just do that—and read, of course.

CA: Would you like to try your hand at writing fiction or something else unlike the books you've done so far?

SPENDER: I've just written *Mrs. Pepys's Diary*, which is a slight venture away from what I've done in the past, because it's using some of my research knowledge to put down what she thought of Samuel and things like that. My agent says I'm dreadful at fiction, so I suppose I've got to believe her and give it up. I *would* like to write some feminist thrillers about women taking over the world and what we'd do with men. I actually did write a novel about an international feminist call-girl service. It was about women taking all this money from men and using it to resource women. I enjoyed doing it, but my agent didn't like it. It does take a lot to get a character from one room to another in a novel.

CA: What are your greatest concerns now for women?

SPENDER: It's such a fragmented world. I worry, worry, worry about women and violence, women and physical abuse. I worry about reproductive technology and what that's going to mean, because it seems to me that once women are no longer necessary for making babies, we might no longer be necessary at all. I worry about third-world women, about black women. I worry about the distribution of the world's resources. I'm certainly not by any stretch of the imagination wealthy, but seeing the resources I and other women like me use up, white women in the Western world, is enough to keep me awake at night. I feel guilty about that frequently. I suppose the issue is not what you've got, which you have little control over, but how you use it. I would hope that I try to use the privilege and resources that I've been given as responsibly as I can. And I would hope that lots of other women would too.

I sound like a Christian missionary when I talk like that. I don't mean to. I once asked Dora Russell, the wife of philosopher Bertrand Russell, what was the meaning of life. She said to look after the planet. If we don't do it, it won't be done, and that's all we've got. I feel very strongly that we've got to look after the planet, do the housekeeping, keep it going, keep ourselves in order, look after each other. That seems to me the most important thing there is. And read a lot of novels!

BIOGRAPHICAL/CRITICAL SOURCES:

PERIODICALS

Antioch Review, summer, 1983.
Chicago Tribune, June 21, 1987.
Ms., July, 1984.
Nation, May 28, 1983.
New Statesman, May 21, 1982, October 1, 1982, May 6, 1983, January 4, 1985.
Observer, April 10, 1983, May 25, 1986.
Times (London), May 1, 1987.
Times Educational Supplement, May 14, 1982, January 7, 1983, June 8, 1984.
Times Literary Supplement, December 24, 1982, June 27, 1986.

—*Sketch by Christa Brelin*

—*Interview by Jean W. Ross*

* * *

SPIEGELMAN, Art 1948-
(Joe Cutrate, Al Flooglebuckle, Skeeter Grant)

PERSONAL: Born February 15, 1948, in Stockholm, Sweden; immigrated to United States; son of Wladek (in sales) and Andzia (Zylberberg) Spiegelman; married Francoise Mouly (a publisher), July 12, 1977; children: Nadja Rachel. *Education:* Attended Harpur College (now State University of New York at Binghamton), 1965-68.

ADDRESSES: Home—New York, N.Y. *Office*—c/o Raw Books and Graphics, 27 Greene St., New York, N.Y. 10013. *Agent*—

Wylie, Aitken & Stone, 250 West 57th St., Suite 2106, New York, N.Y. 10107.

CAREER: Free-lance artist and writer, 1965—; Topps Chewing Gum, Inc., Brooklyn, N.Y., creative consultant, artist, designer, editor, and writer for novelty packaging and bubble-gum cards and stickers, 1966—. Instructor in studio class on comics at San Francisco Academy of Art, 1974-75, and in history and aesthetics of comics at New York School of Visual Arts, 1979—. On advisory board of Swann Foundation. Art work featured in numerous exhibitions at galleries and museums in the United States and abroad, including the New York Cultural Center, the Institute of Contemporary Art in London, and the Seibu Gallery in Tokyo.

AWARDS, HONORS: Annual *Playboy* Editorial Award for best comic strip and Yellow Kid Award (Italy) for best comic strip author, both 1982; Regional Design Award from *Print* magazine, 1983, 1984, and 1985; Joel M. Cavior Award for Jewish Writing, and National Book Critics Circle nomination, both 1986, both for *Maus;* Inkpot Award from San Diego Comics Convention and Stripschappenning Award (Netherlands) for best foreign comics album, both 1987.

WRITINGS:

COMICS

The Complete Mr. Infinity, S. F. Book Co., 1970.
The Viper Vicar of Vice, Villainy, and Vickedness, privately printed by Spiegelman, 1972.
Zip-a-Tune and More Melodies, S. F. Book Co., 1972.
(Compiling editor with Bob Schneider) *Whole Grains: A Book of Quotations,* D. Links, 1972.
Ace Hole, Midge Detective, Apex Novelties, 1974.
Language of Comics, State University of New York at Binghamton, 1974.
(Contributor) Don Donahue and Susan Goodrich, editors, *The Apex Treasury of Underground Comics,* D. Links, 1974.
Breakdowns; From Maus to Now: An Anthology of Strips, Belier Press, 1977.
Work and Turn, Raw Books, 1979.
Every Day Has Its Dog, Raw Books, 1979.
Two-Fisted Painters Action Adventure, Raw Books, 1980.
(Contributor) Nicole Hollander, Skip Morrow, and Ron Wolin, editors, *Drawn Together: Relationships Lampooned, Harpooned, and Cartooned,* Crown, 1983.
Maus: A Survivor's Tale, Pantheon, 1986.
(With wife, Francoise Mouly) *Read Yourself Raw: Comix Anthology for Damned Intellectuals,* Pantheon, 1987.

Contributor to many underground comic books since the 1960s.

Editor, *Douglas Comix,* 1972; contributing editor with Bill Griffith, *Arcade, the Comics Revue,* 1975-76; founding editor with Mouly, *Raw,* 1980—.

WORK IN PROGRESS: A sequel to *Maus* entitled *Maus, Part Two: From Mauschwitz to the Catskills and Beyond;* "From McCay to *Maus,*" a group show of comics that will travel from the Smithsonian Institution in Washington, D.C., to the Cooper-Hewitt Museum in New York City and elsewhere between 1989 and 1990.

SIDELIGHTS: Art Spiegelman is an artist who, as one critic put it, "redefines the comic book." Perhaps no one in the history of the genre has had such an elevating influence on its public image or brought to it more dedication to graphic originality and intellectual substance. "Good comix are nourishing comix," wrote Spiegelman in *The Apex Treasury of Under-*

ground Comics, "unlike the Hostess Twinkies to be found in most children's comic books or in newspaper funny sections. The comix I like, and try to do, can be read slowly and often. . . . I try to make every panel count and sometimes work as long as a month on a page. It's like concentrated orange juice." The nourishment with which Spiegelman has enriched the field as artist, editor, designer, and writer has brought him unparalleled critical esteem and carried the medium itself to a public audience that had never before suspected its creative potential.

Spiegelman's keen eye was set on a career as a cartoonist from as far back as he can remember, and as he reported to the *New York Daily News* magazine in 1986, "except for a part-time job once for three days selling shoe polish when I was fourteen," he has been drawing for a living all his working life. He never had a real taste for comic books, though he supposes that he learned to read from them; his earliest interest was in satire magazines such as *Mad,* and before his teens he was copying pictures from them. It served as merely a pastime only briefly, he reported: "It became an obsession very quickly." At thirteen he was drawing for his school newspaper, and a year later he began selling sports and political cartoons, illustrations, and covers to the *Long Island Post.* His first actual sale came as a fifteen dollar cover for that newspaper, and by then he was hopelessly hooked on the craft.

Spiegelman studied cartooning in high school. He attracted the attention of a syndicate editor with a comic strip he did as a classroom assignment, but after the initial elation wore off Spiegelman decided that it was not in the conventional comic strip genre that his destiny lay. His anarchic spirit was already finding expression in submissions to a variety of cartoon markets and in turning out his own hectographed magazine. Not surprisingly, his parents were less than enthusiastic about his ambitions, preferring that he become a doctor, or—failing that—at least a dentist. "Their logic was great," he recalled in the *New York Daily News.* "They used to tell me that if I became a dentist, I could be secure and at night I could still draw cartoons. But if I became a cartoonist, I couldn't drill anybody's teeth at night."

Spiegelman persevered, nonetheless, and majored in art and philosophy at Harpur College—now State University of New York at Binghamton. There he drew for the college newspaper and began contributing to such periodicals as the *Fast Village Other.* What he didn't place in underground tabloids, he printed up himself and distributed by hand on the street. "I just found myself in the underground press . . . radicalized and psychedelized, just because of when, where, and how old I was," Spiegelman stated in a 1981 *Comics Journal.* Admitting that his work for these alternative publications was derivative at that time, he reflected that "I was trying to do what *other* people defined as underground comics," but that his heart wasn't really in shocking people with sex, violence, drugs, and scatology—the stock-in-trade of the underground press.

Spiegelman retained a healthy taste for simple satire, and while still in college he accepted a commercial job creating novelties for the Topps Chewing Gum company in Brooklyn. A request for an original baseball card drawing led to his meeting with employee Woody Gelman, a major collector of comic strips and a publisher, who was so impressed with Spiegelman that he offered the young fan a summer job a year or so later. Spiegelman's skill at the typewriter and the drawing board resulted in a continuing series of funny cards. In the spirit of *Mad* magazine, he has since generated such innovative material as the "Garbage Pail Kids" bubblegum cards and the

"Wacky Packages," miniature labels wickedly spoofing familiar consumer products with fictitious brand names and slogans like "Rice-a-Phony" and "Neveready" flashlight batteries—"Keeps You in the Dark." As a consultant at Topps, Spiegelman continues designing packages, creating candy and novelty concepts, art directing, or writing captions for bubblegum cards.

By the time Spiegelman left college in 1968, underground comics were evolving into a distinct subgenre, and he became as solidly established in it as that ephemeral stratum permitted. He edited magazines—including *Arcade* with Bill Griffith, and his own *Douglas Comix,* a promotional giveaway for Douglas Communications—and contributed often under his various pseudonyms to many other periodicals such as *Young Lust, Real Pulp, Bizarre Sex,* and *Sleazy Scandals of the Silver Screen.* Spiegelman's art increasingly assumed a graphic identity, and if his readership was not widespread, it was at least passionately devoted. To make a living, however, he did illustrations, book covers, and Topps bubblegum cards. Always fascinated by the possibilities of the comics as an art form, which he feels has a "secret language" of its own, Spiegelman has since 1979 conducted classes on the history and aesthetics of comics at the School of Visual Arts in New York.

In 1980 Spiegelman and his wife, Francoise Mouly, created *Raw,* an annual magazine featuring avant-garde comics. Convinced that "the flaring promise of underground comics had fizzled," they saw a need for a periodical that provided "comics by adults, for adults; comics that weren't under any obligation to be funny, or escapist pulp; comics unselfconsciously redefining what comics should be, by smashing formal and stylistic, as well as cultural and political taboos," explained Spiegelman in the introduction to *Read Yourself Raw*—a selection from the first three issues of their magazine. With the success of the Spiegelman's shoestring publishing venture, aesthetically if not financially, *Raw* has developed into the leading international comics periodical of the avant-garde. Described by Bill Sherman in *Comics Journal* as "a fascinatingly complementary package of prose, art, and experimental comics stripwork," *Raw* has done much to bring a mature and creative intelligence to its medium.

Similarly, *Raw* has provided a new and broader audience for underground comics and has introduced the United States to such noted European cartoonists as Jacques Tardi of France and Joost Swarte of the Netherlands. It has also served as a showcase for Spiegelman's own art and has further extended his reputation. The range of his commerical work has soared beyond bubblegum cards to include such disparate projects as cartoons for *Playboy,* covers for the novels of French existentialist Boris Vian, and illustrations for the *New York Times.* The growing success of *Raw,* a sell-out of twenty thousand copies per year, has exposed Spiegelman's original work to a public wide enough to elevate him from a cult hero of the undergound avant-garde to a substantial figure in mainstream American literature who is both interviewed on television and by the popular press and called on to review and write introductions for books. This lionization has come about largely as the result of a single ongoing work, *Maus,* which was published serially in *Raw* and issued as a trade book by Pantheon in 1982.

Maus originated as a three-page story in a 1972 underground comic book called *Funny Aminals* that restricted its characterizations to the exclusive use of anthropomorphic animals (or aminals). Bored with the cliches of Mickey-Mouse cuteness,

Spiegelman turned to his own experience as the son of Nazi concentration camp survivors and created a moving and scarifying tale of the Holocaust metaphorically featuring cats as Nazis and mice as Jews. Commenting in the *New York Daily News* on his decision to expand *Maus* for publication in *Raw*, Spiegelman recalled: "I told myself it was time to take on something serious," adding, "I wanted to tell a story, but I wanted it to be a story worth telling." He now regards this continuing saga as "the point where my work starts" and is working on a sequel. The true story of the artist's father, and of the younger Spiegelman's relationship with him, *Maus* has evolved into a complex, multi-layered parable rich in psychological insight and historical resonance. The deliberate simplicity of its images, starkly rendered in black and white, has an impact that a more elaborated graphic treatment could never have achieved. The book, which is being translated into more than a dozen languages, became an immediate popular and critical success, winning praise and awards for both its bold artwork and its compelling literary sensitivity. Newspapers ranging from *Rolling Stone* to the *Wall Street Journal* applauded *Maus*, but perhaps more gratifying to Spiegelman is the unstinted admiration the book fostered among the artist's colleagues. Featured on the cover of the volume, for example, are laudatory remarks from cartoonist Jules Feiffer, who called *Maus* "Brilliant, just brilliant," and Edward Sorel, who stated that "Mr. Spiegelman's passionate pen has stretched the boundaries of the comic strip and created a work of immense power."

According to Spiegelman's own assessment of his craft in the 1974 *Apex Treasury of Underground Comics:* "As an art form, the comic strip is just past its infancy. So am I. Maybe we'll grow up together." There is evidence that both the artist and the medium to which he has dedicated his life have richly fulfilled that prediction.

BIOGRAPHICAL/CRITICAL SOURCES:

BOOKS

Donahue, Don and Susan Goodrich, editors, *The Apex Treasury of Underground Comics*, D. Links, 1974.
Spiegelman, Art, *Maus: A Survivor's Tale*, Pantheon, 1986.
Spiegelman, Art and Francoise Mouly, *Read Yourself Raw: Comix Anthology for Damned Intellectuals*, Pantheon, 1987.

PERIODICALS

American Bookseller, May, 1987.
Arrival, spring, 1987.
Art Forum, February, 1987.
Baltimore Jewish Times, October 11, 1986.
Comics Journal, November, 1980, July, 1981, August, 1981, December, 1986.
Detroit News, September 23, 1987.
Los Angeles Times, October 2, 1986.
New Republic, June 22, 1987.
Newsweek, September 22, 1986.
New York Daily News, December 14, 1986.
New York Times, November 10, 1986.
New York Times Book Review, May 26, 1985, December 7, 1986.
People, October 27, 1986.
Village Voice, September 23, 1986.
Washington Post, September 1, 1986.

—*Sketch by Dennis Wepman*

SPIRES, Robert C(ecil) 1936-

PERSONAL: Born December 1, 1936, in Missouri Valley, Iowa; son of Roy C. and Ellen M. (a housewife; maiden name, Epperson) Spires; married Roberta A. Hyde (a schoolteacher), February 2, 1963; children: Jeffrey R., Leslie Ann. *Education:* University of Iowa, B.A., 1959, M.A., 1963, Ph.D., 1968.

ADDRESSES: Home—1802 West 22nd St., Lawrence, Kan. 66046. *Office*— Department of Spanish and Portuguese, University of Kansas, Lawrence, Kan. 66045.

CAREER: Ohio University, Athens, instructor, 1967-68, assistant professor of Spanish, 1968-69; University of Kansas, Lawrence, assistant professor, 1969-74, associate professor, 1974-78, professor of Spanish, 1978—, chairman of department of Spanish and Portuguese, 1982-85, 1987—. *Military service:* U.S. Army, 1959-61.

MEMBER: Modern Language Association of America (member of executive committee on twentieth century Spanish literature), American Association of Teachers of Spanish and Portuguese.

AWARDS, HONORS: Fellow of National Endowment for the Humanities, 1981-82, and U.S.-Spain Joint Committee, 1985-86.

WRITINGS:

(Contributor) Rodolfo Cardona, editor, *Novelistas espanoles de postguerra* (title means "Postwar Spanish Novelists"), Taurus, 1976.
La novela espanola de postguerra: Creacion artistica y experiencia personal (title means "The Postwar Novel: Artistic Creation and Personal Experience"), Collection Planeta/Universities, 1978.
Beyond the Metafictional Mode: Directions in the Modern Spanish Novel, University Press of Kentucky, 1984.
Transparent Simulacra: Spanish Fiction, 1902-1926, University of Missouri Press, in press.

Contributor to Hispanic studies journals.

WORK IN PROGRESS: Research on post-Franco Spanish fiction.

SIDELIGHTS: Robert C. Spires told *CA:* "I view my teaching and my research as inseparable. Publishing is a way of extending the classroom space in which I work. I am interested in how literature does not merely reflect, but in effect transforms into experience the context in which it was created. Because of the unique sociopolitical circumstances of Spain after its civil war I was attracted to the Spanish novel of that period. Next I explored the post-Franco period, again focusing on how the novel transforms sociopolitical reality into an aesthetic experience. My most recent work on the 1902-1926 period was a natural spin-off of my previous work and enabled me to close the circle. Now I want to open that circle as I turn my attention to how the current novelists, particularly the very young ones, search for new modes of expression and new means of transforming reality into a very real fictional experience."

*   *   *

SPIRO, Howard M(arget) 1924-

PERSONAL: Born March 23, 1924, in Cambridge, Mass.; son

of Thomas (a lawyer) and Martha (a housewife; maiden name, Marget) Spiro; married Marian Freelove Wagner (a teacher), March 11, 1951; children: Carolyn Spiro Winn, Pamela, Philip, Martha. *Education:* Harvard University, B.A., 1943, M.D., 1947.

ADDRESSES: Home—260 Millbrook Rd., North Haven, Conn. 06473. *Office*—Department of Internal Medicine, School of Medicine, Yale University, 333 Cedar St., New Haven, Conn. 06510.

CAREER: Affiliated with Peter Bent Brigham Hospital, as intern, 1947-48, resident and clinical fellow, 1948-49, and senior assistant resident, 1948-51; Massachusetts General Hospital, Boston, Mass., resident and clinical fellow, 1953-54; Yale University, New Haven, Conn., instructor, 1955-56, assistant professor, 1956-61, associate professor, 1961-67, professor of medicine, 1967—, chief of Gastrointestinal Section, 1955-82, director of Program for Humanities in Medicine, 1983—, senior fellow of Law-Medicine Program, 1977-83, fellow of Berkeley College, 1966—, executive fellow, 1968-70, director of Yale Affiliated Gastroenterology Program, 1967—. Fellow at Center for Advanced Study in Behavioral Sciences, Stanford, Calif., 1982-83. Member of staff at Yale-New Haven Hospital, Backus Hospital, Griffin Hospital, Gaylord Hospital, Hospital of St. Raphael, New Britain General Hospital, Norwalk Hospital, Park City Hospital, St. Vincent's Medical Center, and Waterbury Hospital. Chairman of Vivian Tappan Research Trust, 1966-80; associate director for patient care, Connecticut Regional Medical Program, 1968; National Foundation for Ileitis and Colitis, vice-president, 1977, chairman of Education Committee, 1981. President of Beaumont Homestead Preservation Trust, 1969-82. *Military service:* U.S. Naval Reserve, active duty, 1943-45. U.S. Army Reserve, active duty, 1951-53.

MEMBER: American Federation for Clinical Research, American Gastroenterological Association, American College of Physicians (governor, 1972-76; master, 1981), American Society for Clinical Investigation, American College of Gastroenterology (governor, 1984-85), Eastern Gut Club, Connecticut Medical Society, New Haven County Medical Society (member of board of governors, 1969-73), Beaumont Medical Club (president, 1969-70), Alpha Omega Alpha.

AWARDS, HONORS: M.A. from Yale University, 1967; Francis Blake Award from Yale University, 1971; named physician of the year by Connecticut Digestive Disease Society, 1973; National Achievement Award from National Foundation for Ileitis and Colitis, 1975; Laureate Award from Connecticut chapter of American College of Physicians, 1986.

WRITINGS:

Clinical Gastroenterology, Macmillan, 1970, 3rd edition, 1983. *Doctors, Patients, and Placebos*, Yale University Press, 1986. (Editor with H. M. Mandell) *When Doctors Get Sick*, Plenum, 1987.

Contributor to medical journals. Editor in chief of *Journal of Clinical Gastroenterology*, 1979—; editor of *G. I. Tract*, 1970-76; associate editor of *Italian Journal of Gastroenterology*, 1980—; book review editor of *Gastroenterology*, 1986—; member of editorial board of *Medical Times*, 1975—, *Medical Heritage*, 1984—, *Humane Medicine*, 1985—, and *Physician and Patient*, 1985—.

WORK IN PROGRESS: Research on "how diagnoses are made" now and how they were made one hundred years ago.

SIDELIGHTS: Howard M. Spiro's book *Doctors, Patients, and Placebos* addresses the value of placebos in medical practice. His detailed analysis reveals that nearly one-third of the patients who have used placebos have benefited, at least psychologically, from these inocuous medications. The doctor's book also covers the historical use of placebos and the practice of medicine from classical times, a study of healing in primitive and non-Western cultures, and the potential for change in approaches to scientific investigation and medical education. Spiro discusses several issues in the philosophy of medicine, including the humane and holistic approaches to medical treatment. According to Alfred H. Katz, a *Los Angeles Times Book Review* critic, these commentaries "reveal Spiro as a cultivated humanist, a well-read social philosopher, as well as a sensitive clinician."

BIOGRAPHICAL/CRITICAL SOURCES:

PERIODICALS

Los Angeles Times Book Review, February 1, 1987.

*   *   *

SROLE, Leo   1908-

PERSONAL: Born October 8, 1908, in Chicago, Ill.; son of William (a milliner) and Rebecca (Epstein) Srole; married Esther Hannah Alpiner (a teacher), December 27, 1941; children: Ira Herschel, Rebecca Yona. *Education:* Harvard University, B.S. (cum laude), 1933; University of Chicago, Ph.D., 1940.

ADDRESSES: Home—151-39 25th Ave., Whitestone, N.Y. 11357. *Office*—100 Haven Ave., North Tower, Apt. 29F, New York, N.Y. 10032.

CAREER: New York University, New York, N.Y., lecturer in anthropology, 1940-41; Hobart College (now Hobart and William Smith Colleges), Geneva, N.Y., professor of sociology and chairman of department, 1941-42; Columbia University, New York City, member of Bureau for Applied Social Research, 1947-48; research director for Anti-Defamation League, B'nai B'rith, 1948-52; Cornell University, School of Medicine, New York City, research professor of sociology, 1952-59; Yeshiva University, Albert Einstein College of Medicine, New York City, research professor of social psychiatry, 1959-61; State University of New York Downstate Medical Center, Brooklyn, N.Y., professor of psychiatry, 1961-65; Columbia University, professor of social sciences in psychiatry, 1965-76, professor emeritus, 1976—. Chief of psychiatric research in social sciences at New York State Psychiatric Institute, 1966-78; extraordinary professor at University of Louvain, 1969; consultant to World Health Organization and Belgian Ministry of Health. *Military service:* U.S. Army Air Forces, 1943-45, military psychologist, became major; U.S. Army, 1945-46, welfare director at displaced persons camp operated by the United Nations Relief and Rehabilitation Administration in Landsberg, Germany, retained rank of major.

MEMBER: International Sociological Association, American Psychiatric Association (honorary fellow), American Sociological Association, American Association of University Professors, Society for the Study of Social Problems, Gerontological Society, Sigma Xi.

WRITINGS:

(With W. Lloyd Warner) *The Social Systems of American Ethnic Groups*, Yale University Press, 1945, reprinted, Greenwood Press, 1976.

(With others) *Mental Health and the Metropolis: The Midtown Manhattan Study*, foreword by Alexander H. Leighton, McGraw, 1962, enlarged and revised edition, two volumes, edited by Srole and Anita Kassen Fischer, Harper, 1975-77.

Mental Health in the Metropolis Revisited: Twenty Years Later, Basic Books, in press.

Contributor to scholarly journals. Past associate editor of *American Sociological Review* and *Journal of Social Issues;* member of editorial board of *Israel Journal of Psychiatry, American Sociological Review* and *Journal of Psychiatric Evaluation and Treatment.*

WORK IN PROGRESS: Community Remarkable of Western World: Accepting the Rejected, publication by Basic Books expected in 1990.

*   *   *

STACEY, Judith   1943-

PERSONAL: Name legally changed; born January 2, 1943, in Irvington, N.J.; daughter of Robert (a meat dealer) and Sandra (a decorator; maiden name, Shapiro) Gisser; married Ira Goldfine, June 27, 1964 (divorced, 1969); married Herb Schreier (a child psychiatrist), June 3, 1980; children: (second marriage) Jacob. *Education:* Attended Syracuse University, 1960-62; University of Michigan, B.A. (with high distinction), 1964; University of Illinois at Chicago, M.A., 1968; further graduate study at University of Chicago, 1968-70; Brandeis University, Ph.D., 1979. *Politics:* "Progressive, feminist." *Religion:* Jewish.

ADDRESSES: Home—Oakland, Calif. *Office*—Department of Sociology, University of California, Davis, Calif. 95616.

CAREER: Richmond College of the City University of New York, Staten Island, N.Y., instructor in education, 1971-73; University of California, Davis, assistant professor, 1978-84, associate professor of sociology, 1984—.

MEMBER: American Sociological Association, Society for the Study of Social Problems, National Women's Studies Association, Phi Beta Kappa.

AWARDS, HONORS: Jessie Bernard Award from American Sociological Association, 1985, for *Patriarchy and Socialist Revolution in China;* fellow of Ford Foundation and American Council of Learned Societies, 1986; Davis Humanitites Institute fellowship, 1988.

WRITINGS:

And Jill Came Tumbling After: Sexism in American Education, Dell, 1974.
Patriarchy and Socialist Revolution in China, University of California Press, 1983.

Contributor to sociology and feminist studies journals. Advisory editor of *Signs* and *Gender and Society;* editorial board member of *Feminist Studies.*

WORK IN PROGRESS: The Postmodern Family: Stories of Gender and Kinship in the Silicon Valley.

SIDELIGHTS: Judith Stacey told *CA:* "I am interested in the relationships between gender and family orders and broad-scale social change because I wish to understand the barriers to gender and social justice. This interest links my research on China and California's Silicon Valley to my essays on feminism and family politics."

STAINES, David   1946-

PERSONAL: Born August 8, 1946, in Toronto, Ontario, Canada; son of Ralph McKenzie (a florist) and Mary Rita (a secretary and accountant; maiden name, Hayes) Staines. *Education:* University of Toronto, B.A., 1967; Harvard University, A.M., 1968, Ph.D., 1973. *Politics:* Liberal. *Religion:* Roman Catholic.

ADDRESSES: Home—12 Galt St., Ottawa, Ontario, Canada K1S 4R4. *Office*—Department of English, University of Ottawa, Ottawa, Ontario, Canada K1N 6N5.

CAREER: Harvard University, Cambridge, Mass., assistant professor of English, 1973-78; University of Ottawa, Ottawa, Ontario, associate professor, 1978-85, professor of English, 1985—.

MEMBER: International Arthurian Society, Mediaeval Academy of America (vice-chairman, 1975-81; chairman of standing committee on centers and regional associations, 1981-87), Modern Language Association of America.

AWARDS, HONORS: Fellow of National Endowment for the Humanities, 1977-78; honorary research fellow at University College, London, 1977-78; fellow of Social Sciences and Humanities Research Council of Canada, 1986-87.

WRITINGS:

(Editor) *The Canadian Imagination: Dimensions of a Literary Culture*, Harvard University Press, 1977.
(Editor) *Responses and Evaluations: Essays on Canada by E. K. Brown*, McClelland & Stewart, 1977.
(Editor) *The Callaghan Symposium: A Reappraisal*, University of Ottawa Press, 1981.
Tennyson's Camelot: The Idylls of the King and Its Medieval Sources, Wilfrid Laurier University Press, 1982.
(Editor with Andrew Garrod) *Illuminations: The Days of Our Youth*, Gage Publishing, 1984.
(Editor) *The Forty-ninth and Other Parallels: Contemporary Canadian Perspectives*, University of Massachusetts Press, 1986.
(Editor) *Stephen Leacock: A Reappraisal*, University of Ottawa Press, 1987.
(Editor with Robert Scholes, Nancy R. Comley, and Carl H. Klaus) *Elements of Literature: Fiction, Poetry, Drama*, Oxford University Press, 1987.

Editor of *Journal of Canadian Poetry.*

WORK IN PROGRESS: A history of the English Canadian novel, two volumes; translating the romances of twelfth-century poet Chretien de Troyes, publication by Indiana University Press expected in 1989.

SIDELIGHTS: David Staines told *CA:* "I began my academic career as a medievalist, focusing on medieval Arthurian literature. My publications include studies of Arthuriana, both medieval and modern. My interest has now turned to the literature of twelfth-century France and fourteenth-century England. In addition, I have become a frequent lecturer and essayist on Canadian literature and culture. As a critic, editor, and scholar I have been a careful observer of the Canadian cultural scene. In my writings there is a consistent vision of Canada as a mature, challenging, and exciting world of the arts. The Canadian preference for a mosaic structure in which all the ethnic and social regions retain their distinctness is central to an understanding of the nation. As a country Canada is not only a mosaic of ethnic cultures but also a mosaic of regions, each with its own sense of identity; the nation, therefore, exists in a dialectic of regional and ethnic tensions.''

*   *   *

STARER, Robert   1924-

PERSONAL: Surname is pronounced "Star-er," not "Stairer"; born January 8, 1924, in Vienna, Austria; came to United States, 1947, naturalized citizen, 1957; son of Nison and Erna (Gottlieb) Starer. Education: Juilliard School, Post Graduate Diploma, 1949.

ADDRESSES: Home—P.O. Box 946, Woodstock, N.Y. 12498. Agent—John Hawkins, 71 West 23rd St., New York, N.Y. 10010.

CAREER: Juilliard School, New York, N.Y., teacher, 1949-74; Brooklyn College of the City University of New York, Brooklyn, N.Y., 1963—, began as professor, became distinguished professor. Distinguished professor at Graduate Center of the City University of New York. Military service: Royal Air Force, 1943-46.

MEMBER: American Society of Composers, Authors, and Publishers.

AWARDS, HONORS: Guggenheim fellow, 1957, 1963; grant from American Academy of Arts and Letters, 1979; recipient of awards, including Fulbright from U.S. Department of State, 1964, Ford Foundation, 1969, and National Endowment of the Arts, 1979, 1983.

WRITINGS:

Rhythmic Training, M.C.A. Music, 1963.
Basic Rhythmic Training, Hal Leonard, 1986.
Continuo: A Life in Music (autobiography), Random House, 1987.

WORK IN PROGRESS: The Music Teacher, a fiction work.

SIDELIGHTS: Composer Robert Starer was trained at the State Academy in Vienna. After the German annexation of Austria in 1938, he went to Palestine, where he attended a conservatory in Jerusalem. Later, as a graduate of the Juilliard School, Starer studied with composer Aaron Copeland.

Continuo, the composer's autobiography, is a group of essays telling of Starer's life in music. The memoir has been well received by critics. In the Washington Post, Jonathan Yardley called Continuo "a book that contains far more wisdom than its slender size would suggest. If it is the story of a life in music, even more it is a journey into a wise, compassionate and expansive mind.'' And Richard Dyer of the Boston Globe held that "each of these [essays] is beautifully organized, penetrating in observation, delightful in characterization, emotional but never sentimental, and leavened with charming anecdote.''

Starer told CA: "I wrote Continuo because many people said to me: 'You have led an interesting life; you should write about it.' I wrote it while I am still in the midst of activities, not when all is over. It is a musical autobiography, not a personal one. I describe people I have known who had an influence on me: teachers, conductors, dancers, choreographers, and writers. I discuss my life as a pianist, accompanist, harpist, and composer in the concert hall as well as on Broadway and for television. I express my views on different aspects of the mu-

sical scene, in particular the estrangement between the composer and his audience. There are anecdotes in the book, from my borrowing a friend's swastika to see Hitler from as near as possible during the Nazi occupation of Vienna, to a waitress in a restaurant telling me how she hated me because she had to use my book Rhythmic Training during her college years. Writing the book gave me great pleasure and helped me formulate my opinions as best as I could.''

BIOGRAPHICAL/CRITICAL SOURCES:

PERIODICALS

Boston Globe, March 17, 1987.
New Yorker, May 18, 1987.
New York Times, February 15, 1987.
New York Times Book Review, June 14, 1987.
Washington Post, February 25, 1987.

*   *   *

STEIN, Calvert   1903-1982

OBITUARY NOTICE—See index for CA sketch: Born April 6, 1903, in Newcastle-on-Tyne, England; immigrated to United States, 1912; naturalized U.S. citizen, 1919; died October 20, 1982. Physician, neuropsychiatrist, educator, editor, and author. After serving for three years as a general practitioner at Livermore Sanatorium in California, Stein became senior resident in psychiatry, neurology, and child guidance at Massachusetts's Monson State Hospital and Springfield Hospital in 1931. Seven years later he established a private practice in counseling and psychosomatic medicine, which he pursued from 1938 to 1975. During that time he continued to serve Springfield Hospital as consulting neuropsychiatrist. In the 1940s he acted as official consultant and examiner for the U.S. Civil Service, the U.S. Railroad Retirement Board, the Veterans Administration, and the U.S. Armed Forces Entrance and Examining Station. For seven years he was consultant to Westover Air Force Base, and in 1980 he became consultant to Balboa Naval Hospital. Stein lectured in neurology and psychiatry at Springfield College, American International College, Tufts University, and the Medical University of South Carolina. His writings include Nothing to Sneeze At, Practical Psychotherapeutic Techniques, Practical Family and Marriage Counseling, Practical Pastoral Counseling, and Psychotherapy in the Bible. Stein was also a contributing editor to Group Psychotherapy for thirteen years.

OBITUARIES AND OTHER SOURCES:

Date of death provided by wife, Lucille Helen Stein.

BOOKS

Who's Who in American Jewry, Standard Who's Who, 1980.

*   *   *

STEPTOE, Patrick C(hristopher)   1913-1988

OBITUARY NOTICE: Born June 9, 1913, in Oxfordshire, England; died of cancer, March 21, 1988, in Canterbury, England. Obstetrician and author. Steptoe, together with his longtime partner, physiologist Robert Edwards, pioneered the technique of in vitro fertilization, making parenthood possible for many infertile couples. After uniting a ripened human egg with sperm outside of a woman's womb and then returning the resultant embryo to the womb for the duration of the pregnancy, Steptoe delivered the first "test tube" baby, Louise

Brown, on July 25, 1978. Since then thousands of children have been born by this method to women who, because of abnormalities of the ovaries or fallopian tubes, could not conceive normally. Steptoe, who at one time was ostracized by the medical establishment for his innovative scientific ideas, was made a fellow of the Royal Society in 1987 for his contributions to medicine. He and Edwards wrote the 1980 book *A Matter of Life.*

OBITUARIES AND OTHER SOURCES:

BOOKS

Current Biography, H. W. Wilson, 1979, June, 1988.

PERIODICALS

Chicago Tribune, March 23, 1988.
Los Angeles Times, March 23, 1988.
New York Times, March 23, 1988.
Times (London), March 23, 1988.

*   *   *

STEVENS, George (Cooper), Jr.   1932-

PERSONAL: Born April 3, 1932, in Los Angeles, Calif.; son of George (a filmmaker) and Yvonne (Shevlin) Stevens; married Elizabeth Guest (an interior designer), July 5, 1965; children: Caroline (stepdaughter), Michael Murrow, David Averell. *Education:* Occidental College, B.S., 1953.

ADDRESSES: Home—3050 Avon Lane, Washington, D.C. 20007. *Office*—American Film Institute, Kennedy Center, Washington, D.C. 20566. *Agent*—Lynn Nesbit, International Creative Management, 40 West 57th St., New York, N.Y. 10019.

CAREER: Director, producer, and writer. Production assistant to his father, George Stevens, for Giant Productions, 1953-54, and to Jack Webb, for Mark VII Ltd., 1956-57; director of television programs "Alfred Hitchcock Presents," "Peter Gunn," and "Phillip Marlowe," 1957-60; associate producer and director with his father, of "The Diary of Anne Frank," 1958-59, and of "The Greatest Story Ever Told," 1960-61; U.S. Information Agency (USIA), director of Motion Picture and Television Service, 1962-67, and producer of documentary films, including "Jacqueline Kennedy's Asian Journey," 1962, "Nine From Little Rock," 1964, and "John F. Kennedy: Years of Lightning, Days of Drums," 1964; American Film Institute (AFI), founding director, 1967-79, co-chairman, 1979—. Chairman of U.S. delegations to international film festivals in Cannes, Moscow, Vienna, and Berlin, 1962-65; executive producer of "The American Film Institute Life Achievement Awards Salute" to John Ford, 1973, James Cagney, 1974, Orson Welles, 1975, William Wyler, 1976, Bette Davis, 1977, and Henry Fonda, 1978, all broadcast by Columbia Broadcasting System, Inc. (CBS-TV); producer of "America at the Movies," a feature film commemorating U.S. Bicentennial, 1976; executive producer of television special "The Stars Salute America's Greatest Movies," 1977; executive producer of television special "Christmas in Washington," broadcast by National Broadcasting Company, Inc. (NBC-TV), 1982—; producer of television special "Normandy to Berlin: A War Remembered," first broadcast by British Broadcasting Corporation (BBC-TV), May, 1985, later broadcast in the United States by Public Broadcasting Service (PBS-TV). Adviser to John F. Kennedy Presidential Library, 1964—; producer of gala openings, including that of the Kentucky Center for the Arts, Louisville, 1983, and the Wortham Center for the Per-

forming Arts, Houston, Texas, 1987; operator of film companies New Liberty Productions and Creative Film Center. *Military service:* U.S. Air Force, 1954-56; served as motion-picture officer; became first lieutenant.

MEMBER: Directors Guild of America, Writers Guild of America, Academy of Motion Picture Arts and Sciences, Academy of Television Arts and Sciences, The Caucus for Producers, Writers, and Directors, American Federation of Television and Radio Artists, Century Association.

AWARDS, HONORS: Stevens's USIA films have received numerous awards, including four Academy Award nominations and one Oscar—the latter in 1966 for "Nine From Little Rock"; Emmy Award from National Academy of Television Arts and Sciences, 1975, for "AFI Salute to James Cagney" and, 1984 and 1986, for "The Kennedy Center Honors"; Writers Guild Award, 1983, for best script of a variety television special, for "AFI Salute to John Huston"; Special Jury Prize from Chicago Film Festival, 1985, Special Award from National Board of Review of Motion Pictures, 1986, and Award of Excellence from Film Advisory Board, 1986, all for "George Stevens: A Filmmaker's Journey."

WRITINGS:

(And director/producer) "George Stevens: A Filmmaker's Journey" (screenplay), Castle Hill Productions, 1984.
(Author of introduction) Max Hastings, *Victory in Europe: D-Day to VE Day in Color* (Book-of-the-Month Club selection), photographs by George Stevens, Weidenfeld & Nicolson, 1985.

TELEVISION SCRIPTS

(And producer) "America Entertains Vice Premier Deng," broadcast from Kennedy Center Opera House, on the occasion of the establishment of diplomatic relations between the People's Republic of China and the United States, over PBS-TV to the United States and by satellite to China, January 19, 1979.
(And co-producer) "The Kennedy Center Honors—A Celebration of the Performing Arts," broadcast by CBS-TV, 1978—.
(And producer) "The American Film Institute Life Achievements Awards Salute," broadcast by CBS-TV, 1979-86, rotating yearly among NBC-TV, American Broadcasting Companies, Inc. (ABC-TV), and CBS-TV, 1986—.

OTHER

Contributor of articles to *New York Times, Washington Post, Los Angeles Times,* London *Sunday Times, Saturday Review, Film Quarterly,* and *American Film.*

WORK IN PROGRESS: Producer and co-screenwriter of "The Ballad of Mary Phagan," a four-hour miniseries to be broadcast on NBC-TV.

SIDELIGHTS: "George Stevens: A Filmmaker's Journey," which George Stevens, Jr., wrote, produced, and directed, opened in 1985 to critical acclaim and a highly successful theatrical release. According to *Film Comment* contributor Ronald Haver, it is "a film of many layers, for it traces the evolution of a man, an artist, an art form, a nation, and a son's love for his father." Narrated by George, Jr., the documentary contains interviews with a number of friends and associates of the elder Stevens, one of Hollywood's most successful and prolific directors. Included also are clips from his feature films, among them "Shane," "A Place in the Sun," "Gunga Din," and "Giant," and rare color footage shot on location. Of special interest is a celluloid record in color of World War II, a war otherwise etched in memory almost exclusively from black-and-white newsreels of the day. As a member of General Dwight D. Eisenhower's special film unit in Europe, the senior Stevens was assigned to film black-and-white footage of the activities of the Sixth Army for the national archives. However, the experienced director, who made home movies as an avocation, took along his own 16mm camera and color film to keep a personal record. Although the five hours of footage lay in rusty cans under a dusty army blanket for almost four decades before his son found it, its colors were still intense and its impact undiminished. Among the landmark events of World War II captured by Stevens's lens were the Allied invasion of Normandy, the liberation of Paris, and the horror of the concentration camp at Dachau.

"George Stevens: A Filmmaker's Journey" garnered considerable critical praise. Reviewers described the son's tribute to his famous father as compelling, splendid, entertaining, quietly passionate, and heartfelt. Writing in the *Los Angeles Times*, Sheila Benson judged the documentary "the real stuff of drama . . . with more that is profoundly moving than the best novel." Furthermore, she complimented Stevens, Jr., on making a film "which at the same time honors a decent man and his work and goes straight to the heart of the film-making passion." *New York Times* film critic Vincent Canby was similarly enthusiastic. He called "George Stevens: A Filmmaker's Journey" "one of the best studies of the work of a single director that exists on film," adding that it is "put together with love, intelligence, wit and, most important of all, a knowledge of film history."

CA INTERVIEW

CA interviewed George Stevens, Jr., by telephone on June 30, 1986, at his office in the Kennedy Center, Washington, D.C.

CA: It's hard to imagine a more favorable circumstance for learning filmmaking than growing up with your father, reading scripts and helping him on such movies as A Place in the Sun, Shane, *and* Giant. *Did you know from early on that you wanted a career in films too?*

STEVENS: I worked with my father during my last summer in high school and during summers in college. I did not have my mind set on a career in motion pictures. I was very interested in writing—I was sports editor of the paper at my college—and I thought I was headed toward journalism. But almost without realizing it, I found myself on the other path.

CA: After two years of military service, during which you directed and produced training films, you went into television. Were there special lessons in television that you might not have gotten anywhere else?

STEVENS: I had a wonderful mentor in Jack Webb, who created the "Dragnet" television series, a very innovative effort. It set a style for television. Of course, it later became a kind of parody of itself, but it was strong and dramatic and original. Jack was an extremely effective organizer and producer-director and I learned a great deal about creating an organization from working with his Mark VII Ltd. Company. I remember he had the wonderful logo for "Dragnet"—Mark VII Ltd., the hammer, the stamp, and the sound—and his stationery was terrific. His offices were efficient and attractive. It gave me

an appetite for having style and efficiency in the operations that I later became connected with.

CA: You've managed to have two careers, one as a private movie and television producer, and another in public service, as director of the Motion Picture and Television Service of the United States Information Agency (1962-1967) and as a moving spirit behind the American Film Institute and its director for twelve years. Was there at some point a conscious decision not to remain solely a private filmmaker?

STEVENS: It was circumstance. In 1961, shortly after President Kennedy was elected, Edward R. Murrow came to Los Angeles in his role as director of the United States Information Agency, and he asked me to come and work with him in Washington as head of the Motion Picture Division of that agency. It was a difficult choice, leaving what I had been doing and also parting company with my father on the project we were working on, "The Greatest Story Ever Told." As important as was Ed Murrow's offering me that new avenue, equally important was my father's urging me to explore it. By that time I had become extremely valuable to him, a close colleague and partner, and my leaving would represent a loss—but he saw the importance of my finding an opportunity out from under his shadow. I always appreciated that paternal wisdom. And, of course, the opening that Ed created in my life allowed me to discover, perhaps at its most exciting time in recent American history, the appeal and satisfaction of public service. I refer to the New Frontier in the [John F.] Kennedy years, when there existed the belief that energetic and effective government could serve the people and the nation.

CA: And a belief that every individual could play a part.

STEVENS: Yes. President Kennedy used to say that each person can make a difference and everyone should try.

CA: One of the functions of the American Film Institute is to archive and preserve films. Before the Institute was founded, were films scattered around in many different places?

STEVENS: It was a mess. The motion pictures made before 1950 were produced on nitrate cellulose film stock. This material tends to deteriorate and disintegrate in time, and, on occasion, to explode or burn. Nearly half of the films that had been made from the very beginning of moviemaking in the United States were lost or missing or had been destroyed. In some instances the movie companies had melted down the negatives to retrieve their silver content. In other cases they had simply junked films because they didn't want the expense of storing them. In other instances there had been fires in which whole vaults of films went up in flames.

There also had never been a systematic national program to preserve motion pictures. There were organzations that had worked at preservation, such as the Museum of Modern Art and George Eastman House, but there was no national coordination or government funding behind it. The preservation of the motion picture heritage of the country became the first major program of the American Film Institute. In the nineteen years that the AFI has been in existence we have accumulated 21,000 films and television programs in the AFI collection in the Library of Congress. It is assured that those films will survive.

CA: Color fading is one of the obvious problems in movie preservation, as everyone knows who has seen old color movies on television or video. Is work being done on this now?

STEVENS: Color fading is an equally troubling situation. Originally color motion pictures were produced in the three-strip Technicolor process, in which three strips of film would run through the camera, representing the different colors, and they would later be blended together into a composite release print. The color stability was excellent. But in the 1950's Eastman Kodak invented a single-strip process that was much less costly, because it required only one strip of film. However, it became apparent later on that the durability of the color of this film was not good. Consequently, most of the films made in Eastman Color during the 1950's and 1960's are losing their color quality. There are ways of dealing with this. One is to make separation negatives onto three strips and the other is cold storage. The various archives—the AFI, the Library of Congress, Eastman House, the Museum of Modern Art, UCLA—are all at work on this problem. A new organization housed within the AFI called the National Center for Film and Video Preservation is the focal point for preservation activities.

CA: Are there less obvious problems involved in movie preservation that we may not observe first-hand or hear so much about?

STEVENS: The new problem—and it's a problem that also represents an opportunity—is the transferring of films to videocassette. In one sense it is a form of film preservation. It makes them accessible to a new audience. The problems associated with it are (1) sometimes the studios transfer incomplete or truncated versions of the films; (2) sometimes the transfers are made from negatives that are not of high quality—that have been scratched or otherwise damaged; and (3) there is an unfortunate new process called colorization by which certain companies want to artificially color black and white films so as to widen what they deem to be their appeal. The American Film Institute at its last board meeting passed a resolution unanimously opposing this practice, noting that some of the more important works of art of this century in this country have been black and white movies, and that "Citizen Kane" and "The Grapes of Wrath" and "A Place in the Sun" and the works of Charlie Chaplin will never be the same if some computer technician adds color to them, any more than a da Vinci drawing would be enhanced by someone's adding a color wash to it.

CA: One of the programs you instituted at the AFI is the "Directing Workshop for Women." Has it helped increasing numbers of women to find opportunities to direct and to get financial backing for their projects?

STEVENS: Yes. We started that about ten years ago. At that time, there were virtually no women directors. I would not want to overstate the effect of our program, but it certainly can be said that it provided a rallying point for the idea that women were equally capable of directing films as men. Many of the women who have been involved in that program over the years have gone on to become directors, and the program provided them both what we might call a place to stand and an opportunity to do their first directing work.

CA: What kinds of people use the American Film Institute for research or special study? Do you get many scholars?

STEVENS: To a certain extent. We have a library in Los Angeles at the Center for Advanced Film Studies campus. That is used by researchers and scholars. And we have a reference facility in the AFI headquaters in the Kennedy Center in Washington that is also used by researchers, scholars, and journalists.

CA: How do you think the availability of movies on video has affected the success of commercial films?

STEVENS: It is my view that we are systematically driving adults away from movie theatres, first because the majority of films being released today are designed for a fourteen to twenty-four-year-old audience, and second, by the breaking down of movie theatres into small cubicles called multiplexes, where very often the screen is small and the projection is marginal. These factors make moviegoing a much less attractive proposition for adults. Consequently, more and more people take the alternative and rent a videocassette and play it on their television screens. As the size of the screen in movie theatres tends to grow smaller and become more comparable to the size of a television screen, the incentive for going to the theatre and paying five dollars to see a movie becomes reduced.

CA: One of the most visible things you've done in your work at the AFI is establish a repertory film center at the Kennedy Center, with the idea that people are becoming more and more interested in "enjoying the riches of the entire history of film, appreciating a given film in terms of its place in the historical continuity of the medium." Has the number of similar theatres increased considerably across the country in the last decade or so?

STEVENS: Yes. We designed the American Film Institute Theater in the Kennedy Center to have all of the qualities I've described as lacking in so many theatres today. Even though it is a relatively small theatre—only 230 seats—the size of the screen in proportion to the audience is large. We have flexible maskings that allow us to show films at the aspect ratio in which they were originally composed—whether that be Cinemascope, 1:85 to 1, or the old Academy aspect ratio that the movies before 1950 were made in. We also have the capability for 70 millimeter. With this format flexibility, we are able to show films exactly as they were originally designed, and that means that people's heads are not cut off just above their eyes. The theatre also has excellent sound and we make every effort to get the best possible prints of the films we show. The concept of the AFI Theater is to maintain for film presentation the same kind of standards that a museum for great painting has. We intend it to serve as an example, and I believe more and more around the country there are facilities that have this kind of quality presentation. The numbers are still relatively limited, but I hope one day every city will have a repertory cinema that presents high quality films properly.

CA: In 1969 you established the AFI's Center for Advanced Film Studies in Hollywood, which you mentioned earlier, a highly respected institution that accepts annually only about a hundred students out of more than five hundred applicants. What kind of qualities does the Center look for in its applicants?

STEVENS: From the very beginning my notion was that we should seek individuals with interesting minds rather than people who were proficient at one or another of the technical aspects of moviemaking. Consequently, we try to determine what the individual will bring to the medium once he or she masters the crafts of moviemaking. So we end up with people who have been playwrights, photographers, and writers along with quite a number who have studied cinema in graduate work in universities.

CA: You majored in English and speech at Occidental College. Do you favor a liberal arts education for people who want to go into movie careers?

STEVENS: I do. I think there's a terrible risk of people becoming preoccupied with movies and moviemaking during their college years, when they have that one-time opportunity to gain an education in history and literature and science. When I'm asked, I generally advise young people to get a wonderful education and then to concentrate on learning the ins and outs of moviemaking.

CA: You've been active in international film festivals. Do you think there are lessons we could learn from the filmmakers of other countries?

STEVENS: Yes. Filmmaking is truly an international art. From the days of [Sergei] Eisenstein in the Soviet Union and [D. W.] Griffith in the United States, filmmakers have been going to school on the fine works of colleagues in other countries. I think that's a continuing process, and a good one.

CA: You paid tribute to your father and his work by writing, directing, and producing the fine 1985 film "George Stevens: A Filmmaker's Journey," which has enjoyed high critical acclaim. Do you have any plans to do a written memoir of your father?

STEVENS: It was the other way around. A publisher had been urging me to write a book about my father, and that caused me to think about his life. While I was contemplating that, it occurred to me that he was a filmmaker and I am a filmmaker and therein was a wonderful opportunity to tell his story in the medium in which he worked and in which he involved me. As for written memoirs, I see that as a last act, hopefully much later on.

CA: In the film on your father, Millie Perkins, who played Anne Frank in "The Diary of Anne Frank," spoke of his ability to treat actors in whatever way was required to get them to do their best work. Could you comment on that?

STEVENS: In "A Filmmaker's Journey," Joel McCrea said something about my father that a number of actors said in different ways. He said that my father had such confidence in himself that he gave the actors confidence in *themselves,* that they knew they could afford to try things they might not otherwise try, because his taste and judgment would be there in the editing room, saving them from doing something with which they wouldn't be pleased when they saw it on the screen. He did not come to the set on the morning they were beginning a new scene and tell the actors what to do. He would get the stage very quiet, and then tell the actors to begin the scene, and let them try to find their way through it. In that way he was able to take advantage of whatever ideas they might bring to it rather than pre-empting those ideas by imposing his own. Also, once the actors tried to make their way through the scene and found difficulties with it—I remember this particularly with Elizabeth Taylor and Montgomery Clift—they were then extremely receptive to what he had to offer.

CA: The valuable wartime archive your father left provided material not only for "A Filmmaker's Journey," but also for the picture book Victory in Europe *and the BBC television documentary "Normandy to Berlin," which was shown here on PBS. Will other segments of the war footage be used for more documentaries or other projects?*

STEVENS: I'm sure they will. I just made available a copy of all of that material to the Imperial War Museum in London, which has one of the great collections of records, memorabilia, photos, and film of the war. I imagine over the years this five hours of color film will be used in many ways to expand the knowledge and perception of World War II.

CA: Your father was making movies at a time when there was a great deal of novelty and excitement in filmmaking. How do you think that time compares with our own?

STEVENS: I think many of us envy that era. In 1935 and 1936 my father made five movies. Today you spend that much time developing a script, taking it from studio to studio, taking it from star to star—simply going through the whole process of trying to "put a picture together" or create a "package." I think this limits the development of filmmakers and it is one reason why we don't have as many filmmakers of the caliber we had a generation ago—and I speak of the time when, if you confine it to directors and producer-directors, my father, John Ford, John Huston, William Wyler, Billy Wilder, Alfred Hitchcock, Howard Hawks, and Frank Capra were all at the top of their game.

CA: You now operate two film companies, New Liberty Productions and the Creative Film Center. How do they differ? What are the main goals of each?

STEVENS: New Liberty Productions is the company in which I produce my commercial ventures. Its name is a modification of the name of the company my father and William Wyler and Frank Capra created when they came home after World War II, Liberty Films. The Creative Film Center is a film company that enables me to do occasional projects of a nonprofit character.

CA: Your ideas and hard work have certainly resulted in institutions that reap long-term benefits not just for the movie industry but for the larger culture as well. Are there new projects in the works that you'd like to talk about, or dreams for the future?

STEVENS: I am happily at work doing the various things that I work on, which include the Kennedy Center Honors, our annual celebration of the great performing artists of the country that takes place each year at the Kennedy Center and is broadcast on CBS. I am working on movie projects and television projects and continuing to enjoy my association with the American Film Institute, which is these days an unpaid, part-time role as co-chairman of the board. And I have learned that the things I do are best served by not talking about them too much before they are actually achieved. Otherwise there becomes too little incentive to go on and do them.

CA: Is there a philosophy that guides your work?

STEVENS: I'm fond of the speech William Faulkner made when he accepted the Nobel Prize. He said that the artist's duty is to lift up men's hearts and help them endure. I've always thought that was a good touchstone for creative people in any of the media.

BIOGRAPHICAL/CRITICAL SOURCES:

PERIODICALS

American Film, July-August, 1985.
Christian Century, July 17-24, 1985.
Commonweal, May 31, 1985.
Film Comment, August, 1985.
Los Angeles Times, April 11, 1985.
Maclean's, May 20, 1985.
New York Times, November 22, 1964, May 3, 1985.
People, February 13, 1978.
Time, May 6, 1985.
Times Literary Supplement, May 15, 1985.
Variety, December 29, 1982, May 22, 1985, September 4, 1985.
Washington Post, May 17, 1985.

—*Interview by Jean W. Ross*

* * *

STIGLER, Stephen M(ack) 1941-

PERSONAL: Born August 10, 1941, in Minneapolis, Minn.; son of George (an economist) and Margaret (Mack) Stigler; married Virginia Lee, June 27, 1964; children: Andrew, Geoffrey, Margaret, Elizabeth. *Education:* Carleton College, B.A., 1963; University of California, Berkeley, Ph.D., 1967.

ADDRESSES: Home—5816 Blackstone Ave., Chicago, Ill. 60637. *Office*— Department of Statistics, University of Chicago, Chicago, Ill. 60637.

CAREER: University of Wisconsin—Madison, assistant professor, 1967-71, associate professor, 1971-75, professor of statistics, 1975-79; University of Chicago, Chicago, Ill., professor of statistics, 1979—. Member of board of trustees of Center for Advanced Study in the Behavioral Sciences.

MEMBER: American Association for the Advancement of Science, American Statistical Association, Institute of Mathematical Statistics, History of Science Society, American Academy of Arts and Sciences (fellow).

WRITINGS:

The History of Statistics: The Measure of Uncertainty Before 1900, Belknap Press, 1986.

Contributor of more than fifty articles to statistics and history journals. Editor of *Journal of the American Statistical Association*, 1979-82.

WORK IN PROGRESS: Research on the history of statistics in the twentieth century and on the application of statistical methods in the geophysical sciences.

BIOGRAPHICAL/CRITICAL SOURCES:

PERIODICALS

New York Times Book Review, October 15, 1986.

* * *

STOWE, Charles E(dwin) Hambrick
See HAMBRICK-STOWE, Charles E(dwin)

* * *

STREET, James H(arry) 1915-1988

OBITUARY NOTICE—See index for *CA* sketch: Born November ber 17, 1915, in New Braunfels, Tex.; died of prostate cancer, June 20, 1988, in Edison, N.J. Economist, educator, statistician, journalist, editor, and author. Street, a professor emeritus of economics at Rutgers University, taught at that institution from 1952 to 1986. Prior to his tenure at Rutgers, Street worked as a reporter and editor for the *New Braunfels Herald*, as an agricultural economist for the U.S. Department of Agriculture, a statistician for the U.S. Forest Service, and an instructor and assistant professor at the University of Pennsylvania and at Haverford College. A one-time Fulbright scholar in Latin America, he lectured at institutions throughout the Americas, serving in 1955 as Smith-Mundt Professor at the National University of Asuncion. Street wrote *The New Revolution in the Cotton Economy: Mechanization and Its Consequences* and co-authored *Urban Planning and Development Centers in Latin America* and *Responsibilities of the Foreign Scholar to the Local Scholarly Community*. He edited *Ideas and Issues in the Social Sciences* and co-edited *Technological Progress in Latin America: The Prospects for Overcoming Dependency* and *Latin America's Economic Development: Institutionalist and Structuralist Perspectives*.

OBITUARIES AND OTHER SOURCES:

BOOKS

Who's Who in America, 44th edition, Marquis, 1986.

PERIODICALS

New York Times, June 22, 1988.

* * *

STROHMEYER, John 1924-

BRIEF ENTRY: Born June 26, 1924, in Cascade, Wis. American educator, journalist, and author. Pulitzer Prize-winning editor of the Bethlehem, Pennsylvania, newspaper *Globe-Times*, Strohmeyer wrote *Crisis in Bethlehem* (Adler & Adler), a 1986 expose of the inefficiency and extravagance that led to the decline of the American steel industry in the world market. Concentrating on the Bethlehem Steel Corporation, one of the top moneymaking companies in the United States at one time but nearly bankrupt today, Strohmeyer cites as contributing to the giant's downfall its management's resistance to modernization, its disregard of European and Japanese innovation, and its directors' self-indulgence. Strohmeyer also faults the steelworkers' demand for excessively high wages and their reluctance to accept cost-cutting modifications, as well as the U.S. Government's economic policies that focus on immediate profit rather than research and development for future stability.

A newspaperman in Bethlehem for thirty-two years before he left the *Globe-Times* in 1984, Strohmeyer began as a night reporter with the paper, became its editor in 1958, and subsequently served as its vice-president and director. He taught journalism in Nairobi, Kenya, Freetown, Sierra Leone, and at Lehigh University and has been a faculty member of the University of Alaska at Anchorage since 1987. *Addresses: Home*— 262 West Langhorne Ave., Bethlehem, Pa. 18017. *Office*— University of Alaska, Anchorage, Ala. 99508. *Agent*—The Sterling Lord Agency, 660 Madison Ave., New York, N.Y. 10021.

BIOGRAPHICAL/CRITICAL SOURCES:

BOOKS

Who's Who in America, 44th edition, Marquis, 1986.

PERIODICALS

Chicago Tribune, March 9, 1987.
New York Times Book Review, October 26, 1986.
Washington Post Book World, January 18, 1987.

* * *

STUTZMAN, Esther M. Friesner
See FRIESNER-STUTZMAN, Esther M.

* * *

SULLIVAN, Mary Ann 1954-

PERSONAL: Born December 1, 1954, in Springfield, Mass.; daughter of John Joseph (a shipping supervisor) and Clara (a seamstress; maiden name, D'Ammoral) Sullivan. *Education:* Framingham State College, B.A., 1978; Norwich University, M.F.A., 1986. *Politics:* Democrat. *Religion:* Roman Catholic.

ADDRESSES: Home—102 William St., Springfield, Mass. 01105. *Office*—Springfield Technical Community College, Springfield, Mass. 01105.

CAREER: Springfield Technical Community College, Springfield, Mass., instructor in English and journalism, 1986—. Free-lance fiction editor, 1984—.

MEMBER: International Women's Writing Guild, Society of Children's Book Writers, Associated Writing Program.

AWARDS, HONORS: Child of War named Notable Children's Book in social studies by National Council of Social Studies, 1985.

WRITINGS:

Child of War, Holiday House, 1984.
"Abbandonato" (short story), published in *Chariton Review,* 1986.

WORK IN PROGRESS: Research on Blessed Margaret of Castello, protagonist of an upcoming novel for adults.

SIDELIGHTS: Mary Ann Sullivan told *CA:* "I have been working endlessly, it seems, on a major novel for adults which develops a form of realism beyond the magical realism given to us by South American writers. In order to portray the miracles of Blessed Margaret, my protagonist, in a 'real' sense, I have been struggling to develop a full-dimensional realism that would encompass the actions of God manifested through man.

"Blessed Margaret of Castello lived in Italy between 1287 and 1320. Research for the novel on her life involves the translation of medieval Latin and Italian documents and trips to Italy.

"I am participating on a panel with medievalists from Mount Holyoke and Harvard University to discuss medieval research problem resolution."

AVOCATIONAL INTERESTS: "I love to swim and also to live in the woods."

* * *

SUNNERS, William 1903-1988
(Lee Keith, Weston Satterly)

OBITUARY NOTICE—See index for *CA* sketch: Born August 11, 1903, in New York, N.Y.; died of congestive heart failure, May 9, 1988, in Brooklyn, N.Y. Educator, editor, and author.

Sunners was best known for the more than one hundred books he wrote about solving puzzles, winning contests, and writing promotional jingles. The subject of a 1979 *New York* magazine article titled "King of Twenty-five Words or Less," Sunners taught school in New York from 1929 to 1960 and served as a consultant and adviser to advertising agencies and newspaper syndicates. Under the pseudonym Lee Keith he wrote *Out-of-the-Place Words* and *How to Solve Contest Picture Puzzles,* and as Weston Satterly he published *Complete Contest Course.* Under his own name he edited *Picture Encyclopedia* and wrote *American Slogans, How to Write Prize Winning Statements,* and *How to Make and Sell Original Crossword Puzzles.*

OBITUARIES AND OTHER SOURCES:

PERIODICALS

New York, March 26, 1979.
New York Times, May 13, 1988.

* * *

SUTHERLAND, John (Patrick) 1920-1988

OBITUARY NOTICE—See index for *CA* sketch: Born June 12, 1920, in Kansas City, Mo.; died after a heart attack, March 16, 1988, in Alexandria, Va. Journalist, editor, and author. A reporter for *U.S. News & World Report* for almost thirty years, Sutherland began in 1952 as a White House correspondent, became senior editor in 1974, and served as congressional correspondent from 1976 to 1980. He then became associate editor of *U.S. News Washington Letter,* retiring in 1985. Sutherland, a former president of the White House Correspondents Association, received the National Press Foundation's Journalism Excellence Award in 1977. Prior to joining *U.S. News & World Report* he worked as an assistant editor for Barrick Publishing Company and as a reporter for the *Wall Street Journal.* His book *Men of Waterloo* was published in 1966.

OBITUARIES AND OTHER SOURCES:

BOOKS

Who's Who in America, 44th edition, Marquis, 1986.

PERIODICALS

Washington Post, March 18, 1988.

* * *

SUTTON, Barry 1919-1988

OBITUARY NOTICE: Born in 1919; died March 16, 1988. Military pilot, reporter, and author. A newspaper reporter in central England prior to World War II, Sutton had a passion for flying that prompted him to join the Royal Air Force Volunteer Reserve (RAFVR). He transferred to the Royal Air Force (RAF) proper when the war broke out and fought against the Germans in France in 1940. Shot down during the Battle of Britain, Sutton was badly burned and hospitalized for a year. After his recuperation he returned to combat, fighting in Burma in 1942 and India in 1944. A recipient of the Distinguished Flying Cross, Sutton retired from the RAF as a group captain in 1956. His writings include two memoirs, *The Way of a Pilot* and *Jungle Pilot.*

OBITUARIES AND OTHER SOURCES:

PERIODICALS

Times (London), March 18, 1988.

SZASZ, Ferenc Morton 1940-

PERSONAL: Born February 14, 1940, in Davenport, Iowa; son of Ferenc Paul (a mechanical engineer) and Mary (a teacher; maiden name, Plummer) Szasz; married Margaret Connell (a historian), August 1, 1969; children: Eric, Chris, Maria. *Education:* Ohio Wesleyan University, B.A., 1962; University of Rochester, Ph.D., 1969. *Religion:* Congregational.

ADDRESSES: Office—Department of History, University of New Mexico, Albuquerque, N.M. 87131.

CAREER: University of New Mexico, Albuquerque, instructor, 1967-69, assistant professor, 1969-76, associate professor, 1976-82, professor of history, 1982—. Fulbright lecturer at University of Exeter, 1985-86.

AWARDS, HONORS: Gasper Percz de Villagra Award from Historical Society of New Mexico, 1985, and Robert G. Athearn Award from Western Historical Society, 1986, both for *The Day the Sun Rose Twice.*

WRITINGS:

The Divided Mind of Protestant America, University of Alabama Press, 1982.

(Editor) *Religion in the West*, Sunflower University Press, 1984.

The Day the Sun Rose Twice, University of New Mexico Press, 1984.

The Protestant Minister in the Great Plains and Mountain West, 1865-1915, University of New Mexico Press, 1988.

Contributor of nearly fifty articles to history journals and popular magazines.

WORK IN PROGRESS: A work on the British mission to Los Alamos, 1943-1945.

SIDELIGHTS: Ferenc Morton Szasz told *CA:* ''*The Day the Sun Rose Twice* details the story of the world's first nuclear explosion at Trinity Site, New Mexico, on July 16, 1945. The world has never been the same since then.''

T

TAM'SI, Tchicaya U
See TCHICAYA, Gerald Felix

*　　*　　*

TANGYE, Nigel (Trevithick)   1909-1988

OBITUARY NOTICE: Born in 1909 in London, England; died June 2, 1988. Pilot, historian, and author of books on aviation, Cornish history, and the sea. Tangye began his writing career as an air correspondent for London's *Evening News* and *Spectator.* His 1938 book *Teach Yourself to Fly* was adopted by the British Air Ministry as a guide for novice service pilots. The author was a wing commander in the Royal Air Force Volunteer Reserve during World War II, a secret agent in Spain, an adviser to filmmaker Alexander Korda, and a hotel proprietor. Tangye's seventeen books include *The House on the Seine, Footsteps on the Beach, From Rock and Tempest, Voyage Into Cornwall's Past,* and a memoir, *Facing the Sea: A Cornishman Remembers.*

OBITUARIES AND OTHER SOURCES:

PERIODICALS

Times (London), June 4, 1988.

*　　*　　*

TATCHELL, Peter   1952-

PERSONAL: Born January 25, 1952, in Melbourne, Australia; son of Gordon (a lathe operator) and Mardi (a factory packer; maiden name, Rhodes) Tatchell. *Education:* West London College, Certificate in Applied Sociology, 1974; Polytechnic of North London, B.Sc. (with honors), 1977. *Politics:* "Left-wing socialist." *Religion:* None.

ADDRESSES: Home and office—45 Arrol House, Rockingham St., London SE1 6QL, England.

CAREER: Free-lance journalist and researcher in Malawi, Papua New Guinea, and New Hebrides, 1977-79; housing adviser and campaigner for the rights of the homeless, 1979-82; free-lance writer and political campaigner, 1982-83; free-lance journalist and writer, 1983—. Labour candidate for Parliament, 1983; member of Campaign for Nuclear Disarmament, Labour Movement Campaign for Palestine, Labour Campaign for Lesbian and Gay Rights, and Socialist Environment and Resources Association; member of executive committee of Vietnam Moratorium Campaign, 1971; member of Malawi Support Committee, 1979-82.

WRITINGS:

The Battle for Bermondsey, Heretic Books, 1983.
(Contributor) Louis Mackay and David Fernbach, editors, *Nuclear-Free Defence*, Heretic Books, 1983.
Democratic Defence: A Non-Nuclear Alternative, GMP, 1985.
AIDS: A Guide to Survival, GMP, 1986.
(Contributor) Warren Middleton, editor, *The Betrayal of Youth*, CL Publications, 1986.

Contributor of articles and reviews to magazines and newspapers.

WORK IN PROGRESS: "Two of the Boys," a filmscript about the struggle of two gay, working-class teenagers to come to terms with a hostile and prejudiced community, for England's Channel Four Television.

SIDELIGHTS: Peter Tatchell told *CA:* "Most of my writings, both fiction and nonfiction, blend a mixture of personal commitment, involvement, and experience with a broader and more general political insight, message, and vision. For me, writing is an instrument for human understanding and liberation.

"*The Battle for Bermondsey* is a personal account of my campaign for election as a Labour member of Parliament in the southeast London constituency of Bermondsey in 1983. The subject of a violent hate campaign by the far Right and of vicious press smears which vilified me as an extremist, foreigner, draft-dodger, homosexual, traitor, and 'nigger-lover,' I told in *The Battle for Bermondsey* the inside story of the dirtiest election in Britain in this century.

"*Democratic Defence: A Non-Nuclear Alternative* proposes an alternative to nuclear weapons that is non-provocative, self-reliant, and democratic. This includes a switch to strictly self-defensive weapon systems; withdrawal from NATO and the remnants of Empire to a nonthreatening home-based defense posture; the reorientation of the armed forces around a Swedish-style guerrilla strategy and citizen's army; the incorporation of nonviolent civilian resistance as a component of defense policy; and a radical democratization of the armed forces.

"*AIDS: A Guide to Survival* brings a message of hope to the many people already exposed to the AIDS virus. No one need

446

face this disease as a passive victim. By fighting back mentally and physically, people with the virus can reduce their chances of developing AIDS, and those who already have AIDS can increase their likelihood of survival. Drawing on studies of immune-deficient cancer patients, my book sets out a comprehensive practical program for strengthening the body's natural defenses by means of diet, exercise, sleep, and relaxation. It explains how to fight AIDS psychologically, using the techniques of meditation and mental imagery, and gives useful advice on how to sustain self-valuation and the will to live.''

BIOGRAPHICAL/CRITICAL SOURCES:

PERIODICALS

London Review of Books, December 22, 1983.
New Statesman, November 4, 1983, April 19, 1985.
Times Literary Supplement, May 17, 1985.

*   *   *

TATHAM, Andrew Francis   1949-

PERSONAL: Born July 31, 1949, in London, England; son of Francis Hugh Currer and Nancy Margaret (Robins) Tatham; married Margaret Yvonne Backhurst (a lecturer), August 12, 1972; children: Hugh Francis, Alice Elizabeth. *Education:* University of Durham, B.A. (with honors), 1971; King's College, London, Ph.D., 1984. *Religion:* Church of England.

ADDRESSES: Office—King's College, University of London, Strand, London WC2R 2LS, England.

CAREER: George Philip Printers Ltd., London, England, editorial assistant, 1972-74; University of London, London, England, map curator at King's College, 1974—. Registrar of National Register of Maps for the Visually Handicapped, 1979—.

MEMBER: International Cartographic Association (British member of Tactile and Low Vision Mapping Commission, 1985—), British Cartographic Society, Society of University Cartographers (editor, 1981-82).

WRITINGS:

(With A. G. Hodgkiss) *Keyguide to Information Sources in Cartography,* Mansell, 1986.
National Register of Maps for the Visually Handicapped, King's College, London, 1986.

*   *   *

TAYLOR, Alec Clifton
See CLIFTON-TAYLOR, Alec

*   *   *

TAYLOR, Clyde Willis   1904-1988

OBITUARY NOTICE: Born November 7, 1904, in Fort Smith, Ark.; died June 3, 1988, in Arnold, Md. Clergyman, missionary, editor, and author. Taylor was founder of the Bethel Bible Institute, pastor of the Central Baptist Church in Quincy, Massachusetts, and an official of the National Association of Evangelicals (NAE), an evangelical unification organization. Prior to joining the NAE staff, he was a missionary in the South American countries of Peru and Colombia. During World War II, Taylor worked to obtain passports and visas for missionaries facing travel restrictions. His writings include *Ecumenical Strategy in Foreign Missions, A Glimpse of World Missions: An Evangelical View,* and *Evangelicals Examine Ecumenicity.*

OBITUARIES AND OTHER SOURCES:

PERIODICALS

Chicago Tribune, June 9, 1988.

*   *   *

TAYLOR, Mark C.   1945-

PERSONAL: Born December 13, 1945; son of Noel A. and Thelma Kathryn (Cooper) Taylor; married Mary-Dinnis Stearns (a computer analyst), June 22, 1968; children: Aaron Stearns, Kirsten Jennie. *Education:* Wesleyan University, B.A., 1968; attended University of Copenhagen, 1971-72, Doktorgrad, 1981; Harvard University, Ph.D., 1973.

ADDRESSES: Home—45 Forest Rd., Williamstown, Mass. 01267. *Office*—Department of Religion, Williams College, P.O. Box 487, Williamstown, Mass. 01267.

CAREER: Williams College, Williamstown, Mass., assistant professor, 1973-78, associate professor, 1978-1981, professor, 1981-86, William R. Kenan, Jr., Professor of Religion, 1986—, director of Center for Humanities and Social Sciences, 1987—.

MEMBER: American Academy of Religion, Modern Language Association of America, Society for Values in Higher Education, Hegel Society of America.

AWARDS, HONORS: Guggenheim fellow, 1978-79; fellow at National Humanities Center, 1982-83; Fulbright travel grant, 1983.

WRITINGS:

Kierkegaard's Pseudonymous Authorship: A Study of Time and the Self, Princeton University Press, 1975.
Religion and the Human Image, Prentice-Hall, 1977.
Journeys to Selfhood: Hegel and Kierkegaard, University of California Press, 1980.
Deconstructing Theology, Scholars Press (New York), 1983.
Erring, University of Chicago Press, 1985.
Deconstruction in Context: Literature and Philosophy, University of Chicago Press, 1986.
Altarity, University of Chicago Press, 1987.
Tears, State University of New York Press, in press.

SIDELIGHTS: Mark C. Taylor told *CA:* ''For many years, my primary concern has been to develop a constructive position in the philosophy of religion and theology. Toward this end, I have developed extensive analyses of major nineteenth- and twentieth-century thinkers. The primary focus of my early work was on Hegel and Kierkegaard. It has long seemed to me that most of the major issues in twentieth-century theology and philosophy of religion were defined by these two philosophers. In my recent work, I have been exploring the implications of contemporary philosophy and literary criticism for theology and religion. Although the connections are not immediately apparent, thinkers like Jacques Derrida, Georges Bataille, and Maurice Blanchot provide a rich resource for religious reflection. Work in this area has brought me into conversation with architects and artists. I expect my future work to extend the kind of cultural analysis that I have begun in my previous books.''

TCHICAYA, Gerald Felix 1931-1988
(Gerald Felix-Tchicaya, Tchicaya U Tam'si, Gerald Felix Tchicaya U Tam'si)

OBITUARY NOTICE: Born August 25, 1931, in Mpili, Moyen Congo (now People's Republic of the Congo); died April 21, 1988. Journalist and poet. The most prolific black poet in France, Tchicaya, who often wrote under the pseudonym U Tam'si, left his native Africa as a teenager and moved to Paris with his family. He wrote about the Congo from the perspective of a black man in voluntary exile. The tone and content of the author's writings were shaped by his memories of Africa; cultural loss, isolation, and dark humor inform most of his poetry. Tchicaya has been compared to Aime Cesaire and Leopold Sedar Senghor, major poets of *negritude*, a conscious pride in Blackness.

Although Tchicaya was a free-lance writer for English and French reviews and editor of the African journal *Congo*, he is most famous for his books of verse written in French, such as *Le Mauvais Sang, Feu de brousse, A triche-coeur, Epitome, Le Ventre,* and *L'Arc musical. Epitome,* published in 1962 and winner of the grand prize for poetry at the 1966 Dakar Festival, is generally recognized as his best work. The 1964 translation of the anthology *Feu de brousse,* published as *Brush Fire,* gave English-speaking readers in the United States, Europe, and Africa greater access to African poetry. Translations of poems from four of the author's collections are available in a volume entitled *Selected Poems.*

OBITUARIES AND OTHER SOURCES:

BOOKS

African Authors: A Companion to Black African Writing, Volume I: *1300-1973,* Black Orpheus Press, 1973.
The Penguin Companion to Classical, Oriental, and African Literature, McGraw, 1969.
Reader's Guide to African Literature, Africana Publishing, 1971.
World Authors: 1970-1975, H. W. Wilson, 1980.

PERIODICALS

Times (London), April 23, 1988.

* * *

TCHICAYA U Tam'si
See TCHICAYA, Gerald Felix

* * *

TEICHGRAEBER, Richard F. III 1950-

PERSONAL: Born January 5, 1950, in Houston, Tex.; married, 1974; children: two. *Education:* Amherst College, B.A., 1971; Brandeis University, Ph.D., 1978.

ADDRESSES: Office—Murphy Institute of Political Economy, 108 Tilton Hall, Tulane University, 6823 St. Charles Ave., New Orleans, La. 70118.

CAREER: Tulane University, New Orleans, La., assistant professor, 1979-86, associate professor of history, 1986—, director of Murphy Institute of Political Economy, 1986—.

MEMBER: American Historical Association, Conference for the Study of Political Thought, Intellectual History Group.

AWARDS, HONORS: Fellow of American Council of Learned Societies, 1987-88.

WRITINGS:

"Free Trade" and Moral Philosophy: Rethinking the Sources of Adam Smith's "Wealth of Nations," Duke University Press, 1987.
(Editor with Gordon Winston) *The Boundaries of Economics,* Cambridge University Press, 1988.

WORK IN PROGRESS: Adam Smith and Tradition: A Reading and Publishing History of the "Wealth of Nations"; American Commerce and American Individualism, a study of Emerson, Thoreau, and Whitman.

BIOGRAPHICAL/CRITICAL SOURCES:

PERIODICALS

Times Literary Supplement, May 22, 1987.

* * *

TEMPLE, Paul
See McCONNELL, James Douglas Rutherford

* * *

TERICH, Thomas A. 1943-

PERSONAL: Born December 12, 1943, in Alhambra, Calif.; married Maureen T. Kelly; children: three. *Education:* California State University, Los Angeles, B.A., 1965, M.A., 1968; Oregon State University, Ph.D., 1973.

ADDRESSES: Office—Department of Geography, Western Washington University, Bellingham, Wash. 98225.

CAREER: Western Washington University, Bellingham, assistant professor, 1973-76, associate professor, 1976-87, professor of geography, 1988—.

WRITINGS:

Living With the Coast of Puget Sound and the Georgia Strait, Duke University Press, 1987.

WORK IN PROGRESS: Research on coastal management and coastal geomorphology.

* * *

TERZIAN, Yervant 1939-

PERSONAL: Born February 9, 1939, in Alexandria, Egypt; immigrated to United States, 1960, naturalized citizen, 1971; son of Bedros and Maria (Kiriakaki) Terzian; married Araxy Hovsepian (a computer analyst), April 16, 1966; children: Sevan, Tamar. *Education:* American University in Cairo, B.Sc., 1960; attended Harvard University, 1961; Indiana University—Bloomington, M.S., 1963, Ph.D., 1965; studied at National Radio Astronomy Observatory, 1963-65.

ADDRESSES: Office—Department of Astronomy, Space Sciences Building, Cornell University, Ithaca, N.Y. 14853.

CAREER: Cornell University, Ithaca, N.Y., research associate and head of scientific services at Arecibo Observatory in Puerto Rico, 1965-67, assistant professor, 1967-72, associate professor, 1972-77, professor of astronomy, 1977—, professor of history and philosophy of science, 1986—, chairman of department of astronomy, 1979—, assistant director of Center for Radiophysics and Space Research, 1968-74, acting director of center, 1979-80, member of National Astronomy and Ionosphere Center, chairman of Symposium on the Highlights of

Modern Astrophysics, 1984. Visiting professor at University of Montreal, 1973-74, University of Thessaloniki, 1974, and University of Florence; Harrow Shapley Lecturer of American Astronomical Society, 1974—. Vice-chairman of New York Astronomical Corp., 1969-78; American member of International Consultative Radio Communications Committee, 1970-76; member of Radio Astronomy Panel of Jet Propulsion Laboratory, 1973—; member of Committee on Radio Frequencies of National Academy of Sciences, 1974-76; invited scientist at U.S.S.R. Academy of Sciences, University of Moscow, and Byurakan Astrophysical Observatory, 1976; head delegate of the National Science Foundation to Astronomical Council of Saudi Arabia, 1977; member of National Aeronautics and Space Administration's International Ultraviolet Explorer Review Panel, 1979-81, and chairman of panel on nebulae, 1982, 1984, and 1987; member of Space Sciences Panel of Science Applications, Inc., 1985.

MEMBER: International Astronomical Union (chairman of Symposium on Planetary Nebulae, 1976-77; chairman of Working Group on Planetary Nebulae, 1985—), International Scientific Radio Union, American Astronomical Society, Society for Scientific Exploration (vice-president, 1987—), Armenian Assembly, Kirkos Professional Organization for Higher Education in Greece (chairman of Task Force on Visiting Scholars, 1975-78), Astronomical Society of New York (vice-president, 1974-78), Sigma Xi (vice-president, 1975-77; president, 1977-78).

AWARDS, HONORS: Danforth associate, 1976; Dicran H. Kabakjian Award for Outstanding Achievement in Science from North American Armenian Student Association, 1985.

WRITINGS:

(Editor and contributor) *Interstellar Ionized Hydrogen*, W. A. Benjamin, 1968.
(Editor and contributor) *Planetary Nebulae: Observations and Theory*, D. Reidel, 1978.
(Editor of English translation) G. A. Gurzadyan, *Flare Stars*, Pergamon, 1980.
(Editor with Elizabeth M. Bilson) *Cosmology and Astrophysics: Essays in Honor of Thomas Gold*, Cornell University Press, 1982.

Member of editorial advisory board of *Encyclopedia of Astronomy and Astrophysics*, 1982—.

CONTRIBUTOR

D. E. Osterbrock and C. R. O'Dell, editors, *Planetary Nebulae*, D. Reidel, 1968.
D. S. Evans, editor, *External Galaxies and Quasi-Stellar Objects*, D. Reidel, 1972.
A. M. Lenchek, editor, *The Physics of Pulsars*, Gordon & Breach, 1972.
Arthur Beer, editor, *Vistas in Astronomy*, Pergamon, 1974.
A. G. W. Cameron, editor, *Fundamentals of Cosmic Physics*, Gordon & Breach, 1974.
F. J. Kerr and S. C. Simonson, editors, *Galactic Radio Astronomy*, D. Reidel, 1974.
P. A. Shaver, editor, *Radio Recombination Lines*, D. Reidel, 1980.
J. M. Dickey, editor, *The Phases of the Interstellar Medium*, NRAO Publications, 1981.
Giuliano Giuricin, Fabio Mardirossian, and other editors, *The Structure and Evolution of Active Galactic Nuclei*, D. Reidel, 1986.

John Kormendy and G. R. Knapp, editors, *Dark Matter in the Universe*, D. Reidel, 1986.
Jun Jugaku and Manuel Peimbert, editors, *Star Forming Regions*, D. Reidel, 1987.
Phyllis Lugger, editor, *Asteroids to Quasars*, Cambridge University Press, 1988.

Contributor to *McGraw-Hill Yearbook of Science and Technology*. Contributor of more than 130 articles to scientific journals.

WORK IN PROGRESS: Radio studies of the late stages of stellar evolution; research on the explosive phases of dying stars.

SIDELIGHTS: Yervant Terzian told *CA:* "I have always wanted to know why there are stars in the sky. I had to work hard to learn physics, mathematics, and astronomy to find out what humans have understood about the cosmos. I am fortunate to live in an era of very fast and spectacular advancements in the nature of the universe. Now I think the most important question is: 'Why is there existence?' It may be possible for science to answer this question.

"I am also very concerned about education, in particular science education and the lack of it. Most people do not understand what science is and what science is not. The most important single item for the happy survival of human beings is education. I am working hard on this issue."

BIOGRAPHICAL/CRITICAL SOURCES:

PERIODICALS

Times Literary Supplement, October 7, 1983.

*   *   *

THELLE, Notto R(eidar)   1941-

PERSONAL: Born March 19, 1941, in Hong Kong; son of Notto Normann (a missionary) and Rannfrid (a missionary and teacher; maiden name, Danielsen) Thelle; married Mona Irene Ramstad (a psychologist), June 19, 1965; children: Rannfrid Irene, Olav Ramstad, Anne Helene, Notto Johannes, Ellen Mari. *Education:* Attended University of Sheffield, 1968-69, and Otani University, 1972-73; University of Oslo, Dr.Theol., 1983; attended Modum Bads Nerve sanatorium, 1985-86. *Religion:* Lutheran.

ADDRESSES: Home—Nordengveien 29, 0755, Oslo 7, Norway. *Office*—University of Oslo, P.O. Box 1023, Blindern, Oslo 3, Norway.

CAREER: Scandinavian East Asia Mission, Kyoto, Japan, missionary, 1969-85; National Christian Council Center for the Study of Japanese Religions, Kyoto, associate director, 1974-85; University of Oslo, Oslo, Norway, professor of theology, 1986—.

WRITINGS:

Buddhism and Christianity in Japan, University of Hawaii Press, 1987.

Editor of *Japanese Religions*, 1974-85, and *Norsk Tidsskrift for Misjon*, 1988—.

WORK IN PROGRESS: "A book, in Nowegian, about experiences and encounters in Japan, related especially to the interfaith dialogue, or encounters between persons committed to different religious faiths."

SIDELIGHTS: Notto R. Thelle told *CA:* "My interest in Japan has especially been the encounter between Christianity and other religions, Buddhist studies, and Japanese studies. As professor of mission studies and ecumenics, I want to motivate students to discover that the center of Christendom is no longer in the West, but in the third world."

* * *

THOBY-MARCELIN, (Emile) Philippe 1904-1975

PERSONAL: Born December 11, 1904, in Port-au-Prince, Haiti; immigrated to United States, c. 1949; died August 13, 1975, in Cazenovia (some sources indicate Syracuse or New York City), N.Y.; son of Emile (a politician, novelist, and literary critic) and Eva (Thoby) Marcelin; married Eva Ponticello. *Education:* Attended Petit Seminaire College Saint-Martial in Port-au-Prince; received law degree.

CAREER: Writer. Served as a public official in the Haitian Ministry of Public Works prior to 1949; Pan American Union, Washington, D.C., French translator, beginning in 1949.

AWARDS, HONORS: Second Latin-American Literary Prize Competition award, 1943, for *Canape-Vert;* Guggenheim fellowship, 1951.

WRITINGS:

POETRY

Lago-Lago, publisher unknown, 1930.
La Negresse adolescente (collection), preface by Leon La-Leau, Impr. La Presse (Haiti), 1932.
Dialogue avec la femme endormie, Editions "La Reserve" (Haiti), 1941.
A fonds perdu, P. Seghers (Paris), 1953.

Also author of *Le Jour et la nuit.*

NOVELS

(With brother, Pierre Marcelin) *Canape-Vert,* Editions de la Maison Francaise, 1944, English translation by Edward Larocque Tinker, Farrar & Rinehart, 1944.
(With P. Marcelin) *La Bete de Musseau,* Editions de la Maison Francaise, 1946, translation by Peter C. Rhodes published as *The Beast of the Haitian Hills,* Rinehart, 1946, new edition with introduction by Thoby-Marcelin, Time Inc., 1964, City Lights, 1986.
(With P. Marcelin) *Le Crayon de Dieu,* La Table Ronde (Paris), 1952, translation by Leonard Thomas from original French manuscript published as *The Pencil of God,* introduction by Edmund Wilson, Houghton, 1951.
(With P. Marcelin) *Tous les hommes sont fous,* publisher unknown, 1970, translation by Eva Thoby-Marcelin published as *All Men Are Mad,* introduction by Edmund Wilson, Farrar, Straus, 1970.

OTHER

Panorama de l'art haitien (art history), Impr. de l'Etat, 1956.
Haiti (art history), Pan American Union, 1959.
(With brother, Pierre Marcelin) *Contes et legendes d'Haiti* (juvenile collection), illustrations by Philippe Degrave, F. Nathan (Paris), 1967, translation by Eva Thoby-Marcelin published as *The Singing Turtle, and Other Tales From Haiti,* illustrations by George Ford, Farrar, Straus, 1971.

SIDELIGHTS: A popular Haitian writer and former poet, Philippe Thoby-Marcelin gained widespread recognition for the

critically acclaimed novels he and his brother Pierre wrote depicting peasant life in their native country. Originally written in French, the books feature a descriptive look at the various customs practiced by Haiti's predominantly black population, especially the voodoo rituals inspired by their African ancestors. Generally, critics described these stories as both entertaining and informative, and most hailed the authors for the clarity and detail distinguishing their lively prose. The brothers' prize-winning *Canape-Vert* holds the distinction of being the first Haitian fiction translated into the English language; as such it served to introduce Western civilization to Haitian literature, and some consider it a classic among the works of Caribbean writers. Voicing similar praise for another of their successful collaborations, Arna Bontemps wrote in the *New York Times Book Review* that *The Beast of the Haitian Hills* is "a poetically conceived account" in which the "skill, grace, and spice of the storytelling are art from a distant and neglected world."

Aside from the international reputation that his writing afforded him, Thoby-Marcelin is credited with both shaping the literary and artistic development of Haiti and preserving its cultural heritage. Most notably, he assumed a major role in the country's renaissance of arts and letters during the 1920s and served as a leading exponent of the avant-garde literary movement in Haiti. As a member of an elite group of intellectuals, Thoby-Marcelin also helped found the *Revue Indigene* magazine, which advocated the exclusive use of the standard French language as opposed to such imitative derivatives as the Creole dialect adopted by most of his countrymen. In effect he nurtured a return to the original folkways of his native land, a concern that prompted his adherence to an old custom of prefixing his surname with his mother's maiden name. Perhaps Thoby-Marcelin's commitment and dedication to perpetuating the rich cultural history of his people contributed to his stature as one of Haiti's most popular and renowned writers.

BIOGRAPHICAL/CRITICAL SOURCES:

PERIODICALS

New York Times Book Review, November 24, 1946.
Village Voice, June 23, 1987.

OBITUARIES:

PERIODICALS

New York Times, August 17, 1975.*

* * *

THOMPSON, China
See LEWIS, Mary (Christianna)

* * *

THOMPSON, Francis Clegg
See MENCKEN, H(enry) L(ouis)

* * *

THOMPSON, George H(yman) 1923-

PERSONAL: Born June 22, 1923, in Tylertown, Miss.; son of Joseph Talbert and Linnie (Simmons) Thompson; married Sharon Lee Wood, November 24, 1960; children: Joseph, George, Curt. *Education:* Hendrix College, B.S., 1948, B.A., 1949; Columbia University, M.A., 1951, Ph.D., 1968.

ADDRESSES: Office—Department of History and Political Science, Hendrix College, P.O. Box 439, Conway, Ark. 72032.

CAREER: Hendrix College, Conway, Ark., assistant professor, 1952-57, associate professor, 1957-68, professor, 1968-80, Elbert L. Eausett Professor of History, 1980—.

MEMBER: American Historical Association, Organization of American Historians, Southern Historical Association.

WRITINGS:

Arkansas and Reconstruction: The Influence of Geography, Economics, and Personality, Kennikat, 1976.
Member of editorial board, *Faulkner County: Its Land and People,* 1986.

BIOGRAPHICAL/CRITICAL SOURCES:

PERIODICALS

Annals of the American Academy of Political and Social Science, July, 1977.
Journal of American History, June, 1977.

*   *   *

THOMSON, John W(illiam)   1940-

PERSONAL: Born October 8, 1940, in Warren, Ohio; son of John C. and Ruth M. Thomson; divorced. *Education:* Wichita State University, B.Mus., 1963, M.Mus., 1965; University of Missouri—Kansas City, D.Mus., 1968.

ADDRESSES: Home—8201 East Harry, No. 404, Wichita, Kan. 67209. *Office*— Department of Music, Wichita State University, Wichita, Kan. 67208.

CAREER: Free-lance keyboardist in Las Vegas, Nev., 1970-72; Kansas State University, Manhattan, assistant professor of music, 1972-76; Wichita State University, Wichita, Kan., assistant professor, 1976-79, associate professor, 1979-87, professor of music, 1988—. Member of board of directors of Wichita Jazz Festival, Inc., 1980—.

MEMBER: American Society of Composers, Authors, and Publishers, Music Educators National Conference, American Federation of Musicians, National Association of Jazz Educators, Kansas Music Education Association.

WRITINGS:

(With Lowell D. Holmes) *Jazz Greats: Getting Better With Age,* Holmes & Meier, 1986.

WORK IN PROGRESS: A book on jazz studies.

SIDELIGHTS: John W. Thomson told *CA* that his book *Jazz Greats* represents an attempt to explore the relationship between creativity and aging or retirement. The author believes that the creativity factor in jazz has been too often overlooked by other scholars. He continued: "All of the subjects of *Jazz Greats* were 'sidemen' with name musicians of many eras. Sidemen are rarely identified individually, but without them the better-known performers would not have been successful. These are the 'backbone' players with many, many famous band leaders and big names.

"All but one of the musicians I spoke with said they were getting better with age, that is, more creative and willing to take chances, musically speaking. Most felt one had to be creative to adapt to aging. Aging is an ongoing condition, and each was living with that thought. But by continuing to play

and enjoy what they were doing they did not seem to dwell on the aging process."

*   *   *

THORUP, Kirsten   1942-

BRIEF ENTRY: Born February 2, 1942, in Gelsted, Fyn, Denmark. Danish literary consultant and author. Thorup's first work of fiction, *Baby* (Gyldendal, 1973; translation published by Louisiana State University Press, 1980), won a 1980 Pegasus Prize for Literature for being judged the best Danish novel written during the 1970s. The work revolves around six working-class characters whose lives cross in a Copenhagen slum. Using a highly detailed, run-on prose style, Thorup illustrates the degradation that the ghetto dwellers encounter daily, including turning to prostitution to pay the rent and being victimized by serious crime.

Following *Baby* Thorup wrote a trilogy of novels about the coming of age of a young country girl in post-World War II Denmark. The first work, *Lille Jonna* (Gyldendal, 1977), recounts the adolescence of the heroine, Jonna, while the second, *Den lange sommer* (title means "The Long Summer"; Gyldendal, 1979), tells of her move from her provincial surroundings to Copenhagen, where she seeks to forge her own identity. The third novel, *Himmel og helvede* (title means "Heaven and Hell"; Gyldendal, c. 1982), begins in 1968 with a twenty-eight-year-old Jonna narrating the exploits of Maria, an eighteen-year-old girl who unwisely weds a bisexual man and becomes involved with a sadomasochistic young girl before marrying Jonna's brother, a respectable man with a social conscience. Thorup has also written poetry, including *Love in Trieste* (Gyldendal, 1969; Curbstone, 1980), a collection focused on the emotional and sexual interactions of a small group of people. Additionally, she is the author of numerous short stories and television and radio plays, and has worked as a literary consultant for various publishing houses. *Addresses: Home*—Copenhagen, Denmark.

BIOGRAPHICAL/CRITICAL SOURCES:

PERIODICALS

Los Angeles Times Book Review, November 30, 1980.
Times Literary Supplement, January 30, 1981.
World Literature Today, winter, 1981, summer, 1981, winter, 1984.

*   *   *

THROWER, Percy John   1913-1988

OBITUARY NOTICE—See index for *CA* sketch: Born January 30, 1913, in Winslow, Buckinghamshire, England; died March 18, 1988. Gardener, editor, and author. Thrower was a well-known horticulturist who made more than twelve hundred radio broadcasts for the British Broadcasting Corporation (BBC) and appeared more than fifteen hundred times on "Gardening Club," "Gardener's World," and "Blue Peter" television programs. He worked as an apprentice gardener and a journeyman gardener in England from 1927 until around 1940, when he became assistant parks superintendent for the County Borough of Derby. From 1945 to 1976 he was parks superintendent for the Borough of Shrewsbury in Shropshire, England, after which he began his own gardening center. In 1974 he received the Victoria Medal of Honour from the Royal Horticultural Society. Thrower edited his *Encyclopaedia of Gardening* in 1962 and wrote several books on the subject, including *In the Flower Garden With Percy Thrower; In Your Greenhouse With Percy Thrower; Bulbs, Corms, and Tubers for Garden, Greenhouse, and Home; Percy Thrower's How to Grow Vegetables and Fruit;* and, with Ronald Webber, his autobiography *My Lifetime of Gardening.*

OBITUARIES AND OTHER SOURCES:

BOOKS

International Authors and Writers Who's Who, 10th edition, International Biographical Centre, 1986.
Thrower, Percy John and Ronald Webber, *My Lifetime of Gardening,* Hamlyn, 1977.

PERIODICALS

Times (London), March 19, 1988.

*   *   *

TODD, Richard (Killingworth)   1949-

PERSONAL: Born September 6, 1949, in London, England; son of Killingworth Richard (a medical practitioner) and Olive Isobel (a medical practitioner; maiden name, Gray) Todd; married Winifred Kooy (a schoolteacher), November 10, 1978; children: Jennifer Isabel, Marina Alexandra. *Education:* Attended University of Wales, University College of Swansea, 1968-69; University of London, B.A. (with first class honors), 1973, Ph.D., 1977.

ADDRESSES: Home—P. Berghoutlaan 40, 2343 PN Oegstgeest, Netherlands. *Office*—Vrye Universiteit (Letteren), PB 7161, 1007 MC Amsterdam, Netherlands.

CAREER: State University of Leyden, Leyden, Netherlands, research assistant, 1976-77; Free University, Amsterdam, Netherlands, assistant professor, 1977-86, associate professor of English, 1986—. Research fellow at Netherlands Institute for Advanced Study, 1984-85; co-director of plays at Leiden English Speaking Theatre and Free University English Speaking Theatre. Lecturer at Indiana University—Bloomington, 1983, 1984, 1986; University of Nebraska at Lincoln, Louisiana State University, and University of Missouri—Columbia, 1984; and at University of Kansas, University of California, Los Angeles, and University of Michigan—Dearborn, 1986.

MEMBER: Society of Authors, Modern Language Association of America, Renaissance Society of America, Iris Murdoch Society.

WRITINGS:

Iris Murdoch: The Shakespearean Interest, Barnes & Noble, 1979.
(Editor with Jacques B. H. Alblas, and contributor) *From Caxton to Beckett: Essays Presented to W. H. Toppen,* Rodopi, 1979.
Iris Murdoch, Methuen, 1984.
(Contributor) Hedwig Bock and Albert Wertheim, editors, *Essays in Contemporary English Fiction,* Max Hueber, 1985.
The Opacity of Signs: Acts of Interpretation in George Herbert's "The Temple," University of Missouri Press, 1986.
(Contributor) Douwe Fokkema and Hans Bertens, editors, *Approaching Postmodernism,* John Benjamins, 1986.
(Editor) *Encounters With Iris Murdoch,* Free University, 1987.
(Contributor) Matei Calinescu and Fokkema, editors, *Exploring Postmodernism,* John Benjamins, 1987.

(Contributor) Theo D'Haen, Helmut Lethen, and Rainer Gruebel, editors, *Convention and Innovation in European and American Literature,* John Benjamins, 1988.
(Contributor) Theo D'Haen, editor, *Postmodernism Fiction International,* Humanities, 1988.

Contributor to and member of editorial board of *Lexicon of Post-War Literatures in English.* Contributor of articles and reviews to literature journals. Co-founder and editor in chief of *FUSE Quarterly.*

WORK IN PROGRESS: Editing a festschrift for Professor Hans Heinrich Meier, with J. L. Mackenzie, publication by Foris expected in 1989; research on the literature of the English Renaissance, with a special interest in Anglo-Dutch relations; research on the contemporary British novel.

SIDELIGHTS: Richard Todd told *CA:* "I gained a temporary appointment at the State University of Leyden in 1976 and an annual series of temporary appointments at the Free University, Amsterdam, in succeeding years. By 1981, when I received tenure in Amsterdam, I had settled down in the Netherlands both domestically and professionally, to the extent of having learned the language and becoming attracted to the relatively egalitarian way of life. We have no long-term plans to move to Britain, although I visit there quite frequently.

"The field of Anglo-Dutch relations in the sixteenth and seventeenth centuries remains underresearched, and the primary materials are of great interest. Although much of this material is in neo-Latin, I believe that there were also (sometimes less direct) vernacular contacts. I have been interested in possible vernacular influences on the psalm translations of Sir Philip Sidney and the Countess of Pembroke (c. 1594-99) and the implications of these influences for a fuller and more European understanding of the nature of Protestantism in the period. More recently I have embarked on work on national stereotyping during the Anglo-Dutch wars in the period 1652 to 1674, with particular reference to Andrew Marvell's *The Character of Holland* (1653), a work that contains word-play strongly suggesting a more than passing acquaintance with the Dutch language on Marvell's part.

"My study of George Herbert, *The Opacity of Signs,* which was published in 1986, is based on my 1976 dissertation. The chance to rethink and rewrite has clarified both the argument and my own convictions concerning Herbert's reception of Augustinian notions of signification.

"The studies *Iris Murdoch: The Shakespearean Interest* and *Iris Murdoch* were commissioned, and arise out of a long-held conviction that she will be considered one of the major British novelists of the second half of the twentieth century. In particular I am fascinated by a particular paradox in her most interesting work: the intellectual control over structure co-exists with her articulate moral convictions concerning freedom in the novelist's conception of character. In *Iris Murdoch: The Shakespearean Interest* I argue that there is a phase in her work in which we can see her making particularly interesting use of Shakespearean comic form in order to explore this paradox. I was asked to provide a more general, systematic, and chronological account of Murdoch's career for *Iris Murdoch,* but my fascination with that paradox still underlies it, although in this book I try to express it in the more general terms of Murdoch's attainment of a 'strong agile realism' that is uniquely her own. In fact I sense that many novelists writing in Britain at the moment are forced to confront an extraordinarily rich literary tradition, and that existence of the various forms that

that confrontation takes is characteristic of the work of the most interesting of them. To my mind it is here that the most fundamental differences between the practice of fiction in Britain (and indeed Europe) as opposed to that in the United States can be found.''

*   *   *

TONKS, A. Ronald   1934-

PERSONAL: Born May 14, 1934, in Vancouver, British Columbia, Canada; immigrated to United States, 1962; son of Alfred J. (a manager) and Gertrude A. (a teacher; maiden name, Kion) Tonks; married Ann Rodgers Morrison (an editor and writer), June 27, 1958; children: A.R. Douglas, Kenneth J.W., Stephen J.M. *Education:* McGill University, B.A., 1955; McMaster University, B.D., 1958; Southern Baptist Theological Seminary, Th.M., 1964, Ph.D., 1968.

ADDRESSES: Office—Historical Commission, Southern Baptist Convention, 901 Commerce St., Nashville, Tenn. 37203.

CAREER: Indiana Central University (now University of Indianapolis), Indianapolis, assistant professor, 1967-70, associate professor of history, 1970-72; Southern Baptist Convention Historical Commission, Nashville, Tenn., research director, 1972-73, assistant executive director, 1974—.

MEMBER: American Historical Association, American Society of Church History, Southern Baptist Historical Society, Canadian Historical Society.

WRITINGS:

Baptists, Meet Your Past, Broadman, 1975.
Faith, Stars, and Stripes, Broadman, 1976.

Contributor to journals. Associate editor of *Baptist History and Heritage,* 1972—.

*   *   *

TORRE, Raoul della
See MENCKEN, H(enry) L(ouis)

*   *   *

TOSI, Henry L(ouis), Jr.   1936-

PERSONAL: Born November 11, 1936, in Martin's Ferry, Ohio; son of Henry Louis (in insurance business) and Rose M. (a housewife; maiden name, Purpura) Tosi; married Rosemary F. Mondlak (a housewife), November 15, 1958; children: Lisa Ann, M. Kathleen, Jennifer Louise. *Education:* Ohio State University, B.Sc., 1958, M.B.A., 1962, Ph.D., 1964.

ADDRESSES: Home—5902 Southwest 36th Way, Gainesville, Fla. 32608. *Office*—Department of Management, University of Florida, Gainesville, Fla. 32611.

CAREER: Libby, McNeill & Libby, Leipsic, Ohio, supervisor of industrial relations, 1960-61; University of Maryland at College Park, assistant professor of management, 1964-67; Michigan State University, East Lansing, professor of management, 1967-78; University of Florida, Gainesville, professor of management, 1978—, chairman of department, 1978-83. Visiting professor at University of California, Irvine, 1974-75, Cornell University, 1984, and Luigi Bocconi University, 1985; adjunct professor at Emory University, 1987. Member of Scientific Evaluation Panel of National Science Founda-

tion's Productivity Improved Research Group, 1984. *Military service:* U.S. Army, personnel specialist, 1958-60.

MEMBER: Academy of Management (fellow; member of executive committee of Organization Behavior Division, 1973-74, chairman of division, 1977-78; member of board of governors, 1975-77; chairman of Research Methodology Interest Group, 1984-85), Midwest Academy of Management (vice-president, 1971-72; president, 1972-73).

AWARDS, HONORS: Visiting scholar at Western Michigan University, 1969; distinguished management scholar at Grand Valley State College, 1974; grants from National Science Foundation, 1983-86 and 1987-88, and University of Florida/Purdue Center for Software Engineering Research, 1987-89.

WRITINGS:

(Editor with R. J. House and M. D. Dunnette, and contributor) *Managerial Compensation and Motivation,* Division of Research, Graduate School of Business, Michigan State University, 1972.
(With Stephen Carroll) *Management by Objectives: Applications and Research,* Macmillan, 1973.
Readings in Management: Contingencies, Structure, and Process, St. Clair Press, 1976.
(With Carroll) *Management: Contingencies, Structure, and Process,* Wiley, 1982.
(With Jerald Young) *Management: Experiences and Demonstrations,* Irwin, 1982.
Theories of Organization, Wiley, 1983.
(Editor with W. Clay Hamner) *Management and Organizational Behavior: A Contingency Approach,* Grid Publishing, 1985.
(With John Rizzo and Carroll) *Managing Organizational Behavior,* Pitman Publishing, 1986.

Editor of *Journal of Business Research,* fall, 1983; co-editor of *Leadership Quarterly;* member of editorial board of *Business Topics,* 1970-78, *Journal of Business Research,* 1975-78, *Academy of Management Review,* 1976-79, *Journal of Library Administration,* 1980—, and *Administrative Science Quarterly,* 1980-87.

CONTRIBUTOR

R. J. House, editor, *Management Development: Design Implementation and Evaluation,* Bureau of Industrial Relations, University of Michigan, 1967.
F. D. Sturdivant and others, editors, *Perspectives in Marketing Management,* Scott, Foresman, 1971.
Elmer Burack and James Walker, editors, *Manpower Planning and Development,* Allyn & Bacon, 1972.
Kenneth Wexley and Gary Yukl, editors, *Organizational Behavior and Industrial Psychology,* Oxford University Press, 1975.
J. Leslie Livingston, editor, *Managerial Accounting: The Behavioral Foundations,* Grid Publishing, 1975.
Walter R. Nord, editor, *Concepts and Controversy in Organizational Behavior,* 2nd edition, Scott, Foresman, 1976.
John James and John Champion, editors, *Critical Incidents in Management,* R. D. Irwin, 1979.
G. M. Dupy and others, editors, *The Enlightened Manager,* Ginn, 1979.
L. E. Boone and D. D. Bowen, editors, *The Great Writings in Management and Organizational Behavior,* PPC Books, 1981.
M. A. Magala, editor, *Understanding Organization,* Ginn, 1982.

J. G. Hunt and others, editors, *Leadership: Beyond Establishment Views,* Southern Illinois University Press, 1982.

Hunt and J. D. Blair, editors, *Leadership on the Future Battlefield,* Pergamon, 1985.

Craig E. Schneier, Richard Beatty, and Harold McEvoy, editors, *Personnel/Human Resource Management Today,* second edition, 1986.

Luis Gomez and David Balkin, editors, *Issues in Compensation,* Prentice-Hall, 1987.

Contributor of more than sixty articles and reviews to personnel and management journals.

WORK IN PROGRESS: Worker Adaptation to New Technologies and Management Practice, publication expected in 1988; *Organizations: An Integrative Model of Structure, Strategy, and Processes,* publication expected in 1988.

*   *   *

TRAVERS, Scott A(ndrew)   1961-

PERSONAL: Born November 12, 1961, in New York, N.Y.; son of Harvey Charles (a chemical engineer) and Barbara (a real estate broker; maiden name, Goldman) Travers. *Education:* Brandeis University, B.A., 1983.

ADDRESSES: Office—Scott Travers Rare Coin Galleries, Inc., FDR Box 1711, New York, N.Y. 10150. *Agent*—Arnold I. Rady, Morgan, Finnegan, Pine, Foley & Lee, 345 Park Ave., New York, N.Y. 10154.

CAREER: Musical Coin Co., New York, N.Y., founder and chairman, 1976-81; Scott Travers Rare Coin Galleries, Inc., New York, N.Y., founder and chairman of board of directors, 1981—, founder of Travers Financial Group and administrator of Scott Travers Elite Collector Program. Organizer of Numismatic Authors' Symposium, 1985; member of board of governors of Institute of Numismatic and Philatelic Studies, Adelphi University, 1980—; state adviser to U.S. Congressional Advisory Board, 1983—; founder of Coin Collector's Survival Conferences, 1984—; charter member of panel of advisers of *Who's Who in Numismatics.* Guest on television and radio programs, including "Good Morning America" and "Saturday Morning Live."

MEMBER: Numismatics International, International Association for Financial Planning, International Banknote Society, American Numismatic Association, Numismatic Literary Guild, American Israel Numismatic Association, Central States Numismatic Society, New England Numismatic Association, Great Eastern Numismatic Association (member of advisory council, 1977—), Michigan State Numismatic Society, Texas Numismatic Association, Florida United Numismatists, Authors Guild.

AWARDS, HONORS: American Numismatic Association, named "outstanding young numismatist," 1978, Melissa Van Grover Exhibit Award, 1978-79, Ray Byrne Literary Award, 1979, for article "Coins Under the Lights"; Roethke Memorial Award from Michigan State Numismatic Society, 1980, for article "The Numismatist and the Magnifying Glass"; book of the year award from Numismatic Literary Guild, 1984, for *The Coin Collector's Survival Manual.*

WRITINGS:

The Coin Collector's Survival Manual, Prentice-Hall, 1984.
The Rare Coin Investment Strategy, Prentice-Hall, 1986.

Contributor to magazines and newspapers, including *Numismatic News, Numismatist,* and *Swiatek Numismatic Report.* Contributing editor of *COINage.*

WORK IN PROGRESS: How to Make a Fortune From Your Pocket Change.

SIDELIGHTS: Scott A. Travers told *CA:* "The future is the primary consideration of everything I write. Vision, commitment, and moral responsibility should go into planning for the future. I believe in tomorrow. I view the future as a time of potential richness and vitality, and the present as a time of potential opportunity or a time to encourage constructive change. But in order to make the most everlasting and significant changes, you have to stand up and be heard. You should not expect to see beneficial results if you don't create the environment in which they can be achieved.

"When I wrote *The Coin Collector's Survival Manual,* I knew that some other coin dealers might not like my strong consumer protection thrust. But I have a stake in the future. I want to see the coin industry prosper and refine its practices through the next generation and beyond. Although there might have been a few things revealed that a select few didn't want revealed, in the long run, public knowledge of this information will make for a stronger coin field.

"Only through the revealing of information will the coin field have a solid future. These revelations, however, must be made in a supportive and constructive environment.

"In writing *The Rare Coin Investment Strategy,* the future of the reader was a crucial consideration. I wanted to tell him or her exactly how to get the best values possible, as well as how to plan for and finance the next generation. I gave practical advice, as well as some philosophical insights.

"I want my writings to help people to think about tomorrow. Too many people are caught in the maze of yesterday's world. Too many people only think about the here-and-now and are willing to let the future fall to happenstance. If I move even one reader to active thinking and planning about what tomorrow might bring, I will have achieved a success. I do not, however, try to instill my points of view. I present objective information and let the reader decide. The best writing is that which shows, not that which tells."

BIOGRAPHICAL/CRITICAL SOURCES:

PERIODICALS

Coin World, August 29, 1984, December 5, 1984, January 30, 1985.
Numismatic News, February 26, 1985.

*   *   *

TREGOE, Benjamin B., Jr.   1927-

PERSONAL: Born December 23, 1927, in San Francisco, Calif.; son of Benjamin B. and Marianne W. Tregoe; married Jeannette S. Gill, August 4, 1956; children: Cynthia, Elizabeth, Benjamin. *Education:* Whittier College, A.B., 1951; Harvard University, Ph.D., 1957.

ADDRESSES: Office—Kepner, Tregoe, Inc., Box 704, Research Rd., Princeton, N.J. 08540.

CAREER: Rand Corp., Santa Monica, Calif., associate social scientist in social psychology, 1955-57; Systems Development Corp., Santa Monica, associate social scientist in social psychology, 1957-58; Kepner, Tregoe, Inc., Princeton, N.J., president, 1958—. Lecturer at University of California, Los Angeles, 1957-58, and University of Southern California, 1957. *Military service:* U.S. Marine Corps, 1947-48.

MEMBER: American Sociological Association.

WRITINGS:

(With Charles H. Kepner) *The Rational Manager: A Systematic Approach to Problem Solving and Decision Making,* McGraw, 1965, 2nd edition, 1976.
(With John W. Zimmerman) *Top Management Strategy: What It Is and How to Make It Work,* Simon & Schuster, 1980.
The New Rational Manager, Princeton Research Press, 1981.

Contributor to business journals.

WORK IN PROGRESS: A book on strategy implementation.

* * *

TRIMBALL, W. H.
   See MENCKEN, H(enry) L(ouis)

* * *

TRISTRAM
   See HOUSMAN, A(lfred) E(dward)

* * *

TROST, Cathy   1951-

PERSONAL: Born March 29, 1951, in Kansas City, Mo.; daughter of Cecil (an auto executive) and Merrilee (a record promoter; maiden name, Buck) Trost; married Paul Magnusson (a journalist), January 1, 1984. *Education:* Michigan State University, B.A., 1973.

ADDRESSES: Home—Washington, D.C. *Office*—*Wall Street Journal,* 1025 Connecticut Ave. N.W., Washington, D.C. 20036. *Agent*—Rafe Sagalyn, 2813 Bellevue Terr., Washington, D.C. 20007.

CAREER: United Press International (UPI), reporter in Detroit, Mich., 1973-75 and San Francisco, Calif., 1975-77; *Detroit Free Press,* Detroit, reporter, 1977-81; editor of *APF Reporter,* quarterly publication of the Alicia Patterson Foundation, 1982-84; *Wall Street Journal,* Washington, D.C., reporter, 1984—.

AWARDS, HONORS: Award from Michigan UPI and from Detroit Press Club for feature writing for story on the effects of television on Michigan families, both 1978; award from Michigan Associated Press and from Michigan UPI for breaking news for story on Vietnamese refugees, both 1979; Alicia Patterson Foundation fellow, 1981.

WRITINGS:

Elements of Risk: The Chemical Industry and Its Threat to America, Times Books, 1984.

SIDELIGHTS: In *Elements of Risk,* reporter Cathy Trost examines the public health controversy in the United States over certain chemical products that have been linked to cancer and other illnesses. The book focuses on two powerful chemicals formerly manufactured by the Dow Chemical Company, the herbicide 2,4,5-T and the parasitic worm killer DBCP. Trost follows two lawsuits filed against Dow by residents of Globe, Arizona, who were exposed to spraying of the dioxin-contam-

inated 2,4,5-T, and workers at a California plant processing DBCP. She allows both the company and the plaintiffs to state their cases in extensive interviews and quotes. The Environmental Protection Agency banned DBCP in 1979, the author notes, and ultimately Dow settled the cases out of court, voluntarily withdrawing 2,4,5-T from the market in 1983 under intense public pressure.

In a *Washington Post* review, Carol Van Strum questioned what she described as Trost's "nearly exclusive focus on these particular lawsuits . . . at the expense of other significant events that likely contributed to Dow's sudden about-face." Among these, Strum noted the impending Vietnam veterans' lawsuit over health problems allegedly caused by Agent Orange defoliant containing dioxin, and litigation by the EPA over pollution in Midland, Michigan, the location of Dow's home plant. The *Post* critic found Trost's survey of the origin and growth of Dow Chemical "a fascinating study of the political and social ramifications of unfettered industrial expansion," however. Overall Strum judged *Elements of Risk* "an informative study of corporate behavior, dramatizing the conflict between corporate and individual rights."

BIOGRAPHICAL/CRITICAL SOURCES:

PERIODICALS

Washington Post, September 11, 1984.

* * *

TSAI, Shih-shan Henry   1940-

PERSONAL: Surname is pronounced "Chai"; born February 1, 1940, in Chia-yi, Taiwan; immigrated to United States, naturalized citizen, 1978; son of A-tsou (a farmer) and Kuei-chi (a housewife; maiden name, Li) Tsai; married Hsiu-chaun Sonia Chang (a research associate), March 29, 1971; children: Shirley, Rocky. *Education:* National Taiwan Normal University, B.A., 1962; University of Oregon, M.A., 1967, Ph.D., 1970.

ADDRESSES: Home—2105 Austin Dr., Fayetteville, Ark. 72703. *Office*—Department of History, University of Arkansas, Fayetteville, Ark. 72701.

CAREER: National Taiwan University, Taipei, Taiwan, visiting associate professor, 1970-71; University of Arkansas, Fayetteville, assistant professor, 1971-76, associate professor, 1976-83, professor of history and chair of Asian studies, 1983-88. Served on editorial board of *Amerasia* journal, 1976-85; University of California, Los Angeles, visiting associate professor, 1979, postdoctoral fellow, 1982; visiting associate professor at University of California, Berkeley, 1981.

MEMBER: Chinese Historical Society of America, Asian Studies Association, Chinese Historical Society, Southwestern Conference on Asian Studies.

AWARDS, HONORS: Grants from Chinese Science Foundation, 1974-75, Arkansas Endowment for the Humanities, 1980, and South Seas Society of Singapore, 1984.

WRITINGS:

Hsi-yang shih-hsueh shih (title means "Western Historiography"), National Institute for Compilation and Translation, Taipei, 1975.
China and Overseas Chinese in the United States, 1868-1911, University of Arkansas Press, 1983.

The Chinese Experience in America, Indiana University Press, 1986.

Contributor of articles to journals in his field, including *Amerasia, Pacific Historical Review, Historian, American Studies,* and *Asian Profile*.

WORK IN PROGRESS: Research on eunuchs in Ming China.

SIDELIGHTS: Shih-shan Tsai told *CA:* "I submitted my first article for publication when I was in high school and got my first royalty. As an undergraduate in college I earned a little spending money by writing short stories and by translating English into Chinese. I continue to write miscellaneous essays for Chinese-language magazines and newspapers."

AVOCATIONAL INTERESTS: "I love to travel and play tennis."

*   *   *

TSE, K. K.   1948-

PERSONAL: Born September 10, 1948, in Hong Kong; son of Lo Pak (a teacher) and Pak Ling (a housewife; maiden name, Tang) Tse; married Helen Cheng (a teacher), September 7, 1974. *Education:* Chinese University of Hong Kong, B.Soc.Sci., 1974; Victoria University of Manchester, M.A., 1975, Ph.D., 1978; Cranfield School of Management, M.B.A., 1982.

ADDRESSES: Home—5 Hatten Rd., 10th Floor, Flat C1, Wisdom Court, Hong Kong. *Office*—11/F Harbour Crystal Centre, 100 Granville Rd., Tsimshatsui, Kowloon, Hong Kong.

CAREER: Lam Soon (Hong Kong) Ltd., Hong Kong, personnel manager, 1979-81; Shui On Group, Hong Kong, assistant general manager of human resources, 1982-86; Shui On Group, Hong Kong, Pat Davie Ltd., executive director, 1986—. Member of Hong Kong Government Social Work Training Advisory Board, 1985—, and Criminal and Law Enforcement Injuries Compensation boards, 1986—.

MEMBER: Hong Kong Management Association, Hong Kong Society of Training and Development, Hong Kong Industrial Relations Association, Association of Hong Kong Scholars, Institute of Personnel Management, Association of Experts for Modernization (secretary general, 1985-86).

WRITINGS:

(With S. L. Wong, K. C. Shek, and wife, Helen Cheng) *At What Cost: Instruction Through the English Medium in Hong Kong Schools*, privately printed, 1973.
Marks & Spencer: Anatomy of Britain's Most Efficiently Managed Company, Pergamon, 1985.
Quality Circles: A New Challenge for Enterprise Management, Commercial Press, 1986.

Contributor to periodicals. Member of editorial board of *Hong Kong Manager*.

WORK IN PROGRESS: A book on human resources development, aimed at the Hong Kong and Mainland China market.

SIDELIGHTS: K. K. Tse told *CA:* "The book on Marks & Spencer is extremely important to me. I am not interested simply in publishing the book, but in the active promotion of an idea that I feel will be of tremendous relevance to Hong Kong and China. In the book I analyze Marks & Spencer's unique and very progressive management policy, which has been successful in providing a crucial link between mass manufacturing and mass retailing. It is my conviction that Hong Kong should play the critical role of linking the world market with the manufacturing hinterland of China, and, in this respect, Marks & Spencer's experience can provide much valuable insight.

"Apart from the English edition of the book, I have already published more than a dozen articles on the subject in Hong Kong and Mainland China in order to promote my idea. The Chinese edition of the book will be widely read inside China, and I hope that it can create a major impact on the Chinese managerial cadres. I have also given numerous talks on the subject to local businessmen, as well as management cadres across the border. Over the next decade, I will be spending much effort in my spare time to have my idea accepted and put into practice."

BIOGRAPHICAL/CRITICAL SOURCES:

PERIODICALS

Times Literary Supplement, May 31, 1985.

*   *   *

TUFTE, Virginia J(ames)   1918-

PERSONAL: Born August 19, 1918, in Meadow Grove, Neb.; daughter of M. D. and Sarah Elizabeth (Bartee) James; married Edward E. Tufte, 1940; children: Edward R. *Education:* University of Nebraska, A.B., 1944; Arizona State University, M.A., 1950; University of California, Los Angeles, M.A., 1962, Ph.D., 1964.

ADDRESSES: Office—Department of English, University of Southern California, University Park, Los Angeles, Calif. 90089.

CAREER: University of Southern California, Los Angeles, assistant professor, 1964-69, associate professor, 1969-74, professor of English, 1974—. Fellow of William Andrews Clark Memorial Library, 1963-64.

MEMBER: Modern Language Association of America, Renaissance Society of America, Phi Beta Kappa.

WRITINGS:

Transformational Grammar: A Guide for Teachers, English Language Service, 1968.
(Editor) *High Wedlock Then Be Honoured: Wedding Poems From Nineteen Countries and Twenty-five Centuries*, Viking, 1970.
The Poetry of Marriage: The Epithalamium in Europe and Its Development in England, University of Southern California Studies in Comparative Literature, 1970.
Grammar as Style, Holt, 1971.
(With Garrett Stewart) *Grammar as Style: Exercises in Creativity*, Holt, 1971.
(Editor with Barbara Myerhoff) *Changing Images of the Family*, Yale University Press, 1979.

Contributor to literature and philology journals.

WORK IN PROGRESS: Visualizing "Paradise Lost": Illustrations of Milton's Epic From Four Centuries, with Wendy Furman.

*   *   *

TUGGLE, Ann Montgomery   1942-

PERSONAL: Born February 26, 1942, in Plainfield, Ill.;

daughter of Leo F. and Lois (Grieff) Kelly. *Education:* Illinois State University, B.S. (cum laude), 1964; Rosary College, M.A.L.S., 1968.

ADDRESSES: Home—29W250 Gary's Mill Rd., West Chicago, Ill. 60185. *Office*—P.O. Box 431, LaGrange, Ill. 60525.

CAREER: District media coordinator for schools in Plainfield, Ill., 1968-78; in-service training specialist in special education for public schools in LaGrange, Ill., 1978-80; district media coordinator for public elementary schools in West Chicago, Ill., 1981-85; Glenbard East High School, Lombard, Ill., chairperson of library media services department, 1985—. Copublisher of *Library Insights, Promotion, and Programs;* past member of Illinois State Library Media Advisory Committee. President of West Chicago Cable Communications Foundation, 1982-85; West Chicago Chamber of Commerce, member of board of directors, 1984, vice-president, 1985.

MEMBER: American Library Association, American Association of School Libraries, Library Administration and Management Association (past chairman of Publications Committee of Public Relations Section), Illinois Library Association (past member of board of directors; past chairperson of Public Relations Committee), Illinois Association for Media in Education (past member of board of directors).

AWARDS, HONORS: Grolier Award for Public Relations from Illinois Library Association, 1976, for Librarians to the People speakers bureau.

WRITINGS:

(Contributor) Kathleen Kelly Rummel and Esther Perica, editors, *Persuasive Public Relations for Libraries,* American Library Association, 1983.
(With Dawn Hansen Heller) *Grand Schemes and Nitty Gritty Details: Library PR That Works,* Libraries Unlimited, 1987.
(With Heller) *Winning Ideas From Winning Schools: Reorganizing Excellence,* ABC-CLIO, 1988.

Contributor to library journals. Co-editor of *Illinois Libraries,* 1978.

WORK IN PROGRESS: A book about application of video production in library settings, publication by Libraries Unlimited expected in 1988.

SIDELIGHTS: Ann Montgomery Tuggle told *CA:* "Library public relations have been sadly neglected for a long time. Librarians assume everyone will see and appreciate their good work, but they need to reach out to a larger audience. Since 1978 I have worked in this field, gaining experience by practical application. My workshops, seminars, and consulting and production work for clients convince me that a strong library program is one that considers the ramifications of everything that is done on the people who are served. It's not enough to just be good; you have to tell someone.

"While library public relations are my primary concern, I also hope to write a novel—a poor man's 'Dallas' based on my personal observations. Fiction is another facet of writing I want to explore."

*   *   *

TULL, Delena   1950-

PERSONAL: Born July 29, 1950, in Chicago, Ill.; daughter of William (an engineer) and Delena (a nurse; maiden name, Nimmo) Tull; married George Oxford Miller (a photographer

and writer), February 24, 1980; stepchildren: Koda, Heather. *Education:* University of Texas at Austin, B.A., 1972, doctoral study, 1981-84, 1986—; Michigan State University, M.S., 1975. *Religion:* Baha'i faith.

ADDRESSES: Home—314 Smith Ln., San Marcos, Tex. 78666.

CAREER: Fenner Arboretum Nature Center, Lansing, Mich., interpretive naturalist, 1972-75; owner of a house painting business, 1975-77; Austin Natural Science Center, Austin, Tex., interpretive naturalist, program coordinator, and plant specialist, 1977-80; Austin Community College, Austin, member of natural sciences faculty, 1980-83; writer, 1983—. Conducts workshops for science teachers and nature centers; public speaker.

MEMBER: National Association for Research in Science Teaching, National Audubon Society, Nature Conservancy, Science Teachers Association of Texas, Texas Native Plant Society, Kappa Delta Pi, Phi Delta Kappa.

WRITINGS:

(With husband, George Oxford Miller) *Texas Parks and Campgrounds,* two volumes, Texas Monthly, 1984.
A Practical Guide to Edible and Useful Plants: Including Recipes, Harmful Plants, Natural Dyes, and Textile Fibers, Texas Monthly, 1987.
(With Miller) *A Field Guide to Texas Wildflowers, Trees, and Shrubs,* Texas Monthly, in press.

Author of "Wild Plant Notebook," a weekly column in *San Marcos Daily Record,* 1986-87. Contributor to magazines, including *Texas Gardener, Mother Earth News,* and *Texas Parks and Wildlife.*

WORK IN PROGRESS: Research on the botanical classifications and concepts of sixth-grade students.

SIDELIGHTS: Delena Tull told *CA:* "My career as a writer developed out of a career as a naturalist or environmental interpreter. My writing has fallen into two categories: that of interpreting the natural world for the lay person, as exemplified by my books, and that of journalistic reporting on human and environmental issues. Upon completion of my doctoral degree in science education, I plan to resume teaching college courses in botany, ecology, and environmental science education, and to conduct research in education. I also plan to be involved in curriculum writing for schools and nature centers.

"As a member of the Baha'i faith, service to humanity and promotion of the unity of humankind are important, lifelong goals. I consider my writing and teaching as natural tools for achieving those goals. I am interested in using my skills to assist in educational and economic development projects, both in the United States and abroad."

*   *   *

TURPIN, Waters Edward   1910-1968

PERSONAL: Born April 9, 1910, in Oxford, Md.; died November 19, 1968; son of Mary Rebecca Henry (a household manager and cook); married Jean Fisher, 1936. *Education:* Morgan College (now Morgan State University), B.A.; Columbia University, M.A., Ph.D.

CAREER: Served as a welfare investigator for the Works Progress Administration in the early 1930s; Storer College, Harper's Ferry, W. Va., professor and football coach, beginning in 1935; Lincoln University, Lincoln University, Pa., professor of English, 1940-49; Morgan State College (now Morgan State University), Baltimore, Md., professor, 1949-68.

AWARDS, HONORS: Rosenwald Fellowship in creative writing, 1941.

WRITINGS:

These Low Grounds (novel), Harper, 1937, McGrath, 1969.
O Canaan! (novel), Doubleday, 1939, AMS Press, 1975.
"Let the Day Perish" (play), first produced in Baltimore, Md., at Morgan State College (now Morgan State University), March 21, 1950.
"Saint Michaels Dawn" (two-act play), first produced in Baltimore at the Little Theater, Morgan State College (now Morgan State University) Christian Center, May 2, 1956.
(Author of lyrics) "Li'l Joe" (opera), first produced in Baltimore at the Chick Webb Memorial Recreation Center, Dunbar High School, May 11, 1957.
The Rootless (novel), Vantage Press, 1957.
(With Nick Aaron Ford) *Basic Skills for Better Writing: A Guide and Practice Book for Those Who Intend to Master the Essentials of Good English*, Putnam, 1959.
(Editor with Ford) *Extending Horizons: Selected Readings for Cultural Enrichment*, Random House, 1969.

Also author of "Long Way Home," a novel left unfinished at time of death. Contributor of short stories and articles to periodicals, including *Morgan State College Bulletin* and *Negro History Bulletin*.

SIDELIGHTS: Waters Edward Turpin was labeled the "progenitor of the Afro-American saga" by Burney Hollis in the *Dictionary of Literary Biography*. Paving the way for authors such as Alex Haley, who chronicled the history of one black family from pre-slavery days in Africa in his best-selling *Roots*, Turpin is best remembered for two of his novels: *These Low Grounds*, praised by reviewer Augusta Tucker in the *New York Times* for its "remarkable and just and fair balance," and *O Canaan!*, lauded as "a realistic and revealing picture of the way of his people" by F. T. March critiquing for the same periodical. Turpin was known to have envisioned a set of five novels concerning different generations of the same family, which would have explored the experience of black people in America from the time of the American Revolution to the 1930s, but his career as an educator and his involvement in other writing projects allowed him to complete only three of the books before his death in 1968.

Turpin's commitment to featuring black experience in his historical novels was formed at an early age, according to Hollis. As a boy growing up in Oxford, Maryland, he enjoyed listening to his maternal grandfather's stories of heroic local blacks "who fought and died for their freedom—the stuff of which legends are made," in Hollis's words. When Turpin was older and was attending secondary school at Morgan Academy, his mother took a job as household manager and cook for novelist Edna Ferber, famed for books such as *Show Boat* and *Cimarron*. Visiting his mother in Ferber's home on weekends and holidays, Turpin became the author's protege. Ferber allowed him the use of her library, introduced him to her acquaintances in the publishing field, and discussed with him whatever writing she was doing at the time. Reported Hollis: "Turpin detected the absence in her writing of black achievers whom he saw as equivalent to the American white frontier pioneers about whom she was writing. . . . [This] fueled his growing determination to tell the story of black pioneers, no less valiant,

adventuresome, or successful than those whom Ferber had immortalized."

Turpin showed his first effort towards this goal, *These Low Grounds*, to Ferber, who praised the manuscript and arranged to send it to its eventual publisher, Harper. Set primarily in eastern Maryland, the novel details four generations of the Prince family, beginning with Martha, whom the Civil War freed from slavery. Martha's descendants rise in social status from lifetime to lifetime, making transitions from bondage to domestic service, farming, and teaching. Though *These Low Grounds* was generally well received by both black and white critics, many objected to what Hollis described as "the overly ambitious scope of [Turpin's] first novel—its having attempted to trace rather sketchily four generations of a family in the confines of 350 pages."

O Canaan!, Turpin's second novel, focuses on the city of Chicago rather than eastern Maryland. Concerning the migration of many southern blacks to a Chicago seen as the biblical promised land of Canaan in the early twentieth century, the book recounts the trials and triumphs of both the Prince family from *These Low Grounds* and the Benson family. The prosperity experienced by blacks who built on the city's south side, the devastation brought by the Great Depression, and the determination of characters like Joe Benson to recover from the ensuing state of disadvantage are all chronicled by Turpin. Hollis declared that "the heroes of *O Canaan* are of mythical and biblical stature, and, more than a family chronicle, the novel is a black odyssey with a hero whose fighting spirit is equal to that of Ulysses." Other critics, such as R. A. Chace in the *Boston Transcript*, found the characters' realism to be more important than their larger-than-life qualities. "More than anything else," Chace argued, "the reader will recognize the common humanity of these people."

In his next effort towards his planned pentology, *The Rootless*, Turpin went backwards in chronology to the time of the American Revolution. The story revolves around the ancestor of the Prince family, a man born on a Maryland slave ship. He grows up and gradually realizes that he is willing to pay any price, even death, to gain his freedom. *The Rootless* also focuses on a family of Maryland slaveowners and, through the characters of Louisa and Mariah Shannon, "debunks, without apology or maudlin sentimentality, the myth of the purity of the southern belle," according to Hollis. More condemnatory of the ways in which whites shaped the black experience than Turpin's previous novels, *The Rootless* was unable to find itself a publisher for many years. Unwilling to soften the content of his novel merely to see it in print, Turpin decided to publish it himself in 1957, about ten years after he finished it. Due to the limited circulation of vanity press publications, there was little critical reaction to *The Rootless*.

Turpin took time out from his projected five-novel set to begin another book to which he gave the tentative title "Long Way Home." Dealing more directly with a theme that had been a strong undercurrent in the Prince family sagas, that of the black woman being forced into a matriarchal role, "Long Way Home" features a heroine named Ella Winters. Ella is pushed into a strange dual role—she becomes the leader of her own family while serving as a domestic laborer for a white family. Centered more firmly on one character than any of his previous books, "Long Way Home" has "considerable thematic and technical integrity and shows promise of being Turpin's best novel," judged Hollis.

Due to shifting priorities and interests, Turpin completed only two sections of "Long Way Home." In addition to collaborating with Nick Aaron Ford on the nonfiction works *Basic Skills for Better Writing* and *Extending Horizons,* Turpin also began to write plays. His first, "Let the Day Perish," takes its title from the biblical story of Job and concerns the hardships of a black family living in Harlem during the Great Depression. Though, as Hollis points out, the play ends on a note of determination and survival, it does not emphasize achievement and success as do Turpin's novels. Another of Turpin's dramas, "Saint Michaels Dawn," portrays the adolescence of famed black lecturer and writer Frederick Douglass.

BIOGRAPHICAL/CRITICAL SOURCES:

BOOKS

Dictionary of Literary Biography, Volume 51: *Afro-American Writers From the Harlem Renaissance to 1940,* Gale, 1987.

PERIODICALS

Boston Transcript, August 19, 1939.
New York Times, September 26, 1937, July 16, 1939.*

—*Sketch by Elizabeth Thomas*

*   *   *

TUTU, Desmond M(pilo)   1931-

PERSONAL: Born October 7, 1931, in Klerksdorp, Witwatersrand, Transvaal, South Africa; son of Zachariah (a school teacher), and Aletta (a domestic servant) Tutu; married Leah Nomalizo Shenxane, July 2, 1955; children: Trevor Thamsanqa, Theresa Thandeka, Naomi Nontombi, Mpho Andrea. *Education:* Bantu Normal College, Pretoria, South Africa, teacher's diploma, 1953; University of South Africa, Johannesburg, B.A., 1954; St. Peter's Theological College, Johannesburg, L.Th., 1960; King's College, London, B.D., 1965, M.Th., 1966.

ADDRESSES: Home—Bishopscourt, Claremont, Cape Province 7700, South Africa. *Office*—c/o Diocesan Office, P.O. Box 1131, Johannesburg 2000, South Africa.

CAREER: Teacher at high schools in Johannesburg, South Africa, 1954-55, and in Krugersdorp, South Africa, 1955-58; ordained as deacon, 1960, and Anglican priest, 1961; St. Alban's Church, Benoni, Johannesburg, curate, 1960-61; St. Mary's Cathedral, Johannesburg, priest, 1961; St. Philip's Church, Alberton, Transvaal, South Africa, curate, 1961-62; St. Alban's Church, Golders Green, London, England, part-time curate, 1962-65; St. Mary's Church, Bletchingley, Surrey, England, part-time curate, 1965-66; lecturer at Federal Theological Seminary, Alice, Cape Province, South Africa, 1967-69; lecturer in theology at University of Botswana, Lesotho, and Swaziland, 1970-72; World Council of Churches' Theological Education Fund, Bromley, Kent, England, associate director, 1972-75; St. Augustine's Church, Grove Park, Kent, England, curate, 1972-75; dean of Johannesburg, Johannesburg, 1975-76; bishop of Lesotho, South Africa, 1976-78; general secretary of South African Council of Churches, 1978-85; assistant Anglican bishop of Johannesburg, 1978-85, bishop, 1984-86; St. Augustine's Parish, Soweto, South Africa, rector, 1981-85; archbishop of Cape Town and Anglican primate of southern Africa, 1986—; social reformer and political activist.

Chaplain at University of Fort Hare, 1967-69; visiting professor at General Theological Seminary, New York, N.Y., 1984;

Richard Feetham Academic Freedom Lecture, University of the Witwatersrand, Johannesburg, 1985. Participant at several international conferences, including the "Salvation Today" conference, Bangkok, Thailand, Anglican Consultative Council, Port of Spain, Trinidad, and the World Council of Churches' 6th Assembly, Vancouver, Canada, 1983. Trustee of Phelps Stoke Fund.

MEMBER: National Association for the Advancement of Colored People.

AWARDS, HONORS: Fellow of King's College, London, 1978; Prix d'Athene from Onassis Foundation, 1980; designated member of International Social Prospects Academy, 1983; Family of Man Gold Medal Award, 1983; Martin Luther King, Jr., Humanitarian Award, 1984; Nobel Peace Prize from Norwegian Nobel Committee, 1984, for "role as unifying leader . . . in the campaign to resolve the problem of apartheid in South Africa"; Sam Ervin Free Speech Award, 1985. Recipient of numerous honorary doctoral degrees, including LL.D. from Harvard University, 1979, D.Th. from Ruhr University, and D.D. from Aberdeen University, 1984.

WRITINGS:

Crying in the Wilderness, Eerdmans, 1982.
Hope and Suffering: Sermons and Speeches, [Johannesburg], 1983, revised edition, edited by William B. Eerdmans, Eerdmans, 1984.
(Author of foreword) Omar Badsha, editor, *South Africa: The Cordoned Heart,* Gallery Press, 1986.
(Contributor) Buti Tlhagale and Itumeleng Mosala, editors, *Hammering Swords Into Ploughshares: Essays in Honor of Archbishop Mpilo Desmond Tutu,* Eerdmans, 1987.

Also author of several articles and reviews.

SIDELIGHTS: As archbishop of Capetown, leader of the Anglican Church in southern Africa, and one of the world's foremost black critics of South Africa's apartheid government, Desmond M. Tutu is "nothing if not impassioned," wrote Joshua Hammer in *People* magazine. "Like all great preachers, his every speech and press conference is a blaze of emotion, his every gesture a drop of oil fueling the oratorical fire. Waving his arms, punching the air like a boxer, the elfin . . . figure draws in his followers with a stream of whispers, shouts and sobs, punctuated with roars of laughter." Yet until he received the Nobel Peace Prize in 1984, Tutu was little known outside his native South Africa.

During the 1970s and into the 1980s, first as general secretary of the South African Council of Churches, then as bishop of Johannesburg, and later as archbishop of Capetown, Tutu has campaigned vigorously for the abolition of apartheid, South Africa's system of government that defines and allocates political power and privileges to different groups of people on the basis of skin color and ethnic background. The vast majority of non-South African political commentators see apartheid as a means of keeping political power in the hands of South African whites—some five million people who constitute fifteen percent of the country's total population. The system does this, critics say, by designating South African blacks as "citizens" of specified areas called independent homelands. The government keeps the black population within each homeland below the total number of whites in South Africa, thus establishing an arbitrarily defined white "majority." Since 1948, when apartheid became official policy of the newly elected National party, the South African government has forced more than four million blacks to relocate to the homelands. Those allowed to remain near white-designated areas live in run-down townships segregated from the whites, and the blacks wishing to work in white areas must apply for a government permit to do so. Incomes average one-sixth of those received by whites for the same job; these black workers are also required to live in single-sexed hostels during the week, leaving their families in the homelands. Despite policy changes made by the government of President Pieter W. Botha, which lifted the ban on interracial marriages and enfranchised people of Asian and mixed descent, black South Africans are still denied the right to vote. It is against these forms of discrimination—economic and racial—that Archbishop Tutu stands.

Tutu's first recollections of the apartheid system in operation came when he was growing up in the western Transvaal mining town of Klerksdorp. He told Marc Cooper and Greg Goldin of *Rolling Stone* that the constant racial taunts of the white boys were not "thought to be out of the ordinary," but as he got older he "began finding things eating away at [him]." Recalling one incident in which he heard his father referred to as "boy," Tutu remarked, "I knew there wasn't a great deal I could do, but it just left me churned. . . . What he must have been feeling . . . being humiliated in the presence of his son. Apartheid has always been the same systematic racial discrimination: it takes away your human dignity and rubs it in the dust and tramples it underfoot." Young Tutu also witnessed the harsh economic realities of the government's discriminatory policies while attending the local school. The white children, for whom the government had arranged free school meals, disliked the institutional food and threw it away, preferring to eat what their mothers packed for them. Many black school children of poor families, recalled Tutu, were reduced to scavenging in the cafeteria's rubbish bins for food during lunch periods.

In 1943 the Tutu family moved to Johannesburg where Desmond's father continued to teach and his mother worked as a cook at a missionary school for the blind. The new surroundings greatly affected young Tutu. Not only was he deeply moved by the dedication and service shown by staff members to the children in the school where his mother worked, but it was here that he first met Father Trevor Huddleston, who became his most influential mentor and friend. A leading British critic of South Africa's apartheid system, Huddleston served as the parish priest in Sophiatown, a black slum district of Johannesburg. In an interview with the *Observer,* Tutu recalled his first meeting with the priest: "I was standing with my mother one day, when this white man in a cassock walked past and doffed his big black hat to her. I couldn't believe it—a white man raising his hat to a simple black labouring woman." Huddleston, who was beginning to build an international reputation as an outspoken opponent of apartheid and whom the South African authorities recognized as one of their most controversial critics, became a close friend of Tutu. When the young African contracted tuberculosis as a teenager and was hospitalized for almost twenty months, Huddleston visited him nearly every day. "Like many people, I came under the spell of Trevor Huddleston. I will never forget his compassion, caring, love and deep spirituality," Tutu told *People* reporters Peter Hawthorne and Dawn Clayton. The impact of Huddleston's friendship on Tutu's later life was immense.

Following full recovery from tuberculosis, Tutu resumed his education, and entered the School of Medicine at Witwatersrand University with the intention of becoming a doctor. When his family could no longer afford the tuition fees, however, he was forced to drop out of medical school and begin training as a teacher instead. Tutu received his B.A. from the University of Johannesburg in 1954 and taught high school in Johannesburg and Krugersdorp until 1957. It was then that Tutu's previous experiences with apartheid and the compassion he felt for his fellow man combined to change and redirect what might otherwise have been an uneventful career. While teaching at Munsieville High School in Krugersdorp, the South African government announced plans to introduce a state-run system of education especially intended for students in black districts. Limiting both the quality and extent of education, the system was considered by many to be deliberately second-rate. Tutu, along with several of his colleagues, found the plan ubiquitous and resigned. As a young man newly married, without a job, and sensing a growing urge to serve his community and country, Tutu, in retrospect, said he felt as if God had grabbed him by the scruff of his neck and, whether it was convenient or not, had sent him off to spread God's word. That same year, inspired by the ideals of his mentor Trevor Huddleston, he began theological studies with the priests of the Community of the Resurrection, the Anglican order to which Huddleston belonged.

Following ordainment as a priest in 1961, Tutu began to establish his career in the Anglican church, working in small parishes in England and South Africa. Concurrently he continued his education and in 1966 received a master's degree in theology from King's College, London. In 1972 he accepted a position in England as associate director of the Theological Education Fund. Thoroughly enjoying his role, he traveled extensively throughout Asia and Africa and presided over the allocation of World Council of Churches scholarships. Thoughts of South Africa and the discrimination faced by his black countrymen seemed to surface continually, however, demanding his consideration. Throughout the early 1970s, tensions increased between an angry black community and a white-dominated government determined to maintain its political powers. Finally, in 1975, Tutu decided to return to his homeland and "contribute what I could to the liberation struggle," he explained to Hawthorne and Clayton. Upon returning, his presence and commitment to the cause of black Africans was felt almost immediately.

As Tutu ascended the ecclesial ranks of the Anglican church—in 1976 he was consecrated bishop of Lesotho, one of the government-designated black homelands—his involvement in the antiapartheid cause assumed an importance concomitant with his position. Choosing always to live in his parish, he closely monitored the feelings of his congregation and the local community; during the 1970s, in an atmosphere of mounting racial tensions, Tutu attempted to pacify angry black youths, encouraging them to seek change through peaceful means. In 1976, he met with black activist Nhato Motlana in an effort to curb the potential violence of youths in the black township of Soweto on the outskirts of Johannesburg. He also wrote to the incumbent South African Prime Minister Balthazar J. Vorster, warning him of the dangerous situation in Soweto. Tutu later claimed that Vorster dismissed his letter as a ploy engineered by political opponents. On June 16, 1976, however, racial tensions exploded into racial violence as black demonstrators met untempered reprisal from white security forces. Six hundred blacks were shot to death in the confrontation.

The tragic consequences of the Soweto riots seemed to mark a watershed in the attention given to the antiapartheid struggle in South Africa. Thereafter the situation received more extensive coverage from the world's press, which supplied the West with explanations of the escalating racial conflict and attempted to expose the possible reasons for it. For Tutu the increasing number of violent confrontations between blacks and security forces marked a change in his perception of his own involvement. Until the Soweto riots, he made himself generally available to discuss the situation with any representative from any side; following the riots he began to use his growing influence and openly initiated peaceful negotiation. This was not done in deference to the government; Tutu had become a highly visible and vocal critic.

By 1978 Tutu had been appointed the first black secretary general of the South African Council of Churches, and his personal attitude toward apartheid had hardened. He felt he could no longer condone the system on either political or moral grounds, and he determinedly set out to promote peaceful change toward a truly democratic system of government in South Africa. As head of the Council Tutu became spokesman for its thirteen million members, thus gaining increased political strength; due to its racial composition—eighty percent black—the Council was an ideal vehicle for voicing political opposition to the apartheid system. Under Tutu's direction the Council not only became openly critical of the South African government, but it also supported a network of anti-government protest. Responsible for paying the legal fees of arrested black protesters, for supporting the families of imprisoned activists, and for financing anti-government demonstrations, the Council did not endear itself to the South African authorities. The South African government began to single out Council leaders—Tutu prominent among them—for criticism, with the help of press agencies that supported government views. In addition Tutu and his colleagues were constantly harrassed with accusations of minor misdemeanors and, through government legislation, were deprived of certain rights of free movement. But in 1979, on two occasions, Tutu openly challenged the government, seriously confronting its credibility in the eyes of the rest of the world.

The first challenge came after the passing of the Group Areas Act, a policy that gave the government the power to forcibly remove blacks from their homes in urban South Africa and relocate them in government designated tribal homelands. The act made it virtually impossible for blacks to continue working at the better-paying city jobs without enduring lengthy and uncomfortable journeys every day or paying to live in one of the government's single-sexed hostels located in the city suburbs. And for those blacks who stayed in the homelands to work, their only hope was to eke out a meager living from very poor farmland. Appalled by the situation and by conditions in the homelands, Tutu compared the South African government with that of Nazi Germany, denouncing the forced relocation of blacks as South Africa's "final solution" to the black "problem." Although he later retracted the wording of his outburst, he continued to protest the policy and chided the government in Pretoria for deliberately starving people in South Africa while it boasted about its grain exports to nearby Zambia.

Tutu voiced his second major condemnation of the South African government before an international audience in autumn of 1979, which probably marks the beginning of his visibility in the world's media. In an interview for a Danish television program, Tutu called on the government of Denmark to cease buying South African coal as a sign of support for the anti-apartheid cause. The appeal moved people in Western countries to consider economic sanction as the ultimate weapon in the battle against apartheid. Concerned citizens, particularly in Europe, had voiced disapproval of South Africa's white

minority government for years, but they had never found an effective means of critical expression that would force the white government to reconsider its policies. Tutu's proposal offered a method that has since become a principal part of the strategy in the worldwide fight against apartheid. It also successfully focused attention upon the real possibility of positive change in South Africa.

Tutu's actions brought him very close to serious government reprisals. Returning from Denmark in 1979, authorities seized his passport, a move generally seen as a warning of possible imprisonment—the fate of two previous government critics, Nelson R. Mandela and Victor Tambo—or expulsion from the country. Tutu ignored the signal, however, and continued his antiapartheid campaign. The South African government eventually returned his passport in January, 1981, but confiscated it again in April. Thereafter Tutu was allowed to travel outside South Africa only with the government's permission and special travel documents that listed his nationality as "undetermined." In August, 1982, the South African government denied Tutu permission to go to New York to receive an honorary doctorate from Columbia University. Since the university does not grant degrees in absentia, Columbia's president traveled to South Africa and personally presented Tutu his degree in a ceremony held in Johannesburg.

It was during a permitted stay in the United States, on October 16, 1984, that Desmond Tutu received word that he was the 1984 Nobel peace laureate. Part of the Nobel citation read: "It is the committee's wish that the Peace Prize now awarded to Desmond Tutu should be regarded not only as a gesture of support to him and to the South African Council of Churches of which he is leader, but also to all individuals and groups in South Africa who, with their concern for human dignity, fraternity and democracy, incite the admiration of the world." According to *Time*, "much of white South Africa reacted grumpily or indifferently to the news." Said Tutu, in response: "You feel humble, you feel proud, elated and you feel sad. One of my greatest sadnesses is that there are many in this country who are not joining in celebrating something that is an honor for this country." Less than a month later, on November 3, 1984, Tutu was elected first Anglican bishop of Johannesburg; he subsequently resigned as secretary general of the South African Council of Churches.

Tutu immediately expanded his efforts to abolish apartheid. He called upon the international community to use diplomatic, political, and economic pressures to convince the South African government in Pretoria to rid itself of apartheid. Maintaining a strong belief in nonviolence, Tutu was positive such actions offered the only viable means of avoiding massive bloodshed. His request caused considerable reaction in the United States. In December, 1984, Tutu traveled to Washington, D.C., to meet with President Ronald Reagan. He tried to persuade the president to impose economic sanctions against South Africa, arguing that such a measure would help put an end to police violence and lead to the release of political prisoners. But Reagan preferred, instead, to remain on friendly terms with Pretoria, believing only diplomacy would produce positive change in South Africa, a policy he called "constructive engagement." The president's stance provoked a nationwide response as hundreds of antiapartheid demonstrators picketed South African consulates and embassies throughout the country. In a well-received speech before a bipartisan congressional committee, Tutu called on the United States to make a stand against racism. In response to the bishop's appeal, increasing numbers of state and local governments, educational institutions, and labor unions began plans to withdraw investments from companies doing business with South Africa. Pretoria viewed the American developments with growing concern.

Over the next several months civil unrest in South Africa escalated from boycotts, strikes, and stone-throwing clashes between township blacks and police to bloody riots symptomatic of civil war. By July, 1985, more than five hundred people had been killed, including four leaders of the largely black nationalist United Democratic Front (UDF) party. Many of the victims were black government employees and town councillors attacked by blacks loyal to UDF, some were blacks who had patronized white businesses, others were killed when police opened fire on rioters. The deteriorating situation prompted President Botha to declare a state of emergency in more than thirty districts throughout the country, including Johannesburg and most of the Transvaal provinces. Invoking the emergency powers of South Africa's 1953 Public Security Act, the government was allowed to impose curfews, arrest and detain suspects for fourteen days without a warrant, interrogate prisoners without the presence of lawyers, and tighten censorship on the press. International response to Botha's move was guarded, but antiapartheid leaders in South Africa were incensed. Asked in a *Newsweek* interview if the state of emergency changed South Africa's situation, Bishop Tutu replied: "Declaring a state of emergency is a typical reaction. It doesn't really change much: it just removes the last vestiges of our rights, and it means that whatever they do to us now, they can do with more impunity."

The government outlawed funeral marches, for example, sensing that the traditionally communal affairs represented subversion and civil disorder. Funeral services, however, were permitted. During one instance in the black township of Daveyton, reported *Time,* police and military units surrounded the tent where family, friends, and community members gathered for the burial service of a young black woman shot and killed during a demonstration. Army troops held guns ready, police dogs were positioned atop armored cars, and helicopters surveyed the area from above. It was the largest display of government force since Botha's declaration of emergency began. The tension mounted as the government forces waited to see if the crowd would, in defiance, march to the cemetery located several blocks away. Just when violence seemed likely to erupt, Bishop Tutu arrived and the atmosphere relaxed immediately. The coffin of the slain girl was brought into the tent and set before the clergyman, who calmly performed the religious service. According to *Time,* "Tutu told the gathering that he had asked the government, 'Please allow us to mourn, to bury our dead with dignity, to share the burden of our sorrow. Do not rub salt in our wounds . . . I appeal to you because we are already hurt, already down. We are humans, not animals. When we have a death, we cry.'" In warning to the authorities, reported *Time,* "the bishop declared, 'I have been a minister for 24 years, and I am not going to start now being told what to preach. I do not want to defy the government. But Scripture says that when there is a conflict between the law of God and the law of man, we must obey the law of God. I will continue to preach as instructed.'" After the completion of the religious service, the police ordered the crowd to disperse, allowing people in vehicles only to go to the cemetery. Tutu pleaded with the police commandant to provide buses, warning that violence could otherwise erupt. After an hour of tense waiting, buses finally arrived and transported the mourners to the cemetery. A potentially bloody confrontation was avoided, order had been maintained, and peace prevailed. Recalling for a *Time* reporter the confrontation with the police commandant, Tutu chuckled and said, "He saluted me. Twice."

During the weeks following the Daveyton incident, international condemnation of Pretoria's declared state of emergency increased. Canada prepared to toughen its limited economic sanctions, the U.S. House of Representatives approved the first imposition of broad economic sanctions against South Africa, and more than a dozen European nations recalled their diplomats in a gesture of disapproval. By the end of 1985, the rand (South Africa's monetary unit) lost fifty percent of its value. President Botha, however, was determined not to succumb to external pressure and his declaration of emergency held firm. Tutu also held firm to his own declaration to rid South Africa of apartheid, and he continued his outspoken appeal for international support of the antiapartheid cause. "We face a catastrophe in this land," warned Tutu, according to *Newsweek.* "Only the action of the international community, by applying pressure, can save us." Speaking in Wales some time later, reported *New Statesman,* Tutu declared, "It is still possible for us to move back from the edge of a precipice if the international community is prepared to intervene decisively." But international action was slow to develop, especially in the United States where President Reagan insisted on maintaining his current policy of deploring the apartheid system while opposing punitive sanctions. Angry with the Reagan administration's attitude, Tutu, according to *Newsweek,* observed: "President Reagan has [imposed sanctions on] Poland, Nicaragua and Libya. He is not opposed to sanctions per se. He is opposed to them when blacks are involved." Tutu also asserted, "In my view, the Reagan administration's support and collaboration with [the South African government] is immoral, evil and totally unchristian. You are either for or against apartheid, and not by rhetoric. You are either on the side of the oppressed or on the side of the oppressor. You can't be neutral."

Over the next several months antiapartheid forces did gain support in the United States when the House of Representatives approved a bill that would impose a trade embargo on South Africa. President Reagan still refused to approve sanctions, however, and promised to veto such a bill. In a speech made in July, 1986, Reagan stated that current U.S. policy toward South Africa would remain unchanged. Tutu's reaction, as disclosed in *Newsweek,* was unusually blunt: "[Tutu] called the speech 'nauseating,' likened Reagan to the 'great white chief of old' and said, 'The West, for my part, can go to hell.'" Pretoria seemed pleased with Reagan's message. Meanwhile the situation in South Africa worsened and Tutu's speeches began to take on fatalistic undertones. Speaking with *Time,* Tutu said: "I think the white ruling class is quite ready to do a Samson on us. That is, they will pull down the pillars, even if it means they perish in the process. They are really scared that we are going to treat them as they treated us."

In early September, 1986, Tutu was elected archbishop of Cape Town and the primate of the Anglican Church for all of southern Africa. Conducting his final service in Johannesburg before his enthronement as archbishop, according to *Time,* Tutu assured his congregation: "Despite all that the powers of the world may do, we are going to be free." But in a British Broadcasting Corporation interview reported by *Time* in April, 1987, President Botha declared, "I am not prepared to sacrifice my rights so that the other man can dominate me with his greater numbers. . . . I never read in the Bible that to be a good Christian means I must commit suicide to please the other man.'' Shortly thereafter, Pretoria toughened its policies against antiapartheid demonstrators even more. According to *Time* the South African government ''announced a new emergency regulation banning South Africans from doing or saying anything to bring about the release of people who have been detained without trial''—an estimated eight thousand, including two thousand minors. The government also declared it ''illegal to participate in 'any campaign, project or action aimed at accomplishing the release' of detainees. Among the forbidden acts . . . are the signing of petitions, the sending of telegrams and even the wearing of political stickers or shirts bearing antidetention slogans.''

Time reported that Tutu and other critics in South Africa ''said they would ignore the restrictions and continue to speak their minds.'' Holding a prayer service to protest Pretoria's action, the archbishop warned: ''Beware when you take on the Church of God. Others have tried and have come a cropper.'' He then added, ''The government has gone crazy. I want to tell them that I am not going to stop calling for the release of detainees in or out of church.'' Governments worldwide, including the United States, also expressed official disapproval. Faced with such widespread opposition, Pretoria retreated somewhat, but they had once again fueled the fires of civil unrest and the antiapartheid cause. Tutu, adhering to his conviction that democracy and freedom can exist in South Africa, continued his campaign for the peaceful liberation of his countrymen.

Many of Tutu's orations have been collected in *Hope and Suffering: Sermons and Speeches*, described as ''vintage Tutu'' by Huston Horn in the *Los Angeles Times Book Review*. ''Tutu's gaze rarely wanders from a benign, visionary South Africa ruled together by blacks and whites,'' explained Horn, and ''the bishop's preachments [still] have contemporary relevance and ring.'' Colman McCarthy of *Washington Post Book World* called the book ''stunning'' and concluded that Bishop Tutu, even without his Nobel, ''would still have been a force that no regime could stop or silence.''

AVOCATIONAL INTERESTS: Music, reading, jogging.

BIOGRAPHICAL/CRITICAL SOURCES:

BOOKS

Tlhagale, Buti and Itumeleng Mosala, editors, *Hammering Swords into Ploughshares: Essays in Honor of Archbishop Mpilo Desmond Tutu*, Eerdmans, 1987.

PERIODICALS

Chicago Tribune, July 7, 1980.
Christian Science Monitor, April 26, 1979, March 28, 1984.
Economist, March 28, 1987, April 18, 1987.
Maclean's, August 12, 1985, April 14, 1986.
Manchester Guardian Weekly, October 28, 1984.
Newsday, October 17, 1984.
New Statesman, May 30, 1986.
Newsweek, October 29, 1984, December 17, 1984, July 29, 1985, August 4, 1986.
New York Times, October 17, 1984.
New York Times Magazine, March 14, 1982.
Observer (London), August 8, 1982, May 8, 1983.
People, December 17, 1984.
Rolling Stone, November 21, 1985.
Time, October 29, 1984, January 14, 1985, August 19, 1985, August 4, 1986, September 15, 1986, April 13, 1987, April 27, 1987.

Washington Post, October 17, 1984, October 19, 1984.

—*Sketch by Jeremy Kane and Linda S. Smouse*

*   *   *

TWIGG, Alan (Robert)   1952-

PERSONAL: Born February 11, 1952, in North Vancouver, British Columbia, Canada; son of Arthur Maitland and Olive Betty Alice Twigg; married Tara Lovene Farnsworth, September 2, 1973; children: Jeremy Jude, Martin Jules.

WRITINGS:

For Openers: Conversations With Twenty-four Canadian Writers, Harbour Publishing, 1981.
Hubert Evans: The First Ninety-three Years, Harbour Publishing, 1985.
Vancouver and Its Writers, Harbour Publishing, 1986.
Vander Zalm: From Immigrant to Premier, Harbour Publishing, 1986.

Contributor of more than a thousand articles and reviews to periodicals.

SIDELIGHTS: Alan Twigg commented: ''Writing truthfully and well is a subversive act.''

*   *   *

TYLER, Patrick (Edward)   1951-

PERSONAL: Born November 6, 1951, in St. Louis, Mo.; son of John Winfred (in retailing) and Isla Lorayne (a nurse) Tyler; married Linda Wagner (a writer of children's books), September 1, 1973; children: Silas O'Connell, Landry DeVere. *Education:* Attended University of Texas at Austin, 1969-70; University of South Carolina—Columbia, A.B., 1973.

ADDRESSES: Home—1750 Lamont St. N.W., Washington, D.C. 20009. *Office*—Washington Post, 1150 15th St. N.W., Washington, D.C. 20071.

CAREER: Allendale County Citizen, Allendale County, S.C., editor, 1974; *Hampton County Guardian*, Hampton, S.C., editor, 1974; *Charlotte News*, Charlotte, N.C., staff reporter, 1975; *St. Petersburg Times*, St. Petersburg, Fla., staff reporter, 1976-78; *Washington Post*, Washington, D.C., investigative reporter, 1980-85, national security correspondent, 1985-86, Middle East correspondent, 1986—.

WRITINGS:

Running Critical: The Silent War, Rickover, and General Dynamics, Harper, 1986.

SIDELIGHTS: Patrick Tyler's *Running Critical: The Silent War, Rickover, and General Dynamics* ''covers, in riveting detail,'' according to reviewer Doug Bandow in the *Los Angeles Times Book Review*, perhaps one of the biggest scandals ever to rock the United States' defense purchasing system. In the late 1960s, Admiral Hyman Rickover informed the U.S. Congress that America needed a new, faster submarine to maintain naval superiority over the Soviet Union. General Dynamics was awarded the job at an unbelievably low bid, writes Tyler. Although the cost overruns on the proposed 688 submarine rose to astronomical proportions over the next few years, both the company and the Navy were committed to the project. The loss to General Dynamics, Tyler reveals, rose to one and one-half billion dollars, an amount that could have bankrupted the company.

General Dynamics began deceptive strategies, outlined in *Running Critical,* to conceal the huge amount and to secure additional funds from the Navy. At the same time it was discovered that Admiral Rickover had, over the previous several years, received expensive gifts and that a top General Dynamics official had appropriated other gratuities. Additionally, according to Tyler, the 688 submarine had been doomed from the start by a design flaw that would prevent it from ever matching the speed of the Soviet craft. In the end, Tyler reports, the development of the submarine and the bailout of General Dynamics cost the United States an estimated one billion dollars.

Tyler's handling of these events was commended by Arthur T. Hadley in the *Washington Post Book World* as "reporting of the highest order, successfully interweaving historical perspective, social setting and the devastation wrought by the hubris of powerful personalities too long unchecked." Bandow concluded that *Running Critical* is "a truly important book, one that simultaneously informs and enthralls."

BIOGRAPHICAL/CRITICAL SOURCES:

PERIODICALS

Los Angeles Times Book Review, October 26, 1986.
Washington Post Book World, October 12, 1986.

*   *   *

TYRRELL, William Blake   1940-

PERSONAL: Born August 30, 1940, in Middletown, N.Y.; son of Blake W. (a truck driver) and Frances (Misner) Tyrrell; married Mary Ann Sapienza (a librarian), July 1, 1967; children: Blake A. *Education:* Hobart and William Smith Colleges, B.A., 1962; University of Pennsylvania, M.A., 1964; University of Washington, Seattle, Ph.C., 1968, Ph.D., 1970.

ADDRESSES: Office—Department of Romance and Classical Languages, A548 Wells Hall, Michigan State University, East Lansing, Mich. 48824.

CAREER: Michigan State University, East Lansing, assistant professor, 1970-75, associate professor, 1975-79, professor of classics, 1979—.

WRITINGS:

Medical Terminology for Medical Students, C. C Thomas, 1978.
A Legal and Historical Commentary to Cicero's oratio pro Rabirio perduellionus reo, A. Hakkert, 1978.
Amazons: A Study in Athenian Mythmaking, Johns Hopkins University Press, 1984.

WORK IN PROGRESS: Research on Greek myths and social institutions.

SIDELIGHTS: William Blake Tyrrell told *CA:* "*Medical Terminology for Medical Students* came from teaching a course on the subject for which no adequate textbook was available.

"My earliest scholarship involved Roman history and criminal law. The commentary derived from my thesis and presented more radical views of the Roman magistracy involved than I realized. Roman law, however, was not a gripping subject.

"When I had to teach a course in mythology, I found my consuming academic interest, vocation, and avocation. The Amazon study began as a footnote which led to an article and became a book. I realized there was more to the subject of Amazons than a footnote and, subsequently, more than an article. The Amazons as a subject provided three years of rapture, but I wouldn't want to meet one."

U

UDELSON, Joseph H. 1943-

PERSONAL: Born July 18, 1943, in Chicago, Ill. *Education:* Bradley University, A.B., 1965; University of Michigan, A.M., 1966; Vanderbilt University, Ph.D., 1975.

ADDRESSES: Office—Department of History and Geography, Tennessee State University, 3500 John A. Meritt Blvd., Nashville, Tenn. 37209-1561.

CAREER: Tennessee State University, Nashville, associate professor of history and geography, 1969—.

WRITINGS:

The Great Television Race: A History of the American Television Industry, 1925-1941, University of Alabama Press, 1982.

WORK IN PROGRESS: A biography on Israel Zangwill.

*　　*　　*

ULLMAN, Edward L(ouis) 1912-1976

OBITUARY NOTICE—See index for *CA* sketch: Born July 24, 1912, in Chicago, Ill.; died April 24, 1976. Geographer, educator, cartographer, editor, and author. For his exceptional contribution to the field of geography, Ullman received citations from the Association of American Geographers in 1958 and from the Italian Geographical Society in 1959. He was a professor of geography at the University of Washington from 1951 to 1976, and he also taught at Washington State College, Indiana University at Bloomington, Harvard University, and institutions in England, Italy, the Soviet Union, and West Germany. During the 1940s Ullman worked as a geography and transportation specialist for U.S. government organizations, such as the Office of Strategic Services, the U.S. Department of State, and the U.S. Maritime Commission. He served at different times as consultant to the *Boston Globe,* Stanford Research Institute, European Productivity Agency, the U.S. Department of Commerce, and Asian Development Bank. In addition to his many contributions to professional journals and books, Ullman wrote *Mobile: Industrial Seaport and Trade Center, American Commodity Flow: A Geographical Interpretation of Rail and Water Traffic Based on Principles of Spatial Interchange,* and *Geography as Spatial Interaction.* With Michael F. Dacey and Harold Brodsky he wrote *The*

Economic Base of American Cities: Profiles for the 101 Metropolitan Areas Over 250,000 Population, Based on Minimum Requirements for 1960, and with R. O. Shreve, H. E. Robison, R. K. Arnold, J. W. Landregan, and J. A. McCuniff he edited the seven-volume *Economic Analysis of Philippine Domestic Transportation.* The geographer also directed the preparation of the 1949 *Boston Globe Map of Metropolitan Boston: Population and Shopping Centers,* and he prepared the 1950 map *U.S. Railroads, Classified According to Capacity and Relative Importance.*

OBITUARIES AND OTHER SOURCES:

BOOKS

American Men and Women of Science: The Physical and Biological Sciences, 13th edition, Bowker, 1976.
Eyre, John D., editor, *A Man for All Regions: The Contributions of Edward L. Ullman to Geography; Papers of the Fourth Carolina Geographical Symposium, 1977,* Department of Geography, University of North Carolina at Chapel Hill, c. 1978.
Who Was Who With World Notables, Volume VII: *1977-1981,* Marquis, 1981.

*　　*　　*

UNSTEAD, R(obert) J(ohn) 1915-1988

OBITUARY NOTICE—See index for *CA* sketch: Born November 21, 1915, in Deal, Kent, England; died May 5, 1988. Educator, publisher, editor, and author. Unstead was best known for his books on history, which he hoped would make the subject appealing for young readers. He was a schoolmaster in St. Albans, England, for four years and a headmaster in Letchworth, England, for ten. The historian retired from teaching in 1957 to become a free-lance author and to direct his own publishing company. His writings include *Looking at History: Britain From Cavemen to the Present Day, Pioneer Homelife in Australia, Living in Samuel Pepys' London, How They Lived in Cities Long Ago, A History of the World,* and the eight-volume *History of the English-Speaking World.* Unstead also edited series of children's reference books for A. & C. Black and reviewed history books for the *Times Literary Supplement.*

OBITUARIES AND OTHER SOURCES:

BOOKS

Who's Who, 140th edition, St. Martin's, 1988.

PERIODICALS

Times (London), May 9, 1988.

*   *   *

UPSHAW, Margaret Mitchell
  See MITCHELL, Margaret (Munnerlyn)

*   *   *

UPTON, L(eslie) F(rancis) S(tokes)   1931-1980

OBITUARY NOTICE—See index for *CA* sketch: Born December 8, 1931, in Leigh-on-Sea, Essex, England; died of cancer, March 29, 1980. Educator, editor, and author. Upton was a professor of history at the University of British Columbia from 1964 until the time of his death. Prior to his tenure at British Columbia he taught history at St. John's College. Upton edited *Diary and Selected Papers of Chief Justice William Smith, 1784-1793, United Empire Loyalists: Men and Myths,* and *Revolutionary Versus Loyalist: The First American Civil War, 1774-1784,* and he wrote *The Loyal Whig: Chief Justice William Smith of New York and Quebec* and *MicMacs and Colonists.*

OBITUARIES AND OTHER SOURCES:

Date of death provided by daughter, Elizabeth A. S. Upton.

*   *   *

URE, Jean
  (Jean Gregory; Ann Colin, Sarah McCulloch, pseudonyms)

PERSONAL: Surname is pronounced "Ewer"; born in Surrey, England; daughter of William (an insurance officer) and Vera (Belsen) Ure; married Leonard Gregory (an actor and writer), 1967. *Education:* Attended Webber-Douglas Academy of Dramatic Art, 1965-67. *Religion:* None.

ADDRESSES: Home—88 Southbridge Rd., Croydon, Surrey CRO 1AF, England. *Agent*—Maggie Noach, 21 Redan St., London W14 0AB, England.

CAREER: Writer. Has also worked as a waitress, cook, washer-up, nursing assistant, newspaper seller, shop assistant, theatre usherette, temporary shorthand-typist, translator, secretary with NATO and UNESCO, and television production assistant.

MEMBER: Society of Authors, Vegan Society, Animal Aid.

AWARDS, HONORS: See You Thursday was chosen one of American Library Association's Best Books for Young Adults, 1983.

WRITINGS:

FOR YOUNG PEOPLE

Dance for Two, Harrap, 1960, reprinted, Goodchild, 1984.
See You Thursday (Junior Literary Guild selection), Kestrel, 1981, Delacorte, 1983.
A Proper Little Nooryeff, Bodley Head, 1982, published in the United States as *What If They Saw Me Now?,* Delacorte, 1984.

If It Weren't for Sebastian, Bodley Head, 1982, Delacorte, 1985.
Hi There, Supermouse, illustrations by Martin White, Hutchinson, 1983, Viking Penguin, 1985; published with illustrations by Ellen Eagle as *Supermouse* (Junior Literary Guild selection), Morrow, 1984.
The You-Two, Hutchinson, 1984, published in the United States with illustrations by Ellen Eagle as *You Two,* Morrow, 1984.
You Win Some, You Lose Some, Bodley Head, 1984, Delacorte, 1987.
After Thursday, Kestrel, 1985, Delacorte, 1987.
Nicola Mimosa, Hutchinson, 1985, published in the United States with illustrations by Ellen Eagle as *The Most Important Thing,* Morrow, 1986.
Megastar, Blackie, 1985.
Swings and Roundabouts, Blackie, 1986.
A Bottled Cherry Angel, Hutchinson, 1986.
Brenda the Bold, illustrations by Glenys Ambrus, Heinemann, 1986.
The Other Side of the Fence, Bodley Head, 1986.

FOR ADULTS

The Other Theatre, Corgi, 1966.
The Test of Love, Corgi, 1968.
If You Speak Love, Corgi, 1972.
Had We But World Enough and Time, Corgi, 1972.
The Farther Off From England, Corgi, 1973.
Daybreak, Corgi, 1974.
All Thy Love, Corgi, 1975.
No Precious Time, Corgi, 1976.
Hear No Evil, Corgi, 1976.
Early Stages, Corgi, 1977.
Dress Rehearsal, Corgi, 1977.
All in a Summer Season, Corgi, 1977.
Curtain Fall, Corgi, 1978.
Bid Time Return, Corgi, 1978.
Masquerade, Corgi, 1979.
A Girl Like That, Corgi, 1979.

GEORGIAN ROMANCES, UNDER PSEUDONYM SARAH McCULLOCH

Not Quite a Lady, Corgi, 1980, Fawcett, 1981.
A Most Insistent Lady, Corgi, 1981.
A Lady for Ludovic, Corgi, 1981.
Merely a Gentleman, Corgi, 1982.
A Perfect Gentleman, Corgi, 1982.

FOR ADULTS, UNDER PSEUDONYM ANN COLIN

A Different Class of Doctor, Corgi, 1980.
Doctor Jamie, Corgi, 1980.

FOR ADULTS, UNDER NAME JEAN GREGORY

Love Beyond Telling, Corgi, 1986.

OTHER

Also translator of books from the French. Contributor of articles to periodicals, including *Vegan* and *Writers' Monthly.*

WORK IN PROGRESS: A novel, *Tea Leaf on the Roof,* for Blackie; a young adult book, *One Green Leaf,* for Bodley Head; a children's book, *War With Old Mouldy,* illustrations by Alice Englander, for Methuen.

SIDELIGHTS: Jean Ure told *CA:* "I would say that the kind of children's books I write are books written from the child's/teenager's point of view as recalled in tranquillity by the adult me. Bearing in mind that we have all been there, I don't think there is any particular need for my kind of writer either to have kids of her own or to have any ongoing contact with kids. This might provide the 'externals,' the 'frills,' as it were, but not the essence, which is the inner workings of the young mind, the young emotions. I try not to ride specific hobby-horses in any of my books, but obviously my own philosophy of life must be reflected. It's hard to sum this up in a few words, but the main thing I aim to do in *all* my junior fiction is to question the status quo, examine received prejudices, get readers thinking for themselves instead of accepting what parents, teachers, politicians tell them; and having thought, to make up their own minds.

"As a writing junkie—namely, a compulsive writer who cannot exist without her daily fix—I obviously need a living by writing; and earning a living by writing fiction means for all practical purposes writing 'genre' fiction. The romantic genre served me very well as an apprenticeship, when I was young and innocent. I learned my craft and worked out my daydreams at the same time. But there are boundaries in all genre fiction, and you overstep these boundaries at your peril—in other words, your editor starts screaming at you—and when I finally started transgressing just a bit too far in the romantic novel field—with characters who *think*, who *talk*, who *philosophize*—I knew the game was up.

"This was the point at which I turned to Georgian romances. For a brief spell I had great fun writing these. They are froth and they are nonsense, but they require a sense of period, a sense of elegance and style, and an ability to play with language that appealed to me. I could no longer write a 'romantic novel' to save my life, but I think I could always with pleasure write the old Georgian. Unfortunately, alas, such are the strange ways of the publishing world, Georgians this decade are not 'in': we do not want any Georgians today. If the fashion changes, then I have lots more plots waiting to be worked out, lots more characters waiting to be set free.

"And so, I turned full circle, back to where I started as a teenager: to junior fiction. I wrote my first published novel when I was fifteen—a pure wish-fulfillment book. I thought at fifteen that this would be my first and last junior book. I was convinced that adults who wrote for kids must be intellectually defective. Well, maybe they are—but now that I'm an adult I love it! The very best thing about writing for children and young people is that there are *no boundaries*, other than those one imposes on oneself. The boundaries I impose are that I should always bear in mind my readers' likely level of *experience*, and that I should never, ever destroy hope. *I* may be cynical and worldly-wise, but it is the precious prerogative of youth to be optimistic. Perhaps this is why I and so many others get a kick out of writing junior fiction. . . . It takes us back to the days when *we* were full of optimism. I guess it's a form of escapism, and why not? So long as, for the readers, it's constructive and helpful escapism, then I'm all for it!"

AVOCATIONAL INTERESTS: Animals, political philosophy, horseback riding, reading, walking.

BIOGRAPHICAL/CRITICAL SOURCES:

PERIODICALS

British Book News, March, 1985.
New Statesman, October 2, 1987.
Observer, November 29, 1981, August 26, 1984.
Times Literary Supplement, April 13, 1984, August 16, 1985, November 28, 1986, September 18, 1987.
Washington Post Book World, May 11, 1986.

*   *   *

U TAM'SI, Gerald Felix Tchicaya
See TCHICAYA, Gerald Felix

*   *   *

U TAM'SI, Tchicaya
See TCHICAYA, Gerald Felix

*   *   *

UTLEY, T(homas) E(dwin)   1921-1988

OBITUARY NOTICE: Born February 1, 1921; died June 21, 1988. Political theorist, journalist, and author. Although Utley was blinded by an illness at the age of nine, he went on to become a highly respected journalist in England for more than four decades. He wrote lead articles for the London *Times,* the *Sunday Times,* and *Observer,* and, during his long tenure with the conservative *Daily Telegraph,* he served as assistant editor and as chief editorial writer. As obituary editor for the *Times* Utley reportedly suggested that his own death notice should read: "Hoist with his own petard," a line from Shakespeare's *Hamlet* meaning destroyed by his own weapon.

Widely known for his conservative views, Utley greatly influenced England's Tory party, a political organization representing business, aristocratic, and professional interests. In his book *Not Guilty: The Conservative Reply,* the author defended "new Conservatism" as an expression of Burkean ideas—that political, social, and religious institutions represent the wisdom of the ages—in the post-World War II era. Utley's other writings include *Essays in Conservatism, Modern Political Thought, Edmund Burke, Enoch Powell: The Man and His Thinking,* and *Lessons of Ulster.*

OBITUARIES AND OTHER SOURCES:

BOOKS

Who's Who, 140th edition, St. Martin's, 1988.

PERIODICALS

Chicago Tribune, June 26, 1988.
Times (London), June 23, 1988.

V

VANDERHAAR, Gerard A(nthony) 1931-

PERSONAL: Born August 15, 1931, in Louisville, Ky.; son of Gerhard August (an artist) and Margaret Mary (a musician; maiden name, Hammerstein) Vanderhaar; married Janice Marie Searles (a social worker), December 22, 1969. *Education:* Providence College, A.B., 1954; Dominican House of Studies, Washington, D.C., S.T.B. (magna cum laude), 1956, S.T.L. (cum laude) and S.T.Lr., 1958; Pontifical University of St. Thomas Aquinas, Rome, Italy, S.T.D. (cum laude), 1965.

*ADDRESSES: Home—*3554 Boxdale, Apt. 3, Memphis, Tenn. 38118. *Office—* Department of Humanities, Christian Brothers College, 650 East Parkway S., Memphis, Tenn. 38104.

CAREER: Christian Brothers College, Memphis, Tenn., instructor in theology, 1958-61; Nazareth College (now Spalding College), Louisville, Ky., assistant professor of theology, 1961-62; St. John's University, Jamaica, N.Y., assistant professor of theology, 1964-65; Providence College, Providence, R.I., associate professor of religious studies, 1965-68; Wesleyan University, Middletown, Conn., assistant professor of religion and member of university ministry, 1968-69; Wisconsin State University (now University of Wisconsin)—Oshkosh, assistant professor of religion, 1969-70; Siena College, Memphis, associate professor of theology and chairman of department, 1970-71; Christian Brothers College, associate professor, 1971-78, professor of humanities, 1978—, chairman of department of religion, 1973-74, and department of humanities, 1974-76 and 1988—, coordinator of Peace Studies Program, 1975—.

Visiting professor at Loyola University, Chicago, Ill., summers, 1971-73. Pax Christi U.S.A., member of national executive council, 1975-79 and 1983-85, chairman, 1979-80, chairman of National Task Force on Nonviolence, 1981-83 and 1987-88; associate executive director of Non-Violent Alternatives of Antwerp, Belgium, 1979-80; member of Pax Christi International Commission of Eastern European Communications, 1980-82, and Commission on Alternatives to Violence, 1981—; co-founder and member of board of directors of Mid-South Peace and Justice Center, 1982-88; member of Consortium on Peace Research, Education, and Development. Member of Wisconsin Committee on Religion in Public Education, 1969-70; co-director of Greater Memphis Consortium, 1970-71; member of the Diocese of Memphis Peace and Justice Commission, 1976-78, and Theological Commission, 1985-87.

MEMBER: American Academy of Religion, American Association of University Professors, Fellowship of Reconciliation, War Resisters League.

AWARDS, HONORS: Distinguished Service Award from United Nations Association, 1981, for aid in publicizing the work of the United Nations.

WRITINGS:

(Author of introduction) Franziskus Stratmann, *The Church and War*, Garland Publishing, 1971.
Christians and Nonviolence in the Nuclear Age, Twenty-Third, 1982.
Enemies: And How to Love Them, Twenty-Third, 1985.
(Editor with Mary Lou Knowacki) *Way of Peace: A Guide to Nonviolence*, Pax Christi, 1987.

Contributor to magazines and newspapers, including *Fellowship* and *Cross Currents*. Former editor of newsletter of Pax Christi U.S.A.

WORK IN PROGRESS: Your Personal Best: The Nonviolent Self, for Twenty-Third.

SIDELIGHTS: Gerard A. Vanderhaar told *CA:* "I'm not a professional writer, although I do write. I'm really a college teacher who belongs to the peace movement and who believes that people can change. If it happened to me, it can happen to anyone. The nuclear threat hanging over our world demands a new way of thinking if we are to survive, much less be creative and prosper. For me that new way is active nonviolence, in the spirit of Mahatma Gandhi and Dr. Martin Luther King, Jr. But that kind of nonviolence will not become national policy until it is first the personal policy of millions of people. So I'm trying to make a nonviolent way of thinking and acting more widely known.

"For a long time it's seemed to me that the way we as a people and as individuals deal with our enemies is at the heart of the matter. So I've made efforts to investigate enemies, and interact with them—in the Soviet Union, Cuba, Nicaragua, and, from another perspective, at the U.S. Army War College.

I'm leery of fanaticism, on whatever side. I believe, with Abraham Lincoln, that I destroy my enemies when I make them my friends. That's a huge job. I'm sure it'll take the rest of my life.''

* * *

Van HELDEN, Albert   1940-

PERSONAL: Born March 7, 1940, in The Hague, Netherlands. *Education:* Stevens Institute of Technology, B.Eng., 1962, M.S., 1964; University of Michigan, M.A., 1967; University of London, Ph.D., 1970.

ADDRESSES: Office—Department of History, Rice University, P.O. Box 1892, Houston, Tex. 77251.

CAREER: Ford Motor Co., Dearborn, Mich., metallurgical engineer, 1964-66; Rice University, Houston, Tex., assistant professor, 1970-75, associate professor, 1975-83, professor of history, 1983—, chairman of department, 1987—.

MEMBER: International Academy of the History of Science, American Association for the Advancement of Science, History of Science Society, British Society for the History of Science.

WRITINGS:

Measuring the Universe, University of Chicago Press, 1985.

Contributor to periodicals.

WORK IN PROGRESS: Telescopic Astronomy, 1608-1750.

BIOGRAPHICAL/CRITICAL SOURCES:

PERIODICALS

Times Literary Supplement, February 7, 1986.

* * *

Van NIMMEN, (Carol) Jane   1937-

PERSONAL: Born December 20, 1937, in Champaign, Ill.; daughter of William Curtis (a geophysicist) and Pauline (a nurse; maiden name, Hall) Adams; married David M. Jones, June 25, 1955 (divorced June, 1960); married Michael Levandowsky, July 23, 1960 (divorced, July, 1965); married Armand Van Nimmen (an economist), August 15, 1967; children: (third marriage) Asha Paulina. *Education:* Attended Wayne State University, 1956-58; Antioch College (now University), A.B., 1960; University of Maryland at College Park, M.A., 1971.

ADDRESSES: Home—2601 36th St. N.W., Washington, D.C. 20007.

CAREER: Detroit News, Detroit, Mich., junior writer, 1956-58; kindergarten teacher at public schools in St. Thomas, Virgin Islands, 1961-62; Columbia University, New York, N.Y., editor, 1963-65; Library of Congress, Washington, D.C., writer and editor, 1966-68; University of Maryland at College Park, museum training fellow, 1969-70, teaching assistant, 1970-71; United Nations kindergarten, New Delhi, India, coordinator, 1972-78; free-lance writer in Dhaka, Bangladesh, 1978-81.

WRITINGS:

(With Leonard Bruno and Robert Rosholt) *The NASA Historical Data Book,* National Aeronautics and Space Administration, 1976.

Lightest Blues: Great Humor From the Thirties, Imago Imprints, 1984.

Author of exhibition catalogs.

WORK IN PROGRESS: Raphael and the Nineteenth-Century Museumgoer; Right Red Returning, a novel.

SIDELIGHTS: Jane Van Nimmen lived in India and Bangladesh from 1972 to 1981. She has studied Sanskrit, Hindi, French, German, and Dutch, and has begun to study Norwegian and Italian. Van Nimmen told *CA:* "Art history research is an adventure game, and I often find clues for my next move by turning the pages of old newspapers and magazines. As more and more of these precious resources go onto microforms, the experience of reading periodicals from the past becomes inevitably dim and mechanical. Reprint editions are an expensive alternative, and putting together selections from the entire run is another way to keep less accessible serials alive in our memory. To share my vivid rediscovery of one such rare periodical I wrote *Lightest Blues,* described by *Publishers Weekly* as 'bitingly satirical pieces and pictures culled from the pages of *Americana,* the iconoclastic art and literature magazine of the early '30s.'

"A former journalist myself, I rely heavily on ephemeral material from the popular press as I explore the 'forgotten nineteenth century,' my special field of inquiry in European art. When I stumbled upon a few issues of *Americana* found in the George Grosz estate, I learned that despite contributions by Grosz, E. E. Cummings, Nathanael West, Al Hirschfeld, Kenneth Burke, and other splendid writers and artists of the 1930s, this feisty little magazine had been all but forgotten. I decided to recreate it for a modern audience. *Publishers Weekly* declared the result 'a curio that will leave no one unmoved,' and the *Foreign Affairs* reviewer described the book as 'a graphic history lesson with many relevant links to today.'

"As I prodded the memories of those wonderful contributors about work done more than fifty years ago, it was not so much writing a book as opening a time capsule. Photographer Robert Disraeli, whose photomontages for *Americana* were the first of their kind in America, parallel to the pioneering work of John Heartfield in Germany, called to the book 'a cultural achievement and a warning to the perceptive that the present is little different from the past' in a letter to the publisher, dated August 10, 1984.

"The novel I am working on also arose from my love of another popular form, the comic strip adventure. The book grew from a projected group of related novellas linked by the theme of travellers in modern China. The main characters are a Belgian population bureaucrat and his American wife, a comic book expert for Sotheby's. During a holiday on the Belgian coast, they step into a TinTin adventure as the husband tries to resume contact with his closest childhood friend, now the leader of a minute Marxist party.

"My long stay in Asia reveals another strong thread in my life—an enduring love of India. It was the goal of my first trip abroad in 1960 and the setting of my first long novel, completed in 1980. I have not yet managed to write about the inexhaustible richness of that culture to my own satisfaction and have shelved that first attempt for revisions and further practice."

BIOGRAPHICAL/CRITICAL SOURCES:

PERIODICALS

Foreign Affairs, September, 1984.

Los Angeles Times Book Review, December, 1984.
Publishers Weekly, May, 1984.

*   *   *

VARNEY, Philip 1943-

PERSONAL: Born December 3, 1943, in Evanston, Ill.; son of F. C. and Mary (Marshall) Varney; married Marsha Malone, April 3, 1971 (divorced in January, 1986); children: Janet. *Education:* University of Arizona, B.Ed., 1966, M.Ed., 1971.

ADDRESSES: 422 North Arcadia Ave., Tucson, Ariz. 85711.

CAREER: Rincon High School, Tucson, Ariz., English teacher, 1966-77, chairman of department, 1977—. Member of faculty at University of Arizona, 1979-84.

MEMBER: National Education Association, Arizona Education Association, Tucson Education Association, Greater Arizona Bicycling Association.

WRITINGS:

Arizona's Best Ghost Towns: A Practical Guide, with own photographs, Northland Press, 1980.
New Mexico's Best Ghost Towns, with own photographs, Northland Press, 1981.

WORK IN PROGRESS: Southern California's Best Ghost Towns, and *Northern California's Best Ghost Towns,* both for University of Oklahoma Press.

SIDELIGHTS: Philip Varney told *CA:* "Exploring ghost towns should be an emotional experience. Part of it is the excitement and even the occasional danger that comes from leaving main roads for hours of backroads travel. Part is the absolute beauty of the desolate places these towns tend to occupy. Part is the infrequent resident who needs to be reassured that you are no threat—that you are, in fact, an asset in his day, a person who hunts for fascinating people as well as interesting places. And part is simply the 'being there,' attempting to draw from your knowledge of the town—the legends, the tall tales, the tragedies—to try to capture how the settlers of these out-of-the-way places might have lived.

"One such emotional experience captures why I explore and write about ghost towns. It happened to me in Dawson, New Mexico, at the site of two disastrous coal mine explosions. After walking around the cemetery of identical crosses, seeing graves of sons in the later disaster near the graves of the fathers who perished in the earlier one, I wrote: 'Ghost town enthusiasts love to wander about mills, peer down shafts, and browse through cabins; and I think that it is rather easy to romanticize the lives of the men who worked the mines or at least to feel rather detached about them as individuals. It's as if we are less concerned with their lives than their leavings. A trip to the Dawson cemetery, then, should be obligatory, for we can see the importance and value of their lives as it is mirrored by their graves. It is a hard person who is not deeply moved by the sight.'"

*   *   *

VARTAN, Vartanig G(arabed) 1923-1988

OBITUARY NOTICE—See index for *CA* sketch: Born June 28, 1923, in Pasadena, Calif.; died of cancer, May 24, 1988. Journalist and novelist. Vartan was a financial writer for the *New York Times* beginning in 1963 and the main writer of the newspaper's "Market Place" column beginning in 1983. He began his journalistic career in 1948 as a reporter for newspapers in Mississippi, then for the United Press in New York City. In 1955 he became a financial writer for the *New York Herald-Tribune,* and from 1957 to 1962 he was a Wall Street columnist for the *Christian Science Monitor.* Vartan wrote two novels, *50 Wall Street* and *The Dinosaur Fund.*

OBITUARIES AND OTHER SOURCES:

BOOKS

Who's Who in America, 44th edition, Marquis, 1986.

PERIODICALS

New York Times, May 25, 1988.

*   *   *

VAUGHAN, Frances E. 1935-

PERSONAL: Born January 1, 1935, in New York, N.Y.; daughter of Frederick V. and Caroline (Willis) Vaughan; children: Reece Robert Clark, Leslie Elizabeth Clark. *Education:* Stanford University, B.A. (with honors), 1956; California State University, Sonoma, M.A., 1969; California School of Professional Psychology, Ph.D., 1973. *Politics:* Democrat. *Religion:* Episcopalian.

ADDRESSES: Office—10 Millwood Ave., Mill Valley, Calif. 94941.

CAREER: California State University, Sonoma, lecturer in psychology, 1969-73; University of California, Extension Division, instructor in psychology at branches in Berkeley, Santa Cruz, Los Angeles, and Riverside, 1973-76; professor of psychology at Institute of Transpersonal Psychology, 1975-84; University of California, Irvine, assistant clinical professor, 1987—. Member of field faculty at Humanistic Psychology Institute, San Francisco, Calif., 1973-77; member of faculty at California School of Professional Psychology, 1974-76; adjunct professor at Union Graduate School West, 1979-81. Private practice of psychology in Mill Valley, Calif., 1974—; member of board of directors of Transpersonal Institute, 1974-81, and of Interlog, 1983-87.

MEMBER: International Center for Integrative Studies, American Psychological Association, Association for Humanistic Psychology (president, 1988-89), Association for Transpersonal Psychology (past president), California Psychological Association, Phi Beta Kappa.

WRITINGS:

Awakening Intuition, Anchor Press, 1979.
(Editor with Roger N. Walsh) *Beyond Ego: Transpersonal Dimensions in Psychology,* J. P. Tarcher, 1980.
(Editor with Walsh) *Accept This Gift: Selections From a Course in Miracles,* J. P. Tarcher, 1983.
The Inward Arc: Healing and Wholeness in Psychotherapy and Spirituality, New Science Library, 1986.
(Editor with Walsh) *A Gift of Peace: Selections From a Course in Miracles,* J. P. Tarcher, 1986.
(Editor with Walsh) *A Gift of Healing: Selections From a Course in Miracles,* J. P. Tarcher, 1988.

Contributor to psychology journals. Member of board of editors of *Journal of Transpersonal Psychology,* 1973—, *Journal of Humanistic Psychology,* and *Re-Vision.*

BIOGRAPHICAL/CRITICAL SOURCES:

PERIODICALS

Virginia Quarterly Review, autumn, 1986.

*   *   *

VAUGHT, Jacque
    See BROGAN, Jacqueline Vaught

*   *   *

VERDI, Marie de
    See MENCKEN, H(enry) L(ouis)

*   *   *

VINEBERG, Arthur (Martin)   1903-1988

OBITUARY NOTICE—See index for CA sketch: Born May 24, 1903, in Montreal, Quebec, Canada; died of pneumonia, March 26, 1988, in Montreal, Quebec, Canada. Surgeon and author. Vineberg developed a procedure for artery transplants soon after completing his service with the Canadian Army Medical Corps during World War II. Adaptations of the Vineberg method, used to maintain blood circulation in the heart muscle, gained acceptance in the 1960s and are currently in wide use. Vineberg worked as a staff surgeon at Bellevue Hospital from 1928 to 1939, then set up a private practice. He became surgeon in charge of cardiac surgery at Royal Victoria Hospital and acted as consultant surgeon to Jewish General Hospital, Queen Mary Veterans Hospital, and Montreal Institute of Cardiology. He contributed articles to the Textbook of Surgery and to medical journals, and he wrote, under different forms of his name, How to Live With Your Heart: The Family Guide to Heart Health and Myocardial Revascularization by Arterial/Ventricular Implants.

OBITUARIES AND OTHER SOURCES:

PERIODICALS

New York Times, March 30, 1988.

*   *   *

von BALTHASAR, Hans Urs   1905-1988

OBITUARY NOTICE: Born August 12, 1905, in Lucerne, Switzerland; died June 26, 1988, in Basel, Switzerland. Clergyman, theologian, and author. Ordained a Roman Catholic priest in 1936, von Balthasar spent most of his life reading and writing theological works. His 1952 essay "The Razing of the Bastions" is regarded as an important influence on the preparation of the 1963 to 1965 Second Vatican Council. Dubbed "one of the century's greatest theologians" by Bishop Otto Wuest of Basel, von Balthasar died two days before he was to be formally elevated to the rank of cardinal on June 28, 1988. Of his seventy-four books, several are available in translation, including Heart of the World, Prayer, A First Glance at Adrienne von Speyr, Elucidations, and Engagement With God.

OBITUARIES AND OTHER SOURCES:

PERIODICALS

Chicago Tribune, June 28, 1988, July 3, 1988.
Los Angeles Times, June 29, 1988.
Washington Post, June 28, 1988.

Von GUNDEN, Heidi Cecilia   1940-

PERSONAL: Born April 13, 1940, in San Diego, Calif.; daughter of Clarence F. Von Gunden (a general contractor) and Evangeline Savage (a teacher). Education: Mount St. Mary's College, B.Mus., 1963; California State University, Los Angeles, M.A., 1971; University of California, San Diego, Ph.D., 1977.

ADDRESSES: Home—2717 Heritage Dr., Champaign, Ill. 61821.

CAREER: Southern Illinois University, Carbondale, assistant professor of music theory and composition, 1975-79; University of Illinois at Urbana-Champaign, Urbana, assistant professor, beginning in 1979, associate professor of music theory and composition, 1985—.

MEMBER: American Society of University Composers, American Women Composers, College Music Society, Pi Kappa Lambda, Phi Kappa Phi.

WRITINGS:

The Music of Pauline Oliveros, Scarecrow, 1983.
The Music of Ben Johnston, Scarecrow, 1986.

Contributor to music journals.

WORK IN PROGRESS: The Music of Lou Harrison, publication by Scarecrow expected in 1990.

SIDELIGHTS: Heidi Celia Von Gunden told CA: "I enjoy writing about contemporary American composers, such as Pauline Oliveros, Ben Johnston, and Lou Harrison. I chose people whose music interests me. Oliveros's sonic meditation, Johnston's use of just intonation, and Harrison's involvement with world music are examples of fascinating research projects. I study the composers' music with the intention of discovering how and why their compositions work and then show my readers how to listen to specific works."

*   *   *

VOUTE, J. Peter   1906-

PERSONAL: Born October 27, 1906, in Amsterdam, Netherlands; immigrated to United States, 1953; naturalized U.S. citizen, 1961; son of Jan Reinier (a lawyer) and Jacoba (a homemaker; maiden name, Portielje) Voute; married Barbara Mary Carrad (a homemaker), November 18, 1931; children: Peter M., Reinier E., C. Antoinette Voute Roeder, Joan C. Education: University of Amsterdam, M.D., 1933. Religion: Episcopalian.

ADDRESSES: Home—132 Valley Dr., Santa Fe, N.M. 87501.

CAREER: Private practice of family medicine in Naarden, Netherlands, 1933-51, and in Eunice, Hagerman, and Las Cruces, N.M., 1953-65; New Mexico Department of Public Health, Santa Fe, district health officer, 1965-71; La Familia Medical Center, Santa Fe, medical director, 1971-78; writer, 1978—. Medical adviser to Santa Fe's Recovery Alcoholics Program; member of advisory board of La Residencia Nursing Home.

MEMBER: American Medical Association, American Academy of Family Physicians.

AWARDS, HONORS: Medal of Merit in Silver from Netherlands Red Cross, for postwar medical relief work in Java, 1945-46.

WRITINGS:

Only a Free Man: War Memories of Two Dutch Doctors, With the Journals of Henry Rynders, Lightning Tree, 1982.
Stranger in New Mexico: A Doctor's Journey, 1951-1986, University of New Mexico Press, 1987.

WORK IN PROGRESS: A novel, tentatively titled *My Son, Jacob* or *The Jewish Orphan.*

SIDELIGHTS: J. Peter Voute told *CA:* "As a retired physician of Dutch descent who practiced medicine during the Nazi occupation in Holland and migrated to the United States in 1953, I decided to tell the story of Medical Contact, the successful resistance movement of the Dutch medical profession against the Nazis. That is the subject of the book *Only a Free Man.*

"Later, after a second medical career of thirty years in New Mexico, I decided to write about my immigration, adaptation to a new homeland and culture, and the incredible progress (both the positive and negative aspects) of medical technology during my fifty years of medical practice. The result was my second book, *Stranger in New Mexico: A Doctor's Journey.*

"My work in progress is the story of a Jewish boy, born in Amsterdam in 1943, who loses his parents in the Holocaust when he is six months old. The woman who adopts him as a baby is a heroine in the resistance movement. She is arrested by the gestapo while caring for Jews in hiding. The woman survives the Mauthausen concentration camp and adopts the baby boy, who grows up to become a world renowned concert violinist. The book should be of interest to people who want to read about Nazi terror and the Holocaust, and certainly to Jews who are sensitive to the drama of a Jewish orphan who grows up learning about the gas chambers and the fate of his parents."

BIOGRAPHICAL/CRITICAL SOURCES:

PERIODICALS

Albuquerque Journal, September 6, 1987.

*   *   *

VROMAN, Mary Elizabeth (Gibson)   1923-1967

PERSONAL: Born in 1923 in Buffalo, N.Y.; died from complications following surgery, April 29, 1967, in New York, N.Y.; married Oliver M. Harper (a dentist). *Education:* Received B.A. from Alabama State Teachers College (now Alabama State University).

ADDRESSES: Home—892 Eastern Parkway, Brooklyn, N.Y.

CAREER: Teacher at Camden Academy, Camden, Ala., and other public schools in Alabama, Chicago, and New York for twenty years. Music and art coordinator for New York board of education "Higher Horizons" program.

MEMBER: Screen Writers Guild, Delta Sigma Theta.

AWARDS, HONORS: Christopher Award for inspirational magazine writing, 1952, for "See How They Run."

WRITINGS:

(And technical advisor) "Bright Road" (screenplay; based on Vroman's short story "See How They Run"), Metro-Goldwyn-Mayer, 1953.

Esther: A Novel, Bantam, 1963.
Shaped to Its Purpose: Delta Sigma Theta, The First Fifty Years, Random House, 1965.
Harlem Summer (young adult novel), illustrations by John Martinez, Putnam, 1967.

Work represented in anthology *Best Short Stories by Negro Writers.* Contributor of nonfiction, short stories, and poetry to *National Education Association Journal, Freedomways,* and *Ladies' Home Journal.*

SIDELIGHTS: During her tragically abridged literary career (she died of post-surgical complications while in her early forties), Mary Elizabeth Vroman portrayed the hard realities of black life without becoming strident. A writer whose race consciousness expressed itself in humanistic terms, Vroman explored how black people, confronted with adversity, managed to "retain their sense of humanity," described Edith Blicksilver in the *Dictionary of Literary Biography,* "and . . . find joy in their lives." Best known for the acclaimed short story "See How They Run" about her teaching experiences in the segregated, rural South, Vroman questioned the effectiveness of "angry stories by angry writers." "I just thought about how much I loved [the children] and tried to put it down on paper," she stated.

Like Vroman, the protagonist of "See How They Run" is an idealistic teacher from the North who is unprepared for the inadequacies of the segregated school system. In charge of forty-three poor black students, Jane Richards shows how caring and perseverance can gradually weaken poverty's powerful grasp. Like the blind mice of the nursery rhyme from which the story's title is taken, the students are urged to flee the privations of their environment through education. First published in the *Ladies' Home Journal,* "See How They Run" won a Christopher Award for its "humanitarian quality." It was later made into the motion picture "Bright Road," and Vroman became the fist black female member of the Screen Writers Guild with her screen adaptation.

Esther, Vroman's first novel, illustrates how breaking free of one's environment is particularly hard for the southern black woman. Lydia Jones, a black midwife bent on providing granddaughter Esther with a nursing education, acknowledges: "a colored woman . . . got to fight for it all the way"; her assertion is borne out by Esther's long, toilsome struggle to join that profession. Yet the younger woman eventually does reach her goal, achieving substantial career success. "The story ends on a note of optimistic brotherhood as both black and white medical personnel cooperate together to aid the victims of ptomaine [poisoning]," Blicksilver related.

In Vroman's young-adult novel, *Harlem Summer,* sixteen-year-old John Brown leaves his Montgomery, Alabama, home to spend the summer living and working in New York's Harlem. Encountering a variety of unfamiliar experiences, the youth discovers "that being a Negro is not as simple as it seemed in the safety of a loving home environment," wrote Dorothy M. Broderick in the *New York Times Book Review;* through new acquaintances John sees how anger, complacency, withdrawal, and pride are used to cope with poverty and degradation. "The novel provides a good range of attitudes and associations within an urban Negro community," one *Saturday Review* critic decided. While noting the novel's sparse plot and melodramatic climax, Broderick agreed, calling *Harlem Summer* "an exciting, provocative story [that] . . . explores the complexities of Negro ghetto life." The reviewer added: "It is in this honest portrayal, without descending to cynicism, that the book lays the groundwork for the reader to move on to 'Go Tell It on the Mountain,' something no other young people's novel has done.''

BIOGRAPHICAL/CRITICAL SOURCES:

BOOKS

Dictionary of Literary Biography, Volume 33: *Afro-American Fiction Writers After 1955,* Gale, 1984.
The Ethnic American Woman: Problems, Protests, Lifestyle, Kendall/Hunt, 1978.

PERIODICALS

Ebony, July, 1952.
Negro American Literature Forum, spring, 1973.
New York Times Book Review, May 7, 1967, May 4, 1969.
Saturday Review, May 13, 1967.

OBITUARIES:

PERIODICALS

New York Times, April 30, 1967.
Publishers Weekly, June 19, 1967.*

W

WACHER, J(ohn) S(tewart)   1927-

PERSONAL: Born August 12, 1927, in Canterbury, England. *Education:* Received B.Sc. from University of London.

CAREER: University of Leicester, Leicester, England, reader in archaeology.

MEMBER: Royal Archaeological Institute, Society for the Promotion of Roman Studies, Society of Antiquaries of London (fellow).

WRITINGS:

The Civitas Capitals of Roman Britain, Leicester University Press, 1966.
Excavations at Brough-on-Humber, 1958-1961, Society of Antiquaries, 1969.
(Contributor) Alice Mary Hadfield, editor, *Cirencester: The Roman Corinium, Gloucestershire,* British Publishing Co., 1970.
The Towns of Roman Britain, University of California Press, 1975.
Roman Britain, Dent, 1978.
The Coming of Rome, Routledge & Kegan Paul, 1979, Scribner, 1980.
(With A. D. McWhirr) *Early Roman Occupation at Cirencester,* Cirencester Excavation Committee, 1982.
(Editor with Brian Hartley) *Rome and Her Northern Provinces: Papers Presented to Sheppard Frere in Honour of His Retirement From the Chair of the Archaeology of the Roman Empire, University of Oxford, 1983,* Alan Sutton, 1983.
(Editor) *The Roman World,* two volumes, Routledge & Kegan Paul, 1987.

Contributor to *Princeton Dictionary of Classical Archaeology.* Contributor to scholarly journals.

BIOGRAPHICAL/CRITICAL SOURCES:

PERIODICALS

Times Literary Supplement, September 12, 1975, September 22, 1978, August 21, 1987.
Virginia Quarterly Review, autumn, 1975.*

WALMAN, Jerome   1937-

PERSONAL: Born June 19, 1937, in Charleston, W.Va.; son of Joe (a business consultant) and Madeline Minnie (a concert pianist; maiden name, Levy) Walman; married Mary Joan Granara (a singer and actress), September 5, 1960. *Education:* Attended West Virginia University, 1955; Boston University, 1958; Berkley School of Music, Boston, 1959.

ADDRESSES: Home—400 East 59th St., Apt. 9F, New York, N.Y. 10022. *Office*—P.O. Box 31, Franklin Delano Roosevelt Station, New York, N.Y. 10150.

CAREER: Psychotherapist in hypnosis and music therapy, 1964—. Musical composer and producer, 1962-63; independent television producer, 1978-88; consultant to New York University Medical School program Network for Learning, 1980, and educational consultant to U.S. Defense Department, 1984; playwright and theatrical producer; part-time lecturer.

MEMBER: Music Therapy International, Memory Improvement and Concentration Center of America, Meditation and Mental Development Center of New York, Parapsychology Center.

AWARDS, HONORS: Honorary doctorate in psychology, 1971; award from *TV World* magazine, 1982, for television show.

WRITINGS:

PLAYS

(With Kenneth Jerome) *Moments* (two-act; first produced in Washington, D.C., at Washington Theater Club, April 1, 1971), Dramatic Publishing, 1983.
"I Murdered Mary Finch One Sunny Day Last Spring" (three-act), first produced in New York City at Nat Horne Musical Theater, 1976.
"Last Call" (three-act), first produced in New York City at 26th Street Theater, 1977.
"TV Mag" (five-act opera), first produced in Los Angeles at Central Theater, 1978.
"Three Very Important Little Men" (three one-act plays), first produced in London at a West End theater, 1983.

OTHER

(Contributor) *Hypnosis and Law,* Matthew Bender, 1986.

Author of *The Walman Educational Systems,* 1985, and *The Walman Diet Book,* 1987.

WORK IN PROGRESS: A work on "the enhancement of food and wine via altered states of hypnosis and/or meditation."

SIDELIGHTS: Jerome Walman told *CA:* "In addition to teaching a wine appreciation course internationally and being a world traveler, I am a food and wine consultant to restaurants, schools, and corporations, and an independent image and artistic consultant."

AVOCATIONAL INTERESTS: Acting, singing, athletic performance enhancement, psychic phenomena.

*   *   *

WALROND, Eric (Derwent)   1898-1966

PERSONAL: Born in 1898 in Georgetown, British Guiana (now Guyana); immigrated to Barbados, 1906, to Panama Canal Zone, c. 1910, to United States, 1918, to Europe, c. 1928; died in 1966 in London, England; married twice; children: Jean, Dorothy, Lucille. *Education:* Attended City College of New York (now of the City University of New York), 1922-24, Columbia University, 1924-26, and University of Wisconsin, 1928.

ADDRESSES: Home—London, England.

CAREER: Worked in the Panama Canal Zone, c. 1916-18, as a clerk for the Health Department of the Canal Commission and as a reporter and sportswriter for *Panama Star and Herald* and aided in the publication of *Workman;* held various secretarial and stenographer positions in New York, N.Y., c. 1918-21; *Brooklyn and Long Island Informer,* New York City, co-owner, editor, and reporter, 1921-23; *Weekly Review,* New York City, associate editor, 1921-23; associate editor of *Negro World,* 1923-25; *Opportunity: Journal of Negro Life,* New York City, business manager, 1925-27.

MEMBER: Eclectic Club, Universal Negro Improvement Association.

AWARDS, HONORS: Received a John Simon Guggenheim Memorial Foundation Award and became a Zona Gale scholar at University of Wisconsin, both in 1928.

WRITINGS:

Tropic Death (short story collection), Boni & Liveright, 1926, Macmillan, 1972.
(Contributor) Van Wyck Brooks and others, editors, *The American Caravan* (anthology), Macaulay, 1927.
(Editor with Rosey E. Pool) *Black and Unknown Bards: A Collection of Negro Poetry,* Hand & Flower Press, 1958.
(Contributor) Richard Bardsdale and Kenneth Kinnaman, editors, *Black Writers of America* (anthology), Macmillan, 1972.

Work represented in anthologies, including *Anthology of American Negro Literature, Dark Symphony, Best Short Stories by Negro Writers, From the Roots,* and *Best Short Stories.* Contributor to periodicals such as *All Star Weekly, Black Man, Crisis, Current History, Dearborn Independent, Independent, Messenger, Negro World, New Age, New Republic, Opportunity, Saturday Review, Saturday Review of Literature, Smart Set, Success,* and *Vanity Fair.*

WORK IN PROGRESS: At the time of his death, Walrond was working on a book about the Panama Canal.

SIDELIGHTS: Eric Walrond migrated to New York City in 1918 at the age of twenty and within a few years established himself as one of the more important young writers associated with the black artistic movement known as the Harlem Renaissance. Initially Walrond concentrated on the subject of racial bigotry, which he personally experienced after arriving in the United States, and his writings reflect both his indignation and disillusionment. *Tropic Death,* his most significant work, however, focuses on and illuminates the multitudinal problems faced by migratory blacks of the Caribbean. A collection of short stories, the book was regarded as an outstanding example of avant-garde writing and drew high praise from contemporary critics.

BIOGRAPHICAL/CRITICAL SOURCES:

BOOKS

Dictionary of Literary Biography, Volume 51: *Afro-American Writers From the Harlem Renaissance to 1940,* Gale, 1987.

PERIODICALS

Savacou 2, September, 1970.*

*   *   *

WALTON, William   1909-

PERSONAL: Born in 1909 in Jacksonville, Ill.; son of J. William (a newspaper publisher) and Helen (Weller) Walton; married Emily Ann Lillie, 1935 (divorced, 1948); children: Frances Walton Buehler, Matthew. *Education:* Attended Illinois College, 1927-29; University of Wisconsin—Madison, A.B., 1931.

ADDRESSES: Home and office—236 West 26th St., New York, N.Y. 10001.

CAREER: Associated Press, journalist in Springfield, Ill., Chicago, Ill., and New York, N.Y., 1935-40; foreign newswriter for *PM* (newspaper), 1940-42; correspondent for *Time* and *Life,* 1942-46; *New Republic,* New York City, Washington editor, 1946-49; painter and free-lance writer, 1949—. Chairman of Fine Arts Commission, Washington, D.C., 1963-70; past foreign editor of *Life.* New York City campaign coordinator for John F. Kennedy, 1960.

MEMBER: American Institute of Architects (honorary member, 1986), Century Club.

AWARDS, HONORS: Bronze Star, 1944, for parachuting into Normandy as a correspondent; L.H.D. from Illinois College, 1946.

WRITINGS:

The Evidence of Washington, Harper, 1968.
(Editor) *A Civil War Courtship: The Letters of Edwin Weller From Antietam to Atlanta,* Doubleday, 1980.

Contributor of articles to periodicals, including *House & Garden* and *Architectural Digest.*

WORK IN PROGRESS: "Some sketchy memoirs."

SIDELIGHTS: William Walton told *CA* that his first book, *The Evidence of Washington,* is about "the pastoral beginnings and the sophisticated present of our capital." His second book, *A Civil War Courtship,* is "a soldier's eyewitness to great events, including Gettysburg and the wilderness—at the same time wooing the girl" who became the author's grandmother.

WARD, Theodore (James)   1902-1983

PERSONAL: Born September 15, 1902, in Thibodeaux, La.; died of a heart attack, May 8, 1983, in Chicago, Ill.; son of Everett (a schoolteacher and book salesman) and Mary Louise (Pierre) Ward; married Mary Sangigian (an office manager), June 15, 1940; children: Elsie Virginia, Laura Louise. *Education:* Attended University of Utah, 1930, and University of Wisconsin, 1931-33.

CAREER: Playwright. Traveled around the United States and worked at various odd jobs, including elevator operator and barbershop porter. WIBA-Radio, Madison, Wis., staff artist, 1931-32; Works Progress Administration (WPA; renamed Work Projects Administration, 1939), Chicago, Ill., recreational director, 1934-38, instructor of dramatics at Lincoln Center, 1937, actor with Federal Theatre Project, 1937-39; Negro Playwrights Co. of Harlem, New York, N.Y., co-founding president, 1940-41; factory laborer and bootblack during early 1940s; writer for Office of War Information, c. 1944; taught adult writing seminars in Chicago and New Orleans, La., after 1960s, and drama classes for children in Chicago, 1963; South Side Center for the Performing Arts, Chicago, founding executive director, 1967-68; playwright-in-residence at Free Southern Theatre, New Orleans, during 1970s.

MEMBER: Dramatists Guild.

AWARDS, HONORS: "Sick and Tiahd" won second prize in Chicago Repertory Company theatre contest, 1937; National Theatre Conference fellowship, 1945-47; Theatre Guild Award, 1947, for play "Our Lan'"; named Negro of the Year, 1947; Guggenheim fellowship, 1947-48, for play "John Brown"; named Outstanding Pioneer of Black Theatre, 1975; DuSable Writers' Seminar and Poetry Festival Award for excellence in drama, 1982.

WRITINGS:

PLAYS

Big White Fog: A Negro Tragedy (first produced at Great Northern Theatre, Chicago, 1983; produced Off-Broadway at Lincoln Theatre, Harlem, 1940), privately printed, c. 1973.
"Our Lan'" (first produced at Henry Street Playhouse in New York, 1947; produced on Broadway, 1947), published in *A Theater in Your Head,* edited by Kenneth Thorpe Rowe, Funk, 1960.

Author of perhaps twenty or thirty other plays, including "Sick and Tiahd" (also as "Sick and Tired"), 1937; "The Daubers," 1953; "Candle in the Wind," 1967; "The Creole"; "John Brown"; "Whole Hog or Nothing"; "Challenge"; "Skin Deep"; "Even the Dead Arise and Shout Hallelujah"; "Falcon of Adowa"; "Throwback"; "Charity"; "The Life of Harriet Tubman"; "Deliver the Goods"; and "John de Conqueror."

Work represented in anthologies, including *Black Drama in America: An Anthology,* edited by Darwin T. Turner, Fawcett, 1971.

OTHER

Contributor of articles to periodicals, including *Current Opinion, Mainstream,* and *Black Theatre.*

Associate editor of *Mainstream.*

SIDELIGHTS: Regarded as "the dean of black dramatists" during his day, Theodore Ward contributed to the advancement of black theatre in the United States and was officially named Outstanding Pioneer of Black Theatre in 1975. His plays, which focus on themes of Negro life, were roundly acclaimed for their innovative depiction of the black experience and for avoiding the use of spirituals and feverish dancing that typically distinguished theatricals about Negro people. According to C. Gerald Fraser in the *New York Times,* former critic Brooks Atkinson once wrote that Ward "'made no concessions to the white man's taste.'" Similarly, Fraser reported that in Errol Hill's opinion Ward consistently endeavored through his work "'to establish heroes for the black race.'"

Between 1934 and 1939 Ward found employment with the Works Progress Administration (WPA), a U.S. Government agency designed to counter rising unemployment during the Great Depression by engaging the jobless in diverse projects. In particular, the program's Federal Theatre Project, which Ward joined in 1937, induced theatrical production and experimentation by impoverished writers. In 1938 it staged Ward's first major work, "Big White Fog." The play's success with Chicago audiences precipitated Ward's joining the newly formed Negro Playwrights Company in New York, where he and fellow members, such as Langston Hughes and Richard Wright, launched their fledgling company with an Off-Broadway production of Ward's "Big White Fog" in 1940. While critics and Ward's contemporaries applauded the play's seriousness and realism, New York theatergoers disapproved of its unrestrained leftist political tone. Consequently, "Big White Fog" closed after sixty-four performances, and the Negro Playwrights Company folded.

Undaunted but wary due to his experience in New York, Ward returned to Chicago for his next play, "Our Lan'." Circumstances including the outbreak of World War II, however, prevented the work from being staged until 1947, when it premiered at a New York playhouse. That same year "Our Lan'" opened on Broadway and ran forty-two shows before closing. Though short-lived, the play's appearance on Broadway distinguished Ward as one of the few black writers to have their work produced there following the end of the Harlem Renaissance of the late 1920s and early 1930s and earned him a 1947 Theatre Guild Award. Variously described as Ward's "best" and "best-known" play, "Our Lan'" was revised by Ward and restaged around 1967 at the Louis Theater in Chicago.

Factors such as a lack of support for the development of black theatre contributed to Ward's limited success as a playwright. In particular, the 1950s proved an increasingly difficult time for him to have his work produced. As a result, most of Ward's ensuing twenty or thirty plays were either short-term runs or not produced at all. Additionally, as some observers pointed out, much of Ward's work proved too radical for audiences of the time and thereby sacrificed popular appeal. In retrospect, critics have since deemed his work a major contribution to the early development of American black theatre, thus judging Ward an undeservedly neglected playwright.

BIOGRAPHICAL/CRITICAL SOURCES:

BOOKS

Abramson, Doris E., *Negro Playwrights in the American Theatre, 1925-1959,* Columbia University Press, 1969.
Flanagan, Hallie, *Arena: The History of the Federal Theatre,* Duell, Sloane & Pierce, 1940.
Nathan, George Jean, editor, *Theatre Book of the Year, 1948-1949,* Knopf, 1949.

OBITUARIES:

BOOKS

The Annual Obituary 1983, St. James Press, 1984.

PERIODICALS

Chicago Tribune, May 12, 1983.
Los Angeles Times, May 14, 1983.
Newsweek, May 23, 1983.
New York Times, May 11, 1983.
Time, May 23, 1983.
Washington Post, May 13, 1983.*

*   *   *

WASHINGTON, Booker T(aliaferro)   1856-1915

PERSONAL: Original name, Booker Taliaferro; later added surname Washington; born into slavery, April 5, 1856, on a plantation near Hale's Ford, Franklin County, Va.; died of arteriosclerosis and extreme exhaustion, November 14, 1915, in Tuskegee, Ala.; buried in a brick tomb, made by students, on a hill overlooking Tuskegee Institute; son of Jane Ferguson (a slave); married Fannie Norton Smith, 1882 (deceased, 1884); married Olivia A. Davidson (an educator), 1885 (deceased, 1889); married Margaret J. Murray (an educator), October 12, 1893; children: (first marriage) Portia Washington Pittman; (second marriage) Booker Taliaferro, Jr., Ernest Davidson. *Education:* Hampton Institute, B.A. (with honors), 1875; Wayland Seminary, M.A., 1879.

CAREER: Worked in the salt furnaces and coal mines of West Virginia as a child, and as a houseboy for General Lewis Ruffner, 1970-72; teacher at a rural school for blacks, Malden, W.Va., 1875-78; Hampton Institute, Hampton, Va., teacher and director of experimental educational program for Indians, 1879-81; Tuskegee Normal and Industrial Institute, Tuskegee, Ala., co-founder, principal, and professor of mental and moral sciences, 1881-1915; writer. Founder of National Negro Business League, 1900, and National Negro Health Week, 1914; adviser to several U.S. presidents, including Theodore Roosevelt and William Howard Taft, on racial and social matters; lecturer on racial and educational subjects.

AWARDS, HONORS: A.M., Harvard University, 1897; LL.D., Dartmouth College, 1901; first black elected to Hall of Fame, New York University, 1945.

WRITINGS:

Black-Belt Diamonds: Gems From the Speeches, Addresses, and Talks to Students of Booker T. Washington, compiled by Victoria Earle Matthews, introduction by Thomas Fortune, Fortune & Scott, 1898, reprinted, Negro Universities Press, 1969.
The Future of the American Negro (essays and speeches), Small, Maynard, 1899, reprinted, Negro Universities Press, 1969.
(With N. B. Wood and Fannie Barrier Williams) *A New Negro for a New Century*, American Publishing House, 1900, reprinted, AMS Press, 1973.
Sowing and Reaping, L. C. Page, 1900, reprinted, Books for Libraries, 1971.
(With Edgar Webber) *The Story of My Life and Work* (autobiography), illustrations by Frank Beard, J. L. Nichols, 1900, revised edition published as *An Autobiography by Booker T. Washington: The Story of My Life and Work*, introduction by J.L.M. Curry, J. L. Nichols, 1901, another revised edition published as *Booker T. Washington's*

Own Story of His Life and Work, supplement by Albon L. Holsey, 1915, reprint of original edition, Negro Universities Press, 1969.
(With Max Bennett Thrasher) *Up From Slavery: An Autobiography*, A. L. Burt, 1901, reprinted, with an introduction by Langston Hughes, Dodd, 1965, reprinted, with an introduction by Booker T. Washington III and illustrations by Denver Gillen, Heritage Press, 1970, reprinted, with illustrations by Bart Forbes, Franklin Library, 1977, abridged edition, Harrap, 1929.
Character Building: Being Addresses Delivered on Sunday Evenings to the Students of Tuskegee Institute by Booker T. Washington, Doubleday, Page, 1902, reprinted, Haskell House, 1972.
(Contributor) *The Negro Problem* (articles), James Pott, 1903, reprinted, AMS Press, 1970.
Working With the Hands (autobiography), illustrations by Frances Benjamin Johnston, Doubleday, Page, 1904, reprinted, Arno, 1970.
(Editor with Emmett J. Scott) *Tuskegee and Its People: Their Ideals and Achievements*, Appleton, 1905, reprinted, Books for Libraries, 1971.
Putting the Most Into Life (addresses), Crowell, 1906.
(With S. Laing Williams) *Frederick Douglass* (biography), G. W. Jacobs, 1907, reprinted, edited by Ellis Paxson Oberholtzer, Argosy-Antiquarian, 1969.
The Negro in Business, Hertel, Jenkins, 1907, reprinted, AMS Press, 1971.
(With W.E.B. Du Bois) *The Negro in the South: His Economic Progress in Relation to His Moral and Religious Development* (addresses), G. W. Jacobs, 1907, reprinted, AMS Press, 1973.
The Story of the Negro: The Rise of the Race From Slavery, two volumes, Doubleday, Page, 1909, reprinted, Negro Universities Press, 1969.
(With Robert E. Park and Emmett J. Scott) *My Larger Education: Being Chapters From My Experience* (autobiography), illustrated with photographs, Doubleday, Page, 1911, reprinted, Mnemosyne Publishing, 1969.
(With Robert E. Park) *The Man Farthest Down: A Record of Observation and Study in Europe*, Doubleday, Page, 1912, reprinted, with an introduction by St. Clair Drake, Transaction Books, 1984.
The Story of Slavery, Hall & McCreary, 1913, reprinted, with biographical sketch by Emmett J. Scott and photographs from Tuskegee Institute, Owen Publishing, 1940.
One Hundred Selected Sayings of Booker T. Washington, compiled by Julia Skinner, Wilson Printing, 1923.
Selected Speeches of Booker T. Washington, edited by son, E. Davidson Washington, Doubleday, Doran, 1932, reprinted, Kraus Reprint, 1976.
Quotations of Booker T. Washington, compiled by E. Davidson Washington, Tuskegee Institute Press, 1938.
The Booker T. Washington Papers, thirteen volumes, University of Illinois Press, 1972-84, Volume I: *The Autobiographical Writings*, Volume II: *1860-1889*, Volume III: *1889-1895*, Volume IV: *1895-1898*, Volume V: *1899-1900*, Volume VI: *1901-1902*, Volume VII: *1903-1904*, all edited by Louis R. Harlan; Volume VIII: *1904-1906*, Volume IX: *1906-1908*, Volume X: *1909-1912*, Volume XI: *1911-1912*, *Volume XII: 1912-1914*, Volume XIII: *1914-1915*, all edited by Louis R. Harlan and Raymond W. Smock.

Author of numerous monographs, including *Education of the Negro*, J. B. Lyon, 1900.

SIDELIGHTS: Booker T. Washington was born near Roanoke, Virginia, at Hale's Farm, where his mother was the slave cook of James Burroughs, a small planter. His father was white and possibly a member of the Burroughs family. As a child Booker swept yards and brought water to slaves working in the fields. Freed after the Civil War, he and his mother went to Malden, West Virginia, to join Washington Ferguson, whom his mother had married during the war. There young Washington helped support the family by working in salt furnaces and coal mines. He taught himself the alphabet, then studied nights with the teacher of a local school for blacks. In 1870 he started doing housework for the owner of the coal mine where he worked at the time. The owner's wife, an austere New Englander, encouraged his studies and instilled in Washington a great regard for education. In 1872 he set out for the Hampton Institute, a school set up by the Virginia legislature for blacks. He walked much of the way and worked menial jobs to earn the fare to complete the five-hundred-mile journey.

Washington spent three years at Hampton, paying for his room and board by working as a janitor. After graduating with honors in 1875, he taught for two years in Malden, then returned to Hampton to teach in a program for American Indians. In 1881, General Samuel Chapman Armstrong, the principal at Hampton, recommended Washington to the Alabama legislature for the job of principal of a new normal school for black students at Tuskegee. Washington was accepted for the position, but when he arrived in Tuskegee he discovered that neither land nor buildings had been acquired for the projected school, nor were there any funds for these purposes. Consequently, Washington began classes with thirty students in a shanty donated by a black church. Soon, however, he was able to borrow money to buy an abandoned plantation nearby and moved the school there.

Convinced that economic strength was the best route to political and social equality for blacks, Washington encouraged Tuskegee students to learn industrial skills. Carpentry, cabinetmaking, printing, shoemaking, and tinsmithing were among the first courses the school offered. Boys also studied farming and dairying, while girls learned cooking and sewing and other skills related to homemaking. Strong empahsis was placed on personal hygiene, manners, and character building. Students followed a rigid schedule of study and work and were required to attend chapel daily and a series of religious services on Sunday. Washington usually conducted the Sunday evening program himself. During his thirty-four-year principalship of Tuskegee, the school's curriculum expanded to include instruction in professions as well as trades. At the time of Washington's death in 1915 Tuskegee had an endowment of $2 million and a staff of 200 members. Nearly 2,000 students were enrolled in the regular courses and about the same number in special courses and the extension division. Among its all-black faculty was the renowned agricultural scientist George Washington Carver.

Although his administration of Tuskegee was Washington's best-known achievement, his work as an educator was only one aspect of his multifaceted career. Washington spent much time raising money for Tuskegee and publicizing the school and its philosophy. His success in securing the praise and financial support of northern philanthropists was remarkable. One of his admirers was industrialist Andrew Carnegie, who thought Washington "one of the most wonderful men . . . who ever has lived." Many other political, intellectual, and religious leaders were almost as laudatory. Washington was also in demand as a speaker, winning national fame on the lecture circuit. His most famous speech was his address at the opening of the Cotton States and International Exposition in Atlanta in September, 1895.

Later known as the Atlanta Compromise, the speech contained the essence of Washington's educational and racial views and was, according to C. Vann Woodward in his review of Louis R. Harlan's biography *Booker T. Washington: The Making of a Black Leader, 1865-1901* for *New Republic*, "his stock speech for the rest of his life." Emphasizing to black members of the audience the imporance of economic power, Washington contended that "the opportunity to earn a dollar in a factory just now is worth infinitely more than the opportunity to spend a dollar in an opera house." Consequently he urged blacks not to strain relations in the South by demanding social equality with whites. To the white members of the audience he promised that "in all things that are purely social we can be as separate as fingers, yet one as the hand in all things essential to mutual progress."

The Atlanta speech, Woodward noted, "contained nothing [Washington] had not said many times before. . . . But in the midst of racial crisis, black disenfranchisement and Populist rebellion in the '90s, the brown orator electrified conservative hopes." Washington was hailed in the white press as leader and spokesman for all American blacks and successor to the prominent abolitionist Frederick Douglass, who had died a few months earlier. His position, however, was denounced by many black leaders, including civil rights activist W.E.B. Du Bois, who objected to Washington's emphasis on vocational training and economic advancement and argued that higher education and political agitation would win equality for blacks. According to August Meier, writing in the *Journal of Negro History,* those blacks who accepted Washington's "accommodation" doctrines "understood that through tact and indirection [Washington] hoped to secure the good will of the white man and the eventual recognition of the constitutional rights of American Negroes."

The contents of Washington's recently released private papers reinforce the latter interpretation of the educator's motives. These documents offer evidence that in spite of the cautious stance that he maintained publicly, Washington was covertly engaged in challenging racial injustices and in improving social and economic conditions for blacks. The prominence he gained by his placating demeanor enabled him to work surreptitiously against segregation and disenfranchisement and to win political appointments that helped advance the cause of racial equality. "In other words," Woodward posited, "he secretly attacked the racial settlement that he publicly sanctioned."

Among Washington's many published works is his autobiography *Up From Slavery,* a rousing account of his life from slave to eminent educator. Often referred to by critics as a classic, its style is simple, direct, and anecdotal. Like his numerous essays and speeches, *Up From Slavery* promotes his racial philosophy and, in Woodward's opinion, "presents [Washington's] experience mythically, teaches 'lessons' and reflects a sunny optimism about black life in America." Woodward added, "It was the classic American success story, 'the Horatio Alger myth in black.'" Praised lavishly and compared to Benjamin Franklin's *Autobiography, Up From Slavery* became a best-seller in the United States and was eventually translated into more than a dozen languages.

MEDIA ADAPTATIONS: Recordings—"Up From Slavery," read by Ossie Davis, Caedmon Records, 1976.

BIOGRAPHICAL/CRITICAL SOURCES:

BOOKS

Bontemps, Arna Wendell, *Young Booker: Booker T. Washington's Early Days,* Dodd, 1972.

Drinker, Frederick E., *Booker T. Washington: The Master Mind of a Child of Slavery,* National Publishing, 1915, reprinted, Negro Universities Press, 1970.

Harlan, Louis R., *Booker T. Washington: The Making of a Black Leader, 1856-1901,* Oxford University Press, 1972.

Harlan, Louis R., *Booker T. Washington: The Wizard of Tuskegee, 1901-1915,* Oxford University Press, 1983.

Hawkins, Hugh, editor, *Booker T. Washington and His Critics: The Problem of Negro Leadership,* Heath, 1962, 2nd edition, 1974.

Matthews, Basil Joseph, *Booker T. Washington, Educator and Interracial Interpreter,* 1948, reprinted, McGrath, 1969.

Meier, August, *Negro Thought in America, 1880-1915: Racial Ideologies in the Age of Booker T. Washington,* University of Michigan Press, 1963.

Scott, Emmett J. and Lyman Beecher Stowe, *Booker T. Washington, Builder of Civilization,* Doubleday, Page, 1916, reprinted, Kraus Reprint, 1972.

Spencer, Samuel R., Jr., *Booker T. Washington and the Negro's Place in American Life,* edited by Oscar Handlin, Little, Brown, 1955, reprinted, 1965.

Thornbrough, Emma Lou, editor, *Booker T. Washington,* Prentice-Hall, 1969.

Weisberger, Bernard A., *Booker T. Washington,* New American Library, 1972.

PERIODICALS

American Heritage, August, 1968.

American Historical Review, January, 1966, December, 1985.

Crisis, August, 1978, February, 1983.

Journal of American History, December, 1985.

Journal of Negro Education, fall, 1977.

Journal of Negro History, January, 1953, October, 1955, January, 1958, April, 1960, April, 1968, July, 1969.

Journal of Southern History, August, 1971, February, 1979, February, 1986.

Nation, November 18, 1915.

Negro History Bulletin, April, 1958.

New Republic, November 11, 1972, July 18, 1983.

New York Review of Books, August 9, 1973.

New York Times Book Review, March 4, 1973, May 22, 1983.

North American Review, August, 1901.

Phylon, September, 1976.

Social Education, May, 1968.

South Atlantic Quarterly, autumn, 1978.

Times Literary Supplement, April 13, 1973, November 15, 1974.*

—*Sketch by Joanne M. Peters*

*   *   *

WASSERMAN, Mark   1946-

PERSONAL: Born January 29, 1946, in Boston, Mass.; son of Herbert (a stockbroker) and Deborah (a homemaker; maiden name, Seevak) Wasserman; married Marlie Parker (an editor), November 24, 1968; children: Aaron, Danielle. *Education:* Duke University, B.A., 1968; University of Chicago, M.A., 1971, Ph.D., 1975.

ADDRESSES: Office—Department of History, Rutgers University, New Brunswick, N.J. 08903.

CAREER: Northern Illinois University, DeKalb, assistant professor of history, 1976-77; Rutgers University, New Brunswick, N.J., assistant professor, 1978-84, associate professor of history, 1984—. Member of board of education of Highland Park, N.J., 1984—.

MEMBER: American Historical Association, Latin American Studies Association, Conference on Latin American History, Association of Borderlands Scholars, Middle Atlantic Council of Latin American Studies, Southeastern Council of Latin American Studies.

AWARDS, HONORS: Tinker Foundation fellowship, 1977; Arthur P. Whitaker Prize from Middle Atlantic Council of Latin American Studies, 1984, for *Capitalists, Caciques, and Revolution.*

WRITINGS:

A History of Latin America, 1st edition, Houghton, 1980, 3rd edition, 1988.

Capitalists, Caciques, and Revolution, University of North Carolina Press, 1984.

WORK IN PROGRESS: Elites in Post-Revolutionary Mexico.

*   *   *

WATKINS, Frances Ellen
See HARPER, Frances Ellen Watkins

*   *   *

WATSON, Irving S.
See MENCKEN, H(enry) L(ouis)

*   *   *

WEIGEL, George   1951-

PERSONAL: Born April 17, 1951, in Baltimore, Md.; son of George Shillow (an insurance executive) and Betsy (a homemaker; maiden name, Schmitz) Weigel; married Joan Balcombe (a homemaker); children: Gwyneth Anne, Monica Ruth. *Education:* St. Mary's Seminary and University, Baltimore, Md., B.A. (magna cum laude), 1973; University of St. Michael's College, Toronto, Ontario, M.A. (summa cum laude), 1975. *Politics:* "Registered Democrat, but constantly wondering why." *Religion:* Roman Catholic.

ADDRESSES: Home—5415 Glenwood Rd., Bethesda, Md. 20817. *Office*—James Madison Foundation, 1030 15th St. N.W., No. 412, Washington, D.C. 20005.

CAREER: Christian Brothers College, Orangeville, Ontario, lecturer in theology, 1974-75; St. Thomas Seminary, Washington, D.C., assistant professor of theology and assistant dean of studies, 1975-77; Religious Education Center, Seattle, Wash., instructor in religion and pastoral theology, 1975-78; World Without War Council of Greater Seattle, Seattle, scholar in residence, 1977-84, founder and director of Cathedral Fellowships in World Affairs, 1980-84, co-director of American Initiatives Project, 1981-84; James Madison Foundation, Washington, D.C., president, 1985—, editor and principal author of *American Purpose,* 1987—, co-director of U.S. Institute of Peace seminar, 1987—. Research fellow at Woodrow Wilson International Center for Scholars, 1984-85; member of executive committee of Institute on Religion and Democracy, 1980—; member of board of directors of Rural Development Institute, 1983—, Puebla Institute, 1987—, and Keston-USA,

1987—; associate of Center on Religion and Society, 1986—; member of Ad Hoc Committee on Religious Liberty, 1987—. Mars Lecturer at Northwestern University, 1984; lecturer on theology, ethics, war, and peace. Member of board of regents of Seattle University, 1981-84; member of advisory committee on ethical values, U.S. Information Agency, 1982-84; member of academic advisory board of Washington Institute for Public Policy Research, 1986—.

AWARDS, HONORS: Grant from National Endowment for the Humanities, 1977-84; senior fellow of Earhart Foundation, 1985-86.

WRITINGS:

Washington's Window on the World: A Guide to World Affairs Organizations and Institutions in Washington State, Frayn Publishing, 1983.
Peace and Freedom: Christian Faith, Democracy, and the Problem of War, Institute on Religion and Democracy, 1983.
Tranquillitas Ordinis: The Present Failure and Future Promise of American Catholic Thought on War and Peace, Oxford University Press, 1987.

Columnist for *Progress,* 1979-86. Contributing editor of *Seattle Weekly,* 1982—; founding member of editorial board of *Crisis;* member of editorial board of *This World.*

CONTRIBUTOR

Raymond D. Gastil, editor, *Freedom in the World 1982,* Greenwood Press, 1982.
Paul M. Cole and William J. Taylor, editors, *The Nuclear Freeze Debate: Arms Control Issues for the 1980s,* Westview, 1983.
John D. Jones and Marc F. Griesbach, editors, *Just War Theory in the Nuclear Age,* University Press of America, 1985.
Charles Reid, editor, *Peace in a Nuclear Age,* Catholic University of America Press, 1987.
Michael A. Scully, editor, *The Best of "This World,"* University Press of America, 1987.

Contributor of articles and reviews to magazines and newspapers, including *Thomist, America, Christian Century, National Catholic Reporter, World Affairs,* and *Eternity.*

WORK IN PROGRESS: A book of essays on the current state of Catholicism in the United States, publication by Paulist Press expected in 1989; editing a book of essays on basic questions in the ethics, war, and peace debate for the 1990s, publication expected in 1989; *Beyond Niebuhr: The Necessity and Limits of Christian Realism* (tentative title), publication expected in 1990.

SIDELIGHTS: George Weigel told *CA:* "My work is an exploration of the relationship between religious conviction, moral reasoning, and public policy, with a focus on foreign affairs and an explicit interest in the debate over war and peace, security and freedom. That work is enthusiastically received by some, deplored by others, but seems to bore no one."

*   *   *

WEIL, Robert   1955-

PERSONAL: Born September 9, 1955, in New York, N.Y.; son of Lothar and Elsbeth (Landmann) Weil. *Education:* Yale University, B.A., 1977.

ADDRESSES: Home—5 Riverside Dr., New York, N.Y. 10023. *Agent*—Wendy Lipkind Agency, 225 East 57th St., New York, N.Y. 10022.

CAREER: Times Books, New York, N.Y., assistant editor, 1979-81; *Omni,* New York City, editor of book division, 1981-87, features editor, 1984-87; senior editor at St. Martin's Press, 1988—.

MEMBER: Phi Beta Kappa.

WRITINGS:

The Yankee Quizbook, Doubleday, 1981.
(Editor) *The Omni Future Almanac,* Crown, 1982.

*   *   *

WEINSTEIN, Nathan
See WEST, Nathanael

*   *   *

WEINSTEIN, Nathan von Wallenstein
See WEST, Nathanael

*   *   *

WEIR, Carol S.   1924-

PERSONAL: Born December 15, 1924, in Oakland, Calif.; daughter of Albert George (a businessman) and Clara (a housewife; maiden name, Armes) Swain; married Benjamin M. Weir (a minister), September 2, 1949; children: Christine Weir Abbyad, Susan Weir Nelson, John, Ann (deceased). *Education:* University of California, Berkeley, B.S., 1947; San Francisco Theological Seminary, M.A., 1970; American University in Beirut, M.A., 1976. *Religion:* Presbyterian.

ADDRESSES: 28 Austin Ave., San Anselmo, Calif. 94960.

CAREER: Public health nurse in San Francisco, Calif., 1946-47; missionary in Lebanon serving on administrative committee concerned with medical work for Presbyterian church, developing health lessons for villagers, and working in women's programing with the National Evangelical church in Beirut, 1947-72; Near East School of Theology, Beirut, assistant professor of Christian education, 1972-85; affiliated with Presbyterian church in Lebanon, campaigning in United States for husband's release, 1985-87; San Francisco Theological Seminary, San Anselmo, Calif., Flora Lamson Hewlett Professor of Evangelism and Mission, 1987—. Instructor at Haigazian College, Beirut, 1981-83, and American University in Beirut, 1983-84. Chairman of board of trustees of American Community School, Beirut, 1980.

WRITINGS:

(With husband, Ben Weir, and Dennis Benson) *Hostage Bound, Hostage Free,* Westminster, 1987.

SIDELIGHTS: Ben Weir had been a Presbyterian missionary in Lebanon for more than thirty years when he was taken hostage by Shiite Muslims in 1984. During nearly five hundred days of her husband's captivity, Carol S. Weir exhausted every avenue that might lead to Ben's release. *Hostage Bound, Hostage Free* is the story of two dedicated Christians, one imprisoned in degrading conditions, the other frustrated by her inability to persuade U.S. Government officials to negotiate with the Lebanese on her husband's behalf. Carol Weir's struggle led her to men like Lieutenant Colonel Oliver North, who refused to negotiate, and Secretary of State George Schultz, who stated that the fundamentalist Muslims were incapable of negotiation. John V. Loudon wrote in *Publishers Weekly:* "Their story, as told in the book . . . , is riddled with ironies that bring home the Catch-22 insanity of Middle East politics."

Weir told *CA:* "While still a part of the Presbyterian church's mission force in Lebanon from 1985 to 1987, I returned to the United States to seek help from our administration for my husband Ben's release. I sought to be a resource on the plight of Palestinians in the Arab world, stressing the need for us as U.S. citizens to seek a more even-handed foreign policy in relation to the Arab world.

"I believe Ben's abduction was in protest of the foreign policy of the United States, perceived by the Lebanese to be against their interests and against them as Moslems. I believe Ben was abducted because he was an American, and it was not against him personally. The trauma and frustration experienced by me while Ben was held captive was sharp and continuous. However, I received support, comfort, and encouragement in Lebanon from neighbors and friends and the Seminary community. In the United States I had the full support of our church's staff who provided pastoral care and became a think tank for approaches we might use to secure Ben's release. My own faith as a Christian and the support of worshipping communities in their love, prayers, and political support were sustaining in our mutual vigil in working for Ben's release and that of the other captives. I continue to be grateful for the work and support of our four children, my father and stepmother, and other family members for their personal encouragement and actions on behalf of Ben and me.

"We wrote our book to help others understand the complexities of the agony and suffering of the people of the Middle East, particularly in Lebanon. So many people had shared in our story that we wanted to give them a more complete account. I hoped readers would become aware of the strength of the church—in spite of its weaknesses—in its faithfulness to community, its concern for individuals, and its message of hope and forgiveness. I pay tribute to the Reverend Frederick Wilson and other collegues and staff of the Presbyterian church who were unstinting in their efforts on our behalf."

BIOGRAPHICAL/CRITICAL SOURCES:

PERIODICALS

Los Angeles Times Book Review, June 28, 1987.
Publishers Weekly, March 6, 1987.

*   *   *

WEISS, Peg

PERSONAL: Born in Denver, Colo.; daughter of Robb (an engineer) and Amy (an English teacher; maiden name, Lemert) Hake; married Volker Weiss (a professor of physics and metallurgy); children: Erick V., Christopher J. *Education:* Syracuse University, B.A. (magna cum laude), 1954, M.A., 1960, Ph.D., 1973; attended University of Munich.

ADDRESSES: Home—238 Scottholm Ter., Syracuse, N.Y. 13224. *Office*—Department of Fine Arts, 441 Hall of Languages, Syracuse University, Syracuse, N.Y.

CAREER: Everson Museum of Art, Syracuse, N.Y., curator of publications, 1974, curator of collections, 1974-79, registrar, 1974-75, chief curator, 1979; Solomon R. Guggenheim Museum, New York, N.Y., guest curator, 1979—. Visiting

assistant professor at Columbia University, 1974-75, and Cornell University, 1983; Syracuse University, adjunct professor, 1974-84, research associate professor, 1984—. Member of Syracuse Landmark Preservation Board.

MEMBER: College Art Association of America, Women in Communications, American Association of Museums, American Society of Aesthetics, Phi Beta Kappa.

AWARDS, HONORS: Scholar of German government, 1956-57; Fulbright scholar, 1967-68; award from Millard Meiss Publication Fund, 1977; named Post-Standard Woman of Achievement in the Arts, 1982; grants from the National Endowment for the Humanities, 1981 and 1986, and from the Smithsonian Institution, 1985 and 1988.

WRITINGS:

Kandinsky in Munich: The Formative Jugendstil Years, Princeton University Press, 1978, revised edition, 1985.
(Editor and contributor) *Adelaide Alsop Robineau: Glory in Porcelain*, Syracuse University Press, 1981.
(Editor and contributor) *Kandinsky in Munich, 1896-1914*, Solomon R. Guggenheim Museum, 1982.
Kandinsky and "Old Russia": An Ethnographic Exploration, Yale University Press, in press.

Guest editor of *Art Journal*, spring, 1983.

CONTRIBUTOR

Laura Corti, editor, *Census: Computerization in the History of Art*, Scuola Normale Superiore Pisa and J. Paul Getty Trust, 1984.
Gabriel Weisberg and Laurinda Dixon, editors, *Elizabeth Gilmore Holt: Source Studies in the History of Art*, Syracuse University Press, 1987.

Contributor to periodicals, including *Syracuse Scholar*, *Art Journal*, *Arts Magazine*, *Heresies*, *Pantheon International Art Journal*, *Burlington Magazine*, and *Art News*.

WORK IN PROGRESS: The Blue Four: A Dialogue With America; The Correspondence of Lyonel Feininger, Alexei Jawlensky, Wassily Kandinsky, and Paul Klee With Galka Scheyer, for University of California Press.

*   *   *

WELLS, Allen   1951-

PERSONAL: Born August 26, 1951, in New York, N.Y.; son of Henry (a cabinetmaker) and Alice (a beautician; maiden name, Hacker) Wells; married Katherine Conant (a housewife), May 1, 1976; children: Anna, Emily, David. *Education:* State University of New York at Binghamton, B.A., 1973; State University of New York at Stony Brook, M.A., 1974, Ph.D., 1979.

ADDRESSES: Home—4 South St., Brunswick, Me. 04011. *Office*—Department of History, Bowdoin College, Brunswick, Me. 04011.

CAREER: Appalachian State University, Boone, N.C., assistant professor, 1979-85, associate professor of Latin American history, 1985-88; Bowdoin College, Brunswick, Me., assistant professor, 1988—. Visiting professor at University of California, San Diego, 1985.

MEMBER: Latin American Studies Association, Conference on Latin American History, Academia Yucatanense de Ciencias y Artes (corresponding member), Southeastern Council of Latin American Studies.

AWARDS, HONORS: Fellow of National Endowment for the Humanities at Harvard University, 1981; grants from Southern Regional Education Board (for Mexico), 1984, National Endowment for the Humanities (for Mexico), 1984, 1987-88, Appalachian State University (for Yucatan), 1984, 1985, and American Philosophical Society (for Yucatan), 1986; Sturgis Leavitt Prize from Southeastern Council of Latin American Studies, 1985, for article "Yucatan: Violence and Social Control on Henequen Plantations," and 1987, for article "Summer of Discontent: Economic Rivalry Among Elite Factions During the Late Porfiriato in Yucatan."

WRITINGS:

(Contributor) Thomas Benjamin and William McNellie, editors, *Other Mexicos: Essays on Regional Mexican History, 1876-1911*, University of New Mexico Press, 1984.
Yucatan's Gilded Age: Haciendas, Henequen, and International Harvester, 1860-1915, University of New Mexico Press, 1985.
(Contributor) William H. Beezley and Judith Ewell, editors, *The Human Tradition in Latin America: The Twentieth Century*, Scholarly Resources, 1987.
(Contributor) Thomas Benjamin and Mark Wasserman, editors, *Mexican Revolutions: Essays on Mexican Regional History, 1910-1929*, University of New Mexico Press, 1988.
(Contributor) Gilbert M. Joseph and Jeffery Brannon, editors, *New Approaches to Mexican Regional History: Changing Patterns of Land, Labor, and Capital in Modern Yucatan*, University of Alabama Press, 1988.

Contributor to biographical dictionaries. Contributor to Latin American studies journals. Editor of *Southeastern Latin Americanist*, 1982-85.

WORK IN PROGRESS: Summer of Discontent, Seasons of Upheaval: Elite Politics and Rural Rebellion in Yucatan, 1890-1915, publication by University of New Mexico Press expected in 1990.

*   *   *

WELLS, Edward
See WELLSTED, W. Raife

*   *   *

WELLSTED, W. Raife 1929-
(Edward Wells)

PERSONAL: Born July 21, 1929, in Hornsea, East Yorkshire, England; son of Charles Gordon (a civil engineer) and Janet (Coote) Wellsted; married Antonia Kirby, May 28, 1955 (divorced, 1979); married Hilary West (a legal secretary), May 26, 1979; children: Adrian, Carole, Dominic. *Education:* Attended South West Essex Technical College, 1948-50. *Religion:* Church of England.

ADDRESSES: Home—513 Ben Jonson House, Barbican, London EC2Y 8DL, England. *Office*—Lieuse Publications Ltd., 6 Hornton Place, London W8 4LZ, England.

CAREER: Cork Manufacturing Group, London, England, company director, 1950-70; Engineering Components Ltd., Slough, England, general sales manager, 1970-74, general manager of Challenger Handling Division, 1974-78; Hunton International, Norwich, England, sales director, 1978-80; self-employed author and researcher, 1980-86; affiliated with Lieuse Publications Ltd., London, England, 1987—. *Military service:* British Army, 1950-67, attached to Territorial Army, 1953-67; became major.

WRITINGS:

(With Stuart Rossiter and John Fowler) *The Stamp Atlas*, Facts on File, 1986.
(Under pseudonym Edward Wells) *Mailshot: History of the Army Postal Service*, Royal Engineers, 1987.
The Stamps of King George V, Lieuse Publications, in press.

Contributor to history and philately journals; contributor to military journals, under pseudonym Edward Wells. Editor of *Postal History International*, 1979-80; editor of *Stamp World*.

WORK IN PROGRESS: A Pictorial and Military History of the West Indies, publication expected in 1991.

SIDELIGHTS: W. Raife Wellsted told *CA:* "The preparation of *The Stamp Atlas* was the original idea of Stuart Rossiter, who died in 1982 with the work only partially complete. The original intent was to deal with every stamp-issuing country and to show the boundary changes since 1840. In the writing this changed slightly, and the resultant book is intended to place the issuing of stamps by each country in its historical perspective. It is the first time anything of this type has been attempted.

"In carrying out the research for the West Indies section of the book, it was apparent that there was no single source that could provide the information needed. Not only that, but the need to use multiple sources led to confusion over dates, places, and people. It was because of this complication and subsequent research for another client into the history of the Leeward Islands that my interest was focused onto the need for an extensive modern history of the West Indies. There are many other areas that have not been fully covered in a historical sense, particularly in relation to the 'Western Connection.' If the work on the West Indies is a success, similar books on southeast Asia, the Himalayas, and west Africa have all been suggested.

"My own personal view is that in these modern times, the work carried out by the Colonial Powers of the nineteenth century tends to be denigrated. While I accept that not all that was done was proper or for altruistic reasons, I do not accept the other side of the coin where everything was done for materialistic reasons or for exploitation. It is my intent to show the balance between these two opposing views.

"I am motivated to produce this complex historical information in a concise form. I have tried to develop a simple informative style, which, in *The Stamp Atlas*, has been well received."

*   *   *

WERTZ, S. K.
See WERTZ, Spencer K.

*   *   *

WERTZ, Spencer K. 1941-
(S. K. Wertz)

PERSONAL: Born October 27, 1941, in Amarillo, Tex.; son

of Ralph E. (a petroleum engineer) and Pauline (a secretary and bookkeeper; maiden name, Tressler) Wertz; married Linda L. Loflin (a benefits analyst), August 12, 1967. *Education:* Texas Christian University, B.A., 1965, M.A., 1966; University of Oklahoma, Ph.D., 1970.

ADDRESSES: Home—2720 Sandage Ave., Fort Worth, Tex. 76109. *Office*—Department of Philsophy, Texas Christian University, P.O. Box 30781, Fort Worth, Tex. 76129.

CAREER: Texas Christian University, Fort Worth, instructor, 1969-71, assistant professor, 1971-75, associate professor, 1975-82, professor of philosophy, 1982—, instructor in wine appreciation in Division of Extended Education, 1975—. Instructor at Austin College, spring, 1969; lecturer in Japan, Europe, Canada, and Mexico.

MEMBER: American Philosophical Association (life member), Philosophic Society for the Study of Sport (president, 1985-86), Southwestern Philosophical Society (president, 1985-86), New Mexico-West Texas Philosophical Society (president, 1980-81), North Texas Philosophical Association (president, 1987-88), Society of Wine Educators (instructor member).

WRITINGS:

Sport Inside Out, Texas Christian University Press, 1985.
Talking a Good Game: Inquiries Into the Principles of Sport, Southern Methodist University Press, in press.

Contributor, under name S. K. Wertz, of more than sixty articles to magazines and journals.

WORK IN PROGRESS: Between Hume's History and Philosophy; a book on the semantics and aesthetics of wine.

SIDELIGHTS: Spencer K. Wertz told *CA:* "I analyze issues in sport and the sports world primarily from the analytic tradition in philosophy, although *Talking a Good Game* is eclectic in its approach. I am interested in analyzing the value structure in sport, and the book traces the change in value structure in sport during this century—from ethical to artistic (including aesthetic, philosophic, and religious) values.

"My current work on David Hume (1711-1776) is a reinterpretation of Hume from the basis that he moved from a personal, individual notion of experience to a general, historical notion of experience.

"My research on wine is to lead to a book on how to analyze and talk about wine. Hopefully this will prove useful to wine educators and their students."

AVOCATIONAL INTERESTS: Tennis (state-ranked player in senior division), gardening.

*   *   *

WEST, Nathanael   1903-1940
(Nathan Weinstein, Nathan von Wallenstein Weinstein)

PERSONAL: Name originally Nathan Weinstein; name legally changed, August 16, 1926; born October 17, 1903, in New York, N.Y.; died following an automobile accident, December 22, 1940, near El Centro, Calif.; buried in Mount Zion Cemetery, Queens, N.Y.; son of Max (a building contractor) and Anna (Wallenstein) Weinstein; married Eileen McKenney, April 19, 1940. *Education:* Attended Tufts College (now University), 1921; Brown University, Ph.B., 1924.

CAREER: Writer. Worked for father's construction firm during early 1920s; Kenmore Hall (residence hotel), New York City, assistant manager, 1927-30; Sutton Club Hotel, New York City, manager, 1930-33; screenwriter for film studios in California, including Columbia, 1933 and 1938, Republic, 1936-38, RKO, 1938, Universal, 1938-39, and RKO, 1939-40.

MEMBER: League of American Writers (member of Hollywood committee), Screen Writers Guild (member of executive board, beginning in 1939), Motion Picture Guild (member of executive board), Motion Picture Artists Committee (member of executive board), Motion Picture Democratic Committee, Hollywood Anti-Nazi League.

WRITINGS:

NOVELS

The Dream Life of Balso Snell, Contact Editions, 1931, recent edition published in *Two Novels by Nathanael West*, Farrar, Straus, 1981.
Miss Lonelyhearts, Liveright, 1933, recent edition published in *Miss Lonelyhearts* [and] *The Day of the Locust*, New Directions, 1969.
A Cool Million: The Dismantling of Lemuel Pitkin, Covici, Friede, 1934, recent edition published in *Two Novels by Nathanael West* (see above).
The Day of the Locust, Random House, 1939, recent edition, Buccaneer, 1981.
The Complete Works of Nathanael West (omnibus volume; contains *The Dream Life of Balso Snell, Miss Lonelyhearts, A Cool Million*, and *The Day of the Locust*), introduction by Alan Ross, Farrar, Straus, 1957, Octagon, 1978.

SCREENPLAYS

(With Jack Natteford) "Ticket to Paradise," Republic, 1936.
(With Lester Cole) "The President's Mystery," Republic, 1936.
(With Lester Cole and Samuel Ornitz) "Follow Your Heart," Republic, 1936.
"Rhythm in the Clouds," Republic, 1937.
(With Samuel Ornitz) "It Could Happen to You," Republic, 1937.
"Born to Be Wild," Republic, 1938.
"I Stole a Million," Universal, 1939.
(With Jerry Cady and Dalton Trumbo) "Five Came Back," RKO, 1939.
(With Whitney Bolton) "The Spirit of Culver," Universal, 1939.
"Men Against the Sky," RKO, 1940.
"Let's Make Music," RKO, 1940.

Also author of unproduced screenplays.

OTHER

(With Joseph Schrank) "Good Hunting" (play), first produced on Broadway at the Hudson Theater, November 21, 1938.
(Under name Nathan Weinstein) *My Island Os Sonnets* (poems), Exposition, 1974.

Also author, with S. J. Perelman, of the unproduced play "Even Stephen."

Contributor of articles, short stories, and poems to periodicals, including *Casements* (under name Nathan von Wallenstein Weinstein), *Americana, Contact, Contempo*, and *Pacific Weekly*. Associate editor of *Contact*, 1931-32, and *Americana*, 1933.

SIDELIGHTS: An American novelist who wrote primarily during the Great Depression of the 1930s, Nathanael West was called "the chief neglected talent of [his] age" by Leslie Fiedler in *Love and Death in the American Novel.* While many of his contemporaries composed straightforward novels about social and economic injustice, West produced an idiosyncratic blend of pathos and comedy, realism and wild unreality. "He too deplored the emptiness of twentieth-century life in the United States," declared Richard B. Gehman in *Atlantic Monthly,* "but he chose to depict that life in terms not of people who were consciously involved in a struggle, but of those who were unconsciously trapped—people who were, in their blindness, so tragic as to be comic figures." Little known to the American public for years after his death, West's work maintained a select following in literary circles. As popular tastes in the novel changed, West's fiction gained a broader audience, and he was widely hailed as a precursor of the "black humor" novelists who wrote in the 1950s, 1960s, and beyond.

Born in 1903 in New York City, West was the son of Jewish immigrants Max Weinstein, a prosperous building contractor, and Anna Wallenstein, who fancied herself a descendant of a German nobleman of the same last name. West's parents were more concerned with status and money than art. His father expected him to enter the family business, and he gave West several Horatio Alger novels—highly popular tales in which honest young men work their way to financial success. But West was a high-school dropout whose friends called him "Pep" because he showed so little energy.

To enroll in Tufts College, West lied about his grades, and when Tufts asked him to leave because of laziness, another student's transcript gained him admission to Brown. There West read widely, but he was better known for his enthusiastic socializing and a biting intellectual wit. When classmate and future journalist Quentin Reynolds pressed him for a graduation speech, West created the story of St. Puce, a flea who lives in the armpit of Christ. During the 1920s West wove St. Puce and similar anecdotes into *The Dream Life of Balso Snell,* a broad parody of the ideals of Western civilization that became his first published novel.

Unsure of his future after he was graduated from Brown in 1924, West convinced relatives to fund a trip to Paris, where he could join other Americans on the city's literary scene. But in 1927, only a few months after he arrived in Europe, the family construction business began to decline—an economic downturn that presaged the Great Depression. West's family recalled him to America, and through their influence he obtained a succession of jobs managing inexpensive residential hotels. Outside the social mainstream West gained an education far different from his college years, and the experience would inspire his most successful novels.

By providing rent-free lodgings to struggling writers, West remained close to the New York literary world. His charity aided the literary critic Edmund Wilson; novelists Robert M. Coates, Erskine Caldwell, and Dashiell Hammett; and playwright Lillian Hellman. West also housed his newlywed sister and her husband, S. J. Perelman, a renowned satirist and a lifelong friend. West became fascinated with the desperate lives of his other tenants: a onetime actress worked as a prostitute; young men headed for work at businesses failing under the impact of the Depression; lonely residents killed time in the lobby reading magazines. At the Sutton Club Hotel six people committed suicide by jumping from the same terrace. When West was especially curious about a lodger, he would steam open the person's mail, sometimes with Hellman's assistance.

One evening Perelman introduced West to an advice columnist for the *Brooklyn Eagle.* She showed the two men a sample of her mail, wondering if it might inspire Perelman to write a comedy. West was deeply moved by the pain and helplessness the letters displayed, and he soon began work on *Miss Lonelyhearts,* the tale of a young advice columnist who destroys himself by becoming personally involved in the miserable lives of his readers. Considered a major advance over *Balso Snell,* *Miss Lonelyhearts* was lauded in the *New Yorker* and the *New York Times Book Review* when it was published in 1933. But sales of the book faltered when its publisher, Liveright, declared bankruptcy.

As the 1930s wore on West became increasingly concerned about his failure to gain either artistic recognition or a steady income from his writing. He joined the staffs of two literary magazines—including *Contact,* where he joined poet William Carlos Williams—but the journals soon folded. When Columbia Pictures offered West a screenwriting job, he eagerly accepted, only to be laid off within a year. Supported by friends he wrote a third novel, *A Cool Million,* which vented his bitterness about the Great Depression by satirizing the myth of success portrayed in Horatio Alger novels. Commentators have since contended that the strength of West's anger damaged the book, which received largely unenthusiastic reviews and sold poorly.

A major Hollywood studio bought the rights to *A Cool Million,* however, and the sale encouraged West to move to California in 1935 for a second try at screenwriting. Several months passed and he was unable to find work, even with the aid of an agent. Hammett had become successful in the movie business, and West repeatedly approached him for help with a job but was greeted with taunts. Moreover, at a time when the major studios were trying to keep unions out of the film industry, West's membership in the Screen Writers Guild hurt his prospects. Depressed and poor, West became desperately afraid that he would always be a failure. Money from Perelman sustained him.

As in New York, West occupied a succession of shabby lodgings, and he began to meet the marginal people of Southern California. He became a confidant of prostitutes and considered compiling their slang into a dictionary. His circle of acquaintances gradually grew to include midgets, petty criminals, and murder investigators. Long before West felt accepted as a Hollywood screenwriter, he was familiar with the industry's stuntmen and laborers.

After a year West found a screenwriting job at Republic, a minor studio known as a factory for formulaic, low-budget films. He adapted readily to this commercial atmosphere, for he saw screenwriting as merely a craft that could support him while he wrote novels and plays. For extra money he eventually teamed with writer Boris Ingster, developing scripts and script ideas that producers purchased eagerly. As biographer Jay Martin explained, Ingster generated conventional story lines and gave them to West, who contributed his flair for distinctive characters and twists of plot.

Immersed in the unglamorous side of Hollywood, West wrote *The Day of the Locust,* his fourth and final book. Unusual among Hollywood novels, it ignores film stars and financiers to concentrate on the obscure, disheartened people who inhabit the town's social fringes. Like *Miss Lonelyhearts,* *Day of the*

Locust was praised in literary circles but ignored by the larger public. Over the course of his lifetime, West earned less than thirteen hundred dollars from his books.

By contrast, the commercial film industry that West scorned in *Day of the Locust* began to appreciate his screenwriting. He continued to write undistinguished films, but now he worked for the higher-paying major studios, particularly Universal and RKO. While his friend F. Scott Fitzgerald, a highly popular novelist during the 1920s, struggled to survive as a screenwriter, West earned a comfortable income for the first time in his life. He bought a pleasant house in the Hollywood hills and married Eileen McKenney, immortalized as the vivacious title character of Ruth McKenney's book *My Sister Eileen.* Eight months later the couple died in a traffic accident when West ran a stop sign.

Near the end of his life West recognized that his writing had always been too unusual to appeal to a broad audience. As Martin quoted him in a letter to Fitzgerald, "Somehow or other I seem to have slipped in between all the 'schools.' My books meet no needs except my own, their circulation is practically private and I'm lucky to be published. And yet I only have a desire to remedy that *before* sitting down to write, once I begin I do it my way. I forget the broad sweep, the big canvas, the shot-gun adjectives, the important people, the significant ideas, the lessons to be taught . . . and go on making what one critic called 'private and unfunny jokes.'"

As James F. Light noted in *Nathanael West: An Interpretative Study,* if "there is any constant pattern in the novels of West, it is the pilgrimage around which each novel centers." He continued: "In each the hero is in search of something in which he can believe and to which he can belong . . . but the result is always the same: tragic disillusionment." In *The Dream Life of Balso Snell,* the title character pursues cultural enlightenment by journeying to the site of ancient Troy, where Trojans and Greeks had clashed thousands of years earlier in a war that inspired the earliest classic of Western literature, Homer's *Iliad.* Snell finds the wooden horse that the Greeks used to invade and conquer Troy. Entering the horse through its anus, he begins a dreamlike journey through Western culture. The artists and philosophers Snell meets, however, are frauds and fools—one is the devoted chronicler of St. Puce. West derides the characters by making them blatantly repulsive, often associating them with excrement.

Commentators have generally agreed that West has a serious point to make in *Balso Snell*—that art and ideas have become too removed from human reality—but they disagreed substantially about the merits of his technique. Admirers observed that West's vivid imagery and his concern with human dreams and delusions anticipate his later works. Detractors, however, said that *Balso Snell* is overstated and contains too many scholarly allusions—mistakes, some suggested, that a recent college graduate might make. In the *New York Times Book Review,* Malcolm Cowley called the book "an elaborate joke . . . that doesn't quite come off."

But West soon transcended his penchant for "gratuitous and perverse humour," as V. S. Pritchett observed in *New Statesman.* In his second novel, *Miss Lonelyhearts,* West "became [both] comic and humane." The title character, whose real name West never reveals, is a young newspaperman assigned to write an advice column. At first Miss Lonelyhearts agrees with his friends that the job is a joke, but the letters he receives are a wrenching mixture of inane comedy and undeniable sorrow. A teenage girl, for instance, laments that no one will ask her on dates because she "was born without a nose"; at the end of her letter, she asks for advice—"ought I to commit suicide?" Miss Lonelyhearts finds himself tangled in a moral dilemma: how can he reconcile himself to the existence of such meaningless suffering?

West depicts the plight of the columnist with "ironic and bitter humor," as T. C. Wilson wrote in the *Saturday Review.* The characters around Miss Lonelyhearts offer him solutions that are too simple for him to accept. While his girlfriend ignores the world's troubles by remaining silly and naive, his editor, Shrike, presents an air of worldly disillusionment edged with sadism. When Miss Lonelyhearts becomes physically ill with anxiety, Shrike visits his bedside to belittle him. Shrike lists the columnist's hopes of escape—art, a place in the country, suave indifference—and dismisses them all with a sneer. Miss Lonelyhearts, Shrike declares, is a "leper-licker." The columnist becomes convinced that he can heal his readers with Christian love, but his efforts are ludicrous and futile. Visiting one troubled couple, he holds hands with the husband and is seduced by the wife. The husband, in a jealous rage, seizes a gun and kills Miss Lonelyhearts—by accident. As T. C. Wilson concluded, "the tragic lives of [West's] characters impress us even more powerfully because they are made to seem stupid and comic."

Miss Lonelyhearts has repeatedly garnered praise for its adept language and its tight dramatic focus. In fifteen short chapters, West chronicles progressive stages of the columnist's emotional disintegration. Pritchett called the book "a selection of hard, diamond-fine miniatures" and noted the "precision" of the author's "poetic images." As Brad Darrach noted in *Time,* "Nothing else in American fiction radiates the compacted fury of this little parable."

West's third novel, *A Cool Million,* is a political satire directed against America's image as a land of prosperity—a predictable target during the Great Depression. Subtitled *The Dismantling of Lemuel Pitkin,* the book chronicles the misadventures of a well-intentioned fool who is physically torn apart as he quests for financial success. As the novel opens, Pitkin gets a loan from Shagpoke Whipple, a dishonest banker who advises him to venture forth from their small town to pursue his fortune. After Pitkin loses his teeth, an eye, his leg, a thumb, and his scalp, he becomes a performing freak in a vaudeville show, entertaining the audience by being beaten on stage. Shot dead by a Communist agent, Pitkin is turned into a martyr by Whipple's Fascist party. Though *A Cool Million* displays West's gift for a colorful plot, most commentators agree that the book is hampered by a heavy-handed use of mock-heroic prose. West seems uninvolved with his characters, biographer Robert Emmet Long averred, and the book "seems surprisingly crude and rambling," especially "in comparison with *Miss Lonelyhearts.*"

By contrast, as Pritchett observed, "*The Day of the Locust* is an advance from fable and from fragments of people, to the courageous full statement of the novel." This novel, he continued, "is mature because the compassion has no theatrical pressure; because now West is now blocking in a sizeable society, and because his gift for inventing extraordinary scenes has expanded." *Day of the Locust* centers on Tod Hackett, a recent Yale art-school graduate who designs sets in Hollywood. Lacking funds, awaiting the inspiration for a painting, he haunts the underside of California life much as West had done. Tod meets Homer Simpson, a timid bookkeeper from Iowa; Adore Loomis, a snide child actor; Abe Kusich, an angry dwarf; and Faye Greener, a flirtatious aspiring actress who arouses the unfulfilled desires of many men she meets, including Tod and Homer.

Frustration becomes the motif of the novel, for as many critics note, West sees California as a deceptive land of promise inhabited by Americans whose dreams have failed to come true. Feeling bored and deceived, these masses occupy their time with idle thrill-seeking. In the climactic episode of the novel, which reviewers found particularly compelling, a crowd assembles outside a movie house to see the pageantry of a Hollywood premiere. Taunted once too often by Adore, the long-suffering Homer erupts in anger and kills him. The crowd becomes a lynch mob, tearing Homer to pieces, and Tod—nearly crushed in the riot—envisions his completed painting. It will be a portrait of apocalypse entitled "The Burning of Los Angeles."

The Day of the Locust has repeatedly been called the best Hollywood novel ever written. "Mr. West has caught the emptiness of Hollywood," wrote Edmund Wilson in *New Republic,* "and he is, as far as I know, the first writer to make this emptiness horrible." And in *Hudson Review,* Daniel Aaron praised West for turning the movie capital into a powerful symbol. "Not an isolated piece of dreamland or a national joke," Aaron wrote, West's Hollywood "is America carried out to its logical conclusion."

Literary critics have generally agreed that West's work is difficult to categorize. Many have linked him to surrealism, a French aesthetic movement of the 1920s and 1930s that stressed the imagery of dreams; others, citing his interest in America's downtrodden, have linked him to naturalism, a more political movement that stressed an individual's helplessness in a hostile society. In an article titled "West's Disease," which appeared in *The Dyer's Hand and Other Essays,* poet W. H. Auden declared that West "is not, strictly speaking, a novelist" because he portrays neither dreams nor society in an accurate fashion. Fiedler praised this characteristic of West's work, calling the author "the inventor of a peculiar kind of book . . . the neo-gothic novel," which derived from West's understanding that "literary truth is not synonymous with fact." Fiedler wrote that such a style, unburdened by the minutiae of factual and psychological detail, "opened up possibilities . . . of capturing the quality of experience in a mass society." He concluded: "Putting down a book by West, a reader is not sure whether he has been presented with a nightmare endowed with the conviction of actuality or with actuality distorted into the semblance of a nightmare; but in either case, he has the sense that he has been presented with a view of a world in which, incredibly, he lives."

As West himself observed, the world he presents is unrelieved by hope. "There is nothing to root for in my books," Martin quoted him. Reviewers have been particularly troubled by West's portrayal of human relationships. In his books friendship and sexual love appear repulsive, inadequate, or ridiculous, for such ideals are overwhelmed by loneliness, despair, and brutality. Some critics call West's world-view a sign of his limitations as a writer, and some suggest that it reflects deep-seated psychological problems. In West's books, wrote biographer Kingsley Widmer, "female sexuality tends to be fascinatingly horrific, women destructive powers demanding hostile responses. . . . West's sex-violence obsessions in his fiction may suggest erotic difficulties in [his] life."

West, however, found nothing abnormal about centering his fiction on brutality. In an essay titled "Some Notes on Violence," he told readers of *Contact* that manuscripts submitted to the magazine generally had this same obsession. "In America," he declared, "violence is idiomatic," so much so that only great violence can attract any attention. As Martin observed, "West's notion of how to express the 'American grain' was to 'do it obviously—cruelly, irresponsible torture, simply, obviously, casually told.'" Sexuality in West's novels was a literary device, according to Victor Comerchero in *Nathanael West: The Ironic Prophet.* "The disorder of the individual mirrors the disorder of the society," Comerchero declared. "Sexual inadequacy is ineffectualness at its most primitive biological level. Tied up in one vivid image are man's social, biological, psychological, and 'metaphysical' inadequacies—man's inadequacy before the 'laws of life.'" West remained true to his artistic vision, but the price he paid was unpopularity. Critics speculated that West's pessimism, coming at a time when America faced the twin burdens of the Great Depression and an impending world war, was simply too painful for his audience to bear.

After West's death his literary reputation languished for many years. But prominent old friends such as Coates and Williams continued to praise him, and in 1947 Daniel Aaron helped begin a broad reassessment of West's work when he praised the novelist in the literary magazine *Partisan Review.* The West revival became extensive in 1957, when the four novels were published in one volume for the first time. Known somewhat inaccurately as the *Complete Works,* the collection received lengthy positive reviews in a wide variety of publications in the United States and England. The first book-length studies of West appeared in the early 1960s, followed by many more works of literary criticism and biography, including Martin's highly detailed *Nathanael West: The Art of His Life.*

As many commentators have observed, West's vivid, brooding humor, so unusual in his own time, became a widespread trend in American literature after World War II. By "the middle decades of the twentieth century," Widmer averred, West had become "one of *the* authors to read." West's followers included Flannery O'Connor, whose novel *Wise Blood* centers on a tormented young Southerner who preaches a new religion called the "Church Without Christ." Literary critics found echoes of West in the works of many postwar American novelists, whose writings often blend comedy, chaos, and pessimism. As Stanley Edgar Hyman wrote in his book *Nathanael West,* the author "was a true pioneer and culture hero, making it possible for the younger symbolists and fantasists who came after him, and who include our best writers, to do with relative ease what he did in defiance of the temper of his time, for so little reward, in isolation and in pain."

MEDIA ADAPTATIONS: Miss Lonelyhearts was adapted by Leonard Praskins for the film "Advice to the Lovelorn," Fox/United Artists, 1933; by Howard Teichmann for a play of the original title, 1957; by Dore Schary for the film "Lonelyhearts," United Artists, 1958; and by Michael Dinner and others for a television play of the original title, Public Broadcasting Service, 1983. *The Day of the Locust* was adapted by Waldo Salt for a film of the same title, Paramount, 1975.

BIOGRAPHICAL/CRITICAL SOURCES:

BOOKS

Auden, W. H., *The Dyer's Hand and Other Essays,* Random House, 1962.

Bloom, Harold, editor, *Nathanael West: Modern Critical Views*, Chelsea House, 1986.

Comerchero, Victor, *Nathanael West: The Ironic Prophet*, Syracuse University Press, 1964.

Dictionary of Literary Biography, Gale, Volume 4: *American Writers in Paris, 1920-1939*, 1980, Volume 9: *American Novelists, 1910-1945*, 1981, Volume 28: *Twentieth-Century American Jewish Fiction Writers*, 1984.

Fiedler, Leslie A., *Love and Death in the American Novel*, revised edition, Stein & Day, 1966.

Hyman, Stanley Edgar, *Nathanael West*, University of Minnesota Press, 1962.

Light, James F., *Nathanael West: An Interpretive Study*, second edition, Northwestern University Press, 1971.

Long, Robert Emmet, *Nathanael West*, Ungar, 1985.

Madden, David, editor, *Nathanael West; The Cheaters and the Cheated: A Collection of Critical Essays*, Everett/Edwards, 1973.

Malin, Irving, *Nathanael West's Novels*, Southern Illinois University Press, 1972.

Martin, Jay, *Nathanael West: The Art of His Life*, Farrar, Straus, 1970.

Martin, Jay, editor, *Nathanael West: A Collection of Critical Essays*, Prentice-Hall, 1971.

Reid, Randall, *The Fiction of Nathanael West: No Redeemer, No Promised Land*, University of Chicago Press, 1967.

Twentieth-Century Literary Criticism, Gale, Volume 1, 1978, Volume 14, 1984.

West, Nathanael, *Miss Lonelyhearts*, introduction by Robert M. Coates, New Directions, 1946.

West, Nathanael, *The Day of the Locust*, introduction by Richard B. Gehman, New Directions, 1950.

West, Nathanael, *The Complete Works of Nathanael West*, introduction by Alan Ross, Farrar, Straus, 1957.

White, William, *Nathanael West: A Comprehensive Bibliography*, Kent State University Press, 1975.

Widmer, Kingsley, *Nathanael West*, Twayne, 1982.

PERIODICALS

Atlantic Monthly, September, 1950, October, 1970.

Ball State University Forum, autumn, 1980.

Commonweal, May 10, 1957, October 23, 1970.

Contact, Volume 1, number 3, 1932.

Hudson Review, winter, 1951.

Massachusetts Review, winter-spring, 1965.

Modern Fiction Studies, summer, 1974.

Nation, July 25, 1934, July 15, 1939, May 4, 1957, August 17, 1970.

New Republic, July 26, 1939, May 23, 1970.

New Statesman, December 7, 1957, October 11, 1968.

Newsweek, September 4, 1950, May 13, 1957, June 29, 1970.

New Yorker, April 15, 1933, May 18, 1957, October 10, 1970.

New York Times, June 2, 1974, February 2, 1987, February 8, 1987.

New York Times Book Review, April 23, 1933, July 1, 1934, May 21, 1939, May 12, 1957.

Partisan Review, January-February, 1947, January-February, 1951, number 3, 1971.

Saturday Review, May 13, 1933, May 20, 1939, May 11, 1957, June 27, 1970.

Spectator, July 19, 1968.

Time, June 17, 1957, August 17, 1970.

Times Literary Supplement, January 24, 1958, April 11, 1958.

Washington Post, January 25, 1983.*

—*Sketch by Thomas Kozikowski*

WHARTON, James
See MENCKEN, H(enry) L(ouis)

*   *   *

WHIPPLE, A(ddison) B(eecher) C(olvin)   1918-

PERSONAL: Born July 15, 1918, in Glens Falls, N.Y.; son of Frank Augustus and Adela (Colvin) Whipple; married Jane M. Banks (an editor and indexer), June 27, 1942; children: Ann Whipple Marr, Christopher. *Education:* Yale University, B.A., 1940; Harvard University, M.A., 1941.

ADDRESSES: Home—Cove Rd., Old Greenwich, Conn. 06870. *Agent*—Julian Bach, Julian Bach Literary Agency, Inc., 747 Third Ave., New York, N.Y. 10017.

CAREER: Time Inc., New York, N.Y., editor of international editions of *Life*, 1955-70, executive editor of Time-Life Books, 1970-75; writer, 1975—. Member of Greenwich Historic District Commission.

MEMBER: Time-Life Alumni Society (president, 1985-87).

WRITINGS:

Yankee Whalers in the South Seas, Doubleday, 1954.

Pirate: Rascals of the Spanish Main, Doubleday, 1957.

Famous Pirates of the New World (juvenile), Random House, 1958.

Tall Ships and Great Captains: A Narrative of Famous Sailing Ships Through the Ages and the Courageous Men Who Sailed, Fought, or Raced Them Across the Seas, Harper, 1960.

Hero of Trafalgar: The Story of Lord Nelson (juvenile), Random House, 1963, published as *All About Nelson*, W. H. Allen, 1966.

The Fatal Gift of Beauty: The Final Years of Byron and Shelley, Harper, 1964.

The Mysterious Voyage of Captain Kidd (juvenile), Landmark, 1970.

Fighting Sail, Time-Life, 1978.

The Whalers, Time-Life, 1979.

The Clipper Ships, Time-Life, 1980.

The Racing Yachts, Time-Life, 1981.

Storm, Time-Life, 1982.

World War II in the Mediterranean, Time-Life, 1982.

Restless Oceans, Time-Life, 1983.

The Challenge, Morrow, 1987.

Contributor to magazines, including *Smithsonian*, *Nautical Quarterly*, and *Reader's Digest*.

WORK IN PROGRESS: Research for a book on the China trade.

SIDELIGHTS: A. B. C. Whipple told *CA:* "I became a journalist and author largely through serendipity. Planning a career as a teacher of English literature, I was lured into journalism, which I found marvelously congenial and rewarding. (Time Inc., of course, had a lot to do with that.) For nearly forty years I reported, wrote, and edited for the weekly *Life* magazine; I edited *Life*'s international editions and then was executive editor of Time-Life Books. Visiting Nantucket Island, I became fascinated by the colorful history of whaling and tangentially in all U.S. maritime history.

"I recommend journalism to all aspiring authors. Not only is it the perfect disipline, but it is also a field of never-ending fascination. Not the least of journalism's advantages is the fact that eventually you can retire from the comparative drudgery of the office without retiring from the stimulation and satisfaction of reporting and writing.''

BIOGRAPHICAL/CRITICAL SOURCES:

PERIODICALS

New York Times Book Review, July 26, 1987.

*   *   *

WHITAKER, Shelagh (Dunwoody)   1930-

PERSONAL: Born January 23, 1930, in Winnipeg, Manitoba, Canada; daughter of James M. (a chartered accountant) and Nora (Bell) Dunwoody; married W. Denis Whitaker (a business executive and author), September 14, 1973; children: Wendy, Barbara, Martha, Jenifer. *Education:* Queen's University, Kingston, Ontario, B.A., 1951.

ADDRESSES: Home—173 Chartwell Rd., Oakville, Ontario, Canada L6J 3Z7. *Agent*—Colbert Agency, Inc., 303 Davenport Rd., Toronto, Ontario, Canada M5R 1K5.

CAREER: Shelagh Whitaker and Associates Ltd. (communications consultants), Oakville, Ontario, president, 1967—.

AWARDS, HONORS: John W. Dafoe Award from the *Winnipeg Free Press* and the University of Manitoba for best book on Canadian International Affairs, 1984, for *Tug of War.*

WRITINGS:

(With husband, W. Denis Whitaker) *Tug of War,* Stoddart, 1984.
(With W. D. Whitaker) *Battle of the Rhineland,* Stoddart, 1988.

Contributor to magazines and newspapers.

SIDELIGHTS: Shelagh Whitaker told *CA:* ''Prior to *Tug of War,* the only books written about the Canadian military contribution to the northwestern European campaign of World War II were regimental histories. It was a privilege to write about the Canadian campaign. The book is based on two hundred interviews with its veterans. Our new book, *Battle of the Rhineland,* glorifies the American, British, and Canadian soldiers who fought and won the war, *despite* their generals. It underlines the fact that the men of three nations fought together to push the German army across the Rhine to defeat.''

BIOGRAPHICAL/CRITICAL SOURCES:

PERIODICALS

Globe and Mail (Toronto), February 23, 1985.

*   *   *

WHITCOMB, Jon   1906-1988

OBITUARY NOTICE—See index for *CA* sketch: Born June 9, 1906, in Weatherford, Okla.; died of heart failure, April 27, 1988, in Menlo Park, Calif. Artist, illustrator, columnist, and author. Whitcomb, who was elected to the Society of Illustrators Hall of Fame in 1973, was best known for his portraits of beautiful women. He was a cover artist and columnist for *Cosmopolitan* and an illustrator for many other magazines, including *Collier's, Ladies' Home Journal,* and *McCall's.* After serving the Navy as an artist during World War II, he helped found the Famous Artists Schools and was a member of the institution's faculty of portrait painting. Whitcomb began his

artistic career in 1928 as a poster artist for Radio-Keith-Orpheum (RKO) Theaters in Chicago, Illinois, then worked as an advertising artist in Ohio. In 1935 he became vice-president of the Charles E. Cooper advertising art company in New York City. Whitcomb wrote and illustrated *How I Make a Picture, Pom-Pom's Christmas, All About Girls,* and *Coco, the Far-Out Poodle.*

OBITUARIES AND OTHER SOURCES:

BOOKS

Who's Who in American Art, 15th edition, Bowker, 1982.

PERIODICALS

New York Times, April 29, 1988.

*   *   *

WHITING, Allen S(uess)   1926-

PERSONAL: Born October 27, 1926, in Perth Amboy, N.J.; son of Leo Robert and Viola (Allen-Suess) Whiting; married Alice Marie Conroy, May 29, 1950; children: Deborah Jean, David Neal, Jeffrey Michael, Jennifer Hollister. *Education:* Cornell University, B.A., 1948; Columbia University, M.A., 1950, certificate in Russian, 1950, Ph.D., 1952.

ADDRESSES: Home—125 Canyon View Dr., Tucson, Ariz. 85704. *Office*—Department of Political Science, University of Arizona, Tucson, Ariz. 85721.

CAREER: Northwestern University, Evanston, Ill., assistant professor of political science, 1951-53; Michigan State University, East Lansing, assistant professor of political science, 1955-57; RAND Corp., Santa Monica, Calif., social scientist, 1957-61; U.S. Department of State, Washington, D.C., special assistant in international relations for Bureau of Intelligence and Research, 1961-62, director of Office of Research and Analysis for the Far East, 1962-66, deputy consul general in Hong Kong, 1966-68; University of Michigan, Ann Arbor, professor of political science, 1968-82; University of Arizona, Tucson, professor of political science, 1982—, director of Center for East Asian Studies, 1982—. Director of National Committee on U.S.-China Relations, 1977—; associate of China Council, 1978—; president of Arizona China Council, 1983—; special commentator on China for CBS-TV and NBC-TV; consultant to Bendix Corp. and National Security Council. *Military service:* U.S. Army, 1945.

MEMBER: Association for Asian Studies, Institute for International Strategic Studies, Council on Foreign Relations, American Political Science Association.

AWARDS, HONORS: Fellow of Social Science Research Council, 1950 and 1974-75, Ford Foundation, 1953-55, and Rockefeller Foundation, 1978; Superior Honor Award from U.S. Department of State, 1965.

WRITINGS:

(With Ernst B. Haas) *Dynamics of International Relations,* McGraw, 1955.
(With Sheng Shih-ts'ai) *Sinkiang: Pawn or Pivot?,* Michigan State University Press, 1958.
Soviet Policies in China, 1917-1924, Stanford University Press, 1968.
China Crosses the Yalu: The Decision to Enter the Korean War, Stanford University Press, 1968.
The Chinese Calculus of Deterrence: India and Indochina, University of Michigan Press, 1975.

China and the United States: What Next?, Foreign Policy Association, 1976.

(With Robert F. Dernberger) *China's Future: Foreign Policy and Economic Development in the Post-Mao Era*, McGraw, 1977.

Chinese Domestic Policies and Foreign Policy in the 1970s, Center for Chinese Studies, University of Michigan, 1979.

Siberian Development and East Asia: Threat or Promise?, Stanford University Press, 1981.

Contributor to political science journals.

BIOGRAPHICAL/CRITICAL SOURCES:

PERIODICALS

Times Literary Supplement, February 27, 1976.

*   *   *

WIENER, Allen J. 1943-

PERSONAL: Born August 14, 1943, in Newark, N.J.; son of Harry (a tavern owner) and Helen (an insurance claims officer; maiden name, Roth) Wiener; married Katherine Ann Zantal (a special education consultant), June 22, 1974; children: Amanda Lee. *Education:* Fairleigh Dickinson University, B.A., 1968; Rutgers University, M.A., 1971, graduate study, 1971-73. *Politics:* "I always manage to vote for the loser."

ADDRESSES: Home—Potomac, Md. *Office*—Washington, D.C. *Agent*—c/o McFarland & Co., P.O. Box 611, Jefferson, N.C. 28640.

CAREER: Morris County Daily Record, Morristown, N.J., news reporter and feature writer, 1968-69; Creative Communications, Inc., Newark, N.J., public relations writer and account executive, 1969-70; Federal Aviation Administration, Washington, D.C., budget analyst, 1973-74; Federal Railroad Administration, Washington, D.C., administrative assistant, 1974-75; U.S. Department of Transportation, Washington, D.C., transportation intern, 1975-76, transportation specialist in Policy Office, 1976—, policy analyst in Maritime and Surface Division of Office of International Transportation and Trade, 1986—. Professional actor on stage and in films, as well as television and radio commercials; radio narrator. Member of board of directors of Georgetown Workshop Theater and Touring Company, 1976-77. *Military service:* U.S. Air Force, education and training specialist, 1961-65.

MEMBER: American Federation of Television and Radio Artists, Screen Actors Guild.

AWARDS, HONORS: Achievement Award from Federal Aviation Administration, 1973.

WRITINGS:

The Beatles: A Recording History, McFarland & Co., 1986, revised edition, in press.

Contributor of articles and reviews to periodicals, including *Goldmine*.

WORK IN PROGRESS: A book on collecting Beatles recordings and variations, publication expected in 1989; two articles about John Lennon for *Goldmine*.

SIDELIGHTS: Allen J. Wiener told *CA* that the research for his book, *The Beatles: A Recording History*, "and the chronological presentation of its results, takes in all known events (involving the Beatles) that exist in recorded form, including

unreleased material, much of which is found on bootleg records. This emphasis on *recordings*, rather than commercially released *records*, may seem a fine distinction, but it is quite significant. Many collectors seek discs, accumulating the same recorded material in all its many physical forms of release (different label variations, cover art, country of origin, and reissues), but I have addressed the collector of *recorded* material, or events in the Beatles' careers that were recorded, including, but not limited to, their released studio work. Collectors focusing on my material do not necessarily care if they obtain every variation of the material's release, once they have at least one copy of the recording. My book catalogs all of these Beatles recordings and then directs the reader to records on which the material can be found.

"Writing is a discipline; it is seldom 'fun' in the strictest sense. You have to sit down and work until you get something started and it begins to take shape. The hardest part is getting started on any project. Just getting words on paper is the key, regardless of what type of writing you are doing or what subject matter you are treating. Once the first draft is done you have something to work with, edit, revise, or reconsider. When you do reference works, your aim is to make the book as complete and accurate as possible. In the case of recordings, this involves the expense and time of obtaining and listening to the recordings, which can take months or years. You also want to organize and design the book so that it is easy to use and allows readers to quickly find the information they need. The key here is a thorough, accurate index."

AVOCATIONAL INTERESTS: Running, rowing, swimming, gardening, reading (especially mysteries), record collecting.

BIOGRAPHICAL/CRITICAL SOURCES:

PERIODICALS

Asbury Park Press, February 1, 1987.
Washington Post, June 4, 1987.

*   *   *

WIKANDER, Matthew H. 1950-

PERSONAL: Born March 21, 1950, in Philadelphia, Pa.; son of Lawrence E. (a librarian) and E. Marie (a librarian; maiden name, Whitlow) Wikander; married Christine Child (a playwright), July 31, 1980. *Education:* Williams College, B.A., 1970; Cambridge University, B.A., 1972; University of Michigan, Ph.D., 1975.

ADDRESSES: Home—2308 Robinwood Ave., Toledo, Ohio 43620. *Office*— Department of English, University of Toledo, Toledo, Ohio 43606.

CAREER: University of Michigan, Ann Arbor, lecturer in drama and director and head of drama program at Residential College, 1974-78; Columbia University, New York, N.Y., assistant professor of English and comparative literature, 1978-87; University of Toledo, Toledo, Ohio, associate professor of English, 1987—.

MEMBER: Modern Language Association of America, Shakespeare Association of America, Northeast Modern Language Association, Midwest Modern Language Association.

AWARDS, HONORS: Marshall scholar in England, 1970-72.

WRITINGS:

The Play of Truth and State: Historical Drama From Shakespeare to Brecht, Johns Hopkins University Press, 1986.

Contributor to literature journals.

WORK IN PROGRESS: Princes to Act and Monarchs to Behold: Royal Performance and Royal Audience, 1600-1789, a study of drama in the courts of James I, Charles I, and Charles II of England, Louis XIV and Louis XV of France, and Gustav III of Sweden, completion expected in 1990.

SIDELIGHTS: Matthew H. Wikander told *CA:* "My interest in historical drama began with a simple question: Why did the history play, as a genre distinct from tragedy and comedy in Renaissance England, disappear after about 1610? And why, when plays on English history became regular stage fare once again in the 1680s, did they invariably take the form of pathetic tragedies concentrating on the private passions of kings and queens in love? Politics played a major role—historical drama attracted the atention of censors on the lookout for contemporary applications—but so, too, did the rise of history as an independent discipline. While Shakespeare could claim to dramatize history as truthfully as his sources chronicled it, the later playwrights appeared to react either resentfully or passively to the authority of the historians from whom they drew their stories. Encouraged by both censors and historians to see history as a political science, dramatists in England came to avoid the public sphere and concentrate upon the private feelings and sufferings of those caught up in great events. This argument makes up the first part of my book *The Play of Truth and State: Historical Drama From Shakespeare to Brecht.*

"In the second part of the book, I sought to examine the historical dramas of some major playwrights from continental Europe: Johann Schiller, Alfred de Musset, Georg Buchner, August Strindberg, and Bertolt Brecht. All of these announce themselves to be in some way indebted to Shakespeare, and all experimented with the form of historical dramas. Using the English experience as a model, I found similar tensions between the authority of the playwright and the authority of the historian in these dramatists: Schiller and Strindberg declared themselves to be chroniclers of higher truths than those of history, while Musset and Buchner portrayed their characters as annihilated by the impersonal force of history. But Brecht, through Karl Marx's critique of historicism, was able to set himself up, as Shakespeare did, as an authority equal to the historian, proclaiming himself and his audience to be historians themselves. The great age of narrative history corresponds to the period between Shakespeare and Brecht as a period in which playwrights wanted to write historical dramas but found the form to be extraordinarily difficult. Brecht, at the end of the period, and Shakespeare, at the beginning, directly involve their audiences in the experience of making sense of the past.

"The study of court drama is especially focused upon one question raised in my work on historical drama: How did changing social conditions and institutions change the ways in which monarchs were portrayed in dramas that could be expected to have monarchs in their audiences? On such occasions, as actors and audiences in the days of Queen Elizabeth and King James in England watched the royal viewer perhaps more attentively than the monarch watched them, who can be said to be the performer and who the audience? Moving from Elizabethan England through France in the age of Louis XIV and XV to Sweden in the age of Gustav III at the very time of the French Revolution, I trace a general pattern: In the Renaissance dramas—both in play scripts and in descriptions of specific performances—the people (actors and members of the audience) keep their eyes on the monarch, fearing his irrational rages, basking in his gracious mercy. But eighteenth-

century drama—specifically the plays of Voltaire and his imitators, among them King Gustav III of Sweden—reverses the paradigm, and the monarch keeps his eyes on the people, fearful of their rage, hopeful of their love. Throughout the period between 1600 and 1789, the drama of England, France, and Sweden repeatedly suggests that playing the king and being the king are activities that are not merely analogous but can also become identical. The implications for our own age of mass media image management are striking."

BIOGRAPHICAL/CRITICAL SOURCES:

PERIODICALS

Times Literary Supplement, January 30, 1987.

*   *   *

WILCOX, James 1949-

BRIEF ENTRY: Born April 4, 1949, in Hammond, La. American short story writer and novelist. Called a writer of "real comic genius" by Anne Tyler in the *New York Times Book Review* and "one of the most promising fiction writers on the national scene" by *Los Angeles Times Book Review* contributor Peter Heinegg, Wilcox wrote three novels set in the fictional small town of Tula Springs, Louisiana, and filled them with eccentric, amiable, and endearing characters caught in absurd and hilarious situations. The first of these, *Modern Baptists* (Dial, 1983), recounts the misadventures of the paunchy and balding Bobby Pickens, assistant manager of Sonny Boy Bargain Store, who falls in love with an eighteen-year-old salesgirl, who in turn lusts after Bobby's ex-convict brother. *North Gladiola* (Harper, 1985), Wilcox's second novel, focuses on the relationships of the menopausal and meddlesome Ethyl Mae Coco with her husband, Louis, a haberdasher losing business to the malls; her six grown children, including one who raises crickets and another who is a professional basket weaver; and the other members of the Pro Arts Quartet, with whom Ethyl plays cello and becomes the object of the second violinist's affections. The third novel, *Miss Undine's Living Room* (Harper, 1987), takes on small-town politics and crime solving when Olive Mackie, who is running for the office of Superintendent of Streets, Parks, and Garbage, must clear the name of her senile and bedridden uncle when his obnoxious nurse is found dead outside of the uncle's window. Wilcox has also contributed numerous short stories to periodicals, including *New Yorker, Avenue,* and *Louisiana Literature. Addresses: Home*—239 East 24th St., No. 9, New York, N.Y. 10010. *Agent*—Amanda Urban, International Creative Management, 40 West 57th St., New York, N.Y. 10019.

BIOGRAPHICAL/CRITICAL SOURCES:

PERIODICALS

Chicago Tribune Book World, July 7, 1985.
Los Angeles Times Book Review, August 17, 1983, October 4, 1987.
New York Times Book Review, July 31, 1983, June 30, 1985, October 18, 1987.
Times Literary Supplement, January 20, 1984.
Washington Post Book World, August 16, 1987.

*   *   *

WILKES, Peter 1937-

PERSONAL: Born August 12, 1937, in Manchester, England; immigrated to the United States, 1974, naturalized citizen,

1980; son of William Arnold and Emily Edith (Robinson) Wilkes; married Norah Hobson (a receptionist), September 6, 1958; children: Simon, Jonathan, Elisabeth. *Education:* Victoria University of Manchester, M.S., 1963, Ph.D., 1967.

ADDRESSES: Office—South Hills Church, 6601 Camden Ave., San Jose, Calif. 95120.

CAREER: Ordained independent Methodist minister, 1958; Victoria University of Manchester, Manchester, England, lecturer in metallurgy, 1964-74; University of Wisconsin—Madison, professor of metallurgic and nuclear engineering, 1974-80; pastor in Milwaukee, Wis., 1980-82; South Hills Community Church, San Jose, Calif., pastor, 1982—.

WRITINGS:

Solid State Theory in Metallurgy, Cambridge University Press, 1973.
Christianity Challenges the University, Inter-Varsity Press, 1981.
Overcoming Anger and Other Dragons of the Soul, Inter-Varsity Press, 1987.
Overcoming the Dragons of the Heart, Inter-Varsity Press, 1988.

WORK IN PROGRESS: A biblical program for spiritual growth.

SIDELIGHTS: Peter Wilkes told *CA:* "I have been blessed (or cursed) with a combination of theological interest and scientific background. In Christianity this inclines me to serious thinking, with a determined effort to apply it in very practical situations. It should by now be obvious to any thinking person that secularism has failed, and Christianity is our only hope. I want to spend my life working toward the practical implications of that.

"Having abandoned my scientific career at God's command after some sixteen months in university teaching, I also want to use my familiarity with campus to serve Christian groups in that setting.

"My writing is an extension of my preaching in that I want to help people understand the Bible and its application to life. I used the theme of dragons to express how we experience the inner struggle with temptations and cumpulsive behavior patterns. The dragons are things like lust, doubt, fear, and legalism. My longing is to help Christians in our sensual society to be gripped with a passion for holiness out of love for Jesus."

*   *   *

WILKIE, Katharine E(lliott) 1904-1980

OBITUARY NOTICE—See index for *CA* sketch: Born February 6, 1904, in Lexington, Ky.; died April 5, 1980. Educator and author. Wilkie, the author of numerous children's books, taught public and private school in Kentucky and for two summers conducted a course in writing children's literature for a University of Kentucky writer's workshop. Her writings include *Zack Taylor: Young Rough and Ready, Mary Todd Lincoln: Girl of the Bluegrass, Maria Mitchell: Stargazer, Pocahontas: Indian Princess, Helen Keller: Handicapped Girl,* and, with Elizabeth R. Moseley, *Atlantis.*

OBITUARIES AND OTHER SOURCES:

Date of death provided by son, Raymond Abell Wilkie, Jr.

WILLEFORD, Charles (Ray III) 1919-1988
(Will Charles)

OBITUARY NOTICE—See index for *CA* sketch: Born January 2, 1919, in Little Rock, Ark.; died after a heart attack, March 27, 1988, in Miami, Fla. U.S. Army sergeant, educator, playwright, and author. Though he is best known for his series of novels featuring homicide detective Hoke Moseley, Willeford wrote in several different genres. His first publication was 1948's *Proletarian Laughter,* a collection of poems, and soon after he wrote the radio serial "The Saga of Mary Miller" for Armed Forces Radio Service and the television play "The Basic Approach" for Canadian Broadcasting Corporation. He also wrote numerous short stories, some of which are collected in *The Machine in Ward Eleven;* a book on literary criticism, titled *New Forms of Ugly: The Immobilized Man in Modern Literature;* and a 1986 autobiography, *Something About a Soldier.* His novels, sometimes written under the pseudonym Will Charles, include *The Burnt Orange Heresy, Miami Blues, Sideswipe,* and *The Way We Die Now.* Willeford served in the U.S. Army for twenty years, retiring in 1956 as master sergeant. Though a high school dropout, he taught humanities at the University of Miami for three years and joined the faculty of Miami-Dade Community College in 1967, becoming associate professor of English in 1970.

OBITUARIES AND OTHER SOURCES:

BOOKS

Willeford, Charles, *Something About a Soldier,* Random House, 1986.
The Writers Directory: 1988-1990, St. James Press, 1988.

PERIODICALS

Chicago Tribune, March 30, 1988.
Los Angeles Times, March 29, 1988.
New York Times, March 29, 1988.
Washington Post, March 29, 1988.

*   *   *

WILLIAMS, Clayton (Wheat) 1895-1983

PERSONAL: Born April 15, 1895, in Fort Stockton, Tex.; died September 9, 1983, in Fort Stockton, Tex.; son of Oscar Waldo (a judge) and Sallie (Wheat) Williams; married Chicora Lee Graham, September 10, 1928; children: Clayton Wheat, Janet (Mrs. Robert W. Pollard). *Education:* Texas A&M University, B.S., 1915.

CAREER: Employed by Chino Copper Co., Santa Rita, N.M., 1916-17; Oil Belt Power Co., Eastland, Tex., electrical engineer, 1919; surveyor in Pecos County, Tex., 1920; highway engineer in New Mexico and Texas, 1921-24; chief engineer for Texon Oil and Land Co. and Group Number One Oil Corp. in Santa Rita, 1924-28; owner and operator of the first ice plant and water works in Crane, Tex., 1927-35; part owner of a ranch in Pecos County, 1935-54; Olix Industries, Austin, Tex., director, 1960-74. County commissioner of Pecos County, 1935-40, 1943-50. *Military service:* U.S. Army, Coast Artillery, 1917-19; served in Europe; became second lieutenant.

WRITINGS:

Never Again, three volumes, Naylor, 1969.
(Compiler) *Animal Tales of the West,* illustrated by Bill Bristow, Naylor, 1974.
Texas' Lost Frontier: Fort Stockton and the Trans-Pecos, 1861-1895, Texas A&M University Press, 1986.*

WILLIAMS, Eric (Eustace)   1911-1981

PERSONAL: Born September 25, 1911, in Port of Spain, Trinidad; died of a heart attack, March 29 (one source says March 31), 1981, in St. Anne, Trinidad; son of Thomas Henry (a postal clerk) and Eliza (Boissiere) Williams; married Elsie Ribeiro c. 1939 (divorced, 1951); married Soy Moyeau c. 1951 (divorced, 1953); married Mayleen Mook-Soong (a dentist), 1957 (divorced c. 1958); children: Alistair, Pamela (first marriage), Erica (second marriage). *Education:* Attended Queen's Royal College, 1922-31; St. Catherine's College, Oxford, B.A. (first class honors), 1935, D.Phil. (first class honors), 1938. *Religion:* Roman Catholic.

CAREER: Queen's Royal College, Port of Spain, Trinidad, acting master, and acting lecturer for the Government Training College for Teachers, 1931; Howard University, Washington, D.C., assistant professor, 1939-44, associate professor, 1944-47, professor of social and political science, 1947-1955; adviser to Trinidad Government, 1954-55; founded People's National Movement (PNM) in Trinidad, 1956; chief minister and minister of finance, planning, and development of Trinidad and Tobago, 1956-61; first prime minister of independent state of Trinidad and Tobago, 1962-81, also minister of external affairs, 1961-64, 1973-74, minister of community development, 1964-67, minister of Tobago affairs, minister of finance, planning, and development, and minister of national security, 1967-71, minister for finance beginning in 1975. Worked for the Anglo-American Caribbean Commission, consultant to the British, 1943-44, secretary of the Agricultural Committee, 1944-46, consultant, 1946-48, deputy chairman of the Caribbean Research Council and member of commission, 1948-55.

MEMBER: Historical Society of Trinidad and Tobago (past president).

AWARDS, HONORS: Julius Rosenwald fellowship, 1940, 1942; D.C.L. from Oxford University, and LL.D. from University of New Brunswick, both 1965.

WRITINGS:

The Negro in the Carribbean, Associates in Negro Folk Education, 1942, Negro Universities Press, 1969.

Capitalism and Slavery, University of North Carolina Press, 1944, Putnam, 1980.

Education in the British West Indies, foreword by John Dewey, Guardian Commercial Printery, 1950.

(Editor) *Documents on British West Indian History,* Trinidad, 1952.

History of the People of Trinidad and Tobago, People's National Movement Publishing, 1962, Praeger, 1964.

Documents of West Indian History, People's National Movement Publishing, 1963.

British Historians and the West Indies, People's National Movement Publishing, 1964, published with preface by Alan Bullock, Scribner, 1967.

Inward Hunger: The Education of a Prime Minister (autobiography), Deutsch, 1969, published with an introduction by Denis Brogan, University of Chicago Press, 1971.

From Columbus to Castro: The History of the Caribbean, 1492-1969, Deutsch, 1970, Harper, 1971.

(Contributor) Roy Boyke, editor, *Patterns of Progress: Trinidad and Tobago; Ten Years of Independence,* Key Caribbean Publications, 1972.

Forged From the Love of Liberty: Selected Speeches of Dr. Eric Williams, compiled by Paul K. Sutton, Longman Caribbean, 1981.

Also author of published political addresses, including *Federation: Two Public Lectures,* 1956; *Perspectives for Our Party,* 1958; *Revision of the Federal Constitution,* 1959; *From Slavery to Chaguaramas,* 1959; *Ghandi: A Broadcast on the 90th Anniversary of the Birth of Mahatma Ghandi,* 1959; *The Approach of Independence: An Address to the Fourth Annual Convention of the People's National Movement,* 1960; *Perspectives for the West Indies,* 1960; *Our Fourth Anniversary: The Last Lap,* 1960; *Responsibilities of the Party Member,* 1960; *Massa Day Done: A Masterpiece of Political and Sociological Analysis,* 1961; *Tagore: Centenary Celebration Address,* 1961; *Reports on the Inter-Governmental Conference: Two Broadcasts by the Premier of Trinidad and Tobago,* 1961; *Message to the Youth of the Nation,* 1962; *Some Thoughts on Economic Aid to Developing Countries,* 1963; *The Future of the West Indies and Guyana,* 1963; *The University: Symbol of Freedom,* 1963; *Trinidad and Tobago and the British Guiana Question,* 1963; *The Developing Nation in the Modern World,* 1965; *Reorganization of the Public Service: Three Speeches,* 1966; *A Review of the Political Scene,* 1966; *Prime Minister's Broadcast to the Nation on the Unemployment Situation in Trinidad and Tobago,* 1967; *Devaluation Speeches,* 1967; *People's National Movement's Perspectives in the World of the Seventies,* 1970; *Some Historical Reflections on the Church in the Caribbean,* 1973; and *The Energy Crisis, 1973-1974,* 1974. Author of pamphlets, including *Economic Problems of Trinidad and Tobago, Constitution Reform in Trinidad and Tobago, The Historical Background of Race Relations in the Caribbean,* and *The Case for Party Politics in Trinidad and Tobago,* all 1955.

SIDELIGHTS: Eric Williams became the first prime minister of Trinidad and Tobago when that two-island nation gained its independence from Great Britain in 1962. Also a respected historian, he taught at Howard University in Washington, D.C., and had published several well-received books on the history of the Caribbean before returning to his native Trinidad to become involved in its politics in 1955. There he founded colonial Trinidad and Tobago's first stable political party, the democratic, socialist People's National Movement (PNM). As the PNM gained in power and popularity, so did Williams. Under his leadership, in 1956 the PNM won a majority of the seats in the colony's legislative council by calling for reforms that included universal and secular education and wider availability of birth control. In accordance with the colonial constitution, the British territorial governor named Williams, as leader of the majority party, chief minister of Trinidad and Tobago. He became prime minister when the colony was made an independent member of the British Commonwealth, and remained his nation's highest official until his death in 1981.

Williams's most famed historical work, *Capitalism and Slavery,* began as his Ph.D. thesis at Oxford University. Labeled "a classic in [its] field" by C. Gerald Fraser in Williams's *New York Times* obituary, the work explored the ways in which slavery contributed to the growth of British capitalism. Williams's scholarship carried over to his political life as well; his public addresses as prime minister given in Port of Spain's Woodford Square, many of which were published, were so full of factual information that the site was nicknamed the "University of Woodford Square."

From Columbus to Castro: The History of the Caribbean, published by Williams in 1970, is "less a history than an interesting and well-written essay on slavery and sugar-cane cultivation and the effects of their interaction on the peoples of the Caribbean," according to a *Times Literary Supplement* reviewer. The work covers the time span beginning when Columbus brought sugar cane from the Canary Islands to the region on his second voyage to the New World and ending with Fidel Castro's rule of Cuba. The *Times Literary Supplement* had particular praise for Williams's handling of "present conditions in the West Indies," and for his "suggestions for the future."

BIOGRAPHICAL/CRITICAL SOURCES:

PERIODICALS

Times Literary Supplement, September 11, 1970.

OBITUARIES:

PERIODICALS

Newsweek, April 13, 1981.
New York Times, March 31, 1981.
Time, April 13, 1981.*

* * *

WILLIAMS, George (Joseph) III 1949-

PERSONAL: Born March 3, 1949, in Springfield, Mass.; son of George Joseph, Jr., and Millie (Dalton) Williams; married Edie Karen Godfrey, September 18, 1976; children: Sarah, Michael. *Education:* Attended Riverside City College, 1967-69; California State University, Fullerton, B.A. in music composition, 1971; University of California, Riverside, B.A. in English, 1974. *Religion:* "Born-again Christian."

ADDRESSES: Office—Tree by the River Publishing, Box 463, Bridgeport, Calif. 93517.

CAREER: Recording engineer in Riverside, Calif., 1977-84; professional author, 1980—.

AWARDS, HONORS: John Stone Award from Riverside City College, 1969; nominated for Pulitzer Prize in Letters, 1987, for *Mark Twain: His Life in Virginia City, Nevada.*

WRITINGS:

PUBLISHED BY TREE BY THE RIVER

Rosa May: The Search for a Mining Camp Legend, 1980.
The Guide to Bodie and Eastern Sierra Historic Sites, 1981.
The Murders at Convict Lake, 1984.
The Redlight Ladies of Virginia City, Nevada, 1984.
Mark Twain: His Life in Virginia City, Nevada, 1986.
Mark Twain: His Adventures at Aurora and Mono Lake, 1986.
Hot Springs of the Eastern Sierra, 1987.
Mark Twain: Jackass Hill and the Jumping Frog, 1987.
On the Road With Mark Twain in California and Nevada, 1988.

PUBLISHED BY MUSIC BUSINESS BOOKS

The Songwriter's Demo Manual and Success Guide, 1984.

WORK IN PROGRESS: A Good Place in Nevada.

SIDELIGHTS: The inspiration for George Williams III's acclaimed first book, *Rosa May: The Search for a Mining Camp Legend*, was a gravestone in an outcast cemetery of a California ghost town. For more than three years the author re-

searched the life of Rosa May, a late nineteenth-century prostitute who died after tending stricken miners during an epidemic. The town where Rosa May is buried, Bodie, was a mining camp in the late 1800s and is now part of the California State Park system. The ghost town is the principal subject of Williams's second book, *The Guide to Bodie and Eastern Sierra Historic Sites*, which provides photos, maps, and travel directions for vacationers.

In addition to his books about the West, Williams has also written a series of books on American author Mark Twain. The books provide biographical and critical information on Twain's life in the West from 1861 to 1868, as well as travel information on historic sites relating to the renowned author.

BIOGRAPHICAL/CRITICAL SOURCES:

PERIODICALS

Kirkus Reviews, May 15, 1986.
Las Vegas Review Journal, January 25, 1981, May 30, 1982.
Los Angeles Times Book Review, January 18, 1981.

* * *

WILLIAMS, Juan 1954-

PERSONAL: Born April 10, 1954, in Colon, Panama; son of Rogelio L. (an accountant) and Alma Geraldine (a secretary; maiden name, Elias) Williams; married Susan Delise (a social worker), July 1, 1978; children: Antonio Mason, Regan Almina. *Education:* Haverford College, B.A., 1976.

ADDRESSES: Home—607 Whittier St. N.W., Washington, D.C. 20012. *Office*—*Washington Post*, 1150 15th St. N.W., Washington, D.C. 20071. *Agent*—Rafe Sagalyn, Raphael Sagalyn, Inc., 2813 Bellevue Ter. N.W., Washington, D.C. 20007.

CAREER: Washington Post, Washington, D.C., columnist and reporter, 1976—.

AWARDS, HONORS: Front Page Award from Washington-Baltimore Newspaper Guild and award from Education Writers of America, both 1979, both for series on public schools in Washington, D.C.; named columnist of the year by *Washingtonian*, 1982; DuSable Museum Award, 1985, for political writing.

WRITINGS:

Eyes on the Prize: America's Civil Rights Years, 1954-1965, Viking, 1987.

SIDELIGHTS: Each chapter of Juan Williams's book *Eyes on the Prize* deals with a specific event or series of events from the civil rights movement of the 1950s and 1960s. The book—produced in conjunction with a six-part public television series of the same title—provides a tribute to the thousands of ordinary people who participated in a movement that was physically strenuous, socially daring, and at times life-threatening. The author has concentrated on the memorable events, such as sit-ins, voting rights campaigns, and bus boycotts, but he does not neglect the lesser-known individuals who have faded from public memory. The book is dedicated to the men and women who lost their lives in the struggle. Roy Reed wrote in the *Washington Post Book World:* "The book is rich in detail on how the movement started, gained momentum and finally engulfed the political system and changed it."

Williams told *CA:* "I became interested in civil rights because of my work as a White House correspondent for the *Washing-*

ton Post during a period of strife between President Ronald Reagan's administration and civil rights groups. I gathered material for the book from extensive interviews, some taped and used in the public television series. Born in 1954, I was too young to participate in the civil rights movement but am inspired by it nonetheless. At the same time, I believe I'm sufficiently dispassionate about the events to see them as historically valuable evidence of democracy at work in modern America. That perspective makes me part of a new generation of black writers who feel less compelled to be advocates and, instead, simply recount the truth of the black American triumph.''

BIOGRAPHICAL/CRITICAL SOURCES:

PERIODICALS

Washington Post Book World, January 11, 1987, February 14, 1988.

* * *

WILLIAMS, Kenneth   1926-1988

OBITUARY NOTICE: Born February 22, 1926, in London, England; died April 15, 1988, in London, England. Actor, comedian, and author. A star of British stage, television, and radio, Williams is best known for his farcical and often risque "Carry On" movies. A whiny, effeminate voice, arched eyebrows, flaring nostrils, and rolling eyes became his comic trademarks. Williams first discovered his gift for comedy as a soldier in the British army entertaining troops during World War II. He was transferred from his position as mapmaker for the Royal Engineers to the Combined Services Entertainment division and toured Malaya and Burma before receiving his first theatrical job at Singapore's Victoria Theatre. Williams's writings include *Acid Drops, Back Drops, I Only Have to Close My Eyes,* and *Just Williams,* a compilation of his diary entries.

OBITUARIES AND OTHER SOURCES:

BOOKS

Who's Who, 139th edition, St. Martin's, 1987.
Who's Who in the Theatre: A Biographical Record of the Contemporary Stage, 17th edition, Gale, 1981.

PERIODICALS

Chicago Tribune, April 17, 1988.
Los Angeles Times, April 16, 1988.
Times (London), April 16, 1988.

* * *

WILLIAMS, Martha E(thelyn)   1934-

PERSONAL: Born September 21, 1934, in Chicago, Ill.; daughter of Harold Milton (a president of a trade association) and Alice Rosemond (a librarian; maiden name, Fox) Williams. *Education:* Barat College, B.A., 1955; Loyola University of Chicago, M.A., 1957.

ADDRESSES: Home—Route 1, Monticello, Ill. 61856. *Office*—Coordinated Science Laboratory, University of Illinois at Urbana-Champaign, 1101 West Springfield St., Urbana, Ill. 61801.

CAREER: Illinois Institute of Technology, Research Institute, Chicago, technical assistant, 1957, assistant chemist, 1957-61, associate chemist, 1961, assistant supervisor of technical

information research, 1961-62, manager of information sciences, 1962-72, manager of Computer Search Center, 1968-72; Illinois Institute of Technology, Chicago, adjunct associate professor of science information, 1965-73, lecturer in chemistry, 1968-70; University of Illinois at Urbana-Champaign, Urbana, professor of information science and director of Information Retrieval Research Laboratory, 1972—, professor of library science, 1973—, affiliate of computer science department, 1979—. Engineering Information, Inc., trustee, 1974-84, director, 1976-88, vice-president, 1979-80, president, 1980-81, chairman of board of directors, 1981-88; National Library of Medicine, member of board of regents, 1979-82, chairman of board of regents, 1981-82. Member of board of advisers of Funding Sources Clearinghouse, 1972-73; member of MIDLNET Technical Committee, 1976-77; member of National Science Foundation Task Force on Science Information Activities, 1977; member of U.S. National Committee for International Federation for Documentation, 1974-75 and 1977-78; chairman of Gordon Research Conference, 1978; consultant to Computer Corp. of America, Environmental Protection Agency, and Solar Energy Research Institute. Lecturer at universities, including American, Case-Western Reserve, Louisiana State, Northern Illinois, Northwestern, Rutgers, Tokyo, Western Illinois, Western Kentucky, Texas at Austin, Wisconsin—Madison, and Washington, Seattle, and at Massachusetts Institute of Technology.

MEMBER: American Association for the Advancement of Science (fellow), American Society for Information Science (member of council, 1971-72; chairman of Committee on Intersociety Cooperation, 1972-73, Networks Committee, 1973-74, and Special Interest Group on Computerized Retrieval Services, 1974-75; president, 1987-88), American Chemical Society, Association for Computing Machinery (chairman of Data Base Committee, 1973), Association for Information and Dissemination Centers (chairman of Cooperative Data Management Committee, 1970-74, and Quality Control Committee, 1972; vice-president, 1971-73; president, 1975-77), Institute for Information Scientists (England; fellow).

AWARDS, HONORS: Award of merit from American Society for Information Science, 1984, for contributions to the field of information science; best paper of the year award from H. W. Wilson Co., 1975, for "Criteria for Evaluation and Selection of Database Services"; travel grants from National Science Foundation, 1972, 1973, and 1976.

WRITINGS:

(With P. A. Llewellyn, Barbara Burroughs, and others) *Properties of Fused-Salt Mixtures,* four volumes, Research Institute, Illinois Institute of Technology, 1964.
(Editor) *Design Guide for Pressurized Gas Systems,* two volumes, Research Institute, Illinois Institute of Technology, 1966.
(Editor) *Permeability Data for Aerospace Applications,* Research Institute, Illinois Institute of Technology, 1968.
(Editor) *Survey on Air Pollution Monitoring Instrumentation,* Research Institute, Illinois Institute of Technology, 1968.
(With E. S. Schwartz and Paul Fanta) *Modern Techniques in Chemical Information,* Research Institute, Illinois Institute of Technology, 1968.
(Contributor) James Mattson, Harry B. Mark, Jr., and Herbert C. MacDonald, editors, *Chemistry and Instrumentation,* Dekker, 1974.
(Contributor) Carlos A. Cuadra, editor, *Annual Review of Information Science and Technology,* Volume IX, American Society for Information Science, 1974.

(With Laurence Lannom and Elaine Tisch-Dunatov) *ASIDIC Survey of Information Centers Using Machine-Readable Databases,* Association of Information and Dissemination Centers, 1976.

(With S. H. Rouse) *Computer-Readable Bibliographic Data Bases: A Directory and Data Sourcebook,* American Society for Information Science, 1976.

(Contributor) E. V. Ludena, N. H. Sabelli, and A. C. Wahl, editors, *Computers in Chemical Education and Research,* Plenum, 1977.

(With Lannom, Rosemary O'Donnell, and Steven Barth) *Computer-Readable Databases: A Directory and Data Sourcebook,* American Society for Information Science, 1979, new edition with Lannom and Carolyn Robbins published as *Computer-Readable Databases, 1982: A Directory and Data Sourcebook,* 1982, 1985 edition, two volumes, American Library Association/Elsevier Science Publishers, 1985.

(Contributor) E. B. Jackson, editor, *Special Librarianship: A New Reader,* Scarecrow, 1980.

(Editor with T. H. Hogan, and contributor) *National Online Meeting Proceedings,* seven volumes, Learned Information, Inc., 1981-87.

Contributor to *Encyclopedia Americana, International Encyclopedia of Communication, Encyclopedia of Chemistry,* and *ALA Yearbook.* Contributor to library and information science journals. Contributing editor of column "Data Bases" in bulletin of the American Society for Information Science, 1974-79; editor of *Annual Review of Information Science and Technology,* 1975—; editor of *Online Review,* 1977—. Member of publications board of Association for Computing Machinery, 1972-77; member of editorial board of *Reference Librarian,* 1980—, and *Information Processing and Management,* 1982—. Member of editorial advisory board of *Data Base,* 1978—, and *Information Today,* 1983—.

* * *

WILLIAMS, Robert G.   1948-

PERSONAL: Born December 30, 1948, in Birmingham, Ala.; son of Charles C. (a lawyer) and Marna (a psychologist; maiden name, Bromberg) Williams. *Education:* Princeton University, B.A., 1971; Stanford University, Ph.D., 1978.

ADDRESSES: Home—1160 Cheryl Dr., Kernersville, N.C. 27284. *Office*— Department of Economics, Guilford College, 5800 West Friendly Ave., Greensboro, N.C. 27410.

CAREER: Brookings Institution, Washington, D.C., research economist, 1973-74; Guilford College, Greensboro, N.C., assistant professor, 1978-83, associate professor of economics, 1984—. *Military service:* U.S. Army, 1973; became captain.

MEMBER: Latin American Studies Association.

WRITINGS:

Export Agriculture and the Crisis in Central America, University of North Carolina Press, 1986.

WORK IN PROGRESS: A book, *Coffee and the State in Central America,* which "will contribute to our understanding of why governments of Central America behave so differently today," publication by University of North Carolina Press expected in 1990.

SIDELIGHTS: Robert G. Williams told *CA:* "I have been researching Central American issues since 1972. My Ph.D.

dissertation, 'The Central American Common Market: Unequal Benefits and Uneven Development,' examines why this drive to industrialize came into being in the 1960s and what forces led to its demise in the early 1970s. When the crisis in Central America heated up in the late 1970s, I turned my attention to agriculture, the heart of the Central American economy. My book *Export Agriculture and the Crisis in Central America* critically examines the U.S. policy of export expansion and military aid as a means of achieving stability in the region. I conclude that by expanding the fortunes of the elite at the expense of the Central American peasantry, this policy combination created ecological and social stress and helped prepare the region for revolution in the late 1970s and 1980s."

* * *

WILLIAMSON, Joseph   1895-1988

OBITUARY NOTICE—See index for *CA* sketch: Born June 15, 1895, in London (one source says Poplar), England; died March 14, 1988. Anglican priest and author. Williamson is remembered for founding the Wellclose Trust, a refuge for needy young women. The priest was ordained by the Church of England in 1925 and soon after served four years in Grahamstown, South Africa. From 1932 to 1952 he was rector of parishes in Warwickshire, Suffolk, and Norfolk, England, and for the next ten years was rector of St. Paul's Cathedral in London, England. During the 1940s Williamson served as chaplain of forces for the British military. The priest wrote *Father Joe: The Autobiography of Joseph Williamson of Poplar and Stepney* and *Friends of Father Joe,* both published in the 1960s.

OBITUARIES AND OTHER SOURCES:

BOOKS

Williamson, Joseph, *Father Joe: The Autobiography of Joseph Williamson of Poplar and Stepney,* Hodder & Stoughton, 1963.

PERIODICALS

Times (London), March 18, 1988.

* * *

WILLS, Millicent A(gatha)   1901(?)-1988

OBITUARY NOTICE: Born c. 1901 in Guyana; died following a long illness, February 28, 1988, in Detroit, Mich. Educator and author. Wills was a teacher for thirty years in Detroit public schools. Dedicating her life to helping young people, Wills set up scholarships for minority students at Northern High and her alma mater, Wayne State University. After retiring in 1972, she wrote two books, *My Journey Into the Past* and *Believe the Works,* both of which describe her life, philosophy, and travels abroad.

OBITUARIES AND OTHER SOURCES:

PERIODICALS

Detroit Free Press, March 5, 1988.

* * *

WILSON, Adrian   1923-1988

OBITUARY NOTICE: Born July 1, 1923, in Ann Arbor, Mich.;

died of congestive heart failure, February 3, 1988, in San Francisco, Calif. Book designer, printer, scholar, and author. A conscientious objector during World War II, Wilson became interested in typography and book design while doing alternative service at a civilian camp in Waldport, Oregon, in 1944. After the war he became an apprentice to several prominent San Francisco printers and went on to set up his own printing press, the Press at Tuscany Alley, in 1960. While researching one of his classic books on printing, Wilson found the earliest known example of printer's copy, the more than five-hundred-year-old Subiaco manuscript of Saint Augustine's *De civitate Dei*. Wilson, the recipient of a MacArthur Foundation grant of more than $200,000, wrote *The Design of Books, Printing for Theater,* and *The Making of the Nuremberg Chronicle.* The author collaborated with his wife, Joyce Lancaster, on other books, including *A Medieval Mirror.*

OBITUARIES AND OTHER SOURCES:

PERIODICALS

New York Times, February 6, 1988.
Publishers Weekly, February 26, 1988.
Times (London), February 5, 1988.

*   *   *

WILSON, Chris(topher Paul) 1949-

PERSONAL: Born November 18, 1949, in London, England; son of Paul Barclay (a farmer) and Joan (a teacher; maiden name, Hesketh) Wilson. *Education:* Sir John Cass College, London, B.Sc., 1971; London School of Economics and Political Science, London, Ph.D., 1973. *Religion:* ''Faltering agnosticism.''

ADDRESSES: Home—3 Florence St., Islington, London N1 2DX, England. *Office*—Department of Communications, Goldsmiths' College, University of London, London SE14 6NW, England.

CAREER: University of London, London, England, research psychologist, 1973; London Hospital, London, research psychologist, 1974-76; Arts Council of Great Britain, London, research psychologist, 1977; Ministry of Agriculture, Fisheries, and Food, London, research psychologist, 1978; University of London, Goldsmiths' College, lecturer, 1979-83, senior lecturer in communications, 1984—, coordinator of creative writing program, 1985—.

WRITINGS:

Jokes (nonfiction), Academic Press, 1979.
Audience to an Audience (nonfiction), Arts Council of Great Britain, 1980.
Gallimauf's Gospel (novel), Harvester, 1986.
Baa (novel), Harvester, 1987.

WORK IN PROGRESS: The Mumblers, a novel; novels about acting and the idiot-savant syndrome, publication expected in 1988; a book on the techniques of fiction writing, publication expected in 1989.

*   *   *

WILSON, William E(dward) 1906-1988

OBITUARY NOTICE—See index for *CA* sketch: Born February 12, 1906, in Evansville, Ind.; died of cancer, May 29, 1988, in Bloomington, Ind. Educator, journalist, and author. Wilson, a professor emeritus at Indiana University at Bloom-

ington, taught English at that institution from 1950 to 1973. He also taught at Brown University and University of Colorado, and for two years he served Fulbright lectureships in Aix-Marseilles, Grenoble, and Nice, France. During the 1920s and 1940s he worked as a journalist for the *Evansville Press,* the *New Bedford Standard* in Massachusetts, and the Baltimore, Maryland, *Evening Sun.* Wilson's many books include *The Wabash, Crescent City, Abe Lincoln of Pigeon Creek, The Angel and the Serpent: The Story of New Harmony, Indiana: A History,* and *Every Man Is My Father.*

OBITUARIES AND OTHER SOURCES:

BOOKS

International Authors and Writers Who's Who, 10th edition, International Biographical Centre, 1986.

PERIODICALS

New York Times, June 4, 1988.

*   *   *

WITHORN, Ann 1947-

PERSONAL: Born February 27, 1947, in Atlanta, Ga.; daughter of Edward W. and Flo (Hogan) Withorn; married George Abbott White (a teacher and writer), June 5, 1971; children: Gwyne Withorn White, Bronwen Withorn White. *Education:* Florida State University, B.A., 1968; Harvard University, M.A., 1970; Brandeis University, Ph.D., 1978. *Politics:* ''Socialist-feminist.'' *Religion:* None.

ADDRESSES: Office—College of Public and Community Service, University of Massachusetts, Downtown Campus, Boston, Mass. 02125.

CAREER: University of Massachusetts, Downtown Campus, Boston, assistant professor, 1977-84, associate professor of social policy, 1984—.

MEMBER: Bertha Capen Reynolds Society.

WRITINGS:

The Circle Game: Services for the Poor in Massachusetts, 1966-1978, University of Massachusetts Press, 1982.
Serving the People: Social Services and Social Change, Columbia University Press, 1984.
(Editor with Rochelle Lefkowitz) *For Crying Out Loud: Women and Poverty in the United States,* Pilgrim Press (New York, N.Y.), 1986.
Fears of Dependence: Conservative Opposition to the Welfare State, University of Wisconsin Press, in press.

SIDELIGHTS: Ann Withorn told *CA:* ''I have been, and still am, intensely interested in creating a viable, serious, socialist-feminist movement in this country. Understanding and transcending our current welfare state is central to that task, so I keep working with women on welfare, with human service workers, and with activist organizers and theoreticians toward achieving that goal. It's hard.''

*   *   *

WITTFOGEL, Karl A(ugust) 1896-1988

OBITUARY NOTICE: Born September 6, 1896, in Woltersdorf, Germany; died of pneumonia, May 25, 1988, in New York, N.Y. Social scientist and author. Wittfogel joined the German Communist party in 1920 and remained a Communist until 1939 when the Russians signed a nonaggression pact with Germany. He fled Germany when Adolf Hitler came to power in 1934, settling in the United States three years later. A respected scholar of the Orient, Wittfogel advanced his thesis of "Asiatic restoration" in Russia in his 1957 book *Oriental Despotism*. According to the author, absolute power in the Orient had been gained through hydraulic monopoly, the control of the water supply by the ruler. His other books on the Orient include *Awakening China, Economy and Society in China,* and *History of Chinese Society.*

OBITUARIES AND OTHER SOURCES:

BOOKS

Biographical Dictionary of Neo-Marxism, Greenwood Press, 1985.
Directory of American Scholars, Volume I: *History,* 8th edition, Bowker, 1982.

PERIODICALS

New York Times, May 26, 1988.
Times (London), June 18, 1988.

*　　　*　　　*

WOOD, Charles Monroe　1944-

PERSONAL: Born November 22, 1944, in Salida, Colo.; son of Roy Milton (a railroad machinist) and Ruth (Avery) Wood; married Jean Ann Fesler, September 4, 1966; children: Leslie Anne. *Education:* University of Denver, B.A., 1966; Boston University, Th.M., 1969; Yale University, M.Phil., 1971, Ph.D., 1972.

ADDRESSES: Office—Perkins School of Theology, Southern Methodist University, Dallas, Tex. 75275.

CAREER: Ordained United Methodist minister, 1967; pastor of United Methodist churches in Colorado and Wyoming, 1972-76; Southern Methodist University, Dallas, Tex., assistant professor, 1976-82, associate professor of theology, 1982—.

MEMBER: American Academy of Religion, American Theological Society.

WRITINGS:

Theory and Religious Understanding: A Critique of the Hermeneutics of Joachim Wach, Scholars Press (Missoula, Mont.), 1975.
The Formation of Christian Understanding: An Essay in Theological Hermeneutics, Westminster, 1981.
Vision and Discernment: An Orientation in Theological Study, Scholars Press (Atlanta, Ga.), 1985.

Contributor to theological journals.

WORK IN PROGRESS: Research on theological education, the Christian doctrine of providence, and theological method.

*　　　*　　　*

WOOD, John A(rmstead, Jr.)　1932-

PERSONAL: Born July 28, 1932, in Roanoke, Va.; son of John Armstead and Lillian Cary (Hall) Wood; married Elisabeth Mathilde Heuser, June 12, 1958 (divorced); children: Crispin S., Georgia K. *Education:* Virginia Polytechnic Institute (now Polytechnic Institute and State University), B.S., 1954; Massachusetts Institute of Technology, Ph.D., 1958; postdoctoral study at Cambridge University, 1959-60.

ADDRESSES: Home—1716 Cambridge St., No. 15, Cambridge, Mass. 02138. *Office*—Harvard-Smithsonian Center for Astrophysics, 60 Garden St., Cambridge, Mass. 02138; and Department of Earth and Planetary Sciences, Harvard University, Cambridge, Mass. 02138.

CAREER: Harvard University, Cambridge, Mass., staff scientist at Smithsonian Institution Astrophysical Observatory, 1959, 1961-62; University of Chicago, Chicago, Ill., research associate at Enrico Fermi Institute for Nuclear Studies, 1962-65; Harvard University, staff scientist at Smithsonian Institution Astrophysical Observatory, 1965—, professor of the practice of geology, 1976—, associate director of Harvard-Smithsonian Center for Astrophysics, 1981-86. Vice-chairman of Lunar Sample Analysis Planning Team, 1971-73.

MEMBER: International Astronomical Union, American Geophysical Union (fellow), Meteoritical Society (fellow; president, 1971-72), American Association for the Advancement of Science (fellow), American Astronomical Society, Geochemical Society.

AWARDS, HONORS: Fellow of American Chemical Society Petroleum Research Fund in England, 1959-60; medal for exceptional scientific achievement from National Aeronautics and Space Administration, 1973, for studies of Apollo lunar samples; J. Lawrence Smith Medal from National Academy of Sciences, 1976, and Frederick E. Leonard Medal from Meteoritical Society, 1980, for meteorite research.

WRITINGS:

Meteorites and the Origin of Planets, McGraw, 1968.
The Solar System, Prentice-Hall, 1979.
(Editor with Sherwood Chang) *The Cosmic History of the Biogenic Elements and Compounds,* Scientific and Technical Information Branch, National Aeronautics and Space Administration, 1985.

Contributor to scientific journals.

WORK IN PROGRESS: "A book on the moon and the history of lunar research since World War II—principally the Apollo program," for Smithsonian Press.

SIDELIGHTS: John A. Wood told *CA:* "I am first and foremost a scientist, not a writer, but in the senior years of my career I seem to be drawn increasingly into writing my thoughts and feelings (as opposed to reporting research results)."

*　　　*　　　*

WOOD, Peter Weston　1953-

PERSONAL: Born February 5, 1953, in New York, N.Y.; son of Guy B. (a songwriter) and Nathalie (a designer; maiden name, Pierce) Wood. *Education:* Fordham University, B.A., 1976; Ohio State University, B.S., 1982.

ADDRESSES: Home—280 West St., Mount Kisco, N.Y. 10549. *Agent*—Kurt Busiek, Scott Meredith Literary Agency, 845 Third Ave., New York, N.Y. 10022.

CAREER: Sales manager at resort in Montauk, N.Y., 1977; Lincoln Hall, Lincolndale, N.Y., counselor, 1978-79; Vanity Fair Corp., New York, N.Y., sales representative, 1979-83; high school English teacher in Columbus, Ohio, 1982-85; White Plains High School, White Plains, N.Y., English teacher and football and baseball coach, 1986—. Sales representative for Nasco, 1984; English teacher at North Adult Learning Center, 1985; artist, with solo exhibitions of his work.

WRITINGS:

"Dog Food Pie" (one-act play), first produced in Lincolndale, N.Y., at Batcher Theater, 1979.
To Swallow a Toad (novel), Donald I. Fine, 1987.

Contributor to magazines, including *Commonweal, Ring,* and *Amateur Boxer.* Also author of full-length play, produced at White Plains High School, 1988.

SIDELIGHTS: Peter Weston Wood commented on his work as a visual artist: "My art work is usually encased within boxes. People also live in boxes. Our days and nights are boxes; our skin is a box. The box symbolizes divisions of space and time—all that defines and limits our experience. The brain is a three-pound machine in a box, and its only liberation is imagination. Imagination has no box. Imagination is my tool. I seek to begin where my consciousness ends."

The author added: "Being a writer is a splendid misery. Spawning characters, plots, and themes from a thin, yellow pencil is tough, very tough. When I write, I bleed. But I've noticed that writing is both the bandage and the knife.

"It's not much fun, writing. I start doing nervous things like pacing floors, staring at walls, and eating the inside of my cheeks. I perspire. But the wonderful truth about putting pencil to paper is that is reveals you to yourself. Words are windows in very specific ways. Sometimes you see that you are thick-headed and have too much bone in your skull. Still, you write. You write because you want your readers to be able to sniff the very protons of your characters' minds. You follow that dream to the very end.

"And at the end, after the fifth rewrite, when your heart is softly pounding in your chest, you can smell the odor of your own strength. You rejoice. You finally can see the force of your own beauty—a book. A beautiful, silent bellow—a book."

Like the protagonist of his novel, Wood began boxing as a teenager. In 1971 he boxed in the New York Golden Gloves finals at Madison Square Garden. The author was a member of the U.S. boxing team that fought in Montreal in 1972, and he represented the United States at the Maccabian Games in Tel Aviv in 1976. *To Swallow a Toad* is, according to *Washington Post* reviewer Chris Mead, "a voice . . . so raw, violent and perfectly limited that the book barks of autobiography."

The novel tells the story of a young boy who begins boxing as a teenager and reaches the New York Golden Gloves finals. It also depicts the inner struggles of a young man from a broken home, coping with loneliness, helplessness, and adolescent confusion. "Author Wood lets the reader know what it feels like to walk into a gym alone for the first time, what it is like to gasp for breath, to be powerless in your own home, confused in school and wanting to be anywhere else but a boxing ring," Mead commented, adding that the book "seems more like life than art." Praising Wood's characters as "unique and believable" and his dialogue as "sharp and revealing," the critic concluded, "*To Swallow a Toad* is an honest voice from a narrator who ordinarily would not speak like this to us."

BIOGRAPHICAL/CRITICAL SOURCES:

PERIODICALS

Washington Post Book World, July 10, 1987.

WOODALL, Mary   1901-1988

OBITUARY NOTICE: Born March 6, 1901, in Chelsea, England; died March 31, 1988. Museum curator, art historian, and author. Director of the Birmingham City Museum and Art Gallery in England beginning in 1956, Woodall was the first woman to assume the top post at a major municipal art gallery. Together with the museum's former director, Trenchard Cox, Woodall worked to broaden Birmingham's collection in the years following World War II. She is credited with expanding the gallery's vision through her wise purchasing of masterpieces and her administrative expertise. An authority on eighteenth-century English painter Thomas Gainsborough, Woodall wrote her doctoral thesis on the artist's landscape paintings. In addition, she authored the biography *Thomas Gainsborough: His Life and Work,* and edited *The Letters of Thomas Gainsborough.*

OBITUARIES AND OTHER SOURCES:

BOOKS

Who's Who, 139th edition, St. Martin's, 1987.
Who's Who in Art, 21st edition, Art Trade Press, 1984.

PERIODICALS

Times (London), April 6, 1988.

*   *   *

WOODMAN, Bill
See WOODMAN, William

*   *   *

WOODMAN, William   1936-
   (Bill Woodman)

PERSONAL: Born October 30, 1936, in Bangor, Maine; son of Frederick Leland (a restorer of antiques) and Ada (a homemaker; maiden name, Scanlin) Woodman; married second wife, Barbara Shelley, 1976 (separated, 1981); children: (first marriage) Jowill; (second marriage) Anne. *Education:* Attended Phoenix School of Design, 1958-60, School of Visual Arts, and Pratt Institute.

ADDRESSES: Home—308 West 105th St., New York, N.Y. 10025. *Office*—373 Broadway, New York, N.Y. 10013.

CAREER: Free-lance cartoonist and illustrator, 1959—. Part-time chartist, 1958-61; also worked as paste-up artist, messenger, furniture mover, and bartender; watercolor paintings exhibited in Maine and at Limited Art Editions, New York, N.Y. *Military service:* U.S. Navy, 1954-57.

AWARDS, HONORS: Honorable mention from Turkey's International Cartoon Contest, 1983.

WRITINGS:

UNDER NAME BILL WOODMAN

Fish and Moose News, Dodd, 1980.
Whose Birthday Is It?, Crowell, 1980.
(Illustrator) Carl Ewald, *The Spider and Other Stories,* Crowell, 1981.
Buzzwords, Simon & Schuster, 1983.

Contributor of cartoons to magazines, including *Cavalier, New Yorker, Playboy, Saturday Review, Esquire,* and *National Lampoon.*

WOODRUFF, Robert W.
   See MENCKEN, H(enry) L(ouis)

*   *   *

WOODS, James M.   1952-

PERSONAL: Born November 28, 1952, in Little Rock, Ark.; son of Henry (a federal judge) and Kathleen (a housewife; maiden name, McCaffrey) Woods; married Rebecca Ann Williams, June 23, 1979. *Education:* University of Dallas, B.A., 1976; Rice University, M.A., 1979; Tulane University, Ph.D., 1983. *Religion:* Roman Catholic.

ADDRESSES: Home—100 North Melrose, Apt. 1506, Natchitoches, La. 71547. *Office*—Louisiana School for Mathematics, Science, and the Arts, Natchitoches, La. 71457.

CAREER: Tulane University, New Orleans, La., instructor in U.S. history, 1979-81; St. Mary's Dominican College, New Orleans, instructor in U.S. history, spring, 1981; University of Arkansas, Little Rock, instructor in U.S. history, summer, 1981; teacher of church history at Jesuit high school in New Orleans, 1981-83; Claflin College, Orangeburg, S.C., assistant professor of history, 1983-85; Northwestern State University, Natchitoches, La., assistant professor of history, 1985-86; Louisiana School for Mathematics, Science, and the Arts, Natchitoches, history teacher, 1986—. Leader of Roman Catholic retreats and seminars throughout the South.

MEMBER: Organization of American Historians, American Catholic Studies Association, Southern Historical Association, Arkansas Historical Association.

WRITINGS:

Rebellion and Realignment: Arkansas's Road to Secession, University of Arkansas Press, 1987.

Contributor of articles and reviews to history journals.

WORK IN PROGRESS: A People Set Apart: A History of the Catholic Church in Arkansas, for Roman Catholic diocese of Little Rock, publication expected in 1993; a historiographical synthesis of southern secession.

SIDELIGHTS: James M. Woods told *CA:* "I have a strong interest in southern secession. I also have some interest in writing a major political biography of Senator Ellison 'Cotton Ed' Smith of South Carolina (1866-1944). I have a strong background in Arkansas history as well, and I am glad to be writing the first history of Arkansas Catholicism. I chose an Arkansas subject for my books because, as a native Arkansan and a student of history, I realized the paucity of published histories of the state. When I was a graduate student at Rice University, historian Frank Vandiver directed me toward a Civil War topic; soon thereafter I discovered that there was no recent or published study of Arkansas from statehood to secession, 1836 to 1861. I believe *Rebellion and Realignment: Arkansas's Road to Secession* fills this gap in the scholarship of the Old South.

"*Rebellion and Realignment* is more than just a narrative of a particular era; it also addresses some of the wider issues raised by recent historians regarding Southern secession. While there have been any number of published state studies of southern disunionism, with some since 1970 being especially significant, Arkansas has been ignored. The most recent studies focused on the lower South—those states which left the Union between Abraham Lincoln's election and his inauguartion. *Rebellion and Realignment* is the first published study of an upper South state which, as late as March, 1861, had rejected disunion. Arkansas did secede after the firing on Fort Sumter and Lincoln's call for troops; it withdrew exactly six months to the day after the 1860 presidential election. There are some upcoming works which will study the secession movement in Virginia, North Carolina, and Tennessee, the other three upper South states.

"Perhaps to fill another historical vacuum I decided to write *A People Set Apart: A History of the Catholic Church in Arkansas,* about the oldest Christian denomination within the state. Catholicism might have arrived with the earliest European settlers and colonists, yet since the early nineteenth century the church's adherents have consistently numbered less than 5 percent of the total population. Despite such small numbers, Arkansas Catholicism has been a real leader in education and social services. Arkansas's second Catholic bishop was one of only two prelates in the world, and the only one in the English-speaking church, to vote against papal infallibility at the First Vatican Council in 1870.

"The title *A People Set Apart* comes from the Jerusalem Bible translation of 1 Peter 2:9. It is meant to symbolize that Arkansas Catholics were a people set apart in two important ways: they were often victims of prejudice from their more numerous Protestant neighbors, and their rural, rather isolated existence is to be contrasted with the urban, ghetto experience of most American Catholics. I believe this work will fill an important lacuna in Arkansas's religious history and the history of the Catholic church in the United States."

*   *   *

WOODS, Sharon   1949-

PERSONAL: Born December 5, 1949, in Chicago, Ill.; daughter of Alice and Fred Taich; married Robert A. Woods (a company president), 1971; children: Shane, Robby, Amber. *Education:* Syracuse University, B.F.A., 1971.

ADDRESSES: Office—Robert A. Woods Construction, Inc., 302 Catron St., Santa Fe, N.Mex. 87501.

CAREER: Art teacher in Santa Fe schools, 1973-78; Robert A. Woods Contruction, Inc., Santa Fe, N.Mex., vice-president, 1978-86, president and architectural designer, 1986—; business partner of Southwest Remodeling Services, 1984—.

WRITINGS:

(With Christine Mather) *Santa Fe Style,* Rizzoli International, 1986.

WORK IN PROGRESS: A book on Santa Fe style floorplans.

*   *   *

WOODWARD, John (O.)   1922(?)-1988

OBITUARY NOTICE: Born c. 1922; died following a long illness, March 13, 1988. Art curator, art historian, and author. Best known for his work as keeper of art at the City of Birmingham Museum in England, Woodward began his career in the art world as an assistant keeper of Western art in Oxford's

Ashmolean Museum. He is credited with an impressive record for acquisitions while at Birmingham, buying for his department works by some of history's most prominent painters, including Pompeo Girolamo Batoni, Sandro Botticelli, Simone Martini, Charles Locke Eastlake, Thomas Gainsborough, and Hilaire Germain Edgar Degas. Woodward's writings include *Tudor and Stuart Drawings* and *British Painting: A Picture History*.

OBITUARIES AND OTHER SOURCES:

PERIODICALS

Times (London), April 11, 1988.

* * *

WRIGHT, Sewall 1889-1988

OBITUARY NOTICE: Born December 21, 1889, in Melrose, Mass.; died of complications from a hip fracture, March 3, 1988, in Madison, Wis. Geneticist and author. Considered the twentieth century's foremost evolutionary theorist, Wright was best known for establishing a mathematical basis for evolution. His experimental work at the University of Chicago and the University of Wisconsin—especially his study of the effects of inbreeding on guinea pigs—has led to important advances in the scientific understanding of human evolution. Wright proposed the theory of "genetic drift," which holds that significant changes in a population's gene pool may occur by chance. His publications include hundreds of scientific articles and *Evolution and the Genetics of Populations: A Treatise*.

OBITUARIES AND OTHER SOURCES:

BOOKS

American Men and Women of Science: The Physical and Biological Sciences, Bowker, 15th edition, 1982.
Who's Who, 140th edition, St. Martin's, 1988.

PERIODICALS

Chicago Tribune, March 9, 1988.
Los Angeles Times, March 5, 1988.
New York Times, March 5, 1988.
Washington Post, March 7, 1988.

* * *

WRIGHT, T(erence) R(oy) 1951-

PERSONAL: Born April 12, 1951, in Rinteln, West Germany; son of H. Roy and Sheila (Goldsmith) Wright; married Gabriele Hentrich (a teacher), September 2, 1978; children: Catherine Elizabeth. *Education:* Christ Church, Oxford, B.A., 1977. *Politics:* Social Democrat. *Religion:* Roman Catholic.

ADDRESSES: Home—14 Woodburn Ave., Fenham, Newcastle upon Tyne NE4 9EZ, England. *Office*—Department of English Literature, University of Newcastle upon Tyne, Newcastle upon Tyne NE1 7RU, England.

CAREER: University of Newcastle upon Tyne, Newcastle upon Tyne, England, lecturer in English literature, 1978—.

MEMBER: American Academy of Religion, Association of University Teachers.

WRITINGS:

(Editor) *John Henry Newman: A Man for Our Time?* Grevatt & Grevatt, 1983.
The Religion of Humanity: The Impact of Comtean Positivism on Victorian Britain, Cambridge University Press, 1986.
Theology and Literature, Basil Blackwell, 1987.
(Editor with David Jasper) *The Critical Spirit and the Will to Believe*, Macmillan, 1988.
Wessexuality: The Erotic World of Thomas Hardy, Macmillan, in press.

Associate editor of *Literature and Theology*.

SIDELIGHTS: In his book *Religion and Humanity*, T. R. Wright stresses that, despite the failure of his secular religion, Auguste Comte's philosophy attracted many intellectual and literary figures whose writings spread the impact of positivism widely throughout Victorian England. Comte's positivist tenets were reflected in the novels of such respected authors as George Eliot and Thomas Hardy. Thinkers like John Stuart Mill were drawn to the philosophy of positivism, and it has even been claimed that Comte's impact on the public provided the impetus for the radical trade union movement of the 1860s. Though there were relatively few dedicated followers of the religion of humanity, it was one of the most widely recognized philosophical movements of its day. Despite its popularity, the secular religion was doomed to failure. It contained too few of the mysteries and rituals of traditional religion to fill the spiritual needs of Victorian society. "T. R. Wright's excellent book," assessed Peter Clarke in the *Times Literary Supplement*, "combines wide reading and thorough research with a restraint in exposition which was exactly what was needed."

Wright told *CA*: "Hardy's Wessex is a world dominated by desire, a shadowy region of distortion and displacement in which men and women weave erotic and fantastic dreams around one another. It is a world that anticipates not only pioneer psychoanalyst Sigmund Freud, Hardy's contemporary, but such radical modern thinkers as Roland Barthes, Michel Foucault, and Jacques Lacan, whose ideas are summarized in the opening chapter.

"From a critical perspective enlightened by these theories I proceed to explore the whole range of Hardy's fiction. I begin with the disguised and distorted autobiography before considering the early romances and fantasies, in which women are seen mainly as erotic objects. Then I turn from the novels of the 1880s, in which the concept of manliness is cruelly undermined, and the grotesque short stories, which dramatize some of the more perverse aspects of desire, to the tragedies of the 1890s, whose heroines finally fall victim to male visions of women. I end with that astonishing farewell to both fiction and desire, *The Well-Beloved*."

BIOGRAPHICAL/CRITICAL SOURCES:

PERIODICALS

Times Literary Supplement, May 23, 1986.

* * *

WULFORST, Harry David 1923-

PERSONAL: Born October 24, 1923, in Brooklyn, N.Y.; son

of Henry Joseph (a business executive) and Grace (Bickell) Wulforst; married Marjorie Gilbert (a director of occupational therapy), July 17, 1948; children: Arthur David, Stephen Walker, Katharine Hilyard. *Education:* New York University, B.S.J., 1948.

ADDRESSES: Home—Quarry Lane, Valley Forge, Pa. 19481.

CAREER: Associate editor of *Electronic Industries* at Caldwell-Clements Publishing Co., 1948-54; began as managing editor and became editor in chief of *Automatic Control* at Reinhold Publishing Co., 1954-60; assistant to the president at Diebold Group (management consultants), 1960-61; Sperry Corp., Blue Bell, Pa., supervisor of trade press relations, 1961-64, manager of public relations, 1964-70, director of public information, 1970-81; free-lance writer, 1981—. Lecturer at Rutgers University, 1956-58.

MEMBER: Public Relations Society of America.

WRITINGS:

Breakthrough to the Computer Age, Scribner, 1982.

The Rocket Makers, Crown, in press.

WORK IN PROGRESS: Groves and Oppenheimer: The Volatile Partnership of a Soldier and a Scientist.

SIDELIGHTS: Harry David Wulforst told *CA:* "The motivation for committing myself to such long-range projects as writing book-length manuscripts stems from a curiosity about the 'beginnings' of some of the major scientific and technological forces that help to shape modern-day life: Computers, for example. Few in the civilized world have not been influenced by them. Yet many of us are not aware of the innovative men and women and the curious sequence of events that produced the world's first computers. Similarly, the high-powered rockets that enable us to explore the far reaches of the Solar System and to send men to the moon are a direct consequence of pioneering experiments in the United States and Germany a half of a century ago. Hopefully, new insights concerning the men and women who lead us into the Nuclear Age will be offered in a work currently in progress."

X-Y

XAVIER I
See HORNE, Frank (Smith)

* * *

YARBROUGH, Camille 1938-

PERSONAL: Born in 1938 in Chicago, Ill. *Education:* Studied acting and voice in United States and Australia; attended Roosevelt University.

CAREER: Employed in dance company of Katherine Dunham; dance instructor at Performing Arts Training center at Southern Illinois University, East St. Louis; provided drama workshops at high schools in New York; drama teacher. Actress in plays, including "To Be Young, Gifted, and Black," "Trumpets of the Lord," "Cities in Bezique," and "Sambo"; in films, including "Shaft," 1973; and in television. Singer on tour in United States, Canada, and South America.

WRITINGS:

Cornrows (poems for children), illustrations by Carole Byard, Coward, McCann & Geoghegan, 1979.

Also author of poetry and songs.

MEDIA ADAPTATIONS: A program of Yarbrough's songs and poetry was presented by Nina Simone at Philharmonic Hall, New York City, in 1972.*

* * *

YEAGER, Leland B(ennett) 1924-

PERSONAL: Born October 4, 1924, in Oak Park, Ill.; son of Leland Edward and Alice Mary (Bennett) Yeager. *Education:* Oberlin College, A.B., 1948; Columbia University, M.A., 1949, Ph.D., 1952.

ADDRESSES: Home—Charlottesville, Va. *Office*—Department of Economics, University of Virginia, Charlottesville, Va. 22901.

CAREER: Texas Agricultural and Mechanical College (now Texas A & M University), College Station, instructor in economics, 1949-50; University of Maryland at College Park, began as instructor, became assistant professor of economics, 1952-57; University of Virginia, Charlottesville, began as as-

sistant professor, became associate professor, 1957-69, Paul Goodloe McIntire Professor of Economics, 1969—, chairman of department, 1968-72. Visiting professor at Southern Methodist University, 1962, and University of California, Los Angeles, 1975. Vice-president and director of Galilee Ltd.; member of board of directors of Virginia Council on Economic Education, 1969—. *Military service:* U.S. Army, 1943-46.

MEMBER: American Association for the Advancement of Science, American Economic Association (member of executive committee, 1965-67; vice-president, 1967-68), American Finance Association, Royal Economic Association, Mont Pelerin Society.

AWARDS, HONORS: Ford Foundation fellow, 1967-68.

WRITINGS:

Free Trade: America's Opportunity, Robert Schalkenbach Foundation, 1954.
(Editor) *In Search of a Monetary Constitution*, Harvard University Press, 1962.
International Monetary Relations: Theory, History, and Policy, Harper, 1966.
(With David G. Tuerck) *Trade Policy and the Price System*, International Textbook Co., 1966.
The International Monetary Mechanism, Holt, 1968.
Proposals for Government Credit Allocation, American Enterprise Institute for Public Policy Research, 1977.
(Co-author) *Experiences With Stopping Inflation*, American Enterprise Institute for Public Policy Research, 1981.
(With Ludwig von Mises) *Nation, State, and Economy: Contributions to the Politics and History of Our Times*, New York University Press, 1983.

BIOGRAPHICAL/CRITICAL SOURCES:

PERIODICALS

American Economic Review, September, 1966.
Economist, May 7, 1966.
Journal of Political Economy, December, 1963.
National Review, June 4, 1963.*

* * *

YORK, Simon
See HEINLEIN, Robert A(nson)

YOSKOWITZ, Irving
See YOUNGER, Irving

* * *

YOUNG, Allan Edward 1939-

PERSONAL: Born June 21, 1939, in Brooklyn, N.Y.; son of Louis W. and Alice D. (Klein) Young; married Eleanor Podheiser, September 16, 1962; children: David, Shari, Alison. *Education:* Harpur College (now State University of New York at Binghamton), B.A., 1961; Columbia University, M.B.A., 1963, Ph.D., 1967.

ADDRESSES: Home—27 Ely Dr., Fayetteville, N.Y. 13066. *Office*—School of Management, Syracuse University, Syracuse, N.Y. 13210.

CAREER: Bernard M. Baruch College of the City University of New York, New York, N.Y., lecturer in economics and finance, 1965-66; Syracuse University, Syracuse, N.Y., assistant professor, 1966-71, associate professor, 1971-74, professor of management, 1974—, director of Small Business Administration-School of Management Internship Program, 1970—, adviser to *Promethean.* Sheriff of Onandaga County; expert witness on financial matters related to securities; consultant to New York State Urban Development Corp., Rinfret-Boston Associates, Syracuse Supply Co., and Securities Industry Association.

MEMBER: American Economic Association, Financial Management Association, Eastern Finance Association (member of board of directors).

AWARDS, HONORS: Prize from New York State Society of Certified Public Accountants, 1963.

WRITINGS:

(With Charles Ellis) *The Repurchase of Common Stock,* Harper, 1971.
The New York Securities Industry: Its Contribution to New York State and City, Securities Industry Association, 1985.
(With Jerome B. Cohen and Sidney M. Robbins) *The Financial Manager,* Publishing Horizons, 1986.

Editor of *Financial Review,* 1976-82, and *Journal of Corporate Finance and Accounting,* 1977-82.

WORK IN PROGRESS: Work on the U.S. and international securities industry.

* * *

YOUNGBLOOD, Ila Dell 1926-

PERSONAL: Born February 21, 1926, in Oklahoma City, Okla.; daughter of Floyd L. (a pharmacist) and Bessie L. (a teacher; maiden name, Parker) Yarbro; married Hugh A. Youngblood, Jr. (a sculptor and foundry worker), June 12, 1948; children: Sue Dell Youngblood Smith. *Education:* University of Oklahoma, B.F.A., 1947, M.A., 1971.

ADDRESSES: Home—3229 North Virginia, Oklahoma City, Okla. 73118. *Agent*—Ellen Levine Literary Agency, 432 Park Ave. S., Suite 1205, New York, N.Y. 10016.

CAREER: Oklahoma City Public Schools, Oklahoma City, Okla., teacher of speech and English, 1947-51; housewife, 1951-63; free-lance writer, 1963-68; *Daily Oklahoman,* Oklahoma City, staff writer, 1971-72; Oklahoma State Department of Education, Oklahoma City, writer and editor, 1972-73; Oklahoma Educational Television Authority, Oklahoma City, director of communications, 1973-74; Central State University, Edmond, Okla., director of news bureau, 1977-81; free-lance writer, 1981.

AWARDS, HONORS: First place award from Educational Public Relations Officers, 1973, for newsletter *Oklahoma Educator;* award for excellence in public information from Corporation for Public Broadcasting, 1975.

WRITINGS:

Bitter Promise (historical novel), Avon, 1982.

Contributor of articles to periodicals and newspapers, including *Orbit, Sports Aviation,* and *National Enquirer.*

WORK IN PROGRESS: A historical novel set in fourteenth-century England; a historical novel set in eleventh-century Scotland; a contemporary novel.

SIDELIGHTS: Ila Dell Youngblood told *CA:* "The only motivation for my writing is a mysterious compulsion that cannot be denied. My husband and I share an enthusiasm for travel and have made four trips to Europe and England. I spent two weeks in London in 1982 doing preliminary research for one of my books, using the facilities of the Guild Hall Library. I did some research for *Bitter Promise* in Paris."

AVOCATIONAL INTERESTS: Gardening and reading.

* * *

YOUNGER, Irving 1932-1988
(Irving Yoskowitz)

OBITUARY NOTICE: Surname originally Yoskowitz; born November 30, 1932, in New York, N.Y.; died of pancreatic cancer, March 13, 1988, in Minneapolis, Minn. Lawyer, educator, and author. Known for his theatrics in the courtroom and on the lecture circuit, Younger is best remembered as a dynamic and innovative law professor who enhanced his lectures on trial techniques with humor, animation, and compelling tales of past cases. In his thirty-year career Younger was an assistant U.S. attorney in Manhattan, a lawyer in private practice, a civil court judge, and a professor of law at several schools, including New York University and Cornell University. In 1981 he left teaching to join the Washington law firm of Williams & Connelly, where he represented the *Washington Post* and *National Enquirer* and was chief counsel in litigation resulting from the collapse of a skywalk in a Kansas City hotel. Younger re-entered the academic world in 1984, holding a professorial post at the University of Minnesota until his death. He wrote *The Art of Cross Examination* and co-authored *Principles of Evidence.*

OBITUARIES AND OTHER SOURCES:

BOOKS

Who's Who in American Law, 4th edition, Marquis, 1985.

PERIODICALS

New York Times, August 27, 1982, March 15, 1988.
Washington Post, March 16, 1988.

YU, Elena S. H.   1947-

PERSONAL: Born June 25, 1947, in Fukien, China. *Education:* University of San Carlos, B.A., 1968; University of Notre Dame, M.A., 1971, Ph.D., 1974.

CAREER: University of St. Thomas, New Brunswick, lecturer in sociology, 1973-74; University of Notre Dame, Notre Dame, Ind., assistant professor of Chinese and fellow of Center for the Study of Man in Contemporary Society, 1974-75; University of Victoria, Victoria, British Columbia, assistant professor of sociology, 1975-78; San Diego State University, San Diego, Calif., adjunct assistant professor of sociology, beginning in 1978. Field director of Vietnamese Refugee Study in the United States at University of Illinois at Chicago Circle, 1978-79.

MEMBER: American Sociological Association, National Council on Family Relations, Gerontological Society, Society for Applied Anthropology, Canadian Association of Sociologists and Anthropologists.

WRITINGS:

(With William T. Liu and Tran Minh Tung) *Interviewing Conduct: A Manual for Training Vietnamese,* Vietnamese Refugee Research Project, 1979.

(With Liu) *Fertility and Kinship in the Philippines: An Ethnographic Study,* University of Notre Dame Press, 1980.

(With Alice K. Murata and Chien Lin) *Bibliography of Pacific/Asian American Materials in the Library of Congress,* Pacific/Asian American Mental Health Research Center, 1982.*

Z

ZELIZER, Viviana A. 1946-

PERSONAL: Born January 19, 1946, in Buenos Aires, Argentina; immigrated to United States, 1967, naturalized citizen, 1976; daughter of Julio S. (a lawyer) and Rosa (Weill) Rotman; married Gerald Zelizer (a rabbi), February 15, 1967; children: Julian. *Education:* Rutgers University, B.A., 1971; Columbia University, M.A. and M.Phil., both 1974, Ph.D., 1977.

ADDRESSES: Office—410 D Milbank, Barnard College, Columbia University, New York, N.Y. 10027.

CAREER: Rutgers University, New Brunswick, N.J., assistant professor of sociology, 1976-78; Columbia University, Barnard College, New York, N.Y., assistant professor, 1978-82, associate professor, 1982-85, professor of sociology, 1985—.

MEMBER: American Sociological Association, Eastern Sociological Association, Phi Beta Kappa.

AWARDS, HONORS: Rockefeller Foundation fellow in humanities, 1980-81; Elizur Wright Award from American Risk and Insurance Association, 1985, for *Morals and Markets;* C. Wright Mills Award from the Society for the Study of Social Problems, 1985, for *Pricing the Priceless Child.*

WRITINGS:

Morals and Markets: The Development of Life Insurance in the United States, Columbia University Press, 1979.
Pricing the Priceless Child: The Changing Social Value of Children, Basic Books, 1985.

Contributor to sociology journals.

WORK IN PROGRESS: Special Dollars: The Social Meaning of Money, a study of the non-economic aspects of money in modern society, for Basic Books.

SIDELIGHTS: According to Neil Postman of the *Washington Post Book World,* Viviana A. Zelizer's book *Pricing the Priceless Child* is "provocative and significant . . . mainly . . . because of her unusual perspective." The author has compared the economic value of the child in the nineteenth century to the economic uselessness of today's children coupled with their enormous emotional value in society. Zelizer has provided a chronology of the changes that occurred between 1870, when children were expected to contribute to the family income and

build moral character at the same time, and 1930, when parents began to insist that children make no economic contribution to family life. When children were elevated to the level of sacred ornaments, however, they lost all economic control of their lives, and Zelizer would like to reverse this trend. Postman found her historical account fascinating; he praised her conclusion as a "wide-ranging and deeply informed discussion of the different positions now being taken on the future of childhood."

BIOGRAPHICAL/CRITICAL SOURCES:

PERIODICALS

Washington Post Book World, June 9, 1985.

* * *

ZIEWACZ, Lawrence E. 1942-

PERSONAL: Surname is pronounced "Zee-*wat*-ta"; born December 23, 1942, in Sault Sainte Marie, Mich.; son of Lawrence J. (a federal civil servant) and Carolina H. (a housewife; maiden name, Dedo) Ziewacz; married Marily Sue Wood (a registered nurse), December 7, 1968; children: Elizabeth, John. *Education:* Attended Michigan College of Mining and Technology, Sault Branch (now Lake Superior State College), 1961-64; Michigan State University, B.A., 1965, M.A., 1966, Ph.D., 1971. *Politics:* Democrat. *Religion:* Roman Catholic.

ADDRESSES: Home—East Lansing, Mich. *Office*—Department of American Thought and Language, 229 Bessey Hall, Michigan State University, East Lansing, Mich. 48824.

CAREER: Lansing Community College, Lansing, Mich., instructor in U.S. history, 1968-70; Edinboro State College, Edinboro, Pa., instructor in U.S. history, 1970-71; Michigan State University, East Lansing, instructor, 1971-74, assistant professor, 1974-79, associate professor, 1979-84, professor of American thought and language, 1984—. Co-chairman of sport sessions of American Culture and Popular Culture National Conventions.

MEMBER: American Historical Association, Organization of American Historians, American Culture Association, Society for the History of Education, Popular Culture Association, Society for the Study of Midwestern Literature and Culture.

WRITINGS:

(With Bruce Rubenstein) *Michigan: A History of the Great Lakes State,* Forum Press, 1981.

(Contributor) William J. Baker and John M. Carroll, editors, *Sports in Modern America,* River City Publishers, 1981.

(Contributor) Gerald R. Baydo, editor, *The Evolution of Mass Culture,* Forum Press, 1981.

(With Douglas Noverr) *The Games They Played: Sports in American History, 1865-1980,* Nelson-Hall, 1983.

(Contributor) Charles E. Babbitt, editor, *The Sociological Galaxy: Sociology Toward the Year 2000,* Beacons Publishing, 1983.

(Editor with Douglas Noverr) *Sport History: Selected Reading Lists and Course Outlines From American Colleges and Universities,* Markus Wiener Publishing, 1986.

(With Bruce Rubenstein) *Three Bullets Sealed His Lips,* Michigan State University Press, 1987.

Assistant editor of "Sports Syllabi" series, Markus Wiener Publishing. Contributor of articles and reviews to history and sociology journals. Associate editor of *Journal of the Great Lakes History Conference,* 1980, and newsletter of Group for the Study of Nationalism.

WORK IN PROGRESS: Research on grand jury investigations of the Michigan legislature during the 1940s.

SIDELIGHTS: Lawrence E. Ziewacz told *CA:* "I have a long-standing interest in Michigan history. My dissertation was about Thomas W. Palmer, a U.S. senator from Detroit. Since I teach writing, I have tried to craft textbooks which are well-written and which would be attractive to a general audience. I have been interested in sports ever since I lettered in sports in high school. I believe that a healthy mind and body go hand in hand. Now I have been able to turn my avocation into a vocation.

"*The Games They Played: Sports in American History, 1865-1980,* co-authored with Douglas Noverr, was written for the purpose of placing sports that have been important to the United States in their proper cultural and historical perspective. It is our view that sports, far from being on the peripheral edge of society, since the Civil War, have often been a 'mirror of society.' Each chapter focuses on the overall cultural scene of each period, focusing on sports, to see where and how prominently they fit into the picture and how they evolve to serve the needs of society. The overall view is followed by a close-up analysis of the most popular sports and the leading sports figures of the period. These popular games have dominated the sports scene and have steadily become more commercialized and more competitive, while at the same time have continued to maintain the cherished national values of fair play, physical discipline, and individual as well as team effort. Previous books dealing with sports and American culture were either by physical education people or by journalists. Douglas Noverr and I believe we were the first to provide both a cultural perspective as well as a historical chronology of events with interpretation.

"*Three Bullets Sealed His Lips,* co-authored with Bruce Rubenstein, deals with the death of Michigan state senator Warren Hooper of Albion, Michigan, on January 11, 1945, several days before he was to testify on legislative corruption. He was shot three times while en route to his Albion home from Lansing, Michigan. The grand jury investigation was a probe of the state legislature with a number of legislators and an ex-lieutenant governor sent to jail. The chief prosecutor, Kim Sigler, was elected governor of Michigan in 1946. Our book attempts to demonstrate who actually killed Hooper and who was behind the killing. Hooper's death has never clearly been solved."

*   *   *

ZWEIG, Ferdynand   1896-1988

OBITUARY NOTICE: Born in 1896 in Krakow, Poland; died June 9, 1988. Economist, sociologist, and author. A highly respected economist best known for his studies of the British working classes, Zweig escaped from his native Poland after the German invasion during World War II. He fled to England where he taught at the Polish university college. After the war, Zweig was commissioned to write a study on spending habits and poverty, whereupon he mingled with the poor on the streets, in public houses, at racetracks, and amusement parks; he claimed his Polish accent allowed him to cross class barriers as no native English sociologist could. His resulting book, *Labour, Life, and Poverty,* was closely followed by *Men in the Pits* and *Economic Ideas and Productivity and the Trade Union.*

When the Polish college was forced to close due to insufficient funding, Zweig took time out to examine his career options at a seaside resort. Information gathered from the people he met during this trip laid the foundation for his book *The British Worker,* the publication of which earned him a reputation as a sympathetic social chronicler. In *The New Acquisitive Society,* Zweig explored the ramifications of the welfare state evolving in England during the mid-1970s, and he discussed Middle Eastern issues in *The Israeli Worker* and *Israel: The Sword and the Harp.*

OBITUARIES AND OTHER SOURCES:

PERIODICALS

Times (London), June 13, 1988.

Contemporary Authors and *Contemporary Authors New Revision Series* Encompass Authors in Every Field—From Established Writers to Individuals Best Known for Their Non-literary Activities:

Novelists

(continued from front endsheets)

Hermann Hesse
Bohumil Hrabel
Aldous Leonard Huxley
LeRoi Jones
Yasunari Kawabata
Yashar Kemal
Thomas Keneally
Jack Kerouac
Jerzy Kosinski
Milan Kundera
Oliver La Farge
Margaret Wemyss
   Laurence
Doris Lessing
Jack London
Alison Lurie
Norman Mailer
Bernard Malamud
Andre Malraux
Vladimir Maximov
Mary McCarthy
Carson McCullers
N. Scott Momady
Brian Moore
Iris Murdoch
Vladimir Nabokov
Shiva Naipaul
V. S. Naipaul
Anais Nin
Joyce Carol Oates
Flannery O'Connor
Juan Carlos Onetti
Walker Percy
Katherine Anne Porter
Chaim Potok
Marcel Proust
Barbara Pym
Thomas Pynchon
Ayn Rand
Erich Maria Remarque
Jean Rhys
Alain Robbe-Grillet
Philip Roth
Gabrielle Roy
Juan Rulfo
Salman Rushdie
Ernesto Sabato
V. Sackville-West
J. D. Salinger

Irwin Shaw
Naoya Shiga
Mikhail Sholokhov
Claude Simon
Upton Sinclair
Isaac Bashevis Singer
Josef Skvorecky
Aleksandr I.
   Solzhenitsyn
Muriel Spark
John Steinbeck
William Styron
Jean Toomer
Anne Tyler
John Updike
Mario Vargas Llosa
Gore Vidal
Kurt Vonnegut, Jr.
Alice Walker
Evelyn Waugh
Fay Weldon
Eudora Welty
Elie Wiesel
P. G. Wodehouse
Herman Wouk
Richard Wright
Marguerite Yourcenar
   . . . and more

Philosophers

Mortimer J. Adler
Theodor W. Adorno
William Barrett
Ernst Bloch
C. D. Broad
Albert Camus
Etienne Henry Gilson
Martin Heidegger
Sidney Hook
Claude Levi-Strauss
Gyorgy Lucas
Gabriel Honore Marcel
Karl R. Popper
Jean-Paul Sartre
   . . . and more

Photographers

Berenice Abbott
Ansel Adams

Antony Armstrong-
   Jones
Eve Arnold
David Bailey
Margaret Bourke-White
Howard Dearstyn
Alfred Eisenstaedt
Ron Galella
Peter Jenkins
David Hume Kennerly
Francesco Scavullo
   . . . and more

Physicians

Virginia Apgar
Christiaan Barnard
Beatrice Bishop Berle
T. Berry Brazelton
Mary S. Calderone
Michael E. DeBakey
Nawal El Saadawi
Henry Jay Heimlich
Milton Helpern
John H. Knowles
Frederick Leboyer
Robert B. Livingston
Elizabeth Miller
Jonathan Miller
William A. Nolen
Ray H. Rosenman
Richard Selzer
Andrew Weil
   . . . and more

Playwrights

Marcel Achard
Edward Albee
Jean Anouilh
Samuel Beckett
Brendan Behan
Andre Brink
Abe Burrows
Paddy Chayefsky
Marc Connelly
Noel Coward
Friedrich Duerrenmatt
Christopher Durang

Lonne Elder III
Max Frisch
Athol Fugard
Charles Fuller
Tsegaye Gabre-Medhin
Frank D. Gilroy
John Guare
Wilson John Haire
Lorraine Hansberry
Moss Hart
Vaclav Havel
Lillian Hellman
Beth Henley
William Motler Inge
Eugene Ionesco
George S. Kaufman
Raymond Evenor
   Lawler
David Mamet
Mark Medoff
Arthur Miller
Jason Miller
Thomas Murphy
Sean O'Casey
Clifford Odets
Harold Pinter
David Rabe
Elmer Rice
Ntozake Shange
Sam Shepard
Neil Simon
Tom Stoppard
John Whiting
Oscar Wilde
Tennessee Williams
   . . . and more

Poets

Ai
Anna Akhmatova
Rafael Alberti
Yehuda Amichai
Jean Arp
John Ashbery
W. H. Auden
John Berryman
Elizabeth Bishop
Paul Blackburn
Robert Bly
Gwendolyn Brooks
Paul Celan

Rene Char
John Ciardi
Cid Corman
e.e. cummings
James Dickey
Diane di Prima
Hilda Doolittle
Alan Dugan
Henry L. Dumas
Robert Duncan
Guenter Eich
T. S. Eliot
Odysseus Elytis
Hans Magnus
   Enzensberger
Lawrence Ferlinghetti
Carolyn Forche
Robert Frost
Allen Ginsberg
Nikki Giovanni
Louise Gluck
Robert Graves
Seamus Heaney
Ralph Hodgson
David Holbrook
Langston Hughes
Ted Hughes
Gyula Illyes
Robinson Jeffers
Galway Kinnell
Thomas Kinsella
Carolyn Kizer
Maxine Kumin
Stanley Kunitz
Philip Lamantia
Philip Larkin
Denise Levertov
Philip Levine
Audre Lorde
Robert Lowell
Hugh MacDiarmid
Archibald MacLeish
Louis MacNeice
Rod McKuen
Samuel Menashe
W. S. Merwin
Czeslaw Milosz
Marco Antonio Montes
   De Oca
Marianne Moore
Pablo Neruda
Christopher Okigbo
Nicanor Parra

Poets
(continued)

Octavio Paz
Lucio Piccolo
Sylvia Plath
Ezra Pound
Pierre Reverdy
Kenneth Rexroth
Adrienne Rich
Theodore Roethke
Muriel Rukeyser
Carl Sandburg
Delmore Schwartz
Giorgos Stylianou
  Seferiades
Anne Sexton
Dame Edith Sitwell
Sydney Goodsir Smith
Gary Snyder
Stephen Spender
Rabindranath Tagore
Dylan Thomas
Mona Van Duyn
Diane Wakoski
Derek Walcott
Robert Penn Warren
Richard Wilbur
William Carlos Williams
Yevgeny Yevtushenko
  . . . and more

Political and
Social Activists

Jane Alpert
Daniel Berrigan
Philip Berrigan
Romulo Betancourt
Stokely Carmichael
Eldridge Cleaver
William Sloan Coffin
Angela Davis
Vine Deloria, Jr.
Bernadette Devlin
W. E. B. DuBois
Dick Gregory
Thomas E. Hayden
Julius W. Hobson
Abbie Hoffman
Martin Luther King, Jr.
Adam Clayton Powell,
  Jr.
Charles Alan Reich
Jerry Rubin
Bobby Seale
Roy Wilkins
  . . . and more

Politicians and
World Leaders

David Ben-Gurion
Willy Brandt
Zbigniew K. Brzezinski
Jimmy Carter
Winston Churchill
Anthony Eden
Millicent Hammond
  Fenwick
Gerald R. Ford
Dag Hammarskjoeld
Jack Kemp
Edward Moore
  Kennedy
Ruhollah Khomeini
Nikita Sergeyevich
  Khrushchev
Henry A. Kissinger
Edward I. Koch
Mao Tse-tung
George S. McGovern
Golda Meir
Jawaharlal Nehru
Richard M. Nixon
Shimon Peres
Ronald Reagan
Anwar Sadat
Margaret Chase Smith
Strom Thurmond
Kurt Waldheim
Harold Wilson
  . . . and more

Print Journalists

Jack Anderson
Russell Baker
Carl Bernstein
Jimmy Breslin
William F. Buckley, Jr.
Herb Caen
Maxine Cheshire
Oriana Fallaci
Sheilah Graham
Bob Greene
Seymour M. Hersh
Haynes Bonner Johnson
Anthony Lewis
A. J. Liebling
Walter Lippmann
Sylvia F. Porter
Mike Royko
William Safire
Susan Sheehan
Hedrick Smith
George Will

Gary Wills
Bob Woodward
  . . . and more

Psychologists

Ernest Becker
Bruno Bettelheim
Joyce Brothers
Erik H. Erikson
Anna Freud
Erich Fromm
Howard E. Gruber
Joan Halifax
Thomas A. Harris
Arthur Janov
Carl Jung
Irene Chamie Kassorla
R. D. Laing
Timothy Leary
John E. Mack
Abraham H. Maslow
Rollo May
Stanley Milgram
Fritz Perls
Jean Piaget
Theodore Isaac Rubin
Lee Salk
Anne Seifert
June Singer
B. F. Skinner
  . . . and more

Publishers

Sylvia Beach
William Maxwell
  Aitken Beaverbrook
Barry Bingham, Jr.
Hedley Donovan
Robert Giroux
Katharine Graham
Richard L. Grossman
William Jovanovich
Howard Kaminsky
Stefan Kanfer
Alfred A. Knopf
James Laughlin
Joseph W. Lippincott
William Loeb
Henry R. Luce
Scott Meredith
Henry Regnery
Barney Rosset
Maisie Ward
Helen Wolff
  . . . and more

Radio
Personalities

Bob Edwards
Garrison Keillor
Larry King
Gary Owens
Susan Stamberg
Studs Terkel
Lowell Thomas
  . . . and more

Religious Figures

William Barclay
Harvey Cox
Henry Dumery
Mircea Eliade
Jerry Falwell
Billy Graham
Andrew M. Greeley
Pope John Paul I
Hans Kueng
Harold S. Kushner
Bernard J. F. Lonergan
Jacques Maritain
Malcolm Muggeridge
William J. Murray III
Reinhold Niebuhr
Norman Vincent Peale
Karl Rahner
Oral Roberts
Robert Schuller
Fulton J. Sheen
Lawrence Joseph
  Shehan
Ruth Carter Stapleton
Paul Tillich
  . . . and more

Romance and
Gothic Writers

Iris Bancroft
Barbara Cartland
Barbara P. Conklin
Janet Dailey
Daphne du Maurier
Anne Eliot
Anne Hampson
Constance Heaven
Georgette Heyer
Victoria Holt
Fannie Hurst
Johanna Lindsey
Norah Lofts

Laurie McBain
Natasha Peters
Paula Schwartz
Kathleen Winsor
Kathleen E. Woodiwiss
  . . . and more

Scholars

Hannah Arendt
Jacob Bronowski
Norman O. Brown
Michel Foucault
Ivan Illich
R. W. B. Lewis
Lewis Mumford
Robert A. Nisbet
Susan Sontag
  . . . and more

Science Fiction
Writers

Poul Anderson
Isaac Asimov
Alfred Bester
James Blish
Ben Bova
Ray Bradbury
C. J. Cherryh
Arthur C. Clarke
Philip K. Dick
Gordon R. Dickson
Harlan Ellison
Joe Haldeman
Robert A. Heinlein
Frank Herbert
Ursula K. Le Guin
Fritz Leiber
Stanislaw Lem
Frank Belknap Long
Anne McCaffrey
Vonda N. McIntyre
Patricia A. McKillip
Michael Moorcock
C. L. Moore
Larry Niven
Andre Norton
Frederik Pohl
Jerry Pournelle
Joanna Russ
Robert Silverberg
Theodore Hamilton
  Sturgeon